Eastern Europe
Comparative Management in Focus:
Joint Ventures in the Commonwealth
of Independent States, Chapter 8
Case: Colgate-Palmolive in Hungary, Part 3

Asia
Comparative Management in Focus:
Global Managers Respond to Economic
Slide in Indonesia, Chapter 2
Case: Managing a Diverse Workforce
in Indonesia, Part 4

South Africa
Comparative Management in Focus:
A New Day Dawns for MNCs in
South Africa, Chapter 3
Case: Colgate-Palmolive in
Post-Apartheid South Africa, Part 1

International Management

INTERNATIONAL
MANAGEMENT
MANAGING ACROSS
BORDERS AND CULTURES

THIRD EDITION

HELEN DERESKY
STATE UNIVERSITY OF NEW YORK–PLATTSBURGH

Prentice Hall
Upper Saddle River, New Jersey 07458

Senior Acquisitions Editor: David Shafer
Editor-in-Chief: Natalie Anderson
Developmental Editor: Ruth Berry
Senior Production Supervisor: Nancy Fenton
Managing Editor: Jennifer Glennon
Executive Marketing Manager: Michael Campbell
Assistant Editor: Michele Foresta
Editorial Assistant: Kim Marsden
*Project coordination, text design, art, photo research,
    and electronic page makeup:* Thompson Steele, Inc.
Design Manager: Regina Hagen
Cover Designer: Leslie Haimes
Print Buyer: Tim McDonald

Library of Congress Cataloging-in-Publication Data
Deresky, Helen.
    International management: managing across borders and cultures/
Helen Deresky.—3rd ed.
        p.   cm.
    Includes bibliographical references and index.
    ISBN 0-321-02829-5
1. International business enterprises—Management.
2. International business enterprises—Management—Case studies.
3. Industrial management.   I. Title.
HD62.4.D47   2000
658'.049—dc21   99-23032
                                                 CIP

Prentice Hall International (UK) Limited, London
Prentice Hall of Australia Pty. Limited, Sydney
Prentice Hall Canada, Inc., Toronto
Prentice Hall Hispanoamericana, S.A., Mexico
Prentice Hall of India Private Limited, New Delhi
Prentice Hall of Japan, Inc., Tokyo
Pearson Education Asia Pte. Ltd. Singapore
Editora Prentice-Hall do Brasil, Ltda., Rio de Janeiro

Printed in the United States of America
10 9 8 7 6 5 4 3

To my husband, John,
and my children, John, Mark, and Lara,
for their love and support

Brief Contents

Contents   ix

Preface   xix

PART 1

Assessing the Environment of International Management   1

Chapter 1: The Challenge of International Management   2

Chapter 2: The Political, Economic, Legal,
            and Technological Environment   27

Chapter 3: Managing Interdependence: Social Responsibility
            and Ethics   54

Comprehensive Cases   87
The Prominant Dr. Rombach • Footwear International • Colgate-Palmolive in
Postapartheid South Africa • La Keisha Washington's Ethical Dilemma Presented
by Nike

PART 2

The Cultural Context of International Management   101

Chapter 4: The Role of Culture in International Management   102

Chapter 5: The Cross-Cultural Communication Environment   138

Chapter 6: Negotiation and Decision Making   166

Comprehensive Cases   202
Deli Rockwool Corp. in the People's Republic of China • Moto: Coming
to America • Euro Disney SCA: Perspectives from Two Cultures

Formulating and Implementing Strategy for International Operations 217

Chapter 7: Strategy Formulation for International Markets 218

Chapter 8: Cross-Border Alliances and Strategy Implementation 255

Chapter 9: Organization Structure and Coordinating Systems 286

Comprehensive Cases 318
Reorganization at AB Telecom (1998) • Johnson Electric • Colgate-Palmolive Hungary • Lee Jing Textile Company, Ltd.

PART 4

Managing Human Resources Around the World 343

Chapter 10: Staffing and Training for Global Operations 344

Chapter 11: Expatriation and Labor Relations in Global HRM 374

Chapter 12: Motivating and Leading 406

Chapter 13: Managing International Teams and Workforce Diversity 438

Comprehensive Cases 468
TDK de Mexico • Solartron • Managing a Diverse Workforce in Indonesia

INTEGRATIVE SECTION

Integrative Term Project 490

Integrative Cases 491

AT&T Consumer Products • Whirlpool's Quest for Global Leadership • Anita Roddick, OBE, and the Body Shop International PLC (1996)

Glossary 557
Booknotes 562
Credits 583
Company Index 588
Subject and Name Index 592

Contents

Preface   xix

About the Author   xxv

PART 1

Assessing the Environment of International Management   1

1   *The Challenge of International Management*   2

OPENING PROFILE
Motorola Joins the Siemens–Toshiba–IBM Alliance: High-Tech
and Cross-Cultural Challenges   3

Developments in the Global Community   5

Globalism   5   •   Regional Trading Blocs—The TRIAD   7   •   Other Regions in the World
9   •   Less Developed Countries   10   •   Privatization   11   •   Information Technology
12   •   Workforce Diversity   13   •   Technology Application: EU Imposes Cross-Border
Electronic Data Privacy   14   •   Small Businesses Go International   15

Multinational Corporations   16

The Challenge of International Management   17   •   The Contingency Role of the
International Manager   17   •   Management Focus: Citibank Gives Advice on Career
Planning   18

The Future of International Management   19

Application and Experiential Exercises   21

Case Study: GE Brings Good Life to Hungary   21

2 The Political, Economic, Legal, and Technological Environment 27

OPENING PROFILE
PepsiCo Loses Fizz After Soviet Disintegration 28

The Political and Economic Environment 29

Political Risk 30 • Political Risk Assessment 31 • Managing Political Risk 34
Managing Terrorism Risk 38 • Economic Risk 38 • Technology Application:
Multicurrency Translation Software Provides a Global Solution for Lam Research 39
Comparative Management in Focus: Global Managers Respond to Economic Slide in
Indonesia 40

The Regulatory Environment 41

Contract Law 42 • Other Regulatory Issues 43

The Technological Environment 44

Management Focus: War Declared on Pirating: *The Lion King* Launched
in Beijing Before Boston 46

Application and Experiential Exercises 49

Case Study: Conflict in Colombia: The Other Oil War 50

3 Managing Interdependence: Social Responsibility and Ethics 54

OPENING PROFILE
The Tobacco Industry's Social Responsibility in Developing Countries 55

The Social Responsibility of MNCs 56

MNC Responsibility Toward Human Rights 60 • Management Focus: Levi Takes a
Stand for Human Rights 61 • Comparative Management in Focus: A New Day Dawns
for MNCs in South Africa 61 • Codes of Conduct 63

Ethics in International Management 65

Questionable Payments 67 • Comparative Management in Focus: Ethics in Europe 69

Managing Interdependence 73

Foreign Subsidiaries in the United States 74 • Managing Subsidiary–Host Country
Interdependence 74 • Comparative Management in Focus: Interdependence: The

NAFTA Perspectives from the South and the North   77   •   Technology Application: High-Tech Jobs Boost Maquiladora-Ville   78   •   Managing Environmental Interdependence   81

Application and Experiential Exercises   84

Case Study: Balancing Human Rights Around the World: Nike and Reebok   85

Comprehensive Cases: The Prominant   Dr. Rombach   87   •   Footwear International   90
Colgate-Palmolive in Postapartheid South Africa   95   •   La Keisha Washington's Ethical Dilemma Presented by Nike   99

PART 2

The Cultural Context of International Management   101

4 | *The Role of Culture in International Management*   102

OPENING PROFILE
Telmex Uses Cultural and Political Understanding to Stymie AT&T and MCI   103

Culture and Its Effects on Organizations   105

Technology Application: As East Meets West, Asia Encounters a User-Unfriendly Interface   107

Cultural Variables and Dimensions   109

Management Focus: Adjusting to American Culture   110   •   Subcultures   111
Cultural Variables   111   •   Value Dimensions   113   •   Hofstede's Value Dimensions   113   •   Geographic Clusters   117   •   Trompenaars' Findings   118
Critical Operational Value Differences   120

Developing Cultural Profiles   123

Comparative Management in Focus: Profiles in Culture   124

Culture and Management Styles Around the World   130

Saudi Arabia   130   •   Chinese Small Family Businesses   131

Application and Experiential Exercises   135

Case Study: Trouble at Computex Corporation   136

5 The Cross-Cultural Communication Environment 138

OPENING PROFILE
Oriental Poker Face: Eastern Deception or Western Inscrutability? 139

The Communication Process 140

Cultural Noise in the Communication Process 141

Technology Application: Technology Communicates Across Borders and Cultures 142
Cultural Variables in the Communication Process 142 • Context 148
Comparative Management in Focus: Communicating with Arabs 149 • Communication
Channels 152

Managing Cross-Cultural Communication 156

Developing Cultural Sensitivity 156 • Careful Encoding 156 • Management Focus:
How 21 Men Got Global in 35 Days: Problem Number One Was Communication 157
Selective Transmission 157 • Careful Decoding of Feedback 158 • Follow-Up
Actions 159

Application and Experiential Exercises 162

Case Study: Elizabeth Visits GPC's French Subsidiary 164

6 Negotiation and Decision Making 166

OPENING PROFILE
The Iraq–U.S. Negotiations 167

Negotiation 168

The Negotiation Process 168

Stage One: Preparation 169 • Comparative Management in Focus: Successful
Negotiators Around the World 170 • Stage Two: Relationship Building 176
Stage Three: Exchanging Task-Related Information 177 • Stage Four: Persuasion 178
Stage Five: Concessions and Agreement 180

Managing Negotiation 180

Comparative Management in Focus: Negotiating with the Chinese 183 • Managing
Conflict Resolution 186

Decision Making 187

Technology Application: Daimler's Stuttgart Command Post Speeds Cross-Border
Decisions for Integration with Chrysler 188 • The Influence of Culture on Decision

Making 189 • Approaches to Decision Making 189 • Comparative Management in Focus: Decision Making in Japanese Companies 191

Application and Experiential Exercises 194

Case Study: Martinez Construction Company in Germany 197

Comprehensive Cases: Deli Rockwool Corp. in the People's Republic of China 202 • Moto: Coming to America 209 • EuroDisney SCA: Perspectives from Two Cultures 212

PART 3

Formulating and Implementing Strategy for International Operations 217

7 | *Strategy Formulation for International Markets* 218

OPENING PROFILE
Global or Local? Comparing FedEx and UPS in China 219

Reasons for Going International 220

Reactive Responses 221 • Proactive Reasons 222

Strategic Formulation Process 223

Management Focus: Unisys: Off and Running in Vietnam 225

Steps in Developing International Strategy 226

Mission and Objectives 226 • Environmental Assessment 226 • Internal Analysis 231 • Competitive Analysis 232 • International Strategic Alternatives 233 Approaches to World Markets 234 • Global Integrative Strategies 235 Management Focus: Matsushita: Way to Go Global and Act Local 236 • Entry Strategy Alternatives 238 • Comparative Management in Focus: Strategic Planning for the EU Market 241 • Technology Application: Dutch Insurance Giant Achmea Prepares for the Borderless Europe 244 • Strategic Choice 245

Application and Experiential Exercises 247

Case Study: Cola Wars: The Venezuelan Coup 248

8 | *Cross-Border Alliances and Stategy Implementation* 255

OPENING PROFILE
The DaimlerChrysler AG Global Alliance 256

Strategic Alliances 257

Cross-Border Alliances: Motivations and Benefits 258 • Challenges in Implementing Global Alliances 259 • Guidelines for Successful Alliances 261 • Comparative Management in Focus: Joint Ventures in the Commonwealth of Independent States 263

Strategic Implementation 266

Managing Performance in International Joint Ventures 267 • Technology Application: Benneton Group Spa Supports Its Worldwide Business with a Technological Edge 268 Government Influences on Strategic Implementation 272 • Cultural Influences on Strategic Implementation 273 • Comparative Management in Focus: Implementing Sino–U.S. Joint Ventures: The Culture Factor 274 • Management Focus: Wal-Mart's Implementation Problems in South America 277

Application and Experiential Exercises 278

Case Study: Ben & Jerry's and Iceverks: Alliance Meltdown in Russia 281

9 | *Organization Structure and Coordinating Systems* 286

OPENING PROFILE
Poland: Reorganizing Structure and Systems Brings New Life to ABB Zamech 287

Organization Structure 288

Evolution and Change in MNC Organizational Structures 289

Integrated Global Structures 291

Organizing for Globalization 293

Comparative Management in Focus: The Overseas Chinese Global Network 294 Organizing to "Be Global, Act Local" 296

Emergent Structural Forms 298

Interorganizational Networks 298 • The Transnational Corporation (TNC) Network Structure 298

Choice of Organizational Form 300

Organizational Change and Design Variables 301

Coordinating and Reporting for Global Operations   305

Monitoring Systems   305   •   Direct Coordinating Mechanisms   306   •   Indirect Coordinating Mechanisms   306   •   Technology Application: Air Express International in Latin America: Old Problems, New Solutions   307   •   Management Focus: McDonald's in Moscow: Control Challenge Extraordinaire!   308

Managing Effective Monitoring Systems   310

The Appropriateness of Monitoring and Reporting Systems   310   •   The Role of Information Systems   311   •   Evaluation Variables Across Countries   312

Application and Experiential Exercises   314

Case Study: Flexit International   314

Comprehensive Cases: Reorganization at AB Telecom (1998)   318   •   Johnson Electric   322 Colgate-Palmolive Hungary   330   •   Lee Jing Textile Company, Ltd.   333

PART 4

Managing Human Resources Around the World   343

10   *Staffing and Training for Global Operations*   344

OPENING PROFILE
Oleg and Mark: Equal Work but Unequal Pay   345

Technology Application: When HRMS Goes Global at British Airways   347

Staffing Philosophies for International Operations   348

Global Selection   353

Problems with Expatriation   354

Training and Development   355

Cross-Cultural Training   356   •   Training Techniques   358   •   Integrating Training with Global Orientation   360   •   Training Host-Country Nationals   360

Expatriate Compensation   361

Management Focus: Careers in Spain and China   362   •   Comparative Management in Focus: Compensation in Russia   367

Application and Experiential Exercises   369

Case Study: Fred Bailey in Japan: An Innocent Abroad   370

11 Expatriation and Labor Relations in Global HRM   374

OPENING PROFILE
Labor Laws for the EC: Ground Rules for the Firing Squad   375

Maintaining Global Human Resources   376

Developing an International Management Cadre   377

Preparation, Adaptation, and Repatriation   377   •   The Role of the Expatriate Spouse
378   •   Expatriate Career Management   378   •   The Role of Repatriation in Developing
a Global Management Cadre   380   •   The Role of Women in International Management
381   •   Technology Application: Booz-Allen & Hamilton Uses Intranet Technology to
Share Knowledge Around the Globe   382   •   Applying Title VII Abroad   384
Minority Groups in Overseas Assignment   384   •   Management Focus: Women in
Foreign Postings   386   •   Sexual Harassment in Overseas Assignment   389

Working Within Local Labor Relations Systems   389

Organized Labor Around the World   390   •   Convergence Versus Divergence in Labor
Systems   394   •   The NAFTA and Labor Relations in Mexico   395   •   Comparative
Management in Focus: Labor Relations in Germany   397   •   Labor Participation in
Management   399   •   Cultural Influences on Labor–Management Practices   400

Application and Experiential Exercises   403

Case Study: Mexican Workers Turn up the Heat at Honeywell   403

12 Motivating and Leading   406

OPENING PROFILE
Starbucks' Java Style Helps Recruit, Motivate, and Retain Leaders in Beijing   407

Motivating   407

Cross-Cultural Research on Motivation   408

The Meaning of Work   408

The Need Hierarchy in the International Context   411   •   Management Focus: Mazda's
Clashing Cultures   413   •   Comparative Management in Focus: Motivation in China
414   •   The Intrinsic–Extrinsic Dichotomy in the International Context   415
Comparative Management in Focus: Motivation in Mexico   417

Reward Systems   421

Management Focus: Ms. Wong: Employee of the Month   422

Leading   422

The Multicultural Leader's Role and Environment   423

Cross-Cultural Research on Leadership   423

Technology Application: Italtel Spa's Leadership Style Empowers Global Employees with Technology   425

Contingency Leadership—The Culture Variable   426

Comparative Management in Focus: Leadership in India   431

The Effective International Leader   433

Application and Experiential Exercises   434

Case Study: Elizabeth's Visit to GPC's Subsidiary in the Philippines   435

13 | *Managing International Teams and Workforce Diversity*   438

OPENING PROFILE

3Com Plant Flies 65 Different National Flags   439

International Management Teams   440

Technology Application: Timberland UK Facilitates Global Team Results   441
Building International Teams   441   •   Management Focus: Airbus: An Exceptional Multicultural Success   443   •   Management Focus: Building Teamwork Across Nine Nations   444

Domestic Multiculturalism: Managing Diversity   445

Building Programs to Value Diversity   446   •   Multicultural Work Teams   449
Maximizing Effectiveness   451   •   Acculturation   453   •   Integrating Immigrants   456
Management Focus: Cultural Integration of Work Groups: A Two-Way Street   458

Application and Experiential Exercises   460

Case Study: Managing Diversity at Luxury Island Resort   465

Comprehensive Cases: TDK de Mexico   468   •   Solartron   475   •   Managing a Diverse Workforce in Indonesia   483

INTEGRATIVE SECTION

Integrative Term Project   490

Intergrative Cases   491

AT&T Consumer Products   491

Whirlpool's Quest for Global Leadership   509

Anita Roddick, OBE, and the Body Shop International PLC (1996)   534

Glossary   557

Booknotes   562

Credits   583

Company Index   588

Subject and Name Index   592

Preface

Managers around the world are, or soon will be, involved to some degree in international business. The escalating level of international involvement and competition in today's business arena mandates that managers develop the skills necessary for effective cross-national interactions and daily operations in foreign subsidiaries. Feedback from companies operating abroad reveals that the cause of expatriate failure is often the ineffective management of intercultural relations, so the fate of expatriate missions depends at least in part on the international manager's cultural skills and sensitivity. Similarly, domestic managers also need "international management" skills because of increasing diversity in their own countries.

In recognition of the growing importance of international business and the need to prepare future managers to operate in a multicultural environment, the American Assembly of the Collegiate Schools of Business (AACSB) has required business schools to internationalize the curriculum. This requirement, along with the demands of the publics that business schools serve, has led schools to recognize that we are now in a global economy and that students need to take courses that will prepare them for international operations. Today, most schools have at least one international course in their curricula, and many offer a major in international business management.

Clearly, the skills needed for effective management of people and processes in an intercultural context are crucial for the twenty-first century. There is thus a pronounced need for a comprehensive textbook that addresses the actual management functions and behaviors required for effective cross-cultural management at both the **organizational/strategic** (macro) level and the **interpersonal** (micro) level. *International Management: Managing Across Borders and Cultures,* Third Edition, fills this need.

This text places the student in the role of a manager of any nationality, encouraging the student to make a truly global perspective in dealing with dynamic management issues in both foreign and diverse domestic environments. Cross-cultural situations are evaluated in the context of global changes—the European Union, the North American Free Trade Agreement (NAFTA), the liberalization of Eastern Europe, and the genesis of the Commonwealth of Independent States—that require new management applications. Throughout, the text emphasizes how the variable of culture interacts with other national and international factors to affect managerial process and behaviors.

This textbook is designed for undergraduate and graduate students majoring in international business or general management and for executive training programs with an international focus. It can also be used by students in an elective international course or a course offered to meet AACSB requirements. Graduate students might be asked to focus more heavily on the comprehensive cases that end each part of the book and to complete the term project in greater detail. It is assumed, though not essential, that most students using *International Management: Managing Across Borders and Cultures* will have taken a basic principles of management course. Although this text is primarily intended for business students, it is also useful for practicing managers and for student majoring in other areas, such as political science or international relations, who would benefit from a background in international management.

Changes to the Third Edition

The third edition contains a number of changes, listed below, that provide a comprehensive framework for international management courses, which in the past have been ill-defined and inconsistently presented. This edition devotes particular attention to strategic management in a globally competitive environment and to the role of culture in motivation, leadership, communication, negotiation, decision making, IHRM practices, and the management of a multicultural workforce abroad or at home.

- **More than half the comprehensive and integrative cases are new**, dealing with management issues in Germany, Japan, Hong Kong, Hungary, Indonesia, and "the world." The most popular cases from the second edition—covering issues in South Africa, Bangladesh, China, France, Taiwan, Mexico, and Kenya—have been retained.
- **A Restructured format** for parts and chapters changes the "principles" approach of the second edition to a more "global" approach. The third edition covers the *process* of management based on both the macro (organizational) level of environment and strategy and on the micro (interpersonal) level of culture and human resources. There are now four parts instead of five:

  Part One: Assessing the Environment of International Management
  Part Two: Understanding the Cultural Context of International Management
  Part Three: Formulating and implementing Strategy for International Operations
  Part Four: Managing Human Resources Around the World

- **A new chapter**, "Cross-Border Alliances and Strategy Implementation," has been added.
- **Consolidation:** The second edition chapters on motivations and leadership have been combined into one chapter (Chapter 12, "Motivating and Leading"), and the second edition chapters on organizing and controlling have also been streamlined (Chapter 9, "Organization Structure and Coordinating Systems").
- **Coverage of social responsibility and ethics** has been moved up from Chapter 14 to Chapter 3, "Managing Interdependence: Social Responsibility and Ethics."
- **New chapter opening profiles** explore topics such as "The DaimlerChrysler AG Global Alliance" and "Global or Local? Contrasting Fedex and UPS in China."
- **A new feature—the Technology Application box**—has been added to each chapter, covering topics such as "EU Imposes Cross-Border Electronic Data Privacy" and "Multicurrency Translation Software Provides a Global Solution for LAM Research."

- **New Comparative Management in Focus** sections on topics, such as "Global Managers Respond to Economic Slide in Indonesia," have been added; expanded and updated sections cover the most recent developments pertaining to the EU, the CIS, NAFTA, and South Africa.
- Several new **Management Focus** boxes, such as "Citibank Gives Advice on Career Planning," and "Careers in Spain and in China," have been added.
- **New chapter-ending cases** include "Balancing Human Rights Around the World: Nike and Reebok," "Cola Wars: The Venezuelan Coup," and "Ben & Jerry's and Iceverks: Alliance Meltdown in Russia."
- **A new feature—Internet Exercises—**are featured on the book's Web site and organized by chapter. Go to http://www.prenhall.com/Deresky
- **New experiential exercises,** covering topics such as multicultural negotiations, Japanese decision-making, partner selection in IJVs, and myths of IM, have been added to the text and Instructor's Manual.
- Information on recent world developments, including events in China and Europe, has been expanded and updated throughout with the inclusion of new data and research results.
- Topics suggested by reviewers, such as **strategic alliances, information technology,** and **expatriation/repatriation,** have been added.
- Selected charts have been simplified to increase student understanding.

Distinctive Text Features

This text offers a complete set of resources for instructors who wish to design a course in international or comparative management without having to collect materials, case studies, and examples from varied sources. Specifically, this text provides—and thus eliminates the need for instructors to search out—the following elements:

Research Base *International Management: Managing Across Borders and Cultures* is as current as possible, both from the perspective of empirical research in the field and that of current events and experiences of companies around the world. The book draws from a spectrum of interdisciplinary research literature and from popular business sources, including the *Journal of International Business Studies, Harvard Business Review, Columbia Journal of World Business, Journal of International Management Studies, International Journal of Psychology, International Journal of Personality and Social Psychology, International Studies of Management and Organization, International Journal of Intercultural Relations, Academy of Management Journal, Academy of Management Review, Administrative Science Quarterly, Management International Review, Research in Organizational Behavior, Journal of Applied Psychology, Organizational Dynamics,* as well as *Business Week,* the *Wall Street Journal,* the Asian and the European versions of the *Wall Street Journal, Fortune,* the *Financial Times* and the *Economist.*

Culture Base Where applicable throughout the text, the variable of culture is discussed in the context of its impact on the managerial function and issues presented.

Comparative Management in Focus Sections In most chapters, these sections illustrate the comparative application in specific countries of the topics discussed. Examples include "The Overseas Chinese: The Cultural Web of Chinese Alliances," "Leadership in India,"

"Communicating with Arabs," "Compensation in Russia," "Strategic Planning for the EC Market," "Joint Ventures in the Commonwealth of Independent States," and "Negotiating with the Chinese."

Management Focus Boxes   These are short boxed sections that illustrate the chapter topics with examples of specific companies, managers, or situations, such as "Levi Takes a Stand for Human Rights," "Ms. Wong: Employee of the Month," and "Women in Foreign Postings."

Technology Application Boxes   These are short boxed sections that illustrate the role to technology as it pertains to the chapter topics; many examples discuss how real companies are currently using technology.

Internet Exercises   Pertaining to selected topics throughout the book, Internet Exercises are provided on the book's Web site to help students explore chapter content in more detail and relate what they've learned to real-world situations. Go to http://www.prenhall.com/Deresky

Chapter Cases   There are two cases for each chapter: an opening profile that presents a real company, person, or situation to set the stage and preview the chapter contents; and an end-of-chapter case study, drawn from an actual situation, that poses a problem for students to resolve by applying their understanding of the subjects covered in the chapter. All chapter-closing cases are followed by discussion questions.

Comprehensive Cases   Three to four longer, comprehensive cases are grouped at the end of each part and challenge students to apply their knowledge from a systems perspective. Students must analyze the case situation and make recommendations for action.

Integrative Cases   Three integrative cases at the end of the book put students in a typical international manager's role of having to make decision and carry out plans from a systems perspective, while taking into account the many interrelated issues discussed in the text.

Integrative Term Project   A term project is outlined at the end of the text to provide a vehicle for research and the application of the course content.

Application and Experiential Exercises   At the end of each chapter there are application and experiential exercises to facilitate active learning through application of chapter concepts and skills.

Other Pedagogical Tools   Throughout the text, tables, charts, figures, real company examples, and vignettes are used to illustrate and clarify the chapter material. The summary of key points gives a review of the material. Discussion questions and application and experiential exercises aid the student's review and understanding of each chapter. A glossary at the end of the book provided definitions for key terms and concepts.

Supplements

International Management: Managing Across Borders and Cultures is supported by a full range of Instructor supplements to facilitate the design and presentation of a comprehensive course.

Instructor's Manual with Test Bank and PowerPoint Exhibit Gallery

Prepared by George Puia of Indiana State University, the Instructor's Manual provides for each chapter a lecture outline, suggested answers to discussion questions and closing case questions, and a "Student Stimulation" activity. Lecture outlines are annotated with suggestions for using the Internet and other media sources. The Instructor's Manual also contains extra experiential exercises for selected chapters; an "Enrichment Resources Directory" that lists print and media sources; summaries and suggested solutions for each of the comprehensive and integrative cases; and sample syllabi.

The **Test Item File** portion of the Instructor's Manual, also written by George Puia, contains a variety of multiple-choice, short answer, and essay questions for every chapter. An electronic version of these questions can be found on the Prentice Hall Custom Test program.

Transparency Masters for all the PowerPoint slides are also included in the Instructor's Manual, making them easily viewable and available for copying.

Instructor's Manual on Disk

The Instructor's Manual material from the print version is available on disk in Word files, allowing professors to add notes for their classroom use.

PowerPoint Slides

Electronic PowerPoint slides are available on disk for each chapter. They contain a variety of text and nontext illustrations and exhibits.

Prentice Hall Custom Test

All the test questions from the Instructor's Manual are available in the Prentice Hall Custom Test program. Custom Test is available in a Windows format that has been upgraded to work in '95, '98, and NT environments. Professors can view, edit, and add questions to accommodate material not covered in the text, or rely on the random generator to develop chapter by chapter tests.

Prentice Hall Custom Video Library for International Management

Created specifically for International Management, this video library includes five 8- to 10-minute videos featuring such well-known companies as Land's End, Yahoo, MTV Europe/Latin America, Nivea, Sabago Shoes, Rollerblade, Kodak, and the World Bank.

Web Site

This text is supplemented with a companion Web site containing valuable resources such as Internet activities and an interactive study guide. For the latest material, please visit the site often at http://www.prenhall.com/Deresky.

Acknowledgments

The author would like to acknowledge, with thanks, the many people who made this text possible. For the third edition, these people include the following:

Dr. Yohannan T. Abraham, Southwest Missouri State University
Bill Archer, Northern Arizona University
Tope A. Bello, East Carolina University
William R. Boulton, Auburn University
Ralph Catalanello, Northern Illinois University
Ann Clarke-Okah, Carleton University
Anne Cowden, California State University, Sacramento
Darla Domke-Damonte, Florida State University
Derrik D'souza, University of North Texas
Colette A. Frayne, California Polytechnic State University
Robert D. Goddard, Appalachian State University
Tom Hannen, College of Notre Dame
Dr. Asterios Kefalas, University of Georgia
James A. Kuhlman, University of South Carolina
Terry Lituchy, Concordia University
Dr. Robert C. Maddox, The University of Tennessee
Xavier Martin, New York University
Dr. Kamlesh T. Mehta, St. Mary's University
Joseph Peyrefitte, Mississippi State University
George Puia, Indiana State University
Joel Rudin, University of Central Oklahoma
John A. Ruhe, Saint Mary's College, Notre Dame
Scott R. Safranski, Saint Louis University
Paul G. Simmonds, Florida State University
Steve L. Sizoo, Eckerd College
Dr. Anne D. Smith, University of New Mexico
Coral R. Snodgrass, Canisius College
Greg Stephens, Texas Christian University
Dr. Melanie S. Treviño, University of Texas, El Paso
Dan Voich, Florida State University
Marion White, James Madison University
Dr. Anatoly Zhuplev, Loyola Marymount University

—Helen Deresky, June 1999

About the Author

Helen Deresky (Ph.D., Concordia University, Montreal) is Professor of Strategic Management and International Management and Director of the International Business Program at the State University of New York, Plattsburgh. She is a Canadian Studies Associate and a member of the U.S.–Canada Business Council. She is a consultant for the Institute for International Business Education, Research, and Training (IBERT). Professor Deresky was born in England and worked and consulted in various industries in Europe for a number of years before settling in the United States and entering academia. Since then, her research interests have been in strategic implementation and also in management in Latin American countries and in Canada, for which she has developed teaching modules under U.S.D.E. research grants. Professor Deresky has published in various journals, including the *Strategic Management Journal, Organizational Dynamics*, and the *Journal of Business Education,* and has presented papers at numerous conferences in the United States and Canada. She consults for regional universities and colleges wishing to internationalize their curricula. She teaches courses in strategic management, small business management, and international management. She developed this text for her course in comparative and multinational corporation management.

PART 1

Assessing the Environment of International Management

Chapter 1

The Challenge of International Management

Chapter 2

The Political, Economic, Legal, and Technological Environment

Chapter 3

Managing Interdependence: Social Responsibility and Ethics

1

The Challenge of International Management

O U T L I N E

Opening Profile: Motorola Joins the Siemens–Toshiba–IBM Alliance: High-Tech and Cross-Cultural Challenges

Developments in the Global Community

Globalism

Regional Trading Blocs—The TRIAD

Other Regions in the World

Less Developed Countries

Privatization

Information Technology

Workforce Diversity

Technology Application: EU Imposes Cross-Border Electronic Data Privacy

Small Businesses Go International

Multinational Corporations

The Challenge of International Management

The Contingency Role of the International Manager

Management Focus: Citibank Gives Advice on Career Planning

The Future of International Management

Summary of Key Points

Discussion Questions

Application Exercise

Experiential Exercise

Internet Resources

Case Study: GE Brings Good Life to Hungary

OPENING PROFILE

Motorola Joins the Siemens–Toshiba–IBM Alliance: High-Tech and Cross-Cultural Challenges

In the small town of East Fishkill, New York, three competing companies from three continents—Siemens AG of Germany, Toshiba Corporation of Japan, and IBM of the United States—formed a research joint venture that, in 1995, developed a 256-Mbit DRAM on a–0.25-micron process with 26-nanosecond access speed. Since then, Motorola has joined the group, which aims to develop future generations of semiconductor chips. This alliance is cutting edge, both in technology and in the scope of its cross-cultural cooperation. The need to share the astronomical costs of research and development as well as productive facilities is the reason that huge international alliances will become more common in the future.

Clearly, the original three-way venture has been successful. But it wasn't always that easy. Obviously, there is no shortage of high-tech expertise in the transborder research facility. But when you put together more than 100 scientists from competitive, culturally diverse backgrounds to work on such a large project, cross-cultural expertise is essential if you want to make progress. And it is just these human issues and differences in work habits among the three parties that hampered progress early on in this venture. For example, the Japanese—used to working in big groups in large rooms where everyone shares information—felt disoriented when in small, individual offices. Toshiba researcher Toru Watanabe explains that, "For us, very important information exchanges are handled in informal situations—just after finishing lunch, while relaxing and discussing baseball. We say, 'I have a new idea—what do you think?' But here, you have to go to someone's office and say, 'do you have a minute?'" Workspace has been a problem for the Siemens employees also. They were shocked to find that most of their offices in East Fishkill were windowless; no one would be asked to work in a windowless office in Germany. Like the Japanese, they were unused to doors having panes of glass in them, and often hung their coats over the glass, annoying IBMers, who could not then tell, before entering, whether the occupant was busy. Overworked managers in Japan close their eyes to rest during meetings whenever the talk doesn't concern them, a practice very disturbing to the Siemens scientists who were talking.

Matt Wordeman, of IBM, had often worked with people in other countries, and appreciated that diverse groups can be very creative. This time, however, he said, it was different. For this project, entire groups of people came with their own company ties, and were thus able to remain separate, causing distrust among the various groups. IBMers complained that the Germans planned too much and that the Japanese—who like to thoroughly review ideas and gain consensus—didn't make clear decisions.

Wordeman feels this is a major reason why the kinds of creative technical leaps he had hoped for were slow to develop. Although most of those involved now realize that such international alliances require joint training in understanding different approaches to work and team building, at the time this didn't occur. Takaaki Tanaka, a Toshiba human resources expert in New York, said that Toshiba gave its employees the usual round of courses on working and living abroad, but they should have had cooperative training efforts with the human resources people from Siemens and IBM. Siemens did brief employees on what it calls America's hamburger style of management.

American managers, Siemens says, prefer to criticize subordinates gently. They start with small talk: "How's the family?" That is the top of the hamburger bun. Then Americans slip in the meat—the criticism. They exit with encouraging words—more bun. With Germans, all you get is the meat. And with the Japanese, it's all the soft stuff—you have to smell the meat. (*Wall Street Journal*, 1992).

Unfortunately, these kinds of cross-cultural clashes caused people to retreat somewhat into their company groupings, with very little informal interaction across company lines. Mr. Roithner, a German engineer, noticed the differences most of all in the evening. Whereas the American engineers and most of the German engineers are usually gone, he says, "Half the Japanese engineers are in the aisles, talking. You can see that real work is going on—unplanned and informal." While the Germans and Japanese are visitors, the Americans are at home, needing to attend PTA meetings, children's activities, and the like, with the result that, for them, socializing after hours is not so easy.

Sources: "Re-memorying the Gang of Four," *PC Week* 12, November 6, 1995, no. 44: N1(1); R. Krause, "IBM, Toshiba, Siemens Plan New Fabs," *Electronic News* 41, no. 2078, August 1, 1995: 1(2); E. S. Browning, "Computer Chip Project Brings Rivals Together, But the Cultures Clash," *Wall Street Journal*, May 3, 1994; "Talk About Your Dream Team," *Business Week*, July 27, 1992; "IBM, Toshiba, Siemens Form Venture to Develop DRAMs for Next Century," *Wall Street Journal*, July 13, 1992; B. R. Schlender, "How Toshiba Makes Alliances Work," *Fortune*, October 4, 1993; L. H. Young, "Managing a Three-Country Team Project," *Electronic Business Buyer*, May 1994.

The International Manager's Role is being shaped by a Triple Revolution—simultaneous upheavals in politics, technology and economics.

—*Business Week*

As we embark on the 21st century, international managers are challenged by sweeping changes in the global arena. Signs of the democratization of the world—and the resulting many faces of capitalism—are all around them: "Chinese capitalists. Russian entrepreneurs. Thabo Mbecki, President of South Africa."[1]

Add to these transitions sweeping economic fluctuations in an economically interdependent world, and the burgeoning use of computers (a global network now totaling 120 million computers), and a dynamic global business environment emerges. Skilled international managers face a complex business environment—full of opportunities but pitted with risks—in which they can make effective business decisions, improve interpersonal relations, and meet societal obligations. Experienced managers thrive in an international context, intuitively understanding how to gain the cooperation of their foreign partners and workers. But it is not so easy—especially when it comes to cross-cultural differences in expectations, behaviors, and work habits—to forge congenial alliances, as illustrated in the Opening Profile of the alliance among Siemens, Toshiba, IBM, and Motorola.

To compete aggressively in the 21st century, firms must make considerable investments overseas—not only capital investment but also investment in well-trained managers with the skills essential to working effectively in a multicultural environment. In any foreign environment, managers need to handle a set of dynamic and fast-changing variables—political, economic, legal, technological, and ecological. Intertwined with these variables, the all-pervasive variable of culture affects every facet of daily management. Culture, therefore, forms the major focus for the interpersonal aspects of the manager's role discussed in this book.

In many instances, rather than a foreign country, the cross-cultural environment of the "international" manager is a multicultural domestic workforce in the manager's own country, calling for special leadership skills to engender a climate of valuing and utilizing multiculturalism. In fact, the ability to manage workforce diversity in any country is a critical skill necessary for international managers in the 21st century.

This chapter introduces you to international management by providing a brief overview of the multifaceted environment in which international managers operate, the challenges they face, and the roles they play—subjects that are discussed in more detail throughout this book.

International management is the process of developing strategies, designing and operating systems, and working with people around the world to ensure sustained competitive advantage. Executives increasingly recognize the importance of specialized international

Italian, and they are wary of giving up too much power to centralized institutions or of giving up their national culture.[9]

International managers face two major tasks. One is strategic (dealt with more fully in Chapter 7): how firms outside Europe can deal with the implications of the EU and of what some have called a "Fortress Europe," that is, a market giving preference to insiders. The other is cultural: how to deal effectively with multiple sets of national cultures, traditions, and customs within Europe, such as differing attitudes about how much time should be spent on work versus leisure activities.

Asia Japan and the Four Tigers—Singapore, Hong Kong, Taiwan, and South Korea, each of which has abundant natural resources and labor—provide most of the capital and expertise for Asia's developing countries.[10] Economists observe a growing integration of the region, with Japan as a catalyst and a dominant—but welcome—partner.

In the 1980s and early 1990s, much of Asia's economic power and competitive edge was attributed to Japan's *keiretsu* and South Korea's *chaebol*. Both are large conglomerates of financially linked groups of companies that play a significant role in their countries' economies. Japanese keiretsus—Mitsubishi and Toyota, to name two of the most powerful—are regarded in Washington as forms of trade barriers: They do business among themselves whenever possible, adding to the huge bilateral trade imbalance between the United States and Japan.[11] Korea's chaebols—Daewoo, Samsung, Hyundai, and so on—earn billions of dollars of revenue each year. But excessive investment in industries with oversupply contributed to the country's debt crisis. Those chaebols are now having to restructure themselves under pressure from the South Korean government, which is transitioning Korea's major industries to the world open market. Some of the conglomerates are forming mergers among themselves and reshaping entire industries.[12]

As the century draws to a close, however, Japan's economic slide has been partially attributed to the closed system of the keiretsu, including political protection and influence for the keiretsu, and dubious financial backing. Indeed, the long-term benefits of Japan's economic model—long revered around the world—have been called into question.

In all, the economic woes in Southeast Asia have severely slowed the growth in the region and, in fact, have had a ripple effect on the sales and earnings of companies around the world.

North America The goal of the North American Free Trade Agreement (NAFTA) among the United States, Canada, and Mexico was to bring faster growth, more jobs, better working conditions, and a cleaner environment for all as a result of increased exports and trade. This trading bloc—"one America"—has 360 million consumers and has the potential for expansion into countries such as Chile, Brazil, and Argentina as trade liberalization among the Latin American countries progresses.[13]

Reflecting optimism about investment opportunities resulting from NAFTA, foreign companies have invested billions in Mexico since 1988. To take advantage of increased trade, American companies have set up new manufacturing facilities in Mexico or extended their manufacturing and assembly operations in the *maquiladoras*—U.S. manufacturing facilities that have operated just south of the Mexican–American border since the 1960s under special tax concessions. The value added by these border companies to Mexico's total exports topped U.S. $10 billion for 1998. Many Mexican and American companies have set up joint ven-

management skills as the workforce (both in the United States and in many other countries) becomes more diverse, and as the level of investment in international business increases. **International business** refers to profit-related activities conducted across national boundaries.[2] The environment for those business activities within which the international manager functions is shaped by major developments in the world, as outlined in the following section.

Developments in the Global Community

Globalism

Economics, not politics, defines the landscape on which all else must operate.[3]

International competitiveness has now evolved to a level of sophistication that many term **globalism**—global competition characterized by networks that bind countries, institutions, and people in an interdependent global economy. The invisible hand of global competition is being propelled by the phenomenon of an increasingly borderless world. As described by Kenichi Ohmae, "The nation-state itself—that artifact of the eighteenth and nineteenth centuries—has begun to crumble, battered by a pent-up storm of political resentment, ethnic prejudice, tribal hatred, and religious animosity."[4]

As a result of global economic integration, extrapolation of current trends will lead to world exports of goods and services of $11 trillion by the year 2005, or 28 percent of world gross domestic product (GDP).[5] Exhibit 1–1 shows the growth in the volume of world merchandise exports and GDP from 1987 to 1997. As reported by the World Trade Organization

EXHIBIT 1–1

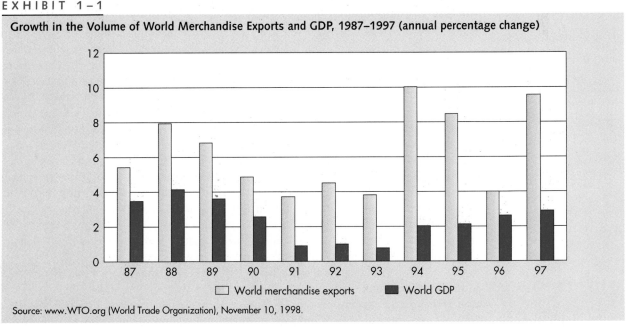

Growth in the Volume of World Merchandise Exports and GDP, 1987–1997 (annual percentage change)

☐ World merchandise exports   ■ World GDP

Source: www.WTO.org (World Trade Organization), November 10, 1998.

8

EXHIBIT 1-2

World Exports of Merchandise and Commercial Services, 1995-1997 (billion dollars and percentage)

	Value U.S. $			Annual % Change		
	1995	1996	1997	1995	1996	1997
Merchandise	4,915	5,125	5,295	20.0	4.0	3.0
Commercial services	1,200	1,270	1,295	15.0	6.0	2.0

Source: www.WTO.org (World Trade Organization), November 10, 1998.

(www.WTO.org), differences in regional output growth rates narrowed in 1997, as economic activity picked up in western Europe and its neighboring transition economies. Note, however, that in Exhibit 1-2, we see that when we state the value of world exports of merchandise ($5,295 billion in 1997) in dollar terms—rather than the volume terms in Exhibit 1-1—the percentage change has gone down. This is because the appreciation of the U.S. dollar vis-à-vis the currencies of major trading nations in western Europe and Asia exerted a strong downward pressure on trade growth rates measured in dollar terms. Thus, although there was an acceleration of world trade growth in real terms in that period, we observe a deceleration in dollar terms. (We discuss more on the effects of currency translations in Chapter 2.) No matter how it is stated, world trade is phenomenal and growing, and is increasingly including the developing nations.

No matter what size, almost all firms around the world are affected to some extent by globalism. They are affected through economic interdependence—as well illustrated by the domino effect on profits and financial markets around the world resulting from financial problems in Asia and Russia in 1997-1998—and by global competition. Firms from any country now compete with your firms both at home and abroad, and domestic competitors are competing on price by outsourcing resources anywhere in the world. It is essential, therefore, for managers to go beyond operating only in their domestic market because if they don't they are already behind the majority of managers who recognize that they must have a global vision for their firms, and that that vision starts with preparing themselves with the skills and tools of managing in a global environment. Companies that desire to remain globally competitive and expand their operations to other countries will have to develop a top management cadre of managers who have experience operating abroad and who understand what it takes to do business in other countries and work with people in and from other cultures.

As another indicator of globalism, foreign direct investment has grown more than three times faster than the world output of goods. The European Union (EU) has now caught up with the United States to share the position of the world's largest investor. Investment by global companies around the world benefits developing economies—through the transfer of financial, technological, and managerial resources, and through the development of local allies, which later become self-sufficient and have other operations.

As for world corporate leadership, as of July 1998, the United States had gained back ground from Japan from previous years. Unfortunately, with Southeast Asian markets in turmoil and Japan's economy continuing to decline, firms in Japan and South Korea were declining considerably in their profitability. European corporations, benefiting from restruc-

turing and mergers and acquisitions as companies positioned themselves for rency (the "euro"), vaulted up the list of the world's largest corporations, ra The 1997 Financial Times 500 Global Companies, ranked by market capita high-tech companies rapidly moving up the list—Intel went from te WorldCom (now MCI–WorldCom) (a communications group) went fr Microsoft has displaced Coca-Cola. Japanese firms such as NTT and Toyo the list, and Japanese banks have been particularly badly hit with the fina region. Those global companies are becoming less and less tied to spe operations and allies are spread around the world, as they source and co activities wherever is most suitable, and as technology allows more flexi

Regional Trading Blocs—The TRIAD

Much of today's world trade takes place within three regional fr Europe, Asia, and North America), called the TRIAD market, groupe inant currencies (the euro, the yen, and the dollar).[7] One researche this new order has had on our perception of national boundaries in

> Today, if you look closely at the world TRIAD companies inhabit, na tively disappeared and, along with them, the economic logic that r demarcation in the first place.[8]

The European Union (EU)

> *We are very conscious about the euro because our main mc*
> *clients that as soon as they are ready, we will be ready [by pri*
> —Willy Lin, Milos Manufacturing, Hong Kong

With 11 of the 15 member states of the European Com rency and monetary policy, the **EU**—a single, borderless Denmark to Portugal—is now a reality. With the **euro** Europe's business environment will be transformed. The v have been adopted to create an internal market with fr among the EU countries. These are the original twelve— Germany, Greece, Ireland, Italy, Luxembourg, Netherl addition, in 1995, of Austria, Finland, and Sweden. N EU leaders have also invited Poland, Hungary, the C Cyprus to begin membership negotiations, and also F Latvia, Bulgaria, Lithuania, and Slovakia. How quickl eastern European economies are brought more in lir the ability of the EU institutions to absorb those cc largest and most integrated common market in the the elimination of internal tariffs and customs, as has not eliminated national pride. Though most F of simply as Europeans, they still think of the

tures, such as the one between Wal-Mart and Cifra, the largest retailers in the United States and Mexico, respectively. The Mexican car industry is expected to double, perhaps triple, by the year 2000. Already known as "Detroit South," the car industry south of the border is taking over more and more factory production for the Big Three carmakers in the United States, taking advantage of lower Mexican wages.[14]

Two-way trade between Mexico and the United States was up more than $12 billion for the first half of 1998. However, the falling peso again threatens trade by making goods produced in the United States more than twice as expensive for Mexican shoppers. In addition, many towns on the U.S.–Mexico border are suffering from traffic gridlock at ports of entry. The infrastructure has not kept up with the increased border traffic as a result of NAFTA. In Canada (the largest trading partner of the United States), Quebec's continued drive for autonomy threatens to fragment economic unity within North America. (Issues surrounding NAFTA are discussed further in Chapter 3.)[15]

Other Regions in the World

Sweeping political, economic, and social changes around the globe present new challenges to international managers. The worldwide move away from Communism, for instance, has had an enormous influence on the world economy; economic freedom is a critical factor in the relative wealth of nations:

> One of the most striking changes today is that almost all nations have suddenly begun to develop decentralized, free-market systems in order to manage a global economy of intense competition, the complexity of high-tech industrialization, and an awakening hunger for freedom.[16]

Central and Eastern Europe   An area greatly affected by these recent developments is the central and eastern European bloc, where Communism proved unworkable and crumbled. World attention is now focused on a new market of 430 million people whose invitingly low wage rates offer investors an unexplored, low-cost manufacturing opportunity. Many impediments remain that will hamper business growth, however, because eastern European countries lack the capitalist structure and systems to reproduce Western management practices easily. As one researcher notes, "Market research is unfamiliar. The closest thing to a market survey that many East Europeans have experienced is a government interrogation."[17] However, growing stability and economic gains in central Europe—Poland, Hungary, and the Czech Republic—are attracting a flood of foreign investment. These include an Opel car plant in southern Poland, expansion by IBM of its disk-drive plant in Hungary, and a new TV plant by Matsushita in the Czech Republic.[18]

The Commonwealth of Independent States (CIS)   Mikhail Gorbachev's goal in the former Soviet Union was to privatize two-thirds of virtually all industry within five years in an attempt to use the capitalist system to save the Soviet Union's failing economy. He named this program *perestroika*.[19] This desperate attempt to move quickly from the crumbling centrally planned economy to a Western free-market economy did produce some results: Fiat offered to buy 30 percent of the VAZ auto works in Togliatti, local investors developed more than 3,000 commercial banks, and new private airlines were formed from the state carrier

Aeroflot. But as economic cures, these limited initiatives did not work fast enough, contributing to the collapse of the entire Soviet state structure and the subsequent formation of the Commonwealth of Independent States (comprising all but two republics that formerly made up the Soviet Union; Georgia and the Baltic states did not join the CIS). Gorbachev's resignation left the republic of Russia, led by Boris Yeltsin, as the dominant power.

Yeltsin's second phase of privatization, in July 1994, began a dramatic restructuring of the Russian economy, as discussed later in this chapter. But as of summer 1998, massive economic problems continued, in spite of continued IMF aid, leading to devaluation of the ruble and Yeltsin's decision to let the ruble float. Steep inflation and political unrest were brewing; liquidity was tight, especially in dollars. Many individuals, businesses, and even government agencies were bartering their goods and services. The planned free-market system remained elusive—caught between state control and robber-baron capitalism.[20]

China   China has enjoyed recent success as an export powerhouse, a status built on its strengths of low costs and a constant flow of capital. Its GDP growth rate, though slowing, was the fastest growth rate in the world for several consecutive years. Reebok, one of many companies around the world that buy from China, "expects costs there to fall as the country develops the ability to provide the raw materials and components that it now imports. Such progress will come slowly, but in the meantime a bowl of rice and $2 a day beat wage rates almost everywhere."[21]

Igniting the expansion has been President Clinton's decision to delink human rights issues (discussed in Chapter 3) from most favored nation (MFN) status—thereby renewing China's MFN status in May 1999. (MFN refers to those favored countries that are allowed to trade with the United States at normal tariff rates; unfavored nations, such as Cuba and Romania, have tariffs of 70 percent or more imposed on many of their products.) As a result, U.S. companies such as Motorola, AT&T, and Chrysler have rapidly expanded their operations in China.[22] Large corporations also bring with them dozens of small companies that provide support for multinationals. Still, the political and commercial risks and the problems of operating in China are great (discussed further in Chapter 2).

Fueling the investment in mainland China and elsewhere in Asia is the tremendous amount of resources and power wielded by the Overseas Chinese—a scattered but tightly bound network of Chinese émigrés living in other parts of Asia and around the world. Acting like an extended family of *guanxi* (personal connections and relationships), their "old-country" culture has brought considerable entrepreneurial venture capital to China. (This topic is discussed in Chapter 9.)

Less Developed Countries

Change in less developed countries (LDCs) has come about more slowly as they struggle with low GNP and low per capita income as well as the burdens of large, relatively unskilled populations and high international debt. Their economic situation and the often unacceptable level of government intervention discourage the foreign investment they need. Many countries in Central and South America, the Middle East, India, and Africa desperately hope to attract foreign investment to stimulate economic growth. For firms willing to take the economic and political risks, there is considerable potential for international business in the

LDCs. Assessing the risk–return tradeoffs and keeping up with political developments in these developing countries are two of the many demands on international managers.

Privatization

The global trend toward privatization—the sale of government-owned operations to private investors—is spreading from western to eastern Europe, and indeed to all corners of the world. This trend comes as world competition escalates and the restraints of socialism are shed in favor of free enterprise.

As discussed earlier, Russia completed its first phase of privatization in mid–1994 after a period of 18 months of trading vouchers for shares in state-owned companies. This phase resulted in 12,000 state companies being transferred to 40 million Russian citizens, and opened the door for foreign investors to buy controlling interests in some industries, such as food, tobacco, and metals.[23, 24] The second phase, started in July 1994, seemed to mark a giant step toward capitalism for Russia by allowing blocks of shares of privatized and remaining state companies to be sold for cash, in the hopes of sparking foreign investment.[25] Unfortunately, to date, privatization has not worked well in Russia because so many companies have not modernized and continue to turn out products that are not competitive in the world market. Russia seems stuck between the old system and the new system, and is falling into a depression.

In Europe, Great Britain continues selling companies, including the entire British rail system. British Gas sold for $7.9 billion, and British Airways sold for $1.4 billion. Spain, France, Italy, and Sweden have also followed the trend toward privatization; however, a recent poll showed that privatization is unpopular in France—only 11 percent of the people want less government control of business.[26, 27]

In eastern Europe, governments, led by Hungary, the Czech Federal Republic, and to a lesser extent, Poland, are having the fire sale of the century. They know they need to privatize industries so as to provide the inflow of capital that will rescue their debt-laden economies after decades of Communist rule.[28] Now, through various incentive schemes, the problems of a country's economic survival are being shifted from the government to new private owners, foreign and domestic. Incentives for foreign companies to invest in Prague businesses, for example, include 100 percent repatriation of profits and two-year tax holidays. Among the larger buyouts that have already occurred are the purchase of Hungary's OZD Steel by Germany's Korf and Metallgesellschaft and, in the car industry, the purchase of the former Czechoslovakia's Skoda and BAZ by Germany's Volkswagen.[29]

The global trend toward capitalism—and the attempts at privatization and deregulation to achieve a capitalist economy even in LDCs—is illustrated by recent developments in various South and Central American countries. In Mexico, the government has privatized some 750 enterprises, including the banking and telephone industries.[30] This type of activity is typical in other Latin American countries:

> In Argentina, the drive is on to privatize state companies; everything from airlines to zoos is on the block. Argentina has already sold off its flag carrier, and its telephone company, and dozens of other assets, including utilities and railways, are up for grabs. Venezuela has sold two banks and is looking for buyers for its telephone company, airline, ports, and even a

Caracas race-course. Brazil, after much delay, has announced plans to float 27 companies. Looking for a cheese factory? Honduras is selling one. Maybe a hotel? Talk to the Bolivian government.[31]

Foreign companies are now welcome in South America as military regimes are being shed, and free-market economics are replacing floundering economic nationalism, state ownership, protectionism, monopolies, subsidies, and price controls as avenues to greater economic growth.[32]

The wave of capitalist sentiment has also spread to Asia. In China, President Jiang Zemin has made state-enterprise reform his priority, though it can hardly be called mass privatization; his plan is to save China's 1,000 largest state enterprises and privatize or dissolve smaller, money-losing ones. His goal is to invigorate Chinese industry so that it can compete in the global economy. As a result, millions of surplus industrial workers will lose their jobs, and those who retain them will no longer receive free lifelong social benefits.[33]

Unfortunately, privatization is not as easy as it sounds. Whether in Pakistan or in Argentina, the problems involved with selling state-owned companies—monsters of inefficiency that have incurred colossal losses over the years—are not easily solved.

Information Technology

From his London office, Richard J. Callahan, the U.S. West International chief,... begins a turbocharged conference call with seven division presidents in five countries. They hash over cellular-phone sales in the Czech Republic, forecast long-distance hookups in Russia, and give a thumbs-up to opening an office in Japan.[34]

Of all the developments propelling international business today, the one that is transforming the international manager's agenda more than any other is **information technology (IT)**. The speed and accuracy of information transmission are changing the nature of the international manager's job by making geographic barriers less relevant. Indeed, the necessity of being able to access IT is being recognized by managers and families around the world, who are giving priority to being "plugged in" over other lifestyle accoutrements. An example is the Hei family of Shanghai (shown in the accompanying photograph), who live in a one-room apartment with no bathroom or cooking facilities. Instead, the family has invested in a PC, cell phone, pager, TV, and VCR. The father runs his printing business with the cell phone; Dan, the son, studies computer science at the university.

Information can no longer be centrally or secretly controlled by governments; political, economic, market, and competitive information is available almost instantly to anyone around the world, permitting informed and accurate decision making. Even cultural barriers are being gradually lowered by the role of information in educating societies about one another. Indeed, as consumers around the world become more aware, through various media, about how people in other countries live, their tastes and preferences begin to converge:

Global brands of colas, blue jeans, athletic shoes and designer ties and handbags are as much on the mind of the taxi driver in Shanghai as they are in the home of the schoolteacher in Stockholm.[35]

The Hei family in Shanghai chooses high-tech conveniences over bathroom and cooking conveniences.

The explosive growth of information technology is both a cause and an effect of globalism. The information revolution is boosting productivity around the world. Such technology also permits managers around the world to hold videoconferences and teleconferences with one another, facilitating instant consultations and decisions and alleviating the necessity for travel. In addition, the use of the Internet is propelling electronic commerce around the world. Internet trade is expected to reach $105 billion by the year 2000. Companies around the world are linked electronically to their employees, customers, distributors, suppliers, and alliance partners in many countries. Technology, in all its forms, gets dispersed around the world by MNCs and their alliance partners in many countries. However, some of the information intended for electronic transmission is currently subject to export controls by a EU directive intended to protect private information about its citizens, as explained in the accompanying Technology Application. So, perhaps IT is not yet "borderless" after all, but rather is subject to the same norms, preferences, and regulations as "human" cross-border interactions.

Workforce Diversity

In many countries around the world, the workforce is becoming increasingly diverse because of the erosion of rigid political boundaries, the rapidity of travel, and the quick spread of information. Propelled by globalism, the world labor force is undergoing considerable change

TECHNOLOGY APPLICATION

EU Imposes Cross-Border Electronic Data Privacy

Most people in the United States have wished for more privacy of personal data; they receive mailings, solicitations, and other information about themselves that make them wonder where that source acquired the personal information. Not so in Europe. In fact, the Europeans are determined that they won't get on any unwanted mailing list from the United States or elsewhere. As of October 25, 1998, when the European Union Directive on Data Protection went into effect, commissioners in Brussels have resolved to prosecute companies and block websites that fail to live up to Europe's standards on data privacy. The directive guarantees European citizens absolute control over data concerning them. A U.S. company wanting personal information must get permission from that person and explain what the information will be used for; the company must also guarantee that the information won't be used for anything else without the person's consent. EU citizens have the right, under this directive, to file suits against a company if they feel it is abusing their private data.

Such protections seem admirable, but free marketers across the ocean are worried about the prospect of Europe being able to regulate the computer databases and the Internet, which are vital to the information economy. They feel that regulations should be agreed upon for a global system. It is a stalemate situation of protection of privacy versus freedom of information,
which is protected by the First Amendment in the United States. At the heart of the standoff is a basic cultural difference: Europeans trust their governments over companies, whereas in the United States, it is the opposite. Already, European inspectors travel to Sioux City, South Dakota, to Citigroup's giant data processing center, where computers store financial information about millions of German credit card holders, to make sure that Citigroup is complying with the privacy data protection law. Citigroup accepted the supervision as a condition to market a credit card in Germany.

U.S. companies are concerned that the EU directive will force them to establish separate data networks for Europe, making it impossible to conduct business as usual with EU member countries. The privacy rules are already having an effect—prohibiting U.S. airlines and hotels, for example, from storing information about their clients that they would normally use to provide better service for them. Third parties to business transactions, such as FedEx delivering a package across the ocean, could also be held responsible. There is considerable concern that the EU directive will imperil the future of electronic commerce.

The question of protection of export of private data is but one of the complexities brought about by the use of technology in international business. For now, on your next trip to Europe, bringing back the contact information that you entered on your laptop computer is illegal!

Source: "Europe's Privacy Cops," *Business Week*, November 2, 1998; "Eurocrats Try to Stop Data at the Border," *Wall Street Journal*, October 30, 1998.

as a result of (1) the increasing movement across borders of workers at all skill levels; (2) the rising average age of employees; and (3) the addition of great numbers of women to the workforce (particularly in developing countries), many with higher levels of education.[36] In the United States, for example, demographic information from the Bureau of Labor Statistics indicates that, in the year 2000, 92 percent of the new entrants to the workforce will be white women or male and female representatives of other racial groups. Minority racial groups—especially Hispanic Americans—and immigrants will already hold 26 percent of U.S. jobs, and white women will hold 47 percent. And by the year 2050 Hispanic Americans will represent 25 percent, and Asian/Pacific Americans 9 percent, of the United States population.

Thus, workforce diversity is becoming a crucial managerial issue. In essence, cross-cultural management worldwide is as much the task of managing multiculturalism at home as it is of managing a workforce in a foreign country. In fact, it often means both: One manages in a foreign environment and, while there, manages a culturally diverse local workforce.

Effective management increasingly depends on the ability to design and implement programs, throughout an organization, that value diversity and pluralism. Such programs enable the organization to enjoy the benefits of multiculturalism, including the possibility of more creativity, innovation, and flexibility; they heighten sensitivity to foreign customers and provide a greater and more varied pool of talent.[37] Valuing diversity, managers are encouraged to explore differences among the company's multicultural personnel and thus to create synergy.[38] Recognizing those benefits, a number of corporations (AT&T, Johnson & Johnson, Xerox) have hired full-time "diversity managers" to make their firms more receptive to and fertile for diverse talents. (Managing a multicultural workforce is covered in Chapter 13.)

Small Businesses Go International

The vast majority (about 98 percent) of businesses in developed economies are small and medium-sized enterprises (**SMEs**), typically referred to as those having fewer than 500 employees. They play a vital role in contributing to their national economies—through employment, new job creation, development of new products and services, and international operations, typically exporting. Though many small businesses are affected by globalism only to the extent that they face competing products from abroad, an increasing number of entrepreneurs are being approached by potential offshore customers, thanks to the burgeoning number of trade shows and federal and state export initiatives. In fact, more than half of U.S. companies with annual revenue under $100 million export their products.[39] Further, one-quarter of all exporting companies employ fewer than 100 people. As small companies expand abroad, international management skills become an important asset to managers other than those in large corporations. The problem is that most small businesses cannot afford to create an international division, and many entrepreneurs are too independent to relinquish power to someone else. But it is very time consuming for an entrepreneur to learn about trade regulations and business practices in other countries, or to travel abroad to hammer out business deals face to face—which is essential in many countries. They are often unable to take the time away from the domestic business and so may turn to export management companies to handle all the details.

For the most part, small businesses are limited by their resources to exporting, but some have tried other strategies. One of these strategies is franchising, which is ideal for small businesses because of the low investment needed in capital and personnel to establish franchise outlets. An example is this author's brother, James Kimber, who started out by owning and operating one hairdressing shop in his hometown of Bexhill, England. His business grew rapidly, first in England and later internationally, as he franchised shops (individually or in groups) in many countries throughout the world—some as far away as Singapore. His Kimber Group became the fourth-largest hairdressing group in the world.

Various types of strategic alliances offer additional ways for a small business with limited resources to internationalize (these strategies are discussed in more detail in Chapters 7 and 8).

Exporting, as we have said, remains the primary means for small businesses to become involved in overseas markets. Small-business exports are rapidly growing; one reason for this is that all kinds of businesses can get involved. One such example is Izabel Lam International; Izabel is an artist who creates silverware based on visions she has when scuba diving. She now sells the silverware worldwide. Lam's early years were fraught with problems in manufacturing and piracy overseas, but she perservered and now designs and sells a wide range of houseware products in all continents—to the tune of $2.5 million in revenues.[40]

Multinational Corporations

Although international business is conducted by organizations both large and small, the bulk of the world's international business is conducted through multinational corporations. In fact, the output of many of these large companies exceeds that of some countries.

A **multinational corporation (MNC)** is a company that engages in production or service activities through its own affiliates in several countries, maintains control over the policies of those affiliates, and manages from a global perspective.[41] An MNC typically derives more than 25 percent of its sales from foreign sources.

Around the world, MNCs are already giants and growing even more gigantic. These big, traditional manufacturing enterprises, with their long planning horizons, are leading the drive toward globalization. Increasingly, too, we are seeing service organizations go global—financial institutions such as Citigroup, retailers such as Wal-Mart, telecommunications companies such as MCI-WorldCom. Leadership in global trends comes from the close involvement of these companies in cross-boundary relationships with suppliers, customers, and venture partners.[42] Conglomerates such as Thailand's Chraroen Pokphand, with revenues of $7.6 billion, have chosen to go global through alliances with foreign players such as Nynex in the telecom market and Wal-Mart in retailing. Some American MNCs (for example, Mobil Oil and Hoover) earn most of their sales outside the United States; Chrysler, IBM, and Coca-Cola earn more than half their profits outside the United States. In addition, many nonprofit organizations—called **multinational enterprises (MNEs)**—such as the Red Cross in Switzerland and the Roman Catholic Church in Italy, operate globally.

Because many MNCs have become complex conglomerates, it is difficult to identify which companies are the parents of which, or which companies own various other companies or properties around the world. Although American MNCs own many foreign firms, a significant number of large American firms are owned by foreign MNCs. Many of these foreign-owned firms have familiar American names, so they are assumed to be American firms—for example, RCA (owned by Thompson SA of France), Green Giant (owned by Grand Metropolitan in England), Vaseline (owned by Unilever, an Anglo–Dutch company), and Tropicana Orange Juice (owned by Canada's Seagram).

Criticism is sometimes levied against the power and role of MNCs around the world, but there is no doubt about the positive influence of the role of globalism and MNCs in bringing about revitalization in developing economies such as in central and eastern Europe. Volkswagen, for example, has decided to drive a pot-holed road in its return to war-torn Sarajevo even though it knows that the usual conditions for investment in a foreign country are still absent. Volkswagen Sarajevo is trying to breathe life back into its operation that ceased in April 1992, as war swept through Bosnia. Before the war, the plant was turning out about 35,000 vehicles a year, as a joint venture with Unis, one of Yugoslavia's industrial con-glomerates. Now VW has taken a 58 percent stake in VW Sarajevo in exchange for prewar debts it was owed by the old joint venture. But the company is starting back up slowly to limit early financial exposure and await redevelopment of the transportation infrastructure, as well as to build markets elsewhere.[43] But in 1999, war in the region again brought risks.

The Challenge of International Management

Whatever the size or nature of a firm, but particularly in the case of MNCs, it is clear that an increasing number of managers are going to deal with international business in the future—both in overseas assignments and in domestic assignments where they have daily interactions with firms in other countries.

In today's business world, you could soon find yourself as an international manager in a foreign subsidiary of a European or American firm, for example, facing on a daily basis all aspects of international management. Or you could end up at the home office coordinating operations with foreign affiliates. Or you could travel to various countries negotiating export sales or negotiating deals with suppliers, customers, or franchise parties. Many different kinds of positions are now available in the global arena, and the importance of experience overseas is becoming a critical ingredient to moving up to high-level positions in global organizations. This aspect of career development is illustrated by the advice offered to potential applicants to Citibank given on their website, as described in the Management Focus "Citibank Gives Advice on Career Planning." Citibank is now part of Citigroup—a global financial and insur-ance institution—since the merger of Citicorp and Travelers Insurance in 1998.

The Contingency Role of the International Manager

Whatever your level of involvement, you need to understand the international business envi-ronment and its influence on the manager's role. International management demands a con-tingency approach to complex and dynamic environments, each of which has its own unique requirements. Those who subscribe to the contingency model, well documented in the man-agement literature, take the view that the choice of an appropriate management system depends on the nature of the people involved, the task, and the environment. Conducting managerial functions effectively is hard enough in a familiar home environment, but doing so in a foreign setting with a unique combination of economic imperatives, traditions, work ethic, and culture is a totally new ballgame for most managers.

Within the larger context of global trends and competition, the rules of the game for the international manager are set by each country (as depicted in Exhibit 1–3): its political and economic agenda, its technological status and level of development, its regulatory environ-ment, its comparative and competitive advantages, and its cultural norms. The astute interna-tional manager will analyze the new environment, anticipate how it may affect the future of the home company, and then develop appropriate strategies and operating styles. As seen in Exhibit 1–3, in the daily operating environment, the manager can then plan and manage operations and people in a way appropriate to specific situational factors, such as local regu-lations and expectations regarding employment and staffing, the availability of skills and technology, norms regarding work output and expectations, and ethical behavior. In other

MANAGEMENT FOCUS

Citibank Gives Advice on Career Planning

Be Mobile: To Get Somewhere, You Have to Go Places!

As Citbank continues to expand globally, there is a growing need for a cadre of professionals with the global perspective to lead the organization. Two-thirds of Citibank's current management team have already had international experience. While living and working in other countries is probably the most direct way to gain a global perspective, there are alternate routes to accomplish this objective. These are well worth exploring if your road to career growth lies over Citibank's global horizons.

A Global Move Is a Good Career Move

Expatriate assignments offer an extraordinary opportunity for experience, learning, and personal and career enrichment. Our goal is to have each expatriate assignment fulfill a business need and to provide each person who accepts an expatriate assignment with professional as well as personal growth opportunities.

Some Career Advantages Offered by an Expatriate Assignment

- Develop a global business outlook and an understanding of how to leverage the bank's global position

- Gain the broader perspective through working in different cultures, geographies, businesses and functions
- Interact with a wide range of customers and work with globally focused managers and colleagues, so you can stretch beyond your current environment and add breadth and depth to your work experience
- Apply your solutions to truly unique problems within different cultures and environments
- Take on new challenges that stretch and develop your skills by requiring you to take educated risks

Other Ways to Gain a Global Perspective

While advantageous for some, international assignments aren't right for everyone. Only you and those close to you can decide if you want to live and work in a different country, and if so, at which point in time. If success on your career path requires international experience and you are unable to take on an international assignment at this time for any reason, there are other ways to gain global exposure. These might include short-term assignments in other locations, jobs that involve cross-border interaction, or a task force made up of a global team.

Source: www.Citibank.com.

words, the role of the international manager involves the same functions as those performed by the domestic manager; however, the nature and performance of those functions will vary according to the unique set of factors in each specific environment.

Our model in Exhibit 1–3 shows the contingency role of the capable international manager whose objective is to perform the managerial functions appropriately within an open system of interacting variables, both in the operating environment and in external environments. This contingency model represents the framework for this book. In the text, Part 1 presents an overview of the major factors in the environment, which interact in a dynamic system and place unique demands and constraints on the manager's role. Part 2 focuses on the cultural context of the manager's role. Part 3 discusses the firm-level decisions the manager must make in planning and implementing strategy for international operations. Part 4 discusses various levels and dimensions of managing human resources around the world.

EXHIBIT 1–3

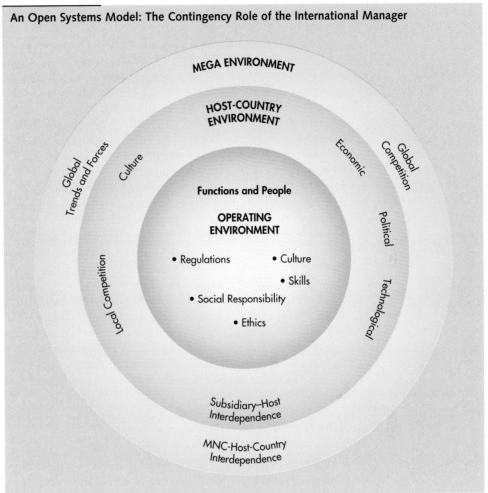

An Open Systems Model: The Contingency Role of the International Manager

MEGA ENVIRONMENT

HOST-COUNTRY ENVIRONMENT

Global Trends and Forces

Culture

Economic

Global Competition

Political

Local Competition

Technological

Functions and People

OPERATING ENVIRONMENT

- Regulations
- Culture
- Skills
- Social Responsibility
- Ethics

Subsidiary–Host Interdependence

MNC-Host-Country Interdependence

The Future of International Management

We cannot predict the future, but some trends are clearly going to continue. One is the mounting pressure on international management to keep pace with the increasing amount of international business and the intensifying competition in the world, both from large trading blocs and from the new developed economies (NDEs). Companies around the world are making serious commitments to meet that competition with considerable international investment.

Another future trend will be the increasingly complex nature of the overall business environment. In a more interdependent world, rapid and unpredictable changes in political, economic, technological, regulatory, and financial variables will provide constant pressures to adapt and to compete. To benefit from future opportunities, astute managers will maintain a global orientation; that is, they will view the world as one giant market where "cooperation and interdependence, not conflict and independence, are prerequisites for survival."[44] Globalization in turn will continue to drive the proliferation of global alliances—more joint ventures, more joint research and development, and more interdependence.

To deal with globalization more effectively, international managers will increasingly organize their corporations into transnational corporations (TNCs). These are MNCs that have truly globalized, viewing the world as one market, operating as a "stateless" corporation, and crossing boundaries to secure functions or resources in the most efficient way. Such corporations produce truly multinational products, as one observer suggests: "A sports car is financed in Japan, designed in Italy, and assembled in Indiana, Mexico and France, using advanced electronic components invented in New Jersey and fabricated in Japan."[45] The term *headquarters* is becoming immaterial; headquarters now cross boundaries whenever expedient, either to sites where operations dictate or to rootless and scattered but integrated networks of information.[46] This latter form of organization—described as "delayered, downsized, and operating through a network of market-sensitive business units"—will have a profound effect on the structure of global business.[47]

As part of this trend, MNCs are becoming entities that exist separately from their originating country and whose success is no longer linked to the economics of that country. An example in the service industry is Citigroup, discussed earlier, which uses global information networks to treat the world as a single market.[48]

Even so, international managers play a powerful role in determining the relative competitiveness of various countries in the global arena. Managers' skills and biases, based on their administrative heritage, will have a subtle influence on strategies and resource allocation.

They will be faced with "more cultures to understand, more social responsibilities to master, more time pressures to juggle, and more relationships to rethink."[49] These pressures are illustrated in this chapter's Case Study, "GE Brings Good Life to Hungary."

Conclusion

Our goal in this book is to bridge the gap from research to practice. We thereby hope to develop your knowledge beyond that of domestic management skills and comparative management theory to the actual practice of effective management in the international, global, and multicultural spheres. To do so, we will study the management of organizational behavior on two levels: (1) the macro, strategic level, which deals with how firms behave in the global arena; and (2) the micro, cross-cultural level, which deals with how managers within those organizations actually do behave and how they should behave on an interpersonal level in international environments. Because "interaction, not merely comparison, is the essence of most managerial action,"[50] we want to examine what happens when people from different nations or cultures work together and how managers can most effectively work with foreign colleagues, clients, and employees.

In the next chapter, we will review factors in the global and host-country environment that set the stage for the kinds of planning and operational decisions you will make as an international manager.

Summary of Key Points

1. Competing in the 21st century requires firms to invest in the increasingly refined managerial skills needed to perform effectively in a multicultural environment. Managers need a global orientation

to meet the challenges of world markets and rapid, fundamental changes in a world of increasing economic interdependence.

2. International management is the process of developing strategies, designing and operating systems, and working with people around the world to ensure sustained competitive advantage.

3. One major direction in world trade is the development of regional free-trade blocs. The TRIAD market refers to the three trade blocs of western Europe, Asia, and North America.

4. New markets and trading opportunities are emerging in eastern Europe (in countries like Hungary and those of the Commonwealth of Independent States), in China, and in less developed countries.

5. Drastic worldwide changes present dynamic challenges to international managers, including the political and economic trend toward the privatization of businesses, rapid advances in information technology, and a growing culturally diverse workforce.

Discussion Questions

1. What is globalism? What has led to this stage of international competitiveness? What are the implications for international management?

2. Explain what is meant by the TRIAD. What will this phenomenon mean to future world trade?

3. What kinds of changes are taking place in eastern Europe, and what are the implications for international management?

4. How is the explosive growth of information technology affecting international management functions?

5. What is the role of small businesses in the global arena? What does this mean for the role of managers? What are the predominant strategies used by small businesses seeking to expand abroad?

6. What are MNCs? What role do they play in world business and in global economic interdependence?

7. What kinds of positions do international managers hold? What kinds of skills and preparation do they need? What factors make their jobs so challenging? What can you do to prepare for a top management position in a global company?

Application Exercise

Research, firsthand or through the library, some companies of any size that have international dealings. What kinds of positions are available? Can you find out what kind of success managers assigned overseas (expatriates) have had? What preparations do the companies offer for international assignments?

Experiential Exercise

In groups of three, choose a country of interest to you. Discuss, list, and present to the class the following:

- Recent developments in that country—and likely future developments—and how they would affect international management
- The kinds of challenges specific to that country that you, as an expatriate manager, would face

Internet Resources

Visit the Deresky companion Web site at http://prenhall.com/Deresky for this chapter's Internet resources.

Case Study

GE Brings Good Life to Hungary

Success sometimes takes time. Hungary (where GE bought Tungsram in 1989) was very difficult. The problem wasn't the people—it was that they didn't understand the market economy. It was

that simple. Today, though, we are a world-class lighting company in Hungary—with at least half of the advanced technology being done there. Patient capital pays off.
—Jack Welch, CEO, General Electric, October 1997[1]

Looking back, the problems seemed overwhelming. The road for George Varga began in 1956, when he fled Hungary to Austria in the midst of the Soviet invasion, leaving his entire family behind. Today, as an American, he is president and chief operating officer of General Electric's joint venture with Tungsram, the top lighting firm in Hungary (see organization charts in Exhibits 1–4 and 1–5). Frequently, Varga wanders through his Hungarian plant, stopping to converse with workers and asking them to *voice* their concerns. This stuns workers accustomed to Communist bosses who expect little more than compliance with company policy. "The mental attitude still disturbs me," says Varga. "Rather than can-do, it's a can't-do attitude.... I wish they would be aggressively positive."[2]

With 40 years of Communism to cut through, Varga's task is not an easy one. Still, breaking into the Hungarian market has distinct advantages. Of all the countries in central and eastern Europe, Hungary is the leader in reforms. The government has offered tax breaks and incentives and has put numerous state-owned companies up for sale—attracting considerable foreign investment. Foreign corporations may purchase up to 100 percent equity in these companies and can appoint foreign managers to run them. When acquiring less than 50 percent in a joint venture, government approval is not needed.

One of these joint ventures took place between the American General Electric Company and Tungsram, a 90-year-old Hungarian company consisting of 12 factories, 3 of which are in the city of Nagykanizsa. Seventy percent of Tungsram's production is exported to hard-currency countries, with products used by corporations as well known as Mercedes-Benz, BMW, and Volvo.[3] Tungsram's workforce is committed, its engineers are talented, and the cost of labor is low. Most important, Tungsram's 7 percent share of western Europe's light bulb market would increase GE's

EXHIBIT 1–4

Tungsram Co. Ltd.—Organization Chart

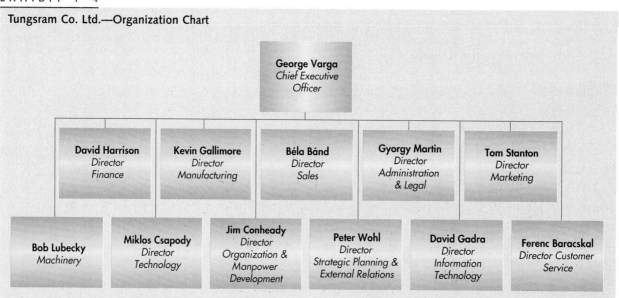

EXHIBIT 1–5

Tungsram Organization and Manpower Development Division

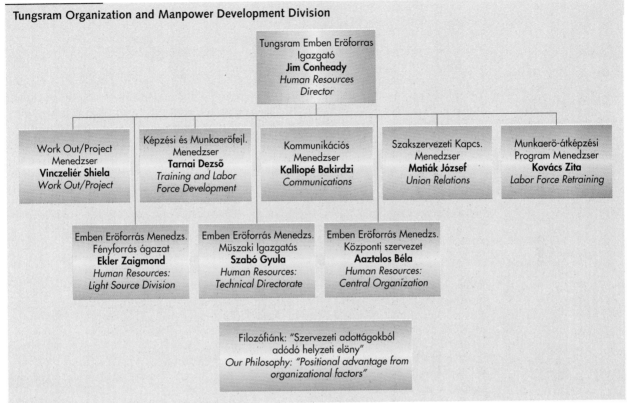

share to almost 10 percent. GE found these benefits attractive and decided to acquire 50.1 percent of Tungsram in November 1989, for $150 million.

GE entered the joint venture with Tungsram with excitement—formulating extensive plans and establishing long- and short-term goals. Among these goals were plans to double Tungsram's advertising budget, decrease the amount of energy used to manufacture its products, and gradually raise prices while increasing the number of high-end products. They also planned on selling or combining several of Tungsram's 12 major plants, thus providing ease in overall management and slashing waste. GE also wanted to conserve capital by increasing production of the components Tungsram purchased from others. Finally, GE's overall goal was to reach a 14 percent market share in western Europe by 1995.

Above all, GE wished to achieve complete technical and cultural integration with Tungsram. Top management proposed creating "twin plants," one in the United States and one in Hungary: namely, the Winchester, Virginia, plant and one of the Nagykanizsa plants.[4] Both plants make incandescent lamps. Employees from Nagykanizsa were to visit the Winchester plant, and vice versa. In this way, if any employee in the Hungarian plant had a problem, he or she could pick up the phone and get help from a coworker in Winchester. The main purpose of this project was to establish personal relationships. Overall, GE wanted to form a strong bond, utilizing the strengths of each corporation without imposing Western philosophies and practices.

The joint venture presented not only many opportunities but a number of problems as well. The Tungsram plants are anything but modern: "One visit to Tungsram by an American production team yielded a list of 112 projects to cut costs and improve efficiency." [5] Tungsram's employees did not know the most basic of capitalist business concepts. In a company with a 40-year history of state ownership, workers are understandably perplexed by the notion of profit. In 1987, taxes took 85 percent of Tungsram's profits to offset economic problems in the government. Even when Tungsram's accountants reported the company's profits, it was clear that their figures were grossly inaccurate. Piles of unpaid bills, inventory reported as sold but found stored in warehouses, and cartons of light bulbs lined with rocks (so that workers could receive bonuses for increasing shipping volumes) accounted for half of what was reported as profits in 1989. [6] Yet another surprise was in store for GE executives when they discovered $3 million worth of unsalable inventory in Tungsram's warehouses in France and Germany.

Operational problems continue to plague GE managers. Methods of conducting business in Tungsram are years behind the times. Accounts are handwritten in ledgers. Payroll envelopes must be hand-filled each week with cash for 17,000 employees because the banking system is not automated. Plans for installing a data system linking all Tungsram's operations have been delayed for more than a year by Hungary's outdated infrastructure. A further complication is the Hungarian bureaucracy—in some areas, Tungsram had as many as 11 layers of management. According to one source, "A purchase order required 24 signatures with a copy going to each person." [7]

On an interpersonal level, GE has had to face the problem of breaking down the autocratic barriers resulting from a centrally planned system. "The most difficult part is the human software," says Varga. [8] Middle managers have no concept of problem solving. They give elaborate speeches about complex problems at daily meetings held by Tungsram but are silent when asked for a solution. One employee discovered that "my [American] boss doesn't want to know everything I'm doing. He tells me, 'If I have to make all your decisions for you, one of us isn't necessary.'" [9] The employees at Tungsram were so used to following instructions in their daily work that it simply was not part of their work culture to come up with their own ideas and to participate in attempts to enhance productivity.

Varga also faced the challenge of cutting the workforce without upsetting the Hungarian labor union. Tungsram and GE each had about 17,000 employees—yet Tungsram had only one-seventh the sales of GE. Annual production in 1989 was worth $2 billion in the United States, compared to $300 million in the Hungarian subsidiary. Varga planned to eliminate 2,000 jobs through normal attrition, but the continuing need to boost employee morale made this difficult.

In the first 18 months, Tungsram was GE's most exciting and significant international venture. In spite of the many obstacles, Tungsram's future looked bright. In 1990, sales rose to about $400 million, up almost one-third from the year before, and GE expanded its equity share to 75 percent. This growth, along with the economic reforms taking place in Hungary, make the venture outlook a positive one.

GE's managers have to move carefully in making the many decisions facing them. After investing $50 million in Tungsram since 1989, they have learned that patience is the most important quality an American manager in Hungary can have. They realize that they must appreciate the Hungarians and their work while gradually introducing Western ideas—a difficult process with workers who have little experience with freedom or responsibility.

The success of the GE–Tungsram joint venture will determine more than the fate of GE in Hungary. It also will influence the decisions that a number of top managers of other American companies will make regarding investment in Hungary. Thus it could very well affect the future of more than 2,000 state-owned Hungarian companies.

In Hungary, said one observer, "Retooling factories is far easier than retooling minds." [10] But if anyone can handle the challenge, Varga can. "Sometimes I feel I spent the past 34 years learning English, going to college, moving ahead at GE, just to prepare for this job," said Varga. [11] Ironically, when Varga climbed through the barbed wire fence separating Austria and Hungary in 1956, he was dodging the rays of Tungsram-made light bulbs.[12]

Tungsram and GE employees have certain characteristics in common. They are talented, proud of their lighting heritage, and confident that by working together they will strengthen and grow in the European and world lighting markets. Tungsram is known to symbolize the merging of "manufacturing tradition with invigorating Western technology and management expertise," a model for joint ventures. The opportunities are limitless.

By April 1992, GE had experienced much less profitability from its joint venture with Tungsram than anticipated and had instituted a number of cost-cutting measures—cutting capital investment by 25 percent and laying off 900 workers across its 11 plants. The problems included inflation in Hungary, an overvalued currency, strong union opposition in reducing the workforce and increasing the production speed, and difficulties in modernizing Tungsram's archaic facilities. Inflation was running at about 35 percent, and the Hungarian government had refused to devalue its currency. Observers note that Western businesses have to exert their own pressure for change because there really isn't a business lobby in Hungary. They note also that the GE–Tungsram joint venture has shown other American businesses some hard truths.

GE's setbacks with Tungsram should dispel any doubts about the difficulty of operating in a country where industry is decades behind the times and government has little experience meeting the needs of free-market enterprises.[13]

In 1993, after a loss of $105 million in 1992, and after 9,000 workers had been laid off, Varga was replaced. As of 1994, GE had boosted its stake in Tungsram to 96.6 percent, giving GE the increased flexibility to manage and invest as they deem necessary. In total, GE has invested $550 million.[14] Market share and profitability increased, and production workers were hired for the first time in 5 years. Getting there meant laying off half of Tungsram's nearly 20,000 workers.[15] The displaced employees were well compensated, well above the Hungarian law. New equipment was also invested to increase productivity by 50 percent. The combination of GE's productivity drive and the scientific resources in Hungary is finally bringing results. As the operation turned profitable and some assembly-line workers were rehired, the question of higher wages loomed. The average hourly wage is $2 for Tungsram workers. Yet, the pay has failed to keep pace with inflation. GE employees may indeed earn wages that are in the top 25 percent in each of the eight plant towns, but in 1993, 36 percent of Tungsram workers lived in families that were on the poverty line.[16] GE continues efforts to build up Tungsram as the cornerstone of its European lighting business.[17]

Case Questions

1. What are the many challenges in starting a joint venture in a former centrally planned nation?
2. What are the advantages to starting a joint venture in Hungary? Do you think GE made the right decision to go ahead with the joint venture?
3. What methods other than creating "twin plants" would you apply to create international teams?
4. What techniques can managers of the joint venture use to encourage employees to improve product quality and express their concerns?
5. What advantages did GE realize in promoting Varga to lead the joint venture in Hungary?

Case Endnotes

1. www.FT.com (*Financial Times*), "Own Words: Jack Welch, General Electric," October 1, 1997.
2. R. Thurow, "Seeing the Light," *Wall Street Journal,* September 20, 1991, R1.
3. F. P. Doyle, "Opportunities for American Business in Hungary," *National Foreign Trade Council,* New York, June 18, 1991.

4. S. Harris, "Dynamo on the Danube," *Monogram* 68, no. 4 (Fall 1990): 18.
5. Thurow, R2.
6. J. Levine, "GE Carves Out a Road East," *Business Week,* August 30, 1990, 32.
7. S. Greenhouse, "Running on Fast-Forward in Budapest," *New York Times,* December 16, 1990, B8.
8. Ibid.
9. Thurow, R2.
10. Thurow, R1.
11. Greenhouse, B8.
12. Thurow, R2.
13. M. L. Johnson, "Business Isn't Easy in Eastern Europe—Just Ask GE," *Investor's Business Daily,* April 7, 1992, 4.
14. G. E. Schares, "GE Gropes for the On-Switch in Hungary," *Business Week,* April 26, 1993, 102–104.
15. J. D. Opie, "GE Succeeded with Hungary Venture," *New York Times,* August 1, 1994, A14.
16. J. Perlez, "GE Finds Tough Going in Hungary," *New York Times,* July 25, 1994, C1.
17. "GE Gropes for the On-Switch in Hungary," *Business Week,* April 26, 1993, 102–103.

Source: Updated by the author from a case written by Chris Buccola and Susan Owens, students at the State University of New York–Plattsburgh, Fall 1991. Copyright ©1993 by Helen Deresky. This case is presented as a basis for class discussion, not to illustrate either effective or ineffective handling of an administrative situation.

2

The Political, Economic, Legal, and Technological Environment

O U T L I N E

Opening Profile: PepsiCo Loses Fizz After Soviet Disintegration

The Political and Economic Environment

Political Risk

Political Risk Assessment

Managing Political Risk

Managing Terrorism Risk

Economic Risk

Technology Application: Multicurrency Translation Software Provides a Global Solution for Lam Research

Comparative Management in Focus: Global Managers Respond to Economic Slide in Indonesia

The Regulatory Environment

Contract Law

Other Regulatory Issues

The Technological Environment

Management Focus: War Declared on Pirating: "The Lion King" Launched in Beijing Before Boston

Summary of Key Points

Discussion Questions

Application Exercises

Experiential Exercise

Internet Resources

Case Study: Conflict in Colombia: The Other Oil War

OPENING PROFILE

PepsiCo Loses Fizz After Soviet Disintegration

When governments deregulate industrial sectors and privatize state entities, corporate managers usually lick their chops. But when entire economic systems collapse overnight, the results can be devastating to companies that have worked out how to operate within that system. That's what happened to PepsiCo Inc. when the Soviet Union collapsed. Almost overnight all the hard-earned skills that the famed retailer of soft drinks, snack foods, and fast-food chains had developed for operating in a centralized command economy counted for nothing. PepsiCo's experiences in the capitalistic world allowed it to recover, but the structures, skills, and careers built up over decades suddenly lost all value and had to be replaced.

PepsiCo's involvement in Russia traces to the famous Kitchen Cabinet debate between Soviet Premier Nikita Kruschev and Richard Nixon, then vice president of the United States. That's when PepsiCo executive Donald Kendall seized the moment to thrust a bottle of Pepsi Cola into the hand of the explosive Russian leader for a famous photo op. Later, as chief executive of PepsiCo, Kendall cultivated ties with Soviet leaders that led to the New York office signing a deal whereby it would provide the Soviet Union with Pepsi concentrate and state-of-the-art bottling technology in return for the inside track to the huge unexploited soft-drink market within the Soviet Empire.

The deal demanded the development of special managerial skills. Pepsi managers based in Vienna supplied the technical skills required to guarantee quality control, covering everything from ensuring that bottle necks were straight to mixing cola concentrate correctly. On the other hand, no marketing or sales staff was required. "We sold everything we could make," says former PepsiCo marketing executive Peter Kendall (no relation to Donald). And if serious situations arose, such as sugar lacking the requisite brix (sweetness) for cola marketing or distribution trucks being diverted to bring in the harvest, Don Kendall had words with his buddies in the Politburo and had the situation cleared up.

SPECIAL SKILLS

The other skill Pepsi developed to a fine art was countertrading. Because the ruble was not convertible, PepsiCo could not get its money out of the country. So it built up credits within the Soviet Union for use in plant expansions and the like, and took Soviet products, most of which were a hard sell in the outside world. These products ranged all the way from Stolichnaya vodka to oceangoing ships. PepsiCo then had to acquire or develop the skills required to find buyers for these products.

PepsiCo never made a great deal of money on its Soviet investments—the dream of quenching the thirst of 350 million thirsty Soviets remained elusive. But it did garner substantial political capital out of showcasing a business deal that could bring East and West together. The Soviet experience also helped Pepsi gain a foothold in another Communist market with even larger potential, namely, China. The skills honed in the Soviet Union generally applied to forging deals with the central and provincial state agencies of the People's Republic. (Although they did not prevent a Chinese joint venture partner from stubbing his political toe by handing out free Pepsi to protesting students in Beijing's Tiananmen Square in 1989.)

What appeared to be finely honed competitive edges were badly dulled when the Soviet Empire dissolved. PepsiCo was seen to be in bed with the discredited former regime. More important, it possessed precisely the wrong skills for a suddenly wide-open market. Managers accustomed to taking two to three years to hammer out deals with centralized stable bureaucracies can't hack it in Russia or eastern Europe these days—not with Western rivals like Coca-Cola pouring in. What's needed are aggressive marketing and sales teams, along with efficient distribution operations. Nor are the financial and negotiating skills employed in counter trade of any benefit; indeed, PepsiCo did not even receive any acclaim from the new regimes for the foreign exchange garnering work performed over all those years.

Whereas Russia is still working out where it wants to go—rendering business difficult for veteran players and newcomers—eastern Europe has established clear new rules that have nothing to do with the old regime's modus operandi. There, Pepsi was once again a novice and burdened with internal organization and focus that no longer made market sense. With no old ways to undo and unlearn, archrival Coca-Cola almost immediately launched a drive for market share. The results were striking. In Hungary, for example, PepsiCo's market share tumbled from 70 to 30 percent almost overnight. A strong counterattack has that share back up to 55 percent, but PepsiCo knows it is in for a serious dogfight to retain reasonable market shares in markets it once owned.

Source: Hugh D. Menzies, "PepsiCo's Soviet Travails," *International Business*, November, 1995, pp. 34–42.

This chapter's Opening Profile illustrates the need for MNCs to be prepared to change their strategies and operations in response to political and economic changes around the world. PepsiCo's situation was rather the opposite of the usual case because the company, used to operating under the old Soviet regime, found itself at a disadvantage when political change led to the need for capitalist techniques. As you read this chapter, consider the many contingencies that astute international managers foresee, plan for, and control—particularly the assessment and management of political and economic risk.

Many interrelated factors—political, economic, legal, technological, and cross-cultural—influence the manager's job and the relative success of the firm's operations in the global arena. The cross-cultural variable is the central focus of this book, whereas the other factors are covered more fully in courses on international economics, international business, international law, and so forth. In this chapter, we will give a brief overview of how these powerful and often interdependent variables play a vital role in the environment in which the manager makes decisions, both strategic and operational.

The Political and Economic Environment

Proactive international firms maintain an up-to-date profile of the political and economic environment of the countries in which they maintain operations (or have plans for future investment). In the early 1990s, the formerly rigid ideological systems of capitalism, communism, and socialism underwent profound changes, and the lines of demarcation between those systems have increasingly blurred. It is now best to measure such systems along a continuum of economic systems—from those that operate primarily according to market forces (such as the United States) to those that use central planning for resource allocation (such as the People's Republic of China). Near the center of the continuum lie the industrialized western European countries and Japan.[1] Less developed countries in Africa, Asia, and Latin America are continuing to develop their market mechanisms and economic systems to improve their economic health.

An important aspect of the political environment is the phenomenon of ethnicity—a driving force behind political instability around the world. In fact, many uprisings and conflicts that are thought to be political are actually expressions of differences among ethnic groupings. Often, religious disputes lie at the heart of those differences. Uprisings based on religion operate both in conjunction with ethnic differences (as probably was the case in the former Yugoslavia) and separate from them (as in Northern Ireland). Many terrorist activities are also based on religious differences, as in the Middle East. Managers must understand the ethnic and religious composition of the host country in order to anticipate problems of general instability as well as those of an operational nature—such as effects on your workforce, on production and access to raw materials, and on your market.[2] For example:

> In Pakistan one must understand the differences between Punjabi and Sindi. In Malaysia it is essential to recognize the special economic relationship between Chinese and Malay. In the Philippines it is important to understand the significant and lead financial role played by the Filipino-Chinese.[3]

Political Risk

> *Increasingly, investors are understanding that projects can be derailed by little "p" political risk ... the death from 1,000 cuts.*[4]

The managers of an international firm need to investigate the political risks to which they expose their company in certain countries—and the implications of those risks for the economic success of the firm. **Political risks** are any governmental action or politically motivated event that could adversely affect the long-run profitability or value of a firm.[5] The Middle East, as we have seen, has traditionally been an unstable area where political risk heavily influences business decisions.

In unstable areas, multinational corporations weigh the risks of nationalization or expropriation. **Nationalization** refers to the forced sale of the MNC's assets to local buyers, with some compensation to the firm, perhaps leaving a minority ownership with the MNC. Nationalization often involves the takeover of an entire industry, as when Middle Eastern countries nationalized foreign oil companies after the OPEC embargo in 1973. **Expropriation**, very rare in the last decade, occurs when the local government seizes the foreign-owned assets of the MNC, providing inadequate compensation; in the case of no compensation, it is called confiscation. In countries that have a proven history of stability and consistency, the political risk to a multinational corporation is relatively low. The risk of expropriation is highest in countries that experience continuous political upheaval, violence, and change, as was the case in Chile in the early 1970s, resulting in the expropriation of many copper-mining companies.

Events that affect all foreign firms doing business in a country or region are called **macro political risk events**. In the Middle East, Iraq's invasion of Kuwait in 1990 abruptly halted all international business with and within both those countries, and caught businesses wholly unprepared. In China, the Tiananmen Square crackdown on student protestors in 1989 interrupted much foreign business in the Far East. After years of increasing international investment in China (the United States had reached the $3-billion mark in direct foreign investment at the time of the crackdown), many companies closed and withdrew their personnel. Concerned about the government's response to student unrest, these businesses were wary about the future.[6]

The political uncertainty and unrest in the newly independent countries of eastern Europe are a prime example of the risk–return tradeoff that companies must assess. In particular, the potential for chaos in the newly formed Commonwealth of Independent States, as it struggles in its transition to a market economy, threatens the remarkable reforms that have transformed the rest of eastern Europe.[7] That risk of chaos has not deterred Japan from setting up bases in eastern Europe to penetrate the European Community market.[8]

In many regions, terrorism poses a severe and random political risk to company personnel and assets, and can, obviously, interrupt the conduct of business. According to Micklous, **terrorism** is "the use, or threat of use, of anxiety-inducing ... violence for ideological or political purposes."[9] The increasing incidence of terrorism, especially in Latin America, concerns MNCs. In particular, the kidnapping of business executives has become quite common, for example, since a guerrilla group in Colombia netted a hefty ransom in 1984 for the return of three engineers employed by Mannesmann Company, a West German contractor. (More details of terrorist activities in Colombia are given in the Case Study at the end of this chapter.)

Those events that affect one industry or company or only a few companies are called **micropolitical risk events**.[10] When Saudi Arabia nationalized its oil industry in 1974, for example, foreign oil companies there were at risk, but other companies in the manufacturing sector remained unaffected. These types of events have become more common than macro-political risk events. Such microaction is often called creeping expropriation, indicating a government's gradual and subtle action against foreign firms.[11] This is when the "death from a 1,000 cuts" comes in—"when you haven't been expropriated, but it takes ten times longer to do anything."[12] Such continuing problems with an investment present more difficulty for foreign firms, typically, than major events that are insurable by political risk insurance agencies. The following list describes seven typical political risk events common today:

1. Expropriation of corporate assets without prompt and adequate compensation
2. Forced sale of equity to host-country nationals, usually at or below depreciated book value
3. Discriminatory treatment against foreign firms in the application of regulations or laws
4. Barriers to repatriation of funds (profits or equity)
5. Loss of technology or other intellectual property (such as patents, trademarks, or trade names)
6. Interference in managerial decision making
7. Dishonesty by government officials, including canceling or altering contractual agreements, extortion demands, and so forth[13]

Political Risk Assessment

International companies must conduct some form of **political risk assessment** to manage their exposure to risk and to minimize financial losses. In the past, few companies saw the need for such assessment; however, since the revolution in Iran, which caused MNCs to lose millions of dollars in assets expropriated by the Khomeini regime, companies have begun to track with much more care the potential relative risk among various countries.[14] Xerox, for example, has established a program, called an Issues Monitoring System, through which it periodically identifies the ten most important political issues in countries where it operates. Local managers in each country assess the potentially destabilizing issues and evaluate their future impact on the company, making suggestions for dealing with possible problems. Xerox then establishes guidelines for each local manager to follow in handling these problems and allocates part of the manager's yearly bonus based on how well the objectives are met. Dow

Chemical also has a program in which it uses line managers trained in political and economic analysis as well as executives in foreign subsidiaries to provide risk analyses of each country.[15]

Risk assessment by multinational corporations usually takes two forms. One is through the use of experts or consultants familiar with the country or region under consideration. For example, Henry Kissinger, former secretary of state under President Nixon and experienced in foreign affairs at the highest levels of government, serves as adviser to the Risk Committee for Foreign Loans for Chase Manhattan Bank.[16] Such consultants, advisers, and committees usually monitor important trends that may portend political change, such as the development of opposition or destabilizing political parties. They then assess the likelihood of political change and develop several plausible scenarios to describe alternative political conditions in the future.[17]

A second and increasingly common means of political risk assessment used by MNCs is the development of their own internal staff and inhouse capabilities. This type of assessment may be accomplished by having staff assigned to foreign subsidiaries or affiliates monitor local political activities or by hiring people with expertise in the political and economic conditions in regions critical to the firm's operations. Frequently, both means are used. The focus must be on monitoring political issues before they become headlines; the ability to minimize the negative effects on the firm—or to be the first to take advantage of opportunities—is greatly reduced once CNN has put out the news.

To monitor political change, for example, large oil companies draw on their overseas divisions for current information, particularly in unstable regions like the Middle East. To assess risk in countries where it operates, Exxon uses its own staff to monitor influential groups—labor unions, politicians, and the military—that might precipitate change.[18]

No matter how sophisticated the methods of political risk assessment become, however, nothing can replace timely information from people on the front line. According to S. J. Kobrin, although "a formal political assessment unit can serve as a focal point that allows full advantage to be taken of multiple information flows, and it can provide the potential for improving patterns of communication,... political assessment is basically a line management function."[19] In other words, sophisticated techniques and consultations are useful as an addition to, but not as a substitute for, the line managers in the foreign subsidiaries, many of whom are host-country nationals. These managers represent the most important resource for current information on the political environment, and how it might affect their firm, because they are uniquely situated at the meeting point of the firm and the host country. Prudent MNCs, however, weigh the subjectivity of these managers' assessments and also realize that similar events will have different effects from one country to another.[20]

An additional technique, the assessment of political risk through the use of computer modeling, is now becoming fairly common. One firm, American Can, uses a program called PRISM (primary risk investment screening matrix). This program digests information from overseas managers and consultants on 200 variables, and reduces them to an index of economic desirability and an index of political and economic stability. Those countries with the most favorable PRISM indices are then considered by American Can for investment.[21] Such a program, of course, is only as good as its input data—which is often of doubtful quality because of inadequate information systems in many countries and because the information is processed subjectively.

To analyze their data on potential risks, some companies attempt to quantify variables into a ranking system for countries. As shown in Exhibit 2–1, they use their staff or outside

EXHIBIT 2–1

Political Risk Assessment—Country X

Subindex	Criteria	Factor Ratings Score Range min.	max.
I.			
Political and economic environment	1. Stability of the political system	3	14
	2. Imminent internal conflicts	0	14
	3. Threats to stability emanating from the outside world	0	12
	4. Degree of control of economic system	5	9
	5. Reliability of the country as a trading partner	4	12
	6. Constitutional guarantees	2	12
	7. Effectiveness of public administration	3	12
	8. Labor relations and social peace	3	15
	Σ	20	100
II.			
Domestic economic conditions	9. Size of population	4	8
	10. Per capita income	2	10
	11. Economic growth during previous five years	2	7
	12. Prospective growth during next three years	3	10
	13. Inflation during previous two years	2	10
	14. Accessibility of domestic capital market to foreigners	3	7
	15. Availability of high-quality local labor	2	8
	16. Possibility of giving employment to foreign nationals	2	8
	17. Availability of energy resources	2	14
	18. Legal requirements concerning environmental protection	4	8
	19. Traffic system and communication channels	2	14
	Σ	28	100
III.			
External economic relations	20. Restrictions imposed on imports	2	10
	21. Restrictions imposed on exports	2	10
	22. Restrictions imposed on foreign investments in the country	3	9
	23. Freedom to set up or engage in partnerships	3	9
	24. Legal protection for brands and products	3	9
III.			
External economic relations	25. Restrictions imposed on monetary transfers	2	8
	26. Revalorizations against the DM during previous five years	2	7
	27. Development of the balance of payments	2	9
	28. Drain on foreign funds through oil and other energy imports	3	14
	29. International financial standing	3	8
	30. Restrictions imposed on the exchange of local money into foreign currencies	2	8
	Σ	27	100
Total Risk Evaluation—Country X:		75	300

Source: E. Dichtl and H. G. Koglmayr, "Country Risk Ratings," Management International Review 26, no. 4 (1986): 6.

consultants to allocate a minimum and a maximum score for criteria they deem important to them (1) on the political and economic environment, (2) on domestic economic conditions, and (3) on external economic relations. The sum of the individual scores for each variable represents a total risk evaluation range for each country.[22] Of course, the relative scores will depend on the type of company, the type of ownership it has in that country, its infrastructure and resource requirements, and so forth. Those scores will also change over time, and so they need to be updated continually in light of new events. Consider, for example, the differences in scores that a company might give to Kuwait now as compared with the early part of 1990.

An actual risk ranking of selected countries for 1997 is shown in Exhibit 2–2 (see pages 36–37).[23] The country risk assessment is a comparative ranking of those countries based on factors such as GDP growth, trade policy, and foreign investment climate—that is, economic, not just political, factors. The comparison is on a scale of 1 to 5, with 5 being the highest ranking, or lowest relative risk. Thus, Russia and Turkey have the most risk in the overall rating of these countries, with Singapore and the Netherlands having relatively low risk.[24]

One drawback of these quantitative systems is that they rely on information based primarily on past events. They are therefore limited in their ability to predict political events in a volatile environment.

Still another method, more rapidly responsive to and predictive of political changes, is called the early-warning system.[25] This system uses lead indicators to predict possible political dangers, such as signs of violence or riots, developing pressure on the MNC to hire more local workers, or pending import–export restrictions.[26] The early-warning analysis is typically separated into macrorisk and microrisk elements.

In addition to assessing the political risk facing a firm, alert managers assess the specific types of impact that such risks may have on the company. For an autonomous international subsidiary, most of the impact from political risks (nationalization, terrorism) will be at the level of the ownership and control of the firm because its acquisition by the host country would provide the state with a fully operational business.[27] For global firms, the primary risks are likely to be from restrictions (on imports, exports, currency, and so forth), with the impact at the level of the firm's transfers (or exchanges) of money, products, or component parts.[28] One study of the relative levels of loss due to sociopolitical causes in the period 1987–1992 concluded that the largest levels of loss were for investments in Czechoslovakia, Yugoslavia, and Saudi Arabia.[29]

Managing Political Risk

After assessing the potential political risk of investing or maintaining current operations in a country, managers face perplexing decisions on managing political risk. On one level, they can decide to suspend their firm's dealings with a certain country at a given point—either by the **avoidance** of investment or by the withdrawal of current investment (that is, by selling or abandoning plants and assets). On another level, if they decide that the risk is relatively low in a particular country or that a high-risk environment is worth the potential returns, they may choose to start (or maintain) operations there and to accommodate that risk through

adaptation to the political regulatory environment. That adaptation can take many forms, each designed to respond to the concerns of a given local area. Some means of adaptation suggested by Taoka and Beeman are given here:

1. *Equity sharing* includes the initiation of joint ventures with nationals (individuals or those in firms, labor unions, or government) to reduce political risks.
2. *Participative management* requires that the firm actively involve nationals, including those in labor organizations or government, in the management of the subsidiary.
3. *Localization of the operation* includes the modification of the subsidiary's name, management style, and so forth, to suit local tastes. Localization seeks to transform the subsidiary from a foreign firm to a national firm.
4. *Development assistance* includes the firm's active involvement in infrastructure development (foreign-exchange generation, local sourcing of materials or parts, management training, technology transfer, securing external debt, and so forth).[30]

In addition to avoidance and adaptation, two other means of risk reduction available to managers are **dependency** and **hedging**. Some means that managers might use to maintain dependency—keeping the subsidiary and the host nation dependent on the parent corporation—are listed here:

1. *Input control* means that the firm maintains control over key inputs, such as raw materials, components, technology, and know-how.
2. *Market control* requires that the firm keep control of the means of distribution (for instance, by only manufacturing components for the parent firm or legally blocking sales outside the host country).
3. *Position control* involves keeping certain key subsidiary management positions in the hands of expatriate or home-office managers.
4. *Staged contribution strategies* mean that the firm plans to increase, in each successive year, the subsidiary's contributions to the host nation (in the form of tax revenues, jobs, infrastructure development, hard-currency generation, and so forth). For this strategy to be most effective, the firm must inform the host nation of these projected contributions as an incentive.[31]

Finally, even if the company cannot diminish or change political risks, it can minimize the losses associated with these events by hedging. Some means of hedging are as follows:

1. *Political risk insurance* is offered by most industrialized countries. In the United States, the Overseas Private Investment Corporation (OPIC) provides coverage for new investments in projects in friendly, less developed countries. Insurance minimizes losses arising from specific risks—such as the inability to repatriate profits, expropriation, nationalization, or confiscation—and from damage as a result of war, terrorism, and so forth.[32] The Foreign Credit Insurance Association (FCIA) also covers political risks caused by war, revolution, currency inconvertibility, and the cancellation of import or export licenses. However, political risk insurance covers only the loss of a firm's assets, not the loss of revenue resulting from expropriation.[33]
2. *Local debt financing* (money borrowed in the host country), where available, helps a firm hedge against being forced out of operation without adequate compensation. In such

EXHIBIT 2–2

Comparative Country Risk Rankings

Country	Overall Rating	Political Risk	GDP Growth	Per Capita Income	Trade Flow with U.S.
Italy	4.13	5	3	5	4
Denmark	4.25	5	3	5	2
Netherlands	4.63	5	3	5	4
Japan	4.19	5	3	5	5
Australia	4.5	5	4	5	4
Ireland	4.38	5	3	5	3
Germany	4.5	5	3	5	5
Sweden	4	5	3	5	3
France	4.38	5	3	5	5
Switzerland	4.5	5	3	5	4
Singapore	4.88	5	5	5	5
Belgium	4.38	5	3	5	4
United Kingdom	4.63	5	3	5	5
Canada	4.38	5	3	4	5
Israel	4	4	4	4	4
Malaysia	3.75	4	4	—	4
Chile	2.88	4	3	—	2
Thailand	3.5	4	4	—	4
South Korea	3.63	4	4	3	5
Spain	3.5	4	3	4	3
Hong Kong	4.5	4	4	5	4
Saudi Arabia	3.38	4	3	2	4
Taiwan	4.13	4	4	4	5
Turkey	2.13	3	—	—	2
South Africa	2.75	3	3	—	2
Argentina	3.25	3	4	3	3
Poland	2.75	3	4	—	2
Indonesia	2.63	3	4	—	3
Philippines	3	3	4	—	4
Costa Rica	2.38	3	3	—	2
Czech Republic	2.75	3	3	—	—
Colombia	3.25	3	4	3	3
India	2.75	3	3	—	3
China	2.88	3	4	—	5
Mexico	3.38	3	3	2	5
Brazil	3	3	4	—	4
Egypt	2.38	2	3	—	2
Venezuela	2.38	2	2	—	4
Peru	2.56	2	4.5	—	2
Russia	2	—	—	2	2

Source: Data from T. Morrison, W. Conaway, J. Douress, Dun & Bradstreet's *Guide to Doing Business Around the World* (Englewood Cliffs, N.J.: Prentice-Hall, 1997).

Country	Monetary Policy	Trade Policy	Protection of Property Rights	Foreign Investment Climate
Italy	4	4	4	4
Denmark	5	4	5	5
Netherlands	5	5	5	5
Japan	5	4	4	2.5
Australia	5	4	5	4
Ireland	5	4	5	5
Germany	5	4	5	4
Sweden	4	4	4	4
France	5	4	5	3
Switzerland	5	4	5	5
Singapore	5	5	4	5
Belgium	5	4	5	4
United Kingdom	5	4	5	5
Canada	5	4	5	4
Israel	3	4	4	5
Malaysia	5	4	4	4
Chile	3	3	3	4
Thailand	5	3	3	4
South Korea	5	3	3	2
Spain	3	4	3	4
Hong Kong	4	5	5	5
Saudi Arabia	5	3	3	3
Taiwan	5	4	4	3
Turkey	—	3	2	4
South Africa	4	3	3	3
Argentina	4	3	3	3
Poland	2	3	3	4
Indonesia	3	2	3	2
Philippines	4	2	4	4
Costa Rica	2	2	3	3
Czech Republic	3	4	3	4
Colombia	4	3	3	3
India	4	2	3	3
China	3	2	2	3
Mexico	4	3	3	4
Brazil	3	3	3	3
Egypt	4	2	2	3
Venezuela	2	2	3	3
Peru	2.5	2.5	3	3
Russia	—	3	3	3

Ranking Scale: 1–5, with 5 = best, or lowest risk.

instances, the firm withholds debt repayment in lieu of sufficient compensation for its business losses.

Multinational corporations also manage political risk through their global strategic choices. Many large companies diversify their operations both by investing in many countries and by operating through joint ventures with a local firm or government or through local licensees. By involving local people, companies, and agencies, firms minimize the risk of negative outcomes due to political events. (We discuss these and other global strategies in Chapter 8.)

Managing Terrorism Risk

Pool Re (U.K. Insurance Mutual) slashes rates by 85% for terrorism risks [in Northern Ireland].

—*Financial Times,* October 1998

Interpreting this quote tells us that the risk premium for companies operating in Northern Ireland was very high before the peace settlement in 1998 if it can now be reduced by 85 percent! How can companies anticipate and discount for this kind of risk in operating in some countries? Can this terrorism risk be "managed"?

As incidents of terrorism accelerate around the world, such as the recent bombings of the U.S. embassies in Tanzania and Kenya, many companies are becoming increasingly aware of the need to manage the risk of terrorism. Both IBM and Exxon try to develop a benevolent image in high-risk countries through charitable contributions to the local community. They also try to maintain low profiles and minimize publicity in the host countries by using discreet corporate signs at the company sites, for instance.[34] Some companies have put together teams to monitor the patterns of terrorism around the world. Kidnappings are common in Latin America (as a means of raising money for political activities). In fact, Mexico has become one of the most dangerous countries in Latin America, with almost a daily occurrence, most involving high kidnappings ransoms. In the Middle East, airplane hijackings, the kidnapping of foreigners, and blackmail (for the release of political prisoners) are common. In western Europe, typically, terrorists aim bombs at U.S. banks and computer companies.[35] Almost all MNCs have stepped up their security measures abroad, hiring consultants in counterterrorism (to train employees to cope with the threat of terrorism) and advising their employees to avoid U.S. airlines when flying overseas.[36]

Economic Risk

In one month, you see your net income wiped out before your eyes.

—John Vondras, U.S. West Manager in Indonesia[37]

Closely connected to a country's political stability is its economic environment—and the relative risk that it may pose to foreign companies. A country's level of economic development generally determines its economic stability and therefore its relative risk to a foreign firm. Most industrialized nations pose little risk of economic instability; less developed nations pose more risk.

A country's ability or intention to meet its financial obligations determines its **economic risk**. The economic risk incurred by a foreign corporation usually falls into one of two main categories; its subsidiary (or other investment) in a specific country may become unprofitable (1) if the government abruptly changes its domestic monetary or fiscal policies or (2) if the government decides to modify its foreign-investment policies. The latter situation would threaten the ability of the company to repatriate its earnings and would create a financial or interest rate risk.[38] Furthermore, the risk of exchange rate volatility results in currency translation exposure to the firm when the balance sheet of the entire corporation is consolidated and may cause a negative cash flow from the foreign subsidiary. Currency translation exposure occurs when the value of one country's currency changes relative to another. For a U.S. company operating in Mexico, for example, the peso devaluation meant that the company's assets in that country were worth less when translated into dollars on the financial statements; on the other hand, the firm's liabilities in Mexico were less also. When exchange rate changes are radical, as with the devaluation of the Russian ruble in 1998, there are repercussions around the world. Not only is it unfortunate for the Russian people whose money suddenly can buy so much less, but it also means that Russian firms do not have enough buying power to buy products from overseas, which means that the sales of foreign companies will go down. On the other hand, foreign companies have more purchasing power in Russia to outsource raw materials, labor, and so on. These days, companies have new tools to assess the impact of currency translation exposure, as detailed in the accompanying Technology Application.

Because every MNC operating overseas exposes itself to some level of economic risk, often affecting its everyday operational profitability, managers constantly reassess the level of risk the company may face in any specific country or region of the world. Four methods of analyzing economic risk, or a country's creditworthiness, are recommended by John Mathis, a

TECHNOLOGY APPLICATION

Multicurrency Translation Software Provides a Global Solution for Lam Research

Lam Research, a leading manufacturer of semiconductor etching equipment, purchased Systems Union's SunSystems software to carry out various currency, financial management, and business functions at its Fremont, California, headquarters and at its offices in Asia and Europe. The software allows Lam Research to automatically consolidate and report in an unlimited number of currencies and charts of accounts for various important activities, such as customer and supplier invoices, bank accounts, fixed assets, inventory, and budgets. The software's multicurrency features can report exposures in any currency and are able to revalue currencies to calculate and post gains and losses by individual currencies. In addition, checks can be paid and invoices raised in a number of currencies and still conform to all international accounting standards, and automatic currency translation in processing these transactions eliminates rekeying data. Furthermore, the software is able to work in the currency of the host nation.

Source: Excerpted from "SunSystems' Multicurrency Software Translates into the Global Solution for Lam Research," *Management Accounting* 79 (September 1997 supp): 8.

professor of international economics who has also served as senior financial policy analyst for the World Bank. These methods are (1) the quantitative approach, (2) the qualitative approach, (3) a combination of both of these approaches, and (4) the checklist approach.

The quantitative method, says Mathis, "attempts to measure statistically a country's ability to honor its debt obligation."[39] This measure is arrived at by assigning different weights to economic variables to produce a composite index used to monitor the country's creditworthiness over time and to make comparisons with other countries. A drawback of this approach is that it does not take into account different stages of development among the countries it compares.

The qualitative approach evaluates a country's economic risk by assessing the competence of its leaders and analyzing the types of policies they are likely to implement. This approach entails a subjective assessment by the researcher in the process of interviewing those leaders and projecting the future direction of the economy.

The checklist approach, explains Mathis, "relies on a few easily measurable and timely criteria believed to reflect or indicate changes in the creditworthiness of the country."[40] Researchers develop various vulnerability indicators that categorize countries in terms of their ability to withstand economic volatility. Most corporations recognize that neither this nor any single approach can provide a comprehensive economic risk profile of a country, and therefore they try to use a combination of approaches.

In 1998, companies around the world were feeling the effects of their exposure to economic risk in Asian countries as their economic decline that began with Thailand in 1997 deepened, and as it appeared that Japan was not taking sufficiently radical steps to turn around its economy. The reverberations, felt around the world in its effects on the earnings of MNCs and on the world's stock markets, reconfirmed for everyone the interdependence of world economies, and clarified the points of interface between world economic issues and business, and indeed that of the individual's welfare. The Comparative Management in Focus section further details this situation.

COMPARATIVE MANAGEMENT IN FOCUS

Global Managers Respond to Economic Slide in Indonesia[41]

As one Asian economy after another appeared to be melting down in 1998, one of the first to fall, and the hardest hit, was Indonesia. The result was devastating for the people in Indonesia since the rupiah lost 75 percent of its value over a period of a few months. Inflation seemed to be out of hand, and there was considerable unrest and rioting. It wasn't long before President Suharto was forced to resign.

Foreign companies operating in Indonesia were also hit hard; their managers struggled with how to respond to the events and how much economic risk to take for the potential long-term rewards of a vast market opening up to foreigners. Japanese and British companies have an even greater investment to date in Indonesia than do American companies, which alone have invested some $9 billion there. Lured by abundant natural resources, companies such as Goodyear Tire & Rubber have long had a presence in Indonesia. Unocal has been there for 30 years and plans to stay. Barry Lane of Unocal notes that, "Major infrastructure projects are so integrated into a country, it's not like we could pack up our bags and leave at any moment." Interdependence of country and foreign investment is further evidenced by

Freeport McMoRan, Inc., which mines copper, gold, and silver in the Irian Jaya province; that region is the company's entire mining resource, and the company is Indonesia's largest corporate taxpayer.

One of the managers caught in the downdraft is U.S. West's top manager in Indonesia, John Vondras, who is in charge of running a 500,000-line telephone system there. His problems were many; as a result of the devaluation of the rupiah, the company was losing a great deal in dollar terms even though the local revenues in rupiahs were up 26 percent. In addition, his joint venture has to repay a $615 million loan in dollars though it earns revenues in rupiahs. "In one month," says Vondras, "you see your net income wiped out before your eyes."[42]

A number of companies, such as a KFC franchise, are in partnership with a member of the Suharto family, often the only entry mode in the past for foreign firms trying to gain a foothold in Indonesia. Other companies, such as General Motors, have been able to get out of this relationship. GM, which has been making cars in Indonesia since 1994, was able to buy out its Indonesian partner, a Suharto half-brother, in 1997. Although the local partner has since gone bankrupt—unable to withstand the Asian economic crisis—GM has been able to keep afloat. Hardship continues, however; in January 1998, GM cars lost two thirds of their dollar value within a few days. GM now makes monthly price revisions in anticipation of currency exchange fluctuations. Other strategies to combat the problem have been to increase the GM cars' local content in order to take advantage of lower local costs. Bill Botwick, president of GM's Indonesian operation, says he is hanging in there for the long run because they expect to have a good market share.

As the IMF pressures the Indonesian government to privatize state-owned companies in the banking, telecommunications, mining, steel, shipbuilding, and aerospace sectors, investment opportunities will become available and help reverse the economic decline. Meanwhile, foreign managers there assess their exposure to continued economic risk compared to the potential long-term market opportunities.

The Regulatory Environment

The prudent international manager consults with legal services, both locally and at her or his headquarters, to comply with host-country regulations and to maintain cooperative long-term relationships in the local area. If the manager waits until a problem arises, little legal recourse may be available outside local interpretation and enforcement. Indeed, this has been the experience of many foreign managers in China, where financial and legal systems remain rudimentary in spite of attempts to show the world a capitalist face. Managers there often simply ignore their debts to foreign companies, as they did under the old socialist system; disregarding their agreements is a way of life in China.[43] The painful lesson to many foreign companies in China is that they are losing millions because Beijing often does not stand behind the commitments of its state-owned enterprises. Although still no guarantee, ways to minimize the risk of massive losses include making sure you get approval from related government offices (national, provincial, and local), making sure you are not going to run amok of long-term government goals, and getting loan guarantees from the headquarters of one of Beijing's main banks.[44] In addition, don't assume there will be legal recourse in China.

Mr. Cheng, an American businessperson who grew up in Hunan, was thrown in jail in China because a Chinese businessman changed his mind about investing in Mr. Cheng's safety-helmet factory in Zhuhai. Only after two months and his son's visit to the U.S. Embassy in Beijing was Mr. Cheng freed. Mr. Cheng asks, "[without even a trial], how could the court render a decision just one hour after Mr. Liu and my general manager had signed a new contract?"[45] Some of the contributing factors, he has realized since then, were the personal connections—*guanxi*—involved, and the fact that some courts offer their services to the business community for profit; in addition, many judges get their jobs through nepotism rather than by virtue of a law degree.

Although the regulatory environment for the international manager consists of the many local laws and the court systems in those countries in which he or she operates, certain other legal issues are covered by international law. International law is the law that governs relationships between sovereign countries, the basic units in the world political system.[46] One such agreement, which regulates international business by spelling out the rights and obligations of the seller and the buyer, is the United Nations Convention on Contracts for the International Sale of Goods (CISG). This convention became law on January 1, 1988, and applies to contracts for the sale of goods between countries that have adopted the convention.

Generally speaking, the manager of the foreign subsidiary or foreign operating division will comply with the host country's legal system. Such systems, derived from common law, civil law, or Islamic law, are a reflection of the country's culture, religion, and traditions. Under **common law**, used in the United States and 26 other countries of English origin or influence, past court decisions act as precedents to the interpretation of the law and to common custom. **Civil law** is based on a comprehensive set of laws organized into a code. Interpretation of these laws is based on reference to codes and statutes. About 70 countries, predominantly in Europe (for example, France and Germany), are ruled by civil law, as is Japan. In Islamic countries, such as Saudi Arabia, the dominant legal system is Islamic law; based on religious beliefs, it dominates all aspects of life. **Islamic law** is followed in approximately 27 countries and combines, in varying degrees, civil, common, and indigenous law.[47]

Contract Law

In China, the old joke goes, a contract is a pause in the negotiation.
—Vanessa Chang, KPMG Peat Marwick[48]

A **contract** is an agreement by the parties concerned to establish a set of rules to govern a business transaction. Contract law plays a major role in international business transactions because of complexities arising from the differences in participating countries' legal systems and because the host government in many developing and Communist countries is often a third party in the contract. Both common-law and civil-law countries enforce contracts although their means of resolving disputes differ. Under civil law, it is assumed that a contract reflects promises that will be enforced without specifying the details in the contract; under common law, the details of promises must be written into the contract to be enforced.[49] Astute international managers recognize that they will have to draft contracts in legal contexts different from their own, and so they prepare themselves accordingly by consulting with experts in international law before going overseas. In China, for example, "The risk is, you could have a contract torn up or changed. We're just going to have to adjust to that in the West," says Robert Broadfoot, who heads the Political & Economic Risk Consultancy in Hong Kong.[50] He says that Western companies think that they can avoid political risk by spelling out every detail in a contract, but "in Asia, there is no shortcut for managing the relationship." In other words, the contract is in the relationship, not on the paper, and the way to ensure the reliability of the agreement is to nurture the relationship.

Even a deal that has been implemented for some time may start to get watered down at a time when you cannot do anything about it. A Japanese-led consortium experienced this problem after it built an expressway in Bangkok. The Thai government later lowered the toll that they had agreed could be charged for use of the road. This is a subtle form of expropriation since a company cannot simply pack up a road and leave.[51] Neglect regarding contract law may leave a firm burdened with an agent who does not perform the expected functions or faced with laws that prevent management from laying off employees (often the case in Belgium, Holland, Germany, Sweden, and elsewhere).[52]

Other Regulatory Issues

Differences in laws and regulations from country to country are numerous and complex. These and other issues in the regulatory environment that concern multinational firms are discussed briefly here.

Countries often impose protectionist policies, such as tariffs, quotas, and other trade restrictions, to give preference to their own products and industries. The Japanese have come under much criticism for protectionism, which they use to limit imports of foreign goods while they continue exporting consumer goods (for example, cars, electronics) on a large scale. The American auto industry continues to ask the U.S. government for protection from Japanese car imports. In fact, as the economic recession dragged on in the early 1990s, Americans began to lay much of the blame on the Japanese and their protectionist policies. In 1992, as General Motors proceeded with its retrenchment strategy of closing down 21 auto plants in North America, those workers who were losing their jobs started a wave of anti-Japanese sentiment. Their anger was fueled by Japanese leaders publicly criticizing American workers and pointing out the inefficiencies of U.S. car manufacturing. Calls to "buy American," however, were thwarted by the difficulty of identifying cars that were truly American-made; the intricate web of car-manufacturing alliances between Japanese and American companies often makes it difficult to distinguish the maker.

A country's tax system influences the attractiveness of investing in that country and affects the relative level of profitability for an MNC. Foreign tax credits, holidays, exemptions, depreciation allowances, and taxation of corporate profits are additional considerations the foreign investor must examine before acting. Many countries have signed tax treaties (or conventions) that define terms such as income, source, and residency, and spell out what constitutes taxable activities.

The level of government involvement in the economic and regulatory environment varies a great deal among countries and has a varying impact on management practices. In Canada, the government has a significant involvement in the economy. It has a powerful role in many industries, including transportation, petrochemicals, fishing, steel, textiles, and building materials—forming partly owned or wholly owned enterprises. Wholly owned businesses are called Crown Corporations (Petro Canada, Ontario Hydro Corporation, Marystown Shipyard, Saskatchewan Telephones, and so forth), many of which are as large as the major private companies. The government's role in the Canadian economy, then, is one of both control and competition.[53] Government policies, subsidies, and regulations directly affect the manager's planning process, as do other major factors in the Canadian legal environment, such as the high proportion of unionized workers (30 percent). In Quebec, the law requiring official bilingualism imposes considerable operating constraints and expenses. For a foreign subsidiary, this regulation forces managers to speak both French and English, and to incur the costs of language training for employees, translators, the administration of bilingual paperwork, and so on.[54]

The Technological Environment

The effects of technology around the world are pervasive—in business and in private lives. In fact, in many parts of the world, whole generations of technological development are being skipped over; for example, many people will go straight to a digital phone without ever having their houses being wired under the analog system. Advances in information technology are bringing about increased productivity—for employees, for companies, and for countries.

Now that we are in a global information society, it is clear that corporations must incorporate into their strategic planning and their everyday operations the accelerating macroenvironmental phenomenon of **technoglobalism**—in which the rapid developments in information and communication technologies (**ICTs**) are propelling globalization and vice versa.[55] Investment-led globalization is leading to global production networks, which result in global diffusion of technology to link parts of the value-added chain in different countries. That chain may comprise parts of the same firm, or it may comprise technology-partnering alliances among two or more firms; either way, technological developments are facilitating, indeed necessitating, the network firm structure that allows flexibility and rapid response to local needs. Clearly there is no ignoring the effects of technology on global trade and business transactions; in addition, the **Internet** is propelling electronic commerce around the world. In fact, the ease of use and pervasiveness of the Internet raises difficult questions about ownership of intellectual property, consumer protection, residence location, taxation, and other issues.[56]

New technology specific to a firm's products represents a key competitive advantage to firms and challenges international businesses to manage the transfer and diffusion of proprietary technology, with its attendant risks. Whether it is a product, a process, or a management technology, an MNC's major concern is the **appropriability of technology**—that is, the ability of the innovating firm to profit from its own technology by protecting it from competitors.[57] This issue of appropriability has led to an ongoing legal clash between Texas Instruments (TI) and Fujitsu. At issue is the original semiconductor "Kilby patent" granted to Texas Instruments in the United States in 1964. Fujitsu's top executive, Hikotary Masunaga, rejects Texas Instruments' patent claims that its semiconductor patent applies to all integrated circuits made, used, or sold in Japan. Despite the use of the semiconductor patent in Japan,

Japanese authorities didn't get around to approving a core part of the patent until October 1989—30 years after the original application—and the patent therefore doesn't expire in Japan until 2001. Fujitsu argues that the new patent covers only specific techniques, now outdated, instead of the broad chip-making concepts.[58] As Schlesinger writes in the *Wall Street Journal,* this legal clash is a typical struggle over the definition and ownership of a technological innovation:

> It's a classic bilateral battle of technological pride. On one side, a struggling U.S. company claims its innovations are responsible for Japanese prowess. On the other, a Japanese behemoth refutes the stereotype of Japanese copycatting, asserting that it has long cut its dependence on U.S. ideas.[59]

The battle is likely to continue for some time, and the outcome will probably affect other companies as well.

An MNC can enjoy many technological benefits from its global operations. Advances resulting from cooperative research and development (R&D) can be transferred among affiliates around the world, and specialized management knowledge can be integrated and shared. However, the risk of technology transfer and pirating is considerable and costly. Although firms face few restrictions on the creation and dissemination of technology in developed countries, less developed countries often impose restrictions on licensing agreements, royalties, and so forth, and have other legal constraints on patent protection.

In Germany, for example, royalties on patents are limited to 10 percent of sales, but the patent and trademark durations are 20 years and 10 years, respectively, with 45 percent the highest tax bracket allowed on royalties. Less developed countries tend to be comparatively more restrictive on the patent and trademark durations and on the range of unpatentable items. Egypt has no limits on royalties, but will patent only production processes, and then only for 15 years.

In most countries, governments use their laws to some extent to control the flow of technology. These controls may be in place for reasons of national security; during the cold war, for example, the United States imposed a trade embargo on transfers of sophisticated microcircuitry to the former Soviet Union because that technology could be used in advanced offensive weapon systems. Other countries, LDCs in particular, use their investment laws to acquire needed technology (usually labor-intensive technology to create jobs), to increase exports, to use local technology, and to train local people.[60]

The most common methods of protecting proprietary technology are the use of patents, trademarks, trade names, copyrights, and trade secrets. Various international conventions do afford some protection in participating countries; more than 80 countries adhere to the International Convention for the Protection of Industrial Property, often referred to as the Paris Union, for the protection of patents. However, restrictions and differences in the rules in some countries not signatory to the Paris Union, as well as industrial espionage, pose continuing problems for firms trying to protect their technology.

One of the risks to a firm's intellectual property is the inappropriate use of the technology by joint venture partners, franchisees, licensees, and employees (especially those who move to other companies). Some countries rigorously enforce employee secrecy agreements. In 1982, the FBI arrested two Hitachi employees who had tried to obtain trade secrets from IBM and

MANAGEMENT FOCUS

War Declared on Pirating: "The Lion King" Launched in Beijing Before Boston

February 4, 1995: Trade war declared by the United States after 20 months of negotiations with China failed to resolve a dispute over the theft of American computer programs, movies, music, and trademarks. The United States threatened to slap over $1 billion worth of import taxes on 35 categories of goods from China. The U.S. movie industry alone has estimated about $1 billion in lost royalties from piracy of their movies. But retaliation was quick, with Chinese officials pledging to raise tariffs 100 percent on many U.S. products, such as video games and compact discs. Tariffs on software products are largely meaningless when they are being pirated and sold for a small fraction of their cost anyway. Although China has strong copyright and patent laws, it doesn't enforce them. The United States has made specific requests such as that China shut down 29 factories that are producing more than 70 million pirated compact discs, laser discs, and CD-ROMs a year. The Tianjin New Star Electronic Company, for example, sold more than 300 Nintendo look-alikes in 1993. New Star's company president is the director of the Chinese Government Ministry of Electronics and Machinery, and the staff is mostly ministry employees; the Ministry receives 20 percent of New Star's profits.

Software piracy is not limited to China—in fact, it is a multimillion-dollar international racket across Taiwan, Singapore, South Korea, Italy, Spain, Mexico, Venezuela, and Saudi Arabia. But at issue is China's lack of protection of the intellectual property rights of American firms—trademarks, copyrights, and patents. A visit to a grocery store there reveals countless American products with the same packaging and design, and little attempt even to change the name, as in the Colgate box—called "Cologate," and Kellogg's well-known rooster trademark, renamed "Kongalu."

February 26, 1995: Officials in Beijing agreed to curb Chinese piracy of intellectual property. Time will tell how well the agreement is implemented. Protection of proprietary technology and intellectual property remains a vital issue in world trade. European and Japanese companies benefited from the U.S. agreement with China without being perceived by China as taking action.

Source: "NBC Nightly News," February 3, 1995; *Associated Press,* February 5, 1995; H. Lincoln, "Huge China Market, a Mirage," *Wall Street Journal,* March 23, 1994; M. Brauchli, "Chinese Flagrantly Copy Trademarks of Foreigners," *Wall Street Journal,* June 20, 1994; "Free Ride in China for America's Pals," *Business Week,* March 13, 1995.

who later pleaded guilty, along with Hitachi, to conspiring to transport stolen IBM property from the United States to Japan. Such incidents led to a crackdown on stolen intellectual property in 1987 by large companies, who are highly dependent on technology. But the pervasive problem of piracy of software, movies, music, and trademarks continues and, in fact, has escalated to a trade war between the United States and China, as described in the Management Focus "War Declared on Pirating: 'The Lion King' Launched in Beijing before Boston."

As another major consideration, international managers will want to evaluate the appropriateness of technology for the local environment—especially in less developed countries. Studying the possible cultural consequences of the transfer of technology, managers must assess whether the local people are ready and willing to change their values, expectations, and behaviors on the job to use new technological methods, whether applied to production, research, marketing, finance, or some other aspect of business. Often, the decision regarding the level of technology transfer is dominated by the host government's regulations or requirements. In some instances, the host country may require that foreign investors import only their most modern machinery and methods so that the local area may benefit from new technology. In other cases, the host country may insist that foreign companies use only labor-intensive processes—this can help reduce high unemployment in the area. When the choice is left to international managers, experts in economic development recommend that managers make an informed choice of appropriate technology; the choice of technology may be capital intensive, labor intensive, or intermediate, but the key is that it should suit the level of development in the area and the needs and expectations of the people who will use it.[61]

As an example of the successful use of appropriate technology, we can point out a small manufacturer of detergent in India called Patel. Patel has taken over three-quarters of the detergent market from Lever, a multinational company whose Surf brand detergent had formerly dominated the market in India. Managers at Patel realized that, although Surf was a high-quality, high-priced product, it was clearly not suitable for a poor country. They set up a chain of stores in which people mixed their own detergent ingredients by hand. This primitive method has enabled Patel to tailor its technology to the conditions and expectations in India and to outsell Lever on the basis of price; its annual sales now exceed $250 million.[62]

Conclusion

In conclusion, a skillful international manager cannot develop a suitable strategic plan or consider an investment abroad without first assessing the environment—political, legal, regulatory, and technological—in which the company will operate. This assessment should result not so much in a comparison of countries as in a comparison of the relative risk and the projected return on investments among these countries. Similarly, for ongoing operations, the subsidiary manager and headquarters management both must continually monitor the environment for potentially unsettling events or undesirable changes that may require the redirection of certain subsidiaries or the entire company. Some of the critical factors affecting the international manager's environment (and therefore requiring monitoring) are listed in Exhibit 2–3.

Clearly, the international manager must assess and manage a number of different kinds of risk in the global environment. When you consider, for example, the effects on MNCs of the Asian economic crisis in the late 1990s, the ability to effectively practice risk management will determine the success of international firms now and in the future:

Environmental risk has become the new frontier in global business. The skills of companies and the measures taken to really manage their exposure to environmental risk on a world scale will soon largely replace their ability to develop, produce and market global brands as the key element in global competitive advantage.[63]

As we shall see, the managerial functions and the daily operations of a firm are also affected by a subtle, but powerful, environmental factor in the host country—that of culture. The pervasive role of culture in international management will be discussed fully in Part 2 and applied throughout the remainder of the text.

In the next chapter, we will assess some more subtle, but critical, factors in the global environment—those of social responsibility and ethical behavior. We will consider such

EXHIBIT 2–3

The Environment of the International Manager

Political Environment	Economic Environment
Form of government	Economic system
Political stability	Stage of development
Foreign policy	Economic stability
State companies	GNP
Role of military	International financial standing
Level of terrorism	Monetary/fiscal policies
Restrictions on imports/exports	Foreign investment
Regulatory Environment	**Technological Environment**
Legal system	Level of technology
Prevailing international laws	Availability of local technical skills
Protectionist laws	Technical requirements of country
Tax laws	Appropriability
Role of contracts	Transfer of technology
Protection for proprietary property	Infrastructure
	Environmental protection

Cultural Environment (see Part 2)

questions as: What is the role of the firm in the future of other societies and their people? What stakeholders do managers need to consider in their strategic and operational decisions in other countries? How do the expectations of firm behavior vary around the world, and should those expectations influence the international manager's decisions? What role does long-term global economic interdependence play in the firm's actions in other countries?

Summary of Key Points

1. International managers must be aware of political risks around the world. Political risks are any governmental actions or politically motivated events that adversely affect the long-run profitability or value of a firm.

2. Political risk assessment by MNCs usually takes two forms: consultation with experts familiar with the area and the development of internal staff capabilities. Political risk can be managed through (1) the avoidance or withdrawal of investment; (2) adaptations to the political regulatory environment; (3) maintaining the host country's dependency on the parent corporation; and (4) hedging potential losses through political risk insurance and local debt financing.

3. Economic risk refers to the ability of a country to meet its financial obligations. The risk is that the government may change its economic policies, thereby making a foreign company unprofitable or unable to repatriate its foreign earnings.

4. The regulatory environment comprises the many different laws and courts of those nations in which a company operates. Most legal systems derive from the common law, civil law, or Islamic law.

5. The appropriability of technology is the ability of the innovating firm to protect its technology from competitors and to obtain economic benefits from that technology. Risks to the appropriability of technology include technology transfer and pirating as well as legal restrictions on the protection of proprietary technology. Intellectual property can be protected through patents, trademarks, trade names, copyrights, and trade secrets.

Discussion Questions

1. Discuss examples of recent macropolitical risk events and the effect they have or might have on a foreign subsidiary. What are micropolitical risk events? Give some examples, and explain how they affect international business.

2. What means can managers use to assess political risk? What do you think is the relative effectiveness of these different methods? At the time you are reading this, what countries or areas do you feel have political risk sufficient to discourage you from doing business there?

3. Can political risk be "managed"? If so, what methods can be used to manage such risk, and how effective are they? Discuss the lengths you would go to manage political risk relative to the kinds of returns you would expect to gain.

4. Discuss the risk of terrorism. What means can managers use to reduce the risk or the effects of terrorism? Where in the world, and from what likely sources, would you anticipate terrorism?

5. Explain what is meant by the economic risk of a nation. Use a specific country as an example. Can economic risk in this country be anticipated? How?

6. Discuss the importance of contracts in international management. What steps must a manager take to ensure a valid and enforceable contract?

7. Discuss the effects of various forms of technology on international business. What role does the Internet play? Where is all this leading us? Explain the meaning of the appropriability of technology. What role does this play in international competitiveness? How can managers protect the proprietary technology of their firms?

Application Exercises

1. Do some further research on the technological environment. What are the recent developments affecting businesses and propelling globalization? What problems have arisen regarding use of the Internet for global business transactions, and how are they being resolved?

2. Consider recent events and the prevailing political and economic conditions in the Commonwealth of Independent States (the former Soviet Union). As a manager who has been considering investment there, how do you assess the political and economic risks at this time? What should be your company's response to this environment?

Experiential Exercise

In groups of three, represent a consulting firm.

You have been hired by a diversified multinational corporation to advise on the political and economic environment in different countries. The company wants to open one or two manufacturing facilities in Europe to take advantage of the EU agreement. Consider a specific type of company and two specific countries in Europe, and present to the class the types of risks that would be involved and what steps the firm could take to manage those risks. Which country do you recommend?

Internet Resources

Visit the Deresky companion Web site at http://prenhall.com/Deresky for this chapter's Internet resources.

Case Study

Conflict in Colombia: The Other Oil War

Colombia is home to numerous multinational corporations that continue to operate in the midst of chaos. These firms contend with the risks of notorious drug cartels, an unstable government, domestic violence, and left-wing insurgents. In the fall of 1998, in fact, Canadian television newscasts and newspapers announced that the CEO of a small Canadian company had turned himself in to a group of kidnappers in Columbia in exchange for one of his managers whom they had held for three months, demanding a ransom. Since he could not come up with the money the kidnappers had demanded, he felt he had no other choice, saying to his manager: "Your shift is up; you can go home now—it's my turn." The kidnappers then raised the ransom money considerably. In early 1999, he was released after the ransom money was raised for him.

Like many developing countries, Colombia traditionally depended on a monocultural economy. Until recently, coffee exports determined the economic prosperity of the country, but coffee plays a lesser role today. Colombia has succeeded in diversifying its exports, and in 1990, oil surpassed coffee as the leading export earner.

In an effort to relinquish the past and to create a more prosperous future, President Cesar Gaviria Trujillo has painstakingly led his country through numerous economic and political reforms. His bold policies came in response to President Bush's Enterprise for the Americas Initiative (EAI). The EAI was intended to create a hemispherewide free-trade zone, from Anchorage to Tierra del Fuego.

Because of its vagueness, the EAI plan has not received much attention and is perceived by some as having unattainable goals. Nevertheless, many Latin American countries are forgoing short-term comforts in hopes of benefiting from new trade policies, debt reduction, and fresh investments. Colombia has surged ahead of other countries in adopting measures to achieve these goals; however, its effort has been stymied by severe internal conflict.

Fierce domestic violence severely undermines Colombia's potential for economic prosperity. The violence within Colombia stems from two entirely different groups with different objectives: drug cartels and left-wing guerrillas. The drug cartels pit the nouveau riche drug barons against the traditional elites and ruling class of Colombia; the left-wing guerrillas have squared off against the government. Despite speculation, there is no evidence that the drug cartels pose any direct threats to MNCs—the new drug barons are simply fighting to gain power and influence, and the old elites are fighting back to preserve their privileges.[1]

The left-wing guerrilla groups, however, do threaten foreign investment. Many MNCs, particularly in the petroleum industry, have become the prime targets of the guerrillas' anti-imperialistic beliefs. Nationalistic sentiment, the driving force behind left-wing guerrilla groups, has led to numerous terrorist acts against foreign oil firms.

Colombia lacks the scientific and technical know-how to properly conduct oil exploration and drilling on its own. In 1948, the government created the state-owned oil company Ecopetrol to oversee continued exploration, foster foreign investment, and obtain a fair share of the profit generated from this valuable resource. Ecopetrol has a monopoly on local production and works directly with MNCs to participate in oil exploration and production.[2] Together, on the average, they pump some 450,000 barrels a day.[3]

Among Latin American countries, Colombia remains a distant third behind Mexico and Venezuela in exporting oil. Historically, Colombia has depended on a number of small oil fields to supply its oil exports. In 1983, however, Occidental Petroleum struck a gusher in what has turned out to be one of the richest deposits in South America. After 40 years of sporadic and marginal results, Colombia uncovered an oil field of significant proportions. The Cano–Limon oil field in the Llanos basin near the Venezuelan border is estimated to contain one billion barrels of recoverable oil. It provides easy-to-drill wells at moderate depths, high production rates, and recoveries that could exceed 50 percent.

Ecopetrol and Its Partners

To maintain exploration and development momentum, Ecopetrol signed a number of association contracts with foreign oil companies in the 1980s, largely to lure foreign investment and to continue exploiting this natural resource. The operator (in Cano–Limon's case, Occidental) assumes all the risks and costs of exploration. Ecopetrol holds 50 percent interest in the Cano–Limon production; Occidental and Royal Dutch/Shell each hold 25 percent.[4]

Guerrilla Activity

Unfortunately, standing between Colombia and an oil bonanza are two battle-hardened guerrilla groups bent on sabotaging the nation's economy—at any cost. Colombia's foremost left-wing guerrilla groups, the FARC (Revolutionary Armed Forces of Colombia) and the ELN (National Liberation Army), are particularly active in the Cano–Limon region. Both groups have been responsible for an incredible number of terrorist actions against petroleum-related MNCs operating in the region since 1985. Bombings and kidnappings are among the most common means of violence against foreign investment. Because Cano–Limon is the largest and most productive oil field now operating in Colombia, Occidental bears the brunt of these terrorist acts. Since its start-up, the company's oleoduct has been bombed at least 125 times, spilling 630,000 barrels and resulting in $500 million in damages and lost oil production.[5] In addition to pipelines, insurgents have destroyed a variety of petroleum-related machinery. Despite heavy security, Occidental's gleaming headquarters in Bogotá was severely damaged by an explosion in 1987.[6]

One of the first instances of terrorist action occurred during the construction of the Cano–Limon–Covenas pipeline in 1984. An engineer and two assistants from Mannesmann (the West German contractor) were kidnapped and ransomed for a hefty fee. Guerrilla groups thus discovered that kidnapping can be quite profitable, encouraging a rash of such acts.[7] The sabotage efforts of the ELN to blow up oil pipelines brought exports to a standstill in November of 1992. The ELN had acted in response to the increased government efforts to patrol oil facilities with the help of counterguerrilla units. In 1992, according to Colombia tallies, the oil pipeline bombings by Marxist guerrillas cost Ecopetrol more than $50 million.[8] More than 80,000 barrels of oil were lost due to 27 terrorist explosions on the Cano–Limon–Covenas pipeline. The bombing of the Cano–Limon–Covenas oil pipeline continued into 1994. It was bombed 39 times in 1993 and five times as of January 24, 1994. In the past nine years, leftist guerrilla squads have dynamited oil pipelines 346 times, spilling slightly more than 1.2 million barrels of crude oil.[9]

Rationale and Concerns of the Insurgents

Evidence to date does not prove that the FARC and the ELN traditionally collaborate in achieving their goals. More recently, however, they have cooperated in waging economic and ecological war on the MNCs in the name of a common goal—nationalism. They feel that Colombia's resources are being exploited by the MNCs and would rather see these resources destroyed than in "enemy hands." *Elenos* (as the guerrillas are commonly called) oppose foreign investments in developing their natural resources of coal and oil. They also do not like the government granting concessions to foreign oil companies, in particular to Occidental.[10] Guerrilla demands include (1) the renegotiation of the association contracts between Ecopetrol and the MNCs (in Colombia's favor) and (2) the return of tax revenue that they allege the MNCs have kept.[11]

In contrast, other guerrilla groups have publicly admitted that they realize Colombia's position. They understand that Colombia does not yet possess the know-how to develop its resources on its own and must seek outside help. Thus they do not entirely oppose foreign participation in the development of their resources but protest the limited portion of the profits that Colombia currently receives.

Response of the MNCs

A decade ago, pacifying the guerrillas simply meant furnishing them with food, medical supplies, consumer goods, and even prostitutes—but times have changed. Guerrillas have found it more profitable to request money from the MNCs to ensure the safe passage of their personnel and goods. The MNCs have capitulated to their demands and have provided protection money to maintain the status quo.[12]

Armand Hammer, the late founder of Occidental Petroleum, once publicly admitted that guerrilla payoffs in Colombia were a normal way of doing business. More recently, the Colombian government has accused Occidental of making payoffs, but the company has denied such allegations. Occidental does admit, however, that it has responded to guerrilla requests for the construction of roads, schools, and hospitals.[13]

Although there is no actual proof of wrongdoing, Ecopetrol's president claims that it is a "recognized fact" that Mannesmann gave in too quickly to guerrilla demands. In an effort to finish the pipeline, Mannesmann paid a hefty $9.8 million for the release of its personnel.[14] The elenos now boast a war chest of $50 million obtained through "war taxes" paid by oil companies and through ransoms for victims of kidnapping. Paying off the guerrillas provides only a short-term solution, however; it allows the MNCs to conduct business, but it also undermines the Colombian government's efforts to solve the problem.

The most dramatic and long-term effects of insurgent-related sabotage are not economic but ecological. In 1987, the seventh World Conference on Oil Spills called Colombia one of the worst offenders in the world, and the situation has only deteriorated since then.[15] The amount of oil spilled in Colombia since 1985 is three times that spilled by the notorious *Exxon Valdez* in Alaska. Guerrilla activity has cost Ecopetrol and its partners more than $723 million in cleanup expenses. One example is the recent attack on a pipeline in northern Colombia resulting in spillage into the river Ite. Also, on August 23, 1991, a 19,000-barrel spill into the Cataumbo River was caused by yet another bombing of the Cano–Limon–Covenas crude pipeline.[16] A study by the Colombian Environment Minister in 1991 found that guerrilla pipeline bombings polluted 375 miles of creeks and rivers and fouled 12,500 acres, ranging from tropical wetlands to Andean watersheds.[17] Sabotage has caused many MNCs to debate whether future ventures in Colombia are worth the price.[18]

Outlook for the MNCs

A significant recent oil find in the Casanare region may double the country's known reserves and spark a renewed oil bonanza.[19]

Insurers have cut back drastically on the amount of coverage they will provide to the MNCs operating in Colombia, viewing the risks there as "predictable" rather than "fortuitous." Their decision is a result of the shift in guerrilla demands over the past decade—from material goods to cash. Insurers cite the Mannesmann case as the turning point in guerrilla demands.[20]

The guerrillas now have a voice in government, but the violence has continued. The two insurgent groups have further complicated matters by forming one body—the CNG (National Guerrilla Coordinating Body). Through this body, the guerrillas have become more efficient in their actions, further straining the MNCs' operations in Colombia. Colombia rebels welcomed plans for peace talks between the Colombian Revolutionary Armed Forces and the government.[21] One of four guerrilla groups at war with the government, the Socialist Renewal Movement (CRS), recently accepted terms for its disarmament and reintegration into civilian society.[22]

Case Questions

1. Do you think Occidental was proactive or reactive when it decided to develop the Cano–Limon oil field? Give reasons for your choice.
2. Do you believe Occidental and Royal Dutch/Shell are responsible for the ecological damage done to Colombia?
3. Should foreign oil companies operating in Colombia play a significant part in future peace talks with the FARC and the ELN?
4. Because the role of MNCs is becoming increasingly important in the developing nations of the world, should they adopt certain guidelines or policies specifically to deal with terrorists?

Case Endnotes

1. "Colombia Cracks Up," *NACLA Report on the Americas* 23, no. 6 (April 1990).
2. J. P. Riva, "Exploration: A Look at the Status of Petroleum in Colombia," *Oil and Gas Journal,* December 18, 1989.
3. J. de Cordoba, "Guerrillas' Oil Pipeline Bombing Clouds Colombia's Quest for Foreign Investment," *Wall Street Journal,* January 9, 1991.
4. Riva.
5. Occidental Petroleum Co., 1986 Annual Report.
6. Cordoba.
7. Ibid.
8. "Colombia Tallies Bomb Costs," *The Oil Daily,* 43, no. 164 (August 26, 1993): 5.
9. J. Brooke, "Colombia Oil Spills Net Fines for All but Rebels," *New York Times,* March 6, 1995.
10. M. Weiskopf, "Terrorism in Colombia: The Other Oil War," *Wall Street Journal,* February 22, 1991.
11. Cordoba.
12. "Is Terror Risk No Longer Insurable?" *Latin American Weekly Report,* August 15, 1991.
13. Cordoba.
14. "Terror Risk."
15. J. Brooke, "Colombia Rebels Turn to Ecological Terrorism," *New York Times,* October 29, 1991.
16. "Colombia," *Oil and Gas Journal,* September 9, 1991.
17. Brooke.
18. Ibid.
19. A. Oppenheimer, "Colombia Spells Relief O-I-L," *Manchester Herald,* July 5, 1991.
20. "Terror Risk."
21. S. Ambrus, "Colombia Rebels Welcome Plan for Peace Talks," *Los Angeles Times,* November 16, 1994, A1.
22. "Colombia: Rebel Group Accepts Peace Terms," *Facts on File, April 21, 1994.*

Source: Updated and adapted by the author from a term project written by Peter Mitchell, student at the State University of New York–Plattsburgh, 1991. Copyright ©1993 by Helen Deresky.

3

Managing Interdependence: Social Responsibility and Ethics

O U T L I N E

Opening Profile: The Tobacco Industry's Social Responsibility in Developing Countries

The Social Responsibility of MNCs

MNC Responsibility Toward Human Rights

Management Focus: Levi Takes a Stand for Human Rights

Comparative Management in Focus: A New Day Dawns for MNCs in South Africa

Codes of Conduct

Ethics in International Management

Questionable Payments

Comparative Management in Focus: Ethics in Europe

Managing Interdependence

Foreign Subsidiaries in the United States

Managing Subsidiary–Host Country Interdependence

Comparative Management in Focus: Interdependence: The NAFTA—Perspectives from the South and the North

Technology Application: High-Tech Jobs Boost Maquiladora-Ville

Managing Environmental Interdependence

Summary of Key Points

Discussion Questions

Application Exercise

Experiential Exercise

Internet Resources

Case Study: Balancing Human Rights Around the World: Nike and Reebok

OPENING PROFILE

The Tobacco Industry's Social Responsibility in Developing Countries

Few developing countries require health warnings on cigarette packages, compared to 95 percent of developed countries. Should tobacco MNCs put warnings on the packages anyway? Should those companies even be promoting cigarettes (and tobacco growing) in LDCs?

Cigarette production and consumption are increasing faster in LDCs than in developed countries, and the primary marketing targets are women and young people. In addition, cigarettes in developing countries usually contain more tar and other harmful chemicals than those in developed nations. Family health and nutrition are doubly affected because the large proportion of a typical household income that pays for cigarettes is then not available for food.

Similarly, should land be used for growing tobacco rather than food? Many believe that tobacco endangers both the health of the people and the economies in developing countries. The tobacco industry, however, argues that (1) tobacco cultivation in LDCs grants higher returns than the cultivation of alternative cash or food crops, (2) 100 million people worldwide depend on tobacco for their livelihood, and (3) people in developing countries have been growing and smoking tobacco for centuries. In addition, exports to LDCs represent an important opportunity for American tobacco companies.

Newton and Ford offer a succinct summary of the ethical dilemma facing tobacco companies:

> Granted that it will help our balance of trade to purvey tobacco to the world, and granted that tobacco has its dangers, perhaps potentially deadly dangers, ought we to sell it? It is not a sufficient answer to cite the long and respectable history of tobacco use, sale and export in our defense. People have been using tobacco for hundreds of years in some places, of course, including smoking cigarettes for the last century and more. But dealing in tobacco now is different: now we know that smoking tobacco can contribute to people's deaths, and that changes the moral picture completely.

> At present, we are selling and promoting American cigarettes abroad; we are encouraging farmers in developing economies to grow tobacco, and sending agronomists to teach them how to do it. There seems to be no problem with receptivity: farmers enjoy growing a high-income crop; governments enjoy the taxes collected on cigarette sales and on the income from the tobacco crops; and the tobacco customers of the developing countries, a large and growing population, enjoy having available to them higher quality products than their indigenous industry could provide. But is this right? Do we have some responsibility to put an end to the trade in human health and disease—no matter how profitable it may be? ...

> What weight should be given to human freedom—the autonomy of the farmers and smokers of LDCs—and what weight should be given to human welfare and to our obligation not to harm our customers? In general, what is the responsibility of the business person in this dilemma? To serve his or her customers, and wait upon the law to make decisions protecting them from harm? Or to take a proactive stance, actively arranging business dealings to do the least harm, and promote the most good, for those affected by those dealings?

This chapter will ask you to consider such issues regarding the social responsibility, ethical behavior, and interdependence of those involved in international business activities.

Source: E. Foote, "Advertising and Tobacco," *Journal of the American Medical Association* 245 (April 1981): 1668; S. Taylor, "Tobacco and Economic Growth in Developing Nations," *Business in the Contemporary World* (Winter 1989); Tobacco industry representatives, "Letters to the Editor: The Tobacco Controversy," *Business in the Contemporary World* (Winter 1989); and L. H. Newton and W. W. Ford, *Taking Sides: Clashing Views on Controversial Issues in Business Ethics and Society* (Guilford, CT: Dushkin, 1990): 297.

G lobal interdependence is a compelling dimension of the global business environment, creating demands on international managers to take a positive stance on issues of social responsibility and ethical behavior, economic development in host countries, and ecological protection around the world.

Managers today are usually quite sensitive to issues of social responsibility and ethical behavior because of pressures from the public, from interest groups, from legal and governmental concerns, and from media coverage. It is less clear where to draw the line between socially responsible behavior and the corporation's other concerns, or between the conflicting expectations of ethical behavior among different countries. In the domestic arena, managers are faced with numerous ethical complexities. In the international arena, such concerns are compounded by the larger numbers of stakeholders involved, including customers, communities, and owners in various countries.

Our discussion will focus separately on issues of social responsibility and ethical behavior, but there is considerable overlap between them. The difference is a matter of scope and degree. Whereas ethics deals with decisions and interactions on an individual level, decisions about social responsibility are broader in scope, tend to be made at a higher level, affect more people, and reflect a general stance taken by a company or a number of decision makers.

The Social Responsibility of MNCs

Multinational corporations have been and—to a lesser extent—continue to be at the center of debate regarding social responsibility, particularly the benefits versus harm wrought by their operations around the world, especially in less developed countries. The criticisms of MNCs have lessened in recent years owing to the decreasing economic differences among countries, by the emergence of LDC multinationals, and by the greater emphasis on social responsibility by MNCs. However, concerns still remain about the exploitation of LDCs, fueled by such incidents as the Union Carbide gas leak in Bhopal, India, in December 1984, which killed 2,500 people and injured more than 200,000 others. Such incidents raise questions about the use of hazardous technology in developing economies.

Issues of social responsibility continue to center on the poverty and lack of equal opportunity around the world, the environment, consumer concerns, and employees' safety and welfare. Many argue that, since MNCs operate in a global context, they should use their capital, skills, and power to play a proactive role in handling worldwide social and economic problems and that, at the least, they should be concerned with host-country welfare. Others argue that MNCs already have a positive impact on LDCs by providing managerial training, investment capital, and new technology, as well as by creating jobs and improving the infrastructure. Certainly, multinational corporations (now often called transnational corporations, or TNCs) constitute a powerful presence in the world economy and often have a greater capacity than local governments to induce change. The sales, debts, and resources of the largest multinationals exceed the gross national product, the public and private debt, and the resources, respectively, of some nations.[1]

The concept of international social responsibility includes the expectation that MNCs concern themselves with the social and economic effects of their decisions. The issue is how far that concern should go and what level of planning and control that concern should take.

Such dilemmas are common for MNC managers. Del Monte managers, for example, realize that growing pineapples in the rich coastal lands of Kenya brings mixed results there. Although badly needed foreign exchange earnings are generated for Kenya, there are adverse effects for poor Kenyans living in the region because less land is available for subsistence agriculture to support them.[2]

Opinions on the level of social responsibility that a domestic firm should demonstrate range from one extreme—the only responsibility of a business is to make a profit, within the confines of the law, in order to produce goods and services and serve its shareholders' interests[3]—to another extreme—companies should anticipate and try to solve problems in society. In between these extremes are varying positions described as socially reactive, in which companies respond, to some degree of currently prevailing social expectations, to the environmental and social costs of their actions.[4] Carroll's classic model illustrates the relationships among the social issues involved, the categories of social responsibilities, and the four levels of the philosophy of reaction, or responsiveness: reaction, defense, accommodation, and proaction.[5] Carroll's model is shown in Exhibit 3–1. The levels of philosophy (proaction, accommodation, and so on), at the top, correspond to the levels of social responsibility on the side in the same order as shown (from top to bottom). Thus, usually a company with a proactive philosophy will put in the extra effort to fulfill discretionary responsibilities, whereas a company with a defensive philosophy will not be concerned beyond its legal

EXHIBIT 3–1

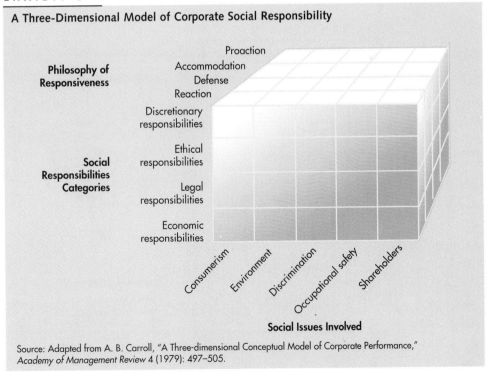

A Three-Dimensional Model of Corporate Social Responsibility

Source: Adapted from A. B. Carroll, "A Three-dimensional Conceptual Model of Corporate Performance," *Academy of Management Review* 4 (1979): 497–505.

responsibilities. In applying those dimensions to the typical social issues facing a corporation, the model suggests that a company with a defensive philosophy toward the social issue of discrimination typically only meets its legal responsibilities as they are brought to bear by outside forces, as compared with a company with a proactive philosophy, which would meet its ethical and discretionary responsibilities by setting up positive programs to value diversity in the company. For example, the Denny's chain of restaurants in the United States was forced by lawsuits in 1997–98 to diversify its management structure, whereas a more proactive stance would have called for that change to be made much earlier, perhaps as the growing diversity of its clientele was noted.

The stance toward social responsibility that a firm should take in its international operations, however, is much more complex—ranging perhaps from assuming some responsibility for economic development in a subsidiary's host country to taking an active role in identifying and solving world problems. The increased complexity regarding social responsibility and ethical behavior of firms across borders is brought about by the additional stakeholders in the firm's activities through operating overseas. As illustrated in Exhibit 3–2, managers are faced with not only considering stakeholders in the host country, but also with weighing their rights against the rights of their domestic stakeholders. Most managerial decisions will have a tradeoff of the rights of these stakeholders—at least in the short term. For example, a decision to discontinue the use of children in Pakistan to sew soccer balls means the company will pay more for adult employees, and therefore reduce the profitability to its owners. That same decision—though taking a stand for human rights according to the social and ethical expec-

EXHIBIT 3–2

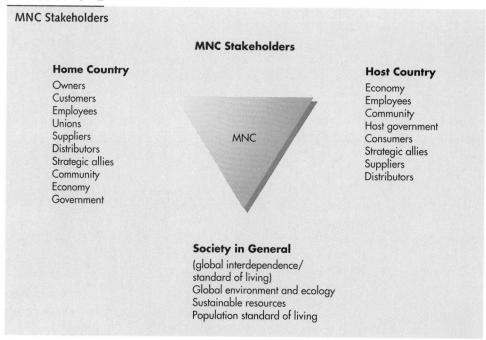

MNC Stakeholders

MNC Stakeholders

Home Country
Owners
Customers
Employees
Unions
Suppliers
Distributors
Strategic allies
Community
Economy
Government

MNC

Host Country
Economy
Employees
Community
Host government
Consumers
Strategic allies
Suppliers
Distributors

Society in General
(global interdependence/
standard of living)
Global environment and ecology
Sustainable resources
Population standard of living

tations in the home country, and bowing to consumers' demands—may mean that those children and their families go hungry or are forced into worse working situations. Another decision to keep jobs at home to satisfy local employees and unions will mean higher prices for consumers and less profit for stakeholders; in addition, if competitors take their jobs to cheaper overseas factories, then a company may go out of business, which will mean no jobs at all for the domestic employees and a loss for the owners.

With the growing awareness of the world's socioeconomic interdependence, global organizations are beginning to recognize the need to reach a consensus on what should constitute moral and ethical behavior. Some think that such consensus is emerging because of the development of a global corporate culture—an integration of the business environments in which firms currently operate.[6] This integration results from the gradual dissolution of traditional boundaries and from the many intricate interconnections among MNCs, internationally linked securities markets, and communication networks.[7]

Although it is very difficult to implement a generalized code of morality and ethics in individual countries, such guidelines do provide a basis of judgment regarding specific situations. Bowie uses the term *moral universalism* to address the need for a moral standard that is accepted by all cultures.[8] He says that this approach to doing business across cultures is far preferable to other approaches, such as **ethnocentrism** or **ethical relativism**. With an ethnocentric approach, a company applies the morality used in its home country—regardless of the host country's system of ethics.

A company subscribing to ethical relativism, on the other hand, simply adopts the local moral code in whatever country it is operating. With this approach, companies run into value conflicts, such as continuing to do business in China despite home-country objections to China's continued violation of human rights. In addition, public pressure in the home country often forces the MNC to act in accordance with ethnocentric value systems anyway. In one instance, public outcry in the United States and most of the world resulted in major companies (IBM, General Motors, Coca-Cola, and Eastman Kodak) either selling or discontinuing their operations in South Africa during the 1980s to protest that country's apartheid policies.

In another instance, a seven-year boycott of Nestlé's baby products and a United Nations code on selling baby formula in LDCs pressured Nestlé to change its marketing strategy for Similac baby formula in 1981. Nestlé had promoted Similac in LDCs as a replacement for breast milk, giving out free samples of the baby formula without proper instructions for preparing it. Public outcry arose over the massive number of infant deaths that resulted primarily from the lack of information about sterilizing the bottles and the water to mix with the formula and from the lack of facilities to do so. In addition, poverty-stricken mothers resorted to overdiluting the formula or not buying any more when the samples ran out; meanwhile, they found that their own breast milk had stopped flowing from lack of use.[9]

More recently, the FDA has been pressuring U.S. manufacturers of silicone-filled breast implants (prohibited in the United States for cosmetic surgery because of health hazards) to adopt a voluntary moratorium on exports. Although Dow Corning has ceased its foreign sales—citing its responsibility to apply the same standards internationally as it does domestically—the other three major manufacturers continue to export the implants, often from their factories in other countries.

The difficulty, even in adopting a stance of moral universalism, is in deciding where to draw the line—which kinds of conflicts of values, asks Wicks, are "conversation stoppers" or "cooperation enders"? Individual managers must at some point decide, based on their own morality, when they feel a situation is simply not right and withdraw their involvement:

> There are practical limitations on our ability to act in the modern world,... but a systematic infringement of basic personal rights is generally grounds for ending cooperation. Less blatant violations, or practices which are not abhorrent to our basic values, are treated as items which are negotiable.[10]

MNC Responsibility Toward Human Rights

Whereas many situations regarding the morality of the MNC's presence or activities in a country are quite clear, other situations are not, especially when dealing with human rights. The role of MNCs in pulling out of South Africa in the 1980s as part of the movement against apartheid has now played out, and many cautiously return to the now multiracial democracy: This is discussed in the next Comparative Management in Focus section. In many other areas of the world, the question of what role MNCs should play regarding human rights is at the forefront.[11] So loud has been the cry about products coming from so-called sweatshops around the world that President Clinton established an Anti-Sweatshop Code of Conduct, which includes a ban on forced labor, abuse, and discrimination and requires companies to provide a healthy and safe work environment and to pay at least the prevailing local minimum wage, among other requirements. A group has been named to monitor compliance; enforcement is difficult, of course, but publicity helps! The Department of Labor publishes the names of companies that comply with the code, including Nike, Reebok, Liz Claiborne, Wal-Mart, and Phillips-Van Heusen.[12] Those companies can be identified on the department's home page website (http://www.gov./nosweat.htm).

What constitutes "human rights" is clouded by the perceptions and priorities of people in different countries. Even though the United States often takes the lead in the charge against what it considers human rights violations around the world, other countries point to the homelessness and high crime statistics in the United States. Often the discussion of human rights centers on Asia because many of the products in the West are imported from there by Western companies using manufacturing facilities located there.[13] It is commonly held in the West that the best chance to gain some ground on human rights issues is for large MNCs and governments around the world to take a unified stance; many global players now question the morality of trading for goods that have been produced by forced labor or child labor.[14] Though laws in the United States ban prison imports, shady deals between the manufacturers and companies acting as intermediaries make it difficult to determine the origin of many products—and make it easy for companies wanting access to cheap products or materials to ignore the law. However, under pressure from their labor unions (and, perhaps, their conscience), a number of large image-conscious companies have established corporate codes of conduct for their buyers, suppliers, and contractors and have instituted strict procedures for auditing their imports.[15] Nike, for instance, now spot-checks all its company-owned factories, and Reebok has audited all its suppliers in Asia (see the end-of-chapter case study). Levi Strauss has gone a step further. After sending teams of investigators around the world, Levi announced a new company policy: "We should not initiate or renew contractual relationships in countries where there are pervasive violations of basic human rights."[16] The Management Focus section "Levi Takes a Stand for Human Rights" offers more insight into Levi's practices.

MANAGEMENT FOCUS

Levi Takes a Stand for Human Rights

Levi Strauss & Co., the world's largest supplier of brand-name apparel, has been exporting jeans and jobs around the world for years, but recently it also decided to export human rights.

During the 1980s, Levi paid little attention to working conditions at its contract factories—until 1991, in fact, when it was informed that a contractor on the island of Saipan was keeping imported Chinese women in conditions of near slavery. The contractor was working them 11 hours a day for 7 days a week, paying them below the local minimum wage. Levi terminated that contract. Following that, the company—which exports about 50 percent of its jeans and shirts overseas—decided to investigate its 400 foreign contractors in 1992: Levi found that about 25 percent of them were treating their workers badly, and child labor was being used in places such as Bangladesh. After that, Levi adopted strict guidelines for its foreign contractors, such as:

- Suppliers must provide safe and healthy conditions that meet Levi's standards.
- Suppliers must pay workers no less than prevailing local wages.
- Company inspectors will make surprise visits to contractors to ensure compliance.

Levi was the first MNC to impose such guidelines, covering the treatment of workers and the environmental impact of production, on its contractors abroad. The company backed up its new stance with threats to cancel contracts with violators. The company inspectors, such as Im Choong Hoe, travel around Southeast Asia to Levi's contracted factories, from Indonesia to Bangladesh—not examining the quality of the products, but looking for health and safety hazards and any abuses of worker rights. But Im Choong Hoe and other inspectors try to work with contractors to improve the situation rather than to impose hardship among the workers. For example, when Im Choong found that one of Levi's contractors in Bangladesh employed children, Levi decided to pay the children while they attended school on the factory site until age 14, rather than insist that the contractor fire them and bring hardship to their families.

In 1993, Levi withdrew its contracts in China and Burma, citing pervasive violation of human rights and continuing labor inequities. Of course, Levi was also concerned with its image in the eyes of its customers. Levi Strauss knew that its brand and reputation would suffer and that customers would not want to buy a shirt made by children in Bangladesh or by forced labor in China. Robert Haas, chairman and CEO of Levi, notes that he has found that decisions focusing only on cost factors don't best serve the long-term interests of the company or its shareholders. Benefits that he feels have accrued from Levi's values-driven approach include improved loyalty, trust, and retention among its employees, business partners, suppliers, and customers, as well as more credibility among leaders in new markets.

Source: F. Gibney, "The Trouble with China," *Newsweek,* May 17, 1993; B. Dumaine, "Exporting Jobs and Ethics," *Fortune,* October 5, 1992; G. P. Zachary, "Levi Tries to Make Sure Contract Plants in Asia Treat Workers Well," *Wall Street Journal,* July 28, 1994; R. D. Haas, "Ethics in the Trenches," *Across the Board* (May 1994): 12–13.

COMPARATIVE MANAGEMENT IN FOCUS

A New Day Dawns for MNCs in South Africa

I am concerned that political apartheid is not replaced with economic apartheid.
—The Rev. Leon Sullivan, South Africa[17]

Those [foreign companies] that stayed connected, win.... Those that didn't, play catch-up.[18]
—*Business Week,* June 1995

During the 1980s, many MNCs (IBM, GM, Coca-Cola, for example) decided to sell or discontinue their operations in South Africa under pressure to take a stand in opposing the government's apartheid policies. This pressure was brought about by the huge lobbying efforts of groups (many of them grassroot groups) in the United States for disinvestment—mainly by pension funds. Such disinvestment and international outcry were the major causal factors leading to the dissolution of apartheid. Pressure from the inside had been exerted by the Reverend Sullivan, author of the Sullivan Principles, which gave guidelines regarding equal employment, pay, training, supervisory positions, conditions, and so forth for blacks, and discussed how to eliminate laws and customs that impeded justice. However, it soon became clear that these principles were insufficient to bring about real change, and the Reverend Sullivan recommended that U.S. firms disinvest.

Later, as president of South Africa, Nelson Mandela encouraged foreign investment to help job creation and economic stability, after decades of discouraging that investment in order to hasten the demise of apartheid. South Africa is the most advanced and productive economy in Africa and has a rapidly expanding economy and modern infrastructure. Foreign investors are allowed to have 100 percent ownership.

The African National Congress (ANC)—now the country's ruling party—is switching from socialist to free-market policies and privatizing state-owned industries such as transportation, electricity, and telecommunications.[19]

Some investors, such as South Korea's Samsung Corp., remain concerned about political instability and potential violence, and are adopting a wait-and-see attitude. Others, such as H. J. Heinz Co., plunged right back in. Heinz's CEO Anthony O'Reilly said that "many people will wait too long and it will be regrettable if they do."[20] PepsiCo Inc. and a group of private U.S. investors returned to South Africa nine years after selling its last bottling operations there in response to international economic sanctions. Its joint venture is run by a team of five South African executives, three of whom are black, and it involves local people in a process of ownership and management. But Pepsi is facing difficulties getting bottling and distribution going again, whereas Coca-Cola, which maintained its presence in South Africa through independent bottlers, now has 75 percent of the market. It is the same story with other companies that disconnected from South Africa—Apple, AT&T, McDonald's—they seem to be fighting a losing battle against competitors that maintained a presence or connection, such as IBM, Ingersolle Rand, and Ford.[21] Of course, because those companies may feel they are at a disadvantage does not mean that they did not do "the right thing" as a global corporation in establishing their integrity for the long term and in gaining respect for their companies around the world.

While investors hesitate and consider the risks of operating in South Africa, the Reverend Sullivan wants a new code of social responsibility for returning American companies. His desire is that American companies concern themselves with their responsibility to protect equal rights, promote education, and provide job training. But South African officials are afraid that such a code of conduct will act as a disincentive to invest and will put American companies at a disadvantage with respect to foreign companies. As Mr. Mthembu of the ANC said, "We will have our own laws protecting the employee. We want business to act in a socially responsible manner. But it is not desirable to put this as a code of conduct."[22] The activities of some MNCs seem to support that confidence. Federal Express, for example, signed with South Africa's XPS Services to ship its packages, and negotiated a contractual agreement that XPS have a ratio of half black managers and half white managers; and

Microsoft contracted South Africa's WorkGroup Systems to distribute its software and train South Africans at its headquarters in Redmond, Washington.[23]

The long-term effects of the different decisions by MNCs regarding their presence in South Africa in the 1980s remains to be seen, but the problem of how to deal with those kinds of dilemmas regarding social responsibility provides a classic example for students of international management.

Although it is not entirely clear which action was most socially responsible in fighting apartheid, it is clear that MNCs in South Africa could not evade an ethical choice of how best to exercise their leverage against apartheid. Those that left thought that by doing so they were taking a stand against apartheid, or at least that they were escaping criticism and future problems. Those firms that chose to stay thought that they could help most by bettering the lot of black people, providing jobs and working with them to fight apartheid in a more positive way. Many, of course, also thought that this was the best economic decision for the company. Those MNCs that stayed often did what they could by following the Sullivan Principles. Others said that the firms that disinvested hurt the very people they were trying to help by removing jobs and training programs for blacks and terminating programs for their social advancement. In any event, the challenge of the 2000s for MNCs in South Africa is to help the people of that country move forward equally to economic stability, while enhancing corporate profitability and global presence.

Codes of Conduct

A considerable number of organizations have developed their own codes of conduct; some have gone further, joining with others around the world to establish standards to improve the quality of life for workers. Companies such as Avon, Sainsbury Plc., Toys 'R' Us, and Otto Versand have joined with the Council on Economic Priorities (CEP) to establish SA8000 (Social Accountability 8000, on the lines of the manufacturing quality standard ISO9000). Their proposed global labor standards would be monitored by outside organizations to certify that plants are meeting those standards, among which are the following:

- Do not use child or forced labor
- Provide a safe working environment
- Respect workers' rights to unionize
- Do not regularly require more than 48-hour work weeks
- Pay wages sufficient to meet workers' basic needs[24]

Moreover, there are four international codes of conduct that provide some consistent guidelines for multinational enterprises (MNEs). These codes were developed by the International Chamber of Commerce, the Organization for Economic Cooperation and Development, the International Labor Organization, and the United Nations Commission on Transnational Corporations. Getz has integrated these four codes and organized their common underlying principles, thereby establishing MNE behavior toward governments, publics, and people, as shown in Exhibit 3–3 (the originating institutions are in parentheses). She concludes, "As international organizations and institutions (including MNEs themselves)

EXHIBIT 3-3

International Codes of Conduct for MNEs

MNE and Host Governments

Economic and developmental policies

- MNEs should consult with governmental authorities and national employers' and workers' organizations to assure that their investments conform to the economic and social development policies of the host country. (ICC; OECD; ILO; UN/CTC)
- MNEs shouid not adversely disturb the balance-of-payments or currency exchange rates of the countries in which they operate. They should try, in consultation with the government, to resolve balance-of-payments and exchange rate difficulties when possible. (ICC; OECD; UN/CTC)
- MNEs should cooperate with governmental policies regarding local equity participation. (ICC; UN/CTC)
- MNEs should not dominate the capital markets of the countries in which they operate. (ICC; UN/CTC)
- MNEs should provide to host government authorities the information necessary for correctly assessing taxes to be paid. (ICC; OECD)
- MNEs should not engage in transfer pricing policies that modify the tax base on which their entities are assessed. (OECD; UN/CTC)
- MNEs should give preference to local sources for components and raw materials if prices and quality are competitive. (ICC; ILO)
- MNEs should reinvest some profits in the countries in which they operate. (ICC)

Laws and regulations

- MNEs are subject to the laws, regulations, and jurisdiction of the countries in which they operate. (ICC; OECD; UN/CTC)
- MNEs should respect the right of every country to exercise control over its natural resources, and to regulate the activities of entities operating within its territory. (ICC; OECD; UN/CTC)
- MNEs should use appropriate international dispute settlement mechanisms, including arbitration, to resolve conflicts with the governments of the countries in which they operate. (ICC; OECD)
- MNEs should not request the intervention of their home governments in disputes with host governments. (UN/CTC)
- MNEs should resolve disputes arising from expropriation by host governments under the domestic law of the host country. (UN/CTC)

Political involvement

- MNEs should refrain from improper or illegal involvement in local political activities. (OECD, UN/CTC)
- MNEs should not pay bribes or render improper benefits to any public servant. (OECD, UN/CTC)
- MNEs should not interfere in intergovernmental relations. (UN/CTC)

MNEs and the Public

Technology transfer

- MNEs should cooperate with governmental authorities in assessing the impact of transfers of technology to developing countries, and should enhance the technological capacities of developing countries. (OECD; UN/CTC)
- MNEs should develop and adapt technologies to the needs and characteristics of the countries in which they operate. (ICC; OECD; ILO)
- MNEs should conduct research and development activities in developing countries, using local resources and personnel to the greatest extent possible. (ICC; UN/CTC)
- When granting licenses for the use of industrial property rights, MNEs should do so on reasonable terms and conditions. (ICC; OECD)
- MNEs should not require payment for the use of technologies of no real value to the enterprise. (ICC)

Environmental protection

- MNEs should respect the laws and regulations concerning environmental protection of the countries in which they operate. (OECD; UN/CTC)
- MNEs should cooperate with host governments and with international organizations in the development of national and international environmental protection standards. (ICC; UN/CTC)
- MNEs should supply to appropriate host governmental authorities, information concerning the environmental impact of the products and processes of their entities. (ICC; UN/CTC)

MNEs and Persons

Consumer protection

- MNEs should respect the laws and regulations of the countries in which they operate with regard to consumer protection. (OECD; UN/CTC)
- MNEs should preserve the safety and health of consumers by disclosure of appropriate information, proper labeling, and accurate advertising. (UN/CTC)

Employment practices

- MNEs should cooperate with host governments' efforts to create employment opportunities in particular localities. (ICC)
- MNEs should support representative employers' organizations. (ICC; ILO)
- MNEs should try to increase employment opportunities and standards in the countries in which they operate. (ILO)
- MNEs should provide stable employment for their employees. (ILO)

EXHIBIT 3–3

International Codes of Conduct for MNEs (Continued)

- MNEs should establish nondiscriminatory employment policies, and promote equal employment opportunities. (OECD; ILO)
- MNEs should give priority to the employment and promotion of nationals of the countries in which they operate. (ILO)
- MNEs should assure that adequate training is provided to all employees. (ILO)
- MNEs should contribute to the managerial and technical training of nationals of the countries in which they operate, and should employ qualified nationals in managerial and professional capacities. (ICC, OECD, UN/CTC)
- MNEs should respect the right of employees to organize for the purpose of collective bargaining. (OECD; ILO)
- MNEs should provide workers' representatives with information necessary to assist in the development of collective agreements. (OECD; ILO)
- MNEs should consult with workers' representatives in all matters directly affecting the interests of labor. (ICC)
- MNEs, in the context of negotiations with workers' representatives, should not threaten to transfer the operating unit to another country. (OECD; ILO)

- MNEs should give advance notice of plant closures, and mitigate the resultant adverse effects. (ICC; OECD; ILO)
- MNEs should cooperate with governments in providing income protection for workers whose employment has been terminated. (ILO)
- MNEs should provide standards of employment equal to or better than those of comparable employers in the countries in which they operate. (ICC; OECD; ILO)
- MNEs should pay, at minimum, basic living wages. (ILO)
- MNEs should maintain the highest standards of safety and health, and should provide adequate information about work-related health hazards. (ILO)

Human rights
- MNEs should respect human rights and fundamental freedoms in the countries in which they operate. (UN/CTC)
- MNEs should not discriminate on the basis of race, color, sex, religion, language, social, national and ethnic origin, or political or other opinion. (UN/CTC)
- MNEs should respect the social and cultural objectives, values, and traditions of the countries in which they operate. (UN/CTC)

International agency sources:
OECD: The Organization for Economic Cooperation and Development Guidelines for Multinational Enterprises.
ILO: The International Labor Office Tripartite Declarations of Principles Concerning Multinational Enterprises and Social Policy.
ICC: The International Chamber of Commerce Guidelines for International Investment.
UN/CTC: The United Nations Universal Declaration of Human Rights.
The UN Code of Conduct on Transnational Corps.

continue to refine the codes, the underlying moral issues will be better identified, and appropriate MNE behavior will be more readily apparent."[25]

Ethics in International Management

The computer is on the dock, it's raining, and you have to pay $100 [bribe] to get it picked up.
—*William C. Norris, Control Data Corp.*

Globalization has multiplied the ethical problems facing organizations. Yet business ethics have not yet globalized. Although domestic American companies may use general guidelines for appropriate behavior based on federal law and the value structure rooted in the nation's Judeo-Christian heritage, such guidelines are not consistently applicable overseas.[26] For an MNC, it is very difficult to reconcile consistent and acceptable behavior around the world with home-country standards. One question, in fact, is whether they even should be reconciled; it seems that the United States is the driving force to legislate moral business conduct overseas.[27]

The term **international business ethics** refers to the business conduct or morals of MNCs in their relationships with individuals and entities.[28] Such behavior is based largely on the cultural value system and the generally accepted ways of doing business in each country or society, as we discuss throughout this book. Those norms, in turn, are based on broadly accepted guidelines from religion, philosophy, the professions, and the legal system. Should managers of MNC subsidiaries, then, base their ethical standards on those of the host country or those of the home country—or can the two be reconciled? What is the moral responsibility of expatriates regarding ethical behavior, and how do these issues affect business objectives? How do expatriates simultaneously balance their responsibility to various stakeholders—to owners, creditors, consumers, employees, suppliers, governments, and societies? The often conflicting objectives of host and home governments and societies also must be balanced.[29] The approach to these dilemmas varies among MNCs from different countries. Whereas the American approach is to treat everyone the same by making moral judgments based on general rules, managers in Japan and Europe tend to make such decisions based on shared values, social ties, and their perception of their obligations.[30] According to many U.S. executives, there is little difference in ethical practices among the United States, Canada, and Northern Europe. In fact, according to Bruce Smart, former U.S. Undersecretary of Commerce for International Trade, the highest ethical standards seem to be practiced by the Canadians, British, Australians, and Germans; as he says, "a kind of noblesse oblige still exists among the business classes in those countries"—compared with the prevailing attitude among many American managers that condones succeeding whatever way you can.[31] Another who experienced few problems with ethical practices in Europe is Donald Petersen, former CEO of Ford Motor Co. But he warns us about underdeveloped countries, in particular those under a dictatorship, where bribery is generally accepted practice. And in Japan, says Petersen, the idea behind "give me the business and I'll give you a gift" is simply an accepted part of Japanese culture.[32]

The biggest single problem for MNCs in their attempt to define a corporatewide ethical posture is the great variation of ethical standards around the world. Many practices that are considered unethical or even illegal in some countries are accepted ways of doing business in others. U.S. companies are often caught between being placed at a disadvantage by refusing to go along with a country's accepted practices, such as bribery, or being subject to criticism at home for using "unethical" tactics to get the job done. Large companies that have refused to participate have led the way in taking a moral stand because of their visibility, their potential impact on the local economy, and after all, their ability to afford such a stance.[33]

Whereas the upper limits of ethical standards for international activities are set by the individual standards of certain leading companies—or, more realistically, by the moral values of their top managers—it is more difficult to set the lower limits of those standards. Laczniak and Naor explain:

> The laws of economically developed countries generally define the lowest common denominator of acceptable behavior for operations in those domestic markets. In an underdeveloped country or a developing country, it would be the actual *degree of enforcement* [italics added] of the law that would, in practice, determine the lower limit of permissible behavior.[34]

The bribery of officials is prohibited by law in many countries, but it still goes on as an accepted practice; often, it is the only way to get anything done. In such cases, the MNC managers have to decide on what standard of behavior they will follow. What about the $100 bribe to get the computer off the rainy dock? According to William Norris, he told them to pay the $100 because to refuse would be taking things too far. Generally, Control Data Corp. did not yield to such pressure, though they say they lost sales as a result.[35]

Questionable Payments

The most we can hope for is that the fallout from the [ex-President] Roh scandal will mean it won't cost us as much this year [for "gifts"].
—Business executive in South Korea. Quoted in *Wall Street Journal,* November 21, 1995

A specific ethical issue for managers in the international arena is that of **questionable payments**. These are business payments that raise significant questions of appropriate moral behavior either in the host nation or in other nations. Such questions arise out of differences in laws, customs, and ethics in various countries, whether the payments in question are political payments, extortion, bribes, sales commissions, or "grease money"—payments to expedite routine transactions.[36] Other common types are payments to speed the clearance of goods at ports of entry and to obtain required certifications. They are called different names: *tokens of appreciation, la mordida* ("the bite," in Mexico), *bastarella* ("little envelope" in Italy), *pot-de-vin* ("jug of wine" in France). For the sake of simplicity, we will categorize all these different types of questionable payments as some form of bribery.

In South Korea, for example, the bribery scandal that has put former President Roh Tae Woo behind bars has spread to the top 30 *chaebols* (which account for 14 percent of gross domestic product), as the investigation continued in early 1996. Any ensuing changes to the close relationship between politics and business in South Korea are likely to reshape, and perhaps slow down, the Korean economy. But executives in those *chaebols* say they still expect to pay the *Huk Kab,* or "rice-cake expenses," which run thousands of dollars, as "holiday gifts" to cabinet ministers as a hedge against disadvantageous treatment.

The dilemma for Americans operating abroad is how much to adhere to their own ethical standards in the face of foreign customs, or how much to follow local ways to be competitive. Certainly, in some societies, gift giving is common to bind social and familial ties, and such gifts incur obligation. However, Americans must be able to distinguish between harmless practices and actual bribery, between genuine relationships and those used as a cover-up. To help Americans distinguish, the **Foreign Corrupt Practices Act (FCPA)** of 1977 was established, which prohibits U.S. companies from making illegal payments or other gifts or political contributions to foreign government officials for the purposes of influencing them in business transactions. The goal was to stop MNCs from contributing to corruption in foreign government and to upgrade the image of the United States and its companies operating overseas. The penalties include severe fines and sometimes imprisonment. Many managers feel the law has given them a more even playing field, and may have therefore been more willing to do business in certain countries where it seemed impossible to do business without bribery and kickbacks. Unfortunately, bribery still continues, mostly on a small scale, where it often goes undetected. But the U.S. government does vigorously pursue and prosecute bribery cases. Even the mighty IBM's Argentine subsidiary has recently been accused of paying a bribe of $249 million to get the contract to install computers at all the branches of Argentina's largest commercial bank, Banco de la Nacion.[37] U.S. companies claim that they are placed at a competitive disadvantage in Latin America and elsewhere because their competitors overseas do not face the same home-country restrictions on bribery.

If we agree with Carson that "accepting a bribe involves the violation of an implicit or explicit promise or understanding associated with one's office or role, and that, therefore, accepting (or giving) a bribe is always prima facie wrong," then our decisions as a manager, salesperson, or whatever are always clear, no matter where we are.[38]

However, if we accept that in some cases—in "morally corrupt contexts," as Philips calls them—"there may be no prima facie duty to adhere to the agreements implicit in one's role or position," then the issue becomes situational and a matter of judgment, with few consistent guidelines.[39] If our perspective, continues Philips, is that "the action purchased from the relevant official does not count as a violation of his [or her] duty," then the American managers or other foreign managers involved are actually victims of extortion rather than guilty of bribery.[40] That is the position taken by Gene Laczniak of Marquette Company, who says that it is just part of the cost of doing business in many countries to pay small bribes to get people just to do their jobs; however, he is against paying bribes to persuade people to make a decision that they would not otherwise have made.[41]

Whatever their professed beliefs, many businesspeople are willing to engage in bribery as an everyday part of meeting their business objectives. Many corporate officials, in fact, avoid any moral issue by simply "turning a blind eye" to what goes on in subsidiaries. Some companies avoid these issues by hiring a local agent who takes care of the paperwork and pays all the so-called fees in return for a salary or consultant's fee.[42] However, though the FCPA does allow "grease" payments to facilitate business in a foreign country, if those payments are lawful there, other payments prohibited by the FCPA are still subject to prosecution even if the company says it did not know that its agents or subsidiaries were making such payments—the so-called reason to know provision.[43, 44]

Critics of the FCPA contend that the law represents an ethnocentric attempt to impose U.S. standards on the rest of the world and puts American firms at a competitive disadvantage.[45] In fact, the United States is the only country prohibiting firms from making payments to secure contracts overseas.[46] In any event, business activities that cannot stand scrutiny, many feel, are clearly unethical, corrupt, and in the long run, corrupting.[47] Bribery fails three important tests of ethical corporate actions: (1) Is it legal? (2) Does it work (in the long run)? (3) Can it be talked about?[48]

Many MNCs have decided to confront concerns about ethical behavior and social responsibility by developing worldwide practices that represent the company's posture. Among those policies are the following:

- Develop worldwide codes of ethics
- Consider ethical issues in strategy development
- Given major, unsolvable, ethical problems, consider withdrawal from the problem market
- Develop periodic "ethical impact" statements[49]

Most of the leadership in developing ethical postures in international activities comes from the United States. Although this move toward ethics and social responsibility is spreading, both in the United States and around the world, problems still abound in many countries.

Heightened global competition encourages companies to seek advantages through questionable tactics. A 1995 Commerce Department study revealed many incidents of improper inducements by companies and governments around the world (such as Germany's Siemens and the European airframe consortium Airbus Industrie) that undercut U.S. companies. Indeed, American companies are not all clean. In October 1995, Lockheed Martin Corporation's former vice president was sentenced to 18 months in prison and fined $125,000 for bribing a member of the Egyptian Parliament to win an order for three C–130 cargo planes.[50] So much for Lockheed's consent decree to refrain from corrupt practices, which they signed 20 years ago following their bribery scandal in Japan.

Japan also continues to have its share of internal problems regarding the ethical behavior of its officials and businesspeople. In the scandal involving Nippon Telephone and Telegraph Company (NTT), the chairman of the board of NTT was involved in obtaining cut-rate stock in a real estate subsidiary of the Recruit Company in exchange for helping the company obtain two U.S. supercomputers. When the stock went public, the chairman and other NTT executives made a lot of money, and they were later arrested and charged with accepting bribes.[51] As the scandal unfolded, it appeared that government members were involved, including the prime minister, Noboru Takeshita, who had received $1.4 million in questionable, albeit legal, donations from the Recruit Company. Takeshita subsequently resigned, as did other government officials, and the incident became known as Recruitgate, in reference to the Watergate scandal that forced President Nixon to resign.[52]

COMPARATIVE MANAGEMENT IN FOCUS

Ethics in Europe

Because of the growing power of the EU market, it is useful to focus on what to expect regarding the ethical approaches of European countries, especially in comparison to the United States. It is interesting to point out, first, that in a 1996 survey of employees of multinational firms and institutions through Transparency International of Berlin, 11 of the 13 countries ranked by those employees as the "least corrupt" were countries in western Europe—the other two countries were New Zealand and Australia.[53]

To find out more about the ethical codes of various MNCs, one study compared 600 large European companies with similar U.S. firms. To ensure that the CEOs in the sample from British, French, formerly West German, and American companies had a common understanding of the characteristics of a corporate code of ethics, the researchers formulated a working definition: "A statement setting down corporate principles, ethics, rules of conduct, codes of practice or company philosophy concerning responsibility to employees, shareholders, consumers, the environment, or any other aspects of society external to the company."[54]

The CEOs were asked whether their companies had codes of ethics and, if so, to supply a copy or give information regarding the issues covered. Bearing in mind that the CEOs who chose to respond to the survey were probably more likely to have codes than those who did not, the results were as follows.

Among the MNCs surveyed who had written codes, 30 percent were in France, 51 percent in the former West Germany, 41 percent in Britain, and 75 percent in the United States. Factoring out European companies that were U.S. subsidiaries, the results changed to 18 percent for France, 47 percent for West Germany, and 31 percent for Britain—showing a clear influence from U.S. parents. Most codes were introduced after 1984.[55] Although the word *ethics* did not often appear in the title, the companies, through these codes, were clearly committing themselves to a set of core values against which to measure their actions. Most also circulated their codes to external interest groups, such as customers and suppliers. Also of interest in this study was the comparative content of those codes of ethics—that is, what subjects they addressed, as shown in Exhibit 3–4.

Some striking differences are that all European company codes address the issue of employee conduct, whereas only 55 percent of U.S. company codes do; more than 80 percent of U.S. codes address the customer, compared to 67 percent of European codes. In addition, whereas the majority of U.S. firms discuss relations with the government and with suppliers, less than 20 percent of European companies broach either topic.

The researchers conclude from this study that (1) there is an "ethics gap" between Europe and the United States and that it will be some years before the number of European companies adopting codes of ethics catches up with the number of American firms with such codes; (2) Europe and the United States differ significantly regarding the relative emphasis on issues covered by their codes of ethics; and (3) most ethical issues transcend national barriers

EXHIBIT 3–4

Comparative Content of Codes of Ethics

Subjects	U.K. n = 33 No	%	France n = 15 No	%	W.G. n = 30 No	%	Total European Countries No	%	United States* n = 118 No	%
Employee conduct	33	100	15	100	30	100	78	100	47	55
Community and environment	21	64	11	73	19	63	51	65	50	42
Customers	18	39	14	93	20	67	52	67	96	81
Shareholders	13	39	11	73	18	60	42	54	NA‡	NA‡
Suppliers and contractors	7	21	2	13	6	20	15	19	101	86
Political interests	4	12	3	20	5	17	12	15	113	96
Innovation and technology	2	6	3	20	18	60	26	33	18	15

*U.S. comparison is based on a survey of the Foundation of the Southwestern Graduate School of Banking (1980).
‡NA = no comparable data available.

Source: Catherine C. Langlois and Bodo B. Schlegelmilch, "Do Corporate Codes of Ethics Reflect National Character? Evidence from Europe and the United States," *Journal of International Business Studies* 21 (4th Quarter 1990): 519–539.

(except for political issues, which reflect legal environments, and attitudes toward employee relations). Overall, the authors found that "European companies emphasize employee responsiveness to company activities, while firms in the U.S. stress company responsiveness to employee requirements of fairness and equity."[56] The question thus arises, could the world ever adopt standardized codes of ethics when such codes actually reflect national environments and national identities? In general, European businesspeople tend to use informal mechanisms of social control in a company and do not believe that a code of conduct would really change the behavior of its employees. Rather than the individualistic approach of Americans, Europeans are more likely to make decisions about their company's responsibilities based on their understanding of the norms of the community.[57]

Codes of conduct give us some idea of the ethical posture of a company—and, overall, of the country. However, when it comes to what people actually do, or don't do, when faced with ethical dilemmas, we need to look at specific situations and try to find out what, if any, different actions managers in various countries take. To do this, one study compared the ethical behavior of 72 French, 70 German, and 124 American managers.[58] The authors used a series of situational vignettes to compare what managers in those countries would do—how likely each manager would be to take the indicated action, and what his or her rationale would be for taking it. (Note that such research tells you only what those managers say they would do.) The situations used in the study (and also used in other books on ethics) represent a range of ethical situations, including (1) coercion and control, (2) conflict of interest, (3) the physical environment, (4) paternalism, and (5) personal integrity. Two examples are presented here. The first asks the managers whether they would pay a bribe, and what their rationale would be:

> Rollfast Bicycle Company has been barred from entering the market in a large Asian country by collusive efforts of the local bicycle manufacturers. Rollfast could expect to net $5 million per year from sales if it could penetrate the market. Last week a businessman from the country contacted the management of Rollfast and stated that he could smooth the way for the company to sell in his country for a price of $500,000.

What are the chances the managers would pay the bribe? On a scale from 0 (definitely would not) to 10 (definitely would), the mean for the U.S. sample was 4.0, for the German sample 5.8, and for the French sample 6.9, indicating that the American managers were significantly less likely to pay the bribe than the European managers. The rationales for their responses are shown in Exhibit 3–5.

In another vignette, a decision must be made regarding a conflict of interest:

> Jack Brown is vice president of marketing for Tangy Spices, a large spice manufacturer. Jack recently joined a business venture with Tangy's director of purchasing to import black pepper from India. Jack's new company is about to sign a five-year contract with Tangy to supply their black pepper needs. The contract is set at a price 3 cents per pound above the current market price for comparable black pepper imports.

Should Brown sign the contract? For this vignette, there was little difference in the mean responses. Managers representing all three countries indicated that they would be unlikely to sign the contract if they were Brown; however, their reasons differed. The U.S. managers' rationale was mostly that signing such a contract would be dishonest or a conflict of interest. The French and German managers' main rationale was that they should look out for their own interest. U.S. managers were thus noticeably more concerned with ethical and legal questions, whereas the French and Germans appeared more concerned with maintaining a successful business posture.[59]

EXHIBIT 3-5

Comparison of French, German, and U.S. Responses to Vignette Number One—Coercion and Control

Rationale for Response	Percent of Respondents		
	French	German	U.S.
Bribe, unethical	9%	9%	23%
Illegal under Corrupt Business Practices Act	3	0	16
Against company policy	3	0	8
Competition forces us to take offer	0	9	3
An acceptable practice in other countries	15	6	22
Is not unethical, just the price paid to do business	55	29	14
No one is hurt	0	2	4
Other	15	45	9
Total	100%	100%	100%
Number of respondents providing rationale	34	65	107

Source: Adapted from Helmut Becker and David J. Fritzsche, "A Comparison of the Ethical Behavior of American, French and German Managers," *Columbia Journal of World Business* (1987): 87–95.

Managers of MNCs need to be aware of the cultural background and ethical stance of other firms when doing business with them. The obvious differences in ethics that distinguish Americans from Europeans, for example, are attributed to the American tradition of liberal individualism. Whereas morality in America tends to be regarded as a personal decision and responsibility, European managers usually consult the opinion of others. They also tend to consider economic and legal implications and the long-term interests of others before making a moral decision, as van Luijk explains: "In the course of this process it may become obscure who exactly is making the final decision, but no uncertainty remains about the fact that an ethically relevant decision has been made."[60]

Such differences in ethical environments are not only relevant to U.S.–European business interactions—they also create confrontation within Europe. For example, the business environment in Italy often poses ethical conflicts to foreign businesspeople who come in contact with organized white-collar crime or corruption in the political system.[61] In May 1993, in fact, France's Renault put on hold its negotiations with Italy's Fiat to go to Italy as a strategic partner in Fiat's auto division, after discovering that nine of the Italian automaker's top executives had been implicated in bribes. Fiat, according to *Business Week*, "was being sucked deeper and deeper into the anticorruption investigation that is reshaping the political and economic face of Italy."[62]

Making the Right Decision   How is a manager operating abroad to know what is the "right" decision when faced with questionable or unfamiliar circumstances of doing business? The first line of defense is to consult the laws of both the home and the host countries, such as the FCPA. If any of those laws would be violated, then you, the manager, must look to some other way to complete the business transaction, or withdraw altogether. Second, you could consult the International Codes of Conduct for MNEs, as shown in Exhibit 3–3. These are broad and cover various areas of social responsibility and ethical behavior; however, though they are comprehensive, many issues are subject to interpretation.

If legal consultation does not provide you with a clear answer about what to do, you should consult the company's code of ethics (if there is one). You, as the manager, should realize that you are not alone in making these kinds of decisions; it is also the responsibility of the company to provide guidelines for the actions and decisions made by its employees. In addition, you are not the first, and certainly not the last, to be faced with this kind of situation—which also sets up a collective experience in the company about what kinds of decisions your colleagues typically make in various circumstances. Those norms or expectations (assuming they are honorable) can supplement the code of ethics or substitute for the lack of a formal code. If your intended action runs contrary to the norms or the formal code, then discontinue that plan. If you are still unsure of what to do, you have the right and the obligation to consult your superiors. Unfortunately, often the situation is not that clear cut, or your boss will tell you to "use your own judgment." Sometimes your superiors back at the home office just want you to complete the transaction to the benefit of the company, and don't want to be involved in what you have to do to get the deal done. It is at this point that, if your dilemma continues, you must fall back to your own moral code of ethics. One way to consider the dilemma is to ask yourself what are the rights of the various stakeholders involved (see Exhibit 3–2), and how should you weigh those rights. First, does the proposed action (a rigged contract bid or a bribe, for example) harm anyone? What are the likely consequences of your decision both in the short run and in the long run? Who would benefit from your contemplated action? What are the benefits to some versus the potential harm to others? In the case of a rigged contract bid through bribery, for example, people are put at a disadvantage, especially over the long term with a pattern of this behavior. This is because if competition is unfair, not only are your competitors harmed by losing the bid, but also the consumers of the products or services are harmed because they will pay more to attain them than they would under an efficient market system. You have to follow your own conscience and decide where to draw the line in the sand in order to operate with integrity—otherwise, the line moves farther and farther away with each transgression. In addition, that which can start with a small bribe or cover-up—here, a matter of personal ethics—can, over time, and in the aggregate of many people covering up, result in a situation of a truly negligent, and perhaps criminal, stance toward social responsibility to society, as that revealed by investigations of the tobacco industry in the United States. Indeed, executives are increasingly being held personally and criminally accountable for their decisions; this is true even for people operating on the board of directors of a company.

Managing Interdependence

Because multinational firms (or other organizations, such as the Red Cross) represent global interdependency, their managers at all levels must recognize that what they do, in the aggregate, has long-term implications for the socioeconomic interdependence of nations. Simply to describe ethical issues as part of the general environment does not address the fact that managers need to control their activities at all levels—from simple, daily business transactions involving local workers, intermediaries, or consumers to global concerns of ecological responsibility—for the future benefit of all concerned. Whatever the situation, the powerful long-term effects of MNC and MNE action (or inaction) should be planned for and controlled—not haphazardly considered part of the side effects of business. The profitability of individual companies depends on a cooperative and constructive attitude toward global interdependence.

Foreign Subsidiaries in the United States

Much of the preceding discussion has related to U.S. subsidiaries around the world. However, to highlight the growing interdependence and changing balance of business power globally, we can also consider foreign subsidiaries in America, for example. Since much criticism about a lack of responsibility has been directed toward MNCs with headquarters in the United States, we need to think of these criticisms from the perspective of a firm headquartered outside the United States. The number of foreign subsidiaries in the United States has grown and continues to grow dramatically; foreign direct investment (FDI) in the United States by other countries is in many cases far more than U.S. investment outward. Americans are thus becoming more sensitive to what they perceive as a lack of control over their own country's business.

Things look very different from the perspective of Americans employed at a subsidiary of some overseas MNC. Interdependence takes on a new meaning when people "over there" are calling the shots regarding strategy, expectations, products, and personnel. Often, resentment by Americans over different ways of doing business by "foreign" companies in the United States inhibits cooperation, which gave rise to the companies' presence in the first place.

Today, managers from all countries must learn new ways, and most MNCs are trying to adapt. Sadahei Kusomoto, president and CEO of the Minolta Corporation, says that Japanese managers in the United States need to recognize that they are "not in Honshu [Japan's largest island] anymore" and that one very different aspect of management in the United States is the idea of corporate social responsibility.[63]

In Japan, corporate social responsibility has traditionally meant that companies take care of their employees, whereas in the United States, the public and private sectors are expected to share the responsibility for the community. Part of the explanation for this difference is that American corporations get tax deductions for corporate philanthropy, whereas Japanese firms do not; nor are Japanese managers familiar with community needs. For these and other reasons, Japanese subsidiaries in the United States have not been active in U.S. philanthropy. However, Kusomoto pinpoints why they should become more involved in the future: "In the long run, failure to play an active role in the community will brand these companies as irresponsible outsiders and dim their prospects for the future."[64]

Whether Kusomoto's motives for change are humanitarian or just good business sense does not really matter. The point is that he recognizes interdependence in globalization and acts accordingly.

Managing Subsidiary–Host Country Interdependence

When managing interdependence, international managers must go beyond general issues of social responsibility and deal with the specific concerns of the MNC subsidiary–host country relationship. Outdated MNC attitudes that focus only on profitability and autonomy are shortsighted and usually result in only short-term realization of those goals; MNCs must learn to accommodate the needs of other organizations and countries:

> Interdependence rather than independence, and cooperation rather than confrontation are at the heart of that accommodation … the journey from independence to interdependence managed badly leads to dependence, and that is an unacceptable destination.[65]

Most of the past criticism levied at MNCs has focused on their activities in LDCs. Their real or perceived lack of responsibility centers on the transfer-in of inappropriate technology, causing unemployment, and the transfer-out of scarce financial and other resources, reducing the capital available for internal development. In their defense, MNCs help LDCs by bringing in new technology and managerial skills, improving the infrastructure, creating jobs, and bringing in investment capital from other countries by exporting products. The infusion of outside capital provides foreign-exchange earnings that can be used for further development. The host government's attitude is often referred to as a love–hate relationship: It wants the economic growth that MNCs can provide but does not want the incursions on national sovereignty or the technological dependence that may result.[66] Most criticisms of MNC subsidiary activities, whether in less developed or more developed countries, are along these lines:

1. MNCs raise their needed capital locally, contributing to a rise in interest rates in host countries.
2. The majority (sometimes even 100 percent) of the stock of most subsidiaries is owned by the parent company. Consequently, host-country people do not have much control over the operations of corporations within their borders.
3. MNCs usually reserve the key managerial and technical positions for expatriates. As a result, they do not contribute to the development of host-country personnel.
4. MNCs do not adapt their technology to the conditions that exist in host countries.
5. MNCs concentrate their research and development activities at home, restricting the transfer of modern technology and know-how to host countries.
6. MNCs give rise to the demand for luxury goods in host countries at the expense of essential consumer goods.
7. MNCs start their foreign operations by purchasing existing firms rather than by developing new productive facilities in host countries.
8. MNCs dominate major industrial sectors, thus contributing to inflation by stimulating demand for scarce resources and earning excessively high profits and fees.
9. MNCs are not accountable to their host nations but respond only to home-country governments; they are not concerned with host-country plans for development.[67]

Specific MNCs have been charged with tax evasion, union busting, and interference in host-country politics. Of course, MNCs have both positive and negative effects on different economies; for every complaint about MNC activities (whether about capital markets, technology transfer, or employment practices), we can identify potential benefits, as shown in Exhibit 3–6.

Numerous conflicts arise between MNC companies or subsidiaries and host countries, including conflicting goals (both economic and noneconomic) and conflicting concerns, such as the security of proprietary technology, patents, or information. Overall, the resulting trade-offs create an interdependent relationship between the subsidiary and the host government,

EXHIBIT 3–6

MNC Benefits and Costs to Host Countries

Benefits	Costs

Capital Market Effects

■ Broader access to outside capital	■ Increased competition for local scarce capital
■ Foreign-exchange earnings	■ Increased interest rates as supply of local capital decreases
■ Import substitution effects allow governments to save foreign exchange for priority projects	■ Capital service effects of balance of payments
■ Risk sharing	

Technology and Production Effects

■ Access to new technology and R&D developments	■ Technology is not always appropriate
■ Infrastructure development and support	■ Plants are often for assembly only and can be dismantled
■ Export diversification	■ Government infrastructure investment is higher than expected benefits

Employment Effects

■ Direct creation of new jobs	■ Limited skill development and creation
■ Opportunities for indigenous management development	■ Competition for scarce skills
■ Income multiplier effects on local community business	■ Low percentage of managerial jobs for local people
	■ Employment instability because of ability to move production operations freely to other countries

Source: R. H. Mason and R. S. Spich, *Management: An International Perspective* (Homewood, IL: Irwin, 1987): 202.

based on relative bargaining power. The power of MNCs is based on their large-scale, worldwide economies, their strategic flexibility, and their control over technology and production location. The bargaining chips of the host governments include their control of raw materials and market access and their ability to set the rules regarding the role of private enterprise, the operation of state-owned firms, and the specific regulations regarding taxes, permissions, and so forth.[68]

MNCs run the risk of their assets becoming hostage to host control, which may take the form of nationalism, protectionism, or governmentalism. Under nationalism, for example, public opinion is rallied in favor of national goals and against foreign influences. Under protectionism, the host institutes a partial or complete closing of borders to withstand competitive foreign products, using tariff and nontariff barriers, such as those used by Japan. Under governmentalism, the government uses its policy-setting role to favor national interests rather than relying on market forces—an example is the decision of Britain to privatize its telephone system.[69]

Ford Motor Company came up against many of these controls when it decided to produce automobiles in Spain. The Spanish government set specific restrictions on sales and export volume: The sales volume was limited to 10 percent of the previous year's total automobile market, and the export volume had to be at least two-thirds of the entire production in Spain. Ford also had to agree that it would not broaden its model lines without the authorization of the government.[70]

The intricacies of the relationship and the relative power of an MNC subsidiary and a host-country government are situation specific. Clearly, such a relationship should be managed for mutual benefit; a long-term, constructive relationship based on the MNC's socially responsive stance should result in progressive strategic success for the MNC and economic progress for the host country. The effective management of subsidiary–host country interdependence must have a long-term perspective. Although temporary strategies to reduce interdependence via controls on the transnational flows by firms (for example, transfer-pricing tactics) or by governments (such as new residency requirements for skilled workers) are often successful in the short run, they result in inefficiencies that must be absorbed by one or both parties, with negative long-term results.[71] In setting up and maintaining subsidiaries, managers are wise to consider the long-term tradeoffs between strategic plans and operational management. By finding out for themselves the pressing local concerns and understanding the sources of past conflicts, they can learn from mistakes and recognize the consequences of the failure to manage problems. Further, managers should implement policies that reflect corporate social responsibility regarding local economic issues, employee welfare, or natural resources.[72] At the least, the failure to manage interdependence effectively results in constraints on strategy. In the worst case, it results in disastrous consequences for the local area, for the subsidiary, and for the global reputation of the company.

The interdependent nature of developing economies and the MNCs operating there is of particular concern when discussing social responsibility because of the tentative and fragile nature of the economic progression in those countries. MNCs need to set a high moral standard and lay the groundwork for future economic development; at the minimum, they should ensure that their actions will do no harm. Some recommendations by De George for MNCs operating in and doing business with developing countries are as follows:

1. Do no intentional harm. This includes respect for the integrity of the ecosystem and consumer safety.
2. Produce more good than harm for the host country.
3. Contribute by their activity to the host country's development.
4. Respect the human rights of their employees.
5. To the extent that local culture does not violate ethical norms, MNCs should respect the local culture and work with and not against it.
6. Pay their fair share of taxes.
7. Cooperate with the local government in developing and enforcing just background (infrastructure) institutions (laws, governmental regulations, unions, and consumer groups) that serve as a means of social control.[73]

One issue that illustrates conflicting concerns about social responsibility and interdependence is the North American Free Trade Agreement (NAFTA), discussed in the following Comparative Management in Focus.

COMPARATIVE MANAGEMENT IN FOCUS

Interdependence: The NAFTA—Perspectives from the South and the North

Maquiladora-ville—The value added by border companies to Mexico's total exports tops U.S. $10 billion for 1998[74]

It may be too soon to judge the long-run success of NAFTA, but early results do reinforce the interdependent nature of the agreement, the three economies (Mexico, United States, and Canada), and the relative level of success attained for business firms, environmental issues, and people. Now, several years since NAFTA took effect—the Mexican border factories have boomed, with employment there rising to more than a million. More important, many of those jobs are now high tech, bringing training and a higher standard of living for many Mexicans, as described in the accompanying Technology Application.

It seems that because of lower labor costs for "foreign" companies, the devalued peso, and the NAFTA-reduced tariff levels, NAFTA has had a mitigating effect on the Mexican economic crisis.[75] Further, in a touch of irony, Asia's currency crisis has caused some global companies to relocate factories from Asia to Mexico. In fact, Mexico has overtaken mainland China as the volume leader of exports of textiles and garments to the United States. But do the trade numbers tell it all? Perhaps we can compare perspectives from south and north of the border by looking at some examples and issues.

---

http://www.technology.com

TECHNOLOGY APPLICATION
High-Tech Jobs Boost Maquiladora-Ville

Border industries—*maquiladoras*—that started as low-skilled assembly operations are increasingly moving up the technological scale. In Juarez, for example, where there are 178,000 workers in 235 plants, Mexican engineers earn about $20,000 a year working for GM's Delphi Automotive Division, which employs 18,000 there and is expanding its R&D capacity to double the number of engineers required.

In the same town, Mr. Gomez, who works for France's Thomson, S.A., oversees technical problems and quality control in a factory of 4,000 workers who turn out 3 million television sets a year. Although his salary is the envy of many Mexican employees, it is considerably less than that of equivalent French or U.S. positions, which is one reason that the region is gaining global prominence for efficiency in manufacturing. Thompson managers have set up a program of continuous training and adaptation to changing technology. Along with programs to reduce worker turnover, such

initiatives have resulted in a steady increase in worker productivity along the border—to about U.S. $12,000 output per worker in Juarez, where the majority of workers still make only about $100 a week. Along with other familiar names such as Philips NV, United Technologies Corp., and Ford, other "foreign" firms such as Samsung, Sony, and Sanyo are making towns like Tijuana the TV-set capital of the world. Samsung, for example, which employs some 7,500 people, is spending $670 million through the year 2000 on a complex to make TV sets, computer monitors, and components in Tijuana.

Although low-tech production is still the most prevalent in Mexico, especially in the textile industry and inexpensive consumer goods, it is clear that the transfer of technological skills and experience to Mexico through firms from around the world will be beneficial for all concerned.

Sources: D. Darlin, "Maquiladora-ville," *Forbes,* May 6, 1996; "The Border," *Business Week,* May 12, 1997; J. Millman, "High-Tech Jobs Transfer to Mexico with Surprising Speed," *Wall Street Journal,* April 9, 1998.

From the South Looking North

It's not like ten years ago, when we wanted to talk to [U.S.] customers and no one would talk to us. Now, big [U.S.] customers are calling us.

—Victor Almeida, CEO, Interceramic[76]

The Almeida family of Interceramic (Internacional de Ceramica SA, Chihuahua, Mexico) always wanted to export to the United States, but it took the heightened interest in Mexico through the NAFTA agreement to really give them their breakthrough.

The manufacturer of glazed floor and wall tile is just one of the many savvy Mexican firms making inroads into the U.S. market. But in many ways it is harder for Mexican managers to go north than for U.S. managers to go south. Though they both face the same sorts of cross-cultural managerial problems, Mexican companies are typically at a competitive disadvantage in the United States because they are not as advanced in technology or efficiency as American firms.

Interceramic, a traditional Mexican family business, had to learn the hard way that business is done differently in the United States. Victor Almeida, the CEO, found that contractors buy most of the tile in the United States, compared to the homeowner in Mexico, and that customers in the United States demanded a much better level of service.[77] He had to convince U.S. distributors that Interceramic had high-quality products and that the company was reliable, and it took some time to find the right U.S. managers to represent the company and interact with people on both sides of the border. He encouraged them to be more like Mexicans by showing their emotions more openly. In addition, he opened offices in Texas so that the export managers could be closer to the customer and thus get more input to custom-design the tiles to suit American tastes. Although it has taken a few years, Mr. Almeida's efforts are now paying off, and he attributes much of that to NAFTA, as well as to his hard work.

But it's a different story for smaller, less efficient firms: Many simply cannot compete with the resources of technology and access to capital that U.S. firms are bringing to Mexico. Corner stores and small businesses are getting driven out by the Wal-Marts and Dunkin' Donuts—the same competitive situation that has hit towns in the United States. Mexican factories are finding it difficult to compete for employees with companies like GM that are offering subsidized housing. However, other businesses, in towns such as Nuevo Laredo, are booming as a result of servicing large companies such as Wal-Mart.

From the North Looking South

If you don't have trustworthy Mexican partners, you can get into trouble here; only idiots try to figure it out themselves.

—R. Heckmann, CEO, U.S. Filter[78]

"For every factory opened in Mexico (whether by Asian, Canadian, European, or American firms), the U.S. wins service, transportation, or distribution jobs."[79] What's more, American firms that supply components to those factories are profiting from the boom south of the border. This is because primary components in products such as VCRs must be made in North American to benefit from NAFTA. U.S. and Mexican companies also benefit from orders for supplies from European and Asian firms.

Although many Canadian and American companies are expanding into Mexico, taking advantage of the increased confidence and opportunities resulting from passage of NAFTA, most firms face an uphill battle because they make incorrect assumptions about the similarity of the market and distribution system. Problems include corruption, American arrogance, red tape on both sides of the border, and misunderstandings about the Mexican culture and how to do business there.

Coupling these problems with those in the infrastructure, it is easy to see why many foreign firms have had difficulties expanding into Mexico, often giving up. It is easier now to get a business phone line, but transportation and mail systems are still behind American expectations, and bill collecting often must be done in person because of numerous problems with the mail and required documentation. Electricity is sometimes cut off without notice, and the legal system is so difficult to figure out that foreigners risk going to jail without being accused of a crime. Mexican partners and alliances seem to be the answer—as even the giant Wal-Mart Stores Inc. found out when it ran into so many distribution problems in Mexico that it decided it would cost no more in the long run to use local distributors.

So why do American companies bother? Typically because they want to take advantage of market expansion opportunities. One example is U.S. Filter, a water-purification company whose target in Mexico is "90 million people who can't trust their tap water, and a slew of companies under government pressure to clean up waste water."[80]

Interdependence: South–North Strategic Alliances

Richard Heckmann, U.S. Filter's CEO, realized early on that alliances with trustworthy Mexican partners provided the answer to many problems and to achieving the interdependent goals of both countries and their firms. He knew, for example, that the political reality was that Mexican officials would favor their ties to Mexican firms and steer bids to those companies. So he contracted a Mexican construction company, Plar SA, with strong political connections. Moreover, in order to reach his smaller potential customers, Mr. Heckmann has formed a joint venture with Enrique Anhalt, a local Mexico City water-purification supplier to 250 manufacturers and other customers with small systems, assuming that when they upgrade they will turn to a local supplier. Plar SA benefits from the deal by getting technical and financial help from U.S. Filter to upgrade its technology.

The environmental cleanup efforts in Mexico clearly exhibit the interdependence of NAFTA and will benefit everyone in the long run. Funding from the United States is helping with projects such as the sewage-treatment plants at 11 cities south of the border. In turn, that business is going to many U.S. environmental services companies, such as San Diego Gas & Electric Co., which is building natural gas pipelines to Mexicali and Tijuana to supply clean fuel to industrial plants.

The auto industry is another agent of massive change in Mexico—building an industrial base south of the border that will help strengthen the Mexican economy. "The auto industry has the unusual ability to ... jump start a middle class," according to David Cole, director of the University of Michigan's automotive studies office.[81] Although the average Ford worker in Hermosillo still earns considerably less than his counterpart in Wayne, Michigan, that wage does represent a considerable increase for Mexican workers. In addition, every new auto plant in Mexico trains thousands of Mexicans, most of them new to factory work. Even though those factors don't console auto workers in the United States who have lost their jobs, it does mean that American auto manufacturers can be more globally competitive.

There is likely to be increasing interdependence among the Americas in the future as agreements open up further trade with other South American countries such as Chile and Brazil. These countries are tearing down their internal trade barriers also, in a wave that may eventually form a free-trade zone from Alaska to Tierra del Fuego. South Americans are realizing that they may get left out in the cold as both the European Community and North America form their own huge markets. As noted by Mr. Grisetti, an Argentine businessman, "If the world is dividing into blocs, we have to form a bloc or disappear … it's a necessity."

Managing Environmental Interdependence

International managers—and all people—can no longer afford to ignore the impact of their activities on the environment. As Ward and Dubois put it,

> Now that mankind is in the process of completing the colonization of the planet, learning to manage it intelligently is an urgent imperative. [People] must accept responsibility for the stewardship of the earth. The word *stewardship* implies, of course, management for the sake of someone else…. As we enter the global phase of human evolution, it becomes obvious that each [person] has two countries, his [or her] own and the planet earth.[82]

Effectively managing environmental interdependence includes considering ecological interdependence as well as the economic and social implications of MNC activities. There is an ever-increasing awareness of, and a mounting concern worldwide about, the effects of global industrialization on the natural environment. This concern was evidenced by the gathering of world leaders at the Earth Summit in Rio de Janeiro in June 1992 to discuss and decide on action for ecological preservation. Government regulations and powerful interest groups are demanding ecological responsibility regarding the use of scarce natural resources and production processes that threaten permanent damage to the planet. MNCs have to deal with each country's different policies and techniques for environmental and health protection. Such variations in approach reflect different levels of industrialization, living standards, government–business relations, philosophies of collective intervention, patterns of industrial competition, and degrees of sophistication in public policy.[83] For an MNC to take advantage of less stringent regulations (or expectations) is not only irresponsible but also invites disaster, as illustrated by the Union Carbide accident in Bhopal.

In recent years, the export of hazardous wastes from developed countries to less developed ones has increased considerably. One instance was the dumping of more than 8,000 drums of waste, including drums filled with polychlorinated biphenyl (PCB), a highly toxic compound, in Koko, Nigeria.[84] Although not all dumping is illegal, the large international trade in hazardous wastes (as a result of the increasing barriers to domestic disposal) raises disturbing questions regarding social responsibility. Although the importer of waste must take some blame, it is the exporter who shoulders the ultimate responsibility for both generation and disposal. Often, companies choose to dispose of hazardous waste in less developed countries to take advantage of weaker regulations and lower costs. Until we have strict international regulation of trade in hazardous wastes, companies should take it upon themselves to monitor their activities, as Singh and Lakhan demand:

> To export these wastes to countries which do not benefit from waste-generating industrial processes or whose citizens do not have lifestyles that generate such wastes is unethical. It is especially unjust to send hazardous wastes to lesser developed countries which lack the technology to minimize the deleterious effects of these substances.[85]

The exporting of pesticides poses a similar problem, with the United States and Germany being the main culprits. The United States exports about 200 million pounds of pesticides each year that are prohibited, restricted, or not registered for use in the United States.[86] One MNC, Monsanto Chemical Corporation, for example, sells DDT to many foreign importers, even though its use in the United States has been essentially banned. Apart from the lack of social responsibility toward the people and the environment in the countries that import DDT, this action is also irresponsible to American citizens because many of their fruits and meat products are imported from those countries.[87]

These are only two of the environmental problems facing countries and large corporations today. According to Graedel and Allenby, the path to truly sustainable development is for corporations to broaden their concept of industrial ecology:

> The concept [of industrial ecology] requires that an industrial system be viewed not in isolation from its surrounding systems, but in concert with them. It is a systems view in which one seeks to optimize the total materials cycle from virgin material, to finished material, to component, to product, to obsolete product, and to ultimate disposal.[88]

Essentially, this perspective supports the idea that environmental citizenship is necessary for a firm's survival as well as responsible social performance.[89]

It is clear then, that MNCs must take the lead in dealing with ecological interdependence by integrating environmental factors into strategic planning. Along with an investment appraisal, a project feasibility study, and operational plans, such planning should include an environmental impact assessment.[90] At the least, MNC managers must deal with the increasing scarcity of natural resources in the next few decades by (1) looking for alternative raw materials, (2) developing new methods of recycling or disposing of used materials, and (3) expanding the use of byproducts.[91]

Multinational corporations already have had a tremendous impact on foreign countries, and this impact will continue to grow and bring about long-lasting changes. Even now, U.S. MNCs alone account for about 10 percent of the world's GNP. Because of interdependence at both the local level and the global level, it is not only moral but also in the best interest of MNCs to establish a single clear posture toward social and ethical responsibilities worldwide and to ensure that it is implemented. In a real sense, foreign firms enter as guests in host countries and must respect the local laws, policies, traditions, and culture as well as those countries' economic and developmental needs.

Conclusion

In conclusion, when research findings and anecdotal evidence indicate differential attitudes toward ethical behavior and social responsibility across cultures, MNCs must take certain steps. For example, they must be careful when placing a foreign manager in a country whose values are incongruent with his or her own because this could lead to conflicts with local managers, governmental bodies, customers, and suppliers. As discussed earlier, expatriates should be oriented to the legal and ethical ramifications of questionable foreign payments, the differences in environmental regulations, and the local expectations of personal integrity, and they should be supported as they attempt to integrate host-country behaviors with the expectations of the company's headquarters.[92]

Social responsibility, ethical behavior, and interdependence are important concerns to be built into management control—not as afterthoughts, but as part of the ongoing process of planning and controlling international operations for the long-term benefit of all.

In Part 2, we will focus on the pervasive and powerful influence of culture in the host-country environment in which the international manager operates. In Chapter 4, we will examine the nature of culture: What are its various dimensions and roots? How does culture affect the behavior and expectations of employees? What are the implications for how managers operating in other countries should behave?

Summary of Key Points

1. The concept of international social responsibility includes the expectation that MNCs should be concerned about the social and economic effects of their decisions regarding activities in other countries.
2. Moral universalism refers to the need for a moral standard that is accepted by all cultures.
3. Concerns about MNC social responsibility revolve around issues of human rights in other countries, such as South Africa and China. Many organizations develop codes of conduct for their approach to business around the world.
4. International business ethics refers to the conduct of MNCs in their relationships to all individuals and entities with whom they come into contact. Ethical behavior is judged and based largely on the cultural value system and the generally accepted ways of doing business in each country or society. MNC managers must decide whether to base their ethical standards on those of the host country or those of the home country and whether these different standards can be reconciled.
5. MNCs must balance their responsibility to various stakeholders, such as owners, creditors, consumers, employees, suppliers, governments, and societies.
6. Questionable payments are those payments that raise significant questions about appropriate moral behavior either in the host nation or other nations. The Foreign Corrupt Practices Act prohibits most questionable payments by U.S. companies doing business in other countries.
7. Managers must control their activities relative to interdependent relationships at all levels, from simple, daily business transactions involving local workers, intermediaries, or consumers to global concerns of ecological responsibility.
8. The MNC–host country relationship is generally a love–hate relationship from the host-country's viewpoint in that it wants the economic growth that the MNC can provide but does not want the dependency and other problems that can result.
9. The failure to manage interdependence effectively will result in constraints on strategy, in the least, or in disastrous consequences for the local area, the subsidiary, and the global reputation of the company.
10. Managing environmental interdependence includes the need to consider ecological interdependence as well as the economic and social implications of MNC activities.

Discussion Questions

1. Discuss the concept of international social responsibility. What role does it play in the relationship between a company and its host country?
2. Discuss the criticisms that have been leveled against MNCs in the past regarding their activities in less developed countries. What counterarguments are there to those criticisms?
3. What does moral universalism mean? Discuss your perspective on this concept. Do you think the goal of moral universalism is possible? Is it advisable?
4. What do you think should be the role of MNCs toward human rights issues in other countries—for example, China or South Africa? What are the major human rights concerns at this time? What ideas do you have for dealing with those problems? What is the role of corporate codes of conduct in dealing with these concerns?
5. What is meant by international business ethics? How does the local culture affect ethical practices? What are the implications of such local norms for ethical decisions by MNC managers?
6. As a manager in a foreign subsidiary, how can you reconcile local expectations of questionable payments with the Foreign Corrupt Practices Act? What is your stance on the problem of "pay-offs"? How does the degree of law enforcement in a particular country affect ethical behavior in business?
7. Explain what is meant by managing interdependence in the global business arena. Discuss the love–hate relationship between MNCs and host countries.
8. What do you think are the responsibilities of MNCs toward the global environment? Give some examples of MNC activities that run counter to the concepts of ecological interdependence and environmental responsibility.

Application Exercise

Do some research to find out the codes of conduct of two MNCs. Compare the issues that they cover and share your findings with the class. After several students have presented their findings, prepare a chart showing the commonalities and differences of content in the codes presented. How do you account for the differences?

Experiential Exercise

Consider the ethical dilemmas in the following situation and decide what you would do. Then meet in small groups and come to a group consensus. Discuss your decisions with the class.

I am CEO of an international trading company in Turkey. One state-owned manufacturing company (Company A) in one of the Middle East countries opened a tender for 15,000 tons PVC granule K value 70. Company A makes all its purchases through tenders. For seven years in that market my company has never been able to do any business with Company A (though we have sold many bulk materials to other state-owned companies in that market). One of our new managers had a connection with the purchasing manager of Company A, who promised to supply us with all of our competitors' bids if we pay him a 2 percent commission on all of our sales to his company. Our area manager accepted this arrangement. He got the competing bids, made our offer, and we got the tender. I learned of this situation when reviewing our income and expenses chart, which showed the 2 percent commission.

What shall I do, given the following: (1) If I refuse to accept the business without any legitimate reasons (presently there are none) my company will be black-listed in that country—where we get about 20 percent of our gross yearly profit. (2) If I accept the business and do not pay the 2 percent commission, the purchasing manager will make much trouble for us when he receives our shipment. I am sure that he will not release our 5 percent bank guarantee letter about the quality and quantity of the material. (3) If I accept the business and pay the 2 percent commission, it will go against everything I have achieved in the 30 years of my career.

You have three ethical problems here: First, your company has won a rigged bid. Second, you must pay the person who rigged it, or he will make life miserable for you. And third, you have to decide what to do with the area manager who accepted this arrangement.

Source: J. Delaney and D. Sockell, "Ethics in the Trenches," *Across the Board* (October 1990): 17.

Internet Resources

Visit the Deresky companion Web site at http://prenhall.com/Deresky for this chapter's Internet resources.

Case Study

Balancing Human Rights Around the World: Nike and Reebok

Nike and Reebok—two major footwear companies familiar to most people—outsource their footwear production around the world. But they each structure the outsourcing process differently.

Nike

Nike managers refer to their company as a "network firm"—one that is connected to other companies that produce their products. Nike employs 8,000 people in management, design, sales, and promotion, and leaves production in the hands of some 75,000 workers around the world, hired by independent contractors. Most of Nike's outsourced goods come from Indonesia and Vietnam, where wages are low and enforcement of labor laws is lax.

Recently, Nike has come under fire for its continuous relationship with some Korean and Vietnamese subcontractors who were accused of mistreating their workers. In Korea, there were reports of women being forced to kneel down and hold their hands up for 25 minutes, and another woman being subjected to having her mouth taped shut because of talking during working hours. In Vietnam, it was reported that a supervisor molested workers, and also that employees, mostly young females, were getting paid about $0.20 an hour and working six days a week (below the minimum wage in Vietnam).

These are just a few of the reported incidents involving Nike's "network firms." But Nike has kept the company out of the spotlight because it does not actually own these factories—it just does business with them. Nike has no plans to change their operations, and the company has used high-profile figures to downplay the problem. John Thompson, Georgetown basketball coach, hired by Nike, viewed a Vietnam plant and stated that he did not see any of the kinds of things he had heard about.

After these reports, Nike joined the list of companies adhering to the Anti-sweatshop Code of Conduct. In May 1998, Nike announced a new Code of Conduct, and it plans to select partners to participate in monitoring practices in Indonesia, China, and Vietnam. The company also announced in the fall of 1998 that it would lift wages for its entry-level factory workers in Indonesia by 22 percent to offset Indonesia's devalued currency.

Reebok

Reebok, a global athletic sports and fitness company, prides itself on its commitment to human rights. The company is also committed to finding partners who will use ethical manufacturing policies. Reebok helped establish the Task Force on Global Manufacturing Practices to organize, research, and develop recommendations for action.

Reebok has set stringent standards for production of their goods: the Reebok Human Rights Production Standards. Reebok will seek compliance with set standards in the selection of subcontractors, contractors, suppliers, and other business partners. Some of these standards include the following, as set out on their home page (http://www.reebok.com):

Working hours/overtime: Reebok seeks only partners that do not require more than 60-hour work weeks ... and it prefers those that use a 48-hour work week.

Forced or compulsory labor: Reebok will not work with or purchase materials from companies that use labor that is required as a means of political coercion as a punishment for holding or expressing political views.

Fair wages: Reebok searches for partners that share their belief in fair wages and benefits. Reebok will not select partners that pay less than minimum wage required by local law or pay their workers less than prevailing local industry practices.

Child labor: Reebok will not work with business partners that employ children in the production of goods (under 14 years of age).

Safe and healthy work environment: Reebok seeks business partners that provide workers with a safe and healthy workplace, and who do not expose workers to hazardous conditions.

Partners: Reebok will seek business partners that allow them full knowledge of the production facilities used and will undertake affirmative measures, such as on-site inspection of production facilities, to implement and monitor these standards.

One example of Reebok's commitment has been in reassessing their soccer ball business. After learning that as much as 20 percent of the soccer ball stitching in Pakistan may have been done by children, Reebok has tried to do their part in ending the poor conditions that have promoted child labor. After soliciting several proposals from soccer ball manufacturers in Pakistan, Reebok signed an agreement with Reed and Associates and Moltex Rubber Works to establish a new manufacturing facility. The terms of the agreement are that all work on the balls will be done inside the plant, and that all workers will be at least 15 years old and will be paid at least the minimum wage in Pakistan.

Case Questions

1. How do you assess the approaches of Nike and of Reebok to outsourcing around the world? Can you apply the term *ethnocentrism* or the term *ethical relativism* to either of these cases? What are your thoughts on the concept of moral universalism as it may pertain to these situations?

2. Do a "stakeholder analysis" for each company separately. Lay out the categories of stakeholders and detail for the "stake" of each party—the rights, obligations, incentives, and motivations. What is, or should be, their role in the dilemma of outsourcing production from countries in which there may be a sweatshop situation?

3. Return to your answers to question 1. Now assess the impact—the changes in stake—that your recommendations would have on each of the stakeholders you identified in question 2. Who benefits and who loses through the use of so-called sweatshops for outsourcing production? What do you think the future holds for this situation?

4. What actions can consumers take to end sweatshops? Do you think they should take action? What would be the results on the various stakeholders? Do you think the negative publicity about Nike has caused positive change in both companies' policies?

Sources: Robert Senser, "Human Rights for Workers Bulletin," http://ourworld.compuserve.com/homepages/HRW/bu10.htm; Reebok: "Reebok Production Standards," http://www.reebok.com/humanrights/products.htm; Reebok home page: http://www.reebok.com; http://www.Nikebiz.com; "A Floor Under Foreign Factories?" *Business Week*, November 2, 1998.

PART ONE
Comprehensive Cases

CASE 1
THE PROMINENT DR. ROMBACH

John had settled comfortably into the soft, leather passenger seat. The big, black Mercedes slipped silently onto the autobahn on the outskirts of Munich. In a few moments the driver, Klaus Ehrwald, was expertly guiding the car at over 120 miles per hour. They were heading for Salzburg, Austria, for a meeting with Dr. Hans Rombach, a prominent cardiovascular surgeon. At this speed it wouldn't take them long to get there.

John Cannon was an American expatriate managing the German subsidiary of International Medical Laboratories (IML), a large American biomedical equipment company specializing in expensive, high-quality heart/lung machines used in open heart surgery. John was a graduate of a prestigious American west coast university where he majored in international business and had been a very successful biotechnology market analyst early in his career. When he joined IML as their marketing product line manager for cardiovascular instrumentation, he was charged with the responsibility of taking the system into the international market. He immediately targeted Western Europe.

The system proved to be an instant success, with Germany the strongest market. It wasn't long until John was appointed the subsidiary manager for Germany and became a quick learner of local business practices. He was

determined to successfully promote the IML system to surgeons in all the clinics and hospitals in the German sales region. He had been living in Munich for over a year now.

He spoke casually about the upcoming meeting with Dr. Rombach to Klaus, his general sales manager. Klaus was a Bavarian native and understood the "Teutonic character" very well.

John: *I've been wanting to meet Dr. Rombach for a long time, Klaus. He has quite a reputation among his peers. What sort of a man is he?*

Klaus: *Pretty typical for a successful European surgeon: arrogant, confident and with a very great opinion of himself. He did one of the very first heart transplants in Austria, and now people come from everywhere to him for routine cardiovascular surgery. He does four or five surgeries a week and makes a fortune. He has really pioneered some new, successful procedures and publishes the results of his work in the very best medical journals. He has an international reputation as both a brilliant surgeon and a very successful entrepreneur at his private clinic.*

John: *What kind of equipment is he using now?*

Klaus: *He's using a Freznus system, German of course. It's not as good as ours, but the company has been around for a long time and he's been using their equipment for years. Like most surgeons, he doesn't like to change equipment once he gets used to it.*

John: *As I recall, we can be very price-competitive with Freznus. Our system sells for about $25,000, and theirs typically sells for over $30,000 when you compare all the same features. Besides, we have a much more stable temperature control system (for controlling blood temperatures during bypass surgery) plus*

---

the very latest technology in the new pump systems. Our overall system is based on U.S. technology, and one of the main subsystems now includes new Swiss-designed pumps which are generally thought to be the most reliable in the world.

Klaus: *Tell it to Dr. Rombach. I've been trying to sell him on our system for a long time, but he continues to use the German system in spite of the price difference and the high-tech image of our equipment. He's very concerned about quality and reliability. I guess he regards the German equipment as being more reliable, or maybe he's just nationalistic.*

As they moved smoothly and swiftly along the autobahn, John thought about the nationalism issue for a while. It was true that many citizens of Europe actively sought out nationally produced products—the French, Germans, and the British in particular. In some cases it was a subconscious sort of thing. In other cases it was very specific. In order to sell capital equipment to the public hospitals and clinics in France, for example, you had to be named on the French-approved supplier list. The only companies which appeared on the list were French companies or perhaps a few foreign firms that had no French competitor.

The Austrians were not quite so tough on foreigners, but they typically favored the German products. John hoped that the current attempt to unite Europe would help to remove some of the traditional barriers to foreign products. He thought carefully about how to approach this issue with Dr. Rombach and decided to let the product speak for itself. After all, the IML system was in use in the most prestigious heart hospitals in the United States and that fact would not be lost on the prominent doctor.

After a brief conversation with Klaus on sales strategy and a technical comparison of the competing systems, they exited the autobahn onto a long, sweeping curve, gearing down smoothly, and soon arrived at the outskirts of Salzburg. Dr. Rombach's clinic was only a few kilometers from the exit. As they approached the clinic, John could not help but admire the gracious old building with its Greek columns. Upon entering, they were struck by the transition from the dusty marble entryway with its classic style of architecture to a modern, gleaming, state-of-the-art medical facility. There was no mistaking the detailed attention to high quality everywhere. Dr. Rombach's office was on the third floor, overlooking the river and the woods beyond. The secretary greeted them efficiently and confirmed their appointment. Yes ... the doctor was in and expecting them.

As they were being ushered into the office, Dr. Rombach swiveled around in his huge chair and rose to welcome them.

Klaus: *Good morning Dr. Rombach. I'd like to introduce my colleague, Herr Cannon.*

Dr. Rombach: *Ah, good morning Herr Ehrwald and Herr Cannon. I suppose you have come to tell me of your new and wonderful American equipment.*

Klaus: *Of course. As always, we wish you to have the very best equipment for your work.*

Dr. Rombach: *Fine, fine ... Let us have some coffee while we chat, and then I shall take you for a tour of our facility and show you our new operating theaters and recovery wing, just finished last month.*

As they began to make conversation, both John and Klaus were careful to avoid any direct mention of their purpose for the visit. All parties knew that they were there to talk about the American equipment, but it could wait until the proper moment. The tour was impressive. State-of-the-art equipment was everywhere; the facilities and laboratories were the most modern John had ever seen. He had recently been in Los Angeles, Houston, and Minneapolis to see the best of the U.S. facilities, as well as the new hospital in Rotterdam, but this clinic was truly incredible. He noted the Freznus equipment in the operating theaters. It seemed oddly dated among all the other high tech equipment.

Dr. Rombach: *We have been able to reduce the stay in our clinic to only four or five days following open heart surgery. Most of the best hospitals around the world require two or three weeks. It's due to our new surgical techniques and postoperative care. We have the highest success rate and the best recovery time in the world. I've just published an article in the* European Medical Review *describing our successful program.*

John: *This is really incredible, Dr. Rombach. To what do you owe your success?*

Dr. Rombach: *Good people, good technology, and good care. There's nothing mystical about good medicine. The technology helps you make good diagnoses and safe surgeries. The people provide the skill, the support, and the care necessary for success. We have also developed some new low-trauma techniques that seem to work very well.*

John's mind was racing. If they could convince Dr. Rombach to use their equipment, they could be a part of every medical advance he reported. Everyone would want to use the same equipment and follow the same techniques pioneered here. John quietly wondered why Klaus had not yet been able to sell him on the IML system. They returned to Dr. Rombach's office for some earnest conversation.

John: *I know you're very busy, Dr. Rombach, so I won't waste your time with a lengthy sales pitch about the IML system. But I did want to be sure that you knew about our recent advances in temperature controls and our new pumping system that uses the Friedreich pumps from Switzerland.*

Dr. Rombach: *Yes, yes ... I know all about them. I was in the Friedreich factory in Zurich just a few months ago. You see, Karl Friedreich is an old friend of mine. I even gave him some ideas on the best way to design the perfusionist's cart.*

John: *Then you know that the IML system has the most reliable pumps in the world.*

Dr. Rombach: *Of course. That's why I'm willing to talk to you about your system.*

John: *I guess you also know that Drs. Shumway, Barnard, and DeBaky also use the IML system. (John was banking on the use of these prominent surgeons' names to impress Dr. Rombach. While they had not specifically endorsed IML, they did indeed use the system.)*

Dr. Rombach: *Yes, I spoke with DeBaky in Houston last year. He seemed satisfied enough with the system. But, he's sort of retired now and is not active as he once was.*

John: *We would very much like to see you using the IML system, too. It's really more cost-effective than your present Freznus system, and with the Friedreich pumps, perhaps even more reliable.*

Dr. Rombach: *Perhaps. I am impressed with your system and may be willing to give it a try, especially if it can help my research. You know, conducting our research is very expensive. Our research methods must use real patients to be of any practical value to other surgeons. This means not only developing new techniques but advising patients, obtaining consents, explaining methods, publishing results, etc. Would your company, IML, be willing to make a contribution to my research fund? This would make my decision to purchase your equipment much easier.*

John: *Um ... contribution to your research fund? Well, I don't know. How much did you have in mind?*

Dr. Rombach: *Well any amount would be helpful, but $25,000 or so would be particularly helpful.*

John's memory flashed to a recent meeting at corporate headquarters. The subject was the various forms of international bribery and the interpretation of the Foreign Corrupt Practices Act (see Exhibit C1–1) as passed by Congress after the Lockheed scandal in Japan. The company was very specific about adherence to the letter of the law of this act and maintained a corporate position of steadfastly refusing to participate in any questionable actions, no matter how they might be presented. Being a leader in the life-saving medical equipment business meant that the company should also be perceived as a leader in maintaining absolute trust in the public eye and unquestioned ethical behavior. Their reputation meant everything, and even the appearance of inappropriate behavior could be disastrous. They had included in their corporate mission the statement "The company does not engage in any sort of activity which might be construed as unethical." Their consistent advice was to "just say no" to any questionable request. But still, John hesitated. Was this really a request for a bribe? After all, Dr. Rombach was the most prominent cardiovascular surgeon in Europe. Everyone knew him—he certainly published a lot of his research. Surely a $25,000 contribution could be made up in future sales of the IML system once the medical community knew that Dr. Rombach was using the IML system in his work. After all, the system produced a 10-percent pre-tax margin so they would only have to sell an extra ten systems to break even. Rombach might even buy three or four himself!

John: *Well, I guess I'll have to think about that. Perhaps I can discuss this with our management and we can get back to you.*

Dr. Rombach: *Of course. My secretary will show you out. Have a safe trip back to Munich.*

Having said that, Dr. Rombach smiled, punched a button on his telephone, and turned his attention to his work on the desk. His secretary appeared immediately and courteously showed them the way to their car.

As Klaus eased the Mercedes back onto the autobahn, John thought about the possibilities. He knew that if he contacted the corporate management, they would never approve such an expenditure. In fact, it might be risky to even ask. They might see him as a questionable representative of IML with regard to ethical issues. He knew that several other Austrian cardiovascular surgeons had purchased

EXHIBIT C1–1

Foreign Corrupt Practices Act—Prohibited Activities

1. Any payment to a foreign official, foreign political party, or candidate for foreign political office, for the purpose of influencing any act or decision to obtain, retain or assist in obtaining business for the company.
2. The maintenance of "off book" accounts or "slush funds."
3. Intentionally making false statements on company books, records and supporting documents, such as payments for services or payments on expense accounts.
4. Engaging in overbilling, underbilling or other practice for the purpose of effecting transactions or improper payments which will not be accurately reflected in the company's books.
5. Making any payment which, in whole or part, is used for purposes other than those designated by the documents supporting or authorizing them.

the IML system without any requests for research funds. Still, John was sure that it made some good business sense to consider it. There was almost $100,000 available in the budget for discretionary spending. It was supposed to be used to promote IML products in whatever way he thought was most effective. He knew he would receive lots of recognition if he could get Dr. Rombach as an IML system customer. He also knew everyone would want to know exactly how he had pulled off such a coup.

John: *Klaus, do you think Freznus makes contributions to Dr. Rombach's research fund?*

Klaus: *Well, I suspect they might. What do you think?*

John: *I don't know what to think. What should we do?*

CASE QUESTIONS

1. How should John Cannon deal with this situation?
2. How does an American expatriate deal with value systems which are not necessarily wrong in a foreign culture but are very different from what is commonly practiced in the United States? What ethical frameworks can we use to evaluate the possible decisions, and what outcomes do they produce? How do we judge which is the best?

CASE 2

FOOTWEAR INTERNATIONAL

John Carlson frowned as he studied the translation of the front-page story from the afternoon's edition of the *Meillat*, a fundamentalist newspaper with close ties to an opposition political party. The story, titled "Footwear's Unpardonable Audacity," suggested that the company had knowingly insulted Islam by including the name of Allah in a design used on the insoles of sandals it was manufacturing. To compound the problem, the paper had run a photograph of one of the offending sandals on the front page. As a result, student groups were calling for public demonstrations against Footwear the next day. As managing director of Footwear Bangladesh, Carlson knew he would have to act quickly to defuse a potentially explosive situation.

FOOTWEAR INTERNATIONAL

Footwear International is a multinational manufacturer and marketer of footwear. Operations span the globe and include more than 83 companies in 70 countries. These include shoe factories, tanneries, engineering plants producing shoe machinery and moulds, product development studios, hosiery factories, quality control laboratories, and approximately 6,300 retail stores and 50,000 independent retailers.

Footwear employs more than 67,000 people and produces and sells in excess of 270 million pairs of shoes every year. The head office acts as a service center and is staffed with specialists drawn from all over the world. These specialists, in areas such as marketing, retailing, product development, communications, store design, electronic data processing, and business administration, travel for much of the year to share their expertise with the various companies. Training and technical education, offered through company-run colleges and the training facility at headquarters, provide the latest skills to employees from around the world.

Although Footwear requires standardization in technology and the design of facilities, it also encourages a high degree of decentralization and autonomy in its operations. The companies are virtually self-governing, which means their allegiance belongs to the countries in which they operate. Each is answerable to a board of directors that includes representatives from the local business community. The concept of "partnership" at the local level has made the company welcome internationally and has allowed it to operate successfully in countries where other multinationals have been unable to survive.

BANGLADESH

With a population approaching 110 million in an area of 143,998 square kilometers (see Exhibit C2–1), Bangladesh is the most densely populated country in the world. It is also among the most impoverished, with a 1987 per capita gross national product of $160 and a high reliance on foreign aid.

EXHIBIT C2–1

Bangladesh

More than 40 percent of the gross domestic product is generated by agriculture, and more than 60 percent of its economically active population works in the agriculture sector. Although the land in Bangladesh is fertile, the country has a tropical monsoon climate and suffers from the ravages of periodic cyclones. In 1988, the country experienced the worst floods in recorded history.

The population of Bangladesh is 85 percent Muslim, and Islam was made the official state religion in 1988. Approximately 95 percent of the population speaks Bengali, with most of the remainder speaking tribal dialects.

Bangladesh has had a turbulent history in the 20th century. Most of the country was part of the British-ruled East Bengal until 1947. In that year, it joined with Assam to become East Pakistan, a province of the newly created country of Pakistan. East Pakistan was separated from the four provinces of West Pakistan by 1,600 kilometers of Indian territory, and although the East was more populous, the national capital was established in West Pakistan. Over the following years, widespread discontent built in the East whose people felt that they received a disproportionately small amount of development funding and were underrepresented in government.

Following a period of unrest starting in 1969, the Awami League, the leading political party in East Pakistan, won an overwhelming victory in local elections held in 1970. The victory promised to give the league, which was pro-independence, control in the National Assembly. To prevent that happening, the national government suspended the convening of the Assembly indefinitely. On March 26, 1971, the Awami League proclaimed the independence of the People's Republic of Bangladesh, and civil war quickly followed. In the ensuing conflict, hundreds of thousands of refugees fled to safety across the border in India. In December, India, which supported the independence of Bangladesh, declared war, and 12 days later Pakistan surrendered. Bangladesh had won its independence, and the capital of the new country was established at Dhaka. In the years immediately following independence, industrial output declined in major industries as the result of the departure of many of the largely non-Bengali financier and managerial class.

Throughout the subsequent years, political stability proved elusive for Bangladesh. Although elections were held, stability was threatened by the terrorist tactics resorted to by opposition groups from both political extremes. Coups and countercoups, assassinations, and suspension of civil liberties became regular occurrences.

Since 1983, Bangladesh had been ruled by the self-proclaimed President General H. M. Ershad. Despite demonstrations in 1987 that led to a state of emergency being declared, Ershad managed to retain power in elections held the following year. The country remains politically volatile, however. Dozens of political parties continually maneuver for position, and alliances and coalitions are the order of the day. The principal opposition party is the Awami League, an alliance of eight political parties. Many of the parties are closely linked with so-called opposition newspapers, which promote their political positions. Strikes and demonstrations are frequent and often result from cooperation among opposition political parties, student groups, and unions.

FOOTWEAR BANGLADESH

Footwear became active in what was then East Bengal in the 1930s. In 1962, the first major investment took place with the construction of a footwear manufacturing facility at Tongi, an industrial town located 30 kilometers north of Dhaka. During the following years, the company expanded its presence in both conventional and unconventional ways. In 1971, the then managing director became a freedom fighter, while continuing to oversee operations. He subsequently became the only foreigner to be decorated by the government with the "Bir Protik" in recognition of both his and the company's contribution to the independence of Bangladesh.

In 1985, Footwear Bangladesh went public and two years later spearheaded the largest private-sector foreign investment in the country, a tannery and footwear factory at Dhamrai. The new tannery produced leather for local Footwear needs and the export market, and the factory produced a variety of footwear for the local market.

By 1988, Footwear Bangladesh employed 1,800 employees and sold through 81 stores and 54 agencies. The company introduced approximately 300 new products a year to the market using their in-house design and development capability. Footwear managers were particularly proud of the capability of the personnel in these departments, all of whom were Bangladeshi.

Annual sales in excess of 10 million pairs of footwear gave the company 15 percent of the national market in 1988. Revenues exceeded $30 million and after-tax profit was approximately $1 million. Financially, the company was considered a medium contributor within the Footwear organization. With a population approaching 110 million, and per capita consumption of one pair of shoes every two

years, Bangladesh was perceived as offering Footwear enormous potential for growth both through consumer education and competitive pressure.

The managing director of Footwear Bangladesh was John Carlson, one of only four foreigners working for the company. The others were the managers of production, marketing, and sales. All had extensive and varied experience within the Footwear organization.

THE INCIDENT

On Thursday, June 22, 1989, John Carlson was shown a copy of that day's *Meillat,* a well-known opposition newspaper with pro-Libyan leanings. Under the headline "Footwear's Unpardonable Audacity," the writer suggested that the design on the insole of one model of sandal produced by the company included the Arabic spelling of the word *Allah* (see Exhibit C2–2). The story went on to suggest that Footwear was under Jewish ownership and to link the alleged offense with the gunning down of many people in

EXHIBIT C2-2

Translation of the Meillat Story*

Unpardonable Audacity of Footwear

In Bangladesh a Sandal with Allah as Footwear trade mark in Arabic designed in calligraphy has been marketed although last year Islam was made the State Religion in Bangladesh. The Sandal in black and white contains Allah in black. Prima facie it appears it has been designed and the Alif "the first letter in Arabic" has been jointly written. Excluding Alif it reads LILLAH. In Bangladesh after the Satan Rushdie's† Satanic Verses which has brought unprecedented demonstration and innumerable strikes (Hartels). This International shoe manufacturing organization under Jewish ownership with the design of Allah has made religious offense. Where for sanctity of Islam one million people of Afghanistan have sacrificed their lives and wherein occupied Palestine many people have been gunned down by Jews for sanctity of Islam in this country the word Allah under this guise has been put under feet.

Last night a group of students from Dhaka university came to Meillat office with a couple of pairs of Sandal. The management staff of Footwear was not available over telephone. This sandal has got two straps made of foam.

*The translation is identical to that which Carlson was given at work.
†Salman Rushdie was the author of the controversial book The Satanic Verses. The author had been sentenced to death, in absentia, by Ayatollah Khomeini, the late leader of Iran, for crimes against Islam.

EXHIBIT C2–3

The Temple Bells and the Design Used on the Sandal

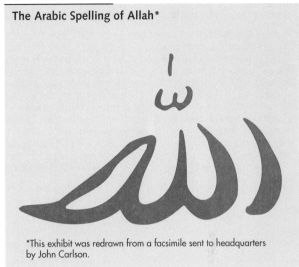

Company
name and
logo*

*The company's name and logo appeared prominently on the insole of the sandal.
Both of the images in the exhibit were redrawn from copies of facsimiles sent to
headquarters by John Carlson.

EXHIBIT C2–4

The Arabic Spelling of Allah*

*This exhibit was redrawn from a facsimile sent to headquarters
by John Carlson.

mitted to her supervisor for consideration and approval (see Exhibit C2–3).

All the employees in the development and marketing department were Muslims. The supervisor reported that the woman who had produced the offending design was a devout Bengali Muslim who spoke and read no Arabic. The same was true of almost all the employees in the department. The supervisor confirmed to Carlson that numerous people in the department had seen the new design prior to its approval, and no one had seen any problem or raised any objection to it. Following the conversation, Carlson compared the design to the word *Allah,* which he had arranged to have written in Arabic (see Exhibit C2–4).

Carlson was perplexed by the article and its timing. The sandals in question were not new to the market and had not been subject to prior complaints. As he reread the translation of the *Meillat* article, he wondered why the Jewish reference had been made when the family that owned Footwear International was Christian. He also wondered if the fact that students from the university had taken the sandals to the paper was significant.

As the day progressed, the situation got worse. Carlson was shown a translation of a proclamation that had been circulated by two youth groups calling for demonstrations against Footwear to be held the next day (see Exhibit C2–5). The proclamation linked Footwear, Salman Rushdie, and the

Palestine by Jews. The story highlighted the fact that the design was on the insole of the sandal and therefore, next to the bottom of the foot, a sign of great disrespect to Muslims.

Carlson immediately contacted the supervisor of the design department and asked for any information he could provide on the design on the sandals. He already knew that they were from a medium-priced line of women's footwear that had the design on the insole changed often as a marketing feature. Following his investigation, the supervisor reported that the design had been based on a set of Chinese temple bells that the designer had purchased in the local market. Pleased by the appearance of the bells, she had used them as the basis for a stylized design, which she sub-

EXHIBIT C2–5

Translation of the Student Group's Proclamation*

The audacity through the use of the name "Allah" in a sandal.

Let Rushdie's Jewish Footwear Company be prohibited in Bangladesh.

Dear people who believe in one God it is announced in the holy Quran Allahs name is above everything but shoe manufacturing Jewish Footwear Shoe Company has used the name Allah and shown disrespect of unprecedented nature and also unpardonable audacity. After the failure of Rushdie's efforts to destroy the beliefs of Muslims in the Quran, Islam and the prophet (SM) who is the writer of Satanic verses the Jewish People have started offending the Muslims. This time it is a fight against Allah. In fact Daud Haider, Salman Rushdie Viking Penguin and Footwear Shoe Company all are supported and financed by Jewish community. Therefore no compromise with them. Even at the cost of our lives we have to protest against this conspiracy.

For this procession and demonstration will be held on 23rd. June Friday after Jumma prayer from Baitul Mukarram Mosque south gate. Please join this procession and announce we will not pardon Footwear Shoe Company's audacity. Footwear Shoe Company has to be prohibited, don't buy Jewish products and Footwear shoes. Be aware Rushdie's partner.

Issued by Bangladesh Islamic Jubashibir (Youth Student Forum) and Bangladesh Islamic Satrashbir (Student Forum)

———
Source: *The translation is identical to that which Carlson was given at work.

Jewish community, and ominously stated that "even at the cost of our lives we have to protest against this conspiracy."

More bad news followed. Calls had been made for charges to be laid against Carlson and four others under a section of the criminal code that forbade "deliberate and malicious acts intended to outrage feelings of any class by insulting its religion or religious believers" (see Exhibit C2–6). A short time later, Carlson received a copy of a statement that had been filed by a local lawyer although no warrants were immediately forthcoming (see Exhibit C2–7).

While he was reviewing the situation, Carlson was interrupted by his secretary. In an excited voice, she

EXHIBIT C2–6

Section 295 of the Criminal Code

295-A. *Deliberate and malicious acts intended to outrage religious feelings of any class by insulting its religion or religious believers.* Whoever, with deliberate and malicious intention of outraging the religious feelings of any class of [the citizens of Bangladesh], by words, either spoken or written, or by visible representations, insults, or attempts to insult the religion or religious beliefs of that class, shall be punished with imprisonment . . .

. . . In order to bring a matter under S. 295-A it is not the mere matter of discourse or the written expression but also the manner of it which has to be looked to. In other words the expressions should be such as are bound to be regarded by any reasonable man as grossly offensive and provocative and maliciously and deliberately intended to outrage the feelings of any class of citizens. . . . If the injurious act was done voluntarily without a lawful excuse, malice may be presumed.

EXHIBIT C2–7

The Statement of the Plaintiff

The plaintiff most respectfully states that:

1) The plaintiff is a lawyer, and a Bangladeshi Citizen and his religion is Islam. He is basically a devout Muslim. According to Islamic tradition he regularly performs his daily work.

2) The first accused of this . . . is the Managing Director of Footwear Shoe Company, the second accused is the Production Manager of the said company, the third accused is the Marketing Manager, the fourth accused is the Calligrapher of the said company and last accused is the Sales Manager of the said company. The said company is an international organization having shoe business in different countries.

3) The accused persons deliberately wanted to outrage the religion of Muslims by engraving the calligraphy of "Allah" in Arabic on a sandal thereby to offend the Religion of majority this Muslim Country. By marketing this sandal with the calligraphy of "Allah" they have offended the religious feelings of millions of Muslims. It is the solemn religious duty and responsibility of every devout Muslim to protect the sanctity of "Allah." The plaintiff first saw the sandal with this calligraphy on 22nd June 1989 at Elephant road shop.

The accused persons collectively and deliberately wanted this calligraphy under the feet thereby to offend the religion of mine and many other Muslims and have committed a crime under provisions of section 295A of the Penal Code. At the time of hearing the evidence will be provided.

Therefore under the provisions of section 295A of the Penal Code the accused persons be issued with warrant of arrest and be brought to court for justice.

The names of the Witnesses

1)
2)
3)

informed him that the prime minister was being quoted as calling the sandal incident an "unforgivable crime." The seriousness of the incident seemed to be escalating rapidly, and Carlson wondered what he should do to try to minimize the damage.

Source: Reproduced by permission of the author. (Copyright © R. William Blake, Faculty of Business Administration, Memorial University of Newfoundland, St. Johns, Canada.)

CASE QUESTIONS

You are in John Carlson's position. Analyze the situation facing Footwear, and prepare a detailed plan of action to deal with your immediate responsibilities as well as the entire situation and a long-term plan. The following suggestions may help you develop your plan:

- Use a stakeholder analysis to assess the role and objectives of various interest groups and evaluate what is going on and why, and to look beyond the immediate situation.
- Consider what role or roles local politics play in the Footwear case, and who are the principal actors in this real-life business drama.
- What issues are of greatest concern to Footwear Bangladesh? To Footwear International?

Note: These events actually happened. Ask your professor for the information on the follow-up events. Do you think this situation could happen again?

CASE 3

COLGATE-PALMOLIVE IN POSTAPARTHEID SOUTH AFRICA

After a month of intense contemplation, Carol Lewis decided to accept the position of head of Colgate-Palmolive Foundation (South Africa). Carol learned in her job interview that the American subsidiary, based in South Africa, was committed to extending its leadership role in generating social responsibility (SR) activities in a postapartheid South Africa (see appendix).

"Ever since 1967, when four dental educators first went into the surrounding black townships to educate residents about teeth that can be strong and healthy through receiving daily care and nourishment, investing in communities where the firm earns its living had been—and would continue to be—integral to its South African mission," Vice President David Moore told her.

Indeed, Carol had studied the American firm and learned that Colgate-Palmolive had achieved an outstanding Category 1 rating on the Sullivan Code for South Africa (see Exhibit C3–1). She discovered that compliance to the code requires a firm to direct 12 percent of its salary budget to social responsibility efforts. And she knew the company meant business about their SR activities. The firm had recently launched the $3 million Colgate-Palmolive Foundation. Many South African firms believed this level of achievement was beyond even their financial reach.

So Carol was glad to have been selected to lead Colgate-Palmolive's SR initiatives. With more than $100 million annual sales and a workforce of 600 employees, she

EXHIBIT C3–1

Signatory Code for South Africa

These were devised in 1977 by the Reverend Leon Sullivan of Philadelphia as a code of conduct for American multinationals in South Africa.

Principle 1
Nonsegregation of the races in all eating, comfort, locker room and work facilities.

Principle 2
Equal and fair employment practices for all employees.

Principle 3
Equal pay for all employees doing equal or comparable work for the same period of time.

Principle 4
Initiation and development of training programs that will prepare blacks, coloured, and Asians in substantial numbers for supervisory, administrative, clerical and technical jobs.

Principle 5
Increasing the number of blacks, coloured, and Asians in management and supervisory positions.

Principle 6
Improving the equality of employees' lives outside the work environment in such areas as housing, transportation, schooling, recreations and health facilities.

Principle 7
Working to eliminate laws and customs that impede social and political justice.

believed that the American firm could continue to build on its stellar track record (see Exhibit C3–2 for Mission Statement).

After a month spent doing MBWA (management by wandering around) on the job, Carol had listened to the opinions of individual and group stakeholders in the firm. She had learned about the kinds of SR initiatives they thought the firm should consider in a postapartheid South Africa.

First, she discovered that Colgate-Palmolive employees were the highest-paid workers in the industry. In fact, she learned that the firm pays employees in excess of stipulations listed in the Sullivan principles.

Second, she learned of the overwhelming support of all employees to the SR initiatives of Colgate-Palmolive. Indeed, she'd been frequently stopped in hallways and on factory floors by employees who thanked her and the company profusely for, among other things, helping their kids with school bursaries, receiving funds for school fees for employees (on the condition they pass their subjects), and nutritional classes. She learned from her briefing by senior management that the primary mission of the firm's SR efforts was to "accelerate economic empowerment through education by developing formal and informal educational skills and motivating communities to become self-sufficient" (see a list and description of specific SR activities of Colgate-Palmolive at conclusion of case). In fact, the firm had "adopted" seven schools that could approach an employee committee with requests for anything from photocopying ink to teacher and pupil upgrading programs.

Third, she learned that Colgate-Palmolive sponsors professional nurses to help daycare centers, schools, and community groups with primary health care education.

Fourth, she learned of the strategic initiative of top management to institute a formal "affirmative action" plan for black employees that would be implemented as a strategy to accelerate economic empowerment and remove any barriers to advancement into senior corporate positions.

Fifth, Carol listened to the appreciative comments from union leaders and community activists about the "social justice" role the firm had performed for its surrounding communities. She learned the firm had become politically active to assist neighboring communities in two ways. First, she discovered that Colgate-Palmolive had provided legal assistance to members of a neighboring squatter camp who had been intimidated by the local town council while steps were being taken to solve the squatter problem. Second, she discovered that although the American firm explicitly advocated nonalignment with any political party, initiatives were in place, at the request of community leaders, to provide "democracy training" as a social justice program. Indeed, materials she studied indicated that the firm sponsored lectures for the community by academics and other experts on specific subjects, such as voting procedures of issues connected with a bill of rights (these courses were offered for both white and black groups and communities).

Finally, Carol found out that the SR projects that "worked" and achieved Colgate-Palmolive's mission were ones in which people who were beneficiaries of the project were actively involved in formulating and implementing each activity. Colgate-Palmolive followed the process of consultation with all stakeholders throughout their SR initiatives.

Carol paused, however, to reflect on a number of disturbing issues that had surfaced in personal interviews with some trade union leaders and community activists. In one of her meetings with trade union shop stewards, they argued that union leaders, not management, should direct and manage Colgate-Palmolive's SR budget since they believed their constituency was the primary stakeholder group who were recipients of the firm's SR activities.

Carol countered that the SR budget should remain with the Foundation since Colgate-Palmolive's unionized workforce comprised only 50 percent of employees and the firm had to ensure fair representation for all employees. Besides, Carol indicated to the shop stewards that the firm's SR activities were for "underprivileged" communities represented by all employee stakeholder race and ethnic groups.

EXHIBIT C3–2

Mission Statement

Colgate-Palmolive is committed, through its social investment program, to support social and socio-economic projects; in particular, those that promote the principles and structures of a non-racial society, equality of opportunity, advancement based on merit and freedom of association and speech.

We are dedicated to the upliftment of the quality of life for all South Africans through education, health and youthful sporting activities, which will encourage self-development and confidence-building to create an improved social climate in the South African community

Carol speculated on another issue that had surfaced with trade union leaders that made her uncomfortable. She wondered about the extent to which union leaders were genuinely interested in the needs of their community. She considered whether, based on her interviews with union leaders, they were more inclined to support issues to gain "political" favor with their followers inside the firm than the company's stakeholders and surrounding communities outside the firm. For example, she remembered a discussion she'd had with union leaders about the best method to provide bursaries to the children of employees. Union leaders pressed hard to have ten bursaries that paid all fees. What's more, the union wanted to announce this decision to employees as a concession they'd obtained from management. On the other hand, she argued for shared responsibility of bursaries where parents paid a nominal amount and Colgate-Palmolive contributed the remainder so that the budget would allow for an additional 20 bursaries and thus provide funding assistance to more in need. She believed this alternative was consistent with the notion that "shared help" is more effective than a "hand-out" in the firm's commitment to economic empowerment for underprivileged communities.

Finally, Carol reflected on an issue that several union representatives had raised during her interviews. Some leaders saw a dilemma for the firm. They pointed out that the firm was self-serving in promoting SR initiatives because a number of products were "sold" under the umbrella of social responsibility activities. For example, one leader described how the firm had supported primary healthcare education activities for a local community. He conceded that parents and children who received healthcare and nutritional hand-outs, posters, and other reading materials featuring a cartoon and logo depicting the "Colgate Smile" were helped by the program. On the other hand, they also received information promoting the "purchase" of oral care products sold by Colgate-Palmolive. He queried her, "Is it right to help underprivileged communities while at the same time also promoting your products to these communities?"

Carol frowned as she considered these issues; then the phone rang and she had to dash out, reminding herself to gain closure on the issues facing her.

CASE QUESTIONS

1. What method did Carol use to probe stakeholder opinion about Colgate-Palmolive's social responsibility initiatives in South Africa? Assume you have arrived from the United States to manage your firm's operations in a foreign country, what are the advantages and disadvantages of using this method to discover what employees think?

2. Colgate-Palmolive is politically active in a postapartheid South Africa as part of its social responsibility initiatives. Should American firms continue their political activism in a postapartheid South African society? What implications does your answer have for U.S. firms conducting similar activities in other countries, or foreign firms conducting similar activities in the United States?

3. If you believe trade union criticisms that Colgate-Palmolive is selling several products in South Africa under the umbrella of social responsibility activities, what ethical issues need to be considered?

4. From your reading of this case, what specific knowledge and skills do you believe American managers need to learn?

APPENDIX

Social Responsibility Activities through Education

Primary School. Colgate-Palmolive was at the forefront of the adopted school initiative in South Africa. In 1977, Kutloanong Primary School in Vosloorus was the first school to receive assistance under this scheme, and Colgate-Palmolive now has five adopted primary schools in Vosloorus and Daveyton, all receiving assistance for teacher upgrade, media equipment, books, sports equipment, and even basics such as electricity and burglar-proofing.

High School. The St. Andrews Outreach and Bridging Program takes disadvantaged children from Daveyton to St. Andrews for additional and remedial tuition. Recreational days and fun events are also organized.

University. Preprimary- to tertiary-level bursaries are offered to employees' dependents. The bursaries, which cover fees and textbooks, are also offered to dependents of retired and deceased employees.

Colgate-Palmolive's assistance to the Academic Support Program at the University of the Witwatersrand is structured to supplement students' lectures, particularly at first-year level.

Colgate-Palmolive recognizes the lack of adequate career guidance material and funds a high school career guidance program at the Medical University of South Africa.

An annual bursary donation is made to Medunsa and awarded by the university to dental students. A number of students also benefit each year from bursary funding to the University of Cape Town.

Forty schools on the East Rand participated in the Deved Trust's Career Guidance Teachers' Program. Regular workshops and visits to industries give the teachers a better perception of the education necessary to enter identified careers.

The foundation supports teacher upgrade programs at the East Rand College of Education, Vista, and Promat. It also funds research surveys undertaken by Amcham's Policy Research Unit into open, nonracial education in East Rand schools. This includes high school teacher training in cultural issues, and symposia for principals from TED and DET schools in the Boksburg area.

As part of their college diploma course, Technikon students are required to undertake six months' practical experience in industry. Colgate-Palmolive has assisted many students to obtain their diplomas in analytical chemistry, chemical engineering, and production management through these six-month practical training periods.

Social Responsibility Activities Through Community Projects

The Colgate-Palmolive Youth for South Africa program, started in January 1993, highlights the positive side of today's young people. It is aimed at encouraging youth groups to become more responsible to their communities, and rewards their efforts in diverse ways, as follows:

- Support is given to the Institute of Natural Resources project in KwaZulu, which includes water purification and basic sanitation work.
- Funding is provided for the St. Anthony's Aged Center in Johannesburg.
- Colgate-Palmolive organizes and manages the nonracial Colgate 15-km Road Race, which attracts more than 4,500 runners each year. A percentage of the entrance money, matched by Colgate-Palmolive, is given to the Retinitis Pigmentosa Organization.
- Assistance is provided to the House of Mercy drug and alcohol rehabilitation center run by St. Anthony's.
- Colgate-Palmolive sponsors the running costs of the St. Francis House for the terminally ill.

- AIDs Education Programs include sponsorship of an AIDs awareness page in school exercise books piloted by the Johannesburg City Council Health Department, as well as in-house programs for Colgate-Palmolive employees.
- The Medunsa/Colgate Mobile Dental Unit provides treatment to underprivileged communities in the northeastern Transvaal.
- Mobile Dental Units provide treatment to underprivileged communities in South Africa. Colgate-Palmolive sponsorship has enabled the Departments of Community Dentistry at the Universities of Witwatersrand, Pretoria, and Medunsa to operate the three units currently providing this much needed service in both rural and urban areas.
- The Business Development Training–East Rand Townships Project offers basic business skills training courses. This program gives opportunities to informal businesses to develop and create additional job opportunities in these areas of high unemployment.
- Colgate-Palmolive supports the nonracial Eagle Tumbling Club, which offers gymnastics and tumbling training to children; it also covers transport and equipment costs.
- The Durban Lifesaver project sponsors the training and equipment needs of black lifesavers.
- Assistance and funding is provided to the Daveyton Physically Handicapped Training Center, where a workshop offers sheltered employment.
- A Mobile Health Clinic has been built, using a bus, and is utilized in the expanding township of Vosloorus.
- Health education programs are provided by medical and dental students at rural clinics as part of the Medunsa–Children's Clinic and Community Program. Funding is provided for a dental clinic located next to the children's medical ward at the provincial hospital adjoining Medunsa, and treatment is given free of charge by final-year Medunsa dental students.

Source: David T. Beaty, School of Business, Hampton University, Virginia, 1994. Used with permission. Copyright ©1995 by David T. Beaty. This case is presented as a basis for educational discussion rather than to illustrate either effective or ineffective handling of an administrative situation.

CASE 4

LA KEISHA WASHINGTON'S ETHICAL DILEMMA PRESENTED BY NIKE

La Keisha Washington had grown up in a small town outside Atlanta, Georgia. She had been an outstanding student throughout her primary education, excelling at all sports, but basketball in particular. Heavily recruited by several colleges for their women's basketball team with full scholarship, she had graduated with honors from the University of Connecticut. Her initial college days had been her first major cultural shock. Here she was at a name school in a state very foreign in its history and ways to her beloved Georgia.

She had majored in business with an eye toward a solid career in management, maybe even sports management with the growing interest in professional women's basketball. Recruited by several top WNBA teams, La Keisha had opted for a good job with Nike. Throughout her career, she had worn Nike products and felt good about affiliating with such an important sports company. Many of her teammates and friends wore all sorts of Nike products, unwilling to consider any other brand names. If they were good enough for Michael Jordan, then they were basically great.

Training for her position took her to Oregon. She had always been a girl of the South and embraced the closeness of a large family. Her family was strong in values, ethical conduct, religious beliefs, and the importance of family. In the mid–1800s, her great-great-great-great grandmother had bought the family out of slavery, a point of great pride to her family. As she arrived for her training, she was excited but a bit anxious. Being away from home in a very different environment was a culture shock. First college and now the West were preparing her for a new world as she represented Nike around the country and, in the future, other nations. She knew she would rely on her own faith and strength to do well, but the beginning was somewhat rocky.

The training went well, and she liked her fellow trainees. They were to be an elite salesforce for Nike in the West. La Keisha was assigned to the New Mexico–Arizona territory, another source of cultural shock, with the anticipation of covering Central and South America in the future. She went from the Northwest pioneer spirit to the land of Native Americans, Mexicans, and Latinos; deserts; and traditions of the Wild West. There were few African Americans in the region, but she made friends quickly at work and settled in within a few months.

Her job took her around the two states to colleges, universities, many retail outlets, and some manufacturing plants. During college, she had little time for reading about current events or becoming involved in campus or community activities. Her time had been divided between basketball and studies. Now she was becoming involved in her work and its relationship to the community. She started to read about Nike, its power and influence around the globe. What she found disturbed her on some levels.

One day La Keisha had been looking for information on buying a kitchen appliance. She decided to check *Consumer Reports* for possible recommendations. In her perusal of a number of issues, she came upon an article in the July 1998 issue entitled "Sweatshops? Just don't do it." It was a commentary on Nike Inc.'s practices of contracting with overseas factories whose employees were treated unfairly, according to reports. Some of the points were of concern to her: Workers were often under 18 or even 16 in many of these plants. Work weeks were from 77 to 84 hours with a pay rate often less than $2.00 a day. Workshifts were between 11 and 12 hours in China with only 2 days off a month. The article noted that analysts have stated that Nike could triple wages and still only need to add no more than a dollar or two to the price of their shoes. The company disagreed with this allegation, but promised to improve the lot of workers over time. The report concluded that what was needed now for all clothing companies were tough standards, independent monitoring of those standards, and labels to assist concerned customers to do the right thing.

The points made in the article really bothered La Keisha. Her family had come from slavery, and this sounded too close to the conditions of those times. Obviously, these were better days, but there was a labor, management, and company issue here. She remembered that her business and society class at UConn had emphasized social responsibility. It was hard to reconcile the allegations of the article with her own values. Before she jumped to too many conclusions, she decided to research her company in greater depth. In hindsight, she realized she should have looked more carefully at Nike in its totality prior to accepting a job, but she had been so enthralled by the idea, she blew off what her professors had said about researching a company prior to accepting an offer.

In her research, La Keisha found that Nike had been under pressure for some time to change its labor policies overseas. In a short headliner piece in the May 25, 1998, issue of *Business Week*, she read that CEO Philip Knight had already been pressured into revamping labor practices and was now putting pressure on other companies to follow his lead. Though the CEO's details for the plan had not been laid out, there was a sense that with the leverage that the Nike name has it would hasten others' compliance. In an early 1998 article in the same trade magazine, she found a story criticizing Nike entitled "Pele vs. Nike."

Having decided in 1997 to target soccer on a global strategy, the impending World Cup Finals in Paris in the summer of 1998 seemed a very lucrative plan. The article stated that Pele, soccer's Babe Ruth and Muhammad Ali rolled into one, and currently the sports minister of Brazil, had complained that Nike was forcing the national team, favored to win its fifth World Cup title, to play "unnecessary" exhibition games. He also charged that there was a great deal of corruption with millions from these games going into the corrupt pockets of Brazilian Football Confederation. Besides drawing Nike into a furious battle, it also created a public relations nightmare. Subsequently, Brazil lost to the French team at the World Cup finals, perhaps compounding the issues raised by Pele. She read also that Adidas, a Germany firm and second only to Nike, was definitely on the rebound and out to beat Nike.

La Keisha talked to some close friends about her concerns. One friend pointed out that *Working Mother* ranked Nike very high as a great place for women to work. Of the 10,818 employees in 1997, 48 percent were women, with 24 percent managers and 14 percent of the corporate board female. This was a consideration for La Keisha because she wanted a family sometime in the future, and she wanted a family-friendly environment to work in. However, Nike did not make the "100 Best Companies to Work in America" by long-time rankers of companies, Levening and Moskowitz. Then when she was stuck in the Portland, Oregon, airport on a trip to Nike headquarters in Beaverton, Oregon, she picked up the June 8, 1998, issue of *The Nation*, a magazine she seldom even looked at. There she found the following poem by Calvin Trillin, "On Nike's Reformation":

> The reputation of the swoosh
> Had lately gotten rather *louche*.
> If Nike factories abuse
> The workers making Nike shoes
> And people hear of those travails,
> It starts to affecting sneaker sales.
> Protesters say, "if you don't heed us,
> We'll do our dunking in Adidas."
> So Nike's CEO, Phil Knight,

> To make the workers' burden light,
> Said Nike will reduce the squalor
> They work all day in for a dollar.

La Keisha was rather at a loss. Should she say anything in her meeting with her supervisor? This was to be her first evaluation of how she was doing. Although she wanted to impress and do well, her ethics and sense of justice were being tried with all this negative information about her beloved company. She did not know if she wanted to stay or go to a company that had a better reputation for good works. Maybe she should push up her exercises and try for the WMBA instead of establishing a steady career track at this time. What should she do? Where could she find guidance? What was at stake? Could she stay in Nike's corporate culture? What did she now think of the marketing strategies used by the company? What did it mean to wear the Nike check now that she knew all she knew? How might all this impact her future with the company?

CASE QUESTIONS

1. What are the political, legal, technical, and social issues La Keisha faces?
2. What do you think she should do?
3. What are the ethical dilemmas within this case?
4. How would you describe social responsibility at Nike?
5. How does Adidas fit into this picture?
6. What do you think Nike should do?
7. What would you do in her shoes?

CASE BIBLIOGRAPHY

1. A. Bernstein, "Nike Finally Does It," *Business Week*, May 25, 1998, 48.
2. *Consumer Reports*, "Sweatshops? Just Don't Do It," July 1998, 26.
3. W. Echikson with I. Katz, "Pele vs. Nike: Guess Who Won't Score," *Business Week*, February 16, 1998, 59.
4. *Business Week*, "Adidas Rebounder," January 12, 1998, 66.
5. M. Moskowitz, "Best Companies for Working Mothers," *Working Mother*, October 17, 1997, 78.
6. C. Trillin, "On Nike's Reformation," *The Nation*, June 8, 1998, 7.

Source: Anne Cowden, School of Business Administration, California State University, Sacramento, 1999. Used with permission.

PART 2

The Cultural Context of International Management

CHAPTER 4

The Role of Culture in International Management

CHAPTER 5

The Cross-Cultural Communication Environment

CHAPTER 6

Negotiation and Decision Making

The Role of Culture in International Management

O U T L I N E

Opening Profile: Telmex Uses Cultural and
Political Understanding to Stymie AT&T
and MCI

Culture and Its Effects on Organizations

Technology Application: As East Meets West,
Asia Encounters a User-Unfriendly Interface

Cultural Variables and Dimensions

Management Focus: Adjusting to American
Culture

Subcultures

Cultural Variables

Value Dimensions

Hofstede's Value Dimensions

Geographic Clusters

Trompenaars' Findings

Critical Operational Value Differences

Developing Cultural Profiles

Comparative Management in Focus: Profiles in
Culture

**Culture and Management Styles Around
the World**

Saudi Arabia

Chinese Small Family Businesses

Summary of Key Points

Discussion Questions

Application Exercises

Experiential Exercises

Internet Resources

Case Study: Trouble at Computex Corporation

OPENING PROFILE

Telmex Uses Cultural and Political Understanding to Stymie AT&T and MCI

We speak to our customers in a language they can understand about benefits they can understand.
—Francisco Camacho, Telmex manager

When U.S. phone giants AT&T and MCI Communications started up long-distance business in Mexico last year, they got a surprising lesson about competition from Telefonos de Mexico SA (Telmex), the former state-owned monopoly. So far, AT&T and MCI (now MCI-Worldcom, Inc. after the merger) have invested a total of about $2 billion in joint ventures in Mexico, but their executives acknowledge that they will not be making money anytime soon. Their combined market share has slipped to about 25 percent from a peak of 28 percent.

Telmex, apparently, has taught them a thing or two about doing business in the developing world, and outfoxed them at every turn in defending its stake in the busy U.S.–Mexico long-distance corridor. Telmex has won out by understanding its markets and its people. The company priced its services aggressively, used its knowledge of Mexico's feeble regulatory and legal systems to its advantage, and engaged in smart marketing. In addition, Telmex, in a joint venture with Sprint, has started encroaching on the U.S. market by selling a specialized long-distance service targeting the 18 million U.S. residents of Mexican descent.

Telmex understands its customers, their needs and lifestyle, better than do AT&T and MCI. As an example, at a regular weekend swap meet in Tucson, which attracts thousands of Mexican–Americans, one of their salespeople, Oscar Nava, from Guaymas in Sonora, attracts passersby with a compelling pitch. He tells a young landscaper named Juan Villegas that an account with Telmex means a phone can be quickly installed in his parents' house on the other side of the border. Mr. Villegas can then pay their bills right in Tucson and avoid sending money home through the costly money-order system most Mexicans use. In addition, the service is much cheaper than accepting collect calls from his parents or using prepaid phone cards, the way Mr. Villegas normally communicates with his family—so he doesn't hesitate to sign up. Mr. Nava understands the importance of family contact and support to the Mexican people, and he understands firsthand the problems with finances and infrastructure that many Mexican people have.

Much of Telmex's success, according to AT&T and MCI executives, is attributable to its mastery of how to operate in a country where influence often counts more than the law. Says Francisco Gil Diaz, President of the MCI–Avantel joint venture, "with weak authorities, toothless rules and slow courts, Telmex manages to get away with everything their imagination conjures up."

Privatized in 1991, Telmex was sold to a stockbroker, Carlos Slim Helu, who has since spent about $14.3 billion to bring Telmex technologically up to date. It is now a far cry from when it was one of Latin America's worst-run state utilities. It is now 90 percent digitalized, and it takes a couple of days to get a line, not several months as in the past. Mr. Slim, the Telmex chairman, says that the U.S. companies' main barrier to success is their own arrogance, and that they did not try to provide a better service for the Mexican people.

Source: Adapted and excerpted from "U.S. Phone Giants Find Telmex Can Be a Bruising Competitor," *Wall Street Journal*, October 23, 1998.

This chapter's Opening Profile describes how understanding of the local culture and business environment can give managers an advantage in competitive industries, and that foreign companies, no matter how big, can ignore those aspects to their peril.

Such differences in culture and the way of life in other countries necessitate that managers develop international expertise to manage on a contingency basis according to the host-country environment. Powerful, interdependent factors in that environment—political, economic, legal, technological, and cultural—influence management strategy, functions, and processes.

A critical skill for managing people and processes in other countries is **cultural savvy**—that is, a working knowledge of the cultural variables affecting management decisions. Managers have often seriously underestimated the significance of cultural factors; according to numerous accounts, many blunders made in international operations can be attributed to a lack of cultural sensitivity.[1] **Cultural sensitivity**, or **cultural empathy**, is an awareness and an honest caring about another individual's culture. Such sensitivity requires the ability to understand the perspective of those living in other (and very different) societies and the willingness to put oneself in another's shoes.

International managers can benefit greatly from understanding the nature, dimensions, and variables of a specific culture and how these affect work and organizational processes. This cultural awareness enables them to develop appropriate policies and determine how to plan, organize, lead, and control in a specific international setting. Such a process of adaptation to the environment is necessary to implement strategy successfully. It also leads to effective interaction in a workforce of increasing cultural diversity, both in the United States and in other countries.

Company reports and management studies make it clear that a lack of cultural sensitivity costs businesses money and opportunities. One study of U.S. multinational corporations found that poor intercultural communication skills still constitute a major management problem; American managers' knowledge of other cultures lags far behind their understanding of other organizational processes.[2] In a synthesis of the research on cross-cultural training, Black and Mendenhall (as mentioned in Chapter 1) found that up to 40 percent of expatriate managers leave their assignments early because of poor performance or poor adjustment to the local environment. About half of those who do remain are considered only marginally effective. Further, they found that cross-cultural differences are the cause of failed negotiations and interactions, resulting in losses to U.S. firms of more than $2 billion a year for failed expatriate assignments alone.[3]

We also have evidence, however, that cross-cultural training is effective in developing skills and enhancing adjustment and performance.[4] In spite of such evidence, little is done by U.S. firms to take advantage of such important research and to incorporate it into their ongoing training programs, whose purpose is ostensibly to prepare managers before sending them overseas. Too often, the importance of such training in developing cultural sensitivity is realized much too late, as seen in the following account of the unhappy marriage between America's AT&T and Italy's Olivetti, the office-equipment maker:

> One top AT&T executive believes that most of the problems in the venture stemmed from cultural differences. "I don't think we or Olivetti spent enough time understanding behavior patterns," says Robert Kayner, AT&T group executive. "We knew the culture was different, but we never really penetrated. We would get angry, and they would get upset." Mr. Kayner says AT&T's attempts to fix the problems, such as delays in deliveries, were transmitted in curt memos that offended Olivetti officials. "They would get an attitude, 'Who are you to tell us what to do,'" he says. Or the Olivetti side would explain its own problems, and AT&T man-

agers would simply respond, "Don't tell me about your problems. Solve them." AT&T executives are the first to admit, now, that one of the greatest challenges of putting a venture together is that partners frequently see the world in very different—and potentially divisive—ways.[5]

In this chapter, we will provide a conceptual framework with which companies and managers can assess relevant cultural variables and develop cultural profiles of various countries. We will then use this framework to consider the probable effects of cultural differences on an organization and their implications for management. To do this, we need to examine the powerful environmental factor of cultural context. First, we will explore the nature of culture, its variables and dimensions, and then we will consider specific differences in cultural values and their implications for the on-the-job behavior of individuals and groups. We will discuss cultural variables in general in this chapter. The impact of culture on specific management functions and processes will be discussed in other chapters as appropriate.

Culture and Its Effects on Organizations

As generally understood, **the culture of a society** comprises the shared values, understandings, assumptions, and goals that are learned from earlier generations, imposed by present members of a society, and passed on to succeeding generations. This shared outlook results, in large part, in common attitudes, codes of conduct, and expectations that subconsciously guide and control certain norms of behavior.[6, 7, 8] One is born into, not with, a given culture, gradually internalizing its subtle effects through the socialization process. Culture results in a basis for living grounded in shared communication, standards, codes of conduct, and expectations.[9] A U.S. manager assigned to a foreign subsidiary, for example, must expect to find large and small differences in the behavior of individuals and groups within that organization. As depicted in Exhibit 4–1, these differences result from the societal, or sociocultural, variables of the culture, such as religion and language, in addition to prevailing national variables, such as economic, legal, and political factors. National and sociocultural variables thus provide the context for the development and perpetuation of cultural variables. These cultural variables, in turn, determine basic attitudes toward work, time, materialism, individualism, and change. Such attitudes affect an individual's motivation and expectations regarding work and group relations, and they ultimately affect the outcomes that can be expected from that individual.

The way these sets of variables can interact is illustrated by a policy change made by KLM Royal Dutch Airlines, where the organizational culture responded to national cultural values and accepted practices. The culture of social responsiveness in the Netherlands was incorporated into business policy when the airline revised its travel benefits policy for families of employees. For some time, many KLM stewards had protested the rule that only immediate family were eligible for low fares on KLM flights. They found it discriminatory that even just-married heterosexual spouses received the benefit, whereas long-term homosexual partners were not eligible. Upon reconsideration, KLM responded that any couple who formally registered as living together, which is a normal legal practice in the Netherlands, would be eligible for the low fares. However, a year had to elapse between partners before a new partner could be registered. By changing its policy, KLM put the emphasis on committed relationships rather than on marital status or sexual preference.[10]

EXHIBIT 4–1

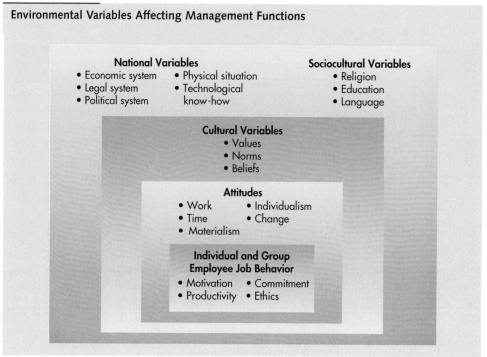

Environmental Variables Affecting Management Functions

National Variables
- Economic system
- Legal system
- Political system
- Physical situation
- Technological know-how

Sociocultural Variables
- Religion
- Education
- Language

Cultural Variables
- Values
- Norms
- Beliefs

Attitudes
- Work
- Time
- Materialism
- Individualism
- Change

Individual and Group Employee Job Behavior
- Motivation
- Productivity
- Commitment
- Ethics

The recent opening of McDonald's in Moscow demonstrates the combined effects of national and cultural variables on work. There, local employees required lengthy training to serve up "Bolshoi Maks" in the "McDonald's way." Unfortunately, Russians are simply not familiar with working under the capitalist system; they have been victims of the inertia brought about by the old system of central planning for so long that productivity still remains low. As a result, Russians have few goods to buy, and the new free-market prices are so high that there is little motivation for them to work for rubles that won't buy anything.[11] (McDonald's in Moscow is further profiled in the Case Study at the end of Chapter 9.)

It is thus clear that cultural variables—shared beliefs, values, and attitudes—can greatly affect organizational processes. In fact, one example of how culture affects organizational processes is frequently evident as the use of technological applications in those processes spreads around the world. The result can be culture–technology clashes, as illustrated in the accompanying Technology Application. Which organizational processes are most affected, and how, is the subject of ongoing cross-cultural management research and debate.[12] Some argue that the effects of culture are more evident at the individual level of personal behavior than at the organizational level, as a result of convergence.[13] Convergence describes the phenomenon of the shifting of individual management styles to become more similar to one another. The convergence argument is based on the belief that the demands of industrialization and worldwide coordination and competition tend to factor out differences in organizational-level processes, such as choice of technology and structure. Redding and Martyn-Johns

TECHNOLOGY APPLICATION

As East Meets West, Asia Encounters a User-Unfriendly Interface

Computers can't replace old-fashioned pedal power at Japan's Fuji Bank Ltd. Bicycles remain a fixture at the bank's branches across Japan, an indispensable way for employees to make their rounds of corporate clients. Fuji, though hardly a technological laggard, has encountered a cultural glitch when it comes to getting corporate clients on line: Companies expect to have a personal relationship with their banker, one nurtured over beers, not over high-speed computer connections.

"It's very difficult to change the way you do business with customers from human interaction to just computer-based," says Satoru Sakauchi, manager at Fuji bank.

Something gets lost in translation when the gospel according to Silicon Valley crosses the Pacific. So-called information technology (IT) often runs head-on into Asia's corporate culture. Rigid office hierarchies that put consensus above individual initiative, a heavy reliance on personal connections and a reluctance to stand apart from the crowd, make many Asian companies slower to embrace the new technologies. And, as Fuji Bank's example shows, exceptions must be made in deference to local custom. So, although IT is being credited for shaping a leaner, meaner corporate America, Asian companies aren't reaping as much from their networking investment.

One of the biggest reasons companies in Asia haven't been using IT to overhaul operations is simple:

They haven't needed to. Economies were booming, labor plentiful. It still can be cheaper to pay an employee for a year's work than to install a network. In less developed countries such as Thailand, Indonesia, and China, it's less expensive to pay an employee than to buy and operate a single personal computer. Asia's business culture also has a powerful impact on cost-cutting. Corporate paternalism has long been a fact of life in Asia—China's old state-run companies housed, clothed, and fed their employees; joining a big Japanese company has long meant a guaranteed job for life. Although such policies are breaking down, their influence still runs deep: Across the region, layoffs remain taboo. Some of the resistance to technology stems from the fact that computing has deep English-language roots. The industry's cultural homeland is California. Americana dominates the Internet. The traditional keyboard even presents hurdles for Asia's brush-based scripts.

So, while the world adjusts to America's latest ideological export, Liz Claiborne, among other multinationals, patiently faxes orders to less adventurous suppliers. And at Fuji Bank, the bikes stay—but with a high-tech twist. Fuji has outfitted each of its 5,000-odd salespeople with a palmtop computer that they load with the latest interest rates and such before heading out. New data on clients gets downloaded into the branch computer when they return.

Source: Excerpted and adapted from Wayne Arnold, "Technology Lost in Translation," *Asian Wall Street Journal*, August 4, 1997.

found, however, that management functions, such as planning and organizing, were affected in different ways by an individual manager's cultural beliefs, such as those concerning morality, causality, and the meaning of time.[14] These factors are discussed in more detail later in this chapter.

The effects of culture on specific management functions are particularly noticeable when we attempt to impose our own values and systems on another society. Exhibit 4–2 gives some examples of the values typical of U.S. culture, compares some common perspectives held by people in other countries, and shows which management functions might be affected, clearly implying the need for the differential management of organizational processes. For example, American managers plan activities, schedule them, and judge their timely completion based

EXHIBIT 4-2

U.S. Values and Possible Alternatives

Aspects of U.S. Culture*	Alternative Aspect	Examples of Management Function Affected
The individual can influence the future (where there is a will there is a way).	Life follows a preordained course, and human action is determined by the will of God.	Planning and scheduling
The individual can change and improve the environment.	People are intended to adjust to the physical environment rather than to alter it.	Organizational environment, morale, and productivity
An individual should be realistic in his or her aspirations.	Ideals are to be pursued regardless of what is "reasonable."	Goal setting and career development
We must work hard to accomplish our objectives (Puritan ethic).	Hard work is not the only prerequisite for success; wisdom, luck, and time are also required.	Motivation and reward system
Commitments should be honored (people will do what they say they will do).	A commitment may be superseded by a conflicting request, or an agreement may only signify intention and have little or no relationship to the capacity for performance.	Negotiating and bargaining
One should effectively use one's time (time is money that can be saved or wasted).	Schedules are important, but only in relation to other priorities.	Long- and short-range planning
A primary obligation of an employee is to the organization.	The individual employee has a primary obligation to his or her family and friends.	Loyalty, commitment, and motivation
The employer or employee can terminate the relationship.	Employment is for a lifetime.	Motivation and commitment to the company
The best-qualified people should be given the positions available.	Family, friendship, and other considerations should determine employment practices.	Employment, promotions, recruiting, selection, and reward

*Aspect here refers to a belief, value, attitude, or assumption that is a part of a culture in that it is shared by a large number of people in that culture.

Source: From *Managing Cultural Differences* by Philip R. Harris and Robert T. Moran, 4th ed. Copyright © 1996 by Gulf Publishing Company, Houston, TX. Used with permission. All rights reserved.

on the belief that people influence and control the future, rather than assuming that events will occur only at the will of Allah, as managers in an Islamic nation might believe.

Many people in the world understand and relate to others only in terms of their own culture. This unconscious reference point of one's own cultural values is called a self-reference criterion.[15] The result of such an attitude is illustrated in the following story:

> Once upon a time there was a great flood, and involved in this flood were two creatures, a monkey and a fish. The monkey, being agile and experienced, was lucky enough to scramble up a tree and escape the raging waters. As he looked down from his safe perch, he saw the poor fish struggling against the swift current. With the very best of intentions, he reached down and lifted the fish from the water. The result was inevitable.[16]

The monkey assumed that its frame of reference applied to the fish and acted accordingly. International managers from all countries thus must understand and adjust to unfamiliar social and commercial practices—especially the practices of that mysterious and unique nation, the United States, as shown in the Management Focus "Adjusting to American Culture."

As a first step toward cultural sensitivity, an international manager should understand his or her own culture. This awareness helps guard against adopting either a parochial or an ethnocentric attitude. **Parochialism** occurs when a Frenchman, for example, expects those from or in another country to automatically fall into patterns of behavior common in France. **Ethnocentrism** describes the attitude of those who operate from the assumption that their ways of doing things are best—no matter where or under what conditions they are applied. Companies both large and small have demonstrated this lack of cultural sensitivity in countless subtle (and not so subtle) ways, with varying disastrous effects.

Procter & Gamble was one such company. In a 1983 Japanese television commercial for Camay soap, a Japanese woman is bathing when her husband walks into the bathroom. She starts telling him about her new beauty soap. Her husband, stroking her shoulder, hints that he has more on his mind than suds. The commercial, which had been popular in Europe, was a disaster in Japan. For the man to intrude on his wife "was considered bad manners," says Edwin L. Artzt, P&G's vice chairman and international chief. "And the Japanese didn't think it was very funny." P&G has learned from its mistakes and is now predicting that foreign sales will generate half of its revenue by the year 2000.[17]

After studying his or her own culture, the manager's next step toward establishing effective cross-cultural relations is to develop cultural sensitivity. Managers not only must be aware of cultural variables and their effects on behavior in the workplace but also must appreciate cultural diversity and understand how to build constructive working relationships anywhere in the world. In the next sections, we will explore cultural variables and dimensions. In later chapters, we will suggest specific ways in which managers can address these variables and dimensions to help build constructive relationships.

Cultural Variables and Dimensions

Given the great variety of cultures and subcultures around the world, how can a student of cross-cultural management, or a manager wishing to be culturally savvy, develop an understanding of the specific nature of a certain people? With such an understanding, how can a manager anticipate the probable effects of an unfamiliar culture within an organizational setting and thereby manage human resources productively and control outcomes?

One approach is to develop a cultural profile for each country or region with which one does or is considering doing business. To develop a cultural profile, one first needs some familiarity with the cultural variables universal to most cultures. From these universal variables, one can identify the specific differences found in each country or people—and hence anticipate their implications for the workplace.

Managers should never assume that they can successfully transplant American, or Japanese, or any other country's styles, practices, expectations, and processes. Instead, they should practice a basic tenet of good management: contingency management. Contingency management requires managers to adapt to the local environment and people, and to manage accordingly.

MANAGEMENT FOCUS

Adjusting to American Culture

A group of Arab oil workers sent to Texas for training found American teaching methods impersonal. Several Japanese workers at a U.S. manufacturing plant had to learn how to put courtesy aside and interrupt conversations when there was trouble. Executives of a Swiss-based multinational company couldn't understand why its American managers demanded more autonomy than their European counterparts.

To all these people, America is a foreign country with a strange corporate culture. Just as Americans doing business abroad must grapple with unfamiliar social and commercial practices, so too must a growing number of European, Asian, and Latin American managers of U.S. subsidiaries struggle with diversity.

"Most people think that culture is manners, food, dress, arts, and crafts," says Clifford Clarke, president of IRI International, a Redwood City, California, consulting company. "They don't realize that how you motivate a guy is culturally determined. Every managerial task is culturally determined."

Occasionally, transferees find that behavior suitable at home may irritate coworkers here. *Living in the U.S.A.*, a recent training film, portrays a Japanese employee angering an American colleague by repeatedly apologizing for a late report; the American expects explanations and solutions. "In America, if you talk around things, people get frustrated with you," says Lennie Copeland, who helped produce the film.

Jose Carlos Villates, a business manager for animal health products at American Cyanamid Company, also had a problem with office protocol. In Puerto Rico and the Dominican Republic, where he was raised, businesspeople would begin meetings with relaxed chitchat. At the company's headquarters in Wayne, New Jersey, however, he says he picks up "signals or body language" that Americans find such sociability a waste of time. Even after 15 months in the United States, Villates feels uncomfortable plunging abruptly into business. "It strikes us as cold-blooded," he says.

Europeans, on the other hand, can be flummoxed by "a deceiving appearance of informality," says French-born André Rude, who counsels international transferees at Hewlett-Packard in Palo Alto, California. "They don't realize the urgency of the request and find themselves in trouble" when work isn't done on time.

Non-American managers don't need to be physically present in the United States to be confused about American ways. Foreign top executives must ponder how to manage and motivate an increasing number of senior-level Americans who oversee their U.S. subsidiaries.

Rodman Drake, a consultant, cites the case of a Swiss-based multinational whose U.S. unit accounted for 30 percent of the company's worldwide sales. The Swiss parent called in consultants to help eliminate the "ongoing friction" between American and Swiss managers over day-to-day pricing, planning, and marketing decisions.

The Swiss were persuaded to allow the American managers more autonomy. They were uncomfortable doing so, however, because they didn't run any of their 70 or 80 other international units that way. "There's more of a macho, cowboy, I'm-in-charge style of operating" in America, in contrast to the collegial approach prevalent in Europe and Asia, Drake explains.

Families of foreign managers can find the United States stressful, too, and many companies try to accommodate them. Utaka Yamaguchi, a Hewlett-Packard engineer, was confident he would adapt to life here during a three-year California assignment, but he worried about his wife, who spoke no English. The company found them an apartment near many other Japanese families, who help Mrs. Yamaguchi with shopping and errands. Meanwhile, she began studying English.

Source: Adapted from "American Culture Is Often a Puzzle for Foreign Managers in the U.S.," *Wall Street Journal*, February 12, 1986, 34.

Subcultures

Managers should recognize, of course, that generalizations in cultural profiles will produce only an approximation, or stereotype, of national character. Many countries, in fact, comprise diverse subcultures whose constituents conform only in varying degrees to the national character. In Canada, distinct subcultures include anglophones and francophones (English-speaking and French-speaking people) and indigenous Canadians. The United States, too, has varying subcultures. While abroad, Americans are almost always dealt with in the context of the stereotypical American, but at home Americans recognize differences among themselves due to ethnic, geographic, or other subcultural backgrounds. Americans should extend the same insight toward people in other countries and be extremely careful not to overgeneralize or oversimplify. For example, although Americans tend to think of Chinese as homogeneous in their culture, there are in fact considerable differences due to regional diversity—including distinct ethnic groups with their own local customs and a multitude of dialects. A study by Ralston, et al. concluded that, although adherence to traditional Confucian values was common to all regions, there were considerable differences among regions on variables such as individualism and openness to change (with Guangzhou and Shanghai ranking the highest on those dimensions, followed by Beijing and Dalian and then Chengdu and Lanzhou).[18] This implies that Chinese in Guangzhou and Shanghai may be somewhat more "Westernized" and more open to doing business with Westerners.

Above all, good managers treat people as individuals, and they consciously avoid any form of stereotyping. However, a cultural profile is a good starting point to help managers develop some tentative expectations—some cultural context—as a backdrop to managing in a specific international setting. It is useful, then, to look at what cultural variables have been studied and what implications can be drawn from the results.

Cultural Variables

As mentioned, to develop cultural profiles, we first need to be familiar with the kinds of universal cultural variables, found in most societies, that make up unique clusters and provide a snapshot of the overall character of a specific group. Although there are countless individual variables, one approach to categorizing interdependent variables is given by Harris and Moran, who identified eight categories that form the subsystems in any society.[19] This systems approach to understanding cultural and national variables—and their effects on work behavior—is consistent with the model shown in Exhibit 4–1. The following sections describe these eight categories and explain their implications.

Kinship   A kinship system is the system adopted by a given society to guide family relationships. Whereas in the United States this system primarily consists of the nuclear family (which is increasingly represented by single-parent families), in many other parts of the world the kinship system consists of an extended family with many members, spanning several generations. This extended, closely knit family, typical in many Eastern nations, may influence corporate activities in cases where family loyalty is given primary consideration—such as when contracts are awarded or when employees are hired (and a family member is always selected over a more suitable candidate from outside the family). In these family-oriented societies, such practices are pervasive and taken for granted. Foreign managers often find themselves locked out of important decisions when dealing with family businesses. If, however, they take the time to learn the local cultural expectations regarding families, they will notice predictable patterns of behavior and be better prepared to deal with them. Such traditional practices are exemplified in the experience of an Asian MBA, educated in the United States, when he presented a more up-to-date business plan to his uncle, the managing director of a medium-sized firm in India:

> The family astrologer attended the meeting and vetoed the plan. Later, the nephew persisted and asked the astrologer to reconsider the plan. The astrologer recommended various ceremonies after which the astral signs would probably bend toward the plan.[20]

Education   The formal or informal education of workers in a foreign firm, received from whatever source, greatly affects the expectations placed on those workers in the workplace. It also influences managers' choices about recruitment and staffing practices, training programs, and leadership styles. Training and development programs, for example, need to be consistent with the general level of educational preparation in that country.

Economy   Whatever the economic system, the means of production and distribution in a society (and the resulting effects on individuals and groups) has a powerful influence on such organizational processes as sourcing, distribution, incentives, and repatriation of capital. At this time of radically changing political systems, it appears that the drastic differences between capitalist and socialist systems will have less effect on MNCs than in the past.

Politics   The system of government in a society, whether democratic, Communist, or dictatorial, imposes varying constraints on an organization and its freedom to do business. It is the manager's job to understand the political system and how it affects organizational processes, to negotiate positions within that system, and to manage effectively the mutual concerns of the host country and guest company. As demonstrated by the difficulties that McDonald's had in training Russian workers for its Moscow restaurant (discussed earlier in the chapter), the political and economic subsystems of a country often dominate other cultural systems.

Religion   The spiritual beliefs of a society are often so powerful that they transcend other cultural aspects. Religion commonly underlies both moral and economic norms. In the United States, the effects of religion in the workplace are limited (other than a generalized belief in hard work, which stems from the Protestant work ethic), whereas in other countries religious beliefs and practices often influence everyday business transactions and on-the-job behaviors. For example, in a long-standing tradition based on the Qur'an and the sayings of Muhammad, Arabs consult with senior members of the ruling families or the community regarding business decisions. Hindus, Buddhists, and some Muslims believe in the concept of destiny, or fate. In Islamic countries, the idea of *inshallah*, that is, "God willing," prevails. In some Western countries, religious organizations, such as the Roman Catholic Church, play a major cultural role through moral and political influence.

One of the ways that the Islamic faith affects the operations of international firms involves the charging of interest:

> The kingdom of Saudi Arabia observes Sharia, which is Islamic law based on both the Qur'an and the Hadith—the traditions of the Prophet Muhammad. Under these codes, interest is

banned, and both the giver and the taker of interest are equally damned. This means that the modern Western banking system is technically illegal. A debate has begun on the interpretation of the concept of interest. The kingdom's religious scholars, the ulema, view all interest, or rib'a, as banned. Some have challenged that interpretation as too restrictive, however, and have called for a more liberal interpretation. Their view is that Muhammad referred only to excessive interest when he condemned usury. Should something come of this debate, it would help establish a legal framework for dealing with Saudi Arabia's banking problems, such as steep drops in profits, and end the legal limbo of Western-style banking in the kingdom.[21]

Associations   Many and various types of associations arise out of the formal and informal groups that make up a society. Whether these associations are based on religious, social, professional, or trade affiliations, managers should be familiar with them and the role they may play in business interactions.

Health   The system of healthcare in a country affects employee productivity, expectations, and attitudes toward physical fitness and its role in the workplace. These expectations will influence managerial decisions regarding healthcare benefits, insurance, physical facilities, sick days, and so forth.

Recreation   Closely associated with other cultural factors, recreation includes the way in which people use their leisure time, as well as their attitudes toward leisure and their choice of whom to socialize with. Workers' attitudes toward recreation can affect their work behavior and their perception of the role of work in their lives.

Value Dimensions

Cultural variables result from unique sets of shared values among different groups of people. Most of the variations between cultures stem from underlying value systems, which cause people to behave differently under similar circumstances. **Values** are a society's ideas about what is good or bad, right or wrong—such as the widespread belief that stealing is immoral and unfair. Values determine how individuals will probably respond in any given circumstance. As a powerful component of a society's culture, values are communicated through the eight subsystems just described and are passed from generation to generation—although interaction and pressure among these subsystems (or more recently from foreign cultures) may provide the impetus for slow change. The dissolution of the Soviet Union and the formation of the Commonwealth of Independent States is an example of extreme political change resulting from internal economic pressures and external encouragement to change.

Hofstede's Value Dimensions

One useful framework for understanding how basic values underlie organizational behavior is proposed by Hofstede, the result of his research on more than 116,000 people in 50 countries. He proposes four value dimensions: (1) power distance, (2) uncertainty avoidance, (3) individualism, and (4) masculinity.[22, 23] We should be cautious when interpreting these results, however, because his research findings are based on a sample drawn from one multinational firm, IBM, and because he does not account for within-country differences in multicultural countries.[24] Although we introduce these value dimensions here to aid in the understanding of different cultures, their relevance and application to management functions will be discussed in later chapters.

The first of these value dimensions, **power distance**, is the level of acceptance by a society of the unequal distribution of power in institutions. In the workplace, inequalities in power are normal, as evidenced in hierarchical boss–subordinate relationships. However, the extent to which subordinates accept unequal power is societally determined. In countries in which people display high power distance (such as Malaysia, the Philippines, and Mexico), employees acknowledge the boss's authority simply by respecting that individual's formal position in the hierarchy, and they seldom bypass the chain of command. This respectful response results, predictably, in a centralized structure and autocratic leadership. In countries where people display low power distance (such as Austria, Denmark, and Israel), superiors and subordinates are apt to regard one another as equal in power, resulting in more harmony and cooperation. Clearly, an autocratic management style is not likely to be well received in low power-distance countries.

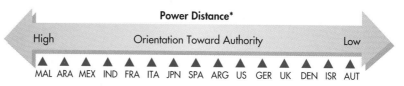

Power Distance*

High   Orientation Toward Authority   Low

MAL ARA MEX IND FRA ITA JPN SPA ARG US GER UK DEN ISR AUT

*Not to scale—indicates relative magnitude.
See Exhibit 4–3 for abbreviations.

The second value dimension, **uncertainty avoidance**, refers to the extent to which people in a society feel threatened by ambiguous situations. Countries with a high level of uncertainty avoidance (such as Japan, Portugal, and Greece) tend to have strict laws and procedures to which their people adhere closely, and there is a strong sense of nationalism. In a business context, this value results in formal rules and procedures designed to provide more security and greater career stability. Managers have a propensity for low-risk decisions, employees exhibit little aggressiveness, and lifetime employment is common. In countries with lower levels of uncertainty avoidance (such as Denmark, Great Britain, and to a lesser extent, the United States), nationalism is less pronounced, and protests and other such activities are tolerated. As a consequence, company activities are less structured and less formal, some managers take more risks, and there is high job mobility.

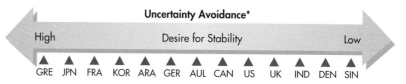

Uncertainty Avoidance*

High   Desire for Stability   Low

GRE JPN FRA KOR ARA GER AUL CAN US UK IND DEN SIN

*Not to scale—indicates relative magnitude.
See Exhibit 4–3 for abbreviations.

The third of Hofstede's value dimensions, **individualism**, refers to the tendency of people to look after themselves and their immediate family only and neglect the needs of

EXHIBIT 4-3

Abbreviations for Countries and Regions in Value Dimension Graphics

ARA	Arab countries (Egypt, Lebanon, Libya, Kuwait, Iraq, Saudi Arabia, U.A.E.)	JAM	Jamaica
		JPN	Japan
ARG	Argentina	KOR	South Korea
AUL	Australia	MAL	Malaysia
AUT	Austria	MEX	Mexico
BRA	Brazil	NET	Netherlands
CAN	Canada	NZL	New Zealand
CHL	Chile	PAK	Pakistan
COL	Colombia	PAN	Panama
COS	Costa Rica	PER	Peru
DEN	Denmark	PHI	Philippines
EAF	East Africa (Kenya, Ethiopia, Zambia)	POR	Portugal
EQA	Ecuador	SAF	South Africa
FIN	Finland	SAL	El Salvador
FRA	France	SIN	Singapore
GBR	Great Britain	SPA	Spain
GER	Germany	SWE	Sweden
GRE	Greece	SWI	Switzerland
GUA	Guatemala	TAI	Taiwan
HOK	Hong Kong	THA	Thailand
IDO	Indonesia	TUR	Turkey
IND	India	URU	Uruguay
IRA	Iran	USA	United States
IRE	Ireland	VEN	Venezuela
ISR	Israel	WAF	West Africa (Nigeria, Ghana, Sierra Leone)
ITA	Italy	YUG	Yugoslavia

society. In countries that prize individualism (such as the United States, Great Britain, and Australia), democracy, individual initiative, and achievement are highly valued; the relationship of the individual to organizations is one of independence on an emotional level, if not on an economic level.

In countries such as Pakistan and Panama, where low individualism prevails—that is, where collectivism predominates—one finds tight social frameworks, emotional dependence on belonging to "the organization," and a strong belief in group decisions. People from a collectivist country, like Japan, believe in the will of the group rather than that of the individual, and their pervasive collectivism exerts control over individual members through social pressure and the fear of humiliation. The society values harmony and saving face, whereas individualistic cultures generally emphasize self-respect, autonomy, and independence. Hiring and promotion practices in collectivist societies are based on paternalism rather than achievement or personal capabilities, which are valued in individualistic societies. Other management practices (such as the use of quality circles in Japanese factories) reflect the emphasis on group decision-making processes in collectivist societies.

Hofstede's findings indicate that most countries scoring high on individualism have both a higher gross national product and a freer political system than those scoring low on individualism—that is, there is a strong relationship among individualism, wealth, and a political system with balanced power. Other studies have found that the output of individuals working in a group setting differs between individualistic and collectivist societies. In the United States, a highly individualistic culture, social loafing is common—that is, people tend to perform less when working as part of a group than when working alone.[25] In a comparative study between the United States and the People's Republic of China (a highly collectivist society), Earley found that the Chinese did not exhibit as much social loafing as the Americans.[26] This result can be attributed to Chinese cultural values, which subordinate personal interests to the greater goal of helping the group succeed.

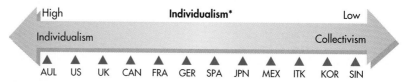

*Not to scale—indicates relative magnitude.
See Exhibit 4–3 for abbreviations.

The fourth value dimension, **masculinity**, refers to the degree of traditionally "masculine" values—assertiveness, materialism, and a lack of concern for others—that prevail in a society. In comparison, femininity emphasizes "feminine" values—a concern for others, for relationships, and for the quality of life. In highly masculine societies (Japan and Austria, for example), women are generally expected to stay home and raise a family. In organizations, one finds considerable job stress, and organizational interests generally encroach on employees' private lives. In countries with low masculinity (such as Switzerland and New Zealand), one finds less conflict and job stress, more women in high-level jobs, and a reduced need for assertiveness. The United States lies somewhat in the middle, according to Hofstede's research. American women typically are encouraged to work and usually are able to get some support for childcare (through daycare centers and maternity leaves).

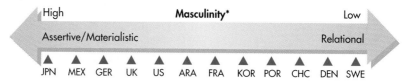

*Not to scale—indicates relative magnitude.
See Exhibit 4–3 for abbreviations.

The four cultural value dimensions proposed by Hofstede do not operate in isolation; rather, they are interdependent and interactive—and thus complex—in their effects on work attitudes and behaviors. Again, managers must remember that the assessment of an entire country on any cultural value dimension is a generalization and thus an oversimplification. Variations will occur according to subcultures, regions, and individuals.

Geographic Clusters

Nath and Sadhu summarized and categorized by geographic region the four value dimensions by Hofstede as well as other cultural dimensions, as shown in Exhibit 4–4.[27]

Based also on a synthesis of Hofstede's research and other cluster studies, Ronen and Shenkar developed eight country clusters grouped according to the similarities found in those studies of employee attitudes toward (1) the importance of work goals, (2) need fulfillment and job satisfaction, (3) managerial and organizational variables, and (4) work role and interpersonal orientation.[28] These country clusters are shown in Exhibit 4–5. In addition, per capita gross national product (GNP) at that time (1985) was used to determine placement in

EXHIBIT 4–4

The Cultural Milieu

Region/Country	Hofstede's Dimensions				Other Dimensions
	Individualism-Collectivism	Power Distance	Uncertainty Avoidance	Masculinity-Femininity	
North America (USA)	Individualism	Low	Medium	Masculine	
Japan	Collectivism	High and low	High	Masculine and feminine	*Amae* (mutual dependence); authority is respected but superior must be a warm leader
Europe:					
Anglo	Individualism	Low/medium	Low/medium	Masculine	
Germanic West Slavic West Urgic	Medium individualism	Low	Medium/high	Medium/high masculine	
Near Eastern Balkanic	Collectivism	High	High	Medium masculine	
Nordic	Medium/high individualism	Low	Low/medium	Feminine	
Latin Europe	Medium/high individualism	High	High	Medium masculine	
East Slavic	Collectivism	Low	Medium	Masculine	
China	Collectivism	Low	Low	Masculine and feminine	Emphasis on tradition, Marxism, Leninism, and Mao Zedong thought
Africa	Collectivism	High	High	Feminine	Colonial traditions; tribal customs
Latin America	Collectivism	High	High	Masculine	Extroverted; prefer orderly customs and procedures

Source: Raghu Nath and Kunal K. Sadhu, "Comparative Analysis, Conclusions, and Future Directions," in *Comparative Management—A Regional View*, ed. Raghu Nath (Cambridge, MA: Balliger Publishing Company, 1988): 273.

EXHIBIT 4–5

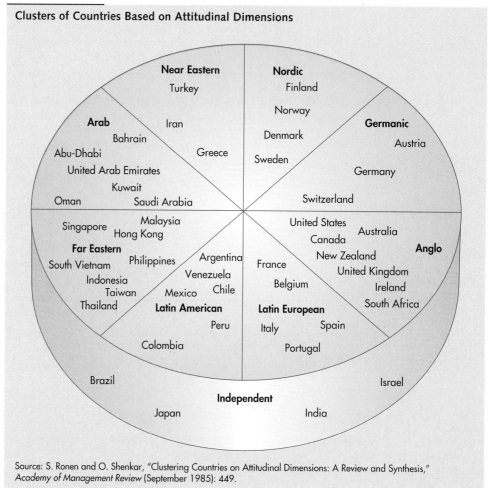

Clusters of Countries Based on Attitudinal Dimensions

Source: S. Ronen and O. Shenkar, "Clustering Countries on Attitudinal Dimensions: A Review and Synthesis," *Academy of Management Review* (September 1985): 449.

the figure, with the most highly developed countries close to the center. This may indicate some relationship between a country's level of development and its generally accepted values and attitudes although the variables are too complex to draw conclusions about any direction of causality among them.

Trompenaar's Findings[29]

Fons Trompenaar also researched value dimensions; his work was spread over a 10-year period, with 15,000 managers from 28 countries, representing 47 national cultures. Some of those dimensions that we are not discussing elsewhere and that affect daily business activities are shown in Exhibit 4–6, along with the descriptions and the placement of nine of the

EXHIBIT 4–6

Trompenaar's Value Dimensions

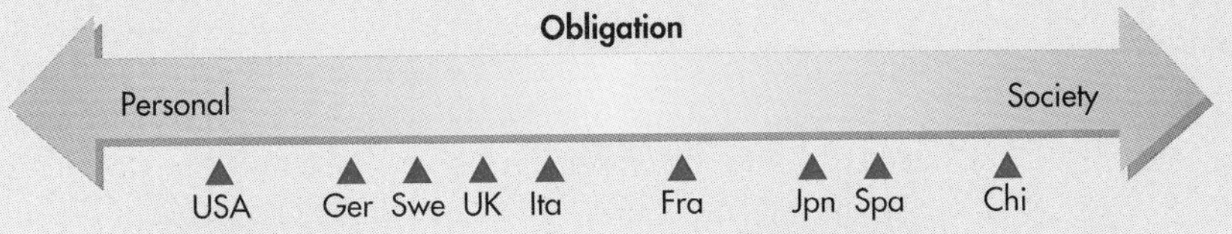

Obligation

Personal ◄──────────────────────────────► Society

USA   Ger Swe UK Ita   Fra   Jpn Spa   Chi

Universalistic
Rules
Legal systems
Contracts
"Higher" obligations
"Objectivity"
One right way

Particularistic
Relationships
Personal systems
Interpersonal trust
Duty to friends, family, etc.
"Relativity"
Many ways

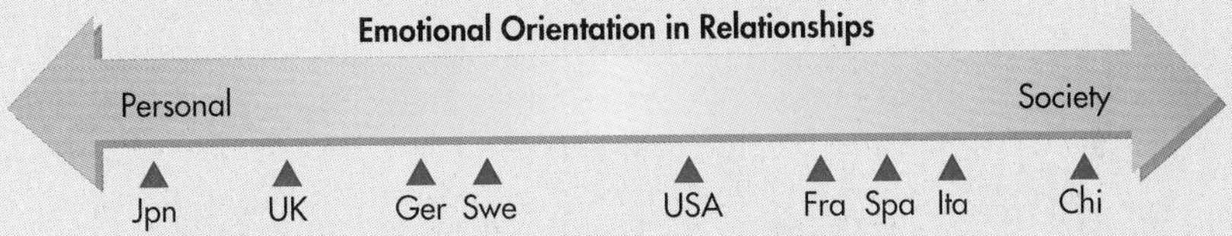

Emotional Orientation in Relationships

Personal ◄──────────────────────────────► Society

Jpn   UK   Ger Swe   USA   Fra Spa Ita   Chi

Neutral
Physical contact reserved for
   close friends and family
Subtle communication
Hard to "read"

Affective
Physical contact more open
   and free
Expressive; vocal
Strong body language

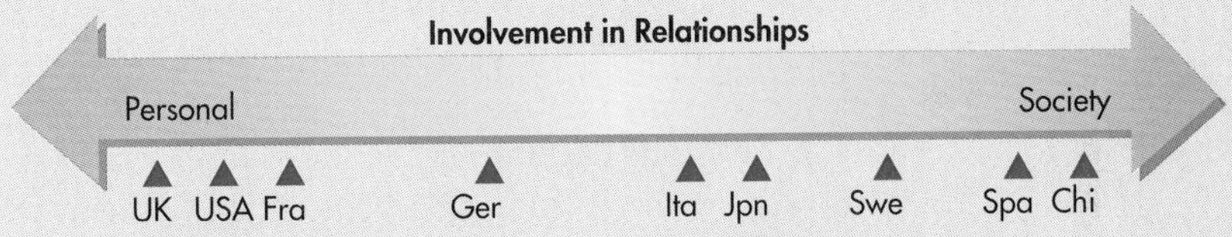

Involvement in Relationships

Personal ◄──────────────────────────────► Society

UK USA Fra   Ger   Ita Jpn   Swe   Spa Chi

Specific
Direct
Confrontational
Open: extrovert
Separate work and private life

Diffuse
Indirect
Avoid direct confrontation
More closed: introvert
Link private and work life

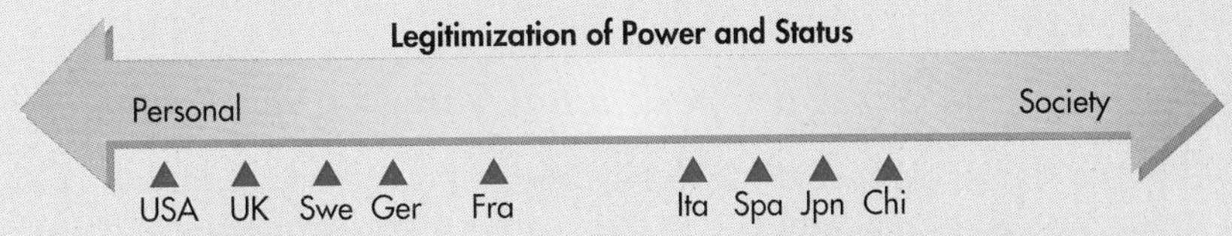

Legitimization of Power and Status

Personal ◄──────────────────────────────► Society

USA UK Swe Ger   Fra   Ita Spa Jpn Chi

Achievement
Status based on competency and
   achievements
Women and minorities visible at more
   levels in workplace
Newcomers, young people, and
   outsiders gain respect if they prove
   themselves

Ascription
Status based on position, age,
   schooling, or other criteria
More homogenous workforce,
   primarily male
Deference based on specific
   criteria

Source: Adapted from Lisa Hoecklin, *Managing Cultural Differences* (Wokingham, England: Addison-Wesley), and The Economist Intelligence Unit, 1995. Based on Trompenaar, 1993.

countries in approximate relative order. If we view the placement of these countries along a range from personal to societal, based on each dimension, some interesting patterns emerge.[30] One can see from the exhibit that the same countries tend to be at similar positions on all dimensions, with the exception of the emotional orientation.

Looking at Trompenaar's dimension of **universalism versus particularism**, the universalistic approach applies rules and systems objectively, without consideration for individual circumstances; whereas the particularistic approach—more common in Asia and in Spain, for example—puts the obligation toward relationships first and is more subjective. Trompenaars found, for example, that people in particularistic societies are more likely to pass on inside information to a friend than those in universalistic societies.

In the **neutral versus affective** dimension, the focus is on the emotional orientation of relationships. The Italians, Mexicans, and Chinese, for example, would openly express emotions even in a business situation, whereas the British and Japanese would consider such displays unprofessional; they, in turn would be regarded as hard to "read."

As for involvement in relationships, people tend to be either **specific or diffuse** (or somewhere along that dimension). Managers in specific-oriented cultures—United States, United Kingdom, France—separate work from personal issues and relationships; they compartmentalize their work and private lives, and they are more open and direct. In diffuse-oriented cultures—Sweden, China—there is spill-over from the work into the personal relationships and vice versa.

The **achievement versus ascription** dimension examines the source of power and status in society. In an achievement society, the source of status and influence is based on individual achievement—how well one performs the job and what level of education and experience one has to offer. Therefore, women, minorities, and young people usually have equal opportunity to attain positions based on their achievements. In an ascription-oriented society, people ascribe status on the basis of class, age, gender, and so on; one is more likely to be born into a position of influence. Hiring in Indonesia, for example, is more likely to be based on who you are than is hiring for a position in Germany or Australia.

It is clear, then, that a lot of what goes on at work can be explained by differences in people's innate value systems, as described by Hofstede and Trompenaars, based on their research. Awareness of such differences and how they influence work behavior can be very useful to you as a future international manager.

Critical Operational Value Differences

After studying various research results about cultural variables, it helps to identify some specific culturally based variables that cause frequent problems for people in international management. Important variables are those involving conflicting orientations toward time, change, material factors, and individualism. We try to understand these operational value differences because they strongly influence a person's attitudes and probable response to work situations.

Time   Managers often experience much conflict and frustration because of differences in the concept of time around the world—that is, differences in temporal values. To Americans and western Europeans, for example, time is a valuable and limited resource, to be saved, scheduled, and spent with precision, lest we waste it. The clock is always running—time is money. Therefore, deadlines and schedules have to be met. When others are not on time for meetings, Germans and Americans feel insulted; when meetings digress from their purpose, they tend to become impatient.

In many parts of the world, however, people view time from different and longer duration perspectives, often based on religious beliefs (such as reincarnation, in which time does not end at death), on a belief in destiny, or on pervasive social attitudes. In Latin America, for example, a common attitude toward time is *mañana*, a word that literally means "tomorrow"; a Latin American person using this word, however, usually means an indefinite time in the near future. Similarly, the word *bukra* in Arabic can mean "tomorrow" or "some time in the future." Although Americans usually regard a deadline as a firm commitment, Arabs often regard a deadline imposed on them as an insult. They feel that important things take a long time and therefore cannot be rushed; to ask an Arab to rush something, then, would imply that you have not given him an important task, or that he would not treat that task with respect. International managers have to be careful not to offend people—or lose contracts or employee cooperation—because they misunderstand the local language of time.

Change Based largely on long-standing religious beliefs, values regarding the acceptance of change and the pace of change can vary immensely among cultures. Western people generally believe that an individual can exert some control over the future and can manipulate events, particularly in a business context—that is, individuals feel they have some internal control. In many non-Western societies, however, control is considered external; people generally believe in destiny, or the will of Allah, and therefore adopt a passive attitude or even feel hostility toward those introducing the "evil" of change. In societies that place great importance on tradition (such as China), one small area of change may threaten an entire way of life. Webber describes just how difficult it is for an Asian male, concerned about tradition, to change his work habits:

> To the Chinese, the introduction of power machinery meant that he had to throw over not only habits of work but a whole ideology; it implied dissatisfaction with his father's way of life in all its aspects. If the old loom must be discarded, then 100 other things must be discarded with it, for there are somehow no adequate substitutes.[31]

International firms are agents of change throughout the world. Some changes are more popular than others; as the photo on the next page shows, McDonald's hamburgers are apparently one change the Chinese are willing to accept.

Material Factors Americans consume resources at a far greater rate than most of the rest of the world. Their attitude toward nature—that it is there to be used for their benefit—differs from the attitudes of Indians or Koreans, for example, whose worship of nature is part of their religious belief.[32] Whereas Westerners often value physical goods and status symbols, many non-Westerners find these things unimportant; they value the aesthetic and the spiritual realm. Such differences in attitude have implications for management functions, such as motivation and reward systems, because the proverbial carrot must be appropriate to the employee's value system. This topic is explored further in Chapter 12.

The New Idea

Source: Courtesy McDonald's Corporation

Individualism   In general, Americans tend to work and conduct their private lives independently, valuing individual achievement, accomplishments, promotions, and wealth above any group goals. In many other countries, individualism is not valued (as previously discussed in the context of Hofstede's work). In China, for example, much more of a "we" consciousness prevails, and the group is the basic building block of social life and work. For the Chinese, conformity and cooperation take precedence over individual achievement, and the emphasis is on the strength of the family or community—the predominant attitude being "we all rise or fall together."

International managers often face conflicts in the workplace as a result of differences in these four basic values of time, change, materialism, and individualism. If these operational value differences and their likely consequences are anticipated, managers can adjust expectations, communications, work organization, schedules, incentive systems, and so forth, to provide for more constructive outcomes for the company and its employees.

Developing Cultural Profiles

Managers can gather considerable information on cultural variables from current research, personal observation, and discussions with people. From these sources, managers can develop cultural profiles of various countries—composite pictures of working environments, people's attitudes, and norms of behavior. As we have previously discussed, these profiles are often highly generalized; many subcultures, of course, may exist within a country. But managers can use these profiles to anticipate drastic differences in the level of motivation, communication, ethics, loyalty, and individual and group productivity that may be encountered in a given country. More such homework may have helped the GM–Daewoo joint venture in Korea, which is coming to an end after years of acrimonious relations. Executives from both sides acknowledge that they "seriously underestimated the obstacles posed to their three-continent car-making experiment by divergent cultures and business aspirations, not to mention the different languages."[33]

It is relatively simple to pull together a descriptive profile for American culture, even though there are regional and individual differences, because researchers have thoroughly studied American culture. The results of one such study by Harris and Moran are shown in Exhibit 4–7, which provides a basis of comparison with other cultures and thus suggests the likely differences in workplace behaviors.

EXHIBIT 4–7

Americans at a Glance

1. *Goal and achievement oriented*—Americans think they can accomplish just about anything, given enough time, money, and technology.
2. *Highly organized and institutionally minded*—Americans prefer a society that is strong institutionally, secure, and tidy or well kept.
3. *Freedom-loving and self-reliant*—Americans fought a revolution and subsequent wars to preserve their concept of democracy, so they resent too much control or interference, especially by government or external forces. They believe in an ideal that all persons are created equal; though they sometimes fail to live that ideal fully, they strive through law to promote equal opportunity and to confront their own racism or prejudice.
   They also idealize the self-made person who rises from poverty and adversity, and think they can influence and create their own futures. Control of one's destiny is popularly expressed as "doing your own thing." Americans think, for the most part, that with determination and initiative, one can achieve whatever one sets out to do and thus fulfill one's individual human potential.
4. *Work oriented and efficient*—Americans possess a strong work ethic, though they are learning in the present generation to enjoy leisure time constructively. They are conscious of time and efficient in doing things. They tinker with gadgets and technological systems, always searching for easier, better, more efficient ways to accomplish tasks.
5. *Friendly and informal*—Americans reject the traditional privileges of royalty and class, but defer to those with affluence and power. Although informal in greeting and dress, they are a noncontact culture (e.g., avoid embracing in public usually) and maintain a certain physical/psychological distance with others (e.g., about 2 feet).
6. *Competitive and aggressive*—Americans in play or business generally are so oriented because of their drives to achieve and succeed. This is partially traced to their heritage of having to overcome a wilderness and hostile elements in their environment.
7. *Values in transition*—Traditional American values of family loyalty, respect and care of the aged, marriage and the nuclear family, patriotism, material acquisition, forthrightness, and the like are undergoing profound reevaluation as people search for new meanings.
8. *Generosity*—Although Americans seemingly emphasize material values, they are a sharing people, as has been demonstrated in the Marshall Plan, foreign aid programs, refugee assistance, and their willingness at home and abroad to espouse a good cause and to help neighbors in need. They tend to be altruistic and some would say naive as a people.

Source: From *Managing Cultural Differences* by Philip R. Harris and Robert T. Moran, 4th ed. Copyright © 1996 by Gulf Publishing Company, Houston, TX. Used with permission. All rights reserved.

It is not so easy, however, to pull together descriptive cultural profiles of peoples in other countries unless one has lived there and been intricately involved with those people. But managers can make a start by using what research and literature is available on a comparative basis. The following Comparative Management in Focus section provides brief, generalized country profiles based on a synthesis of research, primarily from Hofstede[34] and England,[35] as well as numerous other sources.[36] These profiles illustrate how to synthesize information and gain a sense of the character of a society—from which implications may be drawn about how to manage more effectively in that society. More extensive implications and applications related to managerial functions are drawn in later chapters.

COMPARATIVE MANAGEMENT IN FOCUS

Profiles in Culture

Japan

Much of the Japanese culture—and the basis of working relationships—can be explained by the principle of *wa*, "peace and harmony." This principle, embedded in the value they attribute to *amae* ("indulgent love"), probably originated in the Shinto religion, which focuses on spiritual and physical harmony. *Amae* results in *shinyo*, which refers to the mutual confidence, faith, and honor necessary for successful business relationships. Japan ranks high on pragmatism, masculinity, and uncertainty avoidance, and fairly high on power distance. At the same time, much importance is attached to loyalty, empathy, and the guidance of subordinates. The result is a mix of authoritarianism and humanism in the workplace, similar to a family system. These cultural roots are evident in a very homogeneous managerial value system, with strong middle management, strong working relationships, strong seniority systems that stress rank, and an emphasis on looking after employees. The principle of *wa* carries forth into the work group—the building block of Japanese business. The Japanese strongly identify and thus seek to cooperate with their work groups. The emphasis is on participative management; consensus problem solving; and decision making with a patient, long-term perspective. Open expression or conflict is discouraged, and it is of paramount importance to avoid the shame of not fulfilling one's duty. These elements of work culture result in a devotion to work, collective responsibility, and a high degree of employee productivity.

If we extend this cultural profile to its implications for specific behaviors in the workplace, we can draw a comparison with common American behaviors. As shown in Exhibit 4–8, most of those behaviors seem to be opposite to those of their counterparts; it is no wonder that there are many misunderstandings and conflicts in the workplace between Americans and Japanese. For example, a majority of the attitudes and behaviors of many Japanese stems from a high level of collectivism, compared with a high level of individualism common to Americans. This contrast is highlighted in the center of Exhibit 4–8 by "maintain the group," compared with "protect the individual." In addition, the strict social order of the Japanese permeates the workplace in adherence to organizational hierarchy and seniority and in loyalty to the firm. This contrasts markedly with the typical American responses to organizational relationships and duties based on equality. In addition, the often

EXHIBIT 4–8

The American–Japanese Cultural Divide

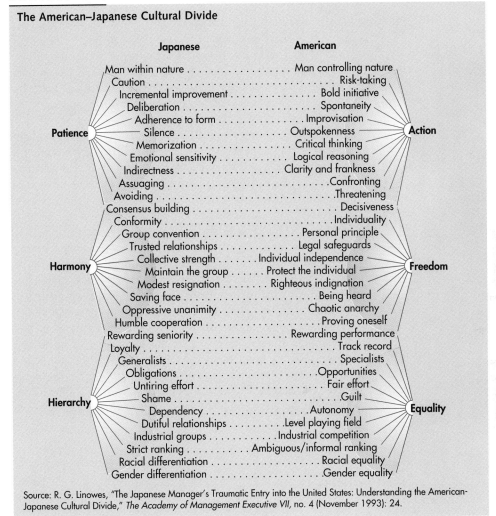

	Japanese	American
	Man within nature	Man controlling nature
	Caution	Risk-taking
	Incremental improvement	Bold initiative
	Deliberation	Spontaneity
	Adherence to form	Improvisation
Patience	Silence	Outspokenness	Action
	Memorization	Critical thinking
	Emotional sensitivity	Logical reasoning
	Indirectness	Clarity and frankness
	Assuaging	Confronting
	Avoiding	Threatening
	Consensus building	Decisiveness
	Conformity	Individuality
	Group convention	Personal principle
	Trusted relationships	Legal safeguards
Harmony	Collective strength	Individual independence	Freedom
	Maintain the group	Protect the individual
	Modest resignation	Righteous indignation
	Saving face	Being heard
	Oppressive unanimity	Chaotic anarchy
	Humble cooperation	Proving oneself
	Rewarding seniority	Rewarding performance
	Loyalty	Track record
	Generalists	Specialists
	Obligations	Opportunities
	Untiring effort	Fair effort
Hierarchy	Shame	Guilt	Equality
	Dependency	Autonomy
	Dutiful relationships	Level playing field
	Industrial groups	Industrial competition
	Strict ranking	Ambiguous/informal ranking
	Racial differentiation	Racial equality
	Gender differentiation	Gender equality

Source: R. G. Linowes, "The Japanese Manager's Traumatic Entry into the United States: Understanding the American-Japanese Cultural Divide," *The Academy of Management Executive VII*, no. 4 (November 1993): 24.

blunt, outspoken American businessperson offends the indirectness and sensitivity of the Japanese for whom the virtue of patience is paramount, causing the silence and avoidance that so frustrates Americans.[37] As a result, Japanese businesspeople tend to think of American organizations as having no spiritual quality and little employee loyalty, and of Americans as assertive, frank, and egotistic. Their American counterparts, in turn, respond with the impression that Japanese businesspeople have little experience and are secretive, arrogant, and cautious.[38]

Germany

The reunited Germany is naturally fairly culturally diverse since the country borders several nations. Generally, Germans rank quite high on Hofstede's dimension of individualism, though their behaviors seem less individualistic than those of Americans. They score fairly high on uncertainty avoidance and masculinity, and have a relatively small need for power distance. These cultural norms show up in the Germans' preference for being around familiar people and situations; they also show up in their propensity to do a detailed evaluation of business deals before committing themselves.

Christianity underlies much of German culture—more than 96 percent of Germans are Catholics or Protestants. This may be why Germans tend to like rule and order in their lives, and why there is a clear public expectation of the acceptable and the unacceptable way to do things. Public signs everywhere in Germany dictate what is allowed or "verboten" (forbidden). Germans are very strict with their use of time, whether for business or pleasure, frowning on inefficiency or on tardiness. In business, Germans tend to be assertive, but they downplay aggression. Decisions are not as centralized as one would expect, with hierarchical processes often giving way to consensus decision making. However, there is strict departmentalization in organizations, with centralized and final authority at the departmental manager level. Hall and Hall describe the German preference for closed doors and private space as evidence of the affinity for compartmentalization in organizations and in their own lives. They also prefer more physical space around them in conversation than do most other Europeans, and privacy in aural distance. In fact, German law prohibits loud noises in public areas on weekend afternoons. Germans are conservative, valuing privacy, politeness, and formality; they usually use last names and titles for all except those close to them.

In negotiations, Germans want detailed information before and during discussions, which can become lengthy. Factors such as voice and speech control are given much weight. But since Germany is a low-context society, communication is explicit, and Americans find negotiations easy to understand.[39]

Korea

Koreans rank high on collectivism and pragmatism, fairly low on masculinity, moderate on power distance, and quite high on uncertainty avoidance. Although greatly influenced by American culture, Koreans are still very much bound to the traditional Confucian teachings of spiritualism and collectivism. Korea and its people have undergone great changes, but the respect for family, authority, formality, class, and rank remain strong. Koreans are quite aggressive and hard working, demonstrative, friendly, and very hospitable. For the most part, they do not subscribe to participative management. Family and personal relationships are important, and connections are vital for business introductions and transactions. Business is based on honor and trust; most contracts are oral. Although achievement and competence are important to Koreans, a driving force in relationships is the priority of guarding both parties' social and professional reputations. Thus, praise predominates, and honest criticism is rare.

Further insight into the differences between American and Korean culture can be derived from the following excerpted letter from Professor Jin K. Kim in Plattsburgh, New York, to his high school friend, MK, in South Korea, who just returned from a visit to the United States. MK, whom Dr. Kim had not seen for 20 years, is planning to immigrate to the United States, and Dr. Kim wants to help ward off his friend's culture shock by telling him about American culture from a Korean perspective.

Dear MK,

I sincerely hope the last leg of your trip home from the five-week fact-finding visit to the United States was pleasant and informative. Although I may not have expressed my sense of exhilaration about your visit through the meager lodging accommodations and "barbaric" foods we provided, it was sheer joy to spend four weeks with you and Kyung-Ok. (Please refrain from hitting the ceiling. My use of your charming wife's name, rather than the usual Korean expression, "your wife" or "your house person," is not an indication of my amorous intentions toward her as any red-blooded Korean man would suspect. Since you are planning to immigrate to this country soon, I thought you might as well begin to get used to the idea of your wife exerting her individuality. Better yet, I thought you should be warned that the moment the plane touches American soil, you will lose your status as the center of your familial universe.) At any rate, please be assured that during your stay here my heart was filled with memories of our three years together in high school when we were young in Pusan.

During your visit, you called me, on several occasions, an American. What prompted you to invoke such a reference is beyond my comprehension. Was it my rusty Korean expressions? Was it my calculating mind? Was it my pitifully subservient (at least when viewed through your cultural lens) role that I was playing in the family life? Or, was it my familiarity with some facets of the American cultural landscape? This may sound bewildering to you, but it is absolutely true that through all the years I have lived in this country, I never truly felt like an American. Sure, on the surface, our family followed closely many ritualistic routines of the American culture: shopping malls, dining out, PTA, Little League, picnics, camping trips, credit card shopping sprees, hot dogs, etc. But mentally I remained stubbornly in the periphery. Naturally, then, my subjective cultural attitudes stayed staunchly Korean. Never did the inner layers of my Korean psyche yield to the invading American cultural vagaries, I thought. So, when you labeled me an American for the first time, I felt a twinge of guilt.

Several years ago, an old Korean friend of mine, who settled in the United States about the same time I did, paid a visit to Korea for the first time in some 15 years. When he went to see his best high school friend, who was now married and had two sons, his friend's wife made a bed for him and her husband in the master bedroom, declaring that she would spend the night with the children. It was not necessarily the sexual connotation of the episode that made my friend blush; he was greatly embarrassed by the circumstance in which he imposed himself to the extent that the couple's privacy had to be violated. For his high school friend and his wife, it was clearly their age-old friendship to which the couple's privacy had to yield. MK, you might empathize rather easily with this Korean couple's state of mind. But it would be a gross mistake even to imagine there may be occasions in your adopted culture when a gesture of friendship breaks the barrier of privacy. Zealously guarding their privacy above all,

Americans are marvelously adept at drawing the line where friendship—that elusive "we" feeling—stops and privacy begins.

Indeed, one of the hardest tasks you will face as an "alien" is how to find that delicate balance between your individuality (for example, privacy) and your collective identity (for example, friendship or membership in social groups). Privacy is not the only issue that stems from this individuality–collectivity continuum. Honesty in interpersonal relationships is another point that may keep you puzzled. Americans are almost brutally honest and frank about issues that belong to public domains; they are not afraid of discussing an embarrassing topic in most graphic details as long as the topic is a matter of public concern. Equally frank and honest gestures are adopted when they discuss their own personal lives once the presumed benefits from such gestures are determined to outweigh the risks involved. Accordingly, it is not uncommon to encounter friends who volunteer personally embarrassing and even shameful information lest you find it out from other sources. Are Americans equally straightforward and forthcoming in laying out heartfelt personal criticisms directed at their friends? Not likely. Their otherwise acute sense of honesty becomes significantly muted when they face the unpleasant task of being negative toward their personal friends. The fear of an emotion-draining confrontation and the virtue of being polite force them to put on a facade or mask. The perfectly accepted social behavior of telling "white lies" is a good example. The social and personal virtues of accepting such lies are grounded in the belief that the potential damage that can be inflicted by directly telling a friend the hurtful truth far outweighs the potential benefit that the friend could gain from it. Instead of telling a hurtful truth directly, Americans use various indirect communication channels to which their friend is likely to be tuned. In other words, they publicize the information in the form of gossip or behind-the-back recriminations until it is transformed into a sort of collective criticism against the target individual. Thus objectified and collectivized, the "truth" ultimately reaches the target individual with a minimal cost of social discomfort on the part of the teller. There is nothing vile or insidious about this communication tactic, since it is deeply rooted in the concern for sustaining social pleasantry for both parties.

This innocuous practice, however, is bound to be perceived as an act of outrageous dishonesty by a person deeply immersed in the Korean culture. In the Korean cultural context, a trusted personal relationship precludes such publicizing prior to direct, "honest" criticism to the individual concerned, no matter what the cost in social and personal unpleasantry. Indeed, as you are well aware, MK, such direct reproach and even recrimination in Korea is in most cases appreciated as a sign of one's utmost love and concern for the target individual. Stressful and emotionally draining as it is, such a frank expression of criticism is done out of "we" feeling. Straight-talking friends did not want me to repeat undesirable acts in front of others, as it would either damage "our reputation" or go against the common interest of "our collective identity." In Korea, the focus is on the self-discipline that forms a basis for the integrity of "our group." In America, on the other hand, the focus is on the feelings of two individuals. From the potential teller's viewpoint, the primary concern is how to maintain social politeness, whereas from the target person's viewpoint, the primary concern is how to maintain self-esteem. Indeed, these two diametrically opposed frames of reference—self-discipline and self-esteem—make one culture collective and the other individualistic.

It is rather amazing that for all the mistakes I must have made in the past 20 years, only one non-Korean American friend gave me such an "honest" criticism. In a sense, this concern for interpersonal politeness conceals their disapproval of my undesirable behavior for a time and ultimately delays the adjustment or realignment of my behavior, since it is likely to take quite a while for the collective judgment to reach me through the "publicized" channels of communication. So many Korean immigrants express their indignation about their American colleagues who smile at them but who criticize them behind their backs. If you ever become a victim of such a perception, MK, please take heart that you are not the only one who feels that pain.

MK—The last facet of the individualism–collectivism continuum likely to cause a great amount of cognitive dissonance in the process of your assimilation to American life is the extent to which you have to assert your individuality to other people. You probably have no difficulty remembering our high school principal, K. W. Park, for whom we had a respect–contempt complex. He used to lecture, almost daily at morning assemblies, on the virtue of being modest. As he preached it, it was a form of the Confucian virtue of self-denial. Our existence or presence among other people, he told us, should not be overly felt through communicated messages (regardless of whether they are done with a tongue or pen). One's existence, we were told, should be noticed by others in the form of our acts and conduct. One is obligated to provide opportunities for others to experience one's existence through what he or she does. Self-initiated effort for public recognition or self-aggrandizement was the most shameful conduct for a person of virtue.

This idea is interesting and noble as a philosophical posture, but when it is practiced in America, it will not get you anywhere in most circumstances. The lack of self-assertion is translated directly into timidity and lack of self-confidence. This is a culture where you must exert your individuality to the extent that it would make our high school principal turn in his grave out of shame and disgust. Blame the size of the territory or the population of this country. You may even blame the fast-paced cadence of life or the social mobility that moves people around at a dizzying speed. Whatever the specific reason might be, Americans are not waiting to experience you or your behaviors as they exist. They want a "documented" version of you that is eloquently summarized, decorated, and certified. What they are looking for is not your raw, unprocessed being with rich texture; rather, it is a slickly processed self, neatly packaged and, most important, conveniently delivered to them. Self-advertising is encouraged almost to the point of pretentiousness. Years ago in Syracuse, I had an occasion to introduce a visiting Korean monk-scholar to a gathering of people who wanted to hear something about Oriental philosophies. After taking an elegantly practiced bow to the crowd, this humble monk declared, "My name is . . . Please teach me, as I do not know anything." It took quite a bit of probing and questioning for us to extract something to chew on from that monk with the mysterious smile. Contrast this with an American colleague of mine applying for a promotion several years ago, who literally hauled in two cabinets full of documented evidence of his scholarly achievements.

The curious journey toward the American end of the individualism–collectivism continuum will be inevitable, I assure you. The real question is whether it will be in your generation, your children's, or their children's. Whenever it happens, it will be a bittersweet revenge for me, since only then will you realize how it feels to be called an American by your best high school chum.

Source: Excerpted from a letter by Dr. Jin K. Kim, State University of New York–Plattsburgh. Copyright ©1993 by Dr. Jin K. Kim. Used with permission of Dr. Kim.

Culture and Management Styles Around the World

As an international manager, once you have researched the culture of a country in which you may be going to work or do business, and developed a cultural profile, it is useful then to apply that information to develop an understanding of the expected management styles and ways of doing business that predominate in that region, or with that type of business setting. Two examples are developed here—those for Saudi Arabia and for Chinese small family businesses.

Saudi Arabia

Understanding how business is conducted in the modern Middle East requires an understanding of the Arab culture since the Arab peoples are the majority there and most of them are Muslim. The Arab culture is intertwined with the pervasive influence of Islam. Even though not all Middle Easterners are Arab, the Arab culture and management style predominates in the Gulf region. Shared culture, religion, and language underlie behavioral similarities throughout the Arab world. Islam "permeates Saudi life—Allah is always present, controls everything, and is frequently referred to in conversation."[40] Employees may spend more than two hours a day in prayer, part of the life patterns that intertwine work with religion, politics, and social life.

Arab history and culture is based on tribalism, with its norms of reciprocity of favors, support, obligation, and identity passed on to the family unit, which is the primary structural model. Family life is based on closer personal ties than in the West. Arabs value personal relationships, honor, and saving face for all concerned; these values take precedence over the work at hand or verbal accuracy. "Outsiders" must realize that establishing a trusting relationship and respect for the Arab social norms have to precede any attempts at business discussions. Honor, pride, and dignity are at the core of "shame" societies such as the Arabs'. As such, shame and honor provide the basis for social control and motivation. Circumstances dictate what is right or wrong and what is acceptable behavior.[41]

Open admission of error is avoided by Arabs at all costs because weakness (*muruwwa*) is a failure to be manly. It is sometimes difficult for Westerners to get at the truth because of the Arab need to avoid showing weakness; instead, a desired, or idealized, situation is painted by Arabs. Shame is also brought on someone who declines to fulfill a request or a favor; therefore, a business arrangement is left open if something has yet to be completed.

The communication style of Middle Eastern societies is high context (that is, implicit and indirect), and their use of time is polychronic—many things can be going on at the same

EXHIBIT 4–9

Behaviors That Will Likely Cause Offense in Saudi Arabia

- Bringing up business subjects until you get to know your host, or you will be considered rude.
- Commenting on a man's wife or female children over 12 years of age.
- Raising colloquial questions that may be common in your country, but possibly misunderstood in Saudi Arabia as an invasion of privacy.
- Using disparaging or swear words and off-color or obscene attempts at humor.
- Engaging in conversations about religion, politics, or Israel.
- Bringing gifts of alcohol or using alcohol, which is prohibited in Saudi Arabia.
- Requesting favors from those in authority or esteem, for it is considered impolite for Arabs to say no.
- Shaking hands too firmly or pumping—gentle or limp handshakes are preferred.
- Pointing your finger at someone or showing the soles of your feet when seated.

Source: P. R. Harris and R. T. Moran, *Managing Cultural Differences*, 4th ed. (Houston: Gulf Publishing, 1996).

time, with constant interruptions commonplace. The imposition of deadlines is considered rude, and business schedules take a back seat to the perspective that events will occur "sometime" when Allah wills (*bukra insha Allah*). Arabs give primary importance to hospitality; they are cordial to business associates and lavish in their entertainment, constantly offering strong black coffee (which you should not refuse) and banquets before considering business transactions. Westerners must realize the importance of personal contacts and networking, socializing and building close relationships and trust, practicing patience regarding schedules, and doing business in person. Exhibit 4–9 gives some selected actions and nonverbal behaviors that may offend Arabs. The relationship between cultural values and norms in Saudi Arabia and managerial behaviors is illustrated in Exhibit 4–10 on the next page.

Chinese Small Family Businesses

The predominance of small businesses in China highlights the need for managers from around the world to gain an understanding of how such businesses operate. Many small businesses—most of which are family or extended-family businesses—become part of the value chain (suppliers, buyers, retailers, and so on) within industries in which "foreign" firms may compete.

The general framework for the Chinese culture is discussed further in Chapter 6. Here we will point out some specifics of Chinese management style and practices in particular as they apply to small businesses. As put forth by Chen, the philosophy and structure of Chinese businesses comprises paternalism, mutual obligation, responsibility, hierarchy, familialism, personalism, and connections.[42] Autocratic leadership is the norm, with the owner using his or her power, but also with a caring about other people that may predominate over efficiency.[43]

According to Lee, major differences between Chinese management styles and those of their Western counterparts are human-centeredness, family-centeredness, centralization of power, and small size.[44] Their human-centered management style puts people ahead of a

EXHIBIT 4–10

The Relationship Between Culture and Managerial Behaviors in Saudi Arabia

Cultural Values	Managerial Behaviors
Tribal and family loyalty	Work group loyalty Paternal sociability Stable employment and a sense of belonging A pleasant workplace Careful selection of employees Nepotism
Arabic language	Business as an intellectual activity Access to employees and peers Management by walking around Conversation as recreation
Close and warm friendships	A person rather than task and money orientation Theory Y management Avoidance of judgment
Islam	Sensitivity to Islamic virtues Observance of the Qur'an and Sharia Work as personal or spiritual growth
Majlis	Consultative management A full and fair hearing Adherence to norms
Honor and shame	Clear guidelines and conflict avoidance Positive reinforcement Training and defined job duties Private correction of mistakes Avoidance of competition
An idealized self	Centralized decision making Assumption of responsibility appropriate to position Empathy and respect for the self-image of others
Polychronic use of time	Right- and left-brain facility A bias for action Patience and flexibility
Independence	Sensitivity to control Interest in the individual
Male domination	Separation of sexes Open work life; closed family life

Source: Robert W. Moore.

business relationship and focuses on friendship, loyalty, and trustworthiness.[45] The family is extremely important in Chinese culture, and small businesses tend to be run like a family.

The centralized power structure in Chinese organizations, unlike those in the West, splits into two distinct levels: At the top is the boss and a few family members, and at the bottom are the employees, with no ranking among the workers.[46]

As Chinese firms in many modern regions in the Pacific Rim seek to modernize and compete locally and globally, there is a tug of war between the old and the new—the traditional Chinese management practices, and the increasingly "imported" Western management

EXHIBIT 4–11

Chinese Management Philosophies: The Old and the New

Old Generation	Young Generation
Claim that they have more experiences	Claim that they have more education
Perceive that their role is to intervene for the workers and help them	Perceive that their role is to hire competent workers and expect them to perform
Believe that it is the boss's responsibility to solve problems	Believe that it is the individual's responsibility to solve problems
Stress that a boss has the obligation to take care of the workers	Stress that workers have responsibility to perform the job well
Emphasize that individuals should conform to majority	Emphasize that individuals should maximize their talents and potentials
Believe that work cannot be divided clearly and like to be involved in everything	Believe that a boss should mind his or her own work and leave the workers to do their job
Perceive that work is more important than designation and organizational structure	Perceive that designation and organizational structure are important in order to get the work done
Believe that managers should help the workers solve their problems	Believe that managers should set objectives and achieve them
Complain that the young generation likes to use complicated management methods	Complain that the old generation does things on ad hoc basis
Perceive that the young generation likes to change and expects immediate results	Perceive that the old generation is static and resistant to change
Worry that the young generation is not experienced in running the business	Frustrated that the old generation still holds on strongly to their power
Emphasize that they have to take care of the old workers in the process of the company's growth	Emphasize that they have to gain acceptance from their peers
Emphasize that ethics are important in business	Emphasize that strategy is important in business
Anticipate that the young generation is going to have many difficulties if they adopt Western concepts of management	Frustrated that the old generation does not let them test out their concepts of management
Believe that one's ability is limited and one should be contented with what one has	Believe that there are a lot of opportunities for achievement and growth

Source: Dr. Jean Lee, "Culture and Management—A Study of Small Chinese Family Business in Singapore," *Journal of Small Business Management* (July 1996).

styles. As discussed by Lee, this struggle is encapsulated in the different management perspectives of the old and young generations, as shown in Exhibit 4–11.

Conclusion

We have examined various cultural values and how managers can understand them with the help of cultural profiles. Now we will turn our attention to the applications of this cultural knowledge to management in an international environment (or, alternatively, in a domestic multicultural environment)—especially as relevant to cross-cultural communication (Chapter 5), negotiation and decision making (Chapter 6), motivating and leading (Chapter 12), and managing workforce diversity (Chapter 13). Culture and communication are essentially synonymous; what happens when people from different cultures communicate, and how can the international manager understand the underlying process and adapt his or her style and expectations accordingly? These questions will be addressed in the next chapter.

Summary of Key Points

1. The culture of a society comprises the shared values, understandings, assumptions, and goals that are passed down through generations and imposed by members of the society.
2. Cultural and national differences strongly influence the attitudes and expectations and therefore the on-the-job behavior of individuals and groups.
3. Managers must develop cultural sensitivity to anticipate and accommodate behavioral differences in different societies.
4. Managers must avoid parochialism, an attitude that assumes one's own management techniques are best in any situation or location and that other people should follow one's patterns of behavior.
5. Harris and Moran take a systems approach to understanding cultural and national variables and their effects on work behavior. They identify eight subsystems of variables: kinship, education, economy, politics, religion, associations, health, and recreation.
6. From his research in 50 countries, Hofstede proposes four underlying value dimensions that help identify and describe the cultural profile of a country and affect organizational processes. These are power distance, uncertainty avoidance, individualism, and masculinity. Through the research of Hofstede and others, we can cluster countries based on intercultural similarities.
7. On-the-job conflicts in international management frequently arise out of conflicting values and orientations regarding time, change, material factors, and individualism.
8. Managers can use research results and personal observations to develop a character sketch, or cultural profile, of a country. This profile can help managers anticipate how to motivate people and coordinate work processes in a particular international context.

Discussion Questions

1. What is meant by the culture of a society, and why is it important that international managers understand it? Do you notice cultural differences among your classmates? How do those differences affect the class environment? Your group projects?
2. Describe the four dimensions of culture proposed by Hofstede. What are the managerial implications of these dimensions?
3. Discuss the types of operational conflicts that could occur in an international context because of different attitudes toward time, change, material factors, and individualism. Give examples relative to specific countries.
4. Give some examples of countries in which the family and its extensions play an important role in the workplace. How are managerial functions affected, and what can a manager do about this influence?
5. Discuss collectivism as it applies to the Japanese workplace. What managerial functions does it affect?

Application Exercises

1. Develop a cultural profile for one of the countries in the following list. Form small groups of students and compare your findings in class with those of another group preparing a profile for another country. Be sure to compare specific findings regarding religion, kinship, recreation, and other subsystems. What are the prevailing attitudes toward time, change, material factors, and individualism?

    Any African country
    People's Republic of China

    England
    Mexico
    France
    India

2. In small groups of students, research Hofstede's findings regarding the four dimensions of power distance, uncertainty avoidance, masculinity, and individualism for one of the pairs of countries listed here. (Your instructor can assign the countries to avoid duplication.) Present your findings to the class. Assume you are a manager of a subsidiary in the foreign country, and explain how differences on these dimensions are likely to affect your management tasks. What suggestions do you have for dealing with these differences in the workplace?

    Germany and Brazil
    Italy and the People's Republic of China
    United States and Russia

Experiential Exercises

1. A large Baltimore manufacturer of cabinet hardware had been working for months to locate a suitable distributor for its products in Europe. Finally invited to present a demonstration to a reputable distributing company in Frankfurt, it sent one of its most promising young executives, Fred Wagner, to make the presentation. Fred not only spoke fluent German but also felt a special interest in this assignment because his paternal grandparents had immigrated to the United States from the Frankfurt area during the 1920s. When Fred arrived at the conference room where he would be making his presentation, he shook hands firmly, greeted everyone with a friendly *guten tag,* and even remembered to bow the head slightly as is the German custom. Fred, a very effective speaker and past president of the Baltimore Toastmasters Club, prefaced his presentation with a few humorous anecdotes to set a relaxed and receptive atmosphere. However, he felt that his presentation was not very well received by the company executives. In fact, his instincts were correct, for the German company chose not to distribute Fred's hardware products.

   What went wrong?

2. Bill Nugent, an international real estate developer from Dallas, had made a 2:30 P.M. appointment with Mr. Abdullah, a high-ranking government official in Riyadh, Saudi Arabia. From the beginning, things did not go well for Bill. First, he was kept waiting until nearly 3:45 before he was ushered into Mr. Abdullah's office. And when he finally did get in, several other men were also in the room. Even though Bill felt that he wanted to get down to business with Mr. Abdullah, he was reluctant to get too specific because he considered much of what they needed to discuss sensitive and private. To add to Bill's sense of frustration, Mr. Abdullah seemed more interested in engaging in meaningless small talk than in dealing with the substantive issues concerning their business.

   How might you help Bill deal with his frustration?

3. Tom Forrest, an up-and-coming executive for a U.S. electronics company, was sent to Japan to work out the details of a joint venture with a Japanese electronics firm. During the first several weeks, Tom felt that the negotiations were proceeding better than he had expected. He found that he had very cordial working relationships with the team of Japanese executives, and in fact, they had agreed on the major policies and strategies governing the new joint venture. During the third week of negotiations, Tom was present at a meeting held to review their progress. The meeting was chaired by the president of the Japanese firm, Mr. Hayakawa, a man in his mid–40s, who had recently taken over the presidency from his 82-year-old grandfather. The new president, who had been involved in most of the negotiations during the preceding weeks, seemed to Tom to be one of the strongest advocates of the plan that had been developed to date. Also attending the meeting was Hayakawa's grandfather, the recently retired president. After the plans had been discussed in some detail, the octogenarian past president proceeded to give a long

soliloquy about how some of the features of this plan violated the traditional practices on which the company had been founded. Much to Tom's amazement, Mr. Hayakawa did nothing to explain or defend the policies and strategies that they had taken weeks to develop. Feeling extremely frustrated, Tom then gave a fairly strong argued defense of the plan. To Tom's further amazement, no one else in the meeting spoke up in defense of the plan. The tension in the air was quite heavy, and the meeting adjourned shortly thereafter. Within days, the Japanese firm completely terminated the negotiations on the joint venture.

How could you help Tom better understand this bewildering situation?

Source: Gary P. Ferraro, *The Cultural Dimensions of International Business*, 2nd ed. (NJ: Prentice Hall, 1994).

Internet Resources

Visit the Deresky companion Web site at http://prenhall.com/Deresky for this chapter's Internet resources.

Case Study

Trouble at Computex Corporation

Mr. Peter Jones
Vice President—Europe
Computex Corporation
San Francisco/USA
Göteborg

The writers of this letter are the headcount of the Sales Department of Computex Sweden, A.S., except for the Sales Manager.

We have decided to bring to your attention a problem which unsolved probably will lead to a situation where the majority among us will leave the company within a rather short period of time. None of us want to be in this situation, and we are approaching you purely as an attempt to save the team to the benefit of ourselves as well as Computex Corporation.

We consider ourselves an experienced, professional, and sales-oriented group of people. Computex Corporation is a company which we are proud to work for. The majority among us have been employed for several years. Consequently, a great number of key customers in different areas of Sweden see us as representatives of Computex Corporation. It is correct to say that the many excellent contacts we have made have been established over years; many of them are friends of ours.

These traits give a very short background because we have never met you. What kind of problem forces us to such a serious step as to contact you?

Problems arise as a result of character traits and behavior of our General Manager, Mr. Miller.

Firstly, we are more and more convinced that we are tools that he is utilizing in order to "climb the ladder." In meetings with us individually, or as a group, he gives visions about the future, how he values us, how he wants to delegate and involve us in business, the importance of cooperation and communication, etc. When it comes to the point, these phrases turn out to be only words.

Mr. Miller loses his temper almost daily, and his outbursts and reactions are not equivalent to the possible error. His mood and views can change almost from hour to hour. This fact causes a situation where we feel uncertain when facing him and consequently are reluctant to do so. Regarding human relationships, his behavior is not acceptable, especially for a manager.

The extent of the experience of this varies within the group due to our location. Some of us are seldom in the office.

Secondly, we have experienced clearly that he has various means of suppressing and discouraging people within the organization.

The new "victim" now is our Sales Manager, Mr. Johansson. Because he is our boss, it is obvious that we regret such a situation, which to a considerable extent influences our working conditions.

There are also other victims among us. It is indeed very difficult to carry through what is stated in our job descriptions.

We feel terribly sorry and wonder how it can be possible for one person almost to ruin a whole organization.

If this group consisted of people less mature, many of us would have left Computex Corporation already. So far only one has left the company due to the above reasons.

From September 1, two new Sales Representatives are joining the company. We regret very much that new employees get their first contact with the company under the present circumstances. An immediate action is therefore required.

It is not our objective to get rid of Mr. Miller as General Manager. Without going into details, we are thankful for what he has done to the company from a business point of view. If he could control his mood, show some respect for his colleagues, keep words, and stick to plans, we believe that we can succeed under his leadership.

We are fully aware of the seriousness of contacting you, and we have been in doubt whether or not to contact you directly before talking to Mr. Miller.

After serious discussions and considerations, we have reached the conclusion that a problem of this nature unfortunately cannot be solved without some sort of action from the superior. If possible, direct confrontation must be avoided. It can only make things worse.

We are hoping for a positive solution.

Six of your Sales Representatives in Sweden

Peter Jones let out a long sigh as he gazed over the letter from Sweden. "What do I do now?" he thought, and began to reflect on the problem. He wondered who was right and who was wrong in this squabble, and he questioned whether he would ever get all the information necessary to make a wise decision. He didn't know much about the Swedes and was unsure whether this was strictly a work problem or a "cross-cultural" problem. "How can I tease those two issues apart?" he asked himself, as he locked his office and made his way down the hallway to the elevator.

As Peter pulled out of the parking garage and onto the street, he began to devise a plan to deal with the problem. "This will be a test of my conflict management skills," he thought. "No doubt about it!" As he merged into the freeway traffic from the on-ramp and began his commute home, he began to wish that he had never sent Miller to Sweden in the first place. "But would Gonzalez or Harris have done any better? Would I have done any better?" Few answers seemed to come to him as he plodded along in the bumper-to-bumper traffic on Interstate 440.

Case Question

You are Peter. How would you deal with this problem now? What should have been done differently in the first place?

5

The Cross-Cultural Communication Environment

O U T L I N E

Opening Profile: Oriental Poker Face: Eastern Deception or Western Inscrutability?

The Communication Process

Cultural Noise in the Communication Process

Technology Application: Technology Communicates Across Borders and Cultures

Cultural Variables in the Communication Process

Context

Comparative Management in Focus: Communicating with Arabs

Communication Channels

Managing Cross-Cultural Communication

Developing Cultural Sensitivity

Careful Encoding

Management Focus: How 21 Men Got Global in 35 Days: Problem Number One Was Communication

Selective Transmission

Careful Decoding of Feedback

Follow-Up Actions

Summary of Key Points

Discussion Questions

Application Exercises

Experiential Exercise

Internet Resources

Case Study: Elizabeth Visits GPC's French Subsidiary

OPENING PROFILE

Oriental Poker Face: Eastern Deception or Western Inscrutability?

Among many English expressions that are likely to offend those of us whose ancestry may be traced to the Far East, two stand out quite menacingly for me: "Oriental poker face" and "idiotic Asian smile." The former refers to the supposedly inscrutable nature of a facial expression that apparently reflects no particular state of mind, whereas the latter pokes fun at a face fixed with a perpetually friendly smile. Westerners' perplexity, when faced with either, arises from the impression that these two diametrically opposed masquerading strategies prevent them from extracting useful information—the type of information that at least they could process with a reasonable measure of confidence—about the feelings of the person before them. An Asian face that projects no signs of emotion, then, seems to most Westerners nothing but a facade. It does not matter whether that face wears an unsightly scowl or a shining ray; a facial expression they cannot interpret poses a genuine threat.

Compassionate and sympathetic to their perplexity as I may be, I am also insulted by the Western insensitivity to the significant roles that subtle signs play in Asian cultures. Every culture has its unique set of modus operandi for communication. Western culture, for example, apparently emphasizes the importance of direct communication. Not only are the communicators taught to look directly at each other when they convey a message, but they are also encouraged to come right to the point of the message. Making bold statements or asking frank questions in a less than diplomatic manner (such as "That was really a very stupid thing to do!" or "Are you interested in me?") is rarely construed as rude or indiscreet. Even embarrassingly blunt questions such as "Senator Hart, have you ever had sexual intercourse with anyone other than your wife?" are tolerated most of the time. Asians, on the other hand, find this direct communicative style quite unnerving. In many social interaction situations, they avoid direct eye contact. They "see" each other without necessarily looking directly at each other, and they gather information about inner states of mind without asking even the most discreet or understated questions. Many times they talk around the main topic and, yet, succeed remarkably well in understanding one another's position. (At least they believe they have developed a reasonably clear understanding.)

To a great extent, Asian communication is listening centered; the ability to listen (and a special talent for detecting various communicative cues) is treated as equally important as, if not more important than, the ability to speak. This contrasts clearly with the American style of communication that puts the utmost emphasis on verbal expression; the speaker carries most of the burden for ensuring that everyone understands his or her message. An Asian listener, however, is prone to blame himself or herself for failing to reach a comprehensive understanding from the few words and gestures performed by the speaker. With this heavier burden placed on the listener, an Asian speaker does not feel obliged to send clearly discernible message cues (at least not nearly so much as he or she is obliged to do in American cultural contexts). Not obligated to express themselves without interruption, Asians use silence as a tool in communication. Silence, by most Western conventions, represents discontinuity of communication, and creates a feeling of discomfort and anxiety. In the Orient, however, silence is not only comfortably tolerated but is considered a desirable form of expression. Far from being a sign of displeasure or animosity, it serves as an integral part of the communication process, used for reflecting upon messages previously exchanged and for carefully crafting thoughts before uttering them.

It is not outlandish at all, then, for Asians to view Americans as unnecessarily talkative and lacking in the ability to simply listen. For the Asian, it is the American who projects a mask of confidence by being overly expressive both verbally and nonverbally. Since the American style of communication places less emphasis on the act of listening than on speaking, Asians suspect that their American counterparts fail to pick up subtle and astute communicative signs in conversation. To a cultural outlook untrained in reading those signs, an inscrutable face represents no more than a menacing or amusing mask.

Source: Dr. Jin Kim, State University of New York–Plattsburgh. Copyright ©1995 by Dr. Jin Kim. Used with permission of Dr. Kim.

Cultural communications are deeper and more complex than spoken or written messages. The essence of effective cross-cultural communication has more to do with releasing the right responses than with sending the "right" messages.[1]

As the Opening Profile suggests, communication is a critical factor in the cross-cultural management issues discussed in this book, particularly those of an interpersonal nature, involving motivation, leadership, group interactions, and negotiation. Culture is conveyed and perpetuated through communication in one form or another. Culture and communication are so intricately intertwined that they are, essentially, synonymous.[2, 3] By understanding this relationship, managers can move toward constructive intercultural management.

Communication, whether in the form of writing, talking, or listening, is an inherent part of a manager's role and takes up the majority of the manager's time on the job. Studies by Mintzberg demonstrate the importance of oral communication; he found that most managers spend between 50 and 90 percent of their time talking to people.[4] The ability of a manager to communicate effectively across cultural boundaries will largely determine the success of international business transactions or the output of a culturally diverse workforce. It is useful, then, to break down the elements involved in the communication process, both to understand the cross-cultural issues at stake and to maximize the process.

The Communication Process

The term **communication** describes the process of sharing meaning by transmitting messages through media such as words, behavior, or material artifacts. Managers communicate to coordinate activities, to disseminate information, to motivate people, and to negotiate future plans. It is of vital importance, then, that the meaning of a particular communication is interpreted by the receiver the way the sender intended. Unfortunately, the communication process, as shown in Exhibit 5–1, involves stages during which the meaning can be distorted.

EXHIBIT 5–1

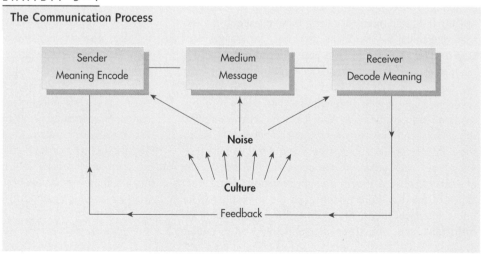

The Communication Process

Anything that serves to undermine the communication of the intended meaning is typically referred to as **noise**.

The primary cause of noise stems from the fact that the sender and the receiver each exist in a unique, private world called his or her life space. The context of that private world, based largely on culture, experience, relations, values, and so forth, determines the interpretation of meaning in communication. People filter, or selectively understand, messages according to what is consistent with their own expectations and perceptions of reality and their values and norms of behavior. The more dissimilar the cultures of those involved, the more likelihood for misinterpretation. In this way, as Samovar, Porter, and Jain state, cultural factors pervade the communication process:

> Culture not only dictates who talks with whom, about what, and how the communication proceeds, it also helps to determine how people encode messages, the meanings they have for messages, and the conditions and circumstances under which various messages may or may not be sent, noticed, or interpreted. In fact, our entire repertory of communicative behaviors is dependent largely on the culture in which we have been raised. Culture, consequently, is the foundation of communication. And, when cultures vary, communication practices also vary.[5]

Communication, therefore, is a complex process of linking up or sharing the perceptual fields of sender and receiver; the perceptive sender builds a bridge to the life space of the receiver.[6] After the receiver interprets the message and draws a conclusion about what the sender meant, he or she will, in most cases, encode and send back a response, making communication a circular process.

The communication process is rapidly changing, however, as a result of technological developments, therefore propelling global business forward at a phenomenal growth rate; these changes are discussed in the accompanying Technology Application.

Cultural Noise in the Communication Process

Because our focus here is on effective cross-cultural communication, we need to understand what cultural variables cause noise in the communication process. This knowledge of **cultural noise** will enable us to take steps to minimize that noise and so improve communication.

When a member of one culture sends a message to a member of another culture, **intercultural communication** takes place. The message contains the meaning intended by the encoder. When it reaches the receiver, however, it undergoes a transformation in which the influence of the decoder's culture becomes part of the meaning.[7] Let's take a look at an example (Exhibit 5–2) of intercultural communication in which the meaning got all mixed up. Note how the attribution of behavior differs for each participant. **Attribution** is the process in which people look for the explanation of another person's behavior. When they realize that they do not understand another, they tend, say Hall and Hall, to blame their confusion on the other's "stupidity, deceit, or craziness."[8]

In the situation depicted in Exhibit 5–2, the Greek employee gets frustrated and resigns after experiencing communication problems with his American boss. How could this outcome have been avoided? We do not have much information about the people or the context of the situation, but we can look at some of the variables that might have been involved and use them as a basis for analysis.

TECHNOLOGY APPLICATION
Technology Communicates Across Borders and Cultures

As business goes global, technology will facilitate human interaction. It will allow people of different languages and cultures to work together seamlessly. Computers will translate language on the fly, allowing multinational and multicultural teams to work together. A file that is sent to people of different languages will ultimately appear in each person's native tongue. But that won't be the only change. The Internet and intranets will allow even more work teams and strategic alliances than we see in today's business world.

"The Internet allows any time, anywhere communication," says Barbara Ells, Industry Analyst at Zona (market) Research, in Redwood City, California. "You can disregard time zones as long as you have a common communication source. And that convenience has huge implications for global business. In the future, we'll see multicultural work teams that share information and collaborate on projects. As a result, language translation tools will become far more important—for web pages, e-mail, word processing, and other functions. It will be essential for information and documents to be accessible worldwide.

In the future, workers will exchange information in many forms: text, images, video, audio, and other media. That will necessitate the use of far more sophisticated tools for managing knowledge and searching for appropriate information. With such a far-flung employee base, most companies are going to rely on human resources to play a larger role in creating a sense of culture and community."

Source: S. Greengard, "How Technology Will Change the Workplace," *Workforce*, 77 (January 1998): 78–79.

Cultural Variables in the Communication Process

Cultural variables that can affect the communication process by influencing a person's perceptions have been identified by Samovar and Porter and discussed by Harris and Moran, Ronen, and others.[9,10,11] These variables are as follows: attitudes, social organization, thought patterns, roles, language (spoken or written), nonverbal communication (including kinesic behavior, proxemics, paralanguage, and object language), and time. Although we discuss these variables separately, their effects are interdependent and inseparable, or, as Hecht, Andersen, and Ribeau put it: "Encoders and decoders process nonverbal cues as a conceptual, multichanneled gestalt."[12]

Attitudes   We all know that our attitudes underlie the way we behave and communicate, and the way we interpret messages from other people. Ethnocentric attitudes are a particular source of noise in cross-cultural communication. In the incident described in Exhibit 5–2, both the American and the Greek are clearly attempting to interpret and convey meaning based on their own experiences of that kind of transaction. The American is probably guilty of stereotyping the Greek employee by quickly jumping to the conclusion that he is unwilling to take responsibility for the task and the scheduling.

This problem, **stereotyping**, occurs when a person assumes that every member of a society or subculture has the same characteristics or traits. Stereotyping is a common cause of misunderstanding in intercultural communication. It is an arbitrary, lazy, and often destructive way to find out about people. A stereotype should be distinguished from a **sociotype**—a

EXHIBIT 5–2

Cultural Noise in International Communication

Behavior		Attribution	
American:	"How long will it take you to finish this report?"	*American:* *Greek:*	I asked him to participate. His behavior makes no sense. He is the boss. Why doesn't he tell me?
Greek:	"I don't know. How long should it take?"	*American:* *Greek:*	He refuses to take responsibility. I asked him for an order.
American:	"You are in the best position to analyze time requirements."	*American:* *Greek:*	I press him to take responsibility for his actions. What nonsense: I'd better give him an answer.
Greek:	"10 days."	*American:*	He lacks the ability to estimate time; this time estimate is totally inadequate.
American:	"Take 15. Is it agreed? You will do it in 15 days?"	*American:* *Greek:*	I offer a contract. These are my orders: 15 days.

In fact, the report needed 30 days of regular work. So the Greek worked day and night, but at the end of the 15th day, he still needed to do one more day's work.

American:	"Where is the report?"	*American:* *Greek:*	I am making sure he fulfills his contract. He is asking for the report.
Greek:	"It will be ready tomorrow."	(Both attribute that it is not ready.)	
American:	"But we agreed it would be ready today."	*American:* *Greek:*	I must teach him to fulfill a contract. The stupid, incompetent boss! Not only did he give me the wrong orders, but he doesn't even appreciate that I did a 30-day job in 16 days.
The Greek hands in his resignation.		The American is surprised.	
		Greek:	I can't work for such a man.

Source: Adapted from H. C. Triandis, *Interpersonal Behavior* (Monterey, CA: Brooks/Cole, 1977): 248; reported in Simcha Ronen, *Comparative and Multinational Management* (New York: John Wiley and Sons, 1986): 101–102.

means of accurately describing members of a group by their traits—which is useful to provide some initial basis for understanding people in a new encounter.[13] Astute managers are aware of the dangers of cultural stereotyping and deal with each person as an individual with whom they may form a unique relationship.

Social Organization   Our perceptions can be influenced by differences in values, approach, or priorities relative to the kinds of social organizations to which we belong. These organizations may be based on one's nation, tribe, or religious sect, or they may consist of the members of a certain profession—examples of such organizations include the Academy of Management or the UAW (United Auto Workers).[14]

Thought Patterns   The logical progression of reasoning varies widely around the world and greatly affects the communication process. Managers cannot assume that others use the same reasoning processes, as illustrated by the experience of a Canadian expatriate in Thailand:

> While in Thailand a Canadian expatriate's car was hit by a Thai motorist who had crossed over the double line while passing another vehicle. After failing to establish that the fault lay

with the Thai driver, the Canadian flagged down a policeman. After several minutes of seemingly futile discussion, the Canadian pointed out the double line in the middle of the road and asked the policeman directly, "What do these lines signify?" The policeman replied, "They indicate the center of the road and are there so I can establish just how far the accident is from that point." The Canadian was silent. It had never occurred to him that the double line might not mean "no passing allowed."[15]

In the Exhibit 5–2 scenario, perhaps the American did not realize that the Greek employee had a different rationale for his time estimate for the job. Because the Greek was not used to having to estimate schedules, he just took a guess, which he felt forced into.

Roles   As discussed in Chapter 12, societies differ considerably in their perception of a manager's role. Much of the difference is attributable to their perception of who should make the decisions and who has responsibility for what. In our example, the American assumes that his role as manager is to delegate responsibility, to foster autonomy, and to practice participative management. He is prescribing the role of the employee without any consideration of whether the employee will understand that role. The Greek's frame of reference leads him to think that the manager is the boss and should give the order about when to have the job completed. He interprets the American's behavior as breaking that frame of reference, and therefore he feels that the boss is "stupid and incompetent" for giving him the wrong order and for not recognizing and appreciating his accomplishment. The manager should have considered what behaviors Greek workers would expect of him and then either played that role or discussed the situation carefully, in a training mode.

Language   Spoken or written language, of course, is a frequent cause of miscommunication, stemming from a person's inability to speak the local language, a poor or too literal translation, a speaker's failure to explain idioms, or a person missing the meaning conveyed through body language or certain symbols. Even among countries that share the same language, there can be problems in the subtleties and nuances inherent in the use of the language, as noted by George Bernard Shaw: "Britain and America are two nations separated by a common language." This problem can exist even within the same country among subcultures or subgroups.[16]

Many international executives tell stories about lost business deals or lost sales because of communication blunders:

> When Pepsi Cola's slogan "Come Alive with Pepsi" was introduced in Germany, the company learned that the literal German translation of "come alive" is "come out of the grave."
> A U.S. airline found a lack of demand for its "rendezvous lounges" on its Boeing 747s flying out of Portugal. They later learned that "rendezvous" in Portuguese refers to a room that is rented for prostitution.[17]

More than just conveying objective information, language also conveys cultural and social understandings from one generation to the next.[18] Examples of how language reflects what is important in a society include the 6,000 different Arabic words used to describe camels and their parts and the 50 or more classifications of snow used by the Inuit Eskimos.

Inasmuch as language conveys culture, technology, and priorities, it also serves to separate and perpetuate subcultures. In India, 14 official and many unofficial languages are used, and more than 800 languages are spoken on the African continent.

Because of increasing workforce diversity around the world, the international business manager will have to deal with a medley of languages. For example, assembly-line workers at the Ford plant in Cologne speak Turkish and Spanish as well as German. In Malaysia, Indonesia, and Thailand, many of the buyers and traders are Chinese. Not all Arabs speak Arabic; in Tunisia and Lebanon, for example, French is the commercial language.[19]

International managers need either a good command of the local language or competent interpreters. The task of accurate translation to bridge cultural gaps is fraught with difficulties, as Schermerhorn discovered in his study of 153 Hong Kong Chinese bilinguals; he found a considerable difference in interpretation and response according to whether the medium used was Chinese or English, even after many experts were involved in the translation process.[20]

Even the direct translation of specific words does not guarantee the congruence of their meaning, as with the word *yes* used by Asians, which usually means only that they have heard you.[21]

Politeness and a desire to say only what the listener wants to hear create noise in the communication process in much of the world. Often, even a clear translation does not help a person understand what is meant because the encoding process has obscured the true message. With the poetic Arab language—replete with exaggeration, elaboration, and repetition—meaning is attributed more to how something is said than to what is said.

In our situation with the American supervisor and Greek employee, it is highly likely that the American could have picked up some cues from the employee's body language, which probably implied problems with the interpretation of meaning. Let's now look at how body language may have created noise in this case.

Nonverbal Communication   Behavior that communicates without words (although it often is accompanied by words) is called **nonverbal communication**. People will usually believe what they see over what they hear—hence the expression, "a picture is worth a thousand words." Studies show that these subtle messages account for between 65 and 93 percent of interpreted communication.[22] The media for such nonverbal communication can be categorized into four types: (1) kinesic behavior, (2) proxemics, (3) paralanguage, and (4) object language.

The term **kinesic behavior** refers to body movements—posture, gestures, facial expressions, and eye contact. Though such actions may be universal, their meaning often is not. Because kinesic systems of meaning are culturally specific and learned, they cannot be generalized across cultures.[23] Most people in the West would not correctly interpret many Chinese facial expressions; sticking out the tongue expresses surprise, a widening of the eyes shows anger, and scratching the ears and cheeks indicates happiness.[24] Research has shown for some time, however, that most people worldwide can recognize displays of the basic emotions of anger, disgust, fear, happiness, sadness, surprise, and contempt.[25, 26]

Many businesspeople and visitors react negatively to what they feel are inappropriate facial expressions, without understanding the cultural meaning behind them. In his studies of cross-cultural negotiations, Graham observed that the Japanese feel uncomfortable when faced with the Americans' eye-to-eye posture. They are taught since childhood to bow their heads out of humility, whereas the automatic response of Americans is "look at me when I'm talking to you!"[27]

Subtle differences in eye behavior (called oculesics) can throw off a communication badly if they are not understood. Eye behavior includes differences not only in eye contact but also in the use of eyes to convey other messages, whether or not that involves mutual gaze. Edward T. Hall, author of the classic *The Silent Language,* explains the differences in eye contact between the British and the Americans. During speech, Americans will look straight at you, whereas the British keep your attention by looking away. They will then look at you when they have finished speaking, which signals that it is your turn to talk. The implicit rationale for this is that you can't interrupt people when they are not looking at you.[28]

It is helpful for managers to be aware of the many cultural expectations regarding posture and how they may be interpreted. In Europe or Asia, relaxed posture in business meetings may be taken as bad manners or the result of poor upbringing. In Korea, you are expected to sit upright, with feet squarely on the floor, and to speak slowly, showing a blending of body and spirit.

Managers can also familiarize themselves with the many different interpretations of hand and finger signals around the world, some of which may even represent obscene gestures. Of course, we cannot expect to change all of our ingrained, natural kinesic behavior, but we can be aware of what it means to others. And we can learn to understand the kinesic behavior of others and the role it plays in their society, as well as how it can affect business transactions. Misunderstanding the meanings of body movements—or an ethnocentric attitude toward the "proper" behavior—can have negative repercussions, as illustrated in the Opening Profile that begins the chapter.

Proxemics deals with the influence of proximity and space on communication—both personal space and office space or layout. Americans expect office layout to provide private space for each person, usually a larger and more private space as one goes up the hierarchy. In much of Asia, the custom is open office space, with people at all levels working and talking in proximity to one another. Space communicates power in both Germany and the United States, evidenced by the desire for a corner office or one on the top floor. The importance of French officials, however, is made clear by a position in the middle of subordinates, communicating that they have a central position in an information network, where they can stay informed and in control.[29]

Do you ever feel vaguely uncomfortable and start slowly moving backward when someone is speaking to you? This is because that person is invading your "bubble"—your personal space. Personal space is culturally patterned, and foreign spatial cues are a common source of misinterpretation. When someone seems aloof or pushy, it often means that he or she is operating under subtly different spacial rules.

Hall and Hall suggest that cultural differences affect the programming of the senses and that space, perceived by all the senses, is regarded as a form of territory to be protected.[30] South Americans, southern and eastern Europeans, Indonesians, and Arabs are **high-contact cultures**, preferring to stand close, touch a great deal, and experience a "close" sensory involvement. On the other hand, North Americans, Asians, and northern Europeans are **low-contact cultures** and prefer much less sensory involvement, standing farther apart and touching far less. They have a "distant" style of body language.[31]

Interestingly, high-contact cultures are mostly located in warmer climates, and low-contact cultures in cooler climates. Americans are relatively nontouching, automatically standing at a distance so that an outstretched arm would touch the other person's ear.[32] Standing any closer than that is regarded as invading intimate space. However, Americans and Canadians certainly expect a warm handshake and maybe a pat on the back for closer friends, though not the very warm double handshake of the Spaniards (clasping the forearm with the left hand). The Japanese, considerably less haptic (touching), do not shake hands; an initial greeting between a Japanese and a Spanish businessperson would be uncomfortable for both parties if they were untrained in cultural haptics.

When considering high- and low-contact cultures, we can trace a correlation between Hofstede's cultural variables of individualism and collectivism and the types of kinesic and proxemic behaviors people display. Generally, people from individualistic cultures are more remote and distant, whereas those from collectivist cultures are interdependent—they tend to work, play, live, and sleep in proximity.[33]

The term **paralanguage** refers to how something is said rather than the content—the rate of speech, the tone and inflection of voice, other noises, laughing, or yawning. The culturally aware manager learns how to interpret subtle differences in paralanguage, including silence. Silence is a powerful communicator. It may be a way of saying no, of being offended, or of waiting for more information to make a decision. Americans, very impatient with silence, don't know how to react. Graham, a researcher on international negotiations, taped a bargaining session held at Toyota's U.S. headquarters in California. The American executive had made a proposal to open a new production facility in Brazil and was waiting for a response from the three Japanese executives, who sat with lowered eyes and hands folded on the table. After about 30 seconds—an eternity to Americans, accustomed to a conversational response time of a few tenths of a second—the American blurted out that they were getting nowhere, and the meeting ended in a stalemate. More sensitivity to cultural differences in communication might have led him to wait longer or perhaps to prompt some further response through another polite question.[34]

The term **object language**, or **material culture**, refers to how we communicate through material artifacts, whether architecture, office design and furniture, clothing, cars, or cosmetics. Material culture communicates what people hold as important. In Mexico, a visiting international executive or salesperson is advised to take time out, before negotiating business, to show appreciation for the surrounding architecture, which is prized by Mexicans.

Time   Another variable that communicates culture is the way people regard and use time (discussed in Chapter 4). To Brazilians, relative punctuality communicates the level of importance of those involved. To Middle Easterners, time is something controlled by the will of Allah.

To initiate effective cross-cultural business interactions, managers should know the difference between **monochronic time systems** and **polychronic time systems**, and how they affect communications. Hall and Hall explain that in monochronic cultures (Switzerland, Germany, and the United States), time is experienced in a linear way, with a past, a present, and a future, and time is treated as something to be spent, saved, made up, or wasted. Classified and compartmentalized, time serves to order life. This attitude is a learned part of Western culture, probably starting with the Industrial Revolution. Monochronic people, found in individualistic cultures, generally concentrate on one thing at a time, adhere to time commitments, and are accustomed to short-term relationships.

In contrast, polychronic systems tolerate many things occurring simultaneously and emphasize involvement with people. Two Latin friends, for example, will put an important conversation ahead of being on time for a business meeting, thus communicating the priority of relationships over material systems. Polychronic people—Latin Americans, Arabs, and

EXHIBIT 5–3

Forms of Nonverbal Communication

- Facial expressions
- Body posture
- Gestures with hands, arms, head, etc.
- Interpersonal distance (proxemics)
- Touching, body contact
- Eye contact
- Clothing, cosmetics, hairstyles, jewelry
- Paralanguage (voice pitch and inflections, rate of speech, and silence)
- Color symbolism
- Attitude toward time and the use of time in business and social interactions
- Food symbolism and social use of meals

those from other collectivist cultures—may focus on several things at once, be highly distractible, and change plans often.[35]

The relationship between time and space also affects communication. Polychronic people, for example, are likely to hold open meetings, moving around and conducting transactions from one party to another, rather than compartmentalizing meeting topics, as do monochronic people.

We can discuss endless nuances and distinctions regarding cultural differences in nonverbal communication. The various forms are listed in Exhibit 5–3; wise intercultural managers will take careful account of the roles that such differences might play.

What aspects of nonverbal communication might have created noise in the interactions between the American supervisor and the Greek employee in Exhibit 5–2? Undoubtedly, there were some cues in the kinesic behavior of each person that could have been picked up. It was the responsibility of the manager, in particular, to notice any indications from the Greek that could have prompted him to change his communication pattern or assumptions. Face-to-face communication permits the sender of the message to get immediate feedback, verbal and nonverbal, and thus to have some idea of how that message is being received and whether additional information is needed. What aspects of the Greek employee's kinesic behavior or paralanguage do you think might have been evident to a more culturally sensitive manager? Did both parties' sense of time affect the communication process?

Context

A major differentiating factor that is a primary cause of noise in the communication process is that of **context**—which, as you will see, actually incorporates many of the variables just discussed. The context in which the communication takes place affects the meaning and interpretation of the interaction. Cultures are known to be high- or low-context cultures, with a relative range in between.[36] In **high-context cultures** (Asia, the Middle East, Africa, and the Mediterranean), feelings and thoughts are not explicitly expressed; instead, one has to read between the lines and interpret meaning from one's general understanding. Two such high-context cultures were just described—those of South Korea and Arab cultures. In such cultures, key information is embedded in the context rather than made explicit. People make assumptions about what the message means through their knowledge of the person or the surroundings. In these cultures, most communication takes place within a context of extensive information networks resulting from close personal relationships. In **low-context cultures** (Germany, Switzerland, Scandinavia, and North America), where personal and business relationships are more separated, communication media have to be more explicit. Feelings and thoughts are expressed in words, and information is more readily available.

In cross-cultural communication between high- and low-context people, a lack of understanding may preclude reaching a solution, and conflict may arise. Germans, for example, will expect considerable detailed information before making a business decision, whereas Arabs will base their decision more on knowledge of the people involved—the information is still there, but it is implicit.

People in high-context cultures expect others to understand unarticulated moods, subtle gestures, and environmental clues that people from low-context cultures simply do not process. Misinterpretation and misunderstanding often result.[37] People from high-context cultures perceive those from low-context cultures as too talkative, too obvious, and redundant. Those from low-context cultures perceive high-context people as nondisclosing, sneaky, and mysterious.[38] Research indicates, for example, that Americans find talkative people more attractive, whereas Koreans, high-context people, perceive less verbal people as more attractive.[39] Finding the right balance between low- and high-context communication can be tricky, as Hall and Hall point out: "Too much information leads people to feel they are being talked down to; too little information can mystify them or make them feel left out."[40] Exhibit 5–4 shows the relative level of context in various countries.

EXHIBIT 5–4

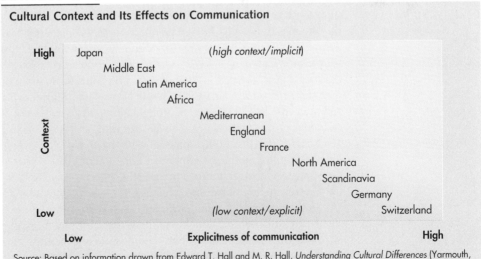

Cultural Context and Its Effects on Communication

High   Japan   (high context/implicit)
            Middle East
                Latin America
                    Africa
                        Mediterranean
                            England
                                France
                                    North America
                                        Scandinavia
                                            Germany
Low   (low context/explicit)   Switzerland

Context

Low   Explicitness of communication   High

Source: Based on information drawn from Edward T. Hall and M. R. Hall, *Understanding Cultural Differences* (Yarmouth, ME: Intercultural Press, 1990); and Martin Rosch, "Communications: Focal Point of Culture," *Management International Review* 27, no. 4 (1987): 60.

The importance of understanding the role of context and nonverbal language to avoid misinterpretation is illustrated in the following Comparative Management in Focus section describing communication between Americans and Arabs.

COMPARATIVE
MANAGEMENT
IN FOCUS

Communicating with Arabs

In the Middle East, the meaning of a communication is implicit and interwoven, and consequently much harder for Americans, accustomed to explicit and specific meanings, to understand.

Arabs are warm, emotional, and quick to explode: "sounding off" is regarded as a safety valve.[41] In fact, the Arabic language aptly communicates the Arabic culture, one of emotional extremes. The language contains the means for overexpression, many adjectives, words that allow for exaggeration, and metaphors to emphasize a position. What is said is often not as important as how it is said.[42] Eloquence and flowery speech are admired for their own sake, regardless of the content. Loud speech is used for dramatic effect.

At the core of Middle Eastern culture are friendship, honor, religion, and traditional hospitality. Family, friends, and connections, very important on all levels in the Middle East, will take precedence over business transactions. Arabs do business with people, not companies, and they make commitments to people, not contracts. A phone call to the right person can help get around seemingly insurmountable obstacles. An Arab expects loyalty from friends, and it is understood that giving and receiving favors is an inherent part of the relationship; no one says no to a request for a favor. A lack of follow-through is assumed to be beyond the friend's control.[43]

Because hospitality is a way of life and highly symbolic, a visitor must be careful not to reject it by declining refreshment or rushing into business discussions. Part of that hospitality is the elaborate system of greetings and the long period of getting acquainted, perhaps the entire first meeting. Although the handshake may seem limp, the rest of the greeting is not. Kissing on the cheeks is common among men, as is handholding between male friends. However, any public display of intimacy between men and women is strictly forbidden by the Arab social code.

Women, in fact, play little or no role in business or entertainment; the Middle East is a male-dominated society, and it is impolite to inquire about women. Other, nonverbal taboos include showing the soles of one's feet and using the left (unclean) hand to eat or pass something. In discussions, a lack of respect is communicated by slouching in a seat or leaning against a wall.

The Arab society also values honor. Harris and Moran explain: "Honor, social prestige, and a secure place in society are brought about when conformity is achieved. When one fails to conform, this is considered to be damning and leads to a degree of shame."[44] Shame results not from just doing something wrong, but from having others find out about that wrongdoing. Establishing a climate of honesty and trust is part of the sense of honor; therefore, considerable tact is needed to avoid conveying any concern or doubt. Arabs tend to be quite introverted until a mutual trust is built, which takes a long time.[45]

In their nonverbal communication, most Arab countries are high-contact cultures. Arabs stand and sit closer and touch people of the same sex more than Westerners. They do not have the same concept of "public" and "private" space, or as Hall puts it: "Not only is the sheer noise level much higher, but the piercing look of the eyes, the touch of the hands, and the mutual bathing in the warm moist breath during conversation represent stepped-up sensory inputs to a level which many Europeans find unbearably intense."[46] On the other hand, the distance preferred by North Americans may leave an Arab suspicious of intentions because of the lack of olfactory contact.[47]

The Muslim expression *bukra insha Allah*—"tomorrow if Allah wills"—explains much about the Arab culture and its approach to business transactions. A cultural clash typically occurs when an American tries to give an Arab a deadline. " 'I am going to Damascus tomorrow morning and will have to have my car tonight,' is a sure way to get the mechanic to stop work," explains Hall, "because to give another person a deadline in this part of the world is to be rude, pushy, and demanding."[48] In such instances, the attitude toward time communicates as loudly as words.

In verbal interactions, managers need to be aware of different patterns of Arab thought and communication. Compared to the direct, linear fashion of American communication, Arabs tend to meander: They start with social talk, discuss business for a while, loop round to social and general issues, then back to business, and so on.[49] American impatience and insistence on sticking to the subject will "cut off their loops," triggering confusion and dysfunction.

Exhibit 5–5 illustrates some of the sources of noise that are likely to interfere in the communication process between Americans and Arabs.

EXHIBIT 5–5

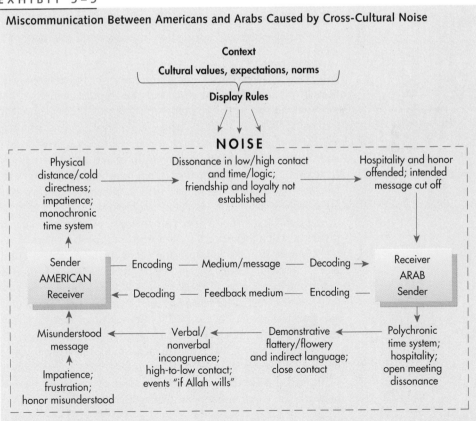

Miscommunication Between Americans and Arabs Caused by Cross-Cultural Noise

For people doing business in the Middle East, the following are some useful guidelines for effective communication:

- Be patient. Recognize the Arab attitude toward time and hospitality—take time to develop friendship and trust since these are prerequisites for any social or business transactions.
- Recognize that people and relationships matter more to Arabs than the job, company, or contract—conduct business personally, not by correspondence or telephone.
- Avoid expressing doubts or criticism when others are present—recognize the importance of honor and dignity to Arabs.
- Adapt to the norms of body language, flowery speech, and circuitous verbal patterns in the Middle East, and don't be impatient to "get to the point."
- Expect many interruptions in meetings, delays in schedules, and changes in plans.[50]

Communication Channels

In addition to the variables related to the sender and the receiver of a message, the variables linked to the channel itself and the context of the message must be taken into consideration. These variables include fast or slow messages and information flows, and different types of media.

Information Systems   Communication in organizations varies according to where and how it originates, the channels and the speed at which it flows, whether it is formal or informal, and so forth. The type of organizational structure, the staffing policies, and the leadership style will affect the nature of an organization's information system.

As an international manager, it is useful to know where and how information originates, and the speed at which it flows, both internally and externally. In centralized organizational structures, as in South America, most information originates from top managers. Workers take less responsibility to keep managers informed than in a typical company in the United States, where delegation results in information flowing from the staff to the managers. In a decision-making system where many people are involved, such as the *ringi* system in Japan, there is a systematic pattern for information flow that the expatriate needs to understand.[51]

Context also affects information flow. In high-context cultures (such as in the Middle East), information spreads rapidly and freely because of the constant close contact and the implicit ties among people and organizations. Information flow is often informal. In low-context cultures (such as Germany or the United States), information is controlled and focused, and thus it does not flow so freely.[52] Compartmentalized roles and office layouts stifle information channels; information sources tend to be more formal.

It is crucial for an expatriate manager to find out how to tap into a firm's informal sources of information. In Japan, employees usually have a drink together on the way home from work, and this becomes an essential source of information. However, such communication networks are based on long-term relationships in Japan (and in other high-context cultures).

The same information may not be readily available to "outsiders." A considerable barrier in Japan separates strangers from familiar friends, a situation that discourages communication.

Americans are more open and talk freely about almost anything, whereas Japanese will disclose little about their inner thoughts or private issues. Americans are willing to have a wide "public self," disclosing their inner reactions verbally and physically. In contrast, the Japanese prefer to keep their responses largely to their "private self." The Japanese expose only a small portion of their thoughts; they reduce, according to Barnlund, "the unpredictability and emotional intensity of personal encounters."[53] Barnlund depicts this difference diagrammatically, as shown in Exhibit 5–6, which illustrates the cultural clash between the public and private selves in intercultural communication between Americans and Japanese. The plus and minus signs indicate the areas of agreement or disagreement (respectively) resulting when each party forces its cultural norms of communication on the other. In the American style, the American's cultural norms of explicit communication impose on the Japanese by invading the person's private self. The Japanese style of implicit communication causes a negative reaction from the American because of what is perceived as too much formality and ambiguity, which wastes time.[54]

Cultural variables in information systems and context underlie the many differences in communication style between Japanese and Americans. Exhibit 5–7 shows some specific differences. The Japanese *ningensei* ("human beingness") style of communication refers to their preference for humanity, reciprocity, a receiver orientation, and an underlying distrust of words and analytic logic.[55] The Japanese believe that true intentions are not readily revealed in words or contracts, but are in fact masked by them. In contrast to the typical American's verbal agility and explicitness, Japanese behaviors and communications are directed to defend and give face for everyone concerned; to do so, they avoid public disagreements at all costs. In cross-cultural negotiations, this last point is essential.

The speed with which we try to use information systems is another key variable that needs attention to avoid misinterpretation and conflict. Americans expect to give and receive information very quickly and clearly, moving through details and stages in a linear fashion to the conclusion. They usually use various media for fast messages—letters giving all the facts and plans up front, faxes, and familiar relationships. In contrast, the French use the slower message channels of deep relationships, culture, and sometimes mediators to exchange information. A French written communication will be tentative, with subsequent letters slowly building up to a new proposal. In fact, the French preference for written communication, even for informal interactions, echoes the formality of their relationships—and results in a slowing down of message transmission that often seems unnecessary to Americans. Jean-Louis Reynal, a plant manager at Citroen, explains that "it wouldn't be too much of an exaggeration to say that, until they are written, until they are entrusted to the blackboard, the notepad, or the flip chart, ideas have no reality for the French manager. You could even say that writing is an indispensable aid to 'being' for us."[56]

In short, it behooves Americans to realize that, because most of the world exchanges information through slower message media, it is wise to schedule more time for transactions, develop patience, and learn to get at needed information in more subtle ways—after building rapport and taking time to observe the local system for exchanging information.

We have seen that cross-cultural misinterpretation can result from noise in the actual transmission of the message—the choice or speed of media. Interpreting the meaning of a

EXHIBIT 5–6

Intercultural Communication Conflicts Between Americans and Japanese

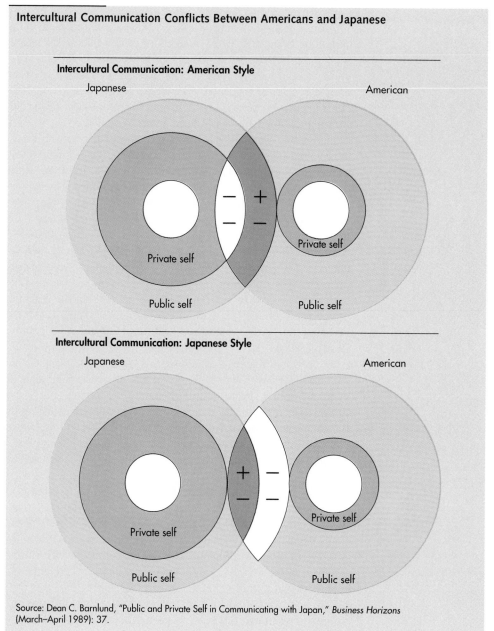

Intercultural Communication: American Style

Japanese

American

Private self

Private self

Public self

Public self

Intercultural Communication: Japanese Style

Japanese

American

Private self

Private self

Public self

Public self

Source: Dean C. Barnlund, "Public and Private Self in Communicating with Japan," *Business Horizons* (March–April 1989): 37.

EXHIBIT 5–7

Differences Between Japanese and American Communication Styles

Japanese *Ningensei* Style of Communication	U.S. Adversarial Style of Communication
1. Indirect verbal and nonverbal communication	1. More direct verbal and nonverbal communication
2. Relationship communication	2. More task communication
3. Discourages confrontational strategies	3. Confrontational strategies more acceptable
4. Strategically ambiguous communication	4. Prefers more to-the-point communication
5. Delayed feedback	5. More immediate feedback
6. Patient, longer term negotiators	6. Shorter term negotiators
7. Uses fewer words	7. Favors verbosity
8. Distrustful of skillful verbal communicators	8. Exalts verbal eloquence
9. Group orientation	9. More individualistic orientation
10. Cautious, tentative	10. More assertive, self-assured
11. Complementary communicators	11. More publicly critical communicators
12. Softer, heartlike logic	12. Harder, analytic logic preferred
13. Sympathetic, empathetic, complex use of pathos	13. Favors logos, reason
14. Expresses and decodes complex relational strategies and nuances	14. Expresses and decodes complex logos, cognitive nuances
15. Avoids decision making in public	15. Frequent decision making in public
16. Makes decisions in private venues, away from public eye	16. Frequent decisions in public at negotiating tables
17. Decisions via *ringi* and *nemawashi* (complete consensus process)	17. Decisions by majority rule and public compromise is more commonplace
18. Uses go-betweens for decision making	18. More extensive use of direct person-to-person, player-to-player interaction for decisions
19. Understatement and hesitation in verbal and nonverbal communication	19. May publicly speak in superlatives, exaggerations, nonverbal projection
20. Uses qualifiers, tentative, humility as communicator	20. Favors fewer qualifiers, more ego-centered
21. Receiver/listening-centered	21. More speaker- and message-centered
22. Inferred meanings, looks beyond words to nuances, nonverbal communication	22. More face-value meaning, more denotative
23. Shy, reserved communicators	23. More publicly self-assertive
24. Distaste for purely business transactions	24. Prefers to "get down to business" or "nitty gritty"
25. Mixes business and social communication	25. Tends to keep business negotiating more separated from social communication
26. Utilizes *matomari* or "hints" for achieving group adjustment and saving face in negotiating	26. More directly verbalizes management's preference at negotiating tables
27. Practices *haragei* or belly logic and communication	27. Practices more linear, discursive, analytical logic; greater reverence for cognitive than for affective

Source: A. Goldman, "The Centrality of 'Ningensei' to Japanese Negotiating and Interpersonal Relationships: Implications for U.S. Japanese Communication," *International Journal of Intercultural Relations* 18, no. 1 (Winter 1994).

message can thus be as much a function of the transmission channel (or medium) as it is of examining the message itself.

Managing Cross-Cultural Communication

Steps toward effective intercultural communication include the development of cultural sensitivity, careful encoding, selective transmission, careful decoding, and appropriate follow-up actions.

Developing Cultural Sensitivity

When acting as a sender, a manager must make it a point to know the receiver and to encode the message in a form that will most likely be understood as intended. On the manager's part, this requires an awareness of his or her own cultural baggage and how it affects the communication process. In other words, what kinds of behaviors does the message imply, and how will they be perceived by the receiver? The way to anticipate the most likely meaning that the receiver will attach to the message is to internalize honest cultural empathy with that person. What is the cultural background—the societal, economic, and organizational context—in which this communication is taking place? What are this person's expectations regarding the situation, what are the two parties' relative positions, and what might develop from this communication? What kinds of transactions and behaviors is this person used to?

Cultural sensitivity (discussed in Chapter 4) is really just a matter of understanding the other person, the context, and how the person will respond to the context. One novel program to raise managers' levels of cultural sensitivity and improve their communication skills has been started by Noel Tichy of the University of Michigan's business school. He gathered an international group of 21 senior executives from major corporations from 5 nations for a 5-week intensive program on worldwide management. The program included traveling to various countries, building rafts, and climbing cliffs as the managers got to know one another. One issue they worked on throughout was that of cross-cultural communication.[57] The Management Focus "How 21 Men Got Global in 35 Days" describes some of the ways they addressed this concern.

Careful Encoding

In translating his or her intended meaning into symbols for cross-cultural communication, the sender must use words, pictures, or gestures that are appropriate to the receiver's frame of reference. Of course, language training is invaluable, but senders should also avoid idioms and regional sayings (such as "go fly a kite" or "foot the bill") in a translation, or even in English when speaking to a non-American who knows little English.

Literal translation, then, is a limited answer to language differences. Even among English-speaking countries, words may have different meanings—as experienced by a U.S. banker in Australia after a business dinner. To show appreciation, he said he was full (interpreted by his hosts as drunk); as the silence spread at the table, he tried to correct himself by saying he was stuffed (a word used locally only in a sexual context).[58] Ways to avoid such problems are to speak slowly and clearly, avoid long sentences and colloquial expressions,

M A N A G E M E N T   F O C U S

How 21 Men Got Global in 35 Days: Problem Number One Was Communication

Stiff and ill at ease at first, the Japanese said little, and some of what they did say was hard to understand. The Americans talked too much and wondered when the Japanese would make a contribution. On the second day, one of the program's faculty—professor Hirotaka Takeuchi from Hitotsubashi University—intervened to clear the air.

First, he suggested that the Japanese might be more comfortable if they made clear how they preferred to be addressed. In an attempt to be jolly good fellows, some had adopted American nicknames on arriving at Ann Arbor. Toshiyoshi Endo, a deputy general manager at Hitachi, had said, "Call me Eddie." But with Takeuchi's prompting, it turned out, he really preferred the more respectful Endo-san.

Then Takeuchi explained to the others why the Japanese spoke so little. Unfamiliarity with English was only the most obvious reason. Unlike Americans, who like to jump in and grab control of a meeting, said Takeuchi, the Japanese prefer to wait and listen; the higher their rank, the more they listen. This group of Japanese were the elite, he explained, and therefore listened a lot. He added that the Japanese

have a not-so-subtle saying: "He who speaks first at a meeting is a dumb ass." Sobered by his implication, the Americans decided to give the Japanese more chance to talk by adopting the two-second rule: When someone else finishes talking, wait two seconds before speaking to give others a chance. The Japanese adopted the athlete's time-out signal, a T formed by both hands extended, to call for explanations when the language became confusing.

After that, the Japanese spoke up more and the Americans quieted down, but communication remained a problem to the end of the five weeks. The lesson: Global leaders will always have to spend time and develop patience to overcome language and cultural barriers. The Japanese will probably never become gabby: "We are a homogeneous people, and we don't have to speak as much as you do here," said Takanaka-san. "When we say one word, we understand ten, but here you have to say ten to understand one."

Source: Adapted and excerpted from Jeremy Main, "How 21 Men Got Global in 35 Days," *Fortune,* November 6, 1989, 71–79.

and explain things in several different ways and through several media, if possible.[59] However, even though English is in common use around the world for business transactions, the manager's efforts to speak the local language will greatly improve the climate. Sometimes people from other cultures resent the assumption by English-speaking executives that everyone else will speak English.

Language translation is only part of the encoding process; the message also is expressed in nonverbal language. In the encoding process, the sender must ensure congruence between the nonverbal and the verbal message. In encoding a message, therefore, it is useful to be as objective as possible and not to rely on personal interpretations. To further clarify their message, managers can hand out written summaries of verbal presentations and use visual aids—graphs or pictures. A good general guide is to move slowly, wait, and take cues from the receivers.

Selective Transmission

The type of medium chosen for the message depends on the nature of the message, its level of importance, the context and expectations of the receiver, the timing involved, and the need for personal interaction, among other factors. Typical media include letters or memos, reports, meetings, telephone calls, teleconferences, or face-to-face conversations. The secret is to find out how communication is transmitted in the local organization—how much is downward versus upward or vertical versus horizontal, how the grapevine (gossip channels) works, and so on. In addition, cultural variables discussed earlier need to be considered: whether the receiver is from a high- or low-context culture, whether he or she is used to explicit or implicit communication, and what speed and routing of messages will be most effective.

For the most part, it is best to use face-to-face interaction for relationship building or for other important transactions, particularly in intercultural communications, because of the lack of familiarity between parties. Personal interactions give the manager the opportunity to get immediate verbal and visual feedback and to make rapid adjustments in the communication process.

International dealings are often long distance, of course, limiting the opportunity for face-to-face communication. However, personal rapport can be established or enhanced through telephone calls or videoconferencing and through trusted contacts. Modern electronic media can be used to break down communication barriers by reducing waiting periods for information, clarifying issues, and allowing instant consultation. Global telecommunications and computer networks are changing the face of cross-cultural communication through the faster dissemination of information within the receiving organization. Ford of Europe uses videoconferencing for engineers in Britain and Germany to consult about quality problems. Through the television screen, they examine one another's engineering diagrams and usually find a solution that gets the factory moving again in a short time.[60]

Careful Decoding of Feedback

Timely and effective feedback channels can also be set up to assess a firm's general communication about the progression of its business and its general management principles. The best means to get accurate feedback is through face-to-face interaction because this allows the manager to hear, see, and sense immediately how a message is being interpreted. When visual feedback on important issues is not possible or appropriate, it is a good idea to use several means of attaining feedback, in particular, employing third parties.

Decoding is the process of translating the received symbols into the interpreted message. The main causes of incongruence are (1) the receiver misinterprets the message, (2) the receiver encodes his or her return message incorrectly, or (3) the sender misinterprets the feedback. Two-way communication is thus essential for important issues so that successive efforts can be made until an understanding has been achieved. Asking other colleagues to help interpret what is going on is often a good way to break a cycle of miscommunication.

Perhaps the most important means to avoiding miscommunication is to practice careful decoding by improving one's listening and observation skills. A good listener practices projective listening, or empathetic listening—listening without interruption or evaluation to the full message of the speaker, attempting to recognize the feelings behind the words and non-verbal cues, and understanding the speaker's perspective.

At the MNC level, avenues of communication and feedback among parent companies and subsidiaries can be kept open through telephone calls, regular meetings and visits, reports, and plans—all of which facilitate cooperation, performance control, and the smooth running of the company. Communication among far-flung operations can be best managed by setting up feedback systems and liaison people. The headquarters people should maintain considerable flexibility in cooperating with local managers and allowing them to deal with the local context as they see fit.

Follow-Up Actions

Managers communicate both through action and inaction. Therefore, to keep open the lines of communication, feedback, and trust, managers must follow through with action on what has been discussed and then agreed upon—typically a contract, which is probably the most important formal business communication. Unfortunately, the issue of contract follow-through is a particularly sensitive one across cultures because of the different interpretations regarding what constitutes a contract (perhaps a handshake, perhaps a full legal document), and what actions should result. Trust, future communications, and future business are based on such interpretations, and it is up to the manager to understand them and to follow through on them.

The management of cross-cultural communication depends largely on a manager's personal abilities and behavior. Those behaviors that researchers indicate to be most important to **intercultural communication effectiveness** (ICE) are listed here, as reviewed by Ruben:

1. Respect (conveyed through eye contact, body posture, voice tone and pitch)
2. Interaction posture (the ability to respond to others in a descriptive, nonevaluative, and non-judgmental way)
3. Orientation to knowledge (recognizing that one's knowledge, perception, and beliefs are valid only for oneself and not for everyone else)
4. Empathy
5. Interaction management
6. Tolerance for ambiguity
7. Other-oriented role behavior (one's capacity to be flexible and to adopt different roles for the sake of greater group cohesion and group communication)[61]

Whether at home or abroad, certain personal capabilities facilitate effective intercultural communication; these abilities can help the expatriate adapt to the host country and enable productive working relations to develop in the long term. Researchers have established a relationship between personality traits and behaviors and the ability to adapt to the host-country's cultural environment.[62] Seldom pointed out, however, is that communication is the mediating factor between those behaviors and the relative level of adaptation the expatriate achieves. The communication process facilitates cross-cultural adaptation—through this process, expatriates learn the dominant communication patterns of the host society. Therefore, we can link those personality factors shown by research to ease adaptation with those necessary for effective intercultural communication.

Kim has consolidated the research findings of these characteristics into two categories: (1) **openness**—traits such as open-mindedness, tolerance for ambiguity, and extrovertedness; and (2) **resilience**—traits such as having an internal locus of control, persistence, a tolerance

EXHIBIT 5-8

A Communication Model of Cross-Cultural Adaptation

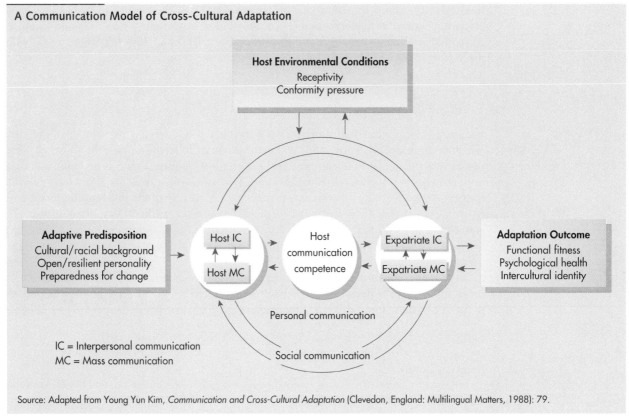

Source: Adapted from Young Yun Kim, *Communication and Cross-Cultural Adaptation* (Clevedon, England: Multilingual Matters, 1988): 79.

of ambiguity, and resourcefulness.[63] These personality factors, along with the expatriate's cultural and racial identity and the level of preparedness for change, compose that person's potential for adaptation. The level of preparedness can be improved by the manager before his or her assignment by gathering information about the host country's verbal and nonverbal communication patterns and norms of behavior. Kim incorporates these factors in a communication model of cross-cultural adaptation. Exhibit 5–8 shows the major variables affecting the level of communication competence achieved between the host and the expatriate. These are the adaptive predisposition of the expatriate and the conditions of receptivity and conformity to pressure in the host environment. These factors affect the process of personal and social communication, and, ultimately, the adaptation outcome. Explains Kim: "Three aspects of strangers' adaptive change—increased functional fitness, psychological health, and intercultural identity—have been identified as direct consequences of prolonged communication–adaptation experiences in the host society."[64] In Chapter 10, we will point out areas where the firm has responsibility to improve the employee and managerial ability to adapt.

In identifying personal and behavioral specifics that facilitate ICE, however, we cannot lose sight of the whole picture. We must remember the basic principle of contingency management, that is, that managers operate in a system of many interacting variables in a dynamic context. Studies show that situational factors—such as the physical environment, time constraints, degree of structure, feelings of boredom or overwork and anonymity—are strong influences on intercultural communication competence.[65]

It is this interdependence of many variables, in fact, that makes it difficult for intercultural researchers to isolate and identify factors for success. Although managers try to understand and control up front as many factors as possible that will lead to management effectiveness, often they find out what works only from the results of their decisions.

Conclusion

Effective intercultural communication is a vital skill for international managers and domestic managers of multicultural workforces. Because we have learned that miscommunication is much more likely to occur among people from different countries or racial backgrounds than among those from similar backgrounds, we try to be alert to how culture is reflected in communication—in particular by developing cultural sensitivity and an awareness of potential sources of cultural noise in the communication process. A successful international manager is thus attuned to these variables and is flexible enough to adjust his or her communication style to best address the intended receivers—that is, to do it "their way."

Cultural variables and the manner in which culture is communicated underlie the processes of negotiation and decision making. How do people around the world negotiate—what are their expectations and their approach to negotiations? What is the importance of understanding negotiation and decision-making processes in other countries? Chapter 6 will address these questions and make suggestions for the international manager to handle these important tasks.

Summary of Key Points

1. Communication is an inherent part of a manager's role, taking up the majority of the manager's time on the job. Effective intercultural communication largely determines the success of international transactions or the output of a culturally diverse workforce.

2. Culture is the foundation of communication, and communication transmits culture. Cultural variables that can affect the communication process by influencing a person's perceptions include attitudes, social organizations, thought patterns, roles, language, nonverbal communication, and time.

3. Language conveys cultural understandings and social norms from one generation to the next. Body language, or nonverbal communication, is behavior that communicates without words. It accounts for 65 to 93 percent of interpreted communication.

4. Types of nonverbal communication around the world are kinesic behavior, proxemics, paralanguage, and object language.

5. Effective cross-cultural communication must take account of whether the receiver is from a country with a monochronic or a polychronic time system.

6. Variables related to channels of communication include high- and low-context cultures, fast or slow messages and information flows, and various types of media.

7. In high-context cultures, feelings and messages are implicit and must be accessed through an understanding of the person and the system. In low-context cultures, feelings and thoughts are expressed, and information is more readily available.

8. The effective management of intercultural communication necessitates the development of cultural sensitivity, careful encoding, selective transmission, careful decoding, and follow-up actions.

9. Certain personal abilities and behaviors facilitate adaptation to the host country through skilled intercultural communication.

<table>
<tr><td>

Discussion Questions

</td><td>

1. How does culture affect the process of attribution in communication?
2. What is stereotyping? Give some examples. How might people stereotype you? How does a socio-type differ from a stereotype?
3. What is the relationship between language and culture? How is it that people from different countries who speak the same language may still miscommunicate?
4. Give some examples of cultural differences in the interpretation of body language. What is the role of such nonverbal communication in business relationships?
5. Explain the differences between monochronic and polychronic time systems. Use some examples to illustrate their differences and the role of time in intercultural communication.
6. Explain the differences between high- and low-context cultures, giving some examples. What are the differential effects on the communication process?
7. Discuss the role of information systems in a company, how and why they vary from country to country, and the effects of these variations.

</td></tr>
</table>

Application Exercises

1. Form groups in your class, multicultural if possible. Have each person make notes about his or her perceptions of (1) Mexican Americans, (2) Native Americans, (3) African Americans, (4) Americans of European descent. Discuss your notes and draw conclusions about common stereotypes. Discuss any differences and why stereotyping occurs.
2. Invite some foreign students to your class. Ask them to bring photographs, slides, and so forth of people and events in their native countries. Have them explain the meanings of various nonverbal cues, such as gestures, dress, voice inflections, architecture, and events. Discuss with them any differences between their explanations and the attributions you assigned to those cues.
3. Interview a faculty member or a businessperson who has worked abroad. Ask him or her to identify factors that facilitated or inhibited adaptation to the host environment. Ask whether more preparation could have eased the transition and what, if anything, that person would do differently before another trip.

Experiential Exercise

Script for Juan Perillo and Jean Moore

Scene I: February 15, San Juan, Puerto Rico

Juan: Welcome back to Puerto Rico, Jean. It is good to have you here in San Juan again. I hope that your trip from Dayton was a smooth one.

Jean: Thank you, Juan. It's nice to be back here where the sun shines. Fred sends his regards and also asked me to tell you how important it is that we work out a firm production schedule for the next three months. But first, how is your family? All doing well, I hope.

Juan: My wife is doing very well, but my daughter, Marianna, broke her arm and has to have surgery to repair the bone. We are very worried about that because the surgeon says she may have to have several operations. It is very difficult to think about my poor little daughter in the operating room. She was out playing with some other children when it happened. You know how roughly children sometimes play with each other. It's really amazing that they don't have more injuries. Why, just last week, my son....

Jean: Of course I'm very sorry to hear about little Marianna, but I'm sure everything will go well with the surgery. Now, shall we start work on the production schedule?

Juan: Oh, yes, of course, we must get started on the production schedule.

Jean: Fred and I thought that June 1 would be a good cutoff date for the first phase of the schedule. And we also thought that 100 A-type computers would be a reasonable goal for that phase. We know that you have some new assemblers whom you are training, and that you've had some problems getting parts from your suppliers in the past few months. But we're sure you have all those problems worked out by now and that you are back to full production capability. So, what do you think? Is 100 A-type computers produced by June 1 a reasonable goal for your people?

Juan: (hesitates a few seconds before replying) You want us to produce 100 of the newly designed A-type computers by June 1? Will we also be producing our usual number of Z-type computers, too?

Jean: Oh, yes. Your regular production schedule would remain the same as it's always been. The only difference is that you would be producing the new A-type computers, too. I mean, after all, you have a lot of new employees, and you have all the new manufacturing and assembling equipment that we have in Dayton. So, you're as ready to make the new product as we are.

Juan: Yes, that's true. We have the new equipment and we've just hired a lot of new assemblers who will be working on the A-type computer. I guess there's no reason we can't meet the production schedule you and Fred have come up with.

Jean: Great, great. I'll tell Fred you agree with our decision and will meet the goal of 100 A-type computers by June 1. He'll be delighted to know that you can deliver what he was hoping for. And, of course, Juan, that means that you'll be doing just as well as the Dayton plant.

Scene II: May 1, San Juan, Puerto Rico

Jean: Hello, Juan. How are things here in Puerto Rico? I'm glad to have the chance to come back and see how things are going.

Juan: Welcome, Jean. It's good to have you here. How is your family?

Jean: Oh, they're fine, just fine. You know, Juan, Fred is really excited about that big order we just got from the Defense Department for 50 A-type computers. They want them by June 10, so we will ship them directly to Washington from San Juan as the computers come off your assembly line. Looks like it's a good thing we set your production goal at 100 A-type computers by June 1, isn't it?

Juan: Um, yes, that was certainly a good idea.

Jean: So, tell me, have you had any problems with the new model? How are your new assemblers working out? Do you have any suggestions for changes in the manufacturing specs? How is the new quality control program working with this model? We're always looking for ways to improve, you know, and we appreciate any ideas you can give us.

Juan: Well, Jean, there is one thing....

Jean: Yes? What is that?

Juan: Well, Jean, we have had a few problems with the new assemblers. Three of them have had serious illnesses in their families and have had to take off several days at a time to nurse a sick child or elderly parent. And another one was involved in a car accident and was in the hospital for several days. And you remember my daughter's surgery? Well, her arm didn't mend properly, and we had to take her to Houston for additional consultations and therapy. But, of course, you and Fred knew about that.

Jean: Yes, we were aware that you had had some personnel problems and that you and your wife had had to go to Houston with Marianna. But what does that have to do with the 50 A-type computers for the Defense Department?

Juan: Well, Jean, because of all these problems, we have had a few delays in the production schedule. Nothing serious, but we are a little bit behind our schedule.

Jean: How far behind is "a little bit"? What are you trying to tell me, Juan? Will you have 50 more A-type computers by June 1 to ship to Washington to fill the Defense Department order?

Juan: Well, I certainly hope we will have that number ready to ship. You know how difficult it can be to predict a precise number for manufacturing, Jean. You probably have many of these same problems in the Dayton plant, don't you?

Exercise Questions

1. What went wrong for Jean in Puerto Rico? Could this have been avoided? What should she have done differently?
2. Replay the roles of Jean and Juan during their conversation, establishing a more constructive communication and management style than Jean did previously.

Source: L. Catlin and T. White, *International Business: Cultural Sourcebook and Case Studies* (Cincinnati, OH: South-Western, Co. 1994).

Internet Resources

Visit the Deresky companion Web site at http://prenhall.com/Deresky for this chapter's Internet resources.

Case Study

Elizabeth Visits GPC's French Subsidiary

Elizabeth Moreno is looking out the window from her business class seat somewhere over the Indian Ocean on Thai Air en route to Paris–Orly International Airport from the Philippines, where she has just spent a week of meetings and problem solving in a pharmaceutical subsidiary of the Global Pharmaceutical Company (GPC). (The Philippines trip is covered in the Chapter 12 case study.)

GPC has the lion's share of the worldwide market in the ethical pharmaceutical products. Ethical drugs are those that can be purchased only through a physician's prescription. In the United States, GPC has research and manufacturing sites in New York, New Jersey, Pennsylvania, and Michigan. The company also has subsidiaries in Canada, Puerto Rico, Australia, Philippines, Brazil, England, and France. GPC has its administrative headquarters in Pennsylvania.

Because of the dispersed geographic locations of its subsidiaries, GPC's top scientists and key managers log thousands of jet miles a year visiting various offices and plants. Its top specialists and executives regularly engage in multisite real-time video and telephone conferences as well as using electronic mail along with faxes, modems, and traditional mail to keep in touch with key personnel.

Despite these technological advances, face-to-face meetings and onsite consultations are used widely. In the case of the French subsidiary, nothing can take the place of face-to-face consultations. The French manager is suspicious of figures in the balance sheet, of the telephone, of his subordinates, of what he reads in the newspaper, and of what Americans tell him in confidence. In contrast, the American trusts all these (Hill 1994, 60). This is the reason GPC regularly sends its scientists and executives to France.

Elizabeth Moreno is one of the key specialists within GPC. Her expertise in chemical processing is widely known not only within her company but also in the pharmaceutical industry worldwide. She has been working at GPC for more than 12 years since finishing her advanced degree in chemistry from a university in the Midwest. While working for GPC, she has been given more and more responsibilities leading to her current position as vice president of chemical development and processing.

From a hectic visit in the Philippines, her next assignment is to visit the French subsidiary plant for one week to study a problem with shelf-life testing of one of its newest antiallergy capsules. It seems that product's active ingredient is degrading sooner than the expiration date. During her stay, she will conduct training for chemists in state-of-the-art techniques for testing as well as training local managers in product statistical quality control. These techniques are now currently used in other GPC locations.

To prepare for her foreign assignments, Elizabeth attended a standard three-hour course given by her company's human resource management department on dealing with cross-cultural issues. Moreover, she recalls reading from a book on French management about the impersonal nature of French business relations. This was so much in contrast with what she just has experienced from her visit in the Philippine subsidiary. The French tend to regard authority as residing in the role and not in the person. It is by the power of the position that a French manager gets things done (Hill 1994, 58). With this knowledge, she knows that her expertise and her position as vice president will see her through the technical aspects of the meetings that are lined up for the few days she will be in Paris.

French managers view their work as an intellectual challenge that requires application of individual brainpower. What matters to them is the opportunity to show one's ability to grasp complex issues, analyze problems, manipulate ideas, and evaluate solutions (Hill 1994, 214).

There are a few challenges for Elizabeth on this assignment. She is not fluent in French. Her only exposure to France and the language was a two-week vacation in Paris she spent with her husband a couple of years ago. But in her highly technical field, the universal language is English. So, she believes that she will not have much difficulty in communicating with the French management to get her assignment successfully completed.

Americans place high value on training and education. In the United States, the field of management has principles that are generally applicable and can be taught and learned. In contrast, the French place more emphasis on the person who can adapt to any situation by virtue of his intellectual quality (Hill 1994, 63). Expertise and intellectual ability are inherent in the individual and simply cannot be acquired through training or education.

It appears that Elizabeth will be encountering very different ways of doing business in France. While she thought about the challenges ahead, her plane landed at the Paris–Orly International Airport. She whisked through customs and immigration without any delays. There was no limousine waiting for her at the arrivals curbside. Instead she took the train to downtown Paris and checked into an apartment hotel that was reserved for her in advance of her arrival.

After a week in Paris, she is expected back in her home office to prepare reports to GPC management about her foreign assignments.

Source: This case was prepared by Edwin J. Portugal, MBA, PhD, who teaches multinational management at State University of New York–Potsdam. It is intended to be used as a basis for discussion on the complexity of multicultural management and not to illustrate effective versus ineffective management styles. Copyright ©1995 by Edwin J. Portugal.

Case Questions

1. What can Elizabeth Moreno do to establish a position of power in front of French managers to help her accomplish her assignment in five days? Explain.
2. What should Elizabeth know about high-context versus low-context cultures in Europe? Explain.
3. What should Elizabeth include in her report, and what should be the manner in which it is communicated, so that future executives and scientists avoid communications pitfalls? Explain.
4. How can technical language differ from everyday language in corporate communications? Explain.
5. How does this business trip compare to her previous trip to the Philippines?

Case Bibliography

Hill, Richard, *Euro-Managers & Martians: The Business Cultures of Europe's Trading Nations* (Brussels: Europublications, Division of Europublic SA/NV, 1994).

6

Negotiation and Decision Making

O U T L I N E

Opening Profile: The Iraq–U.S. Negotiations

Negotiation

The Negotiation Process

Stage One: Preparation

Comparative Management in Focus:
Successful Negotiators Around the World

Stage Two: Relationship Building

Stage Three: Exchanging Task-Related
Information

Stage Four: Persuasion

Stage Five: Concessions and Agreement

Managing Negotiation

Comparative Management in Focus:
Negotiating with the Chinese

Managing Conflict Resolution

Decision Making

Technology Application: Daimler's Stuttgart
Command Post Speeds Cross-Border
Decisions for Integration with Chrysler

The Influence of Culture on Decision Making

Approaches to Decision Making

Comparative Management in Focus: Decision
Making in Japanese Companies

Summary of Key Points

Discussion Questions

Experiential Exercises

Internet Resources

Case Study: Martinez Construction Company in
Germany

OPENING PROFILE

The Iraq–U.S. Negotiations

The breakdown of negotiations between the United States and Iraq in 1991, which led to the Gulf War, culminated in the refusal of Iraq's Foreign Minister Aziz to accept a letter from President Bush to President Hussein. It is useful to examine the cross-cultural interactions that led to this impasse.

Prior to the Geneva meeting between Secretary of State Baker and Foreign Minister Aziz, the U.S. and Iraqi officials behaved in ways that were not expected by their counterparts in Baghdad and Washington. For example, the United States appointed a woman, April Glaspie, as its ambassador. In many Middle Eastern common cultures, the American value of gender equality is not well accepted. The ambassador's gender and her status as a "Westerner" made her a very weak representative in Iraq. Even if she had delivered a clearer (from the Western point of view) message, it would not have been treated as seriously as if it had come from a male. The ambiguity of the message, of course, complicated the issue and signaled to Hussein that the United States was not concerned with his "retaking of Iraq's territory." To him, what was not said by the United States was more important than what was said (high-context communication).

The meeting between U.S. Secretary of State Baker and the Iraqi Foreign Minister Aziz in Geneva was plagued by several common cultural differences (see Halverson in Olsson, 1985). The U.S. approach was as follows: (1) task oriented—demanding Iraq withdraw from Kuwait; (2) abstract—appealing to international law; (3) impersonal—sending a letter from president to president with no personal meetings; (4) definite—demanding Hussein respond or else; and (5) fast paced—setting short time deadlines.

According to Halverson, Easterners such as the Iraqis prefer a different approach to meetings, one that is more holistic, long term, and relational. The Iraqis' approach in Geneva was as follows: (1) group oriented—wanting to get to know the U.S. negotiators; (2) experiential—appealing to past history; (3) personal—asking for direct meetings between the leadership; (4) indefinite—making no commitments without more interaction with the U.S. representatives; and (5) slow paced—rejecting early deadlines. Indeed, some have argued that the United States could not have done a better job of alienating the Iraqis had they tried. And yet the Associated Press (AP) reported that Baker was "genuinely stunned" when Aziz said, "I am sorry, I cannot receive this letter (from President Bush to Saddam Hussein)."

Questions

1. What might Aziz's reasons have been for refusing to accept the Bush letter?
2. Why was Baker stunned when Aziz declined the letter?
3. Do you think that negotiations between Iraq and the United States have improved since this incident? What about the 1998–99 bombings of Iraq sites? Do you think they were based on U.S. officials' perceptions that Hussein is unwilling to live up to the agreements made after the Gulf War? What role do clashing negotiation styles continue to play in this standoff? What has occurred since these bombings?

Source: Paul R. Kimmel, "Cultural Perspectives on International Negotiations," *Journal of Social Issues* 50, no. 1 (1994): 179–196.

Managers negotiate with parties in other countries to make specific plans for strategies (exporting, joint ventures, and so forth). Some initial, exploratory negotiations may have already taken place when the feasibility of various strategic options was being investigated (discussed in Chapters 7 and 8).

Managers must prepare for strategic negotiations; next the operational details must be negotiated—the staffing of key positions, the sourcing of raw materials or component parts, the repatriating of profits, to name a few. As globalism burgeons, the ability to conduct successful cross-cultural negotiations cannot be overemphasized. Failure to negotiate productively will result in lost potential alliances and lost business at worst; confusion and delays at best. Cross-cultural conflicts and misunderstandings are illustrated in this chapter's Opening Profile of the failed negotiations between the United States and Iraq in 1991—a situation that continues today. These are the same problems that plague business negotiations in the Middle East.

During the process of negotiation—whether before, during, or after negotiating sessions—all kinds of decisions are made, both explicitly and implicitly. A consideration of cross-cultural negotiations must therefore include the various decision-making processes that occur around the world. Negotiations cannot be conducted without decisions being made.

This chapter will examine the processes of negotiation and decision making as they apply to international and domestic cross-cultural contexts. Our objective is a better understanding of successful management.

Negotiation

Effecting strategy depends on management's ability to negotiate productively—a skill widely considered one of the most important in international business. In the international arena, cultural differences produce great difficulties in the negotiation process. In fact, ignorance of native bargaining rituals, more than any other single factor, accounts for the United States' unimpressive sales efforts with the Japanese and others.[1] Important differences in the negotiation process from country to country include (1) the amount and type of preparation for a negotiation, (2) the relative emphasis on tasks versus interpersonal relationships, (3) the reliance on general principles rather than specific issues, and (4) the number of people present and the extent of their influence.[2] In every instance, managers need to familiarize themselves with the cultural background and underlying motivations of the negotiators—and the tactics and procedures they use—to control the process, make progress, and therefore maximize company goals.

The word **negotiation** describes the process of discussion between two or more parties aimed at reaching a mutually acceptable agreement. For long-term positive relations, the goal should be to set up a **win–win situation**—that is, to bring about a settlement beneficial to all parties concerned. This process, difficult enough when it takes place among people of similar backgrounds, is even more complex in international negotiations because of differences in cultural values, lifestyles, expectations, verbal and nonverbal language, approaches to formal procedures, and problem-solving techniques. The complexity is heightened when negotiating across borders because of the greater number of stakeholders involved. These stakeholders are illustrated in Exhibit 6–1. In preparing for negotiations, it is critical to avoid **projective cognitive similarity**—that is, the assumption that others perceive, judge, think, and reason in the same way when, in fact, they do not, because of differential cultural and practical influences. Instead, astute negotiators empathetically enter into the private world or cultural space of their counterparts, while willingly sharing their own view of the situation.[3]

The Negotiation Process

The negotiation process comprises five stages, the ordering of which may vary according to the cultural norms; for most people, relationship building is part of a continuous process of preparation in any event: (1) preparation, (2) relationship building, (3) the exchange of task-related information, (4) persuasion, and (5) concessions and agreement.[4, 5, 6] Of course, in

EXHIBIT 6-1

Stakeholders in Cross-Cultural Negotiations

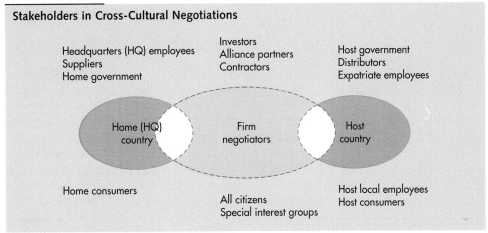

Headquarters (HQ) employees
Suppliers
Home government

Investors
Alliance partners
Contractors

Host government
Distributors
Expatriate employees

Home (HQ) country   Firm negotiators   Host country

Home consumers

All citizens
Special interest groups

Host local employees
Host consumers

reality these are seldom distinct stages, but rather they tend to overlap; negotiators may also revert to an earlier stage temporarily. With that in mind, it is useful to break down the negotiation process into stages to discuss the issues relevant to each stage and what international managers might expect so that they might more successfully manage this process. These stages are shown in Exhibit 6–2 and discussed in the following sections.

Stage One: Preparation

The importance of careful preparation for cross-cultural negotiations cannot be overstated. To the extent that time permits, a distinct advantage can be gained if negotiators familiarize

EXHIBIT 6-2

The Negotiation Process

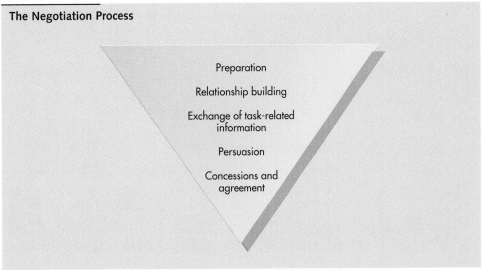

Preparation

Relationship building

Exchange of task-related information

Persuasion

Concessions and agreement

themselves with the entire context and background of their counterparts (no matter where the meetings will take place) in addition to the specific subjects to be negotiated. Because most negotiation problems are caused by differences in culture, language, and environment, hours or days of tactical preparation for negotiation can be wasted if these factors are not carefully considered.[7]

To understand cultural differences in negotiating styles, managers first need to understand their own styles and then determine how their style differs from the norm in other countries. They can do this by comparing profiles of those perceived to be successful negotiators in different countries. Such profiles reflect the value system, attitudes, and expected behaviors inherent in a given society. The following Comparative Management in Focus section shows such profiles for American, Indian, Arab, Swedish, and Italian negotiators, giving some insight into how these negotiators act and how they are perceived by people from different cultural backgrounds.[8] These profiles also give some insight into what to expect from the different negotiators and what they expect from others.

COMPARATIVE MANAGEMENT IN FOCUS

Successful Negotiators Around the World

American Negotiators

According to Casse, a successful American negotiator acts as follows:

1. Knows when to compromise
2. Takes a firm stand at the beginning of the negotiation
3. Refuses to make concessions beforehand
4. Doesn't reveal everything up front
5. Accepts compromises only when the negotiation is deadlocked
6. Sets up the general principles and delegates the detail work to associates
7. Keeps a maximum of options open before negotiation
8. Operates in good faith
9. Respects the "opponents"
10. States his or her position as clearly as possible
11. Knows when he or she wishes a negotiation to move on
12. Is fully briefed about the negotiated issues
13. Has a good sense of timing and is consistent
14. Makes the other party reveal his or her position while keeping his or her own position hidden as long as possible
15. Lets the other negotiator come forward first and looks for the best deal

Indian Negotiators

Indians, says Casse, often follow Gandhi's approach to negotiation, which he called *satyagraha* ("firmness in a good cause"). This approach combines strength with the love of truth. The successful Indian negotiator thus acts as follows:

1. Looks for and says the truth
2. Is not afraid of speaking up and has no fears

3. Exercises self-control ("The weapons of the *satyagraha* are within him.")
4. Seeks solutions that will please all the parties involved ("*Satyagraha* aims to exalt both sides.")
5. Respects the other party ("The opponent must be weaned from error by patience and sympathy. Weaned, not crushed; converted, not annihilated.")
6. Neither uses violence nor insults
7. Is ready to change his or her mind and differ with himself or herself at the risk of being seen as inconsistent and unpredictable
8. Puts things into perspective and switches easily from the small picture to the big one
9. Is humble and trusts the opponent
10. Is able to withdraw, use silence, and learn from within
11. Relies on himself or herself, his or her own resources and strengths
12. Appeals to the other party's spiritual identity ("To communicate, the West moves or talks. The East sits, contemplates, suffers.")
13. Is tenacious, patient, and persistent
14. Learns from the opponent and avoids the use of secrets
15. Goes beyond logical reasoning and trusts his or her instinct as well as faith

Arab Negotiators

Many Arab negotiators, following Islamic tradition, use mediators to settle disputes. A successful Arab mediator acts in the following way:

1. Protects all the parties' honor, self-respect, and dignity
2. Avoids direct confrontations between opponents
3. Is respected and trusted by all
4. Does not put the parties involved in a situation where they have to show weakness or admit defeat
5. Has the necessary prestige to be listened to
6. Is creative enough to come up with honorable solutions for all parties
7. Is impartial and can understand the positions of the various parties without leaning toward one or the other
8. Is able to resist any kind of pressure that the opponents could try to exercise on him
9. Uses references to people who are highly respected by the opponents to persuade them to change their minds on some issues ("Do it for the sake of your father.")
10. Can keep secrets and in so doing gains the confidence of the negotiating parties
11. Controls his temper and emotions (or loses it when and where necessary)
12. Can use conferences as mediating devices
13. Knows that the opponents will have problems in carrying out the decisions made during the negotiation
14. Is able to cope with the Arab disregard for time
15. Understands the impact of Islam on the opponents who believe that they possess the truth, follow the Right Path, and are going to "win" because their cause is just

Swedish Negotiators

A Swedish negotiator, according to Casse, has the following traits:

1. Very quiet and thoughtful
2. Punctual (concerned with time)
3. Extremely polite
4. Straightforward (they get straight down to business)
5. Eager to be productive and efficient
6. Careful, plodding style
7. Down-to-earth and overcautious
8. Rather flexible
9. Able to and quite good at holding back emotions and feelings
10. Slow at reacting to new (unexpected) proposals
11. Informal and familiar
12. Confident
13. Perfectionist
14. Afraid of confrontations
15. Very private

Italian Negotiators

Italians, says Casse, value a negotiator who acts as follows:

1. Has a sense of drama (acting is a main part of the culture)
2. Does not hide his or her emotions (which are partly sincere and partly feigned)
3. Reads facial expressions and gestures very well
4. Has a feeling for history
5. Does not trust anybody
6. Is concerned about the *bella figura* ("good impression") he or she can create among those who watch his or her behavior
7. Believes in the individual's initiatives, not so much in teamwork
8. Is good at being obliging and simpatico at all times
9. Is always on the qui vive ("lookout")
10. Never embraces definite opinions
11. Is able to come up with new ways to immobilize and eventually destroy his or her opponents
12. Handles confrontations of power with subtlety and tact
13. Has a flair for intrigue
14. Knows how to use flattery
15. Can involve other negotiators in complex combinations

Comparing such profiles is useful; Indian negotiators, for example, are humble, patient, respectful of the other parties, and very willing to compromise, whereas Americans are firmer about taking stands. An important difference between Arab negotiators and those from most other countries is that they are mediators, not the parties themselves—direct confrontation is thus impossible. Successful Swedish negotiators are conservative and careful, dealing with factual and detailed information. This profile contrasts with Italian negotiators, who are expressive and exuberant but less straightforward than their Swedish counterparts.

Understanding Negotiating Styles   International managers can benefit from studying differences in negotiating behaviors (and the underlying reasons for them), which can help them recognize what is happening in the negotiating process. Exhibit 6–3 shows some examples of differences among North American, Japanese, and Latin American styles. Brazilians, for example, generally have a spontaneous, passionate, and dynamic style. They are very talkative and particularly use the word *no* extensively—in fact, more than 40 times per half hour, compared with 4.7 times for Americans and only 1.9 times for the Japanese. They also differ markedly from the Americans and Japanese by their use of extensive physical contact.[9]

The Japanese are typically skillful negotiators. They have spent a great deal more time and effort studying American culture and business practices than Americans have spent studying theirs. A typical example of this contrast was apparent at trade negotiations between Japan and the United States in 1994. Charlene Barshefsky—though a tough American international lawyer—had never visited Japan before being sent there as a trade negotiator, and

EXHIBIT 6–3

Comparison of Negotiation Styles—Japanese, North American, and Latin American

Japanese	North American	Latin American
Emotional sensitivity highly valued	Emotional sensitivity not highly valued	Emotional sensitivity valued
Hiding of emotions	Dealing straightforwardly or impersonally	Emotionally passionate
Subtle power plays; conciliation	Litigation not so much as conciliation	Great power plays; use of weakness
Loyalty to employer; employer takes care of employees	Lack of commitment to employer; breaking of ties by either if necessary	Loyalty to employer (who is often family)
Face-saving crucial; decisions often made on basis of saving someone from embarrassment	Decisions made on a cost benefit basis; face-saving does not always matter	Face-saving crucial in decision making to preserve honor, dignity
Decision makers openly influenced by special interests	Decision makers influenced by special interests but often not considered ethical	Execution of special interests of decision expected, condoned
Not argumentative; quiet when right	Argumentative when right or wrong, but impersonal	Argumentative when right or wrong; passionate
What is down in writing must be accurate, valid	Great importance given to documentation as evidential proof	Impatient with documentation as obstacle to understanding general principles
Step-by-step approach to decision making	Methodically organized decision making	Impulsive, spontaneous decision making
Good of group is the ultimate aim	Profit motive or good of individual ultimate aim	What is good for group is good for the individual
Cultivate a good emotional social setting for decision making; get to know decision makers	Decision making impersonal; avoid involvements, conflict of interest	Personalism necessary for good decision making

Source: From Pierre Casse, *Training for the Multicultural Manager: A Practical and Cross-Cultural Approach to the Management of People* (Washington, D.C.: Society for Intercultural Education, Training, and Research, 1982).

had little knowledge of her counterparts. But Mr. Okamatsu, as most Japanese negotiators, is very familiar with America. He lived in New York for three years with his family and has spent many years handling bilateral trade disputes between the two countries. The different styles of Mr. Okamatsu and Ms. Barshefsky are apparent in the negotiations. Ms. Barshefsky wants specific import goals. Mr. Okamatsu wants to talk more about the causes of trade problems rather than set specific targets, which he calls the "cooperative approach." Ms. Barshefsky snaps that the approach is nonsense and "would analyze the past to death, with no link to future change."[10] Such differences in philosophy and style between the two countries reflect ten years of anger and feelings of betrayal in trade negotiations. John Graham, a California professor who has studied international negotiating styles, says that the differences between American and Japanese styles are well illustrated by their respective proverbs: The American believes that "the squeaking wheel gets the grease," and the Japanese say that "the pheasant would not be shot but for its cry."[11] The Japanese are calm, quiet, patient negotiators; they are accustomed to long, detailed negotiating sessions. Whereas Americans often plunge straight to the matter at hand, the Japanese want instead to develop long-term, personal relationships. The Japanese want to get to know those on the other side and will spend some time in **nontask sounding**—general polite conversation and informal communication before meetings (*nemawashi*).

In negotiations, the Japanese culture of politeness and the hiding of emotions can be disconcerting to Americans when they are unable to make straightforward eye contact or when the Japanese maintain smiling faces in serious situations. It is important that Americans understand what is polite and what is offensive to the Japanese (and vice versa). Americans must avoid anything that resembles boasting because the Japanese value humility, and they must avoid physical contact or touching of any sort.[12] Consistent with the culture-based value of maintaining harmony, the Japanese are likely to be evasive or even leave the room rather than give a direct negative answer.[13, 14] Fundamental to the Japanese culture is a concern for the welfare of the group; anything that affects one member or part of society affects the others. Thus, the Japanese view decisions carefully in light of long-term consequences; they use objective, analytic thought patterns; and they take time for reflection.[15]

Further insight into negotiating styles around the world can be gained by comparing the North American, Arab, and Russian styles. As shown in Exhibit 6–4, basic cultural values often shed light on the manner in which information is presented, whether and how concessions will be made, and the general nature and duration of the relationship.

For North Americans, negotiations are businesslike; their **factual appeals** are based on what they believe is objective information, presented with the assumption that it is understood by the other side on a logical basis. Arabs use **affective appeals** based on emotions and subjective feelings; Russians employ **axiomatic appeals**—that is, their appeals are based on the ideals generally accepted in their society. The Russians are tough negotiators; they stall for time until they unnerve Western negotiators by continuously delaying and haggling. Much of this is based on the Russians' different attitude toward time. Because Russians do not subscribe to the Western belief that "time is money," they are more patient, more determined, more dogged negotiators. They try to keep smiles and other expressions of emotion to a minimum to present a calm exterior.[16]

In contrast to the Russians, Arabs are more interested in long-term relationships and therefore are more likely to make concessions. Compared with Westerners, Arabs have a casual approach to deadlines and frequently lack the authority to finalize a deal.[17]

EXHIBIT 6-4

Comparison of Negotiation Styles—North Americans, Arabs, Russians

	North Americans	Arabs	Russians
Primary negotiating style and process	Factual: appeals made to logic	Affective: appeals made to emotions	Axiomatic: appeals made to ideals
Conflict: opponent's arguments countered with . . .	Objective facts	Subjective feelings	Asserted ideals
Making concessions	Small concessions made early to establish a relationship	Concessions made throughout as a part of the bargaining process	Few, if any, small concessions made
Response to opponent's concessions	Usually reciprocate opponent's concessions	Almost always reciprocate opponent's concessions	Opponent's concessions viewed as weakness and almost never reciprocated
Relationship	Short-term	Long-term	No continuing relationship
Authority	Broad	Broad	Limited
Initial position	Moderate	Extreme	Extreme
Deadline	Very important	Casual	Ignored

Source: Adapted from E. S. Glenn, D. Witmeyer, and K. A. Stevenson, "Cultural Styles of Persuasion," *International Journal of Intercultural Relations* 1 (1984).

Variables in the Negotiating Process With all this complexity in negotiating styles, how can a manager sort through the many variables to prepare for negotiations in different countries? Adept negotiators do some research to develop a profile of their counterparts so that they know, in most situations, what to expect, how to prepare, and how to react. Exhibit 6–5 shows 12 variables to consider when preparing to negotiate. These variables can, to a great degree, help managers understand the deep-rooted cultural and national motivations and traditional processes underlying negotiations with people from other countries.

After developing thoughtful profiles of the other party or parties, managers can plan for the actual negotiation meetings. Prior to the meetings, they should find out as much as possible about (1) the kinds of demands that might be made, (2) the composition of the "opposing" team, and (3) the relative authority that the members possess. After this, the managers can gear their negotiation strategy specifically to the other side's firm, allocate roles to different team members, decide on concessions, and prepare an alternative action plan in case a negotiated solution cannot be found.[18]

In some situations, however, the entire negotiation process is something people have to learn from scratch. After the splintering of the Soviet Union into 15 independent republics, managers from the Newmont Mining Corporation of Denver, wishing to form a joint venture to refine gold deposits in Uzbekistan, found themselves at a standstill. Officials in Uzbekistan had never negotiated a business contract and had no one to tell them how to proceed.[19]

Following the preparation and planning stage, usually done at the home office, the core of the actual negotiation takes place on-site in the foreign location (or at the manager's home office if the other team has decided to travel there). In some cases, a compromise on the location for negotiations can signal a cooperative strategy, which Weiss calls "Improvise an approach: Effect Symphony"—a strategy available to negotiators familiar with each others'

EXHIBIT 6-5

Variables in the Negotiation Process

1. *Basic conception of negotiation process:* Is it a competitive process or a problem-solving approach?
2. *Negotiator selection criteria:* Is selection based on experience, status, expertise, personal attributes, or some other characteristic?
3. *Significance of type of issues:* Is it specific, such as price, or is the focus on relationships or the format of talks?
4. *Concern with protocol:* What is the importance of procedures, social behaviors, and so forth in the negotiation process?
5. *Complexity of communicative context:* What degree of reliance is placed on nonverbal cues to interpret information?
6. *Nature of persuasive arguments:* How do the parties attempt to influence each other? Do they rely on rational arguments, on accepted tradition, or on emotion?
7. *Role of individuals' aspirations:* Are motivations based on individual, company, or community goals?
8. *Bases of trust:* Is trust based on past experience, intuition, or rules?
9. *Risk-taking propensity:* How much do the parties try to avoid uncertainty in trading information or making a contract?
10. *Value of time:* What is each party's attitude toward time? How fast should negotiations proceed, and what degree of flexibility is there?
11. *Decision-making system:* How does each team reach decisions—by individual determination, by majority opinion, or by group consensus?
12. *Form of satisfactory agreement:* Is agreement based on trust (perhaps just a handshake), the credibility of the parties, commitment, or a legally binding contract?

Source: Adapted from S. E. Weiss and W. Stripp, *Negotiation with Foreign Business Persons: An Introduction for Americans with Propositions on Six Cultures* (New York University Faculty of Business Administration, February 1985).

culture and willing to put negotiation on an equal footing.[20] Weiss gives the following example of this negotiation strategy:

> For their negotiations over construction of the tunnel under the English Channel, British and French representatives agreed to partition talks and alternate the site between Paris and London. At each site, the negotiators were to use established, local ways, including the language,... thus punctuating approaches by time and space.

In this way, each side was put into the context and the script of the other culture about half the time.

The next stage of negotiation—often given short shrift by Westerners—is that of relationship building; this stage, in fact, usually has either taken place already or is concurrent with other preparations, in most parts of the world.

Stage Two: Relationship Building

The process of relationship building is regarded with much more significance in most parts of the world than it is in America. American negotiators are, generally speaking, objective about the specific matter at hand and usually want to waste no time in getting down to business and making progress. This approach, well understood in the United States, can be disastrous if the foreign negotiators want to take enough time to build trust and respect as a basis for negotiating contracts. In such cases, American efficiency interferes with the patient development of a mutually trusting relationship—the very cornerstone of an Asian business agreement.[21]

In many countries, such as Mexico and China, personal commitments to individuals, rather than the legal system, form the basis for the enforcement of contracts. Effective negotiators allow plenty of time in their schedule for such relationship building with bargaining partners; this process usually takes the form of social events, tours, and ceremonies, along with much light conversation, or nontask sounding, while both sides get to know each other. In such cultures, one patiently waits for the other party to start actual business negotiations, aware that relationship building is, in fact, the first phase of negotiations.[22] It is usually recommended that managers new to such scenarios use an intermediary—someone who already has the trust and respect of the foreign managers and who therefore acts as a "relationship bridge." Middle Easterners, in particular, prefer to negotiate through a trusted intermediary, and for them as well, initial meetings are only for the purpose of getting acquainted. Arabs do business with the person, not the company, and therefore mutual trust must be established.

In their bestseller on negotiation, *Getting to Yes*, Fisher and Ury point out the dangers of not preparing well for negotiations:

> In Persian, the word "compromise" does not have the English meaning of a midway solution which both sides can accept, but only the negative meaning of surrendering one's principles. Also, a "mediator" is a meddler, someone who is barging in uninvited. In 1980, United Nations Secretary-General Kurt Waldheim flew to Iran to deal with the hostage situation. National Iranian radio and television broadcast in Persian a comment he was to have made upon his arrival in Tehran: "I have come as a mediator to work out a compromise." Less than an hour later, his car was being stoned by angry Iranians.[23]

As a bridge to the more formal stages of negotiations, such relationship building is followed by posturing—that is, general discussion that sets the tone for the meetings. This phase should result in a spirit of cooperation; to help ensure this result, negotiators must use words like "respect" and "mutual benefit" rather than language that would suggest arrogance, superiority, or urgency.[24]

Stage Three: Exchanging Task-Related Information

In the next stage, exchanging task-related information, each side typically makes a presentation and states its position; a question-and-answer session usually ensues, and alternatives are discussed. From an American perspective, this represents a straightforward, objective, efficient, and understandable stage. However, Copeland and Griggs point out that negotiators from other countries continue to take a more indirect approach at this stage. Mexican negotiators are usually suspicious and indirect, presenting little substantive material and more lengthy, evasive conversation. French negotiators enjoy debate and conflict, and will often interrupt presentations to argue about an issue even if it has little relevance to the topic being presented. The Chinese also ask many questions of their counterparts, and they delve specifically and repeatedly into the details at hand; conversely, the Chinese presentations contain only vague and ambiguous material. For instance, after about 20 Boeing officials spent 6 weeks presenting masses of literature and technical demonstrations to the Chinese, the Chinese said, "Thank you for your introduction."[25]

The Russians also enter negotiations well prepared and well versed in the specific details of the matter being presented. To answer their (or any other side's) questions, it is generally a good idea to bring along someone with expertise to answer any grueling technical inquiries. Russians also put a lot of emphasis on protocol and expect to deal only with top executives.

Adler suggests that negotiators should focus not only on presenting their situation and needs but also on showing an understanding of their opponents' viewpoint. Focusing on the entire situation confronting each party encourages the negotiators to assess a wider range of alternatives for resolution, rather than limiting themselves to their preconceived, static positions. She suggests that to be most effective, negotiators should prepare for meetings by practicing role reversal.[26]

Stage Four: Persuasion

In the next phase of negotiations, persuasion, the hard bargaining starts. Typically, both parties try to persuade the other to accept more of their position and to give up some of their own. Often, some persuasion has already taken place beforehand in social settings and through mutual contacts. In the Far East, details are likely to be worked out ahead of time through the backdoor approach (*houmani*). For the most part, however, the majority of the persuasion takes place over one or more negotiating sessions. International managers usually find that this process of bargaining and making concessions is fraught with difficulties because of the different uses and interpretations of verbal and nonverbal behaviors. Although variations in such behaviors influence every stage of the negotiation process, they can play a particularly powerful role in persuasion, especially if they are not anticipated.

Studies of negotiating behavior have revealed the use of certain recognizable *tactics*, which skilled negotiators recognize and use. Exhibit 6–6 shows the results of a study comparing the use of various tactics (promises, threats, and so forth) among the Japanese, Americans, and Brazilians. The results indicate that the Japanese and the Americans tend to be more alike in the use of these behaviors, whereas the Japanese and the Brazilians are less alike. For example, the Brazilians use fewer promises and commitments than the Japanese or the Americans (only half as many), but they use commands far more often. The Japanese and the Americans use threats twice as often as the Brazilians, and they use commands only about half as often as the Brazilians. The Brazilians and the Japanese seldom behave similarly.

Other, less savory tactics are sometimes used in international negotiations. Often called *dirty tricks*, these tactics, according to Fisher and Ury, include efforts to mislead "opponents" deliberately.[27] Some negotiators may give wrong or distorted factual information or use the excuse of ambiguous authority: giving conflicting impressions about who in their party has the power to make a commitment. Amid hard bargaining, the prudent international manager will follow up on possibly misleading information before taking action based on trust.

Other rough tactics are designed to put opposing negotiators in a stressful situation physically or psychologically so that they are more likely to give in. These include uncomfortable room temperatures, too-bright lighting, rudeness, interruptions, and other irritations. Specific bargaining pressures include extreme or escalating demands, threats to stop negotiating, calculated delays, and a take-it-or-leave-it attitude. In a survey of 18 U.S.–Korean joint ventures, for example, U.S. executives reported that the behavior of the Koreans during the

EXHIBIT 6-6

Differences Among Japanese, American, and Brazilian Verbal Negotiations Behavior

Bargaining Behaviors and Definition	Frequency per Half-Hour Bargaining Session		
	Japanese	American	Brazilian
Promise. A statement in which the source indicated his or her intention to provide the target with a reinforcing consequence that source anticipates target will evaluate as pleasant, positive, or rewarding.	7	8	3
Threat. Same as promise, except that the reinforcing consequences are thought to be noxious, unpleasant, or punishing.	4	4	2
Recommendation. A statement in which the source predicts that a pleasant environmental consequence will occur to the target. Its occurrence is not under the source's control.	7	4	5
Warning. Same as recommendation, except that the consequences are thought to be unpleasant.	2	1	1
Reward. A statement by the source that is thought to create pleasant consequences for the target.	1	2	2
Punishment. Same as reward, except that the consequences are thought to be unpleasant.	1	3	3
Positive normative appeal. A statement in which the source indicates that the target's past, present, or future behavior was or will be in conformity with social norms.	1	1	0
Negative normative appeal. Same as positive normative appeal, except that the target's behavior is in violation of social norms.	3	1	1
Commitment. A statement by the source to the effect that its future bids will not go below or above a certain level.	15	13	8
Self-disclosure. A statement in which the source reveals information about itself.	34	36	39
Question. A statement in which the source asks the target to reveal information about itself.	20	20	22
Command. A statement in which the source suggests that the target perform a certain behavior.	8	6	14

Source: From John L. Graham, "The Influence of Culture on the Process of Business Negotiations in an Exploratory Study," *Journal of International Business Studies* (Spring 1985): 88.

course of negotiations was often "abusive," resulting in "shouting matches, desk pounding, and chest beating."[28]

International negotiators must keep in mind, however, that what might seem like dirty tricks to Americans is simply the way other cultures conduct negotiations. In some South American countries, for example, it is common to start negotiations with misleading or false information.

The most subtle behaviors in the negotiation process, and often the most difficult to deal with, are usually the nonverbal messages—the use of voice intonation, facial and body expressions, eye contact, dress, and the timing of the discussions. **Nonverbal behaviors** are ingrained aspects of culture used by people in their daily lives; they are not specifically changed for the purposes of negotiation. In a comparative study of the nonverbal negotiating behaviors of Japanese, Americans, and Brazilians, Graham assessed the relative frequency of the use of silent periods, conversational overlaps, facial gazing (staring at people's faces), and touching. He found that the Brazilians interrupted conversation about twice as often as the Japanese and the Americans and used much more touching and facial gazing; needless to say, they scored low on silent periods. The Japanese tended to use more silent periods and interruptions than the Americans, but less facial gazing. The Japanese and the Americans evidenced no touching whatsoever, other than handshaking, during a 30-minute period.[29]

Although we have discussed persuasion as if it were always a distinct stage, it is really the primary purpose underlying all stages of the negotiation process. In particular, persuasion is clearly an integral part of the process of making concessions and arriving at an agreement.

Stage Five: Concessions and Agreement

In the last stage of negotiation, concessions and agreement, tactics vary greatly across cultures. Well-prepared negotiators are aware of various concession strategies and have decided ahead of time what their own concession strategy will be. Familiar with the typical initial positions that various parties are likely to take, they know that the Russians and the Chinese generally open their bargaining with extreme positions, asking for more than they hope to gain, whereas the Swedes usually start with what they are prepared to accept.

Research in the United States indicates that better end results are attained by starting with extreme positions.[30] With this approach, the process of reaching an agreement involves careful timing of the disclosure information and of concessions. Most people who have studied negotiations believe that negotiators should disclose only the information that is necessary at a given point and that they should try to obtain information piece by piece to get the whole picture gradually without giving away their goals or concession strategy. These guidelines will not always work in intercultural negotiations because the American process of addressing issues one at a time, in a linear fashion, is not common in other countries or cultures. Negotiators in the Far East, for example, approach issues in a holistic manner, deciding on the whole deal at the end, rather than making incremental concessions.

Again, at the final stage of agreement and contract, cultural values determine how these agreements will be honored. Whereas Americans take contracts very seriously, Russians often renege on their contracts. The Japanese, on the other hand, consider a formal contract to be somewhat of an insult and a waste of time and money in legal costs since they prefer to operate on the basis of understanding and social trust.[31]

Managing Negotiation

"We faced a lot of naysayers throughout the entire process, and people who thought we could never pull it off."

—Rebecca Mark, Chairperson Enron's International Unit, February 1999

It took three years to February 1999 for Rebecca Mark and her team at Enron's International Unit to bring its Dabhol power plant in India back into operation. In 1996, the Indian government had canceled the partially built plant because of pressure from environmentalists and a derailed economic reform plan that had placed the Dabhol plant as the first foreign-owned power project. But both sides learned from their mistakes, and Ms. Mark's patient and skillful negotiations eventually brought about consensus to reignite economic reform and to get the Dabhol plant going again.[32]

Skillful international managers such as Ms. Mark, then, need to assess many factors when **managing negotiation**. They must understand the position of the other parties in regard to their goals—whether national or corporate—and whether these goals are represented by principles or specific details. They should have the ability to recognize the relative importance attached to completing the task versus developing interpersonal relationships. Managers also need to know the composition of the teams involved, the power allotted to the members, and the extent of the teams' preparation.[33] In addition, they must grasp the significance of personal trust in the relationship. As said earlier, the culture of the parties involved affects their negotiating styles and behavior, and thus the overall process of negotiation. However, whatever the culture, person-related conflicts have been found by research done by Tse, Francis, and Walls to "invite negative, more relation-oriented (versus information-oriented) responses," leading them to conclude that:

> The **software of negotiation**—that is, the nature and the appearance of the relationship between the people pursuing common goals—needs to be carefully addressed in the negotiation process.[34]

This is particularly true when representatives of individual-focused cultures (such as Americans) and group-focused cultures (such as Chinese) are on opposite sides of the table. Many of these cultural-based differences in negotiations in fact came to light in a recent study by Husted of the perceptions of Mexican negotiators of the reasons for the failure of their negotiations with U.S. teams. The summary findings are shown in Exhibit 6–7. However,

EXHIBIT 6–7

Bargaining with the Gringos
Mexican Managers' Perceptions of Causes of Failure of Negotiations with Americans

	Very Important (%)	Important (%)	Moderately Important (%)	Total (%)
Problems with U.S. team				
Lack of authority of U.S. team to make decisions	37.0	20.0	15.0	72.0
U.S. team's failure to resolve doubts of Mexican team	34.0	26.0	14.0	74.0
U.S. team's lack of sincerity	41.0	20.0	9.0	70.0
Eigenvalue: 2.9009/Percent of var.: 26.4/Cum. var.: 26.4				
Negotiation process				
Differences in negotiation styles	26.5	28.4	22.5	77.4
U.S. team quoting unreasonable prices	52.5	17.8	8.9	79.2
Mexican lack of knowledge of delivery system	42.0	19.0	11.0	72.0
Mexican lack of preparation	40.6	21.8	9.9	72.3
Eigenvalue: 2.3577/Percent of var.: 21.4/Cum. var.: 47.8				
Cultural barriers				
Differences in business practices	24.5	29.4	22.5	76.4
Communication barriers	37.3	17.6	12.7	67.6
Eigenvalue: 1.7976/Percent of var.: 16.3/Cum. var.: 64.1				
Language problems	41.2	21.6	5.9	68.7
Eigenvalue: 1.0763/Percent of var.: 9.8/Cum. var.: 73.9				
Price constraints				
Mexican team's inability to lower the price	32.0	22.0	18.0	72.0
Eigenvalue: 1.0433/Percent of var.: 9.5/Cum. var.: 83.4				

Source: Bryan W. Husted, "Bargaining with the Gringos: An Exploratory Study of Negotiations between Mexican and U.S. Firms," *International Executive* 36(5) (September–October 1994): 625–644.

EXHIBIT 6-8

Cross-Cultural Negotiation Variables

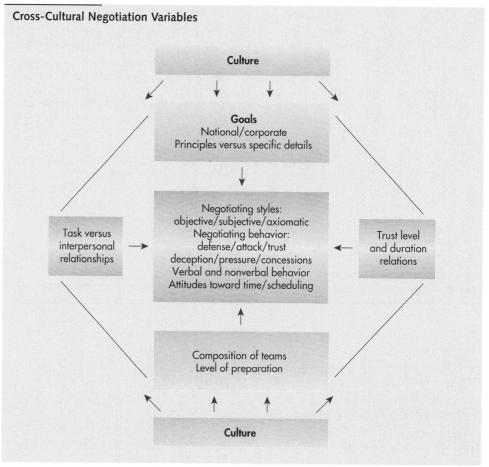

Husted interprets that "many of the perceived differences relate to the typical differences found between high-context and low-context cultures."[35] In other words, the interpretations by the Mexican managers were affected by their high-context culture, with the characteristics of an indirect approach, patience in discussing ideas, and maintenance of dignity. Instead, the low-context Americans conveyed an impatient, cold, blunt communicative style. Rather, to maintain the outward dignity of their Mexican counterparts, Americans need to approach negotiations with Mexicans with patience and tolerance, not attacking ideas that may be taken personally. The relationships among the factors of cross-cultural negotiation that we have discussed in this chapter are illustrated in Exhibit 6–8.

The successful management of intercultural negotiations requires a manager to go beyond a generalized understanding of the issues and variables involved. She or he must (1) gain specific knowledge of the parties in the upcoming meeting, (2) prepare accordingly to adjust to and control the situation, and (3) be innovative.[36]

Research has shown that a problem-solving approach is essential to successful cross-cultural negotiations, whether abroad or in the home office, although the approach works differently in various countries.[37] This problem-solving approach requires that a negotiator treats everyone with respect, avoids making anyone feel uncomfortable, and does not criticize or blame the other parties in a personal way that would make someone feel shame—that is, lose face.

Research by the Huthwaite Research Group reveals how successful negotiators, compared to average negotiators, manage the planning process and their face-to-face behavior. The group found that during the planning process, successful negotiators consider a wider range of options and pay greater attention to areas of common ground. Skillful negotiators also tend to make twice as many comments regarding long-term issues and are more likely to set upper and lower limits regarding specific points. In their face-to-face behavior, skillful negotiators make fewer irritating comments such as "we're making you a generous offer," make counterproposals less frequently, and use fewer reasons to back up arguments. In addition, skilled negotiators practice active listening: asking questions, clarifying their understanding of the issues, and summarizing the issues.[38]

COMPARATIVE MANAGEMENT IN FOCUS

Negotiating with the Chinese

When Westerners attempt business negotiations with representatives from the People's Republic of China, cultural barriers confront both sides. The negotiation process used by the Chinese—although there are variations among the Cantonese, Shanghainese, and northern Chinese—is dramatically different from that of Americans. For instance, the Chinese put much greater emphasis than Americans do on respect and friendship, on saving face, and on group goals.

Businesspeople report two major areas of conflict in negotiating with the Chinese—the amount of detail the Chinese want about product characteristics, and their apparent insincerity about reaching an agreement.[39] In addition, Chinese negotiators frequently have little authority, frustrating Americans who do have the authority and are ready to conclude a deal.[40] This situation arises because Chinese companies report to the government trade corporations, who are involved in the negotiations, often having a representative on the team. The goals of Chinese negotiators remain primarily within the framework of state planning and political ideals. Although China is tending to become more profit oriented, most deals are still negotiated within the confines of the state budget allocation for that project, rather than assessment of profitability or value. It is crucial, then, to find out which officials—national, provincial, local—have the power to make, and keep, a deal. According to James Broering of Arthur Andersen, who does much business in China, "companies have negotiated with government people for months, only to discover that they were dealing with the wrong people"[41]

Research shows that for the Chinese, the negotiation process is greatly affected by three cultural norms: their ingrained politeness and emotional restraint; their emphasis on social obligations; and their belief in the interconnection of work, family, and friendship.[42] Because of the Chinese preference for emotional restraint and saving face, aggressive or emotional attempts at persuasion in negotiation are likely to fail. Instead, the Chinese tendency to avoid open conflict will more likely result in negative strategies such as discontinuing or withdrawing from negotiation."[43] At the heart of this kind of response is the concept of **face**—a concept so important that it is essential for foreigners to understand it to recognize the role that face behavior plays in negotiations. There are two components of face—*lien* and *mientzu: Lien* refers to a person's moral character, the most important thing defining that person, without which one cannot function in society. It can be earned only by fulfilling obligations to others. *Mien-tzu* refers to one's reputation or prestige, earned through accomplishments, bureaucratic or political power.[44] Giving others one's time, gifts, or praise enhances one's own face. In negotiations, it is vital that you do not make it obvious that you have "won" because that means that the other party has "lost" and will lose face. To avoid this, token concessions and other attempts to show respect must be made, and modesty and control must be maintained; otherwise, anyone who feels he or she has "lost face" will not want to deal with you again. The Chinese will later ignore any dealings or incidents that caused them to lose face, maintaining the expected polite behavior out of social consciousness and concern for others. When faced with an embarrassing situation, they will typically smile or laugh in an attempt to save face, responses that are confusing to Western negotiators.[45]

The Chinese emphasis on social obligations underlies their strong orientation toward collective goals. Therefore, appeals to individual members of the Chinese negotiating team, rather than appeals to benefit the group as a whole, will probably backfire. The Confucian emphasis on the kinship system and the hierarchy of work, family, and friends explains the Chinese preference for doing business with familiar, trusted people and trusted companies. "Foreign" negotiators, then, should focus on establishing long-term, trusting relationships, even at the expense of some immediate returns.

Deeply ingrained in the Chinese culture is the importance of harmony for the smooth functioning of society. Harmony is based primarily on personal relationships, trust, and ritual. After the Chinese establish a cordial relationship with foreign negotiators, they use this relationship as a basis for the give-and-take of business discussions. This implicit cultural norm also accounts for the attitude of *guanxi,* which refers to the intricate, pervasive network of personal relations that every Chinese carefully cultivates; it is the primary means of accomplishing things and getting ahead.[46] In other words, *guanxi* establishes obligations to exchange favors in future business activities.[47] Even within the Chinese bureaucracy, *guanxi* prevails over legal interpretations.

Western managers should thus anticipate extended preliminary visiting (relationship building), in which the Chinese expect to learn more about them and their trustworthiness. The Chinese also use this opportunity to convey their own deeply held principles. The Chinese expect Western firms to sacrifice corporate goals and above average profits to Chinese national goals and principles, such as meaningful friendship, Chinese national development, and the growth and enhancement of the Chinese people. Misunderstandings occur when Americans show polite acceptance of these general principles without understanding their significance—because they do not have any obvious relationship to American corporate goals, such as profit. Nor do such principles seem relevant to practical decisions on plant locations, employee practices, or sourcing.[48]

Americans often experience two negotiation stages with the Chinese—the technical and the commercial. During the long technical stage, the Chinese want to hammer out every

detail of the proposed product specifications and technology. If there are two teams of negotiators, it may be several days before the commercial team is actually called in to deal with
aspects of production, marketing, pricing, and so forth. However, the commercial team
should sit in on the first stage to become familiar with the Chinese negotiating style.[49] The
Chinese negotiating team is usually about twice as large as the Western team; about a third of
the time is spent discussing technical specifications, a third is spent on price negotiations,
and a third on the other issues.[50]

The Chinese are among the toughest negotiators in the world—American managers must
anticipate various tactics, such as their delaying techniques and their avoidance of direct, specific answers: both ploys used to exploit the known impatience of Americans. The Chinese
frequently try to put pressure on Americans by "shaming" them, thereby implying that the
Americans are trying to renege on the friendship—the basis of the implicit contract. Whereas
Westerners come to negotiations with specific and segmented goals and find it easy to compromise, the Chinese are reluctant to negotiate details; they find it difficult to compromise
and trade because they have entered negotiations with a broader vision of achieving development goals for China, and they are offended when Westerners don't internalize those goals.[51]
Under these circumstances, the Chinese will adopt a rigid posture, and no agreement or contract is final until the negotiated activities have actually been completed.

Patience, respect, and experience are necessary prerequisites for anyone negotiating in
China. For the best outcomes, older, more experienced people are more acceptable to the
Chinese in cross-cultural negotiations. The Chinese want to deal with the top executive of an
American company, under the assumption that the highest officer has attained that position
by establishing close personal relationships and trust with colleagues and others outside the
organization. Americans tend to send specific technical personnel with experience on the task
at hand; therefore, they have to take care in selecting the most suitable negotiators. In addition, visiting negotiating teams should realize that the Chinese are probably negotiating with
other foreign teams, often at the same time, and will use that setup to play one company's
offer against the others. On an interpersonal level, Western negotiators must also realize that,
though a handshake is polite, physical contact is not acceptable in Chinese social behavior,
nor are personal discussion topics such as one's family. However, it is customary to take small
gifts as tokens of friendship. Pye offers the following additional tips to foreigners conducting
business with the Chinese:[52]

- Practice patience.
- Accept prolonged periods of stalemate.
- Refrain from exaggerated expectations and discount Chinese rhetoric about future
  prospects.
- Expect the Chinese will try to manipulate by shaming.
- Resist the temptation to believe that difficulties may have been caused by one's own mis-
  takes.
- Try to understand Chinese cultural traits, but realize that a foreigner cannot practice
  them better than the Chinese.

Managing Conflict Resolution

Much of the negotiation process is fraught with conflict—explicit or implicit, and such conflict can often lead to a standoff, or a lose–lose situation. This is regrettable, not only for the situation at hand, but because it probably will shut off future opportunities for deals between the parties. Much of the cause of such conflict can be found in cultural differences between the parties—in their expectations, in their behaviors, and particularly in their communication styles.

As discussed in Chapter 5, much of the difference in communication styles is attributable to whether you are part of a high-context or low-context culture (or somewhere in between—see Exhibit 5–6.) In low-context cultures such as that in the United States, conflict is handled directly and explicitly, and also is regarded as separate from the person negotiating—that is, the negotiators draw a distinction between the people involved and the information or opinions they are representing. They also tend to deal on the basis of factual information and logical analysis. That approach to conflict is called **instrumental oriented**.[53] In high-context cultures, such as in the Middle East, the approach to conflict is **expressive oriented**—that is, the situation is handled indirectly and implicitly, and there is no clear delineation of the situation from the person handling it. Those negotiators do not want to get in a confrontational situation because it is regarded as insulting and would cause a loss of "face," so they tend to use evasion and avoidance if they cannot reach agreement through emotional appeals. Their avoidance and inaction conflicts with the expectations of the low-context negotiators who are looking to move ahead with the business at hand and arrive at a solution.

The differences between high- and low-context cultures that often lead to conflict situations are summarized in Exhibit 6–9. As you can see, most of these variables were discussed

EXHIBIT 6–9

Sources of Conflict Between Low-Context and High-Context Cultures

Key Questions	Low-Context Conflict	High-Context Conflict
Why	Analytic, linear logic; instrumental oriented; dichotomy between conflict and conflict parties	Synthetic, spiral logic; expressive oriented; integration of conflict and conflict parties
When	Individualistic oriented; low collective normative expectations; violations of individual expectations create conflict potentials	Group oriented; high collective normative expectations; violations of collective expectations create conflict potentials
What	Revealment; direct, confrontational attitude; action and solution oriented	Concealment; indirect, nonconfrontational attitude; "face" and relationship oriented
How	Explicit communication codes; line-logic style: rational–factual rhetoric; open, direct strategies	Implicit communication codes; point-logic style: intuitive–effective rhetoric; ambiguous, indirect strategies

Source: W. Gudykunst, L. Stewart, and S. Ting-Toomey, *Communication, Culture, and Organizational Processes.* Copyright © 1985 by Sage Publicaitons, Inc. Reprinted by permission of Sage Publications, Inc.

earlier in this chapter or in Chapter 5 on communication. The reason for the overlap is that the subjects of culture and communication are really inseparable, and negotiation differences and conflict situations arise from variables in culture and communication.

The point here is, how can a manager from France, from Japan, or from Brazil, for example, manage conflict situations? The solution, as discussed before, lies mainly in your ability to know and understand the people and the situation you will face. Be prepared by developing an understanding of the cultural context in which you will be operating—what are the expectations of the persons you will be negotiating with? What kinds of communication styles and negotiating tactics should you expect, and how will they differ from your own? It is important to bear in mind your own expectations and negotiating style and to be aware of the other party's expectations about your behavior. Try to consider in advance what it will take to arrive at a win–win solution. Often it helps to use the services of a host-country adviser or mediator who may be able to help with early diffusion of a conflict situation.

Decision Making

Negotiation actually represents the outcome of a series of small and large decisions. The decisions include those made by each party before actual negotiations start—in determining, for example, the position of the company and what fallback proposals it may propose or accept. They also include incremental decisions, made during the negotiation process, on how to react and proceed, when to concede, and on what to agree or disagree. Negotiation can thus be seen as a series of explicit and implicit decisions, and the subjects of negotiation and decision making become interdependent.

For instance, sometimes just the way in which a decision is made during the negotiation process can have a profound influence on the outcome, as this example shows:

> In his first loan negotiation, a banker new to Japan met with seven top Japanese bankers who were seeking a substantial amount of money. After hearing their presentation, the American agreed on the spot. The seven Japanese then conferred among themselves and told the American they would get back to him in a couple of days as to whether they would accept his offer or not. The American banker learned a lesson he never forgot.[54]

The Japanese bankers expected the American to negotiate, to take time to think it over, and to consult with colleagues before giving the final decision. His immediate decision made them suspicious, so they decided to reconsider the deal.

There is no doubt that the speed and manner of decision making affects the negotiation process. In addition, how well negotiated agreements are implemented is affected by the speed and manner of decision making. In that regard, it is clear that the effective use of technology is playing an important role, especially when dealing with complex cross-border agreements in which the hundreds of decision makers involved are separated by time and space. This was the case in implementing DaimlerChrysler AG—the merger of Daimler-Benz AG of Germany and Chrysler Corp. of the United States—in the fall of 1998. (Details of the merger are covered in the Opening Profile for Chapter 8.) Juergen Schrempp (co-CEO with Robert Eaton of Chrysler), emphasized that maintaining momentum was crucial to the merger's success; how that was done is the focus of the accompanying Technology Application.

http://www.technology.com

TECHNOLOGY APPLICATION

Daimler's Stuttgart Command Post Speeds Cross-Border Decisions for Integration with Chrysler

Speed, speed, speed are crucial to the merger's success. Once you slow down, people often lose focus.
—Jüergen E. Schrempp, co-CEO, DaimlerChrysler

In order to maintain momentum and focus on top priorities to implement the DaimlerChrysler AG merger, the "war room" at the Daimler-Benz headquarters in Stuttgart, Germany, is being used to its fullest. Managers in Stuttgart are in constant communication with their counterparts at the Chrysler headquarters in Auburn Hills, Michigan, and also keep track of worldwide events.

The war room hums with state-of-the-art communications technology. Internal Daimler databases, as well as outside news feeds, are available continuously on a bank of six computer screens. A wireless keyboard and mouse can turn a big-screen TV into an oversize display terminal. Videoconference cameras and monitors stand nearby. Clocks around the wall show the time in various cities around the world. An "integration room" with space for 20 is down the hall. Using this, managers in Stuttgart can use video and data feed connections; they write on a giant white board, and their words or diagrams will appear on a computer screen in Auburn Hills. Within two minutes of walking in the room and turning on the lights, an executive can peer into Chrysler's integration room and chat with a counterpart. Frequent videoconferences are held by heads of strategy and planning departments, and by second- and third-tier managers also. Every Friday at 8 A.M. in Auburn Hills and 2 P.M. in Stuttgart, members of the integration team file into their respective integration rooms for a one-hour videoconference to review progress and set the agenda

for the next week. Talking across time zones blurs the concept of the working day; managers on both sides of the ocean end up talking to one another at all hours of the day and night in order to coordinate decisions. When they aren't talking, they are firing reams of data to DaimlerChrysler's Infobase, which keeps track of merger progress using the Lotus Notes software that both companies were already using at headquarters before the merger.

The co-CEOs, Schrempp and Eaton, as well as board members, can keep tabs on progress with a glance at their computers. Most of the initial integration efforts are focusing on finance and purchasing, as well as human resources and information technology; automotive operations will run essentially as they are for the time being. With 421,000 employees, manufacturing facilities in 34 countries, and sales in more than 200 countries, the integration functions so far planned are vast and complex. The status of the work on the 98 priority projects seen as crucial to the merger's success is highlighted with "traffic lights." Green means everything's on schedule; yellow signifies hangups; red means trouble. In addition, all the managers working on a project—whether in Germany or the United States—can tap into the system to see the status of their own projects and to keep informed about their colleagues' work and enter updates on their own activities. Mr. Schrempp felt these capabilities were crucial to the entire process, and would have been unworkable without the management software system.

Source: "DaimlerChrysler: Inside the Megamerger," *Wall Street Journal*, November 13, 1998; *www.businessweek.com*; "Daimler-Benz and Chrysler Plan to Run Main Operations Separately After Merger," *Wall Street Journal*, November 4, 1998; *www.Chrysler.com*; "The DaimlerChrysler Deal: Here Comes the Road Test," *Time*, May 18, 1998; "Gentlemen, Start your Engines," *Fortune*, June 8, 1998; *www.DaimlerChrysler.de*.

The role of decision making in management, however, goes far beyond the finite occasions of negotiations. It is part of the manager's daily routine—from operational-level, programmed decisions requiring minimal time and effort to those nonprogrammed decisions of far broader scope and importance, such as the decision to enter into a joint venture in a foreign country.

The Influence of Culture on Decision Making

It is crucial for international managers to understand the influence of culture on decision-making styles and processes.[55, 56] Culture affects decision making both through the broader context of the nation's institutional culture, which produces collective patterns of decision making, and through culturally based value systems that affect each individual decision maker's perception or interpretation of a situation.[57, 58, 59, 60]

The extent to which decision making is influenced by culture varies among countries. For example, Hitt, Tyler, and Park have found a "more culturally homogenizing influence on the Korean executives' cognitive models" than on those of U.S. executives, whose individualistic tendencies lead to different decision patterns.[61] The ways that culture influences an executive's decisions can be studied by looking at the variables involved in each stage of the rational **decision-making process**. These stages are (1) defining the problem, (2) gathering and analyzing relevant data, (3) considering alternative solutions, (4) deciding on the best solution, and (5) implementing the decision.

One of the major cultural variables affecting decision making is whether a country assumes an **objective approach** or a **subjective approach**. Whereas the Western approach is based on rationality (managers interpret a situation and consider alternative solutions based on objective information), this approach is not common throughout the world. Latin Americans, among others, are more subjective, basing decisions on emotions.

Another cultural variable that greatly influences the decision-making process is the **risk tolerance** of those making the decision. Research shows that people from Belgium, Germany, and Austria have a considerably lower tolerance for risk than people from Japan or the Netherlands—whereas American managers have the highest tolerance for risk.[62]

One important variable in the decision-making process is the manager's perception of the **locus of control** over outcomes—whether that locus is internal or external. Some managers feel that they can plan on certain outcomes because they are in control of events that will direct the future in the desired way. In contrast, other managers believe that such decisions are of no value because they have little control over the future—which lies in the hands of outside forces, such as fate, god, or nature. American managers believe strongly in self-determination and perceive problem situations as something that they can control and that they should change. However, managers in many other countries, Indonesia and Malaysia among them, are resigned to problem situations and do not feel that they can change them. Obviously, these different value systems will result in a great difference in the stages of consideration of alternative actions and choice of solution, often because certain situations may or may not be viewed as problems in the first place.

Another variable that affects the consideration of alternative solutions is how managers feel about staying with familiar solutions or trying new ones. Many managers, particularly those in Europe, value decisions based on past experiences and tend to emphasize quality. Americans, on the other hand, are more future oriented and look toward new ideas to get them there.

Approaches to Decision Making

In addition to affecting different stages of the decision-making process, value systems influence the overall approach of decision makers from various cultures. The relative level of **utilitarianism** versus **moral idealism** in any society affects its overall approach to problems. Generally speaking, utilitarianism strongly guides behavior in the Western world. In fact, research has shown that Canadian executives are more influenced by a short-term, cost–benefit approach to decision making than their Hong Kong counterparts. Canadian managers are considerably more utilitarian than leaders from the People's Republic of China, who approach problems from a standpoint of moral idealism; they consider the problems, alternatives, and solutions from a long-term, societal perspective rather than an individual perspective.[63]

Another important variable in companies' overall approach to decision making is that of autocratic versus participative leadership. In other words, who has the authority to make what kinds of decisions? A country's orientation—whether it is **individualistic** or **collectivist** (as discussed in Chapter 3)—influences the level at which decisions are made. In many countries with hierarchical cultures—Germany, Turkey, and India, among others—the authorization for action has to be passed upward through echelons of management before final decisions can be made. Most employees in these countries simply expect the autocrat, the boss, to do most of the decision making and would not be comfortable otherwise. Even in China, which is a highly collectivist society, employees expect **autocratic leadership** because their value system presupposes the superior to be automatically the most wise. In comparison, in Sweden, decision-making authority is very decentralized. Americans talk a lot about the advisability of such **participative leadership**, but in practice they are probably around the middle between autocratic and participative management styles.

Arab managers have long traditions of consultative decision making, supported by the Koran and the sayings of Muhammad. However, such consultation occurs more on a person-to-person basis than in group meetings, and thus diffuses potential opposition.[64] Although business in the Middle East tends to be transacted in a highly personalized manner, the final decisions are made by the top leaders, who feel that they must impose their will for the company to be successful.[65] In comparison, in cultures like Japan's that emphasize collective harmony, participatory or group decision making predominates, and consensus is important. The best-known example is the bottom-up (rather than top-down) decision-making process used in most Japanese companies, described in more detail in the following Comparative Management in Focus section.

As a summary, Exhibit 6–10 illustrates how all the variables just discussed can affect the steps in the decision-making process.

EXHIBIT 6–10

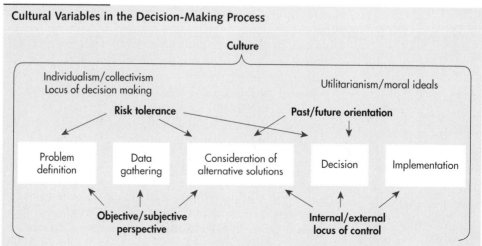

Cultural Variables in the Decision-Making Process

COMPARATIVE MANAGEMENT IN FOCUS

Decision Making in Japanese Companies

Japanese companies are involved in joint ventures throughout the world, especially with American companies. The GM–Toyota joint venture agreement process, for example, was the result of more than two years of negotiation and decision making. In this new company and in similar companies, Americans and Japanese are involved in decision making at all levels on a daily basis. The Japanese decision-making process greatly differs not only from the American process but from that of many other countries—especially at the higher levels of their organizations.

An understanding of the Japanese decision-making process—and indeed of many of their management practices—requires an understanding of their national culture. As previously discussed, much of the Japanese culture, and therefore the basis of Japanese working relationships, can be explained by the principle of *wa,* meaning "peace and harmony." This principle is one aspect of the value they attribute to *amae,* meaning "indulgent love," a concept probably originating in the Shinto religion, which focuses on spiritual and physical harmony. *Amae* results in *shinyo,* which refers to the mutual confidence, faith, and honor required for successful business relationships.[66] The principle of *wa* influences the work group, the basic building block of Japanese work and management. The Japanese identify strongly with their work groups, where the emphasis is on cooperation, participative management, consensus problem solving, and decision making based on a patient, long-term perspective. Open expression or conflict is discouraged, and it is of utmost importance to avoid embarrassment or shame—to lose face—as a result of not fulfilling one's obligations. These elements of work culture generally result in a devotion to work, a collective responsibility for decisions and actions, and a high degree of employee productivity. It is this culture of collectivism and shared responsibility that underlies the Japanese ringi system of decision making.

In the *ringi* system, the process works from the bottom up. Americans are used to a centralized system, where major decisions are made by upper-level managers in a top-down approach typical of individualistic societies. The Japanese process, however, is dispersed throughout the organization, relying on group consensus.

The *ringi* process is one of gaining approval on a proposal by circulating documents to those concerned throughout the company. It usually comprises four steps: proposal, circulation, approval, and record.[67] Usually, the person who originates the written proposal, which is called a *ringi-sho,* has already worked for some time to gain informal consensus and support for the proposal within the section and then from the department head.[68] The next step is to attain a general consensus in the company from those who would be involved in implementation. To this end, department meetings are held, and if necessary, expert opinion is sought. If more information is needed, the proposal goes back to the originator, who finds and adds the required data. In this way, much time and effort—and the input of many people—go into the proposal before it actually becomes formal.[69, 70]

Up to this point, the process has been an informal one to gain consensus, called the *nemawashi* process. Then the more formal authorization procedure begins, called the *ringi* process. The *ringi-sho* is passed up through successive layers of management for approval—the approval made official by seals. In the end, many such seals of approval are gathered, thereby ensuring collective agreement and responsibility and giving the proposal a greater chance of final approval by the president. The whole process is depicted in Exhibit 6–11.

EXHIBIT 6–11

Decision-Making Procedure in Japanese Companies

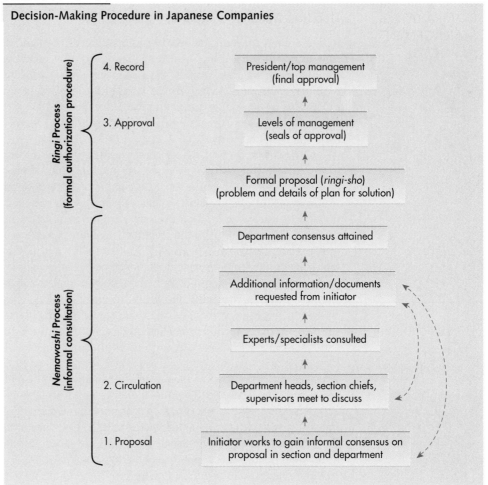

The *ringi* system is cumbersome and very time consuming prior to the implementation stage although implementation is facilitated because of the widespread awareness of and support for the proposal already gained throughout the organization. But its slow progress is problematic when decisions are time-sensitive. This process is the opposite of the top-down decisions made by Americans, which are made quite rapidly and without consultation, but which then take some time to implement because unforeseen practical or support problems often arise.

In addition, another interesting comparison is often made regarding the planning horizon (aimed at short- or long-term goals) in decision making between the American and

Japanese systems. The Japanese spend considerable time in the early stages of the process—defining the issue, considering what the issue is all about, and determining whether there is in fact a need for a decision. They are more likely than Americans to consider an issue in relation to the overall goals and strategy of the company. In this manner, they prudently look at the "big picture" and consider alternative solutions, instead of rushing into quick decisions for immediate solutions, as Americans tend to do.[71]

Of course, in a rapidly changing environment, quick decisions are often necessary—to respond to competitors' actions, a political uprising, and so forth—and it is in such contexts that the *ringi* system sometimes falls short because of its slow response rate. The system is, in fact, designed to manage continuity and to avoid uncertainty, which is considered a threat to group cohesiveness.[72]

Conclusion

It is clear that competitive positioning and long-term successful operations in a global market require a working knowledge of the decision-making and negotiating process of managers from different countries. These processes are complex and often interdependent. Although managers may make decisions that do not involve negotiating, they cannot negotiate without making decisions, however small, or they would not be negotiating. In addition, managers must understand the behavioral aspects of these processes to work effectively with people in other countries or with a culturally diverse workforce in their own country.

With an understanding of the environment and cultural context of international management as background, we move next in Part 3 to planning and implementing strategy for international operations.

Summary of Key Points

1. The ability to negotiate successfully is one of the most important skills in international business. Managers must prepare for certain cultural variables that influence negotiations, including the relative emphasis on task versus interpersonal relationships, the use of general principles versus specific details, the number of people present, and the extent of their influence.

2. The negotiation process typically progresses through the stages of preparation, relationship building, the exchange of task-related information, persuasion, and concessions and agreement. The process of building trusting relationships is a prerequisite to doing business in many parts of the world.

3. Culturally based differences in verbal and nonverbal negotiation behavior influence the negotiation process at every stage. Such tactics and actions include promises, threats, initial concessions, silent periods, interruptions, facial gazing, and touching; some parties resort to various dirty tricks.

4. The effective management of negotiation requires an understanding of the perspectives, values, and agenda of the other parties and the use of a problem-solving approach.
5. Decision making is an important part of the negotiation process as well as an integral part of a manager's daily routine. Culture affects the decision-making process both through a society's institutions and through individuals' risk tolerance, their objective versus subjective perspective, their perception of the locus of control, and their past versus future orientation.

Discussion Questions

1. Discuss the stages in the negotiation process and how culturally based value systems influence these stages. Specifically:
   • Explain the role and relative importance of relationship building in different countries.
   • Discuss the various styles and tactics that can be involved in exchanging task-related information.
   • Describe differences in culturally based styles of persuasion.
   • Discuss the kinds of concession strategies a negotiator might anticipate in various countries.
2. Discuss the relative use of nonverbal behaviors, such as silent periods, interruptions, facial gazing, and touching, by people from various cultural backgrounds. How does this behavior affect the negotiation process in a cross-cultural context?
3. Describe what you would expect in negotiations with the Chinese and how you would handle various situations.
4. What are some of the differences in risk tolerance around the world? What is the role of risk propensity in the decision-making process?
5. Explain how objective versus subjective perspectives influence the decision-making process. What role do you think this variable has played in all the negotiations and decisions between Iraq and the U.N.?
6. Explain differences in culturally based value systems relative to the amount of control a person feels he or she has over future outcomes. How does this belief influence the decision-making process?

Experiential Exercises

A. Multicultural Negotiations Exercise

Goal

To experience, identify, and appreciate the problems associated with negotiating with people of other cultures.

Instructions

1. Eight student volunteers will participate in the role play: four representing a Japanese automobile manufacturer and four representing an American team that has come to sell microchips and other components to the Japanese company. The remainder of the class will observe the negotiations.
2. The eight volunteers will divide up into the two groups and then separate into different rooms, if possible. At that point, they will be given instruction sheets. Neither team can have access to the other's instructions. After dividing up the roles, the teams should meet for 10 to 15 minutes to develop their negotiation strategies based on their instructions (from the instructor's manual).
3. While the teams are preparing, the room will be set up using a rectangular table with four seats on each side. The Japanese side will have three chairs at the table with one chair set up behind the three. The American side of the table will have four chairs side-by-side.

4. After the preparation time is over, the Japanese team will be brought in, so they may greet the Americans when they arrive. At this point, the Americans will be brought in and the role play begins. Time for the negotiations should be 20 to 30 minutes. The rest of the class will act as observers and will be expected to provide feedback during the discussion phase.

5. After the negotiations are completed, the student participants from both sides and the observers will complete their feedback questionnaires. Class discussion of the feedback questions will follow.

Feedback Questions for the Japanese Team

1. What was your biggest frustration during the negotiations?
2. What would you say the goal of the American team was?
3. How would you rate the success of each of the American team members in identifying your team's needs and appealing to them?
    Mr. Jones, Vice-President and Team Leader
    Mr./Mrs. Smith, Manufacturing Engineer
    Mr./Mrs. Nelson, Marketing Analyst
    Mr./Mrs. Frost, Account Executive
4. What would you say the goal of the Japanese team was?
5. What role (decider, influencer, and the like) did each member of the American team play?
    Mr. Jones
    Mr./Ms. Smith
    Mr./Mrs. Nelson
    Mr./Mrs. Frost
6. What strategy should the American team have taken?

Feedback Questions for the American Team

1. What was your biggest frustration during the negotiations?
2. What would you say the goal of the Japanese team was?
3. How would you rate the success of each of the American team members?
    Mr. Jones, Vice-President and Team Leader
    Mr./Mrs. Smith, Manufacturing Engineer
    Mr./Mrs. Nelson, Marketing Analyst
    Mr./Mrs. Frost, Account Executive
4. What would you say the goal of the American team was?
5. What role (decider, influencer, and the like) did each member of the Japanese team play?
    Mr. Ozaka
    Mr. Nishimuro
    Mr. Sheno
    Mr. Kawazaka
6. What strategy should the American team have taken?

Feedback Questions for the Observers

1. What was your biggest frustration during the negotiations?
2. What would you say the goal of the Japanese team was?
3. How would you rate the success of each of the American team members?
    Mr. Jones, Vice-President and Team Leader
    Mr./Mrs. Smith, Manufacturing Engineer

Mr./Mrs. Nelson, Marketing Analyst
Mr./Mrs. Frost, Account Executive
4. What would you say the goal of the American team was?
5. What role (decider, influencer, and the like) did each member of the Japanese team play?
   Mr. Ozaka
   Mr. Nishimuro
   Mr. Sheno
   Mr. Kawazaka
6. What strategy should the American team have taken?

B. Japanese Decision-Making Exercise

Time: Two class meetings

Goal

To allow students to experience the process and results of solving a problem or initiating a project using the Japanese decision processes of *nemawashi* and *ringi*.

Preparation

Review Chapters 5 and 6; study the Comparative Management in Focus section "Decision Making in Japanese Companies," in Chapter 6.

Introduction

The professor explains the exercise and designates or elicits two specific subjects or projects to be resolved by the class. These could be current problems on campus, for example. (One project may be used, but that would mean that half the class would be sitting around waiting during the first stage. Further, by using two projects, each group can experience being a primary group and also a secondary group.)

First Class—Nemawashi

Example for a class of 30
   Stage 1: Three groups of five students meet to draw up a plan to resolve issue No. 1. The other three groups of five meet to draw up a plan to resolve issue No. 2.
   Stage 2: Results for the two projects are switched to the other groups—secondary groups (*Kacho*). The *Kacho* discuss the plan suggested by the primary groups. They may request additional information from the primary groups.
   Stage 3: Groups or individuals may meet outside class as they wish to discuss their assigned project or problem before the second class meeting. Outside experts or sources may be consulted.

Second Class

Formal proposal—Ringi-sho—submitted for project one and project two. Each plan must be signed by all class members, representing a consensus decision. The professor discusses plans with the class to assess the feasibility and likelihood of approval by the university president. Any minor changes are resolved and approval indicated.

Feedback: Ask the class how effective they felt this process to be in their environment and culture. What problems did they encounter? What do they feel about the outcomes compared to other ways in which they would have approached those problems? Would they choose the same decision-making process for another project?

Source: Egidio A. Diodati, assistant professor of Management at Assumption College in Worcester, Massachusetts, in C. Harvey and M. J. Allard, *Understanding Diversity* (New York: HarperCollins Publishers, 1995). Used with permission.

Internet Resources

Visit the Deresky companion Web site at http://prenhall.com/Deresky for this chapter's Internet resources.

Case Study

Martinez Construction Company in Germany

(Martinez Construction & Konstruktion Dreizehn)

Juan Sanchez glanced out the window of the Boeing jetliner and admired the countryside passing below. The overcast skies failed to dampen his enthusiasm for the challenges and opportunities he and his company now faced. Two generations of local services had done little to prepare Martinez Construction for the coming days. Nevertheless, Juan remained confident that once the spirit of cooperation and trust was established, the new German operation would be a success.

Martinez Construction

Martinez Construction is a well-established construction company in eastern Spain. Founded in Barcelona in the mid–1940s, its reputation and quality of service ensured growing profits for decades. However, a recent decline in contracts has resulted in a growing awareness of the dependence the business has on local economic conditions.

Diego Martinez, president and son of the founder of Martinez Construction, now faces a growing certainty that the survival and continued growth of the family business depends upon expansion into the international marketplace. In Barcelona, Diego had met many German tourists. They seemed to enjoy the warm sunshine of Spain. He also knew that many German companies now conducted business in Spain. So, it was natural that when his company started thinking globally they were drawn to the new German states. The recent collapse of Communism and subsequent opening of new markets in eastern Europe provided what seemed like an excellent opportunity for expansion. After all, why shouldn't Martinez Construction take advantage of the cheap labor and raw materials?

More information was needed, however. Martinez Construction representatives contacted banks, commercial departments of foreign consulates, chambers of commerce, and the Treuhandanstalt's Investor Services department. They also depended on accountants, lawyers, consultants, and others to provide advice. After the initial research and discussion of the alternatives with other members of management, Diego has come to the conclusion that the best approach to this venture will be through the acquisition of an existing company from the Treuhandanstalt (THA). This decision was made after concluding that Martinez Construction lacked the resources necessary to risk a greenfield operation. Added to this was the certainty that an alliance with other German companies would not allow Martinez Construction to establish itself as a serious competitor in the international construction market.

Diego chose his brother-in-law and manager of the Barcelona branch of Martinez Construction, Juan Sanchez, to act as the negotiator for the company with the THA. Although Juan is unfamiliar with German business practices, Diego feels that Juan's friendly demeanor and expertise in the needs of the company will ensure the establishment of the necessary trust to build a strong cooperative venture with the THA.

Juan will be accompanied by Diego's nephew and projected manager of the new German acquisition, Miguel Martinez. Miguel is the youngest and most educated of the Martinez managerial staff. His background includes a business degree from a university in the United States, as well as years of employment in the family business. Although lacking in practical managerial experience, it was due largely to his influence that Diego saw the wisdom and necessity of expanding operations abroad. Miguel's opportunity has fueled his optimism despite the challenges he faces in the management of a foreign subsidiary.

Treuhandanstalt

Because of the collapse of Communism in the German Democratic Republic, the two Germanys were finally going to be reunified. The Treuhandanstalt, or THA, was for a short time the world's largest holding company. It was created in what was the German Democratic Republic. The sole purpose of the THA was to find private buyers for some 13,500 businesses and 15,000 parcels of real estate that had previously been owned by the German Democratic Republic. The government knew that the economy in this sector had to be stimulated quickly. There were hopes that many investors would take advantage of the new markets opening up. However, little thought was given to the immensity of the job. No guidelines were issued, which later led to charges of dubious deals, and limited funds were made available to run the agency.

Therefore, any firm wishing to purchase an existing facility in East Germany had no choice in the matter—they had to deal with the THA. The primary job of the THA was to sell the companies, to try to match existing companies with buyers. However, this proved to be an almost impossible task because the THA had insufficient or no information about the financial positions of the companies it was supposed to sell. In some cases, it could not ascertain what companies were to be sold.

The firms wishing to purchase properties through the THA were initially evaluated on the basis of financial soundness. Second, they were evaluated on potential employment opportunity. Next, they were measured according to the cost of restructuring to the buyer. The speed of the sale was, however, the most important issue to the THA. The sooner the THA finished its work, the sooner the economy would improve.

Price was the main aspect of the sales negotiations. Other facets of the negotiations involved guaranteeing jobs for present employees and arranging for the upgrade and improvement of the companies. This meant the investment of a great deal of time and money on the part of the buyer because many of the firms had fallen into disrepair. In fact, some were no longer operable in their present state.

Negotiations

The THA finally found what they considered to be a match for Martinez Construction. It was an existing construction firm, Konstruktion Dreizehn, located in Leipzig, Germany. (Leipzig is a city of about 564,000 people located in the eastern part of Germany.)

From the time of his arrival in Germany, Juan felt that he was having a difficult time just getting acquainted with the Germans. He felt pressured by the THA representatives. The Germans were all business. They didn't seem to have time to get to know Juan personally; rush and urgency to complete the sale was the focus of their approach.

The first meeting was scheduled for 9:00 A.M. Juan and Miguel arrived at 9:15. Juan noticed that the THA representative, Helga Schmidt, seemed quite agitated when they arrived. She didn't even offer them coffee. He wondered what had upset her so much.

When he suggested that they be taken on a tour of the city this morning instead of immediately starting the negotiations, he was reminded of the necessity of proceeding with the negotiations. Even though this displeased Juan, he agreed to start negotiations for the sale.

The Germans presented their proposal to Juan. He was amazed. Every detail was in this contract; and yet the THA had not yet ascertained the financial status and position of the construction firm in Leipzig. For this reason, Juan had expected some sort of flexible agreement. This was especially important since there was no way to determine the extent of future problems given the dearth of available financial analysis. Didn't the Germans know this? If the THA was to be trusted, why bother with this type of contract? He told the Germans exactly what his thoughts were on this subject.

Helga was clearly uncomfortable with Juan's emotional outburst. However, she did see his point and decided to compromise by offering a phased contract, which made Juan more comfortable with the situation. However, the Germans felt lost without the technicalities represented in the original contract.

The negotiations proceeded smoothly from this point. The final contract stated that in two years they would review the original price and recalculate it based on new and presumably more reliable data concerning the true value of the firm. Although there were problems with the negotiations, one thing did impress Juan about the Germans. He really appreciated the way the negotiations were organized. When there was a question, Helga always knew whom to contact. She also knew what forms, reports, and so on, needed to be sent to which department of the THA. Helga, on the other hand, was very uncomfortable with Juan's relaxed manner. However, she did value his genuineness and practicality.

Operations

Miguel Martinez arrived tired but excited in Leipzig. The flight provided ample time to consider his actions in the new German subsidiary. After spending a few days setting up household, Miguel met with the three-member management team sent the month before to begin studying the situation. It was the consensus of the team, and they quickly convinced Miguel, that human resources would be crucial to the recovery of the company. Under the GDR, the company employed approximately 350 workers. The THA had reduced the workforce to 100. Miguel and his team estimated that 50 employees would be sufficient. However, it was not long before they realized that East Germans did not work nearly as well as West Germans. Further confirmation of the effect of the workers' state on the employees was the lack of initiative and the concept of responsibility among the workers. Miguel was frustrated by the unwillingness of the employees to actively participate in the formulation of ideas and implementation of new procedures and policies. More than 40 years of Communism had taught employees to expect all guidance and solutions to come from the top.

Added to the lack of initiative was a fear and distrust of management. This fear was quickly justified when Miguel's new management team investigated a labor union's report criticizing the previous management's hiring practices and competence.

Six months after Miguel's triumphant arrival, his optimism was fading fast. He had just received the latest report concerning the company's financial position, and it was clear that the figures were far from what Martinez Construction had been led to believe. Strict environmental and employee protection regulations forced large investments in plant modifications. Further, there were other costly projects that had not been foreseen during the negotiation process. Cash flow problems were beginning to arise, and this threatened the very existence of the company.

Although reevaluation of the contract was specified after two years, Miguel wondered whether immediate action might be necessary. Sitting in his office overlooking the southern complex of the plant, the heavy rain clouds matched the darkness of his mood.

Appendix 1—A Comparison of Spanish and German Democratic Republic Work Styles
Appendix 2—Negotiating Styles of the Spanish and Germans

Source: Term project by Ann Eubanks and Derek Bonen Clark, graduate students at the State University of New York–Plattsburgh, Spring 1995. Copyright ©1995 by Helen Deresky. This case and the characters represented in it are fictional. The case is presented as a basis for educational discussion rather than to illustrate either effective or ineffective handling of an administrative situation.

Case Questions

1. What was the basis for Martinez Construction's decision to enter the international market? Proactive or reactive? Why?
2. Were the Spanish prepared for the problems faced in the negotiations? If not, what might the Spanish have done to better prepare themselves for the negotiations?
3. How did the Spanish interpret the actions of the Germans?
4. Do you think the Germans were aware of the cultural differences that came to the surface during the negotiations?
5. What might the Spanish have done differently to address the concerns of the employees?
6. What are the diverse problems created by the differences between the Spanish and German cultures? Communist and capitalist cultures?

Appendix 1

A Comparison of Spanish and German Democratic Republic Work Styles
Spanish

- Clear goals not common; work under assumption that goals of past will be goals of future
- Hierarchical society with status based on position; line of authority is top down
- Promotions usually determined by seniority
- Decisions influenced by human factors

German Democratic Republic

- Goals related to politics; what is good for state (society)
- Everyone is equal; however, superiors expected to provide all solutions
- Lifelong employment common; advancement decisions political
- Decisions influenced by what is good for society as a whole

Appendix 2

Negotiating Styles of the Spanish and Germans
Spanish

- Prefer to establish trust by taking time to get to know counterparts
- Don't attach importance to punctuality
- Discuss things at length

- Raise their voices and interrupt speakers during disagreements
- Make decisions based on general principles and leave details undecided

Germans

- Keep business and pleasure separate
- Stress the importance of punctuality
- State facts in a concise manner
- Reserved and formal during discussions
- Exhibit a strong concern for details and exacting contracts

Case Bibliography

This case is based in part on a company discussed in the referenced article by W. R. Frederick and Adolfo de la Fuente Rodriguez; those authors do not indicate the name of the company discussed nor whether it is real or fictional.

Ames, Helen Watley. *Spain is Different* (ME: Intercultural Press, Inc., 1992): 89–96.

Cote, Kevin. "Germany's White Elephant," *Fortune*, June 28, 1991.

Frederick, Richard W. and Adolfo de la Fuente Rodriguez. "A Spanish Acquisition in Eastern Germany: Culture Shock," *Journal of Management Development* 13, no. 2 (March 1994): 42–49.

Hampden-Turner, Charles. "The Boundaries of Business: The Cross-Cultural Quagmir," *Harvard Business Review* (September–October 1991).

Hofstede, G. *Cultures and Organization* (New York: McGraw Hill, 1991): 200–203.

Kanter, Rosabeth Moss. "Transcending Business Boundaries: 12,000 World Managers View Change," *Harvard Business Review* (May–June 1991): 151–164.

Kanter, Rosabeth Moss and Richard Ian Corn. "Do Cultural Differences Make a Business Difference?" *Journal of Management Development* 13, no. 2 (1993): 5–23.

Lacher, Michael A. "Creating and Securing Joint Ventures in Central and Eastern Europe: A Western Perspective," *Site Selection* (June 1994): 554–555.

Meschi, Pierre-Xavier and Alain Roger. "Cultural Context and Social Effectiveness in International Joint Ventures," *Management International Review* 34 (1994): 197–215.

Miller, Karen Lowery, Jeff Javetski, and Peggy Simson. "Europe: The Push East," *Business Week*, November 7, 1994.

Mueller, Franc. "Societal Effect, Organizational Effect, and Globalization," *Organizational Studies* 15, no. 3 (1994): 407–428.

Olie, Rene. "Shades of Culture and Institutions in International Mergers," *Organizational Studies* 15, no. 3 (1994): 381–405.

Torpey, John. "Growing Together, Coming Apart: German Society Since Unification," *Social Education* 57, no. 5, 236–239.

West, Judy F. and Judy C. Nixon. "Cultural Diversity Among American and European Business Persons," paper presented at the annual meeting of the Association of Business Communication International Conference, November 8, 1990.

"Farewell, Sweet Treuhand: Privatisation," *Economist,* 333, 7895 (December 1994): 82–85.

"Fast and Loose: East German Privatisation," *Economist,* 331, 7861, April 30, 1994, 75–76.

"Recognizing and Heeding Cultural Differences Can Be Key to International Business Success," compiled by staff, *Business America* (October 1994).

PART TWO

Comprehensive Cases

CASE 1

DELI ROCKWOOL CORP. IN THE PEOPLE'S REPUBLIC OF CHINA

Prior to President Nixon's historic visit to China and the signing of the Shanghai Communiques in February 1972, trade between the United States and the People's Republic of China (PRC) was negligible. For 1972, total trade between the two countries was only $95.9 million. The normalization of diplomatic and economic relations—and especially the passage by the U.S. Congress on January 24, 1980, of the U.S.–China Trade Agreement granting most-favored nation status to China—and the Chinese open-door policy since 1978 provided great momentum to the development of trade between the two countries. According to U.S. statistics, the bilateral trade reached $45 billion in 1994 making the U.S. China's third largest trading partner exceeded only by Hong Kong and Japan.

Since China, a country with documented history of 4,000 years, was closed to the outside world prior to 1972, it is a newcomer in the international business world. The Chinese way of doing business, though now changing gradually, has been greatly influenced by their country's culture, history, customs, values, and ethics, as well as the political and economic climate, management, and foreign trade administration systems. For nearly 30 years, since 1949, China and the United States had been isolated from each other, so the development of understanding and appreciation for the differences in culture, values, and customs is very helpful in developing business relationships between the two countries.

What follows is a delineation of an American firm's attempt to enter the Chinese market and create for itself a new path for growth after several years of stagnant sales. As is made clear in the case, doing business in the People's Republic of China is very different from doing business in the United States, and as one group of American businesspeople discovered, attempting to reach new horizons in the People's Republic of China can be quite challenging.

BACKGROUND

Shenyang Building Materials Corp. (hereafter referred to as the end user) was headquartered in Shenyang, a city in the northeast of China, and produced different types of building materials, such as bricks, concrete elements, and sanitary wares. It had 1,000 employees and sales of $7 million in 1989. Supported by the local government, and after a preliminary study, management wanted to go ahead with an investment in a rockwool production factory. The project proposal had been approved by the local economic and planning commissions. Since China's economy is centrally planned and foreign trade is monopolized by the government, the end user had no authority to import the machinery and technology directly to produce rockwool. (Rockwool, or mineral wool, is made by blowing a jet of steam through molten rock, such as limestone or siliceous rock, or through slag, and used chiefly for thermal and sound insulation. Fibrous glass is a mass of glass fibers resembling cotton batting or wool used especially for thermal insulation, or fabricated into various products such as acoustic tile or wallboards.)

Yanjing Building Materials Machinery and Technology Import & Export Corp. (hereafter called the buyer) was headquartered in Beijing. It was one of the organizations authorized by the Ministry of Foreign Economic Relation and Trade (MOFERT) to engage in trade with foreign countries. Yanjing Building Materials Machinery and Technology Import & Export Corp. specializes in the import and export of building materials machinery and technology, and is responsible for organizing and conducting the technical and commercial negotiations as well as the signing and execution of contracts on behalf of end users. The buyer sent inquiries to three different foreign suppliers for bidding: Deli in the United States, Toya in Japan, and Horri in Sweden. The preliminary technical discussions had been conducted during a visit by a Buyer delegation to the United States, Japan, and Sweden in January 1989. The commercial negotiations were scheduled to take place in Beijing from November 12 to December 23, 1989, with these three suppliers.

Shenyang is a major city in China with a population of five million. It is also well known for its heavy industry and building materials industries. Located in the northeast of China, the winter period is long, and the temperature can go as low as −30° F. With the rapid growth of the population, the local government worked out a massive construction program to ease the housing shortage problem. All the buildings were constructed with brick and concrete elements, without insulation, which caused a huge waste of heat energy. Considering the rich resources of feldspar, dolomite, and slag in the surrounding areas, the necessary raw materials for rockwool production, the government realized the demand from local and neighboring provinces for this product was potentially enormous. It had listed the development of the insulation industry as one of the priorities in the local development program.

Deli Rockwool Corp., headquartered in West Virginia, is the biggest company in the United States specializing in the design and delivery of rockwool machinery and production technology. The company was founded in 1967 and employs 500 people. Its worldwide sales in 1989 were $37.2 million (see Exhibit C1–1). It supplied more than 30 complete rockwool production lines all over the world except the PRC (see Exhibit C1–2). The sales distribution volume exhibit showed that Asia was an emerging area. The recent market research indicated that with the fast development of China's economy, there would be a huge demand for insulation material for the building construc-

EXHIBIT C1–2

Sales Volume Distribution (by percentage of sales)

	North America	South America	Europe	Asia
1986	52.4%	23.0%	14.8%	10.0%
1987	40.8%	15.0%	22.2%	22.0%
1988	40.7%	11.9%	19.8%	27.6%
1989	32.3%	13.0%	19.9%	34.8%

tion, insulation, and oil-refinery industries. However, China lacked the advanced technology and machinery to produce rockwool. Deli management had defined that as one of the firm's key objectives in entering this market. New strategies were to be developed to position the firm to capture the Chinese market in the future and stimulate the otherwise declining sales volumes and revenues of the company. Deli management was aware that the Japanese firm, Toya, and the Swedish company, Horri, Deli's main competitors in this industry, were simultaneously trying to enter the PRC.

In late 1989, the company received an inquiry from the buyer for a rockwool production line with an annual designed capacity of 15,000 tons. In January 1990, a Chinese delegation headed by Xin Xiaming arrived in America for a plant tour and detailed technical discussions. An exchange of information conducted by fax, telex, and the mail indicated encouraging progress. At the invitation of the buyer, Deli sent a team of four to China in December 1990, for formal commercial negotiations.

It was in the afternoon of December 16, 1990, when the Deli group arrived in Beijing airport. The group consisted of John Gross, vice president of the Marketing Department; Richard Wolf, chief engineer; Arthur Miller, a young lawyer; and Tony Shen. Shen, a recently hired marketing assistant, was born in China and later moved to the United States in 1978 after the Chinese Cultural Revolution. At the airport, the Deli group was met by Wang Hai, director of the Import Department, and Chen Ling, a young interpreter from Yanjiang Building Materials Import and Export Corp. Wang expressed his warmest welcome to the arriving Deli group, "Mr. Xin wants me to convey his apologies to you for not being able to pick you up at the airport because he is at a meeting with the Japanese Toya representatives. But he is looking forward to seeing you at a welcoming banquet this evening."

EXHIBIT C1–1

Sales and Profit

	Sales (million)	Profit (million)
1986	$41.3	$2.25
1987	$40.8	$2.22
1988	$38.4	$2.19
1989	$37.2	$2.17

PART TWO

Before their arrival, John Gross knew that Japanese Toya and Swedish Horri were also bidding for this project, but he did not expect the Chinese to arrange the negotiations with other potential suppliers simultaneously. Two years earlier, Gross had met Xin at an exhibition in Hanover, Germany, where they had become very interested in one another's business activities. In the preceding year, Gross had invited and sponsored the visit of Xin's delegation to Deli's rockwool manufacturing facilities and research center in West Virginia. Xin and his delegation were greatly impressed by Deli's state-of-the-art technology and grateful for the hospitality Gross extended to them. The two men developed a close relationship and expressed a strong mutual interest in developing China's rockwool insulation industry.

On the way to the hotel, Wang enthusiastically recalled the history of Beijing and noted the historical sites of the city, such as the Great Wall, Summer Palace, and Forbidden City. "It is your first time here, you must see the Wall. Do you know in China there is a saying 'You are not a hero unless you have climbed the Wall.'" The Deli group was amused by this expression. Half an hour later, they arrived at the Great Wall–Sheraton Hotel, a five-star hotel located in the eastern part of Beijing, not far from the American Embassy. Gross was surprised to find the hotel so typically American, and to learn that the hotel had built up a part of the Great Wall in its back yard. After check-in, Wang kindly escorted the Deli group to their rooms; within five minutes, their luggage arrived. Pleased by the good service, Gross took out three dollars to tip the bell boy, who said, "No thank you." Gross was obviously puzzled and embarrassed by his refusal and thought that perhaps the amount had been inadequate, until Wang Hai explained in a friendly way, "China is a socialist country. To serve guests is his duty. Tipping is not allowed here. He will be disgraced if he accepts your tip." After the Deli group had settled in, Wang wished them a good rest and said Xin would come to pick them up at 7 P.M. for the banquet.

WELCOMING BANQUET

Punctually at 7 P.M., Xin arrived at the hotel with a delegation of 15 Chinese, of whom Gross recognized two from the Shenyang Building Materials Corp. After shaking hands and exchanging greetings, Xin introduced each of them to the Deli group. They were officials from Shenyang Economic Commission; Shenyang Planning Commission; Bank of China; Shenyang Branch; and the mechanical, electrical, civil, and process engineers from the Shenyang Designing Institute. Since China was a socialist country characterized by central planning, the foreign trade system functioned as an integral part of the national and local economic planning mechanism. The end user had to initiate a project proposal and a feasibility study for approval by the local government authorities responsible for planning, executing, financing, and supervising the economic development program. They would evaluate the priority and feasibility of the proposed project according to the local development program and then grant or deny it accordingly.

A few minutes later, Xin drove the Deli group to a downtown restaurant famous for Chinese Cantonese delicacies. Entering the dining room, the Deli group were surprised to notice not only their place cards on the tables but also Maotai, wine, beer, and cold appetizers. According to a Chinese custom, Xin, the host, was seated facing north, with Gross seated opposite him. The remaining guests were interspersed among the Chinese. Following tea, tiny cups were filled up with Maotai, a premium drink in China containing 60 percent alcohol and normally used to entertain old friends or distinguished guests. To demonstrate the strength of the Maotai, Xin held a lighted match near his cup, and the Maotai immediately ignited. Gross thought to himself: "Good grief, this could fuel a car." Xin gave a welcoming speech expressing his warmest welcome to the Deli group on behalf of his company and lauding the friendship between the two countries. "I hope the negotiation will be conducted in a spirit of friendship and on the basis of mutual benefit and equality, and we wish the negotiations to be successful. Let's *Ganbei* (bottoms up)," Xin enthusiastically proposed. The Chinese applauded, rose, touched their cups with those of the Deli people, and emptied them. Encouraged by his warm words and sensing it was his turn to give a corresponding speech expressing his appreciation for their invitation to China and the excitement of seeing old and new Chinese friends at the banquet, Gross said: "We believe Deli has the best technology and machinery in the world and with all this and our best service, we will no doubt turn your plant into one of the best in the world." Following applause and bottoms up from the Chinese, the representatives from the Shenyang Economic Commission, the Shenyang Planning Commission, the Bank of China, the Designing Institute, and the end user proposed "*Ganbei*" in turn to the Deli group. Aware of Maotai's 60 percent alcohol content, the Deli people tried to drink wine instead but the Chinese, in a friendly manner, refused to allow the substitution. After the fifth course of food and numerous *Ganbeis*, Gross felt he'd had enough; out of curiosity he picked up the menu and to his surprise found seven more courses listed, including dog's meat, duck's paw, and snake soup. He carefully asked Xin whether these were normal Cantonese fare. Xin smiled, replied affirmatively, and to everyone's amusement, explained the varieties of Chinese foods in different regions: "I think the Cantonese food tastes best. The dog's meat is very good during the winter as it produces more heat than any other meat. Have you heard such a saying: 'Cantonese eat all flying animals except airplanes and all climbing animals except a table'?" The Deli team were very impressed by the rich variety of Chinese delicacies. After the seventh course, the food on the plates before the Deli group grew mountainous, but the Chinese continued to urge "Qiang, Qiang," ("please eat more, more, please"). Because it seemed impolite to stop eating and drinking while the Chinese continued to enjoy the meal, the Deli representatives tried to follow the protocol and tasted a bit of every course. The banquet ended with fruit, after which Gross thanked Xin for his kind invitation and most delicious food. To his surprise, Xin replied humbly, "No, no, it is only a simple dinner, hope you don't mind." Gross noticed that the two tables were still laden with unfinished delicacies. He felt confused. "This much food would feed my family for a week," he muttered to himself.

TECHNICAL MEETING

The next day, a meeting was scheduled at the buyer's headquarters. Xin greeted the Deli group at the entrance. Entering the room, the Deli group was surprised to find the flags of both countries on the table. The Chinese arranged themselves on one side of the table while the Deli group was seated opposite them. After tea, Xin proposed the initiation of the meeting. Since he had other important things to attend to, he stated that he could not participate in every meeting but authorized Wang to handle the negotiations. After shaking hands with the Deli people, he left the conference room.

Deli's technology was new to many of the Chinese present, so Wang suggested Deli give a technical presentation. Richard Wolf, Deli's chief engineer, started the presentation, which covered raw materials preparation, feeding, melting, spinning, curing, forming, and packaging. He emphasized the advantages of Deli's melting and spinning technology, and told them how this technology could benefit the end user in terms of raw materials consumption and labor costs in the long run.

Apparently owing to her lack of technical background, the interpreter had difficulty translating the terms used to explain the process and the machinery. She consulted the dictionary or asked Wolf to repeat the technical terms many times. The questions asked by the Chinese engineers also revealed her inadequate translation. The presentation proceeded slowly. Gross started worrying: "What can we do? It is just a start. The tough part comes later. How can the poor girl handle the translation of commercial and legal jargon later on? How can the ideas of both parties be communicated correctly?" During the break, Gross asked Tony Shen whether he could act as translator. Shen said he thought this would not only embarrass Wang but also cause the girl to lose face. Besides, seldom did the Chinese use or trust a foreign interpreter; they always relied on the translation of their own interpreter. "Then what proposal can I make to carry on the negotiation smoothly so as not to embarrass or offend the Chinese?" Gross asked himself.

FIRST ROUND: PRICE NEGOTIATIONS

The negotiations continued in the afternoon and immediately turned to the most sensitive issue—the price. To the surprise of every Deli team member, they found the competitors' quotations on the table before the Chinese negotiators. Wang Hai pointed out that according to Chinese trade practice, quotations from different suppliers shall be fully compared before signing a contract. "The Swedish and Japanese suppliers have agreed to reduce their prices by 20 percent and 15 percent, respectively. We have reviewed Deli's prices and found them on the high side, and the technology transfer fee is unreasonable and especially overvalued. You have already recovered your development costs in your previous machinery and product sales, and we think the technology transfer fee is far greater than is justified. It is unfair that Deli wishes to charge us for both the machinery and technology. We hope Deli can reduce the prices to a competitive level," Wang Hai remarked. Gross endeavored to explain Western business practices and how his company had been investing money for the research and development of new technology. "The technology and machinery offered in the quotation represents the latest innovations and would greatly reduce the end user's labor and use of raw materials and thereby reduce production costs. That is why our fee is different from others, and it would be valued at this level on the world market." The Chinese seemed passive and unenthusiastic. They argued that labor and raw materials were not their major concerns since these were both local and cheap. What concerned them most was that Deli's prices greatly exceeded the end user's approved foreign currency budget.

They explained the difficulties that they would have in applying for any additional hard foreign currency, and that it might take up to six months to get this application approved. If Deli could not reduce its prices to their budget level, they would have to buy from another source. Gross was disappointed not only that the Chinese didn't evaluate the technology in terms of economic efficiency and the benefits it would bring to them in the long run, but also by the Chinese bureaucracy and the red tape necessary to get additional funds approved. The discussion continued for another hour, during which time Gross learned the project had only a $4.2 million foreign currency budget. "We hope you will reconsider the price and quote a more favorable one. Since we will have a meeting with the Japanese supplier tomorrow morning, we have arranged for you to visit the Great Wall and Ming Tombs, and our interpreter will accompany you. Our negotiations are scheduled for the day after tomorrow," Wang said. Gross felt unhappy with this arrangement since his group was here for business and not sightseeing. He was frustrated over the absence of a time schedule; the Chinese had not yet discussed the time frame for the negotiations; his team had to leave China on December 23 to be home for the Christmas holidays.

Back at the hotel, Arthur Miller expressed his worry that since there were almost no commercial secrets in China, the price was virtually "transparent." He doubted whether the Chinese side would keep their contract commitment to protect Deli's technology. Since China had neither the laws nor the regulations to protect industrial properties, nor was it a member of the Convention for the Protection of Industrial Property, "Paris Convention," he pondered what remedies Deli could seek if the Chinese violated the confidentiality clause. If the Chinese copied the technology, not only would Deli's long-term strategy in this market go unrealized, but also all its effort to enter the PRC would come to nothing. Shen told Gross he shared this view, but at the same time the Chinese negotiators regarded a price concession from them as a face-giving act and an indication of Deli's willingness to continue cooperating on this project. A price concession from Deli would be necessary, he said.

SIGHTSEEING TOUR

The Chinese had arranged for the Deli group to visit Baidaling, the best preserved part of the Great Wall and the Ming Tombs. Because they were located to the northwest of Beijing, about 75 kilometers away from the hotel, the trip started early in the morning. On the way to the Wall, the interpreter proudly lectured on the history of the Wall: "The

Great Wall is more than 10,000 *li* (1 kilometer for 2 *lis*) long, and it is one of the few man-made objects that can be observed from the moon." The Wall turns and twists on the mountain ridges, and it has a magnificent view. It is difficult to imagine how the ancient Chinese built it during a time when there were neither modern transportation facilities nor lifting devices. At the foot of the Wall their young interpreter kindly bought each Deli member a certificate proclaiming that they had climbed the Wall. "All of you are heroes now," she laughed. The Deli people were pleased with this interesting certificate.

SECOND ROUND: PRICE NEGOTIATION

Both parties returned to the negotiation table the next morning. After asking Gross about his team's visit to the Wall, Wang immediately turned to the price issue. The room became silent. Obviously, the Chinese were expecting new prices from Gross. Gross proposed a 3 percent reduction on the machinery and 5 percent on the technology, and gave Wang a copy of the new quotation, as shown in Exhibit C1–3, including seaworthy packing. The quotation was valid until February 20, 1991.

To his dismay, the Chinese very quietly studied his new quotation and then responded, "We appreciate your price cuts, but they are still far higher than we expected. For your information, your Japanese competitor agreed to further reduce its price yesterday. To be very honest with you, you are in a disadvantageous position; please reconsider your price. We should solve this issue before we proceed on the contract negotiations. Let's have a break."

Gross was afraid that if he gave the Chinese a new quotation that day, the Chinese might use the concessions won from him to wrest further concessions from the Japanese supplier and then use the Japanese concessions to

EXHIBIT C1–3

Machinery	$3,900,000
Technology transfer	$280,000
Installation and erection	$270,000
Training	$100,000
Spare parts for 2 years	$250,000
	$4,800,000 FOB New York Port, USA

bargain with him again the next day. He was also afraid that if the negotiations continued in this way, it would become a time-consuming and wearying marathon. His team might still be sitting there at Christmas. He also started wondering whether the Chinese were really intending to buy his technology and machinery or simply using Deli to get a better deal from his competitor. The meeting was adjourned for half an hour. To break this deadlock and give the Chinese face to move on with negotiations, Gross promised to try his best to help Wang with the price, but because the final price would depend very much on the payment terms and other contract terms, he suggested both parties continue the negotiations. Wang exchanged his views with his group and then replied, "We will study your proposal; let's meet in the afternoon." Gross noticed the Chinese wished to avoid direct confrontation with him and wanted to solicit comments from their superiors.

CHINESE CONTRACT VERSUS AMERICAN CONTRACT

The negotiations continued in the afternoon. Before the negotiations started, Wang gave Gross and Miller each a Chinese contract form, saying, "Our leader has agreed to your proposal, so let's start discussing the contract terms. This is our standard commercial contract form." Skimming the document quickly, Miller found the form to be exactly the same as the one he had seen three years previously. "But your standard is too simple and outdated and does not incorporate any of the needed adaptations and changes in it. Besides, there are many ambiguities in it. For example, the rights and obligations are too general and uncertain for the guarantee of the acceptance test, your arbitration clause, letter of credit, and remedy for a breach of the contract must be renegotiated. This contract cannot be used for our project. I have prepared the contract from our side, and we can negotiate on this form." Miller then gave Wang two copies of his contract draft. But the Chinese were very adamant and refused to accept Deli's contract form. "I am sorry, our contract form is not negotiable, otherwise our relevant authorities will not approve it. We have signed many agreements on this form. If you have any objection to some terms, we can negotiate these later on," said Wang.

Because the contract form was an important issue, Miller didn't give up, but attempted, by asking questions, to elicit the Chinese reasoning behind their position, and intended to persuade the Chinese to change their minds. To his disappointment, Wang continually repeated the same statement, yet remained unwilling to elucidate the issue. Gross and Miller observed that the Chinese were obviously sensitive about the contract form. Later on, they learned that since the Chinese negotiators were unfamiliar with the U.S. legal system and laws, they were afraid they might be given unfavorable terms or taken advantage of if they accepted a foreign contract. The signed contract was subject to reviews by the government, so Chinese negotiators were afraid that a foreign contract form would not meet approval by the authorities. They would normally firmly insist on using their own standard contract form even though the form didn't incorporate necessary adaptations or changes to reflect the rights and obligations of both parties.

IRREVOCABLE LETTER OF CREDIT VERSUS CONFIRMED IRREVOCABLE LETTER OF CREDIT

Miller was uncertain of China's political stability and its continuing foreign trade policy; he had read recently in a U.S. newspaper that some Chinese companies delayed payments because of the shortage of hard currency. He proposed that the irrevocable letter of credit issued by the Bank of China should be confirmed by a third designated bank. Miller explained how this type of letter of credit worked in the Western countries and tried to convince the Chinese to accept it. Wang politely rejected the proposal: "According to our rules, the confirmed letter of credit is not applicable in China. The Bank of China is owned by our government and, of course, its financial standing can't be questioned. Our bank, unlike the banks in capitalist countries, will not go bankrupt. We have never issued this kind of letter of credit."

Miller was surprised by the different trade practices in China. The Chinese cited undocumented internal rules and regulations that contradicted international business practice. In the United States, parties to a contract were bound only by published laws and regulations to which they had access prior to their decisions. He also found that Chinese organizations had much less independent decision-making power than Western organizations and that many of their decisions would be subject to time-consuming government approvals.

GUARANTEE

At this point, the negotiations shifted to the next topic: the guarantee. The Chinese asked for assurances that Deli would guarantee to do everything possible to ensure that the final product would meet the contract specifications even if repeated and time-consuming tests involving the presence of Deli's technicians in China were required. Miller observed that the guarantee clause the Chinese proposed was too general, and the language used too vague and ambiguous. He demanded specificity concerning the rights and obligations under the guarantee; otherwise, the clause would put Deli under a continuing and vague obligation to repair a bad situation. Such language could serve as a basis for the Chinese to make a claim even though the unsatisfactory products might have resulted from the failure of the Chinese to follow technical instructions carefully, or insufficient supply of power and appropriate raw materials for test runs. "Yes, of course, we will be responsible for our deficiencies from our side, but Deli should be responsible for its faults," Wang said emphatically. "Deli must provide the best machinery and technology as stipulated in the contract to produce the contract products." Obviously, the Chinese misunderstood Miller's position and perceived it as an attempt from Deli's side to avoid any responsibility for quality control. Shen explained to Miller and Gross that given the high costs of failure and limited reward for success in the Chinese system, the Chinese negotiators were generally reluctant to assume what would be seen as normal entrepreneurial risks in the West. So during the contract negotiations, the Chinese emphasized the need for positive outcomes of the project and tried to make the foreign supplier assume most of the risks inherent in the venture, as well as take responsibility as the sole guarantor of the technology.

DISCUSSION AND ARBITRATION VERSUS LITIGATION

The negotiations proceeded to a solution of disputes. On the fourth day, Miller suggested that all disputes or claims relating to this contract should be settled through litigation, but his proposal was immediately declined by the Chinese. Wang insisted that all disputes should be settled through friendly discussion and reconciliation. In case no settlement was reached, the case should be submitted to the China Council for Promotion of International Trade for arbitration in Beijing.

Afraid that the Chinese arbitration organization might act partially or wholly in favor of their own side, Miller proposed a third party, such as the Stockholm Commercial Chamber for arbitration. After a quick exchange with his colleagues, Wang agreed. "We prefer arbitration. No matter what happens, we can always sit down and solve the disputes through friendly discussion or reconciliation. Between friends, everything can be negotiated." Gross noticed that the Chinese were exceptionally cautious with every position and proposal Miller made. He was puzzled by this. Shen explained that the Chinese stressed ethical

and moral obligations rather than legal obligations. The Chinese traditionally and culturally distrusted lawyers, whom they called troublemakers or pettifoggers. They opposed litigation—a face-losing and humiliating act—and were of the opinion that discussion and negotiation could save face for both parties, maintain their self-respect, and preserve the friendship between the two sides. They were reluctant to consider the possibility of a breakdown in the relationship.

ALTERNATIVES

It was already December 21. After four days of negotiations, both groups had gone through most of the contract terms, but the resolution of the pricing issue was still pending. When Gross asked Shen whether "the Chinese were using a stalling tactic to get the best out of us?" Shen suggested, "Since the Chinese place a great deal of importance on personal relationships (guanxi) and you have a good relationship with Mr. Xin, why don't you invite Mr. Xin and Mr. Wang to dinner and settle the price problem face to face across the table?" Gross appreciated his suggestion; he had learned before he came to China that guanxi was a prevalent culture phenomenon, and that it was essential to establish and cultivate guanxi to get business accomplished.

At 7 P.M., Xin and Wang and the interpreter punctually arrived at the hotel. Over dinner, Gross turned the conversation to the price issue. Xin said he had been aware of the progress of negotiations and appreciated Gross's and his team's sincere efforts in the previous days. "Though we admit to some extent your technology is better than the Japanese, their prices are much lower. For your information, the end user has only $3 million for this project, but the Japanese agreed to further reduce their prices below the budget level. China is huge, and the potential market is very big. This project is very important both to you and your competitors. In China, there is a saying: 'Less profits, more projects.' I hope through this project Deli can build up a good reputation in China and our two companies can develop a long-term cooperative relationship. As we are old friends, and as long as you can reduce your prices to our budget level, I will try to persuade the end user to order the machinery and technology from you. The president of the end user was my classmate in high school, and we have a very close relationship."

Gross realized Xin was doing him a favor by giving face and wondered, "What face can I give to him in return? What concession can I make from my side?" To reduce the price to their budget level would mean a negative profit margin for the company; to insist on the present prices would most probably cause him to lose the project to his competitor and eventually let the Japanese establish the first foothold in the Chinese market. Should they go back and wait until the end user's budget had increased even though that would take months or longer? Should he suggest that the Chinese buy the key machinery instead of the whole line in order to meet the budget? But Deli's reputation in this market would be at risk if the machinery from the Chinese failed to perform well with U.S. machinery.

Gross recalled the high hopes everyone at Deli had had for the Chinese project. In a way, the future of the firm seemed to be riding on this deal: Deli's plans called for dominating the market in China. Were those plans sound in the first place, or unrealistic? Should the company sacrifice immediate gain for future growth, or go home and forget the whole thing? Gross found himself in a dilemma. "Doing business in China is more difficult than building the Great Wall!" he murmured under his breath.

Source: This case was prepared by James A. Brunner and Mao Jianhua of The University of Toledo as the basis for class discussion concerning the effects of Chinese customs and negotiation styles upon negotiations for a commercial contract. Used with permission of James A. Brunner. Copyright ©1995 by Brunner.

CASE QUESTIONS

1. Was John Smith's approach correct in his negotiations with the Chinese? If so, how can you explain that the negotiations lasted longer than he expected and the agreement had not been concluded this time?
2. What are some of the fundamental cultural perceptions that separate the Americans from the Chinese and that have contributed to this breakdown?
3. What are some of the distinctive aspects of the Chinese style of negotiating that should have been understood by the American negotiators?
4. What is the significance of the Chinese concepts of face and guanxi, and how do they influence the Chinese in their approach to negotiation?
5. Compare the American and Chinese perceptions on basic cultural values and concepts.
6. What alternatives does John Smith have for dealing with the Chinese? Do you feel that he should endeavor to continue negotiations with the Chinese or shift his attention to other foreign ventures? What other alternatives could be considered?

CASE 2

MOTO: COMING TO AMERICA

Moto arrived in Chicago in the middle of winter, unprepared for the raw wind that swept off the lake. The first day he bought a new coat and fur-lined boots. He was cheered by a helpful salesgirl who smiled as she packed his lined raincoat into a box. Americans were nice, Moto decided. He was not worried about his assignment in America. The land had been purchased, and Moto's responsibility was to hire a contracting company and check on the pricing details. The job seemed straightforward.

Moto's firm, KKD, an auto parts supplier, had spent 1 ½ years researching American building contractors. Allmack had the best record in terms of timely delivery and liaisons with good architects and the best suppliers of raw materials. That night Moto called Mr. Crowell of Allmack, who confirmed the appointment for the next morning. His tone was amiable.

Moto arrived at the Allmack office at nine sharp. He had brought a set of kokeshi dolls for Crowell. The dolls, which his wife had spent a good part of a day picking out, were made from a special maple in the mountains near his family home in Niigata. He would explain that to Crowell later, when they knew each other. Crowell also came from a hilly, snowy place, which was called Vermont.

When the secretary ushered him in, Crowell stood immediately and rounded the desk with an outstretched hand. Squeezing Moto's hand, he roared, "How are you? Long trip from Tokyo. Please sit down, please."

Moto smiled. He reached in his jacket for his card. By the time he presented it, Crowell was back on the other side of the desk. "My card," Moto said seriously.

"Yes, yes," Crowell answered. He put Moto's card in his pocket without a glance.

Moto stared at the floor. This couldn't be happening, he thought. Everything was on that card: KKD, Moto, Michio, Project Director KKD meant University of Tokyo and years of hard work to earn a high recommendation from Dr. Iwasa's laboratory. Crowell had simply put it away.

"Here." Crowell handed his card.

"Oh, John Crowell, Allmack, President," Moto read aloud, slowly trying to recover his equilibrium. "Allmack is famous in Japan."

"You know me," Crowell replied and grinned. "All those faxes. Pleased to meet you, Moto. I have a good feeling about this deal."

Moto smiled and lay Crowell's card on the table in front of him.

"KKD is pleased to do business with Allmack," Moto spoke slowly. He was proud of his English. Not only had he been a top English student in high school and university, but he had also studied English in a *juku* (an afterschool class) for five years. As soon as he received this assignment, he took an intensive six-week course taught by Ms. Black, an American, who also instructed him in American history and customs.

Crowell looked impatient. Moto tried to think of Ms. Black's etiquette lessons as he continued talking about KKD and Allmack's history. "We are the best in the business," Crowell interrupted. "Ask anyone. We build the biggest and best shopping malls in the country."

Moto hesitated. He knew Allmack's record—that's why he was in the room. Surely Crowell knew that. The box of *kokeshi* dolls pressed against his knees. Maybe he should give the gift now. No, he thought, Crowell was still talking about Allmack's achievements. Now Crowell had switched to his own achievements. Moto felt desperate.

"You'll have to come to my house," Crowell continued. "I live in a fantastic house. I had an architect from California build it. He builds for all the stars, and for me." Crowell chuckled. "Built it for my wife. She's the best wife, the very best. I call her my little sweetheart. Gave the wife the house on her birthday. Took her right up to the front door and carried her inside."

Moto shifted his weight. Perhaps if he were quiet, Crowell would change the subject. Then they could pretend the conversation never happened. "Moto-san, what's your first name? Here, we like to be on a first-name basis."

"Michio," Moto whispered.

"Michio-san, you won't get a better price than from me. You can go down the block to Zimmer or Casey, but you got the best deal right here."

"I brought you a present," Moto said, handing him the box of *kokeshi* dolls.

"Thanks," Crowell answered. He looked genuinely pleased as he tore open the paper. Moto looked away while Crowell picked up a *kokeshi* doll in each hand. "They look like Russian dolls. Hey, thanks a lot, my daughter will love them."

Moto pretended that he hadn't heard. I'll help by ignoring him, Moto thought, deeply embarrassed.

Crowell pushed the *kokeshi* dolls aside and pressed a buzzer. "Send George in," he said.

The door opened and a tall, heavyset man with a dark crew cut stepped inside the room.

"George Kubushevsky, this is Moto-san. Michio . . ."

"How do you do?" Kubushevsky's handshake was firm. Moto took out his card.

"Thanks," Kubushevsky said. "Never carry those." He laughed and hooked his thumbs in his belt buckle. Moto nodded. He was curious. Kubushevsky must be a Jewish name—or was it Polish, or maybe even German? In Japan he'd read books about all three groups. He looked at Kubushevsky's bone structure. It was impossible to tell. He was too fat.

"George, make sure you show Michio everything. We want him to see all the suppliers, meet the right people, you understand?"

"Sure." George grinned and left the room.

Moto turned to Crowell. "Is he a real American?" Moto asked.

"A real American? What's that?"

Moto flushed. "Is he first generation?" Moto finished lamely. He remembered reading that Jews, Lebanese, and Armenians were often first generation.

"How do I know? He's just Kubushevsky."

During the next few weeks Moto saw a great deal of Kubushevsky. Each morning he was picked up at nine and taken to a round of suppliers. Kubushevsky gave him a rundown on each supplier before they met. He was amiable and polite, but never really intimate. Moto's response was also to be polite. Once he suggested that they go drinking after work, but Kubushevsky flatly refused, saying that he had to work early the next morning. Moto sighed, remembering briefly his favorite bar and his favorite hostess in Tokyo. Yuko-san must be nearly fifty now, he thought affectionately. She could make him laugh. He wished he were barhopping with his colleagues from his *ringi* group at KKD. Moto regretted that he had not brought more *kokeshi* dolls, since Kubushevsky had not seemed delighted with the present of the KKD pen.

One morning they were driving to a cement outlet.

"George."

"Yes, Michio-san."

Moto paused. He still found it difficult to call Kubushevsky by his first name. "Do you think I could have some papers?"

"What kind of papers?" Kubushevsky's voice was friendly. Unlike Crowell, he kept an even tone. Moto liked that. "I need papers on the past sales of these people."

"We're the best."

"I need records for the past five years on the cement place we are going to visit."

"I told you, Michio-san, I'm taking you to the best! What do you want?"

"I need some records."

"Trust me, I know what I'm doing."

Moto was silent. He didn't know what to say. What did trust have to do with anything? His *ringi* group in Tokyo needed documentation so they could discuss the issues and be involved in the decision. If the decision to go with one supplier or the other was correct, that should be reflected in the figures.

"Just look at what's going on now," George said. "Charts for the last five years, that's history."

Moto remained silent. George pressed his foot to the gas. The car passed one truck, and then another. Moto looked nervously at the climbing speedometer. Suddenly Kubushevsky whistled and released his foot. "All right, Michio-san, I'll get you the damned figures."

"Thanks," Moto said softly.

"After we see the cement people, let's go for a drink."

. . .

Moto looked uneasily at the soft red light bulb that lit the bar. He sipped his beer and ate a few peanuts. Kubushevsky was staring at a tall blonde at the other end of the bar. She seemed to notice him also. Her fingers moved across the rim of the glass.

"George," Moto said gently. "Where are you from, George."

"Here and there," Kubushevsky said idly, still eyeing the blonde.

Moto laughed. "Here and there."

Kubushevsky nodded. "Here and there," he repeated.

"You Americans," Moto said. "You must have a home."

"No home, Michio-san."

The blonde slid her drink down the bar and slipped into the next seat. Kubushevsky turned more toward her.

Moto felt desperate. Last week Crowell had also acted rudely. When Imai, KKD's vice president, was visiting from Japan, Crowell had dropped them both off at a golf course. What was the point?

He drained his beer. Immediately the familiar warmth of the alcohol made him buoyant. "George," he said intimately. "You need a wife. You need a wife like Crowell has."

Kubushevsky turned slowly on his seat. He stared hard at Moto. "You need a muzzle," he said quietly.

"You need a wife," Moto repeated. He had Kubushevsky's full attention now. He poured Kubushevsky another beer. "Drink," he commanded.

Kubushevsky drank. In fact they both drank. Then suddenly Kubushevsky's voice changed. He put his arm around Moto and purred in his ear. "Let me tell you a secret, Moto-san. Crowell's wife is a dog. Crowell is a dog. I'm going to leave Allmack, just as soon as possible. Want to join me, Michio-san?"

Moto's insides froze. Leave Crowell. What was Kubushevsky talking about? He was just getting to know him. They were a team. All those hours in the car together, all those hours staring at cornfields and concrete. What was Kubushevsky talking about? Did Crowell know? What was Kubushevsky insinuating about joining him? "You're drunk, George."

"I know."

"You're very drunk."

"I know."

Moto smiled. The blonde got restless and left the bar. Kubushevsky didn't seem to notice. For the rest of the night he talked about his first wife and his two children, whom he barely saw. He spoke of his job at Allmack and his hopes for a better job in California. They sat at a low table. Moto spoke of his children and distant wife. It felt good to talk. Almost as good as having Yuko next to him.

As they left the bar, Kubushevsky leaned heavily on him. They peed against a stone wall before getting in the car. All the way home Kubushevsky sang a song about a folk hero named Davy Crockett, who "killed himself a bear when he was only three." Moto sang a song from Niigata about the beauty of the snow on the rooftops in winter. Kubushevsky hummed along.

They worked as a team for the next four months. Kubushevsky provided whatever detailed documentation Moto asked for. They went drinking a lot. Sometimes they both felt a little sad, sometimes happy, but Moto mostly felt entirely comfortable. Kubushevsky introduced him to Porter, a large, good-natured man in the steel business who liked to hunt and cook gourmet food; to Andrews, a tiny man who danced the polka as if it were a waltz; and to many others.

Just before the closing, Kubushevsky took him to a bar and told him of a job offer in California. He had tears in his eyes and hugged Moto good-bye. Moto had long since accepted the fact that Kubushevsky would leave.

Two weeks later Moto looked around the conference room at Allmack. Ishii, KKD's president, and Imai had flown in from Tokyo for the signing of the contract for the shopping mall, the culmination of three years of research and months of negotiation. John Crowell stood by his lawyer, Sue Smith. Sue had been on her feet for five hours. Mike Apple, Moto's lawyer, slammed his fist on the table and pointed at the item in question. The lawyers argued a timing detail that Moto was sure had been worked out weeks before. Moto glanced nervously at Ishii and Imai. Ishii's eyes were closed. Imai stared at the table.

Moto shifted uneasily in his seat. Sue was smarter than Mike, he thought. Perhaps a female lawyer wouldn't have been so terrible. While it was not unusual to see females in professional positions in Japan, this was America. Tokyo might have understood. After all, this was America, he repeated to himself. Internationalization required some adjustment. A year ago he would have had total loss of face if confronted with this prolonged, argumentative closing. Today he did not care. He could not explain to Tokyo all he'd learned in that time, all the friends he'd made. When he tried to communicate about business in America, the home office sent him terse notes by fax.

Now the lawyers stood back. President Ishii opened his eyes. Crowell handed a pen to Ishii. They signed the document together. The lawyers smiled. Sue Smith looked satisfied. She should be pleased, Moto thought. Her extensive preparation for the case made him realize again that the Japanese stereotype of the "lazy" American was false. Sue's knowledge of the case was perfect in all details. I'll have to use her next time, Moto thought. She's the smart one. Yes, he thought, his friend Kubushevsky had taught him many things. Suddenly he felt Kubushevsky's large presence. Moto lowered his head in gratitude.

Source: Patricia Gercik, *On Track with the Japanese,* 1992. (New York: Kodansha International, 114 Fifth Ave., NY, NY 10011) (OR Kudanske America)

CASE QUESTIONS

1. What was Moto's purpose and agenda for the first meeting with Crowell? How does he try to implement his agenda?
2. What happened to introduce "noise" in the communication from Moto to Crowell, and then from Crowell to Moto?
3. What was the significance of the doll? What went wrong?
4. Why did Crowell's remarks about Allmack threaten a loss of *face* from Moto's perspective?
5. How did Moto feel about Kubushevsky's behavior early on? How did their relationship change?

CASE 3

EURO DISNEY SCA: PERSPECTIVES FROM TWO CULTURES

Disney consultant Phil Devons has just returned to France. It is January 1994, and he has spent the past week in the United States apprising Michael Eisner, Disney's Chairman, of Euro Disney's poor performance. Since opening in 1992, the park has lost almost $2 billion; Disney, the parent company, has written off $625 million from the venture. Eisner is not pleased with the Euro Disney situation—it is the first time he and the other Disney executives have experienced public failure, and he has charged Devons with developing a plan of action. Devons is unsure of how to go about this. First, he thought, he should find out what went wrong. He set up a meeting to consult with Madame Debois, a French management consultant who has been following Euro Disney since before it opened, to try to understand the perspective from the European point of view.

BACKGROUND

Euro Disney is a joint venture undertaken by Walt Disney Company and several European banks and shareholders. The 5,000-acre theme park is located in Marne-la-Vallee, about 20 miles east of Paris. It opened April 12, 1992, and ran into problems right from the beginning, including considerable bad press from French reporters who called it a "cultural Chernobyl," as well as "Mouseschwitz" and "Eurodismal."

Walt Disney Inc. owns 49 percent of Euro Disney, whereas the other 51 percent is held by European stockholders. Disney has invested more than $175 million but has no legal obligation to Euro Disney; yet it must also be recognized that Disney has never failed in any other business venture. Disney's mission is "to entertain everyone, of every age, from every land." But at Euro Disney, the company has been accused of "sticking too close to the corporate line of homogeneous small world after all" (Wente and Crumley).

THE BEGINNING

Mr. Devons's Perspective

We decided on Marne-la-Vallee because it is at the crossroads of Europe, a few hours from London and most other countries on the continent; 17 million people live within a 6-hour drive. Additionally, our decision was made easier by several government incentives. France wanted Disney; they hoped for some relief to the high unemployment and recession by the theme park, which would employ more than 12,000 people. France extended the RER, Paris's express subway, to reach the park. The government also agreed to make the park a station for the high-speed Train à Grande Vitesse (TGV). This would connect the park to Brussels, which would be only 90 minutes away, and to London, three hours away via the English Channel Tunnel.

Although we were aware that the weather is cold and wet in these parts for a large portion of the year, we believed we could resolve this problem, as we did in Tokyo, which has a similar climate, by making several design modifications such as heating arcades and sheltered walkways, putting fireplaces in shops and restaurants, having shelters over the line areas, and using brighter colors than in our other parks to counter the overcast skies.

We expected at least 11 million visitors in the first year; spending $220 million on a marketing blitz for the opening should have ensured that. Our breakeven point was about seven million visitors, based on an admission price of $51 per adult, $34 per child, and a daily average of $33 per person spent on food and souvenirs. We planned to meet the European demand for fine cuisine and sophisticated souvenirs; overall, we estimated that a family of four would spend, on average, $280 a day. We were confident in our expectations. Our stock rose from $12.75 at the offering, to $29 on March 30, 1993, indicating investor confidence in the park's success. In 1992, the attendance was 10.5 million, and in 1993 it was 9.5 million.

We spared no expense on Euro Disney. The architecture of our hotels and restaurants was first class; the best architects in America were hired to design the park using "entertainment" as our theme; six hotels were constructed within the park. Because of mistakes we made in Florida and Tokyo, we planned to own and operate the hotels and restaurants ourselves, with rates ranging from $110 to $375 a night. Fifty restaurants were built, focusing on high-quality cuisine. But our policy on no alcohol remained firm. "There may have been an assumption that we were innocents abroad, that we were pushovers, but we are very tough negotiators" (Ilott and Williams 1992). Yet the capacity of our hotel is currently only at 74 percent, and the slumping real estate market does not offer any easy exits.

Madame Debois's Perspective

When Euro Disney opened in April of 1992, Europe was in a major recession, and the currency exchange rate for the French franc was weak. This, coupled with Euro Disney's ethnocentric views, greatly influenced the French attitude toward the American theme park and adversely affected attendance. In response to all the concessions that the French government offered Disney, it requested one thing—respect for the French culture. Yet Disney failed to understand and to make adjustments for the differences in negotiating and management styles.

First of all, the park was too expensive—in terms of entrance fees, meal prices, hotel rates, and extra spending on souvenirs. The French considered the average cost for a family too frivolous. Also, there was a negative attitude toward the Americans, which resulted in many French people waiting to see how others felt about the park before they were willing to spend money. As one person commented, "Disney is both crass and seductive. We hate it, but we also want to go there" (Grover and Toy 1992).

Euro Disney executives advertised the park as being big and extravagant. In fact, the company forced this concept of "bigness" onto the French and European public. Europeans found this form of American advertising distasteful; they were not interested in the large size of the park, but rather what it had to offer them personally. Euro Disney's failure to market directly to the French people resulted in lower than expected attendance. "From the outset, the Disney formula, successful everywhere, has proven less than appealing in Europe" (Cohen 1993).

Europeans, especially the French, have set vacation dates; the French vacation during the month of August. For Disney to expect that Europeans would change their vacation habits was extremely arrogant on their part. Other theme parks in Europe close during the winter months. The French do not want to walk around in the cold and the rain when they could be indoors; why do things in the winter that one can do in the summer? The long lines for rides and shows, usually an hour wait, also added to European dissatisfaction with the theme park. Also, Europeans are not generally as enthusiastic about amusement parks as Americans—they regard such entertainment as juvenile, not for adults.

Disney chose France for its access to the European market, but did not suitably design the park for people from surrounding countries, such as the British, the Germans, the Italians, and the Spanish. One British family complained that when they went to the park for a long weekend, they spent about $4,000, were subject to rude employees, and waited in long lines in poor weather only to watch a show entirely in French! For this price the family could have gone to Florida, where it is warm and sunny, the employees are always friendly, and everything is in English. In fact, many Britons decided to forego the Euro Disney experience and continue their vacations in Florida. The souvenirs offered at the park were not only expensive but inappropriate for European demand—they wanted items such as pictures and shirts of Mickey and Minnie. Instead, they got gimmicks such as bottles with ships in them and tortoiseshell knick-knacks. As one English visitor to Euro Disney said, "One imagines it will be perfect, with sunshine and all the little Dalmatians and dwarves running around. Who imagines rain and $6 hamburgers?" (Crumley and Wentz 1993).

By banning alcohol in the park, Euro Disney managers misunderstood the European habit of drinking beer and wine as an integral part of the meal, especially at an average of $41 a meal. Meals were expensive, lines too long, seating inadequate, and no provisions made for serving breakfast. Thus Europeans were misled: served international cuisine, yet prevented from drinking beer and wine. When visiting the park, Europeans wanted American fast food, served fast!

Hotel rates were also too expensive for Europeans. Again, this proves Disney's ignorance, or arrogance, about the European recession. It proved more practical for a family to visit the park during the day and stay in a hotel in Paris overnight. Euro Disney was unprepared for the high demand for breakfast, for the interest in American fast food, and the Europeans' expectation of alcohol in the resort's restaurants.

CAST MEMBERS

Mr. Devons

Disney considers itself to be in the "entertainment business." Thus, our employees are called "cast members" and when working they are on stage. All cast members must go through Disney University, a one-day orientation that covers the company's history and philosophy toward its products and audience. Furthermore, we issue a 13-page manual on dress and manners. We confess that Disney takes a strict approach toward its cast members, but we feel our customers deserve it. "As a matter of fact, the employees are very happy with the standards that we have set forth. They know exactly what they have to do, what they are being judged on, and what we are asking of them. I believe they understand and appreciate this" (Coccoli 1992).

As new members of a community, our goal was to fit in and be regarded as a positive addition to the area. We wouldn't be the top wage payer, but would be in the top third, paying around 15 percent above the minimum wage, from $14,000 to $15,000 a year.

Concerned about employee housing, Disney set up new employees with roommates so they would have an easier time adjusting; we actively searched for vacant apartments and held them for employees, and we constructed 800 units of new housing.

Madame Debois

Many of Euro Disney's "cast members" felt that they were working in a concentration camp and gave the park a nickname, "Mouseschwitz." They objected to rules in the manual prohibiting smoking or chewing gum, facial hair, and hair dyed an unusual shade or color. Although these rules go against normative behavior in Europe, other codes proved rude and discriminatory, such as "wear proper underwear, use deodorant, maintain a height to weight equilibrium." Also, the French tend toward individualism and formality; yet Disney expected them to remain friendly at all times and to greet one another as is a Disney tradition by their first names. But in Europe, everyone addresses others by their title and last name, unless invited to do otherwise.

COMMITMENT

Mr. Devons

Financial performance has not been what we expected. European spending habits, not attendance, turned out to be our problem (about 12 percent less was spent on food and souvenirs than expected). At this point, we are the minority holder (49 percent) in Euro Disney and have a limited investment in the project, so, walking away from this venture is a real option. Walt Disney Inc. cannot afford to continue to invest more money in Euro Disney or take a larger equity share. However, bailing out now would force Disney into an unprecedented admission of failure, and in doing so, we risk damaging our image. Additionally, failure would adversely affect future strategies for expansion, and a tremendous growth opportunity would be lost. Yet it must be known that Mr. Eisner feels that, "Anything is possible today, including closure" (Sims).

On the other hand, we feel confident that by giving French creditors a deadline of March 31, 1994, to compile a plan of action for handling the park's losses, they will come to an agreement because they stand to lose much more.

Madame Debois

Problems arose in Disney's relationship with the 22 European subcontractors who built the park. Owing to frequent changes, subcontractors worked beyond the specifications of the contract, and as of spring 1994, many had not been paid. (It is estimated that Disney owed about $157 million to these contractors, a debt that caused most of them to go out of business.) This led to a growing resentment toward Euro Disney by local companies, but Disney's main concern was staying within budget; it did not focus on building good relations with the host country.

As one subcontractor said, "Working with Disney is like sleeping with an elephant; you spend half the night wondering whether it will roll over and squash you" (Ilott and Williams 1992).

The French government and 60 European banks together own 51 percent of Euro Disney and have invested $960 million in low-interest loans and hundreds of millions in infrastructure. French stakeholders estimate that, for Euro Disney to succeed, 11 billion francs of debt has to be cut. However, the French investors are reluctant to invest more in the park until they have evidence that it will improve. Frankly, without Disney investing more, foreign investors don't have the confidence it will turn around.

The French stakeholders also feel that Disney should take a greater role in this matter even though it is the minority shareholder. The park is a Disney creation, and Walt Disney Inc. has a responsibility to it. The French stakeholders are using Disney's image as leverage to get the company to invest more and to drop some of their management and royalty fees. "A closing of the park would be a humiliation for Disney, and analysts believe that the company will do everything possible to save it" (Cohen 1993).

CONCLUSION

Devons considered the different perspectives Madame Debois had related to him. Because he was concerned, he next planned to consult the major investors. He decided to present to Michael Eisner several feasible options, along with their risks and implications, and then to offer his recommended strategy.

Source: Updated and adapted by the author from a term project by Angela Tallada, Chris Escudero, and Kathleen O'Connor, students at the State University of New York–Plattsburgh, Spring 1994. Copyright ©1995 by Helen Deresky. Information about Euro Disney is drawn from the press sources as cited; the characters of Mr. Devons and Madame Debois and their conversations are fictional.

This case is presented as a basis for class discussion, not to illustrate either effective or ineffective handling of an administrative situation.

CASE QUESTIONS

1. What were the primary problems facing Euro Disney in the early stages?
2. What is Disney's responsibility to the European stakeholders?
3. What were the major factors facing Devons when deciding whether to close or refinance the park?
4. What changes should Devons recommend to improve Euro Disney's poor performance if it remains open?
5. What should Disney do differently when next it enters a foreign market?

CASE BIBLIOGRAPHY

"Blundering Mouse: Euro Disney Is a Hit with Fans, But Parent's Goofs Prompt Park's Losses to Mount," *Wall Street Journal,* March 10, 1994, A12.

Buchan, David and Alice Rawsthorn. "$2 Billion Deal Could Save Disney Park from Closure," *Financial Times,* March 15, 1994, 1.

Burshtein, Karen. "Euro Disney Struggles to Succeed," *Hotel and Motel Management,* May 10, 1993, 3, 25.

Cau, Jean. "Après Mickey, Le Deluge," *Harper's Magazine,* July 1992, 18.

Coccoli, D. "It's A Small World," *Lodging Hospitality,* April 1992, 26–31.

Cohen, Roger. "Euro Disney's Bad News Includes a Sizable Loss," *New York Times,* July 9, 1993, D3.

Cohen, Roger. "Euro Disney '93: $901 Million Loss," *New York Times,* November 11, 1993, 36.

Cohen, Roger. "Euro Disney in Danger of Shutdown," *New York Times,* December 23, 1993, 12.

Coleman, Brian. "Bailout Report Boosts Shares of Euro Disney," *Wall Street Journal,* December 2, 1993, A11.

Coleman, Brian. "Euro Disney Says Audit Won't Delay Restructuring Plan," *Wall Street Journal,* December 1, 1993, A17.

Corliss, Richard, "Voilà!" *Time,* April 20, 1992, 82–84.

Crumley, Richard and Laura Wentz. "Magic Doesn't Translate During Euro Disney Visit," *Advertising Age,* November 1993, 1–3, 1–23.

Dickson, Martin and Alice Rawsthorn. "Walt Disney Prepares to Share the Pain," *Financial Times,* March 15, 1994, 1.

"Disney: A Behind the Scenes Look at Training Techniques," *Hotels,* February 1991, 92.

"Disney's Bungle Book," *International Management,* July–August 1993, 26–27.

Dwyer, Paula and Stewart Toy. "Is Disney Headed for the Euro-Trash Heap?" *International Business,* January 24, 1994, 52.

"Euro Disney Chief Forecasts More Losses," *Financial Times,* March 14, 1994.

"Euro Disney Plans to Slash 950 Jobs to Cut Its Costs," *Wall Street Journal,* October 19, 1993, A17.

"Euro Disney Weathers Fickle French Winter," *Lodging Hospitality,* January 1993, 42.

Gleizes, Fiona and Charles Leerhsen. "And Now, Goofy Goes Gallic," *Newsweek,* April 13, 1992, 67.

Grover, Ronald, Mark Maremont, and Stewart Toy. "Mouse Fever Is About to Strike Europe," *Business Week,* March 30, 1992, 32.

Grover, Ronald, Patrick Oster, and Stewart Toy. "The Mouse Isn't Roaring," *Business Week,* August 24, 1992, 38.

Gumbel, Peter. "Euro Disney Calls on Mary Poppins to Tidy Up Mess at French Resort," *Wall Street Journal,* January 22, 1994, A16.

Gumbel, Peter. "Euro Disney Posts Wide 1st-Period Loss as Creditors Hold Inconclusive Talks," *Wall Street Journal,* February 16, 1994, D3.

Gumbel, Peter. "Marketing Changes Boost Euro Disney as Debt-Restructuring Talks Approach," *Wall Street Journal,* February 22, 1994, A3.

Ilott, Terry and Michael Williams. "Disney Puttin' On the Blitz," *Variety,* March 2, 1992, 1, 80.

Lyman, Rick. "Euro Disney Attendance Is Disappointingly Mickey Mouse," *Journal of Commerce* (August 10, 1993): 9A.

"Mickey Mess," *Time,* June 22, 1992, 30.

"The Not-So-Magic Kingdom," *The Economist,* September 26, 1992, 87.

O'Brien, Tim. "Euro Disneyland: Can They Make It Work?" *Amusement Business,* June 15–21, 1992, 18.

O'Brien, Tim. "Year 1: Euro Disney Keeping Its Chin Up," *Amusement Business,* April 12–18, 1993, 1, 18.

O'Brien, Tim. "Euro Disney's New Attractions Aimed at Increasing Attendance," *Amusement Business,* April 12–18, 1993, 18.

Phillips, Andrew. "Where's the Magic?" *Maclean's,* May 3, 1993, 47.

Rawsthorn, Alice. "Euro Disney Banks Likely to Approve Rescue Plan," *Financial Times,* March 22, 1994, 24.

Rawsthorn, Alice. "Euro Disney Attendance Shows Fall in Second Year," *Financial Times,* March 21, 1994, 17.

Rawsthorn, Alice. "Hopes Rise for $2 Billion Rescue at Euro Disney," *Financial Times,* March 9, 1994, 1.

Rawsthorn, Alice. "Only a Month to Make the Refinancing Fly," *Financial Times,* March 1, 1994, 22.

Rawsthorn, Alice. "Disney Starts Talk with Banks," *Financial Times,* February 15, 1994.

Ridding, John. "Euro Disney Banks Receive Audit Report," *Financial Times,* March 22, 1994, 16.

Russell, Beverly. "Building for Fun," *New Statesman & Society,* April 17, 1992, 35–36.

Sims, Calvin. "Eisner Says Euro Disney May Close," *New York Times,* January 1, 1994, 42.

Turner, Richard. "Disney Records Loss on Charge for Europe Park," *Wall Street Journal,* December 18, 1993, A3.

Turner, Richard. "Disney's Eisner Gives 'D' Grade to Euro Disney," *Wall Street Journal,* December 30, 1993, D6.

Williams, Michael. "Euro Disney Awash in Red Ink," *Variety Europe,* July 19, 1993, 38.

PART 3

Formulating and Implementing Strategy for International Operations

Chapter 7
Strategy Formulation for International Markets

Chapter 8
Cross-Border Alliances and Strategy Implementation

Chapter 9
Organization Structure and Coordinating Systems

7

Strategy Formulation for International Markets

OUTLINE

Opening Profile: Global or Local? Comparing FedEx and UPS in China

Reasons for Going International

Reactive Responses

Proactive Reasons

Strategic Formulation Process

Management Focus: Unisys: Off and Running in Vietnam

Steps in Developing International Strategy

Mission and Objectives

Environmental Assessment

Internal Analysis

Competitive Analysis

International Strategic Alternatives

Approaches to World Markets

Global Integrative Strategies

Management Focus: Matsushita: Way to Go Global and Act Local

Entry Strategy Alternatives

Comparative Management in Focus: Strategic Planning for the EU Market

Technology Application: Dutch Insurance Giant Achmea Prepares for the Borderless Europe

Strategic Choice

Summary of Key Points

Discussion Questions

Application Exercises

Experiential Exercise

Internet Resources

Case Study: Cola Wars: The Venezuelan Coup

OPENING PROFILE

Global or Local? Comparing FedEx and UPS in China

Just how "American" should you be when doing business many cultures away from home? Rarely have two rivals offering similar services answered that question so differently as have Federal Express Corp. and United Parcel Service of America, Inc.

FedEx is trying to paint China red, white, and blue, following the same frontal-assault strategy it employed in the United States in the 1970s and in Europe in the 1980s. While promoting itself with jarring, western-style advertising, FedEx is pouring out money to acquire its own air routes, fly its own aircraft into and out of China, and in partnership with an aggressive local company, build a huge network of purple and orange trucks and distribution centers.

"We're the largest all-cargo (air) carrier in the world, and as a result we've got a pretty good formula for attacking any market," says T. Michael Glenn, executive vice president for marketing at FedEx's parent, FDX Corp. "Whether it's China or Japan or Germany, it really doesn't make any difference." In Asia, FedEx ran a ubiquitous print ad showing the tail of a FedEx plane parked in front of the Forbidden City—a cherished array of imperial buildings that was off limits to the public for five hundred years. "Call FedEx," the ad said. "It's almost forbidden not to."

UPS, by contrast, hopes that Chinese customers won't even notice that it is made in America. Its advertising is understated and old-fashioned even by Chinese standards. Its freight lands in China packed into leased space in the underbellies of planes operated by a Hong Kong airline, Dragonair, or other regional carriers. To deliver packages on the ground, UPS follows the traditional approach of foreign freight companies in China, piggybacking on the operations of Sinotrans, a vast, labyrinthine government-owned transportation company.

These contrasting strategies vividly illustrate two radically different approaches to questions faced by almost any U.S. company striving to expand overseas: Do we partner with entrenched competitors or tackle them head-on? Do we risk the capital to build our own manufacturing and distribution systems or lease someone else's? Who are our customers, the locals or our multinational accounts? How much do we risk to build future market share?

Personal Ties Important

The FedEx style seems to annoy some companies that expect a certain tone in the formal face-to-face sales pitches traditional in China. "I know they're one of the biggest companies in the U.S.A., but that doesn't matter here," says Li Ping, an executive at Chinatex Cotton Yarns & Fabrics Import and Export Corp. in Beijing. "The personal relationship matters most here. You have to talk to customers and make them feel good.... They [FedEx] haven't sent anyone here, so, we don't do business with them."

In more than a dozen major cities in China, FedEx's operations, trucks, and employees look identical to those in the United States. In scores of other cities, FedEx packages are delivered in aqua-blue trucks painted with the logos of both FedEx and its Chinese affiliate. The company says it will add ground service to 20 Chinese cities a year for the foreseeable future. In 1998, it started direct flights between China and Japan, allowing Chinese goods to connect with its direct flights between Osaka, Japan, and its primary U.S. hub in Memphis, Tennessee. "Our focus is on building a network," Mr. Smith says. "Once you have a network in place, if that premise is right, then the growth prospects are huge, and we're going to hopefully have a leadership position."

Adopting the Chinese Way

Meanwhile, 91-year-old UPS, with its giant, mostly ground-based U.S. delivery network and annual revenue of about $22.46 billion, is hewing to its long history of keeping a low profile. So in China, UPS is doing as the Chinese do. Its marketing seeks to build relationships discreetly, on Chinese terms—even though it, too, says multinationals are the core of its initial customer base here.

Monica Yan, an ad executive at China Guoxin Information Corp., switched to UPS from the state-run express-mail service after a UPS account executive came calling at her dank basement office in Beijing. "She came here and explained to me how UPS could be more convenient and not cost so much money, so I decided to use her company," Ms. Yan says.

In promoting itself, UPS emphasizes its global network and stability, virtues that ring true for many Chinese. It also nurtures a Chinese customer base outside China, sponsoring Chinese New Year celebrations in Toronto and Vancouver, where many recent immigrants live.

Lacking its own air service, UPS can't offer customers in China the range of logistical services that FedEx can. But UPS, though avoiding the cheap air cargo that FedEx depends upon to fill out its aircraft, can still skim from the cream of the business, the lucrative document and small-package sector.

Source: Adapted and excerpted from Douglas A. Blackmon and Diane Brady, "Orient Express: Just How Hard Should a U.S. Company Woo a Big Foreign Market?" *Wall Street Journal,* April 6, 1998.

As the Opening Profile on FedEx and UPS illustrates, companies around the world are spending increasing amounts of money and time on international expansion in search of profitable new markets, acquisitions, and alliances—but often spending those resources on very different strategies. Experts predict that those companies with operations in major overseas markets (North America, Europe, and Asia) are far more likely to prosper in the twenty-first century than those without such operations.[1] Because these new international opportunities are far more complex than those in domestic markets, managers must plan carefully—that is, strategically—to benefit from them.

The process by which a firm's managers evaluate the future prospects of the firm and decide on appropriate strategies to achieve long-term objectives is called **strategic planning**.[2] The basic means by which the company competes—its choice of business or businesses in which to operate and the ways in which it differentiates itself from its competitors—is its **strategy**. Almost all successful companies engage in long-range strategic planning, and those with a global orientation position themselves to take full advantage of worldwide trends and opportunities. MNCs, in particular, report that strategic planning is essential to contend with increasing global competition and to coordinate their far-flung operations.

In reality, though, rational strategic planning is often tempered or changed at some point by a more incremental, sometimes messy, process of strategic decision making by some managers. When a new CEO is hired, for example, he or she will often call for a radical change in strategy. That is why new leaders are very carefully chosen on the basis of what they are expected to do. So, while we discuss the rational strategic planning process here, because it is usually the ideal, inclusive method of determining long-term plans, we need to remember that, throughout, there are people making decisions, and their own personal judgment, experiences, and motivations will shape the ultimate strategic direction. The Ben & Jerry's case at the end of Chapter 8, for example, illustrates how the personal interests of the owner became the overriding reason to "go international."

Reasons for Going International

Companies go international for different reasons, some reactive (or defensive) and some proactive (or aggressive). The threat of their own decreased competitiveness is the overriding reason many large companies adopt a strategy of aggressive globalization. To remain competitive, these companies want to move fast to build strong positions in key world markets with products tailored to the common needs of 650 million customers in Europe, America, and Japan.[3] Building on their past success, companies such as IBM are plowing profits back into operations overseas. Europe is now attracting much new investment capital because of both the European Union (EU) and the opening of extensive new markets in eastern Europe. With far-sighted planning, General Motors is already taking advantage of these new opportunities: Its Opel unit has invested more than $500 million on a joint venture to manufacture cars in eastern Germany, and it has won a five-year agreement to supply $1 billion of pollution-control and engine-control parts to Volga Auto Works, the former Soviet Union's largest automaker.[4]

Reactive Responses

International Competition   One of the most common reactive reasons that prompt a company to go overseas is international competition. If left unchallenged, competitors who already have international operations or investments may get so entrenched in foreign markets that it becomes difficult for other companies to enter at a later time. In addition, the lower costs and market power available to these competitors operating globally may give them an advantage domestically.

Trade Barriers   Restrictive trade barriers is another reactive reason companies often switch from exporting to overseas manufacturing. Barriers such as tariffs, quotas, buy-local policies, and other restrictive trade practices can make exports to foreign markets too expensive and too impractical to be competitive. Many firms, for example, want to gain a foothold in Europe—to be regarded as an insider—to counteract the trade barriers and restrictions anticipated at the completion of the EU agreement (discussed further in the Comparative Management in Focus section at the end of this chapter). In part, this fear of "Fortress Europe" is caused by actions such as the EU's block exemption for the franchise industry. This exemption prohibits a franchisor, say, McDonald's, from contracting with a single company, say, Coca-Cola, to supply all its franchisees, as it does in the United States.[5]

Regulations and Restrictions   Similarly, regulations and restrictions by a firm's home government may become so expensive that companies will seek out less restrictive foreign operating environments.[6] Avoiding such regulations prompted U.S. pharmaceutical maker SmithKline and Britain's Beecham to merge. Both thereby guaranteed that they would avoid licensing and regulatory hassles in their largest markets—western Europe and the United States. The merged company is now an insider in both Europe and America.[7]

Customer Demands   Operations in foreign countries frequently start as a response to customer demands or as a solution to logistical problems. Certain foreign customers, for example, may demand that their supplying company operate in their local region so that they have better control over their supplies, forcing the supplier to comply or lose the business. McDonald's is one company that asks its domestic suppliers to follow it to foreign ventures. Meat supplier OSI Industries does just that, with joint ventures in 17 countries, such as Bavaria, so that it can work with local companies making McDonald's hamburgers.[8]

Proactive Reasons

> *From rain forests to remote Chinese villages, the queen of cosmetics (Avon) is cleaning up across the globe.*[9]

Economies of Scale   Careful, long-term strategic planning encourages firms to go international for proactive reasons.[10] One pressing reason for many large firms to expand overseas is to seek economies of scale—that is, to achieve world-scale volume to make the fullest use of modern capital-intensive manufacturing equipment and to amortize staggering research and development costs when facing brief product life cycles.[11] Otis Elevator, for example, developed the Elevonic 411 by means of six research centers in five countries; this international cooperation saved more than $10 million in design costs and cut the development cycle from four years to two. Economies of scale in production are achieved when higher levels of output spread fixed costs over more units, thus lowering the per-unit cost. Gerrit Jeelof, of Holland's Philips Group, contends that "only with a global market can a company afford the large development costs necessary to keep up with advancing technology."[12]

International Markets   When expansion opportunities become limited at home, firms such as McDonald's are often driven to seek expansion through new international markets. A mature product or service with restricted growth in its domestic market often has "new life" in another country, where it will be at an earlier stage of its life cycle. Avon Products Inc., for example, has seen a decline in its U.S. market since its traditional sales and marketing strategy of "Avon calling" (house-to-house sales) now meets with empty houses, due to the increasing number of women who now work outside the home. To make up for this loss, Avon pushed overseas to 26 emerging markets, such as Mexico, Poland, China, India, South Africa, and Vietnam. In Brazil, for instance, Josina Reis Teixeira carries her sample kit to the wooden shacks in the tiny village of Registro, just outside of São Paulo. In some markets, Avon adapts to cultural influences, such as in China, where consumers are suspicious of door-to-door salespeople. There, Avon sets up showrooms in its branch offices in major cities so that women can consult cosmeticians and sample products.[13]

In addition, new markets abroad provide a place to invest surplus profits as well as employ underutilized resources in management, technology, and machinery. When entirely new markets open up, such as in eastern Europe, both experienced firms and those new to international competition usually rush to take advantage of awaiting opportunities. Such was the case with the proactive stance that Unisys took in preparing for and jumping on the newly opened market opportunity in Vietnam.

Resource Access and Cost Savings   Further, resource access and cost savings entice many companies to operate from overseas bases. The availability of raw materials and other resources offers both greater control over inputs and lower transportation costs. Lower labor costs (for production, service, and technical personnel), another major consideration, enable lower unit costs and have proved a vital ingredient to competitiveness for many companies.

Sometimes just the prospect of shifting production overseas improves competitiveness at home. When Xerox Corporation started moving copier-rebuilding operations to

Mexico, the union agreed to needed changes in work style and productivity to keep the jobs at home.[14] Lower operational costs in other areas—power, transportation, and financing—frequently prove attractive. Trinidad, for example, offers abundant inexpensive energy, a skilled and well-educated workforce with labor rates at about one-fourth of U.S. levels, and government incentives for export-oriented ventures that generate foreign exchange.[15]

Incentives   Governments in countries such as Poland seeking new infusions of capital, technology, and know-how willingly provide incentives—tax exemptions, tax holidays, subsidies, loans, and the use of property.[16] Because they both decrease risk and increase profits, these incentives are attractive to foreign companies. One study surveyed 103 experienced managers concerning the relative attractiveness of various incentives for expansion into the Caribbean region (primarily Mexico, Venezuela, Colombia, Dominican Republic, and Guatemala). The results indicate the opinion of those managers about which incentives are most important; however, the most desirable mix would depend on the nature of the particular company and its operations. The first two issues reflect managers' concerns about limiting foreign exchange risk, where restrictions often change overnight and limit the ability of the firm to repatriate profits. Other concerns are those of political instability in countries such as Haiti and Nicaragua, and the possibility of expropriation, and those of tax concessions.[17]

Strategic Formulation Process

Typically, the strategic formulation process is necessary both at the headquarters of the corporation and at each of the subsidiaries. One study, for example, reported that 70 percent of 56 American MNC subsidiaries in Latin America and the Far East operated on planning cycles of five or more years.[18]

The global strategic formulation process, as part of overall corporate strategic management, parallels the process followed in domestic companies. However, the variables, and therefore the process itself, are far more complex because of the greater difficulty in gaining accurate and timely information; the diversity of geographic locations; and the differences in political, legal, cultural, market, and financial processes. These factors introduce a greater level of risk in strategic decisions. However, for firms that have not yet engaged in international operations (as well as for those that do), an ongoing strategic planning process with a global orientation identifies potential opportunities for (1) appropriate market expansion, (2) increased profitability, and (3) new ventures by which the firm can exploit its strategic advantages. Even in the absence of immediate opportunities, monitoring the global environment for trends and competition is important for domestic planning.

The strategic formulation process is part of the **strategic management process** in which most firms engage, either formally or informally. The planning modes range from a proactive, long-range format to a reactive, more seat-of-the-pants method, whereby the day-by-day decisions of key managers, in particular owner-managers, accumulate to what can be discerned retroactively as the new strategic direction.[19] The stages in the strategic management process described here are shown in Exhibit 7–1. In reality, these stages seldom follow such a

EXHIBIT 7–1

The Strategic Management Process

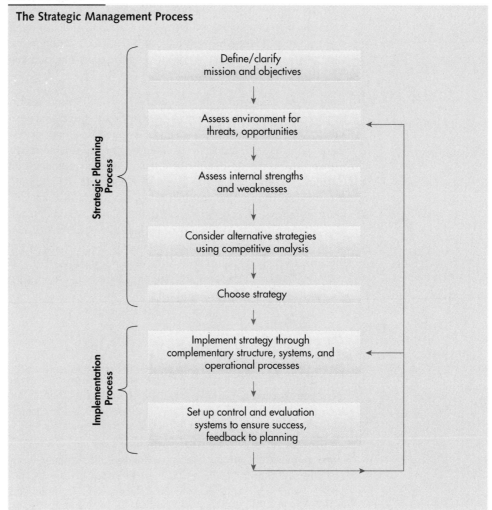

linear format. Rather, the process is continuous and intertwined, with data and results from earlier stages providing information for the next stage.

The first phase of the strategic management process—the planning phase—starts with the company establishing (or clarifying) its mission and its overall objectives. The next two steps compose an assessment of the external environment that the firm faces in the future and an analysis of the firm's relative capabilities to deal successfully with that environment. Strategic alternatives are then considered, and plans are made based on the strategic choice. These five steps constitute the planning phase, which will be further detailed in this chapter.

MANAGEMENT FOCUS

Unisys: Off and Running in Vietnam

In 1993, as it became clear that it was only a matter of time until the United States would lift its 19-year embargo on trade with Vietnam, Roger Stone paid a call on Vietnam's Ministry of Science, Technology, and Communication. Stone, Unisys Corp.'s general manager for Southeast Asia, was with a colleague from Japan's Mitsui Corp., which has been trading in Vietnam for nearly a century.

The ministry was trying to set guidelines for modernizing Vietnam's computer and telephone systems, but it was painfully aware that the country's long isolation meant that few Vietnamese knew much, if anything, about state-of-the-art technology. So Stone made an offer: At no charge to the Vietnamese for its services, Unisys would help the government prepare its information technology strategy.

Over the following six months, Unisys brought 14 experts to Hanoi for varying lengths of time to work with the ministers. The result was a framework, called IT (Information Technology) 2000, to guide the country's decision making in everything from telecommunications standards to technical education. Now the plan is complete, and various government ministries are beginning to make decisions about computer systems, telephone networks, and technical education. And Unisys, in the person of recently appointed Vietnam general manager Maureen Flanagan, is on hand in Hanoi to explain the functions and features of different kinds of hardware, software, and networks. The government was soliciting bids on several computer systems. Unisys expected to win at least one of the contracts.

Such were the stirrings of commercial activity in Vietnam, less than a month after President Clinton's February 3, 1994, lifting of the embargo. Although U.S. companies are now free to resume a full range of trade and investment activities, results in terms of sales and investments will still be some time in coming.

Unisys and Vietnam, in particular, seem made for each other because of Unisys's expertise in telecommunications, banking, government, and airlines. "The correlation between our strengths and the demands of this market is very close," says Stone, who spoke by telephone from Hanoi. "The development of banking and government infrastructure is at the top of the Vietnam government's list. And the telephone company will get as much of the available government funds as almost any other entity in Vietnam."

Vietnam will buy its computer and telephone equipment—like its roads, bridges, cement factories, and power plants—largely with loans and grants from the world's developed nations, which pledged $1.87 billion to Vietnam in November. Additional commitments of at least that amount are expected in each of the next three years, according to Stone.

The Vietnamese government had earmarked about $130 million of the first year's financing for computerization projects, including technology training and computerized management systems for the tax and treasury departments, Stone said.

The state of Vietnam's computerization roughly parallels that of its roads—only 12 percent paved—and indicates both the opportunities and the difficulties created by the country's lack of development. Although government agencies own a few personal computers, they are all standalone devices with no way of sharing information, said Flanagan, who came to Vietnam a year ago for Digital Equipment Corp. and then joined Unisys.

With no obsolete mainframes to worry about, and no installed jumble of incompatible personal computers, the country is free to adopt the most advanced technology from the outset, Stone said.

Source: Andrea Knox, "Off and Running in Vietnam," February 27, 1994. Reprinted with permission from the *Philadelphia Inquirer.*

The second part of the strategic management process is the implementation phase. Successful implementation requires the establishment of the structure, systems, and processes suitable to make the strategy work. These variables, as well as functional-level strategies will be explored in detail in the remaining chapters. At this point, however, note that the strategic planning process by itself does not change the posture of the firm until the plans are implemented. In addition, feedback from the interim and long-term results of such implementation, along with continuous environmental monitoring, flows directly back into the planning process.

Steps in Developing International Strategy

Mission and Objectives

The **mission** of an organization is its overall raison d'être or the function it performs in society. The mission charts the direction of the company and provides a basis for strategic decision making. A company's overall objectives flow from its mission, and both guide the formulation of international corporate strategy. Because we are focusing on issues of international strategy, we will assume that one of the overall objectives of the corporation is some form of international operation (or expansion). The objectives of the firm's international affiliates should also be part of the global corporate objectives. A firm's global objectives usually fall into the areas of marketing, profitability, finance, production, and research and development, among others, as shown in Exhibit 7–2. Goals for market volume and for profitability are usually set higher for international than for domestic operations because of the greater risk involved. In addition, financial objectives on the global level must take into account differing tax regulations in various countries and how to minimize overall losses from exchange rate fluctuations.

Environmental Assessment

After clarifying the corporate mission and objectives, the first major step in weighing international strategic options is the environmental assessment. This assessment includes environmental scanning and continuous monitoring to keep abreast of variables around the world that are pertinent to the firm and that have the potential to shape its future by posing new opportunities (or threats). Firms must adapt to their environment to survive. *How* to adapt is the focus of strategic planning.

The process of gathering information and forecasting relevant trends, competitive actions, and circumstances that will affect operations in geographic areas of potential interest is called **environmental scanning**. This activity should be conducted on three levels—multinational, regional, and national—which are discussed in detail later in this chapter. Scanning should focus on the future interests of the firm and should cover the following major variables (as discussed by Phatak and others):[20]

- *Political instability.* This variable represents a volatile and uncontrollable risk to the multinational corporation, as illustrated by the upheaval in China in recent years. MNCs must carefully assess such risk because it may result in a loss of profitability or even ownership.[21, 22]

EXHIBIT 7–2

Global Corporate Objectives

Marketing

Total company market share—worldwide, regional, national

Annual percentage sales growth

Annual percentage market share growth

Coordination of regional markets for economies of scale

Production

Relative foreign versus domestic production volume

Economies of scale through global production integration

Quality and cost control

Introduction of cost-efficient production methods

Finance

Effective financing of overseas subsidiaries or allies

Taxation—minimizing tax burden globally

Optimum capital structure

Foreign-exchange management

Profitability

Long-term profit growth

Return on investment, equity, and assets

Annual rate of profit growth

Research and Development

Develop new products with global patents

Develop proprietary production technologies

Worldwide research and development labs

- *Currency instability.* This variable represents another risk; inflation and fluctuations in the exchange rates of currencies can dramatically affect profitability when an MNC is operating overseas. In early 1995, for example, both foreign and local firms got a painful reminder of this risk when Mexico devalued its peso, and in 1998, the currency collapse in Indonesia forced President Suharto to resign.
- *Nationalism.* This variable, representing the home government's goals for independence and economic improvement, often influences foreign companies. The home government may impose restrictive policies—import controls, equity requirements, local content requirements, limitations on the repatriation of profits, and so forth. Japan, for example, protects its home markets with these kinds of restrictive policies. Other forms of nationalism may be exerted through the following: (1) pressure from national governments—exemplified by the United States putting pressure on Japan to curtail unfair competition; (2) lax patent and trademark protection laws, as those in

China in recent years, which erode a firm's proprietary technology through insufficient protection; and (3) the suitability of infrastructure, such as roads and telecommunications.

- *International competition.* Conducting an **international competitor analysis** is perhaps the most important task in environmental assessment and strategy formulation. The first step in analyzing the competition is to assess the relevant industry structures as they influence the competitive arena in the particular country (or region) being considered. For example, will the infrastructure support new companies in that industry? Is there room for additional competition? What is the relative supply and demand for the proposed product or service? The ultimate profit potential in the industry in that location will be determined by these kinds of factors.[23]

Managers must specifically assess their current competitors—global and local—for the proposed market. They must ask, what are our competitors' positions, their goals and strategies, their strengths and weaknesses relative to our firm's? What are the likely competitor reactions to our strategic moves? Managers should compare their company with potential international competitors; in fact, it is useful to draw up a competitive position matrix for each potential international market. For example, Exhibit 7–3 analyzes a U.S. specialty seafood firm's competitive profile in Malaysia.[24]

In Exhibit 7–3, the U.S. firm has advantages in financial capability, future growth of resources, and sustainability, but a disadvantage in quickness. It also is at a disadvantage

EXHIBIT 7–3

International Competitor Analysis

A U.S. Firm Compared with Its International Competitors in Malaysian Market

Comparison Criteria	A (U.S. MNC)	B (Korean MNC)	C (Local Malaysian Firm)	D (Japanese MNC)	E (Local Malaysian Firm)
Marketing capability	0	0	0	0	–
Manufacturing capability	0	+	0	0	0
R & D capability	0	0	0	–	0
HRM capability	0	0	0	0	0
Financial capability	+	–	0	0	–
Future growth of resources	+	0	–	0	–
Quickness	–	0	+	–	0
Flexibility/adaptability	0	+	+	0	0
Sustainability	+	0	0	0	–

Key:
+ = firm is better relative to competition.
0 = firm is same as competition.
– = firm is poorer relative to competition.

Source: Diane J. Garsombke, "International Competitor Analysis," *Planning Review* 17, no. 3 (May–June 1989): 42–47.

compared to the Korean MNC in important factors such as manufacturing capability and flexibility/adaptability. Because the other firms seem to have little comparative advantage, the major competitor is likely to be the Korean firm. At this point, then, the U.S. firm can focus in more detail on assessing the Korean firm's relative strengths and weaknesses.

The firm can also choose varying *levels of environmental scanning*. To reduce risk and investment, many firms take on the role of the "follower," meaning that they limit their own investigations; instead, they simply watch their competitors' moves and go where they go, assuming that the competitors have done their homework. Other firms go to considerable lengths to gather data carefully and examine options in the global arena.

Ideally, the firm should conduct global environmental analysis on three different levels: the multinational, regional, and national levels. Analysis on the *multinational level* provides a broad assessment of significant worldwide trends—through identification, forecasting, and monitoring activities. These trends would include the political and economic developments of nations around the world as well as global technological progress. From this information, managers can choose certain appropriate regions of the world to consider further.

Next, at the *regional level,* the analysis focuses in more detail on critical environmental factors to identify opportunities (and risks) for marketing the company's products, services, or technology. For example, one such regional location ripe for investigation by a firm seeking new markets is the European Union.

Having zeroed in on one or more regions, the firm must, as its next step, analyze at the *national level.* Such an analysis explores in depth specific countries within the desired region for economic, legal, political, and cultural factors significant to the company. For example, the analysis could focus on the size and nature of the market, along with any possible operational problems, to consider how best to enter the market. In fact, in many volatile countries, *continuous monitoring* of such environmental factors is a vital part of ongoing strategic planning. In Peru in 1988, inflation had soared to 2000 percent, and leftist terrorists were kidnapping or murdering business leaders. Though key managers fled and many multinational companies pulled out of Peru, Procter & Gamble remained to take advantage of a potentially large market share when competitors left. "Everybody should be dying to come here—you couldn't go to a better business school [than what you learn by managing here]," said Susana Elesperu de Freitas, the 34-year-old Peruvian manager of Procter & Gamble's subsidiary, who was flanked by armed bodyguards wherever she went.[25] Since then, Procter & Gamble, a consumer-products company, has expanded and in 2000 represents a major force in Peru.

This process of environmental scanning, from the broad global level down to the local specifics of entry planning, is illustrated in Exhibit 7–4. The first broad scan of all potential world markets results in the firm being able to eliminate from its list those markets that are closed or insignificant or do not have reasonable entry conditions. The second scan of remaining regions, and then countries, is done in greater detail—perhaps eliminating some based on political instability, for example. Remaining countries are then assessed for competitor strengths, suitability of products, and so on. This analysis leads to serious entry planning in selected countries; managers start to work on operational plans, such as negotiations and legal arrangements.

Sources of Environmental Information

The success of environmental scanning depends on the ability of managers to take an international perspective and to ensure that

EXHIBIT 7–4

International Environmental Scanning Process

Adoption of a global strategic planning perspective

↓

General scan of all markets

↓

First scan—macro

↓

Omit closed markets and insignificant markets
Remaining countries' entry concerns
Can a firm gain entry under reasonable conditions? If not, eliminate

↓

Second scan—greater detail

↓

Check environment constraints—educational, legal, behavioral, social, political
Eliminate countries with undesirable key constraints or put them aside for lower priority consideration

↓

Remaining countries—detailed micro scanning

↓

Data on all key constraints affecting the firm
Visits by key personnel • Get good local legal advice

↓

Competitive analysis

↓

Check out competition (MNC as well as local)
Can the firm compete effectively?
Data analysis on firms and industries

↓

Product line

↓

Which products shall we use as leaders?
Product adaptations necessary? Demand patterns

↓

Serious entry planning

↓

Functional specialists begin detailed work
Staff specialists in action • Linkages with country begin
Zoning, tax questions, negotiations on special arrangements, supplier commitments, etc.

↓

Entry

Source: John Garland, R. N. Farmer, and M. Taylor, *International Dimensions of Business Policy and Strategy,* 2nd ed. (Boston: PWS-Kent, 1990).

their sources of information and business intelligence are global. A variety of public resources are available to provide information. In the United States alone, more than two thousand business information services are available on computer database, tailored to specific industries and regions; other resources include corporate "clipping" services and information packages. However, internal sources of information are usually preferable—especially alert field personnel who, with firsthand observations, can provide up-to-date and relevant information for the firm. Using its own internal resources extensively, Mitsubishi Trading Company employs more than sixty thousand market analysts worldwide, whose job it is to gather, analyze, and feed market information to the parent company.[26] Internal sources of information help to eliminate unreliable information from secondary sources, particularly in developing countries. As Garsombke points out, the "official" data from such countries can be misleading: "Census data can be tampered with by government officials for propaganda purposes or it may be restricted.... In South Korea, for instance, even official figures can be conflicting depending on the source."[27]

Internal Analysis

After the environmental assessment, the second major step in weighing international strategic options is the internal analysis. This analysis determines which areas of the firm's operations represent strengths or weaknesses (currently or potentially) compared to competitors so that the firm may use that information to its strategic advantage.

The internal analysis focuses on the company's resources and operations, as well as global synergies. The strengths and weaknesses of the firm's financial and managerial expertise and functional capabilities are evaluated to determine what **key success factors (KSFs)** the company has and how well they can help the firm exploit foreign opportunities. Those factors increasingly involve superior technological capability (as with Microsoft and Intel), and they involve other strategic advantages such as effective distribution channels (as with Wal-Mart), superior promotion capabilities (Disney), low-cost production and sourcing position (Nike), and superior patent and new product pipeline (Merck).

Using such operational strengths to advantage is exemplified by Japanese car manufacturers: Their production quality and efficiency have catapulted them into world markets. As to their global strategy, they have recognized that their sales and marketing functions have proved to be a competitive weakness in the European car wars, and the Japanese are working on these shortcomings. Japanese automakers—Toyota, Honda, Mazda, and so on—are following Ford and GM in seeking to become more sophisticated marketers throughout Europe.[28]

All companies have strengths and weaknesses. Management's challenge is to identify both and take appropriate action. Many diagnostic tools are available for conducting an **internal resource audit**. Financial ratios, for example, may reveal an inefficient use of assets that is restricting profitability; a salesforce analysis may reveal that the salesforce is an area of distinct competence for the firm. If a company is conducting this audit to determine whether to start international ventures or to improve its ongoing operations abroad, certain operational issues must be taken into account. These issues include (1) the difficulty of obtaining marketing information in many countries, (2) the often poorly developed financial markets, and (3) the complexities of exchange rates and government controls.

Competitive Analysis

At this point, the firm's managers assess its capabilities and key success factors compared to those of its competitors. They must judge the relative current and potential competitive position of firms in that market and location—whether that be a global position or that for a specific country or region. As in a chess game, the firm's managers also need to consider the strategic intent of competing firms and what might be their future moves (strategies). This process enables the strategic planners to determine where the firm has distinctive competencies that will give it strategic advantage as well as what direction might lead the firm into a sustainable competitive advantage—that is, one that will not be immediately eroded by emulation. The result of this process will also help to identify potential problems that can be corrected or that may be significant enough to eliminate further consideration of certain strategies.[29]

This stage of strategic formulation is often called a **SWOT** analysis (an acronym for strengths, weaknesses, opportunities, and threats), in which the firm's capabilities **relative to its competitors'** are assessed as pertinent to the opportunities and threats in the environment for those firms. An example of a SWOT analysis shown in Exhibit 7–5 provides a brief

EXHIBIT 7–5

SWOT Analysis for Philip Morris

Opportunities
70 million smokers
290 million food consumers
Move to free-market system
Growing cigarette consumption
Alliance with meat firms

Threats
Economic instability
Political instability
Inflationary prices
GNP expected to fall
RJR Nabisco, other competitors

Strengths
Financial, production, R&D, marketing
   strengths in world markets
16-year relationship with Russians
German factory for base of
   production, distribution
Product diversification

Weaknesses
Large company—difficulties in
   controls, flexibility
Product-liability lawsuits

Source: Simone Betz and Steven Ellen (Term project at the State University of New York–Plattsburgh, Fall 1991).

overview of some of the major factors considered by Philip Morris (PM) as it recently considered entry into the Commonwealth of Independent States (CIS). The attraction, of course, is the newly opened market of 290 million consumers. Of these, 70 million are smokers and would provide an immediate target market for Philip Morris's cigarette brands. In addition, all 290 million would be a vast potential market for PM's Kraft and General Foods subsidiaries. The next step would be an in-depth assessment of the local and foreign competitors in the region, such as RJR Nabisco.

After its analysis, Philip Morris concluded that the Russian commonwealth presented an attractive opportunity, particularly if the firm could establish a market foothold before RJR Nabisco followed suit.[30] In hindsight, however, Philip Morris might have done some more homework and added other threats to this matrix. After the company set up kiosks to sell packs of Marlboros to people in St. Petersburg in 1992, those booths were blown up overnight—a signal that Russian cigarette distributors didn't want any outside competitors on their turf. Philip Morris subsequently got out of the distribution business. It is also worth noting that, in September 1998, RJR withdrew all operations from Russia as a result of that country's economic problems, after having invested about $520 million. The company was among many who suffered major losses in Russia's latest economic crisis.

Most companies develop their strategy around key strengths, or core competencies. Core competencies represent important corporate resources because, as Prahalad and Hamel explain, they are the "collective learning in the organization, especially how to coordinate diverse production skills and integrate multiple streams of technologies."[31] Core competencies—like Sony's capacity to miniaturize and Philips's optical-media expertise—are usually difficult for competitors to imitate and represent a major focus for strategic development at the corporate level.[32] Canon, for example, has used its core competence in optics to its competitive advantage throughout its diverse businesses—cameras, copiers, and semiconductor lithographic equipment.

Managers must also assess their firm's weaknesses. A company already on shaky ground financially, for example, will not be able to consider an acquisition strategy, or perhaps any growth strategy. Of course, the subjective perceptions, motivations, capabilities, and goals of the managers involved in such diagnoses frequently cloud the decision-making process. The result is that sometimes firms embark on strategies that were contraindicated by objective information because of poor judgment by key players.

International Strategic Alternatives

The fourth major step in the strategic planning process involves considering the advantages (and disadvantages) of various strategic alternatives in light of the competitive analysis. While weighing alternatives, managers need to take into account the goals of their firm and also the competitive status of other firms in the industry.

Depending on the size of the firm, there are two levels of strategic alternatives that a firm must consider. The first level—global strategic alternatives (applicable primarily to MNCs)—determines what overall approach to the global marketplace a firm wishes to take. The second level—entry strategy alternatives—applies to firms of any size; these alternatives determine what specific entry strategy is appropriate for each country in which the firm plans to operate. Entry strategy alternatives will be discussed in a later section. We now turn to the two main global strategic approaches to world markets—globalization and regionalization.

Approaches to World Markets

Globalization   In the last decade, increasing competitive pressures have forced businesses to consider global strategies—to treat the world as an undifferentiated worldwide marketplace. Such strategies are now loosely referred to as globalization—a term that refers to the establishment of worldwide operations and the development of standardized products and marketing. Many, like Porter, have argued that globalization is a competitive imperative for firms in global industries: "In a global industry a firm must in some way integrate its activities on a worldwide basis to capture the linkages among countries. This includes, but requires more than, transferring intangible assets among countries."[33] The rationale behind globalization is to compete by establishing worldwide economies of scale, offshore manufacturing, and international cash flows. The term *globalization,* therefore, is as applicable to organizational structure as it is to strategy. (Organizational structure is discussed further in Chapter 9.)

The pressures to globalize include (1) increasing competitive clout resulting from regional trading blocs; (2) declining tariffs, which encourage trading across borders and open up new markets; and (3) the information technology explosion, which makes the coordination of far-flung operations easier and also increases the commonality of consumer tastes.[34] In addition, the success of Japanese companies with global strategies has set the competitive standard in many industries—most visibly in the automobile industry. Other companies, such as Caterpillar, ICI, and Sony, have fared well with global strategies.

One of the quickest and cheapest ways to develop a global strategy is through *strategic alliances.* Many firms are trying to go global faster by forming alliances with rivals, suppliers, and customers. In fact, the rapidly developing information technologies are spawning cross-national business alliances from short-term virtual corporations to long-term strategic partnerships.[35] (Strategic alliances are discussed further in Chapter 8.)

Globalization is inherently more vulnerable to environmental risk, however, than a regionalization strategy.[36] Global organizations are difficult to manage because doing so requires the coordination of broadly divergent national cultures. It also means, say Morrison, Ricks, and Roth, that firms must lose some of their original identity—they must "denationalize operations and replace home-country loyalties with a system of common corporate values and loyalties."[37] In other words, the globalization strategy necessarily treats all countries similarly, regardless of their differences in cultures and systems. Problems often result, such as lack of local flexibility and responsiveness and neglect of the need for differentiated products. In some recent research into how U.S. companies compete, Morrison et al. discovered that many companies are finding that "globalization is no panacea, and, in fact, global imperatives are being eclipsed by an upsurge in regional pressures."[38] These researchers claim that many companies now feel that regionalization is a more manageable and less risky approach, one that allows them to capitalize on local competencies as long as the parent organization and each subsidiary retain a flexible approach to each other.

Regionalization   For those firms in multidomestic industries—those industries in which competitiveness is determined on a country-by-country basis rather than a global basis—regional strategies are more appropriate than globalization.[39] The **regionalization** (or **multi-local**) strategy is one in which local markets are linked within a region, allowing more local responsiveness and specialization. Top managers within each region decide on their own investment locations, product mixes, and competitive positioning; in other words, they run their subsidiaries as quasi-independent organizations.

As there are pressures to globalize—such as the need for economies of scale to compete on cost—so there are opposing pressures to regionalize, especially for NDEs and LDCs. These localization pressures include unique consumer preferences resulting from cultural or national differences (perhaps something as simple as right-hand drive cars for Japan), domestic subsidies, and new production technologies that facilitate product variation for less cost than before.[40] By "acting local," firms can focus individually in each country or region on the local market needs for product or service characteristics, distribution, customer support, and so on.

As with any management function, the strategic choice regarding where a company should position itself along the globalization–regionalization continuum is contingent on the nature of the industry, the type of company, the company's goals and strengths (or weaknesses), and the nature of its subsidiaries, among many factors. In addition, each company's strategic approach should be unique in adapting to its own environment. Many firms may try to "go global, act local" to trade off the best advantages of each strategy. Matsushita is one firm with considerable expertise at being a "GLOCAL" firm (GLObal, LoCAL), as described in the Management Focus—"Matsushita: Way to Go Global and Act Local."

Global Integrative Strategies

Many MNCs have developed their global operations to the point of being fully integrated—often both vertically and horizontally, including suppliers, productive facilities, marketing and distribution outlets, and contractors around the world. Dell, for example, is a globally integrated company, with worldwide sourcing and a fully integrated production and marketing system. It has factories in Ireland, Malaysia, and Texas, and has an assembly and delivery system from 47 locations around the world. At the same time, it has extreme flexibility; since Dell builds computers to order, it carries very little inventory, and therefore can change its operations at a moment's notice.

Although some companies move very quickly to the stage of global integration—often through merger or acquisition—many companies evolve into multinational corporations by going through the entry strategies in stages, taking varying lengths of time between stages. Typically, a company starts with simple exporting, moves to large-scale exporting with sales branches abroad (or perhaps begins licensing), then proceeds to assembly abroad (either by itself or through contract manufacturing), and eventually evolves to full production abroad with its own subsidiaries.[41] Finally, the MNC will undertake the global integration of its foreign subsidiaries, setting up cooperative activities among them to achieve economies of scale. By this point, the MNC has usually adopted a geocentric orientation, viewing opportunities and entry strategies in the context of an interrelated global market instead of regional or

MANAGEMENT FOCUS

Matsushita: Way to Go Global and Act Local

When you go abroad, don't eat another person's pie.
                                              —Konosuke Matsushita

In 1918, Konosuke Matsushita founded the Matsushita firm, which has become the world's largest consumer electronics firm. Since that time, until his death in 1989, he impressed the world with his leadership in manufacturing high-quality, high-volume, and low-priced products, and in his caring and loyal approach to employees. Matsushita has spent more than 30 years expanding around the world like a bulldozer—unstoppable, but at the same time careful, making few mistakes. Matsushita currently has more than 150 production and R&D bases in 38 countries. Global brands such as Panasonic and National were part of revenues in 1994, with 20 percent in video equipment; 13 percent in home appliances; 12 percent in electronic components; and the rest in entertainment, audio equipment, and kitchen products. Around the world, the workday starts with workers singing the company song about how their work is in noble pursuit of everyone's future welfare.

Yoichi Morishita, current president, has continued Matsushita's success in going global, transplanting high-level manufacturing skills into mini-Matsushitas—factories producing a variety of products in Europe, the Middle East, America, Latin America, and Africa. But though expert at going global, Matsushita has also had to work hard to localize all aspects of its businesses, including procurement of local management; the company was quick to recognize the difficulties in operating in a variety of cultures, political and economic systems, languages, currencies, voltages, and so on. It has encouraged its overseas plants to develop products and marketing plans so as to tailor the home appliances and electronic devices to the needs of local customers, such as designing the cooking controls on microwave ovens differently in Europe to accommodate cooking and food preferences of, for example, both the British and the Germans.

In addition to localizing product design, manufacturing, and marketing strategies, Matsushita has adapted to a variety of different cultures and work habits from Kuala Lumpur, Malaysia, to Beijing. The U.S. company cafeterias in Malaysia, for example, provide different ethnic foods for the diverse employees, whose makeup includes Muslim Malays, ethnic Chinese, and Indians.

Special prayer rooms are set aside for Muslim prayer sessions, allowing two sessions per shift.

Matsushita's founder, Konosuke Matsushita, also founded Matsushita's policy to be a good corporate citizen in every country, when he said, "when you go abroad, don't eat another person's pie." When Matsushita took over a National Semiconductor plant in Puyallup, Washington, for example, Matsushita brought in its no-layoff policy and guaranteed a job for every employee who wanted to stay, even keeping people at their existing salaries when they were assigned to lesser positions. Both sides had to get used to some differences, though, since the company asked for more efficient practices: The Japanese, for instance, had to get used to the fact that, at five o'clock, the Americans go home, whereas in Japan, they stay until the work is finished. In China, the company is working on encouraging teamwork, which the Chinese lack. In addition, Matsushita is trying to accommodate employees' needs by providing them with housing and a preschool for their children. In Malaysia, where Matsushita employs 23,500 people in its 13 new subsidiaries, the company diligently follows its policy of trying to keep the expatriate headcount down and train local managers—only 230 employees there are Japanese.

Much of Matsushita's success is apparently attributable to its "go global, act local" practices and policies, some of which are listed here, as reported in *Fortune*:

- Be a good corporate citizen in every country, respecting cultures, customs, and languages.
- Give overseas operations your best manufacturing technology.
- Keep expatriate headcount down and groom local managers to take over.
- Let plants set their own rules, fine-tuning manufacturing processes to match the skills of workers.
- Develop local R&D to tailor products to markets.
- Encourage competition among overseas outposts and with plants back home.

Source: B. Schlender, "Matsushita Shows How to Go Global," *Fortune,* July 11, 1994; "Tradition Be Damned," *Business Week,* October 31, 1994; "Matsushita: Value-Added Management for Global Partnerships," *Business Week,* July 12, 1993; "Japan's Fallible Firms," *Economist,* February 27, 1993.

EXHIBIT 7–6

Network of Entry Strategies and Alliances

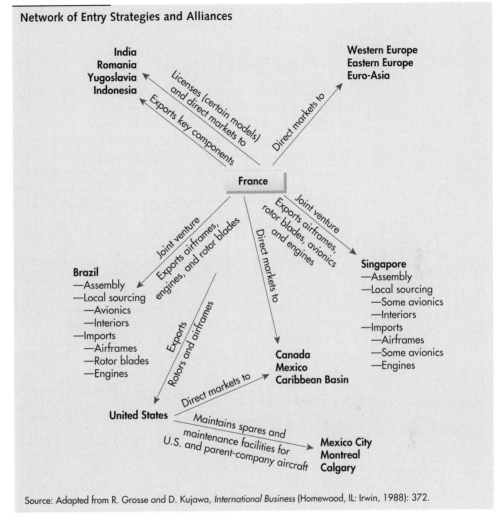

Source: Adapted from R. Grosse and D. Kujawa, *International Business* (Homewood, IL: Irwin, 1988): 372.

national markets. In this way, alternative entry strategies are viewed on an overall portfolio basis to take maximum advantage of potential synergies and leverage arising from operations in multicountry markets.[42]

Exhibit 7–6 illustrates the integrated, concurrent strategies used in the global network of the Helicopter Division of France's Société Nationale Industrielle Aérospatiale. The corporation employs a complex pattern of entry strategies and alliances among plants around the world, involving exporting, licensing, joint ventures, importing, and subassembly and maintenance facilities.[43] For example, the company has joint ventures with Brazil and Singapore and also exports parts to those countries for assembly; it licenses certain models to India and Yugoslavia and also exports to them; and it exports rotors and airframes to the United States, which, in turn, direct markets to Canada and Mexico, and maintains spares and maintenance facilities for operations in those countries.

Entry Strategy Alternatives

For a multinational corporation (or a company considering entry into the international arena), a more specific set of strategic alternatives, often varying by targeted country, focuses on different ways to enter a foreign market. Managers need to consider how potential new markets may best be served by their company in light of the risks and the critical environmental factors associated with their entry strategies. The following sections examine the various entry and ownership strategies available to firms, including exporting, licensing, franchising, contract manufacturing, turnkey operations, management contracts, joint ventures, and fully owned subsidiaries set up by the firm. These alternatives are not mutually exclusive; several may be employed at the same time. They are addressed in order of ascending risk.

Exporting Exporting is a relatively low-risk way to begin international expansion or test out an overseas market. Little investment is involved, and fast withdrawal is relatively easy. Small firms seldom go beyond this stage, and large firms use this avenue for many of their products. Because of their comparative lack of capital resources and marketing clout, exporting is the primary entry strategy used by small businesses to compete on an international level. Jordan Toothbrush, for example, a small company with one plant in Norway and with limited resources, is dependent on good distributors; as Jordan exports around the world, the company recognizes the importance of maintaining good distributor relations. A recent survey by Dun and Bradstreet showed that more than half of small to medium-sized businesses anticipate growth in their export sales in the next few years.[44]

An experienced firm may want to handle its exporting functions by appointing a manager or establishing an export department. Alternatively, an *export management company* (*EMC*) may be retained to take over some or all exporting functions, including dealing with host-country regulations, tariffs, duties, documentation, letters of credit, currency conversion, and so forth. Frequently, it pays to hire a specialist for a given host country.

Certain decisions need special care when managers are setting up an exporting system, particularly the choice of distributor. Many countries have regulations that make it very hard to remove a distributor that proves inefficient. Other critical environmental factors include export–import tariffs and quotas, freight costs, and distance from supplier countries.

Licensing An international licensing agreement grants the rights to a firm in the host country to either produce or sell a product, or both. This agreement involves the transfer of rights to patents, trademarks, or technology for a specified period in return for a fee paid by the licensee. Anheuser-Busch, for instance, has granted licenses to produce and market Budweiser beer in England, Japan, Australia, and Israel, among other countries. Many food-manufacturing MNCs license their products overseas, often under the names of local firms, and products like those of Nike and Disney can be seen around the world under various licensing agreements. Like exporting, licensing is also a relatively low-risk strategy because it requires little investment, and it can be a very useful option in countries where market entry by other means is constrained by regulations or profit-repatriation restrictions.

Licensing is especially suitable for the mature phase of a product's life cycle, when competition is intense, margins decline, and production is relatively standardized.[45] It is also useful for firms with rapidly changing technologies, for those with many diverse product lines, and for small firms with few financial and managerial resources for direct investment abroad. A clear advantage of licensing is that it avoids the tariffs and quotas usually imposed on exports. The most common disadvantage is the licensor's lack of control over the licensee's activities and performance.

Critical environmental factors to consider in licensing are whether sufficient patent and trademark protection is available in the host country, the track record and quality of the licensee, the risk that the licensee may develop its competence to become a direct competitor, the licensee's market territory, and legal limits on the royalty rate structure in the host country.[46]

Franchising Similar to licensing, franchising involves relatively little risk. The franchisor licenses its trademark, products and services, and operating principles to the franchisee for an initial fee and ongoing royalties. Franchises are well known in the domestic fast-food industry; McDonald's, for example, operates primarily on this basis. For a large upfront fee and considerable royalty payments, the franchisee gets the benefit of McDonald's reputation, existing clientele, marketing clout, and management expertise. The "Big M" is well recognized internationally, as are many other fast-food and hotel franchises, such as Holiday Inn. A critical consideration for the franchisor's management is quality control, which becomes more difficult with greater geographic dispersion.

Franchising can be an ideal strategy for small businesses because outlets require little investment in capital or human resources. In fact, through franchising, an entrepreneur can use the resources of franchisees to expand; most of today's large franchises started out with this strategy. An entrepreneur can also use franchisees to enter a new business. Higher costs in entry fees and royalties are offset by the lower risk of an established product, trademark, and customer base, as well as the benefit of the franchisor's experience and techniques.[47]

Contract Manufacturing A common means of using cheaper labor overseas is contract manufacturing, which involves contracting for the production of finished goods or component parts. These goods or components are then imported to the home country, or to other countries, for assembly or sale. Alternatively, they may be sold in the host country. If managers can ensure the reliability and quality of the local contractor and work out adequate means of capital repatriation, this strategy can be a desirable means of quick entry into a country with a low capital investment and none of the problems of local ownership. Firms like Nike use contract manufacturing around the world.

Turnkey Operations In a so-called turnkey operation, a company designs and constructs a facility abroad (such as a dam or chemical plant), trains local personnel, and then turns the key over to local management—for a fee, of course. The Italian company Fiat, for example, constructed an automobile plant in the former Soviet Union under a turnkey agreement. Critical factors for success are the availability of local supplies and labor, reliable infrastructure, and an acceptable means of repatriating profits. There may also be a critical risk exposure if the turnkey contract is with the host government, which is often the case. This situation exposes the company to risks such as contract revocation and the rescission of bank guarantees.

Management Contracts   A management contract gives a foreign company the rights to manage the daily operations of a business, but not to make decisions regarding ownership, financing, or strategic and policy changes.[48] Usually, management contracts are enacted in combination with other agreements, such as joint ventures. By itself, a management contract is a relatively low-risk entry strategy, but it is likely to be short term and to provide limited income unless it leads to another more permanent position in the market.[49]

International Joint Ventures (IJVs)   At a much higher level of investment and risk (though usually less risk than a wholly owned plant), joint ventures present considerable opportunities unattainable through other strategies. A joint venture involves an agreement by two or more companies to produce a product or service together. An IJV ownership is shared, typically by an MNC and a local partner, through agreed-upon proportions of equity. This strategy facilitates an MNC's rapid entry into new markets by means of an already-established partner that has local contacts and familiarity with local operations. IJVs are a common strategy for corporate growth around the world; they also are a means to overcome trade barriers, to achieve significant economies of scale for development of a strong competitive position, to secure access to additional raw materials, to acquire managerial and technological skills, and to share the risk associated with operating in a foreign environment.[50] The joint venture reduces the risks of expropriation and harassment by the host country; indeed, it may be the only means of entry into certain countries, like Mexico and Japan, that stipulate proportions of local ownership and local participation.

In recent years, IJVs have made up about 20 percent of direct investments by MNCs in other countries, including such deals as the robotics venture between Fujitsu and General Electric and the fiber-optic venture between Siemens A.G. and Corning Glass Works.[51] Many companies have set up joint ventures with European companies to gain the status of an "insider" in the European Common Market. Most of these alliances are not just tools of convenience but an important—perhaps critical—means to compete in the global arena.[52] To compete globally, firms have to incur and defray immense fixed costs, and they need partners to help them in this.[53]

Sometimes countries themselves need such alliances to improve economic conditions. The Commonwealth of Independent States (CIS) has recently opened its doors to joint ventures, seeking an infusion of capital and management expertise. Philip Morris, discussed earlier, entered a joint venture with Artovaz, a Russian auto manufacturer, to produce Marlboro cigarettes at a converted plant in Samara.

In a joint venture, the level of relative ownership and specific contributions must be worked out by the partners. The partners must share management and decision making for a successful alliance. The company seeking such a venture must maintain sufficient control, however, because without adequate control, the company's managers may be unable to implement their desired strategies. Initial partner selection and the development of a mutually beneficial working agreement are therefore critical to the success of a joint venture. In addition, managers must ascertain that there will be enough of a "fit" between the partners' objectives, strategies, and resources—financial, human, and technological—to make the venture work. Unfortunately, too often the need for preparation and cooperation is given insufficient attention, resulting in many such marriages ending in divorce. In fact, about 60 percent of IJVs fail, usually because of ineffective managerial decisions regarding the type of IJV, its scope, duration, and administration, as well as careless partner selection.[54] The list of cross-cultural disappointments is getting longer—Chrysler-Mitsubishi and Fiat-Nissan have, according to *Business Week*, "produced as much rancor as rewards." [55] After years of arguments, GM is pulling out of its operations with Korea's Daewoo Motors, citing insufficient care given to their relationship.

International joint ventures are one of many forms of strategic global alliances, further discussed in the next chapter.

Fully Owned Subsidiaries   In countries where a fully owned subsidiary is permitted, an MNC wishing to have total control of its operations can start its own product or service business from scratch, or it may acquire an existing firm in the host country. Philip Morris acquired the Swiss food firm Jacobs Suchard to gain an early inside track in the European Common Market and to continue its diversification away from its aging tobacco business. With this move, PM became the second U.S. company (after Mars) to assure itself a place in Europe's food industry.[56] Such acquisitions by MNCs allow rapid entry into a market with established products and distribution networks, and provide a level of acceptability not likely to be given to a "foreign" firm. These advantages offset, somewhat, the greater level of risk stemming from the larger capital investments, compared with other entry strategies.

At the highest level of risk is the strategy of starting a business from scratch in the host country—that is, establishing a new wholly owned foreign manufacturing or service company or subsidiary, with products aimed at the local market or targeted for export. Japanese automobile manufacturers—Honda, Nissan, and Toyota—have successfully used this strategy in the United States to get around American import quotas.

This strategy exposes the company to the full range of risk, to the extent of its investment in the host country. As evidenced by events in South Africa and China, political instability can be devastating to a wholly owned foreign subsidiary. Add to this risk a number of other critical environmental factors—local attitudes toward foreign ownership, currency stability and repatriation, the threat of expropriation and nationalism—and you have a high-risk entry strategy that must be carefully evaluated and monitored. There are advantages to this strategy, however, such as full control over decision making and efficiency as well as the ability to integrate operations with overall companywide strategy.

Exhibit 7–7 summarizes the advantages and critical success factors of these entry strategies that must be taken into account when selecting one or a combination of strategies depending on the location, the environmental factors and competitive analysis discussed here, and the overall strategy in which the company approaches world markets.

Complex situational factors face the international manager as he or she considers strategic approaches to world markets, along with which entry strategies might be appropriate, as illustrated in the accompanying Comparative Management in Focus—"Strategic Planning for the EU Market."

Strategic Planning for the EU Market[57]

Now that the European Union (EU) common market is a reality—complete with a single currency, the euro, along with the free flow of money, people, goods, and services around its eleven member countries—managers both internal and external to that market must plan their strategies

EXHIBIT 7–7

International Entry Strategies: Advantages and Critical Success Factors

Strategy	Advantages	Critical Success Factors
Exporting	Low risk No long-term assets Easy market access and exit	Choice of distributor Transportation costs Tariffs and quotas
Licensing	No asset ownership risk Fast market access Avoids regulations and tariffs	Quality and trustworthiness of licensee Appropriability of intellectual property Host-country royalty limits
Franchising	Little investment or risk Fast market access Small business expansion	Quality control of franchisee and franchise operations
Contract manufacturing	Limited cost and risk Short-term commitment	Reliability and quality of local contractor Operational control and human rights issues
Turnkey operations	Revenue from skills and technology where FDI restricted	Reliable infrastructure Sufficient local supplies and labor Repatriable profits Reliability of any government partner
Management contracts	Low-risk access to further strategies	Opportunity gain longer-term position

Joint ventures	Insider access to markets
	Share costs and risk
	Leverage partner's skill base technology, local
	  contacts
		Strategic fit and complementarity of partner,
		  markets, products
		Ability to protect technology
		Competitive advantage
		Ability to share control
		Cultural adaptability of partners

Wholly owned subsidiaries	Realize all revenues and control
	Global economies of scale
	Strategic coordination
	Protect technology and skill base
	Acquisition provides rapid market entry into
	  established market
		Ability to assess and control economic, political
		  and currency risk
		Ability to get local acceptance
		Repatriability of profits

accordingly. "Foreign" managers, for example, need to develop an action program to ensure that their products have continued access to the EU and to adapt their marketing efforts to encompass the whole EU. The latter task is difficult, if not impossible, however, because the "citizen of Europe" is a myth; national cultures and tastes cannot be homogenized. With many different languages and distinctive national customs and cultures, companies trying to sell in Europe must thread their way through a maze of varying national preferences. These and other challenges lie ahead, along with numerous opportunities.

UPS is one of many firms experiencing this double-edged sword. Its managers realize that Europe is still virgin territory for service companies, and they expect revenue to grow by 15 percent a year there. However, it has run into many conflicts, both practical and cultural. Some of the surprises "Big Brown" had as it put its brown uniforms on 25,000 Europeans and sprayed brown paint on 10,000 delivery trucks around Europe included indignation in France, when drivers were told they couldn't have wine with lunch; protests in Britain, when drivers' dogs were banned from delivery trucks; dismay in Spain, when it was found that the brown UPS trucks resembled the local hearses; and shock in Germany, when brown shirts were required for the first time since 1945.[58]

Meanwhile, adventurous European businesses are spreading their wings across neighboring countries as they realize that open markets can offer as much growth and profitability as does protectionism—probably more. British Airways, for example, has taken the German market under its wing by buying 49 percent of a local airline and using a new Euroname, Deutsche BA.

For strategic planning, managers around the world must anticipate possible outcomes from the perspective of companies inside as well as outside the new consolidated market. Companies within the EU can gain great advantages by competing in a continental-scale market and thereby avoiding duplication of administrative procedures, production, marketing, and distribution. The Dutch insurance giant Achmea is one such company—competing by being technologically efficient, as described in the accompanying Technology Application. For insiders, a single EU internal market means greater efficiencies and greater economic growth through economies of scale and the removal of barriers, with the consequent lowering of unit costs.

Stiffer competition, however, will result both within the market and outside it, leading to a shakeout of firms; mergers and acquisitions will increase so that larger firms will be strong enough to survive. The eleven "Euroland" countries already have a combined 19 percent of world trade, compared to 17 percent for the United States and 8 percent for Japan, and continued strong growth is projected.

Companies based outside the EU will enjoy the same advantages if they have a subsidiary in at least one member state. But they will potentially feel discrimination simply because they will be outside what for the member states is a domestic market. In other words, the EU may build a protectionist wall—of tariffs, quotas, and competitive tactics—to keep out the United States and Japan. However, the EU will also create opportunities for nonmembers—a market with a potential purchasing power of $2.5 trillion, for instance. Many companies, especially MNCs, will start from a better position than some firms based inside the community because of (1) their superior competitiveness and research and development, (2) an existing foothold in the market, and (3) reduced operating expenses (one subsidiary for the whole EU instead of several). But European harmonized standards, while seeking to eliminate trade barriers within Europe, serve to limit access to EU markets by outside companies through the standardized specifications of products allowed to be sold in Europe. The harmonization laws set minimum standards for exports and imports that are EU-wide. However, those standards also frequently hinder European companies from efficient sourcing of raw materials or component parts from "foreign" companies. Opinions differ about the long-term impact on U.S. firms: The EU could unify its markets, adversely affecting some U.S. industries; market access could be reduced; and demands for reciprocal market access in the United States may ensue.

Others feel that the new single market will provide little threat to and considerable opportunity for Americans. Many U.S. firms (in anticipation of protectionism) have invested in Europe since the beginning of the Common Market in 1958, and they now feel satisfied with their current positions. Indeed, U.S. companies (GE, Dow, 3M, Hewlett-Packard) who already have well-established European presences enjoy the same free flow of goods, services, capital, and people as Europeans.

Those U.S. companies not yet established in Europe must examine the EU internal market to decide on their most effective "European strategy." Many firms are opting for joint ventures with European partners, sacrificing their usual preference of 100 percent ownership (or majority control) to extend operations around Europe. This strategy also opens doors to markets dominated by public procurement, as with the AT&T–Philips venture to produce telecommunications equipment. But for a number of firms—both foreign and European—operating in Europe has become cost prohibitive. The average western European earns more, works fewer hours, takes longer vacations, and receives more social entitlements and job protection than people in Asia and North America. Average hourly manufacturing labor costs in Western Germany, for example, are almost $25, compared to about $16.50 in America and Japan, $11.73 in Spain,

TECHNOLOGY APPLICATION

Dutch Insurance Giant Achmea Prepares for the Borderless Europe

The Challenges

Achmea is the name of a rapidly growing conglomerate of Dutch financial services companies, including insurance companies and financiers. With more than 6,800 employees—a turnover in excess of 12.6 billion guilders and a net profit in 1995 of 471 million guilders—Achmea is one of the leading players in the market. In an integrated Europe, with an atmosphere of increase of scale and disappearing borders, many Dutch companies are opting for far-reaching forms of cooperation in order to remain competitive.

Achmea itself is a member of **Eureko**, an international cross-border European alliance of insurers. But throughout its efforts to expand, the company has not lost sight of the need for cohesion. Within the Achmea group of independently operating business units, maximizing the benefits of synergy receives the highest priority. Levels of performance must be constantly increased and improved to remain ahead of, or at least on terms with, the emerging competition. Achmea has to be more than the sum of its parts. The aim is to create solidarity among the thousands of employees in the various Achmea companies. For instance, synergy awards are presented to people who successfully employ synergy from every corner of the organization and make use of synergy as virtual companies. And the magic glue that holds it together is an unimpeded exchange of relevant information about services and market developments. Optimization of communication has become a strategic objective.

Digital Esperanto (world language)

The world of insurance and financial services has traditionally been dominated by transaction-based mainframe systems. The companies that together form Achmea have a long history of computerization and possess a highly diverse and extensive infrastructure. This is acknowledged in Achmea's IT strategy, and policy is consequently directed toward reducing the diversity in order to simplify the management and exchange of information. Within the Achmea group business unit, AV Holding, the ITC (Information Technology Center) leads the way in implementing the technical aspects of this strategy. ITC looked for a solution capable of enabling communication between the various platforms and locations in the short term: an integral communication system, the successor to the existing e-mail packages. The solution had to be platform independent, facilitate working in shifting groups, and yet be affordable. Given the many requirements, it was a practically impossible task.

The Solution

IBM's Lotus Notes software proved to be the solution. With its platform-independent structure, Notes can be laid like a shelf over all the existing infrastructures. It allows every business unit to maintain its own computer structure and smoothly adds integration of horizontal communication. Notes makes concernwide exchange of information and cooperation in groups possible and feasible.

Source: E-business. IBM Online. www.IBM.com

$5.12 in Singapore, $2.41 in Mexico, and $0.54 in China. Siemens AG of Germany, for example, shifted almost all its semiconductor assembly work from its plants in Germany—where it was not permitted to operate around the clock or on weekends—to a plant in Singapore, where it operates 24 hours a day, 365 days a year, and pays $4.40 a hour for workers.[59]

Suzuki, Toyota, Nissan, and other Japanese companies are also experiencing the dilemma of operating in Europe. They are reluctant to pour yen freely into Europe, but they want to keep a foothold in the market. Suzuki, for example, found that in its Spanish plant it took five times the number of workers and cost 46 percent more to produce a Suzuki Samurai than in Japan.

Strategic Choice

The strategic choice of one or more of the entry strategies will depend on (1) a critical evaluation of the advantages and disadvantages of each in relation to the firm's capabilities, (2) the critical environmental factors, and (3) the contribution that each choice would make to the overall mission and objectives of the company. Exhibit 7–7 summarized the advantages and the critical success factors for each entry strategy discussed. However, when it comes down to a choice of entry strategy or strategies for a particular company, more specific factors relating to that firm's situation must be taken into account. These include factors relating to the firm itself, the industry in which it operates, location factors, and venture-specific factors, as summarized in Exhibit 7–8.

After consideration of the factors for the firm as shown in Exhibit 7–8, as well as what is available and legal in the desired location, some entry strategies will no doubt fall out of the feasibility zone. From those options remaining, then, strategic planners need to decide which factors are more important to the firm than others. One method is to develop a weighted assessment to compare the overall impact of factors, such as those in Exhibit 7–8, relative to the industry, the location, and the specific venture—on each entry strategy. Specific evaluation ratings, of course, would depend on the country conditions at a given time, the nature of the industry, and the focal company.

The choice of entry strategy for McDonald's, for example, varies around the world according to the prevailing conditions in each country. With its 4,700 foreign stores, McDonald's is, according to *Fortune,* "a virtual blueprint for taking a service organization global."[60] CEO Mike Quinlan notes that in Europe, the company prefers wholly owned subsidiaries since European markets are similar to those in the United States and can be run similarly. Those subsidiaries in the United States both operate company-owned stores and license out franchises. Approximately 70 percent of McDonald's stores around the world are franchised. In Asia, joint ventures are preferred so as to take advantage of partners' contacts and local expertise, and their ability to negotiate with bureaucracies such as the Chinese government. Headed by billionaire Den Fujita, McDonald's has more than 1,000 stores in Japan; in China, it had 23 stores in 1994, with more planned, in spite of conflicts with the Chinese government, such as when it made McDonald's move from its leased Tiananmen Square restaurant. In other markets, such as in Saudi Arabia, McDonald's prefers to limit its equity risk by licensing the name—adding strict quality standards—and keeping an option to buy later. Some of McDonald's implementation policies are given in the next chapter.[61]

EXHIBIT 7-8

Factors Affecting Choice of International Entry Mode

Factor Category	Examples
Firm factors	International experience Core competencies Core capabilities National culture of home country Corporate culture Firm strategy, goals, and motivation
Industry factors	Industry globalization Industry growth rate Technical intensity of industry
Location factors	Extent of scale and location economies Country risk Cultural distance Knowledge of local market Potential of local market Competition in local market
Venture-specific factors	Value of firm—assets risked in foreign location Extent to which know-how involved in venture is informal (tacit) Costs of making or enforcing contracts with local partners Size of planned foreign venture Intent to conduct research and development with local partners

Source: *International Management—Concepts and Cases* by A. V. Phatak. Copyright ©1997 South-Western College Publishing, Cincinnati, Ohio, a division of International Thomson Publishing Inc.

Timing Entry and Scheduling Expansions   As with McDonald's, international strategic formulation requires a long-term perspective. Entry strategies, therefore, need to be conceived as part of a well-designed, overall plan. In the past, many companies have decided on a particular means of entry that seemed appropriate at the time, only to find later that it was shortsighted. For instance, if a company initially chooses to license a host-country company to produce a product, then later decides that the market is large enough to warrant its own production facility, this new strategy will no longer be feasible because the local host-country company already owns the rights.[62]

In addition, strategic choices at various levels are often influenced by cultural factors, such as a long-term versus a short-term perspective. Hofstede found that most people in countries such as China and Japan generally had a longer-term horizon than those in Canada and the United States. Whereas Americans, then, might make strategic choices with a heavy emphasis on short-term profits, the Japanese are known to be more patient in sacrificing short-term results in order to build for the future with investment, research and development, and market share.

Conclusion

The process of strategic formulation for global competitiveness is a daunting task in the volatile international arena and is further complicated by the difficulties involved in acquiring timely and credible information. However, early insight into global developments provides a critical advantage in positioning a firm for future success.

When an entry strategy is selected, the international manager focuses on translating strategic plans into actual operations. Often this involves strategic alliances; always it involves functional-level activities for strategic implementation. These subjects are covered in the next chapter.

Summary of Key Points

1. Companies go international for many reasons, including reactive ones, such as international competition, trade barriers, and customer demands. Proactive reasons include seeking economies of scale, new international markets, resource access, cost savings, and local incentives.

2. International expansion and the resulting realized strategy of a firm is the result of intentions from both rational planning and responding to emergent opportunities.

3. The steps in the rational planning process for developing an international corporate strategy include defining the mission and objectives of the firm, scanning the environment for threats and opportunities, assessing the internal strengths and weaknesses of the firm, considering alternative international entry strategies, and deciding on strategy. The strategic management process is completed by putting into place the operational plans necessary to implement the strategy and then setting up control and evaluation procedures.

4. Competitive analysis is an assessment of how a firm's strengths and weaknesses vis-à-vis those of its competitors affect the opportunities and threats in the international environment. Such assessment allows the firm to determine where the company has distinctive competencies that will give it strategic advantage or where problem areas exist.

5. Corporate-level strategic approaches to international competitiveness include globalization and regionalization. Many MNCs have developed to the point of using an integrative global strategy. Entry and ownership strategies include exporting, licensing, franchising, contract manufacturing, turnkey operations, management contracts, joint ventures, and fully owned subsidiaries. Critical environmental and operational factors for implementation must be taken into account.

Discussion Questions

1. Discuss why companies go international, giving specific reactive and proactive reasons.

2. Discuss the ways in which managers arrive at new strategic directions—formal and informal. Which is the best?

3. Explain the process of environmental assessment. What are the major international variables to consider in the scanning process? Discuss the levels of environmental monitoring that should be conducted. How well do you think managers conduct environmental assessment?

4. How can managers assess the potential relative competitive position of their firm in order to decide on new strategic directions?

5. Discuss the relative advantages of globalization versus regionalization.

6. What are the relative merits of the entry strategies discussed in this chapter? What is their role in an integrative global strategy?

7. Discuss the considerations in strategic choice, including the typical stages of the MNC and the need for a long-term global perspective.

Application Exercises

1. Choose a company in the microcomputer industry or a chain in the fast-food industry. In small groups, conduct a multilevel environmental analysis, describing the major variables involved, the relative impact of specific threats and opportunities, and the critical environmental factors to be

considered. The group findings can then be presented to the class, allowing a specific period for each group so that comparison and debate of different group perspectives can follow. Be prepared to state what regions or specific countries you are interested in and give your rationale.

2. In small groups, discuss among yourselves, and then debate with the other groups, the relative merits of the alternative entry strategies for the company and countries you chose in exercise 1. You should be able to make a specific choice and defend that decision.

3. For this exercise, research (individually or in small groups) a company with international operations and find out the kinds of entry strategies the firm has used. Present the information you find, in writing or orally to the class, describing the nature of the company's international operations, its motivations, its entry strategies, the kinds of implementation problems the firm has run into, and how those problems have been dealt with.

Experiential Exercise

In groups of four, develop a strategic analysis for a type of company of interest to your group considering entry into Russia. Which entry strategies seem most appropriate? Share your results with the class.

Internet Resources

Visit the Deresky companion Web site at http://prenhall.com/Deresky for this chapter's Internet resources.

Case Study

Cola Wars: The Venezuelan Coup

Open Case Scenario: Disappointed Pepsi Distributor

Stefano: Hóla señora Ganser, ¿Como estás?
Sra. Ganser: Muy bien gracias, ¿y usted?
Stefano: Muy bien, hoy necesito doscientas botellas de Pepsi para mi tienda.
Sra. Ganser: Lo siento señor, pero tengo solamente Coca-Cola.
Stefano: ¿Qúe? Pero, yo compré trescientas botellas el viernes.
Sra. Ganser: Sí, pero en el fin de semana la embotelladora de Coca-Cola compró a Pepsi. Ahora todas las tiendas en Venezuela solamente pueden comprar Coca-Cola.
Stefano: Ay Díos mío, no tengo ninguna selección de refrescos. ¡Qué tipo de país es este!

Translation

Steve: Hello, Mrs. Ganser, How are you?
Mrs. Ganser: Very well thanks, and you?
Steve: Very good. Today, I need 200 bottles of Pepsi for my store.
Mrs. Ganser: I'm sorry, sir, I have only Coca-Cola.
Steve: What? But I just bought 300 bottles on Friday.
Mrs. Ganser: Yes, but over the weekend Coca-Cola bought Pepsi. Now all the stores in Venezuela can buy only Coca-Cola.
Steve: Oh My God! I have no selection in drinks. What kind of country is this!

Cola Wars

The cola wars have been going on for more than 65 years, since the establishment of Coca-Cola in 1886. Their first shipment was sent abroad in 1900. From the beginning, Coke had a head start in overseas operations. By 1931, they already had bottling operations in Cuba, Panama, Puerto Rico, The Philippines, and Guam (*The Washington Post,* August 24, 1996).

Pepsi was not far behind; by the 1970s, they had captured the Soviet market and scored other international successes, at which time Coke's sales abroad were flat. In 1981, Coca-Cola paid $30 million for a 30 percent equity stake in a Philippine bottler and reversed the 2–1 Pepsi advantage that had previously existed. In 1985, in the United States, Coke suffered legendary humiliation with the launch of New Coke; however, they were quick to replace it with Classic Coke.

By the late 1980s, Coca-Cola had leapt into eastern Europe, where it bought every available bottling plant in East Germany and moved ahead of Pepsi there. By 1995, Coke had customers in 200 countries, and more than 80 percent of its profits came from abroad, compared to 30 percent for Pepsi.

Pepsi was always looking for holes in the cola market where it could gain some market share, while also trying to fend off counterattacks. Its early links in Moscow gave it a 2–1 advantage in eastern Europe, but that advantage has changed with Coke jumping into the markets to grab shares in Moscow and India.

The war continued on in Brazil. Pepsi was obliged to take over BAESA (its largest foreign bottler) because the latter company's overly ambitious expansion program had jeopardized its financial viability. The company faced $400 million in debt and possible bankruptcy. Another Latin American disaster occurred in Venezuela. Pepsi lost out again to Coke when their bottler, the Cisneros Group, defected to Coke, without warning. This defection is the focus of this case study and the cause for analysis of Pepsi's competitive strategy.

Pepsi has attempted everything from celebrity advertising and package changes to introducing fast-food chains in order to keep up with Coke. However, Coke's aggressive strategy seems always to take Pepsi by surprise.

Takeover Events

Roger Enrico, PepsiCo's new CEO, had been on the job for only four months in August of 1996 when the news came. He had received word from Pepsi's regional president in Venezuela, Alberto Uribe, that their longtime bottling partner in Venezuela was terminating their partnership; the partner (Hit de Venezuela) had sold a 50 percent stake in its company to arch-rival Coca-Cola and would be bottling under the Coke brand from now on. This was a catastrophe—the third major blow to PepsiCo in as many weeks. First, there was the problem with their financially plagued franchise in Argentina (BAESA), which had been struggling for years with financial problems because of mismanagement and overextension. Then, in July 1996, PepsiCo went in and took over management to try to salvage what remained of this burdensome yet vital behemoth. Then there was the Puerto Rico scandal, where some questionable accounting practices by their bottler in Puerto Rico were undertaken that sent a shockwave through the company and on to Wall Street. And now this. How could something like this happen? This was PepsiCo's only true conquest in the $350 million-a-year Latin American operation, and in a matter of a few days it was gone. This presented the biggest challenge of Mr. Enrico's 24-year career with Pepsi.

Roger considered Oswaldo Cisneros a close and trusted friend. Oswaldo's family owned Hit de Venezuela (the Venezuelan bottling company) and Oswaldo was in charge of operating it. They had been faithful partners of Pepsi for 47 years. Enrico and Oswaldo had often vacationed together, and their wives were inseparable during their many travels. How could Oswaldo do something so drastic, especially when Pepsi had been in negotiations with him for the past two years, trying to strike an agreement to buy a large part of the Venezuelan operation? He thought Cisneros wanted that, too.

Meanwhile, in Caracas, Venezuela, Oswaldo Cisneros had plenty on his mind. Recently, he had signed an agreement with PepsiCo's arch rival, Coca-Cola, selling Coca-Cola a 50 percent share in the Cisneros bottling operation for $300 million up front, and another $300 million over the next five years. There was one other clincher. Coca-Cola would put up $100 million in a legal defense fund to cover the expected huge costs of court battles with his ex-partner Pepsi since Cisneros did have a contract with PepsiCo through 2003. All this had happened in such a short time that it was hard for him to believe that his family's whole enterprise was about to take on a new identity.

Oswaldo Cisneros grew up under much different circumstances than his old friend Roger Enrico. Oswaldo was born into wealth. His family emigrated from Cuba in the 1930s, and almost from the beginning they were able to do well in their new homeland. All the Cisneros kids were immersed in the soda business from the time they were little, and like their father and uncle, they became quite good at it. Oswaldo was no exception. He nurtured the business and watched it grow into a multibillion-dollar corporation. Now he was about to embark on a new adventure—one that would surely earn him the scorn of Pepsi and his old friend Roger Enrico. Unfortunately, it was the path he felt Pepsi had forced him to take.

Events Leading Up to Defection

The Cisneros empire was aching to expand to other markets, knowing that their own market in Venezuela was saturated. They controlled 85 percent of the soda industry in their country and had no more growth potential unless they could expand into emerging markets. In order to do this, they would need a lot of capital and a strong partner. Oswaldo Cisneros said he approached Pepsi with his offer to sell. Pepsi gave him the runaround for years, offering to buy at only a small fraction of what Cisneros felt it was worth. Pepsi, on the other hand, says that negotiations had been ongoing for only a couple of years and a favorable deal would have soon been reached. Another disillusioning factor for Cisneros was that he felt Pepsi was not going to allow his company to expand into other Latin American countries, instead reserving them for Pepsi's troubled child in Argentina, BAESA. So, Cisneros felt compelled to approach Coca-Cola through an investment banker to see whether Coca-Cola would be interested in a deal. This came as a complete surprise to Roberto Goizueta, chairman and chief executive officer of Coca-Cola, who had no real plans to expand Coca-Cola's market share any further in Venezuela since Pepsi had completely dominated that market for the past five decades. Of course, the possibility of reversing this trend was very appealing since Venezuela was Coca-Cola's only blemish in Latin America, so he decided to take the offer and see what would happen. There were several very secret meetings, which were often argumentative; however, in the end, there was an agreement struck that would be signed in its final form on August 14, 1996.

Meanwhile, at the Pepsi headquarters, there was no apparent reason to be alarmed. Their Venezuelan partner was conducting business as usual, and PepsiCo's corporate team was very busy with a bigger priority—trying to salvage what remained of BAESA, their faltering franchise in Argentina, not to mention the restructuring that had been going on since Roger Enrico had taken over as CEO of Pepsi. Talks had been underway for some time with the Cisneros family to purchase part of their operation, but there seemed to be no need for immediate action, so this was not given top priority.

The Deal

On Wednesday, August 14, 1996, Oswaldo Cisneros and several of his family members and aides arrived at the Atlanta International Airport, and under a veil of complete secrecy were taken to Coca-Cola's headquarters. There, they signed an agreement turning over 50 percent of their bottling operation to Coca-Cola. After the meeting, there was a grand dinner to celebrate the new

$600 million deal. This was a short-lived celebration since there would be an incredible amount of work to do in the next few days.

The Takeover

On Friday, August 16, the last Pepsis were made at Cisneros' 18 bottling plants, and a rapid transformation took place. Several large cargo planes arrived in Venezuela from the United States. They were stocked full of equipment that would be needed to convert the 18 bottling plants from production of Pepsi to that of Coca-Cola. It was a long frenzied weekend, with the old going out the door, and the new coming in. Four thousand trucks had to be repainted with Coke emblems, and many thousands of uniforms had to be distributed. There were also customers to notify, many of whom might not like the idea of this sudden change. By the time Monday rolled around, this logistical, tactical, and technical nightmare, which would have been impossible for most corporations, had been completed. The first Cokes were rolling off the assembly line, and on their way to stores and restaurants by that morning. Coke had now completed its conquest of Latin America, taking the last remaining stronghold of Pepsi.

Monday, August 19, 1996

Roger Enrico had watched in disbelief as the transformation took place. In just three days, Pepsi had gone from an 80 percent market share to zero, and from production of 4 million cases a year to zero. Now the stock market was reacting. Pepsi's shares dove $1.50 a share to $30.125, whereas rival Coke's soared to $51.75, a 52 week high (see Exhibit 7–9). Mr. Enrico knew that because of this defection, there could be rough roads ahead in other parts of the globe if he didn't respond to this crisis appropriately. Other partners might consider defecting unless convinced that Pepsi was still a big player in the cola war, and could meet Coca-Cola toe-to-toe in any fight. If other

EXHIBIT 7–9

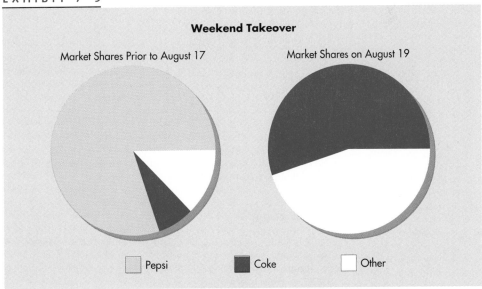

Weekend Takeover

Market Shares Prior to August 17   Market Shares on August 19

Pepsi   Coke   Other

emerging markets perceived that Coke would be a better investment than Pepsi, Pepsi's future in those markets could be very grim. There was also the concern of customers. In Venezuela, millions of loyal customers were without their favorite soft drink. How to reintroduce Pepsi to that market before they started to forget their loyalties was a paramount concern. One final concern was how to convince the stockholders that Pepsi could recover from this financial embarrassment and still give them a good return.

Competitive Situation

It is evident that Coke has adopted a strategy to consciously aim at markets where Pepsi operates. Coke takes over Pepsi's market shares by buying out the bottlers. The following examples demonstrate the takeover strategy that Coke has recently adopted:

- Coca-Cola's independent bottler in Morocco bought the only bottler of rival Pepsi in the African country for $55 million. This was more than Pepsi could imagine paying for the bottler, and as a result, Pepsi had to let Coke take over their market share there. Another case of monopolistic pressure was in South Africa. PepsiCo Inc. operated with a franchise bottler, New Age Beverages, where they owned 25 percent of the operations. Coke held an 81.3 percent share in South Africa, and in May 1997, Pepsi was forced to cease operations with a challenge from Coke's $1 billion beverage market.
- Coca-Cola continued to put Pepsi's shares in peril by purchasing Embotelladora Milca, Nicaragua's largest soft drink bottler. This was one of the few remaining locations where Pepsi accounted for as much as 45 percent of the country's cola market. This share is expected to drop with Coke's recent purchase.
- Coca-Cola was charged with engineering the defection of key PepsiCo employees, bottlers, and consultants in India through "unfair and illegal means."

Some of PepsiCo's critics feel the company should concentrate on the cola industry, improving bottling and distribution setup rather than focusing on snacks and fast-food restaurants. This is debatable, however; Pepsi may be quite content as number 2 in the cola industry considering that their investments in other industries, such as snack foods and restaurants, bring them a greater profit than their cola sales.

The following map (Exhibit 7–10) indicates the areas where Pepsi had a profitable share of the market until Coke came in and used its aggressive strategies to take over the market share.

Case Questions

1. Could Pepsi have done anything differently to stop the defection in Venezuela?
2. What kind of damage control does PepsiCo need to engage in to minimize financial losses and salvage its reputation?
3. What should Pepsi do in the future to ensure that another "Venezuela" does not happen somewhere else in the world?

Case Bibliography

Alexander, Garth. "Shake-Up to Put Sparkle into Pepsi." *Sunday Times,* 26 January 1997: Lexis Nexis. Online.

Bums, Jimmy. "Pepsi Co. Secures $8m Argentina Soccer Deal." *Financial Times* (London), 4 March 1997: 23. Lexis Nexis. Online.

EXHIBIT 7–10

Areas of Coca-Cola's Takeover of Pepsi's Market

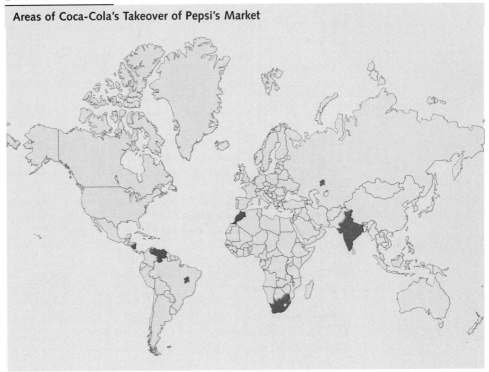

Capos, Claudia. "A Celebration with Fizz: North Carolina Town to Mark Pepsi's 100th Anniversary." *The Boston Globe,* 22 March 1998: MI. Lexis Nexis. Online.

Collins, Glenn. "A Coke Coup in Venezuela Leaves Pepsi High and Dry." *The New York Times,* 17 August 1996: 35. Lexis Nexis. Online.

Collins, Glenn. "Suddenly, Coke Is Winning Cola War in Venezuela." *The Ottawa Citizen,* 24 August 1996: Lexis Nexis. Online.

Collins, Glenn. "Pepsi Co. Wins $94 Million for Defection by Bottler." *The New York Times,* 4 September 1997: 50. Lexis Nexis. Online.

Collins, Glenn. "Pepsi Co. Bottling Operation in South Africa Is Closed." *The New York Times,* 24 May 1997: 34. Lexis Nexis. Online.

Colitt, Ray. "Pepsi Offered Venezuela Foothold." *Financial Times* (London), 20 Aug. 1996: 20. Lexis Nexis. Online.

Dawson, Havis. "Risky Business." *Beverage World,* September 1996: 10. Lexis Nexis. Online.

Deogun, Nikhil and Karp, Jonathan. "Pepsi Sues Coke Unit to Defend Indian Turf." *The Wall Street Journal,* 20 April 1998.

Goering, Laurie. "Coca-Cola Coup Renders Pepsi Flat in Venezuela." *Chicago Tribune,* 29 November 1996: 1. Lexis Nexis. Online.

Hemlock, Doreen. "Brazilian Pepsi Bottler About to Fizz Out." *Sun Sential* (Ft. Lauderdale, Fl.), 7 November 1996: ID. Lexis Nexis. Online.

Jabbonsky, Larry. "Room to Run." *Beverage World,* August 1993: 24. Lexis Nexis. Online.

Jabbonsky, Larry. "The Mexican Resurrection." *Beverage World,* August 1993: 38. Lexis Nexis. Online.

Matthews, Jay. "Coca-Cola and Pepsi Co. Intensify a 65-Year Duel for Soda Supremacy." *The Washington Post*, 24 August 1996: AO 1. Lexis Nexis. Online.

Murphy, Helen. "Cola War Erupts in Mexico." *Corporate Finance*, May 1993: 6–7. Lexis Nexis. Online.

Paulin, David. "Bottled-Up Tension: Pepsi Seeing Red Over Coke's Venezuela Coup." *The Dallas Morning News*, 22 August 1996: 1 0. Lexis Nexis. Online.

Roush, Chris. "Another Loss for Pepsi in Global Competition." *The Atlanta Journal and Constitution*, 18 February 1997: 0 1 E. Lexis Nexis. Online.

Saporito, Bill. "Parched for Growth: Pepsi Had a Grand Plan for Global Expansion. Alas, Coke Was Thirstier." *Time*, 2 September 1996: 48. Lexis Nexis. Online.

Sellers, Patricia. "PepsiCo's New Generation." *Fortune*, April 1996: 1 10. Lexis Nexis. Online.

Swafford, David. "The Fizz That Couldn't Last." *Latin Finance*, November 1996: 36. Lexis Nexis. Online.

Valdmanis, Thor. "Coke Buys Nicaragua's Biggest Bottler." *USA Today*, 22 August 1997: IB. Lexis Nexis. Online.

Nancy Rotenier. "Blue Period." *Forbes*, 12 August 1996: 138. Lexis Nexis. Online.

— "PepsiCo. Begins South American Marathon." *The Financial Times* (London), 13 December 1996: 29. Lexis Nexis. Online.

— "PepsiCo. Finds New Partner in Venezuela." *The Dallas Morning News*, 10 December 1996: 70. Lexis Nexis. Online.

— "PepsiCo. Is Preparing to Return to Venezuela." *The New York Times*, 14 November 1996: 30. Lexis Nexis. Online.

— "Tell Me Your Cola and I'll Tell You Your Party? Well Not Quite." *The New York Times*, 8 November 1992: 16. Lexis Nexis. Online.

Moody's CD Report. PepsiCo Inc., 31 December 1997.

Moody's CD Report. Coca-Cola, 31 December 1997.

Source: Adapted from a term project by Steven Davis, Sandra Ganser, and Adam Isen, students at State University of New York, Plattsburgh. Spring 1998. Copyright ©Helen Deresky, 1998.

8

Cross-Border Alliances and Strategy Implementation

OUTLINE

Opening Profile: The DaimlerChrysler AG Global Alliance

Strategic Alliances

Cross-Border Alliances: Motivations and Benefits

Challenges in Implementing Global Alliances

Guidelines for Successful Alliances

Comparative Management in Focus: Joint Ventures in the Commonwealth of Independent States

Strategic Implementation

Managing Performance in International Joint Ventures

Technology Application: Benneton Group Spa Supports Its Worldwide Business with a Technological Edge

Government Influences on Strategic Implementation

Cultural Influences on Strategic Implementation

Comparative Management in Focus: Implementing Sino–U.S. Joint Ventures: The Culture Factor

Management Focus: Wal-Mart's Implementation Problems in South America

Summary of Key Points

Discussion Questions

Application Exercises

Experiential Exercise: Partner Selection in an International Context

Internet Resources

Case Study: Ben & Jerry's and Iceverks: Alliance Meltdown in Russia

OPENING PROFILE

The DaimlerChrysler AG Global Alliance

*The car business is too capital- and customer-hungry
to care about flags.*

—Time

*By combining and utilizing each other's strengths, we
will have a pre-eminent strategic position in the
global marketplace....*

—Jürgen E. Schrempp, Chairman, Daimler-Benz;
www.Chrysler.com

The $92 billion merger of Daimler-Benz and Chrysler to form DaimlerChrysler Akteingesellschaft represents a triumph of the global economy and the end of car companies as national emblems of industrial might.

Although other automakers have alliances around the world (GM-Opel-Saab; Ford-Mazda-Jaguar; VW-Audi-Rolls-Royce, for example), the sheer size and scope of the DaimlerChrysler AG alliance redefines the industry in its strategic efforts to ensure mutual survival in ongoing global consolidation.

The combined company will have revenues of $130 billion (DM 234 billion) and a complementary product and market mix. Chrysler makes moderately priced cars and light trucks, and has skills in design and product development. Daimler, which makes Mercedes luxury cars and heavy trucks, excels in engineering and technology. Chrysler has strong markets in North America and is weak in western Europe; Daimler's market clout is the reverse. Both companies are doing well in their own markets, but see the alliance as an opportunity for global expansion, not only in Europe and the United States, but also in Latin America, Australia, and elsewhere. The two CEOs announced that they expect immediate growth opportunities by using each other's facilities, capacities, and infrastructure. DaimlerChrysler expects to realize benefits of DM 2.5 billion ($1.4 billion) through the exchange of components and technologies, combined purchasing power, and shared distribution logistics. They expect further synergies to accrue by sharing know-how in engineering and manufacturing.

Jürgen Schrempp, of Daimler-Benz, who will be cochairman and co-CEO ("Vorstandsvorsitzende") with Robert Eaton, CEO of Chrysler, notes that in a consolidating industry that may reduce by half the number of independent manufacturers over the next decade, "The answer can't be joint venture here, joint venture there. We said to ourselves 'we have to find a partner.' Once we did

Daimler's Jürgen Schrempp (left) and Chrysler's Robert Eaton join forces to form the DaimlerChrysler AG Global Alliance.

the studies of Japanese, European, and American companies, it became obvious that Chrysler was the ideal partner" (*Fortune*). Schrempp, 53, will be CEO after serving for three years as co-CEO with Eaton, 58. The merged company will be incorporated in Germany and will have two operational headquarters, one in Stuttgart, Germany, and the other in Auburn Hills, Michigan. Since the actual headquarters will not be in the United States, in reality America's Big Three automakers has become the Big Two. Implementing the merger will be no picnic. These are two giant industrial companies with a total of 421,000 employees. The senior management will have 18 members drawn from both companies. There are complexities of different labor laws and trade policies, as well as different cultures. The company will follow the German mandate that half the 24-member supervisory board (which is a separate board from the board of directors) be labor representatives, with the other 12 from the combined management. This will produce a different working environment. Other differences in the corporate culture will arise from the contrasting profit philosophies of the two companies.

Although Chrysler's past problems have turned it into a lean, profit-focused organization with profit margins of 6.5 percent, Daimler has been content with profit margins of 2 percent. Then there's the difference in executive pay systems, which will likely raise eyebrows in Germany. Last year, Daimler Chairman Jürgen Schrempp's annual compensation was about $2.5 million, whereas Chrysler Chairman Robert Eaton's compensation was more than $16 million.

Despite sticky implementation problems, the globalization advantages are many. In addition to the market expansion opportunities, there are opportunities for major cost cutting, according to the two CEOs. These include combining some of each company's massive R&D operations under one roof and gaining economies of scale through joint purchases of raw materials. The companies also hope to maximize the number of common parts they are using for their cars.

Questions

At the time of this writing, the merger had just been announced; few implementation details had been worked out—or at least they were not made public. As you read this chapter, consider some of the implementation challenges facing this alliance, and discuss them along with the application exercise at the end of the chapter. For example, what are some of the major differences in societal culture between Germans and Americans, and how could they be reconciled in the workplace? What might be the effects of the different corporate cultures? What working relationship could be developed regarding the vastly disparate labor relations systems? (German labor relations are discussed further in Chapter 11.) On the strategic front, what competitive alliances in the global automotive industry may follow this move? Have any been announced since this merger?

Sources: *www.Chrysler.com;* B. Seaman and R. Stodghill, II, "The Daimler–Chrysler Deal: Here Comes the Road Test," *Time,* May 18, 1998; "Gentlemen, Start Your Engines," *Fortune,* June 8, 1998; G. Steinmetz and G. L. White, "Chrysler Pay Draws fire Overseas," *Wall Street Journal,* May 26, 1998.

Strategic Alliances

It is no longer an era in which a single company can dominate any technology or business by itself. The technology has become so advanced, and the markets so complex, that you simply can't expect to be the best at the whole process any longer.
—Fumio Sato, CEO, Toshiba Electronics Co.[1]

Strategic alliances are partnerships between two or more firms that decide they can better pursue their mutual goals by combining their resources—financial, managerial, technological—as well as their existing distinctive competitive advantages. Alliances—often called cooperative strategies—are transition mechanisms that propel the partners' strategy forward in a turbulent environment faster than would be possible for each company alone.[2] Alliances, typically, fall under one of three categories:[3]

- **Joint ventures** occur when two or more companies create an independent company; an example is the Nuumi Corporation, created as a joint venture between Toyota and General Motors, which gave GM access to Toyota's manufacturing expertise and provided Toyota with a manufacturing base in the United States.
- **Equity strategic alliances** occur when two or more partners have different relative ownership shares (equity percentages) in the new venture. As with most global manufacturers, Toyota has equity alliances with suppliers, subassemblers and distributors; most of these are part of their network of internal family and financial links.
- **Nonequity strategic alliances** occur when agreements are carried out through contract rather than ownership sharing. Such contracts are often with a firm's suppliers, distributors, or manufacturers, or they may be for purposes of marketing and information sharing, such as with many airline partnerships.

Global strategic alliances are working partnerships between companies (often more than two) across national boundaries and increasingly across industries. Alliances are also sometimes formed between a company and a foreign government, or among companies and governments. The European Airbus Industrie consortium comprises France's Aerospatiale and Germany's Daimler-Benz Aerospace, each with 37.9 percent of the business; British Aerospace has 20 percent; and Spain's Construcciones Aeronauticas has 4.2 percent.

Alliances may comprise full global partnerships, often joint ventures, in which two or more companies, while retaining their national identity, develop a common, long-term strategy aimed at world leadership. The Daimler–Chrysler alliance is one such global partnership to achieve these kinds of objectives. Whereas such alliances have a broad agenda, others are formed for a narrow and specific function, including production, marketing, research and development, and financing.

Cross-Border Alliances: Motivations and Benefits

Alliances among companies are formed around the world for many reasons, including the following:

1. *To avoid import barriers, licensing requirements, and other protectionist legislation.* Japanese automotive manufacturers, for example, use alliances such as the GM–Toyota venture, or subsidiaries, to produce cars in the United States so as to avoid import quotas.
2. *To share the costs and risks of the research and development of new products and processes.* In the semiconductor industry, for example, where each new generation of memory chips is estimated to cost more than $1 billion to develop, those costs and the fast pace of technological evolution typically require the resources of more than one, or even two, firms. Intel, for example, has alliances with Samsung and NMB Semiconductor for DRAM technology development; Sun Microsystems has partners for its RISC technology, including N.V. Philips, Fujitsu, and Texas Instruments. Toshiba, Japan's third largest electronics company, has more

than two dozen major joint ventures and strategic alliances around the world, including part-ners such as Olivetti, Rhone-Poulenc, and GEC Alstholm in Europe; LSI Logic in Canada; and Samsung in Korea. Fumio Sato, Toshiba's CEO, recognized long ago that a global strategy for a high-tech electronics company such as his necessitated joint ventures and strategic alliances.

3. *To gain access to specific markets,* such as the European Union (EU), where regulations favor domestic companies, which was one of the enticements for Chrysler to ally with Daimler-Benz. Firms around the world are forming strategic alliances with European companies to bolster their chances of competing in the EU and to gain access to markets in eastern European countries as they open up to world business. Chun Joo Bum, chief executive of the Daewoo Electronics unit, acknowledges that he is seeking local partners in Europe for two reasons: (1) to provide sorely needed capital (a problem given Asia's economic woes), and (2) to help navigate Europe's still disparate markets. As Chun Joo Bum says, "I need to localize our management. It is not one market."[4] Market entry into some countries may be attained only through alliances—typically, joint ventures. South Korea, for example, has a limit of 18 percent on foreign investment in South Korean firms.

4. *To reduce political risk while making inroads into a new market.* Maytag Corporation, for example, determined to stay on the right side of the restrictive Chinese government while gaining market access, formed a joint venture with RSD, the Chinese appliance maker, to manufacture and market washing machines and refrigerators. Maytag also invested large amounts in jointly owned refrigeration products facilities to help RSD get into that market. Coca-Cola—a global player with large-scale alliances—is not beyond using some very small-scale alliances to be "political" in China. The company uses senior citizens in the Party's neighborhood committees to sell Coke locally.

5. *To gain rapid entry into a new or consolidating industry and to take advantage of synergies.* Technology is rapidly providing the means for overlapping and merging of traditional indus-tries such as entertainment, computers, and telecommunications in new digital-based sys-tems, creating an information superhighway. As evidenced by such partnerships as the MCI–WorldCom merger in August 1998, such developments are necessitating strategic alliances across industries in order for companies to gain rapid entry into areas in which they have no expertise or manufacturing capabilities. Competition is so fierce that they cannot wait to develop those resources alone. Many of these objectives, such as access to new tech-nology and to new markets, are evident in AT&T's network of alliances around the world, as shown in Exhibit 8–1. Agreements with Japan's NEC, for example, give AT&T access to new semiconductor and chip-making technologies in order to learn how to better integrate com-puters with communications. Another joint venture with Zenith Electronics will allow AT&T to codevelop the next generation of high-definition television (HDTV).[5]

Challenges in Implementing Global Alliances

Effective global alliances are usually tediously slow in the making but can be among the best mechanisms to implement strategies in global markets. In a highly competitive environment, alliances often present a faster and less risky route to globalization than other expansion alter-natives. It is extremely complex to fashion such linkages, however, especially where many

EXHIBIT 8–1

AT&T's Alliance Strategy

Partner	Technology	Intent
NEC	Customized chips, computer-design tools	Learn new core technologies from NEC; sales position in Japan
	Mobile phones	Penetrate cellular phone markets; compatible standards
Mitsubishi	SRAM and gallium–arsenide chips	Increase sales in Japan; learn new semiconductor technologies
Italtel	Telecommunications	Expand beachhead in Europe
N. V. Philips	Circuit boards	Market and technology access; purchased 1990
Lucky-Gold Star	Fibre optics, telecommunications, circuits	Entry into Asian markets; technology sharing agreement
Telefonics	Telecommunications and integrated circuits	Expand European production and marketing
Zenith Technology	High-definition television	Apply and learn digital compression
Intel	Personal computer networks and integrated circuits	Share manufacturing technology and capacity
		Develop UNIX computer operating system for local area networks
Hoya	Photomasks and semiconductor equipment	Develop ion-beam masks and mask design software in Japan and the United States
Mannesmann	Microwave radio gear and cellular phone technology	Serve as OEM supplier to German firm
Go Corp.	Pen-based computers and wireless networks	Set industry standards for telecommunications power and range
Olivetti	Personal computers	Failed in 1988
Eo Corp.	Personal communicator devices	Create new handheld computers
Matsushita	Microprocessors	Encourage new technology standards for Hobbit-based systems
NEC & Toshiba McCaw Cellular	Cellular telephones	Secure downstream market in the United States

Source: D. Lei, "Offensive and Defensive Uses of Alliances," in Heidi Vernon-Wortzel and L. H. Wortzel, *Strategic Management in a Global Economy*, 3rd ed. New York: John Wiley & Sons, 1997.

interconnecting systems are involved, forming intricate networks. Many alliances fail or end up in a takeover in which one partner swallows the other. McKinsey & Company, a consulting firm, surveyed 150 companies that had been in alliances and found that 75 percent of them had been taken over by Japanese partners.[6] Problems with shared ownership, the integration of vastly different structures and systems, the distribution of power between the companies involved, and conflicts in their relative locus of decision making and control are but a few of the organizational issues that must be worked out. But recent economic woes in Asia have turned the tables somewhat, with Western companies having to buy out their financially stressed allies in order for the alliance to survive.

Often, the form of governance chosen for multinational firm alliances greatly influences their success, particularly in technologically intense fields such as pharmaceuticals, computers, and semiconductors. In a study of 153 new alliances, researchers found that the choice of the means of governance—whether a contractual agreement or a joint venture—depended on a desire to control information about proprietary technology.[7] Thus, joint ventures are often the chosen form for such alliances because they provide greater control and coordination in high-technology industries.

Cross-border partnerships, in particular, often become a "race to learn," with the faster learner later dominating the alliance and rewriting its terms. In a real sense, an alliance becomes a new form of competition. In fact, according to researcher David Lei:

> Perhaps the single greatest impediment managers face when seeking to learn or renew sources of competitive advantage is to realize that co-operation can represent another form of un-intended competition, particularly to shape and apply new skills to future products and businesses.[8]

All too often, cross-border allies have difficulty in collaborating effectively, especially in competitively sensitive areas, creating mistrust and secrecy, which then undermine the purpose of the alliance. The difficulty that they are dealing with is the dual nature of strategic alliances—the benefits of cooperation versus the dangers of introducing new competition through sharing their knowledge and technological skills about their mutual product or the manufacturing process. Managers may fear that they will lose the competitive advantage of the firm's proprietary technology or the specific skills that their personnel possess. The cumulative learning that a partner attains through the alliance could potentially be applied to other products or even other industries that are beyond the scope of the alliance, and therefore would hold no benefit to the partner holding the original knowledge.[9] As noted by Lei, the Japanese, in fact, have far outlearned their U.S. allies in developing and applying new technologies to other uses. Examples are in the power equipment industry (for example, Westinghouse-Mitsubishi), the office equipment industry (Kodak-Canon), and the consumer electronics industry (General Electric-Samsung). Some of the tradeoffs of the duality of cross-border ventures are shown in Exhibit 8–2.

Although the benefits of cross-border alliances are enticing, they often mask the many pitfalls. In addition to potential loss of technology and knowledge base, other areas of incompatibility often arise, such as conflicting strategic goals and objectives, cultural clashes, and disputes over management and control systems. Sometimes it takes a while for such problems to become evident, particularly if insufficient homework has been done in meetings between the two sides to work out the implementation details. The alliance between KLM Royal Dutch Airlines and Northwest Airlines linking their hubs in Detroit and Amsterdam, for example, resulted in a bitter feud among the top officials of both companies over methods of running an airline business—the European way or the American way—and over cultural differences between the companies, as well as a power struggle at the top over who should call the shots.[10]

Guidelines for Successful Alliances

There is no doubt that many difficulties arise in cross-border alliances in melding both national and corporate cultures of the parties, in overcoming language and communication barriers, and in building trust between the parties over how to share proprietary assets and management processes. The following basic guidelines serve to minimize potential problems, but nothing is as important as having a long "courtship" with the potential partner to

EXHIBIT 8-2

The Dual Role of Strategic Alliances

Cooperative	Competitive
Economies of scale in tangible assets (e.g., plant and equipment).	Opportunity to learn new intangible skills from partner, often tacit or organization embedded.
Upstream–downstream division of labor among partners.	Accelerate diffusion of industry standards and new technologies to erect barriers to entry.
Fill out product line with components or end products provided by supplier.	Deny technological and learning initiative to partner via outsourcing and long-term supply arrangements.
Limit investment risk when entering new markets or uncertain technological fields via shared resources.	Encircle existing competitors and preempt the rise of new competitors with alliance partners in "proxy wars" to control market access, distribution, and access to new technologies.
Create a "critical mass" to learn and develop new technologies to protect domestic, strategic industries.	Form clusters of learning among suppliers and related firms to avoid or reduce foreign dependence for critical inputs and skills.
Assist short-term corporate restructurings by lowering exit barriers in mature or declining industries.	Alliances serve as experiential platforms to "demature" and transform existing mature industries via new components, technologies, or skills to enhance the value of future growth options.

Source: David Lei, "Offensive and Defensive Uses of Alliances," in Heidi Vernon-Wortzel and L. H. Wortzel, *Strategic Management in Global Economy,* 3rd ed. New York: John Wiley & Sons, 1997.

establish compatibility strategically and interpersonally, and setting up a "prenuptial" plan with the prospective partner. Even setting up some pilot programs on a short-term basis for some of the planned combined activities can highlight areas that may become problematic.

1. Choose a partner with compatible strategic goals and objectives, and one with whom the alliance will result in synergies through the combined markets, technologies, and management cadre.
2. Seek alliances where complementary skills, products, and markets will result. If each partner brings distinctive skills and assets to the venture, there will be reduced potential for direct competition in end products and markets; in addition, each partner will begin the alliance in a balanced relationship.[11]
3. Work out with the partner how you will each deal with proprietary technology or competitively sensitive information—what will be shared and what will not, and how shared technology will be handled. Trust is an essential ingredient of an alliance, particularly in these areas, but this needs to be backed up by contractual agreements.
4. Recognize that most alliances last only a few years and will probably break up once a partner feels that it has incorporated the skills and information it needs to go it alone. With this in mind, you need to "learn thoroughly and rapidly about a partner's technology and management: transfer valuable ideas and practices promptly into one's own operations."[12]

Some of the opportunities and complexities in cross-border alliances are illustrated in the following section on joint ventures in the Commonwealth of Independent States (CIS). Such alliances are further complicated by the different history of the two parties' economic systems and the resulting business practices.

COMPARATIVE MANAGEMENT IN FOCUS

Joint Ventures in the Commonwealth of Independent States

Invest early and move as fast as you can.... Benefit from the firesale prices in the largest market in the world.

I've seen too many westerners fall for the line, "Our license will be arriving any day," which usually means never.

—Vladimir Kvint[13]

These comments reflect both the opportunities and the threats involved in IJVs in the CIS. Those opportunities include abundant natural resources and cheap land; a highly educated and low-cost workforce with high-quality basic research skills; and a huge, relatively untapped market of people who have had little previous opportunity for quality consumer products. Those taking advantage of those opportunities, as of 1998, included 35,000 Western companies that have set up shop in Moscow alone, and more than 20,000 joint ventures in Russia. Of those IJVs, 2,800 are U.S.-Russian. They include Caterpillar, IBM, GE, Ford, Hewlett-Packard, PepsiCo., Eastman Kodak, and AT&T, as well as thousands of smaller IJVs—primarily in software, hotels, and heavy industrial production. Many, like Bell Labs, are involved in research and development, taking advantage of the high level of education and technical capabilities of the Russians.

The roadblocks to successful IJVs in the CIS are many. The overriding concern as of this writing in 1998 is that of impending economic collapse with the devalued ruble, the lack of debt and equity capital, and the nonconvertibility of currency. In fact, the barter system had taken over, with individuals, companies, and governments trading services and goods with no money changing hands. Russian teachers were being paid in vodka. Many foreign companies were losing large amounts of money, and some, such as RJR Nabisco, had withdrawn altogether. Most potential new alliances were put on hold by Western companies. In addition, long-standing problems continued unresolved, including the lack of clear legal protection for investments, contracts, or rights to natural resources, and the lack of efficient infrastructure for sourcing materials, communication, transportation, and living arrangements. Problems involving organized crime—often referred to in the media as "the Mafia," and called "the racket" by Russians—add considerably to the cost of operating businesses such as hotels. When MNCs refuse to pay for "protection," they often suffer, as with the bazooka attack on the bottling plant that Coca-Cola was building in Moscow.

In spite of the continuing political uncertainty and economic risk, joint ventures in the CIS offer great opportunities for both partners. Western companies willing to take the risk can pick up assets very cheaply because of the Russian need for hard currency, capital, new technology, and management skills.[14] Foreigners may now own 100 percent of a venture although to get office space, supplies, and other essentials, it is often necessary to have the local partner own at least half. All registered citizens may now own and operate a business, and the governments in most parts of the CIS are encouraging the privatization of businesses to move rapidly to a market economy—and to stave off economic disaster.

Exhibit 8–3 shows the joint venture relationship between a U.S. firm and a CIS firm, the different goals that they bring to the venture, and the barriers caused by their different operating environments.[15]

EXHIBIT 8–3

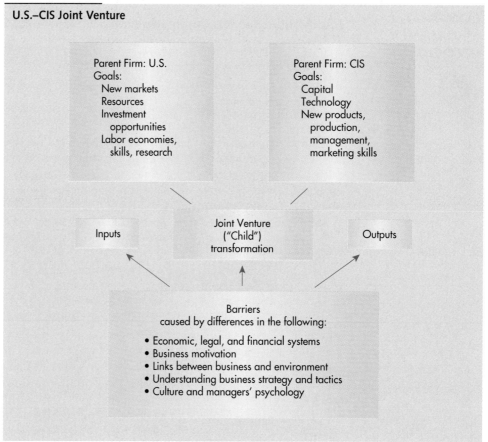

U.S.–CIS Joint Venture

Parent Firm: U.S.
Goals:
   New markets
   Resources
   Investment
      opportunities
   Labor economies,
      skills, research

Parent Firm: CIS
Goals:
   Capital
   Technology
   New products,
      production,
      management,
      marketing skills

Inputs

Joint Venture
("Child")
transformation

Outputs

Barriers
caused by differences in the following:

• Economic, legal, and financial systems
• Business motivation
• Links between business and environment
• Understanding business strategy and tactics
• Culture and managers' psychology

Success requires clearly defined goals, and any proposal must contain solutions to the systemic problems, such as the establishment of efficient supply channels and the repatriation of profits in hard currency. Most managers in the CIS are inexperienced in solving commercial problems based on a capitalist market economy, such as the sourcing of inputs and financing. Western managers will have to teach their joint venture partners about competition, advertising, pricing, distribution networks, and accountability.

Following are four suggestions for foreign companies to minimize the risk of IJVs in the CIS:

1. *Choose the right partner:* The primary reason for IJV failure is a poor match between partners because of lack of compatible goals or strategy, because the CIS partner company is unreliable, or because it lacks the necessary licenses either to produce a product or to export it, or to be involved in development of natural resources. Check with regional government offices about whether the prospective partner has the requisite licenses, appropriate registrations, and reliable bank backing and history; also check on the status of future rights to assets that

were previously under the control of the state, such as those for property or natural resources, or a reserve of shareholdings for future privatization voucher holders. "The choice of a Russian partner can make or break a venture. A local partner may come with risks: you could end up inheriting his 'krysha,' or laundering money (krysha is the Russian term for paying for 'protection')."[16]

Businesspeople must realize that there are established procedures for getting out of disputes with partners, and those procedures take place outside the court system. In Russia, a handshake is more binding than a 100-page legal document, so disputes are best solved quietly—"often using krysha." Paul Tatum, U.S. hotel developer, ignored those procedures to his peril. When he took on his fight for control of the Radisson Slavyanskaya Hotel in 1997, he was gunned down in front of his two bodyguards.

2. *Find the right Russian general manager:* In a survey of 33 successful joint ventures, Lawrence and Vlachoutsicos found that delegating to the right Russian executive is the secret to success for an IJV because that manager is familiar with the local networks and ministries, the suppliers and markets, and the maze of regulatory issues involved. In addition, local managers are part of the culture of the Russian *mir,* or collective; this involves direct bonds of loyalty between managers and employees, hands-on management practices, and wide consultation but top-down final decision making.

3. *Choose the right location:* The political risk of investments in Russia decreases from south to north and west to east, according to the consultant Vladimir Kvint. Because most people in Siberia have stayed far away from communism and the centers of power and political turmoil in the European parts of Russia, investments there and along the Pacific coast are more reliable, and considerable natural resources are available. Now that regional leaders have more autonomy, and some have set up economic zones with tax privileges, Kvint recommends that IJVs branch out, away from Moscow to those areas, and to the Russian far east, where many Japanese IJVs have been set up.

4. *Control the IJV:* To ensure that hard-currency cash flow will be available, it is best to set up the IJV to provide for more operational self-sufficiency than Western managers are used to. This would avoid world suppliers who require hard currency and local suppliers or distributors who provide poor-quality products or services. The venture's best chance of success is to be vertically integrated to retain control of supplies and access to customers. Not only does this avoid some problems of currency convertibility, but it also controls the high chance of shortages of critical materials and supplies. McDonald's, for example, controlled these elements, as well as the quality of its inputs for its three Russian restaurants, by setting up its own farms for potatoes and beef. Other ways to deal with the hard currency problem are (1) to sell products to other foreign businesses within the Commonwealth that hold hard currency; (2) to use IJV rubles to buy raw materials or other products that are marketable in the West—and for which hard currency is paid, as when PepsiCo bought vodka and ships (however, as of 1998, most of Russia—individuals, companies, and government agencies—had reverted to a barter system); and (3) to export products. Of the 33 joint ventures studied by Lawrence and Vlachoutsicos, most had yet to repatriate profits to the West.

There is no doubt that the CIS needs more laws to control business; one less obvious area needing attention is that of cultural differences and how they affect operations.

EXHIBIT 8–4

Potential Problems and Solutions for U.S.–CIS IJVs	
Problems	Solutions
Financial infrastructure: hard currency cash flow and repatriation; capital availability	Reinvest; vertical integration; avoid hard currency deals; get local bank guarantees
Organized crime	Local relationships
Access to materials and supplies; poor quality	Vertical integration, make or supply own
Infrastructure: transportation, communication, banking	Set up operational self-sufficiency where possible
Market access and distribution	Set up alliances; own systems where possible
Operational licenses; rights to assets and resources; liabilities under old system	Validate with central and local authorities before commitment
Political risk	Minimize by locating in New England or Far East if possible
Strategic and reliability conflicts	Explore compatibility and background of partner
Personnel and operational conflicts	Hire local executives and general manager
Motivation; compensation	Give respect; supply goods and services not accessible to employees

Although we refer to the new republics by one name—the Commonwealth of Independent States—it is easy to forget that they are separate republics, each with its own identity, culture, dominant language, ethnic and religious traditions, and economic and labor histories. Different terms are used to differentiate among native Russians (Great Russians), neighboring Ukrainians (Little Russians), and Byelorussians (White Russians). Foreigners need to learn about the particular people in the region where they plan to establish business. Westerners should take time to get to know Russians on a social basis, for example. According to Kvint, "many deals are hatched in saunas between talk of family and philosophy." In particular, it is a mistake to talk down to Russians; they are well educated and advanced in high-technology issues, and they are sensitive to the apparent superiority and wealth of Americans.

Joint ventures in the CIS require a long-term financial and commercial commitment from the foreign partner, including the support of Western on-site personnel. Repatriable profits may not be realized for the first few years of the venture's existence.[17] (See Exhibit 8–4 for additional information.)

Strategic Implementation

Implementation McDonald's Style

- *Form paradigm-busting arrangements with suppliers.*

- *Know a country's culture before you hit the beach.*

- *Hire locals whenever possible.*

- *Maximize autonomy.*

- *Tweak the standard menu only slightly from place to place.*

- *Keep pricing low to build market share. Profits will follow when economies of scale kick in.*[18]

Decisions regarding global alliances and entry strategies must now be put into motion with the next stage of planning—**strategic implementation**. Implementation plans are detailed and pervade the entire organization because they entail setting up overall policies, administrative responsibilities, and schedules throughout the organization to enact the selected strategy and to ensure it works. In the case of a merger or IJV, this process requires compromising and blending procedures among two or more companies and is extremely complex. The importance of the implementation phase of the strategic management process cannot be overemphasized. Until they are put into operation, strategic plans remain abstract ideas—verbal or printed proposals that have no effect on the organization.

Successful implementation requires the orchestration of many variables into a cohesive system that complements the desired strategy—that is, a "system of fits" that will facilitate the actual working of the strategic plan. In this way, the structure, systems, and processes of the firm are coordinated and set into motion by a system of **management by objectives (MBO)**, with the primary objective being the fulfillment of strategy. Managers must review the organizational structure and, if necessary, change it to facilitate the administration of the strategy and to coordinate activities in a particular location with headquarters (as discussed further in Chapter 9). In addition to ensuring the strategy–structure fit, managers must allocate resources to make the strategy work, budgeting money, facilities, equipment, people, and other support. Increasingly, that support necessitates a unified technology infrastructure in order to coordinate diverse businesses around the world and to satisfy the need for current and reliable information. An efficient technology infrastructure can provide a strategic advantage in a globally competitive environment. One example of a company that has recognized and dealt with this support function for strategic implementation is the Benetton Group Spa, headquartered in Italy (see the accompanying Technology Application).

An overarching factor affecting all the other variables necessary for successful implementation is that of leadership; it is people, after all, who make things happen. The firm's leaders must skillfully guide employees and processes in the desired direction. Managers with different combinations of experience, education, abilities, and personality tend to be more suited to implementing certain strategies.[19] In an equity-sharing alliance, sorting out which top managers in each company will be in which position is a sensitive matter. Who in which company will be CEO is usually worked out as part of the initial deal in alliance agreements. Frequently, this problem is settled by setting up joint CEOs, one from each company.

Setting monitoring systems into place to control activities and ensure success completes, but does not end, the strategic management process. Rather, it is a continuous process, using feedback to reevaluate strategy for needed modifications and for updating and recycling plans. In particular, we should consider what is involved in effective management of international joint ventures since they are such a common form of global alliance yet are fraught with implementation challenges.

Managing Performance in International Joint Ventures

Much of the world's international business activity involves international joint ventures (IJVs), in which at least one parent is headquartered outside the venture's country of operation. IJVs require unique controls; ignoring these specific control requisites can limit the parent company's ability to efficiently use its resources, coordinate its activities, and implement its strategy.[20]

TECHNOLOGY APPLICATION
Benneton Group SPA Supports Its Worldwide
Business with a Technological Edge

Benneton brightens its business with AS/400

Although highly diversified, the many divisions that make up the "United Colors of Benetton" share a common thread: the need for current and reliable information. Headquartered in Ponzano Veneto, Italy, Benetton Group Spa is a $2 billion (U.S.) international company operating in 120 countries. More than 7,000 retail outlets sell Benetton's products worldwide. The group consists of 52 companies of varying sizes. Ten are textile producers; 10 are clothing manufacturers; and more than 30 other Benetton companies are engaged in commercial endeavors as diverse as Formula 1 racing, fiber production, spinning, weaving, and shoe manufacturing. Rapid growth over the past several years had led to the progressive integration of many textile businesses supplying raw materials and services. To coordinate these diverse business interests to maximum advantage, the Benetton Group needed a premier technology solution. According to Bruno Zuccaro, vice president of information systems, the company chose the IBM AS/400 Advanced System because of its ease of use, cost effectiveness, and scalability.

AS/400 Advanced System has become the strategic choice for medium-sized Benetton companies in Italy, France, Spain, Hong Kong, Brazil, and Japan.

An international solution   "The reasons for choosing the AS/400 platform were that it is known and supported in almost every country in the world and has a technical reputation beyond reproach" says Zuccaro.

The benefits of using the AS/400 include:

- Lower operating costs
- Automated processes
- Ability to concentrate on core competencies
- Flexibility
- Competitive advantage
- Applications procurement
- Production programming
- Deliveries

- Database and communication management
- Customer item and order management

In addition, Benetton had five key selection criteria that would help it meet its business goals. The company wanted a supplier who would:

- Act as a partner, not just a supplier
- Deliver reliable solutions with the potential to evolve smoothly
- Furnish technical and application competency
- Render system assistance during project development
- Provide excellent references

These criteria played directly to the strengths of AS/400 Advanced System as well as IBM. Says Zuccaro: "AS/400 Advanced System was the right technology platform because it is easy to use and does not require a costly information technology (IT) support staff. And its scalability protects Benetton's current technology investments because the systems can grow as required."

Flexibility on a shared platform   The AS/400 platform addresses two main types of operational needs for Benetton: (1) textile and garment production for associated companies that are "upstream" in the supply chain (that is, producing the products), and (2) commercial applications for associated companies that are "downstream" in the supply chain (that is, engaging in activities such as packaging or wholesaling).

For example, AS/400 Advanced System runs Datatex's Textile Integrated Manufacturing (TIM) package in its textile and garment manufacturing companies. TIM is a highly integrated information system designed exclusively for the textile industry and includes modules such as:

- Inventory
- Procurement
- Production programming
- Deliveries

TECHNOLOGY APPLICATION
(Continued)

For its commercial compares, Benetton uses an inhouse-developed application called Global, a database and communication management system. It delivers services such as:

- Database management services
- Communication management services
- Customer item and order management

Further, each company is responsible for purchasing or developing its own administrative solutions, such as general ledger, according to its own country's needs.

"There is not a common administration software solution for our companies around the world," says Zuccaro. "But we have ensured there are many solution choices available for them by choosing AS/400 Advanced System as our technology."

A unified approach to growth   What sorts of business benefits have flowed to Benetton? According to Zuccaro they include:

- Lower operating and production costs
- Automated processes with greater efficiencies
- Ability to concentrate on core competencies
- Greater flexibility in software solutions
- An overall competitive advantage

"By having a single, reliable technology solution that fits almost any one of our companies like a glove, we are delivering the best technology at the best price to our associates," he says. "Benetton is positioned for growth in its markets, and now has the unified technology infrastructure we need to support that growth."

Source: www.IBM.com IBM Online Case Studies.

International joint venture control can be defined, according to Schaan, as "the process through which a parent company ensures that the way a joint venture is managed conforms to its own interest."[21] Most of a firm's objectives can be achieved by careful attention to control features at the outset of the joint venture, such as the choice of a partner, the establishment of a strategic fit, and the design of the IJV organization.

The most important factor determining IJV success or failure is the choice of a partner. Most problems with IJVs involve the local partner, especially in less developed countries. Despite this fact, many firms rush the process of partner selection because they are anxious to "get on the bandwagon" in an attractive market.[22] In this process, it is vital to establish whether the partners' strategic goals are compatible (discussed in the previous chapter). The strategic context and the competitive environment of the proposed IJV and the parent firm will determine the relative importance of the criteria used to select a partner.[23] IJV performance is also a function of the general fit between the international strategies of the parents, the IJV strategy, and the specific performance goals that the parents adopt.[24] Research has shown that, to facilitate this fit, the partner selection process must determine the specific task-related skills and resources needed from a partner as well as the relative priority of those needs.[25] To do this, managers must analyze their own firm and pinpoint any areas of weakness in task-related skills and resources that can be overcome with the help of the IJV partner.

Organizational design is another major mechanism for factoring in a means of control when an IJV is started. Beamish et al. discuss the important issue of the strategic freedom of an IJV. This refers to the relative amount of decision-making power that a joint venture will have, compared with the parents, in choosing suppliers, product lines, customers, and so on.[26] It is also crucial to consider beforehand the relative management roles each parent will play in the IJV because such decisions result in varying levels of control for different parties. An IJV is usually easier to manage if one parent plays a dominant role and has more decision-making responsibility than the other in daily operations; alternatively, it is easier to manage an IJV if the local general manager has considerable management control, keeping both parents out of most of the daily operations.[27]

International joint ventures are like a marriage: The more issues that can be settled before the merger, the less likely it will be for the partners to break up. Control over the stability and the success of the IJV can be largely built into the initial agreement between the partners. The contract can specify who has what responsibilities and rights in a variety of circumstances, such as the contractual links of the IJV with the parents, the capitalization, and the rights and obligations regarding intellectual property. Exhibit 8–5 lists some of the major areas of allocation of responsibility that can be delineated in the joint venture agreement to lessen the potential for strife later.

Of course, we cannot assume equal ownership of the IJV partners; where ownership is unequal, the partners will claim control and staffing choices proportionate to the ownership share. The choice of the IJV general manager, in particular, will influence the relative allocation of control because that person is responsible for running the IJV and for coordinating relationships with each of the parents.[28]

Where ownership is divided among several partners, the parents are more likely to delegate the daily operations of the IJV to the local IJV management—a move that resolves many potential disputes. In addition, the increased autonomy of the IJV tends to reduce many common human resource problems: staffing friction, blocked communication, and blurred organizational culture, to name a few, which all result from the conflicting goals and working practices of the parent companies.[29] Regardless of the number of parents, one way to avoid such potential problem situations is to provide special training to managers about the unique nature and problems of IJVs.[30]

EXHIBIT 8–5

Control Elements in an IJV Agreement

- Definitions
- Scope of operations
- Management
    Shareholders and supervisory board
    Executive board
    Arrangements in event of deadlock
    Operating management
- Arbitration
- Representations and warranties of each partner

- Organization and capitalization
- Financial arrangements
- Contractual links with parents
- Rights and obligations regarding intellectual property
- Termination agreements
- Force majeur
- Covenants

Source: "Teaming Up for the Nineties—A Guide to International Joint Ventures and Strategic Alliances," Doorley and Collins, 1991, p. 230.

Various studies reveal three complementary and interdependent dimensions of IJV control: (1) the focus of IJV control—the scope of activities over which parents exercise control; (2) the extent, or degree, of IJV control achieved by the parents; and (3) the mechanisms of IJV control used by the parents.[31]

We can conclude from two research studies—Geringer's study of 90 developed country IJVs and Schaan and Beamish's study of 10 IJVs in Mexico—that parent companies tend to focus their efforts on a selected set of activities that they consider important to their strategic goals rather than attempting to monitor all activities.[32, 33] Schaan also found a considerable range of mechanisms for control used by the parent firms in his study (detailed in Exhibit 8–6), including indirect mechanisms such as parent organizational and reporting structure, staffing policies, and close coordination with the IJV general manager (GM). Monitoring the GM typically includes indirect means, perhaps bonuses and career opportunities, and direct mechanisms, such as requiring executive committee approval for specific decisions and budgets. These studies show that a variety of mechanisms are available to parent companies to monitor and guide IJV performance.

The extent of control exercised over an IJV by its parent companies seems to be primarily determined by the decision-making autonomy the parents delegate to the IJV management—which is largely dependent on staffing choices for the top IJV positions and thus on how much confidence the partners have in these managers. In addition, if top managers of the IJV

EXHIBIT 8–6

Control Mechanisms in International Joint Ventures

Ability to make specific decision	Ability to decide on future promotion of JVGM (and other JV managers)
Ability to design:	Feedback; strategy and plan budgets, appropriation
1. Planning process	requests
2. Appropriation requests	JVGM participation in parent's worldwide meetings
Policies and procedures	Relations with JVGM; phone calls, meetings, visits
Ability to set objectives for JVGM	Staffing parent with someone with experience with JV management
Contracts:	MNC level in Mexico
Management	
Technology transfer	Informal meetings with other parent
Marketing	Board
Supplier	Executive committee
Participation in planning or budgeting process	Approval required for:
Parent organization structure	1. Specific decisions
Reporting structure	2. Plans, budgets
Staffing	3. Appropriation requests
Training programs	4. Nomination of JVGM
Staff services	Screening/no objection of parent before ideas or projects are discussed with the other parent
Bonus of JVGM tied to parent results	

Source: J. L. Schaan, "Parent Control and Joint Venture Success: The Case of Mexico, 249," (Unpublished doctoral dissertation, University of Western Ontario, 1983), reprinted in J. Michael Geringer and Louis Herbert, "Control and Performance of International Joint Ventures," *Journal of International Business Studies* 20, no. 2 (Summer 1989).

are from the headquarters of each party, then the more similar their national cultures are, the more compatible their managers will be. This is because there are many areas of control decisions where agreement will be more likely between those of similar cultural backgrounds.[34]

The many activities and issues involved in strategic implementation—such as negotiating, organizing, staffing, leading, communicating, and control—are the subjects of other chapters in this book. Elsewhere, we include discussion of the many variables involved in strategic implementation that are specific to a particular country or region, such as goals, infrastructure, laws, technology, ways of doing business, people, and culture. Here, we take a look at two pervasive influences on strategy implementation—government policy and culture.

Government Influences on Strategic Implementation

There are many areas of influence by host governments on the strategic choice and implementation of foreign firms. The profitability of those firms is greatly influenced, for example, by the level of taxation in the host country and by any restrictions on profit repatriation. Other important influences are government policies on ownership by foreign firms, on labor union rules, on hiring and remuneration practices, on patent and copyright protection, and so on. For the most part, however, if the corporation's managers have done their homework, all these factors are known beforehand and are part of the location and entry strategy decisions. But what hurts is for managers to set up shop in a host country and then experience major economic or governmental policy changes after they have made a considerable investment.

Unpredictable changes in governmental regulations can be a death knell to businesses operating abroad. Although this problem occurs in many countries, one country that is often the subject of concern by foreign firms is China. In a survey of European investment in China, for example, 54 percent of companies questioned said their performance in China was worse than they had anticipated. Caterpillar, Inc. was one of the companies with rapid market growth in producing diesel engines in China in the early 1990s—construction was booming and foreign investment was flooding in. But in 1993, China—afraid that foreign investment was causing inflation—revoked tax breaks and restricted foreign investment. The tables turned on Caterpillar after that because there was not enough domestic demand for their products.[35] In addition, as reported in the *Wall Street Journal*, "the world's auto industry guessed wrong on China."[36] Certainly, the market potential is there—only 1 Chinese out of every 110 has a car—but big problems are causing foreign car ventures to withdraw. Peugeot-Citroen SA of France abandoned their factory in China, and Daimler-Benz AG of Germany withdrew before it even started. Beijing is even worrying GM, which has invested millions in China, including 21 joint ventures and other projects. Out of concern that China cannot handle a surge in cars on its inadequate roads, with little parking and few service stations, the government has stopped an auto-loan program, and many cities can no longer issue license plates for private cars. What's more, Beijing has prohibited government officials below the rank of minister from buying big cars.[37]

Political change, in itself, can, of course, bring about sudden change in strategic implementation of alliances of foreign firms with host country projects. This was evident in May 1998 when President Suharto of Indonesia was ousted following economic problems and currency devaluation. The new government began reviewing and canceling some of the business deals linked with the Suharto family, including the cancellation of two water-supply privatization projects with foreign firms—Britain's Thames Water PLC and France's Suez Lyonnaise des Eaux SA. The Suharto family had developed a considerable fortune from licensing deals, monopolies, government "contracts," and protection from taxes.[38] Alliances with the family were often the only way for foreign companies to gain entry.

Cultural Influences on Strategic Implementation

Culture is one variable that is often overlooked when deciding on entry strategies and alliances, particularly when we perceive the target country to be familiar with us and similar to our own company. However, cultural differences can have a subtle and often negative effect.

As many of Europe's largest MNCs—including Nestlé, Electrolux, Grand Metropolitan, Rhone-Poulenc—experience increasing proportions of their revenues from their positions in the United States, and employ more than 2.9 million Americans, they have decided to shift headquarters of some product lines to the United States. As they have done so, however, there is growing evidence that managing in the United States is not as easy as they anticipated it would be because of their perceived familiarity with the culture. Generally, Rosenzweig has found that European managers appreciate that Americans are pragmatic, open, forthright, and innovative. But they also say that the tendency of Americans to be informal and individualistic means that their need for independence and autonomy on the job aggravates their relationship with the Europeans at or from the head office; Americans simply do not take well to directives from foreign-based headquarters.[39] Rosenzweig has documented some reflections of French managers on their experiences of managing U.S. affiliates:

- "Americans see themselves as the world's leading country, and it's not easy for them to accept having a European in charge."
- "It is difficult for Americans to develop a world perspective. It's hard for them to see that what may optimize the worldwide position may not optimize the U.S. activities...."
- "The horizon of Americans often goes only as far as the U.S. border. As a result, Americans often don't give equal importance to a foreign customer. If a foreign customer has a special need, the response is sometimes: 'It works here, why do they need it to be different?'"
- "It might be said that Americans are the least international of all people, because their home market is too big."

Other European firms have had more successful strategic implementation in their U.S. plants by adapting to American culture and management styles. When Mercedes-Benz of Germany launched its plant in Tuscaloosa, Alabama, U.S. workers and German "trainers" had doubts. Lynn Snow, who works on the door line of the Alabama plant was skeptical whether the Germans and the Americans would mesh well. But now she proudly asserts that they work together determined to build a quality vehicle. Says Jürgen Schrempp, CEO of Mercedes' parent, Daimler-Benz, "'Made in Germany'—we have to change that to 'Made by Mercedes,' and never mind where they are assembled."[40]

The German trainers recognized that the whole concept of building a Mercedes quality car had to be taught to the American workers in a way that would appeal to them. They abandoned the typically German strict hierarchy and instead designed a plant in which any worker could stop the assembly line to correct manufacturing problems. In addition, taking their cue from Japanese rivals, they formed the workers into teams that meet every day with the trainers to problem-solve. Formal uniforms were replaced by casual shirts with personal names on the pocket. To add to the collegiality, get-togethers for a beer after work are common. "The most important thing is to bring together the two cultures," says Andreas Renschler, who has guided the M-Class since it began in 1993. "You have to generate a kind of ownership of the plant."[41] The local community has also embraced the mutual goals, often having beer fests, and including German-language stations on local cable TV.

The impact of cultural differences in management style and expectations is perhaps most noticeable and important when implementing international joint ventures.

The complexity of a joint venture requires that managers from each party learn to compromise in order to create a compatible and productive working environment, particularly when operations are integrated. What are the differences in leadership philosophy, behavior, and systems between the United States and China, for example? The following Comparative Management in Focus explores the opportunities and problems related to Sino–U.S. joint ventures.

COMPARATIVE MANAGEMENT IN FOCUS

Implementing Sino–U.S. Joint Ventures: The Culture Factor

In spite of the increasing attractiveness of Sino–U.S. joint ventures, Western partners are hesitant because of reports about disappointing results. Often, changes in government decisions or philosophy result in foreign companies pulling out of China, as with many of the world's auto manufacturers, as discussed before. But frequently, poor results or disbandment of the venture is caused by poor management of the joint venture, resulting from differences in managerial perspectives and leadership behavior—in particular, with regard to human resource issues and delegation in decision making.[42, 43] Conflicts in role expectations arise because Western managers are used to egalitarian relationships, whereas the Chinese are used to patron–client relationships. The Chinese therefore assume that the West should help less economically developed societies.[44] Exhibits 8–7 and 8–8 show the results of a unique study comparing the perceptions of Chinese and American managers. Baird, Lyles, and Wharton found significant differences in the preferences of those managers for organizational form, work, employment, and reward systems.[45] Responses to their questions regarding the ideal management philosophy within a joint venture (see Exhibit 8–7) show, conclude the researchers, that American managers prefer a more people-oriented approach than Chinese managers:

Chinese managers showed a significant preference for merit rewards and an impersonal, less participative, and more individual style of joint venture management. Americans, by contrast, favored a personal, more participative, team and consensual approach; they favored seniority considerations more than the Chinese although both rated merit highly. The greatest difference was that the Chinese prefer the impersonal to the personal approach.[46]

Contradicting some of their philosophical ideals (indicated in Exhibit 8–7), the American and Chinese managers in the same study described the characteristics of the ideal

EXHIBIT 8–7

Ideal Joint Venture Management Philosophy: U.S.-China

Item	Mean U.S.	Mean China	Discriminant Coefficient
Personal/impersonal	2.48	6.17*	0.77
Participative/directive	2.43	3.79†	0.19
Democratic/authoritarian	3.24	3.83	0.07
Professional/company norms	3.31	4.03	0.08
Obedience/individuality	4.54	5.17	0.10
Seniority/merit	5.73	6.33‡	0.12
Individual/team	5.57	4.27*	–0.23
Consensus/competition	3.54	6.20*	0.37
Collective/individual	3.00	3.67	0.09

*p of t ≤ 0.0001
†p of t ≤ 0.01
‡p of t ≤ 0.05

Responses are on a 7-point scale, e.g., from 1—personal to 7—impersonal.

Source: I. S. Baird, M. A. Lyles, and R. Wharton, "Attitudinal Differences Between American and Chinese Managers Regarding Joint Venture Management," *Management International Review* 30 (Special Issue, 1990): 61.

EXHIBIT 8–8

Ideal Joint Venture Supervisor: U.S.-China

Item	Adjusted Mean		Rank	
	U.S.	China	U.S.	China
Provides positive and negative feedback	1.43	1.66	2	8
Explains expected level of performance	1.00	2.36*	1	11
Detects subtle changes in technology for the joint venture	5.00	5.00	14.5	15
Keeps group attention focused on important matters	1.97	1.97	4	10
Provides rewards for individual efforts	3.38	1.00†	10	7
Considers feelings	5.00	1.43†	14.5	5
Explains the quality of work expected	1.76	1.82	3	9
Encourages career development through informal means	3.70	2.61	11.5	12
Maintains a friendly working relationship	3.92	1.24†	13	3.5
Demands high work performance standards	2.08	1.51	5	7
Believes what we are doing goes beyond making money	2.95	2.86	8	13
Provides employees with opportunities for exposure to other departments and management levels	3.27	1.24†	9	3.5
Keeps employees posted on new developments affecting them	2.41	3.24	6	14
Explains the larger significance of efforts	3.70	1.04†	11.5	2
Holds employees accountable for actions	2.73	1.45*	7	6

*p of t < 0.05
†p of t < 0.001
Scale = 1 strongly agree; 5 strongly disagree.

Source: I. S. Baird, M. A. Lyles, and R. Wharton, "Attitudinal Differences Between American and Chinese Managers Regarding Joint Venture Management," *Management International Review* 30 (Special Issue, 1990): 62.

joint venture supervisor, as shown in Exhibit 8–8. Here, the American managers focused on the importance of the supervisor's responsibility to (1) make performance expectations clear, (2) provide positive and negative feedback, (3) explain the quality of work expected, and (4) focus worker attention on critical tasks. For the Chinese, the ideal supervisor would (1) emphasize individual rewards, (2) explain the larger significance of tasks, (3) maintain friendly working relationships, and (4) provide opportunities for subordinate development. The Chinese and American managers rated the importance of other factors in a more similar way.[47]

These differing expectations and assumptions explain why American managers have encountered problems in relating to Chinese managers and their leadership behaviors. Likewise, they suggest why American managers have often become impatient with their inability to change Chinese behaviors, which are steeped in tradition. The resulting negative repercussions affect the climate and productivity of Sino–U.S. joint ventures. The answer to these problems, as discussed throughout this book, is for managers to familiarize themselves with the cultural expectations that will affect their relationship and to develop a working relationship built on understanding and compromise.

Cultural influences on strategic implementation are often even more pronounced in the service sector because of many added variables, especially the direct contact with the consumer. As described in the accompanying Management Focus, Wal-Mart has not been immune to implementation problems overseas, particularly resulting from culture and lifestyle differences, and infrastructure problems.

Conclusion

Cross-border strategic alliances are becoming increasingly common as innovative companies seek rapid entry into foreign markets and as they try to reduce the risks of going it alone in complex environments. Those companies that do well are those that do their homework and pick complementary strategic partners. Too many, however, get "divorced" because "the devil is in the details"—that is, what seems to be a marriage made in heaven can run into unanticipated problems during actual strategic implementation. The opportunities and problems discussed in this chapter are illustrated in the end-of-chapter case study.

Summary of Key Points

1. Strategic alliances are partnerships with other companies for specific reasons. Cross-border, or global, strategic alliances are working partnerships between companies (often more than two) across national boundaries, and increasingly across industries.
2. Cross-border alliances are formed for many reasons, including market expansion, cost- and technology-sharing, avoiding protectionist legislation, and taking advantage of synergies.
3. Technological advances and the resulting blending of industries, such as those in the telecommunications and entertainment industries, are factors prompting cross-industry alliances.
4. Alliances may be short or long term; they may be full global partnerships, or they may be for more narrow and specific functions, such as research and development sharing.

MANAGEMENT FOCUS

Wal-Mart's Implementation Problems in South America

Wal-Mart Stores, Inc. is finding out that what plays in Peoria isn't necessarily a hit in suburban Sao Paulo. Adapting to local tastes has been one thing. But brutal competition, market conditions that don't play to Wal-Mart's ability to achieve efficiency through economies of scale, and some of its own mistakes have produced red ink. Moreover, the company's insistence on doing things "the Wal-Mart way" has apparently alienated local suppliers and employees.

A lot is riding on Wal-Mart's global expansion drive, which is targeting not only South America, but also China and Indonesia, two other markets full of promise and pitfalls. With opportunities for growth dwindling at home, the company is opening fewer than 100 domestic stores a year, down from as many as 150 in the early 1990s. The current rate of openings can't generate the profit gains Wal-Mart wants, and its main hopes lie overseas.

The performance of Wal-Mart's 16 South American stores may well indicate the future outlook. In Canada and Mexico, many customers were familiar with the company from cross-border shopping trips, and by acquiring local retailers it quickly reached the size necessary to hold down costs. In South America and Asia, by contrast, Wal-Mart is building from scratch in markets already dominated by savvy local and foreign competitors such as Grupo Pao de Acucar SA of Brazil and Carrefour SA of France. As of 1998, losses were mounting in Brazil and Argentina.

Squeezing out costs in its supply chain is crucial to Wal-Mart's formula for "everyday low pricing." But timely delivery of merchandise is a relative concept in the bumper-to-bumper traffic of Sao Paulo, where Wal-Mart depends on suppliers or contract truckers to deliver most of its goods directly to stores. Because it doesn't own its distribution system, it can't control deliveries nearly as well as it does in the

United States, vendors say. Stores in Brazil sometimes process 300 deliveries a day, compared with 7 a day at U.S. locations, and some shipments have mysteriously disappeared somewhere between the port and the store.

Wal-Mart's troubles in South America stem partly from its own mistakes. Analysts say it failed to do its homework before plunging in. Merchandise flubs—such as unsuitable food products and cordless tools, which few South Americans use—were only the beginning. In Brazil, Wal-Mart brought in stock-handling equipment that didn't work with standardized local pallets. It also installed a computerized bookkeeping system that failed to take into account Brazil's wildly complicated tax system. In addition, Wal-Mart has been slow to adapt to Brazil's fast-changing credit culture, under which they needed to recognize postdated checks, which have become the most common form of credit since Brazil stabilized its currency in 1995. The six South American Sam's Club locations got off to a slow start largely because shoppers weren't used to paying a membership fee and don't have enough room at home to store bulk purchases. In Argentina, the clubs have faced another barrier: Small business customers are reluctant to sign up for fear Wal-Mart could provide information to tax authorities on their purchases.

Although Wal-Mart is learning the hard way about local culture and lifestyles (they want soccer balls in South America, not American footballs), and the managers are finding their way around infrastructure problems, they have learned the hard way about the difficulties of strategic implementation in other countries.

Source: Adapted and excerpted from Jonathan Friedland and Louise Lee, "The Wal-Mart Way Sometimes Gets Lost in Translation Overseas," *Wall Street Journal,* October 8, 1997.

5. Alliances often run into trouble in the strategic implementation phase. Problems include loss of technology and knowledge base to the other partner, conflicting strategic goals and objectives, cultural clashes, and disputes over management and control systems.

6. Successful alliances require compatible partners with complementary skills, products, and markets. Extensive preparation is necessary in order to work out how to share management control and technology, and to understand each other's culture.

7. Strategic implementation—also called functional-level strategies—entails setting up overall policies, administrative responsibilities, and schedules throughout the organization. Successful implementation results from setting up the structure, systems and processes of the firm, as well as the functional activities that create a system of fits with the desired strategy.

8. Unanticipated effects on strategic implementation often arise because of differences in national culture and changes in the political arena or in government regulations.

Discussion Questions

1. Discuss the reasons that companies embark on cross-border strategic alliances. What other motivations may prompt such alliances?

2. Why are there an increasing number of mergers with companies in different industries? Give some examples. What industry do you think will be the next for global consolidation?

3. Discuss the problems inherent in developing a cooperative alliance in order to enhance competitive advantage, but also incurring the risk of developing a new competitor.

4. What are the common sources of incompatibility in cross-border alliances? What can be done in order to minimize them?

5. Discuss the economic situation in the CIS with your class. What has changed since this writing? What are the implications for foreign companies to start a joint venture there now?

6. What is involved in strategic implementation? What is meant by "creating a system of fits" with the strategic plan?

7. Explain how the host government may affect strategic implementation—in an alliance or another form of entry strategy.

8. How might the variable of national culture affect strategic implementation? Use the Wal-Mart example to highlight some of these factors.

Application Exercises

1. At the time of writing, the alliance between Daimler and Chrysler featured in the opening case profile had just been announced. By the time you are using this textbook, it should be well under way. How is the alliance doing? Research the events, successes, and problems that DaimlerChrysler AG has experienced so far, and report to the class. Have any of the problems anticipated in the opening case profile been realized at this point? Are the strategic goals, which led to the alliance, being realized to date?

2. Review the Management Focus on Wal-Mart in South America. Research Wal-Mart's operations in South America since 1997, and report to the class. Has Wal-Mart expanded elsewhere in South America? How are their new stores doing? What, if any, problems have they run into?

Experiential Exercise

Partner Selection in an International Context

by Professor Anne Smith

Read the following three scenarios and think about the assigned questions before class. Although the names of the specific telecommunications firms have been disguised, each scenario is based on actual events and real companies in the telecommunications service industry.

Scenario 1: TOOLBOX and FROZEN in Mexico

By October 30, 1990, managers from TOOLBOX (a Baby Bell[1] located in the eastern United States) and FROZEN (a Canadian telecommunications service and equipment provider) had been working for months on a final bid for the Telmex privatization. In two weeks, a final bid was due to the Mexican Ministry of Finance for this privatization; TOOLBOX's consortium was competing against four other groups.

Teléfonos de México (Telmex) was a government-run and -owned telecommunications provider, which included local, long-distance, cellular, and paging services in Mexico. Yet, in late 1989, the Mexican government decided to privatize Telmex. Reasons for Telmex's privatization included its need for new technology and installation expertise and the large pent-up demand for phone service in Mexico (where only one in five households had a phone). In early 1990, managers from TOOLBOX's international subsidiary were in contact with many potential partners such as France Telecom, GTE, FROZEN, and Spain's Telefonica. By June 1990, TOOLBOX and FROZEN had chosen each other to partner and bid on the Telmex privatization. During the past six months, discussions had gone smoothly between the international managers at TOOLBOX and FROZEN. With a local Mexican partner (required by the Mexican government), the managers worked out many details related to their Telmex bid, such as who would be in charge of installations and backlog reduction, who would install new cellular equipment, who would upgrade the marketing and customer service function, and who would select and install the central office switches. A TOOLBOX international manager commented, "We got along extremely well with our neighbors to the north. Not surprisingly, given that we speak the same language, have similar business values … but, basically we liked their international people, which was essential for our largest international deal ever." A FROZEN international manager stated, "It was ironic that our top executive in charge of business development had been a summer intern at TOOLBOX when he was in college. So, he liked our selection of TOOLBOX for this partnering arrangement, even though he was not familiar with the current TOOLBOX top managers." By September 1990, investment bankers estimated that a winning bid would probably top $1.5 billion. On November 15, 1990, all final bids for the privatization would be due. Having worked out the operational details (contingent on a winning bid), managers from TOOLBOX and FROZEN returned to meet with their top managers one final time to get some consensus on a final bid price for Telmex.

Scenario 2: The Geneva Encounter

At the Telecom 1984 convention in Geneva, Robert and Jim (A GEMS senior vice president and a business development manager, respectively) had just finished hearing the keynote address, and were wandering among the numerous exhibits. This convention, hosted every four years in Geneva, included thousands of exhibits of telecommunications services and hardware providers; tens of thousands of people attended. Though GEMS (a Baby Bell in the southwestern United States) did not have a booth at the 1984 convention, Robert and Jim were trying to learn about

[1]Seven Baby Bells (also known as Regional Bell Operating Companies, or RBOCs for short) were created in 1984, when they were divested from AT&T. The term *Baby Bell* is really a misnomer given their large size, between $7 billion to $10 billion in revenues, at divestiture. In 1984, the Baby Bells were granted discrete territories where they offered local telephone service; these seven firms also were allowed to offer cellular service in their local service territories. From the AT&T divestiture settlement, the Baby Bells were allowed to keep the lucrative yellow pages and directory assistance services. Yet, these seven firms had no international activities or significant international managerial experience at divestiture.

international telecommunications providers and activities. On the third day of the conference, Robert and Jim were standing at an exhibit of advanced wireless technologies when they struck up a conversation with another bystander who was from Israel.

"You can get lost in this convention," exclaimed Jim. Daniel from Israel agreed, "Yes, this is my first trip to the Telecom convention, and it is overwhelming.... Tell me about GEMS. How is life freed from Ma Bell?" Robert, Jim, and Daniel continued their conversation over drinks and dinner. They learned that Daniel was an entrepreneur who was involved in many different ventures. One new venture that Daniel was pursuing was yellow pages directories and publishing. Daniel was delighted to meet these high-level executives from GEMS because of the Baby Bell's reputation as high-quality telephone service providers. Several months after the conference, Robert and Jim visited Daniel in Israel to discuss opportunities there. Six months later, GEMS and Daniel's firm were jointly developing software for a computerized directory publishing system in Israel. GEMS had committed people and a very small equity stake ($5 to $10 million) to this venture.

Scenario 3: LAYERS and Jack in UK Cable

In early 1990, LAYERS (another Baby Bell from the western United States) was considering investing in an existing cable television franchise in the United Kingdom. In 1984, pioneer/pilot licenses had been awarded in some cities. Many of these initial licenses were awarded to startup companies run by entrepreneurs with minimal investment capital. Unfortunately, "the 100 percent capital allowances that were seen as vital to make the financial structuring of the cable build a commercial reality" were abolished creating a "break in the industry's development [from 1985–1989] whilst many companies that were interested in UK cable were forced to reexamine their financial requirements."[2]

Jack had obtained one of these early UK cable licenses in 1984, and his investment capital was quickly consumed from installing cable coupled with slow market penetration. By 1986, his efforts toward this venture had waned. In the 1990 Broadcast Act, the government relaxed its rule for cable operators and allowed non-EC control of UK cable companies. This created incentives for current cable operators to sell an equity stake in their ventures. This allowed US and Canadian telephone companies to bring desperately needed cash as well as marketing and installation expertise to these cable ventures. Aware of the impending changes, Jack was once again focusing on his cable operations. He arranged a meeting with several LAYERS international managers in November 1989, in anticipation of the changes. Turning on his charm and sales abilities, Jack explained to the LAYERS' international managers the potential for UK cable television.[3] He also shared with these managers that he was willing to sell a large equity stake in his company to get it growing again. The international managers from LAYERS were impressed by Jack's enthusiasm, but they were even more intrigued by the possibility of learning about the convergence of cable and telephone services from this UK "laboratory." The LAYERS international managers decided that they would discuss this deal with their executive in charge of unregulated activities. By June 1990, LAYERS had an equity stake, estimated to be between $30 and $50 million, in Jack's UK cable venture.

Source: This exercise was written by Professor Anne Smith, University of New Mexico, based on her research of the firms discussed. Copyright 1998 by Professor Anne Smith. Used with permission.

[2]*The Cable Companion,* The Cable Television Association, pp. 1–11, 1–12.

[3]In the UK, cable operators were allowed to offer both cable and telephone service.

Questions to Consider Before Class

Think about these questions from the perspective of the Baby Bell in each scenario:

1. In your opinion, which one of these scenarios should lead to a long-term successful international partnering relationship? Based on what criteria?
2. In your opinion, which one of these scenarios has the least chance of leading to a long-term, successful international partnering relationship? Why?

Internet Resources

Visit the Deresky companion Web site at http://prenhall.com/Deresky for this chapter's Internet resources.

Case Study

Ben & Jerry's and Iceverks: Alliance Meltdown in Russia

In 1988, Ben Cohen, president and cofounder of Ben & Jerry's, took a trip to Karelia, Russia (Vermont's Russian sister state) as a representative from Vermont. During his stay in Karelia, he thought of opening up a Ben & Jerry's scoop shop in Russia in hopes of bringing the United States and Russia together through ice cream diplomacy. After Mr. Cohen's return from Russia, Ben & Jerry's immediately made a joint venture proposal, and in 1989, they completed the preparations for the first step of expanding their business into Russia. The joint venture was to be called Iceverks and would be located in the city of Petrozavodsk in Russia's Karelia region. Ben's mission was to help promote understanding and communication between Russia and the United States. He also wanted to prove that high-quality ice cream could be produced entirely by using Russian employees and ingredients.

Ben & Jerry's initial investment into the joint venture was approximately $500,000 or 50 percent of the total startup fees. The other half of the capital was invested by their Russian partners, who raised 20 percent of it by selling interest to a local bank, Petrobank.

With the joint venture came many problems that Ben & Jerry's managers didn't anticipate. First, they had to find a distribution system, which would be a challenge because Russian systems were undeveloped and inefficient. Second, acceptable suppliers had to be located for their ice cream products. They had to determine whether local resources could provide suitable ingredients to produce high-quality ice cream. But a major ingredient for Ben & Jerry's was their philosophy toward social responsibility and philanthropy. The company gives contributions and support to social issues such as acid rain, rain forest destruction, homelessness, and the disabled. It was important to them to encourage Russians to learn more about recycling technology.

In Karelia, Ben & Jerry's donated 10–15 percent of its profits to disabled children in the community.

Strategic Implementation

Business environment With the collapse of the Soviet Union came political uncertainty for potential foreign investors in the newly democratic Russia. The country had to be rebuilt, and it was questionable what laws would be enacted and what laws would be discarded. Thus, all foreign businesses operating in Russia were doing so under extreme risk. Nevertheless, Ben & Jerry's assumed this risk because their decision to enter Russia was not entirely profit driven. For the most part, they were doing business in Russia for good will, trying to unite two former cold war countries.

As a result of former communist work ideology, skilled managers were in short supply for the Karelia facilities. Managers, as well as subordinates, needed to be trained both in work habits and in Western capitalistic philosophy. Consequently, managers had to be flown in from the United States until the Russians could learn the intricacies of a free market as well as the production of high-quality ice cream.

With the fall of the USSR, the Russian Mafia has gained enormous power. The underworld is thought to control some 40 percent of the Russian economy. U.S. businesses pay as much as 30 percent of their monthly profit for Mafia "protection." This was a major concern for Ben & Jerry's since their company philosophy for doing business in the East is to not give into extortion or bribery.

Production   Ice cream is a popular dessert in Russia—eaten all year-round. Russians in Moscow consume 170 tons of ice cream per year, 98 percent of which is vanilla. Since Russia is the third largest market in the world, the ice cream business represented enormous potential.

To use the Ben & Jerry's logo, ice cream had to be of superior consistency and quality. Karelia's local milk supply had to be reformed to meet Ben & Jerry's requirements; high-grade eggs and sugar had to be located to make Ben & Jerry's ice cream products in Russia consistent to those in the United States; skilled inspectors, who were in short supply, had to be recruited. In addition, since sanitation standards in Russia's dairy industry are not as strict as in the United States, Ben & Jerry's had to license a special plate from the 3M Company that disinfects milk from contaminants such as *E. coli* and coliforms. These plates, called Petffim, react with enzymes produced by bacteria in milk, making it easy to spot contaminants and bacteria growth.

Ben & Jerry's goal was to produce a premium ice cream that Russians could afford. Although their ice cream was slightly more expensive than Russian ice cream, it was still relatively affordable, so they used local suppliers and resources, which reduced cost significantly.

The Ben & Jerry's Company is known for having a wide selection of ice cream flavors. They use a wide variety of ingredients to provide the most satisfying ice cream in the market. But when they introduced some of the American favorite flavors to their new consumers—including Cherry Garcia, Chunky Monkey, and Chocolate Chip Cookie Dough—they ran into problems. The Russians were not accustomed to the chunks of ingredients in the ice cream; they thought it was spoiled or damaged. To adjust to consumer preferences, Ben & Jerry's altered their menu to include more smooth ice creams.

Competition   In 1988, most home refrigerators in Russia had very small freezers—comparable to U.S. models in the 1940s. Thus, ice cream was a dessert commonly sold by street vendors and restaurants for immediate consumption. At this time, street vendors were Ben & Jerry's most substantial competition, selling tons of good-tasting ice cream every day for as little as 35 rubles per unit. However, variety was a weak spot in Russian ice cream—it was vanilla or nothing. Thus, Ben & Jerry's relied on variety and novelty as a competitive advantage.

Local vendors were hostile toward the new Ben & Jerry's facility. Almost all ice cream sold in Petrozavodsk was supplied by a local ice cream monopoly that had ties to the Mafia. Upon hearing of Ben & Jerry's arrival, the local monopoly pressured the dairy not to supply the "outsider" with any cream, forcing them to find a new source of dairy nearly a day's drive away. In addition, they arranged for frequent sanitation inspection visits in an effort to slow Ben & Jerry's operation down and keep them out of the ice cream business in Petrozavodsk.

To add to Ben & Jerry's problems, other imported ice cream products were pushing their way into Karelia, particularly those from nearby Finland and the Czech Republic.

Suppliers   Supply problems plagued Iceverks from 1991 to 1994. Since there were no refrigerated trucks in Russia for their distribution, Ben & Jerry's had to import them. This proved to be time consuming and costly. In addition, there was a lack of refrigeration units in Russian stores, so ice cream would melt and then have to be refrozen, decreasing its quality. In response to this problem, Ben & Jerry's brought in their own refrigerators. They were sold to the stores, or rented, or in some cases, even given to the proprietor of the establishment.

The second problem was the unavailability of many ingredients, such as kahlúa (a cream liqueur) for their White Russian ice cream. The solution was to substitute the kahlúa with vodka, but that altered the flavor of their product.

Conflict in strategic goals In 1993, the Iceverks venture earned about $100,000—a respectable amount for a small distribution operation and franchise in Russia. This unexpected success resulted in conflict and disagreement over expansion between Mr. Morse (head of Ben & Jerry's Russian operation) and Mr. Lukin (one of the Russian partners). Morse felt that they should wait for the right time to expand their Iceverks venture in Russia, and planned this to occur when the demand grew to the point that production was 75 percent of capacity. At that point, they would invest more capital into the venture and expand their market by establishing a distribution network and franchising scoop shops in Moscow and St. Petersburg. They expected this to take about a year. Unfortunately, for ambitious Russian businesspeople who were now getting a taste of real money, this was a year too long. With their newfound capitalistic success, the Russian partners were eager to expand, and Morse's reluctance to do so was a constant frustration for the Russian partners. From the Russians' perspective, they had done all they could in Petrozavodsk. The time to expand was now. This was their country, and they felt that their American partners did not know how to effectively do business on their soil. According to Mr. Lukin, "We didn't know how to make ice cream, and Ben & Jerry's didn't know how to behave in Russia." In addition, the Russian partners received several requests to build other factories throughout Russia, and since loans were available through Russian lending institutions, they saw no reason to delay. "It is difficult to persuade our American partners that our market is—I won't say stable enough—but good enough to move ahead quickly," said Lukin.

Despite their Russian partners' desire to expand, the managers at Ben & Jerry's headquarters preferred to wait for the benefits of nurturing the Iceverks venture before a premature expansion. "We know we have an existing healthy business. If we try to push too hard, we could blow that. I'd rather be a success in Karelia than a failure in Moscow," Mr. Morse said.

In addition to communication problems with Russian partners, the Iceverks venture had to tackle cultural conflicts that affected their performance in the Russian market, primarily in imparting Western business philosophy to the local managers and employees. Simple things like saying "hello" and "thank you" to customers had to be stressed and instilled in every employee's work ethic. In addition, employees had to be trained to keep refrigerators clean and the store sanitary.

Distribution Three years after the joint venture was established, Ben & Jerry's started to sell its product outside Karelia. This growth was slow and overdue, but they believed that "methodical expansion is the recipe for long-term success here." But they soon found out that distribution channels in Russia, such as railroads, were very expensive and prevented them from providing their product at a reasonable price. Distribution in Russia is often controlled by a monopoly, usually with links to organized crime, which means transportation is expensive and arbitrary. Equipment such as refrigerated trucks and warehouses are in short supply, substandard, and expensive.

Partnerships and business contacts in Russia are generally established through friendships and acquaintances. Accordingly, Ben & Jerry's distribution network was established through friends of the Iceverks venture. Iceverks' main distributor, Vessco Co., was headed by a close friend of the Russian partner, which created a favorable business relationship.

Finance   As a joint venture, Ben & Jerry's got a tax break, making its profits tax-free through the end of 1993. After 1993, however, the company would be subjected to tax rates of 30 to 45 percent of earnings.

A major concern for the corporation was the inability to repatriate profits because of the inconvertibility of the ruble. Soviet laws allowed profits to be repatriated in hard currency only if the joint venture produced goods that could be sold abroad for hard currency. Even though rubles were not officially convertible, some Russian banks allowed Ben & Jerry's to buy dollars to wire back to the United States. In 1989, it was almost impossible to estimate the ruble's real value, making it difficult for Ben & Jerry's to value their assets and collateral. When Iceverks was started, the official value of the ruble was $1.65, but its value on the black market at the same time was as little as $0.06. With inflation rates of more than 2,000 percent some years, Ben & Jerry had to periodically adjust their prices. Around that time, prices at other American ventures (such as McDonald's) tripled or quadrupled annually. In one year, for example, the price of Ben & Jerry's cones went up from $0.15 to $0.40 (800 rubles).

Ben & Jerry's produced and sold their ice cream within Russia and used rubles to pay for ingredients, equipment, and salaries. Their revenues were generated partly from their scoop shop operation (in rubles) and partly from selling pints to distributors (in dollars) for sale in Moscow. In the summer of 1993, the Russian government introduced a new law prohibiting the sale of domestically made products wholesale for hard currency. This meant that Ben & Jerry's could no longer sell ice cream to its Moscow distributors for dollars. Rather than deal with the uncertainties of the ruble economy, the Moscow distributors quit, leaving Ben and Jerry's unable to sell its products in Moscow.

Case Questions

1. Was Ben & Jerry's premature in entering a business alliance in Russia?
2. What were the problems that the Iceverks' venture ran into? How would you have handled those problems once they arose?
3. In retrospect, what would you have done differently both in setting up the joint venture and in preparing to expand across Russia?
4. What should Ben & Jerry's do now?

Case Bibliography

1. Dexheimer, Ellen and Dtube, Christine. "A kinder, gentler industry: Dairy companies answer the call of their social conscience; News&Trends" Delta Communication Inc., *Daily Food Magazine,* Vol. 91; No. 5; 13: ISSN: 0888–0050.
2. Steve Liesman. "Ben & Jerry's at a Fork on a Rocky Road," *Wall Street Journal,* 30 July 1994, 35.
3. Jeff Trimble. "Ben & Jerry's big chill," *U.S News & World Report,* 4 April 1988. "Mafia has death grip on Russia," *USA TODAY,* 4 November 1996, 4a. *ww.w.wor.ldaffairsdc.orp,/news./mafia.html.*
4. "Ben&Jerry into low fat, out of Russia, and gone Phisine," Ben & Jerry Homepage, 17 Feb 1998. *http;//www.benjerry.com/international/russia.html.*
5. Neela Banerjee. "Ben & Jerry's is trying to smooth out distribution in Russia as it expands."
6. Betsy McKay. "Ben & Jerry's Post-Cold War Venture Ends in Russia With Ice Cream Melting," *Wall Street Journal,* 7 February 1997, A14.
7. Freadl-liatt. "Da, we have no bananas Karenina; U.S.–Russian ice cream firm succeeding despite crises," *Washington Post,* 26 May 1993.
8. Beth Knobel. "Doing Business," *Los Angeles Times,* 31 August 1993. Pg 2 Column 1: World Report. *www.lexisnexis.com/Universe/docum.*

 9. Richard Andrews. "Do Business in Russia at Their Leisure," Manning Publications Inc., December 1989. Vol. 17; 12; Sec I: 20. *www.lexisnexis.com/Universe./docum.*

10. "Frozen dessert year in review," FIND/SVP, Inc., 20 January 1995, 8, 2, I.

11. Justin Burke. "Russia Gets a Terrible Dip Of Caring Capitalism," *The Christian Science Monitor,* 5 May 1993.

12. "Ice cream diplomacy; Ben & Jerry's super premium ice cream opens shop in Petrozacodsk," Karelia, Soviet Union: Cahners Publishing Company, August, 1991. 92, 8; 66; ISSN: 08880050. *www.lexisnexis.com/.Universe/docum.*

13. Francois Shalom. "Russian Delight: Ben & Jerry's office training exchanges employees," Lexis Nexis, 1 September 1994. DI/BREAK. *www.lexisn xi@s.com/universe/doc.um.*

14. Doeff, Gail. "Russian revelation: Ben & Jerry's Homemade Inc. reports strong market venture in Russia," Delta Communications Inc., January 1994. *www.lexisnexis.com.*

15. Stephen Seplow. "Vermont-style ice cream proves popular to Russian taste buds," *The Houston Chronicle,* 2 May 1993. A 34. *www.lexisnexis,com/Uniyerse./docum.*

16. "Young Professionals," *www.world affairs.com Lnews./mafia.html.*

17. Annelise Anderson. "The Red Mafia: Legacy of Communism," *www.andrsh.stanford.*

18. Reggie Nadelson. "The world in their scoop; Artichoke and Lemon Curd was a big mistake, but Chunky Monkey is a real winner," FIND/SVP, Inc., 14 July 1994, 21.

Source: Adapted by the author from a term paper written by Ryan Gramaglia, Akemi Kikuchi, and Boris Shekhman, students at the State University of New York at Plattsburgh, NY, May 1998. Copyright © Helen Deresky, 1998.

9

Organization Structure and Coordinating Systems

O U T L I N E

Opening Profile: Poland: Reorganizing Structure and Systems Brings New Life to ABB Zamech

Organization Structure

Evolution and Change in MNC Organizational Structures

Integrated Global Structures

Organizing for Globalization

Comparative Management in Focus: The Overseas Chinese Global Network

Organizing to "Be Global, Act Local"

Emergent Structural Forms

Interorganizational Networks

The Transnational Corporation (TNC) Network Structure

Choice of Organizational Form

Organizational Change and Design Variables

Coordinating and Reporting for Global Operations

Monitoring Systems

Direct Coordinating Mechanisms

Indirect Coordinating Mechanisms

Technology Application: Air Express International in Latin America: Old Problems, New Solutions

Management Focus: McDonald's in Moscow: Control Challenge Extraordinaire!

Managing Effective Monitoring Systems

The Appropriateness of Monitoring and Reporting Systems

The Role of Information Systems

Evaluation Variables Across Countries

Summary of Key Points

Discussion Questions

Application Exercises

Experiential Exercise

Internet Resources

Case Study: Flexit International

OPENING   PROFILE

Poland: Reorganizing Structure and Systems Brings New Life to ABB Zamech

In May 1990, Poland's leading manufacturer of steam turbines, transmission gears, marine equipment, and metal castings began a new life as ABB Zamech—a joint venture of ABB (76 percent ownership), the Polish government (19 percent ownership), and the company's employees (5 percent ownership). ABB Zamech employs 4,300 people in the town of Elblag, outside Gdansk. ABB has become the largest Western investor in Poland, and it intends to demonstrate that the philosophy of business and managerial reform it has applied in places like Mannheim, Germany, and Muncie, Indiana, can also work in the troubled economies of eastern Europe. That philosophy has at least four core principles:

1. Immediately reorganize operations into profit centers with well-defined budgets, strict performance targets, and clear lines of authority and accountability.
2. Identify a core group of change agents from local management, give small teams responsibility for championing high-priority programs, and closely monitor results.
3. Transfer ABB expertise from around the world to support the change process, without interfering with it or running it directly.
4. Keep standards high, and demand quick results.

The change program began immediately after the creation of the joint venture. For decades, the company had been organized along functional lines, a structure that blurred managerial authority, confused product-line profitability, and slowed decision making. Within four weeks, ABB Zamech was reorganized into discrete profit centers—each area with a leadership team responsible for its own planning, budgeting, and performance targets, which were used to make staffing decisions and to judge the team's progress.

The reorganization was a crucial first step; the second step was installing ABB's standard financial and control system. For decades, Zamech had been run as a giant overhead machine. Roughly 80 percent of the company's total costs were allocated by central staff accountants rather than traced directly to specific products and services. Managers had no clear idea what their products cost to make, and thus they had no idea which ones made money. Tight financial controls and maximum capital productivity are critical in an economy with interest rates around 40 percent.

Formal reorganization and new control systems, no matter how radical, won't have much of an effect without big changes in who is in charge. Accordingly, ABB made two important decisions. First, there would be no "rescue team" from western Europe—all managerial positions, from the CEO down, would be held by Polish managers from the former Zamech. Second, managers would be selected without regard to rank or seniority; indeed, there would be a premium on young, creative talent. ABB was looking for "hungry wolves"—smart, ambitious change agents who would receive intense training and be the core engine of Zamech's revival. In fact, most of the new leaders came from the ranks of middle management—for instance, the company's top executive, General Manager Pawel Olechnowicz, ran the steel castings department prior to the joint venture's creation.

Next came the process of developing a detailed agenda for reform. The leadership team settled on 11 priority issues, from reorganizing and retraining the salesforce to slashing total cycle times and redesigning the factory layout. To support the change initiatives, ABB created a team of high-level experts from around the world—authorities in functional areas like finance, control, and quality, as well as technology specialists and managers with extensive restructuring experience.

Two steps that ABB had to take to facilitate expertise transfer were training Polish managers in the English language and dealing with the antiquated telephone system in Poland. ABB thus linked Zamech by satellite to its Zurich headquarters for reliable telephone and fax communications. In January 1991, ABB Zamech began electronically transferring quarterly performance reports to Zurich—another big step in making communications more intensive and effective. Once it had created the communications infrastructure, however, ABB had to reckon with a second language barrier—the language of business. To do this, ABB created a "mini MBA program" in Warsaw to introduce the managers to basic business concepts and enable them to transfer these concepts into the ranks.

The change program at ABB Zamech is already generating results. The company is issuing monthly financial reports that conform to ABB standards—a major achievement in light of the simple systems in place before the joint venture. Cycle times for the production of steam turbines have been cut in half and now meet the ABB worldwide average. A task force is implementing a plan to reduce factory space by 20 percent—an important step in streamlining the operation. The program has been so successful, in fact, that ABB is drawing on its Zamech experience in its reform process for its joint ventures with two other Polish manufacturers, Dolmel and Dolmel Drives.

In August 1998, the parent corporation—Asea Brown Boveri AG, which is Europe's largest engineering company, rivaling giants like the United States' General Electric Company—announced restructuring moves in response to the Asian economic crisis. The plan was to change from a regional reporting structure to recasting its various business activities on global lines. Chief Executive Goeran Lindahl stated that "we are streamlining the organization to tap trends toward globalization." This included earlier layoffs in Europe and North America of 16,000 employees, shifting production to the now low-cost countries in Asia. Prior to these changes taking effect, ABB, already a global company with sales of $31.27 billion and 219,000 employees worldwide, had 5,000 profit centers in 140 countries. Its many "home" markets—from Mexico City to Beijing—draw on expertise from around the globe and are part of a "networked" ABB structure with no geographic base. ABB has been successful in creating a transnational management cadre who get global strategies to work with local operations. Their executive committee comprises three Swedes, two Swiss, an American, and a German; only the American and one Swiss live in their native countries.

Source: Adapted and excerpted from William Taylor, "The Logic of Global Business: An Interview with ABB's Percy Barnevik," *Harvard Business Review* (March–April 1991): 91–105; "ABB Fuses Units with One Set of Values," *Wall Street Journal*, October 2, 1996; and C. Fleming and Leslie Lopez, "No Boundaries," *Wall Street Journal*, September 28, 1998, r.16.

There is no permanent organization chart for the world. . . . It is of supreme importance to be ready at all times to take advantage of new opportunities.
—Roberto C. Goizueta, (former) Chairman and CEO, Coca-Cola Company

Strategic plans are abstract sets of decisions that cannot affect a company's competitive position or bottom line until they are implemented. Having decided on the strategic direction for the company, international managers must then consider two of the key variables for implementing strategy—the organization structure and coordinating mechanisms. The relationships among strategy, structure, and coordinating mechanisms are illustrated in this chapter's Opening Profile, which describes ABB-Zamech's dramatic revival of ABB Poland through formal reorganization and new control systems.

Organization Structure

Organizational structures must change to accommodate a firm's evolving internationalization in response to worldwide competition. Considerable research has shown that a firm's structure must be conducive to the implementation of its strategy.[1] In other words, the structure must "fit" the strategy, or it will not work. Managers are faced with how best to attain that fit in organizing the company's systems and tasks.

The design of an organization, as with any other management function, should be contingency based, taking into account the prevailing variables for the company at that specific point in time. Major variables include the firm's strategy, size, and appropriate technology, as well as the environment in those parts of the world where the firm operates. Given the increased complexity of the variables involved in the international context, it is no easy task to design the most suitable organizational structure and subsystems. In fact, research shows that most international managers find that it is easier to determine what to do to compete globally (strategy) than to decide how to develop the organizational capability (structure) to do it.[2] Additional variables affecting structural choices—geographic dispersion as well as differences in time, language, cultural attitudes, and business practices—introduce further layers of complication. We will show how organizational structures need to, and typically do, change to accommodate strategies of increasing internationalization.

Evolution and Change in MNC Organizational Structures

Historically, a firm reorganizes as it internationalizes to accommodate new strategies. The structure typically continues to change over time with growth and with increasing levels of investment or diversity and as a result of the types of entry strategy chosen. **Internationalization** is the process by which a firm gradually changes in response to international competition; domestic market saturation; and the desire for expansion, new markets, and diversification. As discussed in Chapter 7, the firm's managers weigh alternatives and decide on appropriate entry strategies. Perhaps the firm starts by exporting or by acting as a licensor or licensee and then, over time, continues to internationalize by engaging in joint ventures or by establishing service, production, or assembly facilities, or alliances, abroad. At each stage, the firm's managers redesign the organizational structure to optimize the strategy's chances to work, making changes in the firm's tasks and relationships, and designating authority, responsibility, lines of communication, geographic dispersal of units, and so forth. This model of **structural evolution** has become known as the **stages model**, resulting from Stopford's research on 187 U.S. MNCs. Of course, many firms do not follow the stages model because they may start their internationalization at a higher level of involvement—perhaps as a full-blown global joint venture without ever having exported, for example.

Even a mature MNC needs to make structural changes from time to time to facilitate changes in strategy—perhaps a change in strategy from globalization to regionalization (as discussed in Chapter 8) or an effort to improve efficiency or effectiveness. The recent reorganization of Aluminum Company of America (Alcoa), for example, split the company into smaller, more autonomous units. This reorganization gives more focus to growing businesses, such as automotive products, where the market for aluminum is strong. It also enables Alcoa to link businesses with similar functions that are divided geographically—that is, to improve previously insufficient communication between Alcoa's aluminum operations in Brazil and its Australian counterparts.[3]

The typical ways in which firms organize their international activities are shown in the following list. (Larger companies often use several of these structures in different regions or parts of their organization.) After discussing some of these structural forms, we will introduce new, transitional organizational arrangements.

- Domestic structure plus export department
- Domestic structure plus foreign subsidiary

- International division
- Integrated Global Structures:
  Global functional structure
  Global product structure
  Global geographic area structure

As discussed, many firms, especially the smaller ones, start their international involvement by exporting. For this, they may simply use the services of an export management company, or they may reorganize into a simple **domestic structure plus export department**.

To facilitate access to and development of specific foreign markets, the firm can take a further step toward worldwide operations by reorganizing into a **domestic structure plus foreign subsidiary** in one or more countries (as illustrated in Exhibit 9–1). In order for this structure to be effective, subsidiary managers should have a great deal of autonomy and should be able to adapt and respond quickly to serve local markets. This structure works well for a company with one or a few subsidiaries located relatively close to headquarters.

With further market expansion, the firm may then decide to specialize by creating an **international division**, organized along functional, product, or geographic lines. With this structure, the various foreign subsidiaries are under the international division, and subsidiary managers report to its head, typically, the vice president of the international division, who in turn reports directly to the CEO of the corporation. The creation of an international division facilitates the beginning of a global strategy. It permits managers to allocate and coordinate resources for foreign activities under one roof and so enhances the firm's ability to respond, both reactively and proactively, to market opportunities. Some conflicts may arise among the divisions of the firm (1) because more resources and management attention tend to get chan-

EXHIBIT 9–1

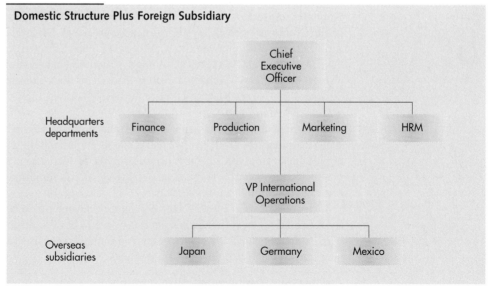

Domestic Structure Plus Foreign Subsidiary

neled toward the international division than toward the domestic divisions, and (2) because of the different orientations of various division managers.[4] Companies such as IBM, PepsiCo, and Gillette have international divisions, called, respectively, IBM World Trade, PepsiCola International, and Gillette International.

Integrated Global Structures

To respond to increased product diversification and to maximize benefits from both domestic and foreign operations, a firm may choose to replace its international division with an integrated global structure. This structure can be organized along functional, product, geographic, or matrix lines.[5]

The **global functional structure** is designed on the basis of the company's functions—production, marketing, finance, and so forth. Foreign operations are integrated into the activities and responsibilities of each department to gain functional specialization and economies of scale. This form of organization is used primarily by small firms with highly centralized systems. It is particularly appropriate for product lines using similar technology and for businesses with a narrow spectrum of customers. This structure results in plants that are highly integrated across products and that serve single or similar markets.[6]

Much of the advantage resulting from economies of scale and functional specialization may be lost if the managers and the work systems become too narrowly defined to have the necessary flexibility to respond to local environments. An alternative structure can be based on product lines.

For firms with diversified product lines (or services) that have different technological bases and that are aimed at dissimilar or dispersed markets, a **global product (divisional) structure** may be more strategically advantageous than a functional structure. In this structure, a single product (or product line) is represented by a separate division. Each division is headed by its own general manager, and each is responsible for its own production and sales functions. Usually, each division is a **strategic business unit (SBU)**, a self-contained business with its own functional departments and accounting systems. The advantages of this organizational form are market concentration, innovation, and responsiveness to new opportunities in a particular environment. It also facilitates diversification and rapid growth, sometimes at the expense of scale economies and functional specialization. William R. Johnson, H. J. Heinz Company CEO, came on board in April 1998 and decided that the company should restructure to implement a global strategy. He changed the focus of the company from a multidomestic international strategy, using the global geographic area structure, to a global strategy, using the global product divisional structure. His goal was further growth overseas by building international operations; this structure also readily incorporated the company's new Specialty Pet Food division for marketing those products around the world.[7] Particularly appropriate in a dynamic and diverse environment, the global product structure is illustrated in Exhibit 9–2.

With the global product (divisional) grouping, however, ongoing difficulties in the coordination of widely dispersed operations may result. One answer to this, particularly for large MNCs, is to reorganize into a global geographic structure.

EXHIBIT 9–2

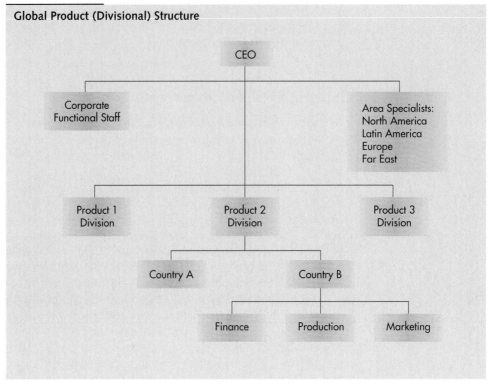

Global Product (Divisional) Structure

In the **global geographic (area) structure**, the most common form of organizing foreign operations, divisions are created to cover geographic regions (see Exhibit 9–3). Each regional manager is then responsible for the operations and performance of the countries within a given region. In this way, country and regional needs and relative market knowledge take precedence over product expertise. Local managers are familiar with the cultural environment, government regulations, and business transactions. In addition, their language skills and local contacts facilitate daily transactions and responsiveness to the market and the customer. Although this is a good structure for consolidating regional expertise, problems of coordination across regions may arise. With the geographic structure, the focus is on marketing since products can be adapted to local requirements. Therefore, marketing-oriented companies, such as Nestle and Unilever, which produce a range of products that can be marketed through similar (or common) channels of distribution to similar customers, will usually opt for this structure. Grouping a number of countries under a region doesn't always work out, however, as experienced by Ford with its European Group; it soon discovered tensions among the units in Germany, Britain, and France resulting from differences in their national systems and culture, and in particular, management styles. Nevertheless, it has pursued its consolidation into five regionalized global centers for the design, manufacture, and marketing of 70 lines of cars around the world.[8] However, there may be further changes on the horizon since Bill Ford, Jr., Chairman of Ford, has let it be known that he is shopping for a global auto business.[9]

EXHIBIT 9-3

Global Geographic Structure

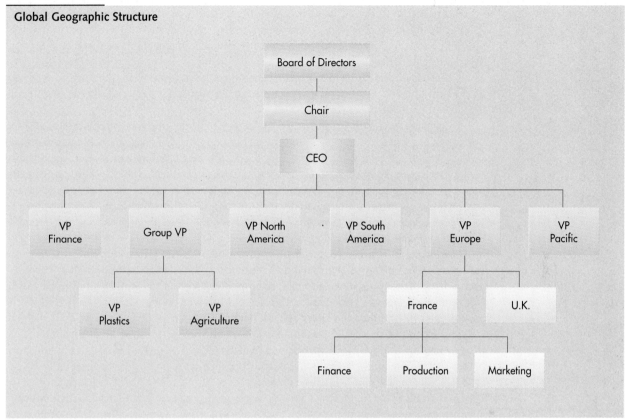

Organizing for Globalization

If you misjudge the market [by globalizing], you are wrong in 15 countries rather than only in one.

—Ford European executive[10]

No matter what the stage of internationalization, a firm's structural choices always involve two opposing forces: the need for **differentiation** (focusing on and specializing in specific markets) and the need for **integration** (coordinating those same markets). The way the firm is organized along the differentiation–integration continuum determines how well strategies—along a localization–globalization continuum—are implemented. This is why the structural imperatives of various strategies such as globalization must be understood to organize appropriate worldwide systems and connections.

As discussed earlier, global trends and competitive forces have put increasing pressure on multinational corporations to adopt a strategy of **globalization**—a specific strategy that treats the world as one market by using a standardized approach to products and markets. Recent examples of companies reorganizing to achieve globalization are the following:[11]

IBM. Big Blue decided in 1994 to move away from its traditional geographic structure to a global structure based on its 14 worldwide industry groups, such as banking, retail, and insurance, shifting power from country managers to centralized industry expert teams. IBM hopes the restructuring will help the company take advantage of global markets and break down internal barriers.

Bristol-Meyers Squibb. The international drug company announced the formation of new worldwide units in 1994 for consumer medicine businesses such as Bufferin, and for its Clairol and hair-care products.

Organizing to facilitate a globalization strategy typically involves rationalization and the development of strategic alliances. To achieve rationalization, managers choose the manufacturing location for each product based on where the best combination of cost, quality, and technology can be attained. This process often involves producing different products or components in different countries; typically, rationalization also means that the product design and marketing programs are essentially the same for all end markets around the world so as to achieve optimal economies of scale. The downside of this strategy is a lack of differentiation and specialization for local markets.

Organizing for global product standardization necessitates close coordination among the various countries involved. It also requires centralized global product responsibility (one manager at headquarters responsible for a specific product around the world), an especially difficult task for multiproduct companies. Henzler and Rall suggest that structural solutions to this problem can be found if companies rethink the roles of their headquarters and their national subsidiaries. Managers should center the overall control of the business at headquarters while treating national subsidiaries as partners in managing the business—perhaps as holding companies responsible for the administration and coordination of cross-divisional activities.[12]

A problem many companies face in the future is that their structurally sophisticated global networks, built to secure cost advantages, leave them exposed to the risk of environmental volatility from all corners of the world. Such companies need to restructure their global operations to reduce the environmental risk that results from multicountry sourcing and supply networks.[13] In other words, the more links in the chain, the more chances for things to go wrong.

Globalization is often achieved through less formal organizational structures and alliances. An example is the powerful global network of the overseas Chinese, as discussed in the following Comparative Management in Focus.

COMPARATIVE MANAGEMENT IN FOCUS

The Overseas Chinese Global Network

The Chinese who left the mother country had to struggle, and that became a culture of its own. Because we have no social security, the Overseas Chinese habit is to save a lot and make a lot of friends.

—Lee Shau Kee, 65, real estate developer, Hong Kong (net worth $6 billion)[14]

Compared to the Japanese *keiretsu* (large industrial groups) the emerging Chinese commonwealth is an interconnected, open system—a new market mechanism for conducting global business.[15] It is now becoming apparent to many business leaders who have finally figured out Japan's keiretsu that they "now need to understand a distinctively Chinese model, where tycoons cut megadeals in a flash and heads of state wheel and deal like CEOs."[16]

The Chinese commonwealth is a form of global network that has become the envy of Western multinationals. It is a network of entrepreneurial relationships spread across continents, though primarily in Asia. What is increasingly being referred to as the "big dragon of Greater China" includes, along with mainland China's 1.3 billion citizens, the more than 55 million Overseas Chinese—most of them from Taiwan, Indonesia, Hong Kong, and Thailand. It is estimated that the Overseas Chinese control $2 trillion in liquid assets and contribute about 80 percent of the capital for the People's Republic of China (PRC); if the Overseas Chinese lived in one country, their gross national product would exceed that of mainland China.[17] In addition, this "bamboo network," which transcends national boundaries, is estimated to contribute about 70 percent of the private sector in Malaysia, Thailand, Indonesia, and the Philippines.[18] Most observers believe that this China-based informal economy is the world leader in economic growth, industrial expansion, and exports. It comprises mostly midsize, family-run firms linked by transnational network channels. "These channels for the movement of information, finance, goods, and capital help to explain the relative flexibility and efficiency of the numerous ongoing informal agreements and transactions that bind together the various parts of the Chinese-based trading area."[19] The network alliances bind together and draw from the substantial pool of financial capital and resources available in the region—including those of entrepreneurial services in Hong Kong; technology and manufacturing capability in Taiwan; outstanding communications in Singapore; and vast endowments of land, resources, and labor in mainland China.[20]

The Overseas Chinese—now models for entrepreneurship, financing, and modernization for the world and, in particular, for Beijing—are refugees from China's poverty, disorder, and communism. Business became the key to survival for those Chinese emigrants faced with uncertainties, hardships, and lack of acceptance in their new lands. The uncertainties, a survivor mentality, and the cultural basis in the Confucian tradition of patriarchical authority have led to a way of doing business that is largely confined to family and trusted friends. This business mentality and approach to life have led to many self-made billionaires among the Overseas Chinese. Among them is Y. C. Wang, the Taiwanese plastics king, who had to leave school after the sixth grade but taught himself what was necessary to develop a new industry. At 77, he still never takes a day off and views personal consumption as undue extravagance. His wife sneaks out his worn suits to the tailor to be copied and sneaks the new ones back into his closet.[21] The network of alliances of the ethnic Chinese is based on *guanxi*—personal connections—among families, business friends, and political associations, often rooted in the traditional clans. Massive amounts of cross-investment and trade are restricted primarily to families and long-standing connections, including those from the province of the PRC from which the overseas Chinese or their ancestors migrated. As examples, Chinese ties in Hong Kong have provided about 90 percent of the investment in the adjacent Guangong; and telephone calls from the special economic zone of Xiamen in the PRC to Taiwan now average 60,000 a month, up from 10 a month 8 years ago.[22] The web of those connections has created an influential network that is the backbone of the East Asian economy.

The history, culture, and personal approach to business of the Overseas Chinese have led to some underlying values, that Kao calls "life-raft" values, which have shaped a distinctive business culture. These values include thrift and a very high savings level, regardless of need, extremely hard work, trust in family before anyone else, adherence to patriarchal authority, investment based strictly on kinship and affiliations, a preference for investment in tangible goods, and an ever-wary outlook on life.[23] It is this shared web of culture and contacts that has spawned an intensely commercial and entrepreneurial network of capitalists and a dominant power in Asia. Two benefits of such a business culture are speed and patience. Because of their knowledge of and trust in their contacts, the Overseas Chinese can smell profits quickly and make decisions even more quickly; a deal to buy a hotel in Asia can be completed in days, whereas it would likely take months in the United States.[24] Patience to invest for the long term is an outcome of closely held ownership and management, often in a single family, so that outside shareholders are not demanding short-term profits. There is no doubt that sharing language and cultural bonds is a vital lubricant for business, especially with people in China, where there are few firm laws that businesspeople can rely on.[25]

Organizing to "Be Global, Act Local"

In their rush to get on the globalization bandwagon, too many firms have sacrificed the ability to respond to local market structures and consumer preferences. Managers are now realizing that—depending on the types of products, markets, and so forth—a compromise must be made along the globalization–localization continuum, and they are experimenting with various structural configurations to "be global and act local." Colgate-Palmolive's organization structure in 1994 illustrates such a compromise. As described by Rosenzweig and illustrated in Exhibit 9–4, the primary operating structure is geographic, that is, localized. The presidents of four major regions—North America, Europe, Latin America, and Asia Pacific—report to the chief operating officer, whereas other developing regions such as Africa, eastern Europe, and the Middle East report to the chief of operations of international business development. Then that person reports to the CEO of Colgate-Palmolive, who oversees the centralized coordinating operations (that is, the "globalized" aspects) for technology, finance, marketing, human resources management, and so on.

Colgate-Palmolive's structure has evolved to this point to complement its evolving strategy. As described by Rosenzweig, at first Colgate-Palmolive structured its international operations on a country-by-country basis, with the foreign subsidiaries each reporting directly to headquarters. With expansion into the 1950s, the structure was changed to a regional one, with regional presidents overseeing subsidiaries. But during the 1970s and 1980s, there was increasing global competition in consumer goods, leading Colgate-Palmolive to strive more for global coordination than relying on geographic decentralization. Toward that end, the company reorganized in 1981, setting up a global business development unit to oversee and coordinate some worldwide operations and launch new products. And, as of 1994, the structure illustrated was a hybrid in order to seek the advantages of global coordination as well as local responsiveness.[26]

Levi Strauss is another example of a company attempting to maximize the advantages of different structural configurations. First, Levi has ensured its ability to respond to local needs in a different way, by allowing its managers to act independently:

> Levi's success turns on its ability to fashion a global strategy that doesn't snuff out local initiative. It's a delicate balancing act, one that often means giving foreign managers the freedom needed to adjust their tactics to meet the changing tastes of their home markets.[27]

EXHIBIT 9-4

Colgate-Palmolive's "Glocal" Organizational Structure

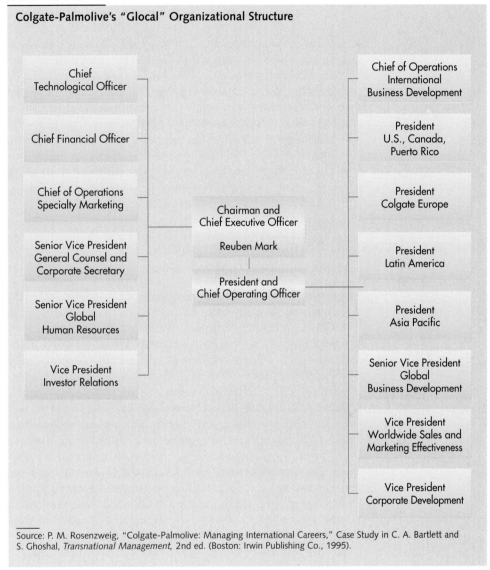

Source: P. M. Rosenzweig, "Colgate-Palmolive: Managing International Careers," Case Study in C. A. Bartlett and S. Ghoshal, *Transnational Management,* 2nd ed. (Boston: Irwin Publishing Co., 1995).

Second, Levi's keeps centralized control of some aspects of its business but decentralizes control to its foreign operations, organized as subsidiaries. These subsidiaries are supplied by a global manufacturing network of Levi plants and contract manufacturers. This approach allows local coordination and the flexibility to respond to ever-changing fashion trends and fads in denim shading.[28]

Another company's plan to go global by acting local does not involve changing the company's basic structure. Fujitsu, a Japanese high-technology conglomerate producing computers, telecommunications equipment, and semiconductors, has found a way to internationalize by proxy. Fujitsu has substantial stakes in two foreign companies that account for nearly half of Fujitsu's overseas revenues. They are Amdahl, a Silicon Valley maker of IBM-compatible mainframes, and International Computers Ltd. (ICL), Britain's biggest computer company. These firms are run by Westerners, who are given free reign to manage and even compete against one another. The plan is doing so well that Fujitsu is looking for similar deals in Europe. As Fujitsu's president, Takuma Yamamoto, explains, "We are doing business in a borderless economy, but there is a rising tide of nationalism, and you have to find ways to avoid conflict. That is one reason we give our partners autonomy."[29]

Although strategy may be the primary means to a company's competitive advantage, the burden of realizing that advantage rests on the organizational structure and design. Because of the difficulties experienced by companies trying to be "glocal" (global and local), researchers are suggesting new, more flexible organizational designs, involving interorganizational networks and transnational design.

Emergent Structural Forms

Interorganizational Networks

Whether the ever-expanding transnational linkages of an MNC consist of different companies, subsidiaries, suppliers, or individuals, they result in relational networks. These networks may adopt very different structures of their own because they operate in different local contexts within their own national environments.[30] By regarding the MNC's overall structure as a network of interconnected relations, we can more realistically consider its organizational design imperatives at both the global and the local levels. Exhibit 9–5 illustrates the network structure of N. V. Philips, a multinational with headquarters in the Netherlands and operating units in 60 countries. These units range from large subsidiaries, which might be among the largest companies in a country, to very small single-function operations, such as the research and development or marketing division for one of Philips's businesses. Some have centralized control at Philips's headquarters; others are quite autonomous.

The network of exchange relationships shown in Exhibit 9–5, say Ghoshal and Bartlett, is as representative of any MNC as it is of Philips. The network framework makes clear that the company's operating units link vastly different environmental and operational contexts based on varied economic, social, and cultural milieus. This complex linkage highlights the intricate task of a giant MNC to rationalize and coordinate its activities globally to achieve an advantageous cost position while tailoring itself to local market conditions (to achieve benefits from differentiation).[31] In fact, N. V. Philips has recently fallen far behind its Japanese competitors in productivity because of its lumbering bureaucratic organization, which it needs to simplify and decentralize.[32]

The Transnational Corporation (TNC) Network Structure

To address the globalization–localization dilemma, firms that have evolved through the multinational form and the global company are now seeking the advantages of horizontal organization in the pursuit of **transnational capability**—that is, the ability to manage across

EXHIBIT 9–5

The Network Structure of N. V. Philips

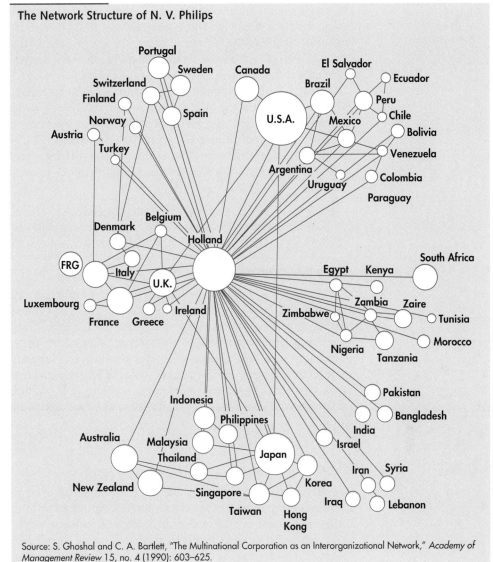

Source: S. Ghoshal and C. A. Bartlett, "The Multinational Corporation as an Interorganizational Network," *Academy of Management Review* 15, no. 4 (1990): 603–625.

national boundaries, retaining local flexibility while achieving global integration.[33] This capability involves linking their foreign operations in a flexible way to each other and to headquarters, thereby leveraging local and central capabilities.[34] ABB (Asea Brown Boveri) is an example of such a decentralized horizontal organization; ABB operates in 140 countries with 1,000 companies with only one management level separating the business units from top management. ABB prides itself in being a truly global company, with 11 board members representing 7 nationalities. Thus, this structure is less a matter of boxes on an organizational chart and more a matter of a network of the company's units and their system of horizontal communication. This involves lateral communication across networks of units and alliances rather than in a hierarchy. The system requires the dispersal of responsibility and decision making to local subsidiaries and alliances. The effectiveness of that localized decision making depends a great deal on the ability and willingness of managers to share current and new learning and technology across the network of units.

Whatever the names given to the organizational forms emerging to deal with global competition and logistics, the MNC organizational structure as we know it, with its hierarchical pyramid, subsidiaries, and world headquarters, is gradually evolving into a more fluid form—often referred to as a Transnational Corporation (TNC)—to adapt to strategic and competitive imperatives. Facilitating this change, Kilmann points out, is the information technology explosion fueled by computers, fax machines, teleconferencing, the Internet, and so forth:

> Competitive companies in the future will be elaborate networks of people and information, each exerting an influence on the other. [These networks will comprise] a small hub of staff connected to each other by their physical proximity, which is electronically connected to global associates who help control assets and negotiate agreements to extend the company's business influence.[35]

In this new global web, the location of a firm's headquarters is unimportant. It may even be, says Reich, "a suite of rooms in an office park near an international airport—a communications center where many of the web's threads intersect."[36] The web is woven by decisions made by managers around the world, both decisions within the company and those between other companies. Various alliances tie together units and subunits in the web. Corning Glass, for instance, changed from its national pyramidlike organization to a global web, giving it the capability of making optical cable through its European partner, Siemens AG, and medical equipment with Ciba-Geigy. These alliances alone generated nearly half of Corning's earnings in 1990.[37]

Choice of Organizational Form

Two major variables in choosing the structure and design of an organization are the opportunities and need for globalization and localization. Exhibit 9–6 depicts alternative structural forms appropriate to each of these variables and to the strategic choices regarding the level and type of international involvement desired by the firm. Exhibit 9–6 thereby updates the evolutionary stages model to reflect alternative organizational responses to more recent environments and to the anticipated competitive environments ahead. The updated model shows that, as the firm progresses from a domestic to an international company—and perhaps later to a multinational and then a global company—its managers adapt the organizational structure to accommodate their relative strategic focus on globalization versus localization, choosing a global product structure, a geographic area structure, or perhaps a matrix form. The model proposes that, as the company becomes larger, more complex, and more sophisticated in its approach to world markets (no matter which structural route it has taken), it may evolve into a TNC. The TNC strategy is to maximize opportunities for both efficiency and local responsiveness by adopting a transnational structure that uses alliances, networks, and

EXHIBIT 9–6

Organizational Alternatives and Development for Global Competition

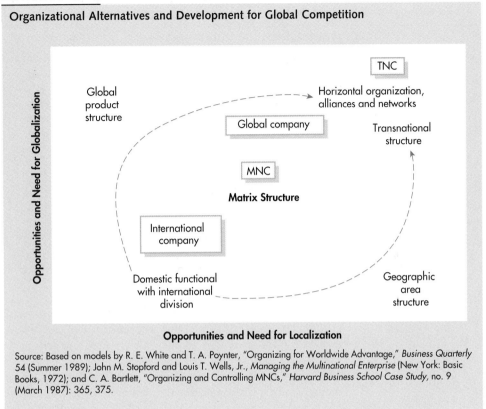

Source: Based on models by R. E. White and T. A. Poynter, "Organizing for Worldwide Advantage," *Business Quarterly* 54 (Summer 1989); John M. Stopford and Louis T. Wells, Jr., *Managing the Multinational Enterprise* (New York: Basic Books, 1972); and C. A. Bartlett, "Organizing and Controlling MNCs," *Harvard Business School Case Study*, no. 9 (March 1987): 365, 375.

horizontal design formats. The relationships between choice of global strategy and the appropriate structural variations necessary to implement each strategic choice are further illustrated in Exhibit 9–7.

Organizational Change and Design Variables

When a company makes drastic changes in its goals, strategy, or scope of operations, it is usually quite clear that a change in organizational structure is called for as well. However, other, less obvious indications of organizational inefficiency also signal a need for structural changes: Conflicts among divisions and subsidiaries over territories or customers, conflicts between overseas units and headquarters staff, complaints regarding overseas customer service, and overlapping responsibilities are some of these warning signals. Exhibit 9–8 lists some indications of the need for change in organizational design.

At persistent signs of ineffective work, a company should analyze its organizational design, systems, and workflow for the possible causes of those problems. The nature and extent of any design changes must reflect the magnitude of the problem. In choosing a new

EXHIBIT 9–7

Global Strategy–Structure Relationships

	Multidomestic Strategy	International Strategy	Globalization Strategy	Transnational Strategy
	Low ◄─────────────────────► Need for Coordination ◄─────────────────────► High			
	Low ◄─────────────────────► Bureaucratic Costs ◄─────────────────────► High			
Centralization of authority	Decentralized to national unit	Core competencies centralized; others decentralized to national units	Centralized at optimal global location	Simultaneously Centralized and Decentralized
Horizontal differentiation	Global area structure	International division structure	Global product group structure	Global Matrix Structure "Matrix in the Mind"
Need for complex integrating mechanisms	Low	Medium	High	Very High
Organizational culture	Not important	Quite Important	Important	Very Important

Source: C. W. L. Hill and E. R. Jones, *Strategic Management*, 3rd ed. (Boston: Houghton Mifflin, 1995): 390.

organizational design or in modifying an existing structure, managers must establish a system of communication and control that will provide for effective decision making. At such times, managers need to localize decision making and integrate widely dispersed and disparate global operations.

Besides determining the behavior of the organization on a macrolevel (in terms of what divisions, subsidiaries, departments, and units are responsible for), the organizational design must determine behavior on a microlevel. For example, the organizational design affects the level at which certain types of decisions will be made. Determining how many and what types of decisions can be made and by whom can have drastic consequences; both the locus and the scope of authority must be carefully considered. This centralization–decentralization variable actually represents a continuum. In the real world, companies are neither totally centralized nor totally decentralized: The level of centralization imposed is a matter of degree. Exhibit 9–9 illustrates this **centralization–decentralization continuum** and the different ways that decision making can be shared between headquarters and local units or subsidiaries. In general, centralized decision making is common for some functions (finance and research and development) that are organized for the entire corporation, whereas other functions (production, marketing, and sales) are more appropriately decentralized. Two key issues are the speed with which the decisions have to be made and whether they primarily affect only a certain subsidiary or other parts of the company as well.

As noted, culture is another factor that complicates decisions on how much to decentralize and how to organize the workflow and the various relationships of authority and responsibility. In Part 4 of this book, we discuss more fully how cultural variables affect people's attitudes about working relationships and about who should have authority over whom. At this point, simply note that cultural variables must be taken into account when designing an organization. Delegating a high level of authority to employees in a country

EXHIBIT 9–8

When Is Change Needed?

- A change in the size of the corporation—due to growth, consolidation, or reduction
- A change in key individuals—which may alter management objectives, interests, and abilities
- A failure to meet goals, capitalize on opportunities, or be innovative
- An inability to get things done on time
- A consistently overworked top management that spends excessive hours on the job
- A belief that costs are extravagant or that budgets are not being met
- Morale problems
- Lengthy hierarchies that inhibit the exercise of strategic control
- Planning that has become increasingly staff-driven and is thus divorced from line management
- Innovation that is stifled by too much administration and monitoring of details
- Uniform solutions that are applied to nonuniform situations. The extreme opposite of this condi-tion—when things that should or could function in a routine manner do not—should also be heeded as a warning. In other words, management by exception has replaced standard operating procedures

The following are a few specific indicators of *international* organizational malaise:

- A shift in the operational scope—perhaps from directing export activities to controlling overseas manufacturing and marketing units, a change in the size of operations on a country, regional, or worldwide basis, or failure of foreign operations to grow in accordance with plans and expectations
- Clashes among divisions, subsidiaries, or individuals over territories or customers in the field
- Divisive conflicts between overseas units and domestic division staff or corporate staff
- Instances wherein centralization leads to a flood of detailed data that is neither fully understood nor properly used by headquarters
- Duplication of administrative personnel and services
- Underutilization of overseas manufacturing or distribution facilities
- Duplication of sales offices and specialized sales account executives
- Proliferation of relatively small legal entities or operating units within a country or geographic area
- An increase in overseas customer service complaints
- Breakdowns in communications within and between organizations
- Unclear lines of reporting and dotted-line relationships, and ill-defined executive responsibilities

Source: Business International Corporation, *New Directions in Multinational Corporate Organization* (New York: Business International Corporation, 1981).

where the workers usually regard "the boss" as the rightful person to make all the decisions is not likely to work well. Clearly, managers must think through the interactions of organiza-tional, staffing, and cultural issues before making final decisions.

In sum, there is no one best way to organize. Contingency theory applies to organiza-tional design as much as to any other aspect of management. The best organizational struc-ture is the one that facilitates the firm's goals and is appropriate to its industry, size, technology, and competitive environment. Structure should be fluid and dynamic—and highly adaptable to the changing needs of the company. The structure should not be allowed

EXHIBIT 9-9

Locus of Decision Making in an International Organization

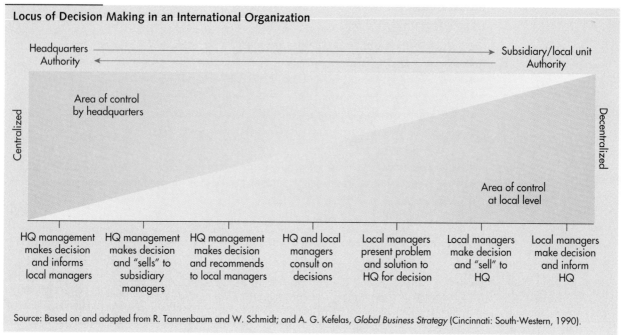

Headquarters Authority ⟶ Subsidiary/local unit Authority

Centralized — Decentralized

Area of control by headquarters

Area of control at local level

| HQ management makes decision and informs local managers | HQ management makes decision and "sells" to subsidiary managers | HQ management makes decision and recommends to local managers | HQ and local managers consult on decisions | Local managers present problem and solution to HQ for decision | Local managers make decision and "sell" to HQ | Local managers make decision and inform HQ |

Source: Based on and adapted from R. Tannenbaum and W. Schmidt; and A. G. Kefelas, *Global Business Strategy* (Cincinnati: South-Western, 1990).

to get bogged down in the **administrative heritage** of the organization (that is, "the way we do things around here," or "what we've always done") to the point that it undermines the very processes that will enable the firm to take advantage of new opportunities.

Most likely, however, the future for MNC structure lies in a global web of networked companies. Ideally, a company tries to organize in a way that will allow it to carry out its strategic goals; the staffing is then done to mesh with those strategic goals and the way the organizational structure has been set up. In reality, however, the existing structural factors often affect strategic decisions, so the end result may be a tradeoff of desired strategy with existing constraints. So too with staffing: "Ideal" staffing plans have to be adjusted to reflect the realities of assigning managers from various sources and the local regulations or cultural variables that make some organizing and staffing decisions more workable than others.

What may at first seem a linear management process of deciding on strategy, then on structure, and then on staffing is actually an interdependent set of factors that must be taken into consideration and worked out as a set of decisions. In the next chapter, we will explore how staffing decisions are—or should be—intricately intertwined with other decisions regarding strategy, structure, and so forth. In fact, a unique set of management cadre and skills in a particular location can be a competitive advantage in itself, and so it may be a smart move to build strategic and organizational decisions around that resource rather than risk losing that advantage. But first let's look at some other processes involved in implementing strategy that are interconnected with coordinating functions through organizational structure.

Coordinating and Reporting for Global Operations

To complement the organization structure, the international manager must design efficient coordinating and reporting systems to ensure that actual performance conforms to expected organizational standards and goals. The challenge is to coordinate far-flung operations in vastly different environments with various work processes; rules; and economic, political, legal, and cultural norms. The feedback from the control process and the information systems should signal any necessary change in strategy, structure, or operations in a timely manner. Often, as in the case of ABB Zamech, the strategy or the coordinating processes, or both need to be changed to reflect conditions in other countries.

Monitoring Systems

The design and application of coordinating and reporting systems for foreign subsidiaries and activities can take any form that management wishes. MNCs usually employ a variety of direct and indirect coordinating and control mechanisms suitable for their organization structure. Some of the typical control methods used for the major organizational structures discussed here are shown in Exhibit 9–10. These are self-explanatory; for example, in the transnational network structure, decision-making control is decentralized to key network nodes, greatly reducing emphasis on bureaucratic control. Output control in this exhibit refers to the assessment of a subsidiary or unit based only on the results attained. Other specific mechanisms are summarized in the following paragraphs.

EXHIBIT 9–10

Control Mechanisms in Multinational Organizational Structures

Multinational Structures	Output Control	Bureaucratic Control	Decision-Making Control	Organization Control
International division structure	Most likely profit control	Must follow company policies	Some centralization possible	Treated like other divisions
Global geographic structure	Profit center most common	Some policies and procedures necessary	Local units have autonomy	Local subsidiary culture often more important
Global product structure	Unit output for supply; sales volume for sales	Tight process controls for product quality and consistency	Centralized at product division headquarters	Possible for some companies but not always necessary
Transnational network structure	Used for supplier units and some independent profit centers	Less important	Few decisions centralized at headquarters; more decisions centralized in key network nodes	Organizational culture transcends national cultures; supports sharing and learning; the most important control mechanism

Source: Adapted from John B. Cullen *Multinational Management* (Cincinnati: South-Western, 1999): 329.

Direct Coordinating Mechanisms

Direct mechanisms that provide the basis for the overall guidance and management of foreign operations include the design of appropriate structures (discussed earlier in this chapter) and the use of effective staffing practices (discussed in Chapter 10). Such decisions proactively set the stage for operations to meet goals rather than troubleshooting deviations or problems after they have occurred. The accompanying Management Focus describes how McDonald's Corp. successfully set up direct control systems in advance of its entry into Moscow.

Other direct mechanisms are visits by head-office personnel and regular meetings. Top executives from headquarters may use periodic visits to subsidiaries to check performance, troubleshoot, and help anticipate future problems. International Telephone and Telegraph Corporation (ITT) holds monthly management meetings at its New York headquarters. Performance data are submitted by each ITT subsidiary general manager from around the world, and problems and solutions are shared.[38] The meetings allow each general manager to keep in touch with his or her associates, with the overall mission and strategy of the organization, and with comparative performance data and new problem-solving techniques. Increasingly, the tools of technology are being applied as direct mechanisms to ensure up front that operations will be carried out as planned, in particular in countries where processes such as efficient infrastructure and goods forwarding cannot be taken for granted. An example of this is the logistics monitoring system set up by Air Express International in Latin America to minimize its many problems there (see the accompanying Technology Application).

Indirect Coordinating Mechanisms

Indirect coordinating mechanisms typically include sales quotas, budgets, and other financial tools, as well as feedback reports, which give information about the sales and financial performance of the subsidiary for the last quarter or year.

Domestic companies invariably rely on budgets and financial statement analyses, but for foreign subsidiaries, financial statements and performance evaluations are complicated by **financial variables in MNC reports**, such as exchange rates, inflation levels, transfer prices, and accounting standards.

To reconcile accounting statements, MNCs usually require three different sets of financial statements from subsidiaries. One set must meet the national accounting standards and procedures prescribed by law in the host country. This set also aids management in comparing subsidiaries in the same country. A second set must be prepared according to the accounting principles and standards required by the home country. This set allows some comparison with other MNC subsidiaries. The third set of statements translates the second set of statements (with certain adjustments) into the currency of the home country for consolidation purposes, in accordance with FASB Ruling Number 52 of 1982. A foreign subsidiary's financial statements must be consolidated line by line with those of the parent company according to the International Accounting Standard Number 3, adopted in the United States.[39]

Researchers have noted comparative differences between the use of direct versus indirect controls among companies headquartered in different countries. One study by Egelhoff examined the practices of 50 U.S., UK, and European MNCs over their foreign subsidiaries. It compared the use of two mechanisms: the assignment of parent-company managers to for-

TECHNOLOGY APPLICATION

Air Express International in Latin America: Old Problems, New Solutions

Air Express International is a leading international freight forwarder, with integrated air, ocean, and ground capabilities. AEI consolidates, documents, and arranges for transportation of its cargo shipments, conveying more than 1.9 million individual freight shipments annually to about 3,000 cities in more than 200 countries. AEI has been serving the Latin American markets for 40 years. However, its operations there continue to be plagued by an insufficiently developed infrastructure and information technology system, and by bureaucratic red tape and customs delays. Those customs delays often require high "fees" to facilitate clearance. Delays are compounded by the problem of theft of cargo waiting at ports, airports, and warehouses for customs clearance. These problems result in difficulty in moving goods quickly, efficiently, and reliably throughout Latin America. But since there is considerable growth opportunity in Latin America for AEI, the firm has developed various means to attempt to control and monitor its operations there, including its logistics database system.

AEI's LOGIS System

The LOGIS system is an electronic database that allows AEI to control and monitor all its operations from its computers. Problems dealing with infrastructure, security, and delays are minimized and sometimes eliminated, and with technological advances, each upgrade of the system provides a lower cost base for AEI through tighter inventory control, scheduling of shipments, and economies of scale through increased demand and customer satisfaction. Some of the services the LOGIS system provides are as follows:

- Air, sea, sea–air, and air–sea transportation monitoring
- Local and international distribution system
- Computerized storage and inventory forwarding control
- Marking, labeling, packaging, and repacking of goods
- Bonded and nonbonded warehousing
- Barcoding
- Hub-to-hub logistics management
- Project cargo handling
- Stuffing and unstuffing of containers
- Off-site warehouse management
- Palletizing, packing, and crating
- Container and conventional haulage
- Air-conditioned and natural ventilated services warehouses
- Pick and pack services trucking

One component of the LOGIS system is electronic data interchange (EDI), which electronically transfers shipping information from ocean carrier to AEI and vice versa. Although this may not be the latest technology for this purpose, it does give customers more control over their shipping flows and enables synchronized production and more efficient shipping schedules.

Guenter Rohrmann, President and CEO of AEI, is using EDI's application to deter thefts at airports, ports, and warehouses. This system will put all trading partners in direct control of monitoring their shipments at every stage. Barcoding and labeling are also planned, as well as a new antitheft device that works as an X-ray machine to monitor stolen merchandise.[40]

eign subsidiaries and the use of performance reporting systems (that is, comparing behavior mechanisms with output reporting systems).[41] The results of this study show that considerable differences exist in practices across MNC nationalities. For example, says Egelhoff:

> U.S. MNCs monitor subsidiary outputs and rely more upon frequently reported performance data than do European MNCs. The latter tend to assign more parent company nationals to key positions in foreign subsidiaries and can count on a higher level of behavior control than their U.S. counterparts.[42]

MANAGEMENT FOCUS

McDonald's in Moscow: Control Challenge Extraordinaire!

When the first McDonald's restaurant finally opened its doors in Moscow's busy Pushkin Square in January 1990, the largest agreement between the former Soviet Union and a food service company became a reality. The 900-seat restaurant has already broken several of McDonald's previous records—30,000 Russians were served on opening day, and 1 million had been served by March. It took 12 years of negotiations by George A. Cohon, president and founder of McDonald's Restaurants of Canada, to open the doors in Pushkin Square. McDonald's has a 49 percent interest in the joint venture with the Moscow City Council Department of Food Service. In all, McDonald's Canada invested $50 million for construction and personnel training for the processing plant and the restaurant. They agreed to reinvest all of their profits in Moscow for a chain of 20 restaurants.

The biggest control problem for McDonald's was that of quality control for its food products. Unlike its Western counterparts, this IJV has had to adopt a strategy of vertical integration for its sourcing of raw materials. To control the quality, distribution, and reliability of its ingredients, McDonald's built a $40 million, 110,000-square-foot plant in a Moscow suburb to process the required beef, milk, buns, vegetables, sauces, and potatoes. The facility includes laboratories for testing to ensure compliance with quality and consistency standards. Peter Frings, an agronomist with McCain Foods Limited, was brought in to introduce the Russian farmers to the nonnative Russet Burbank potato used to make the famous McDonald's fries. Frings and other experts spent several months working on local farms to advise farmers on such aspects as increasing acreage yields and boosting overall quality.

Operational control was a considerable problem for McDonald's in this historic joint venture, specifically in regard to controlling the quality of food and service. The first challenge was the hiring and training of local employees, Craig Sopkowicz, McDonald's quality-control expert, was in charge of this. "We looked for applicants who lived close to the restaurant, among other things, in order to control the timeliness of employees," explains Sopkowicz. Most of the new hires were between 18 and 27 years old; this was usually their first job; teenagers seldom work in Russia because labor laws protect them from conflicts with school work. After selecting the 630-member crew, the all-important training and customer control began. To be flexible when positions changed, the new crew was trained in all aspects of the restaurant's functions—more than 15,000 training hours were logged in by the new staff to ensure control similar to that in Western operations. In addition, Roy Ellis, the personnel specialist, had some concern about the employees' appearance and decided to construct an on-site laundry room. "It's more practical ... and it means we can ensure our standards," explains Ellis. The four Russian managers (Khamzat Khazbulatov, Vladimir Zhurakovskij, Mikhail Sheleznov, and Georgij Smoleevskij) went through the same rigorous training that any other McDonald's manager would, enabling them to manage any of the 11,000 units worldwide. They went to McDonald's Institute of Hamburgerology in Toronto, Canada, for five months—a 1,000-hour program; and from there, they went to Hamburger University in Oakbrook, Illinois, for two weeks training along with 235 managers from around the world. The operating philosophy underlying the training can be summed up as QSC&V—quality, service, cleanliness, and value.

Innovative control procedures take place in front of the counter in the Moscow unit as well as behind the cash registers. To control for the timeliness of service, McDonald's tries to reduce the long waiting lines by hiring private security people to keep order

(Continued)

and by using public address systems to tell patrons how to place orders. In addition to verbal instructions, customers are given picture menus to simplify the ordering process. The Russian menu has also been streamlined to help speed up the service and the decision-making process. McDonald's has combated the growing black market problem by installing a one-door policy—this has eliminated large-scale pilferage, which usually occurs out the back door. A limit of ten Big Macs to each customer helps stop the black market sale to hungry customers anxiously waiting in line.

Top management at McDonald's anticipated difficulties with the setup and daily operations of this IJV and, indeed, had been working toward the opening day for 13 years. Through careful planning for the control of crucial operational factors, they solved the sourcing, distribution, and employment problems inherent in the former Soviet Union.

Adapted by the author from a term paper written by Gil George and Karsten Fetten, students at the State University of New York–Plattsburgh (December 1990). Copyright ©1993 by Helen Deresky.

Sources: "McDonald's Conquers the World," *Fortune*, October 17, 1994, 103–116; J. Daly and D. Rinehart, "The 'Big Mak' Attack," *Maclean's*, February 12, 1990, 50; L. Ehrsam and R. Langan, "Training: The Customer Is Number One" (Press Release prepared by Toronto McDonald's); J. Iams, "Quality Control Vital for Soviet 'Big Mac,'" *Calgary Herald*, January 24, 1990, D4; P. C. Newman, "Cohon's Hamburger Diplomacy," *Maclean's*, May 30, 1988, 44.

Russians line up to sample McDonald's fare in Moscow; 30,000 were served on opening day.

These findings imply that the American system, which measures more quantifiable aspects of a foreign subsidiary, provides the means to compare performance among subsidiaries. The European system, on the other hand, measures more qualitative aspects of a subsidiary and its environment, which vary among subsidiaries—allowing a focus on the unique situation of the subsidiary but making it difficult to compare its performance to other subsidiaries.[43]

Managing Effective Monitoring Systems

Management practices; local constraints; and expectations regarding authority, time, and communication are but a few of the variables likely to affect the **appropriateness of monitoring systems**. How transferable headquarters' practices and goals are probably depends on whether top managers are from the head office, the host country, or a third country. In addition, information systems and evaluation variables must all be considered when deciding on appropriate systems.

The Appropriateness of Monitoring and Reporting Systems

One example of differences in the expectations regarding monitoring practices, and therefore in the need for coordination systems, is indicated by a study of Japanese and American firms. Exhibit 9–11 shows the mean responses of the American and Japanese managers concerning budget control practices in their firms. Ueno and Sekaran say that their research shows that "the U.S. companies, compared to the Japanese companies, tend to use communication and

EXHIBIT 9–11

Mean Responses of American and Japanese Managers Regarding Their Budget Control Practices

Variables	U.S. Mean	Japan Mean
Communication and coordination	4.03	3.70
Planning time horizons	3.51	3.52
Structuring of budgetary processes	2.95	2.90
Budget slack	3.08	2.89
Controllability of budgets	3.42	3.17
Budget performance evaluation time horizons	2.80	3.11

*S.D. = standard deviation.
Response scale: 1–strongly disagree; 2–disagree; 3–neutral; 4–agree; 5–strongly agree

Source: Susumo Ueno and Uma Sekaran, "The Influence of Culture on Budget Control Practices in the U.S.A. and Japan: An Empirical Study," *Journal of International Business Studies* 23 (Winter 1992): 659–674.

coordination more extensively, build budget slack to a greater extent, and use long-term performance evaluations to a lesser extent."[44] Further, Ueno and Sekaran conclude that those differences in reporting systems are attributable to the cultural variable of individualism in American society, compared to collectivism in Japanese society. For example, American managers are more likely to use formal communication and coordination processes, whereas Japanese managers use informal and implicit processes. In addition, American managers, who are evaluated on individual performance, are more likely to build slack into budget calculations for a safety net than their Japanese counterparts, who are evaluated on group performance. The implications of this study are that managers around the world who understand the cultural bases for differences in control practices will be more flexible in working with those systems in other countries.

The Role of Information Systems

Reporting systems such as those described in this chapter require sophisticated information systems to enable them to work properly—not only for competitive purposes, but also for purposes of performance evaluation. Top management must receive accurate and timely information regarding sales, production, and financial results to be able to compare actual performance with goals and to take corrective action where necessary. Most international reporting systems require information feedback at one level or another using financial, personnel, production, or marketing variables.

The specific types of functional reports, their frequency, and the amount of detail required from subsidiaries by headquarters will vary. Neghandi and Wedge surveyed the types of functional reports submitted by 117 MNCs in Germany, Japan, and the United States. They found that U.S. MNCs typically submit about double the number of reports than do German and Japanese MNCs, with the exception of performance reviews. German MNCs submit a few more reports than do Japanese MNCs. U.S. MNCs thus seem to monitor far more through specific functional reports than do German and Japanese MNCs. The Japanese MNCs put far less emphasis on personnel performance reviews than do the U.S. MNCs and the German MNCs—a finding consistent with their culture of group decision making, consensus, and responsibility.

Unfortunately, the accuracy and timeliness of information systems are often less than perfect. This is particularly so in less developed countries, where managers typically operate in conditions of extreme uncertainty. Government information, for example, is often filtered or fabricated; other sources of data for decision making are usually limited. Employees are not used to the kinds of sophisticated information generation, analysis, and reporting systems common in developed countries. Their work norms and sense of necessity and urgency may also compound the problem. In addition, the hardware technology and the ability to manipulate and transmit data are usually limited. The adequacy of **management information systems (MIS)** in foreign affiliates is a sticky problem for headquarters managers in their attempt to maintain efficient coordination of activities and consolidation of results. Another problem is the **noncomparability of performance data across countries**, which hinders the evaluation process.

Evaluation Variables Across Countries

A major problem in the evaluation of the performance of foreign affiliates is the tendency by headquarters managers to judge subsidiary managers as if all the evaluation data were comparable across countries. Unfortunately, many variables can make the evaluation information from one country look very different from that of another country due to circumstances beyond the control of a subsidiary manager. For example, one country may experience considerable inflation, significant fluctuations in the price of raw materials, political uprisings, or governmental actions. These factors are beyond the manager's control and are likely to have a downward effect on profitability—and yet, that manager may in fact have maximized the opportunity for long-term stability and profitability compared with a manager of another subsidiary who was not faced with such adverse conditions. Other variables influencing profitability patterns include transfer pricing, currency devaluation, exchange rate fluctuations, taxes, and expectations of contributions to local economies.

Clearly, one way to ensure more meaningful performance measures is to adjust the financial statements to reflect the uncontrollable variables peculiar to each country where a subsidiary is located. This provides a basis for the true evaluation of the **comparative return on investment (ROI)**, which is an overall control measure. Another way to provide meaningful, long-term performance standards is to take into account other nonfinancial measures. These measures include market share, productivity, sales, relations with the host-country government, public image, employee morale, union relations, and community involvement.[45]

Conclusion

The coordination *process* is the same whether it takes place in a domestic company, a multinational company with a network of foreign affiliates, or a specific IJV. It is the extent, the focus, and the mechanisms used for monitoring systems that differ. More coordination is needed in multinational companies because of uncertain working environments and information systems and because of the variable loci of decision making. These dynamic conditions confound the task of integrating and controlling a worldwide network of subsidiaries, joint ventures, and contractual relationships. Headquarters managers must design appropriate systems to take into account those variables and to evaluate performance.

Summary of Key Points

1. An organization must be designed to facilitate the implementation of strategic goals. Other variables to consider when designing an organization's structure include environmental conditions, the size of the organization, and the appropriate technology. The geographic dispersion of operations as well as differences in time, language, and culture affect structure in the international context.
2. The design of a firm's structure reflects its international entry strategy and tends to change over time with growth and increasing levels of investment, diversity, or both.
3. Global trends are exerting increasing pressure on MNCs to achieve economies of scale through globalization. This involves rationalization and the coordination of strategic alliances.
4. MNCs can be regarded as interorganizational networks of their own dispersed operations and other strategic alliances. Such relational networks may adopt unique structures for their particular environment while also requiring centralized coordination.

5. The transnational structure allows a company to be global and act local by using networks of decentralized units with horizontal communication; this allows local flexibility while achieving global integration.
6. Indications of the need for structural changes include inefficiency, conflicts among units, poor communication, and overlapping responsibilities.
7. Coordinating and monitoring systems are necessary to regulate organizational activities so that actual performance conforms to expected organizational standards and goals. MNCs use a variety of direct and indirect controls.
8. Financial monitoring and evaluation of foreign affiliates is complicated by variables such as exchange rates, levels of inflation, transfer prices, and accounting standards.
9. The design of appropriate monitoring systems must take into account local constraints, management practices and expectations, uncertain information systems, and variables in the evaluation process.
10. Two major problems in reporting for subsidiaries must be considered: (1) inadequate management information systems and (2) the noncomparability across countries of the performance data needed for evaluation purposes.

Discussion Questions

1. What variables have to be considered in designing the organizational structure for international operations? How do these variables interact, and which do you think are most important?
2. Explain the need for an MNC to be global and act local. How can a firm design its organization to enable this?
3. What is a transnational organization? Since many large MNCs are moving toward this format, it is likely that you could at some point be working within this structure. How do you feel about that?
4. Discuss the implications of the relative centralization of authority and decision making at headquarters versus local units or subsidiaries. How would you feel about this variable if you were a subsidiary manager?
5. As an international manager, what would make you suggest restructuring of your firm?
6. What other means of direct and indirect monitoring systems do you suggest in addition to those discussed in this chapter?
7. What are the major variables across countries that must be taken into account in designing appropriate coordinating and reporting systems?
8. What is the role of information systems in the reporting process? Discuss the statement, "Inadequate MIS systems in some foreign affiliates are a control problem for MNCs."
9. Explain the problem of the noncomparability across subsidiaries of the performance data needed for evaluation purposes. What can be done about this problem?

Management Focus: McDonald's in Moscow

1. What other ways are there to control raw material sources besides vertical integration?
2. How can McDonald's reduce the cost and time involved in training for future units?
3. How can McDonald's keep up sales and interest while opening new units in Moscow?
4. How is McDonald's repatriating its profits?
5. What is the role of this McDonald's IJV, and other IJVs, in the transition to a market economy in the Commonwealth of Independent States (CIS)?
6. How would other companies with larger component requirements—for example, automobile manufacturers—control their resources in the CIS?

Application Exercises

1. If you have personal access to a company with international operations, try to conduct some interviews to find out about the personal interactions involved in working with their counterparts abroad. In particular, ask questions about the nature and level of authority and decision making in overseas units compared with headquarters. What kinds of conflicts are experienced? What changes would your interviewees recommend? Alternatively, research what you can on these issues using the Web.

2. Do some research on monitoring and reporting issues facing an MNC with subsidiaries in India. With subsidiaries in the former East Germany. Discuss problem areas and your recommendations to the MNC management on how to control potential problems.

3. Find out about an IJV in the United States. Get some articles from the library, write to the company for information, or if possible, visit the company and ask questions. Present to the class your findings on the company's major control issues—both at the beginning of the venture and now. What is the company doing differently in its control process compared to a typical domestic operation? Are the control procedures having the desired results? What recommendations do you have?

Experiential Exercise

In groups of four, consider a fast-food chain going into eastern Europe. Decide on your initial level of desired international involvement and your entry strategy. Draw up an appropriate organizational design, taking into account strategic goals, relevant variables in the particular countries in which you will have operations, technology used, size of the firm, and so forth. At the next class, present your organization chart and describe the operations and rationale. (You could finalize the chart on an overhead or flip chart before class begins.) What are some of the major control issues to be considered?

Internet Resources

Visit the Deresky companion Web site at http://prenhall.com/Deresky for this chapter's Internet resources.

Case Study

Flexit International

The Flexit Company manufactures and sells athletic conditioning and sports equipment. The primary market is for home use, but approximately 15 percent of the company's profit comes from sales of equipment and spare parts to Aquarius Health Spas Inc. Home use products are sold through sporting goods stores and large retail chain stores such as K mart.

Company History

Flexit began business in 1965 as a small manufacturer of exercise equipment and sold its product—weight sets—to schools and gymnasiums. The product line expanded slowly until the mid–1970s, when the physical fitness craze began. Since 1975, the company has expanded both product line and sales territory. It now sells to the continental 48 states but not to Hawaii or Alaska. However, Flexit's current five-year plan includes exporting to Europe and possible offshore production, as shown in Exhibit 9–12.

The company president, Jim Goodbody, has always taken pride in the company's self-sufficiency. Flexit manufactures all its products although it uses outside transportation (commercial trucking) for distribution to retail and wholesale markets.

EXHIBIT 9–12

Flexit Corporate Goals

1. Remain a leader in the home physical fitness product market in the United States.
2. Expand domestic market share from 38 to 50 percent within five years.
3. Capture a large market share (at least 10 percent) of the European market in five years.
4. Retain control of operations, but consider international alternatives such as offshore production, import of related products for sale in the United States, subsidiary operations, and countertrade.

At present, Flexit has three manufacturing locations in the United States. The home office and original plant are in Ames, Iowa, where four of the eight Flexit products are made. A plant in Oxnard, California, manufactures two products. The newest plant, in Atlanta, makes two fitness products sold to Aquarius Health Spas. All planning for manufacturing, sales, and distribution is done by the president and his staff at the Iowa facility. Company operations are summarized in Exhibit 9–13, and the organization chart is reproduced in Exhibit 9–14.

An International Twist

Market research done by Flexit has indicated a large demand for home athletic products in several European countries. Jim Goodbody would very much like to enter that market and eventually become a dominant company in Europe as well as the United States. However, because Flexit has had no experience in international shipments or doing business in a foreign country, he wants initially to limit involvement in overseas operations to exporting.

The head of Flexit's marketing department traveled to Europe to meet with officials of several firms interested in representing Flexit. He selected Physique Ltd. as best able to contribute to Flexit's overall marketing goals. Physique Ltd. specializes in home physical fitness products, selling and distributing a full line to all European Economic Community countries and to several non-EEC countries. It also sells to several [former] Communist bloc countries on a limited basis. An organization chart for Physique Ltd. is shown in Exhibit 9–15.

Physique Ltd. officials indicated that they see no immediate barriers to handling the Flexit product line. Their distribution channels could easily accommodate the additional products. Physique Ltd. uses rail and truck transportation predominantly and uses air or water services only as necessary.

EXHIBIT 9–13

Flexit Company Operations

1. Each division is responsible for planning each of its product lines. This includes preparing domestic sales forecasts, manufacturing schedules, and inbound and outbound distribution for each product.
2. Raw materials are ordered by each division and trucked to each facility as necessary.
3. All products are manufactured on site. Production schedules are based on sales forecasts from product marketing planners.
4. Outbound distribution of finished products is planned and executed at each division. Shipments are contracted to rail and truck as necessary.
5. The Ames, Iowa, facility includes a manufacturing plant and a corporate staff.

EXHIBIT 9–14

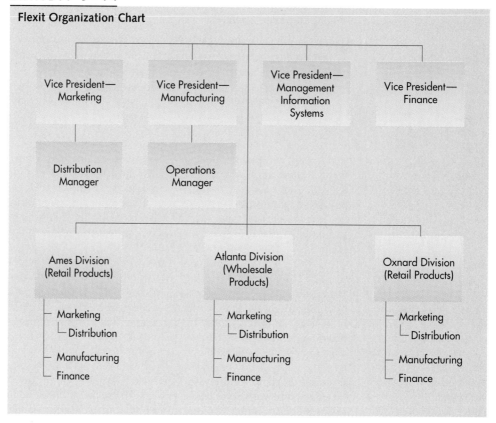

Flexit Organization Chart

Physique Ltd. officials believe that Flexit prices would be competitive even after the Physique Ltd. markup is added. They indicated that they would be very interested in establishing either a countertrade or an export business to the United States using Flexit as their distributor if that would be possible in the future. However, such an agreement was not a condition for Flexit's venture into Europe with Physique Ltd.

The Task at Hand

Jim Goodbody has decided to go ahead with the export operation, using Physique Ltd. as distributor although he has several concerns about the logistics of such an undertaking. Specifically, he is worried that problems may arise because the two companies have different corporate structures. Second, he knows that Flexit managers will be required to take on a number of new tasks. To the head of corporate distribution planning, he gave the broad assignment of determining the best way to get Flexit products to Europe. The only constraint was that he must consult with the head of market planning. The first step taken by the head of corporate distribution planning was to investigate the services offered by freight forwarders. His findings are summarized in Exhibit 9–16.

EXHIBIT 9–15

Physique Ltd. Organization Chart

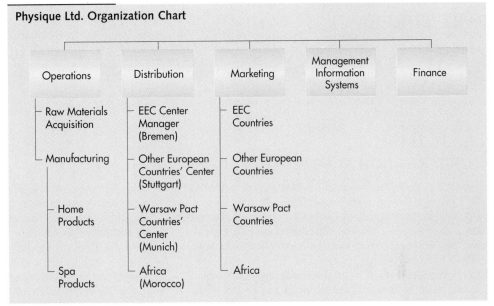

Case Questions

1. Are Flexit's corporate goals realistic for the next five years?
2. Will the existing physical distribution system support the proposed expansion to Europe?
3. Which new tasks can be performed by existing resources, and which must be added or contracted out?
4. What are the benefits and the drawbacks of using an existing distribution channel in Europe?
5. Does the proposed plan have the required flexibility to accommodate expansion for countertrade, import from Europe, offshore production, and subsidiaries in Europe?
6. Is a new organization structure required to support company objectives? What changes do you think should be made? Why? Draw up your recommended new organization chart for Flexit.

EXHIBIT 9–16

Typical Freight Forwarder Services

1. Prepare export documentation.
2. Prepare import documentation for destination.
3. Provide for transportation from the exporter to final destination.
4. Prepare and process bills of lading.
5. Arrange for insurance.
6. Prepare documents in the language of the country and provide for certification.
7. Provide for warehouse storage and services as necessary.
8. Prepare and send shipping statements to banks, other shippers or consignees if necessary.
9. Provide professional assistance on export related matters.
10. In general, coordinate and facilitate the movement of goods from point of origin to point of destination.

PART THREE

Comprehensive Cases

CASE 1

REORGANIZATION AT AB TELECOM (1998)[1]

In early 1998, the top managers at AB Telecom were debating how to change its worldwide organization. AB Telecom is a Canadian telecommunications hardware firm that manufactures fixed wireless systems. This $200 million company earned more than 95 percent of its revenues from outside Canada, with 40 percent coming from Asia in 1997. In 1998, AB Telecom conducted all of its manufacturing and R&D within Canada; much of its market development and project engineering is maintained in its Canadian headquarters.

AB Telecom was founded in 1981 and is publicly traded on several Canadian stock exchanges. It had been profitable since 1990, with an average 7 percent net profitability between 1990 and 1997. Given its strong presence outside Canada, ABT has been awarded the prestigious Canadian Export Award several times by the Canadian government.

AB Telecom's traditional customer is a national telephone company that wants to improve telecommunications to its rural locations. Sixty percent of ABT's sales in 1997 were turnkey projects for national telephone companies. Its structure had been a regional sales and marketing structure, with three regions: Asia/Pacific, Latin America, and Europe/Middle East/Africa. Each region had a headquarters and several sales subsidiaries in different countries. These regional offices had autonomy in booking small deals, but headquarters became involved with deals worth over $2 million. The regional offices are also reliant on some project engineering support provided by the headquarters.

Several significant changes had created a need for top management to review its current structure:

- early signs of economic difficulty in Malaysia and other southeast Asian countries could potentially stall or stop agreed-to projects in this region
- opportunities to use their existing fixed wireless systems for industrial application were growing
- Europe, Middle East, and Africa provided many opportunities for sales to traditional national telephone companies for rural applications
- potential is unknown for its new wireless product for urban data transmissions to telephone companies and new competitors

In March 1998, the CEO, his top management team, and some board members met to discuss how to restructure the company.

Product Applications

Rural Telephony   AB Telecom researches, designs, and manufactures fixed wireless systems mostly for installation in rural and remote areas, to aid in rural telecommunications. ABT manufactures all components required for rural installation. It subcontracts with local contractors to install the systems.

The main application of the AB Telecom product is to connect remote villages and towns to the national telephone system grid. Fixed wireless is a cost-effective solution for many national telephone companies to connect to rural locations; the cost of installing a fixed wireless system is far less than that of laying miles of fiber or copper cable to the same locale. ABT's traditional customers have been national telephone companies.

For this business, ABT considers Alcatel, NEC Japan, and Lucent to be its direct competitors, but the fixed wireless systems are a very small portion of these large multi-

---

[1] This is a real company, but the company name, location and a few aspects of the firm are disguised because of a pledge of confidentiality by the researcher.

EXHIBIT C1-1

AB Telecom at Time of Case

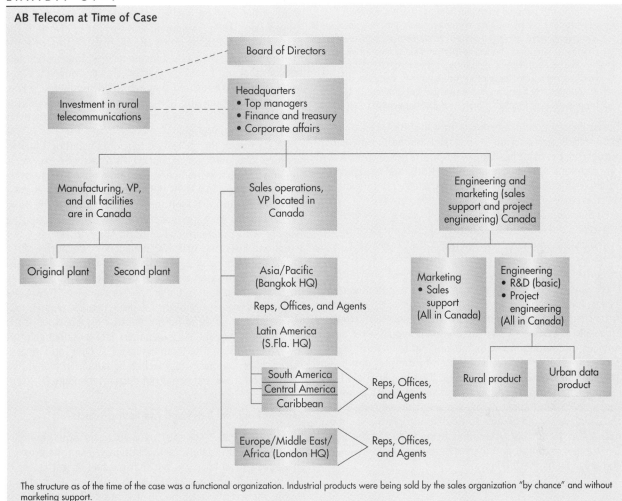

The structure as of the time of the case was a functional organization. Industrial products were being sold by the sales organization "by chance" and without marketing support.

national firms' sales, whereas ABT specializes in the fixed wireless systems and technology.

Industrial Applications   New applications of ABT's wireless systems have been recently recognized. Companies in industries such as oil, gas, and electricity generation require remote sensing of dispersed operations. In early 1998, this type of business had grown to comprise 25 percent of ABT's revenues. Much of this business was developed "by chance," as explained by one top manager:

We realized that the industrial portion of sales could be more significant. The industrial market was not properly marketed to, nor were their needs involved in, our R&D efforts. We realized that this area could become significant if we added more products that customers wanted because we are one of the largest companies selling to this fragmented and diverse market.

This manager went on to explain how industrial customers were developed in one Asian country:

Our industrial customers developed just by chance [in this country]. Now, we have 100 industrial customers.

We had no idea what the customer wanted. Because selling to this national telephone company was slow and government controlled, we stumbled upon the electric companies who were interested. It started off with a change of attention of one salesperson already located in this market, but it developed in a mostly word of mouth way ... this counts for a lot in [this country]. We gained a reputation for being a reliable supplier, but growing this business was not part of a plan ... it just happened.

The estimated potential revenue from this market is around $100 million per year, but it is spread among hundreds of industrial customers. One ABT manager explained, "Tremendous sales and marketing efforts are required to obtain a $5 million order, but once a customer orders and is satisfied, they are more likely to repeat the purchase.... We need more information to develop the business.... It is difficult to find out where the big industrial users are worldwide. ... mostly trial and error," stated one top ABT manager.

Urban Wireless   ABT also had developed and was testing fixed wireless systems in urban settings. The potential customers for this product were telephone companies, both the incumbent telephone company as well as start-up carriers, especially in Europe. A start-up company would offer data services in competition with the original telephone company. The ABT system would be used to transmit data reliably within dense urban settings. This application has required some modification to the original ABT product lines. "With data applications, we are really starting from zero, but we should be able to double or triple them in the future." In 1998, this system was being tested in the U.K. Only a few technical and marketing people were involved and only in a haphazard way.

Investment in Rural License

In 1996, ABT deviated from its sales and delivery of operation systems to invest in the telecommunications infrastructure of a Latin American country. This investment in rural infrastructure in Latin America was a major departure from ABT's short-term, project-oriented, turnkey operations. For several years, top executives had discussed the possibility of pursuing investment as opposed to sales-only deals. This investment was initiated, managed, and controlled by top managers in Montreal, but local managers were hired to help with the installation and operations of this investment.

Top executives outlined several reasons for ABT to pursue an investment in rural telecommunications operations. According to one manager close to this deal, "Many people confuse rural with poverty, but they miss out on a

very good investment and tremendous pent-up demand." Most of the large hardware equipment manufacturers have moved from selling equipment and services to investing and buying up licenses in international markets. As one top manager stated, "It was a difficult decision to invest in rural telecom, but our board of directors was convinced it was a good idea ... we realized that we could supply our equipment at no markup and then sell a 51 percent stake in our investment, perhaps using this to fund future investments in rural telecommunications."

Concerning the challenges inherent in starting this new venture, one manager explained, "We are not experts at running a telephone company; we don't know how to bill or do maintenance." In 1998, ABT hired a local manager away from the national telephone company to run the firm. Consultants with experience with Bell Canada were also helping with the venture. By 1998, ABT had set up 1,000 telephone lines and had 100 employees; the push was to install pay phones, a legal requirement of the license. ABT managers estimated that it would take about 8,000 to 10,000 installed lines to break even, probably in 1999. Once this rural venture establishes a proven track record, ABT managers plan to sell off a portion to a local partner. If this venture is successful, ABT managers are considering future investments in rural telecommunications. One top manager stated, "We are being approached by people in many markets around the world about potential investments."

Current Regional Sales and Marketing Structure

From 1981 until 1988, ABT's Canadian headquarters controlled all of the details of the business. Then, as one top manager explained, "We felt that we had to get closer to the customer, and we went first to Asia because that was where the action was." So, in the late 1980s, ABT placed several sales people in the field in three regions: Asia/Pacific, Latin America, and Europe/Africa/Middle East. In 1997, Asia/Pacific markets were 50 percent of all revenues, Latin America 36 percent, and Europe/Africa/Middle East 19 percent of sales. The United States was not a market for ABT's equipment given the significant rural infrastructure already in place in the United States.

Asia/Pacific   The first subsidiary was in Hong Kong as "an easy way into China," according to a top ABT manager. There were no customers, and it was expensive to maintain an office there. "Because we weren't even paying the light bills, we decided to move the Asia/Pacific headquarters to Manila to save on taxes and expenses, and in order to have access to a skilled labor force." Soon after this move, a sales subsidiary was set up in China, followed by another office in Bangkok after a large project was won there.

By the early 1990s, ABT had more than 60 people on the ground in these three operations. These offices were staffed with technical sales people with an engineering background. They were rewarded on meeting a quota, and they operated autonomously from the headquarters. Their sales efforts centered on selling ABT's equipment and solutions to national telephone companies. These technical sales people placed orders with headquarters and provided service to the firm once the system was installed and in place. Many times, they relied on project engineering for technical details related to a bid or final customer proposal.

In the early 1990s, the Asian headquarters was moved again to Bangkok. As one manager stated, "With these regional offices, we cultivated relationships." If a project or bid was around $1 million, headquarters would rarely get involved. If the order was more strategic (from $5 million to $10 million in size), headquarters would interact closely with sales, working together on pricing, delivery, and technical specifications.

Latin America   The Latin America office was located in south Florida. At first, this region was staffed with sales engineers. Then, managers for different areas within Latin America were brought in to strengthen the region's marketing abilities. In 1998, there were three area managers: one each for South America (included Brazil, Argentina, Colombia, and Peru), Caribbean U.S., and Central America. The total number of engineers and managers in this office was 12 in 1998. Sales support and project engineers were still located in Montreal to support Latin America project bids, technical assistance, or operations. Most of the activity within this area was repeat customers, the national telephone companies. This Latin American sales and marketing area had nothing to do with the 1997 investment in rural telecommunications by ABT. In fact, most of the managers knew very few details about this investment transaction.

With the privatization of many Latin American telephone companies, managers from AB Telecom's Latin American office had developed a close working relationship with Telefonica (Spain's national telephone company) and STET (Italy's national telephone company) because these two companies have purchased significant stakes in many national telephone companies in Latin America. This area had been growing consistently for AB Telecom in the 1990s.

One manager explained how deals are developed in this region: "We follow regulatory changes in countries that are considering privatization. We know that a piece will be rural, and money will be made available for rural according to the bids for this privatization. Our local representatives keep us advised." Another manager explained, "We have not pushed much into the industrial business in Latin America except for one excellent industrial client—an oil company in Venezuela—and this relationship was gained through a technical representative on the ground with this oil company." When asked about how they interact with R&D in Canada, one manager stated, "We don't worry about technology.... we worry about satisfying a need ... we have the best product technically, reflected in our high quality and high price.... this combined with being close to the customer lands us deals ... many of our deals in Latin America are renewals."

One area manager in the Latin American division stated, "The greatest impediment to our international growth is resources—human resources. We are looking for people with language, engineering, project skills, and good interpersonal skills."

Europe/Middle East/Africa   In 1998, the Europe/Middle East/Africa region was the most difficult, according to several managers. This was attributed to too many different regulations and frequencies across this region. Sales subsidiaries have been developed where a strong relationship with a national telephone company existed. Sales subsidiaries had been set up in Nairobi, Saudi Arabia, South Africa, Sweden, and the U.K. The head of this regional structure had recently resigned.

Dilemma

In reviewing the evolution of their structure, top managers recognized that they had moved from a domestic functional structure to a geographic regional sales and marketing structure. They realized that each existing sales subsidiary was organized to develop and maintain a close relationship with the national telephone company of countries within its region, focusing mostly on its rural telephony needs.

Sales persons were not rewarded to develop new markets (such as industrial business or urban data transmission) because they were paid on the basis of meeting quarterly sales quotas. According to one top manager, "They could not focus on such a diverse market as industrial because it is going to take two or three years of working closely with an industrial customer or a new telephone competitor to land a deal, and this just doesn't fit within our reward system of sales persons."

In 1998, traditional Asian markets and telephone companies were beginning to suffer, and top managers anticipated that revenues from these markets would be flat or, worse, fall by the end of the year. There were opportunities to expand their presence in non-Asian markets with their traditional customers or to push for entry into other applications such as industrial and urban data.

Therefore, the top managers were focused on developing a structure to manage the tension within its wireless technology division (traditionally housed in the R&D area in Canada), its current regional structure (responsive to customers needs, cultural differences mostly in its current rural applications), and emerging new customer groups (such as the industrial and urban wireless data products).

CASE QUESTION

How should ABT top managers reorganize to resolve the tensions among the regional organization selling to national telephone customers, new applications for industrial and urban data, and investments in rural telephony?

Source: Case written by Professor Anne Smith, University of New Mexico, based on her research of the firm discussed. ©1998 by Professor Anne Smith. Used with permission.

CASE 2

JOHNSON ELECTRIC*

INTRODUCTION

What do the following brands all have in common: Black and Decker, Toyota, Philips, Sunbeam, Hitachi, Olivetti, and Mercedes-Benz? Answer: They all use micromotors made by Johnson Electric. Headquartered in Hong Kong, Johnson Electric is one of the world's largest micromotor manufacturers producing more than a million AC and DC motors every day. This case study traces the historical development of the Johnson Electric company from its inception in the late 1950s as a small supplier of motors to Hong Kong toymakers, to the number two position in the billion-dollar global micromotor industry.

MICROMOTORS AND SOCIETY

Look around you. How many micromotors are quietly humming nearby? In your house you will find them inside fan heaters, juice extractors, hair dryers, electric shavers, food processors, microwave ovens, coffee grinders, digital video disk players, and VCRs. In your office there is a micromotor spinning the cooling fan that keeps your PC from overheating. Another drives your laser printer, CD-ROM drive, paper shredder, and fax machine. In your car there is a veritable army of micromotors making sure window-wipers work, doors lock, electric aerials go up and down. In a luxury car you may find as many as 80 micromotors hidden behind features such as powered seats, anti-lock braking systems, and air-conditioning units. Finally, what are you wearing that might contain a micromotor? Portable CD-players, even pagers and mobile phones contain micromotors—there's no escaping them. Indeed, given their widespread use in modern society, it is no overstatement to say that our industrialized civilization is largely powered by little motors that spin, shake and squirt.

JOHNSON ELECTRIC'S PRODUCTS

Johnson Electric is the second-largest manufacturer of micromotors in the world with a daily output of just over one million units. While Johnson Electric is a highly focused company offering essentially just one core product, the basic micromotor is targeted at a broad range of applications across a number of different product-markets. Johnson Electric manufactures micromotors for four main product-applications; automotive components, power tools, household appliances, and personal care items. The main applications associated with these core markets are listed in Exhibit C2–1. In addition to its four core product-applications, Johnson Electric has recently begun expanding into two new areas: business equipment (for example,

Source: This case was prepared by Assistant Professor Paul Ellis of Hong Kong Polytechnic University, as a basis for class discussion rather than to illustrate either effective or ineffective handling of an administrative or business situation.

Please address all correspondence to: Assistant Professor Paul Ellis, Department of Business Studies, Hong Kong Polytechnic University, Hung Hom, Kowloon, Hong Kong.

* This case was prepared from secondary sources for the purposes of classroom discussion. An earlier version of this case was awarded First Runner-Up in the First Regional Case Writing Competition (1996) run by the Case Study Group of Hong Kong. The author would like to acknowledge the constructive and valuable feedback provided by two anonymous ACRJ reviewers.

EXHIBIT C2–1

Johnson Electric's Product-Applications

Automotive Equipment

Mirror adjuster, mirror fold, powered roof, windscreen wiper, windscreen washer, flap actuator, aspirator, idle speed control, secondary air pump, throttle valve control, circulation pump, anti-lock braking systems, powered window winder, powered door lock, powered headrest, lumbar support, powered seat, electric aerial, fuel pump, head lamp washer, head lamp wiper, car polisher, car scrubber, windscreen defroster, tyre pump, car vacuum, warning lamp

Household Appliances

Juice extractor, microwave oven, coffee grinder, hand mixer, fan heater, food processor

Power Tools

Circular saws, mini tools, jig saws, drills, screwdriver, impact wrench

Personal Care Appliances

Massager, toothbrush, nail polisher, hair dryer, hair curler, shaver

Source: Company brochures.

EXHIBIT C2–2

Johnson Electric's Sales by Product-Application (1997)

	HK$m	%
Automotive components and accessories	821	32
Home appliances	673	26
Power tools	601	23
Personal care appliances	328	12
Business equipment/multimedia	179	7
Total	2,202,210	100

Source: Johnson Electric (1997), *Annual Report.*

printers by Hewlett-Packard), and audio-visual applications (such as digital video disc players). Sales to business equipment manufacturers increased from 2% to 7% of Johnson Electric's total sales from 1990–1997, fuelled largely by increasing sales of motors to manufacturers of printers and facsimile machines (Exhibit C2–2).

HISTORY OF THE COMPANY

The history and development of the Johnson Electric company is a vignette of Hong Kong's own post-War economic rise. Indeed, the evolution of a small motor-making shop into a multinational competitor parallels Hong Kong's own transformation from a regional entrepôt port to a global services center. And like many of Hong Kong's success stories, this one begins in China.

Within a few years of the Japanese surrender in 1945, China had descended into a state of civil war as Nationalist and Communist armies fought for control of the nation. It was during this turbulent period that Wang Seng Liang, a Shanghai textile industrialist and future founder of Johnson Electric, was forced to flee penniless to Taiwan. From Taiwan, Wang relocated to Hong Kong where he opened a chain of tailor shops.

Hong Kong in the 1950s was, in the true Dickensian sense, both the best and worst of times for a migrant industrialist looking for entrepreneurial opportunities. In 1951 external trade dried up virtually overnight when the United Nations imposed an embargo on trade with the PRC. This embargo had been in response to China's involvement in the Korean Peninsula but the short-term effect on Hong Kong was disastrous. Fortuitously, the cessation of the Colony's 100-year-old entrepôt role stimulated a mini-industrial revolution and within a few years cheap plastics, toys, and textiles, all 'made in Hong Kong,' were beginning to make their mark in foreign markets.

It was during this time that Wang was approached by a local trader who wanted to know if he could produce an inexpensive battery-powered toy boat. Wang was initially enthusiastic because of his manufacturing background. However, after studying the toy in question, Wang decided to just produce the motor. This was because his Shanghai experience had taught him, as son Patrick later explained, 'to build something that doesn't change—toys are fashionable, motors are not.'

Consequently, Johnson Electric was formed in 1959 in response to a local need for electric motors. At that time there were no micromotor manufacturers in Hong Kong and all motors had to be imported from foreign suppliers. The Johnson name was chosen as an anglicized version of the tailor's phrase 'make to an inch' or *zhou xiang* referring both to the exacting precision of tailoring and the name of the chain of tailor-shops owned by Wang and his wife Yik Chun. This was considered appropriate as the start-up capital for the new venture had come from the Wang's tailoring business. At first, Johnson Electric's chief customers were local toy-makers, but in 1969 a joint venture with an

American company saw a shift in emphasis toward the supply of micromotors for various industrial applications, such as automotives.

At about this time the Wangs—demonstrating a pattern of behavior that is common to many typical Chinese family businesses in Hong Kong—sent their four children to the United States to receive a university education. Eldest son Richard Wang Li-Chung earned a Master's degree in electrical engineering at the University of California at Berkeley; daughter Winnie Wang Wing Yee studied at Ohio University; second son Patrick Wang Shui Chung received a Master's degree in electrical engineering from Purdue University; and the youngest, Peter Wang Kin Chung, also studied at Purdue before completing an MBA at Boston University. After their formal education the children began working for the family business. Richard now manages Johnson Electric's worldwide marketing efforts out of an office in Connecticut; Winnie is the executive director in charge of finance; Patrick became managing director of the company in 1982; and Peter has been a non-executive director of the Group since 1982. In early 1996, the elder Wang passed away and Patrick was elected Chairman (and CEO) of the company.

As they were promoted to positions of responsibility within the company, the Wang children began to apply some of what they had learnt whilst studying abroad. In 1984, Johnson Electric floated 70 million shares on the market, largely at the urging of Patrick and Winnie.[*] Another change introduced at the behest of the two eldest sons, was a shift away from standardized, commodity micromotors for low value-added products such as toys, towards more customized, higher value-added motors for products such as home appliances and personal care items.[†]

---

[*] Initially, the family retained 75% of the holdings but by the early 1990s the family's stake had been reduced to 60%. In 1994, Johnson Electric was one of the seven companies added to the Hang Seng Index to replace the migrating Jardine's businesses. Like the delisted companies it replaced, Johnson Electric was by now incorporated in Bermuda. In July 1997, with a market capitalization of HK$8.7 billion, Johnson Electric was one of two firms dropped from the Hang Seng Index in favor of two larger, more mainland-connected firms (with a combined capitalization of more than HK$100 billion).

[†] Although it was the toy industry which led to the demand for Johnson's motors in the first place, by the late 1980s, toy motors accounted for less than 5% of the company's sales, and by the early 1990s sales to toy-makers had fallen to less than 1% of total output.

In addition, the company began to work closely with customers to design application-specific micromotors for new products such as the Kodak disc camera.

In the late 1980s, micromotor sales boomed prompting massive capital investment and a restructuring of the company into a leaner, more responsive organization. The large departments of the 1980s were replaced with 30 small industry-specific teams consisting of workers drawn from a range of disciplines and functions. On one floor in the Hong Kong factory, 150 white-coated engineers and business-types work together in an open-space plan encompassing glass-walled 'interactive centers' where teams hold strategy sessions. Supporting the formal organization, Johnson Electric has attempted to foster a culture where traditional Confucian values, such as loyalty to workers (the company provides benefits such as low interest loans to employees), are combined with Western business practices such as worker empowerment where employees, working in conjunction with customers, have the freedom to make their own decisions without referring to managers. However, the introduction of such initiatives was somewhat problematic given that many of the firm's mainland employees, coming from a society where market reforms are still a novel concept, have little understanding of what a customer actually is. To instill a customer orientation into his organization, CEO Wang admonishes his engineers to 'go back home and watch how their wives or husbands use appliances.' In addition, Johnson Electric brings important customers into the strategy-sessions held by teams working on their projects. In terms of his management philosophy, Patrick Wang has said: 'There is no king around here. My job is basically to create the culture so that professionals can do their job.' To that end Patrick arranges yearly leadership training outings at a US-run Outward Bound camp in Hong Kong where engineers and managers from the factories in China can interact with their Hong Kong counterparts. Patrick himself attends a one-week course every year at the Harvard Business School where he is exposed to new management ideas via case studies and interaction with other executives.

Patrick Wang's ultimate goal is to make Johnson Electric a 'world-class organization.' To achieve this the family-controlled company has sponsored heavy capital investment over the past decade at the expense of dividend payments. In 1987, the company opened a HK$100 million automated plant. Built on reclaimed land at the Tai Po industrial estate in the New Territories, the 25,000 m^2, six-story facility more than doubled the production capacity. Further investment in the mid–1990s in a production facility in Guangdong Province saw the firm's daily output reach

800,000 units. By 1996 the firm had expanded to 14,000 employees up from 1,800 ten years earlier.

The effects of these capital investments can be measured in the productivity growth of the firm. In the mid–1980s Johnson Electric was producing around 150,000 motors a day; by the mid–1990s output had increased more than 500% (Exhibit C2–3). A similar growth rate was evident in the firm's revenue over the same period (Exhibit C2–4). However, profit grew at a much slower rate reflecting both the rising price of raw materials and the firm's heavy and ongoing investment into plant and equipment.

In addition to long-term investments in production capacity, Johnson Electric also invested heavily in research and development (approximately 3% to 4% of annual turnover). This is in stark contrast with the normal practice in Hong Kong where R&D expenditures by firms and government account for around 0.1% of GDP. By way of comparison, Taiwan spends 3.7% of GDP. Indeed, Johnson Electric is, in many ways, atypical of other successful Hong Kong firms. For example, it was, until recently, the only blue-chip company that actually made things: all other Hang Seng Index companies are involved in services-related activities such as property development, finance, shipping, and banking. Johnson Electric is also unusual in terms of its above-average level of female representation on its ten-

member board with two female directors, Wang Yik Chun and Winnie Wang Wing Yee. In contrast, female directors accounted for just 26 of the 450 boardroom posts in Hong Kong's blue-chip companies in early 1997.

INTERNATIONAL MARKETING ACTIVITIES

Johnson Electric is a highly internationalized firm as measured by sales—around 95% of its output is ultimately sold abroad—and by the global dispersion of its value-chain activities. Its Hong Kong headquarters specializes in the design, production, and marketing of micromotors. Apart from Hong Kong, R&D also takes place in facilities located in Germany (in Stuttgart) in order to bring the firm closer to its major European customers. For similar reasons Johnson Electric has also invested in service centers in Japan (in Osaka), China (in Shanghai), and the United States (in Cleveland). Production activities are distributed around the region with facilities located in Hong Kong, Thailand (in Bangnadad, near Bangkok), and principally, China (in Guangdong).

Johnson Electric's foreign market activities began just two years after the company was incorporated, with micromotors exported to toy manufacturers in the UK and the US in the early 1960s. In 1978, the company entered the West

EXHIBIT C2–3

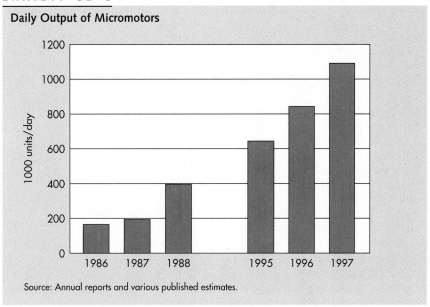

Daily Output of Micromotors

Source: Annual reports and various published estimates.

EXHIBIT C2–4

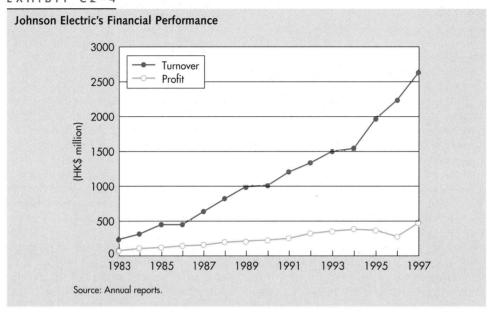

Johnson Electric's Financial Performance

Source: Annual reports.

German market and by the mid–1990s Johnson Electric's motors were exported to more than 20 countries around the world. Johnson Electric's sales by geographical destination are listed in Exhibit C2–5. Around 60% of output is exported directly from the company with the remainder sold to other manufacturers located in Hong Kong and China who then export finished products such as mixers, power-tools, and blenders which contain Johnson Electric micromotors.

As with any industrial good, demand for Johnson Electric's micromotors is derived from the global demand for consumer products such as cars, household appliances, and so on. Thus Johnson Electric's turnover is tied to the consumption levels of those markets in which its customers' products are sold. This explains why the company has actively sought to promote its motors in a number of different markets and for a number of different applications. By leveraging its core product across a number of different product-market environments and by continually developing its motors for new applications, Johnson Electric is able to leverage its core competence on a global scale as well as reduce its exposure to the fluctuations in demand associated with any one particular application. For example, when traditional European and North American markets were depressed by a recession in the early 1990s, sales to both regions nevertheless continued to grow as the com-

pany was able to sell new motors for autos and household appliances in those markets.

Of all the foreign markets that Johnson Electric is active in, two are particularly interesting: Japan and Mexico. Japan has been a tough market for Johnson Electric to enter. Although the company supplies Toyota and various Japanese subcontractors with micromotors, the market has generally resisted the approaches of the *gaijin* (foreign) firm. In the mid–1990s, Japan accounted for only 5–6% of Johnson Electric's total sales. Still, CEO Patrick Wang believes that it is only a matter of time before Japanese

EXHIBIT C2–5

Johnson Electric's Sales by Geographical Destination (% of total sales)

	1990	1997
Hong Kong and China	35	32
Europe	25	29
North America	27	27
Asia-Pacific	13	12

Source: Annual reports.

firms, faced with a loss of competitiveness, will begin to source more components from offshore suppliers. 'Where there is no real value-added, the Japanese will have to give up production.... It took us a long time to become known as Johnson San (a term of respect in Japan) and we still have a way to go in terms of market-share.'

The Japanese Micromotor Market

Why is the Japanese market so important to Johnson Electric? There are several reasons but two are worth noting. First, Japan is the home of rival firm Mabuchi Motors. Although Johnson Electric enjoys the number one position in the four main market segments in which it competes, Mabuchi remains the largest manufacturer in the billion-dollar global micromotor industry. In 1995, Mabuchi produced 1.3 billion micromotors, nearly four times that of Johnson Electric. (The main product-applications served by Mabuchi are listed in Exhibit C2–6). By challenging Mabuchi on its own ground, Johnson Electric engages in an offensive competitive strategy aimed at capturing market-share from its number one rival.

Second, because Johnson Electric's earnings are affected by prices paid for Japanese-sourced parts and components, sales revenue from Japan forms a 'natural hedge' to fluctuations in the value of the yen. In particular, yen-denominated copper-wire purchases can significantly influence the company's bottom-line. (Copper accounts for around half of Johnson Electric's raw materials costs and around a third of overall production costs.) This means that when the price of the yen goes up, so too does the cost of copper. For example, in the financial year 1995, despite a 29% rise in revenue, profit was virtually erased by a 50% increase in the price of copper. Indeed, *any* change in the price of yen induces both an opportunity and a threat to Johnson Electric. Although a rising yen increases the cost of some raw materials, it also gives Johnson Electric a price advantage against its Japanese rivals. For example, sales to Japan increased by 32% in the financial year 1994 as more Japanese car-makers such as Toyota began sourcing components offshore to counter a rising yen. Conversely, when the yen depreciates, Johnson Electric's bottom-line improves in the short-term (with a fall cost of materials), but Japanese-produced goods become cheaper and therefore more attractive to cost-conscious manufacturers in the medium-term. Nevertheless, the general trend over the late 1980s, early 1990s was one of a rising yen leading to a corresponding fall in the volume of micromotors produced in Japan (Exhibit C2–7).

Johnson Electric in Mexico

In the mid–1990s, Johnson Electric established a plant manufacturing micromotors for CD-players in Mexico. In fact, Johnson Electric was just one of more than 100 Asian firms which have invested there in the wake of Mexico's peso crisis. Why Mexico? First, Mexico represents an increasingly affluent market of 90 million consumers. More importantly, however, is Mexico's membership in NAFTA. Investing in low-cost Mexico enables Johnson Electric to gain quota-free access into the world's biggest trading bloc (370 million consumers). It is largely for this reason that Mexico has become, according to Hong Kong-based Trade Commission Federico Chavez, 'the second biggest recipient of foreign investment in the world, after China.'

Prospects in China

While Japan and Mexico have a strategic significance in Johnson Electric's international marketing activities, the best long-term growth prospects for the company are arguably to be found in China. Presently the PRC remains a fairly small consumer market when compared with the industrialized economies of the European Union and North America. China is far more important to Johnson Electric as a production base and as an original equipment manufacturers (OEM) market. For example, Johnson Electric can benefit from the government's policy that requires foreign car manufacturers looking to establish joint ventures within the PRC to use locally-produced components wherever possible.

EXHIBIT C2–6

Mabuchi Motors' Product-Applications

Automotive Equipment
Mirrors, door locks, window washer pumps, idle speed controllers, auto-cruise, air-condition mode actuators, shock absorber adjusters, trunk openers, fuel pumps, fuel tank lid opener, power window lifters

Household and Personal Care Appliances
Hair dryer, shaver, toothbrush, clocks

Others
Printers, CD-ROM drives, cordless power tools, toys, models

Source: Company brochures and promotional material.

EXHIBIT C2–7

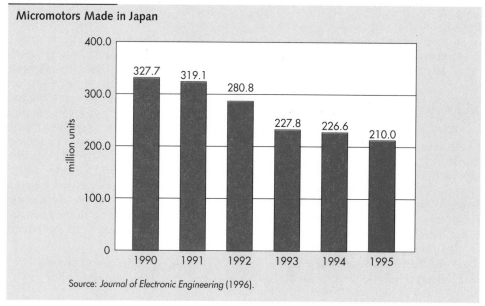

Micromotors Made in Japan

Source: *Journal of Electronic Engineering* (1996).

Nevertheless, as the PRC develops economically, local consumption will increase in a variety of micromotor-related applications. In particular, the emergence of a Chinese middle class will lead to a growing demand for personal care products, household appliances—indeed, products in all four of Johnson Electric's core areas.

Thanks to its long-term investment program in the PRC, Johnson Electric is well-placed to capitalize on the growing demand from the Chinese market. The company established its first mainland factory employing 30 people in 1982, just three years after the PRC re-opened its doors to the world. By the late 1980s most of Johnson Electric's labor-intensive manufacturing activities were being subcontracted to four factories located in Shajing (near the border city of Shenzhen) where labor costs are one-sixth that of Hong Kong. In a pattern typical of many Sino-Hong Kong joint ventures, the Chinese partners would provide land, factory space, and cheap labor, while Johnson Electric would supply the equipment, components, and necessary technical assistance. Components from Hong Kong would be trucked across the border, turned into completed sub-assemblies, and then trucked back into Hong Kong for final assembly, packaging and distribution. By the mid–1990s, with rising rents and labor costs in Hong Kong, around 70% of the company's production took place in Guangdong Province where Johnson Electric now employs 13,000 people.

In addition to its capital investments in China, Johnson Electric has developed excellent *guanxi* (relationships) with joint venture partners and local municipal authorities and has acquired significant experience in dealing with Chinese bureaucracy. The resumption of Chinese sovereignty over Hong Kong has further reduced barriers to business between SAR (Special Administrative Region) firms and Chinese suppliers and buyers. Thus, it is an assumption that Johnson Electric is well-positioned to capitalize on this emerging market. But then, so too are some of Johnson's major competitors. In 1995, 83% of Mabuchi's output came from China while another Japanese rival, Matsushita, made four-fifths of its 100 million motors in China.

Whatever the economic prospects of China as an emerging market and production base, these benefits need to be weighed in light of the PRC's trading relations with other nations. With a good proportion of its motors being sold to American car-makers, Johnson Electric would be adversely affected by the outbreak of a trade war between the United States and China. It is this very possibility that led to Johnson's investment in Thailand. For similar reasons Mabuchi established a subsidiary in Vietnam in February 1996.

To quantify the threat of a Sino-American trade war, it is worth noting that, although the United States accounted for 26% of Johnson Electric's sales in the financial year 1995, only 10% of sales (mostly from motors used for power drills) would be affected. Moreover, if punitive measures were enacted, Johnson Electric could respond by shifting some of its production back to its Tai Po plant in Hong Kong or its Bangnadad plant in Thailand.

THE FUTURE

As with Hong Kong, Johnson Electric's future is inextricably connected to the process of economic reform in China. But at the same time, the company is also sensitive to changing consumption patterns in NAFTA and the European Union. Being exposed to a variety of geographically-dispersed production markets enables the company to leverage its core competency and spread its risk across many environments. Nevertheless, this 'checkerboard' of product market activities continues to present Johnson's management team with significant challenges in terms of identifying emerging opportunities and directing resources toward the company's best growth prospects.

CASE QUESTIONS

1. Explain how various macroenvironmental trends affect the demand for micromotors.
2. Which product-applications are likely to present strong growth prospects for Johnson Electric in the short-to-medium term? Which geographical markets look promising?
3. What are the main kinds of risk faced by Johnson Electric? What has the company done to minimize these risks?
4. Explain the strategic significance of the Japanese market to Johnson Electric.
5. In terms of its management practices, how is Johnson Electric unusual when compared to other Hong Kong Chinese manufacturing firms?

CASE ENDNOTES

1. P. Chan 1996. Micromotor Demand to Use up Johnson Capacity. *South China Morning Post.* August 16: 2.
2. P. Engardio 1995. Live-Wire Management at Johnson Electric. *Business Week.* November 17: 80.
3. P. Engardio and J. Barnathan 1997. Drawing a New Map: Is Intervention the Right Way to Save Manufacturing Sector? *Business Week.* September 6: 42.
4. N. Gopalan 1996. Teamwork Keeps Micromotors Group Running Smoothly. *South China Morning Post.* September 23.
5. *Hong Kong Manager* 1992. Johnson Electric—A Commitment to ISO9000. Nov/Dec: 4–6.
6. E. Iritani 1997. Hong Kong: One Country, Two Systems, but Will It Be Free? *Los Angeles Times.* June 15: 5–6.
7. Johnson Electric Annual Reports 1986–1997.
8. *Journal of Electronic Engineering* 1996. Micromotor Production Continues to Expand in Southeast Asia. January: 16–17.
9. S. Kalathil 1996. Sanction-Proof. *The Asian Wall Street Journal.* May 27.
10. J. Keating 1987. Micromotoring into Maximum Profits. *Asian Business.* January: 18–20.
11. J. Lo 1997. Johnson Electric Capacity to Lift. *South China Morning Post.* August 13: 3.
12. T. Metcalf 1997. Surge of Investment via Trade Bloc's 'Back Door.' *South China Morning Post.* September 16: 31.
13. H. Sender 1994. True to the Core: Johnson Electric Builds Success by Sticking to the Basics. *The Far Eastern Economic Review.* April 7: 70–71.
14. *The Asian Wall Street Journal* 1996. Weaker Yen Helps Some Firms, for Now. August 5: 1.
15. *The Economist* 1996. The Electric-Motor Man. June 22: 68.
16. *The Far Eastern Economic Review* 1997. You Can Go Home Again: Hong Kong Entrepreneurs Revive Their Roots. June 16: 36.
17. A Tanzer 1988. Small Motors, Big Profits. *Forbes.* July 11: 85–86.
18. A Tanzer 1993. The Quick and the Dead. *Forbes.* November 8: 292–293.
19. B. Truscott 1996. Johnson Electric: Fundamentally Sound. *Window.* July 12: 61.
20. *The South China Morning Post* 1995. Johnson to Duck Trade War. January 15: 17.
21. *The South China Morning Post* 1995. Sourcing Strategy Reduces Yen Effect. July 3: 2.
22. *The South China Morning Post* 1996. 'No bias' in Male Domination of Boardrooms. December 22.
23. *The South China Morning Post* 1997. Johnson Electric Outpaces Index. May 21.

CASE 3

COLGATE-PALMOLIVE HUNGARY

SUMMARY

"Colgate-Palmolive Hungary" was written to provide a basis for discussion on the challenges facing a rapidly growing subsidiary in the midst of a turbulent political economic and organizational environment. The parent company, a global consumer products firm experiencing severe competition in the U.S., is looking increasingly to the European and Asian markets to boost its margins. Meanwhile, management at the Hungarian subsidiary must respond strategically to continuing growth in an environment of uncertain economics, changing politics, and increasing competition. Internally, the company faces logistical and organizational structure issues. The myriad of challenges facing the company provides a comprehensive case study for the student of global strategic management.

PARENT COMPANY BACKGROUND

Colgate-Palmolive, headquartered in New York City, is the world's leading manufacturer of oral care products, with more than 40% of the global market share in toothpaste. It is the leading seller of liquid soaps in the U.S. and worldwide. Both product lines are marketed under the company's own name. Deriving 65% of its sales from outside the U.S. and Canada, the company has operations in 75 countries and exports products to 100 others. The U.S. retail environment has become increasingly competitive, exacerbated by the consumer trend towards nonbrand name or generic consumer goods. Retailers have not discouraged this trend, since store brands typically mean higher profit margins. Colgate is responding to the difficult and competitive U.S. retail environment through global expansion and new product introduction.

With its 266 manufacturing, office, distribution, and research facilities worldwide, Colgate-Palmolive has the ability and resources to respond rapidly to changing global trends. The company has come to recognize the importance of the market potential of newly industrializing countries and has initiated, or expanded, operations in such countries as Cambodia, Bulgaria, Tanzania, and Hungary. According to Al Ries, the chairman of a marketing strategy firm, brand equity may be suffering in the U.S., but other countries look to American brands, which can often command premiums over those made by inferior local competitors.

One of the competitive advantages of Colgate internationally is its "bundle book" that contains all the information a Colgate country manager needs to know about a product, including the product attributes and manufacturing formula, standards for packaging, relevant market research and the points that need to be made in advertising. The book creates uniformity of products worldwide and provides a broad strategy for the company's country managers. Specific organizational issues, however, typically are left up to the managers.

Company History

The Colgate-Palmolive Company was formed in 1928 as the result of a merger between the Colgate Company of Jersey City, N.J. (a consumer product firm founded in 1806) and the Palmolive Company of Milwaukee, Wis. (a soap manufacturer founded in 1864 as the B. B. Johnson Soap Company). During the 1930s the company purchased French and German soap makers and opened its first branches in Europe. Post-World War II, the Ajax, Colgate, and Palmolive brands were outselling the European competition. The company expanded to the Far East in the 1950s, and by 1961 foreign sales represented 52% of the total sales.

During the 1960s and 1970s, the company diversified by buying approximately 70 other companies. This diversification strategy, however, proved unsuccessful, and Colgate divested itself of most of these companies during the 1980s. The man behind the divestitures was Reuben Mark, who spent his entire career at Colgate and became chief executive in 1984. That year, Colgate's gross margins were just over 39%, but by 1993 they had increased to nearly 48%. Operating margins more than doubled between 1984 and 1992. The company's financial success over this time period was attributed to Mark's cost-cutting efforts, focus on core businesses with a move towards the higher-margin personal care products, strategic acquisitions within the core businesses, and attention to detail.

In 1987, when Mark launched a reorganization to focus on building Colgate-Palmolive's core businesses (personal care and household products), the company took a $145 million charge against earnings to cover reorganization costs. From 1986 to 1991, the company introduced three new products and acquired eight companies worldwide. In 1991 the company took a one-time $243 million charge to simplify and consolidate global production facilities to capitalize on falling trade barriers. Mark closed or reengineered a number of the company's worldwide plants and by 1993 had brought the number down from 156 to

80. The 1991 restructuring also included reducing the 42,800 worldwide employment force by 20,000. To avoid firing a disproportionate number of minorities or those close to retirement, Mark insisted that he approve all layoff lists.

In the second quarter of 1994, the company experienced problems in the United States. Although worldwide the unit sales volume was up 9% and earnings per share were up 13%, the figures belied the North American results of a 9% unit sales decline in the soap, detergent, and toothpaste businesses, which resulted in a 13% overall decline in U.S. revenues. Mark denied rumors of another major restructuring and instead launched a number of new products in oral and personal care and invested in substantial advertising in the U.S. market.

BACKGROUND ON HUNGARY

Hungary is an Eastern European country with a population of 10.5 million people. Approximately 58% of the population live in urban areas (approximately 2 million in Budapest alone) with the remaining 42 percent residing in the rural regions. The purchasing power of the majority of Hungarians is low compared to Western European standards. For example, it takes the average Hungarian 1.6 hours of work to buy one 75ml tube of Colgate toothpaste, compared to 12 minutes of work for the average German worker.

Despite Hungary's tradition of private ownership under Communism, the transition to a market economy is providing difficult. Only about 10% of communist-era enterprises have been privatized. Although Hungary leads Eastern Europe in foreign investment (60% of joint ventures are with German and Austrian companies) with about $3 billion in direct investment, there have been some problems in making these ventures profitable (e.g., GE/Tungsram) and some cultural conflicts (such as Suzuki's attempt to impose Japanese management methods). On the positive side, private ownership in services is growing quickly and in some fields, such as tourism, is replacing state ownership. Hungary is the most systematic of the Eastern European countries in its attempts to attract foreign capital; banking regulations are being adapted and privatization provisions formulated to facilitate international investors.

The economy of the country has been threatened by Hungary's need to buy oil on the world markets rather than through barter with the Soviet Union as was done prior to the fall of Communism. Following the outbreak of war in Yugoslavia, the unemployment conditions worsened in Hungary with the influx of thousands of Yugoslavian refugees, many with Hungarian family ties. In April of 1992, the Hungarian unemployment rate stood at 9%; it peaked in 1993 at 14% and by July 1994, was hovering at approximately 12% (versus an average 14% for Eastern Europe overall and just above 10% for Western Europe). Hungary's inflation rate for 1994 was 20% and, although high by Western standards, was down from 35 percent in 1991. Despite its economic woes, the nation enjoys one of Eastern Europe's most effective governments.

According to Boston Consulting Group's John Lindquist, most Hungarian companies are poorly managed and structured and suffer from lack of product focus, excessive levels of vertical integration, underdeveloped sales and distribution networks, poor labor productivity, inefficient use of resources, inflexible and overly functional organizational structures and a lack of management and worker incentives.

THE HUNGARIAN SUBSIDIARY

In 1991, Colgate-Palmolive established its Hungarian subsidiary in Budapest with an initial investment of $0.5 million to focus on the marketing and sales of Colgate products imported as finished goods from other European subsidiaries. In 1994, Colgate invested an additional $2.0 million by acquiring a local manufacturer (Fabulon) with a plant located in the small town of Dorog, approximately 45 kilometers from Budapest. Colgate-Palmolive (C-P Hungary) also owns one warehouse in Dorog and leases another in a town near Budapest.

The management at C-P Hungary has targeted three primary objectives to be attained within the next three years: (1) to have C-P Hungary become the best consumer products company in Hungary by year-end 1995, which requires becoming number one or two in the key product categories chosen for investment in the near future; (2) to run a financially healthy and growth-oriented business; and (3) to develop an exciting organization and raise the quality of each function to at least the same level as a comparable subsidiary in Western Europe. The resolution of several issues has been identified as critical to the achievement of the stated objectives. The areas of concern include the competitive environment; external market dynamics; logistics (including the Dorog facility, purchasing, and inventory control); and organizational structure.

COMPETITION

The competition in the consumer products industry in Hungary is very high, with little room for penetration and very low brand loyalty. C-P Hungary's major competitors are Procter & Gamble, Unilever, and Henkel, all of which have larger operations and investments in Hungary than Colgate does. Procter & Gamble began its Hungarian operation in January of 1991 with an investment of $12 million. The company concentrated in manufacturing and sales and established joint ventures in toothpaste filling and diapers. Procter & Gamble's main product lines include detergents, oral care, Pampers, and body care. Unilever began its operations in Hungary in November of 1991 with an acquisition of a local company and an investment of $49 million. The company manufactures its own detergents, liquids, soap, margarine, and butter; product-line focus is on margarine, detergent, toothpaste, body care, and ice cream. The final major competitor is Henkel which began its operations in Hungary in 1988 with several joint ventures in detergents, industrial cleaning, glue, and shoe polish. The company's investment in Hungary totals $30 million, with a focus on detergents, hard surface care, body care, and glue.

MARKET DYNAMICS

Three major market events are impacting C-P Hungary's business: (1) In the consumer products industry, competitive pressures are necessitating significant increases in advertising budgets; (2) political turbulence continues throughout the industry as the result of the May 1994 election of a new socialist government; and (3) bureaucracy remains an issue, as C-P Hungary is faced with time-consuming import limitations.

LOGISTICAL ISSUES

The Dorog Facility

With the acquisition of Fabulon, C-P Hungary inherited a manufacturing plant in Dorog. The plant is well-equipped for filling liquids (e.g., after-shave, gels). The plant management objectives include optimizing investment, developing the facility's flexibility to accommodate low-volume and short-run production, and building on the strength of the present operation by optimizing equipment and developing the workers.

Purchasing

Currently, approximately 70 percent of C-P Hungary's sales are from sourcing finished products from sister subsidiaries. There are existing company guidelines that each subsidiary must follow. Each subsidiary has an appointed inter-company coordinator (ICC). In the Hungarian subsidiary, the ICC is responsible for arranging for the timely supply of finished products to C-P Hungary distribution warehouses for those products which are imported. This individual is also responsible for keeping costs low, maintaining high quality, assuring the quickest delivery possible and maintaining an organized level of paperwork. C-P Hungary has one person running the finished goods purchasing department. Little or no documentation on policy and procedure on purchasing goods exists. A preliminary inter-company purchasing policy was developed, but no follow-up was completed. This lack of proper documentation and total dependence on one individual poses a threat to C-P Hungary with 70% of its business coming from imported finished goods.

Inventory

High levels of safety stock and a high variability between forecasts and actual sales have resulted in unacceptably high levels of inventory for C-P Hungary. There are no sales forecasting systems in place and relatively little historical data available. The inventory problem has been exacerbated by a lack of proper communication among the relevant departments.

ORGANIZATIONAL STRUCTURE

The structure of the organization is in the developmental stage. There has been a recent reorganization of key people and the creation of a new department—the Human Resources Department. Five major departments report to the general manager: Human Resources, General Administration, Finance, Marketing/Sales, and Manufacturing. Only one person handles the Human Resources Department and reports directly to the general manager. The General Administration Department consists of an executive assistant, executive secretary, and a messenger. The Finance Department is headed by the finance director who has reporting to him the assistant financial controller, the MIS manager and the batch accountant. Seven additional positions report to the assistant financial controller. The financial processes and required reports are ill-defined, and fixed costs are not well-managed. The commercial director (Marketing/Sales Department) has six individuals reporting to him: four category managers, one for each of the key product categories (oral care, body care, hard surface care/facial care, and Fabulon), a national sales manager and a sales assistant. The national sales manager in turn has two sales administrators and three area managers reporting to him. Three account salespeople, twelve salespeople, and twelve junior salespeople report to the three area managers. The Manufacturing Department is in the process of being developed, with plans for a director. Once a manufacturing director is in place, an organizational chart for the manufacturing operation will be drawn up and the Dorog facility issues addressed.

CASE QUESTIONS

1. How should operations at the Dorog facility be optimized? How will purchasing and inventory be impacted?

2. Construct an organizational chart reflecting the current C-P Hungary organization. Make any recommended alternatives or modifications, along with a rationale supporting these recommendations.
3. Summarize the strengths, weaknesses, opportunities, and threats facing C-P Hungary.
4. Taking the current environment into consideration, devise a creative strategic plan for the perplexing problems facing the company.

Source: This case was prepared by Professor Mzamo P. Mangaliso, University of Massachusetts, Amherst, Priti R. Patel, and Jann-Marie Halvorsen for class discussion and does not necessarily imply either good or poor management practices.

CASE 4

LEE JING TEXTILE COMPANY, LTD.

INTRODUCTION

In 1993, Lee Jing Textile Company, Ltd. had sales of $3,860 million New Taiwan (NT) dollars (about $148 million), assets of $10,917 million NT (about $420 million), and about 2,500 employees. Lee Jing basically purchases raw cotton from its suppliers, then spins, weaves, and creates dyed fabric. Its primary products are cotton fabric and denim that are sold to customers in Taiwan, Hong Kong, the United States, Germany, Singapore, Malaysia, United Kingdom, Japan, Netherlands, and other parts of the world. Lee Jing is a first-generation company of the Kuo Lee Group, a Taiwanese conglomerate.

Recently, caught in a price squeeze, Lee Jing began downsizing. Like the United States, Japan, and Europe, Taiwan is having fundamental problems with its textile industry because fabric tends to be an undifferentiated product. This means that price often is an overriding consideration; hence, textile companies constantly search for areas where wages are low. Rising wage costs coupled with chronic labor shortages are making the production of fabric at competitive prices very difficult. For the past eight years, the company has been losing a significant amount of money; it needs a strategy to position itself in the world market.

The major challenges facing Lee Jing mean nothing less than the survival of the company. Lee Jing must determine how to best organize itself to tackle this painful transition. Lee Jing hopes that a change in strategy toward high value-added products, superior on-time delivery, and service will distinguish the company from its competitors.

BACKGROUND OF TAIWAN

The Republic of China (ROC) on Taiwan is the formal name for the country of Taiwan, an island southeast of mainland China. Some economics statistics in 1993 sketch the achievement of Taiwan. First, the gross domestic product (GDP) was $206 billion for a population size of 21 million people with a per capita income figure of $10,000 as compared to 1982 when GDP stood at $71.5 billion for 18 million and per capita income of $2,710. Economic growth rate has averaged around 8.7 percent annually for more than 30 years. So dramatic has been the improvement in living conditions, industrial structure, and trade that many call this "Taiwan's Economic Miracle."

After World War II, Taiwan embarked upon an industrial policy that guided its economic development. Specifically, the transition of Taiwan toward becoming a developed country can be broken into six stages. The 1940s witnessed the economic reconstruction of the island, including land reform and the cultivation of emerging industries such as textiles and fertilizers. In the 1950s, Taiwan began an import substitution strategy. This meant high tariffs were placed on consumer commodity imported goods, and Taiwanese firms were encouraged to begin exporting goods.

The 1960s saw the continued rapid growth of light industries. Both textiles and electronics flourished during this period. The 1970s saw a major structural change toward the development of capital- and technology-intensive industries. The government initiated and completed ten national construction projects that benefited

EXHIBIT C4-1

Taiwan

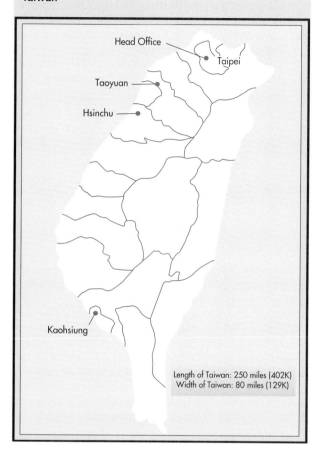

Head Office
Taipei
Taoyuan
Hsinchu
Kaohsiung

Length of Taiwan: 250 miles (402K)
Width of Taiwan: 80 miles (129K)

steel, shipbuilding, petrochemical, electrical power, telecommunication, transportation, and utilities.

The 1980s again saw a shift in industrial policy toward government-supported development of high-tech industries. The Hsinchu Science-based Industrial Park was modeled on the Silicon Valley concept in northern California. The government at this time also took a strong stand on reducing industrial pollution.

The 1990s presents new opportunities and challenges for Taiwan. Specifically, in 1991, the ROC government adopted the Six-Year National Development plan for improving Taiwan's infrastructure and transportation systems. This creates more jobs and upgrades the developing environment for strategic industries. On the other hand, problems facing Taiwan include the 40 percent appreciation of NT dollars since the late 1980s, rising wage costs, insufficient labor force, high cost of land, ecological concerns, and competition from other developing countries. Refer to Exhibit C4-2 for a guide to doing business in Taiwan.

THE TEXTILE INDUSTRY

The word *textile* comes from the Latin "textere," which means to weave, interlace, or intertwine. Earliest known records show some type of clothing existed in prehistoric times, but weaving dates back only to 5000 B.C. Textile fibers can be natural (from animal or plant sources), mineral (such as glass or metallic), man-made (such as rayon or nylon), or a modification or combination of these. Linen is believed to be the oldest textile fabric. Silk dates back to 2640 B.C. with the Chinese, while wool is mentioned in biblical sources. The Crusades and world exploration spread the knowledge of cotton throughout Europe since cotton was found extensively in Mexico, and Central and South America. In 1641, the cotton-based textile industry in England was established, and it rapidly became competitive with wool.

Early civilizations, like the Egyptian, Greek, Roman, and Chinese, all had systems for producing clothes, including hand looms and the hand spindle, but the Middle Ages transformed the industry with the development of the spinning wheel, the horizontal loom, and a process to remove the natural grease from wool to make the fibers.

The Industrial Revolution dramatically expanded the cotton textile industry, especially in Great Britain, from a home operation into a large-scale enterprise consisting of huge mills with mechanized mass production employing 1.5 million people. British cotton mills were supplied by raw material from the United States, and by 1850 these mills were producing more than 2025 million yards per year.

In the early 1800s, U.S. textile mills began operations, mostly in New England, New York, and Pennsylvania, where they flourished until the 1920s. The U.S. textile industry then migrated to the Southern states. In 1925, the man-made fibers of acetate, rayon, and nylon made their first appearance, and became increasingly popular. After World War II, rapid progress in transportation, telecommunications, mass retailing, production, and distribution of clothing again changed the textile industry into a global endeavor. Rotor spinning and shuttleless looms were introduced that greatly increased automation.

The 1960s marked the enormous movement of textile and apparel operations to developing countries, such as

EXHIBIT C4-2

Guide to Doing Business in Taiwan

1. *Develop a Relationship*—Relationships are a very important element of an Asian culture. This relationship or *guanxi* can be instrumental in doing business. While Western cultures emphasize a contract as legally binding, Chinese rely on mutual trust and friendship. Personal friends and business friends are often the same.

2. *Respect Another's "Face"*—Chinese care very much about harmony, and to cause another to "lose face" can mean "losing business." One does not usually criticize another person directly. Thus, there is no disagreement in public. Consensus is important. A straightforward disagreement in public is considered an attack. Try to express opinions indirectly or in private.

3. *Look for a Longer Time Horizon*—Business decisions are based on the long term. Chinese are reluctant to give a big order immediately. They are likely to handle a small order first, even if they lose money. They expect more business in the future. The first several deals provide good opportunity to develop *guanxi*; do not miss them.

4. *Don't Be Surprised at Chinese Hospitality*—The Chinese show tremendous grace and hospitality when they meet people for the first time. Guests are entertained well, and usually given a gift of the occasion. Because of this hospitality, Westerners sometimes become too optimistic about the cooperation that is to follow.

5. *Inquiries About One's Background Are Common*— Chinese people like to inquire about other backgrounds. They will be very happy to know they have something in common. Unfortunately, some inquiries can make Westerners feel uncomfortable and they think their privacy has been invaded.

6. *Negotiations May Be Unclear*—The Chinese tend not to make clear what they really want. They believe that with mutual trust and friendship, people know one another's thoughts instinctively. This can be confusing to Westerners. Negotiation schedules can be delayed, and different conclusions reached.

Taiwan. Although employment in textiles declined in Europe, the United States, and Japan during the past 30 years, the textile industry became a leading employer for many developing countries.

By 1991, the ten leading exporters of textiles and clothing were Hong Kong, Italy, China, Germany, South Korea, Taiwan, France, United States, Belgium/Luxembourg, and the United Kingdom. The top five importers were the United States, Germany, Hong Kong, France, and the United Kingdom. From 1980 to 1990, the fastest-growing exporter of clothing was mainland China.

Yet, the textile industry has also sometimes suffered from a poor image. Besides low wages, even as early as the 17th century, the industry realized that its workers had health problems. The most serious is byssinosis, also known as brown lung. This is a respiratory disorder caused by the dust from cotton and other fibers. Over time (usually several years), breathing becomes more difficult, and the lungs develop a brownish tint. Persons with mild cases experience a chest tightness and shortness of breath on the first day of work after a break (for example, a weekend). More serious cases involve chronic, irreversible lung damage. For some textile manufacturers, there have also been union–management problems, and labor strikes. The movie *Norma Rae* about worker grievances and union organizing is based on a true incident at J.P. Stevens.

The global textile industry has become extremely competitive with supply exceeding demand. Japan, for example, has realized that it can no longer compete in the basic low-end fabric line, and has adopted a value-added product strategy. The Germans have invested heavily in new technologies and labor-saving machinery, whereas the Italians are developing close collaborations with well-known designers. The Taiwan Textile Federation (TTF) established in 1975 and authorized by the Taiwanese Ministry of Economic Affairs attempts to monitor trends in the industry and to provide Taiwanese firms with this information. TTF has a computerized data bank and design center to serve those interested in buying Taiwan textile products. It also negotiates with foreign authorities, administers textile export quotas, and promotes Taiwan textile products internationally.

Numerous Taiwanese textile firms have already moved part of their operations off the island, frequently to mainland China. To curb this outflow of investment to mainland China, the ROC President Lee Teng-Hui has encouraged Taiwanese businesses to adopt a "southern investment" strategy into Singapore, the Philippines, or Indonesia instead. Exhibit C4–3 shows the flow of Taiwanese investment to other parts of Asia.

According to Bruno D. C. Huang, marketing research assistant at Taiwan's World Trade Center, in 1993 more than 1,000 Taiwanese firms were engaged in the textile industry employing about 288,427 workers, down from 459,321 in 1987. In 1993, textiles were still Taiwan's leading export product, followed by electronics in a very close second. In 1992, Far Eastern Textile, Ltd. was the leading Taiwanese textile firm in the cotton industry.

EXHIBIT C4-3

Taiwan's Investment Flow

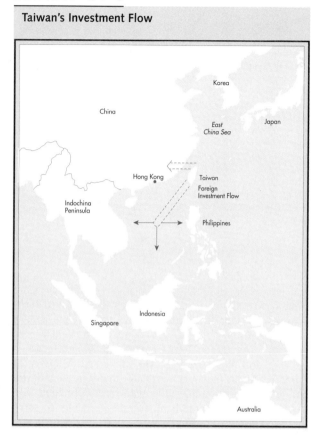

HISTORY OF LEE JING TEXTILES

The company was established in 1949 by Shih-Tei Kuo and Siang-Chun Chang when they migrated from mainland China to Taiwan. The two men brought old equipment from Shanghai and some 30 people who worked for them and set up their first factory in Taoyuan. The original capacity of the plant was 7,508 spindles.

In 1956, Lee Jing built another plant, this one for spinning, and for the next 30 years, Lee Jing alternated between building spinning and weaving plants until they had six spinning, six weaving, and two dyeing mills.

Then in 1980, Lee Jing made a strategic change in its product orientation by adding a higher value-added product. It started the production of denim fabric, including a dyeing and finishing mill. Through the 1980s, the company added new capacity, but closed down older facilities.

The number of employees grew slowly to a high of 5,500 reached in the late 1980s.

Since 1988, the company has been downsizing through increased automation, through the natural attrition from employee turnover of 20 percent, and from layoffs. Laid-off workers receive one month's severance pay for each year of service to Lee Jing. In 1993, Lee Jing employed about 2,500 employees. Until 1986, Lee Jing was quite profitable, but since 1987, Lee Jing has been losing money. From 1991 through 1993, operating costs alone exceeded net revenue. Between the years 1992 and 1993, Lee Jing changed its accounting procedures. Refer to Exhibits C4–4, C4–5, and C4–6 for balance sheet and income statements.

EXHIBIT C4-4

Balance Sheet (in thousands New Taiwan (NT) dollars)

Current Assets	1991	1992	1993
Cash	102,270	63,425	151,925
Short Investment	1,098,922	1,118,811	1,294,153
Notes Receivable	434,322	197,737	151,543
Accounts Receivable	279,099	260,656	162,325
Inventory	1,857,155	1,349,727	1,093,133
Prepaid Items	280,766	108,882	59,661
Other Current Assets	101,166	114,255	67,951
Total Current Assets	4,153,700	3,213,493	2,980,691
Long-Term Investment	3,282,276	3,893,120	4,239,978
Fixed Assets			
Land	377,849	381,006	381,006
Plant & Equipment	1,873,917	1,818,643	1,911,309
Machine Equipment	7,013,020	6,629,838	6,072,387
Transportation Equip.	114,542	113,725	108,781
Other Equipment	105,414	109,602	111,410
	9,484,742	9,052,814	8,584,893
Replacement	109,678	109,679	109,679
Total	9,594,420	9,162,493	8,694,572
Accumulated Depreciation	(5,233,258)	(5,387,411)	(5,332,028)
Unfinished Construction	24,868	26,926	231,630
Net Fixed Assets	4,386,030	3,802,008	3,594,174
Other Assets	1,754	118,414	102,975
Total Assets	$11,823,761	$11,027,035	$10,917,818

Note: Exchange rate 1994: 26 New Taiwan (NT) dollars = $1 U.S.

EXHIBIT C4–5

Balance Sheet (in thousands New Taiwan (NT) dollars)

Current Liabilities	1991	1992	1993
Bank Loans	1,549,670	1,284,093	503,214
Accounts Payable	177,092	95,232	62,713
Other Current Liabilities	1,169,319	953,558	1,728,974
Total Current Liabilities	2,896,080	2,332,883	2,294,901
Long-term Debt	478,810	251,090	89,210
Reserves for Employee Retirement	80,000	23,997	14,939
Other Liabilities	88,413	88,413	164,594
Total Liabilities	3,543,303	2,696,383	2,563,643
Owner Equity			
Capital Stock	4,400,000	4,400,000	4,400,000
Capital Surplus	418,993	487,300	376,520
Retained Earnings	3,461,465	3,443,352	3,576,256
Total Owner Equity	8,280,458	8,330,652	8,354,176
Liabilities & Equity	11,823,761	11,027,035	10,917,818

Note: Exchange rate 1994: 26 New Taiwan (NT) dollars = $1 U.S.

Owing to industry overcapacity and increasing labor costs, Lee Jing began in 1988 to consider moving some operations to other locales. During one three-year period, top executives visited Indonesia, Thailand, Vietnam, Mexico, and Nicaragua. Enlei Lu, one of the company's general managers, went to Nicaragua many times for discussion purposes, including dinner with the president of the country, but too many problems were encountered. For all of their joint ventures, President Chih Nen Wang believes it is necessary for Lee Jing to have 51 percent of the stock for controlling purposes. President Wang has been CEO of Lee Jing for the past three years.

PRODUCTION AND PRODUCTS

Lee Jing has its headquarters in Taipei with factory operations in Taoyuan, Hsinchu, and Kaohsiung, but the latter was closed in 1993. Total land space is 602,489 square meters (about 149 acres) with most land designated for Taoyuan, 405,342 square meters (about 100 acres). Taoyuan has six spinning plants, three weaving plants, and one denim dyeing and finishing plant. The other plant is in

EXHIBIT C4–6

Income Statement (in thousands New Taiwan (NT) dollars)

	1991	1992	1993**
Operating Revenue	$5,410,316	4,472,972	3,880,554
Sales Returns and Allowances	(16,007)	(28,822)	(19,805)
Net Revenue	5,394,309	4,444,150	3,860,749
Operating Cost	5,640,718	4,824,313	3,868,494
Operating Gross	(246,409)	(380,162)	(7,745)
Operating Expenses	395,764	362,025	360,069
Operating Income	(642,173)	(742,187)	(367,814)
Nonoperating Income			
Investment Revenue	743,874	822,542	693,591
Financial Revenue	—	—	33,904
Gain from Inventory Checking	—	—	2,932
Different Estimated Raw Material	—	—	1,490
Dividend Revenue	688	69,888	—
Gain on Sale of Fixed Assets	1,028	68,059	—
Rent Revenue	23,093	25,452	—
Exchange Revenue	37,405	20,484	—
Recovery/Loss of Investment	—	19,890	—
Recovery/Loss of Inventory	20,000	11,000	—
Sales of By-products	16,762	9,752	—
Gain/Sale of LT Investment	14,851	4,070	—
Interest Revenue	32,462	3,091	—
Recovery/Deferred Revenue	551,178	—	—
Recovery/Exporting Loss	38,255	—	—
Other	40,830	19,974	95,787
Total Nonoperating Income	1,520,426	1,074,202	827,704
Nonoperating Expense			
Financial Expense	—	—	166,297
Loss/Selling Assets	—	—	1,343
Loss Checking Inventory	—	—	42
Loss/Inventory Price Reduction	—	—	24,500
Interest Expense	286,752	184,295	—
Loss of Shutdown	54,031	74,204	—
Loss/Selling Fixed Assets	169,841	4,545	57
Loss/Investment	19,890	—	21
Other Loss	—	—	1,549
Other Expense	6,054	6,137	242,557
Total Nonoperating Expenses	536,568	269,181	436,366
Income Before Tax	341,685	62,834	23,524
Tax	—	—	—
Net Income After Tax	341,685	62,834	23,524

**Reporting changed in 1993/Exchange rate 1994: 26 NT dollars = $1 U.S.

Hsinchu, and there is an arrangement for production in mainland China. In 1993, total monthly production was 29,000 bales of yarn, 12 million yards of greige and finished fabrics, including 4 million yards of denim, 300,000 kilograms of knitted fabric, and 30,000 dozen knitted garments, 80 percent of which is for export.

The head office employs about 124 people, with the rest located in Taoyuan and Hsinchu. Lee Jing had been organized functionally, but is moving toward a strategic business unit structure. The organizational chart is shown in Exhibit C4–7.

Lee Jing has four main product lines: yarn, grade piece goods, denim, and finished goods. Yarn and grade piece goods are about 25 and 14 percent of the business, whereas denim and finished cloth are 32 and 28 percent, respectively. Of the yarn, almost 40 percent is differentiated. Grade piece goods are totally undifferentiated. Denim is 50 percent differentiated. The two- to three-year goal is to have 70 percent of the yarn differentiated, 100 percent of grade piece goods differentiated, and 80 percent of the denim differentiated. Eventually, all the undifferentiated fabric will be produced in mainland China, and all the specialized, differentiated goods, R&D, and marketing will be in Taiwan. President Wang wants to make Lee Jing the most profitable textile firm in Taiwan, not necessarily the largest.

As one of the oldest textile firms in Taiwan, the reputation of Lee Jing is very good. Lee Jing could be considered the Ford of the industry—moderate prices, high quality, wide range of products. According to Margaret Li, General Merchandising Manager for Liz Claiborne International in Taiwan, "Lee Jing is one of our 14 piece goods suppliers because they have reasonable prices, their quality of dyeing is good, their shrinkage is consistent, their inspection is very good, they correct defects, and they are very cooperative... Liz Claiborne has very high standards, and if they are one of our suppliers, they have to be good." Other Lee Jing customers include The Gap, Van Heusen, Oxford, Biermann, Mark Spence, and Crew Peabody.

By 1994, Lee Jing successfully applied for and attained ISO 9000. They have also won more than 15 awards from the government for excellence in exporting. In 1981 and 1982, they received the Isikawa award for quality control, and in 1987, received an Industry Pollution Protection award from Taiwan's Environmental Protection Agency (EPA).

Lee Jing is guided by its three statements: (1) people-based permanent operation, (2) quality is first, and (3) kindness and goodwill to all people.

MARKETING OF LEE JING PRODUCTS

According to President Chih Nen Wang, Lee Jing is in a turnaround situation, and faces a lot of competition from third-world countries, such as mainland China, Pakistan, and Indonesia. Cost is a big factor, and owing to accelerating labor costs, Lee Jing cannot make the fabric as cheaply as these other countries because the company must import its raw material, while mainland China and Pakistan produce their own cotton. Further, in 1994, world prices for tradi-

EXHIBIT C4–7

Organizational Chart

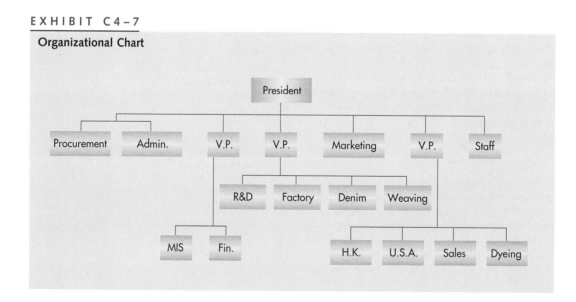

tional undifferentiated fabric were 30 percent lower than in 1984. This was due to industry overcapacity. President Wang indicated that supply runs about 17 percent higher than demand, and he expects the problem of oversupply to continue until 1999.

Hence, in the past three years, Lee Jing has adopted a strategy of product differentiation. President Wang acknowledges that Lee Jing should have begun this new strategy even earlier "about seven or eight years ago when the NT dollar was appreciated." However, he also believes that in 1994, Lee Jing will break even or make a small profit. With this new strategy, in 1993, President Wang established a research and development department of six textile engineers to create differentiated products. Even for differentiated products, the life cycle is only four to six months before a competitor will "copy" the product.

Also in 1993, President Wang created for the first time a marketing department of three people. Richard Tsai, vice general manager, was assigned to head up this department. His focus is both external and internal. Externally, Lee Jing will strengthen its system of gathering market information to assess customer trends and demands. Data will be gathered from papers, magazines, government, Taiwan Textile Federation (TTF), and from visiting customers. Additional activities, such as sales promotions, and an upcoming business trip to New York City to visit twenty piece-goods customers and to emphasize Lee Jing's denim goods items will be performed. Lee Jing has two branch offices, one at 6th Avenue, near the fashion district in Manhattan, and the other in Hong Kong.

Lee Jing has always attended international exhibitions, and it will continue doing this, attending five to six exhibitions per year in the world's major fashion centers. Lee Jing advertises in *Women's Wear Daily* and other major trade publications, but Richard Tsai believes the benefits of such endeavors are hard to evaluate. TTF also introduces customers to Lee Jing, but "developing new customers is very difficult."

Internally, the marketing department has started a series of biweekly seminars in which members of the R&D department from the plant in Taoyuan give presentations to the Lee Jing sales representatives in the Taipei headquarters. The sales personnel were unaware of a number of new Lee Jing products. Lee Jing does have its own trademark.

With the establishment of the R&D and marketing departments, the culture of Lee Jing appears to be changing from a production-driven company to one that is marketing oriented under the leadership of President Wang. One outside source described the culture of Lee Jing as "very conservative."

QUALITY CIRCLES

Lee Jing has been engaged in quality circles since 1981. Initially, 60 quality circles were established, but the number was later reduced to 20. Quality circles are partly voluntary and partly assigned. Each circle has six to ten people who meet twice a year for a quality control campaign that lasts three to four months. Each circle competes to make the best suggestions. Each team makes a presentation with NT12,000 ($480) awarded to the first place team. All participants will each receive NT600 ($24) for the entire campaign.

One quality control project included buying a machine that cost $100,000. The machine's purpose involved measuring "nips" in a piece of fabric. Nips are the tiny balls of thread on the fabric's surface. The ideal fabric has no or few nips. A multiple regression model was developed, and a ten-week experiment drawn-up. The results showed the optimal drawing length of the cotton to satisfy customers' needs while also reducing the amount of waste. One positive outcome was the reduction of customer complaints.

MIS AND THE USE OF COMPUTERS

In terms of their use of computers, Edward Huang, one of Lee Jing's three vice presidents, expressed his opinion that the integration of the system could be improved. Currently, more than 20 people staff their computer department. He stated that too many unnecessary reports are generated. A consultant will be looking at how to integrate their computer system; management believes that the current system is too expensive to maintain and too complicated. They are contemplating a major revision of both hardware and software, but do not plan to outsource their MIS needs.

Systems that are computerized include purchasing material, payroll, personnel, accounting, financing, and warehousing. Production operations are only partly computerized. IBM is their current main computer vendor. Lee Jing has had a computer network system for the past ten years. Prior to their network, communication between headquarters and the plants was carried on via telephone.

INDUSTRIAL SAFETY

At Lee Jing, there is a formal Labor Safety and Hygiene Committee comprising nine managers and seven union workers who meet four times a year. The head of the committee is Edward Huang. The committee has been operating since the plant opened in 1951, but it became formally established in 1975. The committee discusses plant safety and hygiene issues.

PART THREE

From the committee, smaller groups of five people go on two-day inspections and score every Lee Jing plant on a grading sheet. The team checks to see that safety lights are operational, stairs cleared, and hoses for fires functional. Workers are checked to see that long hair is curled and that no one is wearing slippers. Pavements have to be intact. No cigarette butts or cups are to be around. Water fountains and restrooms must be clean. Individuals are rewarded monetarily or punished through fees in the range of NT500 to NT3000 (about $20 to $120).

One issue has been bothering management for quite a while, but they feel somewhat helpless to remedy the situation. Although management is aware of the noise level in the plant, they have been unable to get the workers to wear earplugs. About once a year, a government official conducts a safety training program in the plant to discuss the problems associated with damage to the eardrum, but the program so far appears to be unsuccessful. Management stated that only about 10 percent of the workers wear earplugs, but that from 80 to 90 percent wear face masks (especially those working in the denim dyeing plant). Management asserted that workers think the earplugs are uncomfortable, and that they prevent conversations.

External visits from Taiwanese government agencies include a once-a-year inspection of the boiler, and several visits from the county fire department. The Environmental Protection Agency (EPA) checks randomly for air pollution. The highest fine experienced by Lee Jing was for NT100,000 ($4,000) for water pollution.

In the history of Lee Jing, only one fatality occurred in the mid–1980s when a factory roof crashed during a seasonal typhoon. In accordance with the Taiwanese Labor Safety and Health Act of 1974 (revised 1991), Lee Jing (like other Taiwanese firms) keeps monthly safety records.

At the Taoyuan plant, there is one medical doctor, Dr. Shu Woei Jan, and five other medical personnel. Dr. Jan stated that his facility was established in 1961. Not only does he care for the workers, but the workers' families as well. He sees daily many complaints for head colds and stomachaches. The most frequent industrial accidents are cuts to the hand, mostly the fingers. After four days of absenteeism, industrial cases must be reported to the Bureau of Labor Insurance for compensation. Lee Jing reports about nine to ten cases a year.

Every two years, all plant workers must undergo a minor physical examination. They are checked for their weight, height, ears, eyes, blood pressure, and 11 items in their blood, including hemoglobin and hepatitis A virus. They are also given an X-ray examination for their lungs. Those individuals over 45, or overweight with elevated blood pressure, problems with their eyes, ears, or lungs are rechecked on an annual basis. In 1993, over a one-week period, about 2,215 people participated in the examinations conducted by a local hospital. Between 400 and 600 individuals fell into the annual recheck category.

Dr. Jan showed that in a group of 320 workers, 27 of them had suspicious lung problems and should be monitored for the possibility of brown lung. He also indicated that these people might be changed to another job within the plant. In the same group, there were about 63 people who had some type of hearing defect. Dr. Jan wonders what he should say to management to encourage the use of protective gear. Overall, though, accidents have decreased at Lee Jing due to three factors: (1) workers are more experienced (they have been at the plant longer), (2) there is better equipment and more training, and (3) the quarterly meeting has helped heighten awareness about industrial safety and hygiene.

POLLUTION AND WASTE MINIMIZATION IN TAIWAN

In the 1990s, the issue of pollution has come to the forefront in Taiwan. The west coast of the Taiwan island has one of the highest population densities in the world. The crowded conditions mean many industrial areas are too close to residential areas, and that managing wastes is problematic.

According to Tin-Bai Pan, Deputy General Director of the Industrial Development Bureau of the Ministry of Economic Affairs, in 1991 Taiwan's waste reached 12,000,000 tons per year, 5 percent of which is hazardous. He stated that by 1998, Taiwan needs to build 22 more garbage incinerators, and that Taiwan has aggressively adopted the strategy of industrial waste minimization to "make possible both economic growth and environmental protection."

In the textile industry, how to deal with and treat dye and finishing wastewater is a major issue. The discharge water may be colored, and high or low in pH. Lee Jing already made two major investments in waste water treatment in 1982 and 1988. The first cost approximately NT 60 million ($240,000), whereas the second ran NT50 million ($200,000).

For other waste (scraps of yarn and cotton), Lee Jing has two large incinerators. According to management, maintenance of this equipment is very expensive. In terms of steam, about 30 percent can be reclaimed and recycled.

In Taiwan, Edward Huang believes that Lee Jing is an industry leader in pollution control. Most small- and medium-sized firms do not have such waste minimization equipment, and they rely on the government to pick up and dispose of waste. Management believes they have done as much as they can for environmental protection.

PERSONNEL PRACTICES AND EMPLOYEE SATISFACTION

One issue that concerns Lee Jing is the changing work ethic of the Taiwanese people. According to Enlei Lu, Taiwan's rising affluence has decreased young people's desire to work in a factory. According to Department of Health documents, the median age in Taiwan is almost 28, but for Lee Jing, the average worker ranges in age from 38 to 40 years old. For the past four years, Lee Jing has not been able to hire any college graduates to work in the factory.

Problems of this nature concerned Chih Nen Wang when he assumed the presidency of Lee Jing in 1992. He initiated a major job satisfaction study on 2,275 factory workers in November 1993. This study used the Minnesota Employee Job Satisfaction Inventory as the research tool, which includes five dimensions of jobs, namely, work, pay, promotion, supervision, and coworkers. Since promotion is very rare, this dimension was deleted from the survey. If a respondent's answer for a positive statement is yes, the score for the question would be 3. If the answer is no, the score is 0, whereas 1 means don't know. Using a stratified random sample, 247 questionnaires were distributed with 235 completed. The results are shown as Exhibit C4–8.

Another issue of concern to President Wang is the lack of cross-training. For example, there is no system to rotate the people through different areas. People stay in the factory for 20 years in the same job. In terms of education for managers, recently President Wang and two other top managers began participating in the executive MBA program at the National Chengchi University (NCU). According to President Wang, his involvement with the university has been invaluable to him; it has allowed him to think more "strategically." He plans to send more middle-line managers to NCU in the next five years.

EXHIBIT C4–8

Average Score for the Workers' Satisfaction

1. Work	1.28
2. Supervision	1.54
3. Pay	0.89
4. Coworkers	2.17
5. Overall Satisfaction	1.48

n = 235

FUTURE CHALLENGES

One of the biggest challenges has been the company's transition from its traditional focus on production to more of a marketing emphasis. For example, President Wang wonders to what extent should Lee Jing use outsourcing? Traditionally, Lee Jing yarn has been its own supplier for its product lines, but in 1992 this began to change. Lee Jing now faces a "make or buy" question. Which is better? Which will be more profitable for the company?

Vice president Cheng wonders, how can Lee Jing attract young college graduates to work in the plant to gain experience? Who will be their next generation of managers? Others recognize that the textile volume in Taiwan will probably reduce to one-third. Is Lee Jing positioned to maintain its share of this decreasing market? Cheng asks. Lee Jing appears concerned about worker safety and the environment, but given Taiwan's growing quality-of-life movement, could Lee Jing do an even better job for worker safety and health, and for the environment?

Another challenge for Lee Jing is the development of the land following the closing of the Kaohsiung factory. Lee Jing is looking for opportunities for this piece of property, but the firm is not quite sure what to do. Lee Jing also owns property (about 54,000 square meters) in Kaohsiung that has potential for development. The current price of this land is NT10 billion (or $400 million).

As President Chih Nen Wang looks toward the future, he wonders, what can he do to turn this company around and make it profitable? Or should he just recommend to the board that they leave the textile industry altogether?

Source: Sue Greenfeld, Dept. Management, California State University San Bernardino, and Shun-Ching Horng, National Chengchi University Taipei, Taiwan. This case is presented as the basis for educational discussion rather than to illustrate either effective or ineffective handling of an administrative situation. Presented at North American Case Research Association meeting, November 1994. The names of various participants, the actual company, and its mill locations have been disguised. Used with permission.

CASE QUESTIONS

1. What are the problems associated with the textile industry?
2. What external opportunities and threats does Lee Jing face, and what are the company's strengths and weakness relative to their external environment?
3. What are some of the problems associated with a newly developed country like Taiwan?
4. Based on the case, and your insight into where the

PART THREE

company could prosper, develop a mission statement for the firm.

5. What are some of the issues associated with occupational safety and health at Lee Jing?

6. What are the problems associated with pollution and waste minimization in Taiwan?

CASE BIBLIOGRAPHY

Anson, Robin and Paul Simpson. "World Textile Trade and Production Trends," *Textile Outlook International* (July 1993): 11–28.

Blokker, Niels. *International Regulation of World Trade in Textiles* (Dordrecht, The Netherlands: Martinus Nijhoff Publishers, 1986).

"Byssinosis," *Britannica,* 15th ed., vol. 2 (1986): 698.

"Characteristics and Development of Environmental Technologies in Taiwan Republic of China," n.p., n.d.

Cline, William R. *The Future of World Trade in Textile and Apparel* (Washington, DC: Institute for International Economics, 1987).

Department of Health, *Public Health in Taiwan Area, Republic of China: The Executive Yuan* (March 1993).

Gold, Thomas B. *State and Society in the Taiwan Miracle* (New York: East Gate Books, 1986).

Greenfeld, Sue. "Management's Safety and Health Imperative: Eight Essential Steps to Improving the Work Environment," The Minerva Education Institute Occasional Paper Series, Ref. 9.02 (July 1989). Also in *American Industrial Hygiene Journal* 52 (April 1991): A218–A221.

Khanna, Sri Ram. "Structural Changes in Asian Textiles and Clothing Industries: The Second Migration of Production," *Textile Outlook International* (September 1993): 11–31.

Pan Tin-Bai, Deputy General Director, Industrial Development Bureau, Ministry of Economic Affairs. "Waste Minimization and Industrial Waste Management in Taiwan" (speech to the American Chamber of Commerce, Taipei, Taiwan, December 9, 1993).

Seetoo, Dah Hsian William. "Communication, Negotiation and Management System: The Chinese Style" (unpublished paper), National Chengchi University (April 1994).

"Textiles," *Collier's Encyclopedia,* 22 (1981): 201–225.

Thurow, Lester. *Head to Head: The Coming Economic Battle Among Japan, Europe, and America* (New York: Warner Books, 1993).

PART 4

MANAGING HUMAN RESOURCES AROUND THE WORLD

CHAPTER 10

Staffing and Training for Global Operations

CHAPTER 11

Expatriation and Labor Relations in Global HRM

CHAPTER 12

Motivating and Leading

CHAPTER 13

Managing International Teams and Workforce Diversity

10

Staffing and Training for Global Operations

O U T L I N E

Opening Profile: Oleg and Mark: Equal Work but Unequal Pay

Technology Application: HRMS Goes Global at British Airways

Staffing Philosophies for International Operations

Global Selection

Problems with Expatriation

Training and Development

Cross-Cultural Training

Training Techniques

Integrating Training with Global Orientation

Training Host-Country Nationals

Expatriate Compensation

Management Focus: Careers in Spain and China

Comparative Management in Focus: Compensation in Russia

Summary of Key Points

Discussion Questions

Application Exercises

Experiential Exercise

Internet Resources

Case Study: Fred Bailey in Japan: An Innocent Abroad

OPENING PROFILE

Oleg and Mark: Equal Work but Unequal Pay

Oleg and Mark are project managers at the Moscow subsidiary of a multibillion-dollar international company. Oleg is a Russian local and Mark an American expatriate. Although raised in vastly different countries, they have a lot in common. Both thirty years old, they graduated from top universities in their home countries with degrees in economics, worked for prestigious organizations, went back to graduate school, and now work side by side in the challenging environment of Russia's emerging market economy. They work long hours, have unpredictable schedules, manage difficult relations with vendors and government agencies, and endure the ups and downs in corporate attitudes toward the Russian market. They often work together, attend the same meetings, face similar problems, and send countless faxes and e-mail messages to corporate headquarters in North America. They have an excellent relationship and often help each other. They like what they do, and their boss sees a bright future for both of them.

But when the working day is over, the similarity abruptly ends. Mark drives his Volvo 760 to a lavish four-room apartment in the prestigious South-East district of Moscow, whereas Oleg has to take the subway to the dark apartment in a rundown building downtown that he shares with four roommates. On the weekends, Mark likes to dine out at the fashionable Savoy restaurant, where dinner costs as much as $200; Oleg often has a few beers at a friend's apartment. Three times a year, Mark goes on vacation to western Europe, the Caribbean, or the United States; once a year, Oleg goes to see his parents in Siberia. Neither his car, his apartment, nor his vacation cost Mark anything—they are part of the "hardship package" he receives as compensation for living in Moscow on top of his regular salary of $6,000 U.S. per month. Oleg does not get any "hardship benefits" since he is a local resident and his salary is $200 per month. Says Oleg:

I like my job and I like the people I work with. I think we have a great organization here in Moscow. Most of our expatriates are very open and knowledgeable. I think we learn a lot from each other and the company benefits from having this multinational team.

My compensation? Well, it's a bit frustrating to know that your buddies, who do the same work you do and who you often help, since many of them don't speak Russian, make 30 times more than you do. This summer we had an intern from an American business school, who worked under me. He used to take me out for lunch to hard currency restaurants and pay as much as my monthly salary for it! He was a nice guy, but I don't think our relations were quite normal because I could not even buy a bottle of wine for that lunch, and he knew it.

But at work I don't think about it. I'm too busy to think like that. Sometimes, late at night, some crazy thoughts come to my mind: 'Gee, something must be wrong—they treat you like a second-class citizen, cheap labor, they exploit you.' . . . But the next morning, I am up for work and those thoughts are gone. How long will my patience last? I don't know.

According to the company's managing director for Russia:

Some of our Russian managers, such as Oleg, are equally, if not better qualified than expatriates. They perfectly understand our business and they are truly bilingual, while most of our expatriates can barely speak Russian. We are very fortunate to have these Russian employees—their contribution is hard to overestimate. Compensation? We pay them what the market tells us here in Moscow. Yes, it is extremely low pay according to Western standards, but why should I pay a manager $5,000 if I can hire him for $200? Are they bothered by the inequity? I don't think so. I haven't heard any complaints so far, and I think we have very good relations among Russians and expatriates.

Mark comments:

Oleg is a great guy. We get along well; he helps me a lot, especially with my Russian. Do I feel sorry for him? No, I think he has a bright future. One day he will manage this subsidiary. As far as money goes, we live in a market economy. I was hired in the United States, and what I get is what the job market pays there. It's different in Russia, so Oleg is being compensated differently. And I think he makes more than Russians working for Russian organizations. Plus, one of the reasons why our company is here is the cheap, skilled labor, and we've got to take advantage of this.

Source: Sheila M. Puffer and Stanislav V. Shekshnia, "Compensating Nationals in Post Communist Russia: The Fit Between Culture and Compensation Systems," paper presented at the Annual Academy of International Business Conference, Boston, November 1994. Used with permission.

[In the new millennium], the caliber of the people will be the only source of competitive advantage . . .

—Allan Halcrow, editor, *Personnel Journal*

This chapter's Opening Profile describes a contemporary problem of salary differentials between expatriates and their counterpart host-country managers. There are many challenges to the human resource management function of any organization, domestic or international. However, given the greater complexity of managing international operations, the need to ensure high-quality management is even more critical than in domestic operations.

A vital component of implementing global strategy is **international human resource management (IHRM)**. IHRM is increasingly being recognized as a major determinant of success or failure in international business. In fact, in a highly competitive global economy, where the other factors of production—capital, technology, raw materials, and information—are increasingly able to be duplicated, "the caliber of the people in an organization will be the only source of sustainable competitive advantage available to U.S. companies."[1] Corporations operating overseas need to pay careful attention to this most critical resource—one that also provides control over other resources. Most U.S. multinationals underestimate the importance of the human resource planning function in the selection, training, acculturation, and evaluation of managers assigned abroad. And yet the increasing significance of this resource is evidenced by the numbers. More than 37,000 MNCs are currently in business worldwide. They control some 200,000 foreign affiliates and have in excess of 73 million employees. In the United States, foreign MNCs employ three million Americans, more than 10 percent of the U.S. manufacturing workforce.[2] However, recent advances in technology are enabling firms to effectively and efficiently manage the IHRM function and maximize the firm's international management cadre, as illustrated in the accompanying Technology Application.

At the first level of planning, decisions are required on the staffing policy suitable for a particular kind of business, its global strategy, and its geographic locations. Key issues involve the difficulty of control in geographically dispersed operations, the need for local decision making independent of the home office, and the suitability of managers from alternative sources.

The interdependence of strategy, structure, and staffing is particularly worth noting. Ideally, the desired strategy of the firm should dictate the organizational structure and staffing

TECHNOLOGY APPLICATION
HRMS Goes Global at British Airways

Companies operating in several countries need to globalize their human resource management systems (HRMSs). Compelling reasons for doing so include the need to get an accurate count of the international workforce, to monitor expatriates, to track and analyze employee benefits, to evaluate compensation models, and to streamline payroll. MNCs also need to access data on knowledge and abilities, make up-to-date information easily accessible to line managers, and study career planning and succession planning models. Creating a global HRMS, however, is not an easy task. The different laws, cultures, business practices, and technological limitations of various countries have to be considered.

Michael P. Corey, head of HR Systems for British Airways, knows how challenging it is to coordinate HR management systems when your company has a presence in 83 countries. Without efficient hardware, software, and HR strategies to back it all up, the corporate data highway can easily resemble a one-lane, unpaved roadway in a developing nation: chaotic, crowded, and swarming with obstacles. But Corey is adamant about implementing a system that provides HR with the tools to truly excel. "In an era of intense competition and pressure, at a time when HR must provide value, it's essential to automate and streamline as much as possible," he explains. With more than 50,000 employees working worldwide, and many of them in a different location every day of the week, it's no simple task.

When HR needs to notify employees of a change in benefits or policy, for example, many of the workers are 40,000 feet above the earth. When it needs to track headcount or update employee records, it has to deal with 24 time zones and dozens of languages and cultures. In addition, systems and technologies that work in one place can come to a grinding halt elsewhere. Yet British Airways' automated system handles recruiting, benefits, headcount, basic record keeping, and an array of other functions—cutting across technology platforms and breaking language barriers. Moreover, the system, dubbed ACHORD (Airline Corporate Human and Organisation Resources Database), links to 35 other systems that require staff data within British Airways. Plans are now under way to link to 40 additional business systems.

When a manager in Kuala Lumpur needs information on terminations or company share schemes, it's accessible within seconds. When an HR specialist in New York requires data on pensions or concessional travel arrangements, it's visible in a flash. With a network of IBM mainframe computers linked to PCs and dumb terminals, data flows seamlessly between offices and across national boundaries. What's more, the worldwide network has almost eliminated duplicate data input, paperwork, disks, and delays in processing work. "It fits into the concept of reengineering and making HR accountable and involved in corporate matters," says Corey. "It provides us with a powerful tool."

Source: Adapted from S. Greengard, "When HRMS Goes Global: Managing the Data Highway," *Personnel Journal* (June 1995) 74, no. 6: 90–91.

modes considered most effective for implementing that strategy. In reality, however, there is usually considerable interdependence among those functions. Existing structural constraints often affect strategic decisions; similarly, staffing constraints or unique sets of competences in management come into play in organizational and sometimes strategic decisions. It is thus important to achieve a system of fits among those variables that facilitates strategic implementation.

Staffing Philosophies for International Operations

We found the most successful formula is to hire people in-country and then bring them to our U.S. headquarters to get acquainted and have them interact with our organization.
—Stuart Mathison, Vice President Strategic Planning, Sprint International

Alternative philosophies of managerial staffing abroad are known as the ethnocentric, polycentric, global, and regiocentric approaches. Firms using an **ethnocentric staffing approach** fill key managerial positions with people from headquarters—that is, **parent-country nationals (PCNs)**. Among the advantages of this approach, PCNs are familiar with company goals, products, technology, policies, and procedures—and they know how to get things accomplished through headquarters. This policy is likely to be used where a company notes the inadequacy of local managerial skills and determines a high need to maintain close communication and coordination with headquarters. It is also the preferred choice when the organization has been structured around a centralized approach to globalization, and occurs primarily at the internationalization stage of strategic expansion.

Frequently, companies use PCNs for the top management positions in the foreign subsidiary—in particular, the chief executive officer (CEO) and the chief financial officer (CFO)—to maintain close control. PCNs are usually preferable where a high level of technical capability is required. They are also chosen for new international ventures requiring managerial experience in the parent company and where there is a concern for loyalty to the company rather than to the host country—in cases, for example, where proprietary technology is used extensively.

Disadvantages of the ethnocentric approach include (1) the lack of opportunities or development for local managers, thereby decreasing their morale and their loyalty to the subsidiary, and (2) the poor adaptation and lack of effectiveness of expatriates in foreign countries. Procter & Gamble, for example, routinely appointed managers from its headquarters for foreign assignments for many years. After several unfortunate experiences in Japan, the firm realized that such a practice was insensitive to local cultures and also underused its worldwide pool of management skill.[3] This approach also serves to perpetuate particular personnel selections and other decision-making processes because the same types of people are making the same types of decisions.

With a **polycentric staffing approach**, local managers—**host-country nationals (HCNs)**—are hired to fill key positions in their own country. This approach is more likely to be effective when implementing a multinational strategy. If a company wants to "act local," there are obvious advantages to staffing with HCNs. These managers are naturally familiar with the local culture, language, and ways of doing business, and they already have many contacts in place. HCNs are more likely to be accepted by people both inside and outside the subsidiary, and they provide role models for other upwardly mobile personnel.

As far as cost, it is usually less expensive for a company to hire a local manager than to transfer one from headquarters, frequently with a family and often at a higher rate of pay. Transferring from headquarters is a particularly expensive policy when it turns out that the manager and her or his family do not adjust well and have to be transferred home prematurely. In fact, rather than building their own facilities, some companies acquire foreign firms as a means of obtaining qualified local personnel. Local managers also tend to be instrumental in staving off or more effectively dealing with problems in sensitive political situations. Some countries, in fact, have legal requirements that a specific proportion of the firm's top managers must be citizens of that country.

One disadvantage of a polycentric staffing policy is the difficulty of coordinating activities and goals between the subsidiary and the parent company, including the potentially conflicting loyalties of the local manager. Poor coordination among subsidiaries of a multinational firm could constrain strategic options. An additional drawback of this policy is that the headquarters managers of multinational firms will not gain the overseas experience necessary for any higher positions in the firm that require the understanding and coordination of subsidiary operations.

In the **global staffing approach**, the best managers are recruited from inside or outside the company, regardless of nationality—a practice used for some time by many European multinationals. Recently, as more major U.S. companies adopt a global strategic approach, they are also considering foreign executives for their top positions. In 1992, General Motors hired J. Ignacio Lopez de Arriortua as vice president for worldwide purchasing, Xerox hired Vittorio Cassoni as executive vice president, and Esprit de Corp hired Fritz Ammann as president.[4]

There are several important advantages of a global staffing approach. First, this policy provides a greater pool of qualified and willing applicants from which to choose, which, in time, results in further development of a global executive cadre. As discussed further in Chapter 11, skills and experiences that those managers use and transfer throughout the company result in a pool of shared learning that is necessary for the company to compete globally. Second, where third-country nationals (TCNs) are used to manage subsidiaries, they usually bring more cultural flexibility and adaptability—as well as bilingual or multilingual skills—to a situation than parent-country nationals, especially if they are from a similar cultural background as the host-country coworkers and are accustomed to moving around. In addition, when TCNs are placed in key positions, they are perceived by employees as an acceptable compromise between headquarters and local managers, and this works to reduce resentment. Third, it can be more cost effective to transfer and pay managers from some countries than from others because their pay scale and benefits packages are lower. Indeed, those firms with a truly global staffing orientation are phasing out the entire ethnocentric concept of a home or host country; as part of that focus, the term **transpatriates** is increasingly replacing that of expatriates.[5] Firms such as Philips, Heinz, Unilever, IBM, and ABB have a global staffing approach, which makes them highly visible and seems to indicate a trend.[6]

Generally, it seems that "the more distant geographically and culturally the subsidiary, the more expatriates are used in key positions, especially in less developed countries."[7] Clearly, this situation arises out of concern about uncertainty and the ability to control implementation of the corporation's goals. However, given the generally accepted consensus that staffing, along with structure and systems must fit the desired strategy,[8] firms desiring a truly global posture should adopt a global staffing approach. That is easier said than done. As shown in Exhibit 10–1, such an approach requires the firm to overcome barriers such as the availability and willingness of high-quality managers to transfer frequently around the world, dual-career constraints, time and cost constraints, conflicting requirements of host governments, and ineffective HRM policies.

In a **regiocentric staffing approach**, recruiting is done on a regional basis, say, within Latin America for a position in Chile. This staffing approach can produce a specific mix of PCNs, HCNs, and TCNs, according to the needs of the company or the product strategy.[9]

EXHIBIT 10-1

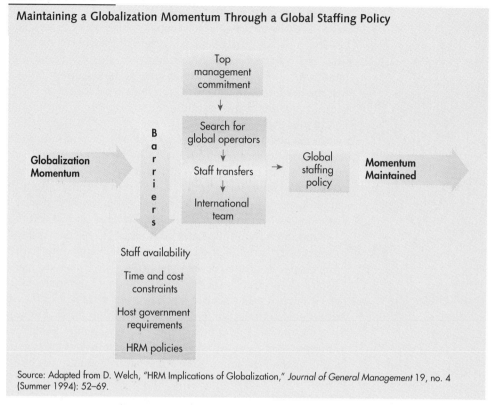

Maintaining a Globalization Momentum Through a Global Staffing Policy

Source: Adapted from D. Welch, "HRM Implications of Globalization," *Journal of General Management* 19, no. 4 (Summer 1994): 52–69.

What factors influence the choice of staffing policy? Among them are the strategy and organizational structure of the firm as well as the factors related to the particular subsidiary (such as the duration of the particular foreign operation, the types of technology used, and the production and marketing techniques necessary). Factors related to the host country also play a part (such as the level of economic and technological development, political stability, regulations regarding ownership and staffing, and the sociocultural setting).[10] As a practical matter, however, the choice often depends on the availability of qualified managers in the host country. Most MNCs use a greater proportion of PCNs (also called **expatriates**) in top management positions, staffing middle and lower management positions with increasing proportions of HCNs as one moves down the organizational hierarchy. The choice of staffing policy has a considerable influence on organizational variables in the subsidiary, such as the locus of decision-making authority, the methods of communication, and the perpetuation of human resource management practices. These variables are illustrated in Exhibit 10–2. The conclusions drawn by researchers some time ago are still valid today. The ethnocentric staffing approach, for example, usually results in a higher level of authority and decision making in headquarters than does the polycentric approach.[11]

EXHIBIT 10-2

Relationships among Strategic Mode, Organizational Variables, and Staffing Orientation

Aspects of the Enterprise	Orientation			
	Ethnocentric	Polycentric	Regiocentric	Global
Primary Strategic Orientation/Stage	International	Multidomestic	Regional	Transnational
Perpetuation (recruiting, staffing, development)	People of home country developed for key positions everywhere in the world	People of local nationality developed for key positions in their own country	Regional people developed for key positions anywhere in the region	Best people everywhere in the world developed for key positions everywhere in the world
Complexity of organization	Complex in home country, simple in subsidiaries	Varied and independent	Highly interdependent on a regional basis	"Global Web": complex, independent, worldwide alliances/network
Authority; decision making	High in headquarters	Relatively low in headquarters	High regional headquarters and/or high collaboration among subsidiaries	Collaboration of headquarters and subsidiaries around the world
Evaluation and control	Home standards applied to people and performance	Determined locally	Determined regionally	Globally integrated
Rewards	High in headquarters; low in subsidiaries	Wide variation; can be high or low rewards for subsidiary performance	Rewards for contribution to regional objectives	Rewards to international and local executives for reaching local and worldwide objectives based on global company goals
Communication; information flow	High volume of orders, commands, advice to subsidiaries	Little to and from headquarters; little among subsidiaries	Little to and from corporate headquarters, but may be high to and from regional headquarters and among countries	Horizontal; network relations
Geographic identification	Nationality of owner	Nationality of host country	Regional company	Truly global company, but identifying with national interests ("glocal")

Source: Updated and adapted by H. Deresky in 1998, from original work by D. A. Heenan and H. V. Perlmutter, *Multinational Organization Development* (Reading, MA: Addison Wesley, 1979): 18–19.

A study by Rochelle Kopp, reported in 1994, found that ethnocentric staffing and policies are associated with a higher incidence of international human resource management problems. Exhibit 10–3A shows the breakdown of staffing among PCNs, HCNs, and TCNs of the 81 Japanese, European, and American companies studied. In addition, Kopp found that Japanese firms scored considerably lower than European and American firms in their practice of implementing policies such as preparing local nationals for advancement and keeping inventory of their managers around the world for development purposes. As a result of these ethnocentric practices, Japanese firms seem to experience various IHRM problems, such as

EXHIBIT 10–3A

Nationality of Top Managers in Overseas Operations

Headquarters Country		% Home-Country Nationals	% Local Nationals	% Third-Country Nationals
Japan	(n = 26)	74%	26%	0.2%
Europe	(n = 21)	48%	44%	8%
U.S.	(n = 20)	31%	49%	18%

Source: R. Kopp, "International Human Resource Policies and Practices in Japanese, European, and United States Multinationals," *Human Resource Management* 33, no. 4 (Winter 1994): 581–599.

high turnover of local employees, more than European and American firms, as shown in Exhibit 10–3B.

Without exception, all phases of human resources management should support the desired strategy of the firm.[12] In the staffing phase, having the right people in the right places at the right times is a key ingredient to success in international operations. An effective managerial cadre can be a distinct competitive advantage for a firm. How the "right" selections are made is the focus of the next section.

EXHIBIT 10–3B

Incidence of International Personnel Problems

Type of Problem	% of Japanese Firms Reporting Problem (n = 34)	% of European Firms Reporting Problem (n = 23)	% of U.S. Firms Reporting Problem (n = 24)
Expatriate-related			
Lack of home-country personnel who have sufficient international management skills	68%	39%	29%
Lack of home-country personnel who want to work abroad	26%	26%	13%
Expatriates experience reentry difficulties (e.g., career disruption) when returning to the home country	24%	39%	42%
Average of expatriate-related problems	39%	35%	28%
Local national staff related			
Difficulty in attracting high-caliber local nationals to work for the firm	44%	26%	21%
High turnover of local employees	32%	9%	4%
Friction and poor communication between home-country expatriates and local employees	32%	9%	13%
Complaints by local employees that they are not able to advance in the company	21%	4%	8%
Local legal challenges to the company's personnel policies	0 (0)	0	8%
Average of local national staff related problems	26%	10%	11%

Source: R. Kopp, "International Human Resource Policies and Practices in Japanese, European, and United States Multinationals," *Human Resource Management* 33, no. 4 (Winter 1994): 581–599.

Global Selection

The initial phase of setting up criteria for global selection, then, is to consider which overall staffing approach or approaches would most likely support the company's strategy—such as HCNs for a localization (multilocal) strategic approach, and transpatriates for globalization. These are typically just starting points using idealized criteria, however; in reality, other factors creep into the process, such as host-country regulations, stage of internationalization, and most often, who is both suitable and available for the position. It is also vital to integrate long-term strategic goals into the selection process and development process, especially when rapid global expansion is intended. Insufficient projection of staffing needs for global assignments will likely result in constrained strategic opportunities because of a shortage of experienced managers suitable to be placed in those positions.

The selection of personnel for overseas assignments is a complex process. The criteria for selection are based on the same success factors as in the domestic setting, but additional criteria must be considered that are related to the specific circumstances of each international position. Unfortunately, many personnel directors have a long-standing, ingrained practice of selecting potential expatriates simply on the basis of their domestic track record and their technical expertise.[13] Too often overlooked is the need to ascertain whether potential expatriates have the necessary cross-cultural awareness and interpersonal skills for the position. It is also important to assess whether the candidate's personal and family situation is such that everyone is likely to adapt to the local culture. There are five categories of success for expatriate managers: job factors, relational dimensions such as cultural empathy and flexibility, motivational state, family situation, and language skills. The relative importance of each factor is highly situational and difficult to establish.[14]

These **expatriate success factors** are based on studies of American expatriates. One could argue that the requisite skills are the same for managers from any country—and particularly so for third-country nationals.

A more flexible approach to maximizing managerial talent, regardless of the source, would certainly be to consider more closely whether the position could be suitably filled by a host-country national, as put forth by Tung, based on her research.[15] This contingency model of selection and training depends on the variables of the particular assignment, such as the length of stay, the similarity with the candidate's own culture, and the level of interaction with local managers in that job. Tung concludes that the more rigorous the selection and training process, the lower the failure rate.

The selection process is set up as a decision tree in which the progression to the next stage of selection or the type of orientation training depends on the assessment of critical factors regarding the job or the candidate at each decision point. The simplest selection process involves choosing a local national since minimal training is necessary regarding the culture or ways of doing business locally. However, to be successful local managers often require additional training regarding the MNC companywide processes, technology, and corporate culture. If the position cannot be filled by a local national, but the job requires a high level of interaction with the local community, there needs to be a very careful screening of candidates from other countries and a vigorous training program.

Most MNCs tend to start out their operations in a particular region by selecting primarily from their own pool of managers. Over time, and with increasing internationalization, they tend to move to a predominantly polycentric or regiocentric policy because of (1) increasing pressure (explicit or implicit) from local governments to hire locals (or sometimes legal restraints on the use of expatriates), and (2) the greater costs of expatriate staffing, particularly when the company has to pay taxes for the parent-company employee in both countries.[16] In addition, in recent years, MNCs have noted an improvement in the level of managerial and technical competence in many countries, negating the chief reason for using a primarily ethnocentric policy in the past. One researcher's comment represents a growing attitude: "All things being equal, a local national who speaks the language, understands the culture and the political system, and is often a member of the local elite should be more effective than an expatriate alien."[17] However, concerns about the need to maintain strategic control over subsidiaries and to develop managers with a global perspective remain a source of debate about staffing policies among human resource management professionals.[18] A globally oriented company such as ABB, for example, has 500 roving transpatriates who are moved every two to three years, thus developing a considerable management cadre with global experience.

For MNCs based in Europe and Asia, human resource policies at all levels of the organization are greatly influenced by the home-country culture and policies. For Japanese subsidiaries in Singapore, Malaysia, and India, for example, promotion from within and expectations of long-term loyalty to and by the firm are culture-based practices transferable to subsidiaries.[19] At Matsushita, however, selection criteria for staffing seem to be similar to those of Western companies. Its candidates are selected on the basis of a set of characteristics the firm calls SMILE: specialty (required skill, knowledge); management ability (particularly motivational ability); international flexibility (adaptability); language facility; and endeavor (perseverance in the face of difficulty).[20]

Problems with Expatriation

Deciding on a staffing policy and selecting suitable managers are logical first steps but do not alone ensure success. When staffing overseas assignments with expatriates, for example, many other reasons besides poor selection can contribute to **expatriate failure** among U.S. multinationals. A large percentage of these failures can be attributed to poor preparation and planning for the entry and reentry transitions of the manager and his or her family. One important variable, for example, often given insufficient attention in the selection, preparation, and support phases, is the suitability and adjustment of the spouse. The inability of the spouse to adjust to the new environment has been found to be a major—in fact, the most frequently cited—reason for expatriate failure in U.S. and European companies.[21] Yet only about half of those companies studied had included the spouse in the interviewing process. In addition, although research shows that human relational skills are critical for overseas work (a fact acknowledged by the companies in a study by Tung), most of the U.S. firms surveyed failed to include this factor in their assessment of candidates.[22, 23] The following is a synthesis of the factors frequently mentioned by researchers and firms as the major causes of expatriate failure:

- Selection based on headquarters criteria rather than assignment needs
- Inadequate preparation, training, and orientation prior to assignment

- Alienation or lack of support from headquarters
- Inability to adapt to local culture and working environment
- Problems with spouse and children—poor adaptation, family unhappiness
- Insufficient compensation and financial support
- Poor programs for career support and repatriation

After careful selection based on the specific assignment and the long-term plans, both of the organization and the candidates, plans must be made for the preparation, training, and development of expatriate managers.

Training and Development

Some 81 percent of companies [around the world] said in 1998 that they expect to send an increasing number of people overseas through 2000. That means more folks confounded by foreign cultures and customs. What's key? Preparation.

—Business Week Online

It is clear that preparation and training for cross-cultural interactions is critical. In earlier discussions of the need for cultural sensitivity by expatriate managers, we noted that reports indicate that up to 40 percent of expatriate managers end their foreign assignments early because of poor performance or an inability to adjust to the local environment.[24] Moreover, about half of those who do remain function at a low level of effectiveness. The direct cost alone of a failed expatriate assignment is estimated to be from $50,000 to $150,000. The indirect costs may be far greater, depending on the position held by the expatriate. Relations with the host-country government and customers may be damaged, resulting in a loss of market share and a poor reception for future PCNs.

Both cross-cultural adjustment problems and practical differences in everyday living present challenges for expatriates and their families. Examples are evident from a 1998 survey of expatriates when they ranked the countries that presented the most challenging assignments to them, along with some pet peeves from their experiences:

China: Adjustment is a continuing problem for expatriates; one complained that at his welcome banquet he was served duck tongue and pigeon head.

Brazil: Expatriates stress that cell phones are essential because home phones don't work.

India: Returning executives complain that the pervasiveness of poverty and street children is overwhelming.

Indonesia: Here you need to plan ahead financially because landlords typically demand rent two to three years in advance.

Japan: Expatriates and their families remain concerned that although there is excellent medical care, Japanese doctors reveal little to their patients.

After these five countries, expatriates rank Russia, Mexico, Saudi Arabia, South Korea, and France also challenging.[25]

Even though cross-cultural training has proved to be effective, less than a third of expatriates are given such training. In a 1997 study by Harvey of 332 U.S. expatriates (dual-career couples), the respondents stated that their MNCs had not provided them with sufficient training or social support during the international assignment.[26] Much of the rationale for this lack of training is an assumption that managerial skills and processes are universal. In a simplistic way, a manager's domestic track record is used as the major selection criterion for an overseas assignment.

In most countries, however, the success of the expatriate is not left so much to chance. Non-U.S. companies provide considerably more training and preparation for expatriates than American companies. Therefore, it is not hard to understand why Japanese expatriates experience significantly fewer incidences of failure than their American counterparts although this may be partially attributable to the lower incidence of families accompanying Japanese assignees. Japanese multinationals typically have recall rates of below 5 percent, signifying that they send abroad managers who are far better prepared and more adept at working and flourishing in a foreign environment.[27] Although this success is largely attributable to training programs, it is also a result of intelligent planning by the human resource management staff in most Japanese organizations, as reported in a study by Tung.[28] This planning begins with a careful selection process for overseas assignments, based on the long-term knowledge of executives and their families. An effective selection process, of course, will eliminate many potential "failures" from the start. Another factor is the longer duration of overseas assignments, averaging almost five years, which allows the Japanese expatriate more time to adjust initially and then to function at capacity. In addition, Japanese expatriates receive considerable support from headquarters and sometimes even from local divisions set up for that purpose. At NEC Corporation, for example, part of the Japanese giant's globalization strategy is its permanent boot camp, with its elaborate training exercises to prepare NEC managers and their families for overseas battle.[29]

The demands on expatriate managers have always been as much a result of the multiple relationships that they have to maintain as they are of the differences in the host-country environment. Those relations include family relations; internal relations with people in the corporation, both locally and globally, especially with headquarters; external relations (suppliers, distributors, allies, customers, local community, and so on); and relations with the host government. It is important to pinpoint any potential problems that an expatriate may experience with those relationships so that these problems may be addressed during predeparture training. Problem recognition is the first stage in the comprehensive plan for developing expatriates shown in Exhibit 10–4. The three areas critical to preparation are cultural training, language instruction, and familiarity with everyday matters.[30] In the model shown in Exhibit 10–4, various development methods are used to address these areas during predeparture training, postarrival training, and reentry training. These methods continue to be valid and used by many organizations. Two-way feedback between the executive and the trainers at each stage helps tailor the level and kinds of training to the individual manager. The desired goal is the increased effectiveness of the expatriate as a result of familiarity with local conditions, cultural awareness, and an appreciation of his or her family's needs in the host country.

Cross-Cultural Training

Although training in language and practical affairs is quite straightforward, cross-cultural training is not; it is complex and deals with deep-rooted behaviors. The actual process of

EXHIBIT 10–4

A Model for Developing Key Expatriate Executives

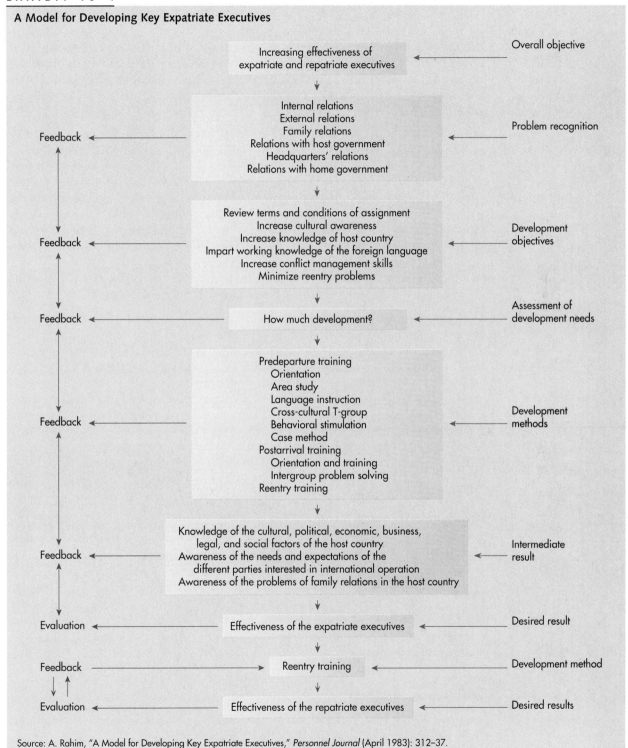

Source: A. Rahim, "A Model for Developing Key Expatriate Executives," *Personnel Journal* (April 1983): 312–37.

cross-cultural training should result in the expatriate learning both content and skills that will improve interactions with host-country individuals by reducing misunderstandings and inappropriate behaviors. Black and Mendenhall suggest that trainers should apply social learning theory to this process by using the behavioral science techniques of incentives and rehearsal until the trainee internalizes the desired behaviors and reproduces them.[31] The result is a state of adjustment, representing the ability to effectively interact with host nationals.[32]

Culture Shock   The goal of this training is to ease the adjustment to the new environment by reducing **culture shock**, a state of disorientation and anxiety about not knowing how to behave in an unfamiliar culture. The cause of culture shock is the trauma people experience in new and different cultures, where they lose the familiar signs and cues that they had used to interact in daily life and where they must learn to cope with a vast array of new cultural cues and expectations.[33] The symptoms of culture shock range from mild irritation to a deep-seated psychological panic or crisis. The inability to work effectively, stress within the family, and hostility toward host nationals are the common dysfunctional results of culture shock—often leading to the manager giving up and going home.

It is helpful to recognize the stages of culture shock to understand what is happening. Culture shock usually progresses through four stages, as described by Oberg:

1. *honeymoon,* when positive attitudes and expectations, excitement, and a tourist feeling prevail (which may last up to several weeks);
2. *irritation and hostility,* the crisis stage when cultural differences result in problems at work, at home, and in daily living. Expatriates and family members feel homesick and disoriented, lashing out at everyone (many never get past this stage);
3. *gradual adjustment,* a period of recovery in which the "patient" gradually becomes able to understand and predict patterns of behavior, use the language, and deal with daily activities, and the family members start to accept their new life; and
4. *biculturalism,* the stage in which the manager and family members grow to accept and appreciate local people and practices, and are able to function effectively in two cultures.[34]

Many never get to the fourth stage—operating acceptably at the third stage—but those who do report that their assignment is positive and growth oriented.

Subculture Shock   Similar to culture shock, though usually less extreme, is the experience of subculture shock. This occurs when a manager is transferred to another part of the country where there are cultural differences—essentially from what she or he perceives to be a "majority" culture to a "minority" one. The shock comes from feeling like an "immigrant" in one's own country and being unprepared for such differences. For instance, someone going from New York to Texas will experience considerable differences in attitudes and lifestyle between those two states. Even moving from one area of Texas—where there are roaming ranches and high technology—to another—where there are Bible-belt attitudes and laws—may unsettle many people.[35]

Training Techniques

Many training techniques are available to assist overseas assignees in the adjustment process. These techniques are classified by Tung as (1) area studies, that is, documentary programs about the country's geography, economics, sociopolitical history, and so forth; (2) culture assimilators, which expose trainees to the kinds of situations they are likely to encounter that are critical to successful interactions; (3) language training; (4) sensitivity training; and (5) field experiences—exposure to people from other cultures within the trainee's own country.[36] Tung recommends using these training methods in a complementary fashion: The trainee has increasing levels of personal involvement as he or she progresses through each method. Documentary and interpersonal approaches have been found comparable, with the most effective intercultural training occurring when trainees become aware of the differences between their own culture and the one they are planning to enter.[37]

Similarly categorizing training methods, Ronen suggests specific techniques, including a field experience called the host-family surrogate, where the MNC pays for and places an expatriate family with a host family as part of an immersion and familiarization program.[38] Exhibit 10–5 shows this and other training methods, some examples of the techniques used for each method, and the purpose of each.

Most training programs take place in the expatriate's own country prior to leaving. Though this is certainly a convenience, the impact of host-country (or in-country) programs can be far greater than those conducted at home because crucial skills, such as overcoming cultural differences in intercultural relationships, can actually be experienced during in-country training rather than simply discussed.[39] In fact, some MNCs are beginning to recognize that there is no substitute for on-the-job training (OJT) in the early stages of the careers of those managers they hope to develop into senior-level global managers. Colgate-Palmolive—whose overseas sales represent two-thirds of its $6 billion in yearly revenue—is one company whose management development programs adhere to this philosophy. After training at headquarters, Colgate employees become associate product managers in the

EXHIBIT 10–5

Training Techniques for Expatriate Preparation

Method	Technique	Purpose
Didactic Informational Training	■ Lectures ■ Reading material ■ Videotapes ■ Movies	Area studies, company operation, parent-country institutions
Intercultural Experiential Workshops	■ Cultural assimilators ■ Simulations ■ Role playing	Culture-general, culture-specific negotiation skills; reduce ethnocentrism
Sensitivity training	■ Communication workshops ■ T groups ■ Outward Bound trips	Self-awareness, communication style, empathy, listening skills, nonjudgmentalism
Field experiences	■ Meeting with ex-PCNs ■ Minicultures ■ Host-family surrogate	Customs, values, beliefs, nonverbal behavior, religion
Language skills	■ Classes ■ Cassettes	Interpersonal communication, job requirements, survival necessities

Source: S. Ronen, "Training the International Assignee," in *Training and Career Development*, ed. I. Goldstein (San Francisco: Jossey-Bass, 1989): 438. Used by permission.

EXHIBIT 10–6

> **Corporate Programs to Develop Global Managers**
>
> - ABB (Asea Brown Boveri) rotates about 500 managers around the world to different countries every two or three years in order to develop a management cadre of transpatriates to support their global strategy.
> - PepsiCo Inc. has an orientation program for its foreign managers by bringing them to the United States for one-year assignments in bottling division plants.
> - Honda of America Manufacturing Inc. gives its U.S. supervisors and managers extensive preparation in Japanese language, culture, and lifestyle, and then sends them to Tokyo for up to three years to the parent company.
> - General Electric likes its engineers and managers to have a global perspective whether or not they are slated to go abroad. The company gives language and cross-cultural training to them so that they are equipped to conduct business with people around the world.[40a]

United States or abroad, and according to John R. Garrison, Manager of Recruitment and Development at Colgate, they must earn their stripes by being prepared to country-hop every few years. In fact, says Garrison, "That's the definition of a global manager: one who has seen several environments firsthand."[40] Exhibit 10–6 shows some other global management development programs for junior employees.

Integrating Training with Global Orientation

In continuing our discussion on strategic fit, it is important to remember that training programs, like staffing approaches, be designed with the company's strategy in mind. Although it is probably impractical to break those programs down into a lot of variations, it is feasible to at least consider the relative level or stage of globalization that the firm has reached because obvious major differences would be appropriate, for example, from the initial export stage to the full global stage. Exhibit 10–7 suggests four stages of rigor and types of training content appropriate for the firm's managers, as well as those for host-country nationals: export, multidomestic, multinational, and global. It is noteworthy, for example, that the training for host-country nationals for a global firm has a considerably higher level of scope and rigor than for the other stages, and borders on the standards for the firm's expatriates.

Training Host-Country Nationals

The continuous training and development of HCNs and TCNs for management positions is also important to the long-term success of multinational corporations. As part of a long-term staffing policy for a subsidiary, the ongoing development of HCNs will facilitate the transition to an indigenization policy. Furthermore, multinational companies like to have well-trained managers with broad international experience available to take charge in many intercultural settings, whether at home or abroad. Such managerial skills are increasingly needed in U.S.–Japanese joint ventures, a good example being G.M.-Toyota in Freemont, California. There, managers as well as employees from both America and Japan learn to work side by side and adjust to a unique blend of country and corporate culture. For the Americans in this

EXHIBIT 10-7

Stage of Globalization and Training Design Issues	
Export Stage	**MNC Stage**
Degree of Rigor: Low to moderate	*Degree of Rigor:* High moderate to high
Content: Emphasis should be on interpersonal skills, local culture, customer values, and business behavior.	*Content:* Emphasis should be on interpersonal skills, two-way technology transfer, corporate value transfer, international strategy, stress management, local culture, and business practices.
Host-Country Nationals: Low to moderate training of host nationals to understand parent country products and policies.	*Host-Country Nationals:* Moderate to high training of host nationals in technical areas, product and service systems, and corporate culture.
MDC Stage	**Global Stage**
Degree of Rigor: Moderate to high	*Degree of Rigor:* High
Content: Emphasis should be on interpersonal skills, local culture, technology transfer, stress management, and business practices and laws.	*Content:* Emphasis should be on global corporate operations and systems, corporate culture transfer, customers, global competitors, and international strategy.
Host-Country Nationals: Low to moderate training of host nationals; primarily focusing on production and service procedures.	*Host-Country Nationals:* High training of host nationals in global organization production and efficiency systems, corporate culture, business systems, and global conduct policies.

Source: J. S. Black, Mark E. Mendenhall, Hal B. Gregersen, and Linda K. Stroh, *Globalizing People Through International Assignments* (Reading, MA: Addison Wesley Longman, 1999).

organization, helping to acculturate the Japanese employees not only demonstrates friendly good will but is a necessary part of securing their own future in the company.

In another common scenario also requiring the management of a mixture of executives and employees, American and European MNCs presently employ Asians as well as Arab locals in their plants and offices in Saudi Arabia, bringing together three cultures: well-educated Asian managers living in a Middle Eastern, highly traditional society and employed by a firm reflecting Western technology and culture. This kind of situation involves the integration of multiple sets of culturally based values, expectations, and work habits.

What are the careers and lifestyles like for modern managers and entrepreneurs in their own countries? Two contrasting career profiles—of Josep Castaner in Olot, Spain, and Liu Jing of Beijing, China—are highlighted in the accompanying Management Focus "Careers in Spain and China."

Expatriate Compensation

The significance of an appropriate compensation and benefit package to attract, retain, and motivate international employees cannot be overemphasized. Compensation is a crucial link

MANAGEMENT FOCUS

Careers in Spain and China

Josep Castaner, Olot, Spain: A Spaniard Seeks Success Amid Siestas

Josep Castaner, a 29-year-old M.B.A., works as a sales manager for a small plastics company in his home town, earning about $53,000 a year and managing a staff of two. He and his wife recently bought a small house and a four-wheel-drive Mitsubishi that they drive into the snow-capped Pyrenees on weekends. He enjoys five weeks of vacation a year and has lunch at his parents' house before taking a quick nap.

In the office, though, Mr. Castaner worries that Europe's Old-World comforts may be stifling his future. While his counterparts in other countries are riding to riches on the computer wave, Mr. Castaner is idling in Europe's technology backwater. His company just installed e-mail last month. Other traditions also die hard: He has to punch a time clock, wear a suit, and listen to weekly lectures from a commanding boss. He has never been offered an ownership stake. While he dreams of launching his own business, finding financing or startup expertise in Spain is next to impossible. "Sometimes I feel like a very qualified secretary," he sighs; "this is not why I got my MBA."

All over the world, young people like Josep are trying to create their own dream. But he and others in Europe find themselves torn. Though reluctant to give up the relaxed traditions of the past, they are increasingly worried that they are falling behind the competition of tomorrow. Even those eager to move into the fast lane find the path blocked by forces resistant to change.

The economy is partly to blame. Europe's 10 percent unemployment is twice as high as America's, and in poorer countries like Spain, joblessness has hit 20 percent. The fabled welfare states in the region force companies to pay heavy costs for layoffs, making them more reluctant to hire new, younger employees.

Tradition is an even bigger barrier. European managers still follow the "escalator" model of career advancement, where employees start at the bottom of a company at an early age and slowly move up the ranks over 20 or 30 years, regardless of results. In Europe, workers who jump from job to job are blackballed as "unstable." In the United States, they are "ambitious." Josep has had frustrating experiences with the "escalator" attitude in previous jobs. Now he is conflicted when weighing the allure of Yankee capitalism against the security of old customs. Like many Europeans, he works close to home, where he was born and where his parents and sisters still live. He bemoans Europe's welfare state but is baffled by America's "hire and fire" policies. Money isn't a career goal. He never works weekends. His career dream, he says, is to help build a company that can last for centuries. He also wants to own a farm.

As the sun sets behind the jagged Pyrenees, Mr. Castaner picks up his wife, Isabel, who works as an economist for a local government, and heads to his parents' house for dinner. A rack of sausage crackles over an open fire as his mother lays out freshly baked bread and wine. Catalan landscape paintings and Catholic icons line the walls.

Liu Jing, Beijing: Startup Capitalist Takes Lonely Road in China

The walls of Liu Jing's design firm—Moli Graphic Design Studios—are dotted with Apple computer logos and the boldly colored brochures he creates for a living. His business card reads "James Lowe." But outside this carefully constructed, 20-square-meter patch of America, Mr. Lowe becomes Liu Jing, back in the China he never left. Printers hand him shoddy work, mumbling excuses about the Chinese climate wearing down their machinery. Middlemen from huge state companies hit him up for bribes. Guards sometimes make it difficult for him to get into his own office, located in a building owned by the state

(Continued)

film production company. At 26 years old, Mr. Liu moves between these two worlds, a loner in each. But he likes that just fine. "I know exactly what I want," he says. "Before I felt alone, but now I'm too busy to think about it." In China, he is a radical, one of a tiny band of young entrepreneurs who are striking out on their own. But Mr. Liu embodies China's best hope to lift the country out of the morass of central planning. The government is counting on the nascent private sector to soak up the tens of millions of state workers being laid off because of economic reforms.

Doing business in China requires Mr. Liu to do no end of creative deal making. Stopping by the office of a U.S. telecommunications company, he offers them some ad hoc computer consulting, a service he provides as a sideline to his design business. In return, the company sells him surplus computer hardware at cut-rate prices. Being resourceful isn't a bonus—it is the best edge Mr. Liu has. He picked up his now-fluent English the same way, on the fly, after some American exchange students visited his high school. "I figured English was a good thing to learn," he says.

Mr. Liu started college intending to be an engineer—an honored but hidebound path in China—but the outside world proved too distracting. He interned at a magazine company started by American expatriates, called *Beijing Scene*. For his first year, he worked for no pay and camped out in a sleeping bag on the office floor. He learned to use Quark, the desktop-publishing software, and he downed sushi and draft beer with his American colleagues. He also learned to speak up the American way, twice threatening to quit and getting a hefty raise in return, he says.

As he embarked on the capitalist path, he lost touch with Chinese friends who took jobs at state companies. The gap widened still further two years later when Mr. Liu left his job to start his computer design firm with his American roommate and a Chinese friend from college. The three spent their savings and borrowed $412,000 from their parents to set up Moli, which means "magic" in Chinese. They even took the unusual step of going legal, applying for a company license, which is proudly displayed in a silver frame on their office wall.

Now a year old, Moli has paid off a third of its debt and counts multinationals, such as Siemens AG of Germany and Sony Corp. of Japan, among its clients. Even in dealing with these established corporations, Mr. Liu puts the minute details of the design contract in writing. Although he acknowledges that enforcing a contract would be difficult in a Chinese court, he believes the document limits the chance that a deal will go bad.

It is precisely Mr. Liu's willingness to brave the perils of business that distinguishes him from most of his countrymen. None of his college friends, for example, wanted to take part in his startup venture. Still, even Mr. Liu can be nostalgic for the days when success could be defined by something other than profits. "When we were little," he says, "it was 'what do you want to do with your life? Do you want to be a scientist?' Maybe it was stupid. But it seemed like there was a higher goal."

But don't get him wrong. Mr. Liu knows how lucky he is to be young in China today. "I've seen the old, and I've seen the new," he says. "I was born in the right era."

Source: Adapted and excerpted from Leslie Chang, "Start-up Capitalist Takes Lonely Road in China," *Wall Street Journal*, June 17, 1998; and Robert Frank, "Catalan Dream: A Spaniard Seeks Success Amid Siestas," *Wall Street Journal*, June 16, 1998.

between strategy and its successful implementation: There must be a fit between compensation and the goals for which the firm wants managers to aim.[41] So that they will not feel exploited, MNC employees need to perceive equity and good will in their compensation and benefits, whether they are PCNs, HCNs, or TCNs. The complexity of providing suitable compensation packages is illustrated in this chapter's Opening Profile. The premature return of expatriates or the unwillingness of managers to take overseas assignments can often be traced to their knowledge that the assignment is detrimental to them financially and usually to their career progression.

From the firm's perspective, the high cost of maintaining appropriate compensation packages for expatriates has led many companies—Colgate-Palmolive, Chase Manhattan Bank, General Motors, and General Electric among them—to cut back on PCN assignments as much as possible. "Transfer a $100,000-a-year American executive to London—and suddenly he [or she] costs the employer $300,000," explains the *Wall Street Journal*. "Move him to Stockholm or Tokyo, and he [or she] easily becomes a million-dollar [manager]."[42]

Designing and maintaining an appropriate compensation package is more complex than it would seem because of the need to consider and reconcile parent- and host-country financial, legal, and customary practices. The difficulty is illustrated in Exhibit 10–8, which shows that although around the world there may be little variation in typical executive salaries at the level of base compensation, there is often a wide variation in net spendable income. American executives may receive more in cash and stock, but they have to spend more for things that foreign companies provide, such as cars, vacations, and entertainment allowances. Examples are shown in the comparison of pay, perks, and expenses for an executive stationed in Frankfurt, Tokyo, and New York. In addition, the manager's purchasing power with that net income is affected by the relative cost of living. The cost of living is considerably higher in most of western Europe than in the United States. In designing compensation and benefit packages for PCNs, then, the challenge to IHRM professionals is to maintain a standard of living for expatriates equivalent to their colleagues at home plus compensating them for any additional costs incurred. This policy is referred to as "keeping the expatriate whole."[43]

To ensure that expatriates do not lose out through their overseas assignment, the **balance sheet approach** is often used to equalize the standard of living between the host country and the home country, and to add some compensation for inconvenience or qualitative loss.[44] This approach is illustrated in Exhibit 10–9. However, there is a recent trend with some companies to base their compensation package on a goal of achieving a standard of living comparable to host-country managers, which does help resolve some of the problems of pay differential illustrated in the Opening Profile. In fact, all eyes are on the new DaimlerChrysler company in Germany, in particular the corporate boards in that country that are wondering how the salary disparity between the two CEOs—Jürgen Schrempp and Robert Eaton—will be resolved. The two CEOs will cochair the new company for three years; then Schrempp will take over. At the time of the merger, Daimler supervisory board chairman Hilmar Kopper said that the company was not planning to match Robert Eaton's 1997 compensation of $10.9 million, which is more than eight times Schrempp's. (CEO compensation in the United States is typically far higher than in other countries.) On the other hand, some "Americanization" seems to be in store for the 1,600 upper-level managers, who will be put under a performance-related pay scale. Though base pay will be lower than Germans usually get, there will be other parts of the package such as stock options and other U.S. imports.[45]

EXHIBIT 10-8

Compensation Score Card

Pay, perks and expenses for a typical vice president of human resources at companies in Frankfurt, Tokyo, and New York.
Note: Currency conversions based on 1992 exchange rates.

	Germany	Japan	U.S.
Base compensation	$105,996	$96,640	$104,100
Fixed bonus	0	7,434	0
Variable bonus	12,720	22,302	18,300
Long-term incentives	0	0	13,950
Total cash compensation	118,716	126,376	136,350
Compulsory benefit contributions	9,346	6,282	5,216
Voluntary benefit contributions	10,297	23,045	18,009
Perquisites	7,268	29,734	0
Total noncash compensation	26,911	59,061	23,225
Total income	145,627	185,437	159,575
Income taxes	34,383	27,015	37,567
Social Security or equivalent	8,377	6,178	5,216
College expenses	7,268	22,302	20,000
Private retirement savings	3,331	3,717	15,000
Housing	46,156	26,018	30,000
Car	3,392	7,434	4,000
Private medical and dependent care	2,271	1,487	3,500
Total expenses	105,178	94,151	115,283
Net spendable income	$ 40,449	$ 91,286	$ 44,292

Perquisites

Perquisites consist of the following in the three countries:

Germany: Reimbursed car expenses: $6,662; annual physical exam: $606.

Japan: Company car and expenses: $14,867; club membership: $5,203; entertainment allowance: $5,947; housing loans: $1,487; business gift allowance: $2,230.

U.S.: None.

Private Retirement Savings

The relatively higher benefits paid out from the combined social security and private pension systems in Germany and Japan mean that less money need be saved for retirement in those countries.

Housing

Here are some typical housing arrangements in the three countries:

Germany: Located in suburbs of Frankfurt/Wiesbaden, single-family home of 1,800 square feet on one-sixth of an acre. Purchase price of $500,000, with a $300,000 mortgage at 8.5% over ten years.

Japan: Small two-story house in western Tokyo (one-hour commute). Living space of 1,500 square feet. Purchase price of $450,000, but current market value of twice that; 20-year mortgage at 6.8% interest.

U.S.: Two-story single-family home of 3,000 square feet, with four or five bedrooms, on an acre, probably in Westchester or Fairfield counties. Purchase price of $350,000; 30-year mortgage at 10% interest.

Car

Costs are based on the following models:

Germany: Mercedes 190E with a purchase price of $21,000 (not including value-added tax).

Japan: Toyota Mark II (two years old) with a purchase price of $18,700.

U.S.: Acura Legend with a purchase price of $25,000.

Private Medical

The comprehensive medical systems in Germany and Japan mean less is required of individual employees. However, the German executive usually splits the contributions for supplemental coverage with the employer.

Source: A. Bennett, "Managers' Incomes Aren't Worlds Apart," *Wall Street Journal*, October 12, 1992.

EXHIBIT 10-9

The Balance Sheet Approach to International Compensation

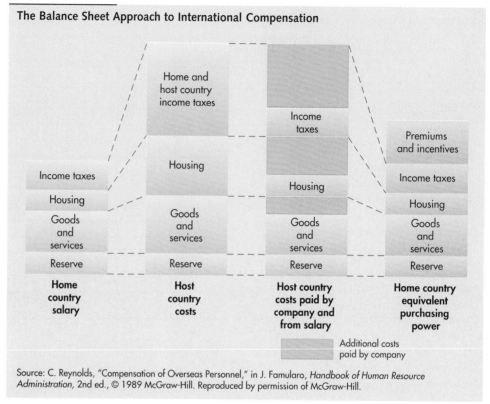

Source: C. Reynolds, "Compensation of Overseas Personnel," in J. Famularo, *Handbook of Human Resource Administration*, 2nd ed., © 1989 McGraw-Hill. Reproduced by permission of McGraw-Hill.

In fairness, the MNC is obliged to make up additional costs the expatriate would incur for taxes, housing, and goods and services. The tax differential is complex and expensive for the company, and generally MNCs use a policy of tax equalization: The company pays any taxes due on any type of additional compensation that the expatriate receives for the assignment; the expatriate pays in taxes only what he or she would be paying at home. The burden of foreign taxes can be lessened, however, by efficient tax planning—a fact often overlooked by small firms. The timing and methods of paying people determine what foreign taxes are incurred; for example, a company can save on taxes by renting an apartment for the employee instead of providing a cash housing allowance.[46] All in all, MNCs have to weigh the many aspects of a complete compensation package, especially at high management levels, to effect a tax equalization policy.

Managing PCN compensation is a complex challenge for companies with overseas operations. Exhibit 10–10 shows the categories that must be considered. All components of the compensation package must be considered in light of both home- and host-country legalities and practices. Most important, to be strategically competitive, the compensation package must be comparatively attractive to the kinds of managers the company wishes to hire or relocate. Some of those managers will, of course, be local managers in the host country. This, too, is a complex situation requiring competitive compensation policies in order to attract,

EXHIBIT 10–10

Components of an Expatriate Compensation Package

Salary
- Home rate/home currency
- Local rate/local currency
- Salary adjustments or promotions—home or local standard
- Bonus—home or local currency, home or local standard
- Stock options
- Inducement payment/hardship premium—percentage of salary or lump sum payment, home/local currency
- Currency protection—discretion or split basis
- Global salary and performance structures

Taxation
- Tax protection
- Tax equalization
- Other services

Benefits
- Home-country program
- Local program
- Social Security program

Allowances
- Cost-of-living allowances
- Housing standard
- Education
- Relocation
- Perquisites
- Home leave
- Shipping and storage

Source: P. J. Dowling and R. S. Schuler, *International Dimensions of Human Resource Management* (Boston: PWS-Kent, 1990).

motivate, and retain the best local managerial talent. In many countries, however, it is a considerable challenge to develop compensation packages appropriate to the local situation and culture while also recognizing the differences between local salaries and those expected by expatriates or transpatriates (that difference itself often being a source of competitive advantage).

COMPARATIVE MANAGEMENT IN FOCUS

Compensation in Russia

How do firms deal with the kinds of situations posed by Mark and Oleg in the Opening Profile? There are many complicating factors involved in compensating Russian nationals: the ongoing transition to a market economy; the past practices and resultant expectations of Russians from their background of employment and compensation in state-owned enterprises; the cultural norms and work behaviors resulting from their social system. Puffer and Shekshnia recommend tailoring compensation packages to the Russian culture and the prevailing economic and market situation. They examined compensation surveys conducted by Otis Elevator Company and the U.S. Embassy in 1992 and 1993. They found that compensation trends of Western firms to Russian nationals typically included three components: a base salary, incentive pay, and a variety of nonmonetary fringe benefits. Puffer and Shekshnia felt that these three components satisfied the prevailing Russian situation and the Russian culture—which they conclude, using Hofstede's categories, to be that of high power distance, high uncertainty avoidance, high collectivism, high femininity, and high short-term orientation. For example, some hard currency and some nonmonetary fringe benefits allow Russian employees to have things that are otherwise simply not available to them because of inflation or nonavailability—in other words, to combat the uncertainty avoidance of the value of basic compensation.[47] However, based on their research and experiences in Russia, Puffer and Shekshnia recommend that Western firms need to design compensation packages that will meet their business objectives as well as reward Russians equitably and appropriately. To achieve this, they give the following recommendations, designed to "reinforce those aspects of Russian culture that help achieve corporate objectives, while reducing the influence of other cultural dimensions that could undermine objectives":[48]

1. Select Russian employees who are achievement oriented and willing to take risks (that is, those who do not fit the cultural profile of the majority of Russian workers).
2. Tie individual bonuses to initiative and personal accountability (to encourage individual goal setting).
3. Organize social events and other group activities.
4. Provide small-group incentives (to encourage team achievement with Western managers).
5. Provide a mix of short- and long-term incentives (to transition to a focus on long-term corporate objectives).
6. Tailor the compensation package to individual preferences (to enjoy choices they have not had before).

Conclusion

The effectiveness of managers at foreign locations is crucial to the success of the firm's operations, particularly because of the lack of proximity to, and control by, headquarters executives. The ability of those expatriates to initiate and maintain cooperative relationships with local people and agencies will determine the long-term success, even viability, of the operation. In a real sense, a company's international cadre represents its most valuable resource. Proactive management of that resource by headquarters will result in having the right people in the right place at the right time, appropriately trained, prepared, and supported. MNCs using these IHRM practices can anticipate the effective management of the foreign operation, the fostering of expatriates' careers, and, ultimately, the enhanced success of the corporation. In the next chapter, we will examine how to fully utilize global human resources.

Summary of Key Points

1. Human resource management is a vital component of implementing global strategy and is increasingly being recognized as a major determinant of success or failure in international business.
2. The main staffing alternatives for international operations are the ethnocentric, polycentric, regiocentric, and global approaches. Each approach has its appropriate uses, according to its advantages and disadvantages.
3. The causes of expatriate failure include the following: poor selection based on inappropriate criteria, inadequate preparation before assignment, alienation from headquarters, inability of manager or family to adapt to local environment, inadequate compensation package, and poor programs for career support and repatriation.
4. The three major areas critical to expatriate preparation are cultural training, language instruction, and familiarity with everyday matters.
5. Common training techniques for potential expatriates include area studies, culture assimilators, language training, sensitivity training, and field experiences.
6. Appropriate and attractive compensation packages must be designed by IHRM staffs to sustain a competitive international management cadre. Compensation packages for host-country managers must be designed to fit the local culture and situation as well as the firm's objectives.

Discussion Questions

1. What are the major alternative staffing approaches for international operations? Explain the relative advantages of each and the conditions under which you would choose one approach over another.
2. Why is the HRM role so much more complex, and important, in the international context?
3. Explain the common causes of expatriate failure. What are the major success factors for expatriates? Explain the role and importance of each.
4. What are the common training techniques for managers going overseas? How should these vary as appropriate to the stage of globalization of the firm?
5. Explain the balance sheet approach to international compensation packages. Why is this approach so important? Discuss the pros and cons of aligning the expatriate compensation package with the host-country colleagues compared to the home country colleagues.

Application Exercises

1. Make a list of the reasons you would want to accept a foreign assignment and a list of reasons you would want to reject it. Do your reasons depend on the location? Compare your list with a classmate's and discuss your reasons.
2. Research a company with operations in several countries and ascertain the staffing policy used for those countries. Try to find out what kinds of training and preparation are provided for expatriates, and what kinds of results the company is experiencing with expatriate training.

Experiential Exercise

This can be done in groups or individually. After the exercise, discuss your proposals with the rest of the class.

You are the expatriate general manager of a British company's subsidiary in Brazil, an automobile component parts manufacturer. You and your family have been in Brazil for seven years, and now you are being reassigned and replaced with another expatriate, Ian Fleming. Ian is bringing his family: Helen, an instructor in computer science, who hopes to find a position; a son, aged 12; and a daughter, aged 14. None of them has lived abroad before. Ian has asked you what he and his family should expect in the new assignment. Remembering all the problems you and your family experienced in the first couple of years of your assignment in Brazil, you want to facilitate their adjustment and have decided to do two things:

1. Write a letter to Ian, telling him what to expect—both on the job and in the community. Tell him about some of the cross-cultural conflicts he may run into with his coworkers and employees, and how he should handle them.
2. Set up some arrangements and support systems for the family and design a support package for them, with a letter to each family member telling him or her what to expect.

Internet Resources

Visit the Deresky companion Web site at http://prenhall.com/Deresky for this chapter's Internet resources.

Case Study

Fred Bailey in Japan: An Innocent Abroad

Fred gazed out the window of his 24th-floor office at the tranquil beauty of the Imperial Palace amid the hustle and bustle of downtown Tokyo. It had been only six months since Fred Bailey had arrived with his wife and two children for this three-year assignment as the director of Kline & Associates' Tokyo office. Kline & Associates was a large multinational consulting firm with offices in 19 countries worldwide. Fred was now trying to decide whether he should simply pack up and tell the home office that he was coming home or whether he should try to somehow convince his wife and himself that they should stay and finish the assignment. Given how excited they all were about the assignment to begin with, it was a mystery to Fred how things had gotten to this point. As he watched the swans glide across the water in the moat that surrounds the Imperial Palace, Fred reflected on the past seven months.

Seven months ago, Dave Steiner, the managing partner of the main office in Boston, asked Fred to lunch to discuss business. To Fred's surprise, the business they discussed was not about the major project that he and his team had just finished; instead, it was about a very big promotion and career move. Fred was offered the position of managing director of the firm's relatively new Tokyo office, which had a staff of 40, including 7 Americans. Most of the Americans in the Tokyo office were either associate consultants or research analysts. Fred would be in charge of the whole office and would report to a senior partner. Steiner implied to Fred that if this assignment went as well as his past projects, it would be the last step before becoming a partner in the firm.

When Fred told his wife about the unbelievable opportunity, he was shocked at her less than enthusiastic response. His wife Jennifer (or Jenny as Fred called her) thought that it would be rather difficult to have the children live and go to school in a foreign country for three years, especially when Christine, the oldest, would be starting middle school next year. Besides, now that the kids were in school, Jenny was thinking about going back to work, at least part time. Jenny had a degree in fashion merchandising from a well-known private university and had worked as an assistant buyer for a large women's clothing store before having the two girls.

Fred explained that the career opportunity was just too good to pass up and that the company's overseas package would make living overseas terrific. The company would pay all the expenses to move whatever the Baileys wanted to take with them. The company had a very nice house in an expensive district of Tokyo that would be provided rent free, and the company would rent their house in Boston during their absence. Moreover, the firm would provide a car and driver, education expenses for the children to attend private schools, and a cost-of-living adjustment and overseas compensation that would nearly triple Fred's gross annual salary. After two days of consideration and discussion, Fred told Steiner he would accept the assignment.

The current Tokyo office managing director was a partner in the firm but had been in the new Tokyo office for less than a year when he was transferred to head up a long-established office in

England. Because the transfer to England was taking place right away, Fred and his family had about three weeks to prepare for the move. Between transferring things at the office to Bob Newcome, who was being promoted to Fred's position, and getting furniture and the like ready to be moved, neither Fred nor his family had much time to really find out much about Japan, other than what was in the encyclopedia.

When the Baileys arrived in Japan, they were greeted at the airport by one of the young Japanese associate consultants and the senior American expatriate. Fred and his family were quite tired from the long trip, and the two-hour ride to Tokyo was a rather quiet one. After a few days of just settling in, Fred spent his first full day at the office.

Fred's first order of business was to have a general meeting with all the employees of associate consultant rank and higher. Although Fred didn't notice it at the time, all the Japanese staff sat together and all the Americans sat together. After Fred introduced himself and his general idea about the potential and future directions of the Tokyo office, he called on a few individuals to get their ideas about how the things for which they were responsible would likely fit into his overall plan. From the Americans, Fred got a mixture of opinions with specific reasons about why certain things might or might not fit well. From the Japanese, he got very vague answers. When Fred pushed to get more specific information, he was surprised to find that a couple of the Japanese simply made a sucking sound as they breathed and said that it was "difficult to say." Fred sensed the meeting was not achieving his objectives, so he thanked everyone for coming and said he looked forward to their all working together to make the Tokyo office the fastest-growing office in the company.

After they had been in Japan about a month, Fred's wife complained to him about the difficulty she had getting certain everyday products like maple syrup, peanut butter, and good-quality beef. She said that when she could get it at one of the specialty stores it cost three and four times what it would cost in the States. She also complained that since the washer and dryer were much too small, she had to spend extra money by sending things out to be dry cleaned. On top of all that, unless she went to the American Club in downtown Tokyo, she never had anyone to talk to. After all, Fred was gone 10 to 16 hours a day. Unfortunately, while Jenny talked, Fred was preoccupied, thinking about a big upcoming meeting between his firm and a significant prospective client, a top-100 Japanese multinational company.

The next day, Fred, along with the lead American consultant for the potential contract, Ralph Webster, and one of the Japanese associate consultants, Kenichi Kurokawa, who spoke perfect English, met with a team from the Japanese firm. The Japanese team consisted of four members: the vice president of administration, the director of international personnel, and two staff specialists. After shaking hands and a few awkward bows, Fred said that he knew the Japanese gentlemen were busy and he didn't want to waste their time so he would get right to the point. Fred then had the other American lay out their firm's proposal for the project and what the project would cost. After the presentation, Fred asked the Japanese what their reaction to the proposal was. The Japanese did not respond immediately, so Fred launched into his summary version of the proposal thinking that the translation might have been insufficient. But again the Japanese had only the vaguest of responses to his direct questions.

The recollection of the frustration of that meeting was enough to shake Fred back to reality. The reality was that in the five months since that first meeting little progress had been made and the contract between the firms was yet to be signed. "I can never seem to get a direct response from Japanese," he thought to himself. This feeling of frustration led him to remember a related incident that happened about a month after this first meeting with this client.

Fred had decided that the reason not much progress was being made with the client was that he and his group just didn't know enough about the client to package the proposal in a way that was appealing to the client. Consequently, he called in the senior American associated with the proposal, Ralph Webster, and asked him to develop a report on the client so that the proposal could be reevaluated and changed where necessary. Jointly, they decided that one of the more promising Japanese research associates, Tashiro Watanabe, would be the best person to take the lead on this report. To impress upon Tashiro the importance of this task and the great potential they saw in him, they decided to have the young Japanese associate meet with both Fred and Ralph. In the meeting, Fred and Ralph laid out the nature and importance of the task, at which point Fred leaned forward in his chair and said to Tashiro, "You can see that this is an important assignment and that we are placing a lot of confidence in you by giving it to you. We need the report by this time next week so that we can revise and represent our proposal. Can you do it?" After a somewhat pregnant pause, Tashiro responded hesitantly, "I'm not sure what to say." At that point, Fred smiled, got up from his chair and walked over to the young Japanese associate, extended his hand, and said, "Hey, there's nothing to say. We're just giving you the opportunity you deserve."

The day before the report was due, Fred asked Ralph how the report was coming. Ralph said that since he had heard nothing from Tashiro he assumed that everything was under control, but that he would double-check. Ralph later ran into one of the American research associates, John Maynard. Ralph knew that John was hired for Japan because of his language ability in Japanese and that, unlike any of the other Americans, John often went out after work with some of the Japanese research associates, including Tashiro. So, Ralph asked John if he knew how Tashiro was coming on the report. John then recounted that last night at the office Tashiro had asked if Americans sometimes fired employees for being late with reports. John had sensed that this was more than a hypothetical question and asked Tashiro why he wanted to know. Tashiro did not respond immediately, and since it was 8:30 in the evening, John suggested they go out for a drink. At first Tashiro resisted, but then John assured him that they would grab a drink at a nearby bar and come right back. At the bar, John got Tashiro to open up.

Tashiro explained the nature of the report that he had been requested to produce. He continued to explain that even though he had worked long into the night every night to complete the report it was just impossible and that he had doubted from the beginning whether he could complete the report in a week.

At this point, Ralph asked John, "Why didn't he say something in the first place?" Ralph didn't wait to hear whether or not John had an answer to his question. He headed straight to Tashiro's desk.

Ralph chewed Tashiro out and then went to Fred explaining that the report would not be ready and that Tashiro, from the start, didn't think it could be. "Then why didn't he say something?" Fred asked. No one had any answers, and the whole thing just left everyone more suspect and uncomfortable with one another.

There were other incidents, big and small, that had made the last two months especially frustrating, but Fred was too tired to remember them all. To Fred it seemed that working with Japanese both inside and outside the firm was like working with people from another planet. Fred felt he just couldn't communicate with them, and he could never figure out what they were thinking. It drove him crazy.

Then on top of all this, Jennifer laid a bombshell on him. She wanted to go home, and yesterday was not soon enough. Even though the kids seemed to be doing all right, Jennifer was tired of Japan—tired of being stared at, of not understanding anybody or being understood, of not being able to find what she wanted at the store, of not being able to drive and read the road signs, of not having anything to watch on television, of not being involved in anything. She wanted to go home and could not think of any reason why they shouldn't. After all, she reasoned, they owed nothing to the company because the company had led them to believe this was just another assignment, like the two years they spent in San Francisco, and it was anything but that!

Fred looked out the window once more, wishing that somehow everything could be fixed, or turned back, or something. Down below the traffic was backed up. Though the traffic lights changed, the cars and trucks didn't seem to be moving. Fortunately, beneath the ground, one of the world's most advanced, efficient, and clean subway systems moved hundreds of thousands of people about the city and to their homes.

Source: J. Stewart Black, in *International Human Resource Management,* eds. M. Mendenhall and Gary Oddou (Boston: PWS-Kent, 1991).

Case Questions

1. You are Fred. What should you do now?
2. Turn back the clock to when Fred was offered the position in Tokyo. What, if anything, should have been done differently, and by whom?

11

Expatriation and Labor Relations in Global HRM

OUTLINE

Opening Profile: Labor Laws for the EC: Ground Rules for the Firing Squad

Maintaining Global Human Resources

Developing a Global Management Cadre

Preparation, Adaptation, and Repatriation

The Role of the Expatriate Spouse

Expatriate Career Management

The Role of Repatriation in Developing a Global Management Cadre

The Role of Women in International Management

Technology Application: Booz-Allen & Hamilton Uses Intranet Technology to Share Knowledge Around the Globe

Applying Title VII Abroad

Minority Groups in Overseas Assignments

Management Focus: Women in Foreign Postings

Sexual Harassment in Overseas Assignments

Working Within Local Labor Relations Systems

Organized Labor Around the World

Convergence Versus Divergence in Labor Systems

The NAFTA and Labor Relations in Mexico

Comparative Management in Focus: Labor Relations in Germany

Labor Participation in Management

Cultural Influences on Labor–Management Practices

Summary of Key Points

Discussion Questions

Application Exercises

Experiential Exercise

Internet Resources

Case Study: Mexican Workers Turn up the Heat at Honeywell

OPENING PROFILE

Labor Laws for the EC: Ground Rules for the Firing Squad

Recent large-scale layoffs have highlighted the ways European countries protect workers. *Financial Times* writers explain the variations.

The French government's reaction to the decision by Hoover to shift some of its production from France to Scotland was to proclaim a further tightening of the rules governing redundancies and plant closures. This was an understandable response from a government facing a national election, but it is not necessarily in the long-term interests of French workers and appears to be running against the European tide.

David Rees, investment location expert at Ernst & Young, says that multinational companies, especially American ones, are starting to add ease of "exit," or at least rationalization, to the list of priorities when making investment location decisions. Within the European Community, that should favor the United Kingdom, Ireland, and Denmark, the three most laissez-faire countries when it comes to closures and sackings. It will count against the southern European economies—Portugal, Spain, Italy, and Greece—which are restrictive and costly, probably one reason why the EC's poorer outer rim has not attracted more investment.

There are many other factors in an investment location decision besides ease of exit, and Rees says it is still only an influence "at the margin." Nevertheless, with the barrier-free single market encouraging companies to concentrate production on one site, as opposed to scattering it around the EC's national markets, such advantages could become increasingly important.

Nevertheless, the debate about whether the UK is winning a legitimate competitive advantage or is undercutting workers' rights across the EC through "social dumping" looks likely to intensify.

Opponents of the UK can take heart from the fact that its advantages are likely to be limited to certain sectors. Most analysts believe the UK will have a competitive advantage in semiskilled manufacturing, if it is not undercut by eastern Europe, but the continuing weakness of its education system will cause it to lose out in higher skill or R&D-based investment.

In the longer run, the current restructuring of the welfare state is likely to shift more cost onto employers and thus undermine the UK's advantage of low nonwage labor costs. Even in the short term, the UK is likely to lose more jobs than it gains from multinational restructuring within Europe precisely because of the ease with which workers can be dismissed.

Hoover decided to move to Scotland even though shedding jobs in France is considerably more costly and complex, a measure of the cost advantage from much lower UK nonwage labor costs.

The French government seems convinced that, at least at this stage in the economic cycle, "locking in" jobs through raising the cost of closure is the most suitable response to multinational restructuring. The new French redundancy law returns the situation to something close to the time prior to 1986 when official approval was still required for large-scale redundancies.

The new law requires official approval of the "social plan" for workers who are losing their jobs. France thus rejoins that large group of EC countries—including Spain, Portugal, Greece, Italy, the Netherlands, and Germany—that give government or workers an effective veto over redundancies, a veto that can be circumvented only with time and money.

There are, however, indications that several countries, most notably Italy and Spain, are starting to recognize that the sky-high cost of dismissal is a disincentive both to international capital and to domestic restructuring. This trend is still weak but will gather momentum when EC growth picks up.

The trend might be strengthened by the introduction of common EC rules on large redundancies that could provide political cover for countries like Spain.

A spate of Hoover-type, beggar-my-neighbor, rows over jobs and investment is just what EC officials have for years been fearing. The Social Charter and its latest manifestation, the Social Chapter, were, in part, meant to soften the process of industrial restructuring within the EC. But as they, quite properly, do not address the question of relative labor costs, they have had no impact on companies like Hoover.

The one EC-wide redundancy rule already in operation requires worker representatives to be given 90 days' notice and proper consultation over larger redundancies. After Hoover, there is also a move to breathe life back into the idea of European works councils—forums for companies operating in more than one EC country where employee representatives must be informed of major corporate plans.

European union leaders say that such councils would have prevented Hoover playing the workers in two different countries off each other.

It is debatable whether a works council would have made much difference in the Hoover case. But it is certain that if compulsory works councils are introduced under the Social Chapter—from which the United Kingdom has opted-out—many U.S. multinationals will be horrified and will be even more likely to concentrate their EC investment in the United Kingdom.

Source: David Goodhart, *Financial Times* (London), February 15, 1993, 8. Reprinted with permission.

If you have to close a plant in Italy, in France, in Spain or in Germany, you have to discuss the possibility with the state, the local communities, the trade unions; everybody feels entitled to intervene . . . even the Church!

—Jacopo Vittorelli, former Deputy Chairman of Pirelli

As illustrated in the Opening Profile and in the preceding quote, the complexity of labor laws around the world presents a considerable challenge for the international manager. Making strategic decisions based partly on labor relations systems around the world, and operating effectively within those local systems, is but one of the many challenges in maintaining global human resources facing managers today.

Maintaining Global Human Resources

A crucial factor in global competitiveness is the ability of the firm to maximize long term its global human resources. To do this, three goals must be attended to:

1. To maximize long-term retention and use of international cadre through career management so that the company can develop a top management team with global experience
2. To understand, value, and promote the role of women and minorities in international management in order to maximize those underutilized resources
3. To work effectively within local labor relations systems

This chapter will address these goals and examine the complexities involved. In the long run, these concerns are interdependent.

Developing a Global Management Cadre

Preparation, Adaptation, and Repatriation

We began to realize that the entire effectiveness of the assignment could be compromised by ignoring the spouse.

—Steve Ford, Corporate Relocations, Hewlett-Packard[1]

Effective human resource management of a company's international cadre does not end with the overseas assignment. It ends with the successful repatriation of the executive into company headquarters. In fact, long-term, proactive management of critical resources should begin with the end of the current assignment in mind—that is, it should begin with plans for the repatriation of the executive as part of his or her career path. The management of the reentry phase of the career cycle is as vital as the management of the cross-cultural entry and training; otherwise, the long-term benefits of that executive's international experience may be negated.[2] Shortsightedly, many companies do little to minimize the potential effects of **reverse culture shock** (return shock). In fact, a survey of companies belonging to the American Society of Personnel Administration International (ASPAI) revealed that only 31 percent had formal repatriation programs for executives, and only 35 percent of those included spouses. In addition, only 22 percent of those had conducted the programs prior to the executive's departure for the assignment.[3] Those American companies without programs had various explanations: a lack of expertise in repatriation training, the cost of the programs, or a lack of a perceived need for such training.

The long-term implications of ineffective repatriation practices are clear—few good managers will be willing to take international assignments because they will see what happened to their colleagues. If a certain manager lost out on promotion opportunities while overseas and is now in fact worse off than before he or she left, the only people willing to take on foreign assignments in the future will be those who have not been able to succeed on the home front or those who think that a stint abroad will be like a vacation. In fact, research has shown that, in many U.S. multinational companies, overseas assignments are commonly seen by employees as negative career moves.[4] However, such moves are seen as positive in most European, Japanese, and Australian companies because they consider international experience necessary for advancement to top management.

In a recent study of dual-career couples, "the perceived impact of the international assignment upon returning to the U.S." was one of the most important issues stated by managers regarding their willingness to relocate overseas.[5]

Reverse culture shock occurs primarily because of the difficulty of reintegration into the organization but also because, generally speaking, the longer a person is away, the more difficult it is to get back into the swing of things. Not only might the manager have been overlooked and lost in the shuffle of a reorganization, but her or his whole family might have lost social contacts or jobs and feel out of step with their contemporaries. These feelings of alienation from what has always been perceived as "home"—because of the loss of contact with family, friends, and daily life—delay the resocialization process. Such a reaction is particularly serious if the family's overall financial situation has been hurt by the assignment and if the spouse's career has also been kept "on hold" while he or she was abroad.

For companies to maximize the long-term use of their international cadre, they need to make sure that the foreign assignment and the reintegration process are positive experiences. This means careful career planning, support while overseas, and the use of the increased experience and skills of returned managers to benefit the home office. Research into the practices of successful U.S., European, Japanese, and Australian MNCs indicates the use of one or more of the following support systems, as recommended by Tung, for a successful repatriation program:

- A mentor program to monitor the expatriate's career path while abroad and upon repatriation
- As an alternative to the mentor program, the establishment of a special organizational unit for the purposes of career planning and continuing guidance for the expatriate
- A system of supplying information and maintaining contacts with the expatriate so that he or she may continue to feel a part of the home organization[6]

The Role of the Expatriate Spouse

Many companies are beginning to recognize the importance of providing support for spouses and children—in particular, because both spouses are often corporate fast trackers and demand that both sets of needs be included on the bargaining table. Firms often use informal means, such as intercompany networking, to help find the accompanying ("trailing") spouse a position in the same location. They know that, with the increasing number of dual-career couples (65 percent in the United States), if the spouse does not find a position, the manager will very likely turn down the assignment. They decline because they can't afford to lose the income, or they worry that it may derail the spouse's career entirely if he or she is out of the workforce for a few years. Indeed, as women continue to move up the corporate ladder, the trailing spouse is often male—estimated at 25 percent in the year 2000.[7] Companies such as Hewlett-Packard, Shell, Medtronic, and Monsanto offer a variety of options to address the dual-career dilemma.

At Procter & Gamble, employees and spouses destined for China are sent to Beijing for two months of language training and cultural familiarization. Nissho Iwai, a Japanese trading company, gets together managers and spouses who are leaving Japan with foreign managers and spouses who are on their way there. In addition, the firm provides a year of language training and information and services for Japanese children to attend schools abroad.[8] Recent research on 321 American expatriate spouses around the world shows that effective cross-cultural adjustment by spouses is more likely (1) when firms seek the spouse's opinion about the international assignment and the expected standard of living, and (2) when the spouse initiates his or her own predeparture training (thereby supplementing the minimal training given by most firms).[9]

Expatriate Career Management

Support services provide timely help for the manager and therefore are part of the effective management of an overseas assignment. The overall transition process experienced by the company's international management cadre over time is shown in Exhibit 11–1. It comprises

EXHIBIT 11–1

The Expatriate Transition Process

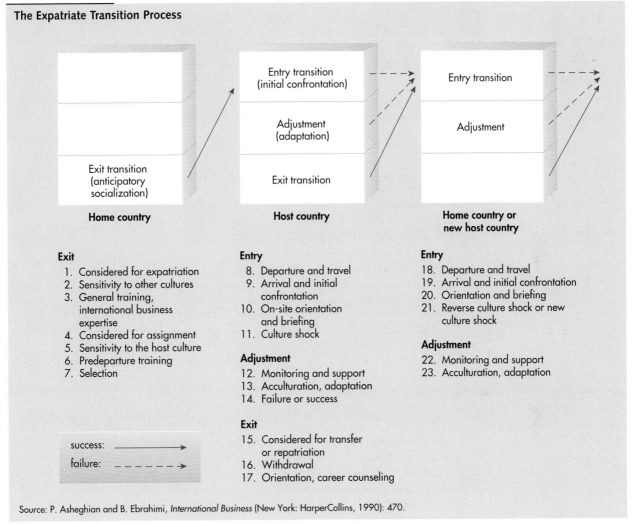

Exit
1. Considered for expatriation
2. Sensitivity to other cultures
3. General training, international business expertise
4. Considered for assignment
5. Sensitivity to the host culture
6. Predeparture training
7. Selection

Entry
8. Departure and travel
9. Arrival and initial confrontation
10. On-site orientation and briefing
11. Culture shock

Adjustment
12. Monitoring and support
13. Acculturation, adaptation
14. Failure or success

Exit
15. Considered for transfer or repatriation
16. Withdrawal
17. Orientation, career counseling

Entry
18. Departure and travel
19. Arrival and initial confrontation
20. Orientation and briefing
21. Reverse culture shock or new culture shock

Adjustment
22. Monitoring and support
23. Acculturation, adaptation

Source: P. Asheghian and B. Ebrahimi, *International Business* (New York: HarperCollins, 1990): 470.

three phases of transition and adjustment that must be managed for successful socialization to a new culture and resocialization back to the old culture. These phases are (1) the exit transition from the home country, the success of which will be determined largely by the quality of preparation the expatriate has received; (2) the entry transition to the host country, in which successful acculturation (or early exit) will depend largely on monitoring and support; and (3) the entry transition back to the home country or to a new host country, in which the level of reverse culture shock and the ease of reacculturation will depend on previous stages of preparation and support.[10] Although we discussed these broad issues earlier, this model offers an interesting overview of the interdependency and the timing of the three transitions.

EXHIBIT 11-2

Skills Learned Abroad

Managerial Skills, Not Technical Skills

Working abroad makes you more knowledgeable about the questions to ask, not the answers.

I learned how to work in two cultures . . . to compromise, not to be a dictator. It's very similar to two domestic cultures . . . like marketing and engineering.

I'm more open-minded . . . more able to deal with a wider range of people . . . because I ran into many other points of view.

Tolerance for Ambiguity

Because I only understood a fraction of what was really going on overseas, maybe 50 percent, I had to make decisions on a fraction of the necessary information. Now I can tolerate nonclosure and ambiguity better.

Things you never thought you'd put up with, you learn to put up with . . . I always thought I was right, until I went overseas.

Multiple Perspective

I learned what it feels like to be a foreigner . . . I could see things from their perspective.

I learned to anticipate . . . it's the role of a diplomat.

Ability to Work with and Manage Others

I increased my tolerance for other people. For the first time, I was the underdog, the minority.

I became a soft-headed screamer. I'm definitely better with others now.

I used to be more ruthless than I am now . . . I was the all-American manager. Now, I stop and realize the human impact more. I use others as resources. I do more communicating with others in the organization.

Source: N. J. Adler, *International Dimensions of Organizational Behavior*, 3rd ed. (Boston: PWS-Kent, 1997).

The Role of Repatriation in Developing a Global Management Cadre

One purpose of the international assignment is that both the manager and the company benefit from the enhanced skills and the experience gained by the expatriate. Many returning executives report an improvement in their managerial skills and self-confidence. Some of these acquired skills, as reported by Adler, are shown in Exhibit 11–2.

In addition to the managerial and cross-cultural skills acquired by expatriates, the company benefits from the knowledge and experience those managers gain about how to do business overseas, and what new technology, local marketing, and competitive information they acquire. At least, the company should benefit from the enhanced management knowledge if it wants to develop a globally oriented and experienced management cadre—an essential ingredient for global competitiveness—in particular where there is a high degree of shared learning among the organization's global managers. If the company cannot retain good returning managers, then their potential shared knowledge is not only lost, but is also conveyed to other organizations that hire these managers, which can be detrimental to the competitive stance of the company. Some companies are becoming quite savvy about how to use technology to utilize shared knowledge to develop their global management cadre, to better service their customers, and—as a side benefit—to store the knowledge and expertise of their managers around the world in case they leave the company; that knowledge, it can be argued, is an asset in which the company has invested large amounts of resources. One such savvy company is Booz-Allen & Hamilton, which instituted a Knowledge On-Line Intranet, as featured in the accompanying Technology Application, on the next page.

In order to gain strategic competitive advantage from its investment in expatriates, any company needs to ensure an effective repatriation process so as to retain the returning managers and utilize their skills in building a core competence for the firm. Unfortunately, this is often not the case because, as discussed before, those companies are negligent or inexperienced in managing the assignment and the repatriation process. Many expatriates leave their companies shortly after their return because they are not put into a position to utilize and acknowledge their contributions, or because they are not incorporated back into the firm's culture, thus experiencing return shock. This makes them seek employment elsewhere, where they will be "appreciated." This scenario has a negative cumulative effect on the firm's management because other managers conclude that an overseas assignment is a death knell on their careers, making it difficult for the firm to convince good managers to take those assignments.

A successful repatriation program, then, starts before the assignment. The company top management must set up a culture that conveys that the organization regards international assignments as an integral part of continuing career development and advancement, and that it values the skills of the returnees. The company's objectives should be reflected in its long-range plans, commitment, and compensation on behalf of the expatriate. GE sets a model for effective expatriate career management. With its 500 expatriates worldwide, it takes care to select only the best managers for overseas jobs and then commits to placing them in specific positions upon reentry.[11] In fact, a study of the IHRM policies of British multinationals indicates that careful planning for foreign assignments pays off. Farsighted policies, along with selection criteria based more on the adaptability of the manager and his or her family to the culture than on technical skills, apparently account for the low expatriate failure rate—estimated at less than 5 percent.[12]

The Role of Women in International Management

Around the world, women are remaking companies, society, and themselves. But in each country, women have achieved different things, fought different battles—and made different sacrifices.[13]

Opportunities for female indigenous employees to move up the managerial ladder in a given culture depend on the values and the expectations regarding the role of women in that society. In Japan, for example, the workplace has traditionally been a male domain as far as managerial careers are concerned (although rapid changes are now taking place). To the older generation, a working married woman represented a loss of face to the husband because it implied that he was not able to support her. Women were usually allowed only clerical positions, under the assumption that they would leave to raise a family and perhaps later return to part-time work. Employers thus made little effort to train them for upper-level positions.[14] As a result, very few women workers have been in supervisory or managerial posts—thus limiting the short-term upward mobility of women through the managerial ranks.[15]

The younger generation and increased global competitiveness have brought some changes to traditional values regarding women's roles in Japan. More than 60 percent of Japanese women are now employed, including half of Japanese mothers.[16] But how and when

TECHNOLOGY APPLICATION
Booz-Allen & Hamilton Uses Intranet Technology to Share Knowledge Around the Globe

Since 1914, senior executives of world-class organizations in both the public and private sectors have selected Booz-Allen & Hamilton to carry out their management and technology consulting assignments. Booz-Allen recently solved a problem for itself that it is often called upon to solve for its clients: how to bridge islands of information that are isolated due to geographical constraints, computing platforms, and different applications.

After eliminating groupware, document management, and homegrown systems as possible solutions, Booz-Allen decided on intranet technology. For its Knowledge On-Line (KOL) intranet, the firm chose Netscape Enterprise Server and Netscape News Server to support a variety of intranet applications, including:

- A database-driven expert skills directory
- A firmwide knowledge repository able to retrieve information in multiple data types
- Employee directories
- Newsgroups that facilitate global project collaboration

Using a series of benchmarks to evaluate intranet solutions vendors, Booz-Allen determined Netscape software to be the best solution. Netscape met the firm's requirements for:

- Industry-leading Web-based server software
- Outstanding performance, reliability, security, and pricing
- Interoperability, application portability, scalability, and systems network management

Booz-Allen has achieved a tremendous return on investment from its intranet, according to an International Data Corporation study.

Booz-Allen & Hamilton relies on its Knowledge On-Line intranet to enhance knowledge sharing among its employees worldwide and to improve client service. By using its intranet to link islands of information separated by geography and platform-specific applications, the renowned consulting firm has enabled its 2,000 private-sector consultants to collect and share firmwide their best thinking and expertise.

Collecting and Sharing Knowledge in Multiple Data Types

One of the most valued applications supported by KOL is a knowledge repository whereby Booz-Allen can capture, classify, and quantify the firm's knowledge and expertise. The idea behind the knowledge repository is to package knowledge within context. Consultants can do a quick search for best practices, frameworks, business intelligence, competitive data, comparative analysis, business tools, and techniques to help them solve client problems as well as locate the leading experts on a topic.

Cyberspace Collaboration

Booz-Allen uses the secure Netscape News Server to let global teams of consultants discuss a variety of company- and noncompany-related topics via message threading and real-time discussion groups.

Consultants all over the world take great advantage of the communicative and collaborative capabilities inherent to KOL. Using the news readers built into Netscape Navigator, consultants can engage in either private or public discourse within Booz-Allen. For more general communication across the entire firm, KOL provides public discussion folders accessible to all users.

Source: Excerpted from Netscape.com case studies.

these cultural changes will affect the number of Japanese women in managerial positions remains to be seen.

The level of discrimination against women in managerial positions has intensified as a result of Japan's recent economic slump. According to a study by Recruit Research Co., 1995 female college graduates are only half as likely to find jobs as males.[17] In fact, Japan's equal employment opportunity law is ineffective because there is no penalty for its violation. One survey of female college students in Tokyo indicated the rampant incidents of rejection and harassment in job interviews because of their gender—such as complaints about legs being too fat or questions about virginity.[18] As a result of the continuing glass ceiling for female managerial opportunities in Japan's male-oriented culture, many women are leaving Japan to advance their careers and enjoy a more enlightened atmosphere in other Asian countries and in Europe and North America. Hong Kong, in particular, has seen a recent increase of more than 25 percent of Japanese women seeking jobs—women such as Michiyo Kozakai, a 28-year-old sales executive at the Hong Kong branch of a Japanese company—a position she feels would have been impossible to attain in Japan. "Japanese women can come here and be themselves," says Yuko Nakanishi, a 29-year-old investment analyst at Ichiyoshi International (H.K.) Ltd. in Hong Kong, who has no plans to return to Japan.[19]

Another traditional norm that still holds women back is the drinking sessions that Japanese managers hold after work, during which a great deal of networking and decision making is done. Most Japanese women are excluded from these sessions because both men and women are uncomfortable with the presence of women in bars. This tradition keeps women out of the information and decision-making loop.

In France, 25.9 percent of managerial positions are held by women.[20] This high rate is undoubtedly supported by the low birthrate (1.8 children) and the daycare system. The French system of subsidized crèches (daycare centers) is synchronized with work hours, and can include a garderie (babysitting service) after hours. In addition, paid maternity leave of from 16 to 18 weeks, with reemployment, is guaranteed by law.[21]

In Germany, the reconciliation of different systems and expectations of women's roles and support in the workplace between the east and the west will take some time to sort out. Women of the former East Germany had as their birthright the right to work and the right to childcare—94 percent of women with children remained in the labor force—but these privileges are being swept away in the transition to a reunited Germany.[22]

In Hong Kong—outwardly a contemporary, westernized society—the ethnic Chinese maintain a strong cultural identity, with a central focus on the family. De Leon and Ho attribute the core value of familism as the critical factor determining the level of success of women's managerial careers in Hong Kong.[23] Although about 20 percent of managers and administrators are women, husbands—and society—expect that the woman's primary commitment and responsibility is to her home and family. In fact, there is no legislation against gender discrimination, considered to be widespread, which deters women's mobility between firms and their opportunities for moving up the managerial ladder.[24] Although success means wealth to the typical Hong Kong Chinese, the cultural ideology of familism inhibits the chances for women to attain positions of power. A woman's work role, rather, is seen as an extension of her female role for the purpose of benefiting the family or community. Now that Hong Kong has returned to Chinese rule, the future of women's role in management is uncertain.[25]

In Singapore, both rapid development and government policy have facilitated the rise of women into about a quarter of all managerial positions, with about 12 percent in the top echelon of wage earner.[26] But in much of the world—for example, in India and Iran—women's choices are restricted to traditional roles involving children, the home, and support activities.

Exhibit 11–3 shows some comparisons of relative levels of employment of women and men in various occupations in selected countries. The lowest levels of female representation in managerial positions of those countries represented are in Pakistan, Israel, and Chile; Japan has a large number of females in professional and technical positions, but few in administrative and managerial positions.

Where women find limitations on managerial opportunities in their own countries, there are obviously even more limitations on their opportunities as expatriates. Overall, more managerial opportunities are available for American women than for women in most other countries. But even for American women, who now fill more than 25 percent of the managerial positions at home, commensurate opportunities are not available to them abroad: About 6 percent of North American expatriate managers are women.[27] The reasons for this anomaly can often be traced to the cultural expectations of the host countries—the same cultural values that keep women in these countries from the managerial ranks. The Management Focus "Women in Foreign Postings" gives some insight into the situation facing American women and minorities aspiring to foreign assignments.

Applying Title VII Abroad

Legally and morally, corporations must make sure they do not exclude women and minorities when staffing overseas positions.[28]

The situation facing U.S. corporations is often a dilemma between responsibility toward their female executives and anticipating problems in the host country due to cultural biases. As international experience becomes critical for promotion into higher-level management positions, those opportunities may be limited to women and minorities if they are denied critical overseas assignments. With the extension of Title VII protection for U.S. citizens working for U.S. companies overseas (except where there is a conflict with foreign law), corporations are placed in a difficult position in countries where cultural perceptions of women's roles result in staffing conflicts.[29] The situation in Nairobi, Kenya, where 97 U.S. companies like GM, Ford, Exxon, Union Carbide, and Xerox have branch offices, is described by Ferraro in his training book as follows:

> That women in Nairobi are generally viewed more negatively than men has important implications for hiring practices and overall team building within the organization. The American multinational corporation is faced with a Hobson's choice in this respect, for accommodation to traditional African views of women will invariably lead to sex discrimination, whereas a policy that aims at treating the sexes with relative equality is likely to lead to personnel problems and a reduction in organizational efficiency.[30]

Minority Groups in Overseas Assignments

An explanation for the lack of expatriates who are female or represent other minority groups does not include their lack of desire to take overseas assignments; studies indicate their

EXHIBIT 11–3

Male–Female Employment by Occupation for Selected Countries

Country	Total		Prof. and Tech.		Adm. and Mgr.		Clerical		Sales		Service		Agriculture		Production	
	M	F	M	F	M	F	M	F	M	F	M	F	M	F	M	F
Canada	7396.50	6109.00	2190.40	2258.40	—	—	391.60	1577.50	720.80	618.40	797.40	1048.40	478.10	127.80	2818.30	478.50
Chile	3406.10	1619.70	205.10	239.30	134.40	33.80	379.70	330.20	319.20	305.20	209.00	429.40	712.40	82.10	1402.20	197.90
Israel*	1090.30	781.10	219.90	256.50	75.10	17.80	86.10	210.90	104.20	63.20	109.20	154.70	51.00	8.80	431.50	65.90
Italy*	12972.00	7030.00	182.00	33.00	868.00	1005.00	1704.00	861.00	1400.00	1409.00	1674.00	1410.00	627.00	293.00	6125.00	1754.00
Japan	38430.00	26140.00	4480.00	3420.00	2160.00	210.00	4950.00	7570.00	5820.00	3620.00	2760.00	3350.00	1980.00	1650.00	16140.00	6220.00
Malaysia	5056.60	2588.40	427.00	329.60	201.20	46.60	379.20	452.80	535.00	299.90	4736.50	372.30	1109.30	430.30	1931.50	656.90
Mexico	23026.80	10854.30	1724.00	1421.00	530.80	131.40	1176.50	1452.80	2841.60	3016.10	3405.10	2142.50	7046.90	1171.30	6271.70	1515.50
Pakistan*	28238.00	4809.00	1222.00	295.00	300.00	12.00	1343.00	34.00	3841.00	120.00	1340.00	168.00	12755.00	3459.00	7437.00	721.00
Philippines	16193.00	9505.00	512.00	915.00	284.00	138.00	479.00	636.00	1140.00	2451.00	1042.00	1268.00	8288.00	2936.00	4424.00	1147.00
Sweden	2061.00	1925.00	509.00	911.00	—	—	261.00	400.00	198.00	179.00	147.00	227.00	97.00	31.00	848.00	178.00
Turkey	141891.00	6486.00	819.00	396.00	438.00	49.00	659.00	357.00	1689.00	166.00	1357.00	195.00	5342.00	4852.00	4502.00	449.00
United States	67377.00	57523.00	10439.00	11602.00	9840.00	7346.00	3776.00	14613.00	7634.00	7485.00	6774.00	10155.00	2916.00	726.00	25998.00	5594.00
Venezuela	5180.03	2489.61	403.12	536.44	201.21	59.87	313.08	467.51	796.96	509.87	495.94	639.34	977.76	36.43	1962.90	238.27

Figures in thousands (000's).

Source: Yearbook of Labor Statistics 1996. Data from 1995; data for those countries with * from 1994.

MANAGEMENT FOCUS

Women in Foreign Postings

When Carla Hills was first nominated for her job as U.S. trade representative, some people had doubts. Many questioned the cultural sensitivity of sending a woman to negotiate with the Japanese. Senator Steven Symms wondered whether she would appear as strong and committed as the "tough men, warriors" who had preceded her.

Such anxieties go to the heart of the debate over who should be doing America's business overseas. In choosing their emissaries, companies are often daunted by stories of submissive Asian wives, racist remarks by Japanese leaders, and laws barring Saudi women from driving. As a result, women, though making small gains, are even rarer among managers abroad than they are at home (see accompanying exhibit).

Those few female executives who have been successful overseas, however, say that many companies still cling to false and outworn notions about other cultures. Although these veteran managers acknowledge that hurdles exist, they say misguided attitudes leave companies unreasonably pessimistic about placing more minorities overseas. Many firms assume, wrongly, that clients will refuse to do business with female representatives. Even executives with international experience agree that there are practical problems for women operating overseas. They cite Saudi Arabia and Pakistan, for example, as places where it doesn't make sense to send a woman.

Conversely, many Americans assume that England is the closest thing to home outside North America. But Americans find that many British men are uncomfortable with female managers. Robert Petzinger, managing director of AT&T's international communications services, recently chose an American women to head a salesforce in London. He acknowledged that five of the men she will manage immediately let him know that he had, in their opinion, "made the wrong choice." Petzinger commented that he told the woman she "faces a challenge."

But even where a culture puts severe restraints on its own women, outsiders may be treated differently, notes Nancy Adler, associate professor at McGill University in Montreal. "You are seen as a foreigner first and then as a woman," she says. "The best predictor of success isn't how they treat their own women, but how they treat other Americans."

Pat Burns, director of industrial development for Madison Public Relations Group, has been doing business in northern Africa and the Mideast since the mid–1970s. On one occasion in Sudan, she was invited into the home of a businessman who brought her a cushion, served her food, and washed her arms with rose water after the meal—all things a man normally would never do for a woman. After the meeting, Burns asked her local agent how the man could have violated accepted rules of conduct. "Oh, it's no problem," she recalls being told, "women do not do business; therefore, you are not a woman."

Ironically, many women feel they have an advantage in business overseas for the same reason they have trouble in business at home: their different upbringing. Consultants say that women are generally more patient than men and more interested in creating harmony and consensus, both highly valued overseas.

As companies address the glass ceiling problem at home, more are pushing the boundaries abroad as well. AT&T, for example, commissioned a 22-country study by Moran to evaluate how women are received in various places and what barriers they might face. Among the findings, it turns out that Chinese businessmen seem less threatened by American women than by American men, and "machismo" is less pervasive in Argentina than in other Latin countries.

Amid such efforts, one of the hardest parts of an overseas assignment for women and minorities

(Continued)

remains: In showing respect and understanding for the local culture, they may have to tolerate attitudes they would not at home. Burns says she has gone out of her way in the Mideast to express respect for a business partner's wife or daughter, or to praise women executives and officials. Still, she says, when a Saudi general recently invited her to visit and asked whether she minded using the women's entrance, she replied, "Not at all."

Source: Adapted from Jolie Solomon, "Women, Minorities and Foreign Postings," *Wall Street Journal*, June 2, 1989, B1.

Sending Women Overseas

A survey of industrial and service companies with international operations revealed that 38 percent of the companies had no female expatriates. The reasons given:

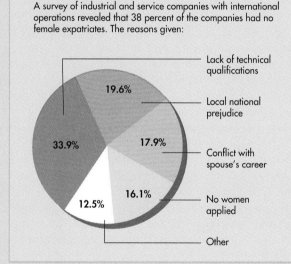

- 19.6% Lack of technical qualifications
- 17.9% Local national prejudice
- 33.9%
- 12.5%
- 16.1% Conflict with spouse's career
- No women applied
- Other

The following shows the geographical breakdown of women assigned overseas:

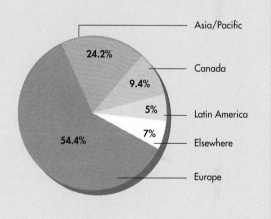

- 24.2% Asia/Pacific
- 9.4% Canada
- 5% Latin America
- 7% Elsewhere
- 54.4% Europe

strong willingness to work abroad. Nor can the situation be explained by their lack of success: For example, a major study by Adler of North American women working as expatriate managers in countries around the world showed that they are, for the most part, successful.[31]

The most difficult job seems to be getting the assignment in the first place. One of the major reasons is that North American executives are reluctant to send minorities abroad because they assume they will be subject to the same culturally based biases as at home, or they assume a lack of understanding and acceptance, particularly in certain countries. Research on 52 female expatriate managers, for example, shows this assumption to be highly questionable. Adler showed, first and foremost, that foreigners are seen as foreigners; further, a woman who is a foreigner (called a *gaijin* in Japan) is not expected to act like a local woman. In fact, Adler and Izraeli say, "Asians see female expatriates as foreigners who happen to be women, not as women who happen to be foreigners." The other women in the study echoed this view. One woman based in Hong Kong noted, "It doesn't make any difference if you are blue, green, purple, or a frog. If you have the best product at the best price, they'll buy."[32]

Most businesspeople affirm that, especially in less developed countries, it is the personal relationship of trust developed between the buyer and the seller that provides the key to business success.

Many female expatriates report, in fact, certain professional advantages to being a woman—in particular, a curiosity about them that provides visibility and sometimes special status.[33] In addition, many women are well suited for expatriate positions because they possess the effective human relationship skills that foster cooperative cross-cultural interactions.

Women and minorities represent a significant resource for overseas assignments that is underutilized by American companies. Adler studied this phenomenon regarding women and recommends that businesses (1) avoid assuming that a female executive will fail because of the way she will be received or because of problems experienced by female spouses; (2) avoid assuming that a woman will not want to go overseas; and (3) give female managers every chance to succeed by giving them the titles, status, and recognition appropriate to the position, as well as sufficient time to be effective.[34] We can assume that the same recommendations would apply when considering assignments for other minority groups.

In addition to the underutilized resource that minority groups and women represent for overseas assignments, firms should avail themselves of the great untapped resource of minority host-country nationals. Women, in particular, are seldom employed in managerial positions by local companies; they are a hiring alternative for foreign employers in countries where cultural conflicts in the workplace can be worked out. In Japan, for example, foreign companies have difficulty attracting well-qualified Japanese men because the culture values long-term relationships between Japanese employers and employees. However, they can draw from a growing pool of college-educated women in Japan by offering these women equal opportunities in recruitment, hiring, and promotion.[35] These firms need to circumvent cultural clashes with Japanese male employees and clients by initially placing the women in positions that give them little contact with Japanese men. IBM Japan, for example, has recently placed female Japanese graduates into its software division; some international banks

Female managers around the world represent a significant pool of resources for effective international human resources management.

have hired women who are fluent in English to manage foreign accounts and deal with foreign clients.[36]

In spite of slow progress for minorities in international management, examples of minority women in top levels in global companies abound. One is Ann Fudge, 47, Executive Vice President of Kraft Foods Coffee and Cereals Division; she also sits on a number of executive boards. Another is Andrea Jung, President and CEO-to-be of Avon Products.

Sexual Harassment in Overseas Assignments

In many Mediterranean and Latin countries, physical contact and sensuality are a common part of socializing.[37]

Sexual harassment is one manifestation of sexual discrimination; however, attitudes about women's rights and behaviors toward them vary greatly in different countries. What are the legal and business implications of international sexual harassment?[38] When a woman on assignment in Mexico, for example, is the target of unwanted sexual advances from her host-country male manager, and is told by her coworkers that it is normal behavior there, what are her rights? Being told that her company's policy protects her overseas does not make the situation any less awkward, or make it any easier to get along with people with whom she must work to make her assignment successful. The dilemma comes down to a question of cultural relativism: "Should an organization operating in a host country with different customs and moral traditions insist that all behavior be measured according to home-country standards?"[39] Here, too, corporations operating abroad have to be very careful. Morally and legally, they must protect their employees wherever they are; however, interpretation of the laws governing sexual harassment abroad is complex, and the issue of where to draw the line while also getting along with host-country employees is a difficult one. In addition, a manager in the host country is not likely to perceive the need to treat a "foreign" female assignee differently from the way he interacts with his own colleagues and employees, and probably would be offended at any suggestion that he should do so.

Working Within Local Labor Relations Systems

An important variable in organizing work and human resources and in strategic planning is that of the labor relations environment and system within which the managers of an MNE will operate in a foreign country. Differences in economic, political, and legal systems result in considerable variation in labor relations systems across countries. As illustrated by the Opening Profile, for example, firms operating in the European Community, or those wishing to operate there, are still dealing with disparate national labor and social systems as the EC directors wrestle with the goal of the harmonization of labor laws.[40] In addition, European businesses continue to be undermined by their poor labor relations and by inflexible regulations. As a result, businesses are having to move jobs overseas to cut labor costs, resulting from a refusal of unions to grant any reduction in employment protection or benefits in order to keep the jobs at home.[41]

The term **labor relations** refers to the process through which managers and workers determine their workplace relationships.[42] This process may be through verbal agreement and job descriptions, or through a union written labor contract that has been reached through negotiation in collective bargaining between workers and managers. The labor contract determines rights regarding workers' pay, benefits, job duties, firing procedures, retirement, layoffs, and so on.

The importance to the international manager of the prevailing labor relations system in a country is that it can constrain the strategic choices and operational activities of a firm operating there. The three main dimensions of the labor–management relationship that the manager will consider are (1) the participation of labor in the affairs of the firm, especially as this affects performance and well-being; (2) the role and impact of unions in the relationship; and (3) the specific human resource policies in terms of recruitment, training, and compensation.[43] Constraints take the form of (1) wage levels that are set by union contracts and leave the foreign firm little flexibility to be globally competitive; (2) limits on the ability of the foreign firm to vary employment levels when necessary; (3) limitations on the global integration of operations of the foreign firm because of incompatibility and the potential for industrial conflict.[44]

Organized Labor Around the World

Exhibit 11–4 is a map showing the relative density of organized labor around the world. But this map does not show the nature of the system in each country. In most countries, a single dominant industrial relations system applies to almost all workers. But in both Canada and the United States there are two systems—one for the organized and one for the unorganized; each, according to Adams, has "different rights and duties of the parties, terms and conditions of employment, and structures and processes of decision making." Basically, in North America, an agent represents unionized employees, whereas unorganized employees can bargain only individually, usually with little capability to affect major strategic decisions or policies or conditions of employment.[45]

The traditional trade union structures in Western industrialized societies have been in the following two categories: industrial unions, representing all grades of employees in a specific industry, and craft unions, based on certain occupational skills. More recently, the structure has been conglomerate unions, representing members in several industries, for example, the metal workers unions in Europe that cut across industries, and general unions, open to most employees within a country.[46] The system of union representation varies among countries. In the United States, most unions are national and represent specific groups of workers—for example, truck drivers or airline pilots—so a company may have to deal with several different national unions. A single U.S. firm—rather than an association of firms representing a worker classification—engages in its own negotiations.[47] In Japan, on the other hand, it is common for a union to represent all workers in a company. In recent years, company unions in Japan have increasingly coordinated their activities, leading to some lengthy strikes.

Industrial labor relations systems across countries can be understood only in the context of the variables in their environment and the sources of origins of unions; these include government regulation of unions, economic and unemployment factors, technological issues, and the influence of religious organizations.[48] Any of the basic processes or concepts of labor unions, therefore, may vary across countries, depending on where and how the parties have their power and achieve their objectives, such as through parliamentary action in Sweden.

For example, collective bargaining in the United States and Canada refers to negotiations between a labor union local and management, whereas in Europe, collective bargaining takes place between the employer's organization and a trade union at the industry level.[49] This difference means that the North American decentralized, plant-level, collective agreements are more detailed than the European industry-wide agreements because of the complexity of negotiating myriad details in multi-employer bargaining. In Germany and Austria, for example, such details are delegated to work councils by legal mandate.[50]

The resulting agreements from bargaining also vary around the world. A written, legally binding agreement for a specific period, common in Northern Europe and North America, is less prevalent in Southern Europe and Britain. In Britain, France, and Italy, bargaining is frequently informal and results in a verbal agreement valid only until one party wishes to renegotiate.[51]

Other variables of the collective bargaining process are the objectives of the bargaining and the enforceability of collective agreements. Because of these differences, managers in MNEs overseas realize that they must adapt their labor relations policies to local conditions and regulations. They also need to bear in mind that, though U.S. union membership has declined by about 50 percent in the last 20 years, in Europe overall membership is still quite high; it, too, has been falling, but from much higher levels.

Most Europeans are covered by collective agreements, whereas most Americans are not. Unions in Europe are part of a national cooperative culture between government, unions, and management, and they hold more power than in the United States. In June 1998, for example, thousands of employees at the state-owned Air France airline staged protests in Paris airports against proposed job and pay cuts, thereby causing the government to back down.[52]

Increasing privatization will make governments less vulnerable to this kind of pressure. It is also interesting to note that there are labor courts in Europe that deal with employment matters separately from unions and works councils. In Japan, labor militancy has long been dead since labor and management agreed 40 years ago on a deal for industrial peace in exchange for job security. Unions in Japan have little official clout, especially amid the Japanese recession. In addition, there is not much to negotiate since wage rates, working hours, job security, health benefits, overtime work, insurance, and so on are legislated. Local working conditions and employment issues are all that's left to negotiate. What's more, the managers and labor union representatives are usually the same people, which serves to limit confrontation, as does the cultural norm of maintaining harmonious relationships.

In the industrialized world, tumbling trade barriers are also reducing the power of trade unions because competitive multinational companies have more freedom to choose alternative productive and sourcing locations. Most new union workers—about 75 percent—will be in emerging nations, like China and Mexico, where wages are low and unions are scarce.[53]

In China, the government ordered all 47,000 foreign firms there to be unionized by mid–1996, and new foreign firms to establish unions in their first year of operation. This was in response to a sharp rise in labor tension and protests about poor working conditions and industrial accidents. The All-China Federation of Trade Unions claimed that "foreign employers often force workers to work overtime, pay no heed to labor-safety regulations and deliberately find fault with the workers as an excuse to cut their wages or fine them."[54] Much of the unrest has been caused by workers who are angry about losing their socialist safety net

EXHIBIT 11–4

Relative Density of Organized Labor Around the World

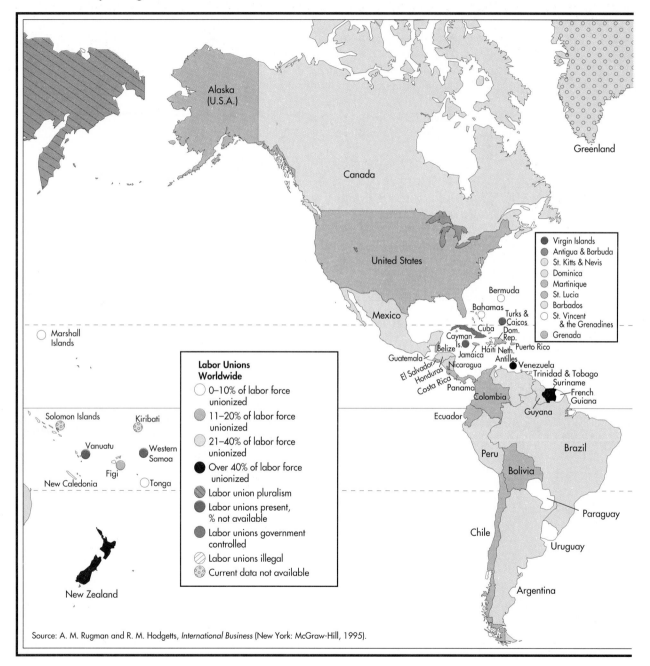

Source: A. M. Rugman and R. M. Hodgetts, *International Business* (New York: McGraw-Hill, 1995).

EXHIBIT 11-4

(continued)

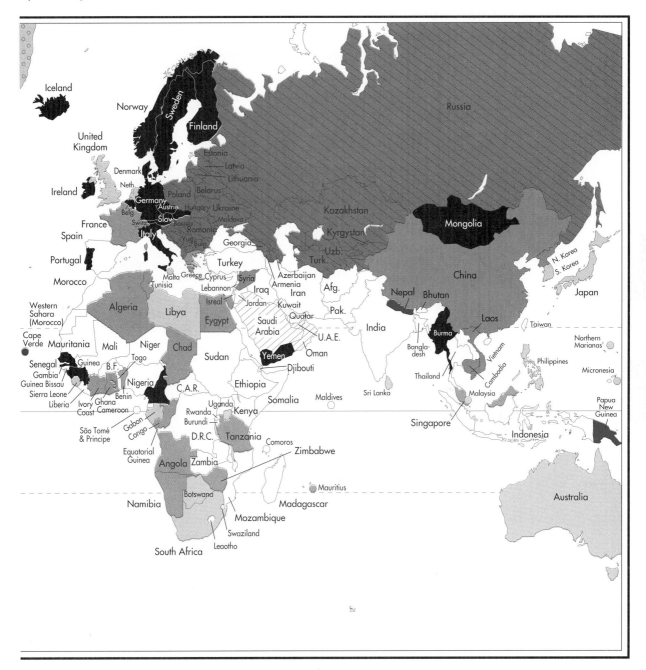

under the government's new economic reforms. Johnson & Johnson's three consumer products manufacturing plants in China were already unionized and have a cooperative relationship with the unions.[55]

Convergence Versus Divergence in Labor Systems

In South Africa, the elimination of apartheid has given rise to a rapidly growing labor movement. The African National Congress is pro-union, and local unions receive assistance from the AFL-CIO branch in Johannesburg.[56]

Although no clear direction is evident at this point, political changes, external competitive forces, increased open trade, and frequent moves of MNCs around the world are forces working toward convergence in labor systems. **Convergence** occurs as the migration of management and workplace practices around the world results in the reduction of workplace disparities from one country to another. This occurs primarily as MNCs seek consistency and coordination among their foreign subsidiaries, and as they act as catalysts for change by "exporting" new forms of work organization and industrial relations practices.[57] It also occurs as harmonization is sought, such as for the EU countries, and as competitive pressures in free-trade zones, such as the NAFTA countries, eventually bring about demands for some equalization of benefits for workers.[58] It would appear that economic globalization is leading to labor transnationalism and will bring about changes in labor rights and democracy around the world.[59] In East European societies in transition to market economies, for example, newly structured industrial relations systems are being created.[60] Trends in industrial relations, such as the flattening of organizations and decline in the role of trade unions, are viewed by many as global developments pointing to convergence in labor systems.[61]

Other pressures toward convergence of labor relations practices around the world come from the activities and monitoring of labor conditions worldwide by various organizations. One of these is the International Labor Organization (ILO)—comprising union, employer, and government representation—whose mission is to ensure that humane conditions of labor are maintained. Other associations of unions in different countries include various international trade secretariats representing workers in specific industries. These include the International Confederation of Free Trade Unions (ICFTU) and the World Confederation of Labor (WCL). The activities and communication channels of these associations provide unions and firms with information about differences in labor conditions around the world.[62] One result of their efforts to provide awareness and changes in labor conditions was the pressure they brought to bear on MNCs operating in South Africa in the late 1980s. The result was the exodus of foreign companies and the eventual repeal of apartheid laws. Now there is a rapidly growing labor union movement there, thanks to the pro-union African National Congress. In fact, the AFL-CIO opened an office in Johannesburg and assists the South African unions.[63]

Political and cultural shifts are also behind the new labor law in South Korea, as the country moves from a system founded on paternalism and authoritarianism to one based on more liberal values.[64]

Although there are forces for convergence in labor relations systems around the world, for the most part, MNCs still adapt their practices to a great extent to the traditions of

EXHIBIT 11–5

Trends in Global Labor Relations Systems

Forces for Global Convergence   <–Current System–>   Forces to Maintain or Establish Divergent Systems

Forces for Global Convergence	Forces to Maintain or Establish Divergent Systems
Global competitiveness	National labor relations systems and traditions
MNC presence or consolidation initiatives	Social systems
Political change	Local regulations and practices
New market economies	Political ideology
Free-trade zones: harmonization (EU), competitive forces (NAFTA)	Cultural norms
Technological standardization, IT	
Declining role of unions	
Agencies monitoring world labor practices	

national industrial relations systems, and there is considerable pressure to do so. Those companies, in fact, act more like local employers, subject to local and country regulations and practices. Although the reasons for continued **divergence** in systems seem fewer, they are very strong; not the least of these are political ideology and the overall social structure and history of industrial practices. It is highly unlikely that China, for example, would accept Western practices that threaten its political ideology. And in the EU, where states are required to maintain parity in wage rates and benefits under the Social Charter of the Maastricht Treaty, there is still a powerful defense of cultural identity and social systems, and considerable resistance by unions to comply with those requirements. Managers in those MNCs also recognize that a considerable gap often exists between the labor laws and the enforcement of those laws—in particular, in less developed countries. Exhibit 11–5 shows the major forces for and against convergence in labor relations systems.

The NAFTA and Labor Relations in Mexico

About 40 percent of the total workforce in Mexico is unionized, with about 80 percent of workers in industrial organizations that employ more than 25 workers unionized. However, government control over union activities is very strong, and although there are some strikes, union control over members remains rather weak.[65] Multinational corporations are required by government regulation to hire Mexican nationals for at least 90 percent of their workforce; preference must be given to Mexicans and to union personnel. However, in reality, the government permits hiring exceptions.[66]

Currently, the only labor issues that are subject to a formal trinational review under the NAFTA labor side pact are minimum wages, child labor, and safety issues. But as illustrated in the end-of-chapter case study, foreign firms like Honeywell operating in Mexico are faced with pressures from various stakeholders in their dealings with unions. In fact, in early 1998, AFL-CIO President John Sweeney flew to Mexico to try "to develop coordinated cross-border

EXHIBIT 11–6

Comparisons of Private-Sector Labor Law Among NAFTA Nations*

	U.S.	Canada	Mexico
Minimum wage (US$)	$4.25/hr.	$3.51/hr.	$0.46/hr. (avg.)
Maximum work week	40 hours (8 × 5)	Varies with province	48 hours (8 × 6)
Pensions	Optional	Required contribution	Optional
Social security (old age)	Required contribution	Required contribution	Required contribution
Social security (disability)	Required contribution	No provision	Required contribution
Healthcare benefits	Optional	Required contribution	Required contribution
Unemployment insurance	Required contribution	Required contribution	No provision
Workers' compensation insurance	Required	Yes, varies with Province	No provision
Pay equity or comparable worth	No provision	Yes in Ontario	No provision
Plant-closing notification	60 days	Yes, varies with province	Yes
Severance pay	Optional	Varies with province	90 days pay
Housing assistance	Optional	Optional	5% base salary
Profit sharing	Optional	Optional	10% net profits
Christmas bonus	Optional	Optional	15-days pay
Holiday leave	Optional	3+ paid holidays	7 paid holidays
Vacation leave	Optional	10 paid days	6+ paid days
Sick leave	Optional	Paid by government after 3 weeks	Paid by government
Maternity leave	Optional	17 weeks + 24 weeks	12 weeks
Gender discrimination	Prohibited	Prohibited	Prohibited
Race or color discrimination	Prohibited	Prohibited	Prohibited
Religious discrimination	Prohibited	Prohibited	Prohibited
National origin discrimination	Prohibited	Prohibited	No provision
Age discrimination	Prohibited	Prohibited	No provision
Disability discrimination	Prohibited	Prohibited	No provision
Marital status discrimination	No provision	Prohibited	No provision

*In all NAFTA countries, states and provinces also have jurisdiction over labor law and may set additional standards.

Source: Institute of International Human Resources, Society for Human Resource Management, *Briefing Paper on the North American Free Trade Agreement,* January 1993.

organizing and bargaining strategies."[67] Although no deals were made at that time, the seeds were sown in the direction of more open union activity and benefits for employees.

Many foreign firms set up production in Mexico at least in part for the lower wages and overall cost of operating there—utilizing the advantages of NAFTA—and the Mexican government wants to continue to attract that investment, as it has for many years before NAFTA. But Mexican workers claim that some of the large U.S. companies in Mexico violate the basic labor rights and cooperate with pro-government labor leaders in Mexico to break up independent unions. MNCs are believed by workers there to routinely use blacklists, physical intimidation, and economic pressure against union organization and independent labor groups that oppose Mexican government policies or the pro-government Confederation of Mexican Workers (CTM). GE, for example, has been accused of firing 11 employees in its Juarez plant who were involved in organizing a campaign for the Authentic Labor Front, Mexico's only independent labor group. The company was also accused of blacklisting union activists (a list of "undesirable employees" that is circulated to other employers). In February 1994, formal complaints were filed to the U.S. National Administration office of the Department of Labor by two U.S. unions—the Teamsters and the United Electrical, Radio, and Machine Workers Union. (U.S. unions have an interest in increasing wages and benefits in Mexico so as to offset some of the reasons that American companies take productive facilities there, along with U.S. jobs.) The Labor Department's National Administrative Office (NAO)—set up by NAFTA to monitor labor policies in the United States, Mexico, and Canada—reviewed complaints that GE may have violated Mexican labor law. That office later ruled that those claims against GE were unsubstantiated; further they ruled that neither that office (the NAO) nor the Mexican counterpart could punish other nations for failing to address union organization rights although they could issue formal complaints.[68]

This incident and others, such as the Honeywell case at the end of this chapter, illustrate the complexities of labor relations when a firm operates in other countries—particularly when there are linkages and interdependence among those countries, such as through NAFTA or the EC. Of interest are the differences in labor law in the private sector among NAFTA nations, shown in Exhibit 11–6. Note, for example, that although the minimum wage in Mexico is far less than that in Canada or the United States, there are a number of costly required benefits for Mexican workers, such as 15-days pay for a Christmas bonus and 90-days severance pay.

COMPARATIVE MANAGEMENT IN FOCUS

Labor Relations in Germany

Codetermination has proved to be efficient, and several northern European countries adopted similar systems, while others, such as the UK, did not. The combined influences made dialogue between management and the workers a natural component of decision making.

—Andre Leysen, Chairman, Supervisory Board, Agla Gebert.[69]

Germany's **codetermination** law (*mitbestimmung*)—which refers to the participation of labor in the management of a firm—mandates representation for unions and salaried employees on the supervisory boards of all large companies, and works councils of employees at every work site. Unions are well integrated into managerial decision making and can make a positive contribution to corporate competitiveness and restructuring; this seems different from the traditional adversarial relationship of unions and management in the United States.[70] However, the fact is that firms, in the form of affiliated organizations of companies, have to contend with negotiating with powerful industrywide unions. Employment conditions that would be negotiated privately in the United States, for example, are subject to federal mandates in Germany—a model unique in Europe.

Union membership in Germany is voluntary, usually with one union for each major industry, and union power is quite strong. Negotiated contracts with firms by the employers' federation stand to be accepted by firms that are members of the federation, or used as a guide for other firms; these contracts therefore result in setting the pay scale for about 90 percent of the country's workers.[71]

The union works councils play an active role in hiring, firing, training, and reassignment during times of reorganization and change.[72] Because of the depth of the works councils' penetration into personnel and work organization matters, as required by law, their role has been termed by some as "co-manager of the internal labor market."[73] This situation has considerable implications for how managers of MNCs plan to operate in Germany. IG Metall, for example, Germany's largest metalworking union, with 2.6 million workers, negotiates guidelines regarding pay, hours, and working conditions on a regional basis. Then works councils use those guidelines to make local agreements. IG Metall's proactive role on change illustrates the evolving role of unions by leading management thinking instead of reacting to it. In addition, management and workers tend to work together because of the structure of the unions.[74] Indeed, Adams suggests that such institutional accord is a powerful factor in changing deeply ingrained cultural traits.

Codetermination has clearly helped modify German managerial style from authoritarian to something more akin to humanitarian, without, it should be noted, altering its capacity for efficiency and effectiveness.[75] This system compares to the lack of integration and active roles for unions in the U.S. auto industry, for example, conditions that limit opportunities for change.

DaimlerChrysler, the new German–American company to be headquartered in Germany, will include a works council in its decision making, as mandated by German law. This will mean that the company's labor representatives will be paying close attention to U.S. attitudes, which may lead to changes in the tone of the collective bargaining processes. The two-tiered system of a supervisory and a management board will remain. It is likely that the company will exert pressure to bring down the high labor costs and taxes in Germany, under the threat of moving its plants elsewhere in order to remain globally competitive. With the DaimlerChrysler company accounting for about 13 percent of the DAX index of 30 German blue-chip stocks, U.S. shareholders and managers in the company will no doubt hold some power to bring about change and reduce operating costs in the company—and perhaps eventually in the country. Pay for German production workers is among the highest in the world, about 150 percent of that in the United States, and about ten times that in Mexico. German workers also have the highest number of paid vacation days in the world, and prefer short work days. The stores are open very little in the evenings or on the weekends. Termination costs are also very high, and include severance pay and retraining costs, as well as time to find another job—and that is assuming that you are successful in terminating the employee in the first place, which is very difficult in Europe. This was brought home to Colgate-Palmolive when it tried to close its factory in Hamburg in 1996. The company offered the 500 employees an average of $40,000 each, but the union wold not accept and eventually Colgate had to pay a much higher (undisclosed) amount.

The German model, according to Rudiger Soltwedel of the Institute for the World Economy at Kiel, holds that competition should be based on factors other than cost.[76] Thus the higher wage level in Germany should be offset by higher-value goods like luxury cars and machine tools, which have been the hallmark of Germany's products. To the extent that the West German unions have established the high-wage, high-skill, and high-value-added production pattern, then, they have also become dependent on the continued presence of that pattern.[77] In recognition of that dependency, German auto firms are remaking themselves after the Japanese model—reducing supplies and cutting costs in order to compete on a global scale. However, this social contract, which has underpinned Germany's manufacturing success, is fraying at the edges as Germany's economy weakens under the $100 billion cost of absorbing East Germany, and under competitive EC pressures.[78]

Labor Participation in Management

Issues of the way work is organized and who makes what decisions are at the core of the differences in labor–management relations around the world. Modern management theory about how to increase productivity involves changes in a variety of employment practices: teamwork, performance-based pay methods, participatory programs, extensive training, and so on.[79] Traditional labor–management relations are changing by virtue of a reshaping of the role of the worker both at the level of the actual work performed and by participation in the decision-making process. MNCs use various methods as appropriate to involve workers in decision making, such as self-management, codetermination, minority board membership, and works councils.[80] In addition, to improve the quality of products and services, as well as the work life of employees, companies variously use techniques such as quality circles, teamwork, and flextime. There is considerable variation around the world in decision-making participation by workers. In western Europe, for example, that variation—typically concerning rights of information, consultation, and codetermination—develops on three levels: [81]

1. The shop-floor level, or direct involvement—for example, the right to be consulted in advance concerning transfers
2. The management level, or through representative bodies—for example, work council participation in setting new policies or changing existing ones
3. The board level—for example, labor membership on the board of directors[82]

The idea of improving productivity and worker satisfaction through teamwork, or small autonomous work groups, has received much attention; this follows the successes of Sweden's advances in industrial democracy with the Saab and Volvo factories in the 1970s and the renowned productive competitiveness of Japan's automobile factories. Such work groups are typically assembly, workshop, or office groups given responsibility for running their own teams, ensuring the quality of their output, solving problems, and so forth.[83]

Studies in the management literature give evidence of increased productivity, lower absenteeism, and fewer defects as a result of incorporating job-enlargement changes and autonomous groups into the organizational design. These studies include 34 companies reviewed by the W. E. Upjohn Institute for Employment Research, with 23 in the United States, 3 in Norway, 2 in (the former) Yugoslavia, 3 in Britain, 2 in Holland, and 1 in Mexico—all indicating positive results.[84]

Work groups in some form are quite common in most market economies, particularly in the automobile industry. Most major automobile companies around the world are experimenting with the quality circle concept. In fact, an OECD (Organization for Economic

Cooperation and Development) report on the worldwide automobile industry noted increased delegation of responsibilities to workers, including preventive maintenance, quality control, and the management of a variety of processes.[85] The report noted that the strongest general trend is the introduction of group work.

There is a trend away from "man–machine relations" toward "team technological system relations." This involves restructuring the production process by setting teams that often number from three to eight people. It represents a move away from assembly-line structures with their isolation and alienating effects.[86]

At Shell Canada's chemical plant in Sarnia, Ontario, for example, intense worker involvement has pushed output as high as 195 percent of design capacity. The new-model local union there has been operating for more than a decade, with workers running the plant through a network of semiautonomous work teams designed jointly by the company and the Energy and Chemical Workers Union (ECWU). The teams—the only two at the plant—are classified as process operators and maintenance technicians, with one process team running the entire plant on each shift.[87] The team members typically can perform 70 percent of the tasks needed to run the plant, and their pay is linked to skill and knowledge, not to job classification or seniority. The members are responsible for the hiring, training, and grievance procedures within their team.

Various economic and cultural reasons lie behind the differences in the rate and form of adoption of teamwork activities around the world. In the United States, for example, most managers still seem reluctant to part with authority, and so team-based work systems are still rare in both union and nonunion plants. The transformation of the U.S. industrial relations system will therefore rely greatly on the willingness of unions to transform themselves into teamwork systems.[88] And in Mexico, the entire labor relations system remains shackled to a decades-long tradition of subservience to government in spite of tough labor laws on the books.[89] At this point, international managers should become familiar with these variations both to learn from the experiences of other countries and to prepare themselves for possible overseas assignments. As an example, the next section will review cultural influences on labor–management practices between Japanese and Mexicans.

Cultural Influences on Labor–Management Practices

Bear in mind that teamwork, decision-making participation of workers, and other labor–management processes are strongly influenced by culture. Hence there is considerable potential conflict when managers attempt to transfer certain labor–management philosophies and practices to another country, especially when there are disparate cultures. For example, if we review some of the basic differences between Japanese and Mexican culture that are likely to affect labor–management practices (shown in Exhibit 11–7), it is not surprising that a number of potential sources of conflict arise when Japanese firms operating in Mexico attempt to use techniques that worked well in Japan. We can see from Exhibit 11–7 that the area of collective decision making and responsibility seems to hold the most potential for culture clash. It seems that the most significant obstacle to Japanese managers' ability to implement their practices is the rigidly hierarchical nature of Mexican culture. The natural state of decision making in Mexico is that power and authority reside at the top of the hierarchy. The

EXHIBIT 11-7

Fundamental Differences Between Japanese and Mexican Culture That Affect Business Organizations

Dimension	Japanese Culture	Mexican Culture
Hierarchical nature	Rigid in rank and most communication; blurred in authority and responsibility	Rigid in all respects
Individualism vs. collectivism	Highly collective culture; loyalty to work group dominates; group harmony very important	Collective relative to family group; don't transfer loyalty to work group; individualistic outside family
Attitudes toward work	Work is sacred duty; acquiring skills, working hard, thriftiness, patience and perseverance are virtues	Work is means to support self and family; leisure more important than work
Time orientation	Balanced perspective; future oriented; monochronic in dealings with outside world	Present oriented; time is imprecise; time commitments become desirable objectives
Approach to problem solving	Holistic, reliance on intuition, pragmatic; consensus important	Reliance on intuition and emotion; individual approach
Fatalism	Fatalism leads to preparation	Fatalism makes planning, disciplined routine unnatural
View of human nature	Intrinsically good	Mixture of good and evil

Source: J. J. Lawrence and Ryh-song Yeh, "The Influence of Mexican Culture on the Use of Japanese Manufacturing Techniques in Mexico," *Management International Review* 34, no. 1 (1994): 49–66.

individualistic approach to work of most Mexicans determines the preference for individual decision making; subordinates are less trusted to make decisions because of the view that human nature is a mixture of good and evil.

In comparison, Japanese managers have a common value system that regards human nature as intrinsically good; in addition, their collective nature and pragmatic approach to problem solving make Japanese managers comfortable with considerable delegation and group decision making.[90]

Conclusion

Managers operating overseas often face unexpected variation—both in a practical sense and a subtle sense—in the labor–management relations and system of worker participation in a country. Those differences influence the decisions of MNE managers both on a strategic level and on a daily operational level. Teamwork, group activities, and other means of decision-making participation by workers are particularly vulnerable to imposition of "foreign" management styles and practices. The international manager should attempt to understand the cultural and societal bases for the prevailing labor–management philosophies and practices before making changes. Some combination of practices can generally be beneficial as long as change is introduced in a participative manner. Successful MNCs—Ford in Germany, GM in Spain, and Bosch in the United States—familiarized their staff with the local industrial relations system and retained industrial relations staff from the host country to aid in the transition.

Summary of Key Points

1. Expatriates and their families usually experience culture shock resulting from transfer anxiety, social dislocation, disorientation, and impatience. Reverse culture shock occurs upon return to the home country.

2. Support programs for expatriates should include information from and contact with the home organization as well as career guidance and support after the overseas assignment.

3. Women represent an underutilized resource in international management; a major reason for this situation is the assumption that culturally based biases may limit the success of female expatriates.

4. Labor relations refers to the process through which managers and workers determine their workplace relationships. The labor relations environment, system, and processes vary around the world.

5. The labor relations system in a country affects how the international manager must plan strategy and organize work and human resources.

6. Coordination of MNE subsidiary activities around the world can be complex because of different labor relations systems, especially within trading blocs such as the NAFTA, or within common markets such as the EC.

7. External competitive forces, increased open trade, and frequent moves of MNCs around the world are forces toward convergence in labor systems; at this time, though, numerous differences among countries still remain.

8. Traditional labor–management relations are changing by reshaping the role of the worker at the level of the actual work performed and, more generally, by participation in the decision-making process.

9. The idea of improving productivity and worker satisfaction through teamwork, or small autonomous work groups, is growing, but implementation depends on the prevailing labor–management relations system.

10. Teamwork, decision-making participation of workers, and other labor–management processes are strongly influenced by culture. Foreign managers who try to transfer their practices and philosophies to another country are likely to experience system conflict based on cultural differences.

Discussion Questions

1. Discuss the role of reverse culture shock in the repatriation process. What can companies do to avoid this problem? What kinds of skills do managers learn from a foreign assignment, and how can the company benefit from them? What is the role of repatriation in the company's global competitive situation?

2. What are the reasons for the small numbers of American female expatriates? What more can companies do to use women and minorities as a resource for international management?

3. Discuss the implications of different labor relations systems around the world for international management. Specifically, what constraints might be realized in strategic planning? What adjustments might need to be made in work organization? What changes in human resource practices might have to be made?

4. How does union representation and collective bargaining differ in Europe from that in the United States? Why are American companies typically in an adversarial relationship with unions, compared to those in Europe? In Japan?

5. What are the forces toward convergence in labor systems around the world? What are the forces against convergence? What do you predict the situation will be in ten years' time?

6. Explain Germany's *mitbestimmung*. What role has this played in that country's world competitiveness?

7. What are the trends in labor participation in management around the world? What kinds of successes and results have been attained in teamwork in different countries?

8. What is the role of culture in labor relations systems? What conflicts are likely to occur with a Mexican subsidiary in Japan?

Application Exercises

1. Interview one of more managers who have held positions overseas. Try to find a man and a woman. Ask them about their experiences both in the working environment and in the foreign country generally. How did they and their families adapt? How did they find the stage of reentry to headquarters, and what were the effects of the assignment on their career progression? What differences do you notice, if any, between the experiences of the male and the female expatriate?
2. Research the union representation and bargaining system in a country not discussed in this chapter, and share your information with the class.
3. Try to find information about a company that has set up a subsidiary abroad (or a joint venture) and find out what differences exist between the labor relations system the company uses in the host country and that in its domestic plants.

Experiential Exercise

Form groups of six students, divided into two teams, one representing union members from a German company and one representing union members from a Mexican company. These companies have recently merged in a joint venture, with the subsidiary to be located in Mexico. These union workers, all line supervisors, will be working together in Mexico. You are to negotiate six major points of agreement regarding union representation, bargaining rights, and worker participation in management, as discussed in this chapter. Present your findings to the other groups in the class and discuss.

Internet Resources

Visit the Deresky companion Web site at http://prenhall.com/Deresky for this chapter's Internet resources.

Case Study

Mexican Workers Turn up the Heat at Honeywell

Honeywell, Inc. is a well-established global company with subsidiaries around the world and more than 78,000 employees. Honeywell began its operations with the development of the thermostat. In 1970, Honeywell bought a segment of computer systems from General Electric (Honeywell Information Systems). This acquisition put them second to IBM in the computer industry. In 1986, Honeywell took its computer section and created a joint venture with Groupe Bull of France and Japan's NEC Corporation.

Honeywell is now a leader in heating controls and alarm systems and a strong competitor in the automation systems market. The current sales focus is on thermostats, automation products, and aerospace and defense equipment. Honeywell's operation in Chihuahua, Mexico, produces thermostats and other building-control products. In November 1993, Honeywell Mexico experienced some labor relations problems, which were becoming common among foreign companies operating there.

Background

The PRI and Relations with Mexican Labor Unions   Compared to U.S. labor unions, most Mexican unions are grouped under the ruling Institutional Revolutionary Party (PRI). However,

American businesspeople working in Mexico say that outside the maquiladora area (just south of the Mexican–American border where U.S. plants operate under special tax considerations), unions do act independently, and these unions have had success in increasing wages.

Labor experts say maquiladora unions operate differently because they are located in a single area, and the owners work together with the managers to keep independent unions out. The general secretary of Stimaches (a metal workers' union) comments that there is a business agreement among companies and official unions to attempt to block the formation of independent unions. President Ernesto Zedillo's pro-business perspective often resulted in actions that held back any pressures to unionize, especially in the maquiladora area.

Mexican Labor Laws   Under article 356 of the Federal Labor Law, a union is defined as "The association of workers or employers for the advancement and defense of their respective interests." Authorization, prior to the organization of the union, is not a requirement.

Article 358 of the Federal Labor Law guarantees a person the right to join a union. The article also states that any barriers to this right are unconstitutional.

Article 370 declares that a union cannot be terminated or suspended. Any reason for doing so must be done through a legal process that demonstrates that the union has been dissolved or does not comply with legal requirements.

The Mexican labor laws hold that all union officers must be recognized by the government before they can take office.

NAFTA Labor Side Pact   Under the NAFTA labor side pact, minimum wages, child labor, and safety issues are the only labor issues that are subject to a formal trinational review.

Influence of U.S. Labor Unions   Prior to the signing of the NAFTA, the AFL-CIO and some of its member unions were the most outspoken critics of the agreement because they thought it would cause a sudden exodus of U.S. firms eager to exploit Mexican low-cost labor, and thus take away American jobs. They were also concerned about the poor working conditions and low wages of Mexican workers. U.S. labor unions feel that the Mexican government and American firms operating in Mexico are not concerned with protecting the rights of Mexican workers.

U.S. labor unions are now using NAFTA labor side pact rules to support their position and the rights of the workers who were fired for trying to start up a union in a maquiladora zone.

President Clinton assured Honeywell workers and U.S. unions that NAFTA will not increase labor rights violations. U.S. labor unions are fully investigating every complaint. U.S. administrative offices set up public hearings to deter American companies from antiunion activities and to achieve a political level for Mexican labor practices. Clinton also supports protection of worker rights on both sides of the border and compliance with the NAFTA labor side pact.

Problems in Chihuahua, Mexico   In November 1993, Honeywell's Mexican operation, which produces thermostats, was charged with violating the rights of at least 20 workers. These charges, leveled by the AFL-CIO, accuse Honeywell of firing workers because they were attempting to organize a union at its Chihuahua, Mexico, maquiladora operation. Ofelia Medrano, a former employee, and Priscilla Wardlow, a Honeywell representative, have two different perspectives on this incident.

Ofelia Medrano was one of the maquiladora workers fired by Honeywell and is the only one demanding reinstatement. She maintains that her dismissal was a direct result of her union activities. Medrano's organizing activities were in response to poor working conditions and low wages. At the Honeywell operation, she was one of 493 workers earning an average of $1.00 per hour making thermostats and other building-control products.

Medrano finds her dismissal, and those of the other 20 workers, illegal because under the Mexican constitution workers have the right to organize and the right of free association.

Priscilla Wardlow, vice president of manufacturing for building controls at Honeywell's head office in Minneapolis, Minnesota, maintains that Medrano was fired for cause, saying that she was bothering other workers and being disruptive. As for the other dismissals, Honeywell maintains that they were part of a planned downsizing of the Mexican plant.

Case Questions

1. Who are the stakeholders in this situation, and what are their respective positions or motivations?
2. Which laws should prevail in this situation, U.S. labor laws or Mexican labor laws?
3. What are the implications for other foreign firms planning operations in Mexico?
4. What issues of social responsibility must Honeywell, Inc. face (refer to Chapter 3)?

Case Bibliography

"U.S. Backs Mexico on Labor Law," *Facts on File,* November 17, 1994, 852.

"Honeywell, Inc.," *International Directory of Company Histories: Electrical & Electronics,* vol. 2 (Chicago: St. James Press, 1988): 40–42.

Ortega, Bob and Dianne Solis. "Honeywell's Firing of Over 20 Women in Mexico May Test Nafta, Unions Say," *Wall Street Journal,* December 9, 1993.

Robberson, Todd. "Mexico's Unions at Issue," *Washington Post,* October 28, 1993.

Rose, Robert L. "NAFTA Side Pact on Labor Laws Faces First Test," *Wall Street Journal,* February 15, 1994.

Shorrock, Tim. "Mexican Laws and Spotlight as U.S. Review Complaints," *U.S. Journal of Commerce and Commercial,* April 19, 1994, 3A.

Shorrock, Tim. "U.S. Hears Charges Tied to Mexican Labor Rights," *U.S. Journal of Commerce and Commercial,* September 13, 1994, 3A.

Shorrock, Tim. "Labor Department to Review Charges of NAFTA Violations," *U.S. Journal of Commerce and Commercial,* April 18, 1994, 3A.

Smith, Geri. "Which Side (of the Border) Are You on? Well, Both," *Business Week,* April 4, 1994, 50.

12

Motivating and Leading

O U T L I N E

Opening Profile: Starbucks' Java Style Helps
Recruit, Motivate, and Retain Leaders in Beijing

MOTIVATING

Cross-Cultural Research on Motivation

The Meaning of Work

The Need Hierarchy in the International
Context

Management Focus: Mazda's Clashing
Cultures

Comparative Management in Focus:
Motivation in China

The Intrinsic–Extrinsic Dichotomy in the
International Context

Comparative Management in Focus:
Motivation in Mexico

Reward Systems

Management Focus: Ms. Wong: Employee of
the Month

LEADING

**The Multicultural Leader's Role and
Environment**

Cross-Cultural Research on Leadership

Technology Application: Italtel Spa's Leadership
Style Empowers Global Employees with
Technology

**Contingency Leadership—The Culture
Variable**

Comparative Management in Focus:
Leadership in India

The Effective International Leader

Summary of Key Points

Discussion Questions

Application Exercises

Experiential Exercises

Internet Resources

Case Study: Elizabeth's Visit to GPC's Subsidiary
in the Philippines

OPENING PROFILE

Starbucks' Java Style Helps Recruit, Motivate, and Retain Leaders in Beijing

Starbucks Coffee International, already operating in London, China, Japan, Singapore, New Zealand, Taiwan, the Philippines, Thailand, and Malaysia, is continuing its aggressive global expansion. It plans to have 500 coffee shops in Europe by the end of 2003. No stranger to training leaders from around the world into the Starbucks' style, the company nevertheless has quite a challenge in recruiting, motivating, and retaining managers for its Beijing outlets—to say nothing of getting a nation of tea drinkers to switch to java.

Starbucks' first challenge is to recruit good managers in a country where the demand for local managers by foreign companies expanding there is far greater than the supply of managers with any experience in capitalist-style companies. Chinese recruits have stressed that they are looking for the opportunity to get training and to advance in global companies more than money; they know that managers with experience in Western organizations can always get a job. The brand's pop-culture reputation is also an attraction to young Beijingers.

In order to expose the recruits to java-style culture as well as to train them for management, Starbucks brings them to Tacoma, Washington for three months to give them a taste of the West-coast lifestyle and the company's informal culture, such as western-style backyard barbecues. Then they are exposed to the art of cappuccino making at a real store before dawn, and taught how to concoct dozens of fancy coffees. They get the same intensive training as anyone else anywhere in the world. One recruit, Mr. Wang, who worked in a large Beijing hotel before finding out how to make a triple grand latte, said that he enjoys the casual atmosphere and respect. The training and culture is very different from the expectations at a traditional state-owned company in China, where the work is strictly defined and has no challenge for employees.

Starbucks has found that motivating their managers in Beijing is multifaceted. They know that people won't switch jobs for money alone if the company gives them an opportunity both to learn and to have a good working environment with a company with a strong reputation. The recruits have expressed their need for trust and participation in an environment where local nationals are traditionally not expected to exercise initiative or authority; in all, what seems to motivate them more than anything else is dignity.

Sources: *www.Starbucks.com*; "Starbucks' Expansion in China is Slated," *Wall Street Journal*, October 5, 1998.

MOTIVATING

In Mexico, everything is a personal matter; but a lot of managers don't get it.
—Robert Hoskins, Manager, Leviton Manufacturing, Juarez

After managers set up a firm's operations by planning strategy, organizing the work and responsibilities, and staffing those operations, they turn their attention to everyday activities. This ongoing behavior of individual people carrying out various daily tasks enables the firm to accomplish its objectives. Getting those people to perform their jobs efficiently and effectively is at the heart of the manager's challenge.

As this chapter's Opening Profile illustrates, motivation—and therefore appropriate leadership style—is affected by many powerful variables (societal, cultural, and political). In China, there is a long history behind workers' assumptions about "the way we do things around here," and a strong culture that determines attitudes toward work. But in the big cities like Beijing, employees are eager to learn Western ways in order to make themselves more marketable. Foreign companies are challenged to find the right mix of old and new in order to motivate and retain good employees.

Our objective in this chapter is to consider motivation and leadership in the context of diverse cultural milieus. We need to know what, if any, differences there are in the societal factors that elicit and maintain behaviors that lead to high employee productivity and job satisfaction. Are effective motivational and leadership techniques universal or culture based?

Cross-Cultural Research on Motivation

Motivation is very much a function of the context of a person's work and personal life. That context is greatly influenced by cultural variables, which affect the attitudes and behaviors of individuals (and groups) on the job. The framework of this context was described in Chapter 4 and illustrated in Exhibit 4–1. In applying Hofstede's research on cultural dimensions of individualism, uncertainty avoidance, masculinity, and power distance, for example, we can make some generalized assumptions about motivation, such as:

- High uncertainty avoidance suggests the need for job security, whereas people with low uncertainty avoidance would probably be motivated by more risky opportunities for variety and fast-track advancement.
- High power distance suggests motivators in the relationship between subordinates and their boss, whereas low power distance implies that people would be more motivated by teamwork and relations with their peers.
- High individualism suggests people would be motivated by opportunities for individual advancement and autonomy; collectivism (low individualism) suggests that motivation will more likely work through appeals to group goals and support.
- High masculinity suggests that most people would be more comfortable with the traditional division of work and roles; in a more feminine culture, the boundaries could be looser, motivating people through more flexible roles and work networks.

In fact, misjudging the importance of these cultural variables in the workplace may result not only in a failure to motivate, but also in demotivation. An example given by Rieger and Wong-Rieger:

> In Thailand, the introduction of an individual merit bonus plan, which runs counter to the societal norm of group cooperation, may result in a decline rather than an increase in productivity from employees who refuse to openly compete with each other.[1]

In considering what motivates people, we have to understand their needs, goals, value systems, and expectations. No matter what their nationality or cultural background, people are driven to fulfill needs and to achieve goals. But what are those needs, what goals do they want to achieve, and what can motivate that drive to satisfy their goals?

The Meaning of Work

Because our focus here is on the needs that affect the working environment, it is important to understand first what work means to people from different backgrounds. For most people, the basic meaning of work is tied to economic necessity (money for food, housing, and so forth) for the individual and for society.[2] However, the additional connotations of work are more subjective, especially about what work provides other than money—achievement, honor, social contacts, and the like.

Another way to view work, though, is through its relationship to the rest of a person's life. The Thais call work *ngan,* which is the same as their word for "play," and they tend to introduce periods of play in their workdays. Most people in China, Germany, and the United States have a positive attitude toward work, though they do not regard it as play. Especially in work-oriented China, seven-day work weeks with long hours and few days off are common.[3]

Studies on the meaning of work in eight countries were carried out by George England and a group of researchers called the Meaning of Work (MOW) International Research Team.[4] Their research sought to determine a person's idea of the relative importance of work compared to that of leisure, community, religion, and family. They called this concept **work centrality**, defined as "the degree of general importance that working has in the life of an individual at any given point in time." The mean score on the work centrality index for the eight countries studied is shown in Exhibit 12–1.

The obvious general implication from these findings is that the higher the mean work centrality score, the more motivated and committed the workers would be. Of even more importance to managers (as an aid to understanding culture-based differences in motivation) are the specific reasons for valuing work. What kinds of needs does the working environment satisfy, and how does this differ among populations?

Some excellent insights into this question were provided by the MOW research team when they asked people in the eight countries to what extent they regarded work as satisfying six different functions. The six functions of work were as follows: (1) provides a needed income, (2) is interesting and satisfying, (3) provides contacts with others, (4) facilitates a way to serve society, (5) keeps one occupied, and (6) gives status and prestige. The results are shown in Exhibit 12–2. Note the similarities of some of these functions with Maslow's need categories and Herzberg's categories of motivators and maintenance factors. Clearly, these studies can help international managers anticipate what attitudes people have toward their work, what aspects of work are meaningful to them in their life context, and therefore, what approach the manager should take in setting up motivation and incentive plans.

In addition to the differences among countries within each category—such as the higher level of interest and satisfaction derived from work by the Israelis as compared with the Germans—it is interesting to note the within-country differences. Although income was clearly the most important factor for all countries, it apparently has a far greater importance than any other factor in Japan. In other countries, like the Netherlands, the relative importance of different factors was more evenly distributed.

The broader implications of such comparisons about what work means to people are derived from considering the total cultural context: The low rating given by the Japanese to the status and prestige found in work, for instance, suggests that those needs are more fully satisfied elsewhere in their lives, such as within the family and community. In the Middle East, religion plays a major role in all aspects of life, including work. The Islamic work ethic is a commitment toward fulfillment, and so business motives are held in the highest regard.[5] The origin of the Islamic work ethic is in the Muslim holy book, the *Qur'an,* and the words of the Prophet Mohammed:

On the day of judgment, the honest Muslim merchant will stand side by side with the martyrs.—Mohammed

EXHIBIT 12–1

The Relative Meaning of Work in Eight Countries

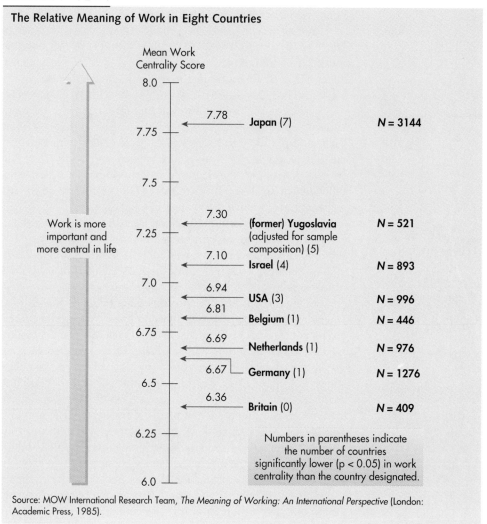

Mean Work Centrality Score

Score	Country	N
7.78	Japan (7)	N = 3144
7.30	(former) Yugoslavia (adjusted for sample composition) (5)	N = 521
7.10	Israel (4)	N = 893
6.94	USA (3)	N = 996
6.81	Belgium (1)	N = 446
6.69	Netherlands (1)	N = 976
6.67	Germany (1)	N = 1276
6.36	Britain (0)	N = 409

Work is more important and more central in life

Numbers in parentheses indicate the number of countries significantly lower ($p < 0.05$) in work centrality than the country designated.

Source: MOW International Research Team, *The Meaning of Working: An International Perspective* (London: Academic Press, 1985).

Muslims feel that work is a virtue and an obligation to establish equilibrium in one's individual and social life. The Arab worker is defined by his or her level of commitment to family, and work is perceived as the determining factor to the ability to enjoy social and family life.[6] A study of 117 managers in Saudi Arabia by Ali found that Arab managers are highly committed to the Islamic work ethic and that there is a moderate tendency toward individualism.[7]

Exhibit 12–3 (p. 412) shows the results of the study and gives more insight into the Islamic work ethic. Another study by Kuroda and Suzuki found that Arabs are serious about their work and that favoritism, give-and-take, and paternalism have no place in the Arab workplace; they compared this attitude to that of the Japanese and Americans who consider friendship to be an integral part of the workplace.[8]

EXHIBIT 12–2

The Perceived Utility of the Functions of Work (Mean Number of Points)

Country	N	Working provides you with an income that is needed	Working is basically interesting and satisfying to you	Working permits you to have interesting contacts with other people	Working is a useful way for you to serve society	Working keeps you occupied	Working gives you status and prestige
Japan	3180	45.4	13.4	14.7	9.3	11.5*	5.6‡
Germany	1264	40.5	16.7	13.1	7.4	11.8	10.1
Belgium	447	35.5	21.3	17.3	10.2	8.7	6.9
Britain	471	34.4	17.9	15.3	10.5	11.0	10.9
Yugoslavia	522	34.1	19.8	9.8	15.1	11.7	9.3
United States	989	33.1	16.8	15.3	11.5	11.3	11.9
Israel	940	31.1	26.2	11.1	13.6	9.4	8.5
Netherlands	979	26.2	23.5	17.9	16.7	10.6	4.9
All countries combined	8792	35.0†	19.5	14.3	11.8	10.8	8.5

Working keeps you occupied was translated in Japan in such a manner that there is real question about how similar its meaning was to that intended.
†The combined totals weight each country equally regardless of sample size.
‡The mean points assigned by a country to the six functions add to approximately 100 points.

Source: Meaning of Work International Research Team, *The Meaning of Working: An International Perspective* (London: Academic Press, 1985).

Other variables affect the perceived meaning of work and how it satisfies various needs, such as the relative wealth of a country.[9] When people have a high standard of living, work can take on a meaning other than simply to provide the basic economic necessities of life. In fact, economic differences among countries were found to explain variation in attitudes toward work in a study by Furnham, Kirkcaldy, and Lynn of more than 12,000 young people from 41 countries on all 5 continents. Specifically, they found that young people in Far and Middle Eastern countries reported highest competitiveness and acquisitiveness for money, whereas those from North and South America scored highest on worth ethic and "mastery" (that is, continuing to struggle to master something).[10] Such studies show the complexity of the underlying reasons for differences in attitudes toward work—cultural, economic, and so on—that must be taken into account when considering what needs and motivations people bring to the workplace. All in all, research shows a considerable cultural variability affecting how work meets employees' needs.

The Need Hierarchy in the International Context

How can a manager know what motivates people in a specific country? One way, certainly, is by drawing on the experiences of others who have worked there; another is by inferring the likely type of motivational structure present by studying what is known about the culture in

EXHIBIT 12–3

The Islamic Work Ethic
Responses by Saudi Arabian Managers

Item	Mean
Islamic Work Ethic	
1. Laziness is a vice.	4.66
2. Dedication to work is a virtue.	4.62
3. Good work benefits both one's self and others.	4.57
4. Justice and generosity in the workplace are necessary conditions for society's welfare.	4.59
5. Producing more than enough to meet one's personal needs contributes to the prosperity of society as a whole.	3.71
6. One should carry work out to the best of one's ability.	4.70
7. Work is not an end in itself but a means to foster personal growth and social relations.	3.97
8. Life has no meaning without work.	4.47
9. More leisure time is good for society.	3.08
10. Human relations in organizations should be emphasized and encouraged.	3.89
11. Work enables man to control nature.	4.06
12. Creative work is a source of happiness and accomplishment.	4.60
13. Any man who works is more likely to get ahead in life.	3.92
14. Work gives one the chance to be independent.	4.35
15. A successful man is the one who meets deadlines at work.	4.17
16. One should constantly work hard to meet responsibilities.	4.25
17. The value of work is derived from the accompanying intention rather than its results.	3.16

On scale of 1–5 (5 highest)

Source: Adapted from Abbas J. Ali, "The Islamic Work Ethic in Arabia," *Journal of Psychology* 126 (5) (1992): 507–519 (513).

that region. Some research and comparative studies about needs in specific countries can provide another piece of the puzzle.

Some researchers have used Maslow's hierarchy of needs to study motivation in other countries. A classic study by Haire, Ghiselli, and Porter surveyed 3,641 managers in 14 countries. They concluded that Maslow's needs, in particular the upper-level ones, are important at the managerial level although the managers reported that the degree to which their needs were fulfilled did not live up to their expectations.[11]

In a similar study, Ronen investigated whether work-related values and needs are similar across nationalities and whether the motivation categories of Maslow and Herzberg apply universally. Studying trained, nonmanagerial male employees (in Germany, Canada, France, Japan, and the United Kingdom), he found that such similarities do exist and that there are common clusters of needs and goals across nationalities. These clusters include (1) job goals, such as working area, work time, physical working conditions, fringe benefits, and job security; (2) relationships with coworkers and supervisors; and (3) work challenges and opportunities for using skills.[12] Ronen concludes that **need clusters** are constant across nationalities and that Maslow's need hierarchy is confirmed by those clusters. In addition, he claims that Herzberg's categories are confirmed by the **cross-national need clusters** in his study.

One clear conclusion is that managers around the world have similar needs but show differing levels of satisfaction of those needs derived from their jobs.[13] Variables other than culture may be at play, however. One of these may be the country's level of economic development: One study of Liberian managers showed that their needs were similar to those of managers in other developing countries (such as in South Africa, Chile, India, and Argentina), but that they had higher needs for security and esteem than managers in more developed countries (such as England and the United States). Whatever the reason, many companies that have started operations in other countries have experienced differences in the apparent needs of the local employees and how they expect work to be recognized. Mazda experienced this problem in its Michigan plant, as discussed in the Management Focus "Mazda's Clashing Cultures."

When considering the cross-cultural applicability of Maslow's theory, then, it is not the needs that are in question as much as the ordering of those needs in the hierarchy. The hierarchy reflects the Western culture where Maslow conducted his study, and different hierarchies might better reflect other cultures. For example, Eastern cultures focus on the needs of

MANAGEMENT FOCUS

Mazda's Clashing Cultures

The experiences of the managers at Mazda's automotive plant in Flat Rock, Michigan, illustrate the motivational difficulties companies experience when managers and workers come from two different worlds—in this case, Japan and the United States. When management started a suggestion program a few years ago, for example, they told the workers that they would get cash awards for their accepted ideas. But these awards turned out to be small—sometimes about $25—compared with the resulting company savings from the suggestion. Workers soon stopped making suggestions; they felt it was not worth it.

Differences between Japanese and American motivational structures stem from cultural differences that affect attitudes about money, work, incentives, performance reviews, and so forth. Japanese firms tend to confer recognition in the form of plaques, attention, and applause. Japanese workers are likely to be insulted by material incentives because such rewards imply that they would work harder to achieve them than they otherwise would. Instead, Japanese firms usually give bonuses and salary raises based on factors such as seniority, gender, and marital status (married men receive the highest compensation) rather than performance, as in the United States. The Japanese stress companywide or groupwide goals, whereas Americans stress individual goals, achievement, and reward.

After learning the differences the hard way, Mazda managers in Flat Rock changed the suggestion system by offering high-priced prizes, such as trips and cars. Since then, they have received many more suggestions—6,918 in 1990 from 3,500 workers. They implemented 4,041 of the suggestions and awarded the first car.

Source: Adapted from R. Eisman, "Employee Motivation: When Cultures Clash," *Incentive* (May 1991): 65–70.

society rather than on those of individuals. Nevis proposes that a hierarchy more accurately reflecting the needs of the Chinese would comprise four levels: (1) belonging, (2) physiological needs, (3) safety, and (4) self-actualization in the service of society.[14] It is difficult to observe or measure the individual needs of a Chinese person because, from childhood, these are intermeshed with the needs of society. Clearly, however, along with culture, the political beliefs at work in China dominate many facets of motivation. The following Comparative Management in Focus takes a closer look at the issue of motivation in the People's Republic of China.

COMPARATIVE MANAGEMENT IN FOCUS

Motivation in China

A gentleman understands what is moral. A base man understands what is advantageous or profitable.

—Confucius

Confucian ethics remain the bedrock of Chinese thought and behavior, perhaps more so in Singapore and Taiwan than in mainland China.[15] To understand motivation in China, you must understand that, from childhood on, the Chinese people are expected to subjugate themselves to the service of the state, and their identity and life goals center on their contribution to it. Therefore, productivity to benefit the overall goals of the state has traditionally been a primary focus.

Since it has been in power, the Chinese Communist party has not been able to eradicate the ancient principle of *mien-tzu* or "face," a basic component of Chinese behavior that refers to a person's social prestige. The Chinese make continuous efforts to preserve the *mien-tzu* of themselves and others—and to avoid the humiliation that otherwise results.[16]

In a collective society such as China, anthropological studies point to the importance of the family or work unit, the father–son relationship (paternalism), and kinship.[17] Emphasis always is on belonging—on, says Serrie, "connecting with others and . . . wishing to be incorporated into a group."[18] From this central motivational need of belonging (Maslow) follow other cultural traits—the need for equity, the avoidance of personal credit for accomplishments, the importance of communal property, and an emphasis on group forces for motivation.[19]

In China, one's work unit defines one's social status; it sets the level of income, healthcare, and old-age pension, and it provides familylike social support, even authorizing marriages.[20] Careful not to do anything to draw any individual recognition or attention, workers try to fit in with the group. Everything is done for the good of the group, and for China.

Traditionally, a pervading sense of harmony and cooperation has existed in China, although the younger generation is showing signs of challenging traditional assumptions and the autocratic government, as evidenced by the uprising in Tiananmen Square in 1989. However, in most of China, particularly in the outlying areas, the boss is still all-powerful, as is the patriarch. Consequently, the worker is expected to be respectful and obedient and to express complete trust, even if the boss is inconsistent or arbitrary in his decisions.[21] In turn, Chinese firms often have a familial-type attitude toward workers, accepting them regardless of the level of skill or performance and relying on top managers or bureaucrats for important decisions.[22, 23]

As the backbone of the industrial system, cadres (managers and technicians) and workers are given exact and detailed prescriptions of what is expected of them as members of a factory, workshop, or work unit.[24] This "rule enforcement" results in conformity at the expense of individual creativity. [25, 26]

Workers are accountable to their group, which is a powerful motivator. Because being "unemployed" is not an option in China, it is important for employees to maintain themselves as cooperating members of the work group.[27] According to Tung, "The principal means of moral encouragement (motivation) used are socialist labor emulation drives (using "model" factories as an example), commendations as pacesetters (giving public recognition), and political indoctrination or education."[28]

China is a rapidly developing nation that realizes its potential; it is now the third largest economy in the world. The government is emphasizing productivity as a way to take advantage of its vast undertapped labor pool, to move closer to a market-based economy, and to compete globally. The government does encourage financial incentives and, in the words of China's constitution, "applies the policy of combining moral encouragement with material reward, with the stress on the former, in order to heighten the citizens' socialist enthusiasm and creativeness in work."[29] The government's modern policy, then, is the socialist principle of "from each according to his or her ability, to each according to his or her *work*." Incentives are based on the work unit's performance (linked to the organization's retained profits) and include wages based on time or piecework, bonuses, subsidies, and welfare benefits.[30, 31] Traditional Chinese societies have been found to "view work as clearly more important than leisure and as contributing to family welfare instead of competing with it."[32, 33] There are, of course, subcultures among Chinese societies and across the vast country of the PRC. [34] It is clear that Western theories are problematic because they focus on specific individual motivational concepts of achievement and self-actualization, whereas many cultures of the world focus more on group relationships.[35]

We will now take a look at other motivation theories and return later to the issue of their applicability in the international context.

The Intrinsic–Extrinsic Dichotomy in the International Context

The intrinsic–extrinsic dichotomy is another useful model (researched by a number of authors) for considering motivation in the workplace. Herzberg's research, for example, found two sets of needs: motivational factors (intrinsic) and maintenance factors (extrinsic).

Results from others' research using Herzberg's model provide some insight into motivation in different countries and also help us determine whether the intrinsic–extrinsic dichotomy is generalizable across cultures. Research on managers in Greece and on workers in general in an Israeli kibbutz indicate that all these people are motivated more by the nature of the work itself; dissatisfactions resulted from the conditions surrounding the work.[36, 37] Another study in Zambia found, in general, the same dichotomy. Work motivation was found to result from the intrinsic factors of the opportunity for growth and the nature of the work and, to some extent, physical provisions; factors that produced dissatisfaction and were not motivators were extrinsic, such as relations with others, fairness in organizational practices, and personal problems.[38]

In addition to research on single countries, Herzberg's theory has been used to compare different countries on the basis of job factors and job satisfaction. A study of MBA candidates from the United States, Australia, Canada, and Singapore, for example, indicated that Herzberg's motivational factors were more important to these prospective managers than hygiene factors.[39] In a broader study of managers from Canada, the United Kingdom, France, and Japan to determine the relative importance of job factors to them and how satisfied they were with those factors, Kanungo and Wright drew a number of interesting conclusions. Interpreting their results, we can draw some overall conclusions: The managers indicated that internally mediated factors (intrinsic, job content factors) were more important than organizationally controlled factors (extrinsic, job context factors). However, they found differences across countries, in particular between the United Kingdom and France, in how much importance the managers placed on job outcomes and also in their relative levels of satisfaction with those outcomes.[40] As a practical application of their research results, Kanungo and Wright suggest the following implications for motivation in the workplace:

> Efforts to improve managerial performance in the UK should focus on job content rather than on job context.... Job enrichment programs are more likely to improve performance in an intrinsically oriented society such as Britain, where satisfaction tends to be derived from the job itself, than in France, where job context factors, such as security and fringe benefits, are more highly valued.[41]

To answer common questions about whether Japanese-style management practices—work groups, quality circles, and long-term employment—make a difference to commitment and job satisfaction, Lincoln studied 8,302 workers in 106 factories in the United States and Japan (though not specifically using Herzberg's factors). He concluded that those practices had similar positive or negative effects on work attitudes in both countries. But though the level of commitment to the company was essentially the same in both samples, the Japanese indicated a lower level of job satisfaction.[42]

The lower level of satisfaction is contrary to popular expectations because of the well-known Japanese environment of teamwork, productivity, long-term employment, and dedication to the company. However, previous research has also found a lower level of job satisfaction in Japan.[43] Lower work satisfaction indicates a higher level of motivation to fulfill personal and company goals (that is, to do better), compared to a lower level of motivation indicated by complacency. As Lincoln points out, however, these research findings could be the result of another cultural variable introducing a measurement bias: the Japanese tendency to "color their evaluations of nearly everything with a large dose of pessimism, humility and understatement" in their persistent quest to do better.[44] This underscores the need to consider carefully all the cultural variables involved in observing or managing motivation.

Clearly, there is a need for more cross-cultural research on motivation, but one can draw the tentative conclusion that managers around the world are motivated more by intrinsic than by extrinsic factors. Considerable doubt remains, however, about the universality of Herzberg's or Maslow's theories because of the inability to take into account all the relevant cultural variables when researching motivation. Different factors have different meaning within the entire cultural context and must be taken into account on a situation-by-situation basis.

The need to consider the entire national and cultural context is shown in the following Comparative Management in Focus, which highlights motivational issues for Mexican workers and indicates the importance to them of what Herzberg calls maintenance factors. As you read, consider whether this situation supports or refutes Herzberg's theory.

**COMPARATIVE
MANAGEMENT
IN FOCUS**

Motivation in Mexico

To get anything done here, the manager has to be more of an instructor, teacher, or father figure than a boss.

—Robert Hoskins, Manager, Leviton Manufacturing, Juarez

It is particularly important for an aspiring international manager to become familiar with Mexican factory workers because of the increasing volume of manufacturing that is being outsourced there.[45]

To understand the cultural milieu in Mexico, we can draw on research that concludes that Latin American societies, including Mexico, rank high on power distance (the acknowledgment of hierarchical authority) and on uncertainty avoidance (a preference for security and formality over risk). In addition, they rank low on individualism, preferring collectivism, which values the good of the group, family, or country over individual achievement.[46] In Mexico, the family is of central importance; loyalty and commitment to the family frequently determines employment, promotion, or special treatment for contracts. Unfortunately, it is this admirable cultural norm that often results in motivation and productivity problems on the job by contributing to very high absenteeism and a turnover rate especially in the maquiladoras. This high turnover and absenteeism are costly to employers, thereby offsetting the advantage of relatively low labor cost per hour. "Family reasons" (taking care of sick relatives or elderly parents) are the most common reasons given for absenteeism and for failing to return to work.[47] Workers often simply do not come back to work after vacations or holidays. In fact, for many Mexican males, the value of work is primarily that it enables them to fulfill their culturally imposed responsibilities as head of household and breadwinner rather than to seek individual achievement.[48] Machismo (sharp role differentiation based on gender) and prestige are important characteristics of the Mexican culture.

As a people, speaking very generally, Mexicans are very proud and patriotic; *respeto* (respect) is important to them, and slights against personal dignity are regarded as a grave provocation.[49] Mexican workers expect to be treated in the same respectful manner that they use toward one another. As noted by one U.S. expatriate, foreign managers must adapt to Mexico's "softer culture"; Mexican workers "need more communication, more relationship-building, and more reassurance than employees in the U.S."[50] The Mexican people are very warm and have a leisurely attitude toward time; face-to-face interaction is best for any kind of business, with time allowed for socializing and appreciating their cultural artifacts, buildings, and so forth. Taking time to celebrate a worker's birthday, for instance, will show that you are a *simpatico* boss and will increase workers' loyalty and effort. The workers' expectations of small considerations that seem inconsequential to U.S. managers should not be discounted. In one maquiladora, when the company stopped providing the annual Halloween candy, the employees filed a grievance to the state arbitration board, Junta de Conciliacion y Arbitraje.

Most managers in Mexico find that the management style that works best there is authoritative and paternal. In fact, paternalism is expected; the manager is regarded as the *patron* (pronounced "pahtrone"), or father figure, whose role it is to take care of the workers as an extended family.[51] Employees expect managers to be the authority; they are the "elite"— power rests with the owner or manager and other prominent community leaders. For the most part, if not told to do it, the workers won't do it; nor will they question the boss or make any decisions for the boss.[52] Nevertheless, employees perceive the manager as a person, not as a concept or a function, and success often depends on the ability of a foreign manager to adopt a personalized management style, such as by greeting all the workers as they come in for their shift.

Generally speaking, many Mexican factory workers doubt their ability to personally influence the outcome of their lives; they are apt to attribute events to the will of God, or to luck, timing, or relationships with higher authority figures. For many, decisions are made on the basis of ideals, emotions, and intuition, rather than objective information. However, there is increasing evidence of individualism and materialism, particularly among the upwardly mobile high-tech and professional Mexican employees.

Corrective discipline and motivation must occur through training examples, cooperation, and, if necessary, subtle shaming. As a disciplinary measure, it is a mistake to insult a Mexican directly; an outright insult implies an insult to the whole family. As a motivation, one must appeal to the pride of the Mexican employees and avoid causing them to feel humiliated. Given that "getting ahead" is often associated more with outside forces than with one's own actions, the motivation and reward system becomes difficult to structure in the usual ways. Past experiences have indicated that, for the most part, motivation through participative decision making is not as effective as that through the more traditional and expected autocratic methods. However, the mutual respect and caring the Mexican people have for one another does lead to positive team spirit needed for the team structure to be used successfully by companies such as GM in its highest-quality plant in the world in Ramos Arizpe, near Saltillo, Mexico.[53] The workers expect that authority will not be abused, but rather that it follow the family model where everyone works together in a dignified manner according to his or her designated role.[54] Any event that may break this harmony, or seem to confront authority, will likely be covered up. This may result in a supervisor hiding defective work, for example, or as in the case of a steel conveyor plant in Puebla, a total worker walkout rather than using the grievance process.[55] Contributing to these kinds of problems is the need to save face for oneself and to respect others' place and honor. Public criticism is regarded as humiliating. Employees like an atmosphere of formality and respect. They typically use flattery and call people by their titles rather than their names to maintain an atmosphere of regard for status and respect.

A context of continuing economic problems and a relatively low standard of living for most workers help explain why Maslow's higher-order needs (self-actualization, achievement, status) are generally not very high on most Mexican workers' list of needs. In discussing compensation, Mariah de Forest, who consults for American firms in Mexico, suggests that:

> Rather than an impersonal wage scale, Mexican workers tend to think in terms of payment now for services rendered now. A daily incentive system with automatic payouts for production exceeding quotas, as well as daily/monthly attendance bonuses, works well.[56]

Because of economic reforms and the peso devaluation, money is now a pressing motivational factor for most employees. Since the enjoyment of life is highly valued by workers, many companies in Mexico provide recreation facilities—a picnic area, a soccer field, and so forth. Bonuses are expected regardless of productivity; in fact, it is the law to give Christmas bonuses of 15-days pay to each worker. Fringe benefits are also important to Mexicans; because most Mexican workers are poor, the company provides the only source of such benefits for them. In particular, benefits that help manage family-related issues are positive motivators for employees to at least turn up for work. To this end, companies often provide on-site healthcare facilities for workers and their families, nurseries, free meals, and even small loans in crisis situations.[57] In addition, those companies that understand the local infrastructure problems often provide a company bus to minimize the pervasive problems of absenteeism and tardiness.

The foregoing statements are broad generalizations about Mexican factory workers. There are increasing numbers of American managers in Mexico since the NAFTA has encouraged more U.S. businesses to move operations there. For firms on American soil, managers may employ many Mexican Americans in an intercultural setting. As the second-largest and second-fastest-growing ethnic group, Mexican Americans represent an important subculture requiring management attention as they take an increasing proportion of the jobs in the United States. Yet, they remain the least assimilated ethnic group in the majority mainstream, partially from economic or occupational causes and partially from choice.[58, 59]

We have discussed some of the research pertinent to motivation in various countries; this research is summarized in Exhibit 12–4.

From the research, it appears that little conclusive information is available to answer a manager's direct question of exactly how to motivate in any particular culture because we cannot assume the universal applicability of the motivational theories, or even concepts, that have been used to research differences among cultures.

In sum, motivation is situational, and savvy managers use all they know about the relevant culture or subculture—consulting frequently with local people—to infer the best means of motivating in that context. Further, tactful managers consciously avoid an ethnocentric attitude, in which they make assumptions about a person's goals, motivation, or work habits based on their own frame of reference, and they do not make negative value judgments about a person's level of motivation because it differs from their own.

Many cultural variables affect people's sense of what is attainable, and thus affect motivation. One, for example, is how much control people believe they have over their environment and their destiny—whether they believe that they can control certain events, not just be at the mercy of external forces. Whereas Americans typically feel a strong internal locus of control, others attribute results to, for example, the will of God (in the case of Muslims) or to the good fortune of being born in the right social class or family (in the case of many Latin Americans). Whereas Americans feel that hard work will get the job done, many Hong Kong Chinese believe that outcomes are determined by *joss*, or luck.[60] Clearly, then, managers must use persuasive strategies to motivate employees when they do not readily connect their personal work behaviors with outcomes or productivity.

The role of culture in the motivational process is shown in Exhibit 12–5. An employee's needs are largely determined by the cultural context of values and attitudes—along with the national variables—in which he or she lives and works; those needs then determine the meaning of work for that employee. The manager's understanding of what work means in

EXHIBIT 12–4

Summary: Selected Studies Pertinent to Motivation

Study	Purpose	Results
Work Goals; Needs		
Furnham, Kirkcaldy, Lynn (1994), 41 countries, 5 continents, 12,000 young people	Relationships among country groups between attitudinal differences and country economic levels	Far/Middle East highest on competitiveness, acquisitiveness for money; Americas highest on work ethic and mastery
MOW Int. Research Team, G. England (1985); 8 countries	Explore relative importance of work; function of work to people	Comparative work centrality score—Japan highest; income most important for all, but differences in other functions across countries
Hofstede (1980); 40 countries (110 later); 60,000 employees and managers	Explore common dimensions to explain differences in goals and attitudes; examine relationship to economic, geographic, cultural variables; job categories	Four cultural dimensions found; wealth, education, religion, account for variance; six clusters; more differences in needs between job categories than countries
Ali (1992), 117 managers in Saudi Arabia	Explores Islamic work ethic and individualism	Strong commitment to Islamic work ethic; moderate individualism
Ronen (1979); 5 countries, 8,934 employees	Examine clusters of work goals across countries	Supports Maslow's need categories and intrinsic-extrinsic dichotomy
Shenkar and Ronen (1987); 163 managers-PRC, Hong Kong, Taiwan, Singapore	Compare work goals	Similar work goals; work more important than leisure; individual recognition of low importance; PRC valued autonomy and cooperation, not self-promotion
Sirota and Greenwood (1971); 25 countries, 13,000 employees	Explore similarities and differences in work goals	Strong traditions affect needs; importance, in order: self-actualization, social, esteem, security, autonomy
Reitz (1975); 8 countries, 736 managers	Compare relative importance of need levels and relationship to education	Similarity of need hierarchy; ranking of self-actualization and security dependent on education level
Herbert, Deresky, and Popp (1986); Mexican American, Anglo American students	Explore personality and work need differences related to integration	Differences in personality scales of work needs—more so for Mexican American males than females
Intrinsic-Extrinsic Dichotomy		
Kanungo and Wright (1983); Canada, United Kingdom, France, Japan; 449 mid-, lower-level managers	Compare importance of job factors, satisfaction	Significant differences across countries, in particular between United Kingdom and France; overall, intrinsic factors more important than extrinsic
Popp, Davis, and Herbert (1986); 165 students, United States, Australia, Canada, Singapore	Compare the relative importance of job factors	Herzberg-type motivational factors more important than maintenance factors
Machungwa and Schmitt (1983); Zambia, 341 employees at all levels	Explore motivation and maintenance factors	Confirm intrinsic-extrinsic dichotomy; work motivation resulted from growth opportunity, nature of work; dissatisfaction resulted from relationships, practices, etc.
White and Leon (1976); Greece, 178 managers	Examine validity of Herzberg's model	Confirm Herzberg's model; relationship of motivational factors to job satisfaction, maintenance factors to dissatisfaction
McCarov (1973); all members of an Israeli kibbutz	Examine validity of Herzberg's model	Confirm Herzberg's model; job satisfaction a result of work itself; dissatisfaction a result of extrinsic conditions
Lincoln (1989); 8,362 workers in 106 factories, United States and Japan	Compare effectiveness of Japanese management practices in Japan and United States	Similar positive or negative effects; Japanese: lower levels of job satisfaction than American

EXHIBIT 12-5

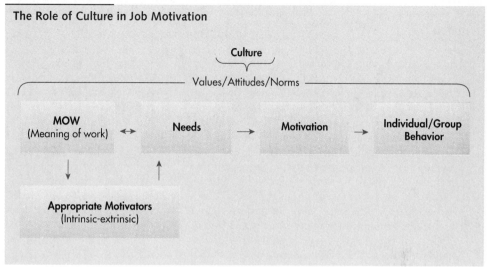

The Role of Culture in Job Motivation

that employee's life can then lead to the design of a culturally appropriate job context and reward system to guide individual and group employee job behavior to meet mutual goals.

Reward Systems

Incentives and rewards are an integral part of motivation in a corporation. Recognizing and understanding different motivational patterns across cultures leads to the design of appropriate reward systems. In the United States, there are common patterns of rewards, varying among levels of the company and types of occupations and based on experience and research with Americans. Rewards usually fall into five categories: financial, social status, job content, career, and professional.[61] The relative emphasis on one or more of these five categories varies from country to country. In Japan, for example, reward systems are based primarily on seniority, and much emphasis is put on the bonus system. In addition, distinction is made there between the regular workforce and the temporary workforce, which usually comprises women expected to leave when they start a family. As is usually the case, the regular workforce receives considerably more rewards than the temporary workforce, both in pay and benefits and in the allocation of interesting jobs.[62] For the regular workforce, the emphasis is on the long-term effectiveness of the employee in terms of behavior, personality, and group output. Rewarding the individual is frowned on in Japan because it encourages competition rather than the desired group cooperation. Therefore, specific cash incentives are usually limited. In Taiwan, recognition and affection are important; company departments compete for praise from top management at their annual celebration.[63]

In contrast, the entire reward system in China is very different from that of most countries. The low wage rates are compensated for by free housing, schools, and medical care. Although egalitarianism still seems to prevail, the recent free-enterprise reform movements have encouraged *duo lao, duo de* (more work, more pay). One important incentive is training,

MANAGEMENT FOCUS

Ms. Wong: Employee of the Month

In some retail stores in China, managers are choosing their "employee of the month." However, this is not an award for exceptional or deserving employees, as is typical in the United States. Rather, they are identifying their worst employees, putting a plaque at that person's work station so that everyone who passes by can see that this is a weak employee. The approach is designed to embarrass that person into doing better work by showing everyone that the employee has let down his or her compatriots with substandard work. Since poor performers cannot generally be fired, management uses a different approach, humiliation, which is particularly devastating to Asians. Many Chinese seem delighted with the practice because retail service in China is extremely poor, and they feel this will improve things.

The worst employees are identified by customers and managerial evaluations. If a customer feels that a clerk has not provided adequate service, the customer has the opportunity to cast a ballot for the clerk as one of the worst employees in the store. The managers then get together, add their own input, and decide which employees to designate as the worst of the month. These awards are given, for example, for rudeness to customers. One clerk showed a customer 11 coats, but none of them pleased her and she grew impatient with the clerk. The sales clerk then told the woman, "Lady, I've never met a customer as rude as you."

That broadside cost the saleswoman dearly. Her customer marched over to the service desk and cast a vote for her as the store's worst assistant. [She] eventually won enough votes to make the designation official, and lost her November bonus—nearly a quarter of her monthly income.

Those who receive this award have to write self-criticisms of their behavior and analyze their actions. In addition, they lose their monthly bonus.

Management seems to be pleased with this negative approach, and plans are afoot to extend the system to include the supervisors. One suggestion on how to identify the "worst supervisor of the month" is to have a ballot box for the sales clerks to vote.

Source: Adapted from Adi Ignatius, "Now If Ms. Wong Insults a Customer, She Gets an Award," *Wall Street Journal,* January 24, 1989, 1, 15.

which gives workers more power.[64] Material incentives are more common now, but another approach used in the past—and one that seems quite negative to Americans—is described in the Management Focus "Ms. Wong: Employee of the Month."

LEADING

The manager's quintessential responsibility is to help his people realize their own highest potential.

—Jacques Maisonrouge, IBM World Trade Corporation

As you read this section on leadership, consider the following questions: To what extent, and how, do leadership styles and practices around the world vary? What are the forces leading to that divergence? Where, and why, will that divergence continue to be the strongest? Is there any evidence for convergence of leadership styles and practices around the world? What are the forces leading to that convergence, and how and where do you think this convergence will occur in the future? What are the implications of these questions for cross-cultural leaders?

The task of helping employees realize their highest potential in the workplace is the essence of leadership. Ideally, leaders aim to achieve the organization's objectives and also those of each employee. Today's global managers realize that increased competition requires them to be open to change and to rethink their old culturally conditioned modes of leadership. Today's managers, say Harris and Moran, must look to the past and the future: "Innovative managers assist people and their social institutions to build upon, yet to transcend, their cultural past."[65]

The Multicultural Leader's Role and Environment

Effective **leadership** involves the ability to inspire and influence the thinking, attitudes, and behavior of people.[66,67] The importance of the leadership role cannot be overemphasized because the leader's interactions strongly influence the motivation and behavior of employees, and ultimately, the entire climate of the organization. The cumulative effects of one or more weak managers can have a significant negative impact on the ability of the organization to meet its objectives.

The multicultural leader tries to maximize leadership effectiveness by juggling several important, and sometimes conflicting, roles as (1) a representative of the parent firm, (2) the manager of the local firm, (3) a resident of the local community, (4) a citizen of either the host country or another country, (5) a member of a profession, and (6) a member of a family.[68,69]

The leader's role comprises the interaction of two sets of variables—the content and the context of leadership. The **content of leadership** consists of the attributes of the leader and the decisions to be made; the **context of leadership** consists of all those variables related to the particular situation.[70] The increased number of variables (political, economic, and cultural) in the context of the managerial job abroad requires astute leadership. Some of the variables in the content and context of the leader's role in foreign settings are shown in Exhibit 12–6. The multicultural leader's role thus blends leadership, communication, motivational, and other managerial skills within unique and ever-changing environments. We will examine the contingent nature of such leadership throughout this section.

An additional factor—that of technology—is becoming increasingly pervasive in its ability to influence the global leader's role and environment, and perhaps will contribute to a lessening of the differences in motivation and leadership around the world. More and more often, companies like Italtel spa, featured in the accompanying Technology Application, are using technology in global leadership techniques to set up systems for their geographically dispersed employees to enable them to expand and coordinate their global operations. In the case of Italtel, this required wide delegation and empowerment of their employees so that they could decentralize.

Cross-Cultural Research on Leadership

Numerous leadership theories variously focus on individual traits, leader behavior, interaction patterns, role relationships, follower perceptions, influence over followers, influence on task goals, and influence on organizational culture.[71,72] Our task in this chapter is to show how the variable of societal culture fits into these theories and what implications can be drawn for international managers as they seek to provide leadership around the world.

EXHIBIT 12-6

Factors Affecting Leadership Abroad

Content	
Attributes of the Person	**Characteristics of Decisions Situation**
Job position knowledge, experience, expectations	Degree of complexity, uncertainty, and risk
Longevity in company, country, functional area	In-country information needs and availability
Intelligence and cultural learning or change ability	Articulation of assumptions and expectations
Personality as demonstrated in values, beliefs, attitudes toward foreign situations	Scope and potential impact on performance
Multiple memberships in work and professional groups	Nature of business partners
Decision and personal work style	Authority and autonomy required
	Required level of participation and acceptance by employees, partners, and government
	Linkage to other decisions
	Past management legacy
	Openness to pubic scrutiny and responsibility

Context	
Attributes of the Job or Position	**Characteristics of the Firm and Business Environment**
Longevity and past success of former role occupants in the position	Firm structure: size, location, technology, tasks, reporting, and communication patterns
Technical requirements of the job	Firm process: decision making, staffing, control system, reward system, information system, means of coordination, integration, and conflict resolution
Relative authority or power	
Physical location (e.g., home office, field office)	
Need for coordination, cooperation, and integration with other units	Firm outputs: products, services, public image, corporate culture, local history, and community relations
Resource availability	
Foreign peer group relations	Business environment: social-cultural, political-economic, and technological aspects of a country or market

Source: R. H. Mason and R. S. Spich, *Management—An International Perspective* (Homewood, IL: Irwin, 1987): 186.

Though the *functions* of leadership are similar across cultures, anthropological studies, such as those by Mead, indicate that leadership is a universal phenomenon and that effective leadership varies across cultures.[73]

In addition to research studies that indicate variations in leadership profiles, the generally accepted image that people in different countries have about what they expect and admire in their leaders tends to become a norm over time, forming an idealized role for these leaders, as discussed in the Management Focus "Authority Figures Must Look and Act the Part."

Most research on American leadership styles describes managerial behaviors on essentially the same dimension, variously termed autocratic versus democratic, participative versus directive, relations-oriented versus task oriented, or initiating structure versus consideration

TECHNOLOGY APPLICATION

Italtel Spa's Leadership Style Empowers Global Employees with Technology

Executive Summary

Company: Italtel spa

Industry: Telecommunications

Business Challenge: To "flatten" the organization and expand globally.

Solution: An intranet based on Netscape products that enables Italtel to share knowledge and product information throughout the company.

Plant operations, antenna functioning, and network traffic are monitored online.

Solution Features: Employees can access Italtel's technical product documentation online.

Employees can book training courses via the intranet.

Reduced costs for information, documentation, and software distribution.

Business Benefits: Network and service monitoring online contributes to improved customer service.

Centralized employee database and single network login for every user dramatically reduces system administration time and costs.

Italtel spa is an international supplier of telecommunications networks that specializes in the design, development, and installation of integrated telecommunications systems. The company employs 16,000 people, 21 percent of whom are involved in research and development. Italtel invests 12 percent of its annual revenues in R&D, addressing a wide range of applications.

Business Challenge

With the globalization of the telecommunications market, Italtel had to expand internationally in order to compete successfully. To do so, Italtel management felt that it should "flatten" the organization, moving from a hierarchical structure to one in which employees are empowered with all the tools and information they need to do their jobs better, thereby improving customer service and time to market.

In addition to the business challenges associated with international expansion, the company faces several technical challenges. Sweeping changes spurred by the convergence of communication and information technologies force Italtel to innovate faster than ever before. As a result, Italtel needs to share knowledge and information and improve communication throughout the company—all within a distributed, extremely heterogeneous computing environment. This environment includes a wide range of client systems, such as Unix workstations and PCs running Windows 3.1, 95, and NT, and servers that include Digital, Hewlett-Packard, IBM, Sun, and Windows NT-based systems. The company needed a new information technology solution that would provide global information access, flexibility, and ease of use. Among the goals for the new system were to create a centralized, easily accessible source for all company information resources, to monitor the company's telecommunications services and network online for better performance, to organize training courses, and to set up working groups in different departments.

Solving the Challenge

Italtel selected key components of the Netscape SuitSpot server software family to deploy an enterprisewide intranet and messaging solution. Netscape Enterprise Server distributes Web-based intranet and Internet services.

Source: www.Netscape.com case studies.

---

continuum.[74–77] These studies were developed in the West, and conclusions regarding employee responses largely reflect the opinions of American workers. The democratic, or participative, leadership style has been recommended as the one more likely to have positive results with most American employees.

Contingency Leadership—The Culture Variable

Modern leadership theory recognizes that no single leadership style works well in all situations.[78] A considerable amount of research, directly or indirectly, supports the notion of cultural contingency in leadership. Much of this research also provides insight into the relative level of preference for autocratic versus participative leadership styles. For example, Hofstede's four cultural dimensions (discussed in Chapter 4) provide a good starting point to study leader–subordinate expectations and relationships. We can assume, for example, that employees in countries that rank high on power distance (India, Mexico, the Philippines) are more likely to prefer an autocratic leadership style and some paternalism because they are more comfortable with a clear distinction between managers and subordinates than with a blurring of decision-making responsibility.

Employees in countries that rank low on power distance (Sweden and Israel) are more likely to prefer a consultative, participative leadership style, and they expect superiors to adhere to that style. Hofstede, in fact, concludes that the participative management approaches recommended by many American researchers can be counterproductive in certain cultures.[79] The crucial fact to grasp about leadership in any culture, he points out, is that it is a complement to **subordinateship** (employee attitudes toward leaders). In other words, perhaps we concentrate too much on leaders and their unlikely ability to change styles at will; much depends on subordinates and their cultural conditioning, and it is that subordinateship to which the leader must respond.[80] Hofstede points out that his research reflects the values of subordinates, not the values of superiors. His descriptions of the types of subordinateship a leader can expect in societies with three different levels of power distance are shown in Exhibit 12–7.

In another part of his research, Hofstede ranked the relative presence of autocratic norms in the following countries, from lowest to highest: Germany, France, Belgium, Japan, Italy, the United States, the Netherlands, Britain, and India. India ranked much higher than the others on autocracy.[81]

Expectations about managerial authority versus participation were also among the managerial behaviors and philosophies studied by Laurent, a French researcher. In a study conducted in nine western European countries, the United States, Indonesia, and Japan, he concluded that national origin significantly affects the perception of what is effective management.[82] For example, Americans and Germans subscribe more to participation than do Italians and Japanese; Indonesians are more comfortable with a strict autocratic structure. Managers in Sweden, the Netherlands, the United States, Denmark, and Great Britain believe that employees should participate in problem solving rather than simply be "fed" all the answers by managers, compared with managers in those countries on the higher end of this scale, such as Italy, Indonesia, and Japan. Laurent's findings about Japan, however, seem to contradict common knowledge about Japan's very participative decision-making culture. In fact, research by Hampden-Turner and Trompenaars places Japan as second highest, after Sweden, in the extent to which leaders delegate authority. Findings regarding the other countries are similar (shown in Exhibit 12–8). However, participative leadership should not mean a lack of initiative or responsibility.

Other classic studies indicate cross-cultural differences in the expectations of leadership behavior. Haire, Ghiselli, and Porter surveyed more than 3,000 managers in 14 countries.

EXHIBIT 12–7

Subordinateship for Three Levels of Power Distance

Small Power Distance	Medium Power Distance (United States)	Large Power Distance
Subordinates have weak dependence needs.	Subordinates have medium dependence needs.	Subordinates have strong dependence needs.
Superiors have weak dependence needs toward their superiors.	Superiors have medium dependence needs toward their superiors.	Superiors have strong dependence needs toward their superiors.
Subordinates expect superiors to consult them and may rebel or strike if superiors are not seen as staying within their legitimate role.	Subordinates expect superiors to consult them but will accept autocratic behavior as well.	Subordinates expect superiors to act autocratically.
Ideal superior to most is a loyal democrat.	Ideal superior to most is a resourceful democrat.	Ideal superior to most is a benevolent autocrat or paternalist.
Laws and rules apply to all, and privileges for superiors are not considered acceptable.	Laws and rules apply to all, but a certain level of privilege for superiors is considered normal.	Everybody expects superiors to enjoy privileges; laws and rules differ for superiors and subordinates.
Status symbols are frowned upon and will easily come under attack from subordinates.	Status symbols for superiors contribute moderately to their authority and will be accepted by subordinates.	Status symbols are very important and contribute strongly to the superior's authority with the subordinates.

Source: Geert Hofstede, "Motivation, Leadership, and Organization: Do American Theories Apply Abroad?" *Organizational Dynamics* (Summer 1980): 42–63. Copyright © Geert Hofstede.

They found that, although managers around the world consistently favored delegation and participation, those managers also had a low appreciation of the capacity and willingness of subordinates to take an active role in the management process.[83]

In addition, several studies of individual countries or areas conclude that a participative leadership style is frequently inappropriate. Managers in Malaysia, Indonesia, Thailand, and the Philippines were found to prefer autocratic leadership, whereas those in Singapore and Hong Kong are less autocratic.[84] Similarly, the Turks have been found to prefer authoritarian leadership, as do the Thais.[85, 86]

In the Middle East, in particular, there is little delegation. A successful company there must have strong managers who make all the decisions and who go unquestioned; much emphasis is placed on the use of power through social contacts and family influence, and the chain of command must be rigidly followed.[87] A comparison of these and other management dimensions between Middle Eastern and Western managers is shown in Exhibit 12–9.

These stereotypical extremes of Middle Eastern and Western leadership styles were exemplified at the highest level by President George Bush and President Saddam Hussein during the 1991 Gulf War, and again in 1998 by President Clinton. Underlying these styles—and the misunderstandings that persist between Arabs and the West—are many cultural and national factors (including differences in religion; logic; and ideas about truth, freedom, honor, trust, family, and friends). Most of these factors are based on elements of Arab history that Westerners find difficult to comprehend. Arabs tend to use the past as their basis of reference, whereas Americans look to the future.

EXHIBIT 12–8

Comparative Leadership Dimensions: Participation and Initiative

Managerial Initiative, Managers' Sense of Drive and Responsibility		Extent to Which Leaders Delegate Authority	
0 = low; 100 = high		0 = low; 100 = high	
USA	73.67	Sweden	75.51
Sweden	72.29	Japan	69.27
Japan	72.20	Norway	68.50
Finland	69.58	USA	66.23
Korea	67.86	Singapore	65.37
Netherlands	67.11	Denmark	64.65
Singapore	66.34	Canada	64.38
Switzerland	65.71	Finland	62.92
Belgium/Lux	65.47	Switzerland	62.20
Ireland	64.76	Netherlands	61.33
France	64.64	Australia	61.22
Austria	62.56	Germany	60.85
Denmark	62.79	New Zealand	60.54
Italy	62.40	Ireland	59.53
Australia	62.04	UK	58.95
Canada	61.56	Belgium/Lux	54.55
Spain	61.55	Austria	54.29
New Zealand	59.46	France	53.62
Greece	58.50	Italy	46.80
UK	58.25	Spain	44.31
Norway	54.50	Portugal	42.56
Portugal	49.74	Greece	37.95

Source: C. Hampden-Turner and A. Trompenaars, *The Seven Cultures of Capitalism* (New York: Doubleday, 1993).

From various accounts, Hussein thinks that his strong leadership means the fulfillment of destiny: Iraq was meant to be the dominant power in the region. Others, however, attest to his use of internal power for personal aggrandizement. His leadership style is, obviously, dictatorial, and to most people in the world he seems a ruthless tyrant and a master of manipulation. However, he is seen as a hero by most Iraqis and by many other Arabs in the region. Participation and delegation in decision making are clearly not among his leadership behaviors, nor is he likely to seek consensus even on radical plans. In contrast, most Western leaders quietly go about team building—consulting widely and building consensus around whatever action they feel should be taken. After Iraq invaded Kuwait in August 1990, President Bush took time to build strong support behind the scenes, forging a powerful alliance among Arabs, Jews, Europeans, Japanese, Chinese, and Soviets. Based on continued support, President Clinton ordered further attacks on Iraq in 1998–99 after Iraq's lack of compliance with agreements made in 1990.

EXHIBIT 12–9

Comparison of Middle Eastern and Western Management Practices

Managerial Function	Middle Eastern Stereotype	Western Stereotype
Organizational design	Highly bureaucratic, overcentralized with power and authority at the top. Vague relationships. Ambiguous and unpredictable organization environments.	Less bureaucratic, more delegation of authority. Relatively decentralized structure.
Patterns of decision making	Ad hoc planning, decisions made at the highest level of management. Unwillingness to take high risk inherent in decision making.	Sophisticated planning techniques, modern tools of decision making, elaborate management information systems.
Performance evaluation and control	Informal control mechanisms, routine checks on performance. Lack of vigorous performance evaluation systems.	Fairly advanced control systems focusing on cost reduction and organizational effectiveness.
Manpower policies	Heavy reliance on personal contacts and gettingindividuals from the "right social origin" to fill major positions.	Sound personnel management policies. Candidates' qualifications are usually the basis for selection decisions.
Leadership	Highly authoritarian tone, rigid instructions. Too many management directives.	Less emphasis on leader's personality, considerable weight on leader's style and performance.
Communication	The tone depends on the communicants. Social position, power, and family influence are ever-present factors. Chain of command must be followed rigidly. People relate to each other tightly and specifically. Friendships are intense and binding.	Stress usually on equality and a minimization of differences. People relate to each other loosely and generally. Friendships not intense and binding.
Management methods	Generally old and outdated.	Generally modern and more scientific.

Source: Copyright © 1980 by The Regents of the University of California. Reprinted from the *California Management Review* 22, no. 3. By permission of The Regents.

The effects of participative leadership can vary even in one location when the employees are from different cultural backgrounds—from which we can conclude that a subordinate's culture is usually a more powerful variable than other factors in the environment. Research that supports this conclusion includes a study conducted in Saudi Arabia that found participative leadership to be more effective with American workers than with Asian and African employees, and a study in a U.S. plant that found that participative leadership resulted in greater satisfaction and communication in American employees than in Mexican employees.[88, 89]

In Exhibit 12–10, we depict our integrative model of the leadership process—pulling together the variables described in this book and in the research on culture, leadership, and motivation—showing the powerful contingency of culture as it affects the leadership role. Reading from left to right, it covers the broad environmental factors through to the outcomes affected by the entire leadership situation. As shown in the exhibit, the broad context in which the manager operates necessitates adjustments in leadership style to all those variables relating to the work and task environment and the people involved. Cultural variables (values, work norms, the locus of control, and so forth), as they affect everyone involved—leader, subordinates, and work groups—then shape the content of the immediate leadership situation.

EXHIBIT 12–10

The Culture Contingency in the Leadership Process: An Integrative Model

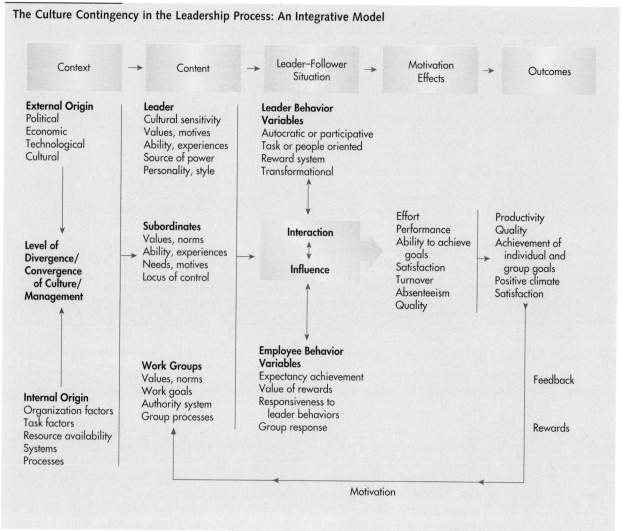

The leader–follower interaction is then further shaped by the leader's choice of behaviors (autocratic, participative, and so on) and the employees' attitudes toward the leader and the incentives. Motivation effects—various levels of effort, performance, and satisfaction—result from these interactions, on an individual and a group level. These effects determine the outcomes for the company (productivity, quality) and for the employees (satisfaction, positive climate). The results and rewards from those outcomes then act as feedback (positive or negative) into the cycle of the motivation and leadership process.

Clearly, then, international managers should take seriously the **culture contingency** in their application of the contingency theory of leadership—meaning that they must adjust their leadership behaviors according to the context, norms, attitudes, and other variables in that society. One example of the complexity of the leadership situation involving obvious contextual as well as cultural factors can be seen from the results of a study of how Russian employees responded to participative management practices of North American managers. It was found that the performance of the Russian workers decreased, which the researchers attributed to a history of employee ideas being ignored by Russian managers, as well as cultural value differences.[90] To gain more insight into comparative leadership situations, the following Comparative Management in Focus highlights the leadership context in India along with the implications for appropriate leadership by expatriates.

COMPARATIVE MANAGEMENT IN FOCUS

Leadership in India

The underlying cultural variable structuring each individual's life in India is the caste system, which extends into organizations in the form of a strict adherence to hierarchy. Indians are disposed to structure all relationships hierarchically; for this reason, they usually work better individually than in groups.[91] Management in India is often autocratic, based on formal authority and charisma. Family norms emphasizing loyalty to the family authority figure underlie the limited decision-making experience and unfamiliarity with responsibility found in some employees. Consequently, decision making is centralized, with much emphasis on rules and a low propensity for risk.[92] In addition, intricate family ties and strong authority figures perpetuate a managerial style of paternalism.

Under the pervasive influences of religion, caste, and family on the life of the Hindu, the Indian culture stresses moral orientation and loyalty, as in the pursuit of *dharma*, one's obligation to society, rather than personal goals. Work tends to be viewed primarily in the context of family or intercaste relationships, rather than being valued for itself.[93]

Since the original source of power is family and friends, nepotism is common both at the lowest and highest levels.[94] Unsurprisingly, power based on expertise frequently takes a back seat to power based on position.[95] In India, it is difficult for nonfamily members to advance into upper management. Such strong cultural influences in managers' origins affect managerial style.

Because of the respect for authority and obedience within the Indian family system, attempts by Indian or American managers to delegate authority often result in confusion and a lack of respect for the manager; Indian employees expect the managers to make the decisions. The norm is to "check with the boss." Any introduction of participative management requires careful training because it is so unlike the cultural norms. Generally, American managers in India need to make connections with the right families, make contact at the highest levels, and provide incentives for middle managers and assistants to help nudge proposals upward.[96]

On the microlevel of leadership—manager to employees—American managers in India are wise to tread slowly while trying to understand the culture and find what works. Various proposals have been put forward to help managers move toward more effective leadership. Tripathi suggests that "indigenous values, such as familism, need to be synthesized with the values of industrial democracy."[97] Similarly, Sinha proposes that, though a leader in India has to be a "nurturant," taking a personal interest in the well-being of each subordinate, he or she can use that nurturance to encourage increasing levels of participation. The manager may accomplish this by guiding and directing subordinates to work hard and maintain a high level of productivity, reinforcing each stage with increased nurturance.[98] According to Sinha and Sinha, a prerequisite to effective cross-cultural leadership in India is to establish work as the "master value." Once this is done, "other social values will reorganize themselves to help realize the master value."[99]

Multiple problems abound on the macrolevel of leadership of a global enterprise in India, as discovered by companies such as Gillette, Rank Xerox, Texas Instruments, and Hewlett-Packard. Investment opportunities are very attractive, with a potential for great sales and a pool of cheap, highly educated, and skilled labor. But even after getting through the entrenched bureaucracy to set up business, managers may face many operating problems because of the undeveloped infrastructure and difficult climate. Gaining control and integrating leadership styles with local managers are additional hurdles. American managers, used to being boss in their own companies, may have difficulty taking orders from Indian partners and prefer to operate at a faster pace.[100] Gill, of Gillette, suggests, "You've got to find the right partner and convince him to give you complete management control."[101] Failure to include an Indian partner or to build local support was behind the cancellation of Enron's $2.8 billion power project in Dabhol, as part of a resurgence of economic nationalism in India in 1995 pending national elections. The project was reinstated in 1999 in other areas, such as telecommunications, liberalization is progressing well, to the benefit of companies such as AT&T, Motorola, and Texas Instruments (TI). It is noteworthy that these companies have Indian joint venture partners and Indian CEOs. TI India's managing director, Srini Rajam, noted that the Bangalore plant was responsible for one-third of TI's design automation for semiconductor products worldwide.[102]

India is expected to be an economic giant someday. Meanwhile, American managers must realize that setting up and running a successful business in India requires astute leadership skills, including integrating and collaborating at all levels of the community for the long term.

As we have said, leadership refers not just to the manager–subordinate relationship, but to the important task of running the whole company, division, or unit for which the manager is responsible. In Japan, for example, in spite of recent economic distress, many companies there continue to provide a model for quality control techniques. One executive, who has worked ten years for Japanese companies, says that a key to Japanese-style success is "to take many small steps, consistently, every day."[103] One of the areas in which Japanese managers use this process of **continuous improvement**—or **kaizen**—is quality control, which has been the hallmark of success for many Japanese industries.

Japanese employees have a great sense of loyalty and duty to the firm, born out of the still common practices of lifetime employment and seniority-based wages and promotions. In fact, hard work and loyalty have resulted in widespread workaholism among Japanese because of "the intense pressures on them to conform and to identify with their corporate 'family.'"[104] Conformity and dedication, instilled since childhood, are illustrated in the photograph "Japanese Loyalty and Conformity," which shows a typical group of employees participating in a company song and creed recitation before work.

For some time, American companies have studied successful Japanese companies for the purpose of emulating management styles to improve productivity, in particular the practice of employee involvement. Recently, increased global competitiveness and further exposure to

Western culture and managerial practices have led Japanese firms to adopt more American practices. This partial blending of management practices indicates a trend toward convergence of leadership styles. Nevertheless, management processes, though ostensibly similar, will usually manifest themselves differently as a function of the entire cultural context in which they are enacted.

The Effective International Leader

What makes an effective international leader, then, is whether the leader has and exercises the appropriate skills to address a given situation. The key **cross-cultural leadership skills** needed, according to Bass, are social perceptual skills, interpersonal competence, effective intelligence, and efficient work habits.[105] Some important information about what managers around the world consider necessary for interpersonal competence is provided by a cross-cultural study of 1,000 managers in 13 countries; in this study, Bass and Burger found seven factors to be linked with interpersonal competence:

1. Preferred awareness (willingness to be aware of others' feelings)
2. Actual awareness (actual understanding of oneself and others)
3. Submissiveness (to rules and authority)
4. Reliance on others (in problem solving)
5. Favoring of group decision making
6. Concern for human relations
7. Cooperative peer relations[106]

As we have discussed, however, the skills and other competences of the leader constitute only one variable of the leadership context. Other variables include the followers, the peers, the superiors, the task, and the environment. Managers must evaluate themselves and the total leadership environment to effect good leadership.

Conclusion

Because leadership and motivation entail constant interactions with others (employees, peers, superiors, outside contacts), cultural influences on these critical management functions are very strong. Certainly, other powerful variables are intricately involved in the international management context, particularly those of economics and politics. Effective leaders carefully examine the entire context and develop a sensitivity to others' values and expectations regarding personal and group interactions, performance, and outcomes—and then act accordingly.

Summary of Key Points

1. Motivation and leadership are factors in the successful implementation of desired strategy. But although many of the basic principles are universal, much of the actual content and process is culture contingent—a function of an individual's needs, value systems, and environmental context.
2. One problem in using content theories, such as those created by Maslow and Herzberg, for cross-cultural research is the assumption of their universal application. Because they were developed in the United states, even the concepts, such as achievement or esteem, may have different meanings in other societies, resulting in a noncomparable basis of research.

3. Implicit in motivating an employee is an understanding of which of the employee's needs are satisfied by work. Studies on the meaning of work indicate considerable cross-cultural differences.

4. Other studies on cross-cultural motivation support Herzberg's two-factor theory. They also indicate, as do studies using Maslow's theory, support for the greater importance of intrinsic factors to motivation, at least on the managerial level. One problem with Herzberg's theory is that it does not account for all relevant cultural variables.

5. A reexamination of motivation relative to Hofstede's dimensions of power distance, uncertainty avoidance, individualism, and masculinity provides another perspective on the cultural contexts that can influence motivational structures.

6. Incentives and reward systems must be designed to reflect the motivational structure and relative cultural emphasis on five categories of rewards: financial, social status, job content, career, and professional.

7. Effective leadership is crucial to the ability of a company to achieve its goals. The challenge is to decide what is effective leadership in different international or mixed-culture situations.

8. The perception of what makes a good leader—both traits and behaviors—varies a great deal from one society to another.

9. Contingency theory is applicable to cross-cultural leadership situations because of the vast number of cultural and national variables that can affect the dynamics of the leadership context. These include leader–subordinate and group relations, which are affected by cultural expectations, values, needs, attitudes, perceptions of risk, and loci of control.

Discussion Questions

1. Discuss the concept of work centrality and its implications for motivation. Use specific country examples and discuss the relative meaning of work in those countries.

2. What are the implications for motivation of Hofstede's research findings on the dimensions of power distance, uncertainty avoidance, individualism, and masculinity?

3. Explain what is meant by the need to design culturally appropriate reward systems. Give some examples.

4. Compare Mexico and China regarding motivational bases. Describe what would be your approach to motivation in these two countries.

5. Describe the variables of content and context in the leadership situation. What additional variables are involved in cross-cultural leadership?

6. Explain the theory of contingency leadership and discuss the role of culture in that theory.

7. How can we use Hofstede's four dimensions—power distance, uncertainty avoidance, individualism, and masculinity—to gain insight into leader–subordinate relationships around the world? Give some specific examples.

8. Describe the autocratic versus democratic leadership dimension. Discuss the cultural contingency in this dimension and give some examples of research findings indicating differences among countries.

Application Exercises

1. Using the material in the chapter on motivation in China and in Mexico, design a suitable organizational reward system for the workers in your company's plants in each of those countries.

2. Choose a country and do some research (and conduct interviews, if possible) to create a cultural profile. Focus on factors affecting behavior in the workplace. Integrate any findings regarding motivation or work attitudes and behaviors. Decide on the type of approach to motivation you would take and the kinds of incentive and reward systems you would set up as manager of a subsidiary in that country. Use the theories on motivation discussed in this chapter to infer motivational structures relative to that society. Then decide what type of leadership style and process you would use. What are the major contingencies that you took into account?

3. Try to interview several people from a specific ethnic subculture in a company or in your college or university regarding values, needs, expectations in the workplace, and so on. Sketch a motivational profile of this subculture and present it to your class for discussion.

Experiential Exercises

1. Bill Higgins had served as the manager of a large U.S. timber company located in a rather remote rain forest in a South American country. Since it began its logging operations in the 1950s, a major problem facing the company has been the recruitment of labor. The only nearby source of labor is the sparsely populated local Indian group in the area. Bill's company has been in direct competition for laborers with a German company operating in the same region. In an attempt to attract the required number of laborers, Bill's company has invested heavily in new housing and offered considerably higher wages than the German company, as well as a guaranteed 40-hour work week. Yet the majority of the available workers continued to work for the German company, despite its substandard housing and minimum hourly wage. Bill finally brought in several U.S. anthropologists who had worked among the local Indians. The answer to Bill's labor recruitment problem was quite simple, but it required looking at the values of the Indian labor force rather than simply building facilities that would appeal to the typical U.S. laborer.

   What did the anthropologists tell Bill?

   Source: Gary P. Ferraro, *The Cultural Dimensions of International Business,* 2nd ed. (NJ: Prentice-Hall, 1994).

2. Meet with another student, preferably one whom you know well. Talk with that person and draw up a list of leadership skills you perceive him or her to possess. Then consider your research and readings regarding cross-cultural leadership. Name two countries where you think the student would be an effective leader and two where you think there would be conflict. Discuss those areas of conflict. Then reverse the procedure to find out more about yourself. Share with the class, if you wish.

Internet Resources

Visit the Deresky companion Web site at http://prenhall.com/Deresky for this chapter's Internet resources.

Case Study

Elizabeth's Visit to GPC's Subsidiary in the Philippines

Elizabeth Moreno is reviewing her notes in midflight somewhere over the vast Pacific Ocean on a 747 jumbo jet en route to the Philippines for her latest assignment. It has been about ten hours since she left her home organization, the Global Pharmaceutical Company (GPC), in rural upstate New York. GPC is the largest ethical pharmaceutical research and manufacturing company worldwide in terms of sales. Ethical drugs are those that can be purchased only through a physician's prescription.

In the United States, GPC has research and manufacturing sites in New York, New Jersey, Pennsylvania, and Michigan. The company also has subsidiaries in Canada, Puerto Rico, Australia, Philippines, Brazil, England, and France. GPC has its administrative headquarters in Pennsylvania. The different subsidiary plants are interlinked technologically. It is normal for various plants to hold multisite real-time video conferences and telephone conferences. Electronic mail along with faxes, modems, and traditional mail are used extensively. Despite these technological advances, face-to-face meetings and on-site consultations are still needed. It is not unusual for GPC's top scientists and key managers to log thousands of air miles a year.

Elizabeth Moreno is one of the key specialists within GPC. Her expertise in chemical processing is widely known not only within her company but also in the pharmaceutical industry worldwide. She has been working at GPC for more than 12 years since finishing her advanced degree in chemistry from a university in the Midwest. While working for GPC, she has been given more and more responsibilities leading to her current position as vice president of chemical development and processing.

Just about a year ago, she was sent by the company to its manufacturing plant in Puerto Rico to advise Puerto Rican management about technical aspects of synthesizing chemicals for eventual use in the production of ethical drugs. She stayed there for a week, and she did not seem to encounter multicultural problems since many of the managers were trained in U.S. universities and were familiar with the corporate policies.

For her latest assignment, she is being sent to the Philippine subsidiary for one week to study a recurrent problem of chemical batches not meeting product specifications and to recommend solutions. During her week's visit, she will conduct training for chemists in state-of-the-art techniques for testing, as well as training for local managers in chemical statistical quality control. These testing techniques are now currently used in other GPC locations.

On the surface, this latest assignment seems perfect for Elizabeth who was born in the Philippines and finished her undergraduate college studies there. She is still fluent in Filipino, which is the official language but is just one of 87 languages spoken. There are more than 7,000 islands scattered in the Philippine archipelago on the South China Sea. Also, Elizabeth had worked as a research analyst at the Asian Development Bank for a couple of years in the Philippines before she started her advanced education in the United States. The Asian Development Bank is an international financial institution that extends financial and technical assistance to developing countries in Asia. While there, she worked directly under the supervision of an American chemical engineer within the department headed by a Nepalese manager and a German research director.

Yet, Elizabeth accepted the assignment to go to the Philippines with some trepidation. Knowing both the American and Philippine culture, she is well aware of the differences between American and Filipino managers. She left the Philippines in 1980 and has not been back since; it has been 15 years. Although she had already finished college when she left the Philippines, she has not had any business dealings with Filipinos. Even her brief work experience in the international organization in the Philippines did not expose her to the Filipino style of management. She does not have firsthand experience dealing with Filipino management. All she knows is what she has read about Filipino management and what she has learned from the standard three-hour crash course given by her company's human resource management department on dealing with cross-cultural issues.

However, she thinks that the difference between what she is used to and what she is expecting will not be much of a problem because in her highly technical field the universal language is English. She believes that she will not have much difficulty in communicating with the Filipino management to get her assignment successfully completed. Also, she thinks she will be able to communicate with ease even outside her official capacity as a technical expert because she can speak the native language.

With only five days to complete all she was sent to do, Elizabeth has a tight schedule to follow. She will have very little time to socialize.

Her plane lands at the Manila International Airport. She whisks through customs and immigration without any delays, and is met at the arrival platform by the company limousine. The driver and she speak English throughout the two-hour drive from the airport in the heavily congested traffic of Metro Manila. It is obvious to her that Manila is different from what it was 15 years ago.

After the initial meeting with the plant managing director and her Filipino counterpart, the vice president of chemical development, Elizabeth knows it is going to be a challenge to stick to her tight schedule and constantly stay with business issues. She wants to immediately tour the facility, talk to the chemists, troubleshoot the problems, and come up with recommendations. However, the Filipino managers have other plans. They are more interested in talking about her life in upstate New York and trying to identify possible mutual acquaintances. For the Filipinos, only when the right and proper climate is established can business discussions get under way. Elizabeth has only five days in the Philippines to accomplish several things, but her Filipino counterparts are more interested in her life in the United States and about showing her around the "new" Philippines.

She finds it difficult to adjust to the highly personalized Philippine society where business is normally done in a warm and pleasant atmosphere. Elizabeth is used to dealing with a set business agenda and discussion points; she is always looking for possible solutions to problems. She is comfortable with non-face-to-face methods of business discussion using teleconferences or videoconferences among the different company sites in the United States.

Elizabeth discovers that to the Filipinos, it is important to cultivate a friend, establish valuable contacts, and develop personal rapport. This is much in contrast to her customary way of dealing with coworkers and upper-level management in her company in the United States.

She is getting frustrated with the snail's pace of progress. She had thought that her life in rural upstate New York was already less hectic than life in the city; the business pace seems considerably slower in the Philippines. She learns quickly that in the Philippines, one must allow ample room for changes in timetables, deadlines, work schedules, and conference appointments.

Her next foreign assignment will take her to a Global Pharmaceutical Company subsidiary in France.

Source: This case was prepared by Edwin J. Portugal, MBA, PhD, who teaches multinational management at the State University of New York at Potsdam. It is intended to be used as a basis for discussion on the complexity of multicultural management and not to illustrate effective versus ineffective management styles. Copyright ©1995 by Edwin J. Portugal.

Case Questions

1. What is the preferred leadership style in the Philippines, Malaysia, Indonesia, and Thailand, and how would knowing this help Elizabeth cope with the Filipino managers? Explain and give examples.
2. Is there a convergence or divergence of leadership practices between American and Asian managers? Explain.
3. Is Elizabeth's gender a factor in dealing with the Filipino managers? Explain.
4. What should Elizabeth know about "high-context" versus "low-context" cultures? Explain.
5. What are your recommendations for Elizabeth Moreno so that she can accomplish her tasks within the five-day schedule in the Philippines?
6. What changes do you recommend in the GPC cross-cultural management training programs for executives bound for foreign assignments?

13

Managing International Teams and Workforce Diversity

OUTLINE

Opening Profile: 3Com Plant Flies 65 Different National Flags

International Management Teams

Technology Application: Timberland UK Facilitates Global Team Results

Building International Teams

Management Focus: Airbus: An Exceptional Multicultural Success

Management Focus: Building Teamwork Across Nine Nations

Domestic Multiculturalism: Managing Diversity

Building Programs to Value Diversity

Multicultural Work Teams

Maximizing Effectiveness

Acculturation

Integrating Immigrants

Management Focus: Cultural Integration of Work Groups: A Two-Way Street

Summary of Key Points

Discussion Questions

Application Exercise

Experiential Exercise

Internet Resources

Case Study: Managing Diversity at Luxury Island Resort

OPENING   PROFILE

3Com Plant Flies 65 Different National Flags

At its Morton Grove, Illinois, factory, 3Com's 65 flags represent the origins of the people who have worked there since it opened in 1995. Now the plant employs 1,200 people—the vast majority immigrants—who speak more than 20 languages, including Tagalog, Gujarati, and Chinese. Thai Chung, a 33-year-old refugee from Vietnam who manages Line 12, says, "If there's a problem, I call over somebody who speaks the person's language to help."

Churning out modems around the clock, 3Com's workers could hardly be more diverse. Urban Asians with multiple college degrees work alongside people only recently arrived from Central American villages. Serbs work with Bosnian Muslims, as well as Iraqis, Peruvians, and South Africans. Managers think that at least a third of their workers wouldn't mind if asked to work at Christmas because they don't celebrate it.

Overcoming language barriers is just one of the challenges. Some immigrants come from countries where you seldom say "please," and certainly not to someone you consider your social inferior. That aloofness can cause hurt feelings, as it does for Eleanor Punay, from the Philippines, who says that where she comes from people say "please" and "thank you" a lot, and that often doesn't happen on the line at 3Com.

Most of the managers don't even try to accommodate cultural differences, instead making it clear that they expect newcomers to adapt to the factory's methods. To make it easy on themselves and the employees, the managers tend to group people on the line according to their common language. The company does continually design and redesign the work to fit the varied workforce, often using signs with picturegraph instructions over the workstations in order to avoid misinterpretation.

The factory also has its own hierarchy, based largely on language ability and background. Those who speak the best English and are the best educated are the most upwardly mobile.

No matter what integration people achieve on the factory floor, it stops in the lunchroom. From a corner table, three Indian women look over the rest of the big dining area. A table near the checkout is occupied almost entirely by African American women; the table next to them by Indian men; and so on. "We share our food," says Jashwanti Bodhanwala, who tugs off a piece of moist, spicy Indian flatbread, and spoons onto it a lump of homemade mango chutney from a plastic container. Asmabahen Patel, sitting opposite her, offers some mustard pickles and says, "Of course, if you weren't here, we'd be speaking Gujarati." One thing the lunch groups do is to facilitate gossip—one of the few places where people relax and swap rumors.

Source: Selected and adapted from T. Aeppel, "A 3Com Factory Hires a Lot of Immigrants, Gets Mix of Languages," *Wall Street Journal,* March 30, 1998.

With the increasingly diverse workforce of the 2000s, managers in today's multicultural organizations will need new skills to realize the full potential of both domestic work teams and cross-border alliances. In this chapter, we will explore how to develop and manage a multicultural workforce within two broad categories: (1) the international management team (comprising people from various countries) and (2) the domestic multicultural work team (comprising people from various racial or ethnic backgrounds within the home country). This subject integrates subjects discussed previously—strategic planning, organizational structure, staffing, communicating, motivation, and leadership—but it is primarily concerned with leadership—how to develop and empower intercultural groups and task forces at all levels of an organization to achieve organizational goals.

International Management Teams

Global teamwork can do more than provide improved market and technological intelligence. It can yield more flexible business planning, stronger commitment to achieving worldwide goals, and closer collaboration in carrying out strategic change.
—Conference Board Report on 30 MNC case studies, Bulletin No. 228

The term **international management teams** describes collections of managers from several countries who must rely on group collaboration if each member is to experience the optimum of success and goal achievement.[1] Whirlpool International, for example, is a U.S.–Dutch joint venture, with administrative headquarters in Comerio, Italy, where it is managed by a Swede and a six-person management team from Sweden, Italy, Holland, the United States, Belgium, and Germany.[2] To achieve the individual and collective goals of the team members, international teams must "provide the means to communicate corporate culture, develop a global perspective, coordinate and integrate the global enterprise, and be responsive to local market needs."[3] The role and importance of international teams increases as the firm progresses in its scope of international activity. Similarly, the manner in which multicultural interaction affects the firm's operations depends on its level of international involvement, its environment, and its strategy. In domestic firms, the effects of cross-cultural teams are limited to internal operations and some external contacts. In international firms that export products and produce some products overseas, multicultural teams and cultural diversity play important roles in the relationships between buyers, sellers, and other intermediaries who are at the boundary of the organization. For multinational firms, the role of multicultural teams again becomes internal to the company; the teams consist of culturally diverse managers and technical people located around the world and also working together within subsidiaries. The team's ability to work together effectively is crucial to the success of the company. In addition, technology facilitates effective and efficient teamwork around the world, as illustrated in the accompanying Technology Application.

International management teams play a vital role in global organizations.

TECHNOLOGY APPLICATION
Timberland UK Facilitates Global Team Results

Timberland's sales conferences (held twice yearly) have always been large, prestigious affairs and a challenge for the company to organize and coordinate. With offices in France, Germany, Spain, Italy, and the UK, it's not hard to see why. Conference organizers would have to travel or use multiple faxes or phone calls to communicate in order to arrange this event—that is, until Timberland found a better way.

Timberland's conference planning team now meets by BT Conference Call four or five times in the two-month period leading up to the event. The number of meetings is not set in stone; in fact, as Claire Cosgrove, Executive Assistant at Timberland Europe points out, "The planning team uses it whenever it is warranted—it is very useful on an ad hoc basis."

BT Conference Call has been so successful in helping arrange this semi-annual event that it has led to applications in other areas of the company. For example, the senior executive teams of Timberland Europe, based in the UK, and Timberland US, based in the United States, use Conference Call for country meetings with management teams in subsidiaries across Europe.

Air travel is costly and often unnecessary for short meetings. Timberland's use of Conference Call allows them to save travel time and expense. "It's a lot more economical to use BT Conference Call than always to travel," says Claire Cosgrove. "It knocks quite a few hours off the time it takes to have a meeting with someone at Timberland US in Boston. There would be really no point in traveling for eight hours to get to a two-hour meeting. So we would lock diaries for a couple of hours over BT Conference Call. It's a simple, efficient method."

Source: www. BritishTelecom.com/cases

For global organizations and alliances, we find the same cross-cultural interactions as in MNCs and, in addition, considerably more interaction with the external environment at all levels of the organization. Therefore, worldwide international teamwork is vital, as are the pockets of cross-cultural teamwork and interactions that take place at many boundaries.[4] For the global company, worldwide competition and markets necessitate international teams for strategy development, both for the organization as a whole and for the local units to respond to their markets.

As shown in Exhibit 13–1, when a firm responds to its global environment with a global strategy and then organizes with a networked "glocal" structure (discussed in Chapter 9), various types of international teams are necessary for global integration and local differentiation. These include headquarters–subsidiary teams and those coordinating alliances outside the organization. In joint ventures, in particular, multicultural teams work at all levels of strategic planning and implementation, as well as on the production and assembly floor.

Building International Teams

The ability to develop effective transnational teams is essential in light of the increasing proliferation of foreign subsidiaries, joint ventures, and other transnational alliances. As noted by David Dotlich of Honeywell Bull Inc. (HBI), an international computer firm, effective international teamwork is essential because cross-cultural "double-talk, double agendas, double priorities, and double interests can present crippling business risks when your storefront stretches for 6000 miles."[5]

EXHIBIT 13–1

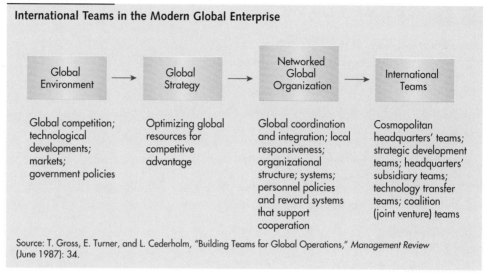

International Teams in the Modern Global Enterprise

Global Environment	→	Global Strategy	→	Networked Global Organization	→	International Teams
Global competition; technological developments; markets; government policies		Optimizing global resources for competitive advantage		Global coordination and integration; local responsiveness; organizational structure; systems; personnel policies and reward systems that support cooperation		Cosmopolitan headquarters' teams; strategic development teams; headquarters' subsidiary teams; technology transfer teams; coalition (joint venture) teams

Source: T. Gross, E. Turner, and L. Cederholm, "Building Teams for Global Operations," *Management Review* (June 1987): 34.

HBI represents a joint venture of NEC (Japan), Campagnie de Machines Bull (France), and Honeywell (United States). To coordinate this joint venture, HBI considered it important to have transnational teams for front-end involvement in strategic planning, engineering design, production, and marketing. Dotlich notes that HBI's primary corporate question is how to integrate a diverse pool of cultural values, traditions, and norms in order to be competitive.[6] HBI tries hard to build consensus to get its transnational managerial teams to appreciate "the common ground on which decisions and actions must be based," which Dotlich calls consensus agendas.

Multinational team management skills are necessary to maximize the potential synergy available through the activities of international teams. Many of the breakdowns in international alliances have been attributed to the inability of management to develop the benefits that can accrue to cross-border teams.

The effectiveness of a team and its ability to integrate with organizational goals depends on the synergy it can attain despite the problems and setbacks that result from the workings of an intercultural group.[7] The advantages of synergy are confirmed by Moran in a survey of managers from two multinational organizations. He found that the respondents could more quickly generate the advantages of cultural diversity in their organizations than the disadvantages. The advantages they listed included a greater opportunity for global competition (by being able to share experiences, technology, and a pool of international managers) and a greater opportunity for cross-cultural understanding and exposure to different viewpoints. The disadvantages they listed included problems resulting from differences in language, communication, and varying managerial styles; complex decision-making processes; fewer promotional opportunities; personality conflicts, often resulting from stereotyping and prejudice; and greater complexity in the workplace.[8]

The synergistic effects of the cross-cultural management of Airbus Industrie, compared with the management problems of the Concorde project, are illustrated in the Management Focus "Airbus: An Exceptional Multicultural Success."

MANAGEMENT FOCUS

Airbus: An Exceptional Multicultural Success

The role of cross-border alliances between firms in the EU countries is vital to the success of the EU's internal market program. But centuries-old cultural barriers will continue to remain, posing many hard questions, such as:

- Will managers, technicians, and executives from France, Germany, Spain, Italy, and other EU countries possess the skills and attitudes to work in multicultural environments?
- Will a true "Euromanager" ever evolve? If not, what will be the consequences for the borderless Europe?

Insights into some of these issues are provided by a recent study of transnational projects in the European aerospace industry. Not surprisingly, Christian Koenig, the French professor responsible for the study, ranks the Franco–British Concorde project a notable failure, while citing the four-nation Airbus project as one of the great success stories of collaborative relationships.

It is fair to say that the Concorde project and Airbus Industrie began with equal potential to draw synergy from diverse groups working together. Why then should one fail and the other succeed?

The foremost reason Concorde was not successful—apart from the oil price rises of the early 1970s—was that problems at the top prevented management from ever tackling the serious disruptions that occur when diverse groups work together.

From the start, Concorde's top management was mired in external and internal politics. Decisions were invariably made at the ministerial level, and managers did not have the power and authority to give the organization the leadership it needed. Moreover, there was a consistent lack of coordination and cooperation between the government partners and industry on either side of the channel.

In contrast, at Airbus, professionals are in charge and have the power to make and implement decisions. From the standpoint of organizational structure, Airbus is far more decentralized. Its decision-making process is relatively short. Unlike Concorde, Airbus is flexible and adapts easily and responds quickly to changes in the external environment.

In addition, the roles of Airbus's British, French, West German, and Spanish partners are all clearly defined, and there are reinforcing mechanisms to keep them together. Top management assists in the integration process but is also sensitive to the roles of the various partners. Executives and technicians from each of the four nations have goals and targets that help transcend the cultural factor. There is a tremendous spirit of teamwork at Airbus and pride among employees in their work.

To successfully produce widebody jets that have seized a significant share of the world's commercial aircraft market, Airbus has had to overcome vast differences in languages, management philosophies and styles, work organizations, and logistics. It has pushed ahead with great efficiency using flow charts that spread over the map of Europe.

As a result, not only has the consortium resurrected the civilian aircraft industry in Europe through the principle of collaboration, with its sensitive and skillful management of cultural diversity, it also has set up a model for European transnational cooperative ventures and clearly demonstrated the benefits that can accrue from international alliances.

Source: Adapted from R. T. Moran, "Airbus: An Exceptional Multicultural Success," *International Management* (February 1989).

What can be done to maximize the potential synergistic effects of international teams? Although this is a relatively new area in the management development field, some firms are recognizing its importance and developing programs to build and refine transnational teamwork. In the Groupe Bull joint venture, for example, considerable attention is being devoted to team-building programs, as discussed in the Management Focus "Building Teamwork Across Nine Nations."

Building Teamwork Across Nine Nations

Just south of Scotland's Grampian Mountains, 26 Groupe Bull executives slid rubber rafts into the swirling waters of the River Spey. But theirs wasn't to be an afternoon of fun and sun. These men from nine nations had just reviewed Bull's business prospects in countries ranging from Albania and Algeria to West Germany and Yemen. The white-water rafting on which they were embarking was to be a metaphor for how they'd have to pull together to navigate some tough months ahead successfully.

Bull believes that team building is essential to global success into the 21st century. Challenges such as this year's outing in Scotland or the ascent of Mont Blanc that Bull chairman and CEO Francis Lorentz led last year are part of a considered strategy. "I think it builds trust quickly. It demonstrates international cooperation. It helps people learn what each other's styles of management behavior are. And it provides a common base of experience," states Dr. Dotlich, executive vice president for corporate resources at Bull's HN Information Systems in Massachusetts, the $2 billion North American arm of France's Groupe Bull.

"The biggest problem with globalization . . . is that all human beings are blinded by their cultural assumptions," says Dr. Dotlich. Because of this realization, Bull does not limit team-building exercises to senior executives. In a variety of two- to five-week education and development sessions, lower-level executives and managers on several continents come together to try to solve problems that go beyond national boundaries. Some recent examples include the design and development of a new UNIX product, the formulation of a worldwide advertising and branding strategy, and the consolidation worldwide of engineering designs.

People are often frustrated by having to develop new relationships and tap new sources of information and expertise. "But the bottom line is that we'll do anything to build a global team," says Dotlich, because Bull believes that to survive and prosper, it cannot afford anything less than a global perspective. Parochial attitudes and bloated bureaucracies are out; enlightened tradeoffs are in. Global organizations are faced with tradeoffs in decisions about sourcing and manufacturing locations, designs, and so forth. Only those global teams that really have trust and interdependency—and are able to see the world as a global business—can make decisions in the company's best interest.

Building teamwork through trust and interdependency will not necessarily achieve the desired results unless other organizational systems are supportive of those results. Reward systems, for example, are typically designed around individual executive accomplishment. Dr. Dotlich notes that they are rarely tied to the achievement of long-range goals. Very little attention is paid to contributions that cross functional boundaries, let alone those that cross national boundaries. Bull offers incentives to executives who join forces and build teams across all lines, and this is a critical criterion around which the company ranks people. Bull encourages its managers to view the world as one market and to pool worldwide resources, and it recruits internationally in the senior ranks and for the board of directors.

Source: J. S. McClenahen, "Not Fun in the Sun: Bull Has a Demanding Program to Build Teamwork," *Industry Week*, October 15, 1990.

How can management find out how well its international teams are performing and what areas need to be improved? The following criteria for evaluating the success of such teams is proposed by Indrei Ratiu of the Intercultural Management Association in Paris:

- Do members work together with a common purpose? Is this purpose something that is spelled out and felt by all to be worth fighting for?

- Has the team developed a common language or procedure? Does it have a common way of doing things, a process for holding meetings?
- Does the team build on what works, learning to identify the positive actions before being overwhelmed by the negatives?
- Does the team attempt to spell out things within the limits of the cultural differences involved, delimiting the mystery level by directness and openness regardless of the cultural origins of participants?
- Do the members recognize the impact of their own cultural programming on individual and group behavior? Do they deal with, not avoid, their differences in order to create synergy?
- Does the team have fun? (Within successful multicultural groups, the cultural differences become a source of continuing surprise, discovery, and amusement rather than irritation or frustration.)[9]

Domestic Multiculturalism: Managing Diversity

Create the dream that all can embrace, and diversity of talent, temperament, ethnicity and gender become valuable.[10]

The potential benefits and difficulties posed by increasing domestic multiculturalism—that is, a culturally diverse workforce and a multicultural marketplace—are crucial challenges for the future that companies must manage in a positive way. Those benefits go beyond issues of social responsibility to the mandate of competitive necessity. The benefits of managing diversity for competitive advantage can be realized in many ways, including: (1) reducing costs of high levels of turnover and absenteeism; (2) facilitating recruitment of scarce labor; (3) increasing sales to members of minority culture groups; (4) promoting team creativity and innovation; (5) improving problem solving; and (6) enhancing organizational flexibility.[11] In addition, experience of working with domestic multiculturalism is good training for managers preparing to operate overseas. In fact, in a recent survey of 15 Fortune 100 company HRM executives, the top three reasons cited for engaging in diversity management were better utilization of talent, increased marketplace understanding, and enhanced breadth of understanding in leadership positions.[12] Overall, those executives stressed workforce diversity as an advantage in pursuing competitive opportunities, rather than as a means to avoid problems. One example of improving sales to minority groups was brought about by Levi Strauss' Hispanic employees. After watching Levi's "501 Blues" television commercials, they asked "Why is that guy walking down the street alone? Doesn't he have any friends?"[13] The employees explained that Hispanic people would respond more readily to scenes of friends and family. So, Levi developed a new series of 501 ads that emphasized camaraderie, in keeping with the Hispanic culture, rather than individuality: The result has been booming sales in the Hispanic community. This new insight is being echoed by many firms. At IBM, Ted Childs, director of workforce diversity, says, "We think it is important for our customers to look inside and see people like them. If they can't, it seems to me that the prospect of them becoming or staying our customers declines."[14] And at MCI, Timothy Price, president of business markets, says, "We don't encourage homogeneity here; the price you pay for conformity is lack of creativity." In addition, foreign-owned companies are also realizing the value in constructive management of their diverse workforce. Mitsubishi, for example, has incurred a $120 million damages settlement resulting from a sexual harassment lawsuit filed by the EEOC and has since set up a comprehensive diversity training program.

Building Programs to Value Diversity

In recognition of the need to take such a competitive stance toward diversity issues, firms are implicitly moving along the evolutionary curve of a human resources management mandate. This evolution has moved from compliance with Equal Employment Opportunity (EEO) laws in the 1960s, to specific affirmative action programs in the 1970s, to attempts to develop a balanced workforce in the corporation in the 1980s. Now, led by progressive firms, the move in the 2000s is toward workforce diversity programs that seek out, include, and value employees from various nontraditional backgrounds.

David Kearns, chairman and CEO of Xerox, warns, "We have to manage diversity right now, and much more so in the future. American business will not be able to survive if we do not have a large, diverse workforce, because those are the demographics."[15] The demographics that Kearns refers to, indicating the increasing representation of various racial groups, immigrants, and women in the workforce, were discussed in Chapter 1. Projections for civilian labor force representation for the year 2005 are shown in Exhibit 13–2; the largest increase will be from Hispanics and Asians. But firms are now expanding the concept of diversity beyond those of race, ethnicity, and gender to include variables such as age and disabilities, and dimensions such as education and language, as shown in Exhibit 13–3. The goal of such an expanded concept of diversity is as explained at Xerox Company, "to create a workplace in which individuals are unencumbered by traditional barriers, stereotypes, and restrictions."[16]

In an era of focusing on so-called minority groups, it is also necessary to realize that the white male worker is an important group to consider and one whose members often feel neglected and threatened by diversity efforts. Even though white males still hold the vast majority of managerial positions, especially at the upper levels, their numbers as profes-

EXHIBIT 13–2

Trends in Civilian Labor Force Participation, 1990–2005

Year	All Workers	Males	Females	Whites	Blacks	Hispanics	Asians
1990	100%	54.7%	45.3%	85.9%	10.8%	7.7%	3.3%
Projected 2005	100	52.6	47.4	83.4	11.8	11.1	7.7

Source: Data from U.S. Bureau of Labor Statistics, *Outlook 1990–2005,* Bulletin 2402 (Washington, D.C.: GPO, 1992): 31–32.

EXHIBIT 13-3

Dimensions of Workforce Diversity

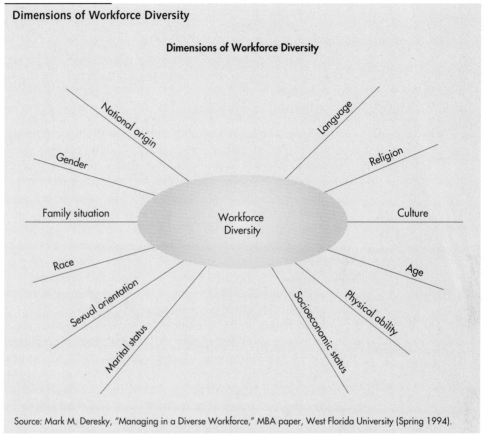

Source: Mark M. Deresky, "Managing in a Diverse Workforce," MBA paper, West Florida University (Spring 1994).

sionals and managers have dropped from 55 to 47 percent. Added to their concerns about demographic changes and their worry about corporate diversity programs is that they will lose out to less qualified workers, or to an equally qualified worker, who is from a less traditional group. Sensitive diversity programs then, like that at Honeywell Inc., specifically include white males and take seriously their concerns and their value to the company.

Clearly, managing diversity is a complex and sensitive task; some broad guidelines for managers that evolve from the foregoing discussion and corporate examples are as follows:

Diversity Program Guidelines

1. Develop and communicate a broad definition of workplace diversity, including all kinds of differences, such as race, gender, age, work, and family issues.
2. Attain visible commitment from top managers to support programs, and communicate to employees the importance of diversity to the firm's competitive stance—that it is not just a matter of sensitivity training. Hold managers accountable for meeting diversity goals.

3. Avoid stereotyping groups of employees by using titles for them; focus instead on what all employees have in common and on each individual's value to the firm.
4. Set up a broad, diverse pool of talented people to be trained and eligible for job promotion or selection; but let it be known that the best person will get the job—and stick by that.
5. Set up regular training programs with the goal to gradually change the corporate culture by educating workers about employee similarities as well as differences and the value those differences bring to the firm.

The composition of the labor force worldwide will also experience similar changes.[17] The implications of multiculturalism in the workforce are profound. At Aramco in Dhahran, Saudi Arabia, for example, professionals from 50 countries work together at all levels. The future competitiveness of corporations, both in the United States and abroad, will depend on their ability to attract and manage such diverse talent effectively.

Managing a culturally diverse workforce—that is, managing diversity—requires managers to understand and value diversity to maximize the potential of the workforce. A number of companies—for example, Xerox, AT&T, Procter & Gamble, and 3M—are training their executives to be aware of and to manage diversity. Paul Nolan, director of corporate training for the Lincoln Savings Bank in New York, says, "I've never seen an ethnic makeup like the one here; the bank's employee mix includes Hispanics, Chinese, East Indians, African Americans and Italian Americans." Lincoln has hired a consulting firm to teach its employees how to understand and better manage such diversity.[18]

Generally, it is clear that many firms are taking various measures that indicate the importance they attach to dealing effectively with the issue of workforce diversity, including creating senior staff positions specifically for that purpose. At GE, for example, Eugene Andrews, Manager Workforce Diversity Division, cites the firm's practices that were implemented to reach their goal "to be recognized as the world's most competitive company due to our ability to value and fully utilize the contributions of all employees from all cultural and social backgrounds":[19]

- Top management commitment and involvement
- Integrated diversity strategy
- Campus recruiting
- Hires expanded at top level to signal commitment and provide role models
- Career management
- Management of work and family issues (for example, childcare and flextime)
- Diversity education and training
- Communications
- Community outreach

The ability to manage diversity is a special skill required of today's managers. The word *manage* does not really mean to "control," as it would seem to imply, but to value diversity—that is, to acknowledge and make use of the different skills and perceptions of people from various backgrounds, and to encourage others to do so. Doing so acknowledges that every culture has something to contribute to the pool of talent necessary to be competitive. Valuing diversity requires that managers create a climate of respect for individual workers and the unique contributions that they can make. When workers come together in committees, task groups, or assembly groups, this climate can create synergistic outcomes.

Multicultural Work Teams

Work teams—whether technical, managerial, or assembly line—form the backbone of the organizational structure for getting work done or decisions made. For each person, work with a work team may compose a small proportion of her or his time or tasks, or it may represent the whole job, as on the assembly line. Of importance to management—and to us here—is how the multicultural composition of such teams, called multicultural work teams, affects the work process, the climate, and ultimately the productivity of the group and company.

One means of assessing the impact of cultural diversity on group processes and outcomes is to consider what happens at each stage of group development. Groups of various kinds usually go through a similar sequence of development known as "forming, storming, norming, and performing."[20] These stages are shown in Exhibit 13–4.

Stage 1: Forming   In the first stage of group formation, members get to know and trust the other group members and try to figure out what kinds of behaviors are expected. In multicultural groups, this stage is likely to be fraught with problems because people tend to distrust anyone unlike themselves—generally because of a lack of understanding. As discussed in Chapter 4, all kinds of verbal and nonverbal behavioral differences can lead to misinterpretation, which in turn leads to mistrust or dislike. Employees' expectations about status, authority, and work division often produce variations in their perception of acceptable interpersonal behavior, thus prolonging the forming process and the ability to focus on the task at hand.

Beginning at this stage, the means of organization, communication, and authority may appear alien to some. For example, centralized networks, which have focal individuals through whom communication must pass, are more accepted in authoritarian cultures. Decentralized networks are more acceptable in democratic cultures. Employees may have difficulty moving from one pattern to another, without even realizing what is causing their unease.[21]

Stage 2: Storming   The key issues of this stage are how the group defines and responds to its task and what type of group structure emerges. Even in homogeneous groups, this is often a period of hostility and conflict as group members have emotional responses to their commitment to the task and to emerging leadership patterns.

EXHIBIT 13–4

Stages of Group Development	
Stage 1: *Forming:*	A period of getting acquainted, testing, and dependence. Members look for cues regarding acceptable interpersonal behaviors.
Stage 2: *Storming:*	Group structure for the task begins to emerge; intragroup conflict and hostility may result.
Stage 3: *Norming:*	Members accept roles and develop cohesion; exchange of task information begins.
Stage 4: *Performing:*	Group focuses on goal attainment; functional roles are accepted and interaction is more effective.

In diverse groups, even greater conflict may arise because members may bring with them varying expectations about who is capable of doing what. Underlying these expectations is the tendency of some people to stereotype others rather than to consider objectively their skills and potential contributions to the group. Some group members may assume that people from economically developed countries are more capable of leadership and complex tasks than people from less developed countries.[22]

In addition, as the group attempts to redefine its task, conflict and stress may arise. This conflict may result from real or perceived attempts at domination by one faction or from different styles of approaching a task.[23]

Stage 3: Norming

The key issue at this stage is the ability of the group to develop cohesion. Cohesion requires everyone to accept his or her own role, as well as the roles of others, and to become united. At this stage, group members establish a consensus on norms of behavior within the group. The achievement of such consensus is a difficult task in a culturally diverse group because norms of behavior are culturally contingent. Much depends on how familiar the members are with working in this kind of situation. Studies have concluded that cultural background has a great influence on how much group pressure is applied to members and to what extent that group pressure produces uniformity. In other words, cultural values determine how group members behave.[24]

This stage is crucial, and its success may depend on whether the group was able to develop mutual trust and respect in the initial stage. If cohesion is not well developed, the group will fragment, be unable to reach consensus on decisions, and ultimately fail to take action.

Stage 4: Performing

If a cohesive group has developed and a working structure is accepted, the group can turn to the actual work stage and concentrate on the problem or task for which it was created. A mature group—one that has worked through its problems and reached a consensus on allocating roles in light of the group's needs for expertise and leadership—should be productive. In a culturally diverse group, this work stage is where the potential for greater productivity lies because of the synergy that may be realized through the blending of a wide range of ideas, approaches, and creative solutions.

The exchange of diverse ideas within multicultural groups helps avoid the tendency toward **groupthink**, a common occurrence when a cohesive group too easily accepts members' decisions without considering other alternatives.[25] At this stage, a mature group can move ahead effectively if its diversity is managed so as to encourage and then to integrate different analytical and decision-making styles. Exhibit 13–5 lists the advantages and disadvantages of group diversity.

In the end, the actual accomplishments of the group are realized at the performing stage: The relative level of effectiveness or productivity depends on how well the group's diversity has been managed. Research shows that culturally diverse groups tend to be either the most or the least effective when compared with the "average" productivity of homogeneous groups.[26] Diverse groups are typically more effective in situations requiring creativity and innovation, in long-term groups, and where members, selected for their expertise, are accorded respect and equal power.[27] The relative effectiveness of cross-cultural groups compared with single-culture groups is illustrated in Exhibit 13–6.

EXHIBIT 13–5

Effects of Multicultural Group Diversity

Advantages	Disadvantages
Full utilization of resources:	*Poor utilization of resources:*
■ Greater pool of skills and talent	■ Members don't acknowledge skills, value of others
■ Broad range of perspectives	■ Poor communication and interpretation in group
■ Richness of ideas, points of view	■ Different norms, behaviors
■ More creativity and innovation	■ Unaccepted management styles
■ Possible solutions to problems	
■ Reduced risk of groupthink	
High personnel development:	*Low personnel development:*
■ Opportunity to share, understand	■ Personality conflicts
■ Learn from others' approaches	■ Lack of trust
■ Learn different experiences and technology	■ Closed to new ideas
■ Role models for motivation of others throughout organization	■ Negative motivation for nondominant group members
	■ Poor role modeling
Increased productivity:	*Decreased productivity:*
■ More effective and creative groups	■ Complexity of group processes
■ Respect, motivation of members	■ Lack of trust or cohesion
■ Greater acceptance in organization of decisions through diverse representation of employees	■ Ineffective discussion and decision-making process
	■ Lack of consensus or action
	■ Low commitment

Source: Based on R. T. Moran, "Cross-Cultural Contact: A Formula for Success in Multicultural Organizations," *International Management* (December 1988): 74; L. Copeland, "Making the Most of Cultural Differences at the Workplace," *Personnel* (June 1988): 52–60; and N. J. Adler, *International Dimensions of Organizational Behavior* (Boston: PWS-Kent, 1991): 135; used by permission.

Maximizing Effectiveness

Much of the potential productivity of diverse work teams depends on the ability of upper management to establish a positive climate for diversity. One way to do this is to set up programs to develop an awareness of cultural differences and their potential value. A reevaluation of the organization's recruiting, training, development, and incentive programs can also ensure that these programs support multiculturalism at all levels. Wang Laboratories, for example, has put more than 1,000 managers—mostly white males—through its training programs on diversity. Wang's program is built on four basic building blocks: (1) an awareness of one's own behavior, (2) a recognition of one's own biases and stereotypes, (3) a focus on job performance, and (4) an avoidance of assumptions.[28]

An important part of creating a positive climate is to show that all people's skills are valued. To do this, managers should develop and promote more minorities and women to upper levels of management. At present, very few such individuals have reached high-level

EXHIBIT 13–6

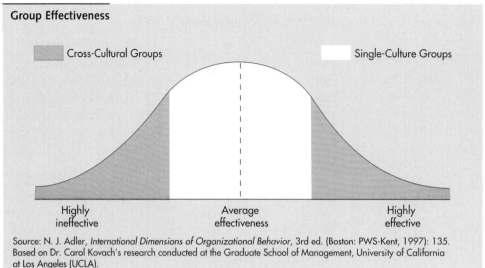

Group Effectiveness

Source: N. J. Adler, *International Dimensions of Organizational Behavior*, 3rd ed. (Boston: PWS-Kent, 1997): 135. Based on Dr. Carol Kovach's research conducted at the Graduate School of Management, University of California at Los Angeles (UCLA).

positions. As a result, according to Joan Green, director of employment opportunity programs at Quaker Oats Company, "People in non-traditional roles try to look like the successful people—white males—with the effect that people whose value to the organization lies in their individuality and creativity lose it when they conform."[29]

One of the problems is that the rules for getting ahead in business are made predominantly by white males. These rules are usually subtle and played out implicitly—on the golf course or over lunch—but they serve to exclude minorities and women from networking and from "the boys' club."[30] Awareness training helps people confront possible prejudicial assumptions and biases, and deal openly with removing those barriers.

Companies around the world are dealing differently with the issue of managing diversity, depending on their location and situation. Honeywell's home base in Minneapolis, for example, is set among the second largest Laotian, Cambodian, and Vietnamese population in the United States. Honeywell is addressing the resulting problems of language and cultural barriers through the development and administration of special courses and groups for Asian American employees.[31]

In Los Angeles, the riots after the Rodney King trial highlighted the diversity of the population in America's large cities and rang a warning bell for the business world, as well as for politicians, about the consequences of failing to manage diversity effectively. Rioters went beyond the streets, severely damaging 1,600 businesses and looting thousands more. Mary McEnrue has researched what companies in Los Angeles are doing to manage diversity in the workforce, noting that:

> [T]he city is an ideal testing ground for managing diversity efforts. More than 100 cultural and ethnic backgrounds currently exist together in Los Angeles. Profound diversity in ethnicity, race, educational background, and country of origin, along with factors of age and

gender, makes the region a massive mosaic. It is also a region with tremendous productivity potential.[32]

McEnrue found that few companies in Los Angeles—of any size or in any location—had done much about managing workforce diversity before the riots. Further, although some got involved in community economic development after the riots, little action has since been taken within those firms to develop corporate policies or programs to address diversity issues. As in previous national surveys, companies acknowledged that diversity is an urgent issue for executives but that they had not yet formulated any plans or committed any resources to deal with it. Unfortunately, many executives in these studies acknowledged that their corporate culture simply was not open to diversity, and that discrimination, and even harassment, of minorities, was evident in their companies.[33] Those firms in Los Angeles that did have diversity management programs in place used a variety of methods, shown in Exhibit 13–7, to modify people's behavior, the environment, the organizational structure, and technology. Various beneficial results were cited, including improved understanding of customer needs, new product development, joint ventures, improved employee relations, an enhanced public image, and lower labor costs.[34]

Acculturation

Underlying these organizational activities designed to maximize effectiveness by valuing diversity is the process of acculturation. **Acculturation** is the transfer of culture from one ethnic group to another; it is the process of gradual adaptation to a new environment by an individual or group, in particular where one or more minority groups are being merged with a majority group.[35] There are four typical modes of acculturation: assimilation, separation, deculturation, and pluralism, as described by Berry.[36]

In **assimilation**, the process of adaptation is one way. Everyone is expected to conform to the values and norms of the dominant culture, resulting in a gradual erosion of the minority groups' cultures. In the United States, for example, success in many companies seems attainable only by behaving like the dominant white men.

The second mode, **separation**, occurs when minority groups are unable or unwilling to adapt to the dominant culture and therefore retain their separate identities. This separation is often reinforced by both the dominant and the minority groups, both in organizations and in communities, as demonstrated by the various "Chinatown" neighborhoods in many large cities in the United States.

The third mode, **deculturation**, occurs when people are in transition between culture groups and tend to lose their cultural identity through insufficient ties to either group.

The term **pluralism** refers to a more constructive mode of acculturation in which there is a two-way integration of groups. The acculturation process is undertaken by both groups to accommodate each other's expectations to a certain extent.

The mode of acculturation that tends to be adopted in an organization depends on a combination of various factors at the individual level, the intergroup level, and the organizational level, as shown in Exhibit 13–8.[37] The term **culture identity structure**, whether at the individual or the organizational level, refers to the nature and relative strength of a culture.

454 • PART FOUR   Managing Human Resources Around the World

EXHIBIT 13-7

Actions Taken by Los Angeles Firms to Manage Workforce Diversity

- Incorporating the issue into the firm's strategic plan.
- Establishing formal links with other organizations such as schools and vendors.
- Engaging in public relations to enhance the company's image.
- Establishing external networking with minority organizations.
- Hiring or appointing a director of diversity.
- Subcontracting work.
- Outsourcing part of operations to offshore sites.
- Changing technology by modifying tools, equipment, and methods.
- Recruiting in nontraditional sites such as eastern Europe.
- Establishing scholarships and summer internship programs.
- Producing "snappy" recruitment brochures.
- Distributing the Workforce 2000 report.
- Holding companywide management awareness training.
- Organizing executive briefings by networks, task forces, focus group members, external consultants, or internal HR people, with follow-through action.
- Trying to anglicize employees.
- Educating managers about cultural mores in standalone training sessions or in existing management training.
- Providing language training for managers, e.g., restaurant Spanish.
- Establishing company-sponsored ESL training.
- Using tuition refund programs.
- Increasing inhouse training for hard-to-hire positions.
- Instituting team-building training for employee groups.
- Establishing a formal secession planning process.
- Instituting formal individual career development training for members of ethnic groups.
- Designing informal or formal mentor programs.
- Changing the performance criteria for managers or employees.
- Creating a salary tie-in or altering bonus payments to measure action on Workforce 2000 issues.

Source: Mary Pat McEnrue, "Managing Diversity: Los Angeles Before and After the Riots," *Organizational Dynamics* (Winter 1993): 18–29.

Pluralism would seem to be the best acculturation mode to enable organizations to benefit from the diversity of their employee pool. Among the factors that can facilitate pluralism are cross-cultural knowledge and understanding, an organizational climate and policies that focus on valuing diversity, and an organizational culture that is tolerant of some differences in values and behaviors.[38] Therefore, companies can promote constructive acculturation through educational programs to promote cross-cultural awareness and by rewarding managers for their various efforts to manage diversity (for example, by including minority-group members on important committees).[39]

The need for this type of pluralistic approach toward acculturation has been highlighted by some recent research on Japanese and American bank employees. Variations in how

EXHIBIT 13-8

Factors Affecting the Modes of Acculturation

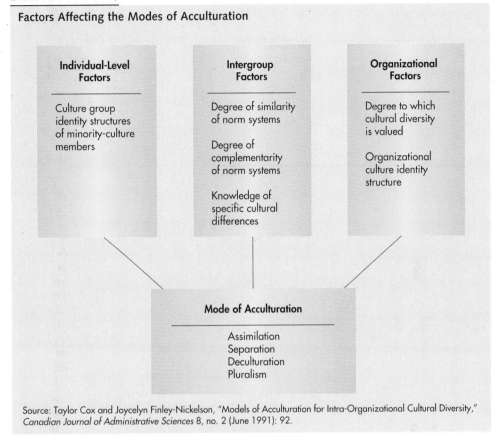

Source: Taylor Cox and Joycelyn Finley-Nickelson, "Models of Acculturation for Intra-Organizational Cultural Diversity," *Canadian Journal of Administrative Sciences* 8, no. 2 (June 1991): 92.

Japanese and Americans conceptualize organizational life have caused major conflicts at Japanese banks in the United States.[40] The research studied what was important in organizational life to Japanese and American employees in banks in their own countries. A statistical analysis of each of the two samples revealed clusters of factors. The connection among those factors shows shared perceptions, or cognitive systems, about organizations.[41] The clusters are shown in Exhibit 13–9. They show various differences between the Japanese and American cognitive maps, or "mind sets," about organizational variables. For example, notice that the Japanese connect their superiors far more with colleagues and with socializing than with authority, as do the Americans. Japanese and Americans thus regard social interactions in organizational life very differently. Americans tend to limit their company relationships to the job context, whereas Japanese extend them to their social life.[42] This difference was, in fact, found to be a major source of conflict in Japanese organizations in the United States, as conveyed by an American manager at a Japanese bank in San Diego: "They [the Japanese] need to realize that the U.S. staff does not view the organization as an extended family. The U.S. staff does not like having to participate in social activities outside of the business place."[43]

EXHIBIT 13-9

Cluster Relationships Among Organizational Factors

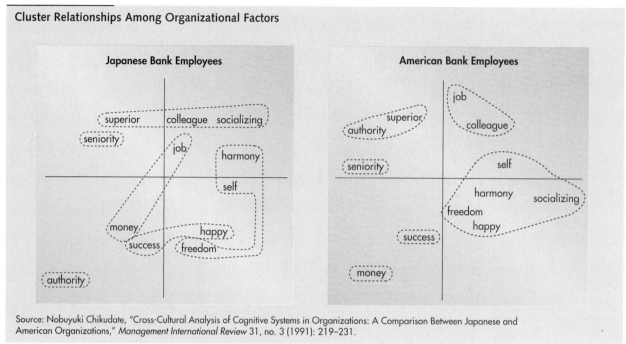

Source: Nobuyuki Chikudate, "Cross-Cultural Analysis of Cognitive Systems in Organizations: A Comparison Between Japanese and American Organizations," *Management International Review* 31, no. 3 (1991): 219–231.

These kinds of differences have implications for managers in intercultural situations. Such managers must find ways to help each party understand the other and adapt to the other's expectations.

Integrating Immigrants

A specific acculturation concern is that of integrating immigrants. Each year, about 1.5 million people around the world emigrate permanently. In cities across Europe, especially in Germany—the main receiving country in Europe, with about 800,000 a year—immigrants make up a large and growing proportion of the workforce. This is true also in U.S. cities such as Los Angeles, New York, and Miami (see Exhibit 13–10).

New waves of immigrants are mainly from Asia and Latin America; as many of them are highly skilled and well educated as are unskilled and little educated.[44] At AT&T's Bell Laboratories, 40 percent of the 200 researchers in one wing are immigrants—just one example of the escalating dependence on immigrants in high-tech industries. Another example is the blend of highly skilled immigrants from various countries building PC motherboards for American Megatrends Company. Recent immigration patterns in Canada also indicate significant increases in immigrants from third-world countries.[45] There are also about 50 million migrant workers around the world, many of whom are "illegals." For a large

EXHIBIT 13–10

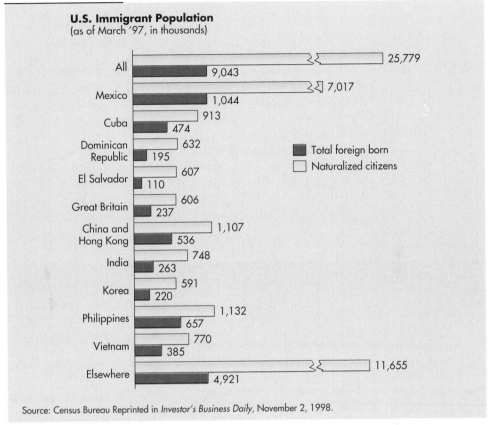

U.S. Immigrant Population
(as of March '97, in thousands)

	Naturalized citizens	Total foreign born
All	25,779	9,043
Mexico	7,017	1,044
Cuba	913	474
Dominican Republic	632	195
El Salvador	607	110
Great Britain	606	237
China and Hong Kong	1,107	536
India	748	263
Korea	591	220
Philippines	1,132	657
Vietnam	770	385
Elsewhere	11,655	4,921

Source: Census Bureau Reprinted in *Investor's Business Daily*, November 2, 1998.

number of companies, therefore, the effective integration of immigrant workers is an immediate means of benefiting from diversity.

Workplace complexities arise from different work norms—for instance, when workers socialize at times when they are expected to be working, or when they have different expectations of supervisory behavior. In addition, immigrants typically need some help outside the company in getting settled in the community.

Oddou offers some suggestions from his research for integrating the foreign born, whom he calls a hidden resource. First, he suggests that, since language can be a considerable barrier in communicating job requirements, companies should facilitate (and reward) training in the host-country language. Second, he suggests that companies share cultures, both by communicating to foreign-born workers—in as many ways as possible—the host-company and community cultural norms, and by making the new employees feel at home by adopting some of their cultural practices, perhaps simply serving some native dishes in the cafeteria. Third, companies should improve their recruiting and placement practices by using bilingual assistants and appropriate bilingual testing techniques to place people where their skills may best be used. Fourth, managers should initiate cross-cultural mentoring—they should ask coworkers to sponsor one or more of the foreign-born employees both on the job and socially until he or she has "settled in." Finally, Oddou suggests that companies take advantage of workforce diversity by exploring additional opportunities to use multicultural workers' skills and perspectives.[46]

Integrating the foreign born requires the efforts of all parties, as described in the Management Focus "Cultural Integration of Work Groups: A Two-Way Street," in which Americans are as much the "integratees" as the integrators, even on their own soil. This cultural exchange is true for all skill levels, from autoworkers to scientists. Honda in Torrance, California, employs 500 U.S. scientists and engineers, and the Nissan engineering center in Plymouth, Michigan, employs 400 U.S. engineers.

The issue of workplace and cultural integration is pervasive throughout all levels of an organization, whether the employees concerned are native to the host country, permanent immigrants, or on a temporary assignment. Sometimes an infusion of "foreigners" may result from a competitive decision by a company; IBM's recent decision to move the headquarters of

MANAGEMENT FOCUS

Cultural Integration of Work Groups: A Two-Way Street

Japanese car plants in America already provide about 20,000 assembly jobs. These plants include Mazda in Michigan, Honda in Ohio, Toyota in Kentucky, Nissan in Tennessee, the Mitsubishi joint venture with Chrysler in Illinois, and the new Subaru–Isuzu plant in Indiana. Additional jobs and a boost to the local economy are not the only changes produced by these plants. Japanese managers train and motivate American workers to adopt Japanese work systems, sending some Americans to Japan for training.

Most employees work in small groups, with those groups on the line responsible for the quality of the work and for finding improvements in the production process. Decision making is passed down to group members over such matters as overtime scheduling and job rotation. Workers are trained to handle every job done by the team, and they are their own efficiency experts, untroubled by managers or time-and-motion study experts hovering over them.

At Nissan, much emphasis is put on team building. Team-building projects are designed to create a cohesive operation based on interpersonal communication. Cooperation and problem solving among teams are also fostered by team-building seminars and by off-site "game days" and similar activities. At all plants, managers promote equality and cooperation among all levels by forgoing the usual seniority perks, by eating in the same cafeteria, and by sharing open offices.

This effort to maintain the team spirit among all workers goes beyond the factories and offices to the local community. In Kentucky, Toyota subsidizes bowling programs for Japanese and American employees to bowl together. In Smyrna, Tennessee, Americans include Nissan's Japanese workers in square dances and other social events. This integration on both the cultural and work levels is regarded by the Japanese and by most of the Americans as beneficial to everyone.

Source: Compiled from L. Krarr, "Japan's Gung-Ho U.S. Car Plants," *Fortune*, January 30, 1989, 98–108; M. Sorg, "They're Going Around in Circles in Smyrna," *Automotive News Detroit Special*, October 7, 1985, D8; and J. Plegue, "Honda's U.S. Factory—Spacious, Spic and Span," *Automotive News*, May 2, 1983.

its $10-billion-a-year communication business to Europe will make 120 American executives foreigners in another country.

We are now witnessing the beginning of a world market for labor, as global competition forces employers to reach across borders to find the skilled workers they need. In the Middle East, for example, many nationalities have been working together for a number of years. In a study of world workforce trends prepared for the U.S. Department of Labor, Professor William B. Johnston of the Hudson Institute concluded, "While much of the world's skilled and unskilled human resources are being produced in the developing world, most of the well-paid jobs are being generated in the cities of the industrialized world."[47] This phenomenon will result, he predicts, in massive relocations of people, especially young, well-educated workers. Countries with growing service-sector jobs, such as Japan, Germany, and the United States, will become magnets, attracting immigrants from countries with good educational systems but poor economies as well as well-educated people dislocated by post-Communist rebuilding in eastern Europe.

Conclusion

The contemporary manager is faced with the responsibility of managing people from culturally diverse backgrounds who work together, either in the form of international management teams or in work groups in a multicultural domestic environment. The effective management of diversity includes encouraging people throughout the organization to value diversity and to take advantage of their different skills and perspectives. The integration of foreign-born employees requires particular care; it is vital to help them to take a permanent and useful place in the workforce.

Summary of Key Points

1. International management teams are collections of managers from several countries who rely on group collaboration for goal achievement.
2. The effectiveness of multicultural teams depends on the synergy they can create despite the setbacks resulting from diverse members working together.
3. The advantages of multicultural teams include greater opportunities for global competition—by sharing experiences, technology, and international managers—and greater opportunities for cross-cultural understanding and exposure to different viewpoints.
4. The disadvantages of multicultural teams include problems resulting from language and communication differences and varying managerial styles; complex decision-making processes; fewer promotional opportunities; personality conflicts; and greater complexity in the workplace.
5. Domestic multiculturalism refers to culturally diverse workforces in home-country companies.
6. Managing diversity—that is, managing a culturally diverse workforce—is a crucial competitive issue for the future. The skills required for this task include understanding and valuing diversity to maximize the potential of the workforce. The benefits of managing diversity include reduction of turnover and absenteeism, recruitment of scarce skills, sales to minority culture groups, team innovation, improved problem solving, and enhanced organizational flexibility.
7. The advantages of multicultural diversity in domestic groups include a fuller use of resources through a wider pool of skills, perspectives, and ideas; better understanding of a multicultural

marketplace; greater innovation and problem solving; and a motivation and commitment in the company resulting from a wider acceptance of decisions.

8. The disadvantages of multicultural diversity in domestic groups include conflicts and a lack of acceptance of ideas resulting from different norms of behavior and managerial styles; limited productivity through a lack of cohesion and an inability to arrive at consensus; and poor motivation because of a lack of trust.

9. Effective means to integrate foreign-born workers include provisions and incentives for language training; culture sharing; improved recruitment and placement techniques that focus on identifying and using the skills of immigrants; and local mentoring programs.

Discussion Questions

1. Discuss the role of international management teams relative to the level of a company's international involvement. Give some examples of the kinds of teams that might be necessary and what issues they would face.

2. Explain what is meant by domestic multiculturalism, and why this is an important management issue for the future. What are the advantages and disadvantages of group diversity? What is entailed in managing diversity?

3. Discuss the effects of cultural diversity on group processes. What are the stages of group development, and how does multiculturalism affect each stage?

4. Discuss some important features of a training and development program that could help maximize the effectiveness of multiculturalism in an organization.

5. As part of managing diversity, what specific steps can managers take to enhance the role of women in a firm? What can companies do to help integrate foreign-born employees?

Application Exercise

Form a culturally diverse group with other students in your class or your college or university. Decide on a problem within the school that you would like to solve. Plan five meetings to address the problem, and then implement the solution. Assign one person as observer to document events and group dynamics. After the task is completed, meet again to discuss the observer's findings and to share reactions. How effective was the team? What problems occurred? Why? How were they addressed? What, if anything, would the group members do differently next time?

Experiential Exercise

The In-Basket Dilemma

Alice L. O'Neill, University of Scranton

Goals

1. To examine the effects of multicultural issues on the practice of management.
2. To learn how to prioritize management decisions and actions that are compounded by multicultural considerations and legal implications.

Description

This in-basket exercise (refer to Exhibit 13–11 for a list of participants) consists of several telephone messages or memos that a manager might find waiting in the office upon return from a

EXHIBIT 13–11

List of Participants

Mike Flynn	Administrator, Birch Acres
Gerald Jones (GJ)	Mike Flynn's secretary
Ms. Jackson	One of the best day-shift RNs
Mr. Rivesio	Hispanic roommate of Mr. James
Mr. James	Black roommate of Mr. Rivesio
Bob French	President, Nursing Home Board
Miss Rodriguez	New Hispanic nursing assistant
Ms. Roth	Director of Nursing (DON)
Ms. Bankroll	Assistant Director of Nursing
Mr. Bascombe	Plant engineer
Mary Jones	Dietitian recruited by Mike Flynn from Northwood when last dietitian retired
Ombudsman	Overseer of resident rights; not a facility member
Department of Health	Inspects and recommends licensure or relicensure; makes unannounced visits and inspections

three-day seminar. Discussion should focus on the multicultural and legal aspects of each situation and on establishing a priority for handling the messages (see Exhibit 13–12).

Directions

1. You are Mike Flynn, the administrator of Birch Acres, a 200-bed long-term care facility.
2. You have just returned from a three-day seminar entitled "The Importance of Understanding Cultural Diversity in Health Care Administration." You are ready to get back to work and are thankful that Birch Acres doesn't have some of the administrative problems that were discussed at the seminar. Gerald Jones, your secretary, greets you with, "Welcome back! There are lots of messages you will need to check out right away."
3. Read the following background information and prioritize the order in which you should act (what should you do first, second, third, and so on).

Mike Flynn

Mike Flynn had been an assistant administrator at Northwood Community Hospital/Skilled Nursing Facility (SNF), a 100-bed nonprofit acute care facility with a 30-bed SNF for 3 years. He had enjoyed working at Northwood, which was near Scranton, Pennsylvania, where he had lived all of his life. Several western European ethnic groups had settled in the area, their ancestors having come here to mine the coal fields, and everyone knew one another or at least someone's relative. There were few minorities, and the families were close-knit and had a real "work ethic," as Mike's father used to say.

Mike's main responsibilities as assistant administrator at Northwood included directing the Employee Relations Department, the Joint Commission on Accreditation of Health Care

EXHIBIT 13–12

Telephone Messages and Memos

Rate priority of action on the line next to the letter from 1 to 15 with 1 being first priority and 15 being last.

Wednesday—8:30 A.M./GJ

A. _____   Ms. Jackson (day RN) called; she wants to see you ASAP. Having baby-sitter problems; can she either come in ½ hr. later on her days to work or can she bring in her children (ages 3 and 4) until somebody can come by to pick them up.

Wednesday—11:00 A.M./GJ

B. _____   Mr. James's (Room 202) family wants to talk to you as soon as you get back. They are VERY upset! They claim that Mr. James's roommate, Mr. Rivesio, is stealing his clothing and a sum of money is missing from his bedside stand. If you don't transfer Mr. Rivesio out of that room immediately they will transfer their father out of the facility (he has private insurance).

Wednesday—11:30 A.M./GJ

C. _____   Mr. Rivesio's wife stopped in to see you. She says that Mr. James's family is discriminating against her husband because he is Hispanic and on welfare, and that Mr. James is hiding his money and telling his family that somebody stole it. She said that the nurses were searching her husband's dresser for the money that Mr. James said was stolen and she's going to sue us.

Thursday—6:00 A.M./GJ

D. _____   Message left on your answering machine that the nursing assistants are talking about unionizing with 1199. Lady's voice—didn't identify herself. Seems that they are unhappy about the nurses here getting a raise when the nursing assistants are the ones that do all the work around here.

Thursday—9:00 A.M./GJ

E. _____   The Ombudsman called. She has received complaints about the food. Nobody seems to care whether the residents like or dislike the food they are served. She will be visiting the facility Monday and will meet with the Residents' Council.

Thursday—1:00 P.M./GJ

F. _____   Carol Roth, Director of Nursing (DON) wants you to have Social Services check about transferring Mrs. Belacastro to another facility. All she does is complain and is abusive to the staff. Why can't she be like Mrs. Chen—the sweet little 80-year-old Chinese lady never complains, even though she has severe pain from terminal bone cancer—in fact, she denies having pain when the nurses ask her about it. If the facility admits any more residents like Mrs. Belacastro, the nurses would revolt—they are already short-staffed.

Thursday—1:00 P.M./GJ

G. _____   Mary Jones, the dietitian called. She's upset about the complaints about the food and that the Ombudsman never notified her that she was coming. Nobody ever complained about the food when she was dietitian at Northwood, she said. She wants to know what should she do.

EXHIBIT 13-12

Telephone Messages and Memos (continued)

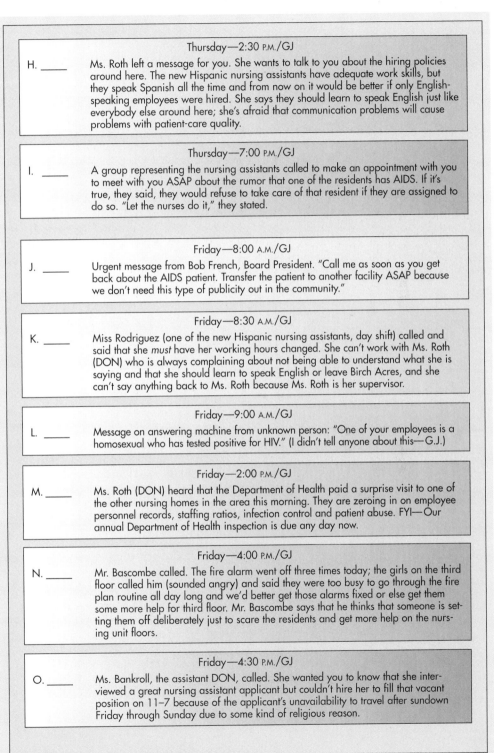

Thursday—2:30 P.M./GJ

H. _____ Ms. Roth left a message for you. She wants to talk to you about the hiring policies around here. The new Hispanic nursing assistants have adequate work skills, but they speak Spanish all the time and from now on it would be better if only English-speaking employees were hired. She says they should learn to speak English just like everybody else around here; she's afraid that communication problems will cause problems with patient-care quality.

Thursday—7:00 P.M./GJ

I. _____ A group representing the nursing assistants called to make an appointment with you to meet with you ASAP about the rumor that one of the residents has AIDS. If it's true, they said, they would refuse to take care of that resident if they are assigned to do so. "Let the nurses do it," they stated.

Friday—8:00 A.M./GJ

J. _____ Urgent message from Bob French, Board President. "Call me as soon as you get back about the AIDS patient. Transfer the patient to another facility ASAP because we don't need this type of publicity out in the community."

Friday—8:30 A.M./GJ

K. _____ Miss Rodriguez (one of the new Hispanic nursing assistants, day shift) called and said that she *must* have her working hours changed. She can't work with Ms. Roth (DON) who is always complaining about not being able to understand what she is saying and that she should learn to speak English or leave Birch Acres, and she can't say anything back to Ms. Roth because Ms. Roth is her supervisor.

Friday—9:00 A.M./GJ

L. _____ Message on answering machine from unknown person: "One of your employees is a homosexual who has tested positive for HIV." (I didn't tell anyone about this—G.J.)

Friday—2:00 P.M./GJ

M. _____ Ms. Roth (DON) heard that the Department of Health paid a surprise visit to one of the other nursing homes in the area this morning. They are zeroing in on employee personnel records, staffing ratios, infection control and patient abuse. FYI—Our annual Department of Health inspection is due any day now.

Friday—4:00 P.M./GJ

N. _____ Mr. Bascombe called. The fire alarm went off three times today; the girls on the third floor called him (sounded angry) and said they were too busy to go through the fire plan routine all day long and we'd better get those alarms fixed or else get them some more help for third floor. Mr. Bascombe says that he thinks that someone is setting them off deliberately just to scare the residents and get more help on the nursing unit floors.

Friday—4:30 P.M./GJ

O. _____ Ms. Bankroll, the assistant DON, called. She wanted you to know that she interviewed a great nursing assistant applicant but couldn't hire her to fill that vacant position on 11-7 because of the applicant's unavailability to travel after sundown Friday through Sunday due to some kind of religious reason.

Organizations (JCAHO) preparedness of Northwood, the plant operations, and overseeing hospital–community relations. He had been involved in two union contract negotiations as well as budgetary preparation for his departments and the entire facility. He had also obtained his nursing home administrator's (NHA) license, following the board's request that each assistant administrator be so licensed. (Pennsylvania state law requires that nursing home administrators be licensed although hospital administrators are not required to be licensed.)

Mike was 31 years old and eager for more administrative challenges. He realized that there would be no upward mobility at Northwood for a few years, so he decided to search for a position that would offer him a chance to prove his administrative capabilities. He applied to Birch Acres for the administrator position. Mike was certain that he could handle the job and he would have no problem relocating on short notice.

Birch Acres

Birch Acres, a 200-bed proprietary long-term care facility, is located in a suburb of Scotsville, Pennsylvania, which has a significant black population, a small Asian population, and over the past three years, an influx of Hispanics into the area. Both the employee component and the residents are representative of the regional population. The facility is not unionized. A majority of the employees are female; several are single parents. One problem that the facility is having is retaining nursing assistants; just as soon as the orientation period is completed, many of the new hires quit and go to work at the local hospital. Two years ago, the facility advertised for an administrator, following the resignation of the one who had been there for ten years. Mike Flynn was hired by the owners following his first interview.

Discussion Questions

Although this in-basket exercise is based in a healthcare setting, problems such as those stated are ones that can occur in any setting. Managers face issues of diversity frequently, many times not realizing the causes or extent of some of those problems. The issues are real and point to the fact that managers must be aware of the need to understand the effects of multicultural diversity on organizational administration.

1. What are the diversity issues in this in-basket exercise?
2. What diverse groups are represented?
3. What legal problems may arise from some of the diversity issues presented?
4. What are some major differences between Northwood Community Hospital/SNF and Birch Acres?
5. What might Mike Flynn have failed to do before he accepted the job at Birch acres?
6. What are the board's responsibilities in the issues presented?
7. What are Mike Flynn's responsibilities to the board in relation to the issues presented?
8. Why are so many of the newly trained nursing assistants going elsewhere to work following the orientation period?
9. What are Carol Roth's (DON) responsibilities concerning the nursing department staffing problems?
10. What actions should be taken to help overcome staffing problems and employee concerns? Who should take these actions?

11. What can be done to address the evident problem of residents who are roommates and who cannot get along satisfactorily?

Source: Alice L. O'Neill, Director, Health Administration Program at the University of Scranton, Scranton, PA. Used with her permission. Copyright ©1995 by Alice L. O'Neill.

Internet Resources

Visit the Deresky companion Web site at http://prenhall.com/Deresky for this chapter's Internet resources.

Case Study

Managing Diversity at Luxury Island Resort

Patricia Atwell had just accepted a position as a human resource consultant for the Luxury Island Resort in California. The resort's profitability was declining, and Patricia had been hired to evaluate the situation and to make recommendations to the local management and the headquarters management. Feeling a little overwhelmed by this task, Patricia pondered where to start.

There had been an extremely high employee turnover rate in the past few years, the quality of the resort's service had declined, and many regular clients were not returning. Patricia decided to start with the clients by interviewing some of them and asking others to fill out a comment slip about the resort. Many clients criticized the poor service from every type of staff member. One regular client said, "This used to be a happy, efficient place. Now I don't even know if I'll come back next year; the atmosphere among the workers seems dismal; nobody ever looks happy." After reviewing the customer comment cards, Patricia decided to investigate staff relations and job performance at the resort.

At the personnel department, Patricia began to investigate trends and practices regarding hiring and placement. In reviewing the files, she noticed that the labor pool had become increasingly diverse in the last few years, reflecting the general labor market trends in that area. The majority of the employees at the resort represented a number of racial and ethnic backgrounds, and many were recent immigrants. Many were unskilled and had little schooling, yet they were placed straight into their jobs. The management and office staff was also quite diversified; yet, even with their higher education and skill level, there was considerable turnover. While glancing through the files, Patricia noticed a letter of resignation in the file of a reservations office clerk, Maria Martinez. Underneath that letter was a copy of a memo from the resort manager to Ms. Martinez, reprimanding her for consuming alcoholic beverages on the premises. Patricia sought out Ms. Martinez and asked her why she was leaving. Ms. Martinez was clearly angry and hurt as she explained that the previous week she had had a bad cold but did not want to miss any work. So she was in the habit of sipping from a bottle of matta, a nonalcoholic barley beverage popular in the Spanish-speaking Caribbean. She said the manager kept walking past her office and looking in at her. The next day she received the reprimand, but when she tried to talk to him about it, he refused to meet with her.

The next day, Patricia decided to get out among the employees—to talk to them and observe them on the job. She started her departmental evaluations in the kitchen, where she found a melange of cultures; the French chef was screaming directions, mostly in French, to his assistants and the waiters, who seemed to be Haitian, Spanish, and Asian. Many seemed confused about what they should do, but did not say anything.

After a cold lunch of chicken à la king, Patricia decided to review the housekeeping department. She observed a new housekeeper who had been hired that day; her name was Teh, and she was a recent immigrant from Taiwan. Teh was given a cleaning cart, an assigned block of rooms, and a key to the rooms; she was told to get to work. That same day there was a customer complaint. Apparently, Teh did not understand the meaning of the sign *Do Not Disturb* and had interrupted someone taking a shower. Patricia chuckled at some of these incidents, yet she knew that, in the aggregate, they were having serious effects. Later, she overheard a manager reprimanding another housekeeper, remarking that she was nothing but a "lazy Mexican." Patricia spoke to the young woman afterward and found out that when the manager noticed her leaning against the wall, she was just waiting for the room occupant to come back out, as he had said he was about to do, so that she could clean the room.

Patricia interviewed a couple of the housekeepers. She asked a variety of questions: What did they perceive the job duties to be? How should they be performed? What could be done to improve the job? The assortment of answers she received perplexed her; each housekeeper perceived the job differently, and each had valid ideas for improvement based on his or her understanding of the job. Patricia asked one Chinese housekeeper why she did not bring her suggestions to her supervisor. She replied, "Oh, no! I could not do that. He will only think my ideas are stupid." At the end of the week, the housekeeping manager passed around a ballot to choose the worker of the week. Patricia was disturbed when she observed two of the Chinese housekeepers throw their ballots in the garbage. When she asked them why they had decided not to vote, they said that they could not make such a difficult decision about their fellow workers.

For the following few days, Patricia practiced her "management by walking around," just trying to quietly observe the staff and their interactions. One thing she noticed was that each day the different ethnic groups could be found socializing only among themselves—outsiders were not welcomed. She observed a group of Chinese workers planning a picnic, but as she approached them, they very politely quieted down. In another section of the resort, a group of Haitian employees was discussing their day at work. Patricia overheard one man remark that he had heard their manager say that he was taking a leave of absence and that the Haitian man was being reviewed for the position—the idea seemed to upset him. Patricia was intrigued by his concern about the possibility of a promotion to supervisor.

After carefully studying the work processes and interactions in the other resort departments, Patricia decided to interview and evaluate the various managers in the resort, both in the hotel and in the various beach and recreation areas. Again she started with the restaurants. The manager said that he did not perceive any problems with his staff. When she mentioned some of her observations, he said that he was busy and that he really did not find anything to be concerned about. Next she approached the manager of housekeeping, Mrs. White, who explained that she set the rules and the duties and that the only real task was for the staff to follow them; if they didn't, she fired them. In consulting with the resort manager, Patricia noticed that he was concerned about declining occupation. However, he explained, he tried not to become involved in employee problems. He said that he hired experienced department managers, and he expected them to be able to handle such problems.

In concluding her evaluation period, Patricia spent a couple of days reviewing her findings from observations, interviews, and questionnaires. Then she drew up her report and recommendations. Next, she set up two meetings—one with all the managers at the resort, and one with the president of the Luxury Island Resorts, the headquarters company that had retained her. She had plenty to discuss at both meetings.

Case Questions

1. You are Patricia Atwell. Evaluate the situation at the resort. What are your conclusions? Draw up a list of recommendations to the resort management and a list of recommendations to the company president.
2. Assuming your recommendations are accepted, outline your plan for implementing them. What specific steps must be taken, by whom, and when? What results do you anticipate?

Source: This case was written by the author and Bethanne Gorenflo, a student at the State University of New York–Plattsburgh (Spring 1993). Copyright ©1993 by Helen Deresky. It is fictional.

PART FOUR

Comprehensive Cases

CASE 1

TDK DE MEXICO

"I want to be the main supplier base of magnets for South and North America," proclaimed Fumio Inouye, general manager of TDK de Mexico, located in Cd. Juarez, a border city of millions close to El Paso, Texas. "To help gain this status, our operating targets need to be met, and that might include expansion of present plant facilities and more automation. Increasingly I feel, though, that people here don't want to see expansion.... They seem to enjoy excuses! Whether you call it Japanese or American management, I cannot accept delays, wastes, and excuses! Culture to me is important only when the process of production and the importance of work are clearly understood. Make no mistake, my parent company (TDK of Japan) wouldn't stand for anything other than making acceptable margins. I am having difficulty in putting the reasons for all the problems on culture.... I refuse to take it as a dumping ground."

PRODUCTION METHODS AND TECHNOLOGY

TDK de Mexico produced ceramic ferrite magnets of various shapes and sizes that were used for speakers, generators, and motors. It was one of the few plants in its area that produced a final product from the raw material. Production was based on job orders—in other words, production was scheduled as TDK de Mexico received orders for X number of Y type of magnet. The raw material used to make the final product was black powder called ferrite powder. The ferrite powder, a critical raw material, was imported although it was available in the Mexican market. But to ensure quality, TDK of Japan insisted on using ferrite powder from Japan. The manufacturing process started by wetting and mixing the powder in large containers. The mixture was dried and then fed into the press machines that gave the shape to the magnets. The shape was determined by the mold inserted into the press machine. All the molds used also came from

Japan. The various molds for the different shapes and sizes were stored at the plant and used as needed.

Two distinct methods were used during the press stage of the production process, the dry method and the wet method. The basic difference between the two was that the wet method, installed at TDK de Mexico in 1983 after Inouye took charge, utilized water during the pressing of the raw material. It made stronger magnets, but it took more time. With the wet method, the worker collected the magnets just pressed and placed them in a temporary drying area before they were baked in the ovens. With the dry method, the worker collected the magnets just pressed, and they were sent straight to the ovens for baking. While collecting the magnets, the worker visually checked each magnet for cracks or other defects. Defective ones were thrown out for scrap. It was important to spot defective magnets at this stage because it was much harder to convert them into scrap after they were baked. All scrap materials were broken down and used again in the raw material mixture.

After pressing, the magnets were mechanically moved through a series of ovens. One set of pressed magnets was placed in the oven every 12 hours. The magnets were baked at progressively higher temperatures from entrance to exit. After their exit from the ovens, the magnets continued moving to a temporary storage area to cool. The ovens presently in use were electrically powered, but there was a plan to convert them to gas ovens to take advantage of the lower cost of gas. Once cooled, each magnet was subject to process inspection by workers. This was one of two main quality control checkpoints in the production process.

Cooled magnets were taken to the scraper machine. The scraper machine smoothed the rough edges and surface of the magnets. The scrapings were collected and used again in the raw material mixture. From the scraper machine, the workers placed the magnets in water to be cleaned. After cleaning, the magnets were sent through the drying machine. At the exit point of the drying machine, the magnets were collected by workers and placed in boxes. The boxes of magnets were taken to the final process department where each magnet was given a final check. This stage was called the shipping inspection, and it represented the second main quality control checkpoint. Quality control and specification requirements adhered to at this stage included measurement of weight, length, and appearance of magnets.

About 85 percent of production was exported to the United States—to TDK of America facilities in Chicago, Los Angeles, New York, and Indiana. The remaining 15 percent was exported to Hong Kong. The sales offices and warehouse facilities in these cities were in charge of all selling, shipping, and billing functions. TDK of America sold most of its products to Briggs and Stratton of Milwaukee, Wisconsin, and to Buehler Products of Kingston, North Carolina.

TDK de Mexico had encountered no bureaucratic delays or customs problems in shipping out final products, even though other companies in the area were having difficulties arranging for timely shipment of their merchandise out of Mexico. Inouye was proud that he had been able to secure the necessary clearances and paperwork for getting the product out of the country without much hassle. His explanation was, "You don't create systems when you simply need some people who can do things for you. You need to get out and find them. You create systems where systems are accepted.... It is not here!"

Hiratzuka, TDK's production manager, commented, "We hear that the Mexican government may change the rules of the game. There are rumors that we may have to buy 20 to 25 percent of our raw materials from Mexican suppliers." He went on, "Other than what the government will and will not do, I think you also need to understand that our primary concern is to attract quality labor, since our production process demands it.... We can't just hire anyone who walks in."

TDK de Mexico had not looked into possible changes in the Mexican government's local procurement rules to any extent, but had expressed its apprehension to Mexican officials if the firm was forced to buy ferrite powder locally. On another issue, Hiratzuka stated, "As you know, border plants in Mexico like ours have a 'no sale' rule where all goods produced must be exported. But the government is considering a compulsory selling rule whereby 20 percent of a border plant's goods must be sold locally." Such a rule was potentially more troublesome to TDK de Mexico because it was not clear that there was much of a market in Mexico for TDK's products.

THE MEXICAN MAQUILADORAS

In 1965, the United States, working in conjunction with the Mexican government, set up the maquiladora program to create jobs for unemployed and underemployed Mexican workers. The idea was to get U.S. companies to open light assembly plants just across the Mexican border and to use cheap Mexican labor to assemble American-made parts into finished goods. In many cases, the components were manufactured in plants located on the U.S. side of the border; this allowed the components to be easily and quickly transported to the Mexican side for final assembly. The effect was to create twin plants a few miles apart—the U.S. plant being used for capital-intensive/skilled-labor operations, and the Mexican plant being used for labor-intensive, assembly operations.

When the finished products were shipped back into the United States, U.S. companies were taxed only on the value added in Mexico (mostly labor costs) rather than on the total value of the goods being imported. When the Mexican government experienced a debt crisis in 1982 and the value of the Mexican peso collapsed against the dollar, cheap Mexican wages triggered a maquiladora explosion. By early 1987, there were more than 630 plants employing more than 178,000 people along the Mexican side of the U.S. border. These plants, known as maquiladoras (or "in-bond" or twin plants), were all engaged in assembling components in Mexico for reexport in the United States and elsewhere and had become an important economic force along the U.S.–Mexican border. Juarez, where TDK de Mexico's plant was located, had a big concentration of maquilas. Exhibit C1–1 presents some of the features of the maquiladoras program.

Maquiladoras operated within a highly volatile political environment, one that affected every aspect of their existence. They were dependent upon the Mexican government continuing to permit raw materials and components to enter duty free and the U.S. government simultaneously permitting finished products to return with duty paid only on the value added in Mexico. Any major change in these policies by either country could shut down most maquiladoras overnight by making assembly operations on the Mexican side of the border uneconomical. Both countries had strong political groups opposed to the maquiladora concept. Opponents labeled such operations sweatshops and claimed that workers were being exploited by capitalistic interests.

The average age of the maquiladora workers was 24, with a relative dearth of workers over 30. Seventy percent were young women and teenage girls. Workers lived under

EXHIBIT C1–1

The Maquiladora Program: Legal and Regulatory Requirements Imposed by the Mexican Government

Foreign investment

As a rule, a foreign company may subscribe and own only up to 49 percent of the stock in Mexican corporations with the exception of maquilas, which may be totally owned by foreigners. Except for wearing apparel, all items may be produced by in-bond assembly enterprises. Wearing apparel, due to the restriction of textile imports into the United States, is subject to a quota.

Import duties

In-bond plants are not required to pay import duties, but the product assembled or manufactured may not be sold in Mexico. Bonds are generally posted by bonding companies and are renewed yearly.

Taxes

The maximum income tax on corporate profits is 42 percent on taxable income of P$$500,000 or more in a fiscal year, and employees' share in profits before taxes is at the rate of 8 percent. There are other taxes such as the Social Security Tax based on salaries earned and state taxes.

Maquiladora versus joint venture

A comparison of the different rules and practices for joint ventures between Mexican and foreign companies is summarized below:

Concept	Maquiladora	Joint Venture
Doing business in Mexico	To operate in Mexico under a maquila program, a company must be incorporated under Mexican laws (i.e., Sociedad Anonima).	To carry out industrial or commercial activities for the Mexican market, a corporation or other recognized corporate entity must be organized.
Equity ownership	100% foreign ownership is allowed	The general rule is that foreigners may not hold more than 49% of the stock of a corporation doing business in the Mexican market. Exceptions to allow higher percentages of foreign ownership, up to 100%, may be authorized by the Mexican government under special circumstances.
Special operating authorizations	To operate under maquila (in-bond) status, the Ministry of Commerce (SOCOFIN) must authorize a maquila program, setting forth the products or activities the company may manufacture/assemble or carry out. Certain commitments must be made, the compliance with which shall be reviewed periodically.	Unless the company intends to work within a branch of regulated industry, a joint venture company may freely operate without the need to obtain any special operating permits.
Importation of equipment	All production equipment may be imported free of all duties, under bond, subject to it being exported once the company ceases to operate under its maquila program.	The importation of equipment for the production of items that are to be sold in the Mexican market requires an import permit to be obtained and normal duties to be paid thereon.
Importation of raw materials	All raw materials and supplies may be imported free of all duties under bond, subject to them being exported within an extendable six-month period, shrinkage and wastage excepted. Under special circumstances, maquiladoras may be authorized to sell up to 20% of a specific product within the Mexican market.	The importation of raw materials and supplies for the production of items that are to be sold in the Mexican market requires an import permit to be obtained and normal duties to be paid thereon. In all cases, import permits are granted on an absolutely discretionary basis. Currently such permits are quite restricted. Under certain conditions, the negotiation of a manufacturing or integration program with the government may be required.

EXHIBIT C1–1, CONTINUED

The Maquiladora Program: Legal and Regulatory Requirements Imposed by the Mexican Government

Concept	Maquiladora	Joint Venture
Currency exchange controls	Any operating expense, including rent, payroll, taxes, etc., must be paid in Mexican pesos that must be obtained from a Mexican bank by selling dollars thereto at the controlled rate of exchange. Fixed assets may be paid for in dollars at the free rate of exchange.	There are no specific exchange controls on domestic transactions. If the company exports, it will, in general, be required to sell foreign currencies received to a Mexican bank at the controlled rate of exchange.
Labor law requirements	Subject to the Federal Labor Law.	Equally subject to the Federal Labor Law.
Acquisition of real estate	Real estate to establish a production facility may be freely bought in the interior of the country. In the border areas or coasts, it may be acquired through a trust.	Same as a maquiladora.
Leasing of real estate	Real estate may be leased under freely negotiated items, up to a maximum of 10 years.	Same as a maquiladora, although the term may be longer.
Immigration requirements	Foreign technical or management personnel are readily granted work visas, subject to very lenient requirements.	Work visas for foreign technical or management personnel are granted on a very limited basis. Requirements for the obtainment thereof are significantly more stringent.
Transfer of technology	For tax purposes it is advisable that a Technical and/or Management Assistance Agreement be executed between the maquiladora and its parent. Such agreement would need to be registered with the National Transfer of Technology Registry (NTTR), which registration would be readily obtained.	If technical or management assistance is granted to a domestic company from a foreign source and royalties or fees are to be paid therefor, an agreement must be registered with the NTTR. To obtain such registration the agreement must meet certain criteria and the amounts which may be charged are limited.
Taxes	A maquiladora is in principle subject to the payment of all Mexican taxes. However, since such operations are intended to be cost centers rather than profit centers, the income taxes to be paid are limited. Also, any value added tax paid by the maquiladora shall be refunded to it upon its request.	A domestic company is subject to all normal taxes such as income tax and value added tax (maximum corporate income tax rate = 42%).

PART FOUR

crowded conditions—the mean household size of maquiladora workers was 7.8 persons. Their wages averaged about $0.80 per hour, barely more than half the 1987 average Mexican manufacturing wage of $1.57 an hour (including benefits). The low wages made it very attractive for mass assembly operations requiring low-skill labor to be located on the Mexican side of the U.S. border. Managers of the maquiladoras expressed a preference for hiring "fresh or unspoiled" workers who had not acquired "bad habits"

in other organizations. The work was so low-skilled that workers received very little training. The turnover rate ran 59 to 100 percent a year in many plants.

However, many of the large multinational companies with maquiladoras paid more than the wage minimums, and their overall compensation package was more attractive than the lowest-paying operations. Some of the multinationals also spent substantial amounts in training and employee development.

The location of twin (or maquiladora) plants along the northern border of Mexico was increasing at a phenomenal speed, and unemployed Mexicans were flocking to northern border towns to fill the rapidly expanding number of job openings. By the end of 1988, it was predicted that maquiladoras would employ 350,000 workers, one-tenth of Mexico's industrial workforce, and that the plants would import $8 billion in U.S. components, add $2 billion in value (mostly labor), and ship $10 billion in finished goods back to the United States for sale in the United States and other world markets. A number of Japanese-based companies had begun to set up maquila operations to handle the production and sale of their products in U.S. markets—TDK de Mexico was one of these companies.

Despite concerns over the maquiladoras, the program was central to the Mexican government's economic revival plans. Mexican leaders were most enthusiastic about a new kind of maquiladora. These were plants built in the interior of Mexico that were geared to exports, like the border plants, but unlike the border operations, they undertook inhouse manufacture of many of the components used in the final assembly process. These plants used higher-skilled employees and paid wages much closer to the average manufacturing wage in Mexico, and they did not rely so heavily on the use of female labor. They also depended more on Mexican companies for raw material supplies and services.

TDK'S INTERNAL MANAGEMENT

TDK de Mexico had 183 employees (158 women and 25 men). Inouye, before he came to TDK de Mexico, operated machines in a Taiwan plant to help gain a better understanding of workers at that level. After his move to Mexico in 1983, Inouye organized the workforce into teams consisting of workers, subleaders, and leaders. Leaders were not entrusted with the job of supervision; all supervisory responsibilities remained with individuals having a title of supervisor. It took an average of two years for a worker to become a subleader. All subleaders at TDK de Mexico were Mexican; they had a median age of 28.2 years. Only three were women.

There were 11 leaders. The specifics of their job were dependent upon their department. Generally, they oversaw workers and machines in their respective departments but were given little authority and were not accountable for achieving set objectives. They were also in charge of training new workers. The leaders at TDK de Mexico had been at the company for an average of 6.4 years. The average time it took to become a leader was about three

years. All the leaders at TDK de Mexico were Mexican. Very few had ever been promoted to the supervisory level.

Five Japanese filled the 12 positions of supervisors and assistant supervisors (Exhibit C1–2). Like the leaders, their jobs varied based on the department they supervised. Primarily their duties included supervision of the leaders as well as the teams under the leaders. They determined production plans for their respective departments. Although there were Mexican nationals in higher positions, all Japanese employees, irrespective of their job titles, reported directly to Inouye. Because most of the Japanese could not speak Spanish, Inouye thought it was wise to have this direct reporting relationship. However, some of the managers of Mexican origin did not accept this line of reasoning (one manager called it "clannish behavior"); their protests to Inouye had not met with much success.

WAGE POLICIES

TDK de Mexico paid higher wages than most other companies located in the Juarez industrial park plants. TDK de Mexico had several pay incentives available to the workers. They received a bonus after 30 days on the job. There was extra pay for overtime, night shifts, weekend work, and also generous incentives for attendance. Yet, Alfred Gomez, personnel manager for TDK de Mexico, stated, "Absenteeism and lateness are becoming problems. In some cases, when a worker decides to leave her job, she just stops coming to work without any notice. One reason for this problem is that the Juarez public health hospital gives out medical excuses to workers to miss work for the slightest illness.... There is very little we can do about it."

TRAINING

TDK had invested a lot of resources in training its employees; most of its training, however, had been confined to leaders and subleaders. Gomez, the head of personnel, did not go through any systematic training need analysis but professed to know "who needed training and who did not by sight." Inouye's position was, "We will spend money on training, of course, but only with those who show promise." Asked how did he see promise, he replied, "I have been working for 25 years.... I know!" A leader who had just finished an inhouse training program on motivation commented, "Whenever we face a major crisis, the six Japanese managers get together with Mr. Inouye and decide what course of action to take. It seems like the

EXHIBIT C1–2

TDK de Mexico Organization Chart

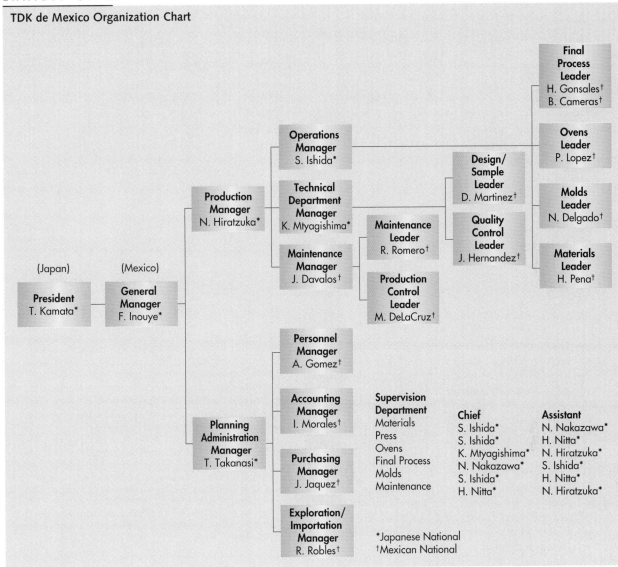

only decisions I am allowed to participate in are of routine nature that are easily solved. What do I do with what I learned from the training sessions?"

FUMIO INOUYE'S CONCERNS

In March 1988, Inouye met with all the managers (Mexican and Japanese) and presented the plant's most recent operating statistics (Exhibit C1–3). He was clearly unhappy with the data. A senior manager from Japanese headquarters also attended the meeting along with two other managers from TDK of America. Inouye laid out several options that could be pursued:

1. Downsize the labor force, to correct for the decline in sales and the increase in expenses.
2. Try to avoid downsizing and try to reduce operating costs by buying ferrite powder locally. Since it was not

EXHIBIT C1-3

Operating Statistics of TDK de Mexico, 1984–1987

	1984	1985	1986	1987
Total sales (U.S. dollars)	$4,168,000	$3,774,000	$3,837,000	$3,168,000*
Employees	112	128	140	183
Sales per person	$ 29,000	$ 22,000	$ 20,000	$ 23,000
Efficiency rate	82%	81%	80%	80%
Labor turnover rate	16%	47%	46%	39%[†]
Selling/administrative expenses	$1,623,000	$1,529,000	$1,698,000	$1,878,000
Cost of raw materials	$1,052,000	$1,071,000	$1,099,000	$1,181,000

Shipping cost = .01¢ per gram or 2%–10% of total costs.

Price of magnets = .05¢ per gram.

Average production for a year = 5,100,000 grams.

Production figure for 1987 = 6,900,000 grams.

Plant is presently at full capacity.

*Based on the then exchange rate.
[†]Other maquilas in the park ranged from 25 to 170 percent per year.

known where and how ferrite powder could be obtained from Mexican sources, Inouye suggested that immediate consideration be given to making the material locally or acquiring a native company.

3. Send some senior managers (Inouye emphasized Mexican nationals) to Japan for further training.

The Mexican managers thought the concerns expressed in the meeting were addressed specifically to them. One Mexican manager said after the meeting, "If these people would live in Mexico and not run to their comfortable homes on the other side of the border after 5 o'clock, maybe they would understand us a little better!"

Several Mexican managers again suggested to Inouye that the Japanese managers learn the language and work closely with the workers. Inouye was sympathetic to the suggestion but questioned whether learning the language was essential. He advised them to examine "the pockets of inefficiency" and lectured them about the value of hard work.

The manager from TDK Japan left with a stern warning for imminent improvement or else. He explained to the casewriter:

> You see, I came over here in late 1983, after spending years in Singapore, Taiwan, and Hong Kong. I don't know how useful it is to have a grand strategy or any

plan per se for an operation like this.... What it boils down to is SHOOTEN (focus), SHITSU (quality), and BUNAI (distribution).... I'm not about to give up because of cultural differences or any such nonsense. Maybe, and just maybe, I will ask these people here: What do you have to do to earn more money! And if the answer is anything but work harder, I have problem!

Inouye began to contemplate what actions he should take.

Source: Adapted from a case prepared by Professor Manab Thakur, California State University, Fresno; reprinted in R. Thompson and R. Strickland, *Strategic Management*, 6th ed. (Homewood, IL: Irwin, 1992). This case is presented for educational discussion purposes, not to illustrate either effective or ineffective handling of an administrative situation.

CASE QUESTIONS

1. What was the strategic importance of the Maquiladoras to U.S. manufacturers? To the Japanese? To the Mexican government? To the Mexican workers? What human resources issues are present?

2. What contingency plan should TDK put in place to prepare for unforeseen changes in the Maquiladoras program?

3. What is your assessment of the manner in which the Japanese were managing the Juarez plant? Were the Japanese treating the Mexican workers fairly? How would you describe the Japanese attitudes toward the Mexican workers? How will the Japanese attitudes and behaviors toward the Mexican workers affect their motivation?

4. What recommendations would you make to Fumio Inouye?

CASE 2
SOLARTRON (C)[1]

DECEMBER 24

Rick Douglas sat at his desk reading the note from Andre Marcil, President of Solartron:

> Pierre and Lise left at 9:45 P.M. and we accomplished quite a bit in the three hours prior to his flight; as usual, when the pressure's on, the work gets done. He looked happy and excited, and I feel that he is going to be a very good addition to the group and that he will definitely help Solartron Kenya really get off the ground.

APRIL 22

As the plane carrying Pierre and Lise lifted off from Kenyatta International Airport, Pierre was both relieved and depressed. What had seemed like such a wonderful opportunity when he joined Solartron Kenya had ended. Now he was leaving Kenya, after less than four months.

The reasons for the early departure were complex and, depending on who you asked, could be attributed in part or in whole to a number of people. It seemed to Pierre that things had gotten off to a bad start from which he had never recovered.

PIERRE BLONDEAU

Pierre Blondeau was a lanky, easygoing solar engineer. His work experience included the preparation of feasibility studies: conducting energy conservation surveys, creating computer simulations, doing field work, and supervising. Pierre's grin and his shaggy hair gave him a boyish appearance that belied his technical competence. At 30, he had already completed a master's degree in solar and mechanical engineering and, although he enjoyed his job with a consulting engineering firm, he was ready for a new challenge.

In recent years, his personal life had been turbulent. Nine months ago, his divorce was finalized. Since that time, he had been living with Lise Rivard, a writer, in a house they had purchased together. Lise was an ardent feminist whose fiery personality and volatility had attracted Pierre the first time they met.

Blondeau had attended a contractors' meeting in Ottawa. During lunch, he got into a discussion with Alain Marcil, sales and marketing manager for Solartron, one of the largest manufacturers of solar systems in Canada. Blondeau had dealt often with Solartron, and was impressed by its products and professionalism. Marcil told him that Solartron was expanding its operations overseas and mentioned that he was looking for an engineer to work for Solartron Kenya, a joint venture that had just been established.

Blondeau was excited by the description of the opportunity. The following week he telephoned Alain's brother, Andre Marcil, Solartron's founder and president, to arrange an interview.

Solartron Kenya

Rick Douglas, Director of the World Three Consultants[2] (WTC), had met Andre Marcil through the offices of the Canadian International Development Agency. The two men discussed the potential for solar energy in Kenya, and Douglas offered an introduction to George Beida, a Kenyan businessman who was very active in housing development. Marcil subsequently made three visits to Kenya; the result was a joint venture agreement with Beida. The agreement called for the creation of two new companies, Solartron Africa (STA), a holding company, and Solartron Kenya (STK), an operating company that would service the Kenyan market. Following the development of STK, the men hoped to expand into other African countries through STA.

During a series of meetings the details of the agreement were finalized. The partners hoped to introduce Solartron's products into Kenya through a three-phase program. Initially, systems would be exported to Kenya; in the second phase, products would be shipped completely knocked down for local assembly; in phase three, all assembly and the bulk of component manufacture would be done locally.

During discussions, Beida made it clear that he considered the provision of an engineer for STK from Solartron to be a very high priority. As he frequently said:

> If we have an engineer from the parent company working for us, our clients will have confidence in us. The type of engineer we really need is a person who can sell—you know, a marketer. Because if it's a question of just producing drawings, we can get the stuff locally and send them to Canada. What we require is a human being with a good personality, you know, good public relations. Because all business as far as I'm concerned, relates to or revolves around charm.

Marcil initially did not understand or share Beida's concern about the credibility of the new company in the eyes of other Kenyan executives:

> Hiring a Canadian for STK would be overkill, and I can't afford to lose a person right now anyway. Harold Kamina (who was to be managing director of STK) is a PhD engineer. Send us a Kenyan and we'll train the person to work with Harold.

But as the discussion progressed, it became clear to Marcil that the presence of a Canadian offered significant advantages to STK in terms of credibility and the availability of technical competence. He agreed to look for a suitable candidate, and Douglas subsequently prepared a memorandum that outlined the type of person Marcil was to look for:

> Someone will be hired to work full time for the company for a part of a year in Kenya. This person should be an engineer, preferably a mechanical engineer, with at least two to three years' experience in industry. He or she must also have good management skills.
>
> The engineering background, although necessary, should be secondary. Management and organization abilities are crucial as this person will play a role in getting the company physically in operation and will assist with the feasibility study.

Marcil started looking for a suitable candidate, and over the next three months he interviewed six people. Among the candidates was Pierre Blondeau.

THE HIRING OF PIERRE BLONDEAU

Andre Marcil was impressed by Blondeau's background and the initiative he had shown in requesting an interview. The two men were immediately comfortable with each other, and as the discussion progressed, Andre became convinced

that Blondeau was the most impressive candidate he had met and would be a great asset to STK. At the conclusion of the meeting, he offered Blondeau the job and suggested he talk it over with Lise before making a decision.

Lise was Blondeau's major concern. She had been reserved when he first mentioned the idea of moving to Africa but was unwilling to be separated from him for the 6 to 12 months he would be away. If he decided to accept, she would go with him.

English was the business language of Kenya and most people spoke it. Although Blondeau spoke fluent English, Lise spoke little; her native French was a language seldom heard in Kenya. This, combined with the anticipated cultural and social changes, dampened her enthusiasm for the adventure.

Blondeau wanted very much to accept the offer. After discussing the options with Lise, he informed Marcil that he would accept if Solartron agreed to provide return airfare for both him and Lise, and if English lessons could be arranged for Lise in Nairobi. He discussed Lise's hesitancy with Marcil, and it was agreed that if she did not enjoy Nairobi, she would return home alone.

Marcil was extremely pleased to have hired someone as qualified as Blondeau. In a final meeting, the two men agreed on the terms of employment and signed a contract.

In a subsequent letter to Rick Douglas, Marcil said of Blondeau:

> We have come to the conclusion that he offers the most potential for the position as manager of Solartron Kenya. His background and experience in solar engineering are quite strong, and to me, this was a nonnegotiable. On the management side, even though he has been responsible for some important projects, he will have to be supervised and directed quite closely, at least to get the organization going.

The terms of the agreement called for Blondeau to work in Solartron's Ottawa facility two or three days a week until mid-December. This would allow him to familiarize himself with the company's products and processes and the details of the African operation. He was to start work in Nairobi on January 1.

THE BRIEFING

Rick Douglas and Andre Marcil had agreed that the person chosen to work for STK would spend two or three days talking with members of the World Three Consultants. The purpose of the visit would be to brief the person on the geography, history, and culture of Kenya. Shortly after accepting the job, Blondeau agreed that he and Lise would spend two days with the consultants. Last-minute scheduling problems resulted in the couple arriving late, and it became necessary to compress the briefings into a day and a half.

The focus of the briefings was primarily on the country. There was little said about the job. Since it was a startup situation, everything would need to be done and anything could be expected to happen. Rick Douglas met first with the pair, giving them an overview of the work of WTC and its involvement with Solartron. He talked at length of his experiences in Africa and of the differences to be expected, and the opportunities enjoyed. His love for the country was evident in his animated discussion of life in Kenya.

In his briefings, Rick's colleague, Bob Allan, took a somewhat harder line. He dwelled at length on the problems of living in a developing country, of coping with being a minority, with language hassles and security problems, with wondering how to deal with a houseboy, and the myriad other small things that can frustrate Westerners. During the afternoon, Lise was visibly tired and her limited ability with English made it difficult for her to follow the discussion. After two hours, she retired for a nap, rejoining the others for supper and the evening talks.

The briefings were generally positive and painted a picture of Kenya as a beautiful and stable country offering an expatriate a good standard of living, and the opportunity to visit some of the finest game parks and resorts in Africa. Balancing this, however, was a warning to Lise and Pierre that there would inevitably be difficulties, and that flexibility would be necessary if they were to make the most of the experience.

Bob Allan had mixed feelings about their visit:

> Pierre was a pleasant person and obviously strong technically, but he was short on management skills. Lise seemed largely uninterested in the briefings and was unsure whether she should go with him.

Allan mentioned his misgivings about Lise to Douglas, who agreed with his concerns but hesitated to mention them to Marcil. Solartron Kenya had won a contract to install 500 domestic hot water systems the previous week, and intense pressure was coming from STK to get someone out there. He felt that the pair could cope, and that the language lessons he had arranged for Lise would allow her to interact in local society and help her enjoy her time in Africa.

DECEMBER 29

As the KLM flight commenced its final approach to Kenyatta International Airport, Pierre Blondeau wondered what the coming weeks would bring. He and Lise had spent the previous week vacationing in Amsterdam and, although tired after the overnight flight, he was excited at the prospect of actually arriving in Africa and the challenge of his new position.

Blondeau had high expectations of Kenya. Marcil had said they would spend the month of January at River Court, a spacious three-bedroom apartment used by the World Three Consultants. During that time, they would choose their apartment to be furnished from curtains to cutlery. A houseboy came along with the home. Although local transportation would not be immediately available, Blondeau was to purchase a station wagon or pickup truck for STK and use it as his own outside working hours; even used cars were expensive in Kenya, and it was thought impractical for him to buy one for a one-year appointment. Having the use of the STK vehicle would give Blondeau and Lise the freedom to explore Kenya in their free time.

Blondeau was looking forward to his new job. Marcil had given him a job description and he was eager to see STK make the transition into a successful operating company. After a few days off to get settled and celebrate New Year's, he expected to be at his desk bright and early Monday morning.

ERICA BECK

Erica Beck was looking forward to meeting Pierre and Lise. As WTC's resident consultant in Nairobi, she had been actively involved in the process that had led to the establishment of STK. Since the awarding of the contract for 500 domestic hot water systems in October, her involvement had been almost full time as she assisted STK's managing director, Harold Kamina, with a wide range of activities. Erica was not an engineer, and although she had found the activities of the previous months highly stimulating, she had other projects underway that needed her attention. With Pierre's arrival, she would be able to bow out of day-to-day involvement with STK.

At age 33, Erica was a veteran of Africa. She previously had lived four years in Swaziland where she established a cooperative garment manufacturing plant. During this time, she had traveled widely and had developed a deep affection for the continent and its people.

On her return to North America from Africa, Erica enrolled in an MBA program. On graduation, she joined WTC and was sent to represent the company in Nairobi.

Erica had discussed Pierre and Lise at length with Rick Douglas during his recent visit to Nairobi. To ensure a smooth transition for the couple, he asked her to arrange for a suitable apartment and to help them through the first weeks in the country.

In late November, Erica started looking for an apartment. Her intention was to locate the pair in a middle-class area with a mixed population and easy access to public transportation. Such an apartment would be reasonably priced and offer a diverse and interesting cultural experience.

Although Erica had located two apartments to fit her criteria, both had been ruled unsuitable by George Beida. After persistent questioning by Erica, he made it clear that he felt Blondeau should be free to choose his own apartment. He also had Erica telex Solartron to suggest the couple bring their own linens since those available in Kenya were expensive and low quality.

December had flown by, and now Erica was at the airport waiting for Blondeau and Lise to complete entry formalities. Although she knew how tiring the overnight flight from Europe could be, Erica was expecting the couple to be excited, positive, and enthusiastic about their arrival in Kenya.

Blondeau and Lise appeared tired as they struggled out of customs under the weight of their baggage. Erica's initial impression was that Pierre was easygoing, but that Lise seemed a little distant. After introducing herself, she led the way to her Volkswagen, which, it soon became obvious, was too small to hold all of their luggage. As Erica and Pierre discussed alternatives, Erica was surprised to see Harold Kamina pull up in his Mercedes.

HAROLD KAMINA

Although he knew that Erica Beck would be meeting Pierre and Lise, Harold Kamina had decided to drive to the airport to welcome them to Kenya.

Kamina was excited at the prospect of meeting Pierre Blondeau. As managing director of STK, he had been under tremendous pressure to get the new company operational. Since the awarding of the contract, he found it something of a struggle to get the installation of the 500 domestic hot water systems running smoothly. Solartron Kenya had added inordinately to his workload; nor did his other obligations leave him the time he needed to devote to the startup. In addition to a refrigeration contracting company, he owned a bakery and a heavy equipment distributorship, both of which required a lot of attention.

As he drove to the airport, Kamina was preoccupied with his latest dilemma; Solartron Kenya had no solar collectors available for installation at Lubango. Although a container destined for the project had arrived the previous week, Kamina had been horrified to discover that no Société Générale du Surveillance (SGS) inspection certificate had been obtained prior to shipment from Canada. Now Kenya customs were refusing to clear it, and it was possible the container would have to be returned. Although his crews were at work installing water storage tanks on the Lubango houses, it would be necessary to start adding the collectors to complete the systems very soon. As an interim measure, Kamina had hoped to borrow some collectors from the Canadian High Commission, which had arranged to bring a container full of systems into Kenya as a diplomatic shipment prior to the World Energy Show in August. The systems were destined for installation on Canadian staff quarter housing and at the International School of Kenya. The container contained more systems than these projects required, and the school's system had yet to be installed. Kamina expected another container to arrive in three weeks; meanwhile, pressure mounted from the project engineers for Kamina to meet his installation commitments. To date, he had been unable to convince the High Commission to release the excess systems to him; he was hoping Blondeau might be able to resolve the problem. Kamina also wanted Blondeau to prepare an inventory of the contents of the container because much of the copper piping had "disappeared" since arriving in Kenya.

Bringing in an engineer from Canada had been important to Kamina:

I felt very strongly that we had to have a representative from the manufacturing company. Somebody had to be there to represent the interests of the parent company and see to things on their behalf because it is a joint venture. That's one point. The other point, which was crucial to me, was that we needed a technical person just for sheer credibility. When we go to sell ourselves, to present ourselves, we also wanted to say, this fellow is the manufacturer of the equipment. If I'm the client, I don't want to talk to a middleman. Also, a technical person would support somebody in charge of administration. So you need a technical arm to lean on, apart from somebody local. This is why we needed two engineers, one expatriate and one local. This is just a market feeling from the business point of view. From the technical point, I can assure you there is nothing I could not do, if I could only have a week or two training. Technically, it's quite ordinary; it's more or less following the rules of the game and adapting from one environment to another. We have a young man eminently suited for that. So technically, even for installation, we don't require help from Canada. We require support in design, not for domestic equipment, but for industrial projects. But as I say, the idea of a Canadian was for the transitional period.

There are so many huge problems setting up a new company ... for example, trying to translate North American business and manufacturing procedures into local terms. This is the first stage of a three-stage project. So this person's role was really to set up all this and also do business for us—look for clients and things like that and oversee our installations.

Kamina arrived at the airport as Erica and Pierre were discussing what to do with the baggage. Enthusiastically pumping Blondeau's hand, he welcomed the pair to Kenya and immediately started discussing the problems facing STK. Quickly taking charge of the situation, he had bundled the remainder of the bags into his car and, taking Blondeau with him, headed for River Court, leaving Erica and Lise to follow in the Volkswagen.

On the drive to River Court, Erica began to feel apprehensive about Lise, who was incensed at having been separated from Pierre and whose general conversation seemed to indicate an inflexible attitude. Would this cause problems in the very traditional Kenyan culture, Erica wondered. It was still pretty much a man's world. Women's lib had not yet arrived in Kenya, and no one knew better than Erica the amount of effort, thought, and flexibility it took to adapt. The couple visibly brightened on seeing the River Court apartment, but their smiles disappeared when Erica told them they would have to vacate in two days. Blondeau had expected to have a month at River Court, during which time he could search for an apartment, and the prospect of finding an apartment so quickly sounded unappealing to him.

Less than an hour later the phone rang. Kamina, now back at the office, was pressing Pierre to come to work. Pierre hung up totally perplexed. He expected to have some time off to settle in and had been surprised when Kamina talked business in the car. Now it appeared he was not to have any time off at all.

Erica felt strongly that Pierre and Lise should go to the office, if only for half an hour, just to be polite. Despite her efforts, Lise refused, and although Pierre went, he did so reluctantly.

SETTLING-IN PROBLEMS

Pierre and Lise's introduction to their new lifestyle was far from tranquil. Although there were numerous minor problems and irritants, these were overshadowed by major prob-

lems that developed in four areas: housing, transportation, working conditions, and personal life.

Housing

From the moment Erica Beck explained they would have to leave River Court within two days, Blondeau thought of nothing but housing:

I expected to spend a month in River Court, which would have left us enough time to find a place with no rush. The company was supposed to take charge of providing all the furniture and everything because I didn't carry that stuff—you see I was expecting to have everything when I arrived here. He said Erica would be staying the month at River Court also. This was also a delicate point. I didn't know Erica at all, you see. I liked her; she was okay. But when you have to live together, there may be some friction. It really was a gamble to get two different people together, and if you force them to live together, it may be too much.

Harold Kamina commented:

When they arrived, they were put up in a flat whose lease was running out in two days. So within those two days, we moved them to another flat. They said it was not suitable, so we said, "Okay, we will now move you to another place." Which is where they are now. So, there was just a question of three or four days in this transition. But I think they didn't take very well to it.

Pierre Blondeau was not impressed by the apartment search:

Erica arranged everything with Beida. We went to three different places and they were all too far away from the city center, so we decided to go for the apartment that was downtown and ready, but there were no household goods, just the furniture, and nothing to cook with.

George Beida commented:

I said, "What would you wish? Where would you like to live?" He said, "You know my wife's not working. I would like to live downtown." "Downtown," I said, "in what type of accommodation?" He said he would like two bedrooms. I said, "Why two bedrooms?" He replied, "Because when Andre comes, we would like him to stay there." I didn't believe that, but it's not the issue. Then, I said, "In Nairobi, we don't have anything like that downtown. There are very few places downtown anyway. However, we do have a two-bedroom flat, which will be ready in February. It's on top of Nairobi

House near the theatre, near the restaurants, next to everything. It's not ready yet, but there's a one-bedroom flat in the same building. Go and look at it! If you like it, and you want to stay there, being inconvenienced for one month, then you can move upstairs into the two-bedroom flat. Then you'll be downtown and your wife will have no problem with transportation." He went to look at it. He didn't even come back to the office. He just went and moved his things there. So I figured the guy was happy.

But Pierre and Lise were soon back in the housing market:

We couldn't stand it for more than one week. It was very noisy. The buses around there clattered day and night. It was small and dark, and I saw big cockroaches running around. Dirty, dirty—cockroaches and everything.

We then found a place that was 2 kilometers outside of the city, but at least there was bus service and it was a serviced apartment. During the first week, I had to buy some household goods, and we argued because the company didn't want to reimburse me.

George Beida was perplexed by Blondeau's behavior:

Then he decided he didn't want downtown anymore. I said, "Okay, go look at furniture you want for the flat." But halfway through, I knew this would never work. He said Andre promised him cutlery. Andre promised him, you know. He was promised linen and so on and so forth. I knew that was not correct. Because when I talked with Erica, I said, "Erica, can you ask those two to bring their own linen because it's cheaper in Canada?" Anyway, I didn't bother to argue about it, and I knew the problem would never be solved. I could not let my partner down. So, I said, "Okay, if you were promised that, what else were you promised? A fellow to clean your flat? Well, okay, we will provide that too. The only thing—downtown is not possible." It's a fact, there are few flats in downtown Nairobi. So I took him in my car. We went to look for serviced apartments, which had cutlery and staff. I said, "Look at this. If you like it, you move in as soon as you want to move in." He said he would take Lise to see it. He said they liked it, so they moved in. And even then, he was not satisfied. Things were not right. You know, the color was not right. He should have said so when they first went there. He can't expect me to go to decide on the color. He went to the flat. He said he was happy, comfortable.

Transportation

While the accommodation was being settled, Blondeau had started work. Progress on the Lubango installations was at a standstill while STK and Blondeau tried to borrow collectors

from the container imported by the Canadian High Commission. He was also involved in conducting an inventory of the contents of the container, a significant portion of which had disappeared. Blondeau's work required him to be mobile and the lack of his own vehicle quickly replaced the housing issue as a point of contention:

Andre told me I was supposed to purchase a car for the company. He told me I could use it for my personal use and when I was working it would be used for company purposes. The first weekend I was able to borrow Kenya Construction's Volkswagen and Mr. Beida told me, no problem, you can take the Volkswagen every night to travel back and forth. But the next week the car broke down and there was no alternative solution. He kept telling me, you will get your own vehicle in two weeks anyway and then it was at the end of the month, and after that it was another two weeks and so on. The Volkswagen was used by the people in Kenya Construction and if one of them had a meeting, he might come back at 7:00 P.M., so I would spend all my time here waiting for the vehicle. I couldn't plan. I'd make an appointment with someone and then realize I had no transportation.

Harold Kamina was not sympathetic to Blondeau:

Each time there was a problem, it really swung around the vehicle, so much that all his memos related to that. These are pool vehicles you know—you can't have them to yourself. So whether he wanted something for himself exclusively, we don't know. Maybe he was promised a vehicle and he interpreted it too literally.

George Beida commented:

When he said he needed a car, we provided him with a car. Then the car broke down. He came to the office immediately and asked for another. I said, "How can we provide another car? We don't have cars all over." We started seeing the problem coming. The company was not yet finalized, so we could not borrow money. In fact, we could not start operating the company without the Foreign Investment License, which we were still waiting for. So I told him, "Listen! Anything we do before the formalities are finalized will cause problems." Because our problem is that we started operating, we started doing business, before we were finalized. So it became a big issue. For example, he said he needed a car to go shopping at night. How can he say that? It's all crazy! There is no shopping at night in Kenya. Anyway, he had a car. If it broke down it had to be repaired. And so it went on. Quite frankly, I started losing interest because I started seeing this man was not going to fit in here. So what's the point in buying a car when that money could be used to clear the solar heaters at the port? He should have understood. He was very negative.

Harold Kamina:

The vehicle was available. During working hours, he might not have it to himself, but to come in to work and to go to his house, he had it. He had it everyday, everyday. When it broke down, he took it so badly. But even a new vehicle has to go to the garage sometime.

Working Conditions

Although the technical aspects of his new job were much as he had anticipated, Blondeau was surprised by the administration he was expected to handle:

Andre gave me a priority list and a job instruction list that included, of course, technical stuff, but also managing, marketing, administration, keeping the inventory and everything. I don't think I realized all the implications of that because it is really a big task to ask someone who has a technical background to be a good administrator at the same time.

He told me there would be staff to do most of the work. I was just to be able to understand what they were doing. When I arrived here, I realized that there was not much staff. I thought that the partners here were going to be more involved in the administration.

I didn't suspect that I would spend so much energy just to get things going, to get the proper tools to do my job and try to convince the directors that I was here to work and that I needed some tools to do that.

To add to Blondeau's frustration, he had been sent home to his apartment to work for three weeks, shortly after his arrival, because he did not have a work permit. Harold Kamina explained:

Before we got approval for the permit, he could not come here to work. So he stayed away for about three weeks until we got approval.

By the time approval was received, Blondeau had decided to leave STK, and Kamina then decided he did not want to put up the security bond and pay for the permit for such a short period:

For his dependent and himself, we would have to put up a bond of $3,000. We can't put that much up for three months; it doesn't make sense. But he took offense to things like that.

With a shortage of collectors and STK short on working capital as it waited for official approval from the Foreign Investment Review Committee, Blondeau felt constrained in what he could accomplish. He also found that he could not get away as easily as he wished. He discovered that his expectations were unacceptable to Kamina, who said:

And then he wanted to be excused from working on Saturdays because he wanted to see the country. We said, "No, we work on Saturdays here. Even if you don't work Saturdays in Canada, we cannot afford not to. We can't help it!" But all the same, he still had to go up country almost every weekend.

Pierre Blondeau commented:

When I arrived here and I realized that I couldn't get these things, at least for the first few months, I wondered how I could go on safari and enjoy myself. When you decide to come to Africa, I think there is the challenge of the job, but there is also your personal life to consider; you want to be able to travel and enjoy the country. It is a new country to discover.

Personal Life

Blondeau's frustration at his situation did not greatly move George Beida, who had been unimpressed from their first meeting:

He was shaggy, disorganized.... The way he was dressed, he looked like a hippie traveling around. When he arrived, we had a problem with the solar collectors being held by the Canadian High Commission, and we were waiting for him to sort it out. The day he arrived he said, "You know, I'm very tired. I'd like to relax for a few days before I do anything." And you know, sure as hell, he had to take four or five days off before he'd look at it. His attitude was not right.

Pierre Blondeau had a different view of the situation:

Rick Douglas told me I would have at least a week off to get familiar with the country and the people. But almost the moment I was off the plane, they required me in the office because they had some problems on a deadline. I could have refused because my contract didn't start until January 1, but I was in a bad position, and I also had to come to the office to solve my lodging problems.

Beida was also concerned about Lise:

I called the man and said, "Listen, we're going to have a lot of problems. You have a young wife. She cannot be expected to be sitting at home doing nothing. Even my wife cannot sit at home doing nothing. So either she gets involved in some voluntary organizations or something else. She's French—she could go to the French Embassy or the French cultural center and find out what can be done there; or be involved in the university. Something— so that she's busy. Otherwise, she will be looking at the watch for you. Is there anything I can help with?" I even tried introducing them to people around, but it just couldn't work. It just couldn't work.

Despite the attempts of Beida and Beck to draw Lise out and make her feel more comfortable, she remained aloof and made little effort to develop friends or socialize in the local community. She seemed to spend most of her time in the flat writing, and Beida felt certain that she was behind much of Blondeau's discontent.

> One weekend I invited Pierre and Lise to my house for lunch. I had some visitors, including some cabinet ministers. During lunch, Lise asked if she could see me. I said, "Sure, why not? Come to my office." So she's the one who came in, in fact, to tell me—to give me a lecture about the apartment. This is why I knew it would not work. The bloody fellow should have told me himself. Unfortunately for me, I managed it badly. I should have kicked her out of my office. Because after that, he started writing me letters also.

Blondeau's frustration with the housing and transportation problems was increased by his contact with other expatriates:

> I met people from France, from Brazil, from all sorts of places, and most of them told me that they enjoyed Kenya. So I tried to discover why they did, and most of them said that they could not afford the same standard of living anywhere else. I feel that I live much better when I am in Canada. I have my own transport. I don't have to beg to get it. I don't have to account to anybody. I have a house that I like.

By mid-February, Blondeau and Lise had decided to leave Africa. Pierre Blondeau explained his decision.

> I would say an accumulation of frustrations made me decide to go back, I didn't see any way that things would really improve. I just felt I had had enough and also there were some other adaptation problems, because we came as a couple and for the man it is usually easier because you have work—you have a job—at least you know how to spend your time for eight hours a day. Lise didn't speak much English, which added to the difficulty.
>
> Also, we didn't know many people and you have to live a certain time in a place before getting to know people. At night, we didn't have much to do. There weren't many movies, and if you don't like going to nightclubs it restricts activities. As you live in a place, you find more and more to do, but I think for Lise, it was a lot harder than for me. But I had difficulties as well; I'm not so sure that even if I had gone there alone . . . I maybe would have left early anyway.

George Beida commented:

> He saw himself coming here, quite frankly, much more to see the country than to do the work. I think his problem is culture shock more than anything else, and I think the major problem is that he's highly dominated by his lady.

Harold Kamina was more concerned with the Lubango project:

> I would like really to see Solartron coming up with a replacement for Blondeau as soon as possible because we are in a critical stage where the next twelve months will mean a pruning away of certain companies involved in the energy field.

The experience with Blondeau had frustrated Andre Marcil. He was uncertain as to what to attribute the early return, but he was sure on one thing: the brief stay had cost a lot of money with little to show for it. Now he sat at his desk rereading a telex from George Beida. The tone of the telex was urgent and the message was clear. Beida and Kamina both felt it was crucial to the survival of STK that a replacement for Blondeau be sent immediately. Marcil's instinctive reaction was that such a step was unnecessary and costly. Despite his reluctance, however, he respected his partners' views and wanted the venture to succeed. If he decided to replace Blondeau, he wondered, what should he do differently?

Source: Henry W. Lane and Lorna L. Wright prepared this case solely to provide material for class discussion. The authors do not intend to illustrate either effective or ineffective handling of a managerial situation. The authors may have disguised certain names and other identifying information to protect confidentiality. Ivey Management Services prohibits any form of reproduction, storage or transmittal without its written permission. This material is not covered under authorization from CanCopy or any reproduction rights organization. To order copies or request permission to reproduce materials, contact Ivey Publishing, Ivey Management Services, c/o Richard Ivey School of Business, The University of Western Ontario, London, Ontario, Canada, N6A 3K7; phone (519) 661-3208, fax (519) 661-3882, e-mail cases@ivey.uwo.ca

CASE QUESTIONS

1. Why did Pierre return to Canada prematurely? What went wrong and who or what was to blame? Separate the individual and the company issues or reasons. What part do the situational factors of this kind of venture in a developing country play? Who are the major stakeholders in this venture?

2. Evaluate who should fill the position that Pierre has vacated—both immediately and in the long term—so that this project does not fall apart. What are the constraints on a small company trying to break into the international marketplace?

3. How would you recommend improving on the IHRM process or correcting the deficiencies that you see?

4. What are the implications of this case to you as an individual and potential expatriate?

CASE 3

MANAGING A DIVERSE WORKFORCE IN INDONESIA

INDONESIAN ENTERPRISES

Paul Korsvald, the general manager of a large Norwegian paper company's subsidiary, Indonesian Enterprises, had several decisions to make before the day was over. His first decision was whether to build a small mosque next to his corrugated carton plant near Jakarta, Java. Among the Indonesian Enterprise workers, 34 were Chinese and were primarily Confucians and Buddhists, 4 were Javanese Christians, and 2 of Indian extraction were Hindus. The other 352 plant workers and supervisors and the 48 office managers, and workers under him said they were Muslims (see Appendix). Many, however, were not strict followers. They practiced an Islam that had been blended with Hindu, Buddhist, and other beliefs. Jim Sterba (*The Wall Street Journal,* September 29, 1987) observes:

> Islam is different in the world's largest Moslem nation, Indonesia. It has a sense of humor. It doesn't seem so stern and insistent. It is more tolerant than Islam elsewhere.

This toleration was attributed by scholars to Indonesia's vast diverse land and population. The country, comprising 13,677 islands of which 6,000 are populated and covering 3,200 miles, has a population of more than 180 million people of 366 different ethnic groups. Although 250 different languages are spoken, Bhasa Indonesia is the official language taught in the schools. Half of the population was Javanese and two thirds of all Indonesians lived in Java, which constituted 7% of the land mass.

Friday is the holiest day of the week for Muslims, and the company was required by custom to permit workers, especially the men, to attend noon prayers and collective recitals of the Koran. Although government offices closed at 11:00 A.M. on Fridays, Indonesian Enterprises' policy was to close the plant and offices from 11:30 A.M. until 2:30 A.M. only. Paul Korsvald observed that typically fewer than 20 Muslim factory and office workers returned to work on Friday. Many excuses were given by the others such as it was impossible to catch a bus or services were longer than expected.

Source: "Managing a Diverse Work Force in Indonesia" by John E. Walsh, Jr. from *International Business Case Studies,* ed. Robert T. Moran, David O. Braaten, and John E. Walsh, Jr. Copyright ©1994 by Gulf Publishing Company. Used with permission. All rights reserved.

Actually, after services was a time for workers to visit with friends to gossip and learn what had taken place during the week. It was also a time to bargain, barter, and buy a variety of goods and food sold near the mosque.

What bothered Paul Korsvald most was the loss in production output and paying people for not working. The average monthly salary for factory workers was approximately US$100; for office workers, it was US$150 for a six-day work week. The day began at 7:00 A.M. and ended at 3:30 P.M. including an hour-and-a-half for lunch.

How could he meet the religious needs of the Muslims and non-Muslims without losing production output and keeping costs down? To build a mosque would cost about US$30,000. Four thousand dollars of this would be spent to purchase and transport sacred stones from Mecca. If Korsvald decided to buy the mosque, he would then have to obtain the services of the local hadji (one who had made the pilgrimage to Mecca) for US$15 to bless the ground before construction began. In addition, he would be required to purchase a goat for sacrifice for about US$20. The goat's head would be buried near the mosque; the remainder given to the workers for a feast. He would also have to provide onions and green peppers to be placed on a stick to keep the rains away on the opening day of the mosque.

If he decided not to build the mosque, Paul Korsvald could also continue the current practice or he could rent seven buses for three hours, at a cost of US$50 per bus. While the buses would probably arrive on time to take the employees to the mosque, Korsvald was unsure if employees would return to the factory on the buses.

THE POSSIBLE PURCHASE OF CALL OR PRAYER CALL CLOCKS

Korsvald was faced with another dilemma as well: whether to buy from Maruem Murakemi and Company, Ltd. either ten semi-automatic prayer call clocks or fully automatic prayer call clocks, or some combination of the two. Good Muslims are required to pray five times a day, first in the morning when they arise, before lunch, mid-afternoon, after sunset and before retiring. This schedule did not have to be followed to the letter, for according to the Koran, "When ye journey about the earth, it is no crime to you that you come short in prayer if you fear that those that disbelieve will set upon you." Typically, employees would pray whenever they had spare time. However, by not praying at the prescribed times, some of the reward was lost. According to Muslim tradition, every corner of Allah's universe was equally pure, so the employees would spread their prayer rugs wherever they were when they decided to pray. Standing erect with their hands on either side of their face and their thumbs touching the lobes of their ears, they would begin, "God is most great." Still standing, they would continue with the opening Ayat (passage from the holy Koran):

> Praise belongs to God, Lord of the Worlds,
> The Compassionate, the Merciful.
> King of the day of Judgment.
> Tis thee we worship and thee we ask for help.
> Guide us in the straight path.
> The path of those whom thou hast favored.
> Not the path of those who incur thine anger
> Nor of those who go astray.

Unfortunately for Paul Korsvald, the prayers continued from noon to afternoon, because each Muslim employee would wait until he or she had spare time. If Paul Korsvald bought the semi-automatic clocks for US$30 and the fully automatic for US$35 and placed them in prominent locations throughout the plant and office, the clocks could be synchronized to proclaim an Azan (prayer call) ten minutes before noon and at 2:40 in the afternoon.

Another option existed. He could eliminate the lunch hour, the practice of the Dutch-owned companies, and end the working day at 2:00 P.M. Rather than buy the clocks, he would make it known through supervisors that plant operations would cease ten minutes before noon for prayers.

THE NEED TO INCREASE PRODUCTIVITY DURING RAMADAN

A third decision confronting Korsvald dealt with solving the problem of low productivity of employees during Ramadan, the holy month of fasting and the ninth month in the Arabian calendar. In this month, Muhammed, according to Muslim tradition, received the holy Koran from God as guidance for his people and made his hyiria from Mecca to Medina. From dawn to dusk, during this period Muslims abstain from food and drink. Among those automatically exempted were the sick, the very old, very young, pregnant and nursing women, soldiers in war, and persons on long trips. Although no one in Indonesia is legally compelled to fast, many Muslim employees did.

When Ramadan fell during the hottest season, fasting took its toll. Employees, observing tradition, were noticeably nervous, excitable, and prone to flare-ups of temper. Korsvald estimated that productivity in the plant and office declined 20–30%. Korsvald had identified three options to address this issue and suspected there were others. First, he could start the plant at 3:30 in the afternoon and end at midnight. Second, he could close the plant for two weeks and require employees to take their vacations during this time. Third, he could require only those Muslim employees who were fasting to take vacations.

SELECTING THE MANAGER OF THE ACCOUNTING DEPARTMENT

A fourth decision had nothing to do with religion. He had to decide whether Mr. Abukar, a native Javan, or Mr. James Lee, an Indonesian of Chinese nationality, should be appointed to the position of manager of the accounting department. In Norway, promotion decisions were primarily based upon employee's prior work performance. However, discussions with other Western general managers operating in Java and researchers from *Business International* revealed a consensus that decisions on promotions in Indonesia placed more importance on ethnic background, personalities, and individual circumstances. Thus, managers in Indonesia had to consider whether a prospective manager was Javanese, an outer islander, Chinese, or Indian. Although Indonesia's motto is "Unity in Diversity," it made a difference for instance if a prospective manager was Javanese, Sumatran, or Moluccan.

The Javanese are considered an agrarian-based conservative people proud of their traditions and strong family ties. They value harmony and sensitivity to others, characteristics that historians attribute to feudal influences. Additionally, they are reluctant to convey information that could displease business associations or cause conflicts.

The outer Islanders, the Bataks of Sumatra and the Moluccans, are more prone to say what they think. The Dutch set up large tobacco, rubber, and palm oil estates in Northern Sumatra, so modern agricultural developments were concentrated there. Because these products were produced primarily for export in contrast to rice production in Java, which is consumed locally, natives possessed greater experience in international trade. The straightforwardness of the outer islanders complemented the style of Western managers, resulting in a disproportionate number of outer islanders holding key positions in foreign companies in Java.

While the Chinese accounted for less than 2% of the population, they played a key role in business and owned, according to reliable sources, more than 50% of the nation's private capital. Despite high levels of education and administration experience, they were excluded from the bureaucracy and the military, which was dominated by the Javanese.

The official ideology of the Indonesian government was Pancasila, which consisted of five principles affirming belief in one God, humanitarianism, national unity, democracy, and social justice. A balance between national unity and social justice proved difficult. Any foreign company having too many Chinese executives would be vulnerable to resentment from indigenous Indonesians (pribumi) workers, and the Indonesian government might intervene and press for social justice. While Indians were also vulnerable to resentment they were too small a group to constitute a threat.

Paul Korsvald had many issues to consider. James Lee was older, and age was important to Indonesians. He was unquestionably the best qualified of the two, technically and in managerial experience. He had more years of work experience with the company. Lee, fearing a backlash from the pribumi staff, might fail to give them firm orders to take disciplinary actions when needed.

On the other hand, Mr. Abukar was reasonably competent technically, pleasant to all employees and well-liked by the Indonesian accounting staff. He came from a respectable family, with several relatives working as lower level executives in the government. Further, the promotion would help him financially, because he had a large family to support. In the past, he had been extremely loyal to the company. He had been reluctant, however, to assume authority, make decisions, and work overtime. Due to a dearth of pribumi managers, it would not be difficult for Mr. Abukar to find another job at a higher salary.

Korsvald could seek a consensus (manufakat) of his key executives through tedious consultation (muskawarah). Whatever choice this consensus brought about, he risked shaming the candidate (malu) in front of others if he did not handle the promotion well. Under no circumstances did he want to create malu.

THE NEED TO FORMULATE POLICIES

His last decision was how to formulate a policy covering responsibilities of his employees to achieve results, to reduce kickbacks, and to determine under what circumstances loans would be made to employees.

The frequent cases of stomach ulcers and heart attacks among European and American managers in Indonesia, he thought, resulted from their failure to counteract djamkeret ("dj" pronounced like "j") or rubber time. He observed that Indonesians could not be rushed and would leave an employer who tried to make them move faster or work

harder. When asked, "When will the job be finished," adherents to djamkeret would simply reply, "sometime during the next few days." Modern plants with international commitments could not operate this way. So, he needed a policy that could dampen the excuses of djamkeret.

European companies operating in Asia have been offering bribes and kickbacks since the 1600s when the British East India Company won duty-free treatment for its exports by giving Mongol rulers expensive gifts including rare paintings and carvings. Korsvald, however, had difficulty adjusting to the succession of kickbacks and payoffs necessary to conduct business in Indonesia. On one occasion, his sales manager had to send twelve bottles of scotch for a party given by a purchasing agent of a large corporate customer. On another, he had to give US$10,000 to the large corporate customer's local director. In the latter case, he was surprised to receive a silver tray as a gift from the local director. Last year on Christmas morning, he awoke to find a Christmas tree brightly lit and heavy with gleaming ornaments. On it was a card from another company's director to whom he had been forced to make kickbacks for years. "Muslim economics require that the wealth of her people be widely shared," he mused, "it insists that acquisitions and competitiveness be balanced by fair play and compassion."

In addition to kickbacks to customers, many foreign businessmen in Indonesia felt it was necessary to place someone in power in the Indonesian government associated with their company. It was rumored the family of the president of Indonesia owned shares in 15 companies including a hotel, a flour mill, and two cement factories. The president's brother strongly denied any favoritism and added that several charitable foundations were set up with business earnings.

Trading on influence was not considered corrupt unless it involved excesses. To maintain a low profile, distant relatives of top military and government officials were placed as heads or directors of companies rather than members of their immediate families.

Korsvald observed that the Chinese were adaptable. If they had to give gifts to generals or make deposits to an official's Singapore bank account and become friends for life, they did so. According to Barry Newman in *The Wall Street Journal,* April 14, 1978):

> The strategy of gift giving has been perfected by Cukongs of Indonesia, about 30 moneyed Chinese who have made fortunes for themselves and, as it happens, for the country's ruling elite. "We don't worry," says a manager in one of their many companies. "We have information first hand. We know what's going on." Occasionally, when there is money to be made, a

Cukong will take a fellow Chinese for a ride on his coat-tails.

Korsvald wondered if kickbacks and payoffs to high officials known as the "untouchables" should be continued by his company. Frequently, he had trouble determining whether middlemen who received bribes from the company to give to his ranking officials still had influence. He was never sure how much to pay or if he was paying the right person. His experience in Indonesia convinced him that establishing good personal relations and trust did not always entail a payoff.

Lower-level civil servants continually practiced the ancient Indonesian form of social commerce called the "sticky handshake." Traditionally, funds acquired through extortion were called "smooth money," "lubricating money" or "rule 2000" (it will cost you 2,000 rupiahs). More recently, they have been labeled "illegal levies" and were required for everything from processing a passport to exporting corrugated boxes. It would be almost impossible to stop "illegal levies," because low-level civil servants needed them to live. Nevertheless, the National Command for the Restoration of Security and Order, a government body, was, at present, trying to ban illegal levies. The response was a combination of outrage and jealousy from civil servants who believed that the higher-ups were taking more and not spreading it around. Although Indonesian Enterprises' workers were better paid than civil servants, they, too, sought ways to increase their incomes. Any items the company had in stock that could be sold easily, like glue and starch, had to be closely monitored and physically secured, or they would be stolen.

Korsvald knew compassion was necessary and could produce practical results each morning. He provided free bottles of "vitasoy," soy bean milk processed in Indonesia by the Hong Kong Soy Bean Products Company of Hong Kong, to mitigate the effects on his employees of malnutrition and tuberculosis, both common ailments in Indonesia. The result was an increase in worker productivity.

Sometimes, though, his compassion created problems. He gave 25 corrugated boxes to one employee who said he wanted the boxes for moving to a new home. Later, he discovered that the boxes were sold to a woman going to Pakistan. When Korsvald confronted the employee, the employee became nervous and started to cry. "My wife was sick and I needed the money," the employee sobbed, "I'm not a criminal." Korsvald knew it would be difficult to fire the employee because of strict Indonesian labor laws, so he returned the money to the woman and treated the payment as an advance loan to the employee. Later, the employee sent flowers to Korsvald.

He wondered about what other policies he should prepare for purchasing and advancing loans. Should his purchasing agent be responsible for all purchases up to a certain amount, say $300 in Indonesian rupiahs? Should the purchasing agent be able to further delegate authority to other departments? Should he let a policy on advance loans be made by the comptroller? Weren't there inherent dangers?

In one Western company in Jakarta, when loan policies were delegated to a pribumi comptroller, salary advances had more than quadrupled. The chief executive called in the comptroller to find out if the report was in error. It was not.

The comptroller said that, rather than follow the policy blindly, cases were judged individually. The company's new chief engineer needed a large sum of money to pay three years' rent advance for the house he had just leased and such advances were normal in Jakarta. A one-year advance in pay was made to an older employee who was making his pilgrimage to Mecca (Haj), which every devout Muslim was required to do at least once in his or her life. While the comptroller gave explanations for each advance in salary, the chief executive noticed a loan of four months' salary to a recently hired factory worker. When the comptroller was questioned about this advance he said, "The man is my brother-in-law, and my wife would be embarrassed if I didn't grant him this favor."

Korsvald wanted policies that would prevent such a problem from occurring in Indonesian Enterprises.

APPENDIX: ISLAM AND THE KORAN

The word *Islam* literally means submission to the will of anybody, but in a religious sense it is properly defined as acceptance of what has been ordered or commanded by God via a man named Muhammed. The principles that regulate the life of Muslims in their relationship with God are called the Five Pillars of Islam. The first pillar is Islam's creed, "There is no God but Allah and Muhammed is his prophet." The second pillar is prayer and Muslims are required to be constant in prayer which under normal conditions means praying five times a day. The third pillar of Islam is charity. Those with money should help those who are less fortunate. The fourth pillar is the observance of Ramadan the ninth month of the Arabian Calendar. Ramadan commemorates God's making Muhammed a prophet and ten years later Muhammed's Hijiah flight from Mecca to Medina. The fifth pillar of Islam is pilgrimage. Once during a lifetime a Muslim is expected to visit Mecca.

The word *Koran* literally means "that which is read," but to Muslims it is the sacred book that contains the word of God as revealed to Muhammed. The book consists of 114 chapters, 6,000 verses, and over 80,000 words. There is no specific order except the shorter chapters are at the beginning. It contains information pertaining to prophets and the people to whom they were sent. It also contains laws, dogmas, and ethical ideas. In addition, it is considered by Muslims as a first-rate piece of literature. Many Muslim writers copy its style which they consider a miracle of eloquence. In many parts it is rhymed and unlike ordinary prose, it is chanted rather than read. During daily prayers Muslims usually recite the opening chapter of the Koran and any other part they like.

CASE QUESTIONS

1. Why do workers often fail to return to work after attending services at the Mosque on Friday? What should be done to correct the problem?
2. What alternatives exist to stop interruptions at work resulting from workers' prayer ritual?
3. How can the problem of lost output and decreased worker efficiency during Ramadan be solved?
4. Which employee should be promoted to manager of the accounting department? Why? What negative effects may occur as a result of this choice, and what actions can be taken to mitigate these consequences?
5. How can Paul Korsvald eliminate or at least lessen "djamkeret," or "rubber time"? Evaluate Korsvald's handling of the situation involving the employee who misused the corrugated boxes.

PART FOUR

INTEGRATIVE SECTION

INTEGRATIVE TERM PROJECT

INTEGRATIVE CASES

Integrative Term Project

This project requires research, imagination, and logic in applying the content of this course and book.

In groups of three to five students, create an imaginary company that you have been operating in the domestic arena for some time. Your group represents top management, and you have decided it is time to go international.

- Describe your company and its operations, relative size, and so forth. Give reasons for your decision to go international.
- Decide on an appropriate country in which to operate, and give your rationale for this choice.
- State your planned entry strategy, and give your reasons for this strategy.
- Describe the environment in which you will operate and the critical operational factors that you must consider and how they will affect your company.
- Give a cultural profile of the local area in which you will be operating. What are the workers going to be like? What kind of reception do you anticipate from local governments, suppliers, distributors, and so on?
- Draw up an organization chart showing the company and its overseas operations, and describe why you have chosen this structure.
- Decide on the staffing policy you will use for top-level managers, and give your rationale for this policy.
- Describe the kinds of leadership and motivational systems you think would be most effective in this environment. Give your rationale.
- Discuss the kinds of communication problems your managers might face in the host-country working environment. How should they prepare for and deal with them?
- Explain any special control issues that concern you for this overseas operation. How do you plan to deal with them?
- Identify the concerns of the host country and the local community regarding your operations there. What plans do you have to deal with their concerns and to ensure a long-term cooperative relationship?

Integrative Cases

CASE 1

AT&T CONSUMER PRODUCTS

In the fall of 1988, Nick Stevens, the vice president of manufacturing at AT&T Consumer Products, had to select a site for a new answering systems manufacturing facility. He was inclined to choose Mexico, but he had not ruled out Malaysia or the United States.

As Stevens pondered the many factors that would affect his decision, he could not help reflecting on the profound changes that had occurred at AT&T in recent years. AT&T in 1988 was vastly different from the company he had joined 22 years earlier. Some changes were clearly reflected on the organizational chart, others involved new policies, but the most challenging ones related to AT&T's role in society, and Stevens had to consider all these factors in making his decision.

HISTORY

Like Singer with its sewing machines and Gillette with its razors, American Telegraph and Telephone was an American icon. Long known as Ma Bell, AT&T had been the world's largest corporation. In the early 1980s, it had more than $150 billion in assets, and its annual revenues of $70 billion represented almost 2 percent of the U.S. gross national product. Until January 1984, AT&T employed one million people and had more than three million shareholders (see Exhibit IC1–1).

Alexander Graham Bell, who patented the telephone in 1876, founded the Bell Telephone Company in 1877. Though Bell was credited with inventing the telephone, it was Theodore Vail who created the Bell System. Vail, one of the first managers hired by the founders of what would become AT&T, stated as early as 1879 that AT&T's goal was "one system, one policy, universal service." [1] Since Vail's time and until the 1984 divestiture, AT&T's annual reports consistently reiterated a commitment to furnishing "the best possible service at the lowest possible cost." [2]

Vail devised an organizational structure that lasted for a century without fundamental change. Local telephone companies, known as Bell Operating Companies, were organized as nominally independent subsidiaries. They provided local telephone service and access to the long-distance network (see Exhibit IC1–2). They also billed customers for long distance and international service provided by the AT&T Long Lines Department.

Western Electric Manufacturing Company was founded in Cleveland in 1869 as an electric-equipment shop. In the 1870s, it became a mecca for inventors. In 1881, Bell Telephone bought an interest in Western Electric, and the following year, it formally became the manufacturer of Bell telephones and equipment.

In addition to producing or procuring practically all Bell System telephone equipment, Western Electric developed the high vacuum electronic amplifying tube that made possible coast-to-coast telephone calls and cleared the way for radio broadcasting, sound motion pictures, and television; it produced the first air-to-ground radio telephones; made and installed one of the pioneer commercial radio broadcasting systems, WEAF in New York; developed the first motion-picture sound system; built all the radar used by the U.S. armed forces in World War II; and in the space age, built the Nike missile systems, the DEW line radar defense system, the Sentinel and Safeguard antiballistic missile systems, and much of the communications and control equipment for the U.S. space program.

Western Electric was the largest component of the Bell System. Had it not been wholly owned by AT&T, Western Electric would have been the 12th largest industrial company in the United States. At its height, Western Electric operated 23 major plants scattered around the United States from Atlanta, Georgia, to Phoenix, Arizona, to North Andover, Massachusetts.

EXHIBIT IC1–1

Seven-Year Summary of Selected AT&T Financial Data (dollars in millions; except per share amounts)

	1982	1983	1/1/84	1984	1985	1986[a]	1987	1988[a]
Results of Operations								
Total revenues	$70,022	$72,357		$33,187	$34,496	$34,213	$33,773	$35,218
Total costs and expenses	50,678	57,338		30,892	31,476	33,847	30,252	38,276
Net Income (loss)	7,279	249		1,370	1,557	139	2,044	(1,669)
Dividends on preferred shares	142	127		112	110	86	23	1
Income (loss) applicable to common shares	7,137	122		1,258	1,447	53	2,021	(1,670)
Earnings (loss) per common share	$8.06	$6.00		$1.25	$1.37	$0.05	$1.88	($1.55)
Dividends declared per common share	5.81	6.10		1.20	1.20	1.20	1.20	1.20
Assets and Capital								
Property, plant and equipment-net			$20,569	$21,343	$22,262	$21,101	$20,808	$15,280
Total assets	$150,004	$140,229	35,545	39,773	40,688	39,534	39,473	35,152
Long-term debt including capital leases			9,137	8,718	7,794	7,660	7,919	8,128
Common shareowners' equity			12,368	13,763	14,633	13,550	14,455	11,465
Other Information (data at year end except 1/84)								
Market price per share	$62.86	$63.02	$17.88	$19.50	$25.00	$25.00	$27.00	$28.75
Employees	1,000,000		373,000	365,200	337,600	316,900	303,000	304,700

[a]1988 data was significantly affected by a charge for accelerated digitization program costs; 1986 data was significantly affected by major charges for business restructuring, an accounting change and other charges.

EXHIBIT IC1–2

Pre-divestiture AT&T

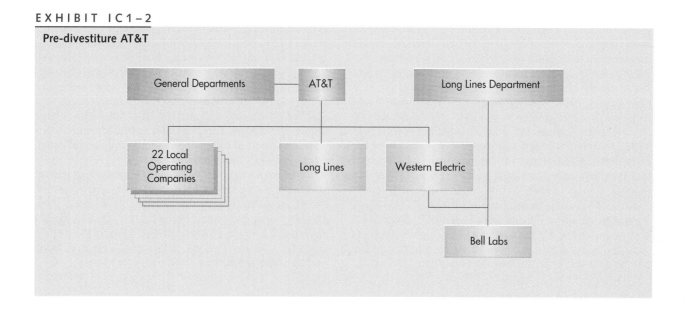

Bell Telephone Laboratories was formed out of the Western Electric engineering research department in 1925. It was equally owned by Western Electric and AT&T. Bell Labs developed and designed the equipment that Western Electric manufactured and the Bell System used. Originally a small organization, Bell Labs grew into a giant as a result of World War II military hardware requirements. Before divestiture, it had 25,000 employees, an annual budget of $2 billion, and employed 20,000 PhDs. It maintained 17 locations in 9 states. Its inventions included the electrical digital computer (1937), transistors (1947), lasers (1958), the communications satellite Telstar (1962), radar, semiconductors, fiber optics, and electronic switching equipment.

REGULATORY HISTORY

In 1934, the United States Congress created the Federal Communications Commission (FCC) to regulate the telephone industry. Its mission was "to make available, so far as possible, to all the people of the United States a rapid, efficient, nationwide and worldwide wire and radio communications service with adequate facilities at reasonable charges." Under FCC regulation, each Bell Operating Company was guaranteed an area of operation without competition and assured a certain maximum profit margin. Local operating companies were required to serve anyone within their operating area who requested telephone service. Charges for local telephone service were subject to state or local government approval.

As of the late 1960s, all telephone sets, private branch exchanges, and other standard equipment used in residences or by businesses were owned by the telephone company and leased to users. Nearly all telephone equipment (referred to as customer premises equipment, CPE, by the telephone industry) was manufactured by Western Electric and sold to the operating companies.

Carterfone   In 1968, the FCC issued its *Carterfone* decision. This case arose when AT&T refused to permit the *Carterfone*, a non-Bell device that linked mobile car radios with the national telephone network, to be connected to the Bell System. AT&T threatened service termination to anyone connecting the device to the network, arguing that non-Bell equipment could harm the system. When Tom Carter appealed to the FCC, the commission ruled in his favor and ordered AT&T to allow customers to connect their own telephone equipment to the Bell System. However, customers were required to lease a protective device from AT&T to link the non-Bell device and the Bell System telephone line.

Many consumers and competitive telephone equipment manufacturers complained that the protective devices constituted a barrier to competition, intended to protect AT&T's monopoly. In 1972, the FCC reexamined its *Carterfone* ruling and held that any equipment could be connected to the network without a protective device, if it had been certified as safe for use on the network. This decision became effective in 1980.

1982 Modified Final Judgment Decree   In January 1982, AT&T and the U.S. Department of Justice announced that they had reached a settlement of the government's longstanding antitrust case against the company. The 1974 lawsuit had charged AT&T with monopolizing the market for telephone equipment and long-distance service. The government maintained that as long as AT&T controlled the local circuits that provided the only access to most consumers, competition could not exist in long-distance service, data services, private branch exchanges, key telephone systems, large telephone switching machines, or other telephone equipment and services.

The settlement, which became known as the Modified Final Judgment called for the divestiture of the Bell Operating Companies by AT&T on January 1, 1984. The 22 BOCs would be regrouped under 7 separate and independent Regional Bell Operating Companies and restricted to providing local telephone service. They could not offer long-distance services and would be barred from manufacturing telephone equipment. They could, however, sell telephone equipment manufactured by others.

Under the terms of the settlement, AT&T would retain part of Bell Labs, all of Western Electric, and its long-distance and customer premises equipment operations. The settlement forbade AT&T's use of the "Bell" name, except for Bell Laboratories. It permitted AT&T to enter other electronics businesses, including computers. Many observers expected the settlement to initiate a great commercial contest between IBM and AT&T in the telecommunications and computing fields.

THE NEW AT&T

Organizational Structure   In anticipation of divestiture, AT&T's vertically integrated, functional organizational structure was replaced by an organizational structure built around the lines of business in which the company would now be engaged. Each line of business would be responsible for its own profitability and its contribution to AT&T's revenues.

Two sectors were created and given responsibility for the overall management of resources to support the lines of

EXHIBIT IC1–3

Post-divestiture AT&T

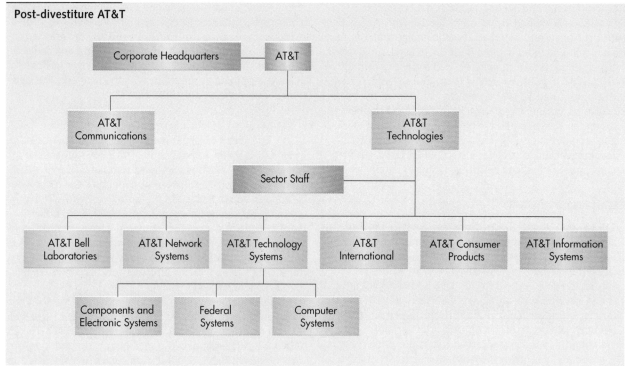

business. AT&T Communications would handle the long-distance service, and AT&T Technologies encompassed the unregulated parts of the business and included AT&T Consumer Products (see Exhibit IC1–3).

Regulation   After 1984, only telephone equipment was fully deregulated. All telephone services remained under federal and state regulation. For example, AT&T's prices for long-distance services still had to be approved by the FCC.

Labor   Before divestiture, three unions represented more than two-thirds of the Bell System's one million workers. The Communications Workers of America (CWA) represented 675,000 AT&T workers, the International Brotherhood of Electrical Workers (IBEW) represented 100,000 AT&T workers, and the Telecommunications International Union (TIU) represented 50,000 AT&T workers.

On August 7, 1983, after the antitrust settlement was announced but before it became effective, a nationwide strike

against the Bell System began after the unions representing Bell System employees rejected the Bell Systems' wage package. The strike was the first since a six-day walkout in 1971. Beyond the wage dispute, the pending January 1984 divestiture of AT&T's 22 operating companies had cast a shadow across the bargaining table. The unions pushed for an "employment security" package that would provide training and retraining for members and protect jobs after divestiture. AT&T, faced with nonunion competition in a deregulated environment, was trying to control costs and maintain maximum flexibility in the way it utilized its workforce.

After 22 days, AT&T and the unions reached an accord. In addition to wage increases for each of the three years of the contract, AT&T agreed to increases in retirement pay, better pension protection for workers transferred to lower-paying jobs, and additional training, transfer rights, and retraining for laid-off workers.

After divestiture, the unionized workers were spread throughout AT&T and the divested Bell Operating

Companies. Of AT&T's 375,000 workers remaining after divestiture, 63.6 percent were members of a union.

Range of Businesses   After divestiture, AT&T described its primary business as "moving and managing information." It provided consumers with basic long-distance service, special calling plans, and other miscellaneous services. AT&T also sold and leased telephones and answering systems to consumers. To businesses, the company offered communications and networked computer systems and telemarketing services. It also provided communications services and products and computer systems to all levels of government in the United States and abroad.

Dealings with the U.S. Government   AT&T's largest customer was the U.S. government. It sold its full range of customized and standard products to such agencies as the U.S. Army, Navy, and Air Force, and the Federal Aviation Administration. AT&T also managed Sandia National Laboratories as a service to the U.S. government on a nonprofit, no-fee basis. Sandia was one of the United States's largest research and development engineering facilities, with projects in areas such as the safety, security, and control of weapons systems, and the development of new energy sources.

International Activities, Joint Ventures, and Alliances   AT&T did business in more than 40 countries and had approximately 21,000 employees outside the United States. It was involved in numerous joint ventures and alliances, both in the United States and abroad. For example, it had agreements and alliances with British Telecom, France Telecom, and Kokusai Denshin Denwa of Japan. It had an agreement to share technology with Mitsubishi and to make and market worldwide a static random access memory chip. AT&T was also cooperating with NEC in Japan on a wide range of semiconductor products and technologies. AT&T also had an agreement with Zenith to codevelop an all-digital, high-definition television system using AT&T's microchips and video compression research and Zenith's television technology.

AT&T CONSUMER PRODUCTS

Although consumers were permitted as early as 1980 to connect non-Bell telephone equipment to the Bell System, the market for residential telephones did not take off until 1983, when leasing charges were listed separately from service charges on consumers' bills. The unbundling of leasing charges alerted consumers to the economic benefits of owning their own telephones. In 1983, retail telephone sales jumped 230 percent to about $1.1 billion.[3] In the first nine months of 1983, imports of telephones from Taiwan, Hong Kong, Japan, and Korea increased 568 percent over the same period in 1982, to 25.7 million telephones.[4]

The imported telephones were unlike the old U.S.-manufactured electromechanical telephones that were built to operate over a 30-year depreciation period. Some were one-piece models selling for as little as $20. Japanese companies, led by Matsushita under the Panasonic label, introduced feature-laden electronic telephones with integrated chips that made possible the inclusion of a variety of features at a reasonable cost.

The onslaught of new competition spelled trouble for AT&T Consumer Products (CP). This unit, formed after the telephone equipment market was deregulated, had never sold as much as a telephone cord before 1983. Moreover, AT&T's telephones were never designed to be marketable. In many ways, AT&T's attitudes toward its customers had been "we make it, you take it." Its telephones had cost $20 to make, while a repair call cost $60, so AT&T's goal had been to make highly reliable telephones, even if they were somewhat overengineered. As Jim Bercaw, a 35-year AT&T veteran described it: "We would bring pellets and metal in the back door, and send telephones out of the front door. We even made our own screws."

In the face of daunting competition, declining revenues, and unacceptable profit levels, CP consolidated its residential telephone production in AT&T's Shreveport, Louisiana, facility and spent tens of millions of dollars to upgrade and automate the facility. After the expense of integrating new technology and methods, CP discovered that its labor costs were still too high. A McKinsey & Company competitive analog study revealed that CP was out of line with its competitors on all points and scores, including such critical areas as cost of goods sold and SO&A. In fact, the cost of goods sold was 90 percent of revenues, and CP executives reasoned that it had to be at 65 percent in order to be competitive. In late 1984, AT&T corporate leaders told CP management to "fix the business or exit the business."

CP soon began making changes. In recalling their impact on its people, Ken Bertaccini, a 25-year veteran of AT&T and President of CP since 1985, said:

> On January 1, 1984, our people went from a world of guaranteed customers, guaranteed profits and guaranteed jobs—to the much less certain world of a fiercely

competitive consumer electronics world—with the only guarantee of success coming from excellent and sustained performance.

CP'S COMPETITORS

In the mid–1980s, there were three types of competitors in the telephone equipment market: (1) telephone companies, (2) consumer electronic companies, and (3) housewares companies. The telephone companies included AT&T, other traditional providers of service and equipment, such as GTE and ITT, and some of the divested Bell Operating Companies. As providers of telephone services, these companies had a strategic interest in the telephone equipment market. But like AT&T, these companies were, for the most part, unfamiliar with the world of competitive consumer marketing.

The consumer electronic companies ranged from sophisticated Japanese manufacturers like Matsushita and Sony, which offered full lines of consumer products, to smaller, specialized companies like Code-A-Phone, Unisonic, and PhoneMate. The consumer electronic companies were market-driven competitors with well-developed distribution networks and considerable expertise in designing products for the consumer market.

Consumer electronics companies' interest in the market was based on long-term possibilities and not just short-term profit and loss. As homes became more and more automated, telephones seemed likely to take on more the role of a home computer terminal. Therefore, the consumer electronics companies wanted the telephone terminal business as a platform for new generations of higher value-added products.

The housewares companies were primarily represented in the telephone equipment market by General Electric. It had a good reputation for reliability and quality and significant experience designing, marketing, and distributing consumer products.

Matsushita, a $40 billion Japanese company that manufactured under the Panasonic label, was CP's most formidable competitor. Panasonic was the predominant residential telephone vendor in Japan. Its strategy had been to provide products that competed with the market leader, but offered marginally more functions for the price. Matsushita manufactured its telephone products entirely in Japan. It used a highly automated manufacturing process and did not subcontract any of its production. Because of the volume of business it did and the wide range of associated products it manufactured, Matsushita was able to operate its manufacturing operations at full capacity year round.

CP'S SURVIVAL PERIOD: 1985–1986

Establishing a Foundation and Culture for CP   CP's management realized that it had to be transformed from a regulated monopoly to a highly flexible organization that not only accepted change, but embraced it. "Business Passion" and "Shared Values" were established as the new foundation of CP. They were created to provide the basis and guidelines for all CP decisions and actions. Said Nick Stevens, CP's vice president of manufacturing: "The passion is truly part of the decision process, and there is seldom a decision not made in its frame of reference."

"Business Passion," depicted in Exhibit IC1–4, signified CP's commitment to "Be the Best" for its owners, customers and people. CP referred to its workers as "people." Executives strongly discouraged the use of the term *employees*, and they incurred a fine for using what they called the "E-word." Management believed that to achieve long-term success it had to weigh equally the effect of each business decision on all three stakeholder groups. The pyramid in the background of the "Business Passion" graphically represents the relationship between the "Business Passion" and "Shared Values."

CP's "Shared Values" described what the business was and aspired to be. On an individual level, the business wanted to create an environment of caring, trust, love,[5] integrity, and respect. On a business level, CP wanted to create an environment that valued commitment, quality, and innovations and achieved excellence in everything it did. CP managers placed a significant part of their compensation "at risk," making it dependent upon the unit's performance.

CP made what its executives called a "huge" investment in its people. It developed education programs as well as honor and recognition programs. Everyone had the opportunity for two weeks of business education each year. There were also several recognition events each year. Spouses or guests were invited to an annual event honoring CP's top performers.

Creating an Organizational Structure   CP's organizational structure was redesigned to promote flexibility and market focus. The nine product lines were turned into Strategic Business Units (SBUs).[6] Product managers and representatives from all relevant functional areas (e.g., sales, finance, etc.) formed an SBU. These SBUs operated as profit centers.

Between 1985 and 1988, the number of executive-level managers was reduced from 40 to 16. The workforce was reduced by almost half. In 1985, CP had as many as six layers of supervision between its operational levels and its president. In 1988, CP had as few as three. A comprehensive measurement system was also developed and imple-

EXHIBIT IC1–4

AT&T Consumer Product Business Foundation: Business Passion and Shared Values

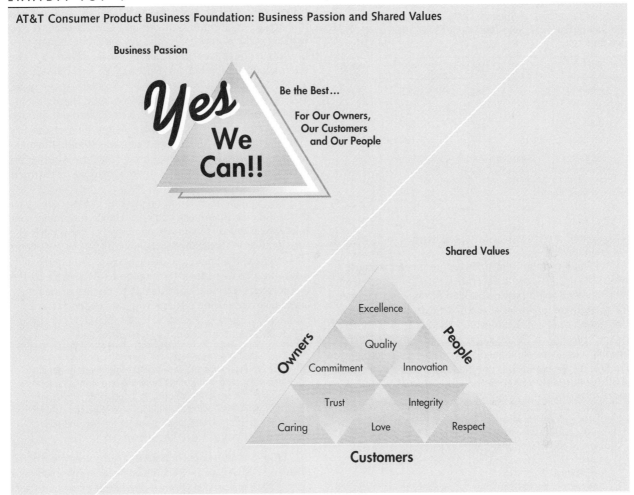

mented. The system focused on assessing owner, customer, and people satisfaction on a regular basis by looking at profits, needs, and attitudes, respectively.

Developing a Business Strategy In late 1984, Jim Bercaw, who was vice president of manufacturing at the time, was told to develop a "global manufacturing plan." To that end, he traveled to the Far East. His trip revealed that all of CP's competitors were manufacturing in Asia. He later said: "I have a second-fastest-gun-in-the-West philosophy. If you can't be the fastest gun in the West, it is better to travel in crowds."

With all its competitors in Asia, CP decided that it also had to move its manufacturing operation there. At the same time, it decided to contract out the remainder of its manufacturing

requirements to Asian original equipment manufacturers (OEMs). After 1986, CP no longer had any U.S. production of residential telephone equipment (see Exhibit IC1–5).

THE DECISION TO MOVE OFFSHORE

Choosing a Location CP chose Singapore as the site of its first offshore manufacturing operation. The facility would first manufacture corded and then cordless telephones. Singapore, an island nation in Southeast Asia, was founded as an *entrepôt* because of its strategic position and excellent natural harbor. In 1988, however, manufacturing employed almost a third of the labor force, and the

INTEGRATIVE CASES

EXHIBIT IC1–5

U.S. Manufacturers' Shipments, Exports, and Imports of Telephone Sets, Selected Years, 1978–1988 (millions of dollars)

	1978	1982	1988
Shipments	$824	$1,065	$359
Exports	10	24	56
Imports	42	149	1,408
Apparent consumption	856	1,190	1,703

Source: United States Bureau of Census, "Selected Electronic and Associated Products, 1979, 1983," series MA36N, and "Communications Equipment, 1988," series MA36P.

Singaporean government played a major role in managing the economy.

CP management chose Singapore in part because it was an English-speaking country and its Economic Development Board provided a kind of one-stop shopping for foreign companies that wanted to do business there. Corruption was not a problem: "The place was squeaky clean," recalled a CP manager. In addition, an existing building was available immediately for lease. According to Jim Bercaw, Singapore was not the lowest cost option, but it was considerably cheaper than the United States. Jim Bercaw described the decision this way:

It was a jiffy quick decision. In January 1985, we began to negotiate, in March 1985, we received budgetary and financial approval. In May 1985, we buttonholed a lease in an existing factory. By January 1986, we shipped our first product.

Logically, the decision to go to Singapore and sacrifice 500 jobs to save 10,000 jobs was a "no-brainer." However, culturally the decision created a struggle around taking jobs from our own facility out of America.[7]

We also had to decide what kind of facility we wanted Singapore to be. We knew we wanted to attract the right kind of people there. We wanted to treat our people well. The labor rate was not crucial because the gap was so large. We wanted the facility to be world-class. And, we had a notion, that at some point we wanted the factory to be solely operated by Singaporeans. We did not want to create an American factory in Singapore.

The move to Singapore reduced CP's labor costs 90 percent and its overhead costs 40 percent. Overall, CP saved 30 percent of its manufacturing costs by moving to Singapore, even after accounting for tariffs and transportation costs.

Impact on Labor In 1985, the Shreveport Western Electric plant employed between 6,000 and 7,000 workers and was the largest employer in northwestern Louisiana. Some 750 workers at the plant were involved in the production of telephones. These workers were represented by the International Brotherhood of Electrical Workers (IBEW).

In July 1985, AT&T laid off 875 workers at the plant, 100 of whom made residential telephones. The remaining 650 residential telephone workers were phased out through later layoffs, transfers, or attrition. At the time of the July 1985 layoffs, AT&T announced that it was shifting the manufacture of residential telephones from the Shreveport facility to a new leased building in Singapore to cut costs and remain competitive.

The Singapore announcement came in the second year of the union's three-year contract. Under the union contract, union workers were not permitted to strike while the contract was in force. The local union officials in Shreveport characterized the union as extremely vocal and unified in its opposition to the move to Singapore. According to the union local, AT&T did not attempt to discuss or negotiate alternatives to moving offshore with the union.

In recalling this period, Ken Bertaccini said:

The decision to downsize was very difficult but clear. It cost American jobs and sacrificed the livelihoods of people who were part of the AT&T family. It meant moving jobs to parts of the world without any associations or relationships with AT&T. Patriotic emotions were involved, as well as the pain of looking great people in the eye and telling them that they would no longer have jobs.

Laid-off workers received Trade Readjustment Payments, as well as the benefits outlined in the union contract. These included severance pay based on years of service as well as extended medical benefits.

During the 1986 contract talks, the union negotiated retraining programs for its membership to help prepare them for life after AT&T. An Enhanced Training Opportunity Program was adopted that provided educational opportunities for workers, including computer training and classes at community colleges.

EXCELLENCE PERIOD: 1987–1988

When Nick Stevens joined CP in November 1987, he noticed that the Singapore facility had strayed from its original manufacturing strategy. Stevens decided CP needed another manufacturing location. The new facility would focus exclusively on manufacturing corded telephones.

According to Nick Stevens, the new location had to be able to sustain a world-class facility. Geographic proximity to Singapore, the cost and availability of labor, government incentive packages, and infrastructure were all among the criteria considered by Stevens. Ultimately, he decided on Bangkok, Thailand.

Thailand, known earlier as Siam, was one of the world's largest producers of rubber. Thai was spoken by approximately 97 percent of the population and was the official language, although English was used in government and commerce. Manufacturing accounted for about one-fifth of the country's gross national product and employed about 11 percent of the workforce. In the late 1980s, the country had one of the highest rates of economic growth in the world.

In February 1988, Stevens presented his Bangkok proposal to the AT&T Board and received approval. By June 1988, the facility was announced in Bangkok.

Answering System Market In 1987, CP adopted a five-year plan to make CP's answering systems the market share leader by 1992. As early as 1985, industry experts predicted a robust market for telephone answering systems. Unit sales in 1986 exceeded four million (see Exhibit IC1–6).

The answering systems market had two segments: adjuncts and integrated. Adjunct answering systems did not include a telephone, but integrated systems did. In both segments, the strongest competitors were Panasonic, PhoneMate, and GE/Thompson. The market set the price for answering systems, and there were no real differences in the margins between the segments. In both segments, however, low-end products (those with less features) commanded smaller margins. In general, the market for answering systems was in affluent countries. In 1987, the largest market by far was the United States. Europe, especially Germany, was expected to develop in future years.

CP's goal for answering systems required it to look for another site for an answering systems manufacturing facility. Stevens's goal for 1988 was to explore the opportunities in Mexico and Europe. In June 1988, he saw an item in the *Wall Street Journal* advertising a seminar in Tucson, Arizona, on Mexican *maquiladoras*.[8] The seminar included a side trip into Nogales and Hermisillo, Mexico, to tour various *maquiladora* operations (see Exhibit IC1–7).

MEXICO

Mexico was the third largest country in Latin America, after Brazil and Argentina. In 1988, more than 83.5 million people lived in Mexico, making it the 11th most populous country in the world. Officially known as the United States of Mexico, it was organized into 31 states and a *distrito federal*. It shared a 2,000 mile border with the United States of America.

Although Mexico secured its independence from Spain in 1821, it was the Mexican Revolution in 1910 that initiated a period of dramatic social change. A new constitution was adopted in 1917 that restricted foreign economic control and gave workers new protections. In 1929, the *Partido Revolucionario Institucional* (PRI) was formed. Since its founding, it never lost an election. Rapid industrial growth after 1940 improved living standards for much of Mexico. Import substitution, which entailed manufacturing locally what had been previously imported, and aggressive promotion of Mexican products for Mexican consumption were adopted as the country's strategy for development.

Unrest in the late 1960s spurred increased government investment in the infrastructure as well as increased spending on social programs. Despite these aggressive policies, the six-year term (from 1970 to 1976) of President Luis Echeverrea Alvarez was marked by 30 percent annual inflation, budget deficits, and political unrest.

In the late 1970s, major new oil fields were discovered in Mexico that gave it easy access to foreign credit at low interest rates. Public debt nearly doubled between 1979 and 1981 from US$40 billion to US$78 billion. Despite the growth in government expenditures, by the end of the 1970s, about 50 percent of all Mexican households lacked running water and sewage services, 25 percent lacked electricity, and 22 percent had neither running water, sewer services, nor electricity. Twenty percent of the population suffered from malnutrition, and 45 percent of the population did not receive adequate health care.[9]

The decline of world oil prices in the early 1980s, as well as a sharp rise in world interest rates, plunged Mexico

EXHIBIT IC1–6

Growth of U.S. Telephone Equipment Markets, 1984–1988 (millions of current dollars, 1990)

Type of Market	1984	1985	1986	1987	1988
Telephone sets—corded	$1,200	$1,585	$1,685	$1,750	$1,825
Telephone sets—cordless	410	305	410	438	474
Answering systems	298	371	535	557	634

Source: North American Telecommunications Association, *Telecommunications Market Review and Forecast* (1990 Edition): 12, 144, 154, 162, 178.

INTEGERATIVE CASES

EXHIBIT IC1–7

Map of Mexico

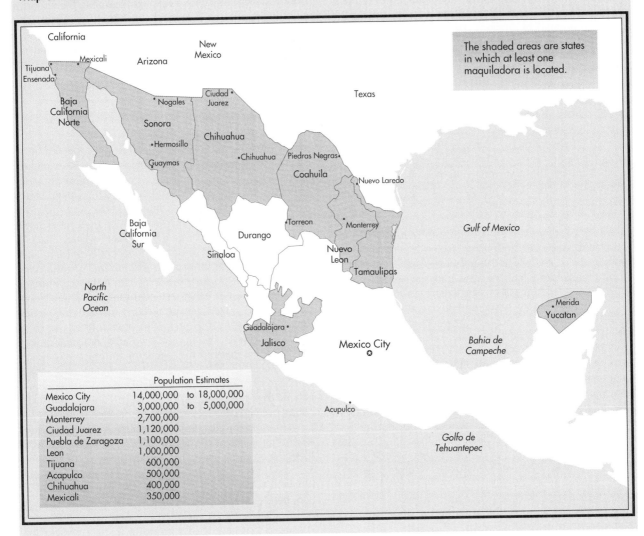

The shaded areas are states in which at least one maquiladora is located.

Population Estimates			
Mexico City	14,000,000	to	18,000,000
Guadalajara	3,000,000	to	5,000,000
Monterrey	2,700,000		
Ciudad Juarez	1,120,000		
Puebla de Zaragoza	1,100,000		
Leon	1,000,000		
Tijuana	600,000		
Acapulco	500,000		
Chihuahua	400,000		
Mexicali	350,000		

into economic crisis. In August 1982, Mexico announced that it could not meet the interest payments on its foreign debt of US$88 billion. In September, banks were nationalized, and new currency controls were put in place.

In December 1982, foreign debt exceeded US$91 billion. Mexico turned to the International Monetary Fund (IMF) for assistance. The government budget was slashed, food subsidies were eliminated, and the peso was sharply devalued. The combination of inflation and the peso devaluation substantially reduced the real wages of workers (see Exhibit IC1–8). In 1986, in exchange for new foreign loan agreements with the IMF, the World Bank, and its commercial bank creditors, Mexico agreed to major reforms of its economic policies, including liberalization of foreign investment, reductions in public spending, tax reform, and divestiture of state-owned enterprises.

EXHIBIT IC1-8

Hourly Compensation of Production Workers in Manufacturing

Country	Wages (US$ per hour worked)								
	1980	1981	1982	1983	1984	1985	1986	1987	1988
United States	$9.84	$10.84	$11.64	$12.10	$12.51	$12.96	$13.21	$13.40	$13.85
Japan	5.61	6.18	5.70	6.13	6.34	6.43	9.31	10.83	12.80
Singapore	1.49	1.79	1.96	2.21	2.46	2.47	2.23	2.31	2.67
Hong Kong	1.51	1.55	1.67	1.52	1.58	1.73	1.88	2.09	2.40
Taiwan	1.00	1.18	1.22	1.27	1.42	1.50	1.73	2.26	2.82
Thailand	NA	NA	NA	NA	NA	NA	NA	NA	1.40
Brazil	1.38	1.64	1.86	1.26	1.07	1.12	1.47	1.38	1.46
Mexico	NA	3.71	2.54	1.85	2.04	1.60	1.09	1.06	1.32
Malaysia	NA	NA	NA	NA	NA	NA	NA	NA	1.60

Note: Hourly compensation is defined as (1) all payments made directly to the worker, pay for time worked, pay for time not worked, all bonuses and other special payments, and the costs of payments in kind, and (2) employer contributions to legally required insurance programs and contractual and private benefit plans.

Source: Except Malaysia and Thailand, 1980, 1984–1988, United States Department of Labor, Bureau of Labor Statistics, May 1991, Report 803: 1981–1983, unpublished data from United States Department of Labor Bureau of Labor Statistics, Office of Productivity and Technology. Malaysia and Thailand, 1988, Bank Swiss.

In July 1988, Carlos Salinas de Gortari, the PRI's candidate, won the presidency with 50.4 percent of the vote,[10] amid widespread charges of irregularities in the polling. Cuauhtemoc Cárdenas, the son of the Mexican president who had nationalized the oil companies in 1938, had mounted a strong campaign against the PRI. Cárdenas was critical of the PRI for abandoning Mexico's history of national self-determination. According to the PRI, Cárdenas won 31.1 percent of the vote in the election, including four states and the *distrito federal*. However, many Mexicans believe that Cárdenas actually won the election. As president, Salinas renegotiated the foreign debt, continued the austerity plan, and continued privatizing government-owned businesses.

Maquiladoras

In 1965, the government of Mexico initiated the Border Industrialization Program. The program permitted foreign corporations to establish wholly owned subsidiary operations in Mexico. Under the program, the subsidiary could import into Mexico duty free, machinery, raw materials, and component parts to be used in processing or assembling

goods in Mexico.[11] So long as the end product was exported, Mexican duties were not levied on the imported components. Under the laws of the United States and most industrialized countries, when the imported components are exported back to their country of origin in the form of finished products, only the value added in Mexico—labor, overhead, raw materials—and not the value of the imported raw materials or components—was subject to duty.[12] Operations established under this program were commonly known as *maquiladoras, maquilas,* or in-bond assembly operations.[13]

Maquiladora or *maquila* is derived from the Spanish verb *"maquilar,"* which means to measure or take payment for grinding corn. In colonial times, the *maquila* was the portion of flour that the miller kept as payment for grinding the corn. In the 1980s, *maquiladora* or *maquila* referred to the system under which foreign companies provide the corn (for example, electronic components), Mexico keeps its portion for assembling or processing (for example, foreign currency changed into pesos for wages and production costs), and the assembled goods return to their country of origin with a duty paid only on the value added in Mexico.

Twin plant is another term often associated with *maquilas*. Originally, the Border Industrialization Program envisioned the establishment of complementary plants across the border from one another. The Mexican twin was intended to provide labor-intensive assembly of components fabricated in the United States. The assembled components would then be shipped to the twin in the United States where they would be finished, inspected, distributed, and sold. However, in most cases, the complementary U.S. plant was not located along the border but elsewhere within the United States at preexisting facilities. In 1987, fewer than 10 percent of all Mexican *maquilas* had a U.S. twin.[14]

The Border Industrialization Program was adopted to provide permanent employment for Mexico's rapidly growing population along the U.S.–Mexico border. The program sought to create jobs by attracting foreign manufacturing facilities that would not compete directly with domestic Mexican producers. The program also attempted to absorb migrant agricultural workers displaced by the expiration of the U.S. Bracero Program.[15] To address the problems resulting from the end of the Bracero Program, the law initially required that all foreign owned assembly operations be located within a 20-kilometer strip along the U.S.–Mexican border. New regulations were adopted in 1977 that permitted *maquilas* to locate in the economically depressed interior regions of Mexico. In 1983, the Mexican government extended the program to all regions of Mexico. However, by 1986, over 88 percent of all *maquila* operations were still concentrated along the border. *Maquiladoras*

located near the border accounted for approximately 87 percent of the total *maquiladora* workforce.[16]

The number of *maquiladoras* grew from 12 in 1965 to over 1,450 in 1988.[17] Over the same period, the number of *maquiladora* workers grew from 3,000 to over 361,800 (see Exhibit IC1–9). The type of *maquila* production had also changed. In 1965 and 1966, the vast majority of *maquiladoras* were textile firms. In 1988, *maquiladora* production included automobiles and auto parts, electronics, telecommunications equipment, and scientific instruments.

Beginning in the early 1980s, a substantial number of major U.S. multinationals, including many Fortune 500 companies, established *maquiladoras*. Several European and Japanese firms also established *maquiladoras* or employed subcontractors to perform their assembly in Mexico. In 1987, there were 20 Japanese *maquiladoras* in Mexico. The most prominent Japanese manufacturers operating *maquiladora* facilities were Sanyo, Sony, Toshiba, Hitachi, Matsushita, and TDK.[18]

MAQUILADORAS FOR MEXICO

Impact on the Economy Mexico earned foreign exchange on the value added to products assembled or processed in Mexico and then exported (see Exhibits IC1–9 and IC1–10). In fewer than 25 years, the *maquiladora* industry had become Mexico's second largest industry after oil and oil-

EXHIBIT IC1–9

Selected Data on the Maquiladoras

	1980	1981	1982	1983	1984	1985	1986	1987	1988
Number of firms	620	605	585	600	672	760	891	1,125	1,450
Average annual employment (000)	119.5	131	127	151	200	212	250	305	362
Imported materials (million $)	1,750	2,227	1,979	2,823	3,749	3,825	4,351	5,507	7,808
Exported material (million $)	2,523	3,202	2,830	3,641	4,904	5,092	5,646	7,105	10,146
Value added (million $)	773	975	851	818	1,155	1,267	1,295	1,598	2,337
Wages, salaries, loans	458	596	463	385	595	660	586	739	1,141
Domestic raw materials and packaging	30	29	26	37	51	36	54	86	132
Utilities and other expenses	129	153	174	183	206	238	295	314	388
Miscellaneous expenses	155	197	189	213	303	334	360	458	676

Note: Figures may not add up due to rounding

Source: Banco de Mexico, "La Industria Maquiladora de Exportación, 1980–1986," mimeo. Mexico, 1987; 1987 and 1988, INEGI, "Advances de Informacion Economica—Industria Maquiladora de Exportación," November 1988 and November 1989.

EXHIBIT IC1-10

Selected Data on Mexico's Balance of Payments

	1980	1981	1982	1983	1984	1985	1986	1987	1988
Merchandise exports	16,070	19,940	21,230	22,312	24,196	21,663	16,031	20,655	20,566
Merchandise imports	(18,900)	(24,040)	(14,435)	(8,550)	(11,255)	(13,212)	(11,432)	(12,222)	(18,898)
Trade balance	(2,830)	(4,100)	6,795	13,762	12,941	8,451	4,599	8,433	1,668
Foreign direct investment	2,090	2,540	1,655	461	390	491	1,160	1,796	635
Current account balance	(8,160)	(1,390)	(6,307)	5,403	4,194	1,130	(1,673)	3,968	(2,443)

Source: Balance of Payments Statistics Vol. 41, Yearbook, Part 1 (IMF: 1990).

Trade Balance, also known as Balance of Trade, is a country's exports of goods minus its imports of goods.

Foreign Direct Investment is the acquisition of physical assets outside the home country with substantial management control (usually defined as 10 percent or more of the ownership of a company) held by the parent corporation of the home country.

Current Account Balance is the net of the country's imports, exports, services and government unilateral transfers (sums sent outside the home country by the government for foreign aid, emergency relief, etc.).

Balance of Payments is the record of the goods and services an economy has received from and provided to the rest of the world and of the changes in the economy's claims on and liabilities to the rest of the world.

Source: Michael G. Rukstad (ed.), *Macroeconomic Decision Making in the World Economy: Text and Cases* (FL: Holt, Rinehart and Winston, Inc., 1989): 485.

related production. In 1987, the *maquiladora* industry accounted for approximately 44 percent of Mexican exports to the United States. That year, *maquiladoras* contributed approximately US$1.6 billion in foreign exchange earnings. Between 1982 and 1987, the industry created 178,000 new jobs out of a total of 408,000 jobs created over this period.[19]

Impact on the Environment   It was estimated that *maquiladoras* generated more than 20 million tons of hazardous waste annually. Such wastes included corrosive acids and bases, sludge from electroplating processes, cyanide solutions, paint sludge and thinners, and heavy metals such as cadmium, chromium, lead, mercury, and silver.[20] Under the Mexican law that had regulated *maquiladoras* since 1983, hazardous wastes had to be returned to their country of origin.[21] American owned *maquiladoras* had to comply with both Mexican and U.S. laws regulating hazardous waste disposal. U.S. law required would-be generators of hazardous waste to obtain an EPA identification number. In addition, *maquiladoras* that planned to transport hazardous waste for off-site treatment, storage, or disposal within the United States had to prepare a manifest. Each time the waste changed hands, the manifest had to be signed. Biennial reports were required to be submitted to the EPA by all companies shipping hazardous waste to the United States.

EPA records showed that in 1987 only 20 out of more than 1,000 U.S. *maquiladoras* returned their hazardous waste to the United States.[22] A study by the Texas Center for Policy Studies found that in a 2 ½ year period only 33 of the approximately 600 *maquiladoras* in the Texas–Mexico border area had filed the required notices for return of their hazardous wastes to the United States.[23] A November 1990 study by the Secretaria de Desarrollo Urbano y Ecología (the Ministry of Urban Development and Ecology or SEDUE), the Mexican Government's equivalent of the U.S. Environmental Protection Agency, revealed that only 19 percent of the plants using toxic materials could show that they had disposed of wastes properly.[24] Other studies revealed that primary sources of drinking water in the border area had been contaminated with industrial solvents and other chemicals.[25]

Historically, Mexico had less stringent environmental standards than the United States and lax enforcement of its standards.[26] In a 1988 survey of *maquiladoras* in Mexicali, a Mexican city near the California border, by El Colegio de la Frontera Norte, 10 percent of the 100 *maquiladoras* surveyed freely admitted that "environmental legislation" in Mexico was one of the main factors in their decision to leave the United States and relocate in Mexico. Seventeen percent of those surveyed considered it a factor of importance.[27]

INTEGERATIVE CASES

In 1988, Mexico enacted the General Law on Ecological Balance and Environmental Protection. The administrator of the U.S. Environmental Protection Agency said about the law:

> ...what we know about Mexico's 1988 comprehensive environmental law indicates that it may be sufficiently stringent to rebut the "pollution haven" argument. Properly enforced, the law should result in greatly improved environmental protection.[28]

SEDUE was the federal Mexican agency charged with enforcing the 1988 environmental law. Its annual budget for pollution control was approximately US $3.1 million. In contrast, in the same year, the annual budget for pollution control in Texas was US$50 million. In Ciudad Juarez, a Mexican state near El Paso, Texas, there was one Mexican federal inspector for more than 300 maquiladora plants and all Mexican domestic industry.[29]

Most of the maquiladoras were clustered around Tijuana–San Diego in California and Ciudad Juarez–El Paso in Texas. The resulting population growth in these cities severely strained the water supply and infrastructure. A 1981 University of Mexico study on border resources found that the aquifer under El Paso–Ciudad Juarez was being depleted faster than it was being replenished. In the lower Rio Grande Valley, closer to the Gulf of Mexico, municipal and industrial needs were expected to reduce drastically the water available for crop irrigation by the year 2000.[30]

Wages and Working Conditions The Mexican Constitution and federal Mexican labor law set forth the minimum rights and benefits to which Mexican workers were entitled. The law regulated employment conditions such as work schedules, overtime, vacation periods, legal holidays, payment of salaries, employment of women and minors, occupational risks, and minimum wages. Article Three of Mexico's federal labor law provided:

> Work is a social right and social obligation. It is not an article of commerce; it requires respect for the freedom and dignity of the person performing it and it shall be carried out under conditions protecting the life, the health, and a decent standard of living for the worker and his family.[31]

Mexican workers also had the right to unionize. In major Mexican cities, nearly all workers were members of a union. Under Mexican law, the union had the right to approve or disapprove an employer's hiring decisions.

A survey conducted by the International Trade Commission found that U.S. companies viewed the Mexican minimum wage as the major attraction of foreign investment in Mexico[32] (see Exhibit IC1–11). Minimum wages in Mexico were set by commissions comprised of members of the government, organized labor, and private industry. These commissions set the minimum wage for 86 different unskilled and skilled occupational classifications in 11 different economic zones in Mexico. The highest minimum wages had traditionally been along the northern border.[33]

Base maquiladora wages averaged about $3.50 to $4.00 per day for production workers[34] (see Exhibit IC1–11). According to the American Friends Service Committee, comparable Mexican manufacturers in major cities paid two to three times maquiladora wages.[35] Common fringe benefits, such as attendance bonuses and transportation subsidies, could raise the wage from $7 to $9 per day. Attendance bonuses were in response to the 10 to 35 percent turnover rate that came to characterize maquiladoras. The average hourly wages paid to maquiladora workers placed strict limits on their purchasing power. In the town of Matamoros, for example, the average worker had to work an hour and a half to buy a half gallon of milk, three hours to buy a box of cereal, five and a half hours to buy two pounds of beef, and 17 hours to buy a toddler-size dress.[36]

Limited studies of maquiladora working conditions indicated that employees experienced many work-related health and safety problems. Eye disease and the weakening of the optic nerve were prevalent among electronics

EXHIBIT IC1–11

Average Hourly Compensation Cost for Maquiladora Workers

Year	Compensation
1980	$1.42
1981	1.67
1982	1.23
1983	0.91
1984	1.06
1985	1.07
1986	0.80
1987	0.75
1988	0.80

Source: 1980–1986, U.S. International Tariff Commission (USTIC), *The Use and Economic Impact of TSUS Items 806.30 and 807*, Publication No. 2053 (Washington, D.C.: USTIC, January 1988): 8–9; 1987 and 1988, Leslie Sklair; *Assembling for Development* (Boston: Urwin Hyman, Inc., 1989): 72.

workers. Among textile workers, inadequate seating was associated with the development of lumbago.[37]

In a Tijuana, Mexico *maquiladora* of one of CP's Asian competitors, the casewriter observed an assembly line of workers, 98 percent of whom were women, hunched over a moving conveyor belt that carried printed circuit boards (PCBs) in various stages of completion. The plant made cable boxes and tuners. The women workers sat on nonergonomic stools while placing capacitors or other minute components on PCBs. Some workers used magnifying glasses to place components on the printed circuit boards. Some women soldered or tested PCBs. Testing was done by manually manipulating a component on a PCB or by staring at a computer screen as the PCB was tested by a machine.

The *maquiladora* employed a handful of male workers. These workers attended the automated processes in the plant, though there seemed to be little for them to do. No women were assigned to the machines. All employees worked a nine and one-half hour day, from 8:00 A.M. to 6:00 P.M., with a half-hour break for lunch. Outside the plant a trailer was used for the storage of hazardous waste.

Half of Mexico's population was below the age of 18. Although it was illegal in Mexico to hire children under 14, the Mexico City Assembly estimated that between 5 million to 10 million children were employed illegally, often in hazardous jobs.[38] The *Wall Street Journal* profiled Vincente Guerrero, a 12-year-old Mexican boy who had been compelled to leave the 6th grade to work in a shoe factory.[39]

> ...Vincente spends most of his time ... smearing glue onto the soles of shoes with his hands. The glue he dips his fingers into is marked "toxic substances ... prolonged or repeated inhalation causes grave health damage; do not leave in the reach of minors." All [the boys who work in the factory] ignore the warning.
>
> Impossible to ignore is the sharp, sickening odor of the glue. The only ventilation in the factory is from slits in the wall where bricks were removed from a window near Vincente that opens only halfway. Just a matter of weeks after he started working, Vincente was home in bed with a cough, burning eyes and nausea.
>
> When a teacher came by the factory to chide school dropouts [the plant superintendent's 13-year old son] rebuked her. "I'm earning 180,000 pesos a week," he said. "What do you make?" The teacher, whose weekly salary is 120,000 could say nothing.[40]

Estimates placed the savings, compared to average *maquiladora* wages, from hiring younger (ages 14–18) and less skilled workers at 30%–40%.

Some critics charged that *maquiladoras* had disrupted the social and family structure of Mexican society by dis-

EXHIBIT IC1-12

Distribution of Men and Women in the Maquila Workforce in 1986

Various Manufacturing Activities	Men	Women
Electrical and electronic machinery and equipment	9,610	29,001
Furniture and fixtures	5,803	1,910
Nonelectrical equipment and parts	1,857	897
Footwear and leather products	1,776	2,052
Transportation equipment and accessories	17,850	23,144
Total industry	64,812	139,076

Source: USTC, Publication No. 2053, January 1988, 8–11.

criminating against Mexican males, the traditional breadwinners, and hiring predominantly women. The critics also contended that women were preferred over men because they were more docile, politically unaware, inexperienced, and less demanding. In the 1970s, women comprised 23 percent of the Mexican labor force overall but 72.3 percent of the *maquila* industry[41] (see Exhibit IC1–12).

Living Conditions   In the Mexican border towns, many *maquiladora* workers lived in dwellings fashioned from cardboard and scraps of wood taken from *maquiladora* trash bins. Some of the cardboard had once contained polyvinyl chloride; written on the cardboard walls were warnings that the former contents could release hazardous fumes. The workers' water supply was stored in 55-gallon drums also found in *maquiladora* trash bins. The drums contained labels indicating that they formerly contained fluorocarbon solvents whose vapors are harmful if inhaled.

MAQUILADORAS AND THE UNITED STATES

Impact on the Economy   Advocates argued that *maquiladoras* help keep U.S. manufacturing internationally competitive, saving jobs that would otherwise be lost if U.S. manufacturers went to the Far East, since *maquiladoras* primarily use components made in the United States. According to a U.S. Department of Commerce report, nearly 75,000 U.S. workers were employed during 1986 to produce and ship $2.9 billion worth of components and raw materials used annually by *maquiladoras*.[42]

Organized labor in the United States contended that *maquiladoras* take jobs out of the United States—some of which could be held by the estimated 27 million workers and unemployed people in the United States who were functional illiterates. The Communications Workers of America (CWA) estimated that had there been no increase in foreign production by U.S. companies, more than 20,000 of the 120,000 jobs lost in the telecommunications industry since 1981 would have been saved.[43] In 1988, the jobless rate in the U.S. electronics industry was 86 percent higher than it was in 1979. In the five years between January 1979 and January 1984, employment for production workers manufacturing telephone and telegraph equipment declined in the United States by 23.4 percent.[44]

Maquiladora workers tended to shop in US border towns which returned a portion of their *maquila* wages to the United States. Studies have suggested that *maquila* workers spent more than half of their wages in the United States, mainly in the stores and shopping malls of the U.S. border towns.[45]

Impact on the Environment The *maquiladoras* brought rapid development on the U.S. side of the border. The pace of development outstripped the ability of the region to absorb it. Mexican officials have complained that growing development on the U.S. side of the border threatened surface-water supplies promised to Mexico under a 1944 treaty. A legal advisor to the Mexican Foreign Ministry believed that by the mid–1990s the United States would be unable to deliver the volume of water promised Mexico.[46] The primary source of drinking water on the Texas border was the Rio Grande, which was consistently drunk dry.[47]

Not only was there a shortage of water, but the water that was available was frequently contaminated. Most Mexican border towns did not have sewage treatment plants. Ciudad Juarez dumped all its raw sewage into a canal that paralleled the Rio Grande. A study in San Elizario, Texas, showed that everyone there had been exposed to hepatitis at least once by the time he or she was 20 years old.[48] More than 20 million gallons of untreated sewage and chemicals ran into the Tijuana River each day. Some ended up on the Imperial Beach on the California coast, which has been closed for ten years.[49] Recreational use of the Rio Grande below Laredo, Texas, has long been considered unsafe because its sister city in Mexico, Nuevo Laredo, dumps about 25 million gallons of untreated sewage into the river every day.[50]

The air quality along the border had also been affected. On the Mexican side of the border across from El Paso, Texas, firewood was the chief cooking and heating fuel for most of the 1.2 million residents of Ciudad Juarez, Mexico. Rubber tires were burned in kilns that made decorative tiles. Along with pollution from motor vehicles and industry, the smoke from these fires produced an acrid cloud over both cities under certain weather conditions.[51]

CONSIDERATIONS ON PLANT LOCATION

In late 1988, Stevens enrolled in the seminar advertised in the *Wall Street Journal* and toured the *maquiladora* operations situated around the U.S.–Mexico border. Stevens described his reactions to the tour: "I did not like what I saw. I saw exploitation in the form of sweatshops, I saw wage inflation, horrible environmental conditions, and huge workforce turnover." CP management had also heard that bribery and corruption were a way of life in Mexico.

Stevens was considering other sites in Mexico including Monterrey, Hermisillo, Chihuahua, and Guadalajara. He was also considering locations outside Mexico: Malaysia, a U.S. greenfield operation in Texas, and a U.S. AT&T "factory-within-a-factory" operation. A plant outside the United States would employ approximately 1,800 people at full capacity of 3.5 million units per year. The work week would average 45 hours.

Projections indicated that a *maquiladora* plant in the border region was the lowest cost option. (See Exhibit IC1–13.) Wages elsewhere in Mexico were likely to be higher—by 15%–20%, for example, in Guadalajara. Expenditures on pollution controls were another cost issue. Complying with U.S. "good citizen" standards with on-site

EXHIBIT IC1–13

Initial Estimates of Average Cost per Unit at Alternative Sites (labor costed at average maquilidora rates)

	Existing AT&T Factory				
	Greenfield	Full	Incremental	Malaysia	Mexico
Landed Cost[a]	$47.33	$52.33	$51.89	$41.48	$39.44
Additional Cost[b]	.72	−.66	.65	3.40	2.96
Total cost	$48.04	$52.99	$52.54	$44.89	$42.39
Incremental carrying costs			0.49		
					$45.37

[a] Landed Cost includes material, labor, and overhead.
[b] Additional Cost includes transportation fees, duties, asset tax, and a charge for AT&T's internal hurdle rate.

Data has been disguised. The essential relationships have, however, been preserved.

facilities would add $2–$3 million to the estimates in Exhibit IC1–13 during the first few years. However, a number of companies avoided those expenditures by paying local firms relatively small amounts to dispose of waste—though some of these disposal firms did not actually comply with Mexican laws and regulations.

Malaysia offered several advantages. AT&T had significant experience in Asia, as well as infrastructure and support systems in the area, and the Malaysian Industrial Development Authority offered, like Singapore, a central, one-stop shopping opportunity for foreign companies. On the negative side, Stevens was concerned about putting too many eggs in one basket in Asia and feared that Malaysian wages and salaries would rise as more companies moved there.

At the time Stevens was considering where to locate CP's new manufacturing facility, AT&T's senior management was reviewing its capital budgeting process. It seemed it would be more difficult to get approval for the current project than for the Singapore and Thailand operations.

Wherever the plant was located, it would be devoted to manufacturing answering systems. Electronic components, printed circuit boards, power adapters, pellets, and cardboard boxes would be brought into the plant. The plant would make the body of the answering systems in-house using plastic injection molding. Completed answering systems would leave the plant boxed and ready to ship.

Even if the project were approved, Stevens and CP management still had to reach decisions on wages and benefits, the profile of its workforce in terms of gender, age, and educational background, the sourcing of components, as well as a host of other issues.

Source: Research Associate Wilda White prepared this case under the supervision of Professor Joseph Badaracco as the basis for class discussion rather than to illustrate either effective or ineffective handling of an administrative situation. Copyright ©1992 by the President and Fellows of Harvard College. To order copies or request permission to reproduce materials, Call 1-800-545-7685, or write the Publishing Division, Harvard Business School, Boston, MA 02163, or go to http://www.hbsp.harvard.edu/ No part of this publication may be reproduced, stored in a retrieval system, used in a spreadsheet, or transmitted in any form or by any means—electronic, mechanical, photocopying, recording, or otherwise—without the permission of Harvard Business School. Rev. October 19, 1994.

CASE QUESTIONS

1. Should AT&T build its telephone answering machine plant in Mexico? Justify your answer.
2. What decisions should Nick Stevens make about wage levels, benefits, waste management, teenage workers, gender-based hiring, and bribery in the event he chooses a Mexican site?
3. What obligations, if any, do AT&T managers have to their U.S. employees or the United States?

CASE ENDNOTES

1. Robert W. Garnet, *The Telephone Enterprise: The Evolution of the Bell System's Horizontal Structure, 1878–1909* (Baltimore: Johns Hopkins University Press, 1985): 173.
2. Ibid.
3. "The Big and Bruising Business of Selling Telephones," *Business Week*, March 12, 1984, 103.
4. Ibid.
5. "Love" had not always been a part of CP's "Shared Values." After extensive discussion, it was included in 1989 in order to deepen, in the words of one manager, "CP's commitment to live up to its personal values of caring, trust, and respect." This decision was reinforced by the outpouring of support for a CP executive who successfully battled cancer during the mid-1980s.
6. CP's product lines were (1) leased telephones, (2) corded telephones, (3) cordless telephones, (4) answering systems, (5) special needs systems (communications products for people with hearing, speech, motion, and vision impairments), (6) telephone accessories, (7) home security systems, and (8) public pay telephones.
7. Approximately 10,000 people worked throughout CP. According to CP management, these jobs were at risk if CP did not make competitively priced telephones.
8. A *maquiladora* is a plant that assembles components that are usually imported into the home country of the *maquiladora* duty free. The assembled components are then reexported. On reexport, a duty is paid only on the value of the labor that assembled the components and the value of any other home-country inputs.
9. Helen Shapiro, "Mexico: Escaping from the Debt Crisis?" (Cambridge, MA: President and Fellows of Harvard College, 1991), p. 6.
10. In comparison, de la Madrid received 71.6 percent of the vote in 1982 and López Portillo received 95 percent of the vote in 1976. M. Deiai Baer, "Electoral Trends," in *Prospects for Mexico*, ed. George W. Grayson (Washington, DC: Center for the Study of Foreign Affairs, Foreign Service Institute, Department of State, 1988), p. 43.

INTEGERATIVE CASES

11. Without the provisions of the Border Industrialization Program, products could not be imported into Mexico without an import license. After Mexico joined the General Agreement on Tariffs and Trade (GATT) in 1986, tariffs at an initial level of 50 percent were substituted for import licenses. At the end of 1987, the tariff ceiling for most items was lowered to 20 percent. Import licenses are still required for electronic and computer equipment and automotive imports. Sidney Weintraub, *Transforming the Mexico Economy: The Salinas Scenerio* (Washington, DC: National Planning Association, 1990), p. 5.

12. In the United States, tariff items 806.30 and 807.00 permit the portion of the product made of U.S. components to reenter the United States duty free.

13. All *maquiladora* facilities that export the assembled products are part of the "In-Bond Industry." The in-bond feature of the BIP requires that an importing *maquiladora* plant guarantee the payment of duties on imported materials that would otherwise be due. The guarantee usually consists of a surety bond. After processing, if the assembled products are exported, the bond is canceled.

14. U.S. International Tariff Commission (USTIC), *The Use and Economic Impact of TSUS Items 806.30 and 807*, Publication No. 2053 (Washington, DC: U.S. International Trade Commission, January 1988), pp. 8–12.

15. The Bracero, or Mexican Labor Program, allowed migrant Mexican workers to enter the United States on a temporary (seasonal) basis from 1942 through 1964. It was initiated to alleviate labor shortages in the U.S. agricultural and railroad industries during World War II. The Bracero Program attracted to the border unemployed workers from the Mexican interior who were seeking the guaranteed U.S. minimum wage. The railroad portion of the program ended in 1946. The agricultural program expired in 1964. A large segment of the border population became dependent on income earned by Braceros in the United States.

16. U.S. International Tariff Commission (USTIC), *The Use and Economic Impact of TSUS Items 806.30 and 807*, Publication No. 2053 (Washington, DC: U.S. International Trade Commission, January 1988), p. 84.

17. Khosrow Fatemi, ed., *The Maquiladora Industry: Economic Solution or Problem?* (New York: Praeger Publishers, 1990), pp. 4 and 28.

18. U.S. International Tariff Commission (USTIC), *The Use and Economic Impact of TSUS Items 806.30 and 807*, Publication No. 2053 (Washington, DC: U.S. International Trade Commission, January 1988), pp. 8–12.

19. Instituto Nacional de Estadfstica, Geograffa e Informtica (INEGI), National Income and Product Accounts, 1988.

20. Douglas Alexander and Roberto L. Fernandez, "Environmental Regulation of Business in Mexico," *Doing Business in Mexico* (New York: Matthew Bender, 1990), pp. 79–29, 79–30.

21. 1982 Decree for Promotion of the Maquiladora Industry (Diario Oficial, August 15, 1983), Art. 26.

22. "Transfrontier Health and Environmental Risks," *Natural Resources Journal* (Winter 1990), p. 177.

23. Remarks of Mary E. Kelly, Executive Director, Texas Center for Policy Studies, before the Senate Finance Committee, February 20, 1991, p. 3.

24. "Border Industry's Nasty Byproduct Imperils Trade," *New York Times,* March 31, 1991, 16, col. 3.

25. Ibid., p. 4.

26. "The Texas Border: Whose Dirt?" *The Economist,* August 18, 1990, pp. 24–25.

27. "Transfrontier Health and Environmental Risks," *Natural Resources Journal* (Winter 1990), p. 177.

28. William K. Reilly, "Mexico's Environment Will Improve With Free Trade," *Wall Street Journal,* April 19, 1991, A15, col. 2.

29. Remarks of Mary E. Kelly, Executive Director, Texas Center for Policy Studies before the Senate Finance Committee, February 20, 1991, p. 6–7.

30. "The Texas Border: Whose Dirt?" *The Economist,* August 18, 1990, pp. 24–25.

31. Commercial, Business and Trade Laws, Mexico, F. Labor Law (Title first to ninth) (United States of America: Oceana Publications, Inc., 1983): p. 3.

32. U.S. International Tariff Commission (USTC), *The Use and Economic Impact of TSUS Items 806.30 and 807*, Publication No. 2053 (Washington, DC: U.S. International Trade Commission, January 1988).

33. Barbara Chrispin, "Manpower Development in the Maquiladora Industry: Reaching Maturity" in Khosrow Faterni ed., *The Maquiladora Industry: Economic Solution or Problem?* (New York: Praeger Publishers, 1990), p. 75.

34. Ibid., p. 76.

35. *Background and Perspectives on the U.S.–Mexico–Canada Free Trade Talks* (Pennsylvania: American Friends Service Committee, April 10, 1991), p. 6.

36. Simon Billenness and Kate Simpson, "Franklin's Insight," September 1992, Boston MA., p. 8.

37. Judith Ann Warner, "The Sociological Impact of the Maquiladoras" in Khosrow Fatemi ed., *The Maquiladora Industry: Economic Solution or Problem?* (New York: Praeger, 1990): 193. Lumbago is pain in the lower back (lumbar region) often caused by muscle strain.
38. Matt Moffett, "Working Children: Underage Laborers Fill Mexican Factories, Stir U.S. Trade Debate," *Wall Street Journal*, April 8, 1991, 1, col. 1.
39. Ibid.
40. Ibid., A14, col. 1.
41. Leslie Sklair, *Assembling for Development: The Maquila Industry in Mexico and the United States* (Boston: Unwin Hyman, 1989), pp. 165–166.
42. U.S. International Tariff Commission (USTIC), *The Use and Economic Impact of TSUS Items 806.30 and 807*, Publication No. 2053 (Washington, DC: U.S. International Trade Commission, January 1988), pp. 8–15.
43. John Cavanagh, Lance Compa, et al., *Trade's Hidden Costs: Worker Rights in a Changing World Economy*

(Washington, DC: International Labor Rights Education & Research Fund, 1988), p. 21.
44. Full Employment Action Council, "Economic Dislocation and Structural Unemployment: The Plight of America's Basic Industries," September 6, 1985.
45. Leslie Sklair, "Mexico's Maquiladora Programme," in George Philip (ed.), *The Mexican Economy* (London: Routledge, 1988), p. 299.
46. "The Natural Limits to Growth," *The Economist*, April 20, 1991, p. 24.
47. Ibid.
48. "Border Industry's Nasty Byproduct Imperils Trade," *New York Times*, March 31, 1991, 16, col 3.
49. "The Texas Border: Whose Dirt?" *The Economist*, August 18, 1990, p. 24.
50. "Border Industry's Nasty Byproduct Imperils Trade," *New York Times*, March 31, 1991, p. 16, col. 3.
51. "Border Industry's Nasty Byproduct Imperils Trade," *New York Times*, March 31, 1991, p. 16, col. 3.

CASE 2

WHIRLPOOL'S QUEST FOR GLOBAL LEADERSHIP

In the Chairman's Letter of Whirlpool Corporation's *1995 Annual Report,* David R. Whitwam, Chairman of the Board and Chief Executive Officer, stated his disappointment with the Company's recent performance:

> On a relative basis, 1995 was a good year for Whirlpool Corporation and we continued to strengthen our position as the global leader in the major home appliance industry. That said, we should have done better. On an operating basis, and compared to our own very high performance expectations, the year was disappointing—for me, our global team and you, our shareholders.[1]

He attributed this disappointing performance partly to manufacturing inefficiencies and start-up costs of a new refrigerator in the United States, partly to restructuring difficulties in Europe, as well as raw materials cost increases combined with minimal growth or even declining demand in North America and Europe. This statement was quite a change in tone compared to his pronouncement a year earlier, when at the same place he had boldly stated that the

company had achieved both primary objectives—to produce "strong, short-term results" and to "building competitive advantage by continuing our expanding worldwide enterprise at all levels, and to leverage its best practices and Whirlpool's cumulative size."[2] (For key performance data see Exhibit IC2–1.)

THE U.S. APPLIANCE INDUSTRY

Home appliances were generally classified as laundry (washers and dryers), refrigeration (refrigerators and freezers), cooking (ranges and ovens), and other appliances (dishwashers, disposals, and trash compactors). Many appliance manufacturers also made floor care goods such as floor polishers and vacuum cleaners.

Manufacturing operations consisted mainly of preparation of a metal frame to which the appropriate components were attached in automated assembly lines and by manual assembly. Manufacturing costs comprised about 65% to 75% of total operating cost, with labor representing less than 10% of total cost. Optimal sized assembly plants had an annual capacity of about 500,000 units for most appliances except microwave ovens. Unlike other industries such as textiles, variable costs played an important role in the

Source: This case was prepared by Professor Arieh A. Ullmann of Binghamton University. Copyright ©1995 by Arieh A. Ullmann. Reprinted by permission.

INTEGERATIVE CASES

EXHIBIT IC2-1

Key Performance Measures: Whirlpool Corporation

Year	Earnings per Share[1]	Return on Equity[2]	Total Return to Shareholders[3]	P/E Ratio
1990	$1.04	5.1%	2.8%	22.6
1991	2.45	11.6	6.7	15.9
1992	2.90	13.1	17.0	15.4
1993	3.19	14.2	25.8	20.8
1994	2.10	9.4	12.0	23.9
1995	2.80	11.6	20.8	19.0

Notes:

1. Earnings from continuing operations before accounting change.

2. Earnings from continuing operations before accounting change divided by average shareholders' equity.

3. Five-year annualized.

cost structure; changes in raw materials and component costs were also significant. Component production was fairly scale-sensitive. Doubling compressor output for refrigerators, for instance, reduced unit costs by 10%–15%. There were also some scale economies in assembly but the introduction of robotics tended to reduce them while improving quality and performance consistency and enhancing flexibility.

Distribution of major appliances occurred either directly through contract sales to home builders and to other appliance manufacturers predominantly or indirectly through local builder suppliers. Traditionally, these customers were very cost conscious and thus preferred less expensive appliance brands. Retail sales represented the second distribution channel, with national chain stores and mass merchandisers such as department, furniture, discount, and appliance stores acting as intermediaries. The consolidation of appliance distributors during the past 10 years led to the current situation where about 45% of the total appliance volume was being sold through 10 powerful mega-retailers with Sears leading with a market share of about 29%. A third, less visible channel was the commercial market such as laundromats, hospitals, hotels, and other institutions.

Industry Structure

Since World War II, when over 250 firms manufactured appliances, several merger waves had consolidated the industry while sales grew and prices held. The most recent consolidation occurred in 1986 when, within less than 1 year Electrolux purchased White Consolidated, Whirlpool acquired KitchenAid and Roper, and Maytag bought Jenn-Air and Magic Chef. Maytag's acquisition of Jenn-Air and Magic Chef increased its overall revenues by giving it brand name appliances at various price points. Likewise, Whirlpool's acquisition of KitchenAid and Roper, respectively, broadened Whirlpool's presence at the high end and low end of the market. By the end of 1995, the number of domestic manufacturers varied by type of product between 4 for dishwashers and 15 for home refrigeration and room air conditioning equipment.

In the 1980s, the market continued to grow, primarily because of booming sales of microwave ovens, which tripled from 1980 to 1989, while washers and dryers increased in sales 34% and 52%, respectively. Appliance manufacturers realized that they must offer a complete line of appliances even if they did not manufacture all of them themselves, which was one reason for the merger activity and practice of interfirm sourcing. For example, Whirlpool made trash compactors for Frigidaire (Electrolux/White Consolidated); General Electric manufactured microwave ovens for Caloric (Raytheon) and Jenn-Air and Magic Chef (Maytag).

By 1995, five major competitors controlled 98% of the core appliance market, each of which offered a broad range of product categories and brands targeted to different customer segments. With 35% domestic market share, Whirlpool was ahead of GE (29.3%), a reversal of the leadership position compared to 5 years earlier. Whirlpool was especially strong in washers and dryers (1995: 53% share), whereas GE was ahead in refrigerators and ranges. In terms of overall market share, Maytag followed (14.4%), then Electrolux (13.5%), and Raytheon (6.2%), respectively.

Throughout the 1980s and into the 1990s competition in the United States was fierce. Industry demand depended on the state of the economy, disposable income levels, interest rates, housing starts, and consumers' ability to defer purchases. Saturation levels remained high and steady; over 70% of households had washers and over 65% dryers (see Exhibit IC2–2). Refrigerator demand stagnated while sales of electric ranges slowed as sales of the microwave oven boomed. Microwave sales, which had jumped from 3.5 million units in 1980 to over 10 million by 1989, started leveling out while sales of ranges dropped off drastically due to market maturation.

Factors of Competition

In this environment all rivals worked hard at keeping costs down. Had the appliance manufacturers been making automobiles, the price of a Chevrolet Caprice would have risen

EXHIBIT IC2-2

Global Home Appliance Industry: Saturation Levels by Region, Demand, and Market Growth, 1994–2004

	North America	Europe[1]	Latin America	Asia
Home Appliances				
Refrigerators	100%	100%	70%	30%
Cooking equipment	100	96	90	—
Clothes washers	74	82	40	20
Clothes dryers	70	18	—	—
Dishwashers	51	30	—	—
Microwave ovens	80	40	—	—
Room air conditioners	41	—	5	8
Compactors	5	—	10	8
Freezers	40	40	—	—
Population (million)	380	1,100	380	2,900
Annual demand (million units)	46	75	17	56
Estimated annual growth rate	3%	3%	6%–8%	8%–9%

Note:

1. Includes Eastern Europe, Africa, and the Middle East.

Source: Whirlpool Corporation, 1994 Annual Report.

from $7,209 in 1980 to $9,500 in 1990, not $17,370. Over 4 years, Electrolux spent over $500 million to upgrade old plants and build new ones for its acquisition, White Consolidated Industries. General Electric automated its Louisville, Kentucky, plant which, over 10 years, halved the work force and raised output by 30%.

Toward the end of the 1980s, it became even more important to lower costs, monitor margins, and achieve economies of scale. The Big Five were renovating and enlarging existing facilities. Maytag built new facilities in the South to take advantage of lower cost, non-union labor. Others built twin plants on the Mexican border to profit from cheap labor. A third trend was toward focus factories where each plant produced one product category only, covering all price points.

Also, all competitors started to push into the high-end segment of the market, which was more stable and profitable. Once the domain of Maytag, it became increasingly crowded with the appearance of GE's Monogram line, Whirlpool's acquisition of KitchenAid, and White's Euroflair models. Quality became an important feature in the competitive game. Maytag used it effectively in its famous ad of

the lonely repairman. Defect rates dropped from 20 per 100 appliances made in 1980 to 10 twelve years later. Relationships with suppliers changed as companies used fewer of them than in years past. Contracts were set up over longer terms to improve quality and keep costs low with just-in-time deliveries.

A recent development was the demand by the powerful distributors for faster delivery. Distributors sought to curtail inventory costs, their biggest expense. As a consequence, manufacturers started to improve delivery systems. For instance, General Electric created its Premier Plus Program, which guaranteed 3-day delivery. Sales departments were reorganized so that one sales representative would cover all of a manufacturer's brands of a given product category. Customer information services via 800-telephone numbers were also strengthened.

Innovation

Two developments—government regulation and advances in computer software—combined with intense competition accelerated product innovation. New energy standards to

INTEGERATIVE CASES

be enforced under the 1987 National Appliance Energy Conservation Act limited energy consumption of new appliances with the objective of reducing energy usage in appliances by 25% every 5 years. At the same time, the possible ban on ozone-depleting chlorofluorocarbons (CFCs) in refrigerators by 1995 was forcing the industry to redesign its refrigerators. Pressures were also exerted to change washer and dishwasher designs to reduce water consumption and noise levels. In 1989, the Super Efficient Refrigerator Program, Inc. (SERP) offered a $30 million award for a refrigerator prototype free of CFCs and at least 25% more energy efficient than the 1993 federal standards. The winner had to manufacture and sell over 250,000 refrigerators between January 1994 and July 1997.

As the industry globalized, more stringent government regulations outside the United States became a issue. For example, there was a concern that the more stringent environmental standards prevailing in the European Community would become law in the United States as well. Although Whirlpool supported the more stringent standards, their competitors, notably GE, opposed them.

Regarding advances in computer technology, new programs using fuzzy logic or neural networks that mimicked the human brain's ability to detect patterns were being introduced in many industries, including white goods. In Asia the use of elevators, washers, and refrigerators using fuzzy logic to recognize usage patterns was already widespread. In late 1992, AEG Hausgeräte AG, then a subsidiary of Daimler-Benz's AEG unit, introduced a washer that used fuzzy logic to control water consumption automatically, depending on the size of the load, and to sense how much dirt remained in clothes.

There were also other innovations. In the late 1980s, new technologies in cooking surfaces were introduced: ceramic–glass units, solid elements, and modular grill configurations. Other new customer-oriented features included the self-cleaning oven, automatic ice cube makers, self-defrosting refrigerators, pilotless gas ranges, and appliances that could be preset. Also, manufacturers worked hard to reduce the noise level of dishwashers and washing machines. Consumers became more concerned with the way appliances looked. Sleek European styling, with its smooth lines, rounded corners, and a built-in look with electronic controls, became fashionable. Another trend was the white-on-white look, which suggested superior cleanability and made the kitchen look larger.

Outlook

For the future, demand in the United States continued to look unattractive, with growth rates estimated at 3% based on a 1994 demand of 46 million units (Exhibit IC2–2). At the prevailing saturation levels, demand was restricted mostly to replacement purchases (79%) with the remainder going to new housing and new household formation. The industry was so competitive that no single manufacturer could keep an innovation to itself for more than a year without a patent. One of the competitors summarized the situation in the North American appliance industry as follows:

> In the 1980s, four manufacturers accounted for almost all major home appliance sales in the United States, a market where approximately 40 million appliances are sold annually. Each was a tough, seasoned competitor fighting for greater sales in a market predicted to grow little in the decade ahead.[3]

THE GLOBALIZATION OF THE APPLIANCE INDUSTRY

Foreign Competition

The white goods industry was as American as baseball and apple pie. In 1992, 98% of the dishwashers, washing machines, dryers, refrigerators, freezers, and ranges sold in the United States were made domestically. Exports represented about 5% of shipments. The manufacturing plants of the industry's leaders were located in places such as Newton, Iowa (Maytag), Benton Harbor, Michigan (Whirlpool), and Columbus, Ohio (White Consolidated Industries). Each of the Big Four was nearer a corn stalk than a parking meter. Combined, these companies practically owned the market for each major appliance, with one exception—microwave ovens. These represented the lion's share of imports, which made up about 17% of total appliance sales.

The acquisition of White Consolidated Industries by A.B. Electrolux of Sweden in 1986 marked a major change in the industry. Until then, foreign competition in the United States was largely restricted to imports of microwave ovens, a segment controlled by Far East competitors from Korea (Goldstar, Samsung) and Japan (Sharp, Matsushita). Aware of the fate of other industries, many expected that it was only a matter of time before these companies would expand from their beachhead in microwave ovens and compact appliances into other segments.

Europe

Of prime attractiveness to the U.S. manufacturers was Europe. Since 1985, Western Europe had rapidly moved toward a unified market of some 320 million consumers, which was not nearly as saturated as Canada and the United States (Exhibit IC2–2). Appliance demand was expected to grow at 5% annually. Political changes in Eastern Europe integrated these countries into the world trade system and thus added to Europe's long-term attractiveness.

During the 1970s and 1980s, the European white goods industry had experienced a consolidation similar to that in the United States. According to Whirlpool, in 1995 the number of manufacturers in Western Europe was 35, most of whom produced a limited range of products for specific geographic regions.[4] However, since the late 1980s, six companies—Electrolux Zanussi, Philips Bauknecht, Bosch-Siemens, Merloni-Indesit, Thompson, and AEG—had controlled 70% of market (excluding microwave ovens and room air conditioners). Until the mid 1980s, most companies were either producing and selling in only one national market or exporting to a limited extent to many European markets from one country. Observed Whirlpool's CEO Whitwam: "What strikes me most is how similar the U.S. and European industries are."[5] Research by Whirlpool also indicated that washers were basically alike in working components around the globe.[6]

The European market was very segmented and consumer preferences differed greatly from country to country with regard to almost every type of appliance. The French preferred to cook their food at high temperatures, splattering grease on oven walls. Thus oven ranges manufactured for France should have self-cleaning ability. However, this feature was not a requirement in Germany where lower cooking temperatures were the norm. Unlike Americans who preferred to stuff as many clothes into the washer as possible, Europeans overwhelmingly preferred smaller built-in models. Northern Europeans liked large refrigerators because they preferred to shop only once a week; consumers in southern Europe preferred small ones because they visited open-air markets daily. Northerners liked their freezers at the bottom of the refrigerators, southerners at the top. In France, 80% of washing machines were top-loaders; elsewhere in Western Europe, 90% were front-loaders. Also, European washers frequently contained heating elements, and the typical European homemaker preferred to wash towels at 95° Celsius. Gas ranges were common throughout Europe, except for Germany where 90% of all ranges sold were electric.

Given this situation, some observers were skeptical about the possibility of establishing pan-European models that would yield a sustainable competitive advantage through manufacturing, procurement, and marketing efficiencies. They claimed that the European market was actually made up of many smaller individual markets corresponding to the respective countries. Furthermore, they reasoned, many of these national markets featured strong competitors.

Distribution of white goods in Europe was different from that in North America. The larger channel, known as the retail trade, comprised independent retailers, many of whom were organized through buying groups or as multiple-store chains. The second channel, the kitchen trade, primarily comprised kitchen specialists that sold consumers entire kitchen packages. The kitchen trade was focused mainly on built-in units and not involved in laundry appliances.

A.B. Electrolux was a force in practically all of Europe with an overall 25% market share. Over 20 years this $14-billion multinational from Sweden had undertaken more than 200 acquisitions in 40 countries spanning five businesses: household appliances, forestry and garden products, industrial products, metal and mining, and commercial services. Its expertise in managing acquisitions and integrating the newly acquired units into the organization was unequaled. For example, in 1983, Electrolux took over a money-losing Italian white goods manufacturer with 30,000 employees, 50 factories, and a dozen foreign sales companies. Within 4 years the Swedes had turned a company which in 1983 lost L120 billion into an efficient organization netting L60 billion. The acquisitions of Zanussi of Italy, Tricity in Britain, and three Spanish companies in anticipation of the changes in Western Europe marked the beginning of a new era in this mature industry as Electrolux sought to establish a pan-European approach to the appliance market, followed by exploring trans-Atlantic opportunities. However, in 1993 Electrolux's pan-European strategy ran into trouble. The recession, combined with Europe's market fragmentation, reduced profits far below the targeted 5% margin.

In Germany Bauknecht (Philips), Siemens-Bosch, and AEG-Telefunken were dominant; in Britain GEC's Hotpoint, and in France Thomson-Brandt were forces to be reckoned with. Merloni from Italy pursued a different approach by flooding Europe with machines produced in Italy with lower-cost labor. In 1987, Merloni gobbled up Indesit, an Italian producer in financial trouble, in order to enlarge its manufacturing base and take advantage of Indesit's marketing position in many European countries. In the late 1980s, no brand had more than 5% of the overall market, even though the top 10 producers generated 80% of the volume.

In 1989, the Americans landed in Europe. General Electric formed an appliance joint venture with Britain's General Electric Corporation (GEC), which had a strong presence in the low-priced segment of the European market, especially in the United Kingdom, and thus complemented GE's high-end European products. In the same year, Maytag acquired the Hoover Division through the purchase of Chicago Pacific. In the United Kingdom, Hoover, best known for its vacuum cleaners, also produced washers, dryers, and dishwashers, which, however, encountered acceptance problems in other European markets. Hoover was also present in Australia and, through a trading company, serviced other parts of the world. In 1989, also, Whirlpool and N.V. Philips of the Netherlands formed a joint venture that included all of Philips's European appliance division. Thus, within a short time, the Americans closed the gap relative to the geographic scope of Electrolux. In spite of concerns about differing consumer preferences in Europe, the largest U.S. appliance manufacturers established themselves before the 1992 EU Program became a reality. European Community rules required 60% local content to avoid tariffs, which, combined with the fear of a "Fortress Europe" protected by Communitywide tariffs after 1992, excluded exports as a viable strategy.

Within a very short time further agreements followed, greatly reducing the number of independent competitors in Europe. AEG started cooperating with Electrolux in washer and dishwasher production and development and, in 1994, became part of Electrolux; Bosch-Siemens formed an alliance with Maytag; the European Economic Interest Group combined several manufacturers with France's Thompson-Brandt as the leader. In spite of this trend toward consolidation in the early 1990s, Whirlpool estimated the number of European manufacturers of home appliances to be about 100.[7]

Asia

Asia, the world's second largest home appliance market, was likely to experience rapid economic growth in the near future primarily thanks to the booming economies of the Pacific Rim countries. Home appliance shipments were expected to grow at least 6% per annum through the 1990s (Exhibit IC2–2). The biggest promise, of course, were the huge markets of the world's most populous states—China and India. However, income levels in these two markets were only approaching levels at which people could afford appliances. The Asian market was dominated by some 50 widely diversified Asian manufacturers, primarily from Japan, Korea, and Taiwan, with no clear leader emerging yet. Matsushita, the market leader, held less than a 10% market share outside Japan.

Consumer preferences in Asia were quite different from those in North America and Europe and varied widely from country to country. For example, typical Asian refrigerators ranged from 6 cu. ft to 10 cu. ft due to the lack of space. Since owning a refrigerator represented a status symbol, refrigerators were often placed in the living room. Such a prominent display created a demand for stylish colors and finishes. In India, for example, refrigerators in bright red or blue were popular. In terms of technology, both direct-cool and forced-air models were common in Asia, whereas in Europe direct-cool prevailed and in North America the forced-air version was preferred. Clothes washers had to be portable because living quarters tended to be small and because usually there was no basement to keep washers permanently hooked up to a water supply and drain. Often they were stored in an outside hallway and moved into the bathroom and kitchen for use. Also, they had to be delivered to large apartment blocks with no elevators and thus had to be carried up many flights of stairs. Therefore washers tended to be designed as lightweight products on wheels equipped with handles for easy relocation. Technological designs varied, even though vertical-axis machines dominated. The clothes themselves also represented a challenge because they ranged from the yards of fabric used in Indian saris to simple cotton dress and Western-style clothing. Clothes dryers were virtually unknown. Washing habits were different, too. For instance, Japanese usually washed with cold water. But in order to get their clothes clean Japanese machines have soak cycles that can range from 30 minutes to several hours. Two-burner, tabletop cooking units were used in contrast to the ranges used in North America and Europe, reflecting the differences in cooking styles. In addition, kitchens were much smaller and baking was virtually unknown, as were dishwashers. In air-conditioning, split-system units were the dominant version in Asia. In regions where air conditioners were used the better part of the year, consumers didn't want to block limited window space. Split-system units were installed high on the wall, often out of reach, making remote controls an important feature.

Latin America

Another market promising attractive growth in appliances was Latin America, once these countries could emerge from decades of political instability, economic mismanagement, and hyperinflation (Exhibit IC2–2). Indeed, much of this was happening in the 1990s, accompanied by efforts to lower tariffs, which would stimulate trade. In 1994, the white goods industry in Latin America comprised about 65 competitors. Whirlpool expected appliance shipments to expand at a faster pace than in North America and Europe.[8]

WHIRLPOOL CORPORATION

Company Background

In early 1996, Whirlpool Corporation, headquartered in Benton Harbor, Michigan, was one of the world's leading manufacturers and marketers of major home appliances. The company's plants were located in 12 countries, and it distributed its products in over 140 countries under 28 brand names (see Exhibit IC2–3). Fifteen years earlier Whirlpool executives had perceived the world primarily as consisting of the U.S. and Canadian markets, with some marginal sales in Latin America and limited export opportunities. However, the company had transformed itself and now recognized that the world encompassed four major regions: North America with 46 million units sold annually (1994) consisting of Canada, Mexico, and the United States; Europe with 50 million units (Western, Central and Eastern Europe, Africa, and the Middle East); Asia with 56 million units; and Latin America with 17 million units (the Caribbean, and Central and South America).

Located 2 hours by car from Chicago, Whirlpool was founded in St. Joseph, Michigan, in 1911 as the Nineteen Hundred Corporation. At the time, it was producing motor-driven wringer washers under the name Upton Machine, with the hope of selling them in quantities to large distributors. In 1916, the first order from Sears, Roebuck and Co. marked the beginning of an enduring relationship with Sears, which became its oldest and largest customer, representing 20% of Whirlpool's 1995 sales. In 1948, the Whirlpool brand automatic washer was introduced. This established the dual distribution system—one product line for Sears, the other for Nineteen Hundred. The Nineteen Hundred Corporation was renamed Whirlpool in 1950, and automatic dryers were added to the company's product line. In 1955, Whirlpool merged with Seeger Refrigerator Co. of St. Paul, Minnesota, and the Estate range and air conditioning divisions of R.C.A. In 1957, Whirlpool entered the foreign market through the purchase of equity interest in Multibras S.A. of Sao Paulo, Brazil, later renamed Brastemp S.A. In 1967, Whirlpool was the first competitor in the industry to take advantage of AT&T's new 800-number service and created the Cool-Line Telephone Service, which provided customers a toll-free number to call for answers to questions and help with service.

In the mid 1980s, the limited growth potential of its established markets motivated Whirlpool to undertake a major examination of the industry. Top management decided "to remain focused on major home appliances but to expand into markets not already served by Whirlpool."[9] In 1986, the KitchenAid division of Hobart Corporation was purchased from Dart & Kraft, which marked Whirlpool's entry into the upscale segment of the appliance market as well as into small appliances. In the same year, Whirlpool sold its central heating and cooling business to Inter-City Gas Corp. of Canada. In 1985 Whirlpool purchased the assets of Mastercraft Industries Corp., a Denver-based manufacturer of kitchen cabinets. A year later a second cabinet maker, St. Charles Manufacturing Co., was acquired through the newly formed Whirlpool Kitchens, Inc. However, in March 1989, Whirlpool Kitchens was sold due to lack of fit.

North American Appliance Group

The North American Appliance Group (NAAG) was formed in 1989 from operations in the United States, Canada, and Mexico (see Exhibit IC2–4). After several plant closings and a reshuffling of product lines between plants, a streamlined organization with a unified strategy was formed, originally around four brands. In 1992, Whirlpool reorganized its North American operations behind a strategy to create a "dominant consumer franchise" (DCF). For Whirlpool, a DCF existed "when consumers insist on our brands for reasons other than price, when they view our products as clearly superior to other appliances, [and] when they demonstrate strong loyalty in their future purchase decisions."[10] Such a strategy required, above all, a better understanding of consumer needs; merely improving product quality and keeping costs low was deemed necessary but not sufficient. The objective was to become more customer focused, which entailed a functional organization dealing with four core processes: product management, brand management, trade partner management, and logistics. Unlike the traditional functional organization, the new approach

EXHIBIT IC2-3

Milestones of Whirlpool's Globalization

1957 • Whirlpool invested in Brazilian appliance market through purchase of equity interest in Multibras S.A., renamed Brastemp S.A. in 1972.

1969 • Entered the Canadian appliance market through a 52% equity interest in Inglis, Ltd. Sole ownership established in 1990.

1976 • Increased investment in Brazil through purchase of equity interests in Consul S.A., an appliance manufacturer, and Embraco S.A., a maker of compressors.

1986 • Purchased majority interest in Aspera S.r.l. of Fiat S.p.A., a manufacturer of compressors, located in Turin and Riva, Italy.

1987 • Entered the Indian appliance market through TVS Whirlpool Limited, a 33% each joint venture company formed with Sundaram-Clayton Limited of Madras.
 • Ownership in Inglis, Ltd., increased to 72%.

1988 • Vitromatic, S.A. de C.V., formed with Vitro, S.A., of Monterrey, Nuevo Leon, to manufacture and market major home appliances for Mexican and export markets. Whirlpool had a 49% interest.
 • Operated a maquiladora, Componentes de Reynosa, in Reynosa, Tamaulipas, to manufacture components for final assembly in the United States.

1989 • Whirlpool and N.V. Philips of the Netherlands consummated an agreement under which Whirlpool acquired a 53% interest in a joint venture company made up of Philips's former major domestic appliance division. The new company, Whirlpool International B.V. (WIBV), was to manufacture and market appliances in Western Europe. The joint venture brand names were Bauknecht, Philips, Ignis, and Laden.
 • North American Appliance Group (NAAG) formed from streamlined U.S., Canadian, and Mexican operations.
 • Affiliates in Brazil, India, and Mexico completed construction of facilities and started producing the "world washer."

1990 • Program launched to market appliances in Europe under the dual brands Philips and Whirlpool.
 • Formed a joint venture company with Matsushita Electric Industrial Co. of Japan to produce vacuum cleaners for the North American market.
 • Created Whirlpool Overseas Corporation as a wholly-owned subsidiary to conduct industrial and marketing activities outside North America and Western Europe.
 • Inglis, Ltd., became a wholly-owned subsidiary.

1991 • Acquired remaining interest in WIBV from Philips Electronics N.V.
 • Created two new global business units: Whirlpool Compressor Operations and Whirlpool Microwave Cooking Business.

1992 • Created Whirlpool Tatramat in the Slovak Republic. Whirlpool Tatramat a.s. would manufacture clothes washers for Slovakia and neighboring countries and import other WIBV major appliances for sale.
 • Began gradual phaseout of dual-branded advertising to sole Whirlpool brand by removing the Philips name in Europe.
 • Assumed control of SAGAD S.A. of Argentina from Philips.
 • Reorganized Whirlpool Europe and changed its name from WIBV to WEBV.
 • Created a global small-appliance business unit.

1993 • Reorganized NAAG.
 • Replaced WOC with two separate regional organizations in Latin America and Asia.
 • Started implementation of a new Asian strategy with Tokyo as headquarters and regional offices in Singapore, Hong Kong, and Tokyo.
 • Opened sales subsidiaries in Greece, Poland, and the Czech Republic.
 • Inglis, Ltd., became Canada's leading home appliance manufacturer.
 • Streamlined European operations with WEBV selling its Spanish refrigerator plant to IAR/Sital of Italy.

1994 • In May Whirlpool announced joint venture with Teco Electric & Machinery Co., Ltd., of Taiwan to market and distribute home appliances in Taiwan.
 • Whirlpool became a stand-alone brand in Europe.
 • Brazilian affiliates Consul and Brastemp merged to form Multibras.
 • Acquired controlling interest in Kelvinator of India, Ltd., and assumed controlling interest in TVS Whirlpool, Ltd.
 • Asian headquarters moved to Singapore; number of regions increased from three to four.
 • Exited vacuum cleaner business by selling its minority interest in the joint venture with Matsushita.
 • Acquired majority ownership in SMC Microwave Products Co., Ltd., and Beijing Whirlpool Snowflake Electric Appliance Company, Ltd.
 • Created the Microwave Oven Business Unit as a global business unit.

1995 • Formed South American sales company.
 • New joint venture formed to produce washers called The Whirlpool Narcissus (Shanghai) Co., Ltd.
 • Acquired majority interest in Raybo Air Conditioner Manufacturing Company.
 • Obtained approval for a joint venture with Sehnzhen Petrochemical Holdings Co. to produce air conditioners.
 • Created the Global Air Treatment Unit as a global business unit.

EXHIBIT IC2–4

North American Appliance Group in Early 1996: Whirlpool Corporation

Principal Products	Major Brand Names	Principal Locations	Sales Offices
Automatic dryers	Acros[1]	**Corporate, Regional, and Research and Engineering Center**	**United States**
Automatic washers	Admiral (Canada)	Benton Harbor, Michigan	Atlanta
Built-in ovens	Chambers	**Subsidiaries**	Boston
Dehumidifiers	Crolls[1]	Inglis, Ltd., Mississauga, Ontario	Charlotte
Dishwashers	Coolerator	Whirlpool Financial Corp., Benton Harbor, Michigan	Chicago
Freezers	Estate	**Affiliate**	Dallas
Ice makers	Inglis	Vitromatic S.A. de C.V., Monterrey, Mexico	Dayton
Microwave ovens	KitchenAid	**Manufacturing Facilities**	Denver
Ranges	Roper	Benton Harbor, Michigan	Kansas City
Refrigerators	Speed Queen (Canada)	Celaya, Mexico	Knoxville
Room air conditioners	Supermatic[1]	Clyde, Ohio	Little Rock
Trash compactors	Whirlpool	Evansville, Indiana	Los Angeles
		Findlay, Ohio	Miami
		Fort Smith, Arkansas	Minneapolis
		Greenville, Ohio	New York City
		Lavergne, Tennessee	Orlando
		Marion, Ohio	Philadelphia
		Mexico City, Mexico	Pittsburgh
		Montmagny, Quebec	Santurce (Puerto Rico)
		Monterrey, Mexico	San Francisco
		Oxford, Mississippi	Seattle
		Puebla, Mexico	**Canada**
		Reynosa, Mexico	Laval, Quebec
		Tulsa, Oklahoma	Mississauga, Ontario
			Vancouver, British Columbia
			Mexico
			Guadalajara, Jalisco
			Mexico City, Distrito Federal
			Monterrey, Nuevo León

Note:
1. Affiliate owned.

employed cross-functional teams within each function with product business teams at the center.

To support its DCF strategy, Whirlpool announced a multitude of new products aimed at six discrete appliance consumer segments labeled: (1) the traditionalist, (2) the housework rebel, (3) the achiever, (4) the self-assured, (5) the proven conservative, and (6) the homebound survivor.[11] KitchenAid brand appliances were marketed to upscale consumers who looked for style and substance, typically found among achievers; Whirlpool was positioned as the brand that helped consumers manage their homes better—for instance housework rebels. Roper brand appliances were value-priced and offered basic styling and features and were a good match for the self-assured. The Estate brand line was limited to a few high-volume models and distributed through warehouse club outlets. The Kenmore Appliance Group was dedicated to serve Whirlpool's single largest customer—Sears, Roebuck and Co.

In June 1993, Whirlpool was named the winner in the $30 million Super Efficient Refrigerator Program, a success that CEO Whitwam attributed to the multidisciplinary team that had been assembled from all over the world. The SERP models eliminated CFCs completely by using a different refrigerant. Also, a different, environmentally safe blowing agent was used to expand foam insulation between the walls of the refrigerator liner and cabinet. Energy efficiency gains were achieved through better insulation, a high-efficiency compressor, and an improved condenser fan motor in conjunction with a microchip-controlled adaptive defrost control that incorporated fuzzy logic. Whirlpool had entered the SERP contest because it was consistent with the company's strategy to exceed customer expectations. Jeff Fettig, Vice-President, Group Marketing and Sales for NAAG, commented, "The SERP program allowed us to accelerate the development process and bring these products to the market sooner. Future products will be designed with these consumer expectations [regarding environmental friendliness] in mind, giving people even more reason to ask for a Whirlpool-built product next time they are in the market for a major home appliance." [12]

After an energy-efficient refrigerator with a CFC-free sealed system was launched in March 1994, the company announced that it would introduce a new clothes washer in 1996 that would use a third of the water and energy of a conventional washer. The company hoped that consumers would be willing "to pay a premium price for the new washer." [13] In its *1993 Annual Report,* Whirlpool announced that, since 1988, NAAG had increased its regional market share by nearly a third with help from Inglis, Ltd., the Canadian subsidiary, and Vitromatic S.A., the Mexican affiliate.

In late 1994, Whirlpool initiated a major restructuring initiative, closing plants and reducing headcount in an effort to reduce costs. In 1995, Montgomery Ward, the second largest home appliance retailer in the United States, became a Whirlpool customer.

Whirlpool's Globalization

In 1995, Whirlpool's efforts to establish a global presence were more than 10 years old. Already, in its *1984 Annual Report,* Whirlpool had announced that it had concluded a 2-year study and adopted a plan for the next 5 years. Among the steps mentioned were developing new international strategies and adding sound new businesses that would complement existing strengths. The strategy was based on the assumption that, in spite of the differences in

consumer habits and preferences, it was possible to gain competitive advantage by leveraging a global presence in the various regional markets. In the *1987 Annual Report,* CEO Whitwam had elaborated on the company's rationale for globalization:

> The U.S. appliance market has limited growth opportunities, a high concentration of domestic competitors and increasing foreign competition. Further, the U.S. represents only about 25% of the worldwide potential for major appliance sales.
>
> Most importantly, our vision can no longer be limited to our domestic borders because national borders no longer define market boundaries. The marketplace for products and services is more global than ever before and growing more so every day.
>
> Consumers in major industrialized countries are living increasingly similar lifestyles and have increasingly similar expectations of what consumer products must do for them. As purchasing patterns become more alike, we think that companies that operate on a broad global scale can leverage their strengths better than those which only serve an individual national market. Very likely, appliance manufacturing will always have to be done regionally. Yet the ability to leverage many of the strengths of a company on an international basis is possible only if that company operates globally. [14]

Whirlpool Trading Corporation was formed to consolidate existing international activities and explore new ventures. In January 1985, the company increased its equity interest in Inglis, which dated back to 1969, from 48% to more than 50%. In the following year, Aspera S.r.l. in Torino, Italy, a large compressor maker, was purchased from Fiat.

In the late 1950s, Whirlpool had undertaken its first expansion beyond the U.S. borders when it entered Brazil, followed by Canada in 1969 (see Exhibit IC2–3). In 1976, Whirlpool strengthened its position in Brazil. However, globalization truly took shape in the 1980s when Whirlpool added Mexico, India, and Europe through a series of joint ventures. The moves in South America and Asia were motivated by the expectation that climbing disposable incomes in these continents would result in a growing demand for appliances that would "at least partially mirror the American consumer boom of the 1950s and 1960s." [15]

Among Whirlpool's top management, David R. Whitwam was known as a champion of Whirlpool's globalization. Whitwam had succeeded Jack Sparks who had retired in 1987 after 47 years of service, including 5 as CEO. Sparks had given Whirlpool the focus it had lacked. It was not an easy task to follow in the footsteps of such a distinguished leader.

Born in Madison, Wisconsin, Whitwam graduated from the University of Wisconsin with a B.S. in economics with honors. After 8 years in the U.S. Army and the Wisconsin National Guard, he joined Whirlpool as a marketing management trainee in July 1968. One year later he was named territory sales manager for the South California sales division, and from there job descriptions did not change, only the locations. Whitwam spent time in New York and then in southern California.

Whitwam moved to corporate headquarters in 1977 when he was named Merchandising Manager for Range Products. From that post came a promotion to Director of Builder Marketing and then Vice-President, Whirlpool Sales, in 1983. In 1985, he was elected to the company's Board of Directors. On December 1, 1987, he assumed his current position as President, CEO, and Chairman of the Board of Whirlpool Corporation. Since then, he has transformed a domestically oriented $4 billion company into an $8 billion global force. Whirlpool's Corporate Vision, which was displayed in many of its publications and throughout its facilities, clearly communicated this orientation:

> Whirlpool, in its chosen lines of business, will grow with new opportunities and be the leader in an ever-changing global market. We will be driven by our commitment to continuous quality improvement and to exceeding all of our customers' expectations. We will gain competitive advantage through this, and by building on our existing strengths and developing new competencies. We will be market driven, efficient and profitable. Our success will make Whirlpool a company that worldwide customers, employees and other stakeholders can depend on.

Whirlpool Europe B.V.

Among those most strongly convinced of the promise of the European market was David Whitwam: "The only people who say you can't have a pan-European brand are the people who don't have one themselves." [16] On August 18, 1988, Whirlpool announced a joint venture with N.V. Philips, the second largest appliance manufacturer in Europe behind Electrolux with a broad presence in many markets throughout Europe and Latin America. The deal was for a 53% interest in Philips's worldwide Major Domestic Appliance Division for $361 million in cash; the new company was called Whirlpool International B.V. In July 1991, Whirlpool exercised its option to purchase from Philips the remaining interest in WIBV and changed the name to Whirlpool Europe B.V. (WEBV) (see Exhibit IC2–5). By 1994, with 13% market share, WEBV occupied the third position in

Europe behind Electrolux (25%) and Bosch Siemens (15%). For financial information see Exhibits IC2–6 and IC2–7.

Soon after the formation of WIBV, Philips's decentralized organization was phased out and WIBV was split into customer-focused business units. Brands were positioned to fit the niches and conditions in Europe, an approach employed earlier in the United States. Bauknecht—Philips's most profitable brand—was aimed at the high end of the market, the dual-branded Philips/Whirlpool at the middle, and Ignis at the lower end. Later, in 1995, Whirlpool terminated its successful brand-transfer effort that had cost $110 million and dropped the Philips brand name. The Bauknecht and Philips/Whirlpool Appliance Groups received the centralized sales and marketing functions, respectively, which supported all of Whirlpool's European brands. National sales subsidiaries were consolidated into three sales regions to take advantage of the growing European cross-border trade. The marketing function included separate, brand-oriented components to strengthen brand identity while at the same time ensuring coordination internally. Manufacturing and technology activities were reorganized around product groups and development centers, with Germany focusing on laundry and dishwashing products and Italy on refrigeration and cooking. Key support functions (consumer services, information technology, logistics, and planning) were maintained as separate, centrally managed entities. Distribution was reconfigured toward a pan-European approach, and 10 of 28 finished goods warehouses were closed. Explained WEBV president Hank Bowman, "The idea is to put systems support in place so we can deliver products more accurately and in a more timely manner." [17] WEBV also assumed responsibility for the Middle East and Africa, which accounted for $100 million in sales, mainly in the form of kits in an attempt to boost local content and thus preempt the emergence of domestic-content rules. In late 1994, yet another reorganization was started to streamline operations on a pan-European basis in conjunction with similar efforts in North America in the hope of achieving annual cost savings of about $150 million, starting in 1997.

In 1992, WIBV started a 4-year effort to redesign its products to increase manufacturing efficiency, improve product quality, and increase customer satisfaction. The goal was to renew the entire product line by 1996. Whirlpool had identified what it called a "value gap" in Europe. When benchmarking the European industry's performance against best-in-class North American and Asian players, managers found that European producers delivered significantly lower levels of customer satisfaction. Also, Europeans paid more

EXHIBIT IC2-5

Europe B.V. in 1996: Whirlpool Corporation

Principal Products	Major Brand Names	Principal Locations
Automatic dryers	Bauknecht	**European Operations Center**
Automatic washers	Ignis	Comerio, Italy
Dishwashers	Laden	**Subsidiaries**
Freezers	Whirlpool	Whirlpool Europe B.V., Eindhoven, Netherlands
Microwave ovens		Whirlpool Tatramat a.s., Poprad, Slovakia
Ranges		**Manufacturing Facilities**
Refrigerators		Amiens, France
		Calw, Germany
		Cassinetta, Italy
		Naples, Italy
		Neunkirchen, Germany
		Norrköping, Sweden
		Poprad, Slovakia
		Schorndorf, Germany
		Siena, Italy
		Trento, Italy
		Sales Offices
		Athens, Greece
		Barcelona, Spain
		Brussels, Belgium
		Budapest, Hungary
		Comerio, Italy
		Dublin, Ireland
		Eindhoven, Netherlands
		Espoo, Finland
		Herlev, Denmark
		Lenzburg, Switzerland
		Lisbon, Portugal
		London, United Kingdom
		Moscow, Russia
		Oslo, Norway
		Paris, France
		Poprad, Slovak Republic
		Prague, Czech Republic
		Stockholm, Sweden
		Stuttgart, Germany
		Vienna, Austria
		Warsaw, Poland

EXHIBIT IC2-6

Business Unit Revenues and Operating Profit: Whirlpool Corporation (Dollar amounts in millions)

Year Ending December 31	1995	1994	1993
Revenues			
North America	$5,093	$5,048	$4,559
Europe	2,502	2,373	2,225
Latin America	271	329	303
Asia	376	205	151
Other	(5)	(6)	130
Total appliance business	$8,163	$7,949	$7,368
Operating Profit			
North America	$ 445	$ 522	$ 474
Europe	92	163	139
Latin America	26	49	43
Asia	(50)	(22)	(5)
Restructuring[1]	—	(248)	(23)
Business dispositions[2]	—	60	(8)
Other	(147)	(154)	(116)
Total appliance business	$366	$370	$504

Notes:

1. Consolidation and reorganization of European and North American operations in 1993 and 1994 and closure of two North American manufacturing facilities in 1994.

2. In 1994, the minority interest in Matsushita Floor Care Company was sold, as were the European compressor operations (to its Brazilian affiliate Embraco) and its refrigerator plant in Barcelona.

for their appliances than did their U.S. counterparts. Explained Ivan Menezes, Vice-President, Group Marketing, WEBV, "When Whirlpool first came to Europe, the typical appliance cost 50 percent to 100 percent more in terms of daily income. In the U.S., for example, a typical consumer could, in 1991, earn the necessary dollars for a dishwasher in 3.8 days, whereas in Europe, it would have taken 7.5 days. Today that gap has closed by 15 percent to 20 percent for all appliances." [18]

A global outlook was forged in the management team. Managers were rotated between Europe and the United States to foster global thinking. The first time this move paid off was in 1991 when the VIP Crisp microwave oven, developed by a new "advanced global technology unit" in Norrköping, Sweden, was introduced and quickly became Europe's best-selling model. The VIP Crisp had a heated base plate that allows Italians to bake crisp pizza crusts and

the British to fry eggs. Subsequently, the company started to import the VIP Crisp to the United States.

WEBV also made a series of moves to establish itself in the emerging markets of Central and Eastern Europe, which in 1991 represented about 11% of the world appliance market and promised attractive growth opportunities over the long term. Bauknecht was the first to set up a distribution system in East Germany after the opening of the border. In early 1992, WEBV developed distribution networks in the entire region and established a wholly-owned sales subsidiary in Hungary. In May 1992, Whirlpool took a 43.8% minority investment in Whirlpool/Tatramat a.s., a joint venture in the Slovak Republic, which manufactured and sold automatic washers and marketed products assembled at other WEBV locations. In 1994, WEBV took a controlling interest in this joint venture. A year earlier, sales subsidiaries had been opened in Poland and the Czech Republic, adding

INTEGERATIVE CASES

EXHIBIT IC2–7

Business Segment Information: Whirlpool Corporation
(Dollar amounts in millions)

Segment	North America	Europe	Other and (Eliminations)
Net Sales			
1995	$5,093	$2,502	$ 586
1994	5,048	2,451	450
1993	4,547	2,410	411
1992	4,471	2,645	185
1991	4,224	2,479	54
1990	4,157	2,405	43
Operating Profit			
1995	$ 314	$ 90	$ (38)
1994	311	43	16
1993	341	129	34
1992	359	101	19
1991	314	82	(3)
1990	269	86	(6)
Identifiable Assets			
1995	$2,031	$2,104	$2,033
1994	2,046	1,824	1,410
1993	1,742	1,758	1,154
1992	3,511	1,917	690
1991	3,672	2,284	489
1990	3,216	1,905	493
Depreciation Expense			
1995	$ 140	$ 105	$ 8
1994	141	98	4
1993	137	101	1
1992	142	132	1
1991	129	104	—
1990	140	107	—
Net Capital Expenditures			
1995	$ 262	$ 186	$ 29
1994	269	135	12
1993	188	116	3
1992	174	111	3
1991	183	104	—
1990	158	106	1

to WEBV's position in Eastern Europe, and Greece in South-eastern Europe, followed by Russia in 1995. Expansions into Romania and Bulgaria were planned for 1996.

Latin American Appliance Group

Whirlpool's foray overseas started in Latin America when, in 1958, the company purchased equity interest in Multibras S.A. of Brazil, a manufacturer of major appliances. Whirlpool's strategy in Latin America called for taking full advantage of this large emerging market by optimally positioning its brands across the entire spectrum, based on in-depth consumer research in an attempt to cultivate "customers for life."

In the crucial Brazilian market, which accounted for about half of all appliances sold in Latin America in 1994, Whirlpool held equity positions in three Brazilian companies: (1) Multibras, which in 1994 merged three sister appliance makers into one organization and with annual sales of $800 million held the market leader position in Brazil; (2) Embraco, which was one of the world's largest manufacturers of compressors and exported to 50 countries on four continents; and (3) Brasmotor S.A., which was a holding company with a majority interest in Multibras and a minority interest in Embraco. Whirlpool claimed that, based on its own research, it had the second highest brand recognition after Coca-Cola.

In January 1992, Whirlpool strengthened its position in South America by taking over control of SAGAD, Philips's white goods operation in Argentina. Except for Brazil and Argentina, the South American Sales Company, a subsidiary of LAAG, was responsible for sales throughout the region.

Originally, Whirlpool's Latin American operations were part of the Whirlpool Overseas Corporation (WOC), formed in Spring 1990 as a wholly-owned subsidiary to conduct marketing and industrial activities outside North America and Europe. It included U.S. Export Sales, the Overseas Business Group acquired from Philips in the WIBV transaction, and three wholly-owned sales companies in Hong Kong, Thailand, and Australia. Industrial activities encompassed technology sale and transfer, kit and component sales, joint venture manufacturing, and project management for affiliates.

Key responsibilities of WOC also included feeding new technologies from Whirlpool's bases in North America and Europe to its other units; ensuring optimal brand positioning in each country and analyzing specific appliance design for their suitability to various markets. Conditions could vary greatly from country to country. For instance, the company

sold so-called giant ovens in Africa and the Middle East. These ovens were 39 in. and 42 in. wide compared to the standard 30 in. size in the United States and were large enough to roast a sheep or goat.

In 1993, after exhaustive and detailed analysis of world markets, the company decided that its global business interests would be better served by establishing two stand-alone business units, one for Latin America called LAAG, and the other the Whirlpool Asian Appliance Group for Whirlpool's Asian operations. (See Exhibits IC2–8 and IC2–9.)

Whirlpool Asian Appliance Group

When Whirlpool began to pursue perceived business opportunities in Asia, it was not new to the market. It had exported home appliances to the region for over 30 years from the United States. Thanks to the acquisition of Philips's appliance business, it gained broadened access to Asian markets. However, Whirlpool realized that a viable position in Asia implied more than selling imports from NAAG and WEBV, having kits assembled by licensees, or by having appliances built to specification by local manufacturers.

Whirlpool's Asian strategy rested on the "Five Ps"—*partnerships, products, processes, people,* and a *pan-Asian*

EXHIBIT IC2–8

Latin American Appliance Group in 1996: Whirlpool Corporation

Principal Products	Major Brand Names	Principal Locations
Automatic washers	Brastemp[1]	**Regional Headquarters**
Dishwashers	Consul[1]	Sao Paulo, Brazil
Dryers	Eslabon de Lujo	**Subsidiaries**
Freezers	Semer[1]	Latin American Sales and Service Company, Miami
Microwave ovens	Whirlpool	
Ranges		South American Sales Company, Grand Cayman
Refrigerators		
Room air conditioners		Whirlpool Argentina S.A., Buenos Aires, Argentina

Note:
1. Affiliate owned.

EXHIBIT IC2-9

Asian Appliance Group in 1996: Whirlpool Corporation

Principal Products	Major Brand Names	Principal Locations
Automatic washers Microwave ovens Refrigerators Room air conditioners	Bauknecht Ignis KitchenAid Raybo Roper Whirlpool **Under license** Kelvinator (India) Narcissus SMC Snowflake TVS	**Regional Headquarters and Technology Center** Singapore **Regional Offices** Hong Kong New Delhi, India Singapore **Subsidiaries** Beijing Whirlpool Snowflake Electric Appliance Co., Ltd., Beijing Kelvinator of India, New Delhi, India Whirlpool Narcissus (Shanghai) Co., Ltd., Shanghai, China Whirlpool Washing Machines, Ltd., Madras, India **Affiliates** Great Teco Whirlpool, Ltd., Taipei, Taiwan Beijing Embraco Snowflake Compressor Co., Ltd., Beijing, China **Manufacturing Facilities** Beijing, China Faridabad, India Pondicherry, India Shanghai, China Shenzhen, China Shunde, China **Sales Offices:** Auckland, New Zealand Bangkok, Thailand Guanzhow, China Ho Chi Minh City, Vietnam Hong Kong New Delhi, India Noble Park, Australia Petaling Jaya, Malaysia Shanghai, China Seoul, South Korea Singapore Tokyo, Japan

approach. The strategy was broken into three phases: start-up, building, and market leadership. Based on extensive market research, Whirlpool decided to base its foray into Asia on four specific appliance products—the so-called "T–4" of refrigerators, clothes washers, microwave ovens, and air conditioners. For a household with no appliances, a refrigerator was usually the first appliance purchased when incomes rose. A clothes washer came next. Air conditioners were important because of the prevailing heat and humidity in much of the region. Microwave ovens had become a truly global appliance with essentially standardized features and design. Whirlpool focused its efforts on China and India, the most populous countries. Market entry was supposed to occur through joint ventures, to be followed later by "greenfield" plants. Based on commonalties identified in the region, Whirlpool planned to use a pan-Asian platform, modified for specific areas to meet regional preferences. In contrast to other regions, only one brand name—Whirlpool—would be used since the market was not considered mature enough to allow for a multibrand approach.

In 1987, Whirlpool created a joint venture in India with Sundaram-Clayton, Ltd., called TVS Whirlpool, Ltd., which began producing semiautomatic clothes washers, the so-called "World Washer," and twin-tub washers for the Indian market.

Whirlpool's Asian expansion gained momentum in 1993 with the creation of the Whirlpool Asian Appliance Group (WAAG) (Exhibit IC2–9) supported by a $10-million investment. A regional headquarters was established in Tokyo and later moved to Singapore, which also became the home of a pan-Asian marketing, product development, and technology center. The Asian market was further subdivided first into three, then four, operating regions: Greater China, based in Hong Kong (Peoples Republic and Hong Kong); South Asia, based in Delhi (India, Pakistan, and surrounding markets); North Asia, based in Tokyo (Japan, Korea, the Philippines, and Taiwan), and Southeast Asia, based in Singapore (Australia and New Zealand).

In 1994, Whirlpool's investment in Asia jumped to over $200 million. The company announced a joint venture with Teco Electric & Machinery Co., Ltd., to market and distribute home appliances in Taiwan as an insider. In February 1995, Whirlpool acquired a controlling interest in Kelvinator of India, Ltd., one of the largest manufacturers and marketers of refrigerators in that country. Also, Whirlpool obtained a controlling interest and day-to-day management of its existing Indian-based venture, TVS Whirlpool, Ltd. In its *1995 Annual Report,* the company announced that in the forthcoming year it would create an efficient, customer-responsive "Whirlpool of India" organization.

Also, China became the center of a series of joint ventures combined with plant expansions and upgrades. These moves marked an important milestone in that they completed Whirlpool's T–4 strategy in China (see Exhibit IC2–9).

Essential for the long-term strategy was the creation of a technology center in Singapore where a new generation of products would be designed for the Asian market and which could tap into Whirlpool's global expertise. As in Latin America, the Worldwide Excellence System was adapted to regional circumstances and provided a strong integrating mechanism. To accelerate the process, Whirlpool assembled global product teams, offered foreign assignments within the global organization to key personnel, and started hiring aggressively within the region.

ORCHESTRATING THE STRATEGY GLOBALLY

Even though Whirlpool by the end of 1995 was a global force, its U.S. exports were less than 10% of gross revenues. As Whirlpool expanded its geographic reach (see Exhibit IC2–10), it became crucial for the company to lay the groundwork for utilizing effectively its experience worldwide in product technology and manufacturing processes and transferring it quickly to wherever it was needed and thereby leverage its global presence to gain sustainable competitive advantage. For this purpose, a number of projects and organizational functions and arrangements were put in place.

Global Business Units

Two product groups were managed and organized on a global platform. The Microwave Oven Business Unit managed microwave oven production and development activities globally with manufacturing and product development facilities in Norrköping, Sweden, and a second, low-cost source in development in Shunde, China. Whirlpool claimed that once the Shunde facility started operating, it would be one of the world's top five microwave oven manufacturers.

In late 1995, Whirlpool created the Global Air Treatment Unit, which relied on the LaVergne Division in Tennessee and Shenzhen Whirlpool Raybo Air-Conditioner Industrial Co., Ltd., which had become part of the Company a few months before. An aggressive growth strategy had been formulated that anticipated quadrupling volume in the first half of 1996 relative to the same period a year earlier.

In addition, Whirlpool Financial Corporation, established in 1957, served manufacturers, retailers, and consumers in the United States, Canada, and Europe. With assets

EXHIBIT IC2–10

Changes in Global Presence, 1988–1995: Whirlpool Corporation

	1988	1995
Revenues	$4.41 billion	$8.35 billion
Market position	Leader in North America; affiliates in Brazil, Canada, India, and Mexico	No.1 in North America, No.1 in Latin America, No.3 in Europe, Largest Western appliance company in Asia
Manufacturing locations (including affiliates)	4	12
Brands (including affiliates)	14	28
Market presence	—	>140 (in more than 140 countries)
Employees	29,110	45,435

exceeding $1.9 billion in 1995, it provided inventory and consumer financing to support product sales from the point of manufacture through the market channel to the consumer.

The World Washer

The "World Washer" represented an effort to create a lightweight compact washer with few parts that could be produced in developing countries where manufacturing technology was not advanced and could be sold at a price that put it within reach of many more households than the designs marketed in the industrialized world. The goal of the World Washer effort was to develop a complete product, process, and facility design package versatile enough to satisfy conditions and market requirements in various countries but with low initial investment requirements. At the same time, the World Washer was to establish a beachhead especially against the Far Eastern rivals. Not everybody in the industry shared Whirlpool's vision of global products. Commented Lawrence A. Johnson, a corporate officer of General Electric's Appliance Division, "We're not in an industry where global products work well. ... There is also no such thing as a global brand, and it's unlikely that there will be. It's hard to change decades of brand commitment." [19]

As the name indicated, a common design was envisaged for India, Brazil, and Mexico where the washer was to be produced and marketed. Originally the plan was to replicate the project design in each of the three countries. It

eventually proved necessary to develop three slightly different variations. Costs also varied widely, further affecting both product and process decisions. "In India, for example, material costs may run as much as 200 to 800 percent higher than elsewhere, while labor and overhead costs are comparatively minimal," added Lawrence J. Kremer, Senior Vice-President, Global Technology and Operations. [20]

The plants also varied subtly from each other, although the goals were identical—minimizing facility investment and avoiding big finish systems and welding stations that required extensive machinery for materials cleanup and environmental safety. In Brazil the plant was designed as a creative convection cooling system to address the high humidity and constructed of precast concrete. In India, the new facility was built in Pondicherry, just 12° north of the equator. Although the plant looked similar to the one in Brazil—except for the overhead fans—the method of construction was different. Concrete was hand mixed on location, then carried in wicker baskets to forms constructed next to the building site. The Indian construction crew cast the concrete, allowed it to cure, and then five or six men raised each 3-ton slab into place using chain, block, and tackle.

Worldwide Excellence System

Established in 1991, the Worldwide Excellence System (WES) was the company's blueprint for how it approached quality, customers, and continuous improvement world-

EXHIBIT IC2–11

Worldwide Excellence System: Whirlpool Corporation

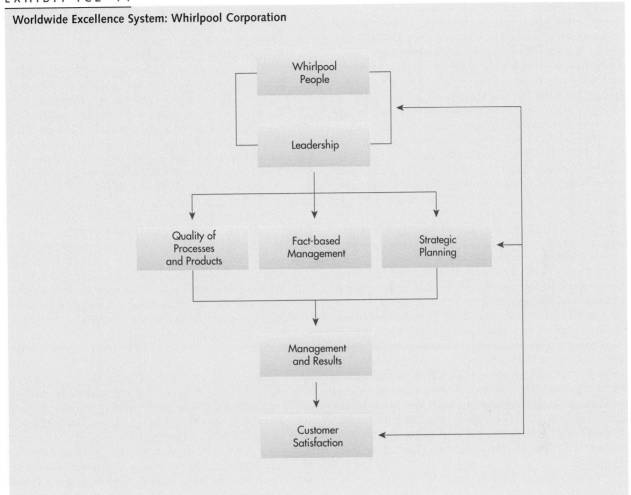

wide. WES combined elements of other well-known quality systems: ISO 9000, the Deming approach used in Asia, and the Baldrige system used in the United States. Like the Baldrige system, WES used a point system to measure success of implementing the program. WES had seven categories (see Exhibit IC2–11). The Whirlpool People and Leadership categories described the involvement of people at all levels in moving the corporation to excellence. Fact-Based Management, Strategic Planning, and Quality of Process and Products outlined the major internal processes for achieving excellence. Measurement and Results explained the methods used to determine what customers

expected and to assess how well they were being satisfied. The continuous monitoring of Customer Satisfaction was used for unending improvement of activities and processes.

Technology Organization

Several of Whirlpool's functions were organized to take advantage of the company's technical know-how scattered around the globe. The goal was to develop advanced, innovative products and move them to market quickly and competitively. As mentioned previously, an early success in this area occurred in late 1991 when the VIP Crisp microwave oven, developed in Norrköping, Sweden, was introduced and quickly became Europe's best-selling model.

A Global Procurement organization bought all materials and components needed by the company's appliance production facilities. From procurement centers in the United States, Italy, and Singapore, it bought finished products, commodities sourced on a regional or global basis, and standardized parts and components. Most other parts and materials were sourced from suppliers located near the production facilities where they were used. In developing countries, this often implied educating and assisting local suppliers in attaining Whirlpool standards.

The Corporate Technology Development group developed product and process technology capabilities and provided technical services to Whirlpool businesses. Although centrally managed from the corporation's technology center in Benton Harbor, technology development activities were geographically dispersed in Europe, Asia, and North America.

An Advanced Product Concepts unit looked beyond current product needs for appliances Whirlpool was making. It was responsible for developing new product concepts that were identified through market research.

The Advanced Manufacturing Concepts team was responsible for bringing new manufacturing processes into the corporation and identifying and developing simulation tools and best practices to be used on a global basis.

A Strategic Assessment and Support organization identified and evaluated non-traditional new product opportunities in cooperation with other units of Whirlpool. It also established corporate policy regarding product safety and computer-aided design and manufacturing; it addressed environmental and regulatory issues and intellectual property rights.

THE RACE FOR GLOBAL DOMINANCE

Whirlpool was by no means alone in its efforts to establish a global position of strength. Everybody in the industry was pursuing similar strategies. Electrolux, the leader in Europe, continued to expand aggressively, using its strong pan-European and local brands. Plans included establishing market share leadership in Central and Eastern Europe by the year 2000. A $100 million investment in China included a joint venture to manufacture water purifiers, another for compressors, and a vacuum-cleaner plant. Vacuum-cleaner manufacturing capacity was also increased in South Africa. In India, Electrolux established itself through acquisitions of majority holdings in production facilities for refrigerators and washing machines. In Thailand, Indonesia, Malaysia, and Singapore, the Swedish giant rapidly developed a strong position through a network of retailers. In Latin America, the company recently had acquired a minority interest in Brazil's second-largest white goods manufacturer, Refripar.

Besides trying to strengthen its position in North America through its alliance with Maytag where it hoped to sell its distinctively European designs beyond the export of 40,000 dishwashers, Bosch-Siemens Hausgeräte GmbH (BSHG) also vied for a larger share in other regions. In China, BSHG had acquired a majority interest in Wuxi Little Swan Co., a leading manufacturer of laundry appliances. In Brazil, BSHG had purchased Continental 2001, a large appliance producer with sales of $294 million. In Eastern Europe, it had recently completed the construction of a washing machine factory in Lodz, Poland.

General Electric Appliances, a $6 billion giant in 1994, was also working hard to establish itself as a global player: "We're focusing our efforts on the world's fastest growing markets, including India, China, Southeast Asia, and South America. . . . We're also strengthening our alliances in Mexico and India, and we developed a number of new products specifically for global markets," explained J. Richard Stonesifer, GEA's President and CEO.[21]

EPILOGUE

For fiscal year 1995, Whirlpool reported per share earnings of $2.80, up from a year earlier but still below the 1993 high. For a summary of financial results see Exhibits IC2–12, IC2–13, and IC2–14. A combination of events and trends had contributed to these results. First, in North America, product shipments had declined by 1.4% and operating profits had dropped by 16%. In Europe, rising raw material costs, fierce competition, and a shift by consumers to cheaper brands and models reduced Whirlpool's shipments by 2% while the industry grew by 1%. Volume in Latin America was up thanks to robust growth in Brazil in contrast to Argentina where industry shipments plummeted by as much as 50% because of the Mexican collapse. Whirlpool Asia reported an operating loss due to continuing expansion while shipments increased by 193% and revenues by 83%, respectively. David Whitwam said that the company was ahead of schedule in its restructuring effort in Europe and North America and that he anticipated significant improvements in operating efficiency for 1996. Evidently, Whirlpool felt good about its position in the industry, as indicated by the quote in his 1995 Letter to Shareholders, in spite of the lackluster short-term results.

EXHIBIT IC2–12

Eleven-Year Consolidated Financial Review: Whirlpool Corporation (Dollar amounts in millions, except per-share data)

Year Ending December 31	1995	1994	1993	1992	1991	1990	1989	1988	1987	1986	1985	1984
Consolidated Operations												
Net sales	$8,163	$7,949	$7,368	$7,097	$6,550	$6,424	$6,138	$4,306	$4,104	$3,928	$3,465	$3,128
Financial services	184	155	165	204	207	181	136	107	94	76	67	63
Total revenues	$8,347	$8,104	$7,533	$7,301	$6,757	$6,605	$6,274	$4,413	$4,198	$4,004	$3,532	$3,191
Operating profit	$ 396	$ 397	$ 482	$ 479	$ 393	$ 349	$ 411	$ 261	$296	$326	$295	$288
Earnings from continuing operations before income taxes and other items	242	292	375	372	304	220	308	233	280	329	321	326
Earnings from continuing operations before accounting change	209	158	231	205	170	72	187	161	187	202	182	190
Net earnings	209	158	51	205	170	72	187	94	192	200	182	190
Net capital expenditures	480	418	309	288	287	265	208	166	223	217	178	135
Depreciation	282	246	241	275	233	247	222	143	133	120	89	72
Dividends paid	100	90	85	77	76	76	76	76	79	76	73	73
Consolidated Financial Position												
Current assets	$3,541	$3,078	$2,708	$2,740	$2,920	$2,900	$2,889	$1,827	$1,690	$1,654	$1,410	$1,302
Current liabilities	3,829	2,988	2,763	2,887	2,931	2,651	2,251	1,374	1,246	1,006	781	671
Working capital	(288)	90	(55)	(147)	(11)	249	638	453	444	648	629	632
Property, plant and equipment—net	1,779	1,440	1,319	1,325	1,400	1,349	1,288	820	779	677	514	398
Total assets	7,800	6,655	6,047	6,118	6,445	5,614	5,354	3,410	3,137	2,856	2,207	1,901
Long-term debt	983	885	840	1,215	1,528	874	982	474	367	298	125	91
Total debt—appliance business	1,635	965	850	1,198	1,330	1,026	1,125	441	383	194	64	53
Shareholders' equity	1,877	1,723	1,648	1,600	1,515	1,424	1,421	1,321	1,304	1,350	1,207	1,096
Per Share Data												
Earnings from continuing operations before accounting change	$2.80	$2.10	$3.19	$2.90	$2.45	$1.04	$2.70	$2.33	$2.61	$2.72	$2.49	$2.59
Net earnings	2.80	2.10	0.67	2.90	2.45	1.04	2.70	1.36	2.68	2.70	2.49	2.59
Dividends	1.36	1.22	1.19	1.10	1.10	1.10	1.10	1.10	1.10	1.03	1.00	1.00
Book value	25.08	22.83	22.80	22.67	21.78	20.51	20.49	19.06	18.83	18.21	16.46	14.97
Closing stock price—NYSE	53¼	50¼	66½	44⅝	38⅞	23½	33	24¾	24⅜	33⅞	24 11/16	23¼

EXHIBIT IC2-13

Income Statement: Whirlpool Corporation (Dollar amounts in millions, except per-share data)

Year Ending December 31	Whirlpool Corporation (Consolidated)			Supplemental Consolidating Data Whirlpool with WFC on an Equity Basis			Whirlpool Financial Corporation (WFC)		
	1995	1994	1993	1995	1994	1993	1995	1994	1993
Revenues									
Net sales	$8,163	$7,949	$7,368	$8,163	$7,949	$7,368	$—	$—	$—
Financial services	184	155	165	—	—	—	219	184	193
	8,347	8,104	7,533	8,163	7,949	7,368	219	184	193
Expenses									
Cost of products sold	6,245	5,952	5,503	6,245	5,952	5,503	—	—	—
Selling and administrative	1,609	1,490	1,433	1,521	1,415	1,305	123	104	155
Financial services interest	66	51	59	—	—	—	79	63	72
Intangible amortization	31	24	25	31	24	25	—	—	—
Gain on dispositions	—	(60)	—	—	(60)	—	—	—	—
Restructuring costs	—	250	31	—	248	31	—	2	—
	7,951	7,707	7,051	7,797	7,579	6,864	202	169	227
Operating profit (Loss)	396	397	482	366	370	504	17	15	(34)
Other income (expense)									
Interest and sundry	(13)	9	6	(23)	3	19	11	8	(9)
Interest expense	(141)	(114)	(113)	(129)	(104)	(105)	—	—	—
Earnings (loss) before income taxes, other items, and accounting change	242	292	375	214	269	418	28	23	(43)
Income taxes	100	176	148	90	169	167	10	7	(19)
Earnings (loss) before equity earnings, minority interests, and accounting change	142	116	227	124	100	251	18	16	(24)
Equity in WFC	—	—	—	14	11	(28)	—	—	—
Equity in affiliated companies	72	59	16	72	59	16	—	—	—
Minority interests	(5)	(17)	(12)	(1)	(12)	(10)	(4)	(5)	(2)
Net earnings (loss) before cumulative effect of accounting change	209	158	231	209	158	229	14	11	(26)
Cumulative effect of accounting change for postretirement benefits	—	—	(180)	—	—	(178)	—	—	(2)
Net earnings (loss)	$ 209	$ 158	$ 51	$ 209	$ 158	$ 51	$ 14	$ 11	$(28)
Per share of common stock									
Primary earnings before accounting change	2.80	2.10	3.19						
Primary earnings	2.80	2.10	0.67						
Fully diluted earnings before accounting change	2.76	2.09	3.11						
Fully diluted earnings	2.76	2.09	0.67						
Cash dividends	1.36	1.22	1.19						
Average number of common shares outstanding (millions)	74.8	75.5	72.3						

Source: Whirlpool Corporation, 1995 Annual Report, p. 37.

Balance Sheet: Whirlpool Corporation
(Dollar amounts in millions)

| | Whirlpool Corporation (Consolidated) | | Supplemental Consolidating Data | | | |
| | | | Whirlpool with WFC on an Equity Basis | | Whirlpool Financial Corporation (WFC) | |
Year Ending December 31	1995	1994	1995	1994	1995	1994
Assets						
Current assets						
Cash and equivalents	$ 149	$ 72	$ 125	$ 51	$ 24	$ 21
Trade receivables, less allowances of $39 in 1995 and $38 in 1994	1,031	1,001	1,031	1,001	—	—
Financing receivables and leases, less allowances	1,086	866	—	—	1,086	866
Inventories	1,029	838	1,029	838	—	—
Prepaid expenses and other	152	197	141	183	11	14
Deferred income taxes	94	104	94	104	—	—
Total current assets	3,541	3,078	2,420	2,177	1,121	901
Other assets						
Investment in affiliated companies	425	370	425	370	—	—
Investment in WFC	—	—	269	253	—	—
Financing receivables and leases, less allowances	772	717	—	—	772	717
Intangibles, net	931	730	931	730	—	—
Deferred income taxes	153	171	153	171	—	—
Other	199	149	199	149	—	—
	2,480	2,137	1,977	1,673	772	717
Property, plant and equipment						
Land	97	73	97	73	—	—
Buildings	710	610	710	610	—	—
Machinery and equipment	2,855	2,418	2,831	2,392	24	26
Accumulated depreciation	(1,883)	(1,661)	(1,867)	(1,645)	(16)	(16)
	1,779	1,440	1,771	1,430	8	10
Total assets	$7,800	$6,655	$6,168	$5,280	$1,901	$1,628
Liabilities and Shareholders' Equity						
Current liabilities						
Notes payable	$ 1,939	$ 1,162	$ 709	$ 226	$ 1,230	$ 936
Accounts payable	977	843	896	795	81	48
Employee compensation	232	201	222	192	10	9
Accrued expenses	552	629	552	620	—	9
Restructuring costs	70	114	70	112	—	2
Current maturities of long-term debt	59	39	56	36	3	3
Total current liabilities	3,829	2,988	2,505	1,981	1,324	1,007
Other liabilities						
Deferred income taxes	234	221	114	110	120	111
Postemployment benefits	517	481	517	481	—	—
Other liabilities	181	262	181	262	—	—
Long-term debt	983	885	870	703	113	182
	1,915	1,849	1,682	1,556	233	293
Minority interests	179	95	104	20	75	75
Shareholders' equity						
Common stock, $1 par value: 250 million shares authorized, 81 million and 80 million shares issued in 1995 and 1994	81	80	81	80	8	8
Paid-in capital	229	214	229	214	26	26
Retained earnings	1,863	1,754	1,863	1,754	234	220
Unearned restricted stock	(8)	(8)	(8)	(8)	—	—
Cumulative translation adjustments	(53)	(93)	(53)	(93)	1	(1)
Treasury stock - 6 million shares at cost in 1995 and 1994	(235)	(224)	(235)	(224)	—	—
Total shareholders' equity	1,877	1,723	1,877	1,723	269	253
Total liabilities and shareholders' equity	$ 7,800	$ 6,655	$ 6,168	$ 5,280	$ 1,901	$ 1,628

Source: Whirlpool Corporation, 1995 Annual Report, pp. 38–39.

CASE QUESTIONS

1. Do a SWOT analysis of Whirlpool at the time of the case.
2. What are the major strategic factors facing Whirlpool?
3. What are the foundations of Whirlpool's competitive advantage? Why was Whirlpool able to go from a position of "one in the pack" to that of a leader in its industry?
4. Have Whirlpool's core competences changed over time? How?
5. Discuss Whirlpool's strategic approach to worldwide expansion. Does it make sense? Are alternative approaches more appropriate? What are the benefits? Risks?
6. Why are Whirlpool's microwave oven and air conditioners configured as global business units and not integrated into the regional structure?
7. Is Whirlpool's assertion of the strategic advantages of being a global competitor justified?
8. Since Whirlpool seems to be convinced of the necessity of becoming a global player, how important is it to be a first mover?
9. Is CEO Whitwam right when he claims that the U.S. and European white goods industries are very similar?
10. What are the reasons for the mergers and acquisitions in the U.S. and European appliance industry?
11. Should Whirlpool be happy with its acquisition of Philips's home appliance business? Did Whirlpool overpay?
12. How satisfied should Mr. Whitwam be with his company's progress in Asia?
13. What do you think that Whirlpool should do next now that it is present in all major regions of the world?

CASE BIBLIOGRAPHY

A. M. "Fleet of Foot." *Appliance Manufacturer* (May 1994), pp. 35–38.
Appliance (June 1991).
"A Portrait of the U.S. Appliance Industry 1992." *Appliance* (September 1992).
Appliance Manufacturer (February 1990), pp. 36–37.
Babyak, R. J. "Strategic Imperative." *Appliance Manufacturer*, Special section (February 1995), pp. 19–24.
Botskor, I., M. Chaouli, and B. Müller. "Boom mit Grauwerten." *Wirtschaftswoche* (May 28, 1993), pp. 64–75.
Bower, J. L., and N. Dossabhoy. "Note on the Major Home Appliance Industry in 1984 (Condensed). Case #385–211, Harvard Business School (mimeo).
Bray, H. "Plugging into the World." *Detroit Free Press* (May 17, 1993), pp. 10F–11F.
Bylinsky, G. "Computers That Learn By Doing." *Fortune* (September 6, 1993), pp. 96–102.
DuPont, T. "The Appliance Giant Has a New President and a Global Vision." *The Weekly Home Furnishings Newspaper* (July 2, 1987), p. 1.
DuPont, T. "Whirlpool's New Brand Name." *The Weekly Home Furnishings Newspaper* (April 11, 1988).
Echikson, W. "The Trick to Selling in Europe." *Fortune* (September 20, 1993), p. 82.
Fisher, J. D. "Home Appliance Industry." *Value Line* (December 22, 1989), p. 132.
Ghoshal, S., and P. Haspeslagh. "The Acquisition and Integration of Zanussi by Electrolux: A Case Study.," *European Management Journal* (December 1990), pp. 414–433.
Hunger, D. J. "The Major Home Appliance Industry in 1990: From U.S. to Global." (mimeo, 1990).
Jackson, T. "European Competition Hurts Whirlpool." *Financial Times* (October 14–15), p. 6.
Jancsurak, J. "Holistic Strategy Pays Off." *Appliance Manufacturer*, Special section (February 1995), pp. 3–6.
Jancsurak, J. "Big Plans for Europe's Big Three." *Appliance Manufacturer* (April 1995), pp. 26–30.
Jancsurak, J. "Wanted: Customers for Life." *Appliance Manufacturer*, Special section (February 1995), pp. 36–37.
Maruca, R. F. "The Right Way to Go Global." An Interview with Whirlpool CEO David Whitwam." *Harvard Business Review* (March–April 1994), pp. 135–145.
Naj, A. K. "Air Conditioners Learn to Sense if You're Cool." *Wall Street Journal* (August 31, 1993), p. B1.
R. J. B. "Demystifying the Asian Consumer," *Appliance Manufacturer*, Special section (February 1995), pp. 25–27.
R. J. B. "Multifaceted Strategy." *Appliance Manufacturer*, Special section (February 1995), pp. 28–29.
Schiller, Z. "The Great Refrigerator Race." *Business Week* (July 5, 1993), pp. 78–81.

Schiller, Z. "GE Has a Lean, Mean Washing Machine." *Business Week* (November 20, 1995), pp. 97–98.

Standard & Poor's. "Waiting for the Next Replacement Cycle." *Industry Surveys* (November 1991), pp. T102–T105.

Standard & Poor's. "Poised for a Moderate Recovery." *Industry Surveys* (November 1992), pp. T96–T101.

Treece, J. B. "The Great Refrigerator Race." *Business Week* (July 15, 1993), pp. 78–81.

Weiner, S. "Growing Pains," *Forbes* (October 29, 1990), p. 40–41.

Whirlpool Corporation. *1987–1995 Annual Reports.*

Whirlpool Corporation. Form 10-K (1992, 1994, and 1995).

Whirlpool Corporation. *1992 Proxy Statement.*

Whirlpool Corporation. *Profile* (1994 and 1995).

Whirlpool Corporation. "Whirlpool 'World Washer' Being Marketed in Three Emerging Countries." News Release (undated).

Whirlpool Corporation. "Whirlpool Corporation Named Winner in $30 Million Super-Efficient Refrigerator Competition."(undated).

Zeller, W. "A Tough Market Has Whirlpool in a Spin." *Business Week* (May 2, 1988), pp. 121–122.

CASE ENDNOTES

1. Whirlpool Corporation, *1995 Annual Report,* p. 4.
2. Whirlpool Corporation, *1994 Annual Report,* p. 2.
3. Whirlpool Corporation, *Profile* (1995).
4. Whirlpool Corporation, Form 10-K, (1994).
5. T. A. Stewart, "A Heartland Industry Takes on the World," *Fortune* (March 2, 1990), pp. 110–112.
6. S. Kindel, "World Washer: Why Whirlpool Leads in Appliance: Not Some Japanese Outfit," *Financial World* (March 20, 1990), pp. 42–46.
7. Whirlpool Corporation, Form 10-K (1992).
8. Whirlpool Corporation, *1992 Annual Report.*
9. Whirlpool Corporation, *Profile (1994).*
10. Whirlpool Corporation, *1994 Annual Report,* p. 9.
11. A. M., "Fleet of Foot," *Appliance Manufacturer* (May 1991), pp. 35–38.
12. Whirlpool Corporation, *World Washer News Release.*
13. Whirlpool Corporation, *1994 Annual Report,* p. 10.
14. Whirlpool Corporation, *1987 Annual Report,* p. 5.
15. Whirlpool Corporation, *1989 Annual Report,* p. 9.
16. T. A. Stewart, "A Heartland Industry Takes on the World."
17. R. Tierney, "Whirlpool Magic," *World Trade* (May 1993).
18. J. Jancsurak, "Marketing: Phase 2," *Appliance Manufacturer* (February 1995), pp. 8–10.
19. N. C. Remich, Jr., "Speed Saves the Day," *Appliance Manufacturer,* Special section (July 1995), p. 129.
20. Whirlpool Corporation, *World Washer News Release.*
21. N. C. Remich, Jr., "A Kentucky Thoroughbred That Is Running Strong," *Appliance Manufacturer,* Special section, (July 1995), pp. 3–6.

INTEGERATIVE CASES

CASE 3

ANITA RODDICK, OBE, AND THE BODY SHOP INTERNATIONAL PLC (1996)

Since 1984, the year The Body Shop went public, as far as I am concerned the business has existed for one reason only—to allow us to use our success to act as a force for social change, to contribute the education and consciousness-raising of our staff, to assist development in the Third World, and above all, to help protect the environment. What we are trying to do is to create a new business paradigm, simply showing that business can have a human face and a social conscience.

Anita Roddick, OBE, Founder
and Chief Executive Officer

On March 5, 1996, CEO Anita Roddick and her husband, Chairman Gordon Roddick, of The Body Shop International PLC, abandoned plans to take the company private.[1] Rumors that the Roddicks were taking the company private had been circulating since November 1995. Reports at that time indicated that the Roddicks felt a private company could address their environmental concerns much more efficiently than a public company, given the pressures of the stock market.[2]

According to advisers to the Roddicks, one idea under active consideration involved turning the business into a charitable trust.[3] However, Anita and Gordon, owners of 25.3% of the company, said taking the company private would have saddled it with growth-impairing debt.[4]

Also in 1996, The Body Shop released the results of its first *Social Audit* (see summary in Exhibit IC3–1). To collect the views of key stakeholder groups, The Body Shop drew both on its own experience of environmental reporting and on systems developed by the New Economics Foundation, a think-tank which verified the company's audit and disclosure processes. Approximately 200 staff members took part in 18 focus groups, called Values Meetings, between October 1994 and April 1995. The concerns and issues raised in these meetings were used in a staff questionnaire designed by the Institute for Employment Studies. Employees were given an hour off work to complete the questionnaire, which achieved a 72% response rate.[5]

While 93% of employees either agreed or strongly agreed that The Body Shop lives up to its mission on the issues of environmental responsibility and animal testing, 29% of shareholders either disagreed or strongly disagreed that the company enjoys the trust of the financial community.[6]

Faced with the results of the social audit and a realization of the amount of debt entailed in taking the company private, Anita and Gordon looked for ways to satisfy their desire to operate an environmentally sensitive firm while maximizing shareholder interests.

ANITA RODDICK: THE ENTREPRENEUR

I certainly had no ambition to start a big international company. I did not want to change the world; I just wanted to survive and be able to feed my children.

Anita Roddick, OBE

In 1942, Anita Perellas was born to Italian immigrant parents and grew up working in the family-owned cafe, the Clifton Cafe, in Littlehampton, West Sussex, England. She wanted to be an actress, but her mother, Gilda, wanted her to be a teacher. Her mother told her to "be special"...[and] "be anything but mediocre."[7] She received a degree in education from Newton Park College of Education at Bath. In 1963, her senior year, she received a 3-month scholarship to Israel, which enabled her to do research for her thesis, "The British Mandate in Palestine."

After graduation, she taught for a brief time at a local junior school. She then accepted a position in Paris with the International Herald Tribune as a librarian. Her next position was with the United Nations International Labour Organization in Geneva. She worked on women's rights in

This case was prepared by Professor Thomas L. Wheelen of the University of South Florida, Ellie A. Fogarty, Business Librarian, and Professor Joyce P. Vincelette of Trenton State College. This case may not be reproduced in any form without written permission of the copyright holder. Copyright ©1996 by Thomas L. Wheelen. Reprinted by permission.

EXHIBIT IC3–1

Results of Social Audit—The Good News and the Bad News: The Body Shop

Employees	Franchisees	Customers
93% agreed or strongly agreed that The Body Shop lives up to its mission on the issues of environmental responsibility and animal testing.	**94%** of UK and **73%** of US franchisees agreed or strongly agreed that The Body Shop campaigns effectively on human rights, environmental protection, and animal testing.	The Body Shop scored an average of **7.5 out of 10** for campaigning effectively on human rights, environmental protection, and animal protection.
79% agreed or strongly agreed that working for The Body Shop has raised their awareness of pressing global issues.	**90%** of UK and **80%** of US franchisees felt that the company provides reliable and honest information to them on social issues.	The Body Shop scored an average of **9 out of 10** for its stance against animal testing among British customers.
23% *felt the best way for them to develop their career was to change companies.*	**More than one-fifth** *of UK and US franchisees expressed no opinion on the majority of issues related to doing business with The Body Shop.*	*Many customers in the UK and US are still confused by what is natural.*
53% *disagreed or strongly disagreed that the behaviour and decision-making of managers was consistent throughout the company.*	**43%** of UK and **64%** of US franchisees disagreed that The Body Shop's sales divisions communicated their long-term strategy clearly to the franchisees.	*UK customer complaints rose from* **18.3** *per 100,000 transactions in 1992/93 to* **20.9** *per 100,000 transactions in 1994/1995.*

Suppliers	Shareholders	Community Involvement
95% agree or strongly agree that the Body Shop takes active steps to make its business more environmentally responsible.	**90%** agreed or strongly agreed that The Body Shop takes active steps to make its business more environmentally responsible.	In 1994/95 The Body Shop's directly employed staff gave an estimated **19,500** hours to projects in the community.
Prompt payment, clarity of delivery and purchase order requirements, and fairness of quality assurance arrangements were all recognized by **80%** or more.	**78%** were satisfied with the information they receive on The Body Shop's financial performance.	**87%** of recipients of funding from The Body Shop Foundation agreed or strongly agreed that The Body Shop takes active steps to make its business more environmentally responsible.
One-fifth *disagreed or strongly disagreed that The Body Shop's purchasing and logistics functions are well structured and efficient.*	**29%** *disagreed or strongly disagreed that the company enjoys the trust of the financial community.*	**75%** *of The Body Shop employees do not participate actively in the community volunteering program.*
8% *claimed to have experienced ethically corrupt behavior in their dealings with individual members of The Body Shop staff.*	**33%** *had no opinion or disagreed that The Body Shop has a clear long-term business strategy.*	**Nearly half the recipients** *of funding disagreed or strongly disagreed that it was easy to identify the right decision makers in The Body Shop Foundation.*

Source: The Body Shop.

Third World countries. She said of her United Nations experience that she learned "the extraordinary power of networking, but I was appalled by the money that was squandered on red tape and all the wining and dining that was going on with no apparent check on expenses. I found it offensive to see all of those fat cats discussing problems in the Third World over four-course lunches at the United Nations Club."[8]

With the money saved from her United Nations position, she decided to satisfy her quest to travel. She boarded a boat bound for Tahiti via the Panama Canal and then went on to visit Africa. During her travels, she developed a deep interest in and curiosity about the beauty practices of women that she encountered. She focused on the effectiveness and simplicity of these beauty practices.

INTEGERATIVE CASES

536 • Integrative Cases

After returning to England, she met Gordon Roddick at El Cubana, her family-owned club. He was an adventurer, who loved to travel and write poetry. They married in Reno, Nevada, on a trip to San Francisco to visit friends in 1970. After the birth of their two daughters, Justine in 1969 and Samantha in 1971, they decided to settle down. They purchased a Victorian hotel, the St. Winifred Hotel, in Littlehampton, which required substantial renovations. They resided in part of the hotel while renovating the guest quarters. The next Roddick enterprise was the Paddington Restaurant in the center of Littlehampton. They borrowed £10,000 from the bank to lease and renovate the restuarant.[9] This was a time-consuming enterprise for the couple. They had no social or family life while running the Paddington and residing in and staffing the St. Winifred Hotel. Anita said, "We did not have time for each other and our marriage was beginning to suffer as a result, exacerbated by the fact we had no privacy, being at St. Winifred's was like living in a commune with a lot of elderly people. And despite all the leisure time we had sacrificed, we were not making much money. All we were doing was surviving."[10] Paddington became the most popular place in the town, especially on a Saturday night. Gordon crawling into bed one night said, "This is killing us,"… [and] "I can't cope with it any more. Let's pack it in."[11]

In 1976, Gordon and Anita agreed that Gordon should fulfill his dream of riding horseback across the Americas from Buenos Aires to New York City. The 5,300 mile horseback trek would take about 2 years to complete. Anita said, "I have admired people who want to be remarkable, who follow their beliefs and passions, who make grand gestures."[12] Anita wanted a real home life, which as entrepreneurs they never had, and she wanted to spend some time with her children, who were 4 and 6. She needed a business to survive and feed the children, so they decided she needed to open a shop.

THE BODY SHOP

Anita decided to sell naturally based cosmetics in five sizes so that her customers had a choice. She felt that "people tend not to trust their gut instincts enough, especially about those things that irritate them, but the fact is that if something irritates you it is a pretty good indication that there are other people who feel the same. Irritation was a great source of energy and creativity."[13] She had been dissatisfied with the purchase of body lotion, since most stores sell only one size.[14] Her dissatisfaction led her to question why she could not buy cosmetics by weight or bulk, like groceries or vegetables, and why a customer could not buy a small size of a cream or lotion, to try it out before buying a big bottle. These were simple enough questions, but at the time there were no sensible answers.[15] She and Gordon discussed her concept for a shop where she could sell cosmetic products in a cheap container and in different sizes. He liked the concept. Anita decided to sell products made from "natural ingredients." The environmental green movement had not yet started.

She obtained a £4,000 bank loan (approximately $6,000) to open the first Body Shop at 22 Kensington Gardens, Brighton. The shop opened Saturday, March 26, 1976, at nine o'clock. By noon, Anita had to call Gordon and ask him to come to the shop and work. At six o'clock, they closed the shop and counted the daily receipts: exactly £130. She had a goal of £300 of weekly receipts to cover her living costs.[16]

Just before she opened the shop, she encountered opposition over the shop name, The Body Shop. The name came from the generic name for auto repair shops in the United States. Two nearby funeral homes threatened to sue her over the shop's name. She contacted the local newspaper about the pending lawsuits. The article on her plight helped draw attention to her new shop. Based on this experience, she developed a company policy of never spending a cent on advertising.[17] It has been estimated that The Body Shop receives £2,000,000 of free publicity each year based on the company's and Anita's position on key social problems. The shop's logo was designed by a local art student at a cost of £25.

Anita based the design of The Body Shop on "a Second World War mentality (shortages, utility goods, and rationing) imposed by sheer necessity and the fact that I had no money. But I had a very clear image in my mind of the kind of style I wanted to create: I wanted it to look a bit like a country store in a spaghetti western."[18]

The first products—all 25 of them—were composed of natural ingredients that Anita could gather and mix together herself rather inexpensively. The cheapest bottles she could find were those used by hospitals to collect urine samples and she offered to fill any bottle the customer would bring in. The labels were plain and simple, as they still are, and handwritten. The store also carried knickknacks to fill space, including cards, books, and jewelry; sometimes this merchandise accounted for 60% of the turnover. She developed loyal clients.

Perhaps because Anita sprayed Strawberry Essence on the sidewalks in the hope that potential customers would follow it, the first store did well. After a successful summer, Anita decided to open a second store in Chichester and approached the bank for a £4,000 loan. She was turned down because she had no track record. So she turned to a friend, Ian McGlinn, who owned a local garage. Ian received a 50% interest in the company for his investment.[19] In 1995,

he owned 52,366,768 (27.6%) of the ordinary shares. The Roddicks owed 48,237,136 shares. Ian played no role in the management of the company. Anita felt that "to succeed you have to believe in something with such a passion that it becomes a reality."[20] This was one of the two principal reasons for the company's initial success. The other was that Anita had to survive while Gordon was away. Exhibit IC3–2 shows a timeline of the key events in the company's life.

EXHIBIT IC3–2

A Timeline: The Body Shop

1976   Anita Roddick opens the first branch of The Body Shop in Brighton on England's south coast.

1977   The first franchise of The Body Shop opens in Bognor Regis, England.

1978   The first branch opens outside the United Kingdom in Brussels, Belgium.

1984   The Body Shop goes public. With a placing of 95p ($1.38), shares close at £1.65 ($2.39) on the first day of dealing.

1985   The Body Shop runs its first in-shop campaign, "Save the Whale," with Greenpeace.

1986   The Body Shop launches its cosmetic range, called Colourings, and Mostly Men, a skin care line for men.

1987   The Body Shop establishes its first Trade Not Aid initiative in Nepal.

1988   The first U.S. branch of The Body Shop opens in New York.
Soapworks, a soap-making plant for The Body Shop, opens in Easterhouse, Scotland.
Queen awards Anita Roddick the Order of the British Empire (OBE).

1989   One million people sign The Body Shop's petition to "Stop the Burning" in the Amazon rain forest.
Anita receives the United Nations' Global 500 Environment Award.

1990   2.6 million people sign The Body Shop's "Against Animal Testing" petition.
The Body Shop launches its Eastern European Drive of volunteers to renovate three orphanages in Halaucesti, Romania.
The Body Shop opens in Tokyo, Japan.

1991   *The Big Issue*, a paper sold by and for the homeless, is launched by The Body Shop in London.
Anita is awarded the World Vision Award by the Centre for World Development Education in recognition of Trade Not Aid initiative.
The Body Shop marks Amnesty International's 30th anniversary with a campaign to increase membership.

1992   The Body Shop's voter registration drive in the United States signs up more than 33,000 voters.
The Company publishes the results of the first environmental audit, *The Green Book* in the United Kingdom.
The Body Shop opens its first American community-based shop on 125th Street, Harlem.

1993   The Body Shop opens its 1,000th shop.
The American "Reuse/Refill/Recycle" campaign increases awareness of the refill and recycling services available at The Body Shop.
The Body Shop USA joins with other corporations in signing the CERES Principles, an environmental code of conduct.
The Body Shop USA joined forces with the Ms. Foundation to support the first annual Take Our Daughters to Work Day.
The Body Shop USA is honored by the NAACP for excellence in minority economic development.
The "Protect & Respect" project, on AIDS education and awareness is launched.

1994   The Body Shop launches its biggest ever international campaign in 30 markets and more than 900 shops to gain public support influencing the U.N. Convention on International Trade in Endangered Species to enforce regulations governing trade in endangered species.

Source: The Body Shop, "This Is the Body Shop" (November 1994), pp. 3–4.

In 1995, the company (1) worked to increase trade with its existing partners; (2) established new trading relationships; (3) adopted the Trading Charter (see Exhibit 3) as the basis on which it did business; and (4) set clear guidelines for expanding its links with communities.[21] The company had a team of nine people dedicated to fair trade. Jacque McDonald joined the company in 1995 to head this team. The Body Shop had over 1210 shops in 45 countries (see Exhibit IC3–4), traded in 23 languages worldwide, and sold over 550 different products. The company Trading Charter and Mission recognized that human rights and civil rights were at the heart of responsible business.

FRANCHISING AS A GROWTH STRATEGY

A friend's daughter, Chris Green, wanted to open her own shop in Hove. The Roddicks thought it was a great idea and agreed. Their only interest was in having her selling products. There were no fees or contracts. Another friend, Aidre, wanted to open a shop with her parents in Bognor Regis. They gave her the same deal.

Gordon had returned home before these two shops were opened. He could see the growth potential of the business, but no bank wanted to lend them money.

Gordon hired a lawyer to develop a franchising contract. The formula was based on a license to use The Body Shop name and to sell its products, and the franchisee would put up the money. In 1978, the first franchise outside the United Kingdom was opened in Brussels. The franchise fee was £300.[22] The fee in 1995 was £10,000. All the initial franchises were owned by women. Anita felt that "men were good at the science and vocabulary of business, at talking about economic theory and profits and loss figures (some women are, too, of course). But I could also see that women were better at dealing with people, caring and being passionate about what they are doing."[23]

During this time, the company was developing its own style of "respond[ing] to needs rather than creating them."[24] The company was run in an informal way as a large, extended family. Anita understood the concept of developing a niche around a competitive advantage. She said, "A true key to success is knowing what features set you apart from the competitor."[25] And also, "We had stuck closely to a policy of being open and honest about out products, and it was paying dividends among our customers who were increasingly irritated by the patently dishonest

advertising of the cosmetics industry. Women in the eighties were less and less inclined to fall for the 'buy this mixture of oil and water and you will be a movie star' pitch dreamed up in the expensive offices of advertising agencies."[26]

By 1982, the Roddicks were exercising much stricter control over what could and could not be done in the shop. They had learned, from experience, that it was absolutely essential to maintain a strong identity.[27] The company opened shops at the rate of two a month. They had shops in Iceland, Denmark, Finland, Holland, and Ireland.

During these early franchising years, the biggest mistake management made was offering three choices of shop styles to franchisees—dark green, dark mahogany stain, or stripped pine. Anita quickly recognized that the shops looked different and that they had lost their distinctiveness. So she persuaded all the shops to return to the dark green.[28]

Anita kept strict control over the franchising process. At times, there were 5,000 franchise applications in process. The franchise process included a home visit, a personality test, and an assessment of the applicant's attitude toward people and the environment. The process could take 3 years to complete. In the final interview with Anita, she was known to ask unexpected questions ("How would you like to die?" "Who is your favorite heroine in literature?") This type of applicant process could ensure that the franchisee would adhere to the principles and image of The Body Shop. After being selected to own a franchise, an owner underwent extensive training on products, store operations, and merchandising techniques. In 1985, The Body Shop Training School opened. The curriculum focused on human development and consciousness-raising. Anita said, "Conventional retailers trained for a sale; we trained for knowledge. They trained with an eye on the balance sheet; we trained with an eye on the soul."[29] The courses centered on "educating" the participant, not training. In the customer care course, the teacher tries to "encourage the staff to treat customers as potential friends, to say hello, smile, make eye contact and to offer advice if it was wanted, to thank them and always to invite them back."[30] She viewed money spent on staff training as an investment, not as an expense.

Sometimes, Anita's passion for a project or a specific issue was not received by the company's staff or franchisees with the same perception or commitment. After presenting a community project at a prison, Gordon said, "I could see they [staff] didn't like it," and he went on to say, "They thought you were blackmailing them emotionally."[31]

EXHIBIT IC3-3

Trading Charter and Mission: The Body Shop

Our Trading Charter

The way we trade creates profits with principles.

We aim to achieve commercial success by meeting our customers' needs through the provision of high quality, good value products with exceptional service and relevant information which enables customers to make informed and responsible choices.

Our trading relationships of every kind—with customers, franchisees and suppliers—will be commercially viable, mutually beneficial and based on trust and respect.

Our trading principles reflect our core values.

We aim to ensure that human and civil rights, as set out in the Universal Declaration of Human Rights, are respected throughout our business activities. We will establish a framework based on this declaration to include criteria for workers' rights embracing a safe, healthy working environment, fair wages, no discrimination on the basis of race, creed, sex, or sexual orientation, or physical coercion of any kind.

We will support long term, sustainable relationships with communities in need.

We will pay special attention to those minority groups, women and disadvantaged peoples who are socially and economically marginalized.

We will use environmentally sustainable resources wherever technically and economically viable. Our purchasing will be based on a system of screening and investigation of the ecological credentials of our finished products, ingredients, packaging and suppliers.

We will promote animal protection throughout our business activities. We are against animal testing in the cosmetics and toiletries industry. We will not test ingredients or products on animals, nor will we commission others to do so on our behalf. We will use our purchasing power to stop suppliers' animal testing.

We will institute appropriate monitoring, auditing and disclosure mechanisms to ensure our accountability and demonstrate our compliance with these principles.

Direct Trading: Our Mission

The Body Shop believes that all trading should be viewed as an exercise in ethics. This is the attitude we seek to apply to all goods and services within the Company and its retail shops.

Our ethical trading program helps create livelihoods for economically stressed communities, mostly in the majority world. Although trading with such communities is currently just a

small percentage of all our trade, we intend to increase this practice wherever possible.

Fair Prices. The Body Shop will pay for the products it purchases. While our program aims to benefit the primary producers directly, we also recognize the value of commercial intermediaries. Where world market prices are applicable, we commit ourselves to pay these prices or more.

Partnership. Both sides must benefit commercially. We aim to develop long-term relationships if possible, and plan to work in partnership to solve potential problems. We aim to help our trade partners achieve self reliance.

Community Benefits. The Company will work with a variety of trading partners—cooperatives, family businesses, tribal councils—with the intention of benefiting the individual worker as much as possible. We can't control the dispersal of community benefits that we provide. That process is determined by local needs, which may mean anything from funds managed by consensus to direct payments to individual producers.

Respect. Our trading relationships are based on respect. The guidelines we are developing for sustainable development ensure that we respect all environments and cultures that may be affected by our trade. Wherever possible, we use renewable natural materials, and skills which are appropriate to local cultures.

Cooperation. The Body Shop is committed to an open relationship with other fair trade organizations and places great emphasis on maintaining dialogue with organizations that are helping to define the path to sustainable development.

Accountability. We believe it is essential that our trading policy be measurable, audited and open to scrutiny, and we are energetically seeking the mechanisms to achieve that goal. We already use an open approach to assess our impact on the environment and to promote our opposition to animal testing in the cosmetics industry by monitoring our suppliers.

Our trading practices are not the solution to everyone's needs. We simply see them as one component of the help we feel qualified to give. We will also help trading partners to broadly assess the likely social and environmental impact of developing trade.

In committing itself to the above aims, The Body Shop believes it is creating a trading policy that will satisfy the needs of our business, our trading partners and our customers. Letting consumers know that neither places nor peoples have been exploited in getting our products to market helps The Body Shop customer make informed, responsible choices.

Source: The Body Shop, handouts.

INTEGERATIVE CASES

EXHIBIT IC3-4

Shop Locations by Regions: The Body Shop

| | Number of Shops | | | First Shop |
	February 1995	February 1994	February 1993	Opening
Europe				
Austria	12	9	8	1979
Belgium	14	11	8	1978
Cyprus	2	1	1	1983
Denmark	14	15	11	1981
Eire	9	10	10	1981
Finland	20	17	15	1981
France	26	25	16	1982
Germany	53	43	37	1983
Gibraltar	1	1	1	1988
Greece	37	28	23	1979
Holland	48	47	40	1982
Iceland	2	2	2	1980
Italy	44	38	37	1984
Luxembourg	2	2	2	1991
Malta	1	1	1	1987
Norway	17	14	15	1985
Portugal	9	8	8	1986
Spain	54	52	33	1986
Sweden	41	40	34	1979
Switzerland	24	21	19	1983
Total Shops	430	385	321	
United Kingdom				
Total Shops	243	239	233	1976
Asia				
Bahrain	2	1	1	1985
Brunei	2	1		1993
Hong Kong	10	9	8	1984
Indonesia	5	4	2	1990
Japan	36	22	11	1990
Kuwait	2	2	2	1986
Macau	2	1		1993
Malaysia	14	11	10	1984
Oman	2	2	2	1986
Qatar	1	1	1	1987
Saudi Arabia	18	13	10	1987
Singapore	9	9	11	1983
Taiwan	9	6	5	1988
Thailand	3	2		1993
UAE	4	4	2	1983
Total Shops	119	88	65	

(continued)

EXHIBIT IC3-4

(Continued)

	Number of Shops			First Shop Opening
	February 1995	February 1994	February 1993	
Australia and New Zealand				
Australia	53	48	43	1983
New Zealand	9	9	7	1989
Total Shops	62	57	50	
America Excluding USA				
Antigua	1	1	1	1987
Bahamas	3	3	4	1985
Bermuda	2	1	1	1987
Canada	112	106	104	1980
Cayman Islands	1	1	1	1989
Mexico	2	2		1993
Total Shops	121	114	111	
USA				
Total Shops	235	170	120	1988
Grand Total Shops	1,208	1,053	900	

Other information:
1. Company shops are located as follows:
   USA 90, UK 43, Singapore 9.
2. Number of countries: 45.
3. Number of languages we trade in: 23.

Source: The Body Shop, *1995* and *1994 Annual Reports*, p. 15 and p. 7.

ANITA RODDICK'S PHILOSOPHY AND PERSONAL VALUES TRANSLATED INTO CORPORATE CULTURE AND CITIZENSHIP

The following are some of Anita's most salient quotes on the issues of our time.

It is immoral to trade on fear. It is immoral to make women feel dissatisfied with their bodies. It is immoral to deceive a customer by making miracle claims for a product. It is immoral to use a photograph of a glowing sixteen-year-old to sell a (beauty) cream aimed at preventing wrinkles in a forty-year-old.[32]

I think all business practices would improve immeasurably if they were guided by "feminine" principles—qualities like love and care and intuition.[33]

I honestly believe I would not have succeeded if I had been taught about business.[34]

We communicate with passion and passion persuades.[35]

I learned there was nothing more important to life than love and work.[36]

Passion persuades and by God I was passionate about what I was selling.[37]

In a society in which politicians no longer lead by example, ethical conduct is unfashionable, and the media does not give people real information on what is happening in the world, what fascinates me is the concept of turning our shops into centers of education.[38]

You can be proud to work for the Body Shop and boy, does that have an effect on morale and motivation.[39]

I have never been able to separate Body Shop values from my personal values.[40]

I think the leadership of a company should encourage the next generation not just to follow, but to overtake.[41]

When you take the high moral road it is difficult for anyone to object without sounding like a fool.[42]

Whenever we wanted to persuade our staff to support a particular project we always tried to break their hearts.[43]

You have to look at leadership through the eyes of the followers and you have to live the message. What I have learned is that people become motivated when you guide them to the source of their own power and when you make heroes out of employees who personify what you want to see in the organization.[44]

I do not believe women have a chance in hell of achieving their desired status and power in business within the foreseeable future. My daughters might see it, but I won't.[45]

If you have a company with itsy-bitsy vision you have an itsy-bitsy company.[46]

The thought that every day might be my last, and the desire to make the most of every moment, drives me on.[47]

These were the statements of a unique woman, who had a strong personal value system that she clearly articulated. She saw herself as a concerned citizen of the world, who continuously searched and developed solutions for its problems; a leader in the green political movement; a very successful business leader; a spokesperson for those without a voice in the world arena; a wife, a mother, and a daughter. She served the needs of the underprivileged and the environment. Anita was a trader. She said, "I am not rushing around the world as some kind of loony do-gooder; first and foremost I am a trader looking for a trade."[48]

In 1988, Anita was knighted by Queen Elizabeth into the Order of the British Empire (OBE).

NORTH AMERICAN MARKET

By 1987, the company had received about 10,000 letters from Americans inquiring about franchising opportunities and asking when stores would be opened so they could purchase products.

Before opening the first store, the Roddicks negotiated for the trademark for The Body Shop. Two companies, owned by the Saunders and Short families, held the rights between them to "The Body Shop" name. Their trademark covered the United States and Japan, which represented 40% of the world's consumers. Gordon negotiated to buy the rights in both countries for $3,500,000.

The first shop was opened in New York on Broadway and 8th Street on July 1, 1988. A few weeks before opening, there was much questioning whether The Body Shop could succeed in the United States without advertising. A Harvard Business School professor was quoted in the *Wall Street Journal,* saying that the company needed, "at minimum," a major launch advertising campaign. Anita had the quote reprinted on a postcard with her response: "I'll never hire anyone from the Harvard Business School."[49]

The first shop was an instant success, and over the next 2 years 13 more company-owned shops were opened. Initially, the company had a hard time trying to locate in malls because it was an unknown. Management asked the company's mail-order customers, who lived within a 110-mile radius of a proposed shop, for a letter-writing campaign. It was very successful. The first franchised store in the United States was opened in Washington, D.C., in 1990. As of February 25, 1995, there were 235 shops in the United States. The company expected to open 40 shops in fiscal year 1996. Retail sales were £91.1 million ($144.8 million) and £72.2 million ($114.9 million) for 1995 and 1994, respectively.

MISSION STATEMENT

The company's mission statement dedicated its business to the pursuit of social and environmental change:

To creatively balance the financial and human needs of our stakeholders: employees, customers, franchisees, suppliers and shareholders.

To courageously ensure that our business is ecologically sustainable, meeting the needs of the present without compromising the future.

To meaningfully contribute to local, national and international communities in which we trade, by adopting a code of conduct which ensures care, honesty, fairness and respect.

To passionately campaign for the protection of the environment and human and civil rights, and against animal testing within the cosmetics and toiletries industry.

To tirelessly work to narrow the gap between principle and practice, while making fun, passion and care part of our daily lives.[50]

CORPORATE GOVERNANCE

Board of Directors

The *1995 Annual Report* stated the Directors' responsibilities as follows:

The Directors were required by company law to prepare financial statements for each financial year which give a true and fair view of the state of affairs of the Company and the Group and of the profit or loss of the Group for that period.

In preparing those financial statements, the Directors were required to

- select suitable accounting policies and then apply them consistently;
- make judgments and estimates that are reasonable and prudent;
- state whether applicable accounting standards have been followed, subject to any material departures disclosed and explained in the financial statements; and
- prepare the financial statements on the going-concern basis unless it is inappropriate to presume that the company will continue in business.

The Directors were responsible for maintaining proper accounting records that disclose with reasonable accuracy at any time the financial position of the company and to enable it to ensure that the financial statements comply with the Companies Act. They were also responsible for safeguarding the assets of the company and hence for taking reasonable steps for the prevention and detection of fraud and other irregularities.[51]

There were 11 board members, of whom 5 were appointed during fiscal year 1995. In 1995, the first nonexecutives were appointed. The board members are:[52]

Anita L. Roddick, OBE	Chief Executive
T. Gordon Roddick	Chairman
Stuart A. Rose	Managing Director
Eric G. Helyer	Executive

Jilly C. Forster	Executive
Michael J. Ross	Executive
Jane Reid (appointed 7/94)	Executive
Jeremy A. Kett (appointed 7/94)	Executive
Terry G. Hartin (appointed 7/94)	Executive
Penny Hughes (appointed 10/94)	Non-Executive
Aldo Papone (appointed 10/94)	Non-Executive

The following are profiles of the two nonexecutive directors.

Penny Hughes became President of Coca-Cola Great Britain and Ireland in 1992. She was promoted to the Board of Coca-Cola in 1989. She held marketing positions with the Milk Marketing Board and Procter and Gamble. She is a member of the Board of Business in the Environment. The Body Shop anticipated that her skills in marketing, franchise management, and delivering consumer satisfaction would contribute to the continued development of the Body Shop as a truly global enterprise.[53]

Aldo Papone is the retired Chairman and Chief Executive Officer of American Express Travel Related Services Company. He stepped down in 1990 but has remained closely involved with the company. In addition to the American Express Board, Aldo currently serves on the boards of the American Express Bank, the software company IMRS, and the National Corporate Theater Fund. Aldo is an expert on marketing and branding strategies which would add greatly to The Body Shop's marketing strategy.[54]

The company has been actively searching for nonexecutives for the past few years. The company executives were committed to making more nonexecutive appointments.

Remuneration for the Executive Directors in 1995 was as follows:[55]

Name	Salary	Benefits	Total
A. L. Roddick	£122,608	£17,984	£140,592
T. G. Roddick	122,641	16,083	138,724
S. A. Rose	216,827	3,107	219,934
E. G. Helyer	91,526	3,784	95,307
M. J. Ross	129,000	8,663	137,663
J. Reid	89,681	5,213	94,894
J. A. Kett	64,897	888	65,785
T. G. Hartin	57,720	3,308	61,028
J. C. Forster	100,300	7,224	107,524

Note: Amounts are in British pounds.

During 1995, a 3% basic pay increase was given to the Executive Directors. No bonus was paid to the Executive

Directors, except the Christmas bonus of £200 maximum paid to all the staff.

Executive Directors' share holdings in 1995 were as follows:[56]

Name	Number of Shares	% of Total Stock Issued
A. L. Roddick	24,010,456	12.6%
T. G. Roddick	24,226,680	12.7%
E. G. Helyer	74,600	[1]
M. J. Ross	2,000	[1]
T. G. Hartin	2,765	[1]

Note: 1. Less than .001 percent

Ian McGlinn, who had loaned £6,000 to Anita to open her second shop, owned 52,366,768 (27.6%) ordinary shares. The EMR Corporation and Fidelity International Limited owned 7,261,657 (3.8%) ordinary shares, and the Prudential Corporation owned 6,586,146 (3.5%) ordinary shares.

Gordon Roddick said that "the Board is determined to ensure that The Body Shop's values are integrated into all aspects of the company. The Values Meetings have been incredibly important in focusing our attention on what needs to be done to achieve that objective."[57] He went on to say:

> One result of the meetings was a higher profile role for the Company Care Team, a five-person group who are taking responsibility for The Body Shop's performance as a caring employer. The team co-ordinates childcare through our Family Care, and launched, in April 1994, a program offering financial help with childcare for our company shop staff. A counselor provides a 24-hour confidential counseling service for employees and their families.[58]

STRATEGIC MANAGERS

Anita said about Gordon and her roles that

> Gordon rarely accompanies me on shop visits because we are each more comfortable in our chosen roles of high profile and low profile. Outsiders often think Gordon as a shadowy figure but that is certainly not how he is viewed within The Body Shop. He is well known to everyone, much loved and deeply respected as the real strength of the company. Our relationship bequeathed a very distinct management style to the company—loosely structured, collaborative, imaginative and improvisatory, rather than by the book—which matured as the company expanded. I think Gordon provides a sense of constancy and continuity while I bounce around breaking the rules, pushing back the boundaries of possibility and shooting off my mouth. We rarely argue ... [and] never

about values. His calm presence and enormous influence are rarely taken into account by critics, who see The Body Shop as a flaky organization led by a madwoman with fuzzy hair.[59]

GROUP STRUCTURE AND ORGANIZATION

The Body Shop International PLC consists of three groups—*retail subsidiaries, operating subsidiaries,* and *other subsidiaries* (see Exhibit IC3–5). The operating structure is shown in Exhibit IC3–6.

Marketing and Advertising

The company had no marketing or advertising department. In 1979, Janis Raven was hired to handle public relations. She helped publicize the company's image and stances on public social issues. An analyst felt that the lack of an advertising and marketing budget had contributed to low repeat customer sales. Customers came in looking for a gift for a friend or out of curiosity. Once a customer satisfied his or her need, there seemed to be little incentive for the customer to come back. Product Information Manuals (PIMs) were available to all customers and staff to increase their knowledge or answer questions about every Body Shop product. These manuals contained information about how the products were made, listing ingredients and the uses for each product. Many potential customers were not sure what products the company offers.

Anita Roddick used regular visits by regional managers to keep tight control over shop layout, window displays, PIM handouts, and operating style. Anita viewed marketing as hype; instead she wanted to establish credibility by educating the customer. She viewed the shop as the company's primary marketing tool. In 1990, The Body Shop was nominated to the United Kingdom Marketing Hall of Fame.

PRODUCT DEVELOPMENT AND PRODUCTION

In 1995, the company introduced 15 new products, over 26 shades, 17 shade extensions in eyeshadows and lipsticks, and base products for darker skins. New products introduced were Lightening Touch and Lip Treats, the company's first cosmetic products developed specifically for dry skin and more mature skin. A number of new products were being developed to cater to individual preferences within international markets. The company informed its customers of the risk of overexposure to the sun and how to protect the skin. This was done in association with Marie Curie

EXHIBIT IC3–5

Group Structure: The Body Shop International PLC

Exercises control of the Group and provides a number of services including product development, environmental, legal, design, and corporate communication functions.

Retail Subsidiaries	Operating Subsidiaries	Other Subsidiaries
The Body Shop Worldwide, Ltd. Responsible for all retail activities outside the United Kingdom and United States	**The Body Shop Supply Company, Ltd.** Manufactures bottle products and controls distribution to all retail outlets	**Jacaranda Productions, Ltd. (80% owned)** Video production for the Group and third parties
The Body Shop UK Retail Company, Ltd. Responsible for all U.K. retail activities	**Cos-tec, Ltd.** Manufactures color cosmetic, skin care, and toiletry products	**Normaland, Ltd. (100% owned)** Owns the franchise agreement for two U.K. outlets
The Body Shop, Inc. (90% owned) Responsible for all U.S. retail activities	**Soapworks, Ltd.** Manufactures soap products	**The Body Shop Film Co. (100% owned)** Finances the film and television series
The Body Shop Singapore Pte, Ltd. Responsible for all retail activities in Singapore	**Colourings, Ltd.** Controls marketing of color cosmetic products	**Skin Health Care Preparations, Inc. (100% owned)** Holds The Body Shop trademark in the United States and Japan
The Body Shop Norway A/S Responsible for company shops in Norway		

Source: The Body Shop, 1994 Annual Report, p. 6.

Cancer Care in the United Kingdom. In 1994, the company published *The Body Shop Book,* which was a comprehensive illustration of essential steps in skin, hair, and body care.

The company concentrated its development programs on skin care. During 1995, the company released six new skin care products, based on tea oil and developed originally for the Australian market. These products were introduced first in the United Kingdom, and then in other international markets. Research for the future focused on products for customers with skin problems and particularly the teenaged market.

The company was addressing the individual needs of markets for fragrances. New products were developed and introduced in Germany, the United States, and the Middle East. One of the company's innovative products was Play Soap, a moldable children's bath soap available in two fragrances. The unique process for producing Play Soap was a collaborative effort by Soapworks and Cos-tec. In 1995, The Body Shop Supply Company, Ltd., manufactured 7,992 tons of bulk skin and hair products at the Watersmead plant. The

company's Homebrew area produced over 100 tons of natural infusions for use in the company's products.

Soapworks, located in Easterhouse, Scotland, an historically high unemployment city, employed over 120 people. When Soapworks was founded, the company made a commitment to donate 25% of its cumulative after-tax profits to local community projects. In 1994, 13 local community projects received support from these funds. Soapworks manufactured 35 million soaps in 1995, an increase of 7 million over 1994.

Cos-tec manufactured color cosmetics and some products packaged in tubs, jars, and tubes. During 1995, it produced 63 tons of lipstick, an increase of 29 tons over the previous year, and 207 tons of powder products, including blushers and eyeshadows.

Anita spent up to 5 months a year traveling the world looking for new product ideas and ingredients. Her samples were brought back to Watersmead where they were analyzed for their potential and durability. The department

INTEGERATIVE CASES

EXHITIB IC3–6

Operating Structure: The Body Shop International PLC

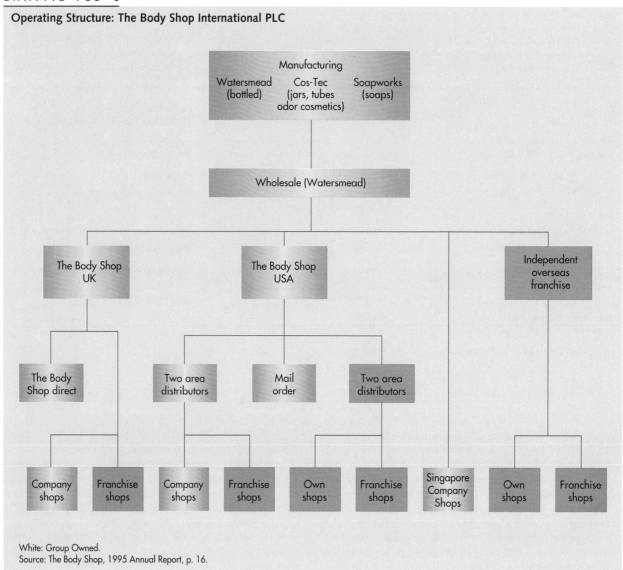

White: Group Owned.
Source: The Body Shop, 1995 Annual Report, p. 16.

was backed by anthropological and ethnobotanical research in traditional uses of plants, herbs, fruits, flowers, seeds, and nuts.

HUMAN RESOURCES MANAGEMENT

Most of the employees in the company were women under 30. Anita constantly worked at communication within the company. Each shop had a bulletin board, a fax machine, and a video player with which she provided the staff a continuous stream of information concerning new products, causes that she supported, or status reports on her latest trip. The in-house video production company produced "Talking Shop," which was a monthly multilingual video magazine. It also produced training tapes and documentaries on social campaigns.

Anita encouraged upward communication through a suggestion system, DODGI (The Department of Damned Good Ideas) and through regularly scheduled meetings of a cross section of staff, often at her home. She set up the "Red Letter" system so that an employee could directly communicate with a Director and bypass the normal chain of communication.

She believed in educating her employees and customers. In 1985, The Body Shop Training Center was opened in London and began offering courses on the company's products and philosophy, customer services, and hair and skin care problems. Sessions were held on key social issues such as AIDs, aging, management by humor, drug and alcohol abuse, and urban survival. She discussed the idea of opening a business college. She said, "You can train dogs and you can train horses, but we wanted to educate and help the people realize their potential."[60]

The Body Shop empowered its staff. It encouraged debate, encouraged employees to speak out and state their views. Anita wanted her staff to be personally involved in social campaigns. She said, "One of the risks of corporate campaigning is that the staff start to fall in love with doing good and forget about trading."[61]

Anita had problems recruiting staff for the New Jersey headquarters because employees were not willing or able to embrace the company's culture. She went on to say, "Most of them came from conventional, moribund jobs and seemed confused by the idea of a company being quirky or zany or contemptuous of mediocrity. I could never seem to get their adrenaline surging. We are a company in which image, design, style and creativity are of paramount importance, but we were unable to find employees who appreciate these qualities."[62] In 1993, U.S. headquarters was moved to Wake Forest, North Carolina.

The company created "the Company Care Team, a five-person group who are taking responsibility for The Body Shop's performance as a caring employer. The team coordinated childcare through the company's Family Centre, and through the launch in April 1994 of programs offering financial help with childcare for all company staff. A counselor service provided 24-hour confidential counseling services for employees and their families."[63]

GLOBAL CORPORATE CITIZENSHIP

The company clearly stated its position on the key global issue of corporate citizenship.[64]

Human and Civil Rights   The Body Shop is committed to supporting and promoting social and environmental change

for the better. We recognize that human and civil rights are at the very heart of such change.

We're All in This Together   Working with organizations like Amnesty International, Human Rights Watch, the Unrepresented Nations and Peoples Organization and the Foundation for Ethnobiology, The Body Shop has tried to promote awareness of our responsibility as human beings. What happens to one of us affects us all. We can no longer pretend it is none of our business if people suffer, whether they're on the other side of the world or in our own backyards. Here are a few successful examples of work by The Body Shop in both those areas:

- In 1990, The Body Shop started a relief drive to fund volunteers to renovate orphanages in Romania, where thousands of children had been abandoned under the regime of dictator Nicolae Ceacescu. The Project has been so successful that we've now extended it to Albania.
- In 1993, the Body Shop Foundation donated £162,000 ($234,900) to Rights and Wrongs, a weekly human rights television series created by Globalvision Inc. on a non-profit basis. By focusing on the human rights revolution around the world, the series explained how interrelated many of our problems are.
- In 1993 our biggest campaign in the U.S. focused attention on people living with HIV and AIDS. Working with groups like the American Red Cross, the San Francisco AIDS Foundation, the Gay Men's Health Crisis and the National Leadership Coalition on AIDS, we developed a multi-faceted campaign, focusing particularly on women and teenagers who are the fastest growing risk groups for HIV infection. Using the theme "Protest & Respect," our campaign included a new corporate policy on life threatening illness; training for all our employees; educational materials on safer sex and living with HIV and AIDS for distribution in our shops; outreach to local community groups; and funding support for organizations which assist people with HIV and AIDS.
- The Body Shop Foundation was founded in 1989. The company donated £480,000 to the foundation in 1995.[65]

Against Animal Testing   The Body Shop is against animal testing of ingredients and products in the cosmetics industry. We do not test our products or ingredients on animals. Nor do we commission others to test on our behalf. We never have and we never will.

We will never endorse the use of animal tests in the cosmetics or toiletries industry. However, no cosmetics company can claim that its manufactured ingredients have never been tested on animals by somebody at some stage for someone. We support a complete ban on the testing of both finished cosmetic products and individual ingredients used in cosmetic products.

We work with leading animal welfare organizations to lobby for a complete ban on animal testing of cosmetic ingredients and products. We also encourage our ingredient suppliers and those who want to become our suppliers to stop animal testing by making our position on animal testing clear to them. We require our suppliers of raw materials to provide written confirmation every six months that any material they supply to us has not been tested by them for the cosmetics industry for the last five years.

The "5 year rolling rule" is the most effective mechanism for change. Every six months, our technical information specialists send out hundreds of declarations requiring all our suppliers to certify the last date of any animal testing they have conducted on behalf of the cosmetics industry on any ingredient which they supply to us.

If a supplier fails to complete the form, the company is pursued until we get the information we need. If no declaration is forth coming, or if the company reports conducting an animal test for any part of the cosmetics industry within the last five years, we immediately stop buying the ingredient from that supplier and look for alternative suppliers who have not tested on animals within the previous five years. If no supplier can be found who meets the 5 year rule, we will try to reformulate the product without that ingredient. If we cannot reformulate, we will stop making the product.

Some companies who adopt an against-animal-testing policy take a "fixed cut off date" stance, declaring they will not use an ingredient which comes into existence after a specific date. This position does little to persuade ingredient suppliers, who continue to develop new ingredients, to stop animal testing. A "fixed cut off date" company provides no market for new ingredients, forcing suppliers to continue dealing with those cosmetic companies which require tests. In addition, the extent to which a company's suppliers adhere to its rule may be questionable since most "cut-off" date companies never recheck with their suppliers to see if previously untested ingredients have been re-tested.

The Body Shop polices the 5 year rule. It's not just the rule itself that provokes the changes we want. It's the policing with regard to each ingredient. As our ingredient suppliers trade with new customs and in new markets, they are confronted by additional demands for animal testing. Our twice yearly declarations ensure they continue to meet our requirements.

We rely upon a number of alternative techniques to help assess a product's safety. At The Body Shop, customer safety is paramount. We believe (as do many experts) that the reliability of animal testing is questionable. In developing products we use natural ingredients, like bananas and Brazil nut oil, as well as others with a long history of safe human usage. Our ingredients and/or finished products are subject to in-vitro testing methods such as Eytex, human patch testing, SPF testing and analytical procedures.

Working for the World's Wildlife All around the world animals are in danger of extinction as their food sources are threatened, their natural habitats diminish and environmental degradation takes its toll. The Body Shop takes action on several fronts to keep this critical issue in the public eye.

The Body Shop has a long established commitment to helping endangered species. Over the years, The Body Shop and its franchisees have raised hundreds of thousands of dollars, locally, nationally and internationally, to support a host of campaigns and projects. We also work hard to inform the public and influence governments the world over, to protect the environment and stop the illegal trade in endangered species.

Care for the Environment The Body Shop believes it just isn't possible for any business to claim to be environmentally friendly, because all commerce involves some environmental impact. But at The Body Shop, we take responsibility for the waste we create. We aim to avoid excessive packaging, to refill our bottles and to recycle our packaging and use raw ingredients from renewable sources whenever technically and economically feasible.

The most accessible aspect of our environmental practice for customers is our refill service. Customers bring back their empty, clean containers and we refill them with the same product at a discount. This conserves resources, reduces waste and saves money. We also accept our packaging back for recycling. At the same time, we're always searching for new ways to reduce our impact on the environment. In the United Kingdom we are investing in wind energy with the ultimate aim of putting back into the national grid as much electricity as we take out.

In the United States, we've yet to achieve the level of environmental management reached in the UK and, unsurprisingly, we've had some growing pains which we've done our best to minimize. For instance, we discovered that because of regulations in some states, our larger bottles required special labels to comply with the state's recycling program. So we used a special stick-on label while we phased out stock of that particular bottle.

A New Kind of Audit   To create a framework for our environmental commitment, we have introduced an annual environmental audit pursuant to European Community Eco-management and Audit Regulation at our UK headquarters. The results of the audit are publicly available. [See Exhibit 1 for results of first Social Audit.] By setting targets to meet on a yearly basis, the audit process is a constant challenge to our commitment, as well as a campaigning platform for us and a role model for other companies. And it's a constant reminder to staff that good environment housekeeping is everyone's business.

Having relocated our headquarters to Wake Forest, NC from Cedar Knolls, NJ we are now committed to publishing a comprehensive and externally verified environmental audit statement like "The Green Book" which is published annually in the UK. Our internal reviews have helped us identify problems to work on and get our staff more involved in environmental management as well.

We are beginning to execute environmental reviews at our principal subsidiaries, retail outlets and overseas franchises. All will be subject to independent examinations which will eventually result in separately accountable environmental management procedures.[66]

In 1995, the company commissioned Professor Kirk Hanson, a leading American professor in business ethics and social responsibility at the Graduate School of Business of Stanford University, to conduct an independent evaluation of the company's social performance and make recommendations for improvements.[67]

A Brief Summary of Our Environmental Policy

1. Think Globally as a constant reminder of our responsibility to protect the environment.
2. Achieve Excellence by setting clear targets and time scales within which to meet them.
3. Search for Sustainability by using renewable resources wherever feasible and conserving natural resources where renewable options aren't available.
4. Manage Growth by letting our business decisions be guided as much by their environmental implications as by economics.
5. Manage Energy by working towards replacing what we must use with renewable resources.
6. Manage Waste by adopting a four-tier approach: reduce, reuse, recycle and as last resort, dispose by the safest and most responsible means possible.
7. Control Pollution by protecting the quality of land, air and water on which we depend.
8. Operate Safely by minimizing risk at every level of our operations: for staff, for customers and for the community in which the business operates.
9. Obey the Law by complying with environmental laws at all times.
10. Raise Awareness by continuously educating our staff and our customers.

Community Outreach   The Body Shop believes that businesses should give something back to the communities in which they trade. We try to do that in a number of different ways.

Harlem   We opened our 120th American shop on 125th Street in Harlem in 1992. Staffed in part by residents of the community, this shop is helping to contribute to the economic revitalization of the Harlem community. Fifty percent of the post-interest, pre-tax profits from the shop are placed in a fund which will be used to open other community-based shops around the country, while the other 50% is given to a fund (monitored by an advisory group of local community leaders) for Harlem community projects.

Community Projects   We encourage all of our employees to do volunteer work and allow them four hours each month of paid time to do it! Community projects are as diverse as our staff and the communities in which we trade. They range from Adopt-a-Highway clean ups, to delivering meals to homebound people with AIDS, to working with children who have been physically abused, to serving meals to the homeless.

Local Events   In addition to regular community projects work, our employees frequently help out with local events. Recent projects have included a Harlem street fair, participation in AIDS walkathons and benefit dances to raise money for the Kayapo Indians in Brazil. Many shops do makeovers, foot and hand massages and aromatherapy massages and donate the proceeds to local organizations. And staff also frequently give talks to various community groups on a wide range of topics—from endangered species to how The Body Shop does business to the rights of indigenous people.[68]

GLOBAL OPERATIONS AND FINANCIAL RESULTS

Turnover

Turnover was a combination of retail sales, excluding sales taxes at company-owned shops, wholesale revenue for goods sold in the United Kingdom and overseas, and sales to third parties by Cos-tec and Jacaranda.[69]

The *Annual Report* stated that "the growth in turnover was achieved through higher retail sales in all markets and higher exports, including sales to overseas subsidiaries, increased by 16 percent to £75.8 million."[70]

Retail Sales

Worldwide retail sales were £500.0 million, £432.7 million, and £371.5 million, and turnover was £219.7 million, £195.4 million, and £168.3 million for 1995, 1994, and 1993, respectively. International sales were 70% and 68% of total sales in 1995 and 1994, respectively. Retail sales by region were as follows:[71]

Retail Sales by Region
(British Pound amounts in millions)

Region	1995	1994	Change	Percentage of Retail Sales
United Kingdom	£148.9	£140.5	6%	30%
Europe (excluding U.K.)	131.0	112.4	17	26
United States	91.1	72.2	26	18
Americas (excluding the United States)	46.5	43.9	6	10
Asia	50.8	33.7	51	10
Australia and New Zealand	31.8	30.0	6	6
Totals	£500.1	£432.7		

Fourteen new shops were opened in Japan during 1995. They contributed to an Asian growth rate of 51% but only 10% of total worldwide sales.

Worldwide, comparable shop sales showed growth of 3% during 1995, compared to 5% in 1994. In 1993, the comparable store sales were down by 6% from the previous year. The turnaround was achieved by a more concentrated retail approach.

Customer transactions, which company executives felt were "the best indicator of volume within our shops,"[72] showed a 12% growth during 1995 to 78.6 million. The average transaction per customer was approximately £6.40. Customer transaction growth rates from 1994 to 1995 by geographic region were (1) United Kingdom, 43%; (2) Europe (excluding U.K.), 23%; (3) United States, 13%; (4) Americas (excluding the United States), 9%; (5) Asia, 6%; and Australia and New Zealand, 6%.

Operating Profits

The operating profits of the company's six geographic regions were as follows:[73]

Operating Profit by Region
(British pound amounts in millions)

Region	1995	1994	Change	Percentage of 1995 Operating Profit
United Kingdom	£12.9	£11.4	13%	37%
Europe	6.7	5.9	14	20
United States	4.9	6.2	(21)	14
Americas (excluding the United States)	2.8	2.4	13	16
Asia	5.6	2.4	133	8
Australia and New Zealand	001.6	001.8	(11%)	5
Total	£34.5	£30.1		

Management Analysis by Regions

This section presents management analyses of operations by geographic regions, as reported in the company's 1995 *Annual Report*.[74]

United Kingdom The company acted as the head franchisee in the United Kingdom, managing wholesale and retail activities. Four shops were opened during the 1995 financial year, giving a total of 243 shops at year-end. Of these, 179 were franchised, 21 were operated on a partnership basis, and 43 were company-owned. The company anticipated a similar level of new store openings in 1996. Refer to the following table for details.

Region: United Kingdom	1995	1994	1993
Shops at year end	243	239	233
Shop openings	4	6	23

Category	British Pound	amounts in millions	Change
Retail sales	£148.9	£140.5	6%
Turnover	96.5	91.1	6
Operating profit	12.9	11.4	13

Total retail sales grew by 6% in the year to February 1995, compared to 4% in the previous year. The company's focus on achieving improved growth in existing stores continued, with comparable store sales improving from a level position in 1994 to growth of 4% in the year to February 1995.

The growth in turnover of 6% was in line with retail sales growth. Growth in operating profit benefited from the overall increase in gross margin.

During 1995, 35 stores were upgraded as part of an initiative to update existing shops in the United Kingdom. A new signage system was implemented in all shops, designed to give better directional and sales information to customers. In addition, the company has been trialing an updated lighting system, a new shop fascia, central floor promotional units, and a new color cosmetics stand.

United States   The company's subsidiary, The Body Shop, Inc., functioned as the head franchisee for the United States. The head office, filling facilities, and main distribution center were based in Wake Forest, North Carolina.

The rate of shop openings accelerated, with 65 new stores opened during 1995 and the number of company-owned shops increased by 39 to 90 at year-end. During 1996, the company expected to open some 40 new stores, as it concentrated resources on reversing the decline in comparable store sales. Refer to the following table for details.

Region: United States	1995	1994	1993
Shops at year end	235	170	120
Shop openings	65	50	42

Category	U.S. dollar amounts in millions		Change
Retail sales	$144.8	$114.9	26%
Turnover	93.6	75.1	17

Category	British pound amounts in millions		Change
Retail sales	£91.1	£72.2	26%
Turnover	58.8	50.4	17
Operating profit	4.9	6.2	21

Total retail sales showed 26% growth for 1995 on the larger base, compared to 47% in the previous year. Comparable store sales showed a decline of 3% in 1995, compared to growth of 7% experienced in 1994.

The Body Shop opened its first store in the United States in 1988. At that time, there was no significant competition of a similar nature. Since then, and particularly in 1994 and 1995, a large number of competitors have opened in the personal care market sector. The Body Shop's expansion had also been rapid, and, as a result, the quality of the products offered at retail in the United States and the operational management of the stores suffered.

All major management functions were in place in the United States, with Terry Hartin, one of the main board directors, taking on the role of Chief Operating Officer in the United States. The focus was on improving retail offer-ings and the standards in stores in order to reverse the decline in comparable store sales. Staff training and promotional activity levels within the shops were being increased in order to appeal to U.S. customers more effectively.

Turnover in the United States was 25% higher when expressed in dollars, but, due to the change in the rate used for translation, the increase in the pound sterling value of turnover was 17%. This growth in turnover was lower than anticipated. As a result, the operating profit showed a decline of 21%. The U.S. operating profit was a combination of the margin realized in the United Kingdom on supplying goods to the United States together with the margin arising from wholesale and retail activities within the United States.

Europe (excluding the U.K.)   Excluding the United States, Europe had the highest level of store openings in 1995, with 10 in Germany, 9 in Greece, and 6 in Italy. The opening rate in Europe was accelerating in 1996, with some 50 new store openings. Refer to the following table for details.

Region: Europe	1995	1994	1993
Shops at year end	430	385	321
Shop openings	45	64	71

Category	British pound amounts in millions		Change
Retail sales	£131.0	£112.4	17%
Turnover	32.0	30.9	4
Operating profit	6.7	5.9	14

Retail sales showed 17% growth compared to 24% in 1994. Comparable store sales showed 4% growth, a lower average than the 8% recorded in 1994. Greece and Germany continued to show good growth, while some other countries (such as Holland and Spain) experienced declines in comparable store sales following the higher rates of store openings in 1994.

The company was looking to build comparable store growth in a number of ways, including customer building programs, retail experimentation, and the opening of flag-ship stores in some key cities.

Turnover was 4% higher than in 1994, with the lower growth partly reflecting a full year of trading following the sale of the Group's 66% share in Eastwick Trading BV in November 1993. The underlying growth in exports to Europe was 17%.

Other than the United Kingdom, Europe had the largest profit contribution, up 145% from 1994.

In October 1994, the company refranchised its business in Norway to an independent head franchisee.

Asia Retail sales grew by 51% in 1995, with Japan showing particularly strong growth (14 new stores were opened). The Body Shop built on its growing presence in the Tokyo and Osaka regions and opened shops in the Nagoya region. Japan was its sixth largest market in terms of retail sales, and the company anticipated that it would become the fourth largest in 1996. Refer to the following table for details.

Region: Asia	1995	1994	1993
Shops at year end	119	88	65
Shop openings	31	23	18

Category	British pound amounts in millions		Change
Retail sales	£50.8	£33.7	51%
Turnover	17.3	8.1	114
Operating profit	5.6	2.4	133

Store openings in Asia were expected to accelerate in 1996. Of the approximately 50 new shops to be opened, about half would be in Japan.

Comparable store sales in Asia showed a steady growth of 10% in 1995, a strong improvement on the previous year when comparable store sales grew by only 1%. Performance in Japan benefited from growing brand awareness as The Body Shop's presence increased. Hong Kong showed good growth, and the store in Singapore performed well.

The growth in both turnover and operating profit from Asia was driven by the growth in retail sales and the impact of the changes made in Southeast Asia.

Americas (excluding the United States) Given the relative maturity of the store base in Canada, The Body Shop was working hard at fueling growth through marketing its products more effectively. Store openings were expected to remain at about the same level in 1996. Refer to the following table for details.

Region: Americas (excluding the United States)	1995	1994	1993
Shops at year end	121	114	111
Shop openings	7	3	12

Category	British pound amounts in millions		Change
Retail Sales	£46.5	£43.9	6%
Turnover	9.7	8.6	13
Operating profit	2.8	2.4	17

Retail sales were 6% higher in 1995 than in 1994. Turnover showed an increase of 13% in 1995. The margin was slightly higher, giving a 17% improvement in operating profit.

Australia and New Zealand Retail sales were 6% higher in 1995 than in the previous year. Comparable store sales were

1% lower, compared to 5% growth in 1994. The deterioration was largely due to a poor performance in New Zealand, where comparable store sales were down by 8%. Store openings in the region were expected to occur at a similar rate in 1996. Refer to the following table for details.

Region: Australia and New Zealand	1995	1994	1993
Shops at year end	62	57	50
Shop openings	5	7	7

Category	British pound amounts in millions		Change
Retail sales	£31.8	£30.0	6%
Turnover	5.4	6.3	(14)
Operating profit	1.6	1.8	(11)

Both turnover and profit were lower than 1994 due to stock adjustments at the company's head franchisee's warehouse, following the relocation of its manufacturing and distribution facilities in March, 1994.

International In the other 43 countries in which The Body Shop traded, wholesale and retail activities were carried out by independent franchisees. Retail sales across the 43 countries grew by 18% in 1995 compared to 20% in 1994. Refer to the following table for details.

Region: International	1995	1994
Shops at year end	732	644
Shop openings	88	97

Category	British pound amounts in millions		Change
Retail sales	£260.1	£220.0	18%
Turnover	64.4	53.9	19
Operating profit	16.7	12.5	34

Turnover increased by 19%, or broadly in line with growth in retail sales. Operating profit was 34% higher, reflecting higher wholesale volumes. Although the number of countries in which The Body Shop trades did not increase during 1995, the company continued to research new markets, particularly in Asia.

Exhibits IC3–7 and IC3–8 show the company's balance sheets and consolidated profit and loss accounts.

CASE QUESTIONS

1. Do a strategic analysis of The Body Shop. Include an assessment of the path of evolution of The Body Shop as a global company and its growth through franchising.
2. What role has been played by the social concerns of the founder, Anita Roddick? What role should they play in the future?

EXHIBIT IC3–7

Balance Sheets: The Body Shop
(British pound amounts in millions)

Year Ending February 25	Group		Company	
	1995	1994	1995	1994
Fixed assets				
Intangible assets	£ 2.2	£ 3.7	£ 2.2	£ 3.7
Tangible assets	73.6	67.9	50.5	49.2
Investments	0.5	0.0	13.0	12.7
	76.3	71.6	65.7	65.6
Current assets				
Stocks	38.6	34.6	21.1	18.0
Debtors	44.5	37.2	52.5	38.8
Cash at bank and in hand	29.0	24.9	24.3	22.0
	112.1	96.7	97.9	78.8
Creditors: Amounts falling due within one year	51.2	35.6	41.1	32.0
Net current assets	60.9	61.1	56.8	46.8
Total assets less current liabilities	137.2	132.7	122.5	112.4
Creditors: amounts falling due after more than one year	23.7	32.4	0.7	1.9
Provisions for liabilities and charges				
Deferred tax	2.9	3.4	3.9	4.2
Total assets	£110.6	£96.9	£117.9	£106.3
Capital and reserves				
Called up share amount	9.5	9.4	9.5	9.4
Share premium account	37.0	35.7	37.0	35.7
Profit and loss account	64.1	51.8	71.4	61.2
Total capital and reserves	£110.6	£96.9	£117.9	£106.3

Notes:

1. These financial statements were approved by the Board on 9 May 1995.

2. Notes were deleted.

Source: The Body Shop, *1995 Annual Report,* p. 29.

INTEGERATIVE CASES

EXHIBIT IC3–8

Consolidated Profit and Loss Account: The Body Shop
(British pound amounts in millions, except per-ordinary share data)

Year Ending February 25	1995	1994
Turnover[1]	£219.7	£195.4
Cost of sales	89.6	89.5
Gross profit	130.1	105.9
Net operating expenses	95.6	75.8
Operating profit	34.5	30.1
Profit on disposal of subsidiary undertaking		1.1
	34.5	31.2
Interest payable (net)	1	1.5
Profit on ordinary activities before tax	33.5	29.7
Tax on profit on ordinary activities	11.7	10.1
	21.8	19.6
Minority interests		0.2
Profit for the financial year	21.8	19.4
Dividends paid and proposed	4.5	3.8
Retained profit	£ 17.3	£ 15.6
Earnings per ordinary share	£ 11.5	£ 10.3
Adjusted earnings per ordinary share	£ 11.5	£ 10.1

Notes:

1. Turnover represents the total amounts receivable in the ordinary course of business for goods sold and services provided and excludes sales between companies in the Group, discount given, Value Added Tax (VAT), and other sales taxes.

2. Other notes were deleted.

Source: The Body Shop, 1995 *Annual Report*, p. 28.

3. Evaluate the strategic planning of The Body Shop as part of the global cosmetics industry.
4. Evaluate (at the time of the case) the financial position, the organizational design, and the future prospects for The Body Shop.
5. Develop a strategic plan for the next 10 years.

NOTES

1. "Body Shop Chief Abandons Plans to Take Firm Private," *Wall Street Journal,* March 5, 1996, p. A10.

2. James Fallon, "Roddicks May Take Body Shop Private," *WWD,* November 3, 1995, p. 4.
3. "UK Company News: Body Shop Downgraded After Warnings," *Financial Times,* January 18, 1996, p. 25.
4. "Body Shop Chief Abandons Plans," p. A10.
5. Anat Arkin, "Open Business Is Good for Business," *People Management,* January 11, 1996, p. 24.
6. *The Body Shop Social Audit.* http://www.the-body-shop.com February 28, 1996.
7. Anita Roddick, *The Body Shop,* (New York: Crown,), 1991, p. 43.

8. *Ibid.*, p. 52.
9. *Ibid.*, pp. 55–62.
10. *Ibid.*, p. 66.
11. *Ibid.*
12. *Ibid.*, p. 67.
13. *Ibid.*, p. 68.
14. *Ibid.*
15. *Ibid.*
16. *Ibid.*, p. 77.
17. *Ibid.*, p. 68.
18. *Ibid.*, p. 74.
19. *Ibid.*, pp. 85–86.
20. *Ibid.*, p. 86.
21. The Body Shop, *1995 Annual Report*, p. 8.
22. *Ibid.*, p. 92.
23. *Ibid.*, pp. 94–95.
24. *Ibid.*, pp. 96–97.
25. *Ibid.*, p. 101.
26. *Ibid.*
27. *Ibid.*, p. 100.
28. *Ibid.*
29. *Ibid.*, p. 143.
30. *Ibid.*, p. 144.
31. *Ibid.*, p. 153.
32. *Ibid.*, p. 15.
33. *Ibid.*, p. 17.
34. *Ibid.*, p. 20.
35. *Ibid.*, p. 25.
36. *Ibid.*, p. 49.
37. *Ibid.*, p. 81.
38. *Ibid.*, p. 108.
39. *Ibid.*, p. 115.
40. *Ibid.*, p. 123.
41. *Ibid.*, p. 226.
42. *Ibid.*, p. 158.
43. *Ibid.*, p. 178.
44. *Ibid.*, p. 214.
45. *Ibid.*, p. 217.
46. *Ibid.*, p. 223.
47. *Ibid.*, p. 231.
48. *Ibid.*, p. 181.
49. *Ibid.*, p. 137.
50. The Body Shop, *Our Reason for Being* (handout).
51. The Body Shop, *1995 Annual Report*, p. 25.
52. *Ibid.*, p. 23.
53. *Ibid.*, p. 24.
54. *Ibid.*
55. *Ibid.*, p. 36.
56. *Ibid.*
57. The Body Shop, *1994 Annual Report*, p. 23.
58. *Ibid.*, p. 22.
59. Anita Roddick, pp. 235–236.
60. *Ibid.*, p. 143.
61. *Ibid.*, p. 125.
62. *Ibid.*, p. 135.
63. The Body Shop, *1994 Annual Report*, p. 22.
64. The Body Shop, *This Is The Body Shop*, November 1994, p. 57. All five paragraphs were taken directly from this source.
65. The Body Shop, *1995 Annual Report*, p. 11.
66. The Body Shop, *This Is The Body Shop*, pp. 6–8. All 16 paragraphs were taken directly from this source.
67. The Body Shop, *1995 Annual Report*, p. 3. The first 6 words were added and the rest taken directly from the source.
68. The Body Shop, *This Is The Body Shop*, pp. 8–9. All 5 paragraphs taken directly from this source.
69. The Body Shop, *1995 Annual Report*, pp. 17–22.
70. *Ibid.*
71. *Ibid.*, pp. 18–20.
72. *Ibid.*, pp. 17–22.
73. *Ibid.*, pp. 18–20.
74. *Ibid.*

Glossary

acculturation   The process of cultural change and adaptation among groups, in particular where one or more minority groups are being merged with a majority group.

affective appeals   Negotiation appeals based on emotions and subjective feelings.

appropriability of technology   The ability of an innovating firm to protect its technology from competitors and to obtain economic benefits from that technology.

assimilation   A one-way process of adaptation in which people are expected to conform to the values and norms of the dominant culture, causing gradual erosion of minority groups' cultures.

attribution   The process in which a person looks for the explanation of another person's behavior.

axiomatic appeals   Negotiation appeals based on the ideals generally accepted in a society.

balance sheet approach   An approach to the compensation of expatriates that equalizes the standard of living between the host and home countries, plus compensation for inconvenience.

chaebol   South Korea's large industrial conglomerates of financially linked, and often family-linked, groups of companies that do business among themselves whenever possible—for example, Daewoo.

codetermination   The participation of labor in the management of a firm.

collective bargaining   In the United States—negotiations between a labor union local and management; in Sweden and Germany, for example, negotiations between the employer's organization and a trade union at the industry level.

collectivism   The tendency of a society toward tight social frameworks, emotional dependence on belonging to an organization, and a strong belief in group decisions.

comparative advantage   A mutual benefit in the exchange of goods between countries, where each country exports those products in which it is relatively more efficient in production than other countries.

competitive advantage of nations   The existence of conditions that give a country an advantage in a specific industry or in producing a particular good or service.

context in cultures (low to high)   Low-context cultures, such as Germany, tend to use explicit means of communication in words and readily available information; high-context cultures, such as those in the Middle East, use more implicit means of communication, in which information is embedded in the nonverbal context and understanding of the people.

control system appropriateness   The use of control systems that are individually tailored to the practices and expectations of the host-country personnel.

convergence (of management styles, techniques, and so forth)   The phenomenon of increasing similarity of leadership styles resulting from a blending of cultures and business practices through international institutions, as opposed to the **divergence** of leadership styles necessary for different cultures and practices.

core competencies   Important corporate resources or skills that bring competitive advantages.

creeping expropriation   A government's gradual and subtle action against foreign firms.

creeping incrementalism   A process of increasing commitment of resources to one or more geographic regions.

cross-cultural management (research), or comparative management (research)   That field of management that studies the behavior of people interacting within and among organizations around the world.

cultural noise   Cultural variables that undermine the communications of intended meaning.

cultural sensitivity (cultural empathy)   A sense of awareness and caring about the culture of other people.

culture   The shared values, understandings, assumptions, and goals that over time are passed on and imposed by members of a group or society.

culture shock   A state of disorientation and anxiety that results from not knowing how to behave in an unfamiliar culture.

culture-specific reward systems   Motivational and compensation approaches that reflect different motivational patterns across cultures.

deculturation   The process by which people in transition between culture groups lose their cultural identity through insufficient ties to either group.

degree of enforcement   The relative degree of enforcement, in a particular country, of the law regarding business behavior, which therefore determines the lower limit of permissible behavior.

direct control   The control of foreign subsidiaries and operations through the use of appropriate international staffing and structure policies and meetings with home-country executives (as compared with **indirect control**).

divergence   see **convergence**.

domestic multiculturalism   The diverse makeup of the workforce comprising people from several different cultures in the home (domestic) company.

economic risk   The level of uncertainty about the ability of a country to meet its financial obligations.

environmental assessment   The continuous process of gathering and evaluating information about variables and events around the world that may pose threats or opportunities to the firm.

ethical relativism   An approach to social responsibility in which a country adopts the moral code of its host country.

ethnocentric staffing approach   An approach that fills key managerial positions abroad with persons from headquarters—that is, with parent-country nationals (PCNs).

ethnocentrism   The belief that the management techniques used in one's own country are best no matter where or with whom they are applied.

expatriate   One who works and lives in a foreign country but remains a citizen of the country where the employing organization is headquartered.

expropriation   The seizure by a local government of the foreign-owned assets of an MNC with inadequate or no compensation.

Foreign Corrupt Practices Act   A 1977 law that prohibits most questionable payments by U.S. companies doing business in other countries.

franchising   An international entry strategy by which a firm (the franchiser) licenses its trademark, products, or services and operating principles to the franchisee in a host country for an initial fee and ongoing royalties.

fully owned subsidiary   An overseas operation started or bought by a firm that has total ownership and control; starting or buying such an operation is often used as an entry strategy.

generalizability of leadership styles   The ability (or lack of ability) to generalize leadership theory, research results, and effective leadership practices from one country to another.

geocentric staffing approach   A staffing approach in which the best managers are recruited throughout the company or outside the company, regardless of nationality—often, third-country nationals (TCNs) are recruited.

global corporate culture   An integration of the business environments in which firms currently operate, resulting from a dissolution of traditional boundaries and from increasing links among MNCs.

globalism   Global competition characterized by networks of international linkages that bind countries, institutions, and people in an interdependent global economy and a one-world market.

globalization   The global strategy of the integration of worldwide operations and the development of standardized products and marketing approaches.

global strategic alliances   Working partnerships that are formed around MNCs across national boundaries and often across industries.

governmentalism   The tendency of a government to use its policy-setting role to favor national interests rather than relying on market forces.

horizontal organization (dynamic network)   A structural approach that enables the flexibility to be global and act local through horizontal coordination, shared power, and decision making across international units and teams.

indirect control   The control of foreign operations through the use of reports, budgets, financial controls, and so forth (see **direct control**).

individualism   The tendency of people to look after themselves and their immediate family only and to value democracy, individual initiative, and personal achievement.

integration of immigrant workers   Providing programs to integrate the foreign-born into the workplace and local community.

intercultural communication   This type of communication occurs when a member of one culture sends a message to a receiver who is a member of another culture.

international business   The profit-related activities conducted across national boundaries.

international business ethics   The business conduct or morals of MNCs in their relationships to all individuals and entities with whom they come in contact.

international codes of conduct   The codes of conduct of four major international institutions that provide some consistent guidelines for multinational enterprises relative to their moral approach to business behavior around the world.

international competitor analysis   The process of assessing the competitive positions, goals, strategies, strengths, and weaknesses of competitors relative to one's own firm.

internationalization   The process by which a firm gradually changes in response to the imperatives of international competition, domestic market saturation, desire for expansion, new markets, and diversification.

international management   The process of planning, organizing, leading, and controlling in a multicultural or cross-cultural environment.

international management teams   Collections of managers from several countries who must rely on group collaboration if each member is to achieve success.

international social responsibility   The expectation that MNCs should be concerned about the social and economic effects of their decisions regarding activities in other countries.

joint venture   An overseas business owned and controlled by two or more partners; starting such a venture is often used as an entry strategy.

keiretsu   Large Japanese conglomerates of financially linked, and often family-linked, groups of companies, such as Mitsubishi, that do business among themselves whenever possible.

kibun   Feelings and attitudes (Korean word).

labor relations   The process through which managers and workers determine their workplace relationships.

licensing   An international entry strategy by which a firm grants the rights to a firm in the host country to produce or sell a product.

locus of decision making (locus of control)   The relative level of decentralization in an organization, that is, the level at which decisions of varying importance can be made—ranging from all decisions made at headquarters to all made at the local subsidiary.

love–hate relationship   An expression describing a common attitude of host governments toward MNC investment in their country—they love the economic growth that the MNC brings but hate the incursions on their independence and sovereignty.

managing diversity   The effective management of a culturally diverse workforce through understanding and valuing diversity; achieved by acknowledging and using the different skills and perceptions of people from various backgrounds and encouraging others to do so.

managing environmental interdependence   The process by which international managers accept and enact their role in the preservation of ecological balance on the earth.

managing interdependence   The effective management of a long-term MNC subsidiary–host country relationship through cooperation and consideration for host concerns.

maquiladoras   U.S. manufacturing or assembly facilities operating just south of the U.S.–Mexico border under special tax considerations.

masculinity   The degree to which traditionally "masculine" values—assertiveness, materialism, and the like—prevail in a society.

MIS inadequacy   The inability to gather timely and accurate information necessary for international management, especially in less developed countries.

monochronic cultures   Those cultures in which time is experienced and used in a linear way; there is a past, present, and future, and time is treated as something to be spent, saved, wasted, and so on (as compared with **polychronic cultures**).

moral idealism   The relative emphasis on long-term, ethical, and moral criteria for decisions versus short-term, cost–benefit criteria (see **utilitarianism**).

moral universalism   A moral standard toward social responsibility accepted by all cultures.

multicultural leader   A person who is effective in inspiring and influencing the thinking, attitudes, and behavior of people from various cultural backgrounds.

multinational corporation (MNC)   A corporation that engages in production or service activities through its own affiliates in several countries, maintains control over the policies of those affiliates, and manages from a global perspective.

nationalism   The practice by a country of rallying public opinion in favor of national goals and against foreign influences.

nationalization   The forced sale of the MNC's assets to local buyers with some compensation to the firm, perhaps leaving a minority ownership with the MNC; often involves the takeover of an entire industry, such as the oil industry.

negotiation   The process by which two or more parties meet to try to reach agreement regarding conflicting interests.

noncomparability of performance data across countries   The control problem caused by the difficulty of comparing performance data across various countries because of the variables that make that information appear different.

nontask sounding (*nemawashi*)   General polite conversation and informal communication before meetings.

nonverbal communication (body language)   The transfer of meaning through the use of body language, time, and space.

objective–subjective decision-making approach   The relative level of rationality and objectivity used in making decisions versus the level of subjective factors, such as emotions and ideals.

open systems model   The view that all factors inside and outside a firm—environment, organization, and management—work together as a dynamic, interdependent system.

parochialism   The expectation that "foreigners" should automatically fall into host-country patterns of behavior.

pluralism   A process of acculturation in which there is a two-way integration of cultural groups.

political risk   The potential for governmental actions or politically motivated events to occur in a country that will adversely affect the long-run profitability or value of a firm.

polycentric staffing approach   An MNC policy of using local host-country nationals (HCNs) to fill key positions in the host country.

polychronic cultures   Those cultures that welcome the simultaneous occurrence of many things and emphasize involvement with people over specific time commitments or compartmentalized activities (as compared with **monochronic cultures**).

posturing   General discussion that sets the tone for negotiation meetings.

power distance   The extent to which subordinates accept unequal power and a hierarchical system in a company.

privatization   The sale of government-owned operations to private investors.

projective cognitive similarity   The assumption that others perceive, judge, think, and reason in the same way.

protectionism   A country's use of tariff and nontariff barriers to partially or completely close its borders to various imported products that would compete with domestic products.

quality control circle (QC circle)   A group of workers who meet regularly to find ways to improve the quality of work.

questionable payments   Business payments that raise significant ethical issues about appropriate moral behavior in either a host nation or other nations.

regiocentric staffing approach   An approach in which recruiting for international managers is done on a regional basis and may comprise a specific mix of PCNs, HCNs, and TCNs.

regionalization   The global corporate strategy that links markets within regions and allows managers in each region to formulate their own regional strategy and cooperate as quasi-independent subsidiaries.

regulatory environment   The many laws and courts of the nation in which an international manager works.

relationship building   The process of getting to know one's contacts in a host country and building mutual trust before embarking on business discussions and transactions.

repatriation   The process of the reintegration of expatriates into the headquarters organization and career ladder as well as into the social environment.

self-reference criterion   An unconscious reference to one's own cultural values; understanding and relating to others only from one's own cultural frame of reference.

separation   The retention of distinct identities by minority groups unwilling or unable to adapt to the dominant culture.

stereotyping   The assumption that every member of a society or subculture has the same characteristics or traits, without regard to individual differences.

strategic alliances (global)   Working partnerships between MNCs across national boundaries and often across industries.

strategic freedom of an IJV   The relative amount of control that an international joint venture will have, compared with the parents, in choosing suppliers, product lines, customers, and so on.

strategic implementation   The process by which strategic plans are realized through the establishment of a system of fits throughout an organization with the desired strategy—for example, in organizational structure, staffing, and operations.

strategic planning   The process by which a firm's managers consider the future prospects for their company and evaluate and decide on strategy to achieve long-term objectives.

strategy   The basic means by which a company competes—the choice of business or businesses in which it operates and how it differentiates itself from its competitors in those businesses.

structural evolution   The stages of change in an organizational structure that follow the evolution of the internationalization process.

subsidiary   A business incorporated in a foreign country in which the parent corporation holds an ownership position.

synergy   The greater level of effectiveness that can result from combined group effort than from the total of each individual's efforts alone.

technoglobalism   A phenomenon in which the rapid developments in information and communication technologies (CTSs) are propelling globalization and vice versa.

terrorism   The use of, or threat to use, violence for ideological or political purposes.

total quality management (TQM)   A philosophy practiced by an entire organization working together with an interdepartmental collective responsibility for the quality of products and services.

transnational corporations (TNCs)   Multinational corporations that are truly globalizing by viewing the world as one market and crossing boundaries for whatever functions or resources are most efficiently available; structural coordination reflects the ability to integrate globally while retaining local flexibility.

uncertainty avoidance   The extent to which people feel threatened by ambiguous situations; in a company, this results in formal rules and processes to provide more security.

utilitarianism   The relative emphasis on short-term, cost–benefit (utilitarian) criteria for decisions versus those of long-term, ethical, and moral concerns (see **moral idealism**).

values   A person or group's ideas and convictions about what is important, good or bad, right or wrong.

work centrality   The degree of general importance that working has in the life of an individual at any given time.

workforce diversity   The phenomenon of increasing ethnic diversity in the workforce in the United States and many other countries because of diverse populations and joint ventures; this results in intercultural working environments in domestic companies.

Booknotes

CHAPTER 1: THE CHALLENGE OF INTERNATIONAL MANAGEMENT

1. "The Triple Revolution," 21st Century Capitalism, *Business Week,* 1995 Special Issue.
2. S. H. Robock and K. Simmonds, *International Business and Multinational Enterprises,* 4th ed. (Homewood, IL: Irwin, 1989).
3. K. Ohmae, "Putting Global Logic First," *Harvard Business Review* (January–February 1995): 119–125.
4. Ibid.
5. *Business Week,* August 31, 1998.
6. Jeremy Kahn, "The Fortune Global 500," *Fortune,* August 3, 1998.
7. K. Ohmae, *The Borderless World* (New York: Harper Business, 1990).
8. Ibid.
9. P. Gumbel, "Customs of the Countries," *Wall Street Journal,* September 30, 1994.
10. *Wall Street Journal,* February 28, 1995.
11. "Japan: All in the Family," *Newsweek,* June 10, 1991.
12. "South Korean Chaebol Enter Series of Mergers," *Wall Street Journal,* September 4, 1998.
13. A. R. Dowd, "Viva Free Trade with Mexico," *Fortune,* June 17, 1991; Bob Davis, "World Business," *Wall Street Journal,* September 24, 1992, R1.
14. "Detroit South," *Business Week,* March 16, 1992.
15. C. F. Doran, "Canada's Role in North America," *Current History* 90, no. 560 (December 1991): 401–404.
16. W. E. Halal and A. I. Nikitin, "One World: The Coming Synthesis of New Capitalism and a New Socialism," *Futurist* (November–December 1990): 8–14.
17. J. A. Quelch, E. Joachimsthaler, and J. L. Nueno, "After the Wall: Marketing Guidelines for Eastern Europe," *Sloan Management Review* (Winter 1991): 82–93.
18. "Piling into Central Europe," *Business Week,* July 1, 1996.
19. A. Imse, Associated Press, "USSR Industry Can Be Sold to Soviets, Foreigners," *Plattsburgh Press-Republican* (July 1991).
20. B. W. Nelan, "Yeltsin's Desperate Gamble," *Time,* August 1998.
21. F. S. Worthy, "Making It in China," *Fortune,* June 17, 1991.
22. "China's Gates Swing Open," *Business Week,* June 13, 1994.
23. "Russia's State Sell-off: 'It's Sink-or-Swim Time,'" *Business Week,* July 7, 1994, 46.
24. Ibid.
25. Ibid.
26. S. Tully, "Europe Goes Wild over Privatization," *Fortune,* March 2, 1987, 68–70.
27. "Twenty-First Century Capitalism, Tearing up Today's Organizational Chart," *Business Week,* 1995 Special Edition.
28. G. Schares, "Eastern Europe Tries to Stoke Up Its Fire Sale," *Business Week,* October 21, 1991.
29. "Eastward Ho! The Pioneers Plunge In," *Business Week,* April 15, 1991.
30. S. W. Sanderson and R. H. Hayes, "Mexico—Opening Ahead of Eastern Europe," *Harvard Business Review* (September–October 1990).
31. T. Kamm, "Going Private: South Americans Push Sales of Assets in Swing to Capitalism," *Wall Street Journal,* July 9, 1991, A1.
32. Ibid.
33. M. Forney, P. Yatsko, "No More Free Lunch," *Far Eastern Economic Review,"* October 16, 1997, 62–63.
34. UPI Newswire, November 7, 1995.
35. K. Ohmae.
36. W. B. Johnston, "Global Work Force 2000: The New World Labor Market," *Harvard Business Review* (March–April 1991): 115–127.
37. N. J. Adler, "Cross-Cultural Management: Issues to Be Faced," *International Studies of Management and Organization* 13 (Spring–Summer 1983): 7–45.
38. E. Joy Mighty, "Valuing Workforce Diversity: A Model of Organizational Change," *Canadian Journal of Administrative Sciences* 8, no. 2 (June 1991): 64–70.
39. S. N. Mehta, "Small Companies Look to Cultivate Foreign Business," *Business Week,* July 7, 1994.

40. W. Dowell, "Silverware from Beneath the Sea," *Time,* December 8, 1997.

41. F. R. Root, *International Trade and Investment,* 5th ed. (Cincinnati: South-Western, 1984): 426–427.

42. Rosabeth Moss Kanter, "Transcending Business Boundaries: 12,000 World Managers View Change," *Harvard Business Review* (May–June 1991): 151–164. "Need for Global Orientation," *Management International Review* 30 (1990/91): 5–18.

43. K. Ohmae, *Beyond National Borders: Reflections on Japan and the World* (New York: Harper Business, 1991).

44. R. Reich, "The Myth of 'Made in the USA,'" *Wall Street Journal,* July 5, 1991.

45. W. J. Holstein, "The Stateless Corporation," *Business Week,* May 16, 1990, 98–105.

46. C. C. Snow, R. E. Miles, and H. J. Coleman, Jr., "Managing 21st Century Network Organizations," *Organizational Dynamics* (Winter 1992): 5–20.

47. L. Uvhitelle, "U.S. Businesses Loosen Link to Mother Country," *New York Times,* May 21, 1989, 1, 12.

48. J. Main, "How to Go Global—and Why," *Fortune,* August 28, 1989, 70.

49. Kanter.

50. N. J. Adler, R. Doktor, and S. G. Redding, "From the Atlantic to the Pacific Century: Cross-Cultural Management Reviewed," *Journal of Management* 12, no. 2 (1986): 295–318.

CHAPTER 2: THE POLITICAL, ECONOMIC, LEGAL, AND TECHNOLOGICAL ENVIRONMENT

1. M. C. Schnitzer, M. L. Liebrenz, and K. W. Kubin, *International Business* (Cincinnati, OH: South-Western, 1985).

2. B. Weiner, president of Probe International, "What Executives Should Know About Political Risks," *Management Review* (January 1991): 19–22.

3. Ibid.

4. S. H. Robock and K. Simmonds, *International Business and Multinational Enterprises,* 4th ed. (Homewood, IL: Irwin, 1989): 378.

5. Ibid.

6. D. F. Simon, "After Tiananmen: What Is the Future for Foreign Business in China?" *California Management Review* (Winter 1990): 106–108.

7. A. Clark, "Japan Goes to Europe," *World Monitor* (April 1990): 36–40.

8. Ibid.

9. E. F. Micklous, "Tracking the Growth and Prevalence of International Terrorism," in *Managing Terrorism: Strategies for the Corporate Executive,* ed. P. J. Montana and G. S. Roukis (Westport, CT: Quorum Books, 1983): 3.

10. Robock and Simmonds.

11. G. M. Taoka and D. R. Beeman, *International Business* (New York: HarperCollins, 1991).

12. Rahul Jacob, "Asian Infrastructure: The Biggest Bet on Earth," *Fortune,* October 31, 1994, 139–146.

13. D. R. Beeman, "An Empirical Analysis of the Beliefs Held by the International Executives of United States Firms Regarding Political Risks and Risk Reduction Methods in Developing Nations" (unpublished doctoral diss., Indiana University Graduate School of Business, 1978), reprinted in G. M. Taoka and D. R. Beeman, *International Business* (New York: HarperCollins, 1991): 36–41.

14. J. V. Micallef, "Political Risk Assessment," *Columbia Journal of World Business* 16, no. 2 (Summer 1981): 47–52.

15. T. W. Shreeve, "Be Prepared for Political Changes Abroad," *Harvard Business Review* (July-August 1984): 111–118.

16. L. Kraar, "The Multinationals Get Smarter About Political Risks," *Fortune,* March 24, 1980, 86–97.

17. R. H. Mason and R. S. Spich, *Management: An International Perspective* (Homewood, IL: Irwin, 1987).

18. A. C. Shapiro, "Managing Political Risk: A Policy Assessment," *Columbia Journal of World Business* 16, no. 3 (Fall 1981): 63–69.

19. S. J. Kobrin, "Assessing Political Risk Overseas," *Wharton Magazine* (Winter 1981–82): 25–31.

20. Ibid.

21. Schnitzer, Liebrenz, and Kubin.

22. C. Erol, "An Exploratory Model of Political Risk Assessment and the Decision Process of Foreign Direct Investment," *International Studies of Management and Organization* (Summer 1985): 75–90.

23. T. Morrison, W. Conaway, J. Bouress, *Dun & Bradstreet's Guide to Doing Business Around the World* (Englewood Cliffs: Prentice-Hall, 1997).

24. Ibid.

25. J. D. Simon, "Political Risk Assessment: Past Trends and Future Prospects," *Columbia Journal of World Business* 17, no. 3 (Fall 1982): 62–70.

26. Schnitzer, Liebrenz, and Kubin.

27. P. Smith Ring, S. A. Lenway, and M. Govekar, "Management of the Political Imperative in International

Business," *Strategic Management Journal* 11 (1990): 141–151.

28. Ibid.

29. L. D. Howell and B. Chaddick, "Models of Political Risk for Foreign Investment and Trade," *Columbia Journal of World Business,* Fall 1994.

30. Taoka and Beeman.

31. Ibid.

32. Overseas Private Investment Corporation, *Investment Insurance Handbook,* 4.

33. Schnitzer, Liebrenz, and Kubin.

34. B. O'Reilly, "Business Copes with Terrorism," *Fortune,* January 6, 1986, 48.

35. Ibid.

36. J. Dahl, "Firms Warn Workers Traveling Abroad," *Wall Street Journal,* April 10, 1989, B1.

37. A. Paul, "Indonesia," *Fortune,* April 13, 1998.

38. F. John Mathis, "International Risk Analysis," in *Global Business Management in the 1990s,* ed. R. T. Moran (Washington, DC: Beacham, 1990): 33–44.

39. Mathis, 40.

40. Ibid.

41. Much of this section is drawn from A. Paul, "Indonesia," *Fortune,* April 13, 1998.

42. Ibid.

43. "Why Sweet Deals are Going Sour in China," *Business Week,* December 19, 1994, 50–51.

44. Loeb.

45. P. Hui-Ho Cheng, "A Business Risk in China: Jail," *Asian Wall Street Journal,* April 22, 1994.

46. M. Litka, *International Dimensions of the Legal Environment of Business* (Boston: PWS-Kent, 1988): 5.

47. Ibid.

48. Jacob.

49. Litka.

50. Jacob.

51. Ibid.

52. R. J. Radway, "Foreign Contract Agreements," in *Global Business Management in the 1990s,* ed. R. T. Moran (Washington, DC: Beacham, 1990): 93–103.

53. S. P. Robbins and R. Stuart-Kotze, *Management* (Scarborough, Ontario: Prentice-Hall, Canada, 1990): 4–11.

54. Ibid.

55. Sylvia Ostry, "Technological Productivity and the Multinational Enterprise," *Journal of International Business Studies* 29, 1 (1st quarter, 1998) 85–99.

56. Ibid.

57. S. Magee, "Information and Multinational Corporations: An Appropriability Theory of Direct Foreign Investment," in *New International Economic Order,* ed. J. Bhagwati (Cambridge, MA: MIT Press, 1977).

58. J. M. Schlesinger, "Money and Honor Are Stakes in Battle Waged by Texas Instruments, Fujitsu," *Wall Street Journal,* July 22, 1991.

59. Ibid.

60. E. Barton, "Technology Controls," in *Global Business Management in the 1990s,* ed. R. T. Moran (Washington, DC: Beacham, 1990); H. Norman and P. Blair, "The Coming Growth in Appropriate Technology," *Harvard Business Review* (November–December 1982).

61. "Where Technology Is the Appropriate Word," *Economist,* April 18, 1987, 83.

62. "How to Sell Soap in India," *Economist,* September 1988, 82.

63. B. James, "Reducing the Risks of Globalization," *Long-Range Planning* 23, no. 1 (1990): 80–88.

CHAPTER 3: MANAGING INTERDEPENDENCE: SOCIAL RESPONSIBILITY AND ETHICS]

1. J. C. Laya, "Economic Development Issues," in *Multinational Managers and Host Government Interactions,* Lee A. Tavis, ed. (South Bend, IN: University of Notre Dame Press, 1988).

2. John A. Quelch and James E. Austin, "Should Multinationals Invest in Africa?" *Sloan Management Review* (Spring 1993): 107–119.

3. Milton Friedman, *Capitalism and Freedom* (Chicago: University of Chicago Press, 1962).

4. S. Prakash Sethi, "A Conceptual Framework for Environmental Analysis of Social Issues and Evaluation of Business Response Patterns," *Academy of Management Review* (January 1979): 63–74.

5. A. B. Carroll, "A Three Dimensional Conceptual Model of Corporate Performance," *Academy of Management Review* 4 (1979): 497–505.

6. John Dobson, "The Role of Ethics in Global Corporate Culture," *Journal of Business Ethics* 9 (1990): 481–488.

7. Ibid.

8. N. Bowie, "The Moral Obligations of Multinational Corporations," in *Problems of International Justice,* ed. Luper-Fay (New York: Westview Press, 1987): 97–113.

9. "Killer in a Bottle," *Economist* 279, no. 7184, May 9, 1981, 50.

10. A. C. Wicks, "Norman Bowie and Richard Rorty on Multinationals: Does Business Ethics Need 'Metaphysical Comfort'?" *Journal of Business Ethics* 9 (1990): 191–200.

11. *Financial Times,* March 16, 1994.

12. Joanna Ramey, "Clinton Urges Industry to Enlist in the War Against Sweatshops," www.labordepartment.com, April 15, 1997.

13. *Asian Wall Street Journal,* April 8, 1994.

14. *Business Week,* June 6, 1994.

15. "Staunching the Flow of China's Gulag Exports," *Business Week,* April 13, 1992.

16. J. Carlton, "Ties with China Will Be Severed by Levi Strauss," *Wall Street Journal,* May 5, 1993, A3.

17. *New York Times,* June 7, 1994.

18. "Doing Worse by Doing Good?" *Business Week,* June 12, 1995.

19. *Business Week,* January 21, 1994.

20. *New York Times,* June 6, 1994.

21. *Business Week,* June 12, 1995.

22. *New York Times,* June 6, 1994.

23. *Business Week,* May 27, 1992.

24. "Sweatshop Police," *Business Week,* October 20, 1997.

25. Kathleen A. Getz, "International Codes of Conduct: An Analysis of Ethical Reasoning," *Journal of Business Ethics* 9 (1990): 567–577.

26. Gene R. Laczniak and Jacob Naor, "Global Ethics: Wrestling with the Corporate Conscience," *Business* (July–August–September 1985): 3–10.

27. D. Vogel, "Is U.S. Business Obsessed with Ethics?" *Across the Board* (November–December, 1993): 31–33; A. Singer, "Ethics—Are Standards Lower Overseas?" *Across the Board* (September 1991): 31–34.

28. Parviz Asheghian and Bahman Ebrahimi, *International Business* (New York: Harper and Row, 1990).

29. Ibid.

30. Vogel.

31. Singer.

32. Ibid.

33. J. G. Kaikati and W. A. Label, "American Bribery Legislation: An Obstacle to International Marketing," *Journal of Marketing* (Fall 1980): 38–43.

34. Laczniak and Naor, 152.

35. Singer.

36. G. A. Steiner and J. F. Steiner, *Business, Government and Society,* 6th ed. (New York: McGraw-Hill, 1991).

37. Larry Luxner, "IBM Feeling Blue in Argentina," *Multinational Monitor* 17, no. 10 (October 1996): 14(4).

38. T. L. Carson, "Bribery and Implicit Agreements: A Reply to Philips," *Journal of Business Ethics* 6 (1987): 123–125.

39. M. Philips, "Bribery," *Ethics* 94 (July 1984).

40. Ibid.

41. Singer.

42. L. H. Newton and M. M. Ford, *Taking Sides* (Guilford, CT: Dushkin, 1990).

43. Ibid.

44. K. Gillespie, "Middle East Response to the U.S. Foreign Corrupt Practices Act," *California Management Review* (Summer 1987): 9.

45. K. M. Bartol and D. C. Martin, *Management* (New York: McGraw-Hill, 1991).

46. Vogel.

47. A. Cadbury, *Harvard Business Review* (September–October 1987): 63–73.

48. M. E. Shannon, "Coping with Extortion and Bribery," in *Multinational Managers and Host Government Interactions,* Lee A. Tavis, ed. (South Bend, IN: University of Notre Dame Press, 1988).

49. Laczniak and Naor.

50. "A World of Greased Palms," *Business Week,* November 6, 1995.

51. D. E. Sanger, "Nippon Telegraph Executive Demoted for Role in Scandal," *New York Times,* December 10, 1988.

52. Susan Chira, "Another Top Official in Japan Loses Post in Wake of Scandal," *New York Times,* January 25, 1989, 1, 5; "Remember the Recruit Scandal? Well …" *Business Week,* January 8, 1990, 52.

53. "Commercial Corruption," *Wall Street Journal,* January 2, 1997.

54. J. Melrose-Woodman and I. Kverndal, *Towards Social Responsibility: Company Codes of Ethics and Practice* (British Institute of Management Survey Reports, no. 28, 1976).

55. Catherine C. Langlois and Bodo B. Schlegelmilch, "Do Corporate Codes of Ethics Reflect National Character? Evidence from Europe and the United States," *Journal of International Business Studies* 21 (4th Quarter 1990): 519–539.

56. Ibid.

57. Vogel.

58. Helmut Becker and D. J. Fritzsche, "A Comparison of the Ethical Behavior of American, French and German Managers," *Columbia Journal of World Business* (Winter 1987): 87–95.

59. Ibid.

60. Henk J. L. van Luijk, "Recent Developments in European Business Ethics," *Journal of Business Ethics* 9 (1990): 537–544.

61. Mario Unnia, "Business Ethics in Italy: The State of the Art," *Journal of Business Ethics* 9 (1990): 551–554.

62. "Fiat's Right Turn," *Business Week,* May 3, 1993, 38.

63. Sadehei Kusomoto, "We're Not in Honshu Anymore," *Across the Board* (June 1989): 49–50.

64. Ibid.

65. P. W. Beamish et al., *International Management* (Homewood, IL: Irwin, 1991).

66. J. N. Behrman, *National Interests and the Multinational Enterprise* (Englewood Cliffs, NJ: Prentice-Hall, 1970): 31.

67. Adapted from P. Asheghian and B. Ebrahimi, *International Business* (New York: Harper and Row, 1990): 640–641.

68. R. Grosse and D. Kujawa, *International Business* (Homewood, IL: Irwin, 1988): 705.

69. R. H. Mason and R. S. Spich, *Management, An International Perspective* (Homewood, IL: Irwin, 1987).

70. Yves L. Doz and C. K. Prahalad, "How MNCs Cope with Host Government Intervention," *Harvard Business Review* (March–April 1980).

71. Mason and Spich.

72. Simcha Ronen, *Comparative and Multinational Management* (New York: John Wiley and Sons, 1986): 502–503.

73. R. T. De George, *Competing with Integrity in International Business* (New York: Oxford University Press, 1993) 3–4.

74. *Wall Street Journal,* April 9, 1998.

75. "Two Years Later, the Promises Used to Sell NAFTA Haven't Come True, but Its Foes Were Wrong, Too," *Wall Street Journal,* October 26, 1995.

76. *Wall Street Journal,* October 28, 1994.

77. Ibid.

78. Ibid.

79. "The Border," *Business Week,* May, 1997.

80. Ibid.

81. *Wall Street Journal,* June 29, 1994.

82. B. Ward and R. Dubois, *Only One Earth* (New York: Ballantine Books, 1972).

83. Ronen.

84. S. Tifft, "Who Gets the Garbage," *Time,* July 4, 1988, 42–43.

85. Jang B. Singh and V. C. Lakhan, "Business Ethics and the International Trade in Hazardous Wastes," *Journal of Business Ethics* 8 (1989): 889–899.

86. R. A. Peterson and M. H. Sauber, "International Marketing Ethics: Is There a Need for a Code?" (paper presented at the International Studies Association Southwest, Houston, TX, March 16–19, 1984).

87. M. Reza Vaghefi, S. K. Paulson, and W. H. Tomlinson, *International Business Theory and Practice* (New York: Taylor and Francis, 1991): 249–250.

88. T. E. Graedel and B. R. Allenby, *Industrial Ecology* (Englewood Cliffs, NJ: Prentice-Hall, 1995).

89. M. Sharfman, Book Review of Graedel and Allenby, *Academy of Management Review* 20, no. 4 (1995): 1090–1107.

90. Ronen.

91. Asheghian and Ebrahimi.

92. Becker and Fritzsche.

CHAPTER 4: THE ROLE OF CULTURE IN INTERNATIONAL MANAGEMENT

1. David A. Ricks, *Big Business Blunders: Mistakes in Multinational Marketing* (Homewood, IL: Dow-Jones-Irwin, 1983).

2. Betty Ann Korzenny, "Cross-Cultural Issues in the Process of Sending U.S. Employees of Multinational Corporations for Overseas Service" (paper presented at the annual meetings of the Speech Communications Association, San Antonio, TX, 1979).

3. J. Stewart Black and Mark Mendenhall, "Cross-Cultural Training Effectiveness: A Review and a Theoretical Framework for Future Research," *Academy of Management Review* 15, no. 1 (1990): 113–136.

4. Ibid.

5. Adapted from Bernard Wysocki, Jr., "Global Reach: Cross-Border Alliances Become Favorite Way to Crack New Markets," *Wall Street Journal,* March 26, 1990, A1, A4.

6. Geert Hofstede, *Cultures's Consequences: International Differences in Work-Related Values* (Beverly Hills, CA: Sage Publications, 1980): 25.

7. E. T. Hall, *The Silent Language* (Greenwich, CT: Fawcett, 1959).

8. For a more detailed definition, see A. L. Kroeber and C. Kluckholhn, "A Critical Review of Concepts and Definitions," in *Peabody Museum Papers* 47, no. 1 (Cambridge, MA: Harvard University Press, 1952): 181.

9. David Dressler and Donald Carns, *Sociology, The Study of Human Interaction* (New York: Knopf, 1969): 56–57.

10. K. David, "Organizational Processes for Intercultural Management" (paper presented at the Strategic Management Association, San Francisco, CA, 1989).

11. George Melloan, "Big Macs Yes, But Don't Wait Up for Russian Capitalism," *Wall Street Journal,* February 2, 1990, A15.

12. Lane Kelley, Arthur Whatley, and Reginald Worthley, "Assessing the Effects of Culture on Managerial Attitudes: A Three-Culture Test," *Journal of International Business Studies* (Summer 1987): 17–31.

13. J. D. Child, "Culture, Contingency and Capitalism in the Cross-National Study of Organizations," in *Research in Organizational Behavior,* ed. L. L. Cummings and B. M. Shaw (Greenwich, CT: JAI Publishers, 1981): 303–356.

14. G. S. Redding and T. A. Martyn-Johns, "Paradigm Differences and Their Relation to Management, with Reference to South-East Asia," in *Organizational Functioning in a Cross-Cultural Perspective* (Kent, OH: Kent State University Press, 1979).

15. James A. Lee, "Cultural Analysis in Overseas Operations," *Harvard Business Review* (March–April, 1966).

16. E. T. Hall, "The Silent Language in Overseas Business," *Harvard Business Review* (May–June 1960).

17. "One Big Market," *Wall Street Journal,* February 6, 1989, 16.

18. D. A. Ralston, Yu Kai-Ceng, Xun Wang, R. H. Terpstra, and He Wel, "An Analysis of Managerial Work Values Across the Six Regions of China" (paper presented at the *Academy of International Business,* Boston, November 1994).

19. Philip R. Harris and Robert T. Moran, *Managing Cultural Differences* (Houston, TX: Gulf Publishing, 1987).

20. K. David, "Field Research," in *The Cultural Environment of International Business,* 3rd ed., ed. V. Terpstra and K. David (Cincinnati, OH: South-Western, 1991): 176.

21. "Sharia Loosens Its Grip," *Euromoney,* May 1987, 137–138.

22. Geert Hofstede, "National Cultures in Four Dimensions," *International Studies of Management and Organization* (Spring–Summer 1983).

23. Simcha Ronen and Oded Shenkar, "Clustering Countries on Attitudinal Dimensions: A Review and Synthesis," *Academy of Management Review* 10, no. 3 (1985): 435–454.

24. Alfred M. Jaeger, "Organization Development and National Culture: Where's the Fit?" *Academy of Management Review* 11, no. 1 (January 1986): 178–190.

25. Elizabeth Weldon and Elisa L. Mustari, "Felt Dispensability in Groups of Coactors: The Effects of Shared Responsibility on Cognitive Effort" (unpublished manuscript, Kellogg Graduate School of Management, Northwestern University).

26. P. Christopher Earley, "Social Loafing and Collectivism: A Comparison of the United States and the People's Republic of China," *Administrative Science Quarterly* 34 (1989): 565–581.

27. Raghu Nath and Kunal K. Sadhu, "Comparative Analysis, Conclusions, and Future Directions," in *Comparative Management—A Regional View,* ed. Raghu Nath (Cambridge, MA: Ballinger Publishing, 1988).

28. Simcha Ronen and Oded Shenkar, "Clustering Countries on Attitudinal Dimensions: A Review and Synthesis," *Academy of Management Review* 10, no. 3 (1985): 435–454.

29. F. Trompenaars, *Riding the Waves of Culture* (London: Nicholas Brealey, 1993).

30. L. Hoeklin, *Managing Cultural Differences: Strategies for Competitive Advantage* (Reading, MA: Addison-Wesley, 1995).

31. Ross A. Webber, *Culture and Management, Text and Reading in Comparative Management* (Homewood, IL: Irwin, 1969): 186.

32. Arvind V. Phatak, *International Dimensions of Management,* 2nd ed. (Boston: PWS-Kent, 1989).

33. D. Darlin and J. B. White, "GM Venture in Korea Nears End, Betraying Firm's Fond Hopes," *Wall Street Journal,* January 16, 1992, 1.

34. Geert Hofstede, *Culture's Consequences: International Differences in Work-Related Values* (Beverly Hills, CA: Sage Publications, 1980).

35. George W. England, "Managers and Their Value Systems: A Five-Country Comparative Study," *Columbia Journal of World Business* (Summer 1978): 35–44.

36. Lennie Copeland and Lewis Griggs, *Going International* (New York: Random House, 1985); Boye De Mente, *Japanese Etiquette and Ethics in Business* (Lincolnwood, IL: NTC Business Books, 1989); Boye De Mente, *Korean Etiquette and Ethics in Business* (Lincolnwood, IL: NTC Business Books, 1989); George W. England and R. Lee, "Organizational Goals and Expected Behavior Among American, Japanese, and Korean Managers: A Comparative Study," *Academy of Management Journal* 14, no. 4 (1971): 425–438; R. L. Tung, *Business Negotiations with the Japanese* (Lexington, MA: Lexington Books, 1984); W. G. Ouchi and A. M. Jaeger,

"Theory Z Organization: Stability in the Midst of Mobility," *Academy of Management Review* 3, no. 2 (1978): 305–314; T. Seth, "Management and Its Environment in India," in *Management in an International Context,* eds. Joseph L. Massie and J. Luytjes (New York: Harper and Row, 1972): 201–225; Nam-Won Suh, "Management and Its Environment in Korea," in *Management in an International Context,* eds. Joseph L. Massie and Jan Luytjes (New York: Harper and Row, 1972): 226–244; Philip R. Harris and Robert T. Moran, *Managing Cultural Differences* (Houston, TX: Gulf Publishing, 1991); Fernando Quezada and James E. Boyce, "Latin America," in *Comparative Management,* ed. Raghu Nath (Cambridge, MA: Ballinger Publishing, 1988): 245–270; Simcha Ronen, *Comparative and Multinational Management* (New York: John Wiley and Sons, 1986); and V. Terpstra and K. David, *The Cultural Environment of International Business,* 3rd ed. (Cincinnati, OH: South-Western, 1991).

37. R. G. Linowes, "The Japanese Manager's Traumatic Entry in the United States: Understanding the American–Japanese Cultural Divide," *Academy of Management Review,* 1993, 21–38.

38. Ibid.

39. Some of the information on Germany follows a discussion by M. J. Gannon, *Understanding Global Cultures* (Thousand Oaks, CA: Sage Publications, 1994).

40. P. R. Haris and R. T. Moran, *Managing Cultural Differences* 4th ed. (Houston, TX: Gulf Publishing, 1996).

41. Robert Moore, "Saudi Arabia," Chapter 11, in ... . (lost reference).

42. M. Chen, *Asian Management Systems: Chinese, Japanese and Korean Styles of Business* (New York: Routledge, 1995).

43. Anne Marie Francesco and Barry Allen Gold, *International Organizational Behavior* (Upper Saddle River, NJ: Prentice-Hall, 1997).

44. J. Lee, "Culture and Management—A Study of Small Chinese Family Business in Singapore," *Journal of Small Business Management* (July 1996).

45. R. Sheng, "Outsiders' Perception of the Chinese," *Columbia Journal of World Business* 14, no. 2 (Summer): 16–22.

46. Lee.

CHAPTER 5: THE CROSS-CULTURAL COMMUNICATION ENVIRONMENT

1. E. T. Hall and M. R. Hall, *Understanding Cultural Differences* (Yarmouth, ME: Intercultural Press, 1990): 4.

2. Ibid.

3. K. Wolfson and W. B. Pearce, "A Cross-Cultural Comparison of the Implications of Self-Discovery on Conversation Logics," *Communication Quarterly* 31 (1983): 249–256.

4. H. Mintzberg, *The Nature of Managerial Work* (New York: Harper and Row, 1973).

5. L. A. Samovar, R. E. Porter, and N. C. Jain, *Understanding Intercultural Communication* (Belmont, CA: Wadsworth, 1981).

6. P. R. Harris and R. T. Moran, *Managing Cultural Differences,* 3rd ed. (Houston, TX: Gulf Publishing, 1991).

7. Samovar, Porter, and Jain.

8. Hall and Hall, 15.

9. L. A. Samovar and R. E. Porter, *International Communication: A Reader* (Belmont, CA: Wadsworth, 1988).

10. Harris and Moran.

11. Simcha Ronen, *Comparative and Multinational Management* (New York: John Wiley and Sons, 1986).

12. M. L. Hecht, P. A. Andersen, and S. A. Ribeau, "The Cultural Dimensions of Nonverbal Communication," in *Handbook of International and Intercultural Communication,* eds. M. K. Asante and W. B. Gudykunst (Newbury Park, CA: Sage Publications, 1989), 163–185.

13. H. C. Triandis, *Interpersonal Behavior* (Monterey, CA: Brooks/Cole, 1977).

14. Harris and Moran.

15. Adapted from N. Adler, *International Dimensions of Organizational Behavior,* 2nd ed. (Boston: PWS-Kent, 1991); based on M. Martin, *Adaptation to a Foreign Environment* (Ottawa: Canadian International Development Agency, to be published).

16. L. A. Samovar, Porter, and Jain.

17. D. A. Ricks, *Big Business Blunders: Mistakes in Multinational Marketing* (Homewood, IL: Dow-Jones-Irwin, 1983).

18. Vern Terpstra and K. David, *The Cultural Environment of International Business,* 3rd ed. (Cincinnati, OH: South-Western, 1991).

19. L. Copeland and L. Griggs, *Going International* (New York: Random House, 1985).

20. J. R. Schermerhorn, "Language Effects in Cross-Cultural Management Research: An Empirical Study and a Word of Caution," *National Academy of Management Proceedings* (1987): 103.

21. Copeland and Griggs.

22. R. L. Daft, *Organizational Theory and Design,* 3rd ed. (St. Paul, MN: West Publishing, 1989).

23. Ronen.
24. O. Klineberg, "Emotional Expression in Chinese Literature," *Journal of Abnormal and Social Psychology* 33 (1983): 517–530.
25. P. Ekman and W. V. Friesen, "Constants Across Cultures in the Face and Emotion," *Journal of Personality and Social Psychology* 17 (1971): 124–129.
26. P. Ekman and W. V. Friesen, "A New Pancultural Expression of Emotion," *Motivation and Emotion* 10 (1986): 159–168.
27. J. Pfeiffer, "How Not to Lose the Trade Wars by Cultural Gaffes," *Smithsonian* 18, no. 10, January 1988.
28. E. T. Hall, *The Silent Language* (New York: Doubleday, 1959).
29. Hall and Hall.
30. Ibid.
31. N. M. Sussman and H. M. Rosenfeld, "Influence of Culture, Language, and Sex on Conversational Distance," *Journal of Personality and Social Psychology* 42 (1982): 66–74.
32. Copeland and Griggs.
33. Hecht, Andersen, and Ribeau.
34. Pfeiffer.
35. Hall and Hall.
36. Ibid.
37. Hecht, Andersen, and Ribeau.
38. P. A. Andersen, "Explaining Differences in Nonverbal Communication," in *Intercultural Communication: A Reader,* eds. L. A. Samovar and R. E. Porter (Belmont, CA: Wadsworth, 1988).
39. S. Scott Elliot, A. D. Jensen, and M. McDonough, "Perceptions of Reticence: A Cross-Cultural Investigation," in *Communication Yearbook* 5, ed. M. Burgoon (New Brunswick, NJ: Transaction, 1982).
40. Hall and Hall.
41. R. Axtell, ed., *Dos and Taboos Around the World,* 2nd ed. (New York: John Wiley and Sons, 1985).
42. Copeland and Griggs.
43. M. K. Nydell, *Understanding Arabs* (Yarmouth, ME: Intercultural Press, 1987).
44. Harris and Moran.
45. E. T. Hall, *The Hidden Dimension* (New York: Doubleday, 1966): 15.
46. A. Almaney and A. Alwan, *Communicating with the Arabs* (Prospect Heights, IL: Waveland, 1982).
47. E. T. Hall, "The Silent Language in Overseas Business," *Harvard Business Review* (May–June 1960).
48. Ibid.
49. Based largely on the work of Nydell; R. T. Moran and P. R. Harris, *Managing Cultural Synergy* (Houston, TX: Gulf Publishing, 1982): 81–82.
50. Ibid.
51. Copeland and Griggs.
52. Hall and Hall.
53. D. C. Barnlund, "Public and Private Self in Communicating with Japan," *Business Horizons* (March–April 1989): 32–40.
54. Hall and Hall.
55. A. Goldman, "The Centrality of Ningensei to Japanese Negotiating and Interpersonal Relationships: Implications for U.S.–Japanese Communication," *International Journal of Intercultural Relations* 18, no. 1 (Winter 1994).
56. Jean-Louis Barsoux and Peter Lawrence, "The Making of a French Manager," *Harvard Business Review* (July–August 1991): 58–67.
57. J. Main, "How 21 Men Got Global in 35 Days," *Fortune,* November 6, 1989, 71–79.
58. D. Ricks, *Big Business Blunders* (Homewood, IL: Dow-Jones-Irwin, 1983).
59. Adler.
60. P. G. W. Keen, "Sorry, Wrong Number," *Business Month,* January 1990, 62–67.
61. R. B. Ruben, "Human Communication and Cross-Cultural Effectiveness," in *Intercultural Communication: A Reader,* eds. L. Samovar and R. Porter (Belmont, CA: Wadsworth, 1985): 339.
62. D. Ruben and B. D. Ruben, "Cross-Cultural Personnel Selection Criteria, Issues and Methods," in *Handbook of Intercultural Training: vol. 1, Issues in Theory and Design,* eds. D. Landis and R. W. Brislin (New York: Pergamon, 1983): 155–175.
63. Young Yun Kim, *Communication and Cross-Cultural Adaptation: An Integrative Theory* (Clevedon, England: Multilingual Matters, 1988).
64. Ibid.
65. R. W. Brislin, *Cross-Cultural Encounters: Face-to-Face Interaction* (New York: Pergamon, 1981).

CHAPTER 6: NEGOTIATION AND DECISION MAKING

1. John Pfeiffer, "How Not to Lose the Trade Wars by Cultural Gaffes," *Smithsonian* 18, no. 10 (January 1988): 145–156.
2. Nancy J. Adler, *International Dimensions of Organizational Behavior,* 2nd ed. (Boston: PWS-Kent), 1997.

3. Philip R. Harris and Robert T. Moran, *Managing Cultural Differences,* 4th ed. (Houston, TX: Gulf Publishing), 1996.

4. John L. Graham, and Roy A. Herberger, Jr., "Negotiators Abroad—Don't Shoot from the Hip," *Harvard Business Review* (July–August 1983): 160–168.

5. Adler.

6. John L. Graham, "A Hidden Cause of America's Trade Deficit with Japan," *Columbia Journal of World Business* (Fall 1981): 5–15.

7. Phillip D. Grub, "Cultural Keys to Successful Negotiating," in *Global Business Management in the 1990s,* ed. F. Ghader et al. (Washington, DC: Beacham, 1990): 24–32.

8. These profiles are adapted from Pierre Casse, *Managing Intercultural Negotiations: Guidelines for Trainers and Negotiators* (Washington, DC: Society for Intercultural Education, Training, and Research, 1985).

9. Pfeiffer.

10. *Wall Street Journal,* February 2, 1994.

11. John L. Graham, "Brazilian, Japanese, and American Business Negotiations," *Journal of International Business Studies* (Spring–Summer 1983): 47–61.

12. T. Flannigan, "Successful Negotiating with the Japanese," *Small Business Reports* 15, no. 6 (June 1990): 47–52.

13. Graham, 1983.

14. Boye De Mente, *Japanese Etiquette and Ethics in Business* (Lincolnwood, IL: NTC Business Books, 1989).

15. Robert H. Doktor, "Asian and American CEOs: A Comparative Study," *Organizational Dynamics* (Winter 1990): 49.

16. Harris and Moran, 461.

17. Adler, 181.

18. R. Fisher and W. Ury, *Getting to Yes* (Boston: Houghton Mifflin, 1981).

19. "Soviet Breakup Stymies Foreign Firms," *Wall Street Journal,* January 23, 1992.

20. S. Weiss, "Negotiating with 'Romans,'" *Sloan Management Review* (Winter 1994): 51–61.

21. John A. Reeder, "When West Meets East: Cultural Aspects of Doing Business in Asia," *Business Horizons* (January–February 1987): 72.

22. Adler, 197.

23. Fisher and Ury.

24. Lennie Copeland and Lewis Griggs, *Going International* (New York: Random House, 1985): 85.

25. Ibid.

26. Adler, 197–198.

27. Fisher and Ury.

28. Tung.

29. John L. Graham, "The Influence of Culture on Business Negotiations," *Journal of International Business Studies* 16, no. 1 (Spring 1985): 81–96.

30. S. S. Komorita and A. R. Brenner, "Bargaining and Concession Making under Bilateral Monopoly," *Journal of Personality and Social Psychology* 9 (1968): 15–20.

31. G. Fisher, *International Negotiation: A Cross-Cultural Perspective* (Chicago: Intercultural Press, 1980).

32. J. Karp and K. Kramhold, "Enron's Plant in India Was Dead; This Month, It Will Go on Stream," *Wall Street Journal,* February 5, 1999.

33. Adler, 179–217.

34. D. K. Tse, J. Francis, and J. Walls, "Cultural Differences in Conducting Intra- and Inter-Cultural Negotiations: A Sino-Canadian Comparison," *Journal of International Business Studies* (3rd Quarter 1994): 537–555.

35. B. W. Husted, "Bargaining with the Gringos: An Exploratory Study of Negotiations between Mexican and U.S. Firms," *International Executive* 36, no. 5 (September–October 1994): 625–644.

36. Pierre Casse, *Training for the Cross-Cultural Mind,* 2nd ed. (Washington, DC: Society for Intercultural Education, Training, and Research, 1981).

37. Nigel Campbell, John L. Graham, Alain Jolibert, and Hans Meissner, "Marketing Negotiations in France, Germany, the United Kingdom, and the United States," *Journal of Marketing* 52 (April 1988): 49–63.

38. Neil Rackham, "The Behavior of Successful Negotiators" (Reston, VA: Huthwaite Research Group, 1976, 1982).

39. R. L. Tung, *U.S.–China Trade Negotiations* (New York: Pergamon Press, 1982).

40. Joan H. Coll, "Sino-American Cultural Differences: The Key to Closing a Business Venture with the Chinese," *Mid-Atlantic Journal of Business* 25, no. 2, 3 (December 1988/January 1989): 15–19.

41. M. Loeb, "China: A Time for Caution," *Fortune,* February 20, 1995, 129–130.

42. O. Shenkar and S. Ronen, "The Cultural Context of Negotiations: The Implications of Chinese Interpersonal Norms," *Journal of Applied Behavioral Science* 23, no. 2 (1987): 263–275.

43. Tse et al.

44. J. Brunner, teaching notes, The University of Toledo.

45. Ibid.

46. Joanna M. Banthin and Leigh Stelzer, "Ethical Dilemmas in Negotiating Across Cultures: Problems in Commercial Negotiations between American Businessmen and the PRC" (paper presented at 1st International Conference on East–West Joint Ventures, October 19–20, 1989, State University of New York–Plattsburgh); and J. M. Banthin and L. Stelzer, "'Opening' China: Negotiation Strategies when East Meets West," *The Mid-Atlantic Journal of Business* 25, no. 2, 3 (December 1988/January 1989).

47. Brunner.

48. Ibid.

49. Boye De Mente, *Chinese Etiquette and Ethics in Business* (Lincolnwood, IL: NTC Business Books, 1989): 115–123.

50. S. Stewart and C. F. Keown, "Talking with the Dragon: Negotiating in the People's Republic of China," *Columbia Journal of World Business* 24, no. 3 (Fall 1989): 68–72.

51. Banthin and Stelzer, "'Opening' China."

52. Lucian Pye, *Chinese Commercial Negotiating Style* (Cambridge, MA: Oelgeschlager, Gunn and Hain, 1982).

53. W. B. Gudykunst, W. B. and Ting Tomey, S., *Culture and Interpersonal Communication* (Newbury Park, CA: Sage Publications, 1988).

54. L. Copeland and L. Griggs, *Going International* (New York: Random House, 1985): 80.

55. E. F. Jackofsky and John W. Slocum, Jr., "CEO Roles across Cultures," in *The Executive Effect: Concepts and Methods for Studying Top Managers,* ed. D. C. Hambrick (Greenwich, CT: JAI Publishers, 1988): 67–99.

56. J. D. Boulgarides and M. D. Oh, "A Comparison of Japanese, Korean and American Managerial Decision Styles," *Leadership and Organization Development Journal* 6 (1985): 9–11.

57. M. A. Hitt, B. B. Tyler, and Daewoo Park, "A Cross-Cultural Examination of Strategic Decision Models: Comparison of Korean and U.S. Executives," in *Best Papers Proceedings of the 50th Annual Meeting of the Academy of Management* (San Francisco, CA, August 12–15, 1990): 111–115.

58. G. Fisher, *International Negotiation: A Cross-Cultural Perspective* (Chicago: Intercultural Press, 1980).

59. G. W. England, "Managers and Their Value Systems: A Five-Country Comparative Study," *Columbia Journal of World Business* 13, no. 2 (Summer 1978).

60. W. Whitely and G. W. England, "Variability in Common Dimensions of Managerial Values Due to Value Orientation and Country Differences," *Personnel Psychology* 33 (1980): 77–89.

61. Hitt, Tyler, and Park, 114.

62. B. M. Bass and P. C. Burger, *Assessment of Managers: An International Comparison* (New York: Free Press, 1979): 91.

63. D. K. Tse, R. W. Belk, and Nan Zhan, "Learning to Consume: A Longitudinal and Cross-Cultural Content Analysis of Print Advertisements from Hong Kong, People's Republic of China and Taiwan," *Journal of Consumer Research* (forthcoming).

64. Copeland and Griggs.

65. M. K. Badawy, "Styles of Mideastern Managers," *California Management Review* 22 (1980): 51–58.

66. De Mente, *Japanese Etiquette.*

67. N. Namiki and S. P. Sethi, "Japan," in *Comparative Management—A Regional View,* ed. R. Nath (Cambridge, MA: Ballinger Publishing, 1988): 74–76.

68. De Mente, *Japanese Etiquette,* 80.

69. S. Naoto, *Management and Industrial Structure in Japan* (New York: Pergamon Press, 1981).

70. Namiki Sethi.

71. Harris and Moran, 397.

72. S. P. Sethi and N. Namiki, "Japanese-Style Consensus Decision-Making in Matrix Management: Problems and Prospects of Adaptation," in *Matrix Management Systems Handbook,* ed. D. I. Cleland (New York: Van Nostrand, 1984): 431–456.

CHAPTER 7: STRATEGY FORMULATION FOR INTERNATIONAL MARKETS

1. Bernard Wysocki, Jr., "U.S. Firms Increase Overseas Investments," *Wall Street Journal,* April 9, 1990.

2. K. R. Andrews, *The Concept of Corporate Strategy* (Homewood, IL: Dow-Jones-Irwin, 1979).

3. Herbert Henzler and Wilhelm Rall, "Facing Up to the Globalization Challenge," *McKinsey Quarterly* (Winter 1986): 52–68.

4. J. B. White, "GM to Supply Cars to Soviet Firm," *Wall Street Journal,* June 8, 1990.

5. Daniel Oliver, "Antitrust as a 1992 Fortress," *Wall Street Journal,* April 24, 1989.

6. Betty Jane Punnett, *Experiencing International Management* (Boston: PWS-Kent, 1989).

7. "The Stateless Corporation," *Business Week,* May 14, 1990, 100–101.

8. A. E. Serwer, "McDonald's Conquers the World," *Fortune,* October 17, 1994.

9. "The Avon Lady of the Amazon," *Business Week,* October 24, 1994.

10. Henzler and Rall.

11. Ibid.

12. G. Melloan, "Global Manufacturing Is an Intricate Game," *Wall Street Journal,* November 29, 1988.

13. "The Avon Lady of the Amazon," *Business Week,* October 24, 1994.

14. "The Stateless Corporation."

15. "Trinidad and Tobago," *Wall Street Journal,* May 23, 1990, special advertising section.

16. Robert Weigand, "International Investments: Weighing the Incentives," *Harvard Business Review* (July–August 1983): C1.

17. M. McCarthy, M. Pointer, D. Ricks, and R. Rolfe, "Managers' Views on Potential Investment Opportunities," *Business Horizons* (July–August 1993): 54–58.

18. Anant R. Negandhi, *International Management* (Boston: Allyn and Bacon, 1987): 230.

19. Henry Mintzberg, "Strategy Making in Three Modes," *California Management Review* (Winter 1973): 44–53.

20. Arvind V. Phatak, *International Dimensions of Management,* 2nd ed. (Boston: PWS-Kent, 1989).

21. Joseph V. Micallef, "Political Risk Assessment," *Columbia Journal of World Business* 16 (Summer 1981): 47–52.

22. Mark Fitzpatrick, "The Definition and Assessment of Political Risk in International Business: A Review of the Literature," *Academy of Management Review* 8 (1983): 249.

23. M. Porter, *Competitive Strategy* (New York: Free Press, 1980).

24. D. J. Garsombke, "International Competitor Analysis," *Planning Review* 17, no. 3 (May–June 1989): 42–47.

25. A. Swasy, "Procter & Gamble Fixes Aim on Tough Market: The Latin Americans," *Wall Street Journal,* June 15, 1990.

26. W. H. Davidson, "The Role of Global Scanning in Business Planning," *Organizational Dynamics* 19 (Winter 1991).

27. Garsombke.

28. Joann S. Lublin, "Japanese Auto Makers Speed into Europe," *Wall Street Journal,* June 6, 1990.

29. Andrews.

30. Simone Betz and Steven Ellen. Term project at the State University of New York–Plattsburgh (Fall 1991).

31. C. K. Prahalad and Gary Hamel, "The Core Competence of the Corporation," *Harvard Business Review* (May–June 1990): 79–91.

32. Ibid.

33. M. E. Porter, "Changing Patterns of International Competition," in *The Competitive Challenge,* ed. D. J. Teece (Boston: Ballinger, 1987): 29–30.

34. P. W. Beamish et al., *International Management* (Homewood, IL: Irwin, 1991).

35. N. S. Levinson and M. Asahi, "Cross-National Alliances and Interorganizational Learning," *Organizational Dynamics* (Autumn 1995): 50–62.

36. Barrie James, "Reducing the Risks of Globalization," *Long Range Planning* 25, no. 1 (1990): 80–88.

37. A. J. Morrison, D. A. Ricks, and K. Roth, "Globalization Versus Regionalization: Which Way for the Multinational?" *Organizational Dynamics* 19 (Winter 1991).

38. Ibid.

39. G. M. Taoka and D. R. Beeman, *International Business* (New York: HarperCollins, 1991).

40. Beamish et al.

41. Phatak.

42. Yoram Wind and Susan Douglas, "International Portfolio Analysis and Strategy: The Challenge of the 1980s," *Journal of International Business Studies* (Fall 1991): 69–82.

43. R. Gross and D. Kujawa, *International Business* (Homewood, IL: Irwin, 1989): 372.

44. "Small Businesses Take Part in Export Boom," *Investor's Daily,* July 10, 1991.

45. John Garland, Richard N. Farmer, and Marilyn Taylor, *International Dimensions of Business Policy and Strategy,* 2nd ed. (Boston: PWS-Kent, 1990): 106.

46. Phatak, 58.

47. R. J. Radway, "International Franchising," in *Global Business Management in the 1990s,* ed. R. T. Moran (Washington, DC: Beacham, 1990): 137.

48. Franklin R. Root, *Entry Strategies for International Markets* (Lexington, MA: Lexington Books, 1987).

49. Ibid.

50. S. Zahra and G. Elhagrasey, "Strategic Management of IJVs," *European Management Journal* 12, no. 1 (1994): 83–93.

51. Dorothy B. Christelow, "International Joint Ventures: How Important Are They?" *Columbia Journal of World Business* (Summer 1987): 7–13.

52. Ibid.

53. Kenichi Ohmae, "The Global Logic of Strategic Alliances," *Harvard Business Review* (March–April 1989): 143–154.

54. Zahra and Elhagrasey.

55. "The Partners," *Business Week,* February 10, 1992.

56. John Templeman and Richard A. Melcher, "Supermarket Darwinism: The Survival of the Fattest," *Business Week,* July 9, 1990.

57. Many of the facts and opinions in this section are from the following sources: R. Hudson, "Investing in Euroland," *Wall Street Journal, World Business R.25.,* September 28,

1998; Dana Milbank, "Can Europe Deliver?" *Wall Street Journal,* September 30, 1994; Tamar Almor and Seer Hirsch, "Outsider's Response to Europe 1992: Theoretical Considerations and Empirical Evidence," *Journal of International Business Studies* 26, no. 2 (2nd Quarter 1995): 223–237; S. Tully, "Europe 1992—More Unity Than You Think," *Fortune,* August 17, 1992; S. Lee, "An Impossible Dream?" *Forbes,* July 25, 1988; R. E. Gut, "The Impact of the European Community's 1992 Project," *Vital Speeches of the Day* 65, no. 2, November 1, 1988; D. Oliver, "Antitrust as a 1992 Fortress," *Wall Street Journal,* April 24, 1989; C. W. Verity, "U.S. Business Needs to Prepare Now for Europe's Single Internal Market," *Business America,* August 1, 1988; L. H. Clark, Jr., "Europe '92? It's Mostly a Break for the Americans," *Wall Street Journal,* May 21, 1990; Barbara Toman, "Now Comes the Hard Part: Marketing," in "World Business Special Report," *Wall Street Journal,* September 22, 1989.

58. Milbank.

59. Ibid.

60. A. E. Serwer, "McDonald's Conquers the World," *Fortune,* October 17, 1994.

61. K. R. Harrigan, "Joint Ventures and Global Strategies," *Columbia Journal of World Business* 19, no. 2 (Summer 1984): 7–13.

62. Ibid.

CHAPTER 8: CROSS-BORDER ALLIANCES AND STRATEGY IMPLEMENTATION

1. B. R. Schlender, "How Toshiba Makes Alliances Work," *Fortune,* October 4, 1993, 116–120.

2. D. Lei and J. W. Slocum, Jr., "Global Strategic Alliances: Payoffs and Pitfalls," *Organizational Dynamics* (Winter 1991).

3. M. A. Hitt, R. D. Ireland, and R. E. Hoskisson, *Strategic Management* (Cincinatti, OH: South-Western, 1999).

4. J. E. Hilsenrath, "Tiger Trouble," *Wall Street Journal,* September 28, 1998, R17.

5. D. Lei, "Offensive and Defensive Uses of Alliances," in Heidi Vernon-Wortzel and L. H. Wortzel, *Strategic Management in a Global Economy,* 3rd ed. (New York: John Wiley and Sons, 1997).

6. J. Main, "Making Global Alliances Work," *Fortune,* December 17, 1990.

7. R. N. Osborn and C. C. Baughn, "Forms of Interorganizational Governance for Multinational Alliances," *Academy of Management Journal* 33, no. 3 (1990): 503–519.

8. Lei, 1997.

9. Lei, 1997.

10. T. L. Wheelen and J. D. Hunger, *Strategic Management and Business Policy,* 6th ed. (Reading, MA: Addison-Wesley, 1998).

11. Lei 1997.

12. T. L. Wheelen and J. D. Hunger.

13. Vladimir Kvint, consultant at Arthur Anderson & Co., New York, originally from Siberia.

14. S. B. Novikov, "Soviet-American Joint Ventures: The Problems of Establishment and Activities." Paper presented to the 1st International Conference on East–West Joint Ventures, State University of New York–Plattsburgh, October 19–20, 1989.

15. K. R. Harrigan, "Joint Ventures and Global Strategies," *Columbia Journal of World Business* 19, no. 2. (Summer 1984): 7–13.

16. M. Brzezinski, "Foreigners Learn to Play by Russia's Rules," *Wall Street Journal,* May 14, 1998.

17. M. Brzezinski, "Foreigners Learn to Play by Russia's Rules," *Wall Street Journal,* August 14, 1998; Vladimir Kvint, "Don't Give up on Russia," *Harvard Business Review* (March–April 1994): 62–73; "The Russian Investment Dilemma: Perspectives," *Harvard Business Review* (May–June 1994): 35–44; Robert Starr, "Structuring Investments in the CIS," *Columbia Journal of World Business* (Fall 1993): 12–19; Paul Lawrence and Charalambos Vlachoutsicos, "Joint Ventures in Russia: Put the Locals in Charge," *Harvard Business Review* (January–February 1993): 44–54. "Investments in the CIS," *Columbia Journal of World Business* (Fall 1993): 12–19; Paul Lawrence and Charalambos Vlachoutsicos, "Joint Ventures in Russia: Put the Locals in Charge," *Harvard Business Review* (January–February 1993): 44–54.

18. A. E. Serwer, "McDonald's Conquers the World," *Fortune,* October 17, 1994.

19. Theodore Herbert and Helen Deresky, "Should General Managers Match Their Strategies?" *Organizational Dynamics* 15, no. 3 (Winter, 1987).

20. E. Anderson and H. Gatignon, "Modes of Foreign Entry: A Transaction Cost Analysis and Propositions," *Journal of International Business Studies* (Fall 1986): 1–26.

21. J. L. Schaan, "Parent Control and Joint Venture Success: The Case of Mexico" (unpublished doctoral dissertation, University of Western Ontario, 1983).

22. H. W. Lane and P. W. Beamish, "Cross-Cultural Cooperative Behavior in Joint Ventures in Less Developed Countries," *Management International Review* 30 (Special Issue 1990): 87–102.

23. J. M. Geringer, "Strategic Determinants of Partner Selection Criteria in International Joint Ventures," *Journal*

of International Business Studies (First Quarter 1991): 41–62.

24. J. M. Geringer and L. Hebert, "Control and Performance of International Joint Ventures," *Journal of International Business Studies* 20, no. 2 (Summer 1989).

25. Geringer.

26. P. W. Beamish et al., *International Management* (Homewood, IL: Irwin, 1991).

27. J. P. Killing, *Strategies for Joint Venture Success* (New York: Praeger, 1983).

28. J. L. Schaan and P. W. Beamish, "Joint Venture General Managers in Less Developed Countries," in *Cooperative Strategies in International Business*, eds. F. Contractor and P. Lorange (Toronto: Lexington Books, 1988): 279–299.

29. Oded Shenkar and Yoram Zeira, "International Joint Ventures: A Tough Test for HR," *Personnel* (January 1990): 26–31.

30. Ibid.

31. J. M. Geringer and L. Hebert, "Control and Performance of International Joint Ventures," *Journal of International Business Studies* 20, no. 2 (Summer 1989): 235–254.

32. M. Geringer, "Criteria for Selecting Partners for Joint Ventures in Industrialized Market Economies" (doctoral dissertation, University of Washington, Seattle, 1986).

33. J. L. Schaan and P. W. Beamish.

34. R. Mead, International Management (Cambridge, MA: Blackwell Publishers, 1994).

35. Lisa Shuchman, "Reality Check," *Wall Street Journal,* April 30, 1998.

36. C. S. Smith, "GM Bets Billions on Shaky Car Market in China," *Wall Street Journal,* May 10, 1998.

37. Ibid.

38. Pura, "Backlash Builds Against Suharto-Lined Firms," *Wall Street Journal,* May 27, 1998.

39. P. Rosenzweig, "Why Is Managing in the United States so difficult for European Firms?" *European Management Journal* 12, no. 1. (1994): 31–38.

40. "In Alabama, the Soul of a new Mercedes?" *Business Week,* March 31, 1997.

41. Ibid.

42. W. H. Davidson, "Creating and Managing Joint Ventures in China," *California Management Review* 29 (1987): 77–94.

43. J. A. Nelson and J. A. Reeder, "Labor Relations in China," *California Management Review* 27 (1985): 13–32.

44. P. B. Alexander and D. M. Bossman, "A Cross-Cultural Model of Negotiation: Strong Group vs. Weak Group Culture as the Context of Joint Venture Negotiations,"

Proceedings of the Academy of Management Meetings, Orlando, Florida, August 1990).

45. I. S. Baird, M. A. Lyles, and R. Wharton, "Attitiudinal Differences Between American and Chinese Managers Regarding Joint Venture Management," *Management International Review* (Special Issue, 1990): 53–68.

46. Ibid.

47. Ibid.

CHAPTER 9: ORGANIZATION STRUCTURE AND COORDINATING SYSTEMS

1. A. D. Chandler, *Strategy and Structure: Chapters in the History of the American Industrial Enterprise* (Cambridge, MA: MIT Press, 1962); R. E. Miles et al., "Organizational Strategy, Structure, and Process," *Academy of Management Review* 3, no. 3 (July 1978): 546–562; and J. Woodward, *Industrial Organization: Theory and Practice* (Oxford Univeristy Press, 1965).

2. C. A. Bartlett and S. Ghoshal, *Managing Across Borders* (Boston: Harvard Business School Press, 1989).

3. D. Milbank, "Alcoa Chairman Plans to Begin Reorganization," *Wall Street Journal,* August 9, 1991.

4. P. Asheghian and B. Ebrahimi, *International Business* (New York: Harper and Row, 1990).

5. Asheghian and Ebrahimi.

6. R. H. Mason and R. S. Spich, *Management—An International Perspective* (Homewood, IL: Irwin, 1987).

7. "Heinz's Johnson to Divest Operations, Scrap Management of Firm by Regions," *Wall Street Journal,* December 8, 1997, B22.

8. A. Taylor III, "Ford's Really Big Leap at the Future," *Fortune,* September 18, 1995, 134–144.

9. www.businessweek.com, September 28, 1998.

10. "Borderless Management," *Business Week,* May 23, 1994.

11. Ibid.; "Power at Multinationals Shifts to Home Office," *The Wall Street Journal,* September 9, 1994; "Big Blue Wants the World to Know Who's Boss," *Business Week,* September 26, 1994.

12. H. Henzler and W. Rall, "Facing up to the Globalization Challenge," *McKinsey Quarterly* (Fall 1986): 52–68.

13. T. Levitt, "The Globalization of Markets," *Harvard Business Review* (May–June 1983): 92–102; and S. P. Douglas and Yoram Wind, "The Myth of Globalization," *Columbia Journal of World Business* (Winter 1987): 19–29.

14. L. Kraar, "The Overseas Chinese," *Fortune,* October 31, 1994.

15. J. Kao, "The Worldwide Web of Chinese Business," *Harvard Business Review* (March–April 1993): 24–35.

16. "Asia's Wealth," *Business Week,* November 29, 1993.

17. Kao.

18. "The New Power in Asia," *Fortune*, October 31, 1994.

19. M. Weidenbaum, "The Rise of Great China: A New Economic Superpower," in *Annual Editions*, 1995/96, (Guilford, CT: Dushkin 1996): 180–185.

20. Weidenbaum.

21. Ibid.

22. Kraar.

23. Weidenbaum.

24. Kao.

25. Kraar.

26. P. M. Rosenzweig, "Colgate-Palmolive: Managing International Careers," Harvard Business School Case.

27. "For Levi's, A Flattering Fit Overseas," *Business Week*, November 5, 1990, 76–77.

28. Ibid.

29. B. R. Schlender, "How Fujitsu Will Tackle the Giants," *Fortune*, July 1, 1991.

30. S. Ghoshal and C. A. Bartlett, "The Multinational Corporation as an Interorganizational Network," *Academy of Management Review* 15, no. 4. (1990): 603–625.

31. R. E. White and T. A. Poynter, "Organizing for Worldwide Advantage," *Business Quarterly* 54 (Summer 1989): 84–89.

32. B. Hagerty, "Philips to Eliminate 35,000 to 45,000 Jobs by End of 1991," *Wall Street Journal*, October 26, 1990, A12.

33. C. A. Bartlett and S. Ghoshal, "Organizing for Worldwide Effectiveness: The Transnational Solution," *California Management Review* (Fall 1988): 54–74.

34. Ibid., 66.

35. R. H. Kilmann, "A Networked Company That Embraces the World," *Information Strategy* 6 (Spring 1990): 23–26.

36. R. B. Reich, "Who Is Them?" *Harvard Business Review* (March–April 1991): 77–88.

37. Ibid.

38. A. V. Phatak, *International Dimensions of Management*, 2nd ed. (Boston: PWS-Kent, 1989).

39. Ibid.

40. www.aeilogistics.com; AEICorp Form 10K; G. Rohrmann, CEO AEI Corp., press release, www.aeilogistics.com, August 1997; S. Macko, "Security Problems in Latin America," *ENN Daily Report*, August 24, 1996, on www.emergency.com/ ltn-scty.htm; M. Marr, Vice President, AEI Ocean Services, on www.aeilogistics.com/commentaries/98outlook.html.

41. W. G. Egelhoff, "Patterns of Control in U.S., U.K., and European Multinational Corporations," *Journal of International Business Studies* (Fall 1984): 73–83.

42. Ibid.

43. Ibid.

44. S. Ueno and U. Sekaran, "The Influence of Culture on Budget Control Practices in the U.S.A. and Japan: An Empirical Study," *Journal of International Business Studies* 23 (Winter 1992): 659–674.

45. Phatak.

CHAPTER 10: STAFFING AND TRAINING FOR GLOBAL OPERATIONS

1. J. L. Laabs, "HR Pioneers Explore the Road Less Traveled," *Personnel Journal* (February 1996): 70–72, 74, 77–78.

2. Ibid.

3. C. A. Bartlett and S. Ghoshal, "Matrix Management: Not a Structure, a Frame of Mind," *Harvard Business Review* (July–August 1990).

4. J. S. Lublin, "Foreign Accents Proliferate in Top Ranks as U.S. Companies Find Talent Abroad," *Wall Street Journal*, May 21, 1992.

5. S. J. Kobrin, "Is There a Relationship Between a Geocentric Mind-Set and Multinational Strategy?" *Journal of International Business Studies* (3rd Quarter 1994); N. J. Adler and S. Bartholomew, "Managing Globally Competent People," *Academy of Management Executive*, August 6, 1992, 52–65; P. Dowling and R. S. Schuler, *International Dimensions of Human Resource Management* (Boston: PWS-Kent, 1990).

6. G. Hedlund, "Who Manages the Global Corporation" (unpublished working paper, Stockholm School of Economics, 1990).

7. D. Welch, "HRM Implications of Globalization," *Journal of General Management* 19, no. 4 (Summer 1994): 52–69.

8. T. T. Herbert and H. Deresky, "Should General Managers Match Their Business Strategies?" *Organizational Dynamics* 15, no. 3 (Winter 1987); "Senior Management Implications of Strategic Human Resource Management Programs," *Proceedings of the Association of Human Resource Management and Organizational Behavior Conference*, New Orleans, November 1986.

9. Heenan and Perlmutter.

10. S. B. Prasad and Y. K. Krishna Shetty, *An Introduction to Multinational Management* (Englewood Cliffs, NJ: Prentice-Hall, 1979).

11. Rochelle Kopp, "International Human Resource Policies and Practices in Japanese, European, and United States Multinationals," *Human Resource Management* 33, no. 4. (Winter 1994): 581–599.

12. Herbert and Deresky.

13. M. Mendenhall and G. Oddou, "The Dimensions of Expatriate Acculturation: A Review," *Academy of Management Review* 10, no. 1 (1985): 39–47.

14. Ronen; R. L. Tung, "Selection and Training of Personnel for Overseas Assignments," *Columbia Journal of World Business* (Spring 1981): 68–78.

15. Tung, "Overseas Assignments."

16. P. J. Dowling and R. S. Schuler, *International Dimensions of Human Resource Management* (Boston: PWS-Kent, 1990).

17. S. J. Kobrin, "Expatriate Reduction and Strategic Control in American Multinational Corporations," *Human Resource Management* 27, no. 1 (1988): 63–75.

18. P. J. Dowling, "Hot Issues Overseas," *Personnel Administrator* 34, no. 1 (1989): 66–72.

19. Hem C. Jain, "Human Resource Management in Selected Japanese Firms, the Foreign Subsidiaries and Locally Owned Counterparts," *International Labour Review* 129, no. 1 (1990): 73–84.

20. Bartlett and Ghoshal.

21. Tung, "U.S., European, and Japanese Multinationals."

22. R. D. Hays, "Expatriate Selection: Insuring Success and Avoiding Failure," *Journal of International Business Studies* 5, no. 1 (1974): 25–37.

23. Tung, "U.S., European, and Japanese Multinationals."

24. J. S. Black, "Work Role Transitions: A Study of American Expatriate Managers in Japan," *Journal of International Business Studies* 19 (1988): 277–294.

25. "They're Sending You Where?" www.businessweek.com.

26. M. Harvey, "Dual-Career Expatriates: Expectations, Adjustment and Satisfaction with International Relocation," *Journal of International Business Studies,* 28, no. 3 (1997).

27. Tung, "U.S., European, and Japanese Multinationals."

28. Ibid.

29. B. Wysocki, Jr., "Prior Adjustment: Japanese Executives Going Overseas Take Anti-Shock Courses," *Wall Street Journal,* December 4, 1987.

30. Mendenhall and Oddou.

31. J. S. Black and M. Mendenhall, "Cross-Cultural Training Effectiveness: A Review and a Theoretical Framework for Future Research," *Academy of Management Review* 15, no. 1 (1990): 113–136.

32. D. Landlis and R. Brislin, *Handbook on Intercultural Training* 1 (New York: Pergamon Press, 1983).

33. K. Oberg, "Culture Shock: Adjustments to New Cultural Environments," *Practical Anthropology* (July–August 1960): 177–182.

34. Ibid.

35. Ibid.

36. P. R. Harris and R. T. Moran, *Managing Cultural Differences,* 4th ed (Houston, TX: Gulf Publishing, 1996): 139.

37. Tung, "Overseas Assignments."

38. P. C. Earley, "Intercultural Training for Managers: A Comparison of Documentary and Interpersonal Methods," *Academy of Management Journal* 30, no. 4 (December 1987): 685–698.

39. Ronen.

40. Kealey, 81.

41. J. S. Lublin, "Younger Managers Learn Global Skills," *Wall Street Journal,* March 31, 1992.

42. Herbert and Deresky, "Senior Management Implications."

43. T. F. O'Boyle, "Little Benefit to Careers Seen in Foreign Stints," *Wall Street Journal,* December 11, 1989.

44. B. W. Teague, *Compensating Key Personnel Overseas* (New York: Conference Board, 1972).

45. C. Reynolds, "Compensation of Overseas Personnel," in *Handbook of Human Resource Administration,* 2nd ed., ed. J. J. Famularo (New York: McGraw-Hill, 1986).

46. "A Secret Weapon for German Reform," *Business Week,* October 12, 1998.

47. M. Selz, "Hiring the Right Manager Overseas," *Wall Street Journal,* February 27, 1992.

48. Sheila M. Puffer and Stanislav V. Shekshnia, "Compensating Nationals in Post-Communist Russia: The Fit Between Culture and Compensation Systems" (paper presented at the Annual Academy of International Business Conference, Boston, November 1994).

CHAPTER 11: EXPATRIATION AND LABOR RELATIONS IN GLOBAL HRM

1. Charlene M. Solomon, "One Assignment, Two Lives," *Personnel Journal,* May 1996, 36–47.

2. N. J. Adler, *International Dimensions of Organizational Behavior,* 2nd ed. (Boston: PWS-Kent, 1991); M. Mendenhall, E. Dunbar, and G. Oddou, "Expatriate Selection, Training, and Career-Pathing: A Review and Critique," *Human Resource Management* 26 (1987): 331–345.

3. M. G. Harvey, "Repatriation of Corporate Executives: An Empirical Study," *Journal of International Business Studies* 20 (Spring 1989): 131–144.

4. Tung, "Career Issues in International Assignments," *Academy of Management Executive* 2, no. 3 (1988): 241–244.

5. M. Harvey, "Dual-Career Expatriates: Expectations, Adjustments and Satisfaction with International Relocation," *Journal of International Business Studies* 28, no. 3 (1997): 627.

6. Ibid.

7. Solomon.

8. R. Pascoe, *Surviving Overseas: The Wife's Guide to Successful Living Abroad* (Singapore: Times Publishing, 1992); R. Pascoe, "Employers Ignore Expatriate Wives at Their Own Peril," *Wall Street Journal,* March 29, 1992.

9. J. S. Black and H. B. Gregersen, "The Other Half of the Picture: Antecedents of Spouse Cross-Cultural Adjustment," *Journal of International Business Studies* (3rd Quarter 1992): 461–477.

10. Based on D. C. Feldman, "The Multinational Socialization of Organization Members," *Academy of Management Review* 6, no. 2 (April 1981): 309–318.

11. T. F. O'Boyle, "Little Benefit to Careers Seen in Foreign Stints," *Wall Street Journal,* December 11, 1989.

12. J. Hamill, "Expatriate Policies in British Multinationals," *Journal of General Management* 14, no. 4 (Summer 1989): 18–33.

13. *Wall Street Journal,* July 26, 1995.

14. M. Kaminski and J. Paiz, "Japanese Women in Management: Where Are They?" *Human Resource Management* 23, no. 2 (Fall 1984): 277–292.

15. P. Lansing and K. Ready, "Hiring Women Managers in Japan: An Alternative for Foreign Employers," *California Management Review* 26, no. 4 (1988): 112–127.

16. "Japan's Working Mothers," *Japan Report* 37, no. 5 (August 1991).

17. *Wall Street Journal,* September 9, 1994.

18. Ibid.

19. Ibid.

20. Helene Alexandre, *Les Femmes Cadres* (Paris: APEC, 1990).

21. Nancy Adler and Dafna N. Izraeli, eds., *Competitive Frontiers: Women Managers in a Global Economy* (Cambridge, MA: Blackwell, 1993).

22. Ariane Berthoin Antal and Camilla Krebsbach-Gnath, in Adler and Izraeli.

23. Corinna T. de Leon and Suk-ching Ho, "The Third Identity of Modern Chinese Women: Women Managers in Hong Kong," in Adler and Izraeli.

24. Ibid.

25. Ibid.

26. N. J. Adler and D. N. Izraeli.

27. "Women in Business: A Global Report Card," *Wall Street Journal,* July 26, 1995.

28. W. Scheibal, "When Cultures Clash: Applying Title VII Abroad," *Business Horizons,* September–October 1995.

29. Ibid.

30. G. P. Ferraro, *The Cultural Dimension of International Business* (Englewood Cliffs, NJ: Prentice-Hall, 1994).

31. N. J. Adler and D. N. Izraeli, *Women in Management Worldwide* (Armonk, NY: M. E. Sharpe, 1988): 245.

32. Ibid.

33. M. Jelinek and N. J. Adler, "Women: World-Class Managers for Global Competition," *Academy of Management Executive* 11, no. 1 (February 1988): 11–19.

34. Adler and Izraeli, 246.

35. P. Lansing and K. Ready, "Hiring Women Managers in Japan: An Alternative for Foreign Employers," *California Management Review* 26, no. 4 (1988): 112–127.

36. Ibid.

37. W. Hardman and J. Heidelberg, "When Sexual Harassment is a Foreign Affair," *Personnel Journal,* April 1996, 91–97.

38. Ibid.

39. Ibid.

40. P. J. Dowling, R. S. Schuler, and D. E. Welch, *International Dimensions of Human Resource Management,* 2nd ed. (Belmont, CA: Wadsworth, 1994).

41. "Taking the Pledge," *The Economist,* November 23, 1996, S15(2).

42. R. M. Hodgetts and F. Luthans, *International Management,* 2nd ed. (New York: McGraw-Hill, 1994).

43. M. R. Czinkota, I. A. Ronkainen, and M. H. Moffett, *International Business,* 3rd ed. (New York: Dryden Press, 1994).

44. C. K. Prahalad and Y. L. Doz, *The Multinational Mission: Balancing Local Demands and Global Vision* (New York: The Free Press, 1987).

45. R. J. Adams, *Industrial Relations Under Liberal Democracy* (University of South Carolina Press, 1995).

46. Dowling, Schuler, and Welch.

47. J. S. Daniels and L. H. Radebaugh, *International Business,* 6th ed. (Reading, MA: Addison-Wesley, 1992).

48. M. Poole, *Industrial Relations: Origins and Patterns of National Diversity* (London: Routledge, 1986).

49. Dowling, Schuler, and Welch.

50. Adams.

51. Ibid.

52. "Unions Feel the Beat," *U.S. News and World Report,* January 24, 1994.

53. Ibid.

54. "World Wire: China to Unionize Foreign Firms," *Wall Street Journal,* May 1, 1994.

55. Ibid.

56. J. T. Barrett, "Trade Unions in South Africa: Dramatic Change After Apartheid Ends," *Monthly Labor Review* 119, no. 5 (May 1996): 37.

57. M. M. Lucio and S. Weston, "New Management Practices in a Multinational Corporation: The Restructuring of Worker Representation and Rights?" *Industrial Relations Journal* 25, no. 2: 110–121.

58. Ibid.

59. D. B. Cornfield, "Labor Transnationalism?" *Work and Occupations* 24, no. 3 (August 1997): 278(10).

60. R. Martin, A. Vidinova, S. Hill, "Industrial Relations in Transition Economies: Emergent Industrial Relations Institutions in Bulgaria," *British Journal of Industrial Relations* 34, no. 1 (March 1996): 3.

61. "Labour Relations: Themes for the 21st Century," *British Journal of Industrial Relations* 33, no. 4 (December 1995): 515.

62. Daniels and Radebaugh.

63. J. T. Barrett.

64. "Culture Clash: South Korea," *The Economist,* January 11, 1997, 35.

65. A. M. Rugman and R. M. Hodgetts, *International Business* (New York: McGraw-Hill, 1995.)

66. Ibid.

67. This section drawn from a term project by Joy Kennley and Tim Lemos, students at the State University of New York–Plattsburgh, Spring 1995; and articles by Tim Shorrock, such as "GE, Honeywell Are Focus of NAFTA Labor Complaints," *Journal of Commerce and Commercial* 399, no. 2814 (February 15, 1994).

68. Daniels and Radebaugh.

69. R. Calori and B. Dufour, "Management European Style," *Academy of Management Executive* 9, no. 3 (August 1995).

70. J. Hoerr, "What Should Unions Do?" *Harvard Business Review* (May–June 1991): 30–45.

71. Hodgetts and Luthans.

72. Hoerr.

73. H. C. Katz, "The Decentralization of Collective Bargaining: A Literature Review and Comparative Analysis," *Industrial and Labor Relations Review* 47, no. 1 (October 1993).

74. Hoerr.

75. Adams.

76. "The Perils of Cosy Corporatism," *The Economist,* May 21, 1994.

77. Wofgang Streeck, "More Uncertainties: German Unions Facing 1992," *Industrial Relations* (Fall 1991): 30–33.

78. "Germany's Economic Future Is on the Bargaining Table," *Business Week,* March 30, 1992.

79. Katz.

80. Czinkota, Ronkainen, and Moffett.

81. Ibid.

82. Industrial Democracy in Europe International Research Group, *Industrial Democracy in Europe* (Oxford, England: Clarendon Press, 1981): chapter 14.

83. R. E. Cole, *Strategies for Learning: Small-Group Activities in American, Japanese and Swedish Industry* (Berkeley, CA: University of California Press, 1989).

84. W. E. Upjohn Institute for Employment Research, *Work in America* (Cambridge, MA: MIT Press, 1973).

85. Organization for Economic Cooperation and Development Report (1984): 37–39, reported in Cole.

86. Ibid.

87. Hoerr.

88. Ibid.

89. "Unions Shout, but Have Little Clout," *Wall Street Journal,* January 5, 1995.

90. J. J. Lawrence and Ryh-song Yeh, "The Influence of Mexican Culture on the Use of Japanese Manufacturing Techniques in Mexico," *Management International Review* 34, no. 1 (1994): 49–66.

CHAPTER 12: MOTIVATING AND LEADING

1. F. Rieger and D. Wong-Rieger, "A Configuration Model of National Influence Applied to Southeast Asian Organizations," *Proceedings of the Research Conference on Business in Southeast Asia,* May 12–13, 1990, University of Michigan.

2. H. R. Kaplan and C. Tausky, "Humanism in Organization: A Critical Appraisal," in *A Sociological Reader on Complex Organizations,* 3rd ed., eds. A. Etzioni and E. W. Lehman (New York: Holt, Rinehart and Winston, 1980): 44–55.

3. M. J. Gannon & Associates, *Understanding Global Cultures: Metaphorical Journeys Through 17 Countries* (Beverly Hills, CA: Sage Publications, 1994).

4. Meaning of Work International Research Team, *The Meaning of Working: An International Perspective* (New York: Academic Press, 1985).

5. D. Siddiqui and A. Alkhafaji, *The Gulf War: Implications for Global Businesses and Media* (Apollo, PA: Closson Press, 1992): 133–135.

6. Ibid.

7. A. Ali, "The Islamic Work Ethic in Arabia," *Journal of Psychology,* 126 (1992): 507–519.

8. Yasamusa Kuroda and Tatsuzo Suzuki, "A Comparative Analysis of the Arab Culture: Arabic, English and Japanese Language and Values" (paper presented at the 5th Congress

of the International Association of Middle Eastern Studies, Tunis, September 20–24, 1991; quoted in Siddiqui.

9. J. R. Hinrichs, "Cross-National Analysis of Work Attitudes" (paper presented at the American Psychological Association Meeting, Chicago, 1975).

10. A. Furnham, B. D. Kirkcaldy, and R. Lynn, "National Attitudes to Competitiveness, Money, and Work Among Young People: First, Second, and Third World Differences," *Human Relations* 47, no. 1 (1994): 119–132.

11. M. Haire, E. E. Ghiselli, and L. W. Porter, "Cultural Patterns in the Role of the Manager," *Industrial Relations* 12, no. 2 (February 1963): 95–117.

12. S. Ronen, *Comparative and Multinational Management* (New York: John Wiley and Sons, 1986).

13. M. Haire, E. E. Ghiselli, and L. W. Porter, "Cultural Patterns in the Role of the Manager," *Industrial Relations* 12, no. 2 (February 1963): 95–117.

14. E. C. Nevis, "Cultural Assumptions and Productivity: The United States and China," *Sloan Management Review* 24, no. 3 (Spring 1983): 17–29.

15. Boye De Mente, *Chinese Etiquette and Ethics in Business* (Lincolnwood, IL: NTC Business Books, 1989).

16. Ibid.

17. Geert Hofstede, *Culture's Consequences: International Differences in Work-Related Values* (Beverly Hills, CA: Sage Publications, 1980).

18. H. Serrie, "Chinese Business and Management Behavior and the Hsu Attributes," in *Anthropology and International Business, Studies in Third World Societies* (Williamsburg, VA: Department of Anthropology, College of William and Mary, 1986); C. H. Hui, "Development and Validation of an Individualism–Collectivism Scale," *Technical Report, ONR–31.*

19. Nevis.

20. S. M. Goldstein, K. Sears, and R. C. Bush, "China Council of the Asia Society," in *The PRC—A Basic Handbook,* 4th ed. (USA: The Asia Society, 1984).

21. Serrie.

22. W. H. Davidson, "Creating and Managing Joint Ventures in China," *California Management Review* 29 (1987): 77–94.

23. M. A. Von Glinow and M. B. Teagarden, "The Transfer of Human Resource Management Technology in Sino-U.S. Cooperative Ventures: Problems and Solutions," *Human Resource Management* 27 (1988): 101–129.

24. R. L. Tung, "Patterns of Motivation in Chinese Industrial Enterprises," *Academy of Management Review* 6, no. 3 (1981): 481–489.

25. F. Katz and R. Kahn, *The Social Psychology of Organizations* (New York: John Wiley and Sons, 1978); R. R. Blake and J. S. Mouton, "Motivating Human Productivity in the People's Republic of China," *Group and Organization Studies* 4, no. 2 (June 1979): 162.

26. Ibid.

27. Blake and Mouton.

28. Tung, 486.

29. *Constitution of the People's Republic of China,* Article 10 (1878).

30. Z. Lin, "Initial Reform in China's Economic Structure," *Social Sciences in China* 3 (1980): 172–194.

31. Tung.

32. O. Shenkar and S. Ronen, "Structure and Importance of Work Goals Among Managers in the PRC," *Academy of Management Journal* 30, no. 3 (1987): 564–576.

33. L. Pye, *Chinese Commercial Negotiating Style* (Cambridge, MA: Oelgeschlager, Gunn and Hain, 1982).

34. Ibid.

35. S. G. Redding, "Some Perceptions of Psychological Needs Among Managers in South East Asia," in *Basic Problems in Cross-Cultural Psychology,* ed. Y. H. Poortinga (Amsterdam: Swets and Zeitlinger, 1977): 338–343.

36. D. D. White and J. Leon, "The Two-Factor Theory: New Questions, New Answers," *National Academy of Management Proceedings* (1976): 358.

37. D. Macarov, "Work Patterns and Satisfactions in an Israeli Kibbutz: A Test of the Herzberg Hypothesis," *Personnel Psychology* (Autumn 1973): 483–493.

38. P. D. Machungwa and N. Schmitt, "Work Motivation in a Developing Country," *Journal of Applied Psychology* (February 1983): 31–42.

39. G. E. Popp, H. J. Davis, and T. T. Herbert, "An International Study of Intrinsic Motivation Composition," *Management International Review* 26, no. 3 (1986): 28–35.

40. R. N. Kanungo and R. W. Wright, "A Cross-Cultural Study of Managerial Job Attitudes," *Journal of International Business Studies* (Fall 1983): 115–129.

41. Ibid., 127–128.

42. J. R. Lincoln, "Employee Work Attitudes and Management Practice in the U.S. and Japan: Evidence from a Large Comparative Survey," *California Management Review* 32, no. 1 (Fall 1989): 89–106.

43. J. R. Lincoln and K. McBride, "Japanese Industrial Organization in Comparative Perspective," *Annual Review of Sociology* 13 (1987): 289–312.

44. Lincoln.

45. "Detroit South," *Business Week,* March 16, 1992.

46. Hofstede.

47. M. B. Teagarden, M. C. Butler, and M. Von Glinow, "Mexico's Maquiladora Industry: Where Strategic Human Resource Management Makes a Difference," *Organizational Dynamics* (Winter 1992): 34–47.

48. T. T. Herbert, H. Deresky, and G. E. Popp, "On the Potential for Assimilation and Integration of Sub-Culture Members into the U.S. Business System: The Micro-Cultural Effects of the Mexican-American National Origin, Culture, and Personality," *Proceedings of the International Business Association Conference* (London, November 1986).

49. John Condon, *Good Neighbors: Communication with the Mexicans* (Yarmouth, ME: Intercultural Press, 1985).

50. G. K. Stephens and C. R. Greer, "Doing Business in Mexico: Understanding Cultural Differences," *Organizational Dynamics* (Summer 1995): 39–55.

51. Teagarden, Butler, and Von Glinow.

52. Stephens and Greer.

53. Ibid.

54. Mariah E. de Forest, "Thinking of a Plant in Mexico?" *Academy of Management Executive* 8, no. 1 (1994): 33–40.

55. Ibid.

56. Ibid.

57. Teagarden, Butler, and Von Glinow.

58. Herbert, Deresky, and Popp.

59. Ibid., 15.

60. R. S. Bhagat and S. J. McQuaid, "Role of Subjective Culture in Organizations: A Review and Direction for Future Research," *Journal of Applied Psychology Monograph* 67, no. 5 (1982): 669.

61. M. A. Von Glinow and M. B. Teagarden, "The Transfer of Human Resource Management Technology in Sino-U.S. Cooperative Ventures: Problems and Solutions," *Human Resource Management* 27, no. 2 (1988): 201–229.

62. M. A. Von Glinow and Byung Jae Chung, "Comparative HRM Practices in the U.S., Japan, Korea and the PRC," in *Research in Personnel and HRM, A Research Annual: International HRM,* eds. A. Nedd, G. R. Ferris, and K. M. Rowland (London: JAI Press, 1989).

63. L. Copeland and L. Griggs, *Going International* (New York: Random House, 1985): 131.

64. Ibid., 168.

65. P. R. Harris and R. T. Moran, *Managing Cultural Differences,* 3rd ed. (Houston, TX: Gulf Publishing, 1991).

66. J. W. Gardner, *John W. Gardner on Leadership* (New York: Free Press, 1989).

67. W. Bennis and B. Nanus, *Leaders* (New York: Harper and Row, 1985).

68. R. D. Robinson, *Internationalization of Business* (Hinsdale, IL: Drysden Press, 1984): 117.

69. R. H. Mason and R. S. Spich, *Management—An International Perspective* (Homewood: IL: Irwin, 1987).

70. Ibid., 184.

71. Gary Yukl, "Managerial Leadership: A Review of Theory and Research," *Journal of Management* 15, no. 2 (1989): 251–289.

72. B. M. Bass, *Bass & Stogdill's Handbook of Leadership* (New York: Free Press, 1990).

73. See, for example, M. Mead, *Sex and Temperament in Three Primitive Societies* (New York: Morrow, 1935); and M. Mead et al., *Cooperation and Competition Among Primitive Peoples* (New York: McGraw-Hill, 1937).

74. D. McGregor, *The Human Side of Enterprise* (New York: McGraw-Hill, 1960).

75. See, for example, R. M. Stogdill, *Manual for the Leader Behavior Description Questionnaire—Form XII* (Columbus: Ohio State University, Bureau of Business Research, 1963).

76. R. R. Blake and J. S. Mouton, *The New Managerial Grid* (Houston, TX: Gulf Publishing, 1978).

77. R. Likert, *The Human Organization* (New York: McGraw-Hill, 1967).

78. F. E. Fiedler, "Engineering the Job to Fit the Manager," *Harvard Business Review* 43, no. 5 (1965): 115–122.

79. Geert Hofstede, "Motivation, Leadership and Organization: Do American Theories Apply Abroad?" *Organizational Dynamics* (Summer 1980): 42–63.

80. Ibid.

81. Geert Hofstede, "Value Systems in Forty Countries," *Proceedings of the 4th International Congress of the International Association for Cross-Cultural Psychology* (1978).

82. Andre Laurent, "The Cultural Diversity of Western Conceptions of Management," *International Studies of Management and Organization* 13, no. 1–2 (Spring–Summer 1983): 75–96.

83. M. Haire, E. E. Ghiselli, and L. W. Porter, *Managerial Thinking: An International Study* (New York: John Wiley and Sons, 1966).

84. S. G. Redding and T. W. Case, "Managerial Beliefs Among Asian Managers," *Proceedings of the Academy of Management,* 1975.

85. I. Kenis, "A Cross-Cultural Study of Personality and Leadership," *Group and Organization Studies* 2 (1977): 49–60.

86. F. C. Deyo, "The Cultural Patterning of Organizational Development: A Comparative Case Study of Thailand and Chinese Industrial Enterprises," *Human Organization* 37 (1978): 68–72.

87. M. K. Badawy, "Styles of Mid-Eastern Managers," *California Management Review* (Spring 1980): 57.

88. A. A. Algattan, *Test of the Path-Goal Theory of Leadership in the Multinational Domain* (paper presented at the Academy of Management Conference, San Diego, 1985).

89. J. P. Howell and P. W. Dorfman, *A Comparative Study of Leadership and Its Substitutes in a Mixed Cultural Work Setting* (unpublished manuscript, 1988).

90. D. H. Welsh, F. Luthans, and S. M. Sommer, "Managing Russian Factory Workers: The Impact of U.S.-Based Behavioral and Participative Techniquess," *Academy of Management Journal* 36 (1993): 58–79.

91. Jai B. P. Sinha and D. Sinha, "Role of Social Values in Indian Organizations," *International Journal of Psychology* 25 (1990): 705–715.

92. Hofstede, "Motivation, Leadership and Organization."

93. Jai B. P. Sinha, "A Model of Effective Leadership Styles in India," *International Studies of Management and Organization* (Summer–Fall 1984): 86–98.

94. Ibid.

95. B. M. Bass and P. C. Burger, *Assessment of Managers: An International Comparison* (New York: Free Press, 1979).

96. L. Copeland and L. Griggs, *Going International* (New York: Random House, 1985): 236.

97. R. C. Tripathi, "Interplay of Values in the Functioning of Indian Organizations," *International Journal of Psychology* 25 (1990): 715–734.

98. Sinha.

99. Sinha and Sinha.

100. A. Spaeth, "India Beckons—and Frustrates: The Country Needs Foreign Investment, but Investors May Find That Hard to Believe," *Wall Street Journal*, September 22, 1989, R23–R25.

101. Ibid.

102. S. S. Rao, "Yankee, Be Good," *Financial World*, November 7, 1995, 54–68.

103. J. J. Curran, "Why Japan Will Emerge Stronger," *Fortune*, May 18, 1992.

104. Kuniyasu Sakai, "The Feudal World of Japanese Manufacturing," *Harvard Business Review* (November–December 1990): 38–47.

105. Bass.

106. Bass and Burger.

CHAPTER 13: MANAGING INTERNATIONAL TEAMS AND WORKFORCE DIVERSITY

1. Based on W. Dyer, *Team Building* (Reading, MA: Addison-Wesley, 1987).

2. R. B. Reich, "Who Is Them?" *Harvard Business Review* (March–April 1991): 77–88.

3. T. Gross, E. Turner, and L. Cederholm, "Building Teams for Global Operations," *Management Review* (June 1987): 32–36.

4. Based largely on N. J. Adler, *International Dimensions of Organizational Behavior* (Boston: PWS-Kent, 1991).

5. T. Brown, "Building a Transnational Team," *Industry Week*, May 16, 1988, 13.

6. Ibid.

7. R. T. Moran, "Cross-Cultural Contact: A Formula for Success in Multicultural Organizations," *International Management* (December 1988): 74.

8. Ibid.

9. I. Ratiu, "International Consulting News," in *Managing Cultural Differences*, 3rd ed., eds. P. R. Harris and R. T. Moran (Houston, TX: Gulf Publishing, 1991).

10. L. S. Lewan, "Diversity in the Workplace," *Human Resource Management* (June 1990): 42–45.

11. T. Cox and S. Blake, "Managing Cultural Diversity: Implications for Organizational Competitiveness," *Executive* 5 (1991): 45–56.

12. J. R. W. Joplin and C. S. Daus, "Challenges of Leading a Diverse Workforce," *Academy of Management Executive* 11, no. 3 (August 1997).

13. "Managing By Values," *Business Week*, August 1, 1994.

14. "How to Make Diversity Pay," *Fortune*, August 8, 1994.

15. J. Braham, "No, You Don't Manage Everyone the Same," *Industry Week*, February 6, 1989, 28–35.

16. Speech by Xerox Company Diversity Manager at the 1994 meeting of the Middle Atlantic Association of Colleges of Business Administration, New York.

17. W. B. Johnston, "Global Work Force 2000: The New World Labor Market," *Harvard Business Review* (March–April 1991): 115–127.

18. A. Edwards, "Cultural Diversity in Today's Corporation," *Working Woman*, January 1991, 45–51.

19. Speech by E. Andrews, Manager Workforce Diversity Division, General Electric Company, at the 1994 meeting of the Middle Atlantic Association of Colleges of Business Administration, New York.

20. B. W. Turkman, "Development Sequence in Small Groups," *Psychological Bulletin* 63 (1965): 384–399.

21. Simcha Ronen, *Comparative and Multinational Management* (New York: John Wiley and Sons, 1986): 108.

22. S. Ferrari, "Human Behavior in International Groups," *Management International Review* 12, no. 6 (1972): 31–35.

23. R. Hayles, "Costs and Benefits of Integrating Persons from Diverse Cultures into Organizations" (paper presented at the 21st International Congress of Applied Psychology, Edinburgh, Scotland, July 1982); quoted in Adler.

24. R. Shuter, "Cross-Cultural Small Group Research: A Review, an Analysis and a Theory," *International Journal of Intercultural Relations* 1 (1977): 91–104.

25. I. L. Janis, *Groupthink*, 2nd ed. (Boston: Houghton-Mifflin, 1982).

26. C. Kovach, "Some Notes for Observing Group Processes in Small Task-Oriented Groups" (Graduate School of Management, UCLA, 1976); quoted in Adler.

27. Adler; W. E. Watson, K. Kumar, and L. K. Michaelsen, "Cultural Diversity's Impact on Interaction Process and Performance: Comparing Homogeneous and Diverse Task Groups," *Academy of Management Journal* 36 (June 1993): 590–602.

28. Braham.

29. L. Copeland, "Making the Most of Cultural Differences in the Workplace," *Personnel* (June 1988): 52–60.

30. R. T. Jones, "How Do You Manage a Diverse Workforce?" *Training and Development Journal* (February 1989): 13–21.

31. Ibid.

32. Mary Pat McEnrue, "Managing Diversity: Los Angeles Before and After the Riots," *Organizational Dynamics* (Winter 1993): 18–29.

33. Ibid.

34. Ibid.

35. J. W. Berry, "Social and Cultural Change," in *Handbook of Cross-Cultural Psychology*, eds. H. C. Triandis and R. W. Brislin (Boston: Allyn and Bacon, 1980).

36. J. W. Berry, "Cultural Relations in Plural Society: Alternatives to Segregation and Their Sociopsychological Implications," in *Groups in Contact*, eds. N. Miller and M. Brewer (New York: Academic Press, 1984).

37. Taylor Cox and Joycelyn Finley-Nickelson, "Models of Acculturation for Intra-Organizational Cultural Diversity," *Canadian Journal of Administrative Sciences* 8, no. 2 (June 1991): 90–100.

38. Ibid.

39. T. Cox, "The Multicultural Organization," *The Executive* 5, no. 2 (1991): 34–47.

40. A. Omens, S. R. Jenner, and J. R. Beatty, "Intercultural Perceptions in U.S. Subsidiaries," *International Journal of Intercultural Relations* 11 (1987): 249–264.

41. Nobuyuki Chikudate, "Cross-Cultural Analysis of Cognitive Systems in Organizations: A Comparison Between Japanese and American Organizations," *Management International Review* 31 (1991/3): 219–231.

42. Ibid.

43. Omens, Jenner, and Beatty.

44. "The Immigrants," *Business Week*, July 13, 1992.

45. Statistics Canada, *Profile of the Immigrant Population, Canada, Provinces and Territories* (Ontario: Ministry of Supply and Services, 1988).

46. G. Oddou, "Unlocking a Hidden Resource: Integrating the Foreign-Born," in *Readings and Cases in International Human Resource Management*, eds. M. Mendenhall and G. Oddou (Boston: PWS-Kent, 1991).

47. Johnston.

Credits

Used with permission. All rights reserved. **125** Exhibit 4–8 from R. G. Linowes, "The Japanese Manager's Traumatic Entry into the United States: Understanding the American–Japanese Cultural Divide," *The Academy of Management Executives,* Vol. VII, No. 4, November 1993, p. 24. Reprinted by permission. **127** "Letter to MK" excerpted from a letter by Dr. Jin K. Sim, State University of New York–Plattsburgh. Copyright © 1993 by Dr. Jin K. Kim. **131** Exhibit 4–9 from *Managing Cultural Differences* by Philip R. Harris and Robert T. Moran. Copyright © 1991 by Gulf Publishing Company, Houston, TX. Used with permission. All rights reserved. **133** Exhibit 4–11 from Dr. Jean Lee, "Culture and Management—A Study of Small Chinese Family Business in Singapore," *Journal of Small Business Management,* July 1996. Reprinted by permission. **136** Case Study from Martin Hilb, case study from the Institut Fuhrung und Personalmangement der Hochschule St. Gallen as reprinted in M. Mendenhall and G. Oddou, *International Human Resource Management,* pp. 341–343, 1991 PWS-Kent. Reprinted by permission of Martin Hilb. **139** Opening Profile from Dr. Jin Kim, "Oriental Poker Face: Deception or Western Inscrutability?" Copyright © 1995 by Dr. Jin Kim, State University of New York–Plattsburgh. **142** Technology Application from S. Greengard, "How Technology Will Change the Workplace," *Workforce,* v. 77 (Jan 1998), p. 78-79. **154** Exhibit 5–6 reprinted from *Business Horizons,* March–April 1989. Copyright 1989 by Indiana University Kelly School of Business. Used with permission. **155** Exhibit 5–7 from A. Goldman, "The Centrality of 'Ningensei' to Japanese Negotiating and Interpersonal Relationships: Implications for U.S. Japanese Communication," *International Journal of Intercultural Relations* 18, no. 1 (Winter 1994). **157** Management Focus adapted and excerpted from Jeremy Main, "How 21 Men Got Global in 35 Days," *Fortune,* November 6, 1989, 71–79. Reprinted with permission of *Fortune Magazine.* **160** Exhibit 5–8 adapted from Young Yun Kim, *Communication and Cross-Cultural Adaptation* (Clevedon, England: Multilingual Matters, 1988): 79. Reprinted by permission. **162** Experiential Exercise reproduced *from International Business: Cultural Sourcebook and Case Studies,* by L. Catlin and T. White with the permission of South-Western College Publishing, a division of International Thomson Publishing, Inc. Copyright © 1994. All rights reserved. **164** Case Study from Edwin J. Portugal, MBA, Ph.D, State Univeristy of New York–Potsdam. Copyright © 1995 by Edwin J. Portugal. Reprinted by permission of the author. **175** Exhibit 6–4 reprinted from *International Journal of Intercultural Relations,* Volume 1, E. S. Glenn, D. Witmeyer, and K. A. Stevenson, "Cultural Styles of Persuasion." Copyright 1984, with permission from Elsevier Science. **176** Exhibit 6–5 adapted from S. E. Weiss and W. Stripp, *Negotiation with Foreign Business Persons: An Introduction for Americans with Propositions on Six Cultures,* (New York University Faculty of Business Administration, February 1985). **179** Exhibit 6–6 from John L. Graham, "The Influence of Culture on the Process of Business Negotiations in an Exploratory Study," *Journal of International Business Studies* (Spring 1985): 88. **181** Exhibit 6–7 from Bryan W. Husted, "Bargaining with the Gringos: An Exploratory Study of Negotiations between Mexican and U.S. Firms," *International Executive* 36(5) (September-October 1994): 625-644. Reprinted by permission of John Wiley & Sons, Inc. **186** Exhibit 6–9 from W. Gudykunst, L. Stewart, and S. Ting-Toomey, *Communication, Culture, and Organizational Processes.* Copyright © 1985 by Sage Publications, Inc. Reprinted by permission of Sage Publications, Inc. **194** from C. Harvey/M. Allard, Understanding Diversity: Cases, Readings and Exercises, (adapted from pages 274–277), © 1995 Addison Wesley Longman, Inc., Reprinted by permission of Addison Wesley Longman. **202** Comprehensive Case from James A. Brunner and Mao Jianhua, "Deli Rockwool Corp. in the Poeple's Republic of China." Copyright © 1995 James A. Brunner. Reprinted with permission of the author. **209** Comprehensive Case by Patricia Gercik excerpted from "On Track with Japanese." New York: Kodansha 1992. Reprinted by permission of Kodansha America Inc. **212** Comprehensive Case updated and adapted from a term project by Angela Tallada, Chris Escudero and Kathleen O'Connor, students at the State University of New York–Plattsburgh, Spring 1994. Copyrght © 1995 by Helen Deresky. **219** Opening Profile reprinted by permission of the *Wall Street Journal,* © 1998 Dow Jones & Company, Inc. All Rights Reserved Worldwide. **225** Management Focus from: Andrea Knox, "Off and Running in Vietnam," February 27, 1994. Reprinted with permission from the *Philadelphia Inquirer.* **228** Exhibit 7–3 from Diane J. Garsombke, "International Competitor Analysis," reprinted from *Planning Forum,* May/June 1989 with permission from The Planning Forum, The International Society for Strategic Management Planning. **230** Exhibit 7–4 from J. Garland, R.N. Farmer and M. Taylor, International Dimensions of Business Policy and Strategy, 2nd ed. (PWS-Kent, 1990). **232** Exhibit 7–5 from a term project by Simone Betz and Steven Ellen at the State University of New York–Plattsburgh, Fall 1991. Copyright © Helen Deresky. **236** Management Focus adapted and compiled from B. Schlender, "Matsushita Shows How to Go Global," *Fortune,* July 11, 1994; "Tradition Be Damned," *Business Week,* October 31, 1994; "Matsushita: Value-Added Management for Global Partnerships," *Business Week,* July 12, 1993; "Japan's Fallible Firms," *Economist,* February 27, 1993. **237** Exhibit 7–6 from R. Grosse and D. Kujawa, *International Business,* p. 372. (Homewood, IL: Irwin, 1988). Reproduced with permission of the McGraw-Hill Companies. **244** Technology Application from E-business, IBM Online. **246** Exhibit 7–8 from G. Hofstede, Cultures and Organizations: Software of the Mind (London: McGraw-Hill, 1991). Reprinted with permission of

Technology Application courtesy of British Telecommuications PLC. **442** Exhibit 13–1 reprinted from *Management Review,* June 1987. Copyright © 1987 American Managment Association International. Reprinted by permission of American Managment Association International, New York, NY. All rights reserved. http://www.amanet.org. **443** Management Focus adapted from R. T. Moran, "Airbus: An Exceptional Multicultural Success," *International Management* (February 1989). **444** Management Focus from J. S. McClenahen, "Not Fun in the Sun: Bull has a Demanding Program to Build Teamwork." Reprinted from *Industry Week,* October 15, 1990. Copyright Penton Publishing, Inc., Cleveland, Ohio. **447** Exhibit 13–3 from Mark M. Dereksy, "Managing in a Diverse Workforce," MBA Paper, West Florida University, Spring 1994. **451** Exhibit 13–5 based on R. T. Moran, "Cross-Cultural Contact: A Formula for Success in Multicultural Organizations," *International Managment* (December 1988): 74; L. Copeland, "Making the Most of Cultural Differences at the Workplace," *Personnel* (June 1988): 52-60; and N. J. Adler, International Dimensions of Organizational Behavior (Boston: PWS-Kent, 1991): 135. **452** Exhibit 13–6 reproduced from International Dimensions of Organizational Behavior, 2/e by Nancy Adler with the permission of South-Western College Publishing a division of International Thomson Publishing. Copyright © 1991. All Rights Reserved. **454** Exhibit 13–7 reprinted from *Organizational Dynamics,* Winter 1993. Copyright © 1993 American Management Association International. Reprinted by permission of American Management Association International, New York, NY. All rights reserved. http://www.amanet.org. **455** Exhibit 13–8 from Taylor Cox and Joycelyn Finley-Nickelson, "Models of Accumulation ofr Intra-Organizational Cultural Diversity," *Canadian Journal of Administrative Sciences,* Vol. 8, No. 2, June 1991; 92. Reprinted by permission of the Administrative Sciences Association of Canada. **456** Exhibit 13–9 from Nobuyuki Chikudate, "Cross-Cultural Analysis of Cognitive Systems in Organizations: A Comparison Between Japanese and American Organizations," *Management International Review* 31, no. 3 (1991): 219-231. Reprinted with permission. **457** Exhibit 13–10 from Census Bureau, reprinted in *Investors Business Daily* 11/2/98. **458** Management Focus compiled from L. Krarr, "Japan's Gung-Ho U.S. Car Plants," *Fortune,* January 30, 1989, 98-108; M. Sorg, "They're Going Around in Circles in Smyrna," *Automotive News Detroit Special,* October 7, 1985, D8; and J. Plegue, "Honda's U.S. Factory—Spacious, Spic and Span," *Automotive News,* May 2, 1983. Reprinted by permission of *Fortune Magazine.* **460** "The In-Basket Dilemma," by Alice L. O'Niell. Reprinted with permission of the author. **468** Comprehensive Case by Professor Manab Thakur, California State Univeristy Fresno; reprinted in R. Thompson and R. Strickland, *Strategic Management,* 6th ed. (Homewood, IL: Irwin, 1992). This case is presented for educational discussion purposes, not to illustrate either effective or ineffective handling of an administrative situation. **475** Comprehensive Case, "Solartron," prepared by Henry W. Lane and Lorna L. Wright. Copyright © 1982, the University of Western Ontario, revised 95/12/04. Reprinted by permission of Ivey Publishing. **483** Comprehensive Case from *International Business Case Studies,* by Moran, Braaten, and Walsh. Copyright © 1994 by Gulf Publishing Company. Used with permission. All rights reserved. **491** Comprehensive Case. Research Associate Wilda White prepared this case under the supervision of Professor Joseph Badaracco as the basis for class discussion rather than to illustrate either effective or ineffective handling of an administrative situation. Copyright © 1992 by the President and Fellows of Harvard College. **509** Comprehensive Case by Professor Arieh A. Ullman, "Whirlpool's Quest for Global Leadership." Reprinted by permission. **534** Comprehensive Case. This case was prepared by Professor Thomas L. Wheelen of the University of Florida, Ellie A. Fogarty, Business Librarian, and Professor Joyce P. Vincelette of Trenton State College. Copyright © by Thomas L. Wheelen. Reprinted by permission.

Company Index

A.B. Electrolux Corporation, 513. *See also* Electrolux Company
ABB Zamech Corporation, 287–288, 305, 349, 354
Achmea Insurance, 243, 244
Adidas, 100
AEG Hausgerate AG, 512, 513
AEG-Telefunken Corporation, 513
Aeroflot, 9–10
Aerospatiale, 258
Agla Gebert Corporation, 397
Airbus Industrie, 69, 442, 443
Air Express International, 306, 307
Air France, 391
Allmack Corporation, 209
Alstholm Corporation. *See* GEC Alstholm Corporation
Aluminum Company of America (Alcoa), 289
Amdahl Corporation, 298
American Can Company, 32
American Cyanamid Company, 110
American Megatrends Company, 456
Anheuser-Busch Company, 238
Apple Corporation, 62
Aramco Corporation, 448
Arthur Andersen Company, 183
Artovaz Corporation, 240
Asea Brown Boveri (ABB) AG, 288, 299–300, 360
Aspera S.r.I., 518
AT&T, 10, 15, 62, 103, 259, 260, 263, 432. *See also* Bell Telephone Laboratories
    diversity management at, 448
    joint ventures of, 104–105, 244
    layoffs at, 498
    women employed by, 386
AT&T Communications, 494
AT&T Consumer Products, 491–509
AT&T Technologies, 494
Audi Corporation, 256
Avon Products, Inc., 63, 222, 389

BAESA Company, 249, 250
Banco de Nation, 68
Bauknecht Company, 519, 521
BAZ Corporation, 11
Beecham Corporation, 221
Bell Operating Companies, 279, 491, 493, 494–495, 496
Bell Telephone Laboratories, 263, 456, 493
Benetton Group Spa, 267, 268–269
Ben & Jerry's, 220, 281–284
Biermann Company, 338
BMW Corporation, 22
Body Shop International PLC, 534–555
Boeing, 144, 177–178
Booz-Allen & Hamilton, 381, 382
Bosch-Siemens Corporation, 513, 514, 519
Bosch-Siemens Hausgerate GmbH, 528
Boston Consulting Group, 331
Brasmotor S.A., 523
Brastemp S.A. Corporation, 515
Briggs and Stratton, 469
Bristol-Meyers Squibb, 294
British Aerospace, 258
British Airways, 11, 243, 347
British Gas Company, 11
British Telecom, 495
Buehler Products, 469

Caloric Company, 510
Campagnie de Machines Bull, 442
Canon Corporation, 233, 261
Carrefour SA, 277
Caterpillar, Inc., 234, 263, 272
Chase Manhattan Bank, 32, 364
Chicago Pacific Corporation, 514
China Guoxin Information Corporation, 219
Chinatex Cotton Yarns & Fabrics Import and Export Corporation, 219
Chraroen-Pokphand, 16
Chrysler Corporation, 10, 16, 187, 188, 241, 258, 259, 458. *See also* DaimlerChrysler AG
Ciba-Geigy Corporation, 300
Cifra Company, 9
Cisneros Group, 249–251
Citibank Corporation, 17, 18
Citicorp Corporation, 17
Citigroup Corporation, 14, 16, 17, 20
Citroen Corporation, 153
Coca-Cola Company, 7, 16, 28, 29, 59, 61, 259, 263, 288
    cola wars of, 248–252
    in South Africa, 62
Code-A-Phone Company, 496
Colgate-Palmolive Company, 95–98, 296, 297, 364, 398
    Hungarian operation of, 330–333
    management deveopment by, 359–360
Construcciones Aeronauticas, 258
Control Data Corporation, 65, 67
Corning Glass Works, 240, 300
Cos-tec Corporation, 545, 550
Crew Peabody Company, 338

Daewoo Motors, 8, 123, 241, 259
Daimler-Benz Aerospace, 258
Daimler-Benz AG, 272
Daimler-Benz Corporation, 273, 512
DaimlerChrysler AG, 187, 188, 256–257, 258, 259, 278, 364, 398
Dart & Kraft Company, 515
Deli Rockwool Corporation, 202–209
Dell Computer Corporation, 235
Del Monte Company, 57
Denny's Restaurants, 58
Deutsche BA, 243
Digital Equipment Corporation, 225
Disney Corporation, 212–215, 231, 238
Dolmel Corporation, 288
Dolmel Drives Corporation, 288
Dow Chemical Corporation, 31–32
Dow Corning Company, 59

Dow Corporation, 243
Dunkin' Donuts, 79

Eastman Kodak Corporation, 59, 263
Ecopetrol Corporation, 50, 51, 52
Electrolux Company, 273, 510, 511, 512, 513, 514, 519, 528
Electrolux Zanussi Corporation, 513
Embotelladora Milca, 252
Embraco Corporation, 523
Enron Corporation, 180–181, 432
Eo Corporation, 260
Ernst & Young, 375
Esprit de Corp, 349
Estate Company, 517
Euro Disney, 212–215
Exxon Corporation, 38, 384

Fabulon Company, 331, 332
FDX Corporation, 219
Federal Express (FedEx) Corporation, 14, 62, 219–220
Fiat Corporation, 9, 72, 241
Ford Motor Company, 62, 66, 76, 78, 80, 145, 231, 256, 263, 293, 384, 401
   European Group, 292
   videoconferencing by, 158
Foreign Credit Insurance Association (FCIA), 35
France Telecom, 495
Freeport McMoRan, Inc., 41
Frigidaire Corporation, 510
Fuji Bank Ltd., 107
Fujitsu Corporation, 44–45, 240, 258, 297–298

Gap, The, 338
GEC Alstholm Corporation, 259
GEC Hotpoint Corporation, 513
General Electric Appliances, 528
General Electric Corporation, 240, 243, 364, 397, 403, 448, 496, 510, 511, 512, 514, 526
   expatriate career management by, 381
   global perspective of, 360
   joint ventures of, 261, 263
   Hungarian operation of, 21–25, 331
General Foods, 233
General Motors Corporation, 41, 43, 59, 61, 231, 349, 364, 384, 401, 418
   Delphi Automotive Division, 78, 79
   joint ventures of, 123, 191, 241, 256,

258, 272, 360
   Opel unit of, 221
GE/Thompson Company, 499
Gillette Corporation, 432
Gillette International, 291
Go Corporation, 260
Goldstar Corporation, 512
Goodyear Tire & Rubber Company, 40
Grand Metropolitan Corporation, 16, 273
Green Giant Company, 16
Groupe Bull, 403, 443, 444
Grupo Pao de Acucar SA, 277
GTE Corporation, 496

H. J. Heinz Company, 62, 291, 349
Henkel Corporation, 331, 332
Hewlett-Packard Corporation, 110, 243, 263, 323, 377, 378, 432
Hitachi Corporation, 45–46, 502
Hit de Venezuela, 249
Hobart Corporation, 515
Holiday Inns, 239
Honda Corporation, 231, 241
Honda of America Manufacturing Inc., 360
Honeywell, Inc., 395, 397, 403–405, 442, 447, 452
Honeywell Bull Inc., 441–442
Hoover Corporation, 16, 514
Horri Corporation, 203
Hotpoint Corporation. See GEC Hotpoint Corporation
Hoya Corporation, 260
Huthwaite Research Group, 183
Hyundai Corporation, 8

IBM Corporation, 16, 45–46, 59, 61, 62, 113, 244, 263, 339, 349, 445, 458–459
   Argentina subsidiary, 68
   global structure of, 294
   joint ventures of, 3–4
   overseas operations of, 9, 38, 221
IBM Japan, 388–389
IBM World Trade Corporation, 291, 422
Iceverks, 281–284
Ichiyoshi International Ltd., 383
ICI Corporation, 234
Ignis, 519
Indonesian Enterprises, 483–487
Ingersolle Rand Corporation, 62
Inglis, Ltd., 518

Intel Corporation, 231, 258, 260
Interceramic Corporation, 79
Inter-City Gas Corporation, 515
International Computers Ltd., 298
International Data Corporation, 382
International Telephone and Telegraph (ITT) Corporation, 496
IRI International, 110
Isuzu Corporation, 458
Italtel Spa, 260, 423, 425
Izabel Lam International, 16

J. P. Stevens Company, 335
Jacaranda Corporation, 550
Jacobs Suchard Corporation, 241
Jaguar Corporation, 256
Jenn-Air Company, 510
Johnson Electric Corporation, 322–329
Johnson & Johnson Corporation, 15, 394
Jordan Toothbrush Company, 238

Kenmore Appliance Group, 517
KFC, 41
Kimber Group, 15
KitchenAid Company, 510, 511, 515, 517
KKD Corporation, 209
KLM Royal Dutch Airlines, 105, 261
Kodak Corporation, 261
Kokusai Denshin Denwa, 495
Korf Corporation, 11
Kraft Foods, 233, 389
Kuo Lee Group, 333

Lam Research Corporation, 39
Latin American Appliance Group (Whirlpool), 523
Lee Jing Textile Company, 333–342
Lever Corporation, 47
Levi Strauss Corporation, 60–61, 296–297, 445
Leviton Manufacturing, 407, 417
Lincoln Savings Bank, 448
Liz Claiborne Company, 60, 107
Liz Claiborne International, 338
Lockheed Martin Corporation, 69
LSI Logic, 259
Lucky-Gold Star Corporation, 260

Mabuchi Motors, 327, 328
Madison Public Relations Group, 386
Magic Chef Company, 510
Mannesmann Company, 31, 51, 52, 260

Mark Spence Company, 338
Marquette Company, 68
Mars Company, 241
Marystown Shipyard, 44
Mastercraft Industries Corporation, 515
Matsushita Corporation, 9, 235, 236, 260, 328, 354, 495, 496, 502, 512
Maytag Corporation, 259, 510, 511, 512, 528
Mazda Corporation, 231, 256, 413, 458
McCain Foods Limited, 308
McCaw Cellular, 260
McDonald's Corporation, 62, 121, 221, 222, 245, 265, 306, 313
    franchises of, 239
    Moscow operation of, 106, 112, 308–309
MCI Communications, 103, 445–446
MCI-Worldcom, Inc., 7, 16, 103, 259
McKinsey & Company, 260, 495
Medtronic Corporation, 378
Mercedes-Benz Corporation, 22, 273–274
Merck Corporation, 231
Merloni-Indesit Corporation, 513–514
Metallgessellschaft Corporation, 11
Microsoft Corporation, 7, 63, 231
Minolta Corporation, 74
Mitsubishi Corporation, 8, 241, 260, 261, 446, 458, 495
Mitsubishi Trading Company, 231
Mitsui Corporation, 225
Mobil Oil Corporation, 16
Moli Graphic Design Studios, 362, 363
Moltex Rubber Works, 86
Monsanto Chemical Corporation, 82, 378
Montgomery Ward, 518
Motorola Corporation, 3–4, 10, 432
Multibras S.A. Corporation, 515, 523

N.V. Philips Corporation, 78, 244, 258, 260, 349, 514, 519, 523
    network structure of, 298, 299
Nabisco. See RJR Nabisco
National Corporation, 236
NEC Corporation, 259, 260, 356, 403, 442, 495
Nestle Corporation, 59, 273, 292
New Age Beverages, 252
Newmont Mining Corporation, 175
Nike Inc., 60, 85, 99–100, 231, 238
Nineteen Hundred Corporation, 515
Nintendo Corporation, 46
Nippon Telephone and Telegraph (NTT) Company, 69

Nissan Corporation, 241, 241, 245, 458, 458
NMB Semiconductor, 258
North American Appliance Group (Whirlpool), 515–518
Northwest Airlines, 261
Nuumi Corporation, 258
Nynex Corporation, 16

Occidental Petroleum Company, 50, 51, 52
Olivetti Corporation, 104–105, 259, 260
Ontario Hydro Corporation, 44
Opel Company, 9, 221, 256
OSI Industries, 221
Otis Elevator Company, 222, 368
Otto Versand Company, 63
Overseas Private Investment Corporation (OPIC), 35
Oxford Company, 338
OZD Steel, 11

Panasonic Corporation, 236, 495, 496, 499
PepsiCo Inc., 62, 144, 248–252, 263, 265, 360
    Russian operation of, 28–29
PepsiCola International, 291
Petro Canada, 44
Peugeot-Citroen SA, 272
Philip's Group, 222
Philip Morris Company, 232, 233, 240, 241
Philips Bauknecht Corporation, 513
Phillips-Van Heusen Company, 60
PhoneMate Company, 496, 499
Pirelli Corporation, 376
Plar SA Company, 80
Political & Economic Risk Consultancy, 43
Procter & Gamble, 109, 229, 331, 332, 348, 378, 448

Quaker Oats Company, 452

Radisson Hotels, 265
Rank Xerox Corporation, 432
Raytheon Company, 510
RCA Corporation, 16
Recruit Company, 69
Recruit Research Company, 383
Red Cross, 73
Reebok Corporation, 10, 60, 85–86
Reed and Associates, 86

Refripar Corporation, 528
Renault Corporation, 72
Rhone-Poulenc Corporation, 259, 273
RJR Nabisco, 233, 263
Rolls-Royce Corporation, 256
Roper Company, 510, 517
RSD Appliances, 259

Saab Corporation, 256, 399
Sainsbury Plc., 63
Samsung Corporation, 8, 62, 78, 258, 259, 261, 512
Sandia National Laboratories, 495
San Diego Gas & Electric Company, 80
Sanyo Corporation, 78, 502
Saskatchewan Telephone, 44
Seagram Corporation, 16
Sears, Roebuck and Company, 515, 517
Seeger Refrigerator Company, 515
Sharp Corporation, 512
Shell Corporation, 378, 400
Shenyang Building Materials Corporation, 202
Shenzhen Whirlpool Raybo Air-Conditioner Industrial Company, Ltd., 525
Siemens AG Corporation, 3–4, 69, 240, 245, 300, 363
Skoda Corporation, 11
SmithKline Corporation, 221
Soapworks Corporation, 545
Société Nationale Industrielle Aérospatiale, 237
Solartron Corporation, 475–482
Sony Corporation, 78, 234, 363, 496, 502
Sprint International, 348
St. Charles Manufacturing Company, 515
Starbucks Coffee International, 407
STET Company, 321
Stolichnaya Company, 28
Subaru Corporation, 458
Suez Lyonnaise des Eaux SA, 273
Sundaram-Clayton, Ltd., 525
Sun Microsystems, 258
Suzuki Corporation, 245, 331
Systems Union Company, 39

TDK de Mexico, 468–475, 502
Teco Electric & Machinery Company, Ltd., 525
Telefonica, 321
Telefonics Corporation, 260
Telefonos de Mexico SA (Telmex), 103
Telefunken Corporation, 513

Texas Instruments (TI), 44–45, 258, 432
Thames Water PLC, 273
Thompson-Brandt Corporation, 514
Thompson Corporation, 513
Thompson SA Corporation, 16
Thomson, S.A., 78
Thomson-Brandt Corporation, 513
3Com Corporation, 439
3M Corporation, 243, 282, 448
Tianjin New Star Electronics Company, 46
Timberland Corporation, 441
Toshiba Electronics Corporation, 3–4, 257, 258–259, 260, 502
Toya Corporation, 203
Toyota Corporation, 8, 231, 241, 245, 326, 327 360, 458
    bargaining by, 147
    joint venture of, 191, 258
Toys 'R' Us, 63
Transparency International Corporation, 69
Traveler's Insurance Corporation, 17
Tricity Corporation, 513
Tropicana Orange Juice Company, 16
Tungsram Corporation, 21–25, 331
TVS Whirlpool, Ltd., 525

U. S. Filter Company, 79, 80
U.S. West International Corporation, 12, 38

Unilever Corporation, 16, 292, 331, 332, 349
Union Carbide Corporation, 56, 81, 384
Unisonic Company, 496
Unisys Corporation, 222, 225
United Parcel Service (UPS), 219–220, 242–243
United Technologies Corporation, 78
Unocal Corporation, 40
Upton Machine Company, 515

Van Heusen Company, 338
Vaseline Corporation, 16
VAZ Corporation, 9
Vessco Company, 283
Vitromatic S.A. Company, 518
Volga Auto Works, 221
Volkswagen Corporation, 11, 256
    Sarajevo, 16–17
Volvo Corporation, 22, 399

W. E. Upjohn Institute for Employment Research, 399
Wal-Mart Company, 9, 16, 60, 79, 80, 231, 276, 277, 278
Walt Disney Inc., 212–215
Wang Laboratories, 451
Western Electric Manufacturing Company, 491–493, 498
Westinghouse Corporation, 261

Whirlpool Asian Appliance Group, 523–525
Whirlpool Corporation, 509–533. See also TVS Whirlpool, Ltd.
Whirlpool Europe B.V., 519–523
Whirlpool Financial Corporation, 525–526
Whirlpool International, 440
Whirlpool Kitchens, Inc., 515
Whirlpool Overseas Corporation, 523
Whirlpool/Tatramat a.s., 521
Whirlpool Trading Corporation, 518
White Consolidated Industries, 510, 511, 512
WorkGroup Systems, 63
World Bank, 40
Wuxi Little Swan Company, 528

Xerox Corporation, 15, 31, 222–223, 349, 384, 446, 448
XPS Services, 62

Yanjing Building Materials Machinery and Technology Import & Export Corporation, 202–203

Zanussi Corporation, 513
Zenith Electronics Corporation, 259, 495
Zenith Technology, 260
Zona Research, 142

Subject and Name Index

Absenteeism, of Mexican workers, 417
Abuse, in negotiation, 178–179
Accommodation, in social responsibility, 57–58, 75
Accomplishment, American valuing of, 122
Accountability, in cosmetics industry, 539
Accounting, in coordinating global operations, 306–310
Acculturation, 453–456
    factors affecting, 455
Achievement
    American valuing of, 122, 123
    as value dimension, 119, 120
Adaptation to environment
    cross-cultural, 159–161
    managing political risk through, 34–35
    in organizational designs, 303–304
Adjustment, of expatriates, 378–380
Adler, Nancy, 386, 387
Administration, of skilled nursing facility, 460–464
Administrative heritage of organizations, 304
Advantage, in strategic planning, 233–234
Adversarial communication style, of Americans, 153, 155
Advertising, in cosmetics industry, 536, 544
Affective appeals, in negotiation, 174–175
Affectiveness, as value dimension, 119, 120
Affirmative action laws, 446
Africa
    high-context cultures in, 148–149
    women managers in, 384, 386
African National Congress (ANC), 62
    labor relations and, 394
Aggressiveness
    of Americans, 123
    in going international, 220–221, 222–223
    of Koreans, 126

Agreement
    in international joint ventures, 270–272
    in negotiating with China, 183
    in negotiation, 168, 169, 176, 180
Airbus airliner, 443
Aircraft industry, in France, 237–238
Airline industry
    Dutch, 105
    in European Union, 243
    human resource management in, 347
    managing international teams in, 443
Alcohol
    Arab proscription of, 131
    in Japanese negotiations, 211
    and Japanese women managers, 383
    during negotiations with China, 204–205
Alienation, of expatriates, 355, 377–378
Allah
    and acceptance of change, 121
    in footwear logo, 92–95
    in Moslem culture, 107–108, 112–113, 130–131, 151, 483–487
Allan, Bob, 477
Alliances, 256–276. *See also* International joint ventures; Joint ventures; Partnerships; Strategic alliances
    globalization through, 15–16, 234
    management of international, 443
    U.S.-German, 256–257
Almeida, Victor, 79
Almeida family, 79
Altruism, American, 123
Amae value, 124
    in decision making, 191
Ambiguity
    in cross-cultural communication, 159–161
    expatriate-learned tolerance for, 380
    in negotiations with China, 207
American corporations
    ethics in international business and, 65–73

    foreign-owned corporations posing as, 16
American culture, 123
Americanization, in compensation packages, 364
American Society of Personnel Administration International (ASPAI), 377
Ammann, Fritz, 349
Andrews, Eugene, 448
Anhalt, Enrique, 80
Animal testing, in cosmetics industry, 547–548
Anti-Sweatshop Code of Conduct, 60, 85
Antitrust actions, 493
Apartheid
    case study concerning, 95–98
    multinational corporations and, 61–63
Appropriability of technology, 44–45
Appropriateness of monitoring systems, 310–311
Arabic language
    communication problems with, 145
    nuances of, 149
Arabic negotiating style, 171, 172, 174–175
Arabic work ethic, 409–410, 412
Arbitration, in negotiations with China, 208
Argentina
    bribery in, 68
    cola wars in, 249
    privatization in, 11
Arnold, Wayne, 107
Artzt, Edwin L., 109
AS/400 Advanced System platform, for Italian spa business, 268–269
Ascription, as value dimension, 119, 120
Asia
    acceptance of change in, 121
    Chinese commonwealth organization in, 295–296
    computers in banking in, 107

contract law in, 42–43
corporate leadership in, 6–7
cosmetics industry in, 552
economic growth of, 5–6
economic risk in, 40
expatriate women managers in, 387–388
family as cultural variable in, 111–112
high-context cultures in, 148–149
home appliance industry in, 514, 523–525
human rights in, 60
integrating immigrants from, 456
joint ventures in, 245
leadership styles in, 427
NAFTA and currency crisis in, 78
privatization in, 12
proxemics of employees in, 146
as regional trading bloc, 7, 8, 10
successful negotiating style in, 180
telecommunications industry in, 496–498
telecommunications joint venture in, 318, 320–321
transportation industry in, 219–220
U.S. cultural values and, 139
workplace safety in, 61
Aspirations, in negotiation, 176
Assertiveness
of Germans, 126
Korean versus American, 129
as value dimension, 116
Assimilation, in acculturation, 453
Associations, as cultural variable, 113
Astrologers, in Eastern cultures, 112
Attainability, in employee motivation, 419
Attitudes, in cross-cultural communication, 142–143
Attitudinal dimensions, geography of, 117–118
Attribution, in intercultural communication, 141–142, 143
Atwell, Patricia, 465–466
Australia
cosmetics industry in, 552
international business ethics in, 66
Authentic Labor Front, 397
Authoritarianism
in Chinese business, 132
in Chinese culture, 131
in Japan, 124
of Mexican managers, 417–418
Authority
delegation of, 426–433

in Indian management, 431
in Mexican management, 400–401
in organizational structure, 302–304
as value dimension, 114
Autocratic leadership
in Chinese employee motivation, 414
in decision making, 190
participative leadership versus, 426–433
Automation, in textile industry, 336–337
Automobile industry
in case study, 209–212
cultural work-ethic differences in, 413
in European Union, 245
in Germany, 256–257
international joint ventures in, 240–241
in Japan, 231
in Mexico, 9, 80–81
in Spain, 76
turnkey operations in, 239
unions in German, 398–399
work groups in, 399–400
Autonomy, of partners, 297–298
Avoidance of investment, managing political risk through, 34–35
Awami League, 91, 92
Axiomatic appeals, in negotiation, 174–175
Aziz, Tariq, 167

Backdoor approach, in negotiation, 178
Backgrounds, in doing business in Taiwan, 335
Baker, James, 167
Balance sheet approach, to expatriate compensation, 364–367
"Bamboo network," 294–296
Bangladesh
case study in, 90–95
child labor in, 61
independence of, 91
Banking industry
acculturation in, 454–456
computers in Japanese, 107
Bargaining, in negotiation, 178–179
Barshefsky, Charlene, 173–174
Bastarella, 67
Beck, Erica, 477–478, 479
Beida, George, 475–476, 479–481, 481–482
Belgium, work ethic in, 410, 411
Bell, Alexander Graham, 491
Bercaw, Jim, 498

Bertaccini, Ken, 495–496, 498
Biculturalism stage, of culture shock, 358
Bicycles, in Japanese banking, 107
Bilingual testing techniques, 457–458
Biomedical equipment, case study concerning, 87–90
Blacklisting, of union activists, 397
Blackmail
by Colombian guerrillas, 52
managing risk of, 38
Blondeau, Pierre, 475–482
Body language
Arabic, 148–152
in communication, 145–147
cultural signals in, 110
Bonuses
for Japanese employees, 421
for Mexican employees, 419
Border Industrialization Program, maquiladoras in, 501–502
Border industries. See Maquiladoras
Bosses, power distance of, 114
Botwick, Bill, 41
Bowman, Hank, 519
Brazil
cola wars in, 249
expatriate training for, 355
successful negotiating style in, 178, 179
Breast implants, ethics of exportation of, 59
Bribery, 65. See also Questionable payments
American prosecution in cases of, 67–68
American versus European managers' attitudes toward, 71–72
case studies of, 87–90, 485–486
codes of conduct proscribing, 64
legal prohibition of, 66–67
in U.S.-Russian joint ventures, 282
Broadfoot, Robert, 43
Broering, James, 183
BT Conference Call, 442
Budget control, 310–311
Building materials industry, case study of negotiations with China in, 202–9
Bureaucratic control, of multinational organizational structures, 305
Burma, human rights violations by, 61
Burns, Pat, 386
Bush, George Herbert Walker, 50, 167, 427–428
Business executives
kidnappings of, 31
model for developing expatriate, 357
in staffing abroad, 348–352

Business relationships
building, 158
contracts and, 43
in doing business in Taiwan, 335

Callahan, Richard J., 12
Canada
collective bargaining in, 391
cosmetics industry in, 552
decision making in, 190
employee participation in
management in, 400
expatriate manager in Kenya from,
475–482
fast-food joint venture with Russia,
308–309
governmental involvement in business
in, 43–44
integrating immigrants to, 456
international business ethics in, 66
international joint ventures in, 277
labor laws in, 396
as low-contact culture, 146–147
miscommunication involving
expatriate from, 143–144
NAFTA as benefiting, 77–81
in North American regional trade
bloc, 8–9
organized and unorganized labor in,
390
and Russian fast-food industry, 308
subcultures in, 111
telecommunications joint venture in,
318–322
Cano–Limon–Covenas oil pipeline,
destruction of, 51, 52
Cano–Limon oil field, 51
Capitalism, privatization and the global
trend toward, 11–12
Cárdenas, Cuauhtemoc, 501
Career rewards, 421
Careers, in international management, 18,
376, 377–389
Carroll, A. B., 57
Carroll's model of social responsibility,
57–58
Cars, for expatriates, 365
Carterfone decision, 493
Cassoni, Vittorio, 349
Castaner, Josep, 361
career profile in Spain of, 362
Caste, in Indian management, 431
Causality, cultural differences in meaning
of, 107, 108
Centralization, in Chinese business,
131–133

Centralization–decentralization continuum,
in organizational structure, 302–4
Chaebols, 8
bribery scandals of, 67
Challenges, as motivation to work, 413
Chang, Vanessa, 42
Change
in American culture, 123
cultural differences in acceptance of,
121, 122
in organizational design, 289–293,
300–304, 314–317
Chang Siang-Chun, 336
Charitable contributions, terrorism risk
management by local, 38
Checklist approach, to economic risk
analysis, 39–40
Chihuahua, Mexico, labor unrest in,
404–405
Child labor, 86
in Bangladesh, 61
in case study, 99–100
Chinese, 61
codes of conduct prohibiting, 63
ethical and social considerations of,
58–59
Children, of expatriates, 378
Childs, Ted, 445
Chile, expropriation in, 30
China. See also Overseas Chinese
acceptance of change in, 121, 122
adverse regulatory environment in,
41–42
American women managers in, 386
collectivism in, 122
contract law in, 42–43
decision making in, 190
doing business in, 28, 131–133,
202–209, 362–363
economic development of, 10
employee motivation in, 414–415
expanding into markets in, 222
expatriate training for, 355
globalized business organization in,
294–296
human rights violations by, 59, 61
international joint ventures in, 272,
274–276
language problems in, 145
licensing in, 245
macropolitical risk events in, 30
management careers in, 362–363
micromotor industry joint venture in,
324–325, 327–329
motivation in coffee business in, 407
no unemployment in, 415

piracy of intellectual property by, 46
political instability in, 226
privatization in, 12
reward systems in, 421–422
small family businesses in, 131–133
strategic alliances in, 259
subcultures in, 111
successful negotiating style in,
177–178, 180, 181
successful negotiation with, 183–185
transportation industry in, 219–220
unionization of foreign firms in, 391–394
U.S. negotiations with, 202–209
work ethic in, 409
Chinese facial expressions, 145
Choices, in strategic planning, 245–246
Christianity, in German culture, 126
Chun Joo Bum, 259
Cigarette consumption, in less developed
countries, 55
Cisneros, Oswaldo, 249–250, 250–251
Civil law, 42
contracts and, 42
Clarke, Clifford, 110
Clinton, William Jefferson, 60, 225, 404,
428
China policies of, 10
Cluster relationships. See also Country
clusters; Need clusters
in acculturation, 455–456
CNG (National Guerrilla Coordinating
Body), 53
Codes of conduct, 85
anti-sweatshop, 60
for multinational enterprises, 63–65
utility of, 71
Codes of ethics, for multinational
corporations, 69–72
Codetermination, in German labor laws,
397–399
Coffee business, motivating leadership in,
407
Coffee exports, in Colombian economy, 50
Cohen, Ben, 281
Cohon, George A., 308
Cola wars, case study of, 248–252, 253
Cole, David, 80
Collective agreements, 391
Collective bargaining, 391
Collectivism
in Chinese employee motivation, 414
in decision making, 190
of Germans, 126
in Japan, 124
in Japanese versus Mexican labor
relations, 401

of Koreans, 126
Korean versus American, 128–130
within Latin American countries, 417
in negotiating with China, 184
as value dimension, 115–116, 117
Colombia
kidnapping of executives in, 31, 50
risks for international business in, 50–53
Commands, in negotiation, 179
Commercial stage, in negotiating with China, 184–185
Commitment, in negotiation, 179
Common law, 42
contracts and, 42
Commonwealth of Independent States (CIS). *See also* Russia; Soviet Union
cultural diversity of, 266
economic development of, 9–10
in international joint ventures, 240, 263–266
rise of, 113
SWOT analysis of, 233
Communication, 140–141. *See also* Cross-cultural communication
environment
careful, 156–157
defined, 140
intercultural, 141–142
among Mexican workers, 417
nonverbal, 142, 145–147, 148
oral, 140
Communication channels, in cross-cultural communication, 152–156
Communications media, 157–158
Communication style
Asian versus American, 139
Japanese versus American, 153, 154–155
Middle Eastern, 130–131
Communism
in eastern and central Europe, 9
Overseas Chinese network and, 295
privatization following, 11, 21–25
Communist countries, contract law in, 42–43
Community projects, social responsibility through, 98, 549
Comparative return on investment (ROI), 312
Compartmentalization, of Germans, 126
Compensation. *See also* Wages
in cosmetics industry, 543–544
for expatriates, 361–368
for Russian managers, 345, 367–368
for U.S. expatriates in Russia, 345

Competition
bribery as advantageous in, 68
cooperation transformed into, 261, 262
global, 5, 6
going international and, 221, 228
in home appliance industry, 510–511, 512
in micromotor industry, 327–329
questionable business practices in, 68–69
in soap industry, 331–332
in telecommunications industry, 495–497
understanding local culture as advantage in, 103–105
in U.S.-Russian joint ventures, 282
Competitive analysis, in strategic planning, 232–233
Competitiveness
of Americans, 123
expatriates as improving, 381
Complexity, in negotiation, 176
Compromise, in negotiation, 177
Computer industry
in China, 362–363
globalization in, 294
Computers
better intercultural communication with, 142
in home appliance industry, 512
in human resource management, 347
for Italian spa business, 268–269, 425
in Japanese banking system, 107
in knowledge sharing, 382
in Puerto Rican case study, 162–164
speeding up negotiation with, 188
in textile industry, 339
Concern for others, as value dimension, 116
Concessions, in negotiation, 168, 169, 180
Concorde airliner, 443
Confederation of Mexican Workers (CTM), 397
Conference calling, 442
Confiscation, as political risk, 30
Conflict, in U.S.-Russian joint ventures, 283
Conflict avoidance, in negotiating with China, 183–184
Conflict resolution, in negotiation, 186–187
Confucianism, 111
in Chinese business, 324
in employee motivation, 414–415

of Koreans, 126
in negotiating with China, 184
Overseas Chinese network and, 295
Conglomerates, globalization of, 16
Consumer protection, codes of conduct for, 64
Content, of leadership, 423, 424, 429–431
Context
as affecting information flow, 152
in communication, 148–152
of leadership, 423, 424, 429–431
Contingency leadership, 426–433
Contingency management
culture in, 109
organizational design for, 288–289
Contingency model, of international management, 17–19
Continuous improvement, quality control in Japan through, 432–433
Continuous monitoring, in international competitor analysis, 229
Contract law, 42–43
Contract manufacturing, as international market entry strategy, 239, 242
Contracts, 42
enforcement of, 177
in negotiations with China, 207
Control
in decision making, 189
in international joint ventures, 269–272
managing monitoring systems for, 310–312
mechanisms for organizational, 305–310
in U.S.-Russian joint ventures, 265
Convergence
in labor systems, 394–395
of management styles, 106
Cooperation. *See also* Alliances
in Chinese employee motivation, 414, 415
in cosmetics industry, 539
in international management, 19–20
in social responsibility, 75
transformed into competition, 261, 262
Coordination, of global operations, 305–310
Copeland, Lennie, 110
Corey, Michael P., 347
Corporate leadership, 6–7
Cosgrove, Claire, 442
Cosmetics industry, environmental protection in, 534–554

Cost savings, going international for, 222–223
Cost sharing, strategic alliances for, 258–259
Council on Economic Priorities (CEP), labor standards by, 63
Counterterrorism, 38
Country clusters, of cultural value dimensions, 117–118
Court system, in China, 41–42
Craft unions, 390
Creeping expropriation, 31
Crime
  as human rights issue, 60
  in Russia, 263–266
Criticism
  among Koreans, 126
  Korean versus American, 128–130
  in Mexican work ethic, 418
Cross-border alliances. See Alliances; Strategic alliances
Cross-cultural adaptation, 159–161
Cross-cultural communication environment, 3–4, 139–161
  Arabic and American, 149–152
  Asian and American, 139
  communication channels in, 152–156
  communication in, 140–141
  context in, 148–152
  cultural noise in, 141–156
  cultural variables in, 142–148
  feedback channels in, 158–159
  management of, 156–161
  Philippine and French, 164–165
  Puerto Rican and American, 162–164
  selective transmission in, 157–158
  sending "right" messages in, 140
Cross-cultural differences
  in case study, 136–137
  as cause of business failure, 104–105
  critical, 120–122
  in leadership functions and styles, 423–425, 426–433
  as management problem, 4–5, 15, 28–29, 29–47, 47–48
  in management styles, 105–109
Cross-cultural management, 20
Cross-cultural mentoring, 458
Cross-cultural negotiation, 167–168, 169, 181–187
  case study of, 194–197
  variables in, 181–182
Cross-cultural training, 355–361
  acquired by expatriates, 380
  effectiveness of, 104–105
Cross-national need clusters, 413

Crown Corporations, 44
CRS (Socialist Renewal Movement), 53
Cultural differences, 103–134
  communication problems arising from, 141
  critical, 120–122
  in employee motivation, 415–421
  as management problem, 4–5, 136–137, 357–358, 439
  in negotiating styles, 169–180
  in work ethic, 408–411, 411–414
Cultural empathy, 104
Cultural environment, 105–109
Cultural haptics, 147
Cultural noise
  in Arab-American business, 151–152
  in communication, 141–156
Cultural profiles
  of Americans, 123
  of Arabs, 130–131
  of Chinese, 131–133
  for countries, 109
  of Germans, 126
  of Japanese, 124–125
  of South Koreans, 126–130
  variables in, 111–113
Cultural savvy, 104
Cultural sensitivity, 104
  acquiring, 109, 156
Cultural values, 113. See also Value dimensions
  American and alternative, 108
  self-reference criteria as, 108–109
Cultural variables, 106–109, 111–113
  chart of, 106
  in communication, 142–148
  in decision making, 190
  in leadership, 429–431
  sociological descriptions of, 109–122
Culture, 4, 103–134
  as barrier to integrating immigrants, 457
  case study concerning, 136–137
  competitive advantages in understanding local, 103–105
  defined, 105
  dimensions and variables of, 109–122
  effects on communication of, 141
  effects on leadership functions and styles, 423–425, 426–433
  effects on organizations of, 105–109
  in globalization, 302–303
  international business ethics and, 66
  in international joint ventures, 273–276
  in job motivation, 419–421

  in labor–management philosophies, 400–401
  management styles and, 130–133
  profiles of, 123–130
Culture contingency, leadership and, 430–431
Culture identity structure, 453
Culture shock
  for expatriates, 358, 377–378, 378–380
  reverse, 377
Currency devaluation
  as economic risk, 39
  in Russia, 263
Currency instability, going international and, 227
Currency translation exposure, as economic risk, 39
Customer demands, going international and, 221

Daycare system, in France, 383
DDT pesticide, ethics of exporting, 82
Deadlines
  in Arab business, 131, 151
  cultural differences in acceptance of, 120–121
Decentralization, in globalization, 299–300, 302–304
Decision making, 187–193
  approaches to, 189–193
  ethics in, 72–73
  by Germans, 126
  locus of control in, 189, 304
  in management, 188
  in negotiation, 176
  during negotiation, 187
  process of, 189
  staffing and, 350
Decision-making control, in multinational organizational structures, 305
Decoding, in communication, 158–159
Deculturation, in acculturation, 453
Defense
  going international as, 220, 221
  in social responsibility, 57–58
de Forest, Mariah, 418
Degree of enforcement, of laws, 66
Delayered organization, 20
Delegation of authority, by leaders, 426–433
Dependency, managing political risk through, 35
Development
  of expatriates, 355–361
  of personnel, 451

Developmental policies
    codes of conduct in, 64
    in negotiating with China, 185
Development assistance, managing
        political risk through, 35
Dharma, in Indian management, 431
Didactic method, for expatriate
        preparation, 359
Differentiation, in globalization, 293
Diffuseness, as value dimension, 119, 120
Dimensions
    cultural, 109–122
    value, 113
Direct coordinating mechanisms, for
        managing global operations, 306
Dirty tricks, in negotiation, 178–179
Disadvantages, in strategic planning,
        233–234
Discipline, in Mexican work ethic, 418
Discrimination
    against women managers abroad, 384
    against women managers in Japan, 383
Distribution
    in home appliance industry, 510
    as joint venture problem, 281
    in U.S.-Russian joint ventures, 283
Divergence, in labor systems, 394–395
Diversity managers, 13–15
    in case study, 483–487
Diversity of cultures, 111
    in Commonwealth of Independent
        States, 266
Diversity of workforce
    in globalization, 13–15, 439–459
    language problems from, 145
    maximizing effectiveness of, 483–487
Diversity programs, 447–448
Djamkeret, 485
Domestic environment
    managing diversity in, 445–459
    in risk assessment, 33, 34
Domestic structure plus export depart-
        ment, as organizational form, 289, 290
Domestic structure plus foreign subsidiary,
        as organizational form, 289, 290
Dotlich, David, 441, 444
Douglas, Rick, 475, 476–477
Downsizing, 20
Drake, Rodman, 110
Drug cartels, Colombian economy and,
        50–53
Duo lao, duo de (more work, more pay)
        system, 421–422

Early-warning system, of risk assessment, 34
Earth Summit in Rio de Janeiro, 81

Ease of exit, 375
Eaton, Robert, 256–257, 364
Echeverrea Alvarez, Luis, 499
Economic environment
    in risk assessment, 33, 34
    risks resulting from, 38–41
Economic policies, codes of conduct in, 64
Economic risk, 39
    managing, 38–41
    in U.S.-Russian joint ventures,
        263–266, 284
Economics, local
    as cultural variable, 112
    as management problem, 29–41
    in risk assessment, 32–34
    and tobacco industry, 55
Economies of scale
    going international and, 222
    in mergers, 257
Education
    as cultural variable, 112
    social responsibility through, 97–98
Efficiency
    of Americans, 123
    of Germans, 126
Egypt
    ethics scandals in, 69
    patent laws in, 45
Eisner, Michael, 212, 215
Electricity, in Mexico, 80
Electronic data interchange (EDI), 307
Electronics industry. *See also* Micromotors
    integration in, 235
    in Japan, 236
    strategic alliances in, 258–259
    telecommunications industry and,
        496
Elenos, 51, 52
Elesperu de Freitas, Susana, 229
Ells, Barbara, 142
ELN (National Liberation Army), 51–52
Embarrassment, as Chinese motivational
        factor, 422
Emotional orientation in relationships, as
        value dimension, 119, 120
Empathy, in cross-cultural
        communication, 159–161
Employee of the month, in China, 422
Employees
    career advancement of, 362–363
    in central Europe, 25
    Chinese humiliation of worst, 422
    codes of ethics toward, 71
    computer-based knowledge sharing
        about, 382
    costs of dismissing, 375–376

in Japan, 432–433
    leaders of, 422–423
    management participation by,
        397–399, 399–400, 400–401
    in Mexico, 417–419
    motivation of, 407–408, 408–421,
        421–422
    multicultural management of,
        439–459
    obligations of, 108
    proxemics among, 146
    ratio of male to female, by country,
        385
    in skilled nursing facility, 460–464
    in textile industry, 341
    women as, 381–384, 385, 386–387,
        387–389
Employee training
    for expatriate positions, 355–361
    in U.S.-Russian joint ventures, 283
Employers, obligations of, 108
Employment practices, codes of conduct
        for, 64–65
Encoding, in communication, 156–157
Endo, Toshiyoshi, 157
Energy and Chemical Workers Union
        (ECWU), 400
Enforcement, degree of, 66
England. *See* Great Britain
England, George, 409
English Channel tunnel, negotiations over,
        176
Enrico, Roger, 249, 250, 251
Enterprise for the Americas Initiative
        (EAI), 50
Entertainment, during negotiations with
        China, 204–205, 206
Entertainment industry, case study in,
        212–215
Entry transition, of expatriates, 378–380
Environment. See also Cross-cultural com-
        munication environment; Cultural
        environment; Domestic environment;
        Economic environment; Political envi-
        ronment; Regulatory environment;
        Technological environment as factor
        affecting leadership, 424
Environmental assessment, in strategic
        planning, 226–231
Environmental interdependence, 81–82
Environmental protection
    codes of conduct for, 64, 503–504
    in cosmetics industry, 534–554
    maquiladoras and, 506
Environmental Protection Agency (EPA),
        340

Environmental scanning
    information sources for, 229–231
    levels of, 229
    process of, 230
    in strategic planning, 226–229
Equal Employment Opportunity (EEO)
    laws, 446
Equite strategic alliances, 258
Equity sharing, managing political risk
    through, 35
Error, Arab aversion to admitting, 130
Ershad, H. M., 92
Escalator model of career advancement,
    362
Ethical relativism, 59
Ethics
    case studies concerning, 87–100
    developing global policies for, 68–69
    interdependence and social responsi-
    bility and, 56, 58–59, 82–83
    international business, 66
    in international management, 58–60,
    65–73
    making the right decision and, 72–73
    of promoting tobacco industry, 55
    in western Europe, 69–72
Ethics gap, between United States and
    Europe, 70–71
Ethnicity, political problems caused by,
    29–30
Ethnocentricity, in body language, 146
Ethnocentric staffing approach, 348, 350,
    351
Ethnocentrism, 59, 109
Euro currency, 241
    establishment of, 7–8
Europe
    career advancement in, 362
    codetermination in labor laws in,
    397–399
    collective bargaining in, 391
    cosmetics industry in, 551
    home appliance industry in, 513–514,
    519–523
    integrating immigrants from, 456
    labor unions in, 391
    organizational staffing in, 351–352
    telecommunications joint venture in,
    321
Europe, central, economic development
    of, 9
Europe, eastern
    cola wars in, 249
    doing business in, 29
    economic development of, 9
    expanding into markets in, 222
    as high-contact culture, 146

political risk in, 30–31, 34
privatization in, 11
soap industry joint venture in,
    330–333
Europe, western
    concept of time in, 120–121, 147
    corporate leadership in, 6–7
    economic growth of, 5–6
    ethics in, 69–72
    informational privacy in, 14
    international business ethics in, 66
    international joint ventures in,
    273–274
    leadership styles in, 426–427
    low-context cultures in, 149
    U.S. cultural values and, 110
    U.S. negotiation with, 212–215
European Community (EC). See European
    Union (EU)
European subsidiaries, monitoring of,
    305–310, 331–333
European Union (EU), 7–8
    cross-border electronic data privacy
    in, 14
    ethics in, 69–72
    as foreign investor, 6
    going international and, 221
    labor laws in, 375–376
    managing international teams in, 443
    organized labor in, 389
    strategic planning for, 241–245
European Union Directive on Data
    Protection, 14
Evaluation variables, 312
    for gauging team success, 444–445
Exchange-rate risk, 39
Exchanging task-related information, in
    negotiation, 168, 169, 177–178
Exit, ease of, 375
Exit transition, of expatriates, 378–380
Expatriate failure, 354–355, 356
Expatriates. See also Parent-country
    nationals (PCNs)
    alienation of, 355, 377–378
    career management for, 378–380
    in case study, 370–373
    compensation for, 361–368
    international business ethics for, 66
    international managers as, 18
    lack of cultural sensitivity among, 104
    personnel problems with, 352
    preventing loss to firms of, 381
    repatriation of, 377–378, 380–381
    reverse culture shock among, 377
    selection of, 353–355
    skills learned abroad by, 380
    spouses of, 370–373, 378

transition process for, 379
    as transpatriates, 349
    U.S. in Russia, 345–346
    women as, 381–384
Expatriate success factors, 353, 356
Experience, in negotiating with China, 185
Exporting, as international market entry
    strategy, 238, 242
Exporting companies, globalism and, 15, 16
Export management companies (EMCs), 238
Expressive oriented approach, to conflict
    resolution, 186–187
Expropriation, 30
    creeping, 31
External economic relations, in risk
    assessment, 33
Extortion
    forced bribery payments as, 68
    in U.S.-Russian joint ventures, 282
Extrinsic maintenance factors, 415–421
Eye contact, 145–146
    among Arabs, 150–151

Face. See also Losing face; Saving face
    in Chinese employee motivation, 414
    in doing business in Taiwan, 335
    in Mexican work ethic, 418
    in negotiating with China, 184
Factual appeals, in negotiation, 174–175
Family
    among Arabs, 130, 132, 149
    in Chinese culture, 131–132
    as cultural variable, 111–112
    in Indian management, 431
    among Koreans, 126
    among Mexicans, 417
    in negotiating with China, 183–184
FARC (Revolutionary Armed Forces of
    Colombia), 51–52
Fast-food industry, in Russia, 106, 308–309
Fatalism, in Japanese versus Mexican labor
    relations, 401
Favoritism, in workplace, 410
Federal Communications Commission
    (FCC), 493
Feedback channels, 158–159
Femininity
    in U.S.-Iraqi negotiations, 167
    as value dimension, 117
Fettig, Jeff, 518
Field experiences, in expatriate preparation,
    359
Filtering, of communications, 141
Finance
    as global corporate objective, 227
    in U.S.-Russian joint ventures, 284
Financial rewards, 421

Financial risk, 39
    in going international, 227, 231–232
Financial statements
    in coordinating global operations,
        306–310
    evaluation variables for, 312
Financial Times 500 Global Companies, 7
Financial variables, in multinational
        corporation reports, 306–310
Firing. See Termination
Firm factors, in strategic planning choices,
        246
Fiscal policy change, local, as economic
        risk, 39
Flanagan, Maureen, 225
Flattery, in Mexican work ethic, 418
Flexibility, in cross-cultural
        communication, 159
Food industry, globalization in, 291
Footwear industry, case studies concern-
        ing, 85–86, 90–95, 99–100
Forced labor, 86
    ethics of, 60
Ford, Bill, Jr., 292
Ford, Steve, 377
Foreign Corrupt Practices Act (FCPA) of
        1977, 67, 89
    on bribery, 68
    prohibited activities in, 90
Foreign Credit Insurance Association
        (FCIA), political risk insurance
        through, 35
Foreign direct investment (FDI), in United
        States, 74
Foreign exchange, in going international,
        223
Foreign investment, by global firms, 6
Foreign investment policy, local, as
        economic risk, 39
Forming stage of group development, 449
France
    case study in, 164–165
    codes of ethics in, 69–72
    global alliances with, 237–238
    improving managerial performance in,
        416
    negotiating style in, 176, 177
    proxemics of employees in, 146
    U.S. cultural values and, 153
    U.S. negotiation with, 212–215
    women managers in, 383
Franchising
    in cosmetics industry, 538–541
    as international market entry strategy,
        239, 242, 245
    of small and medium-size enterprises,
        15

Freedom, American valuing of, 123
Free trade
    in the Americas, 50
    in European Union, 7–8
    in North America, 7, 8–9
French culture, in case study, 212–215
Friendship
    in Arab business, 132, 149–150
    in negotiating with China, 183–184
    in negotiating with Japan, 209–212
    in Philippine business, 436–437
    in U.S.-Russian joint ventures, 283
    in workplace, 410
Fringe benefits, for Mexican employees,
        419
Frings, Peter, 308
Fudge, Ann, 389
Fujita, Den, 245
Fully owned subsidiaries, as international
        market entry strategy, 241, 242, 245

Garment industry, globalization in,
        296–297
Garrison, John R., 360
Gaviria Trujilo, Cesar, 50
General Law on Ecological Balance and
        Environmental Protection, 504
Generosity, American, 123
Geography
    of cultural value dimensions,
        117–118, 118–120
    in organizational design, 289
Germany
    American miscommunication in, 144
    automobile industry in, 188, 256–257
    case study in, 87–90
    codes of ethics in, 69–72
    cultural profile of, 126
    decision making in, 188, 190
    ethics scandals in, 69
    informational privacy in, 14
    integrating immigrants to, 456
    international joint ventures by,
        273–274
    labor relations in, 397–399
    low-context culture in, 149
    micromotor industry joint venture in,
        325–326
    negotiation in, 197–201
    patent law in, 45
    performance monitoring in, 311
    proxemics of employees in, 146
    U.S. cultural values and, 126
    women managers in, 383
    work ethic in, 409, 410, 411
Getting to Yes (Fisher & Ury), 177
Gil Diaz, Francisco, 103

Glaspie, April, 167
Glass industry, global networks in, 300
Glenn, T. Michael, 219
Global community, trade developments in,
        5–16
Global divisional structure, as
        organizational form, 291–292
Global firms
    effects of world trade growth on, 6–7
    management problems facing, 4–5
Global functional structure, as
        organizational form, 290, 291
Global geographic area structure, as orga-
        nizational form, 290, 291, 292–293
Global integration, 235–238
Globalism, 5–7
    corporate objectives in, 227
    in cosmetics industry, 547–554
    defined, 5
    ethical problems resulting from,
        65–73
    ethical relativism in, 59
    in home appliance industry, 525–531
    information technology in, 12–13
    and multinational corporations,
        16–17
    privatization in, 11–12
    risks in, 30–41
    role of international managers in,
        17–19
    of small and medium-size enterprises,
        15–16
    social responsibility in, 58–59
    in strategic planning, 235–238
    technology and, 44–47
    workforce diversity in, 13–15
Globalization, 293
    as approach to world markets, 234
    case studies in, 314–317, 318–341
    expatriate selection in, 353–355
    of home appliance industry, 512–515,
        516, 517, 518–525
    international management teams in,
        441–445
    maintaining human resources in,
        376–389
    organizing for, 293–298, 300–304
    staffing for, 348–352
    of telecommunications industry,
        491–507
Globalization strategy, 302
Global managers, development of,
        359–360
Global orientation, training for, 360
Global product structure, as organizational
        form, 290, 291–292
Global staffing approach, 349, 350, 351

Global strategic alliances, 258
Glocal (global, local) firms, 235, 236, 296–298, 441, 442
Goals, in employee motivation, 408–421
Goizueta, Roberto C., 288
Gorbachev, Mikhail, 9, 10
Governance, in strategic alliances, 260–261
Government. *See also* Regulatory environment
    in codes of conduct, 64
    corruption in foreign, 67–68
    in international business ethics, 66
    in international joint ventures, 272–273
    Mexican, 499–501
    protectionism by, 43
    taxation by, 43
    telecommunications industry and, 493–495
Governmentalism, of host country toward foreign subsidiary, 76
Gradual adjustment stage, of culture shock, 358, 378–380
Graham, John, 174
Grease money, 67
Great Britain
    codes of ethics in, 69–72
    cosmetics industry in, 550–551
    eye contact behavior in, 146
    improving managerial performance in, 416
    international joint ventures in, 280
    labor laws in, 375–376
    micromotor industry joint venture in, 325–326
    negotiating style in, 176
    privatization in, 11
    repatriation of expatriates in, 381
    women managers in, 386
    work ethic in, 410, 411
Greeks, American miscommunication with, 141, 142, 143, 144, 145, 148
Green, Chris, 538
Green, Joan, 452
Gross domestic product (GDP)
    of China, 10
    cultural value dimensions and, 117–118
    growth in, 5–6
    individualism and, 116
    of less developed countries, 10
Gross national product (GNP). *See* Gross domestic product (GDP)
Group development, stages of, 449–451
Groups. *See* Collectivism; Minority groups; Socializing; Work groups

Groupthink, 450
Guangong, Hong Kong and, 295
Guanxi, 10, 42
    in joint venture with China, 328
    in negotiating with China, 184, 208
    among Overseas Chinese, 295
Guarantees, in negotiations with China, 207–208
Guerrillas, Colombian economy and, 50–53

Haas, Robert, 61
Hall, Edward T., 146
"Hamburger" management style, 3
Hamburger University, 308
Hammer, Armand, 52
Hardship packages, for expatriates, 345
Harmony
    in Chinese employee motivation, 414
    in Mexican work ethic, 418
    in negotiating with China, 184
Hazardous wastes
    ethics of exporting, 81–82
    from maquiladoras, 503–504
    in textile industry, 340–341
Headquarters
    in international management, 20, 300, 304
    in staffing, 348
    in Switzerland, 287–288
Health
    as cultural variable, 113
    in textile industry, 340
Health industry
    in case study, 95–98
    management in, 460–464
Health warnings, on cigarette packages, 55
Heavy industry
    globalized reorganization in Polish, 287–288
    U.S.-Russian joint ventures in, 263
Heckmann, Richard, 79, 80
Hedging, managing political risk through, 35–38
Hei family, 12, 13
Helu, Carlos Slim, 103
Herzberg's motivation categories, 411–414
    intrinsic–extrinsic dichotomy in, 415–421
Hierarchy
    in Japanese versus Mexican labor relations, 401
    of needs, 411–414
High-contact cultures, 146–147
    Arabs as, 150–151
High-context cultures, 148–149, 150
    low-context cultures versus, 186–187
    negotiation with, 181–182

High-tech firms
    economic growth of, 7
    globalization among, 297–298
Hijackings, managing risk of, 38
Hills, Carla, 386
Hiring practices, individualism and collectivism and, 115–116
Hofstede's value dimensions, 113–117
    chart of, 117
    in employee motivation, 408
Home appliance industry
    global leadership in, 509–531
    micromotors for, 324–325
Homelessness, as human rights issue, 60
Honesty, Korean versus American, 128–129
Honeymoon stage, of culture shock, 358
Hong Kong
    in Asian trading bloc, 8
    decision making in, 190
    language problems in, 145
    micromotors joint venture in, 322–329
    Overseas Chinese network in, 295
    transportation industry in, 219
    women managers in, 383
Honor, in Arab society, 132, 150
Horizontal organization, in globalization, 299–300, 302
Hoskins, Robert, 407
Hospitality
    among Arabs, 131, 149–150
    in doing business in Taiwan, 335
Host countries
    benefits of multinational corporations to, 76
    foreign subsidiaries in, 74–81
Host-country nationals (HCNs)
    compensation for, 364
    staffing international organizations with, 348–349, 350
    training of, 360–361
Hotel industry, U.S.-Russian joint ventures in, 263
Houmani, 178
Housing, for expatriates, 365, 366, 479–480
Hsinchu Science-based Industrial Park, 334
Huang, Bruno D. C., 335
Huang, Edward, 339, 340–341
Hughes, Penny, 543
Huk Kab money, 67
Humanism, in Japan, 124
Human nature, in Japanese versus Mexican labor relations, 401
Human resource management systems (HRMSs), 347

Human resources (HR). *See also* Staffing
  in cosmetics industry, 546–547
  management of, 346–347, 375–401
Human rights
  case study involving, 85–86
  codes of conduct for, 65
  in international management, 58–60
  responsibility of multinational
    corporations toward, 60–63
Humiliation, for poor performance, 422
Hungary. *See also* Europe, central
  business case study in, 21–25
  doing business in, 29
  soap industry joint venture in,
    330–333
Hussein, Saddam, 167, 427–428

Ice cream business, international joint
    venture in, 281–284
IG Metall, 398
Illegal activity, codes of conduct
    proscribing, 64
Illegal immigrants, 456
Im Choong Hoe, 61
Immigrants
  illegal, 456
  integration of, 456–459
  in resort industry, 465–466
  U.S. population of, 457
Imports, human rights audits of, 60, 61,
    61
Incentives
  in Chinese employee motivation, 415,
    421–422
  for going international, 223
  of reward system, 421–422
Income taxes, for expatriates, 365, 366
India
  appropriateness of technology in, 47
  attitude toward nature in, 121
  decision making in, 190
  expatriate training for, 355
  hazardous technology in, 56, 81
  leadership style in, 431–432
  successful negotiating style in,
    170–171, 172, 180
  work ethic in, 431–432
Indirect coordinating mechanisms, for
    managing global operations, 306–310
Individualism
  cultural differences in, 122
  in decision making, 190
  in employee motivation, 408
  in Germany, 126
  in Japanese versus Mexican labor
    relations, 401
  Korean versus American, 127–130

  within Latin American countries, 417
  as value dimension, 113, 114–116, 117
Indonesia
  decision making in, 189
  economic risk in, 38, 40–41
  expatriate training for, 355
  as high-contact culture, 146
  human rights inspections in, 61
  international joint ventures in,
    272–273
  managing Norwegian paper factory in,
    483–487
  Overseas Chinese network in, 295,
    484–485
Industrial Revolution, textile industry and,
    334
Industrial unions, 390
Industry factors, in strategic planning
    choices, 246
Inflation, multinational corporations as
    causing, 75
Informality, of Americans, 123
Informal meetings, 3
Information. *See* Task-related information
Information and communication
    technologies (ICTs), 44
Information systems
  in cross-cultural communication,
    152–156
  for performance monitoring, 311
Information technology (IT)
  effects of European privacy rules on, 14
  in globalization, 12–13
  in Japanese banking system, 107
  Vietnamese market for, 225
Infrastructure
  problems with Mexican, 80
  Vietnamese market for, 225
Inhouse risk assessment, 32
Initiative, of leaders, 428
Innovation, in home appliance industry,
    511–512
Inouye, Fumio, 468–474
Input control, managing political risk
    through, 35
Inscrutability
  of Japanese, 153
  of Orientals, 139
Inshallah, in Moslem culture, 112–113,
    151
Institute of Hamburgerology, 308
Institutional Revolutionary Party (PRI), 501
  history of, 499
  in Mexican labor relations, 403–405
Instrumental oriented approach, to
    conflict resolution, 186–187
Insults, directed at Mexicans, 418

Insurance industry, in European Union,
    243, 244
Integrated global structures, as organiza-
    tional forms, 290, 291–293
Integration
  in globalization, 293
  of immigrants, 456–459
  of training with global orientation, 360
Integration rooms, 188
Integrative model of leadership process,
    429–431
Integrative strategies, for globalization,
    235–238
Intellectual property
  Chinese piracy of, 46
  protection of, 44–47
Intercultural communication, 141
Intercultural communication effectiveness
    (ICE), 159–161
Intercultural method, for expatriate
    preparation, 359
Interdependence
  in building teamwork, 444
  of cultural value dimensions,
    116–117
  ethical behavior and social responsi-
    bility and, 56, 58–59, 82–83
  in international joint ventures, 271–272
  in international management, 19–20
  management of, 73–82
Interest, in Moslem culture, 113
Interest-rate risk, 39
Internal analysis, in strategic planning,
    231–232
Internal resource audits, in going
    international, 231–232
International business, 5
  as agent of change, 121
  comparison of work-motivational
    factors in, 415–421
  effects of technology on, 44–47
  evaluating profitability of, 312
  monitoring, 305–310, 310–312
  political and economic problems
    facing, 29–41
  reasons for entering, 220–223
  strategies for entering, 220–247,
    248–252
International business environment,
    understanding, 17–20
International business ethics, 66
International Chamber of Commerce
    (ICC), codes of conduct by, 63–65
International competitor analysis, 228–229
International Confederation of Free Trade
    Unions (ICFTU), in convergence of
    labor relations, 394

International Convention for the
    Protection of Industrial Property
    (Paris Union), 45, 206
International division, as organizational
    form, 290–291
International human resource
    management (IHRM), 346–347
Internationalization, 289
    organizational designs for, 289–293
International joint ventures (IJVs), 3–4.
    See also Alliances; Joint ventures;
        Partnerships
    as international market entry strategy,
        240–241, 242, 245
    managing performance of, 267–272
    in Poland, 287–288
    as strategic alliances, 258
    in U.S.-Canadian-Russian fast food,
        308–309
International Labor Organization (ILO)
    codes of conduct by, 63–65
    in convergence of labor relations, 394
International management, 4–5
    appropriateness of technology in, 46–47
    case studies in, 318–341
    critical cultural value differences and,
        120–122
    culture in, 103–134
    ethics in, 65–73
    future of, 17–20
    local environmental considerations in,
        47–48
    social responsibility in, 58–59
    women in, 381–384, 385, 386–387,
        387–389
International management teams, 440–445
    building, 441–445
    defined, 440
International managers
    bribery payments by, 68
    European Union and, 8
    problems facing, 4–5, 17–20
International markets, expansion into, 222
International Monetary Fund (IMF),
        Indonesian fiscal problems and, 41
International strategic alternatives, in
        strategic planning, 233–234
International strategy
    in globalization, 302
    staffing in, 351
Internet
    better intercultural communication
        via, 142
    effects on globalization of, 44
    European regulation of, 14
Interorganizational networks, 298

Interpersonal relationships
    building, 158
    in case study, 475–482
    in cultural values, 119, 120
    in doing business in Taiwan, 335
    in transportation industry, 219–220
Intranets, 382
Intrinsic motivational factors, 415–421
Investment
    in cross-cultural managers, 4
    foreign, 6
    managing political risk through, 34–35
    in Taiwan, 335–336
Involvement in relationships, as value
        dimension, 119, 120
Iran
    political risk in, 31
    U.S. hostage negotiations with, 177
Iraq
    Middle East leadership of, 428
    U.S. negotiations with, 167
Irritation and hostility stage, of culture
        shock, 358
Islam, five pillars of, 486
Islamic faith. *See* Moslems
Islamic law, 42
    in case study, 92–95
Islamic negotiation style, 171
Israel, work ethic in, 410, 411
Issues Monitoring System, assessing
        political risk with, 31–32
Italy
    cross-cultural differences between
        U.S. and, 104–105
    strategic implementation and
        planning in, 267, 268–269
    successful negotiating style in, 172,
        173
    turnkey operations from, 239

Jan Shu Woei, 340
Japan
    in Asian trading bloc, 8
    budget control practices in, 310–311
    collectivism in, 115–116
    computers in banking in, 107
    contract law in, 43
    corporate leadership in, 6–7
    cultural profile of, 124–125
    decision making in, 187, 191–193,
        194–197
    economic risk in, 40
    electronics industry in, 236
    employees in, 432–433
    ethics scandals in, 69
    expatriate in Mexico from, 468–474

    expatriate training for, 355, 356,
        370–373
    expatriate women managers in,
        387–388
    eye contact discomfort in, 145–146
    as fast learner, 261
    globalization in, 234
    haptic culture of, 147
    husband-wife relationship in, 109
    improving managerial performance in,
        416
    international business ethics in, 66
    international joint ventures in, 240
    international patent litigation
        involving, 44–45
    labor–management practices in,
        400–401
    leadership style in, 426, 432–433
    micromotor industry joint venture in,
        325–327, 328
    nationalism of, 227
    negotiations between China and, 204,
        206
    organizational information flow in,
        152–153
    organizational staffing in, 351–352
    paralanguage in, 147
    performance monitoring in, 311
    protectionism of, 43, 76
    quality control in, 432–433
    reward system in, 421
    selling soap in, 109
    social responsibility in, 74
    subsidiaries in U.S. from, 74
    successful negotiating style in,
        173–174, 178, 179
    trade unions in, 390
    U.S. cultural values and, 110,
        124–125, 153, 154–155, 157
    U.S. negotiation with, 168, 173–174,
        187, 209–212
    women employees in, 381–384,
        388–389
    work ethic in, 410, 411, 413
Japanese, successful negotiating style in,
        180
Japanese employees, American
        acculturation of, 454–456
Jeelof, Gerrit, 222
Jews, Moslems versus, 92–95
Jiang Zemin, 12
Job content rewards, 421
Johnson, Lawrence A., 526
Johnson, William R., 291
Joint ventures, 3–4. *See also* Alliances;
        International joint ventures (IJVs);

Partnerships
American-Hungarian, 21–25
as international market entry strategy, 242, 245
maquiladoras and, 470–471
patent protection in, 45–46
as strategic alliances, 258
U.S.-Mexican, 8–9
Joss, in work outcomes, 419
Jung, Andrea, 389

Kaizen, in Japanese quality control, 432–433
Kamina, Harold, 477, 478–479
Kayner, Robert, 104–105
Kearns, David, 446
Keiretsus, 8, 294
Kendall, Donald, 28
Kendall, Peter, 28
Kenya
ethics of pineapple-growing in, 57
solar energy industry case study in, 475–482
Key success factors (KSFs), in going international, 231
Khazbulatov, Khamzat, 308
Kickbacks. *See* Questionable payments
Kidnapping
managing risk of, 38
as political risk, 31
"Kilby patent," international litigation involving, 44–45
Kim, Jin K., letter from, 126–130
Kimber, James, 15
Kinesic behavior, 142, 145–146
Kinship, as cultural variable, 111–112
Knight, Philip, 100
Knowledge, in cross-cultural communication, 159
Knowledge On-Line (KOL) intranet, 382
Knowledge sharing, computers in, 382, 425
Kobrin, S. J., 32
Koenig, Christian, 443
Kopp, Rochelle, 351–352
Kopper, Hilmar, 364
Koran, 486–487
Korea. *See* South Korea
Korsvald, Paul, 483–487
Kozakai, Michiyo, 383
Kremer, Lawrence J., 526
Kruschev, Nikita, 28
Krysha money, 265
Kuo Shih-Teh, 336
Kusomoto, Sadahei, 74

Kuwait, 428
macropolitical risk events in, 30
U.S.-Iraqi negotiations over, 167
Kvint, Vladimir, 263

Labor laws
in European Union, 375–376
for maquiladoras, 470–471
in Mexico, 404, 470–471
in NAFTA countries, 395–397
in strategic planning, 376, 389–401
Labor–management practices, comparison of Japanese and Mexican, 400–401
Labor relations, 375–401. *See also* Child labor; Employees; Forced labor; Human resources (HR)
defined, 389
systems of, 389–401
trends in global, 394–395
Labor side pacts, in Mexico, 404
Labor standards
for multinational enterprises, 63
in telecommunications industry, 494–495, 498
Lack of concern for others, as value dimension, 116
Lac.zniak, Gene, 68
Lam, Izabel, 16
La mordida, 67
Lane, Barry, 40
Language
in Arab business, 132
as barrier to integrating immigrants, 457
as business problem, 44, 156–157, 287–288, 439, 476
in cross-cultural communication, 142, 144–145
in Philippines, 436
Language skills, in expatriate preparation, 359
Latin America. *See also* South America
American women managers in, 386
bribery in, 68
cola wars in, 249
concept of time in, 121, 147–148
cosmetics industry in, 552
expanding into markets in, 222
free trade in, 50
as high-contact culture, 146
home appliance industry in, 515, 523
incentives for expanding into, 223
integrating immigrants from, 456
kidnappings in, 38
monitoring transportation business in, 307

motivating employees in, 417
political risk in, 31
sexual harassment of women expatriates in, 389
successful negotiating style in, 173
telecommunications industry in, 499
telecommunications joint venture in, 321
U.S. cultural values and, 110
Law. *See also* Civil law; Islamic law; Labor laws; Regulatory environment
Chinese business, 41–42
codes of conduct and, 64
compliance with local, 42
contract, 42–43
ethics and degree of enforcement of, 66
German, 126
international business ethics and, 66, 72
need for more Russian, 265–266
Lawsuits, in cosmetics industry, 536
Leader–follower interaction, 430
Leaders
physical appearance of, 424
role and environment of, 423
Leadership, 422–433. *See also* Autocratic leadership; Corporate leadership; Participative leadership
American style of, 424–425
content of, 423, 424
context of, 423, 424, 429–431
contingency, 426–433
effective, 423
factors affecting overseas, 424
in home appliance industry, 509–531
in India, 431–432
integrative model of, 429–431
motivation in, 407–408
purpose of, 422–423
style of, 426–433
Learning, by partners in alliances, 261
Lee Shau Kee, 294
Lee Teng-Hui, 335
Less developed countries (LDCs)
cigarette consumption in, 55
economic development of, 10–11
ethically marketing baby formula in, 59
ethics of exporting hazardous waste to, 81–82
international business ethics in, 66
multinational corporations in, 75–77
privatization in, 11
social responsibility toward, 56
technology acquisition by, 45
technology transfer to, 46–47

Letters of credit, in negotiations with China, 207
Leysen, Andre, 397
Li, Margaret, 338
Licensing, as international market entry strategy, 238–239, 242, 245
Lien concept, in negotiating with China, 184
"Life-raft" values, 295–296
Life spaces, 141, 146
Lighting business, in Hungary, 21–25
Lin, Wally, 7
Lindahl, Goeran, 288
Lindquist, John, 331
Li Ping, 219
Litigation, in negotiations with China, 208
Liu Jing, 361
    career profile in China of, 362–363
Living in the U.S.A., 110
Loafing. See Social loafing
Local debt financing, managing political risk through, 35–38
Localization of operations. See also Glocal (global, local) firms
    in globalization, 300–301
    managing political risk through, 35
Location factors
    in cosmetics industry, 539–541
    in strategic planning choices, 246, 265, 506–507
Locus of control, in decision making, 189, 304
LOGIS system, for monitoring global operations, 307
Long-distance telephony, for Mexico, 103
Lopez de Arriortua, J. Ignacio, 349
Lorentz, Francis, 444
Los Angeles, California, cultural diversity in, 452–453, 454
Losing face
    in negotiating with China, 184, 205
    working women in Japan as, 381
Low-contact cultures, 146–147
Low-context cultures, 148–149, 150
    high-context cultures versus, 186–187
    negotiation with, 181–182
Loyalty
    among Arabs, 149
    in Chinese business, 132
    of Japanese employees, 432–433
Luck, in work outcomes, 419
Lu Enlei, 337, 341

Machismo, of Mexican workers, 417
Macromanagement, in India, 432
Macropolitical risk events, 30–31

Magnet manufacturing, in case study, 468–474
Mail systems, in Mexico, 80
Maintenance factors, in employee motivation, 415–421
Maisonrouge, Jacques, 422
Majlis, in Arab business, 132
Malaise, indicators of organizational, 303
Malaysia
    decision making in, 189
    ethnicity in, 30
    international competitor analysis of, 228–229
    Overseas Chinese network in, 295
    in telecommunications industry, 507
Management. See also Contingency management; Cross-cultural management; International management; Leadership; Multicultural management; Participative management; Strategic management
    in cosmetics industry, 543–544
    direct coordinating mechanisms for, 306
    of global home appliance business, 509–531
    of human resources, 346–347
    in India, 431–432
    indirect coordinating mechanisms for, 306–310
    in Indonesia (case study), 483–487
    of international joint ventures, 270–272
    of international teams, 439–459
    in Japan, 124–125
    of Japanese Mexican subsidiary, 472, 473–474
    of Mexican telecommunications business, 491–507
    Middle Eastern versus Western, 429
    monitoring systems for, 305
    participation of labor in, 397–399, 399–400, 400–401
    in Russian fast-food industry, 308–309
    of skilled nursing facility, 460–464
    of solar energy business, 475–482
    in telecommunications industry, 493–495
Management by objectives (MBO), 267
Management by wandering around (MBWA), 96
Management cadre, developing global, 377–389
Management contracts, as international market entry strategy, 240, 242
Management information systems (MIS), 311

Management styles. See also Leadership
    in China, 41–42
    Chinese versus American, 131–133
    convergence of, 106
    cross-cultural clashes between, 3–4, 105–109
    cross-cultural clashes in, 110
    for Mexican businesses, 417–418
Managerial skills, acquired by expatriates, 380
Managers. See also Leadership
    acquisition of cultural sensitivity by, 156
    application of cultural profiles by, 130–133
    bribery payments by, 68
    compensation for expatriate, 361–368
    cross-cultural interactions between, 3–4
    cultural differences in concept of time and, 120–121
    cultural sensitivity of successful, 103–105, 439
    decision making by, 188, 189
    development of cultural profiles by, 123–130
    finding correct Russian, 265
    in India, 431–432
    international organized labor and, 390–394
    labor relations and, 389–390
    motivation of employees by, 407–408, 411–414
    nationalities of top, 352
    negotiation by, 167–168
    oral communication by, 140
    roles of, 144
    Russian shortage of, 282
    selection of expatriate, 353–355
    as successful cross-cultural negotiators, 181–187
    training of expatriate, 355–361
    uncertainty avoidance by, 114
    in U.S.-Chinese joint ventures, 274–276
    in U.S.-Russian joint ventures, 264
    women as, 381–384, 385, 386–387, 387–389
    world trade growth and, 6
Managing negotiation, 180–187
Mandela, Nelson, 62
Man–machine relations, 400
Maquiladoras, 8–9, 77, 78
    history of, 469–472, 501–502
    management of (case study), 499–507
    motivation among, 417
    unionization and, 404

Marcil, Andre, 475–477, 482
Mark, Rebecca, 180
Mark, Reuben, 330, 331
Market access, strategic alliances for, 259
Market control
    going international and, 222
    managing political risk through, 35
Market entry, strategic alliances for rapid, 259
Market entry alternatives, in strategic planning, 238–245
Marketing
    in cosmetics industry, 544
    as global corporate objective, 227
    in textile industry, 338–339
Martinez, Maria, 465–466
Masculinity
    in Arab business, 132, 150, 167
    in employee motivation, 408
    in Japan, 124
    of Koreans, 126
    as value dimension, 113, 116, 117
Maslow's hierarchy of needs
    intrinsic–extrinsic dichotomy and, 415–421
    in motivation to work, 411–414
Master value, work in India as, 432
Masunaga, Hikotary, 44–45
Material culture, 147
Materialism
    cultural differences in, 121
    as value dimension, 116
Mathis, John, 39–40
Mathison, Stuart, 348
Matrix structure, of organizational forms, 300–304
Matsushita, Konosuke, 236
McDonald, Jacque, 538
McEnrue, Mary, 452–453
McGlinn, Ian, 537, 544
Meaning of work (MOW), 408–421
Meaning of Work International Research Team, 409
Mediators, in Arab negotiations, 171, 177
Medical compensation, for expatriates, 365
Medrano, Ofelia, 404
Meetings, cross-cultural, 3–4
Menezes, Ivan, 521
Mergers, negotiating U.S.-German, 188, 256–257
Mexico, 500
    automobile industry in, 80–81
    economic and logistic problems in, 80
    economic problems in, 9, 499–507
    economic risk in, 39

failed negotiations between U.S. and, 181–182
international joint ventures in, 240, 277, 279
Japanese magnet manufacturing in, 468–474
labor laws in, 396
labor–management practices in, 400–401
labor relations and NAFTA in, 395–397, 403–405
micromotor industry joint venture in, 326–327
motivating employees in, 407, 417–419
NAFTA as benefiting, 77–81
in North American regional trade bloc, 8–9
object language in, 147
oil industry in, 50
sexual harassment of women expatriates in, 389
successful negotiating style in, 177
technology transfer to, 78, 79
telecommunications industry in, 499–507
telephones in, 80, 103
terrorism risk in, 38
textile industry in, 78
tile manufacturing in, 79
unionization in, 391
water-purification business in, 80
Micromanagement, in India, 431–432
Micromotors, in case study, 322–329
Micropolitical risk events, 31
Middle East. See also Saudi Arabia
    business between United States and, 151–152
    decision making in, 190
    high-context cultures in, 148–149, 149–152
    leadership styles in, 427–428
    management practices in, 429
    resolution of negotiation conflicts with, 186
    successful negotiating style in, 171, 177
    terrorism risk in, 38
Mien-tzu concept
    in Chinese employee motivation, 414
    in negotiating with China, 184
Minority groups, 446–447
    in case study, 99–100
    expatriates representing, 384–389
    in labor force, 14
    as underutilized human resource, 376, 388–389

Miscommunication, 141–156
Misleading information, in negotiation, 178–179
Mission, in strategic planning, 226, 227, 542–543
Modem manufacturing, 439
Modesty, Korean versus American, 129
Monitoring. See also Continuous monitoring of global operations, 305–310, 314–317
Monitoring systems, 305, 307. See also Issues Monitoring System
    appropriateness of, 310–312
    U.S. versus European, 305–310
Monochronic time systems, 147–148
Moral idealism, in decision making, 189–190
Morality
    cultural differences in, 107
    international business ethics and, 59–60, 66
    in negotiating with China, 184
Moral universalism, 59–60
Moreno, Elizabeth, 435–437
Morishita, Yoichi, 236
Morocco, cola wars in, 252
Moslems. See also Islamic law
    concept of time among, 121, 147–148
    cultural values of, 107–108, 130–131
    leadership styles among, 427–428
    versus Jews, 92–95
    work ethic of, 409–410, 412, 419, 483–487
Most favored nation (MFN) status, for China, 10
Motivation, 407–421
    categories of, 411–414
    in China, 414–415
    in coffee business, 407
    cross-cultural research on, 408, 419–421
    culture in, 110
    doing meaningful work and, 408–411
    in foreign cultures, 411–415
    intrinsic–extrinsic model of, 415–421
    leadership and, 407–408
    in Mexico, 407, 417–419, 417–419
    reward systems for, 421–422
    studies of, 420
Movie industry, international piracy in, 46
Muhammed, 486–487
Multicultural leaders, 423
Multicultural management, 4–5, 156–161, 439–459
    role of leaders in, 423
Multicurrency translation software, 39

Multidomestic strategy
    in globalization, 302
    staffing in, 351
Multilocal strategy
    for globalization, 235, 236
Multinational corporations (MNCs), 16–17
    changing strategies and operations for,
        29
    codes of ethics for, 69–72
    coordinating global operations of,
        305–310
    cultural sensitivity of successful,
        103–105
    ease of exit for, 375
    economic risk management by, 38–41
    environmental management by, 81–82
    evolution of organizational designs of,
        289–293
    expatriate compensation by, 361–368
    expatriate selection by, 353–355
    expatriate training by, 355–361
    feedback channels between, 158–159
    global integration of, 235–238
    guidelines for socially responsible
        behavior by, 77
    human resource management by,
        346–347
    information technology and, 13
    interdependence management by,
        73–82
    international business ethics for, 65–73
    in international joint ventures, 240–241
    interorganizational networking
        among, 298–300
    operating in Colombia, 50–53
    participation of labor in management
        of, 397–399, 399–400, 400–401
    performance monitoring in, 311
    political risk assessment by, 31–34
    political risk management by, 34–38
    regulatory environments for, 41–44
    responsibility toward human rights,
        60–63
    social responsibility of, 56–65, 82–83
    in South Africa, 61–63
    technological environment for, 44–47
    terrorism risk management by, 38
    as transnational corporations, 20
Multinational enterprises (MNEs), 16
    codes of conduct for, 63–65
Multinational global environmental
    analysis, 229
Muruwwa, 130

Nakanishi, Yuko, 383
National Administrative Office (NAO),
    397

National Chengchi University (NCU), 341
National global environmental analysis,
    229
Nationalism
    of Colombian guerrillas, 51–52
    going international and, 227–228
    of host country toward foreign
        subsidiary, 76
Nationalization, 30
Nation-states, 5
Natural cosmetics, 536–538
Nature. See also Environmental protection
    U.S. attitude toward, 121
Nava, Oscar, 103
Need clusters, 413
Need hierarchy, in motivation to work,
    411–414, 415–421
Negative normative appeal, in negotiation,
    179
Negotiating styles, cultural differences in,
    169–180
Negotiation, 167–187, 193
    conflict resolution in, 186–187
    cross-cultural, 167–168, 169
    defined, 168
    in doing business in Taiwan, 335
    management of, 180–187
    problems in, 181–182
    process of, 168–180
    software of, 181
    variables in, 175–176
Nemawashi, 174
    in decision making, 191, 192, 196
Nepotism
    in Eastern cultures, 111–112
    in Indian management, 431
Netherlands
    airline industry in, 105
    work ethic in, 410, 411
Netscape Navigator, 382
Netscape SuitSpot, 425
Network firms, 85
    transnational corporations as, 298–300
Networking
    American, 152–153
    Chinese, 294–296
    interorganizational, 298
    Italian, 425
    Japanese, 152–153
Network structures, 298–300
Neutrality, as value dimension, 119, 120
New developed economies (NDEs),
    international management in, 19
Newman, Barry, 485–486
Ngan, 409
Nigeria, dumping of hazardous waste in,
    81–82

Ningensei communication style, 153, 155
Nixon, Richard Milhous, 28
Noise, in communication, 141, 143
Nolan, Paul, 448
Noncomparability of performance data
    across countries, 311
Nonequity strategic alliances, 258
Nonprofit organizations, globalization of,
    16
Nontask sounding, 174
Nonverbal behavior, in negotiation, 179
Nonverbal communication
    among Arabs, 150–151
    as business problem, 157
    cross-cultural, 142, 145–147, 148
Norming stage of group development,
    449, 450
Norris, William C., 65, 67
North America
    cosmetics industry in, 542
    as free trade bloc, 7
    home appliance industry in, 515–518
    low-context cultures in, 149
    as regional trading bloc, 8–9
    successful negotiating style in, 173,
        174, 175
North American Free Trade Agreement
    (NAFTA), 8–9, 327, 419
    interdependence under, 77–81
    labor relations and, 395–397, 403–405
Norway, managing paper factory in
    Indonesia from, 483–487
Notes software, for insurance industry,
    244
Nuclear family, 111

Objective approach
    to decision making, 189
    in strategic planning, 226, 227
Object language, 142, 147
Obligation
    in Chinese culture, 131
    in negotiating with China, 183–184,
        208
    as value dimension, 119, 120
Oculesics, 145–146
Office space, as power signal, 146
Ohmae, Kenichi, 5
Oil companies
    in Colombia, 50–53
    political risk assessment by, 32
Olechnowicz, Pawel, 287
Olfactory contact, among Arabs, 150–151
On-the-job training (OJT), in expatriate
    preparation, 359
Openness, in cross-cultural
    communication, 159–160

Opportunities
in joint ventures with Russia, 263–266
as motivation to work, 413
organizing for, 300–301
readiness to take advantage of, 288
in SWOT analysis, 232–233
Oral communication, 140
cross-cultural, 142, 144–145
Organizational design, 287–312
case studies in, 318–341
contingency-based, 288–289
evolution and change in, 289–293, 314–317
geography in, 289
for globalization, 293–298, 301–304
in international joint ventures, 269–270
of transnational corporations, 298–300, 300–301
Organizational forms, 300–304
Organization control, in multinational organizational structures, 305
Organization for Economic Cooperation and Development (OECD)
codes of conduct by, 63–65
Organizations. *See also* Multinational corporations (MNCs); Multinational enterprises (MNEs); Nonprofit organizations
choosing forms of, 300–304
coordination of, 305–310
globalization of, 293–298, 305–310
information flow in, 152
monitoring of, 305–310, 310–312, 314–317
structural changes in, 289–293
structural forms of, 289–293, 298–300
structure of, 288–289, 318–341
structure of Polish, 287–288
in telecommunications industry, 493–495
Organized crime, in Russia, 263–266
Organized labor
geography of (map), 392–393
maquiladoras and, 505–506
overseas, 389–401
Original equipment manufacturers (OEM) market, China as, 327–328
Output control, in multinational organizational structures, 305
Overseas assignments, positive and negative aspects of, 377–378
Overseas Chinese
global network of, 294–296
in Indonesia, 484–485

Overseas Private Investment Corporation (OPIC), political risk insurance through, 35

Pakistan
breakaway of Bangladesh from, 91
child labor in, 58–59, 86
ethnicity in, 30
low individualism in, 115
women managers in, 386
Panama, low individualism in, 115
Pancasila ideology, 485
Papone, Aldo, 543
Paralanguage, 142, 147
Parent companies, in international joint ventures, 271–272
Parent-country nationals (PCNs). *See also* Expatriates
compensation for, 364–367
staffing international organizations with, 348, 349, 350
Paris Union. *See* International Convention for the Protection of Industrial Property (Paris Union)
Parochialism, 109
Participation, of leaders, 428
Participative leadership, 425
autocratic leadership versus, 426–433
in decision making, 190
Participative management, managing political risk through, 35
Particularism, as value dimension, 119, 120
Partner selection, 278–281
in international joint ventures, 269
Partnerships, 86. *See also* Alliances; International joint ventures (IJVs); Joint ventures
autonomy in, 297–298
in case study, 90–95
in cosmetics industry, 539
courtships in, 261–262, 278–281
fate of unequal, 261
in Indian business, 432
in Indonesian business, 41
in U.S.-Russian joint ventures, 264–265
Patent protection
China and lack of, 227–228
in joint ventures, 45–46
licensing and, 239
for technological innovations, 44–45
Paternalism
in Chinese culture, 131
in Chinese employee motivation, 414
of Mexican managers, 417–418
as value dimension, 115–116
in workplace, 410

Patience, in negotiating with China, 185
Pele, 100
People's Republic of China (PRC). *See* China
Perestroika, 9
Performance
Chinese humiliation for poor, 422
systems for monitoring, 310–312
Performing stage of group development, 449, 450–451
Perquisites, for expatriates, 365, 366
Personal space
among Arabs, 150–151
cultural patterns in, 146
Personnel problems, 352
Personnel selection, for overseas assignments, 353–355
Persuasion, in negotiation, 168, 169, 176, 178–180
Peru
environmental risks in, 229
terrorism in, 229
Petersen, Donald, 66
Petzinger, Robert, 386
Pharmaceutical industry
case study in, 435–437
globalization in, 294
Philippines
case studies in, 164–165, 435–437
doing business in, 436–437
ethnicity in, 30
Overseas Chinese network in, 295
Philosophy
in cosmetics industry, 541–542
international business ethics and, 66
of international organization staffing, 348–352
labor–management, 400–401
old and new Chinese management, 133
for reorganizing, 287
in social responsibility, 57–58
in U.S.-Chinese joint ventures, 274–276
Piracy, of intellectual property, 46
Planning cycles, in international management, 223
Plastics industry, globalization in, 295
Play, work as, 409
Pluralism, in acculturation, 453, 454–456
Poland
incentives for expanding into, 223
restructuring organizations in, 287–288
Politeness
in Japanese negotiations, 174, 210–211
Korean versus American, 128–130
language problems from, 145
in negotiating with China, 183–184
Political change, international joint ventures and, 272–273

Political environment
    in international management, 47–48
    maquiladoras in, 469–472
    for Mexican telecommunications
        industry, 499–501
    in risk assessment, 33, 34
Political risk, 30
    assessing, 31–34
    contracts and, 42–43
    in going international, 226
    as management problem, 30–31
    managing, 34–38
    in South Africa, 62
    strategic alliances to reduce, 259
    in U.S.-Russian joint ventures,
        263–266, 281–284
Political risk insurance, managing political
    risk through, 35
Politics, local
    codes of conduct for, 64
    as cultural variable, 112
    as management problem, 29–41
Pollution
    in textile industry, 340–341
    through guerrilla actions, 52
Polycentric staffing approach, 348–349,
    350, 351
Polychlorinated biphenyl (PCB), ethics of
    dumping, 81
Polychronic time systems, 147–148
Portugal, American miscommunication in,
    144
Position control, managing political risk
    through, 35
Positive normative appeal, in negotiation,
    179
Posture
    in body language, 146
    in cross-cultural communication, 159
Pot-de-vin, 67
Poverty, in central Europe, 25
Power
    in case study, 164–165
    in Chinese culture, 131
    in relationships between host country
        and foreign subsidiary, 76–77
Power distance
    in employee motivation, 408
    in Indian management, 431
    of Koreans, 126
    within Latin American countries, 417
    from leaders to subordinates, 427
    as value dimension, 113–114, 117,
        119, 120
Pragmatism
    in Japan, 124
    of Koreans, 126

Premature expansion, in U.S.-Russian
    joint ventures, 283
Preparation
    of expatriates, 355–361, 377–378
    for negotiation, 168, 169, 169–176
Price, in negotiating with China, 205–206,
    206–207
Pride, in Mexican work ethic, 418
PRISM (primary risk investment screening
    matrix), risk assessment with, 32
Prison imports, laws against, 60
Privacy
    in Arab culture, 131
    of electronic data, 14
    in German culture, 126
    in U.S. versus Korean culture,
        127–128
Private space, as power signal, 146
Privatization, 11–12
    in Commonwealth of Independent
        States, 9–10
    labor relations and, 391
Proaction
    of German labor unions, 398
    in going international, 220–221,
        222–223
    in social responsibility, 57–58
Production
    in cosmetics industry, 544–546
    as global corporate objective, 227
    in textile industry, 337–338
    in U.S.-Russian joint ventures, 282
Productivity
    from group diversity, 451
    in Japan, 124
Professional rewards, 421
Profitability
    evaluation variables for, 312
    as global corporate objective, 227
Projective cognitive similarity, in
    negotiation, 168
Promises, in negotiation, 179
Promotions
    American valuing of, 122
    in case study, 484–485
    individualism and collectivism and,
        115–116
Proprietary technology
    protection of, 45–46
    strategic alliances to control, 260–261
Protectionism, 43
    in European Union, 243
    of host country toward foreign
        subsidiary, 76
    strategic alliances to avoid, 258
Protection money, in U.S.-Russian joint
    ventures, 263, 265, 282

Protestant work ethic, 112
    in German culture, 126
Protocol, in negotiation, 176
Proxemics, 142, 146–147
Proxy, internationalization by, 297–298
Publicity, in cosmetics industry, 536
Puerto Rico, case studies in, 162–164, 436
Punay, Eleanor, 439
Punishments, in negotiation, 179
Puritan ethic, 108

Qualitative approach, to economic risk
    analysis, 39–40
Quality circles, in textile industry
    organization, 339
Quality control
    in home appliance industry, 525–527
    in Japan, 432–433
    in textile industry organization, 339
    in U.S.-Russian joint ventures, 282
Quantitative approach, to economic risk
    analysis, 39–40
Questionable payments, 67. See also
        Bribery
    in case study, 485–486
    case study involving, 87–90
    as ethical issue, 67–69
Questions, in negotiation, 179
Quinlan, Mike, 245

Ramadan, 484, 486–487
Ratiu, Indrei, 444–445
Raven, Janis, 544
Reacculturation, of expatriates, 378–380
Reaction
    in going international, 220, 221
    in social responsibility, 57–58
Recommendations, in negotiation, 179
Recreation
    as cultural variable, 113
    for Mexican employees, 418–419
Rees, David, 375
Regiocentric staffing approach, 349, 351
Regional global environmental analysis,
    229
Regionalization, as approach to world
    markets, 235, 236
Regional trading blocs, 7–11
Regular workforce, in Japan, 421
Regulatory environment
    codes of conduct for, 64
    going international and, 221
    in international management, 47–48
    in risk assessment, 41–44
    in telecommunications industry,
        493–495
Reis Teixeira, Josina, 222

Relationship building
    as motivation to work, 412–413
    in negotiating with China, 184
    for negotiation, 168, 169, 176–177
Relaxed posture, body language of, 146
Religion
    in Arab business, 132
    business problems caused by, 92–95,
        483–487
    and cultural differences in acceptance
        of change, 121
    as cultural variable, 112–113
    in Germany, 126
    in Indian management, 431
    international business ethics and, 66
    legal problems caused by, 42
    in Mexican work ethic, 418
    in Moslem work ethic, 409–410
    political problems caused by, 29–30
    in South Korea, 126
Repatriation, of expatriates, 377–378,
    380–381
Reporting, in global operations, 305–310
Reporting systems
    appropriateness of, 310–311
    information systems as, 311
Republic of China (ROC). See Taiwan
Research and development (R&D)
    benefits of, 45
    as global corporate objective, 227
    strategic alliances to promote, 258–259
Resilience, in cross-cultural
    communication, 159–160
Resocialization, of expatriates, 377–378,
    378–380
Resort industry, management in, 465–466
Resource access, going international for,
    222–223
Respect
    in cosmetics industry, 539
    in cross-cultural communication, 159
    among Mexican workers, 417
    in negotiating with China, 185
    in negotiation, 177
Responsiveness, in social responsibility,
    57–58
Restraint, in negotiating with China,
    183–184
Restrictions, going international and, 221
Retailing
    in China, 422
    international joint ventures in, 277
Retirement savings, for expatriates, 365
Return on investment (ROI), comparative,
    312
Return shock. See Reverse culture shock
Reverse culture shock, 377, 381

Rewards
    in Chinese employee motivation, 415
    in Mexican employee motivation,
        418, 419
    in negotiation, 179
Reward systems, 421–422
Reynal, Jean-Louis, 153
Ringi-sho, 191, 196
Ringi system, 152
    in decision making, 191–193, 196–197
Rioting, diversity and, 452–453
Risk. See also Economic risk; Financial
        risk; Political risk
    in joint ventures with Russia, 263–266
    strategic alliances for sharing, 258–259
Risk events, 30–41
    in Colombian business, 50–53
    in going international, 226–228
    in international management, 47–48
    ratings of countries by, 34, 36–37
    in turnkey operations, 239–240
    types of, 31
    uncertainty avoidance and, 114
Risk taking, in negotiation, 176
Risk tolerance, in decision making, 189
Rivard, Lise, 475, 476–477, 477–478,
    479–480, 481–482
Roddick, Anita, 534–554
    biography of, 534–536
Roddick, T. Gordon, 534, 536, 538, 544
Rodney King trial, diversity and, 452–453
Roh Tae Woo, 67
Roles, in cross-cultural communication,
    142, 144
Roman Catholic Church
    cultural values of, 112
    in German culture, 126
Rude, André, 110
Rule enforcement, in Chinese employee
    motivation, 415
Rural telephony, in case study, 318–319,
    320
Rushdie, Salman, 92, 93–94
Russia. See also Commonwealth of
        Independent States (CIS); Soviet
        Union
    cola wars in, 249
    compensation in, 367–368
    doing business in, 28–29
    economic development of, 9–10
    economic risk in, 39
    fast-food industry in, 106
    ice cream business joint venture in,
        281–284
    monitoring fast-food industry in,
        308–309
    privatization in, 11

    successful negotiating style in,
        174–175, 178
    SWOT analysis of, 233
    U.S. expatriate manager in, 345–346
Russian Mafia, 263, 282

Safety in workplace, 61, 86
    codes of conduct on, 63
    ethics of, 60
    in textile industry, 339–340
Sakauchi, Satoru, 107
Salinas de Gortari, Carlos, 501
Sato, Fumio, 257
Satyagraha negotiating style, 170–171
Saudi Arabia. See also Arabic language;
        Middle East
    decision making in, 190
    employing local managers in, 361
    as high-contact culture, 146
    high-context culture in, 148–149,
        149–152
    leadership style in, 429
    licensing in, 245
    micropolitical risks in, 31, 34
    offensive behaviors in (table), 131
    successful negotiating style in, 171,
        172, 174–175
    U.S. cultural values and, 110, 130–131
    women managers in, 386, 387
    work ethic in, 410, 412
Saving face
    among Arabs, 130
    in negotiating with China, 184,
        208–209
Scheduling, of international market entry,
    246
Schrempp, Jürgen E., 188, 256–257, 273,
    364
Scotland
    labor laws in, 375
    managing international teams in, 444
Security measures, managing risk of
    terrorism through, 38
SEDUE environmental protection agency,
    504
Selection criteria, in negotiation, 176
Selective transmission, in cross-cultural
    communication, 157–158
Self-advertising, Korean versus American,
    129
Self-confidence
    acquired by expatriates, 380
    Korean versus American, 129
Self-criticism, of Chinese employees, 422
Self-discipline, Korean versus American,
    129
Self-disclosure, in negotiation, 179

Self-esteem
    in Arab society, 132
    Korean versus American, 129
Self-reference criteria, 108–109
    U.S. and Japanese, 154
Self-reliance
    American valuing of, 123
    Korean versus American, 128–129
Semiconductor patents, international
        litigation involving, 44–45
Seniority
    in Japan, 124
    rewards based on, 421
Sensitivity training, for expatriate
        preparation, 359
Separation, in acculturation, 453
Sexual harassment
    of expatriates, 389
    lawsuit over, 446
Shame, in negotiating with China, 185
Shame society, Arabs as, 130–131, 132,
        150
Shaw, George Bernard, 144
Sheleznov, Mikhail, 308
Shinyo value, 124
    in decision making, 191
Silence
    in Asian communication, 139
    in paralanguage, 147
Silent Language, The (Hall), 146
Similac baby formula, ethically marketing
        in less developed countries, 59
Singapore
    in Asian trading bloc, 8
    competition with European Union in,
        245
    employee motivation in, 414
    Overseas Chinese network in, 295
    telecommunications industry in,
        497–498
    women managers in, 383–384
Skilled nursing facility, in case study,
        460–464
Small and medium-size enterprises (SMEs)
    globalization of, 15–16
    international market entry strategies
        for, 238–245
Smart, Bruce, 66
SMILE characteristics, for expatriate
        selection, 354
Smith, Anne, 278–281
Smoleevskij, Georgij, 308
Snow, Lynn, 273
Soap industry
    globalizational restructuring in, 330–333
    globalization in, 296, 297
    in Hungary, 330–333

    in Japan, 109
    in South Africa, 95–98
Soccer, in case study, 100
Social audits, in cosmetics industry, 534,
        535, 549
Social Chapter, 375–376
Social Charter, 375
Socialism, privatization following, 11
Socialization, 105
    of expatriates, 378–380
Socializing
    among Arabs, 131
    cross-cultural, 3–4, 110
    Korean versus American, 128–129
Social loafing, in individualistic and
        collectivist societies, 116
Social organization, in cross-cultural
        communication, 142, 143
Social responsibility (SR)
    case study in South African, 95–98
    categories of, 57
    corporate stakeholders and, 58–59
    in cosmetics industry, 549
    ethical behavior and interdependence
        and, 56, 58–59, 82–83
    in international context, 58–59
    Japanese versus American, 74
    of multinational corporations,
        56–65
    in South Africa, 61–63
    three-dimensional model of, 57
Social status
    in Japan, 124–125
    as value dimension, 119, 120
Social status rewards, 421
Society
    culture of, 105
    values in, 113
Sociotypes, 142–143
Software
    for insurance industry, 244
    U.S.-Russian joint ventures in, 263
Software of negotiation, 181
Solar energy industry, in case study,
        475–482
Soltwedel, Rudiger, 398
South Africa
    apartheid and multinational
        corporations in, 61–63
    case study in, 95–98
    cola wars in, 252
    labor relations in, 394
    signatory code for, 95
South America. See also Latin America
    freeing of trade between North
        America and, 81
    international joint ventures in, 277

    and North American regional trade
        bloc, 8
    privatization in, 11–12
Southeast Asia, economic problems in, 8
South Korea
    in Asian trading bloc, 8
    attitude toward nature in, 121
    bribery scandals in, 67
    corporate leadership in, 6–7
    high-context culture in, 148–149
    human rights issues in, 85
    international competitor analysis of,
        228–229
    investment in South Africa by, 62
    U.S. cultural values and, 127–130
Soviet Union. See also Commonwealth of
        Independent States (CIS); Russia
    collapse of, 28, 113, 281–284
    doing business in, 28, 29
    embargoes on technological transfers
        to, 45
    turnkey operations in, 239
Space
    proxemics of, 146
    time and, 148
Spain
    automobile industry in, 76
    doing business in, 362
    haptic culture of, 147
    management careers in, 362
    negotiations between Germany and,
        197–201
Sparks, Jack, 518
Specificity, as value dimension, 119, 120
Speed
    in creating global alliances, 259–260
    in negotiation, 188
Spiritual beliefs. See Religion
Spoken language. See also Oral
        communication
    in cross-cultural communication, 142,
        144–145
Sports industry, case study in, 314–317
Spouses, of expatriates, 370–373, 378
Stability, as value dimension, 114
Staffing, 345–368
    case study of, 370–373
    changes in, 304
    global personnel selection in, 353–355
    personnel problems in, 352
    philosophies of, 348–352
Staged contribution strategies, managing
        political risk through, 35
Stages model
    for culture shock, 358
    for organizational change, 289–291
    training design issues in, 361

Stakeholders
in case study, 95–98
in cross-cultural negotiation, 169
social responsibility versus rights of, 58–59
Stateless corporations, 20
State-owned companies, selling off, 11–12
State planning, in negotiating with China, 183
Sterba, Jim, 483
Stereotypes, 111, 142–143, 448
of leaders, 427–428, 429
Stevens, Nick, 491, 498–499, 506–507
Stewardship, as environmental management, 81
Storming stage of group development, 449–450
Strategic alliances, 257–266
defined, 257
dual role of, 262
equity, 258
global, 258
in globalization, 234, 237
guidelines for, 261–266
nonequity, 258
problems in implementing, 259–261, 266–276
reasons for creating cross-border, 258–259, 260
types of, 257–258
Strategic business units (SBUs), 291
Strategic implementation, 266–276
cultural influences on, 273–276
defined, 267
government influences on, 272–273
managing joint ventures and, 267–272
Strategic management, 20, 219–247
in case study, 248–252
in cosmetics industry, 544
managing political risk through, 38
process of, 223–226
in telecommunications industry, 496–507
Strategic planning, 220, 223–226
choices in, 245–246
labor laws in, 376
relationship of organizational structure to, 301–304
steps in, 226–246
Strategy, defined, 220
Strengths, in SWOT analysis, 232–233
Structural evolution model, 289–291
Structure
of home appliance industry, 510
of organizations, 288–312, 318–341, 493–495

Subcultures, 111
language problems among, 144–145
Subculture shock, 358
Subjective approach, to decision making, 189
Subordinateship, leadership and, 426, 427
Subsidiaries
foreign, 74
fully owned, 241
interdependence of host countries and, 74–81
monitoring of, 305–310, 331–333
Suggestion programs, in employee motivation, 413
Suharto family, 40–41
international joint ventures and, 272–273
Sullivan, Reverend Leon, 62, 95
Sullivan Principles, 62, 63
statement of, 95
Supervisors, in U.S.-Chinese joint ventures, 274–276
Suppliers, in U.S.-Russian joint ventures, 282–283
Survival, in international management, 19–20
Sweatshops
in case study, 99–100
as human rights issue, 60
Sweden
in case study, 136–137
labor unions in, 390
negotiations between China and, 204
successful negotiating style in, 172, 172–173
Sweeney, John, 395–396
Switzerland
international joint ventures in, 279–280
low-context culture in, 149
as organizational headquarters, 287–288
SWOT (strengths, weaknesses, opportunities, threats) analysis, 232–233
Symms, Steven, 386
Synergy, 244
in international teamwork, 442–444
strategic alliances for, 259
Systems approach, to categorizing cultures, 111–113

Tactics
in negotiating with China, 185
in negotiation, 178–179
Taiwan
in Asian trading bloc, 8
doing business in, 335
employee motivation in, 414
history of, 333–334

micromotor joint venture in, 324–325
Overseas Chinese network in, 295
reward system in, 421
textile industry joint venture in, 333–341
Taiwan Textile Federation (TTF), 335, 339
Takeovers, case study of, 248–252
Takeuchi, Hirotaka, 157
Tanaka, Takaaki, 3
Tariffs
under NAFTA, 78
retaliatory, 46, 76
Task-related information
acquired by expatriates, 380
in negotiation, 168, 169, 177–178
Tatum, Paul, 265
Taxation, 43. See also Income taxes
by Colombian guerrillas, 52
of maquiladoras, 470
Tax treaties, 43
Team-based work systems, 399–400
Teamsters Union, 397
Team technological system relations, 400
Teamwork
gauging successful, 444–445
international, 439–459
between management and employees, 399–400
among Mexican employees, 418
multicultural, 449–451
Technical stage, in negotiating with China, 184–185, 205
Technoglobalism, 44
Technological environment
business effects of, 44–47
cultural dimensions of, 106
Technology
for better intercultural communication, 142
for better negotiation, 187–188
consulting with intranet knowledge-based systems, 382
in home appliance industry, 527–528
in human resource management, 347
for Italian spa business, 268–269
knowledge acquired by expatriates, 380–381
leadership and, 423
Technology transfer
codes of conduct for, 64
to less developed countries, 46–47
to Mexico, 78, 79
multinational corporations and selective, 75
Telecommunications industry
case studies in, 318–322, 491–507
direct coordinating mechanisms in, 306

international joint ventures in, 279–281, 318–322
knowledge sharing in, 425
strategic alliances in, 260
U.S.-Russian joint ventures in, 263
Telephones
in case study, 460–464
in Mexico, 80, 103
Temporary workforce, in Japan, 421
Termination
of employees, 375–376
of Mexican workers, 404–405
Termination costs, in Germany, 398
Terrorism, 31
in Bangladesh, 91–92
business problems caused by, 30
in Colombia, 50–53
managing risk of, 38
Textile industry
case study in, 333–341
globalizational restructuring in, 333–341
history of, 334–335
micromotor industry from, 323–324
technology in Italian, 268–269
Textile Integrated Manufacturing (TIM) package, 268–269
Thai Chung, 439
Thailand
economic risk in, 40
miscommunication in, 143–144
motivation of employees in, 408
Overseas Chinese network in, 295
Third-country nationals (TCNs)
compensation for, 364
staffing international organizations with, 349
training of, 360–361
Thought patterns, in cross-cultural communication, 142, 143–144
Threats
in negotiation, 179
in SWOT analysis, 232–233
Tichy, Noel, 156
Tile manufacturing, 79
Time
American concept of, 123, 147
Arab concept of, 130–131, 132, 147–148, 171
cultural differences in meaning of, 107, 108, 120–121, 142, 147–148
in doing business in Taiwan, 335
German concept of, 126, 147
in Japanese versus Mexican labor relations, 401
Latin American concept of, 147–148
Moslem concept of, 483–484, 485

in negotiation, 176
Russian concept of, 174
space and, 148
Swedish concept of, 172
Timing, of international market entry, 246
Tipping, in China, 204
Title VII protection, international application of, 384
Tobacco industry, ethics of promoting, 55
Tokens of appreciation, 67
Toy industry, micromotor industry from, 323–324
Trade barriers
going international and, 221
unionization and, 391
Trademark protection
China and lack of, 227–228
licensing and, 239
Trade secrets, theft of, 45–46
Trade war
piracy of intellectual property as, 46
U.S.-Chinese, 328–329
Trading charter, in cosmetics industry, 539
Tradition, in career advancement, 362
Training. See Cross-cultural training; Employee training
in cosmetics industry, 538
for maquiladoras, 472–473
Training techniques, for expatriate preparation, 358–360
Transborder joint ventures, 3–4
Transition process, for expatriates, 378–380
Translation, in cross-cultural communication, 156–157
Transnational capability, in globalization, 298–300
Transnational corporations (TNCs). See also Multinational corporations (MNCs)
in international management, 20
network structures of, 298–300
organizational forms for, 300–304
social responsibility of, 56–65
Transnational strategy
in globalization, 302
staffing in, 351
Transpatriates, expatriates as, 349
Transportation, for expatriates, 480–481
Transportation industry
American versus Chinese, 219–220
in European Union, 242–243
monitoring in, 307
TRIAD market, 7–9
Tribalism, in Arab culture, 130, 132
Trompenaars, Fons, 118
leadership studies of, 427–428

Trompenaars's value dimensions, 118–120
chart of, 119
Trust, in building teamwork, 444
Trustworthiness
in Chinese business, 132
in negotiation, 176, 177
Truth
Arab versions of, 130–131
Korean versus American versions of, 128
Tsai, Richard, 339
Turkey, decision making in, 190
Turnkey operations, as international market entry strategy, 239–240, 242
Turnover rate
coping with high, 465–466
of Mexican workers, 417

Ulema, 113
Uncertainty avoidance
in employee motivation, 408
in Japan, 124
of Koreans, 126
within Latin American countries, 417
as value dimension, 113, 114, 117
Unemployment, in China, 415
Unionization, 390. See also Labor relations
codes of conduct on, 63
in Europe, 391
of foreign firms in China, 391–394
in Germany, 397–399
in Mexico, 403–405
worldwide extent of (map), 392–393
Union works councils, in Germany, 398
United Electrical, Radio, and Machine Workers Union, 397
United Kingdom. See Great Britain; Scotland
United Nations, 534–535
United Nations Commission on Transnational Corporations (UN/CTC) codes of conduct by, 63–65
United Nations Convention on Contracts for the International Sale of Goods (CISG), 42
United Nations Universal Declaration of Human Rights, codes of conduct from, 64–65
United States. See also American corporations
acculturation in, 453–456
American versus Japanese communication style, 153, 154–155, 157
anti-apartheid movement in, 62
Asian view of, 139

budget control practices in, 310–311

business between Arabs and, 151–152

Chinese piracy of movies made in, 46

codes of ethics in, 69–72

collective bargaining in, 391

concept of time in, 120–121, 147

corporate leadership of, 6–7

cosmetics industry in, 551

cultural profile of Americans, 123

cultural values of, 107–109, 110

cultural values of (table), 108

decision making in, 189, 192–193, 194–197

economic growth of, 5–6

embargoes on technological transfers from, 45

ethics of, versus Europe, 69–72

European Union and, 6

expanding into Vietnamese markets, 225

expatriate in Japan from, 370–373

expatriate in Russia from, 345–346

expected leadership behavior in, 426–431

export of hazardous materials by, 82

eye contact behavior in, 145–146

failed negotiations between Mexico and, 181–182

family as cultural variable in, 111–112

fast-food joint venture with Russia, 308–309

foreign subsidiaries in, 74

franchises in, 245

French cultural values and, 153

hazardous waste from Mexico in, 503–504

home appliance industry in, 509–512

hostage negotiations with Iran, 177

ice cream business joint venture with Russia, 281–284

individualism in, 114–116, 122

informational privacy and, 14

integrating immigrants to, 456–459

international business ethics in, 66

international joint ventures by, 272–273, 273–276, 279–281

international patent litigation involving, 44–45

Japanese leadership style versus that of, 432–433

Japanese magnet manufacturing in, 469

joint venture of Mexico and, 8–9

joint venture of Russia with, 263–266

joint ventures of Hungary and, 21–25, 330–333

Korean impressions of, 127–130

labor laws in, 396

leadership style in, 424–425

as low-contact culture, 146–147

low-context culture in, 149

maquiladoras and, 505–506

materialism in, 121

Mexican labor relations and NAFTA and, 395–397, 403–405

micromotor industry joint venture in, 325–326

miscommunication with Germany, 144

miscommunication with Greeks, 141, 142, 143, 144, 145, 148

miscommunication with Portugal, 144

as moral driving force in international business, 65

multicultural diversity in, 451–453

NAFTA as benefiting, 77–81

negotiations with Iraq, 167

negotiation with China, 202–209

negotiation with Germany, 188, 256–257

negotiation with Japan, 168, 173–174, 187, 209–212

in North American regional trade bloc, 8–9

organizational information flow in, 152–153

organizational staffing in, 351–352

organized and unorganized labor in, 390

paralanguage in, 147

performance monitoring in, 311

as promoter of human rights issues, 60

proxemics of employees in, 146

reaction to Japanese protection by, 43

regulation of telecommunications industry by, 493

repatriation of expatriates from, 377–378

resolution of negotiation conflicts with, 186

reward systems in, 421–422

subculture shock in, 358

subcultures in, 111

successful negotiating style in, 170, 172, 176–177, 178, 179, 180, 181

successful negotiation between China and, 183–185

support for tobacco industry in, 55

system for monitoring subsidiaries by, 305–310

team-based work systems in, 400

transportation industry in, 219–220

women managers in, 384

work ethic in, 409, 410, 411, 413, 419

Universalism, as value dimension, 119, 120

Urban wireless, in case study, 320

Uribe, Alberto, 249

Utilitarianism, in decision making, 189–190

Value dimensions, 113

country abbreviations for charts of, 115

critical operational differences in, 120–122

geographic clustering of, 117–118, 118–120

Hofstede's, 113–117

Trompenaars's, 118–120

Values. *See* Cultural values

Varga, George, 22–25

Variables. *See also* Cultural variables

in employee motivation, 408–411

evaluation, 312

in globalization, 301–304

in leadership, 429–431

in meaning of work, 408–411

in negotiation, 175–176, 181, 182

in risk assessment, 32–34

in workforce diversity, 447

Venezuela

oil industry in, 50–51

takeover case study in, 248–252

Venture-specific factors, in strategic planning choices, 246

Videoconferencing, 188

Vietnam

expanding into markets in, 222, 225

human rights issues in, 85

Villates, Jose Carlos, 110

Villegas, Juan, 103

Violence, Colombian economy and, 50–53

Vittorelli, Jacopo, 376

Vondras, John, 38, 41

Wages, 86. *See also* Compensation

codes of conduct on, 63

in Europe, 397–398

in European Union, 244–245

for maquiladoras, 472, 504–505

Waldheim, Kurt, 177

Wang, Y. C., 295
Wang Chih Neh, 337, 338, 339, 341
Wang family, 323–324
Wang Kin Chung, Peter, 324
Wang Li-Chung, Richard, 324
Wang Seng Liang, 323–324
Wang Shui Chung, Patrick, 324, 326–327
Wang Wing Yee, Winnie, 324, 325
Wang Yik Chun, 323, 325
Wa principle, 124
    in decision making, 191
Wardlow, Priscilla, 404–405
Warnings, in negotiation, 179
Watanabe, Toru, 3
Water-purification business, in Mexico, 80
Weakness
    Arab aversion to, 130
    in SWOT analysis, 232–233
Wealth, American valuing of, 122
Welch, Jack, 21
West Germany. *See* Germany
White goods. *See* Home appliance industry
White male employees, diversity programs versus, 446–447
Whitwam, David R., 509, 513, 519
    biography of, 518–519
Windows, in offices, 3
Win–win situations, 168
Withdrawal of investment, managing political risk through, 34
Women
    cultural masculinity and, 116
    in foreign postings, 386–387
    as Hong Kong joint venture executives, 325

in international management, 381–384, 385, 386–387, 387–389, 475–482
    sexual harassment of, 389
    as spouses of expatriates, 378
    status of Arab, 131, 132, 150, 167
    status of Korean, 127
    as underutilized human resource, 376, 381–384, 388–389
Wordeman, Matt, 3
Work
    meaning of, 408–421
    rewarding good, 421–422
Work centrality, 409
    chart of, 410
Work ethic, 408–421
    of Americans, 112, 123, 236, 409, 410, 411, 413, 419
    cultural differences in, 408–411, 411–414
    in India, 431–432
    in Japan, 124, 236, 410
    of Moslems, 409–410, 412, 419
Workforce diversity
    advantages and disadvantages of, 451
    dimensions of, 447
    in globalization, 13–15, 439–459
    language problems from, 145
    maximizing effectiveness of, 451–453, 483–487
Work groups, 399–400
    in Canada, 400
    of immigrants, 458
    in Japan, 124
Work habits
    differences between, 3–4
    in European Union, 244
Working conditions

for expatriates, 481
    in Mexican maquiladoras, 504–505
Working styles, cross-cultural clashes between, 3–4
Workplace safety, 61, 86
    codes of conduct on, 63
    ethics of, 60
    in textile industry, 339–340
Work teams, multicultural, 449–451
Work weeks, 86
    codes of conduct on, 63
World Confederation of Labor (WCL)
    in convergence of labor relations, 394
World GDP, growth in, 5–6
World markets, in strategic planning, 234–235
World merchandise exports, 6
    growth in, 5
World trade, growth in, 5–6
World War II, Taiwan after, 333–334
World Washer, 526
Worldwide Excellence System (WES), 526–527
Written language, in cross-cultural communication, 142, 144–145

Xiamen economic zone, 295

Yamaguchi, Utaka, 110
Yamamoto, Takuma, 298
Yan, Monica, 219–220
Yeltsin, Boris, 10
Yugoslavia, work ethic in, 410, 411

Zedillo, Ernesto, 404
Zhurakovskij, Vladimir, 308
Zuccaro, Bruno, 268, 269